THE CONCISE OXFORD COMPANION TO
ECONOMICS
IN INDIA

Praise for *The Oxford Companion to Economics in India*

'... a unique and important guide to the dynamic Indian economy, and also a collection of penetrating essays by many of the world's true experts.'

STEPHEN P. COHEN
Senior Fellow, Foreign Policy Studies, The Brookings Institution

'... essential reading for anyone seeking to understand India's economic and political economy.'

ASHUTOSH VARSHNEY
Professor, Department of Political Science, Brown University

'India's first companion to economics is certainly among the more impressive additions to the catalogue of Indian encyclopedias.'

The Financial Express

'This unique volume is an indispensable and innovative addition to the library of economics, not only for economists but also those whose lives are affected by economics.'

India Today

'Too many economists may spoil the broth, but they can certainly produce a good encyclopedia on the economy!'

Outlook

'... [This volume has] addressed the long-felt need for an authentic guide that would encourage the study of economics, which had been neglected ...'

The Hindu

THE CONCISE OXFORD COMPANION TO
ECONOMICS
IN INDIA

EDITED BY
KAUSHIK BASU
ANNEMIE MAERTENS

OXFORD
UNIVERSITY PRESS

OXFORD
UNIVERSITY PRESS

YMCA Library Building, Jai Singh Road, New Delhi 110 001

Oxford University Press is a department of the University of Oxford. It furthers the
University's objective of excellence in research, scholarship, and education
by publishing worldwide in

Oxford   New York

Auckland   Cape Town   Dar es Salaam   Hong Kong   Karachi
Kuala Lumpur   Madrid   Melbourne   Mexico City   Nairobi
New Delhi   Shanghai   Taipei   Toronto

With offices in

Argentina   Austria   Brazil   Chile   Czech Republic   France   Greece
Guatemala   Hungary   Italy   Japan   Poland   Portugal   Singapore
South Korea   Switzerland   Thailand   Turkey   Ukraine   Vietnam

Oxford is a registered trademark of Oxford University Press
in the UK and in certain other countries

Published in India
by Oxford University Press, New Delhi

© Oxford University Press 2010

The moral rights of the author have been asserted
Database right Oxford University Press (maker)

First published 2010

ISBN-13: 978-019-806313-1
ISBN-10: 019-806313-X

Typeset in Adobe Jenson Pro 10.5/12.6
by Eleven Arts, Keshav Puram, Delhi 110 035
Printed and bound in India at Repro India Ltd., Mumbai
Published by Oxford University Press
YMCA Library Building, Jai Singh Road, New Delhi 110 001

CONTENTS

INTRODUCTION

This book owes its origin to the success of the *Oxford Companion to Economics in India* published in 2007 by Oxford University Press. The first print run was sold out in the same year, and a reprint was in the market by early 2008. A lot of the demand came from around the world. It was evident that the genesis of this demand lay in the sudden rise of the Indian economy and the appearance of India as a global player, and also the absence of any comparable compendium or encyclopedia on this subject.

While we do not have formal statistics on this, given the high price of the book (even though we were told that on a per-kilogram basis it was not that expensive), it seemed likely that students in India and maybe even in the industrialized world were not able to afford the book. Hence, it was felt by some of us who were engaged in the project that we should use the original *Companion* as a template and produce a more student-friendly, concise version of the same book. The *Concise Oxford Companion to Economics in India* is the outcome.

In editing this book, we decided to retain the entries from the original book which were relevant to the kinds of topics that students learning about the Indian economy would wish to have on hand, and we decided to add a few new topics, which had either gained salience in the years since the publication of the *Companion*, such as the financial crisis of 2007–9 and the accompanying recession, or became clear to us with the advantage of hindsight that they should have been there, to start with, in the *Companion*. Hence, we commissioned some new entries especially for this book. In addition, the entries are now clustered thematically to make for easier reading for those interested in special aspects of the economy.

Both of us editors do research on the Indian economy. We have often found that, despite the spread of the internet and web search engines, there is no substitute to having some of the basic statistics on hand as hard copy. One great value of the *Economic Survey* that comes out each year from the Ministry of Finance is the data appendix at the end. This led to the decision to add a short appendix with some basic data on the Indian economy—its performance over time and in comparison with other nations. For this we scoured various sources—from India and from international organizations such as the World Bank—and pulled together statistics on some of the most salient aspects of India's economy. We believe that this will be of value to students of the Indian economy, policymakers, and economic journalists. The appendix carrying these statistics appears at the end of the book.

Experts on the Indian economy are a vanishing tribe, and for good reason. The complexity of the economy has grown to such enormous proportions that its comprehension is beyond the capacity of any single human mind. And the complexity continues to grow, as the economy gathers steam. But, of course, policies have to be crafted, taxes designed, subsidies doled out or rolled in, exchange rates propped up or allowed to flag, and laws pertaining to the economy enacted, amended, or repealed. Given the multifarious tasks that Indian policymakers have to contend with, there is a growing need to collate and coordinate information and wisdom that is scattered across a large number of institutions and individuals. The *Concise Oxford Companion to Economics in India* and its predecessor, the *Oxford Companion to Economics in India*, are our response to this pressing need of our times.

When, in 1992, India's most famous stock market scam—the Harshad Mehta scandal—broke, an economist and a top official of the Government of India admitted that he did not even know the meanings of the many things that the evil genius of Harshad Mehta had manipulated. No one can blame him. Likewise, the global financial crisis of 2007–9, and the subsequent recession, has brought into the limelight topics and complexities which are very difficult for the lay person (and occasionally even experts—and policymakers) to fully understand.

Anybody interested in the Indian economy, whether a researcher, a policymaker, a corporate manager, or a ground-level activist, will appreciate the need for a reference source, where one can find most of the basic information and ideas concerning the Indian economy and the best of contemporary thinking on the subject. This book is our effort to meet this need.

In his essay, 'Economic Possibilities for our Grandchildren', John Maynard Keynes, no-doubt slightly dizzy from the then-recent rapid advances in economics, had predicted that within the next few decades all the major problems of the economy would be solved, and economics would cease to be an important subject. For once, the self-assured Maynard Keynes was completely wrong. Implicit in that observation was a view of the economy as a static object, waiting to be dissected and diagnosed. In reality, the complexity of the economy grows in step with our understanding of it. As we have a scientific breakthrough and begin to fathom some of this complexity, that very understanding enables our entrepreneurs, managers, consumers, and workers to discover new strategies and actions and that, in turn, gives rise to newer complexities in the economy. Hence, like Sukumar Ray's famous character, Chandidas' uncle, who when setting out on long journeys dangled his favourite foods in front of him, from a mast anchored to his own shoulders, in economics, unlike in the natural sciences, our investigation and the object of our investigation move pretty much in tandem.

Even as this book is being written and edited, the economy of India is evolving into an ever more complex organism. This is a perennial process. Hence, a project like this book, while it has its intellectual excitement, also has its preordained frustrations, because one knows that it can never be comprehensive and never be able to live up totally to the task.

In taking up this large project, we felt that the book had to achieve three tasks. It had to be a reasonably comprehensive reference volume on the basic facts and uniformities that gird the contemporary Indian economy, a record of the best contemporary thinking on the subject, and geared to the interests of students of India's development. Hence, we have tried to include among the contributors leading thinkers, scribes, industrialists, policymakers, and politicians; we have also called upon some fresh PhDs who would have empathy for the student reader trying to understand the Indian economy. The list of authors who figure in the pages that follow must make amply clear that the response has been overwhelming.

Since the mid-1990s not only has the overall economy of India surged, with growth rates frequently crossing the 7 per cent per annum mark and, in the early years of this decade, rising above 8 per cent, but there is also a clear and evident increase in the sophistication of our scholars and researchers. The old polarization of the 'left' and the 'right,' where people took up positions not from facts and deductive reasoning, but from their chosen texts and pre-committed opinions, is less evident today. Barring a few diehards at both ends, most analysts approach the subject much more scientifically. We wanted the best of this new opinion, irrespective of ideology, to be represented in this book. And to that extent the book is aimed at those interested in not just policy but also in the conundrums of the economy as an intellectual challenge *per se*. Moreover, this reference volume is meant to span not just the recent cover stories of India's high growth, leadership role in software and information technology and outsourcing success, but also the backwaters—the widespread poverty, farmer suicides, child labour, and the large and impoverished informal sector, where a vast majority of India's labourers work.

There is virtual consensus that, while India has grown rapidly over the last decade and poverty, as measured by the percentage of population living below the poverty line, has declined, inequality—whether it be regional or personal—has worsened and employment has not grown in step with the growth of the labour force. Understanding the bases of these seeming anomalies is extremely important. A huge rise in inequality can create political upheavals, which can in turn spell doom for growth. Moreover, there are many (the present authors included) who consider such huge inequalities to be innately unconscionable even if the disadvantaged are too weak to protest and destabilize the economy.

But even if one were not trying to think of policies to avoid such a predicament, understanding the diverse changes in India is an intellectual challenge of no mean proportion. Is the growth in inequality a consequence of economic liberalization or a necessary concomitant of global changes, and, hence, largely beyond the reach of national governments? Are movements in stock prices reflections of underlying strengths and weaknesses of the economy or the moods and machinations of investors and speculators? This book is aimed at providing readers with the basic facts and ideas that will help them form their own opinion about these difficult questions.

Big books like this, by their sheer weight in the hands of the reader, raise expectations that are virtually impossible to fulfill. There are invariably topics and entries that disappoint by their omission. The decision of what to omit and what to include can actually be very challenging. In crossing over from the original *Oxford Companion* to the *Concise Oxford Companion* we tried to make some amendments to the selection based on what we have learned about reader interest in the last two years since the publication of the *Oxford Companion*.

The pleasures of editing a mammoth volume like this outweigh the not-inconsiderable costs. For one, there is an enormous amount of learning-by-doing and this happens effortlessly as one reads and edits the manuscript. Then there is the pleasure of human interaction. It has been a pleasure for both of us editors working with the Oxford University Press team. At Cornell University we were aided by numerous friends, faculty, and students. We thank them all.

Finally, we owe a very special thanks to the Board of Advisors—T.C.A. Anant, Pranab Bardhan, Jean Drèze, Dilip Mookherjee, and Govinda Rao—that helped with the original *Oxford Companion*. These individuals of outstanding and varied intellectual strengths were called upon liberally at several stages—about what kinds of entries to include and what to omit, about possible authors, and also to have them read and comment on several of the entries. The *Concise Oxford Companion* used this valuable input and then built upon it to produce a book of reference that, we hope, will be of value to all students of the Indian economy.

KAUSHIK BASU
ANNEMIE MAERTENS

BACKDROP

Corporate Ownership and Performance

Whether ownership characteristics of firms are related to their performance is an extensively debated and researched issue in the academic literature. Existing work in this area can be broadly classified into two groups. The first set of studies has focused on public and private ownership forms at aggregate level, while the second set has been more micro-theoretic in nature and has tried to link differences in performance of mainly private-sector firms to their underlying equity ownership structures.

The debate on public versus private ownership often highlights two extreme positions. At one end is the 'ownership always matters' view subscribed to by the property rights and public choice theorists who maintain that private firms would necessarily outperform public firms. The reason for this, according to the property rights theorists, is that shareholders of private firms can easily sell their shares in case of poor performance which is not the case for public firms. The potential for takeover and the consequent loss in reputation and income always force private-sector managers to perform. Public choice theorists point to specific X-inefficiency factors like lack of well-defined and fixed objectives for managers, presence of

special interests groups, and political rent seeking in public firms that cause them to underperform vis-à-vis private firms. The other extreme position in this debate is the 'no difference in efficiency' view, where some argue that the link between the market for corporate control and superior private enterprise efficiency can be weak because of possible free-rider problems in takeover activity, given that private firms are often owned largely by small shareholders. Some others point to the 'primacy of competition over ownership', arguing that product market competition, through creating the necessary pressure on managers of public firms too, can eliminate any performance differential between public and private firms.

Studies that look at the relationship between ownership structure and performance of private-sector firms originate in the corporate governance literature. These studies are rooted in the observation that modern-day corporations are owned by a large number of small, dispersed shareholders and have to be managed or controlled by professional managers. This separation between ownership and control often breeds managerial opportunism where managers take actions such as expanding firm size beyond optimal level, consuming perquisites, or satisfying managerial hubris, all of which increase their private returns but are inconsistent with shareholder value maximization. Given such agency costs, that is costs imposed by managerial opportunism, various internal and external mechanisms are recommended for aligning the interest of managers and shareholders. Equity ownership is one such crucial internal mechanism. For example, giving managers significant equity ownership may lead to the 'convergence' of managerial and shareholder objectives leading to maximization of firm value. Likewise, a few large shareholders, as compared to dispersed ones, can have the power and incentives to monitor managers effectively. However, in the case of private ownership too, the questions regarding ownership and performance take on conflicting dimensions such as whether large shareholders necessarily increase firm value or instead use their controlling power to pursue objectives that benefit them at the expense of minority shareholders.

Existing empirical evidence on the ownership–performance issue, both with respect to developed and developing countries, closely mirrors the diversity in theoretical opinion, and is largely inconclusive. The diversity of findings across countries and over time has increasingly strengthened the viewpoint that 'institutions matter' in determining the relationship between ownership and performance. For instance, it is argued that the institutional specificities of developing countries, such as less active capital and takeover markets or the absence of a well-developed managerial market, can impact the costs and benefits of different types of ownership in unique ways. Thus findings on ownership and performance in developed countries may not necessarily hold in the context of developing countries.

EMPIRICAL EVIDENCE ON OWNERSHIP AND PERFORMANCE IN INDIA
The literature on ownership and performance in India, as in the case of many developing

countries, is relatively recent and can, in line with the background discussion, be split into two sets. The first set consists of studies comparing the performance of the public sector with the private sector. Most of these studies use the 'dummy variable approach' where the *average* performance of one ownership group is compared with that of the other, without considering their detailed ownership structure. The second set, focusing mainly on private-sector firms, links the structure of their equity ownership across different types of shareholders to their performance.

PUBLIC VERSUS PRIVATE FIRMS
The relative performance of public- and private-sector firms in India for the period 1989–2004 is shown in Figure 1. Private-sector firms are classified into (Indian) private firms and foreign firms operating in India. Performance is measured in terms of mean return-on-assets (ROA) calculated as profits before depreciation, interest, and taxes divided by total assets. This period witnessed the deregulation and liberalization of the Indian economy, starting in the mid-1980s and gathering momentum after the adoption of the structural reforms programme in July 1991. Additionally, while the blueprint of industrial policy in post-Independence India had accorded the public sector 'commanding heights', India's economic transition since the 1990s has been marked by an increasing levelling of the playing field between the private and public sectors.

As the figure shows, foreign firms have performed better than domestic firms, which in turn have outperformed public firms during this sixteen-year period. The mean ROA of the three ownership groups for the period has been 13.53 per cent, 10.02 per cent, and 7.61 per cent respectively.

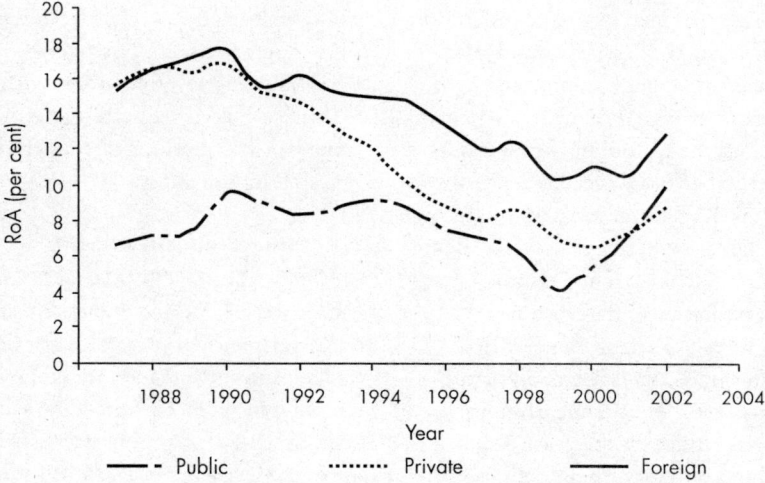

Figure 1   Trends in Return-on-Assets

However, a striking feature of Figure 1 is that, though the relative ranking of the ownership groups has remained unchanged over the years, their performance differentials have narrowed considerably with almost near convergence in the later years, suggesting that in a deregulating economy competition can be a significant driver of economic performance, with ownership becoming less important. Unlike the univariate trends displayed in Figure 1, a multivariate framework controls for other factors like size, industry affiliation, and age that can also affect performance and uses robust quantitative analyses to draw conclusions.

Considering the pre-deregulation years 1973–89, characterized by little competition among the different ownership groups, and using industry-level data, Majumdar (1998) finds that private- and mixed-sector firms had higher efficiency compared to public-sector firms. However, support for primacy of competition over ownership is also found in the study—the gap between private and public firms is shown to narrow as the economy was being deregulated and measures to reform underperforming public-

sector firms were being adopted. While there is a dearth of firm-level evidence on the relative performance of public and private firms, evidence that private firms may not be unambiguously superior to public firms is found in a case study of the Indian banking industry (Sarkar et al. 1998) conducted for a cross-section of public, domestic private, and foreign banks around the initial reform years 1993–4 and 1994–5. The study found, consistent with the property rights hypothesis, that the relative performance of different ownership groups is correlated with the extent of their links with the market for corporate control, with foreign banks performing better than traded private banks which outperformed non-traded private banks. Non-traded private banks, however, had no significant differences in performance, either with respect to profitability or efficiency vis-à-vis public-sector banks. A follow-up analysis by Bhaumik and Dimova (2004), examining whether ownership continues to matter in any way following further deregulation and entry of private-sector banks, was conducted for the period 1995–6 to 2000–1. Consistent with the role of competition envisaged in the 'no difference in performance' view, the study found that ownership was no longer a significant determinant of performance; instead, greater competition has caused public-sector banks to eliminate the performance/efficiency gap that existed vis-à-vis domestic private-sector and foreign banks.

An increasingly researched issue in recent years that has offered some insights on the relevance of ownership in performance in India is the analysis of partial privatization, that is the divestiture of a part of the equity by the government without giving up management control. Between 1991, the inception year of the divestment programme, and 2001, forty public-sector firms across different industries were partially privatized. While several studies have analysed the performance effects of such divestments, the first detailed statistical investigation of the ownership effects of partial privatization using firm-level data for the period 1990–2000 is found in Gupta (2005). As Gupta argues, examining partial privatization helps separate the agency cost determinants and the political determinants of public-sector performance since under partial privatization, while agency costs are mitigated through the market for corporate control, political control still remains with the government. After controlling for 'cherry picking', that is the fact that the better firms are more likely to be chosen for privatization, Gupta finds partial privatization having a positive impact on profitability, productivity, and investment. One aspect not considered by the study is that many of the divested firms had also been granted managerial autonomy by the government under the memorandum of understanding (MOU) scheme introduced in 1988–9. Given that managerial autonomy through performance contracts and

distancing the government from day-to-day operations can positively impact performance as several studies with respect to Chinese enterprises attest to, the effect of partial privatization may be less than that suggested by the study.

OWNERSHIP STRUCTURES AND PERFORMANCE OF PRIVATE-SECTOR FIRMS

Empirical work linking ownership structure and performance of private-sector firms has been gaining currency in India following the increasing focus on corporate governance issues. With the adoption of the structural reforms programme in 1991, as India became more integrated with the world market and more companies started tapping external sources of finance from the debt and capital markets, public concern started zeroing in on understanding how ownership structures of firms are organized and their implications for performance, how firms are governed by their shareholders, whether minority shareholders are protected from expropriation by the majority, and whether large blockholders like banks and institutional investors are active in governance. While the number of published works in India analysing the link between ownership structures and performance in private-sector firms is relatively small compared to the repository of such works in developed countries, these studies nonetheless provide some interesting insights.

The ownership structure of private-sector firms and the associated corporate governance system in India, as presented in Table 1, are by and large a hybrid of the 'outsider systems' of the US and UK and the 'insider systems' of continental Europe and Japan (Sarkar and Sarkar 2000). Also, like for their counterparts in East Asia, Japan, and several European countries, concentrated ownership structure in India is the norm rather than the exception.

Table 1 Distribution of Equity Ownership of Listed Companies

Ownership types	India (1996)	US (1996)	UK (1996)	Germany (1996)	Japan (2001)
Financial sector	9.8	46.0	68.0	39.0	40.0
– Banks/financial institutions	3.6	7.0	10.0	10.0	30.0
– Insurance + pension funds	2.1	28.0	50.0	12.0	10.0
– Mutual/investment funds	4.1	12.0	8.0	8.0	0.0
Non-financial sector	90.2	54.0	32.0	70.0	60.0
– Non-financial corporations	23.8	0.0	1.0	42.0	22.0
– Individuals	56.3	49.0	21.0	15.0	20.0
– Foreign	10.1	5.0	9.0	9.0	18.0
– Government	0.0	0.0	1.0	4.0	1.0
Total	100.0	100.0	100.0	100.0	100.0

Sources: M. Maher and T. Anderson. 2002. 'Corporate Governance: Effects on Firms Performance and Economic Growth', in J. McCahery, P. Moerland, T. Raaijnakers, and L. Renneboog, eds, *Corporate Governance Regimes: Convergence and Diversity*, New Delhi, Oxford University Press, updates by Jayati Sarkar and Subrata Sarkar. 2000. 'Large Shareholder Activism in Corporate Governance in Developing Countries: Evidence from India', *International Review of Finance*, 1(3): 161–94.

Note: The distribution for India is based on a sample of 1567 private listed manufacturing companies. Due to rounding, figures may not add up to the total.

Equity holdings by non-financial corporations, which are primarily inter-corporate cross-holdings, are much higher in India than in the US and UK and are more comparable to the situation in Germany and Japan. However, the participation of the small investor in corporate equity is at comparable levels with the US, with India having the largest number of listed companies in the world. While different types of financial corporations in India separately hold much smaller blocks in comparison to those in other countries, given that nearly all of these institutions are government controlled, together they form a significant block in the equity ownership of Indian companies. The participation of institutional investors like mutual funds and insurance companies which are nearly fully owned by the government in India is comparable to the extent of their participation in Japan and Germany, but much less in scope than that in the US.

What implications does this ownership composition have on firm performance? A handful of studies using both linear and non-linear specifications of the relationship between ownership composition and firm performance provides valuable insights on this issue—Chhibber and Majumdar (1999), Khanna and Palepu (2000), and Sarkar and Sarkar (2000). While the study by Chhibber and Majumdar (1999) primarily analyses the relation between foreign ownership and company performance, the other two examine the effect of other blockholders also, namely domestic and foreign financial institutions and directors on company value. A general finding across these studies is that foreign equity ownership is beneficial for performance. While Khanna and Palepu (2000), postulating a linear relationship between concentrated ownership and firm value, find no evidence of a beneficial impact of equity ownership by domestic financial institutions or directors on company value,

Sarkar and Sarkar (2000) find evidence of a piece-wise linear relationship between the different equity owners. In the latter study, shareholding by directors, who are in many cases de facto owners of family-dominated companies, positively impacts company value once their holdings cross a threshold (25 per cent), a result that is consistent with that of some well-cited studies in the US. The study also finds effective monitoring by financial institutions once they have substantial equity holdings. Further, this monitoring is reinforced by the extent of debt holdings by these institutions. The overall evidence points to the positive role that can be played by blockholders in mitigating managerial agency problems in developing countries like India that are characterized by weak legal protection.

While large shareholders are found to play a beneficial role in influencing performance across Indian firms in general, this picture somewhat changes when the role of such shareholders is considered specifically with respect to firms affiliated to business groups. One key governance issue in the case of such firms is whether controlling shareholders expropriate minority shareholders by transferring corporate resources from companies where they have low ownership or cash flow rights to companies where they have higher ownership rights leading to lowering of company value in the former sets of companies. Such 'tunnelling' of resources is possible because group firms are often organized in terms of pyramids with complex cross-holdings among member companies enabling promoters to have 'effective control' over companies 'on top of the pyramid' in spite of their having low ownership rights in them. Transfer of resources from the top of the pyramid hurts the promoters too, but that is overcompensated by the gains they reap from the companies lower down the pyramid where they have higher ownership rights. Bertrand et al. (2002) document this phenomenon of 'tunnelling' in the case of India and conduct a series of estimations to provide empirically robust evidence of group firms transferring unexpected increases in their profits to member firms, with the extent of transfer depending on the ownership rights of the owners in the recipient firms.

In conclusion, a common feature of existing ownership performance studies in India as it is in the majority of such studies elsewhere, is that the ownership structure of firms is taken as given, that is exogenous, and its effect on performance is then examined. However, a growing body of research suggests that ownership structures may themselves evolve in response to differences in performance and other firm characteristics. Empirical studies using sophisticated econometric techniques that account for this simultaneous determination of ownership and performance should be able to corroborate these theoretical predictions. Findings of these studies taken together with the existing evidence can throw valuable light on the ongoing privatization debate in India regarding whether privatization would matter in the first place and, if so, the type of ownership structure that will maximize post-privatization performance.

JAYATI SARKAR AND
SUBRATA SARKAR

REFERENCES

Bertrand, Marianne, Paras Mehta, and Sendhil Mullainathan. 2002. 'Ferreting out Tunneling: An Application to Indian Business Groups', The Quarterly Journal of Economics, 117(1): 121–48.

Bhaumik, Sumon Kumar and Ralitza Dimova. 2004. 'How Important is Ownership in a Market with Level Playing Field? The Indian Banking Sector Revisited', Journal of Comparative Economics, 32(1): 165–80.

Chhibber, P.K. and S.K. Majumdar. 1999.
    'Foreign Ownership and Profitability:
    Property Rights, Control, and the
    Performance of Firms in Indian Industry',
    Journal of Law and Economics, 42(1):
    209–39.

Gupta, Nandini. 2005. 'Partial Privatization and
    Firm Performance', *The Journal of Finance*,
    60(2): 987–1015.

Khanna, Tarun and Krishna Palepu. 2000.
    'Emerging Market Business Groups, Foreign
    Investors and Corporate Governance', in
    Randall Morck, ed., NBER volume on
    Concentrated Ownership, Chicago, University
    of Chicago Press.

Majumdar, Sumit K. 1998. 'Assessing
    Comparative Efficiency of the State-owned,
    Mixed, and Private Sectors in Indian
    Industry', *Public Choice*, 96(1–2): 1–24.

Sarkar, Jayati and Subrata Sarkar. 2000.
    'Large Shareholder Activism in Corporate
    Governance in Developing Countries:
    Evidence from India', *International Review of
    Finance*, 1(3): 161–94.

Sarkar, Jayati, Subrata Sarkar, and Sumon
    Bhaumik. 1998. 'Does Ownership Always
    Matter? Evidence from the Indian Banking
    Industry', *Journal of Comparative Economics*,
    26(2): 262–81.

Corruption

TYPES

Kautilya's *Arthashastra*, written around
2000 years ago, discusses corruption and its
control. Indians have also made important
contributions to recent scholarly and policy
discussion on corruption.

As is done here, corruption is usually
defined as the misuse of public office for
private gain. Common manifestations of
corruption are bribes in cash or kind taken
by politicians or bureaucrats either in return
for illegal favours (voluntary bribes) or for
refraining from using official power to cause
harm (coercive bribes). With voluntary
bribes, both bribe giver and taker benefit at
the cost of the public. Coercive bribes benefit
bribe takers at the expense of bribe givers.
Threats of harassment generally provide the
inducement to pay coercive bribes.

Besides bribes, nepotism and misuse
or theft of public property by responsible
officials are other common types of
corruption. The *Arthashastra* lists forty
ways in which public officials can steal
government money or harass citizens.

In 2002, Transparency International (TI)
surveyed individuals in South Asia who had
recently used one of seven public services (in
decreasing order of corruption encountered
by respondents, these were the police, judicial
services, land administration, education,
power, tax departments, and health services).
The survey found many types of corruption-
prone activities in different sectors. Types
most often encountered by the 5157 Indian
respondents ranged from the notorious 'hafta'
or periodic bribe to the police by businesses
to avoid harassment, to bribes for admissions
or continued service in health, education,
and power, and bribes to ensure low tax
assessment.

It is likely that survey respondents would
have been less forthcoming about voluntary
bribes as compared to coercive bribes.
Nevertheless, the survey suggests that bribes
in India are largely coercive, with voluntary
bribes being important only for taxes. Even
for taxes, other studies have found coercive
bribes to obtain refunds and clearances and
to release goods at warehouses and check
posts to be important. A second significant
finding of the TI survey is that most bribes
are paid directly to officials rather than
to middlemen. One exception to this is
property registration in Andhra Pradesh
(Caseley 2004).

The World Bank's World Business
Environment Survey (WBES) in 2001–2
provides important qualitative information
about bribes by companies. According to

respondents, in India bribe amounts are known in advance to companies around two-thirds of the time, allowing bribe costs to be accounted for in business plans. On the other hand, payment of bribes only ensures that promised favours will be delivered a quarter of the time. According to Bardhan (1997) inability to deliver promised favours in centralized bureaucracies often results from the need to get approvals from multiple officials.

Regarding stealing of public property, studies in India have focused on siphoning of public funds for infrastructure works such as irrigation and roads, for social and anti-poverty services, and from publicly funded loans to the poor. For example, Bhatia and Drèze (1998) document how heads of village administration (*sarpanches*) collude with development officials to misappropriate around 20 per cent of funds for village-level development works. The Central Vigilance Commission (CVC), a government anti-corruption agency, has recently begun to report other cases of misappropriation.

Some Indian policy writings point to large-scale corruption in government recruitment and transfers to 'lucrative' positions and in awarding public procurement contracts (see Vittal 2002). These types of corruption involve both politicians and bureaucrats. While bribes for postings do not immediately affect ordinary citizens, officers who have paid for posts later indulge in bribe taking to make good their 'investment'.

EXTENT AND DISTRIBUTION
TI's Corruption Perceptions Index for 2004, based on surveys of foreign business executives, ranks India as the fifty-sixth most corrupt of the 146 countries covered. This high corruption rating is repeated in earlier TI surveys as also in surveys of groups other than foreign executives.

Regarding the distribution of corruption, percentages of Indian respondents in the 2002 TI survey encountering corruption ranged from 100 for the police and courts to just fifteen for both tax and health services. However, other studies have found a much higher incidence of bribes among taxpayers, particularly business firms and companies. For companies, the WBES suggests that over 50 per cent commonly pay bribes.

The TI study has one unexpected finding. A large proportion of bribes paid were to *officer-level* staff, like police officers, doctors, land revenue surveyors, tax officers, teachers, and school management, rather than to subordinate staff. A partial exception was the judicial services, where the incidence of bribes to judges and public prosecutors was much lower than that to court officials.

On willingness of citizens to pay voluntary bribes, surveys fail to adequately distinguish between coercive and voluntary bribes. Limited available evidence suggests two trends. First, other things being equal, the willingness to pay voluntary bribes has increased secularly since India's Independence. Second, however, given fewer government controls, increased private-sector alternatives, and reduced tax rates, the extent of corruption and quantum of bribes have both decreased, especially in deregulated sectors.

On the size of bribes, various surveys taken together suggest that bribes range from 10 to 20 per cent of legal sums involved. This appears to be low compared to countries at similar levels of development. So though the *incidence* of corruption in India may be high, additional costs of corruption are probably not. Even so, recent events such as the 'Tehelka expose' of alleged bribe taking by politicians (see Vittal 2002), and the huge payments for lucrative postings in other anecdotal evidence, suggest that bribes can be large in absolute terms if the benefits from purchased favours are themselves large. Bardhan (1997) refers to the tendency in some countries for voluntary bribes to be much lower than bribers' benefits as the 'Tullock paradox'.

CAUSES

Economic analysis of causes of corruption by Indian authors has focused mainly on proximate institutional determinants, taking as given willingness to pay and receive bribes. One major research concern is with the impact on corruption of *incentives*—reward and punishment structures—of corrupt officials dealing with dishonest citizens. This concern with incentives dates back to the *Arthashastra*. Recent research has helped identify desirable practical design features of joint systems of performance-based rewards and corruption penalties (see Mookherjee 1997).

Related research focuses on the impact of supervisory hierarchies, where supervisors are themselves corruptible, given different reward and punishment structures. For example, Sanyal (2000) models a hierarchy of corruptible tax auditors employed to detect tax evasion by dishonest taxpayers. Auditors earn rewards for detecting and reporting evasion but are fined if, instead, they accept a bribe that is detected by a supervisor (if the auditor and supervisor do not collude). He finds that more supervisory levels in the hierarchy increase tax revenue, with the extent of increase depending on the size of rewards and intrinsic abilities of auditors and supervisors to detect tax evasion or bribe taking. While this research has increased understanding about hierarchies, its practical impact is still limited.

Partly informed by this research, some Indian policy analysts stress the corruption-reducing impact of performance incentives and institutions to promote accountability, such as independent audits and vigilance. Related policy analysis suggests that higher collusion costs of bureaus like tax departments organized along functional lines make them less corruption prone than those where groups of taxpayers are assigned to a single tax inspector.

That corruption causes further corruption or other economic crimes is an important observation. This has been pointed out while discussing government recruitment and postings. To take another example, businesses must evade taxes to generate unaccounted money for bribes: there is anecdotal evidence of entire departments set up to deal with government regulators in some prominent companies. So reduced hidden business costs are one important effect of deregulation.

CONSEQUENCES

One clear economic consequence of corruption is reduced government revenue, adversely affecting the government's ability to deliver public services or, alternatively, accentuating macroeconomic instability when deficit financing is resorted to.

The other side of the coin, the negative impact of corruption on the effectiveness of government services and their unit costs, can be inferred from the discussion in the preceding pages. Sporadic evidence on the magnitude of these costs is available in various reports of the Comptroller and Auditor General of India (CAG). Rajiv Gandhi once said that only 15 paise of each rupee spent on anti-poverty programmes actually reaches the poor (Vittal 2002). Clearly, only a part of the remaining 85 paise is directly misappropriated. The important insight of Banerjee (1997) is that corruption is also *indirectly* responsible for high delivery costs since corrupt bureaucrats have the incentive to generate excessive red tape which adds to costs.

Ineffective anti-poverty services adversely affect poverty alleviation. The negative impact of corruption on business costs has also been pointed out. This adversely affects international competitiveness. Bardhan's (1997) review of the negative impact of corruption on efficient resource allocation, investment, particularly foreign investment, and economic growth suggests that these costs are appreciable. Once again, as Bardhan discusses, efficiency and growth costs are not limited to direct costs. Indirect cost channels include reduced information-transmitting efficiency of markets, since corruption is necessarily secretive; business uncertainty since corrupt favours are not always delivered; and further uncertainty since corrupt courts cannot be relied upon to uphold property rights and enforce contracts. Another indirect channel identified in Indian writing is the two-way link between corruption and unaccounted wealth. Conspicuous consumption from 'black' wealth and curtailed investment opportunities further reduce growth. The overhang of black wealth from the pre-liberalization period is also thought to reduce the growth benefits of liberalization, since black money cannot always flow to sectors with the highest returns.

Continuing corruption eventually reduces respect for the rule of law and honesty in public life. Evidence from cross-country studies suggests that the rule of law is an important determinant of economic growth. Though this decline should have large economic costs, no estimate is yet available for India.

THE NATURE AND EFFECTIVENESS OF ANTI-CORRUPTION INSTITUTIONS IN INDIA

The only sure way to incorruptibility is changed individual values and social norms, making corruption unacceptable. Since how to achieve this is not well understood, a widely accepted second-best strategy is to improve institutions of governance. Important improvements include few, transparent regulations; transparency through institutions to effectively implement legislated rights to information about government activity; institutions promoting accountability including independent audit of government bureaus; a free press and civil society involvement in public education and government monitoring; effective citizens' grievance redressal channels; and performance incentives for government servants. A reduced government role through privatization and deregulation can itself bring down corruption though, as a telling example in Bardhan (1997) makes clear, indiscriminate privatization of even corrupt government functions is not advisable.

Unfortunately, existing anti-corruption institutions in India are yet to attain this best-practice ideal, though some significant initiatives exist. Instead, governance reform in India has focused mainly on privatization and, second, automating government departments and procedures. Concurrent institutional reform to ensure that information and transparency advantages of automation actually result in improved performance and reduced corruption is largely absent.

While India's legal framework has important enabling laws including the Prevention of Corruption Act and Right to Information Acts in several states, their implementation is grossly inadequate. Even in cases where court action is initiated, rulings take a long time and are often inconclusive. Existing anti-corruption agencies such as the CVC and, in part, the CAG have had limited success in curbing public corruption. The setting up of a key agency, the Lok Pal (the central ombudsman), has been pending for decades.

There have been some successes in civil society monitoring to combat corruption. Prominent examples are institutionalized public hearings by the Mazdoor Kisan Shakti Sangathan in Rajasthan (Bhatia and Drèze 1998) and survey-based public service report cards for different public agencies conducted by some NGOs.

Despite the limited overall success to date, the relative effectiveness of India's democracy is often seen to be a check on the severity of corruption. As Bardhan suggests, corruption is also likely to decline as India develops.

ARINDAM DAS-GUPTA

REFERENCES

Banerjee, Abhijit V. 1997. 'A Theory of Misgovernance', *Quarterly Journal of Economics*, 112(4): 1289–1332.

Bardhan, Pranab. 1997. 'Corruption and Development: A Review of Issues', *Journal of Economic Literature*, 35: 1320–46.

Bhatia, Bela and Jean Drèze. 1998. 'Campaign in Rural India', Berlin: Transparency International, http://www.transparency.org/working_papers/bhatia-dreze/bhatia-dreze.html (accessed in February 2005).

Caseley, Jonathan. 2004. 'Public Sector Reform and Corruption: CARD Façade in Andhra Pradesh', *Economic and Political Weekly*, 39, 13 March: 1151–6.

Mookherjee, Dilip. 1997. 'Incentive Reform in Developing Country Bureaucracies: Lessons from Tax Administration', in B. Pleskovic and J. Stiglitz, eds, *Annual World Bank Conference on Development Economics, 1997*, Washington D.C., World Bank.

Sanyal, Amal. 2000. 'Audit Hierarchy in a Corrupt Tax Administration', *Journal of Comparative Economics*, 28(2): 364–78.

Vittal, N. (Central Vigilance Commissioner). 2002. 'Initiatives for Tackling Corruption in Public Life in India', Paper presented at the International Video Link Session with British and Indian Participants, British Council, New Delhi.

Data Sets

India stands out among its peers in the breadth and depth of data gathered and disseminated. The richness and credibility of these data is testified by the generations of researchers across the globe who have worked on Indian data. This achievement is rooted in the need, felt in the earliest post-Independence years, for creating a strong statistical system for economic planning (Government of India 2001a). With the establishment of the Central Statistical Unit in 1949 and the Directorate of the National Sample Survey in 1950, India has seen regular, systematic collection of nationwide statistics, often through household and firm surveys. This activity has been remarkable in scale and scope.

In recent years, the availability of these data has improved tremendously. To give an example, any researcher can easily purchase detailed Census or National Sample Survey data, or download the latest agricultural statistics from official websites. In addition to these official data, there is easy access to several datasets which were collected or compiled by other public or private agencies.

Without claiming to be exhaustive, this entry gives a brief outline of these data, focusing on prominent household- and enterprise-level data sets, most of which are in the public domain. Major sources of statistics on wages, prices, production, agricultural conditions, finance, education, health, and nutrition are also discussed. Some of the databases covered here have been dealt with in detail in Chandrashekhar and Tilak (2001).

HOUSEHOLD DATA
National Sample Survey Organisation (NSSO)
The NSSO is the nodal agency for conducting surveys for the Government of India. The NSSO has conducted nationwide

multi-subject integrated socio-economic sample surveys of rural and urban areas since 1950. The wide variety of subjects covered by the NSS can be classified under five broad categories: household surveys covering socio-economic aspects, including the regular employment–unemployment surveys and consumption expenditure surveys; surveys on landholding, livestock, and agriculture; establishment surveys; enterprise surveys; and village surveys (Government of India 2001b). Large, 'thick' sample consumption and employment–unemployment surveys are conducted on a quinquennial basis. Annual surveys involve smaller, 'thin' samples and are based on different sampling designs. Decennial surveys are collected on unorganized enterprises in the non-agricultural sector, landholdings, and livestock enterprises, and on population, births, deaths, disability, morbidity, fertility, maternity and child care, and family planning (Government of India 2001b). Unit-level data sets from 1983 onwards are in the public domain; the data are available after a gap of approximately one–two years. Published reports can be accessed at http://mospi.gov.in.

Consumption Surveys: Consumption surveys form the basis of official poverty estimates in India. Consumption surveys are conducted annually on a small sample basis; larger sample surveys are conducted every five years. The survey collects comprehensive data on a household's consumption of goods and services as well as its socio-economic characteristics. Households are asked to state the value and quantity of goods consumed, as well as the source of consumption. Prior to the 55th round conducted in 1999, these surveys measured consumption using a thirty-day recall period for all items of consumption. Since the 55th round, changes in the recall period for low frequency items such as education,

health, durables, clothing, and footwear have raised concerns about the comparability of consumption, poverty, and inequality measures over time (see Sen 2000; Sen and Himanshu 2004a, 2004b; Deaton and Drèze 2002; Deaton and Kozel 2005, for further details).

Employment–Unemployment Surveys: These five-yearly surveys canvass household-level data on the employment status and wage labour earnings of individual members, as well as various socio-economic characteristics. The NSSO also collects annual information on employment and unemployment within the annual small sample consumption expenditure surveys. In a number of earlier rounds, the NSSO experimented with concepts and methodologies before settling on their current approach, which has remained more or less unchanged since the 27th round (in 1972–3). Official employment statistics are based on the usual activity principal status approach. Since 1977–8, these surveys have also been the source for the Rural Labour Enquiry and Agricultural Labour Enquiry.

Population Census
The decennial population census of India contains a snapshot of the demographic and socio-economic profile of the population of India. The first census was conducted in 1872; the design, conduct, and scope of the census have altered substantially since its inception and, in particular, since the Census Act of 1948 delegated the responsibility for the systematic collection of population data to the Office of the Registrar General and Census Commissioner. The census collects information on economic activity and socio-economic characteristics and village-level amenities. For the earlier years, detailed tables containing population profiles at a disaggregated level have been published in a hard-copy format. Since 1991 detailed tables

have been made available in both soft as well as hard copy format. The census has recently released unit-level data at the 5 per cent and 10 per cent sample. Further details can be found at http://www.censusindia.gov.in.

National Council of Applied Economic Research (NCAER)

Additional Rural Incomes Survey (ARIS)/ Rural Economic Development Survey (REDS): The ARIS/REDS panel data set covers 259 villages in 17 states between 1969 and 1999. The ARIS data set was designed to constitute a nationally representative sample of Indian households in 1969. It covers 4756 households for three crop years from 1968–9 and contains questions on economic, demographic, and village-level characteristics. The REDS data, collected in 1982 and 1999, contain more detailed measures of household-level consumption, investment, and income-generating activities, and also a detailed demographic module covering all adult women in the sample. Households in the REDS data can be linked up to those in the 1971 ARIS data to form a panel. The 1999 round of the data set is one of the first to capture all surviving as well as all split-off households. A further unique feature of the 1999 data is the inclusion of a module capturing data on all siblings and children of the household head, whether present in the village or not. The data are available online at http://adfdell.pstc.brown.edu/arisreds_data/.

India Human Development Survey: This household-level nationally representative survey contains a wide range of questions covering social and economic conditions; 41,554 households in 1503 villages and 971 urban areas are covered; village, school, and medical infrastructure are captured in separate surveys. Household-level data are publicly available online at tp://www.ihds.umd.edu.

International Crop Research Institute in the Semi-Arid Tropics (ICRISAT)

Village Level Studies (VLS) is a high-frequency panel data set initiated in 1975 in six villages in Andhra Pradesh and Maharashtra. The survey was further expanded to include two villages—one in Gujarat (in 1980) and the other in Madhya Pradesh (in 1981). Information from forty households was collected in each village using twelve questionnaires designed to cover the key aspects of income-generating and consumption activities of agricultural households (Walker and Ryan 1990). Data on transactions, income, and consumption was collected on a three–four weekly basis, whilst data on assets was collected on a yearly basis. Four of the six original ICRISAT villages were revisited in 1992; ICRISAT resumed annual data collection on the six original villages in 2002 and the three–four weekly data collection resumed in 2005, at which point all split-off households were captured. The data are available for download online at www.economics.ox.ac.uk/members/stefan.dercon/icrisat/ICRISAT/usingthedata.html.

National Family Health Survey (NFHS)

Since the first survey conducted in 1992–3, two more rounds of this nationally representative survey have been conducted in 1998–9 and 2005–6. The survey collects information on population, health, and nutrition, with an emphasis on women and young children. NFHS-3 additionally covered HIV/AIDS. State and national-level reports are available in soft- and hard-copy format. The unit-level data are publicly available for download through the Demographic and Health Survey website at ww.measuredhs.com.

Living Standards Measurement Survey (LSMS)

The LSMS of household and village characteristics was conducted by the World

Bank in 1997–8. A total of 2250 households were interviewed in 120 villages drawn from a sample of twenty-five districts in Uttar Pradesh and Bihar (World Bank 1998). A follow-up survey conducted in 2008 covers a sub-sample of the original households in Uttar Pradesh. Household data includes information on economic activities, health, education, expenditures, and production. The data from the first wave are available for download online from the World Bank website at www.worldbank.org/lsms/

FIRM DATA
Economic Census

The Economic Census enumerates all establishments engaged in the production or distribution of goods and services other than for the sole purpose of self-consumption (Government of India 2005). The census is conducted by the Central Statistical Organisation (CSO), a department in the Ministry of Statistics and Programme Implementation, Government of India. It covers all establishments without hired workers ('Own Account Establishments', or household enterprises), as well as those with hired workers ('Directory and Non-Directory Establishments'), the only major exception being those engaged in crop production and plantation. Since the main purpose of the census is to establish a frame which can be used for more detailed surveys of enterprises, it has a short questionnaire which primarily collects information on enterprises ownership, type of activity, and number of hired and unpaid workers, all disaggregated by gender.

The CSO has conducted five Economic Censuses since 1977. Unit-level data from the Third, Fourth and Fifth Economic Censuses (conducted in 1990, 1998, and 2005, respectively) are publicly available (http://mospi.gov.in/ecdt.htm).

Annual Survey of Industries (ASI)

The ASI is a large plant-level survey conducted nationwide by the CSO. The ASI frame comprises all industrial units ('factories') employing more than twenty workers (or more than ten workers if they use power) which, as required by the Factories Act, are registered with the Chief Inspector of Factories in each state. Thus, the ASI is representative of manufacturing units registered under the Factories Act, and does not cover the informal manufacturing sector.

The ASI frame is divided into a 'census sector' and a 'sample sector'. All factories employing more than 100 workers are covered in the census sector, and smaller factories are covered in the sample sector. Originally, nearly half of all units in the sample sector were covered every year. This sampling rate dropped to about one-third in 1987–8 and to one-fifth in 2004–5. The sample sector is stratified by state and industry, which ensures that the survey includes factories from more than 3000 state-industry groups.

Unit-level ASI data sets for the years 1974 through 2000 are in the public domain and are available at http://mospi. nic.in/mospi_asi.htm. New ASI data are usually made available after a lag of two to three years.

Prowess

Prowess is a publicly available panel data set on public limited companies, compiled by the Centre for Monitoring Indian Economy (CMIE). The panel, which begins in 1989, has data on all the companies listed on the major stock exchanges of India, and on large and medium-sized unlisted companies, including central public sector enterprises. Apart from annual financial data, Prowess has information on plant location, products, inputs, the history of capital changes, bonus and dividends, and stock prices. It also provides descriptive variables such as industry classification, year of incorporation, and group affiliation.

Surveys of Unorganized Manufacturing (NSSO)

A publicly available, unique source of information on informal manufacturing activity in a developing country, the Surveys of Unorganized Manufacturing collect nationally representative data on the 'unorganized manufacturing sector', or all units not registered under the Factories Act (available at http://mospi. nic.in/nsso_4aug2008/web/nsso.htm). By fully covering household enterprises and establishments hiring fewer than ten workers, they serve to fill the gap in the ASI's coverage of manufacturing activity. Using the Economic Censuses as frames, the NSSO has conducted four such surveys, in 1989, 1994, 2000, and 2005. These surveys sampled enterprises from nearly every district in India by stratifying at the district level and collected data on the nature of activity, revenue, expenses, employment, compensation, fixed assets, and borrowing.

Surveys of Service Sector Enterprises (NSSO)

Apart from Surveys of Unorganized Manufacturing enterprises, the NSSO has periodically used the Economic Census frames to survey service-sector enterprises nationwide. There have been two NSSO 'Surveys of Unorganized Services', in 1979–80 and 2001–2. These surveys covered all household and non-household establishments in the services sector, except those in trade and finance. There have also been three surveys of small trading units, in 1985–6, 1990–1, and 1997. These 'Surveys of Non-Directory and Own Account Trade Establishments' covered all wholesale and retail enterprises employing fewer than six workers, including household enterprises. Unit-level data from all NSSO service sector

surveys conducted in the 1990s and later are available publicly at http://mospi.nic. in/nsso_4aug2008/web/nsso.htm.

World Bank Enterprise Survey

In recent years, the World Bank has conducted standardized 'Enterprise Surveys' in several developing countries, including one in India in 2005 (http://www. enterprisesurveys.org). This publicly available survey covers registered establishments in manufacturing and services. Compared to the ASI, it has a small sample size and limited geographical coverage. However, it collects unique firm-level information on many elements of the 'business climate', such as infrastructure and regulations.

OTHER MAJOR DATA SOURCES

Agriculture, Climate and the Environment

World Bank India Agricultural and Climate Data: This publicly available data set is a compilation of officially published Government of India statistics, and contains district-level data for the years 1957–8 through 1986–7 (available at http://ipl. econ.duke.edu/dthomas/dev_data/ datafiles/india_agric_climate.htm). It covers 271 districts, as defined by 1961 boundaries, in thirteen states (Haryana, Punjab, Uttar Pradesh, Gujarat, Rajasthan, Bihar, Orissa, West Bengal, Andhra Pradesh, Tamil Nadu, Karnataka, Maharashtra, and Madhya Pradesh). It has information on area, production, and prices of twenty crops, including areas under high-yielding varieties of major crops. It also contains data on agricultural wages, and on the price and quantity of agricultural inputs, such as fertilizers, bullocks, and tractors. Soil characteristics and thirty-year averages of rainfall and temperature are also included.

'Maryland Indian District Database': This is a similar compilation of district-level data

from census and agricultural sources between 1961 and 1991 (available at http://www.bsos.umd.edu/socy/vanneman/districts/index.html).

Environment: Detailed data (starting in 1871) on rainfall, temperature, and other environmental variables by meteorological stations and subdivisions are available at the Indian Institute of Tropical Meteorology (http://www.tropmet.res.in). The Central Groundwater Board publishes estimates of groundwater resources at district level, categorizations of the depletion of groundwater resources at *taluk* level, as well as maps capturing the hydro-geological features of India (http://www.cgwb.gov.in). Further water-related statistics are published by the Central Water Commission (www.cwc.nic.in). The Ministry of Water Resources publishes data on groundwater contamination, river basins, water resources, water pollution, and water quality (http://www.wrmin.nic.in).

Cost of Cultivation Surveys: A continuation of the Farm Management Studies of the 1960s and 1970s, these surveys have been the responsibility of the Directorate of Economics and Statistics in the Ministry of Agriculture since 1971. They collect data by season on twenty-eight crops in nineteen states, covering almost 9000 households (available at http://www.dacnet.nic.in/eands/Activities.htm).

Agricultural and Livestock Census: Since 1970–1, agricultural censuses have been conducted at five-year intervals. The census collects information relating to the number and area of operational holdings, livestock, and agricultural implements and machinery. Census reports are available at http://agcensus.nic.in.

Minor Irrigation Census: The Ministry of Water Resources has conducted three censuses of minor irrigation projects in

1986–7, 1993–4, and 2000–1. Published reports can be found online at http://wrmin.nic.in/.

Educational Statistics

All India School Education Survey (AISES): Conducted by the National Council for Educational Research and Training (NCERT), it covers the availability of schooling facilities in rural habitations, physical and educational facilities in schools, incentive schemes and beneficiaries, medium of instruction and languages taught, enrolment (including that of scheduled castes, scheduled tribes, girls, and educationally-backward minority communities), teachers and their qualifications, library, laboratory, ancillary staff, and subject-wise enrolment at the secondary stage of education. The data as well as published reports are publicly available. The last round for which the data are available is the 2002 (7th) round (http://7thsurvey.ncert.nic.in/index.htm).

District Information System for Education (DISE): Available since 1995, and managed by the National Institute of Educational Planning and Administration (NIEPA), this public data set provides information on schooling characteristics at district level (www.dise.in).

Annual Status of Education Report (ASER): The ASER Centre has been conducting surveys on the learning abilities of primary school children since 2005. State and national report cards are available online at http://www.asercentre.org.

Health and Nutrition (other than NFHS)

District-Level Household and Facility Survey (DLHS): The DLHS is conducted and disseminated by the Ministry of Health and Family Welfare, in collaboration with International Institute of Population Sciences. Previously known as Reproductive and Child Health (RCH) survey, it has information on immunization coverage, institutional delivery, and contraceptive prevalence. Detailed data are made available after the reports are released (http://www.rchiips.org/index.html).

Nutritional and Diet Assessment Surveys: These surveys have been conducted by the National Nutrition Monitoring Board since 1975. Although the detailed data are not in the public domain, the published reports are accessible at http://www.nnmbindia.org.

Price Data
Three consumer price indices and one wholesale price index are available for India.

Wholesale Price Index (WPI): Collected and disseminated by the Office of the Economic Adviser (Ministry of Commerce and Industry), this is the main source of information on inflation in the Indian economy. The data are available on a weekly basis for various commodity groups, but there is no state- or sector-wise break-up (http://eaindustry.nic.in).

Consumer Price Index for Agricultural Labourers (CPIAL): This index (along with the consumer price index for rural labourers) is brought out by the Labour Bureau on a monthly basis. It is based on price data collected from various rural centres, and is the only price index for rural areas. Recent data can be accessed at www.labourbureau.nic.in.

Consumer Price Index for Industrial Workers (CPIIW): The CPIIW is the urban counterpart of the CPIAL. It is available on a monthly basis for various urban centres, and it is possible to generate state-level indices using centre weights. The CPIAL and CPIIW are also brought out as annual reports, though with a lag. Recent data can be accessed at www.labourbureau.nic.in.

Consumer Price Index for Urban Non-manual Employees (CPIUNME): This is relevant to urban non-manual employees, and can also be used to index the salaries of public-sector employees. It is available on a monthly basis, but stands discontinued since April 2008.

Wage Data Other than the NSS
Wage Rates in Rural India: This new series of wage data is published by the NSSO and Labour Bureau and has been collected since 1986–7, as part of the effort to amass information for the new series of consumer price indices beginning 1986–7. It has been published monthly in the *Indian Labour Journal* since April 1998. The data are presented for 11 agricultural and seven non-agricultural operations, by sex and age-group. Annual reports are also available at www.labourbureau.nic.in.

Agricultural Wages in India: The oldest wage series available in India, it is collected and disseminated by the Ministry of Agriculture, and contains district-wise data on wages in various agricultural operations. It is published in a monthly publication of the ministry called *Agricultural Situation in India*, and after scrutiny and verification, in the annual *Agricultural Wages in India*.

CACP (Commission for Agricultural Cost and Prices): In reports on the cost of cultivation, the CACP provides data on wages by crops and agricultural season. Reports are available at www.dacnet.nic.in/cacp.

Other
World Bank India Poverty Data Set: It contains poverty and inequality indicators, along with wages, state domestic product, price indices, and other state characteristics. The series ends in 1993 but is being updated (http://go.worldbank.org/SWGZB45DN0).

National Habitation Survey: Conducted and disseminated by the Department of Water, this survey provides information on various village facilities such as schools and health centres, and on water quality in habitations.

Election Data: Detailed data by constituencies and contestants is available at the Election Commission of India for all the elections since independence, including state assembly elections (www.eci.gov.in). The Centre for the Study of Developing Societies (CSDS) collects pre- and post-poll data for national- and state-level generation elections (http://www.csds.in/). The CSDS data is not yet in the public domain.

Reserve Bank of India (RBI): The RBI's Database on the Indian Economy (http://dbie.rbi.org.in/) contains macroeconomic time-series data on areas such as money and banking, public finance, consumption, savings, and investment. Also available at the RBI's website are recent issues of several RBI publications containing data on banking. For example, *Statistical Tables Relating to Banks of India* contain data on the number of offices, assets, liabilities, deposits, and advances of banks, disaggregated by state or by rural/urban location. *Branch Banking Statistics* have district-wise data on the number of branches of commercial banks.

REENA BADIANI, SIDDHARTH
SHARMA, AND HIMANSHU

REFERENCES

Chandrashekhar, C.P. and J.B.G. Tilak. 2001. *India's Socio-economic Database: Surveys of Selected Areas*, New Delhi, Tulika.

Deaton, Angus and Jean Drèze. 2002. 'Poverty and Inequality in India, A Re-examination', *Economic and Political Weekly*, 37(36).

Deaton, Angus and Valerie Kozel. 2005. *The Great Indian Poverty Debate*, New Delhi, MacMillan.

Government of India. 2001a. *Report of the National Statistical Commission*.

Government of India. 2001b. *Concepts and Definitions Used in NSS*, Golden Jubilee Publication, Government of India, Ministry of Statistics and Programme Implementation, National Sample Survey Organisation.

Government of India. 2005. *Economic Census 2005: All India Report*. Government of India, Ministry of Statistics and Programme Implementation, Central Statistical Organisation.

Sen, Abhijit. 2000. 'Estimates of Consumer Expenditure and Its Distribution: Statistical Priorities after NSS 55th Round', *Economic and Political Weekly*, 16–22 December.

Sen, Abhijit and Himanshu. 2004a. 'Poverty and Inequality in India-I', *Economic and Political Weekly*, 18 September.

_____. 2004b. 'Poverty and Inequality in India: Widening Disparities in the 1990s', *Economic and Political Weekly*, 2 September.

Walker, Thomas S. and James G. Ryan. 1990. *Village and Household Economies in India's Semi-arid Tropics*, Baltimore, John Hopkins University Press.

World Bank. 1998. 'Survey of Living Conditions, Uttar Pradesh and Bihar: Introduction to the Datasets'.

Democracy and Social Welfare

QUESTIONS

The relation between democracy and social welfare raises two rather different types of questions. There is, first, the immediately *practical* issue of the pursuit of social welfare: does democracy help that pursuit or hinder the enhancement of social welfare? The second issue is more *conceptual*, and in many ways more difficult. Given the well-known problems in arriving at any cogent and coherent notion of social welfare, we have to ask whether democracy might help to resolve these difficulties.

The last question is almost exactly what Kenneth Arrow asked in his famous book *Social Choice and Individual Values* (1951), as a response to the growing scepticism about not only the cogency but also the reach of what was then on-going welfare economics, which was well reflected in Jan Graaff's superbly nihilistic assessment in his *Theoretical Welfare Economics* (1947). In fact, however, Arrow's discovery of the famous 'impossibility theorem'—to be discussed presently—added further gloom to pre-existing pessimism, as it seemed to take welfare economics out of an inhospitable frying pan into an annihilating fire. We have to ask whether that pessimism reflected a correct reading of the analytical work of Arrow and also how the relationship between democracy and social welfare now looks, after half a century of active work in social choice theory, to a great extent inspired by Arrow's pioneering move.

These questions are of considerable practical importance for the history of modern India, and, not surprisingly, they have attracted the attention of a great many Indian intellectuals—primarily economists but also others. Following India's independence from British rule in 1947, the newly independent country chose a resolutely democratic constitution. There was, at that time, no other poor country in the world with a democratic political system. The leaders of new India were also much occupied, indeed obsessed, with promoting economic and social development in the country and the idea of social welfare was constantly invoked in direct and indirect ways. It is interesting to ask: how do democracy and development relate empirically as well as conceptually, at the sixtieth anniversary of the birth of a democratic India?

PRACTICAL CONNECTIONS

While the champions of democracy have been reticent to suggest that Indian democracy would itself promote development and enhancement of social welfare (they saw both as good but separate goals), the detractors of democracy were soon quite willing to diagnose what they saw as serious tensions. The advocates of a practical split—'do you want democracy or do you want development?'—often came from East Asian countries, and their voice grew in influence as several of these countries became immensely successful in promoting economic growth without pursuing democracy. The observation of a handful of such examples led rapidly to something of a general theory: democracies do quite badly in facilitating development, compared with what authoritarian regimes can achieve. Didn't South Korea, Singapore, Taiwan, and Hong Kong achieve astonishingly fast economic progress without fulfilling the basic requirements of democratic governance? And after the economic reforms in China in 1979, didn't authoritarian China fare a lot better in terms of economic growth than democratic India?

To deal with these issues, we have to pay particular attention both to the content of what can be called development and to the interpretation of democracy (in particular to the respective roles of voting and of public reasoning). The assessment of development cannot be divorced from the lives that people can lead and the real freedoms that they enjoy. Development can scarcely be seen merely in terms of enhancement of inanimate objects of convenience, such as a rise in the gross national product (GNP) (or in personal incomes), or industrialization—important as they may be as means to the real ends. Their value must depend on what they do to the lives and freedoms of the people involved, which must be central to the idea of development.

If development is seen in this way, then it becomes immediately clear that the relation between development and democracy has to be seen partly in terms of their constitutive connection, rather than only through their external linkages. Even though the question has often been asked as to whether political freedom is 'conducive to development', we must not miss the crucial recognition that political liberties and democratic rights are *among* the 'constituent components' of development. Their relevance for development does not have to be established indirectly through their contribution to the growth of GNP.

However, after acknowledging this central connection, we also have to subject democracy to consequential analysis, since there are *other* kinds of freedoms as well—other than political liberties and civil rights—to which attention must be paid. We must be concerned, for example, with economic poverty. We do, therefore, have reason to be interested in economic growth, seen even in the rather limited terms of growth of GNP or GDP (gross domestic product) per head, since raising real income can clear the way for the really important achievements. For example, the general connection between economic growth and poverty removal is fairly well established now, supplemented by distributional concerns.

The much articulated scepticism about the compatibility of democracy and rapid economic growth was based on some selected cross-country comparisons, focusing particularly on rapidly growing East Asia, on one side, and India, on the other, with its long history of modest growth of GNP, hovering around 3 per cent per annum. However, fuller cross-country comparisons, for what they are worth (and they cannot be worth less than basing a conclusion on a handful of selected inter-country contrasts), have not provided empirical support for the belief that democracy is inimical to economic growth.[1] And while India used to be cited as living proof that democratic countries are destined to grow much more slowly than authoritarian ones, now that India's economic growth has become much faster (this began in the 1980s but was firmly consolidated through the economic reforms of the 1990s), it becomes hard to use India as the quintessential example of the slowness of economic progress under democratic governance. India is no less democratic today than it was in the 1960s or 1970s. Indeed, the evidence is overwhelming that growth is helped by the supportiveness of the economic climate rather than by the ruthlessness of the political system.

All this challenges the 'development-versus-democracy school', but it would also seem to suggest that there was wisdom in the reticence of the advocates of democracy in India in not basing their case on the contribution of democracy to economic growth, but on the importance of democracy itself as a part of good living. As far as economic growth is concerned, this would call for good economic policies, not bad political fierceness. But what must also be noted here is that despite the dominance of befuddled economic policies in India for many decades, the democratic system itself allowed some of the necessary reforms that could make economic growth much faster.

Furthermore, we have to go beyond economic growth to understand the fuller demands of development and of the economic components of social welfare. Attention must be paid to the extensive evidence that democracy and political and civil rights tend to enhance

[1] Recent publications by Adam Przeworski and Robert J. Barro easily come to mind.

freedoms of other kinds (such as economic security) through giving voice, at least in many circumstances, to the deprived and the vulnerable. The fact that no major famine has ever occurred in a functioning democratic country with regular elections, active opposition parties, basic freedom of speech, and a relatively free media (even when the country is very poor and in a seriously adverse food situation) merely illustrates the most elementary aspect of the protective power of political liberty. Though Indian democracy has many imperfections, the political incentives generated by it have been adequate to eliminate major famines right from the time of Independence (the last famine was four years before that, in 1943), unlike in China which did have the largest famine in recorded history in 1959–62, the mortality from which is estimated to be around 30 million. The history of famines has had close links with colonialism (as in British India or Ireland), one-party states (as in the Soviet Union in the 1930s, or in China or Cambodia later on), and military dictatorships (as in Ethiopia or Somalia). The very recent famines, such as those in North Korea and Sudan, have also occurred in non-democratic authoritarian regimes.

It is worth mentioning in this context that doubts about the reach of this proposition have sometimes been raised by referring to the fact that there have been famines, or at least conditions approximating famines, in a few countries that have started having political elections of a democratic kind. Niger is sometimes cited as an example of this kind of contrary case. The point to recognize here, as *The New York Times* noted in an editorial in August 2005, is that the presumed connection with famine prevention applies specifically to *functioning* democracies; the adoption of a voting format is not itself adequate for the rationale of the process. The direct penalties

of a famine are borne only by the suffering public and not by the ruling government. The rulers never starve. However, when a government is accountable to the public, and when there is free news reporting and uncensored public criticism, then the government too has good reasons to do its best to eradicate famines.

The protective power of democracy in providing security is, in fact, much more extensive than famine prevention alone. The poor in booming South Korea or Indonesia may not have given much thought to democracy when the economic fortunes of all seemed to go up and up together in the 1980s and early 1990s, but when the economic crises came (and divided they fell) in the late 1990s, democracy and political and civil rights were desperately missed by those whose economic means and lives were unusually battered. Democracy suddenly became a central issue in these countries, with South Korea taking a major lead, and it led to the consolidation of democracy elsewhere as well, including in Thailand.

India has certainly benefited from the protective role of democracy in giving the rulers excellent political incentive to act supportively when disasters threaten. However, the practice of democracy in India is still quite imperfect. Democracy gives an opportunity to the opposition to press for policy change even when the problem is chronic and has had a long history rather than acute and sudden, as in the case of famines. The weakness of Indian social policies on school education, basic healthcare, elementary nutrition, essential land reform, and gender equity reflects deficiencies of politically engaged public reasoning and social pressure, not just mistaken public policies.

Democratic freedoms can certainly be used to make it more embarrassing for the state and central governments to continue with these neglects. The process, however, is not automatic and requires activism on the part of politically engaged citizens. The connection between democracy and the pursuit of social welfare, while largely positive, cannot be entirely left to institutional virtuosity. It calls for active work of human agency in using the institutional opportunities for pursuing important ends.[2]

CONCEPTUAL LINKS

I turn now to the conceptual linkage between democracy and social welfare, going beyond the empirical connections. Arrow's impossibility theorem was formulated at exactly the time when newly independent India was adopting its democratic constitution. The theorem and related results have fascinated a great many Indian academics (in addition, of course, to academics elsewhere). Arrow (1951) thought it natural to give expression to the basic democratic thought that the assessment of social welfare must be based on individual preferences about alternative states of affairs, and the connection must respect what he took to be some elementary conditions linking the two, such as (1) if everyone prefers some state to another then the former must be higher in social welfare than the latter, (2) if everyone's ranking of two states remains the same, then so must be the social ranking of the two, (3) and no person alone can determine the social ranking irrespective of the preferences of others.[3]

Arrow himself did not draw any clearly anti-democratic conclusion from his analytical findings, but that became the common reading of his mathematical result. Perhaps the most weighty expression of that negative conclusion can be found in the writings of William Riker, a leading political analyst in the field of democracy, particularly in his forcefully argued book, *Liberalism against Populism* (1980). Riker argued that there are two rationales for democratic process—what he calls 'populist' and 'liberal'. The former linked democracy to the identification and pursuit of social goals (such as social welfare), and this, Riker argued, has been proved to be incoherent by social choice results, particularly Arrow's. The latter view of democracy (the 'liberal' one, that is), which Riker argued was immune to Arrow's impossibility result, does not seek to establish any general social goal like social welfare, but only demands certain basic processes of making acceptable social decisions, such as removing oppressive authorities. He was, therefore, in favour of delinking democracy and the goal of social welfare, and seeing democracy instead as merely demanding certain basic requirements of social choosability.

The question we have to ask, then, is this: are the impossibility results of social choice theory (Arrow's and related ones) best understood as showing the incoherence of an aggregated ordering (representing social welfare or something like that) based on democratic aggregation of individual

---

[2] These lines of enquiry are pursued further at a conceptual level in Sen (1999) and in the context of India in Basu (2004).

[3] The examples of the conditions imposed by Arrow are made simpler in this statement based on later works, mainly Sen (1970) and Pattanaik (1971). This is an area where the Indian contribution to the global debate and scientific advance has been substantial with contributions from Rajat Deb, Bhaskar Dutta, Ashok Guha, Satish Jain, Tapas Majumdar, Manimay Sengupta, and S. Subramanian. Studies of other economic problems, particularly of development economics, by leading Indian theorists have also been richly informed by social choice perspectives, well illustrated by the works of Kaushik Basu, Ravi Kanbur, Mukul Majumdar, Tapan Mitra, Dilip Mookherjee, and Debraj Ray.

preferences? The answer, I fear, is: no, not at all. The first point to note is that even when we drop the idea of social welfare or social good (and what Riker calls 'popular will'), we can get exactly similar impossibility results to Arrow's, merely with the idea that democratic choice should satisfy certain basic conditions of choosability (like Riker's), even without trying to derive a ranking of social welfare. Indeed, Arrow's conditions can be readily translated into such conditions of choosability for democratic governance (closely in line with Riker's 'liberal' requirements) and we would still get an impossibility. It turns out that the idea of a social goal, or that of an aggregate ranking of social welfare, is entirely redundant in getting over the impasse (see Sen 1993).

The second point to note here is that the main contribution of results like Arrow's is to demonstrate the possibility that general principles of social decisions that initially look plausible enough could turn out to be quite problematic since they may, in fact, conflict with the combined consequences of other general principles which also look plausible enough. We tend to think—if only implicitly—of principles in terms of their plausibility in a few particular cases which focus our attention on those ideas, but once the principles are formulated in very general terms—covering inter alia a great many cases other than those that motivated our interest in those principles—we can run into unforeseen difficulties. We then have to decide what has to give and why. Whether we think of social decisions in terms of some kind of a social ordering or a partial ranking (as in what Riker calls the 'populist' reading—a rather unfortunate term), or in the form of conditions of choosability (what he sees as the 'liberal' reading), we have to face problems of consistency between plausible—or apparently plausible—general principles.

But those conflicts can, of course, be precisely the subject matter of public reasoning. If it turns out, for example, that in order to safeguard the liberties of all, we have to cultivate tolerance of each other, then that is a public-reasoning justification of cultivating tolerance. Democracy is not only an arena of coming to terms with diverse— and possibly conflicting—demands on society and governance, it is also the arena in which such conflicts can be addressed not just through some mechanical procedure of voting, but through interactive societal discussion and public reasoning.

This has a historical connection too. When, in the history of India, visionary political leaders in the form of Emperor Ashoka in the third century BC or Emperor Akbar in the late sixteenth century argued for public discussion to resolve differences, they certainly were not aware of any 'impossibility results' that would be formulated many centuries later. But they did understand that society cannot work harmoniously, nor can the goals of different members of society all be taken into account, except through interactive public discussion.

If interest in public discussion is strong in Arrow's own work (many of them outside social choice theory),[4] the eighteenth-century pioneers of mathematical politics, in particular Marquis de Condorcet, were strongly involved in wanting a society with active dialogues and public encounters. Indeed, Condorcet's insistence on the importance of women's education was linked, among other things, to his recognition of the need for women's voice in public affairs. That basic connection between public reasoning, on the one hand, and the demands of

[4]References must also be made here to the powerful contributions of James Buchanan in emphasizing the role of public discussion and give and take for public choice.

democracy, on the other, is central not just to the practical task of making democracy more effective (this was discussed in the last section), but also to the conceptual problem of basing an adequately articulated idea of social welfare on the demands of democratic governance.

The connection between democracy and social welfare—both conceptual and practical—is, thus, not a mechanical entity, but a constructive process that turns critically on the role of inclusive and unfettered public discussion and political action, which is, of course, central to the philosophy of democracy. This is, as should be obvious, an entirely general point, not specific to India at all, and yet, given its history, the connection is particularly significant for India. Its record of successes as well as failures, so far, has been closely linked with the force and effectiveness with which public reasoning has been used in India. There is something of importance here, I would argue, for India's future as well.

AMARTYA SEN

REFERENCES

Arrow, K.J. 1951. *Social Choice and Individual Values*, New York, Wiley.

Basu, K. ed. 2004. *India's Emerging Economy: Performance and Prospects in the 1990s and Beyond*, Cambridge, MA, MIT Press; New Delhi, Oxford University Press.

Graaff, J. de v. 1947. *Theoretical Welfare Economics*, Cambridge, Cambridge University Press.

Pattanaik, P.K. 1971. *Voting and Collective Choice*, Cambridge, Cambridge University Press.

Riker, W.H. 1980. *Liberalism against Populism*, San Francisco, W. H. Freeman.

Sen, A. 1970. *Collective Choice and Social Welfare*, San Francisco, Holden-Day.

———. 1993. 'Internal Consistency of Choice', *Econometrica*, 61.

———. 1999. *Development as Freedom*, New York, Alfred Knopf; New Delhi, Oxford University Press, 2000.

Growth Experience[1]

India's economic performance during the first three decades since Independence was christened the 'Hindu' rate of growth, a term connoting a disappointing but not disastrous outcome, and playing on the cliché of acquiescence in the present that the religion supposedly imparts, because of a greater emphasis on the hereafter.

That cliché, of course, is gradually lapsing into disuse thanks to the remarkable transformation in India during the last twenty-five years. Since 1980, its economic growth rate has more than doubled, rising from 1.7 per cent (in per capita terms) in 1950–80 to nearly 4 per cent thereafter. Shackled by the socialist policies and the 'license-permit-quota raj' (to use Rajaji's memorable phrase) of the past, India used to serve as an exemplar of development strategies gone wrong. It has now become the latest poster child for how economic growth can be unleashed with a turn towards free markets and open trade. India has yet to catch up with China's growth rates (or China's level of income), but thanks to its solid democratic institutions and impressive performance in information technology, the country is increasingly vying with China as the country of the future.

This entry describes and analyses the Indian growth experience from two perspectives. First, it documents the facts on India's *aggregate* growth performance over time and presents a view on when and why it turned around. Second, it lists the facts relating to *growth across the states* within India, and offers explanations for the variation in state-level economic growth. Lastly, it raises some questions for the future, relating to aggregate and state-level growth.

[1]This entry draws extensively upon Rodrik and Subramanian (2004, 2005) and Kochhar et al. (2006).

AGGREGATE GROWTH

The most striking fact about India's growth has been the remarkable turnaround in nearly all measures of growth performance since 1980 (Figure 1). Output per capita, output per worker, as well as total factor productivity accelerated sharply after 1980. For example, total factor productivity (TFP), which grew at about 0.3 per cent per annum during the 1960–80 period, grew at close to 2 per cent per annum in the following two decades.

A growth accounting decomposition also shows that the contribution of growth of TFP to overall labour productivity growth, which was meagre prior to 1980 was exceptionally high—about 60 per cent—between 1980 and 2000, a performance that was only surpassed by China (Table 1). Indian per capita income growth since 1980 has therefore been extensive—motored by productivity—and

hence sustainable in the future, rather than based on capital accumulation (or deferred gratification), which runs into the limits imposed by diminishing returns to capital. From being a caricature of inefficiency, India has become the model for high and efficient growth.

This turnaround has also been true at the level of the three major sectors, especially manufacturing and services (Table 1). Agricultural growth accelerated by about 2.7 per cent between the 1970s and 1980s, and manufacturing and services posted growth rates of over 6 per cent in the 1980s and 1990s compared to about 2–3 per cent in the years before that.

The surge in Indian growth after 1980 was accompanied by a reduction in the instability of growth. The standard deviation in the growth of output per worker which was 3.7 pre-1980 declined

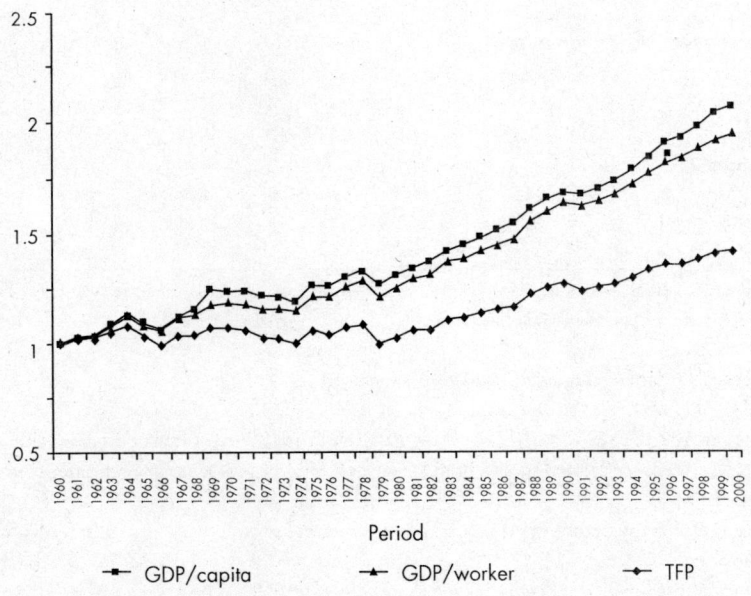

Figure 1   Economic Performance in India 1960–2000
(log scale, 1960=1)

Source: Dani Rodrik and Arvind Subramanian. 2005. 'From Hindu Growth to Productivity Surge: The Mystery of the Indian Growth Transition', *IMF Staff Papers*, 52(2).

Table 1   India: Aggregated and Sectoral Growth Accounting (annual average growth rates, unless otherwise specified)

	1960–70	1970–80	1980–90	1990–9
Bosworth–Collins (B–C)				
Output	3.84	2.98	5.85	5.59
Output per worker (Q/L)	1.87	0.69	3.90	3.27
Capital per worker	0.83	0.61	1.06	1.32
Education	0.29	0.58	0.32	0.34
Total factor productivity (TFP)	0.74	−0.50	2.49	1.57
IMF				
Output	3.75	3.16	5.64	5.61
Output per worker	1.77	0.86	3.69	3.30
Total factor productivity 1/	1.17	0.47	2.89	2.44
Total factor productivity 2/	−0.94	−2.07	1.28	0.94
Disaggregated growth of Q/L based on current employment shares				
Agriculture 3/	1.20	0.13	2.57	1.29
Manufacturing 4/		2.00	6.30	6.00
Services (B–C) 5/		2.12	6.32	6.57
Services (IMF) 6/		3.14	5.30	6.69
Growth rate of aggregate Q/L with base-period employment share as weights				
Aggregate (B–C)		0.69	3.66	3.08
Aggregate (IMF)		0.86	3.49	3.11
Contribution of labour-shifts to aggregate Q/L growth				
Aggregate (B–C)	n.a.		0.24	0.19
Aggregate (IMF)	n.a.		0.20	0.19
Employment Share 7/		1975	1985	1995
Agriculture		70.8	64.4	60.8
Industry		12.4	15.2	15.8
Services		16.8	20.4	23.4

Sources: Dani Rodrik and S. Subramanian. 2005. 'From Hindu Growth to Productivity Surge: The Mystery of the Indian Growth Transition', *IMF Staff Papers*, 52(2).

1. Based on labour force

2. Based on average years of schooling of population above 15 years of age

3. From World Bank's *World Development Indicators*

4. For the 1980s and 1990s, data from IMF Working Paper; for the 1970s, estimate based on Ahluwalia (1995)

5. Calculated as a residual by deducting weighted average sectoral productivity growth rates from B–C agg. Q/L growth rate

6. Calculated as a residual by deducting weighted average sectoral productivity growth rates from IMF agg. Q/L growth rate

7. Obtained from Ghose (1999). His number for 1977–8 is extrapolated backward to 1975 by applying the trend between 1977–8 and 1983 and his number for 1993–4 is extrapolated forward to 1995 by applying the trend between 1987–8 and 1993–4.

Note: Bosworth–Collins (B–C) is from B. Bosworth and S. Collins. 2003. 'The Empirics of Growth: An Update', Brookings paper on Economic Activity, Brookings Institution: 113–206.

sharply to 1.9 per cent thereafter, a performance that surpassed that of nearly every other country. Thus, in the period after 1980, India has had very high but also very stable growth.

The improvement in India's performance since the 1980s is also confirmed by cross-national evidence in the form of Barro-type cross-country growth regressions for the periods 1960–80 and 1980–99. These regressions suggest that, after controlling for policies, endowments, and initial income, India grew 0.7 per cent per year slower than the average country in the 1960–80 period, but grew 2.1 per cent per year faster than the average country in the 1980–99 period. These results indicate that India's turnaround is not a consequence merely of catching up. In the cross-section, the magnitude of overperformance in the latter period has been substantial and exceeds the magnitude of underperformance in the 1960–80 period (Rodrik and Subramanian 2005).

How can this 'reversal of fortune' around 1980 be explained, especially since in the conventional rendition of the Indian economic story, serious reforms and the break with the dirigiste past occurred when India experienced a serious external crisis in 1991, at least ten years after the turnaround?

A number of plausible explanations can easily be ruled out. External liberalization could not have been a factor because the Indian trade regime actually became more restrictive during the 1980s, and the full impact of trade reforms implemented in the 1990s was only felt at the end of the 1990s. Very little internal reform, of product and labour markets, was witnessed in the 1980s, and the only serious effort in this area—the delicensing of Indian manufacturing—started late in the 1980s and was fairly limited in scope; in other words, it was 'too little, too late' to explain the turnaround in performance.

Another strand of opinion (Ahluwalia 2000; Srinivasan and Tendulkar 2003) downplays what happened in the 1980s, arguing that 'the fiscal expansionism of the 1980s, accompanied by some liberalization of controls on economic activity, generated real GDP growth of more than 5.8 per cent a year. This expansionism, however, was not sustainable and led to the macroeconomic crisis of 1991' (Srinivasan and Tendulkar 2003: 9).

This Keynesian-run-amok explanation is, at first blush, supported by the data. During the 1970s, the average consolidated government deficit averaged 5 per cent of GDP. During the 1980s, this had soared to 9 per cent, an annual increase of 4 percentage points. But it is not clear how demand (fiscal) expansion can explain a large and sustained rise in *trend productivity*. After all, Latin America went on a fiscal binge in the 1970s without experiencing a corresponding improvement in supply-side performance.

The only possible explanation would rely on sustained differences in capacity utilization across time. One way to control for such a demand-induced increase in productivity is to compute the productivity aggregates incorporating changes in capacity utilization. One consistent estimate for the 1970s and 1980s (World Bank 1995) implies an increase in capacity utilization of about 2.7 per cent, which would have the effect of reducing measured TFP growth in the 1980s by about 1 per cent per year. Even on the strong assumption that all this change in capacity is demand induced, the turnaround in TFP growth between the 1970s and 1980s would remain substantial (about 2–2.2 per cent per year).

An alternative explanation comprises three elements. First, there was an attitudinal change on the part of the government in the 1980s, signalling a shift in favour of the private sector, with this shift validated in a very haphazard and gradual manner through actual policy changes. Second, this shift and the limited policy changes were *pro-business* rather than *pro-competition*, aimed primarily at benefiting incumbents in the formal industrial and commercial sectors. Third, these small shifts elicited a large productivity response because India was far away from its income possibility frontier.

Sometime in the early 1980s there was a significant attitudinal change towards the private sector on the part of the national government, led by Indira Gandhi's Congress party. The Congress went from being hostile to private business to mildly supportive, and eventually quite supportive. This change was inaugurated with the return of a much-chastened Indira Gandhi to political power in the 1980s after a three-year rule by the Janata party.

As already noted, there were few significant policy changes in the early 1980s, and the changes later on (beginning in 1985) were restricted largely to some internal liberalization relating to the relaxation of industrial licensing. The limited nature of these changes, as well as the form that they took, is best understood by appreciating the political logic of Indira Gandhi's (and later Rajiv Gandhi's) efforts. These were aimed to gather support from the business establishment rather than to alienate it. Hence there was more action where business support existed—for example in reducing taxes, easing access to imported capital inputs, or liberalizing capacity restrictions—than where it did not—for example in external liberalization.

I make a distinction here between a *pro-market* and *pro-business* orientation. The former focuses on removing impediments to markets and aims to achieve this through economic liberalization. It favours entrants and consumers. A pro-business orientation, on the other hand, is one that focuses on

raising the profitability of the established industrial and commercial establishments. It tends to favour incumbents and producers. Nevertheless, this shift towards a pro-business orientation was the essential trigger that set off the boom of the 1980s.

That an attitudinal change on the part of the national leadership could have such a strong impact on growth is in turn grounded in India's initial conditions. India has very strong political and economic institutions for a country at its income level. It is a democracy where the rule of law generally prevails and property rights are adequately protected. Judged by cross-country norms, it ought to have a level of income that is several times higher (see Rodrik and Subramanian 2004: Table 3). The implication is that relatively minor changes in the policy environment can produce a large growth impact. The suspension of the national government's hostility to the private sector could be interpreted as one such change, something that left little paper trail in actual policies but had an important impact on investors' psychology.

STATE-LEVEL GROWTH

Prior to 1980, the growth rate of the Indian states was mediocre but relatively uniform. After 1980, however, the fortunes of the states diverged considerably (Ahluwalia 2000). Figure 2 plots the log of per capita GDP for all states for every ten years beginning in 1960. From 1980 onwards, there is both an upward trend in the average as well as a wider spread in the distribution of incomes. A more formal test of convergence between states for the four decades suggests that there is clear evidence of fortunes diverging in the 1980s but especially in the 1990s and beyond.

What explains this divergent pattern of growth across states in India? Prior to 1960, it is difficult to explain this variation because

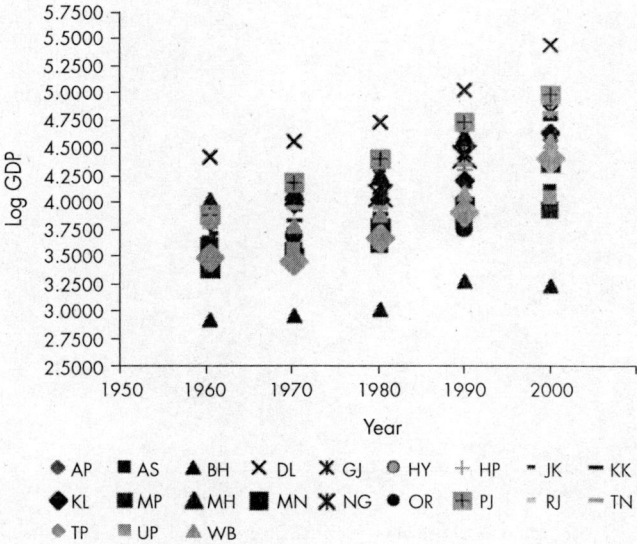

Figure 2   Divergence across States 1960–2000

Source: Dani Rodrik and Arvind Subramanian. 2005. 'From Hindu Growth to Productivity Surge: The Mystery of the Indian Growth Transition', *IMF Staff Papers*, 52(2).

economic decision-making was largely centralized. After 1980, however, some clearer patterns become evident. It appears that two sets of factors played a role. First, different states had different pre-existing capabilities. But these remained latent and could not find expression until the economic environment changed. The trigger—the second set—was the liberalization begun in 1980, and especially the decentralization of economic power that was forced by the changing political landscape after 1980. Thus it was the interaction between pre-existing capabilities and the twin triggers of liberalization and decentralization that explains how the different states fared.

What was this pre-existing capability? It turns out that this capability was something more than a state's level of development or educational level or geography. It is best captured by how diversified a state's manufacturing base was. This diversified base is probably a proxy for some generalized

capability—human capital, entrepreneurial spirit, organizational capital—that could exploit a favourable economic environment.

Figure 3 illustrates this capability at work. It plots the Herfindahl coefficient of concentration within manufacturing in the different states in the early 1980s against their subsequent overall growth rates. The relationship is strongly negative; that is, the less concentrated the manufacturing base to begin with (or the more diversified it was), the faster the subsequent growth. This relationship is confirmed more formally in Kochhar et al. (2006).

Consider next the triggers of liberalization and decentralization. While the formal reforms at the centre received tremendous publicity, perhaps less noticed was the growing decentralization of policy. The Congress party had held power without a break at the centre since Independence, but the aura of invincibility surrounding it started waning soon after Indira Gandhi lost

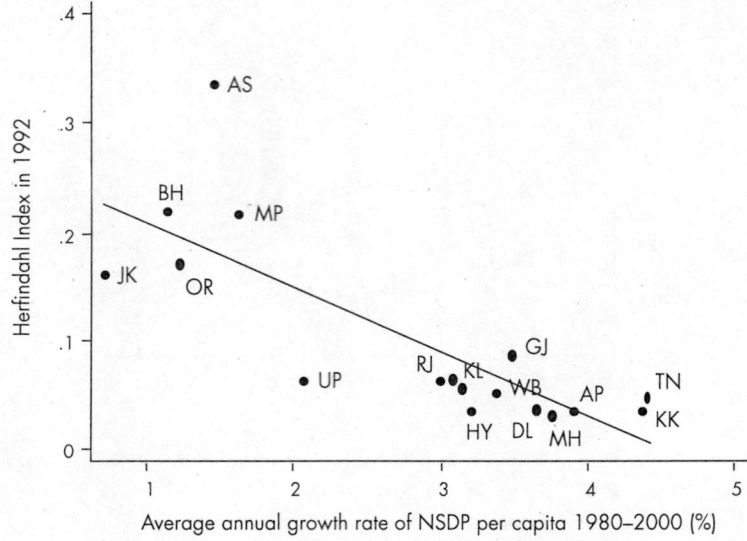

Figure 3   Diversification and States' Growth

Source: Kalpana Kochhar, Utsav Kumar, Raghuram Rajan, Arvind Subramanian, and Ioannis Tokatlidas. 2006. 'India's Pattern of Development: What Happened, What Follows', *Journal of Monetary Economics*, 53(5): 981–1019.
Notes: NSDP is the net state domestic product. For each state, the Herfindahl Index measures concentration of value added across three-digit industries in 1982; the lower the index, the lower the concentration, or the higher the diversification.

the post-Emergency election in 1977. Also, even though the Congress party returned to power at the centre through much of the 1980s, a number of states were captured by the opposition, often by regional or even single state parties.

No longer could a regional leader be confident that the centre—especially if the party in power was different from that running the state—would dole out its bounty fairly across states, and over time. Also, the parties in power could change, so that implicit agreements reached by prior governments might not be honoured by subsequent governments. Simply put, the centrifugal forces created by the dispersion of political power in India did not sit well with the enormous centralization of economic power, and the inter-state cross-subsidies the centre effected through its investment

strategy. Something had to give, and it was the centralization of economic power.

Greater economic decentralization meant states could differentiate themselves, not least in their ability to attract private-sector investment. This was, of course, facilitated by the gradual dismantling of the industrial licensing system that used regional equity as one of the primary criteria guiding industrial investments. Further contributing to differentiation over this period was the rising trend in private investment, as well as the falling trend in public investment, with private investment likely to be more sensitive to differences in policies across states.

The decentralization dynamic is most visible in the divergence in economic performance across states that was illustrated in Figure 2. The decentralization dynamic can be seen in yet another way: if decentralization

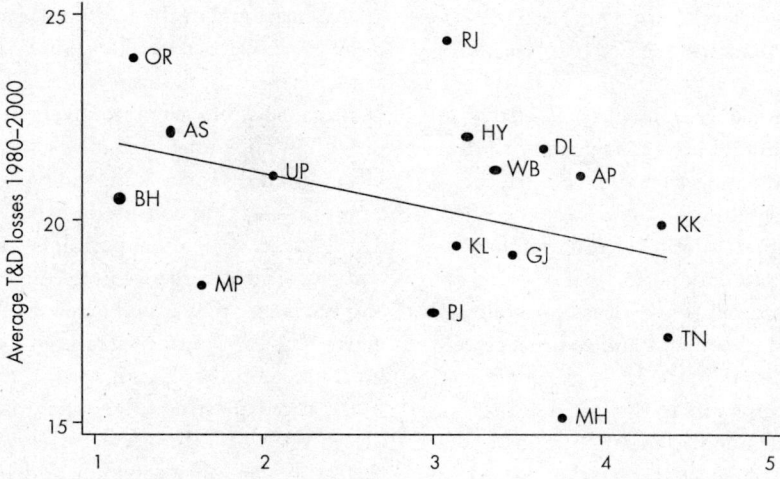

Figure 4   Institutions and States' Growth

Source: Kalpana Kochhar, Utsav Kumar, Raghuram Rajan, Arvind Subramanian, and Ioannis Tokatlidas. 2006. 'India's Pattern of Development: What Happened, What Follows', *Journal of Monetary Economics*, 53(5): 981–1019.
Notes: NSDP is the net state domestic product. Institutions are proxied by transmission and distribution (T&D) losses of the State Electricity Boards, which is the fraction of electrical power generated but not paid for, measured as a per cent of availability.

was indeed important, then states' economic performance should be more closely tied to state-level policies and institutions in the post-1980s period than before. After all, if the pre-1980s era was about the centre deciding, for example, where and how much electricity capacity to instal, there is little that the states could have done to affect economic performance within their borders. This is exactly what the evidence shows. For example, when state-level growth is related to state-level policies and institutions, the latter are found to have no role in explaining growth prior to 1980 but a robust role in explaining post-1980s, especially post-1990s, growth. This is illustrated in Figure 4.

As a measure of state policies and institutions affecting the quality of infrastructure and the business environment, the transmission and distribution losses (T&D losses) of state-level Electricity Boards (as a fraction of generating capacity)

are used. T&D losses refer to power that is generated but not paid for—in part because some of it is lost naturally along power lines in the process of transmission and distribution, but also in part because it is stolen. In areas where T&D losses are high, the quality of power, as reflected in the voltage as well as reliability, is low. Thus T&D losses are not directly related to capacity, but are determined by state-level political decisions. They broadly reflect the quality of both infrastructure and institutions (politicians turning a blind eye to power theft by their constituencies, or politicians' unwillingness to enforce laws, as well as viability and level of corruption in State Electricity Boards).

As Figure 4 shows, there is a negative correlation between the average T&D losses in 1980–2000 in a state and its growth during that period. Formal regression analysis confirms this tighter relationship between state-level institutions and state-level performance for the 1990s (Kochhar et al. 2006).[2]

Economic development results from the interaction of growth triggers with the right fundamentals that allow the triggers to be exploited. In the conventional view of the Indian development process, there was a long and dark period—the period of controls and import substitution—followed by the burst of sunlight and reforms since 1991. The boom in the IT sector first awakened observers to the fact that the dark age was not all dark, that important cumulative elements (the fundamentals) were being built up that yielded rewards with a lag, and that these fundamentals were as important as the triggers that sparked the IT boom.

The fundamentals were not just the pools of skilled human capital built through the technology, management, and research institutes—a sort of import substitution effort in skilled human capital development—that were integral to the Nehruvian vision. They went beyond and consisted of the meta institutions of democracy, rule of law, free press, and technocratic bureaucracy that recent research shows are crucial to economic development.

Looking ahead, a big uncertainty relates to the quality of these institutions. While the scope of state activities is desirably shrinking, there are core functions that need an effective, competent state. The Nehruvian meta institutions have been buffeted and weakened by the vicissitudes of vested interests, time, and politics. While transparency has increased dramatically, there seems to be less and less accountability of key public institutions.

[2]The relationship between state-level growth and institutions is robust to alternative ways of measuring the quality of institutions (see Kochhar et al. 2006).

Institutional decline will not just need to be averted at national level but also at the level of the states. Higher growth in India is leading to more divergent growth, with some key states—Bihar, Uttar Pradesh, Rajasthan, and Madhya Pradesh—lagging considerably behind. These are also the most populous states and any large divergence between political and economic power will assert itself—negatively—for example through demands for inefficient distribution.

So a key question is how the process of divergence within India can be reversed. In theory, free mobility of capital and labour should facilitate convergence. But capital will not flow into the lagging states, which are stuck in a governance trap. Because basic state functions such law and order, an efficient bureaucracy, and competent courts have not been provided, they have remained poor, which in turn has led to exit of the middle class and the skilled, leading to a further hollowing out of state capabilities. If this continues, the process of arresting divergence could take the form of large labour *outflows* from the backward states. This would create its own tensions. Averting them by creating the conditions for greater economic convergence across states and skill groups will be a big challenge for India in the years ahead.

ARVIND SUBRAMANIAN

REFERENCES

Ahluwalia, Montek. 2000. 'Economic Performance of States in the Post Reforms Period', *Economic and Political Weekly*, 6 May: 1637–48.

Bosworth, B. and S. Collins. 2002. 'Economic Reforms in India since 1991: Has Gradualism Worked', *Journal of Economic Perspectives*, 16(7): 67–88.

Ghosh, A.K. 1999. 'Current Issues of Employment Policy in India', *Economic and Political Weekly*, 4 (Sept.): 2592–608.

Rodrik, Dani and Arvind Subramanian. 2004.
    'Why India Can Grow at Seven per cent a
    Year or More? Projections and Reflections',
    Economic and Political Weekly.
————. 2005. 'From Hindu Growth to
    Productivity Surge: The Mystery of the
    Indian Growth Transition,' *IMF Staff Papers*,
    52(2).
Kochhar, Kalpana, Utsav Kumar, Raghuram Rajan,
    Arvind Subramanian, and Ioannis Tokatlidis.
    2006. 'India's Pattern of Development: What
    Happened, What Follows', *Journal of Monetary
    Economics*, 53(5): 981–1019.
Srinivasan, T.N. and S. Tendulkar. 2003.
    Reintegrating India with the World Economy,
    Washington, Institute for International
    Economics.
World Bank. 1995. 'India: Recent Economic
    Developments and Prospects', Country
    Report, Washington D.C.

India's Growth Turnaround

From 1950 to 1980, Indian real gross
domestic product (GDP) grew at an annual
average rate of 3.6 per cent (1.5 per cent in
per capita terms). From 1990 to 2007 the
growth rate averaged 6.4 per cent (4.1 per
cent in per capita terms).[1] The shift to a
higher growth path during the course of the
1980s is referred to as the Indian growth
turnaround. Fast growth in India since the
early 1980s has placed it amongst the top
nine rapidly growing economies in the world
(Ahmed and Varshney 2009).[2]

India's growth turnaround is illustrated
in Figure 1. This plots aggregate real GDP

growth from 1950 to 2008 against the
estimated probability of being in a high
growth regime using Hamilton's (1994)
Markov Switching Model.[3] The model
estimates two distinct regimes: a first sub-
period from 1950 to 1981 over which the
estimated average real GDP growth rate is
3.7 per cent; and a second regime during
which the estimated average growth rate is
6 per cent. The model suggests that there
was a relatively short transition period in
the early 1980s, with an estimated 100
per cent probability of being in the high
growth regime by the mid-1980s. More
recently, between 2003–4 and 2007–8, real
GDP growth increased further, averaging
8.8 per cent.[4]

The identification of a turnaround in
the early 1980s by the Hamilton model
is consistent with a range of studies using
aggregate data (see Rodrik and Subramanian
2005; Balakrishnan and Parameswaran
2007). More recent work using disaggregated
data (Ghate and Wright 2009) points to a
rather later data in the mid-1980s, suggesting
a conflict between both approaches. We
discuss the contrast between these two
attempts to time the turnaround in more
detail later; but the key issue on which all
studies agree is that, at some point during
the 1980s, there was an increase in growth,
which, from the 1990s, was not only of
statistical but also of massive economic

[1]These numbers reflect simple averages and
are measured in 1999–2000 prices. The per capita
averages for the 1990–2007 period are until 2004,
the latest year for which population numbers are
available on the Penn World Tables.

[2]Brad De Long at UC Berkeley first pointed out
that India's growth acceleration started in the early
1980s. Subsequently, there was a race to explain this
acceleration.

[3]Regimes are generated using a Markov
switching model (see Hamilton 1994). The model
was estimated using EM algorithm-based GAUSS
codes by Hamilton. We use the Markov switching
model as an illustrative technique.

[4]The year 1980–1 is also identified as
breakpoint when we undertake the same exercise
with real GDP measured in 1993–4 prices. This
suggests that India's growth transition in the early
1980s does not depend on the price series one
uses. Interestingly, 1991–2 is not identified as a
breakpoint using 1993–4 prices, although it is using
1999–2000 prices.

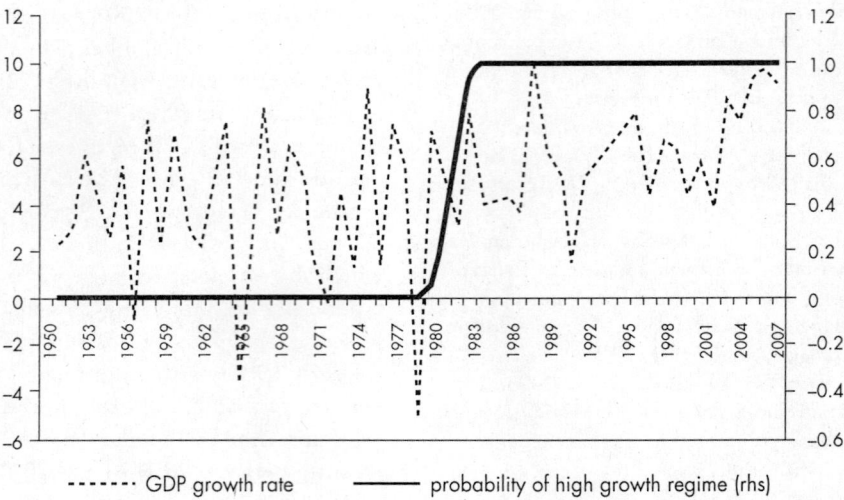

Figure 1   Indian GDP Growth Rate against the Probability of a
High GDP Growth Regime

significance. What has puzzled many contributors to the literature is that analysis of aggregate data suggests a pickup in growth during the early 1980s, *before* most of the major policy changes.[5]

The low growth in the first phase is pejoratively referred to as the Hindu rate of growth, a period in which import duties were among the highest in the world, foreign direct investment (FDI) was prohibited in many sectors of the economy, and there was extensive regulation of interest rates. During this period Indian GDP per capita growth was, at best, in line with the long-run average growth rates in most rich countries: there was minimal, if any, tendency to converge. While this performance was better than many African countries, it was clearly in marked contrast to the extremely rapid rates of convergence of the East Asian Tigers during this period.

[5]While a few significant pro-market reforms took place in the mid-1980s, the bulk of economic reforms—which shifted India to an outward-looking, incentive-based private-sector economy—were enacted after the balance of payments (BOP) crisis of 1991.

The upward shift in India's growth path during the 1980s is significant for two reasons: the turnaround happened well before the BOP crisis of 1991 and the large-scale macroeconomic reforms that ensued.

The second puzzling aspect about India's growth turnaround is that it was not driven by manufactured exports and, therefore, has little in common with the East Asian economic miracle. In particular, there was no industrial policy targeted towards developing specific industries. It was the service sector that led the increase in the overall growth rate in the early 1980s. Since many components of services are income related (such as financial services, business services, and hotels and restaurants) and begin to increase only after a certain stage in development, the fact that India's service sector created the impulse for the growth turnaround is puzzling.

While there is a reasonable degree of consensus amongst economists on the timing of India's growth turnaround, there is less agreement about its causes. What is indisputable is that something happened during the 1980s that opened the door to a rise in growth. The challenge facing growth economists is to weave a logically consistent story on the timing and causes of India's growth turnaround.

TOTAL FACTOR PRODUCTIVITY (TFP) OR POLICIES?

In an influential paper, Rodrik and Subramanian (2005) argue that Indira Gandhi, substantially chastened by her 1977 electoral defeat, became significantly more 'pro-business' after coming back to power in 1980. This 'attitudinal shift' led to more investment which increased manufacturing output dramatically. This led to a growth pickup in 1980. In their view, aggregate productivity measured by TFP growth is driven by an attitudinal shift towards pro-business policies. This contrasts with the role that directly observable policies, such as trade liberalization, would have on a growth shift.[6] The Rodrik–Subramanian story is essentially a manufacturing sector driven explanation of India's growth turnaround.

The above story, however, is generally known to be problematical. This is because of the unlikely finding that a small manufacturing sector (roughly 9 per cent of GDP in the early 1980s) would raise the aggregate growth rate by 2 percentage points. The implied multiplier effects would have to be fantastically large for this to occur. This seems highly implausible, especially since the share of registered manufacturing

to GDP in the early 1980s was very small (roughly 8 per cent of GDP).

Balakrishnan and Paramewswaran (2007) use the multiple structural break test approach of Bai and Perron (1998) to look at breaks in sectoral growth rates since 1950. They find that agriculture growth increases (permanently) during the mid-1960s. This is followed by a take-off in the service sector in the mid-1970s. Finally, manufacturing output growth breaks in 1982–3, after the break in overall growth which they place as early as 1979. Based on the timing of these recursive sectoral breaks, they suggest that the manufacturing sector is not responsible for a shift to a higher growth path, rather it is has been led by growth shifts in other sectors.[7] This discussion suggests that framing the debate on India's growth turnaround as driven either by TFP shifts or a change in policies is problematical. The shift in manufacturing growth occurring after the shift in overall growth is also verified by Figure 2: using the regime switching approach, the break in manufacturing occurs in 1986–7, well after the estimated upward shift in aggregate growth (see Figure 1) with the growth rate of manufacturing output amounting to 4.8 per cent in the period 1964–86 and

[6]Rodrik and Subramanian distinguish between pro-business policies and pro-market policies. Examples of pro-business polices are easing restrictions on capacity expansion for incumbents, removing price controls, and reducing corporate taxes; trade liberalization is an example of a market-oriented policy. They conclude that a shift towards a pro-business orientation can be an essential trigger that sets off growth accelerations.

[7]Balakrishnan and Parameswaran argue that because of the drought of the mid-1960s, there was a huge decline in food grain production. There was also extremely poor management of the macro-economy leaving little foreign exchange to import food. The crisis ultimately induced a green revolution and saw large public investments in the agriculture sector. The resource flow into the sector led to a growth shift in agriculture. This explains the impulse in agriculture in the mid-1960s. The problem with this narrative is that it does not address the endogeneity problem surrounding public investment. An interesting open research question is whether inter-sectoral linkages from the manufacturing sector are greater than those from the service sector.

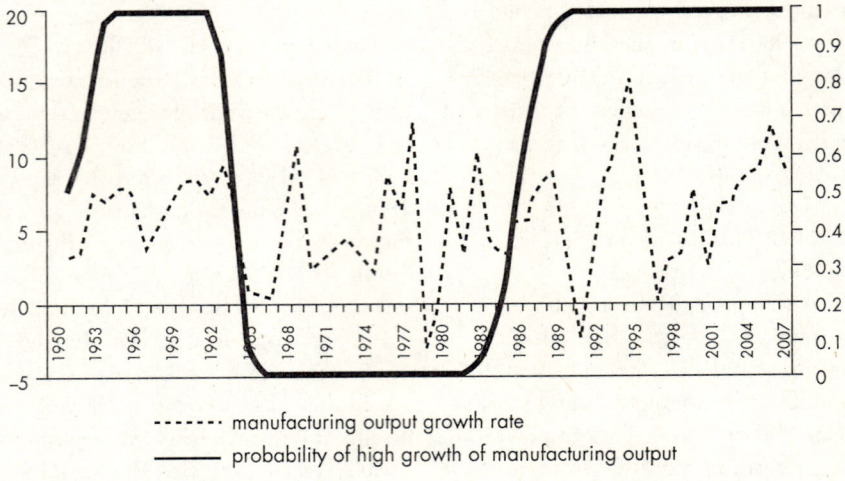

----- manufacturing output growth rate
——— probability of high growth of manufacturing output

Figure 2   Growth Rate of Manufacturing Output against the Probability of
High Growth of Manufacturing Output

6.5 per cent between 1987 and 2007 (and before 1964).[8]

Balakrishnan and Parameswaran's approach for determining turning points is (itself) not without criticism. Basu (2008) argues that a common problem that applies to the existing empirical literature on the Indian growth turnaround is the special nature of the period 1979–80, which saw a sharp contraction in Indian real GDP growth (−5.2 per cent). The approach followed by Balakrishnan and Parameswaran (2007)—by essentially fitting linear segments to a fluctuating growth pattern—would find a propensity for the break to appear before 1979–80.[9]

A possible reconciliation of the TFP versus policy debate is that while a few key

trade reforms were legislatively enacted in the mid-1980s, they started to get debated in the early 1980s. Because investment is forward looking, the anticipated effects of policy changes led to India's growth turnaround prior to the enactment of the reforms. For instance, the removal of capacity constraints would allow firms to produce at higher or full capacity with the same inputs, leading to an increase in the rate of growth of productivity. The need for future research is to understand more clearly the disaggregated mechanisms that induced the Indian growth turnaround.[10]

[8]Both Rodrik and Subramanian (2005) and Balakrishnan and Parameswaran (2007) use the multiple structural break tests of Bai and Perron (1998). This possibly explains why they obtain a similar breakpoint (early 1980s) in aggregate real GDP growth.

[9]Basu (2008) finds that if 1979–80 is discounted, the break in trend occurs in 1975–6. This suggests that the 1979–80 breakpoint is a statistical construct without much policy significance.

[10]In an interesting discussion, Kotwal et al. (2009) suggest that technology transfers in the early and mid-1980s allowed cheaper and easier access to imported machinery made possible by trade liberalization, unleashing a process of creative destruction in which the efficient firms—who upgraded their technology—drove out the inefficient firms. This raised the overall productivity of factors in the economy as factors got reallocated more productively. Rising industrial and service-sector productivity also had secondary effects: it attracted labour from agriculture. This raised wages for the workers left behind in agriculture.

THE V FACTOR

Recent work by Ghate and Wright (2009) suggests that the turning point in Indian growth was not in the early 1980s, as most other studies have assumed, but in the mid-1980s. In this respect the Ghate and Wright approach appears to resolve the puzzle discussed by Rodrik and Subramanian (2005), who, using aggregate data, concluded that the turnaround in growth came in the early 1980s, well before any observable shift in policy. Instead of using an aggregate GDP series, Ghate and Wright use factor analysis on state-level sectoral time series data for fourteen sectors in fifteen states—at 1993–4 prices—to identify common patterns in the growth shifts of Indian states. A significant advantage of the common factor representation is that one does not need to impose a particular date for the turnaround in growth. Nor does one need to impose that it be a deterministic shift, as in standard econometric representations of structural breaks; nor even that all series participate in the shift at identical dates.

Apart from random fluctuations, Ghate and Wright find that two factors drive these time series: one is a nearly deterministic straight-line growth factor, and the other exhibits a V shape, which the authors refer to as the V factor. The apex of the V is in 1987 when reforms to open up the economy started to take place.[11] In fact, the time profile of the V is strongly correlated with the pattern of trade liberalization, as summarized by the effective tariff rate (see Ghate and Wright 2009: figure 7).[12]

While the common nature of the growth turnaround, as identified by the V factor, appears to correspond to a common shift in trade policy, the disparate impact of the V factor across major Indian states presents something of a puzzle. Table 1 examines this issue by showing correlations between identifiable state characteristics shortly before the turnaround, and their estimated V factor loadings. The table provides both negative and some (weaker) positive results. On the negative side, it allows us to dispose

Table 1   State Characteristics and State V factor Loadings

State characteristics	Correlation with average state V factor loading
A Rich State Club?	
Log real ouput per capita 1985	–0.07
Solow Variables	
Fixed investment, % of NSDP 1981	–0.42
Log population 1981	0.09
Population growth 1971–81	–0.22
Public Spending	
Development expenditures as a percentage of NSDP 1981	0.17
Supply-side Characteristics	
Share of registered manufacturing 1985	0.18
Electricity generation, kwh per capita, 1981	–0.19
Share of agriculture, % 1985	–0.68
Literacy rate 1981	0.49
Urban population, %	0.32

Note: NSDP is net state domestic product.

[11]Figure 1 shows that up until at least the mid-1980s growth of GDP remained within the range of variation observed in the first regime. Aggregate data do not, therefore, appear to conflict markedly with the null hypothesis that the switch actually occurred as late as, say, 1987, the date identified by Ghate and Wright (2009), using disaggregated data.

[12]Other major internal liberalization measures that were implemented in 1985 and 1986 involved

(a) eliminating the licensing of twenty-five categories of industries, (b) extending de-licensing to large companies in twenty-two industries that were previously restricted by the Monopolies and Restrictive Trade Practices Act and Foreign Exchange Regulation Act, and (c) allowing companies that had reached 80 per cent capacity utilization to expand their capacity up to 133 per cent of that reached in any of the previous years (see Rodrik and Subramanian 2005).

of some candidate explanations: (a) the turnaround in growth was not restricted to a club of richer states: initial income levels were unrelated to the magnitude of the response to the V factor; (b) explanations based on differences in key magnitudes in a standard Solow-style growth model (saving, investment population growth rate and level) also do not show any systematic differences (the sign of the investment correlation is perverse—the correlation with population growth is of the correct sign but very low); (c) the direct contribution of the public sector to the turnaround appears to have been at best weak, and possibly perverse: there was essentially a zero correlation between the initial values of development spending and the subsequent impact of the V factor; and (d) total public spending actually had a V factor loading which was somewhat negatively correlated with the overall state loading (that is, 'V states'—those with a positive loading on the V factor—tended if anything to have slowdowns in growth of public spending after the turnaround in overall growth).

The bottom block of the table provides evidence of some proxies for supply-side characteristics of individual states. The table shows that 'V states' tended to be somewhat more literate and somewhat more urbanized, and (the strongest correlation shown) had lower shares of agriculture.

Table 1 also shows that there was essentially no link between V factor loadings and the share of registered manufacturing, which played an important role in Rodrik and Subramanian's (2005) explanation of the turnaround. This suggests that while registered manufacturing may, in line with Rodrik and Subramanian's analysis, have been a catalyst for growth in the early 1980s, it was far from being an engine of growth over the longer term.

THE GROWTH TURNAROUND AND IMPLICATIONS FOR DIVERGENCE

The V factor provides evidence of a highly pervasive, but by no means universal shift in behaviour in India during the course of the 1980s. Can we reconcile this evidence with any underlying economic model? One way to think about this is to consider a general model of convergence of the form

$$\Delta(y^i_{t+1} - y^{US}_{t+1}) = \alpha_i (y^{US}_t + s_{it} + s^{India}_t - y_{it}) + \Delta TFP^i_{t+1} - \Delta TFP^{US}_{t+1} + \varepsilon_{it+1}$$

where y_{it} is log output per capita for state i, the s_{it} and s^{India}_t variables captures factors that determine steady-state output relative to the frontier represented by y^{US}_t; log output per capita in the United States, for individual states and for India as a whole; TFP_{it} and TFP^{US}_t is growth rate of TFP in state i and in the United States and ε_{it} captures short-run cyclical factors.

The simple framework of the equation offers a range of possible ways of accounting for the all-India pattern. It seems reasonable to argue that the sum of the last three terms on the right-hand side of the above equation is unlikely to provide an adequate explanation of longer-term trends. In standard Cobb-Douglas type technology models TFP growth shocks are common across all economies and hence cancel out precisely. But even if they are country specific, such relative shocks might reasonably be assumed to have a stationary distribution. The same applies to the short-term error term, (ε_{it}). Thus we need to look for an explanation somewhere in the first term.

One possible interpretation of the earlier period was that the bracketed 'convergence' term (the term multiplied by α_i) was on average close to zero—that is, most, or possibly all, Indian states were conditional upon the s_{it} and s^{India}_t processes, fairly close to their steady-state values. The downward drift in most states' relative output levels would, according to this interpretation, be understood either as a succession of bad relative TFP growth shocks, or possibly as a downward drift in s_t^{India}.

It is harder to continue the logic of this explanation after the growth turnaround. The evidence of the V factor, and its correlation with the measure of trade liberalization in Ghate and Wright (2009), suggests very strongly that the impetus for the turnaround was common across all states, hence it is reasonable to attribute it to changes in the common Indian steady state factor, s_t^{India}. Given the subsequent dramatic changes in rates of convergence, then, conditional upon a reasonable degree of stability in the other elements on the right-hand side of the equation, the implied changes in s_t^{India} must have been quite dramatic. Rodrik and Subramanian (2005) argue that this is plausible because India was well away from its production possibility frontier.

But since these changes were common across states, the puzzle presented by the differential impact of the V factor is why any such shift in s_t^{India} did not have largely symmetric effects across the states. There is one possible explanation which reconciles both the all-India and state-wise evidence. The analysis of these shifts has implicitly assumed that the state-specific rates of convergence, α_i, were both strictly positive and reasonably similar across states. But an alternative explanation would attribute the pattern of the evidence largely to the α_i themselves. According to this interpretation, and consistent with the arguments of Rodrik and Subramanian, the bracketed expression in the first term was *not* necessarily close to zero in the first period; but failure to converge to the global frontier was largely due to the α_i being so close to zero that

differences between actual and steady state income levels had essentially no impact. The turnaround in growth and its differential pattern would then be attributed to some combination of a common shift in s_t^{India} and state-wise differences in the α_i. A differential impact of the all-India shock might be attributed to different values of α_i; with non-V states, by implication, having α_i values extremely close to zero, thus closing off any convergence response.

AGENDA FOR FUTURE RESEARCH

Research on India's growth turnaround needs to move beyond its empiricist nature and towards a theoretical model of India's growth pattern. Given India's economic planning history and the empirical evidence it would be natural to think of the main counterfactual as openness to trade, that is, what would India's growth path have looked like if the many opportunities for trade had been acted upon? However, an alternative counterfactual relates to India's abysmal record in primary education to which the Mahalanobis plan gave little attention (Balakrishnan 2008). The rate of growth induced by higher human capital accumulation might have vastly changed the growth pattern of India.

Looking forward, probably the most crucial factor is whether the Indian turnaround is sufficiently robust that it will be sustained, and whether India will follow the East Asian precedent of rapid convergence (albeit from a very low base) towards per capita income levels of rich countries at the technological frontier. To the extent that, for example, while the 'V factor' of Ghate and Wright (2009) appears strongly correlated with tariff reductions, there are arguably only modest further gains that can arise from this source, since tariffs are now steadily approaching the levels in most OECD countries. The key issue looking forward, therefore, is that having shifted to a higher growth path (whatever the initial impetus or catalyst may have been), will this growth path prove self-sustaining?

CHETAN GHATE, STEPHEN WRIGHT, AND TATIANA FIC*

REFERENCES
Ahmed, Sadiq and A. Varshney. 2009. 'Battles Half Won: The Political Economy of India's Growth and Economic Policy since Independence', Commission on Growth and Development, Working Paper No. 15.
Bai, Jushan and P. Perron. 1998. 'Estimating and Testing Linear Models with Multiple Structural Changes', *Econometrica*, 66(1): 47–78.
Basu, Kaushik. 2008. 'The Enigma of India's Arrival: A Review of Arvind Virmani's "Propelling India: From Social Stagnation to Global Power"', *Journal of Economic Literature*, 46(2): 396–406.
Balakrishan, Pulapare. 2008. 'Visible Hand: Public Policy and Economic Growth in the Nehru Era', *The Indian Economic Journal*, 56(1), April–June: 11–35.
Balakrishnan, Pulapare, and M. Parameswaran. 2007. 'Understanding Economic Growth in India: A Prerequisite', *Economic and Political Weekly*, 42(27–8): 2915–22.
Ghate, Chetan and S. Wright. 2009. 'The V-Factor: Distribution, Timing, and Correlates of the Great Indian Growth Turnaround', *Jena Economic Research Papers in Economics 2009–10*, Max Planck Institute of Economics.
Hamilton, James. 1994. *Time Series Analysis*, Princeton University Press.
Kotwal, Ashok, B. Ramaswami, and W. Wadhwa. 2009. 'Economic Liberalization and Indian Economic Growth: What's the Evidence?', mimeo, Indian Statistical Institute, Delhi Centre.
Rodrik, Dani and A. Subramanian. 2005. 'From Hindu Growth to Productivity Surge: The Mystery of the Indian Growth Transition', *IMF Staff Papers*, 52(2): 193–228.

*We are grateful to Kaushik Basu and Pulapare Balakrishnan for helpful comments.

Law and Legal System in India

The expressions 'law' and 'legal system' should be defined, as they are both used in more than one sense. In the sense used here, 'law' means statutory law and 'legal system' means the framework used for resolving disputes. But more explanation is needed. In the legal system, the bar (lawyers) and the judiciary also have a role to play. All disputes don't necessarily have to go through a process of adjudication. Conciliation, mediation, and arbitration are possibilities. The words 'conciliation' and 'mediation' are often used synonymously. However, there is a difference. Conciliation is an attempt to resolve the dispute before it becomes formal. It is nipped in the bud. Mediation is intervention when there is a formal dispute. When this mediation becomes a little more formalized, with a legal agreement stipulating who will mediate as a third party, we have arbitration. If none of this works, there is no choice but to resort to courts. There are around 10,000 courts—one Supreme Court, eighteen high courts, and the remainder known as lower courts. Courts have to follow prescribed procedures and major statutes on procedures are the Indian Evidence Act 1872, the Limitation Act 1963, the Civil Procedure Code 1908, and the Criminal Procedure Code 1973. In addition, there are tribunals for specific purposes, such as land tribunals, industrial tribunals, tax tribunals, service tribunals, the Company Law Board, water pollution tribunals, and air pollution tribunals. Other quasi-judicial bodies include the MRTP (Monopolies and Restrictive Trade Practices) Commission or forums under the Consumer Protection Act 1986. Tribunals and other quasi-judicial forums don't necessarily have to follow the rigid procedure followed by courts.

STATUTORY LAW REFORM

The law and the legal system should continuously change and adapt. However, since 1991, there has been an additional trigger because of economic reforms. The legal system must provide an adequate structure of incentives and deterrents for a market-based economy to function. Globalization also requires a legal system that conforms to global norms. Some recent initiatives for statutory law reform are directly linked to WTO (World Trade Organization) agreements, intellectual property being a case in point. It must also be mentioned here that legal services might be opened up under fresh WTO negotiations. Other initiatives, such as in infrastructure or the financial sector, are directly linked to privatization, opening up to competition, and removal of historical government monopolies. However, over and above this, old statutes must change. India does not follow the legal principle known as desuetude, which simply means that all statutes are for a prescribed period of time and once this is over, statutes die a natural death, unless a fresh review establishes the need for their continuance. Therefore, dysfunctional and old statutes continue on the books unless they are specifically repealed.

How many statutes are there? This is difficult to answer, because there are both central and state-level statutes. There is also a counting problem. For instance, there may be a new statute that amends an existing statute. Is this going to be counted once or twice? Subject to this, there are between 3000 and 3500 central statutes. The earliest two go back to the year 1836 and these are the Bengal Indigo Contracts Act and the Bengal Districts Act. Thanks to computerization and use of information technology, it is now reasonably easy to access central statutes, that is a listing of titles as well as the text. For instance, they are available on the Ministry of Law and Justice's website (under the head India Code) and private organizations have brought out CDs. Even hard copy versions are available. Unfortunately, this accessibility has not yet extended to all states. Consequently, no one has a handle on how many state-level statutes there are. Figures between 25,000 and 30,000 float around, but may be an exaggeration. A few states have listings of titles on their websites (not the text) and in a few more, hard copy versions have been published. These suggest that something like 15,000 may be a more reasonable figure.

The first element of statutory law reform is to scrap dysfunctional statutes. For the 3000 to 3500 central statutes, this identification has been made. The most visible of these identification exercises was the Jain Commission on Review of Administrative Law, which submitted a report in 1998. This commission identified around 1300 statutes for outright repeal. Based partly on the recommendations of this commission, around 350 central statutes were repealed in 2001–2. It is always easier to repeal a statute in its entirety. Part of the problem is that a statute often has dysfunctional and old sections that need repeal. The entire statute cannot be junked. Unfortunately, not much has been done to repeal old statutes at state level. Some have been repealed in Gujarat and an exercise has been undertaken to identify old ones in Rajasthan. Ideally, all states should have permanent Law Commissions.

Second, statutory law reform should have an element of unification and harmonization. Statutes have been enacted at various points in time in the same area, without taking cognizance of what already exists. Labour legislation is an example. There are forty-seven different central Acts that directly deal with labour and many more that deal indirectly. Among the forty-seven, the Fatal Accidents Act was enacted in 1855 and the Public Liability Insurance Act was enacted in 1991. Given this time span, it stands to reason that concepts and definitions will disagree. Within labour law, there is lack of unanimity about definitions of wages, workman, employee, factory, industry, and child labour. Case law also differs, causing further confusion. Banking law is another example of such lack of harmonization. There is thus a case for unifying and harmonizing.

Third, there is the issue of over-legislation. India is over-legislated and undergoverned. Over-legislation is correlated with the problem of reducing unnecessary state intervention, and with reforms views on what the state should do have changed. For example, controls used by the state under the Essential Commodities Act of 1955 are no longer relevant, or necessary, or even desirable. Incidentally, several such controls date to shortages under Second World War conditions. Temporary legislation under the Defence of India Rules, 1939 became permanent. Another spate of redundant economic legislation dates to the period between 1969 and 1976. Laws on bank, coalmine, and general insurance nationalization, the MRTP Act, the Contract Labour (Regulation and Abolition) Act, the former Foreign Exchange Regulation Act (FERA), the Urban Land (Ceiling and Regulation) Act, and the Foreign Contribution (Regulation) Act are of this vintage. With views on statute intervention changing, these statutes have become redundant.

Fourth, despite the existence of thousands of statutes, there are areas where laws don't exist. Credit cards, automatic teller machines (ATMs), hire purchase and leasing, electronic data interchanges (EDI), some areas of intellectual property, regulatory bodies, or the government's liability in tort are instances. Statutory law reform must fill the gaps.

ADMINISTRATIVE LAW

The most important constraint on efficient decision making is not statutory, but administrative law.[1] These rules, orders, and regulations are not even published. Even when they are, the language is not citizen friendly, the Plain English movement having left India untouched. The last time such a collation of administrative law was attempted was in 1966.

The labour market can be used to illustrate the difference between statutory law and administrative law. In labour markets, reduced state intervention is primarily interpreted as reduced intervention in industrial relations. Most problems relate to the Industrial Disputes Act (IDA), especially Chapter V-B. These concern lay-offs, retrenchments, and closures and Chapter V-B requires prior permission from the 'appropriate' government before such action can take place. This permission is never obtained. Therefore, labour markets become rigid and employers adopt artificially high capital intensity and circumvent the legislation. Given the other provisions of labour legislation, the requirement of governmental permission can be dispensed with, without adversely affecting the interests of labour. This is a valid point and the IDA invariably figures when labour market reform is mentioned. However, the IDA only covers the organized labour force (8 per cent of the total) and, within that, only enterprises that employ more than 100 workers (2.17 per cent of the labour force).

In contrast, administrative law relating to labour issues covers many more people.

[1]The body of rules, regulations, orders, and decisions created by administrative agencies of government (Barrons Law Dictionary © 2003).

Twenty-nine different inspectors can descend under forty-seven statutes. A system of a single inspector for all labour laws does not exist. While grave violations are ignored, minor errors provide scope for harassment. Rules under the Factories Act, framed in 1948, provide for whitewashing of factories. Distemper won't do. Earthen pots filled with water are required. Water coolers won't suffice. Red-painted buckets filled with sand are required. Fire extinguishers won't do. Nor are documentation requirements or time periods for which records have to be kept standardized. And so on. Such procedural problems characterize all three stages of an enterprise's operations, entry, functioning, and exit, and impose transactions costs that render Indian business uncompetitive. Part of the problem with administrative decisions is that they leave a large degree of discretion, often at petty functionary levels, and thereby encourage corruption and rent seeking. Corruption is not distributionally neutral and has an anti-poor bias. The answer lies in removing scope for discretion and discretionary abuse. But that is part of the agenda of pending reforms, often at state level.

SPEED OF DISPUTE RESOLUTION

The legal system will not be credible without speedy dispute resolution. There are 20 million cases pending in lower courts, more than 3 million in high courts. With the Supreme Court included, the pendency figure inches close to 25 million. And this is the backlog only in courts. With tribunals and other quasi-judicial forums included, backlog figures approach 35 million. Two-thirds of the backlog consists of criminal cases, and in criminal cases the rate of conviction is less than 6 per cent. In lower courts, more than 800,000 cases are more than ten years old, with special concentration in states like Gujarat, Madhya Pradesh, Maharashtra, UP, and West Bengal.

In high courts, more than 450,000 cases are more than ten years old, with special concentration in Allahabad and Kolkata. The figure on undertrials is subject to some dispute. But of the figure of around 300,000 that is cited, three-fourths are undertrials, many of whom are in jail and accused of petty offences, having been in jail for longer than the maximum mandatory sentences for those petty crimes. On an average, it takes more than twenty years to resolve a dispute. This doesn't make redressal credible.

There are 26 Supreme Court judges, 540 high court judges, and 900 subordinate judges (including 336 district judges). These are the maximum numbers of allowable judges. In reality, most courts have vacancies. Not surprisingly, the total number of judges in India is on the low side. For every million population, the United States has 107 judges, Canada 75.2, Britain 50.9, and Australia 41.6. The figure for India is slightly over ten. There are 450,000 lawyers, all of whom are regulated by the Advocates Act of 1961. In addition, 2000 judicial officers are posted in various tribunals. Tribunals came up because they were thought to be faster than the court system, being free of cumbersome procedures. However, things have turned out differently. Perhaps the most important reason is that there is no finality about decisions taken in tribunals, as there is always scope for appeal to high courts and the Supreme Court. In the late 1970s, to provide cheap legal services to the poor, the system of *lok adalats* was started. The Legal Services Authorities Act 1989 was enacted to give statutory backing to lok adalats. The experience varies across states.

How does one ensure speedy redressal? There are many aspects, some of which concern the improvement of procedures in the subordinate and appellate courts. Various reports of the Law Commission have highlighted these issues. These reports have also focused on problems concerning the bar and the judiciary. If one visualizes demand and supply curves for dispute resolution, these traditional remedies involve a shift of the supply curve to the right.

But first, let us mention demand-side solutions and these involve a shift of the demand curve to the left. When highlighting the backlog in courts, one has adjudication in mind. But adjudication is only one way of resolving disputes. There are other dispute-resolution mechanisms like conciliation, mediation, and arbitration. If these can be made more efficient, the demand for adjudication will decrease. One of the problems with conciliation and mediation has been a lack of credible conciliators and mediators. Historically, arbitration has never taken off because it has not been freed from the apron strings of courts. A relatively new Arbitration and Conciliation Act was passed in 1996 and has made arbitration more efficient, as systems have become less open-ended.

One must also mention the role of government as a litigant. Government litigation crowds out the private citizen from civil courts. This is especially so for appeals, which often fail. A sample survey found that in Karnataka, the government was a litigant in 65 per cent of civil cases. A large chunk of government litigation was in the form of appeals against lower court judgements and the survey found that 95 per cent of government appeals fail. Apart from being a commentary on the quality of government legal counsel, such statistics also underline the procedure followed in appealing. Appeals have automaticity. That apart, the government is often a litigant on both sides. There are also too many general appeals.

The inefficient indirect tax system also leads to many court cases. For instance, the Supreme Court has adjudicated whether lemons, chillies, green ginger, betel leaf, turmeric, and coconut are vegetables! Once there is standardization and unification of taxes, especially indirect taxes, such cases should decrease.

However, court cases will not disappear even if demand is reduced. Therefore, the efficiency of disposal also needs to improve. Many of the problems are procedural and delays are possible at each of the four stages a civil suit, say, goes through—pre-trial, trial, appellate, and execution. An amendment to the Civil Procedure Code, enacted in 2002, should improve matters in civil cases. In 2003, a committee submitted a report on reforming the criminal justice system. Once those recommendations are accepted, the Criminal Procedure Code, the Indian Evidence Act, and the Limitation Act can be amended. Some fast track courts have also been introduced in selected districts, specially directed towards old and criminal cases. The criminal justice system cannot be dramatically improved without addressing the issue of police reform. Between 1979 and 1981, there were eight reports of the National Police Commission. In 1998 there was the Ribeiro Committee and in 2000 there was the Padmanabhaiah Committee. The issue of police reform has been examined in such detail that no further examination is needed. It is a question of implementing the recommendations. After all, the Police Act dates back to the year 1861. Indeed, the Prisons Act also goes back to 1894, and the recommendations of the All India Committee on Jail Reforms, going all the way back to 1980–3, have again not been implemented. And while on jails and undertrials, information technology is a tool that has been used only up to a fraction of its true potential. How many of the 1200 plus jails have experimented with video recording of evidence? How many have held courts within jail premises? Both ease pressures on the police.

Many suggestions about the functioning of the judiciary have been reiterated in more than one Law Commission report, apart from the Justice Shah Committee Report in 1972 and the Justice Satish Chandra Committee Report in 1986. The argument for more judges and more benches is a valid one, although there is the issue of vacancies not being filled on time and sitting Judges being co-opted to head commissions of inquiry. However, with the same number of judges, it is possible to improve productivity by using modern technology and the Supreme Court has demonstrated how this can be done. There is also the issue of imposing working norms and accountability for judges. For instance, increasing the number of working days and cutting down on long vacations is equivalent to increasing the number of judges by 25 per cent. More than one retired Chief Justice has alluded to corruption in the judiciary. Accountability and transparency norms cannot, and should not, be imposed on the judiciary from outside. And the same principle also applies to the bar.

The scenario is thus quite depressing. The only silver lining is that there is now much greater awareness about the need to reform the law and the legal system, with the political economy of vested interests being less serious than in many other purely economic reform areas.

BIBEK DEBROY

National Income

The conceptual background, recommendations of the National Income Committee, methods of construction of the available time series on national income, the pattern of economic growth, sources of growth, and India's relative position over the past century will be the subject matter of this entry.

National income and net national product (NNP) are synonymous. NNP is the value of the total output of the economy calculated without double counting, that is, GNP (gross national product), less allowance for depreciation (D) of the capital assets used in the production process. Hence NNP = GNP − D. GNP may be distinguished from GDP (gross domestic product). National product is what is produced by normal residents of the country within the country or abroad. Domestic product is what is produced within the country by normal residents and foreigners. There has been a shift of interest first from NNP to GNP, and subsequently to GDP in academic discussions and official publications.

GDP can be calculated by totalling gross value added, that is, value of gross output minus value of raw materials. This method of calculation is known as the 'output' or 'value added' approach. Alternatively GDP can be calculated by summing up the returns to the different factors of production—labour, capital, and enterpreneurship. That is GDP = wages and salaries + rent + profit. This method is known as the income approach. GDP at factor cost equals GDP at market prices minus taxes plus subsidies and other transfer payments. The variant, GDP at factor cost, is the commonly used measure of national income.

National income calculated from the relevant monetary magnitudes for the year in question is referred to as national income at current prices. For inter-temporal analysis, national income at constant prices is the appropriate measure. The contribution of each sector is valued at the base-year prices to obtain the real output of the sector. The sum of the real outputs for different sectors is taken as the national income at constant prices. Such a method may not be entirely satisfactory. However, it may be better than using some overall price index as a deflator.

There are various complexities, qualifications, and ambiguities in applying the general principles for the practical calculation of national income aggregates. The data requirements are very heavy. The quality of the estimates depends on the accuracy of the data sets and appropriateness of the data adjustment procedures.

RECOMMENDATIONS OF THE NATIONAL INCOME COMMITTEE

India has a long tradition of national income estimation by individual scholars. Sivasubramonian (2000: 426–7) briefly reviews the exercises by Naoroji for 1867–8, Atkinson for 1875 and 1895, and Digby for 1898–9. He lists twenty-nine point estimates by different scholars for individual years covering the period 1900–46. Several of these estimates did not cover the Native States, their geographical coverage being limited to British India. Some estimates excluded the service sector. The estimates for a given year are not comparable on account of the differences in concepts, geographical coverage, and data bases. The quality of most of them leaves much to be much desired.

Recognizing the importance of national income data for policy formulation and development planning, the Government of India had set up the National Income Committee (NIC) in 1949 with P.C. Mahalanobis as Chairman and D.R. Gadgil and V.K.R.V. Rao as members. The committee had the benefit of advice of Simon Kuznets, J.R.N. Stone, and J.B.D. Derksen. It prepared the first set of official estimates of national income (NNP) for 1948–9 to 1950–1 at current and constant (1948–9) prices. It identified the data gaps and made a number of recommendations for improvements in data bases and for the promotion of further work and research on national income. It drew up a framework for national accounts. The NIC thus laid the foundations for the estimation of national income and related aggregates in India on sound lines. The methodology adopted by the NIC was on the lines of the approach devised by V.K.R.V. Rao for his estimate for British India for 1931–2.

OFFICIAL ESTIMATES FOR THE POST-INDEPENDENCE ERA

Official estimates of national income and related aggregates are available from the year 1948–9 onwards. The NIC methodology was adopted and refinements were introduced continually. The Central Statistical Organisation (CSO), Government of India, has been in-charge of the preparation and publication of the estimates. The scope of the estimates has been progressively widened. Since 1975, the estimates have been published under the title, National Accounts Statistics (NAS). The base year of the estimates at constant prices was changed several times, from 1948–9 to 1960–1 in 1967, 1970–1 in 1978, 1980–1 in 1988, 1993–4 in 1999, and 1999–2000 in 2006. The 1993–4 base-year series was extended backwards and the 'Back Series', 1950–1 to 1992–3 was published in 2001. A detailed review of the methodology and databases is undertaken whenever the base-year is changed. Workforce estimates available from the decennial population censuses and quinquennial surveys on employment and unemployment conducted by the National Sample Survey Organisation (NSSO) are utilized in the revision of the series. The 1993–4 and 1999–2000 base-year series incorporated several of the recommendations of the 1993 System of National Accounts (1993 SNA) framed by the UN.

For compiling the estimates of GDP, the economy is divided into three broad sectors, agriculture (primary), industry (secondary), and services (tertiary). The value-added or output approach is adopted for the subsectors agriculture, forestry and logging, fishing, mining and quarrying, registered manufacturing, and construction. The income approach is used for the other subsectors.

The domestic product estimates at factor cost by industry of origin fall into two broad categories depending upon the nature of the database: direct estimates and indirect estimates. The direct estimates are based on regularly available annual data. Indirect estimation is resorted to when regular annual data are not available. In such cases, periodic benchmark survey-based estimates are constructed for the survey year and are extrapolated backward or forward on the basis of physical indicator of activity in the sector.

Direct estimates mostly relate to the 'organized' sector while indirect estimates relate to the 'unorganized' sector. 'Direct estimates' have a lower margin of error than 'indirect estimates'. The share of 'direct estimates' in aggregate GDP rose from 57.6 per cent in the 1970–1 base series to 63.7 per cent in the 1980–1 base series and further to 89.6 per cent in the 1993–4 base series. For certain sectors, the share of direct estimates was as low as 26.6 per cent (forestry sector).

A very detailed and informative review of the methodology and data aspects of the 1993–4 base-year series of the NAS is provided in Volume II of the Report of the National Statistical Commission headed by C. Rangarajan. The Report, which was submitted in 2001, contained a critical account of the decline in the quality and reliability of the basic data sets and recommended several improvements. However, the CSO (2006) brochure on the New Series of the NAS does not refer to the status in regard to the implementation of the recommendations of the Rangarajan Commission. Shetty (2006) notes that in the 1999–2000 series progress has been made in updating the database for the services sector. But the quality of data for the agriculture and industry sectors continues to be unsatisfactory. The CSO has a major task to perform in this regard.

The NAS white paper of the CSO presents current and constant price aggregates of GDP and NDP by economic activity, consumption expenditure, saving, capital formation, capital stock, public-sector transactions, and disaggregated statements, as well as four consolidated accounts of the nation.

TIME SERIES ESTIMATES: 1900–1946

The credit for constructing a continuous and long time series of national income estimates for the period 1900–1 to 1946–7 for undivided India including Native States goes to Sivasubramonian (2000) who presented his series in his PhD dissertation completed at the Delhi School of Economics in 1965. The concepts and methods employed by him were broadly similar to those adopted by V.K.R.V. Rao and the National Income Committee. He published his revised series in 2000 taking into account the suggestions and criticisms of well-known economists Heston and Maddison among others. This is the best available series for the first half of the twentieth century.

For the estimation of national income by industrial origin, the economy was divided into three broad sectors: primary, secondary, and tertiary. Each of these sectors was further subdivided into a number of subsectors and their contribution was estimated separately. The 'value-added' approach was followed for all the subsectors in the primary sector and for the mining, large-scale industry, and house property subsectors. The 'income' approach was adopted for the rest of the subsectors. Net factor income from abroad was estimated separately and added to net domestic product (NDP) to obtain NNP. For constant price series, the year 1938–9 was selected as base year.

PATTERN OF ECONOMIC GROWTH

Economic growth, usually measured in terms of the growth in GDP of a country, has received considerable attention during the past two decades or so. The growth performance of the Indian economy and its three broad sectors since 1900 is summarized in Table 1. Several important features of growth are noteworthy. First, in the pre-Independence period from 1900 to 1947, the average annual rate of growth was a mere 0.9 per cent and per capita growth was close to zero. The dominant agricultural sector fared the worst. Second, there was considerable acceleration of growth to around 3.5 per cent a year during 1951–80, but per capita income growth was only about 1.5 per cent. Third, there was further acceleration of growth in the 1980s and 1990s to 5.6 per cent and per capita

growth to 3.5 per cent a year. Fourth, during the very recent period 2001–7, growth increased by about two percentage points to 7.7 per cent. Fifth, in the post-reform period beginning in 1991–2, growth was led by the services sector which recorded growth rates of 7.6 per cent in the 1990s and 9.0 per cent a year in the most recent six-year period. Rakshit (2007) attempts an insightful and detailed analysis of this phenomenon. He examines the demand and supply factors behind India's 'services revolution' and the relative role of agriculture and industry vis-à-vis that of services in the growth process. He notes that the most important factor on the supply side has been growth in total factor productivity (TFP).

SOURCES OF GROWTH

The sources of growth in organized manufacturing and agriculture have been analysed in many studies during the past four decades or so. In recent years several studies for the aggregate economy have been attempted. Bosworth et al. (2007) and Krishna (2007) list the relevant bibliography. The special merit of Bosworth et al. (2007) is that it covers the three

Table 1 Average Growth Rates of GDP by Sector 1900–1 to 2006–7

Sector	1900–1 to 1946–7	1951–2 to 1980–1	1981–2 to 1990–1	1991–2 to 2000–1	2001–2 to 2006–7
(1)	(2)	(3)	(4)	(5)	(6)
Agriculture	0.4	2.5	3.5	2.7	2.9
Industry	1.5	5.3	7.1	5.7	7.9
Services	1.7	4.6	6.8	7.6	9.0
Total GDP	0.9	3.6	5.6	5.6	7.7
Per Capita GDP	0.1	1.4	3.4	3.5	5.8

Sources: S. Sivasubramonian. 2000. *The National Income of India in the Twentieth Century*, New Delhi, Oxford University Press; CSO 2001; www.mospi.gov.i

Notes: 1. The growth rates in columns (2) relate to undivided India.

2. The growth rates for the years 2005–6 and 2006–7 used for column (6) are QE (quick estimate) and RE (revised estimates) respectively.

Table 2   Sources of Economic Growth by Sector: 1960–81, 1985–2005
(annual percentage rate of change)

Sector/Period	GDP	GDP per worker	Contribution of			
			Capital	Land	Education	TFP
(1)	(2)	(3)	(4)	(5)	(6)	(7)
Total Economy						
1960–81	3.4	1.3	1.0	–0.2	0.2	0.2
1981–2005	5.8	3.8	1.4	0.0	0.4	2.0
Agriculture						
1960–81	1.9	0.1	0.2	–0.2	0.1	–0.1
1981–2005	2.8	1.8	0.5	–0.1	0.3	1.1
Industry						
1960–81	4.7	1.6	1.8	–	0.3	–0.4
1981–2005	6.4	2.9	1.6	–	0.3	1.0
Services						
1960–81	4.9	2.0	1.1	–	0.5	0.4
1981–2005	7.6	4.0	0.7	–	0.4	2.9

Source: B. Bosworth, S. Collins, and A. Virmani. 2007. 'Sources of Growth in the Indian Economy',
NBER Working Paper No. 12901, February: Tables 3 and 4.

broad sectors in a unified framework and incorporates the most recent data revisions. The relevant results of the study are given in Table 2. Two sub-periods are distinguished: 1960–81 and 1981–2005.

At the aggregate economy level, while the first period achieved negligible TFP growth (0.2 per cent a year), the second period registered a TFP growth of 2.0 per cent a year, accounting for more than one-third of GDP growth. TFP growth was most impressive in the services sector (2.9 per cent a year) in the period 1981–2005. Agriculture and industry too fared better in this period. However, the contribution of TFP to output growth in industry was quite meagre at about 15 per cent.

INCOME LEVELS IN INDIA AND CHINA

In Table 3, Indian per capita GDP is compared with that of China and the world at three time points, 1913, 1950, and 1998. In 1913, Indian's per capita GDP was 29 per cent higher than China's and it was 44 per cent of world per capita

Table 3   India, China, and the World
1913, 1950, 1998
(per capita GDP in 1990 PPP dollars)

	1913	1950	1998
India	673	619	1760
China	522	439	3117
World	1510	2114	5709
India–China relative	1.29	1.41	0.56
India–world relative	0.44	0.29	0.31

Source: A. Maddison. 2002. 'Introduction: Measuring Asian Performance', in A. Maddison et al., eds, *The Asian Economies in the Twentieth Century*, Cheltenham, Edward Elgar.
Note: The GDP estimates are converted by a purchasing power converter (ICP Geary Khamis PPP).

GDP. In 1950, India further improved its position vis-à-vis China, although it suffered a decline in relation to the world. At the end of the twentieth century in 1998, India's position improved slightly in the world at large but deteriorated sharply in comparison with China. In light of the growth rates of GDP observed since 1998, it can be stated that although India has improved its position in the world, the India–China gap has widened.

K.L. KRISHNA

REFERENCES

Bosworth, B., S. Collins, and A. Virmani. 2007. 'Sources of Growth in the Indian Economy', NBER Working Paper No. 12901, February.

Government of India. 2001. *Report of the National Statistical Commission*, New Delhi.

Central Statistical Organisation. 2001. *National Accounts Statistics, Back Series, 1950–51 to 1992–93*, and *National Accounts Statistics, 2001*.

—————. 2006. *New Series of National Accounts Statistics* (Base Year 1999–2000), Government of India.

Krishna, K.L. 2007. 'What Do We Know about the Sources of Economic Growth in India?' in A. Vaidyanathan and K. L. Krishna, eds, *Institutions and Markets in India's Development*, New Delhi, Oxford University Press.

Sivasubramonian, S. 2000. *The National Income of India in the Twentieth Century*, New Delhi, Oxford University Press.

Rakshit, M. 2007. 'Services Led Growth: The Indian Experience', *Money and Finance*, 3(1), February.

Shetty, S.L. 2006. 'Revision of National Accounts Statistics: A Welcome Step, Good in Parts', *Economic and Political Weekly*, 41(23), 10–16 June.

Political Economy

Political economy refers to the distribution of political and economic power in a given society and how that influences the directions of development and policies that bear on the latter. In India, where the vast masses of people are poor and often socially disadvantaged, a relatively small minority holds much of the power, although in recent years democratic expansion has started to loosen the grip of elite control.

In terms of economic interests the groups that have often been identified as powerful include large and medium business houses, large and medium farmers, the upper echelons of the salaried class, and the top layer of unionized labour. There have been learned, and sometimes intense, debates, particularly among Marxist scholars, on the nature of class formation and mode of production in India. Since empirical data on different categories are often limited to size groups of landholdings, or to asset-holding groups and to corporate market shares, it is not easy to clearly demarcate the different economic interest groups, and it is even more difficult to delineate the cross-cutting cleavages of economic and social stratification. And on how the groups get organized and exercise their power, we usually have mostly anecdotal and case-study evidence. We have more quantitative evidence on wealth distribution, which, of course, is highly unequal in India. According to National Sample Survey data, in 1991 while more than half of the households had less than Rs 50,000 in assets (physical, including land, and financial), only about 10 per cent of rural households and 14 per cent of urban households had assets exceeding Rs 2.5 lakh. (The Market Information Survey of Households carried out by the National Council of Applied Economic Research [NCAER], suggests that in terms of income, about 12 per cent of households in India in 1998–9 had annual income of above Rs 1.05 lakh, while 40 per cent of households had annual income less than Rs 35,000.)

But the inequality in human capital (e.g. education) is much more than in physical or financial capital. According to World Bank estimates, inequality in adult schooling years among people in India is much higher than that in not just Sri Lanka, China, Vietnam, or Indonesia, but also than most Latin American countries including

Brazil and Mexico. The gulf between the educated and the uneducated in India is largely reflected in the social and economic disparity between those who do manual work and those who do not. This is the big dividing line in India, and is much too frozen over time, as education (particularly at secondary level and above), which is the main route of inter-generational mobility, is available (or affordable) to a small group of people, whose boundaries expand much too slowly. In terms of occupation categories, the earlier-mentioned NCAER data suggest that salary earners, professionals, and businessmen constituted the heads of about 22 per cent of households in 1998–9 (since this excludes some unmeasured number of those described as cultivators who may also avoid manual work, the actual proportion of households with heads in non-manual occupations is likely to be higher). Since the overwhelming majority of manual workers are not organized, they hold little political power as workers. Of course, they are at election times often mobilized as social groups (divided along caste, community, religion, or regional lines) that give them some intermittent collective electoral power.

Even when social and economic interest groups (belonging largely, say, to the top two deciles of population) are influential, their influence is somewhat dissipated by extreme fragmentation. In terms of social and economic divisions the Indian elite may be more fragmented than the elite in most other countries, reflecting the fact that India has one of the world's most heterogeneous societies. This gives rise to what political scientists call a 'collective action' problem, that is the actors find it difficult to get their act together. It is more difficult for them to agree on a goal, and even when they agree on one, it is difficult for them to coordinate their actions to achieve that goal. This becomes a particularly acute political–economic problem in the matter of long-term public investment in infrastructure (power, roads, transport, telecommunication, ports, irrigation, etc.). Infrastructure is widely regarded as the crucial bottleneck for Indian economic growth, and the Indian elite is to largely benefit from any improvement in infrastructure. Yet substantial public investment in infrastructure that takes a relatively long time to fructify may require, in the current situation of fiscal deficits, giving up on the part of the elite of government subsidies or benefits of underpriced public goods and services (like water, electricity, fertilizer, cooking gas, and university education), or of major raises in salary or perks in government jobs. But coordinating on short-run sacrifices or curbing particularistic demands on the public fisc (it has been estimated that about two-thirds of all government subsidies go to the relatively rich) for the sake of long-term elite goals has been very difficult to achieve in India. Over the years this collective action problem has become more severe. As more and more of hitherto subordinate social groups have come up to be politically important, particularly at state level (in a welcome expansion of political equality and democracy in India), the sources of demands on the polity have become more diverse. In the first two decades after Independence the massive countrywide organization of the Congress party used to coordinate the transactional negotiations among different groups and leaders in different parts of the country. That organization has fallen into disarray. The proliferation of small and regional parties and their increasing importance for the survival of coalition governments at the centre have often meant that catering to particularistic demands overrides coordination for the long haul. At any given moment an important election somewhere in the country is never too far off, and the short-run issues trump the long-run ones.

When the interest groups are socially and economically fragmented, pulling in different directions with none dominating the whole show, state policies get buffeted around, and any steps towards economic reform are likely to be halting and hesitant. But such fragmentation may also give the state somewhat more autonomy, in the sense that it does not have to march to the tune of one dominant interest group, and an astute political leadership can play off one group against the other to some extent and earn its own rent in the form of special power and privileges. In any case, as the old debates among Marxist scholars on the 'relative autonomy of the state' made clear, in most countries the state leadership retains a great deal of potency as an organizational actor in goal formulation, agenda setting, and policy execution, even when it acts within the broad constraints of interest group politics. In India over the years the state has accumulated a great deal of power in direct ownership and regulation of the economy, and in spite of economic liberalization still controls the production, assets, and employment in large parts of the organized non-agricultural sectors. There is a growing body of public opinion that the state should reorient its role away from public ownership and control of business enterprises and more towards health, education, and other basic social services for the poor, and even when the state is to be the major funding agency for some of these services, it does not necessarily mean that the actual provision of the services has to be bureaucratically managed instead of being contracted out to the private sector or as some form of private–public partnership. But the political implementation of this view in India has been slow.

The paradox is that while the state in India has been powerful (and often heavy-handed) in its regulatory and interventionist role, it will not be described as what the political economy literature calls a 'strong state'. The latter essentially refers to a state that can credibly commit to, for example, a long-term policy and not deviate from it under short-term populist pressures. In the recent history of development, South Korea in the 1960s and 1970s is often cited as an example of a strong state which stuck to its commitment, for example, to export performance as a pre-announced criterion for helping industries, thus using international market discipline in raising cost and quality consciousness in an economy otherwise marked by a great deal of state intervention. Of course, South Korea was then an authoritarian state, and one may think democracies are prone to succumb more to populist pressures. But authoritarianism is neither necessary nor sufficient for credible commitment. That it is not necessary is illustrated by democratic Japan and the Scandinavian countries often successfully committing to pre-announced long-term policies; that it is not sufficient is, of course, amply illustrated by many African authoritarian regimes. But the success of Japan and Scandinavian countries as 'strong' democratic states and the failure of democratic India to be one may have something to do with the fact that social homogeneity and relative economic equality in the former enable them to resolve some collective action problems more easily and coordinate on long-term policies in a way that is much more difficult for extremely heterogeneous and unequal India.

But there is clearly a trade-off between credibility and accountability in state affairs. The institutional insulation that may be required to follow through on commitments may over time make the leadership impervious to the felt (and changing) needs and demands of common people. Even well-intentioned state-directed technocratic development projects, which do not involve the people at ground level but simply treat them as objects of the development process, often end up primarily as conduits of largesse for elite groups—middlemen, contractors, officials, and politicians—and very little reaches the intended beneficiaries. Even when a significant amount reaches the latter, the benefits are sometimes of the wrong kind, inappropriate technologically and unsustainable environmentally, corrosive of local institutions of community bonding and self-help, and always leaving untapped the large reservoir of local initiative, ingenuity and information.

Of course, accountability can be exercised through the periodic elections in which common people give their verdict on politicians' performance, and the Indian electorate has been quite assertive in throwing out incumbents. But general elections constitute a rather blunt instrument for economic performance monitoring. Elections are fought on multidimensional platforms, and even vital economic issues often do not get salience in electoral mobilization. A particular leader who is perceived to uphold a hitherto marginalized caste group's dignity may win election after election, even though the same leader's policy neglect may be responsible for the dismal education and health environment of most children in that caste group.

One can say that federalism and decentralization are ways of making the state more responsive to local needs. The rise of regional parties and the strength of local autonomy movements at state level certainly reflect that, although the major Indian states are larger than most countries in the world, and as such the state governments are still quite distant from local communities, Indian federalism is currently afflicted by two major dilemmas. One is that while the regional governments are becoming more

important in national politics, their fiscal dependence on the central government is steadily increasing: catering to the various particularistic demands, many of them are near fiscal bankruptcy which certainly limits their economic power and ability to carry out various important social service functions. The other dilemma is that with economic liberalization and increased regional competition, the disparity between economically advanced and backward states is growing: the advanced states increasingly resent the redistributive functions of Indian federalism (through the dispensations of the Finance Commission and the Planning Commission) that to them look like rewarding inefficiency and creating dependency, and yet no Indian polity can ignore the fact that some of the populous backward states hold a very large number of seats in the Lok Sabha and a coalition government is unlikely to survive any large-scale withdrawal of their support. How the Indian polity tackles these two dilemmas will shape the political economy of Indian federalism in the near future.

The seventy-third and seventy-fourth constitutional amendments in the early 1990s have given some potency to the movement towards decentralization below state level, all the way down to *gram panchayats*. While this is a major step towards local accountability, as yet effective decentralization is largely absent in most parts of India (outside three or four states). Very few administrative functions (and even fewer sources of independent finance) have been devolved to the local governments, and state-level bureaucrats and politicians still largely hold sway. That in states like Kerala and West Bengal this decentralization has been somewhat more effective than in other states has much to do with the fact that prior land reforms and political awareness movements in these two states have made capture of local governments by the oligarchic local elites somewhat more difficult. While fiscally responsible and locally accountable governments at panchayat level remain one of the major ways of deepening Indian democracy, much will depend on how far we can proceed in our campaigns for land reform to weaken the powers of the local oligarchy, expansion of education, a more vigorous devolution of finances to the local governments, and regular auditing and activation of local non-governmental organizations (NGOs) and media as watchdogs on local-level corruption. There is some evidence that the active freedom-of-information movement and reservation of panchayat leadership positions for women and scheduled castes is having some salutary effects in this respect in some areas.

PRANAB BARDHAN

Savings and Investment

India is a high savings economy when viewed in international perspective. Reflecting India's savings growth, investment has been high. The economy's savings and investment rates have recently shot up to over 35 per cent of the gross domestic product (GDP). This is remarkable when one considers India's per capita income in a cross-country comparison. India's high savings–investment profile was achieved in the early years through policy change, including nationalization of banks in 1969 that multiplied the number of bank branches in rural India, facilitating and increasing financial savings. It was also the result of the beneficial effects of growing incomes on household savings and investment. However, the spurt in the 2000s mainly reflects a growth in private business savings as well as reduction in government deficit as a

consequence of the Fiscal Responsibility and Budget Management (FRBM) Act 2003. Also, the ratio of physical to financial assets has registered an increase after decades of impressive growth in financial assets.

During the early Five Year Plans, the government, considering itself the engine of growth, took a leading role in investment in core strategic, infrastructure, and industrial sectors, confining private-sector activity to only the residual sectors. Further, private-sector activity was circumscribed through licensing and controls such as a restrictive exit policy. Public-sector activity was considered so important that most financial savings instruments—banks, contractual savings institutions such as pension and provident funds, and mutual funds—were stipulated, or strongly encouraged through the tax structure, to invest predominantly in government. A high incremental capital–output ratio implied low marginal efficiency of investment and a lower than achievable rate of economic growth.

The dismantling of the supremacy of the public sector in commandeering financial resources gathered pace with India's 1991 financial crisis. Steadily the financial sector was liberalized together with a gradual removal of licences and controls on private-sector activity. Banks could lend more liberally, with a scaling back of directed lending, and at deregulated interest rates, while micro-finance was encouraged at the same time. Foreign banks could open branches, catering to the private sector. Foreign direct investment (FDI), virtually impossible during the early Plans, was welcomed in specified sectors. Even disinvestment from non-performing as well as profitable public-sector enterprises became acceptable as a concept and was attempted by successive governments, albeit with limited success.

The story recounted in the preceding paragraphs is the one that possibly represents, by and large, the prevailing view. While history—including economic history—is an analytical interpretation of human events, it should nevertheless be considered with perspicuity. Those economies that did not opt for a planning framework in East Asia or Latin America in the post-Second World War era, may have experienced economic growth rates initially higher than India's. This reflected their exclusive export orientation, while India favoured the costlier option of self-sufficiency. But their strategic interests had to be set aside. Not those of India. In hindsight, the choice by the founding fathers of a development path that enabled rapid growth of the large industrial sector through public investment and meticulous management of the nation's scarce resources turns out to have been justified in today's international environment in which a nation's strategic global reach is crucial.

Like every overdrawn policy structure, however, this stance had outlived its purpose by 1991 and the moment had arrived for it to be dismantled in order to energize much-needed private-sector investment and economic activity. There has been a jump in gross domestic investment in the 2000s, from 23.8 per cent of GDP in 2000–1 to over 27 per cent in 2003–4 and 35.1 per cent in 2006–7. Private-sector activity comprised the major increase, private corporate investment rising by 53 per cent, 41 per cent, and (possibly) 25–30 per cent, in 2004–5, 2005–6, and 2006–7 respectively (Government of India 2005; Chanduri 2007)

A comparison of the evolution of public and private savings rates is useful in assessing the rise in public consumption pari passu with the decline in public investment. Total gross domestic savings (that is before mortgage and other loans) in proportion to GDP more than tripled in modern India's economic experience, from 10.3 per

cent of GDP in 1950–5 to 21.6 per cent in 1976–80, surging to 24.1 per cent in 1991–6 (Athukorala and Sen 2002). They continued to rise, to 28.1 per cent in 2003–4 and, remarkably, to 34.7 per cent in 2006–7 (Chanduri 2007) subject to some statistical questions (Balakrishnan and Suresh Babu 2007). The public-sector component of savings was always small, indicating that the public sector was barely meeting its own revenue expenditures. Of course some of it may well have been due to development expenditure. But, as administration and interest expenses climbed, dissavings emerged in 1998–9 and peaked in 2001–2. Thus the public savings ratios to GDP were 1.7 per cent in 1950–5, 4.3 per cent in 1976–80, 1.7 per cent in 1991–6, –2.7 per cent in 2001–2, and –0.3 per cent in 2003–4. A turnaround began after this with the central government strictly adhering to the roadmap for reduction in both the fiscal and revenue deficits, with many state governments following suit.

Private-sector savings have thus represented the overwhelming share of savings, even exceeding total savings since 1998–9. Of this, household savings have far exceeded private corporate savings, the former typically comprising 85 per cent of private savings since the mid-1990s. They were even higher at near 90 per cent but, as private corporate savings improved, there was a remix in the composition. Nevertheless, private corporate savings are still only about one-seventh of household savings. There remains no doubt, therefore, that households have been the overwhelming source of India's savings.

This savings growth was propelled by the expansion in the opportunity to save in non-physical assets as population per bank branch fell from 90,000 in the mid-1950s to 14,000 in the early 1990s. Household financial savings experienced phenomenal growth from 1.6 per cent of GDP in 1950–5 to 10.3 per cent in 1991–6, and then remained stable at about 10.6 per cent. The share of financial savings in total household savings also grew commensurately, from 21.7 per cent in 1950–5 to 38.0 per cent in 1976–80 and 54.2 per cent in 1991–6. It declined somewhat, to 47.3 per cent, in the 2000–4 period with relatively faster growth in physical assets.

Empirical evidence points to various favourable influences on savings including the maintenance of positive real interest rates (the nominal rate being mainly administered), a low inflation rate within an anti-inflation policy framework, positive economic growth (even if somewhat low by Asian standards), and a steady rise in per capita income (though perhaps slow, reflecting the rate of growth of population). But it is clearly the growth in financial intermediation that stands out most as the main driver of savings. On the negative side, a worsening of the terms of trade—relative price of exports over imports—as well as remittances from abroad appear to have wielded adverse influence.

Authors have postulated a robust relationship between economic growth and capital accumulation. For example, Chandra and Sandilands (2001) have claimed that growth has been the causal factor in capital accumulation. While public investment has been mainly policy driven, private investment has had a long-term relationship with GDP and economic growth. Athukorala and Sen (2002) also find that increased availability of credit and lowered cost of capital encouraged private corporate investment, in particular during the reform-oriented 1990s, once again bringing to the fore the role played by the financial sector in the savings–investment process. Interestingly, based on such evidence, the cutback in public investment during the 1991–4 fiscal

tightening seems to have affected private corporate investment adversely, pointing to a possible complementary relationship, and reflecting a widely prevalent view that relative inadequacy in the public provision of economic infrastructure has stunted growth in private investment.

The transmission mechanisms and channels that converted financial policy into instruments for successful investment performance have been detailed in various studies. The role of directed credit in safeguarding investment in priority sectors has been mentioned. With time, as the need emerged for an efficient financial architecture, institutional changes comprising an array of financial reforms were undertaken. Improving the allocative efficiency of resources by deregulating lending rates assisted private investment to penetrate further. At the other end, financial intermediation in the informal sector has also served as a catalyst in unlocking investment funds for those who would not have had access to loanable funds otherwise.

Government has played a crucial role in the development, regulation, and functioning of life insurance and provident funds as long-term savings instruments. It has also accessed, for its own needs, these contractual savings that comprised more than 30 per cent of financial savings by the 1990s. Indeed, experts have opined that such funds have been pre-empted by the public sector. While liberalization of the sector has occurred subsequently, rigidities remain. The capital market, on the other hand, has been a major vehicle for converting savings into private investment. It has experienced phenomenal growth and the risk and exigencies associated with its formative years have been controlled with the establishment and functioning of an appropriate regulatory authority. There has been significant growth in the derivatives market, over-the-counter derivatives playing a role in mitigating the risks of banks, corporations, and financial entities. Foreign institutional investors are being allowed flexibility, albeit regulated, to submit appropriate collateral when trading in derivatives.

With the opening up of the economy, an additional source of funds has been capital inflows. External-sector policy and monetary policy have been closely coordinated. Capital inflows have generally been absorbed in the country's reserves despite their monetary impact, in order to avoid an untoward currency appreciation, with the objective of maintaining export competitiveness. High investment has been an enabling factor in the export-led growth, with a supportive tax structure as its backdrop.

Recently, some modifications have taken place. To recall, in 2003–4, there was a small current account surplus (excess productive capacity) which has now turned into a small deficit, though considerably smaller than the large capital inflows. Thus much of the spurt in investment has been financed from domestic savings. The strength of the rupee has led to its appreciation, and a free float cannot be ruled out in the future. Such a policy would also counteract any demand-driven inflation that has been a short-term, yet nagging, phenomenon in 2006–7.

To conclude, what has been the nature of economic processes in India in terms of savings, investment, and economic growth? Was it demand driven as John Maynard Keynes viewed the world, where an x amount of expenditure—whether backed always by savings or not—would lead, through spin-off effects, to yx amount of income where y was a multiple of x? Was it the neo-classical process associated with the names of Robert M. Solow and T.W. Swan who emphasized the role of savings—translated into investment—for economic growth? Was it economic growth

and rising incomes that triggered savings and investment, in line with the hypothesis propounded by Arthur W. Lewis based on the concept of capitalist surplus? Or was it technological innovation that shifted up the trajectory of the growth path and endogenized technical change itself, as Paul Romer and other contemporary economists have theorized?

Each of these linkages partially explains India's economic processes. During the early Plans, India opted for an expenditure-oriented development strategy based on imported technology in mega infrastructure projects. At the same time, specific policy measures facilitated a rapid growth in savings. As economic growth occurred and incomes rose, further enhancement in savings and investment was realized. As the economy was liberalized and opened in recent years, unrestricted importation of new technology in the manufacturing sector such as textiles and automobiles shifted upward the trend rate of growth, while the share of international trade in GDP grew significantly.

For the immediate future, there continues to be a need for higher public investment. India's annual growth rates have reached 9 per cent in the last three years up to 2006–7. But agriculture has reached only 1.5–2.0 per cent growth, compared to 10–11 per cent for manufacturing and services. As the majority of arable land remains unirrigated, agricultural-sector growth is determined by the vagaries of the monsoon. Volatility in agricultural growth translates also into unwarranted variations in overall growth. Investment in irrigation, perhaps in a public–private partnership, is imperative to lift India out of the limiting effects of its agricultural cycles. Investment is also needed in other economic infrastructure including highways, ports, internal waterways, railways, and, last but not least, utilities including electricity and gas. These challenges can be met by even higher private—both household and corporate—savings, continued reduction in public-sector dissaving, and judicious accessing of funds from international capital markets.

PARTHASARATHI SHOME

REFERENCES

Athukorala, Prema-Chandra and Kunal Sen. 2002. *Savings, Investment and Growth in India*, Oxford University Press, New Delhi.

Balakrishnan, Pulapre and M. Suresh Babu. 2007. 'Trends in Savings, Investment and Consumption', *Economic and Political Weekly*, Mumbai, 42(18), 5 May.

Bernardi, Luigi, Angela Fraschini, and Parthasarathi Shome, eds. 2006. *Tax Systems and Tax Reforms in South and East Asia*, Oxford, Routledge.

Chandra, Ramesh and Roger J. Sandilands. 2001. 'Does Investment Cause Growth? A Test of Endogenous Demand-Driven Theory of Growth Applied to India 1950–96', United Kingdom, University of Strathclyde, mimeo.

Chanduri, Saumitra. 2007. 'Sustainability of Economic Growth', *Economic Times*, New Delhi, 29 June.

Government of India. 2005a. *Economic Survey 2004–05*, New Delhi, Ministry of Finance.

———. 2005b. *Mid-Year Review*, December, New Delhi, Ministry of Finance, Economic Division.

Shome, Parthasarathi. 2002. *India's Fiscal Matters*, New Delhi, Oxford University Press.

AGRICULTURE, RURAL ECONOMY, AND NATURAL RESOURCES

Agriculture Development

Agriculture plays a pivotal role in the Indian economy. Although its contribution to gross domestic product (GDP) is now less than one-fourth, it provides employment to nearly 60 per cent of the Indian workforce. Also, the forward and backward linkage effects of agriculture growth increase the incomes in the non-agriculture sector. The growth of some commercial crops has significant potential for promoting exports of agricultural commodities and bringing about faster development of agro-based industries.

Thus agriculture not only contributes to overall growth of the economy but also reduces poverty by providing employment and food security to the majority of the population in the country.

The objective of this entry is to examine the performance and policy issues in Indian agriculture since Independence with emphasis on the last two decades. It is divided into four sections. The second section deals with performance while the third section briefly examines policies since Independence. The last section is devoted to a discussion of policy changes needed for higher growth in agriculture.

PERFORMANCE OF AGRICULTURE

One of the paradoxes of the Indian economy is that the decline in the share of agricultural workers in total workers has been slower than the decline in the share of agriculture in the GDP. For example, the share of agriculture and allied activities in the GDP declined from 57.7 per cent in 1950–1 to 22 per cent in 2002–3 (Table 1). The share of agriculture in total workers, however, declined slowly from 75.9 per cent in 1961 to 59.9 per cent in 1999–2000 (Table 2).

Table 1 Share of Agriculture GDP in Total GDP: All India (at 1993–4 prices)

Year	Agriculture, forestry, and fishing	Agriculture*
1950–1	57.7	50.2
1960–1	53.0	47.3
1980–1	39.7	35.8
2002–3	22.0	20.0

Source: 'National Accounts Statistics of India: 1950–51 to 2002–03', Economic and Political Weekly Research Foundation, December 2004, Mumbai.
Note: *Refers to crop production and livestock.

Table 2 Share of Agriculture in Total Employment: All India

Year	Agriculture, forestry, and fishing	Crop production and plantations	Livestock
1961	75.9	73.5	2.0
1999–2000	59.9	54.3	4.1

Source: K. Sundaram. 2001. 'Employment and Poverty in 1990s', Economic and Political Weekly, 11 August: 3039–49.

Between 1961 and 1999–2000, there was a decline of 30 percentage points in the share of agriculture in GDP while the decline in share of agriculture in employment was of only 15 percentage points. As a result, the gap between labour productivity in agriculture and non-agriculture increased rapidly.

In terms of growth, the performance of agriculture in the post-Independence era has been impressive as compared to the pre-Independence period. The all crop output growth of around 2.7 per cent per annum in the post-Independence period (during 1949–50 to 1999–2000) was much higher than the negligible growth rate of around 0.4 per cent per annum in the first half of the last century. As a result, India achieved self-sufficiency in food grains at national level.

The highest growth rate of GDP from agriculture and allied activities of more than 3 per cent per annum was recorded in the 1980s (Table 3). In the post-reform period, it declined to 2.76 per cent per annum. The deceleration in the growth rate of GDP from agriculture between the first half of the 1990s and the later period is glaring. It is a matter of concern that during the 1997–8 to 2004–5 period, agriculture growth was only 1.6 per cent per annum (Table 3).

Table 3 Growth Rates in Agriculture GDP: All India

Period	Growth rate (per cent per annum)
1950–5 to 1964–5	2.51
1967–8 to 1980–1	2.20
1980–1 to 1990–1	3.07
1992–3 to 2001–2	2.76
1992–3 to 1996–7	3.85
1997–8 to 2004–5	1.60

Source: National Accounts Statistics. Various years. Central Statistical Organisation, Government of India.
Note: GDP is in 1980–1 constant prices from 1950–1 to 1980–1; in 1993–4 constant prices for the period 1980–1 to 2004–5.

Extensive cultivation has characterized Indian agriculture during the pre-1965 era, and intensive cultivation in the post-green revolution period. There has been significant increase in the use of modern inputs in Indian agriculture. During the period 1950–1 to 2003–4, the percentage of net irrigated area to net cultivated area increased from around 17 to 41. During the same period, fertilizer consumption showed a significant rise from less than 1 kg/ha to 90 kg/ha. Similarly, the percentage of area under high-yielding varieties (HYVs) to cereals cropped area has risen from 15 in 1970–1 to 75 in the late 1990s. The share of agriculture in electricity consumption also rose from 4 per cent in 1950–1 to nearly 30 per cent in recent years. All this led to a significant increase in agricultural output over time.

Output of all crops increased at a compound growth rate of 3.15 per cent per annum during 1949–50 to 1964–5, significantly led by area expansion (Table 4). There has not been any significant increase in agricultural growth in the post-green revolution period. However, the sources of growth have changed from area expansion in the pre-green revolution period to yield growth in the later periods. Yield growth at 2.56 per cent per annum was the highest in the 1980s. However, it declined significantly to 1.31 per cent in the 1990s.

The aggregate output growth at national level hides a great deal of variation in the performance of different crops and regions. While wheat has recorded high and accelerated rates of yield increases, others like coarse cereals and pulses have not. Food grains and non-food grains recorded the highest growth rates in output as well as yields in the 1980s. In the 1990s, growth rate decelerated for both food grains and non-food grains. Increasing commercialization of agriculture started in a significant way in the 1980s.

Table 4   Compound Growth Rates of Area, Output, and Yield: All India

Period	All crops			Food grains			Non-food grains		
	Area	Output	Yield	Area	Output	Yield	Area	Output	Yield
1949–50 to 1964–5	1.58	3.15	1.21	1.35	2.82	1.36	2.44	3.74	0.89
1967–8 to 1980–1	0.51	2.19	1.28	0.38	2.15	1.33	0.94	2.26	1.19
1980–1 to 1989–90	0.10	3.19	2.56	−0.23	2.85	2.74	1.12	3.77	2.31
1990–1 to 1999–2000	0.25	2.28	1.31	−0.17	1.94	1.52	1.37	2.78	1.04

Source: Ministry of Agriculture, Government of India.

There are large regional disparities in output across regions (see Vaidyanathan 1994). Certain regions such as Punjab, Haryana, western Uttar Pradesh, parts of Andhra Pradesh, and Tamil Nadu have benefited more during the initial phase of the green revolution than others. This had accentuated regional disparities in the immediate post-green revolution period. An important feature of the 1980s and the early 1990s, however, is that there has been much more equitable spread of agricultural growth. According to Bhalla and Singh (1997) the period 1980–3 to 1990–3 marks a turning point (in terms of growth) in India's agricultural development. After performing poorly during the early years of the green revolution, many of the states where poverty is widespread—Assam, Bihar, Orissa, Madhya Pradesh, and West Bengal—have shown significant growth in the 1980s. Oilseeds have also gained in the dry belt of Rajasthan, Madhya Pradesh, Karnataka, and Maharashtra.

During the post-reform period, in response to the growing domestic and export demand for non-cereal items of food, there has been a discernible shift in the allocation of resources in Indian agriculture in the recent period away from cereals, particularly coarse cereals, to dairy farming, poultry, edible oils, meat, fish, vegetables, fruits, etc. These enterprises, being labour intensive, are suited to smallholders and lead to a rise in wage employment. Besides they are environment friendly, as they are

generally less land and water intensive, and there is also a rise in incomes of farmers growing high value products. There have, however, been some disturbing trends in the post-reform period. Apart from stagnant or declining public investment, the post-reform period has witnessed a decline in institutional credit for small and marginal farmers, increasing risk and uncertainty in agriculture due to globalization and the World Trade Organization (WTO), increase in farmer suicides, less emphasis on research and extension, and rise in regional disparities.

POLICIES SINCE INDEPENDENCE

At the outset it may be mentioned that agriculture is a 'state subject' under the Constitution of India. However, the central government plays a crucial role in shaping agricultural policies. Although Indian agriculture is in private hands, government policies have greatly influenced its pace and character.

Broadly, agricultural development policies over time can be divided into four sets of policy packages: (a) institutional reforms; (b) public investment policies; (c) incentive policies; and (d) reforms and globalization policies. The relative importance of the first three sets has varied over time.

Thus, during the first three Five Year Plans (1950–65), the institutional reforms and public investment packages dominated. The central and state governments enacted a number of laws regarding land reforms. These laws mainly relate to three aspects:

abolition of zamindari system, land ceiling and redistribution of land, and tenancy reforms. The government was successful in abolishing the zamindari or intermediary system after paying compensation to the zamindars. The land ceiling laws were not effective although there was redistribution of some land to the beneficiaries. The tenancy reforms were more successful in two states, West Bengal in the east and Kerala in the south, than in others. West Bengal succeeded in giving ownership rights to tenants, particularly sharecroppers (bargardars). Some efforts were made to consolidate fragmented holdings in India since Independence. In some parts of north and north-west India these efforts were relatively successful.

There was significant public investment in agriculture during 1950–65. To achieve the objective of self-sufficiency in food grains, there was massive investment particularly in constructing irrigation reservoirs and distribution systems. Another important policy during this period was the expansion of institutional credit which helped reduce informal sources that had been exploitative in respect of interest rates and terms and conditions.

During the 1967–90 period, incentive policies for adoption of new technology and public investment policies dominated government strategy in agriculture. After the humiliating experience with import of food grains in the mid-1960s, there was a vigorous drive for achieving self-sufficiency in food grains by stepping up public investment in irrigation and introduction of new technology through incentives. There was a need to increase domestic food production at a faster rate by much higher productivity without upsetting the agrarian structure. Luckily at that time new high-yielding dwarf varieties of wheat and rice were available in Mexico and the Philippines respectively. Yields increased significantly for wheat

initially and later for rice. This breakthrough is popularly known as the 'green revolution'. The productivity improvement associated with the green revolution is best described as forest- or land-saving agriculture. It may be noted that without the green revolution it would not have been possible to lift the production potential of Indian agriculture.

As mentioned earlier, inter-regional variations increased in the initial phase of the green revolution as it was limited to a few states like Punjab, Haryana, and Uttar Pradesh. However,

unlike in the first decade of the green revolution, the experience in the eighties indicates that the green revolution is spreading to new areas, particularly to the eastern and western regions; the new technology is being increasingly adopted by the small farmers; there is a decline in the relative prices of food grains; and the real wages in agriculture have started rising, especially in the less developed regions [Rao 1994: 63].

Incentive policies focused on both inputs and output. Subsidies for inputs like irrigation, credit, fertilizers, and power increased significantly in the 1970s and 1980s. The objective of the subsidies is to provide inputs at low prices to protect farmer interests and encourage diffusion of new technology. Similarly, on the output side, there has been a comprehensive long-term procurement-cum-distribution policy in the post-green revolution period. The government announces the support prices at sowing time and agrees to buy all the grains offered for sale at this price. To support these operations, institutions like the Food Corporation of India (FCI) and the Agricultural Prices Commission (APC) were established in the mid-1960s.

In the post-reform period, economic reforms in India since 1991 have improved the incentive framework and agriculture has benefited from reduction in protection to industry. The terms of trade for agriculture have improved and private investment has increased. Export of commodities, particularly cereals, has risen and there has been some progress on market reforms in terms of removing domestic and external controls. However, there were also concerns about agriculture and food security in the 1990s. There has been emphasis on price factors at the cost of non-price factors like research and extension, irrigation, and credit. Economic reforms have largely neglected the agricultural sector and only in the last few years have domestic and external trade reforms in the sector started.

Trade policies in India during the last five decades have been highly interventionist and discriminating against agriculture. There has been pessimism regarding international trade in agriculture.

Trade liberalization in agriculture has been faster towards the end of the 1990s in tune with WTO agreements. There has been considerable progress in the liberalization of export controls, and quantitative controls on imports and on decontrol of domestic trade.

Lifting of quantitative restrictions on imports since April 2000 has resulted in a number of agricultural imports, which include fruits, ketchups, and meat products. But monitoring of imports for 300 sensitive products shows that so far such imports constitute only a small proportion of total agricultural imports in the country. Thus the expectation of significant imports due to trade liberalization has not been fulfilled. India has considerable flexibility to counter the flooding of the Indian market by cheap agricultural imports through imposition of tariffs (bound rates) under the WTO.

POLICY CHANGES NEEDED FOR HIGHER GROWTH

There has been concern regarding agricultural growth in India since the mid-1990s. The growth rate of agriculture during 1997–9 to 2004–5 was only around 1.6 per cent per annum. Yield growth also declined significantly in the 1990s. It is important to realize the full potential of agriculture not only for higher overall growth but also to reduce poverty in India. Many policy issues are being discussed in this regard.

A paradoxical situation existed in 2002. Around 60 to 65 million metric tonnes of food grains were held as stock while 260 million people lived below the poverty line. Continuous increases in procurement price have led to the accumulation of stocks far above the levels required. The steep increases in procurement price have discouraged the private sector from holding stocks, made exports uncompetitive, and reduced the domestic consumption of food grains, particularly by the poor. The performance of the public distribution system (PDS) has also not been satisfactory. There is need for reforms in procurement price, buffer stock, and distribution policies (see Vyas 2003).

Public investment in agriculture, particularly in irrigation, and research and extension is needed for higher growth. There seems to be some trade-off between input subsidies and public investment in agriculture. The problem of mounting subsidies and their effect in terms of crowding out public agricultural investment has been highlighted in the Tenth Plan document. Input subsidies (on power, fertilizers, and irrigation) have been rising while public investment has been declining. Therefore reduction in input subsidies is important for raising public investment. Investment in rural infrastructure is more important for agricultural growth and rural development than trade liberalization per se. There has to be greater focus on dryland marginal areas for higher returns.

The growth rate of agricultural credit for small and marginal farmers declined in the 1990s as compared to the 1980s. At the same time, there was no decline of growth in credit for large farmers. The credit system must reach marginal and small farmers. In recent years, farmer suicides have increased in some states. Most of the studies have, rightly, identified household indebtedness as the main reason for suicides. Indebtedness is due to increase in the input intensity of agriculture. Increase in institutional credit and crop insurance for reducing the risks are important for helping farmers. However, since crop insurance is difficult to implement, it is better to reduce risks through other means.

The yield growth for many crops has declined in the 1990s. Technology plays an important role in improving yields. A fresh look at the priorities of the Indian agricultural research system is necessary in light of the emerging prospects. It is known that India spends only 0.5 per cent of GDP on agricultural research as compared to more than 1 per cent in other developing countries. There is considerable potential for raising the effectiveness of these outlays by reordering the priorities in agricultural research and redefining the relative roles of the public and private sectors in research and extension. The returns to investment on research and extension will be much higher than those to other investments.

Management of water is going to be crucial for raising living standards in rural areas. Watershed development can be sustained in the long run only through social mobilization and capacity building. Conservation of surface and ground water can be improved when water and power are priced according to the volume of consumption. Community involvement is essential in setting the user charges as well as for assessing individual consumption.

Institutional reforms are important, particularly in the domain of public systems, for sustained technical progress and output growth in agriculture. There is limited scope for privatizing irrigation, research and extension, and other infrastructure facilities.

Problems such as land degradation, chemicalization of agriculture, waterlogging, and groundwater depletion are affecting the country's land and water resources. Institutions are needed for better management of land and water in order to have sustainable agriculture.

The reforms in the industrial sector that started in 1991 benefited agriculture by shifting the terms of trade in favour of agriculture. However, the full benefits for agriculture can be expected to materialize when reforms directly affecting agriculture, such as removal of restrictions on domestic trade and processing, stepping up public investment in agriculture, and reforms in the management of infrastructure, are put in place.

India does not have to change its food policies relating to minimum support price, buffer stock, and the PDS due to the WTO. The actual tariffs for most of the commodities in India are much lower than the Uruguay Round bound rates. As such, it can easily check edible oil imports by raising its tariff. There is, however, need for taking timely measures within the existing tariff bindings to restrict imports, which affect producers' livelihoods. Indian agriculture is now exposed to international price volatility. In the negotiations, India along with other third world countries should keep up pressure on developed countries to reduce their subsidies.

As international trade in agricultural commodities is likely to be liberalized further, a greater preparedness is required to face the competition in the international market. Standards are fast becoming an important factor in global trade particularly regarding sanitary and phyto sanitary (SPS) measures. In order to compete in the world trade and exploit the full potential of trade liberalization, India should streamline its domestic reforms, infrastructure, and institutions.

The shift in consumption patterns also indicates that there is need for crop diversification and improvements in allied activities like livestock and fisheries. This will also improve employment opportunities. Similarly, reforms should be undertaken for the growth of the rural non-farm sector. The rigidities in rural non-farm employment have to be removed in order to bring about rural transformation. The very low educational levels in rural areas limit access to better-paid employment, leaving rural workers with low skills, low productivity, and, therefore, probably low wage jobs. Education, infrastructure, credit, etc. have to be improved in order to raise the productivity of rural non-farm employment. The policy changes in the food and agricultural sector and in the rural non-farm sector are expected to reduce rural poverty through rural transformation.

S. MAHENDRA DEV

REFERENCES

Bhalla, G.S. and Gurmail Singh. 1997. 'Recent Developments in Indian Agriculture: A State Level Analysis', *Economic and Political Weekly*, 32(13), 29 March–4 April.

Rao, C.H.H. 1994. *Agricultural Growth, Rural Poverty and Environmental Degradation in India*, New Delhi, Oxford University Press.

Vaidyanathan, A. 1994. 'Performance of Indian Agriculture since Independence', in K. Basu, ed., *Agrarian Questions*, New Delhi, Oxford University Press.

Vyas, V.S. 2003. *India's Agrarian Structure, Economic Policies and Sustainable Development: Variations on a Theme*, New Delhi, Academic Foundation.

Contract Farming

Contract farming can be described broadly as an institutional arrangement between farm and firm to produce and transact agricultural commodities on predetermined terms.

The core of contract farming arrangements is some form of commitment, oral or written, on the part of the farmer to provide a commodity of a particular quality and quantity, grown according to specified methods agreed upon before sowing, with a corresponding commitment on the part of the firm to buy that produce at a pre-fixed price. Such an agreement could also involve the firm providing production support through, for example, the supply of inputs and technical advice. This is not the typical arrangement in most developing countries, where farmers make production decisions independently and the produce then passes through many hands before reaching the final buyer.

In theory, contract farming offers farmers an opportunity to link up with a buyer and fix a price even before sowing, thus offering a kind of insurance—not only against price fluctuations, but also against the prospect of not finding a buyer. For firms, the attractiveness of contracting derives from being able to procure timely supplies of quality produce without having to take on the responsibility of managing cultivation on factory-owned farms. It offers an advantage over the spot market too, where supply is usually uncertain and produce might be of variable quality. Further, the direct link between firm and farm implies disintermediation or the elimination of trader-middlemen, saving on transaction costs. In principle, therefore, contract farming is regarded a win–win arrangement with both the farmer and firm standing to benefit.

CONTRACT FARMING IN INDIA: HISTORY AND POLICY

In India, contract farming goes back to the colonial era when indigo, opium, tobacco, and cotton were sourced from cultivators using forms of marketing contracts. In the post-Independence era, commercial seed production by seed companies that emerged in the 1960s, private and public, has invariably been organized around some kind of contract production. Seed potato and cotton stand out as examples where seed multiplication for firms is undertaken on a large scale by contract farmers. Milk production in the cooperative sector, too, has been along these lines, following Operation Flood in the 1970s. Private-sector milk processors have largely been content following this model. Sugarcane is often cited as a prominent example of contract farming, where the state mandates a command area around sugar mills for procurement on pre-specified terms.

Clearly, contract farming is not a new phenomenon. Yet, a recent wave of industrialization of agriculture in developing countries is precipitating a vigorous shift in favour of contract farming on a scale that is probably unprecedented. Changing tastes of consumers, higher demand for processed foods, and globalization of the agro-industry have, each in their own way, contributed to this redefining of producer–processor relationships in developing countries.

India is no exception. The years since the mid-1990s have seen dramatic change in the institutional landscape of Indian agriculture and could well signify a watershed. To understand why this ongoing transformation

is noteworthy, it is useful to step back to look at the recent history of agricultural policy in India.

Ever since Independence, transactions in farm commodities have been regulated heavily, notably through the Essential Commodities Act (ECA) and the Agricultural Produce Marketing Committees Act (APMC Act). The ECA imposes restrictions on storage and movement of certain 'essential' commodities by private parties, mainly to protect consumers. The APMC Act, on the other hand, mandated that purchases of certain agricultural commodities be through government-regulated markets (mandis) with the payment of designated commissions and marketing fees. Furthermore, the Land Ceiling Act proscribed firms from owning and operating large-scale factory-farms. Together, these severely circumscribed private sector participation in agriculture.

Though the APMC Act was designed to protect farmers' interests, it perversely rendered farmers dependent on middlemen—who were financiers, information brokers, and traders, all rolled into one. This dependency often turned exploitative; farmers received but a fraction of the price paid by the final consumer, with middlemen cornering a large part of the rest. Over time, critics felt that APMC Act and the ECA had perhaps overextended their reach, compromising farmers and consumers in favour of trader-middlemen.

Since 1991, with economy-wide reforms, three broad trends began to put severe pressure on these policies that were perceived to be anachronistic, inefficient, and iniquitous. First, with the growth of private-sector participation and export orientation in the processing industries following delicensing, control over the source of feedstock to ensure quality and traceability became desirable. Second, the emergence of supermarkets and modern retail chains necessitated a steady supply of fresh produce of consistently good quality (Gulati 2007). Third, against a background of a silent collapse of state extension systems and rising input subsidies to agriculture, the state began to disengage from traditional forms of policy intervention seeking to create spaces for the private sector within agriculture. Contract farming began to feature prominently in this effort.

In 2000, as part of what was termed a 'Rainbow Revolution', the National Agricultural Policy stated: 'Private sector participation will be promoted through contract farming and land leasing arrangements to allow accelerated technology transfer, capital inflow, and assured market for crop production ...' Soon after, in 2003 a Model Act (The State Agricultural Produce Marketing Development & Regulation Act) outlined a framework for contract farming operations that would safeguard the interests of both firms and farmers equitably. It also paved the way for private market yards, direct buying and selling, among other things. This was later complemented by the creation of Agri-Export Zones (AEZ) across the country, where firms involved in agri-processing for exports would benefit from tax breaks and specific infrastructural facilities. Contract farming in high-value crops also became part of a larger strategy for diversification, weaning farmers away from the rice–wheat system that so dominated Indian agriculture.

In India, agriculture is a state subject so that substantive policy levers in the country work within individual states. Some states, like Tamil Nadu, had always permitted contract farming. Others were already providing space for such arrangements in select sectors such as horticulture. It was, however, Punjab that led the way, when it permitted PepsiCo take up tomato contracting for its processing plant in 1989. Soon after, contracting in high-value commodities, such as *basmati*, spices, chillies, flowers, and fruits began in many states. By the late 1990s, the basket of contract crops already included 'exotic' commodities like baby corn and cut flowers.

Several states followed suit. According to the Economic Survey of 2009, barring a few states, most have reformed the APMC Act, albeit to different degrees. Some states have, however, desisted from deep reform. For example, in 2008 Metro Cash and Carry's APMC licence was renewed in West Bengal only under the condition that it would not pursue contract farming.

EXTENT AND SPREAD

While the precise implications of these reforms for private marketing remain unclear, overall it has provided firms a broader space for operations than ever before. Contract farming schemes now embrace a wider range of crops and new geographies.

The true extent of contract farming in India is largely unknown since there is no formal recording system. It is clear, however, that a rich mosaic of corporate, civil society, and state actors has entered the fray, across the country (though less in the east and north-east), seeking to source produce for processing and retail. These arrangements are polymorphic, differing greatly in the nature of actors, relationship intensity, degree of formality, and specific terms and scale of operation. Some contract with as few as fifty farmers, others with so many farmers that they contract with agents or intermediaries, who then contract with farmers. The development of contract farming in India is still in flux. Mortality of contract schemes is high but rarely recorded and it is unclear how many initiatives survive beyond a few seasons.

Contract farming has endured best in high-value, niche commodities, especially for the export market, and where a well-functioning, competing, domestic market does not exist. Gherkins offer the best example. Introduced into peninsular India in the early 1990s by pickling plants in the region, gherkins are almost entirely sourced through contracts. By Triennium Ending 2008, India accounted for as much as 15 per cent of the world's exports of pickled gherkins. Similarly, large swathes of land, especially in Karnataka, are now under high-value medicinal plants and herbs, ashwagandha, aloe vera, coleus, stevia, and so on, for nutraceutical firms. Certified organic supply chains have emerged too for which a whole range of spices and horticultural produce are now contracted (for example in Uttarakhand).

Contract farming finds least traction when it emerges against a strong alternate domestic market or when too many partners hold the arrangement together. Many rice and wheat contract farming efforts by private-sector banks and firms folded up after initial experiments. Cotton contract farming schemes in states such as Tamil Nadu are fast fading into Corporate Social Responsibility initiatives. In other instances, state-supported schemes for jatropha and oil palm did not take off. In many of these cases, production risks were high and disagreements over pricing led to disgruntled farmers shifting out of the crop.

Despite some commonalities, the relative success of a scheme depends ultimately on the particular relationship between the firm and farmers and factors in the external environment. There are numerous examples of successful schemes that have stabilized and are now over a decade old, despite having competing markets and competitors—wheat and soy contracts for flour making in Madhya Pradesh and Uttar Pradesh, sunflower and safflower for oil in western and central India, and marigold and papaya for extracts in Karnataka and Tamil Nadu.

The broiler industry in the states of Andhra Pradesh, Maharashtra, and Tamil Nadu is today almost entirely integrated through contract farming, led by Godrej Agrovet Ltd., Suguna Poultry, and Ventakeshwara Hatcheries Pvt. Ltd. In fact, the industry's embrace of contract farming virtually rescued the poultry sector in Tamil Nadu, at a time when price volatility and poultry disease had dismantled the livelihoods of small poultry farmers.

More recently, a few firms have successfully acted as back-end integrators for retailers based in Europe and the USA, contracting for fresh produce in north-western India.

Apart from retailers and processors, many contract farming schemes have been initiated by input manufacturers, especially of fertilizers and pesticides (for example, Rallis), along with partners who take responsibility for buy-back. Banks, like ICICI and the State Bank of India, have partnered contracting firms in multi-partite arrangements to provide crop loans and working capital, with the contract itself as collateral.

Some state governments too have been proactive, engaging hands-on in tri-partite contract farming ventures with agribusinesses and banks, acting sometimes as guarantors, sometimes as relationship managers. For example, the Punjab Agro-Industries Corporation founded in 1996 has partnered a number of agribusinesses in implementing projects. Tamil Nadu adopted a public–private tripartite model for cotton contract farming in 2004–5. Karnataka actively promoted gherkins and grape clusters in the state with great success. States such as Andhra Pradesh and Mizoram have attempted to replicate the sugarcane model for oil palm contract farming, mandating farmers to supply fresh fruit bunches to privately owned mills at administered prices.

Non-governmental organizations have been involved as well, mediating contractual relationships between groups of small farmers and agribusinesses as with BASIX (for chipping potato contracts with Frito Lays India Ltd. in Jharkhand) and PRADAN (also in Jharkhand).

Sometimes contracting is just one element of a broader and deeper relationship with the farmer. This model, now called 'open-source intermediation' involves establishing rural business hubs, where a multiplicity of farmers' needs is addressed under a single roof. ITC's Choupal Fresh and DCM Shriram Consolidated Ltd. (DSCL)'s Hariyali Kisan Bazaar are two such ventures, which offer to buy back produce from farmers without obligations to do so.

IMPACT: THE GOOD AND THE BAD

A majority of studies on income gains from contracting in India suggest that contract farmers earn substantially higher profits than non-contract farmers (anywhere between 1.2 to 4 times depending on the commodity and scheme). These gains come partly from savings in transactions costs (estimated at 60–90 per cent for dairy, vegetables, and poultry) and sometimes through productivity gains. Often contracting firms introduce new methods of cultivation or technologies (drip irrigation, new cultivars, etc.) which reduce unit production costs contributing to improved relative profit efficiency. There is some documented evidence of this for livestock and tomato contract farmers. Contract farming is also known to reduce certain risks. In poultry contracting, for instance, farmers transferred 88 per cent of production and marketing risks to the firm, implying that contracting reduces the

volatility growers would have faced if they had produced for alternate markets (Birthal et al. 2005).

Despite these observed benefits, contract farming often brings attendant risks. The chief problem stems from enforcement issues. In the context of agriculture, it is virtually impossible to fashion a contract that provides for all possible contingencies in a way that is verifiable by a third party. Further, the very idea of a contract carries little meaning in a context where few farmers understand the document they are supposed to sign. This has allowed fly-by-night operators to dupe farmers of their lands (as is known to have happened in Orissa).

Even if it were possible to write out complete, verifiable contracts, the proverbially slow legal machinery in India implies huge costs, especially when firms contract with a large number of farmers. For the farmer, recourse to legal redress is practically out of reach. Interestingly, among agribusinesses in India, contract farming is referred to with many epithets—corporate-linked farming, relationship farming, even contact farming! Each of these terms negates the idea of formal contracts. Indeed, one written contract carries a clause that reads: 'This agreement is based on mutual trust and belief' (Singh and Ashokan 2005).

Weak enforcement then gives latitude to both farmers and firms to renege on the contract. Farmers typically divert contract produce to buyers who pay more, or use contract inputs for non-contract crops. Firms establish non-transparent quality standards, reject produce arbitrarily, and alter prices when the produce is delivered. On occasion, when they have enough supply, they do not turn up at all. In general, farmers are in a weaker position, relative to the firm, unless there is a viable alternate market and one where collusion among buyers is not possible.

There are also relevant questions about corporate commitment, or rather the lack of it, to long-term ecological and social consequences of these arrangements. Since most contract farming schemes tap into unpaid family labour, it often bids women and children from other activities into the contract farm in ways that might not be entirely desirable. Even where contract farms use hired labour, thus generating a positive employment effect, the conditions of work leave much to be desired (Singh 2003). For high-input use crops, farmers often report that it depletes soil quality, with lingering impacts on yields. Gherkin farmers in Tamil Nadu report that they often have to replace the topsoil for plots that have grown gherkins. Often, firms respond by moving on to contract from another region. There have also been documented instances of inappropriate advice extended to farmers by contracting firms, destroying standing crops. On the other hand, many farmers report that they benefit from technical advice from the firms, not just for the contract crops but for other crops as well.

THE FUTURE OF CONTRACT FARMING

It is apparent that farm–firm relationships tend to be fragile and fraught with friction. Enduring partnerships between farm and firm are difficult to build and to maintain these requires exceptional effort by the firm. Many firms have had to absorb large losses in order to build trust and persuade the farmer of the firm's commitment. For the farmer, the relationship has to hold significantly greater rewards than alternatives they have and not expose them to a new set of risks.

Given the difficulties in sustaining contractual relationships, the equivocal impact of contract farming, and its selective success, contract farming cannot serve as a broad-based strategy for rural development

(see also Minot 2007). Further, evidence on farmer participation in contract farming schemes suggests that small resource-poor farmers may not always participate. In most cases, selection is spatially skewed. It is time-variant as well, with high levels of farmer attrition. This suggests that the instrumentality of contract farming in delivering technology, access to markets and finance or in enabling small farmers take advantage of opportunities in high-value agriculture is probably overstated.

Yet, the pressure to enable firms to contract for produce is likely to grow stronger in the near future. How should the state respond to this challenge?

On the one hand, weak enforcement mechanisms are prompting several firms to take their contract farming operations to other countries in Southeast Asia and Africa. Yet, establishing a single legal framework that provides for fair contracts and an effective redressal mechanism is unlikely to encourage formal contract farming. From a business standpoint, firms face an expensive system that does not offer predicable dispute resolution and one that is prone to supporting farmers. Indeed, indications are that mandating state overseeing of private contracts might further informalize contract farming where firms end up pole-vaulting the law.

In this scenario, public policy should focus on the context of contract farming rather than contract farming itself. While providing a recommendatory framework is important, states should ensure that farmers' titles to land are secure to guard against unscrupulous operators. Public policy should focus sharply on zones that are excluded by agribusinesses and in regions where they do operate, the state should work to expand farmers' choice set in terms of cropping options, marketing channels, and so on, so that they are not caught in a relationship that creates dependency. Part of this involves provision of public goods like irrigation, power, infrastructure, market information, and extension, so that farmers face fewer constraints while making decisions. This might be the best way to ensure that the benefits of contract farming filter through without its costs.

SUDHA NARAYANAN

REFERENCES

Birthal, Pratap S., P.K. Joshi, and Ashok Gulati. 2005. 'Vertical Coordination in High-Value Commodities Implications for Smallholders', MTID Discussion Paper 85, International Food Policy Research Institute, Washington D.C.

Gulati, Ashok. 2007. 'Agribusiness' in Kaushik Basu (ed.), *The Oxford Companion to Economics in India*, New Delhi, Oxford University Press.

Minot, Nicholas. 2007. 'Contract Farming in Developing Countries: Patterns, Impact, and Policy Implications', Case Study #6–3 in Per Pinstrup-Andersen and Fuzhi Cheng, eds, *Food Policy for Developing Countries: The Role of Government in the Global Food System*, Ithaca, NY, Cornell University Press.

Singh, Sukhpal. 2003. 'Contract Farming in India: Impacts on Women and Child Workers', Gatekeeper Series No.111, IIED, UK.

Singh, Gurdev and S.R. Ashokan. 2005. *Contract Farming in India: Text and Cases*, New Delhi, Oxford & IBH Publishing Co. Pvt. Ltd.

Dams

At Independence, in 1947, there were fewer than 300 large dams in India. By the year 2000, the number had grown to over 4000, more than half of them built between 1971 and 1989. India ranks third in the world in dam building, after the US and China. While some of these dams were built primarily for flood control, water supply, and hydroelectric power generation, the primary purpose of most Indian dams (96 per cent) remains irrigation. In fact, large-dam construction has been the main form of investment in irrigation undertaken by the Indian government. But, starting in the 1980s, public investment in large dams in India has been the subject of a sustained controversy—epitomized by the Sardar Sarovar Project—centring on the balance between the social, environmental, and economic costs of dams and their benefits. This entry analyses the economic impact of large irrigation dams in India, focusing on both their aggregate productivity effects and their distributional effects.

Given that the economic gains and losses from dams, like those from many other public investments, often accrue unevenly to different groups in society, one way to begin is to identify the putative winners and losers. Most irrigation dams in India are embankment dams. That is, they consist of a wall built across a river valley to impound water so as to form a reservoir upstream and a system of spillways and gates to bypass the wall so as to maintain normal river flow and convey water to a network of canals feeding irrigated regions downstream. The upstream areas that feed the dam and those submerged by its reservoir make up its 'catchment' area, and the downstream areas fed by its irrigation canals make up its 'command' area. Before any mitigating effects of resettlement and compensation, whether a household stands to gain or lose depends on its location relative to the placement of the dam. People living in the catchment area, who lose property and livelihood but gain little, if anything, from irrigation, tend to lose out, while people living in the command area, who bear little of the social cost but gain the most from irrigation, typically gain.

Proponents of large dams focus on the aggregate productivity benefits, emphasizing the role of dams in enabling irrigation and, even though this is controversial, in recharging the water table, which had been lowered by overuse of underground water sources for irrigation. Between 1951 and 2000, India's production of food grains increased fourfold, from 51 million tonnes to about 200 million tonnes. This not only stopped the importation of food grains, with attendant saving in foreign exchange, but left India with a marginal food grain surplus. Proponents point to the fact that about two-thirds of this increase was in irrigated areas, and that by the year 2000, areas irrigated by dams constituted 35 per cent of irrigated land in India. The most optimistic estimates attribute 25 per cent of the increase in food grain production to dam-irrigated areas. But it is incorrect to attribute the entire production gains in dam-irrigated areas to dams. First, the increase in irrigation coincided with increased uptake of other inputs and technologies, such as high-yielding varieties (HYVs) beginning in the 1960s, fertilizers, machinery, and multicropping. Even though the contribution of these cannot be readily disentangled, we can surmise that it lowers the proportion of the productivity increase due to irrigation alone. Second, there are other methods of harvesting water for irrigation, and so some of the dam-irrigated areas would still have been irrigated even if the dams had not been built.

Indeed, other methods of harvesting water for irrigation, such as groundwater and small dykes, remain pervasive in India. Even so, proponents of large dams have argued that these cannot be relied upon to meet the needs of India's large and growing population. Moreover, it has been argued, these forms of water harvesting are not cost-effective and do not have the added advantages of hydropower generation and flood management.

Opponents of large dams, on the other hand, emphasize the social costs of dams.

They point out that the economic gains accrue disproportionately to people living in the command areas. The losses, on the contrary, are suffered disproportionately by people living in the catchment areas. Dam construction and submersion lead to significant loss of arable farmland and forest. Waterlogging and increased salinity reduce agricultural productivity in the vicinity of the reservoir. Policies to ensure adequate flow into the reservoir sometimes prohibit water harvesting in the catchment area, reducing agricultural productivity even more. Large-scale impounding of water increases exposure to vector-borne diseases, such as malaria, schistosomiasis, filariasis, and river blindness. Furthermore, the Indian government's compensation policy towards the displaced remains insufficient in many cases. In particular, since the compensation is based on the amount of land owned, landless households were typically not compensated at all. Nor were people compensated for loss of income or subsistence derived from communal holdings, such as common grasslands and forests. Although dams may also increase economic activity in the catchment area—through construction and economic activity around the reservoir, such as tourism and fishing—these increases are either temporary or depend on the ability to learn new trades, and often cannot compensate for the loss of familiar livelihood.

Ultimately, both the aggregate economic impact of dams and their distributional impact remain complicated empirical questions. As has already been stated, whether a household accrues net losses or gains depends in part on the placement of the dam. That, in turn, depends on several factors including the political and financial power of the local governments; the relative strengths of proponent and opponent civic organizations; and the potential of improved agricultural productivity in the would-be command region. All these factors may have direct impact on both agricultural production and poverty quite independently of the construction of the dam. As such, a simple comparison of the areas in the command or the catchment sites of dams and other areas does not directly inform us about the impact of dams, since these areas are likely to differ along these other salient dimensions, and it is difficult to disentangle their effect and the effect of the dams.

One specific determinant of dam placement, however, is geographic suitability. Dam location is strongly influenced by river gradient. A river flowing at a moderately positive gradient favours irrigation dams; higher water levels upstream facilitate water storage and diversion into irrigation canals. Consequently, within states, new dams tend to be built in those regions that have a river flowing at a moderate incline. After one accounts for the impact of the overal hilliness of the district and the availability of rivers, the gradient of the rivers is unlikely to have a direct impact on changes in agricultural productivity or other district-level outcomes before and after a state builds new dams. It is possible, therefore, to use the variation in dam construction induced by differences in river gradient across districts within Indian states to determine the impact of large dams.

In Duflo and Pande (2005), we use this strategy to estimate the impact of dam construction on district agriculture and poverty outcomes. We find that agricultural productivity in the catchment areas is unaffected, but poverty and vulnerability to rain shocks increase. Poverty increases in terms of both the headcount ratio (the fraction of rural population with consumption levels below the poverty line) and the poverty gap (how much income would be needed to bring the poor to a consumption level equal to the poverty line). In the command areas, irrigation and agricultural productivity increase, and poverty and vulnerability to rainfall shocks decline.

A cost–benefit analysis suggests that dams are, on average, only marginally cost-effective, although there is large variation from dam to dam. We also estimate that large dams increased all-India agricultural productivity by about 9 per cent, a figure close to the World Commission on Dams' estimate of 10 per cent, which has been criticized as too low by proponents of dams.

The increase in poverty in the catchment areas suggests that even though losers are clearly identified as those who live in the vicinity and upstream of the dam, they are rarely adequately compensated. This finding suggests that losers do not have the instutional capacity to negotiate higher compensation. To explore this further, we took a cue from Banerjee and Iyer (2005), who show that Indian districts where the British colonial authorities had delegated the setting and collection of land taxes to a class of landlords, tend to have less collective action and public good provision than districts where the individual cultivator paid the taxes directly to the colonial authorities. We found that, while the impact of dams on production is similar in both types of districts, the increase in poverty due to big dams is twice as large in districts where taxation had been delegated to landlords. Our findings are consistent with the view that where the relationship between the elite and the losers is adversarial and where the civic organizations advocating the cause of the losers are relatively weak or non-existent, losers are less likely to have been compensated. The fact that historically disadvantaged groups are disproportionately represented among the displaced (scheduled tribes represent 8 per cent of the population, but 47 per cent of the displaced) also suggests inadequate capacity to negotiate higher compensation. Planning authorities facing groups that have poor capacity to negotiate may not adequately account for the costs of resettlement and compensation, overestimating the economic viability of a dam, which may also increase poverty.

Large dam construction has been an important and expensive undertaking for the Indian government. While dams have enhanced agricultural productivity in India, there is no evidence that they have been very cost-effective, and they have significantly adverse distributional implications. The case of large dams suggests strongly that distributional implications of public policies should be central to any evaluation. Clearly, the case of large dams suggests the need to understand the institutions and power structures that led to the implementation of these projects.

ESTHER DUFLO AND ROHINI PANDE

REFERENCES
Banerjee, A. and L. Iyer. 2005. 'History, Institutions, and Economic Performance: The Legacy of Colonial Land Tenure Systems in India', *American Economic Review*, 95(4), pp. 1190–213.
Biswas, A. and C. Tortajada. 2001. 'Development and Large Dams: A Global Perspective', *International Journal of Water Resources Development*: 9–21.
Duflo, Esther and R. Pande. 2005. 'Dams', mimeo. MIT Poverty Action Lab.
Thakkar, H. 2000. *Assessment of Irrigation in India*, World Commission on Dams.
World Commission on Dams. 2000. *Large Dams: India's Experience*, World Commission on Dams.

Energy

The role of energy in India's economic growth and its importance to Indian society have undergone substantial changes in the past. When India became independent in 1947, its total installed capacity for power generation was a mere 1362 megawatts, which meant that electricity was not available even in many towns and cities, and rural areas certainly could not aspire to any form of electric power. The transport sector was based on energy from human and animal sources including bicycles, bullock carts, and horse-drawn carriages. Most inter-city and long-distance travel was undertaken, however, on a modern and extensive railway system. Fuels for cooking in most households included fuelwood, charcoal, and to a lesser extent kerosene oil. Since then there has been a major expansion in the supply of electricity and modern fuels, but in rural areas an overwhelming dependence on biomass fuels, particularly for cooking, remains a widespread reality. In assessing the role of energy in India's current economy and society, it is important to understand the structural relationship between energy and other activities in the economy. To a large extent, given the growth and modernization of several sectors in India, the role of energy mirrors the linkages and historical evolution experienced in other parts of the world.

The role of energy in economic growth and development really drew the attention of economists after the oil price shock of 1973–4, when a great deal of competitive work was carried out by economists such as Dale Jorgenson and E.W. Berndt (1990) as indeed was the case with a number of engineering studies that essentially analysed energy on the basis of bottom-up models that linked energy consumption with production and consumption activities based on specified technologies for processes as well as energy-using devices. On the other hand, the emphasis in economic studies was largely on the formulation of production functions and empirical estimation of relationships, on the basis of which future predictions could be made and policy options evaluated. Some of this work has recently been revisited by the International Energy Agency (IEA) and briefly described in the 2004 World Energy Outlook. The conclusion was reached that in every country studied except China the combination of capital, labour, and energy contributed more to economic growth than did productivity increases. The analysis also indicated that energy contributed significantly to economic growth in all countries and was the leading driver of growth in Brazil, Turkey, and Korea. On the other hand, its contribution was smaller in India, China, and the United States. A separation of the contribution of factors of production and productivity to gross domestic product (GDP) growth in selected countries is shown in Table 1. Energy, in the short run, is a complement to capital, but over a period of time it is generally a substitute.

The analysis indicates that the role of energy in driving economic growth is highly variable. In a historical context this is brought out clearly by Figure 1, which shows the path traversed by different countries over time in terms of their energy–GDP relationships.

With hindsight it can be seen that the countries that industrialized earliest pursued a highly energy-intensive pattern of growth, largely because in the initial stages of industrialization emphasis was placed on basic mineral industries and heavy manufacturing. It was only later that the services sector, which largely exhibits lower energy intensity, grew and developed. It can also be observed that countries that industrialized later had the benefit of technological choices which in some cases were much more energy efficient than for those that industrialized earlier. The choice of energy technologies would be determined in most cases by the relative prices of energy as well as domestic resource endowments, because national decision making has generally tended to favour the exploitation of local energy resources rather than relying on large-scale imports, for reasons of energy security.

There are still several prevailing myths about the linkage between energy consumption and economic growth, which are driven by an aggregation of engineering

Table 1 Contribution of Factors of Production and Productivity to GDP Growth in Selected Countries 1980–2001

	Average annual GDP growth (%)	Contribution of factors of production and productivity to GDP growth (% of GDP growth)			
		Energy	Labour	Capital	Total factor productivity
Brazil	2.4	77	20	11	–8
China	9.6	13	7	26	54
India	5.6	15	22	19	43
Indonesia	5.1	19	34	12	35
Korea	7.2	50	11	16	23
Mexico	2.2	30	60	6	4
Turkey	3.7	71	17	15	–3
United States	3.2	11	24	18	47

Sources: IEA analysis based on IEA databases and World Bank. 2004. *World Development Indicators 2004*, Washington D.C., World Bank.

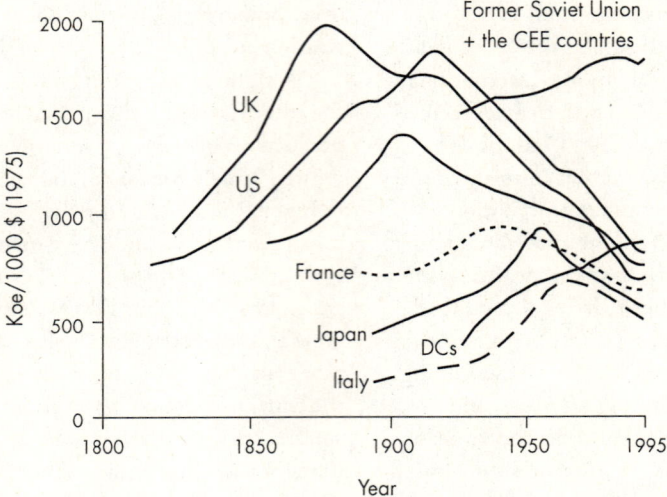

Figure 1

models that generally view the quantity of energy required for economic activities as fixed for specific levels of production. In actual fact, a country has a significant range of choices not only in devising policies that would result in a specific mix of economic activities but also in a range of technologies that would provide an input in the sectors that are favoured for production and consumption. Hence there are not only opportunities for substitution between capital, labour, energy, and the use of raw materials in the exercise of long-term decisions but also in the choice of energy sources used as inputs for preferred sets of economic activities. If we accept this view then there is reason to think of energy policy as not merely an aggregation of policies for supply of power, petroleum, natural gas, etc. but as a clearly defined integrated approach for influencing choices for the use of energy versus other factors of production as well as for choices involving different forms of energy. In today's context the Indian energy scene shows several examples of this reality. For instance, the failure of supply of

electric power in the requisite quantity and quality leads to consumers setting up their own power-production units of various sizes ranging from small generating devices installed by shopkeepers and households to large captive power-generation units installed by industry. The cumulative effect of these individual decisions has generally been a greater dependence on oil products, because many of these devices use oil products. Hence it can be concluded that in situation where consumers, including those involved in manufacturing activities, can make choices of this nature, the state of supply of one form of energy has implications for other forms as well.

On the Indian policymaking front, for several years now there has been a lack of a composite or integrated energy policy. This follows largely from the fact that the rigidities of the centralized planning process that were in evidence right through the 1980s are not as dominant any longer. The second reason is the fragmentation that has taken place in energy decision making with separate ministries dealing with power, petroleum and natural gas, coal and non-conventional energy sources, and atomic energy respectively. Recently the Government of India has established an Energy Coordination Committee to be chaired by the Prime Minister and with members drawn from ministers dealing with various aspects of energy and some of the major consuming sectors. The role of the consuming sectors in determining India's energy future is paramount. Consequently, the definition of the country's energy policy presupposes a clear definition of a transport policy as well as a housing policy, to quote only two examples of major consuming sectors. A country cannot pursue a coordinated approach in defining an energy policy without a comprehensive inclusion of choices covering the major energy-consuming sectors of the economy. An integrated view of energy policy in the past has generally come from committees established for the purpose that come up with policy recommendations for the energy sector as a whole, but these ad hoc and short-term initiatives have failed to alter the fragmented decision making in the sector. This could be the case with the recently established Energy Coordination Committee also unless the Committee is served by on-going and comprehensive analysis of global as well as national developments in the energy sector as well as those sectors that have direct implications for energy decision making.

Several objectives should define India's energy future. The most important of these would be the provision of adequate energy for all at least cost. This would require major reform of energy supply utilities and organizations, involving major restructuring and opening up of these organizations to competitive forces to bring about efficiency improvements. There would also be need for ensuring access to global opportunities and the removal of barriers that in the past have provided protection to domestic industry in coal as well as oil and natural gas. In this context opportunities for supply of natural gas from countries such as Iran and Myanmar would be of great value, particularly given some of the physical constraints in mining of coal and the implied cost of transportation from domestic coal mines to major consuming sectors.

In today's context, and to effectively address future prospects, India's energy policy should be guided by the following objectives:

1. Ensuring secure supply of hydrocarbon fuels. This would require a shift to natural gas and ownership or control of oil resources in other parts of the world combined with a move towards greater efficiency gains in the use of oil within the country.

2. Early reform of the energy supply industry, particularly the power sector, throughout the country, such that it is able to attract private capital in different segments of this industry and by which it is able to provide adequate and reliable power for all customers. The intended reforms in the power sector have been dragging and are now long overdue. The competitiveness of Indian industry is likely to be adversely affected unless some resolute steps are taken to bring about higher efficiency and operational improvements in the power sector.

3. There is a notable lack of a far-sighted rural energy policy, because of which the growing population of India not only in rural areas, but also in the slums of towns and cities depends only on the consumption of poor-quality biomass for cooking purposes. Quite apart from the hardship this imposes largely on women for collection of fuelwood, the

use of inferior biomass in ill-designed
stoves has harmful health effects,
particularly for women and children,
on account of exposure to harmful
emissions from cooking.

4. A mix of effective regulation and market
signals through appropriate pricing
is required to ensure efficient use of
energy and the adoption of appropriate
technologies in the major energy-
consuming sectors of the economy, such
as in the case of transport and the rapidly
growing construction and housing sectors.
In the case of transport, mechanisms need
to be devised by which major expansion
of public transport takes place for intra-
city travel and a major upgradation of the
Indian railways for inter-city travel. As
a result of the stagnation in the railway
system the share of both freight and
passenger transport has been shifting
from rail to road for several decades
now with adverse implications for the
efficiency of energy use.

These objectives, if properly incorporated
in decision making, would require a fiscal
regime involving appropriate taxation and
pricing measures. These would then result
in overall efficiency gains for the Indian
economy and an effective lowering of costs
of energy as a factor of production. In a
rapidly globalizing world, if India has to
register high rates of growth, the low cost
of energy would be an essential prerequisite
and imperative. So would be a diversification
of sources particularly against threats to
energy security that could affect the country
in the not-too-distant future.

R.K. PACHAURI

REFERENCES
Dale W. Jorgenson. 1990. 'Productivity and
Economic Growth', in E. Berndt and
J. Triplett, eds, *Fifty Years of Economic
Measurement*, Studies in Income and
Wealth, vol. 54, Chicago, IL: Reprinted with
permission of the University of Chicago
Press_http://post.economics.harvard.edu/
faculty/jorgenson/colwork/prods2.html
International Energy Agency. 2004. *World Energy
Outlook: Energy and Development*, Paris,
International Energy Agency.
Pachauri, R.K. 1983. 'Third World Energy
Policies: The Urban–Rural Divide', *Energy
Policy*, 11(3), September.
TERI. 2002. *Defining an Integrated Energy
Strategy for India: Ensuring Security, Sufficiency,
and Sustainability*, New Delhi, TERI.

Environment Policy

India has achieved notable economic growth
during the last six decades. However, as the
country enters the new millennium poised to
attain gross domestic product (GDP) growth
in excess of 8 per cent per annum, it is
confronted with the spectre of environmental
pollution and natural resource degradation.

Environmental pollution refers to
release of pollutants, which are unwanted
by-products of production processes, in
water, air, or on land, in quantities in excess
of the assimilative capacity of the receiving
media. Natural resource degradation refers
to the decrease in the quality or quantity
of nature's services. It is associated with
deforestation, soil erosion, land degradation,
erosion of wetlands, mangroves and
coastal ecosystems, threat to wildlife, and
loss of biodiversity. Environmental policy
collectively refers to strategies and actions
needed to address these distinct but related
problems. In addition to these immediate
and direct problems, it also refers to steps
necessary to address the threat of global
warming in the coming decades. This entry
traces the evolution of policy in respect of
environmental pollution.

During the first twenty-five years after
Independence, environmental concerns

got neglected due to the perceived need of urgent industrialization. Environmental policymaking began in earnest only in the 1970s when disappearing forests and the deteriorating quality of water and air compelled attention. The first systematic assessment of India's environment was undertaken by the Planning Commission in 1971. This was in part spurred by a request from the UN to its members to report on the state of their environment in preparation for the Stockholm Conference in 1972. As a follow up, the government set up the National Committee on Environment Planning and Coordination. This was possibly the first institutional arrangement for formally addressing environmental concerns. It is interesting to note, in passing, that the Indian Constitution did not originally contain explicit provisions on environmental protection. It was amended in 1976, and by way of the forty-second amendment, it made environmental protection a fundamental duty of citizens and an obligation on the part of the state. To address a wider set of emerging problems, the Department of Environment was established in 1980, and a full-fledged Ministry of Environment and Forests (MOEF) in 1985. This ministry is currently the apex body for making policy and initiating supportive legislation in respect of environmental matters. Dwivedi (1997) gives a detailed description of the evolution of early thinking and institutions on environmental policy.

The first major environmental legislation was the Water (Prevention and Control of Pollution) Act of 1974. It led to the establishment of State Pollution Control Boards (SPCBs) to set and enforce effluent standards. A Central Pollution Control Board (CPCB) was set up to coordinate the activities of state boards and to advise the central government. The Act made it mandatory for industries which were likely to discharge effluents in water bodies to obtain consent from the SPCBs prior to being set up. Defaulters could be punished with fines, imprisonment, or orders to close down. A tax was levied on the use of water in specified industries, under the Water (Pollution and Control) Cess Act of 1977, to raise financial resources for the boards and to help conserve water. Subsequently, the Air (Prevention and Control of Pollution) Act of 1981 extended the regulatory framework of water pollution to cover air pollution. It became obligatory for industries operating within specified air pollution control areas to obtain prior consent.

The regulatory framework for water and air pollution control proved to be quite ineffective. The SPCBs were perpetually short of funds. They lacked technical expertise and manpower to effectively monitor pollution. Many of them did not even have access to laboratories for testing of water samples. They basically aimed at end-of-the-pipe treatment through installation of specific devices. Often it was enough for a polluting entity just to instal a device to demonstrate compliance. It did not matter whether it actually worked or not. The financial and political clout of polluters also made enforcement difficult. Not surprisingly, these boards could launch very few successful prosecutions against the defaulters in the first decade of their existence. Over time, the volume of pollution increased manifold and its nature became more complex. New sources and newer forms of pollutants, particularly hazardous chemicals, emerged which were dangerous even in miniscule quantities. With restrictions on release in air and water, pollutants started getting diverted to land posing threat to underground water. Soon, the SPCBs found themselves incapable of handling the situation. The Bhopal gas tragedy of 1984 demonstrated this in a dramatic way.

The Environment Protection Act of 1986 (EPA) was enacted to deal with the new catastrophic reality brought home by that tragedy. It was a significant piece of legislation in many ways. It extended the authority of the central government to legislate for the entire country. It took a comprehensive view of the environment and extended the scope of regulation to cover almost all forms of pollution. The government used the Act to frame wide-ranging laws for pollution control, hazardous substance regulation, environmental impact assessment, and the protection of the coasts and other ecologically fragile areas. For pollution control, the government notified detailed standards for discharge of effluents, emissions, and noise. Hazardous waste management rules were designed to fix responsibility on persons generating the waste which, therefore, required a permit to regulate its handling and disposal. For a specified list of industries, government made Environment Impact Assessment (EIA) mandatory prior to their being set up. This would involve, apart from submission of an environment management plan, the holding of a public hearing where affected parties got a chance to voice their concerns. The government also notified specific prohibitions and regulations concerning development in ecologically sensitive areas. For example, Coastal Zone Regulations were notified to control development activity, including tourism, within a strip of 500 m from the sea shore, along the entire Indian coast. The Act gave the SPCBs vast administrative powers to compel compliance with the laws directly instead of having to go to courts as previously. It also gave the CPCB overriding authority over the SPCBs. A development of the utmost importance was that the Act gave citizens the right to initiate proceedings against the defaulting industries and the boards. Divan and

Rosencrantz (2001) provide a detailed and a very lucid description of the evolution of environmental policy from a legal point of view.

By the end of the 1980s, India had an extensive body of laws and rules on environment protection. It also had an elaborate institutional set-up in place. However, these were unable to arrest the deteriorating trend in environment. This was due both to the nature of the regulatory regime and poor enforcement of laws. Even though the EPA considerably expanded the scope of regulation, it in effect continued to be an extension of water and air pollution control. The basic approach continued to be technological fixes, which were ex post in nature and, consequently, tended to take care of the symptoms rather than the causes. Polluters were viewed as adversaries and compliance was enforced through coercion rather than cooperation. Policies were often ad hoc responses to problems that were neglected till they became unbearable or precipitated a crisis. It is ironical that even though the country had a very comprehensive framework for investment planning, environmental considerations were not integrated into it. In the late 1960s an industrial estates programme was started, where clusters of industries could share infrastructural facilities. It is a telling example of lack of foresight that, in many of them, no provision was made for common effluent treatment plants. An oft-cited explanation for poor performance of environmental laws has been lack of adequate funds given the size of the problem. Multiplicity of jurisdiction has also been cited as a source of delays in taking timely action.

At a more basic level, the poor performance of environmental laws, as all other laws, has been attributed to India being a 'soft state', a state characterized by weak institutions, a high degree of corruption, and absence of well-developed social norms. In such a state decisions that go against the vested interests of industry, bureaucracy, or politicians are hard to make and do not get implemented.

However, contrary to the above pessimistic assessment, solutions have in fact been found to many seemingly impossible problems. This is thanks to the Indian judiciary, which has played a critical role in giving teeth to environmental law and in ensuring administrative accountability. Political scientists call this a case of third-party enforcement. The Supreme Court in particular has intervened in environmental matters by allowing citizens' initiatives in the form of public interest litigation and also by taking suo moto cognizance of actions injurious to environment. Not confining itself to mere interpretation of laws, it has at various times stepped in directly to compel enforcement on a variety of issues. It has ordered stretches of rivers to be cleaned up by installation of effluent treatment plants and polluting factories to be shut down or moved out of urban areas. To combat noise pollution, it has imposed restrictions on use of loudspeakers even from religious places, a very thorny issue politically. In one of the more dramatic cases, in the highly polluted capital city of New Delhi, it successfully forced the entire diesel-based public transport system to switch to compressed natural gas. This was a technologically complex and politically difficult problem that had defied solution for long. To inculcate social norms it has directed that ecology and environment be taught in schools and colleges. Judicial activism has often been criticized for intruding into executive territory. Yet it has been so effective that when the SPCBs found themselves powerless against influential people, they actually encouraged public interest litigation. Unfortunately, there are diminishing returns to judicial intervention. While the air in Delhi got cleaned in response

to its intervention, the water in the river Yamuna did not. Ten years ago the Supreme Court had order installation of common effluent treatment plants. The order was complied with. The plants were installed but not put into operation. They have since been rusting. The greatest contribution of judicial intervention has been a heightened awareness of environmental problems in the society. There are now a large number of citizens and non-governmental organizations (NGOs) who are exerting pressure on state agencies through media and the courts.

The effect of this pressure is visible, at least on paper, in the policy statements issued by the Government of India in recent years. The Policy Statement on Pollution released in February 1992 acknowledged the increasing trend in pollution. It also recognized the limitations of the earlier piece-meal approach in arresting it. In its place, it advocated integration of environmental considerations into decision making at all levels. It promised to move towards prevention of pollution at source, making polluters pay for the pollution and for the clean-up costs, and encouraging public participation in decision making. In the Environmental Action Plan of 1993, the government took this commitment a step further by identifying priority areas for industrial pollution, with emphasis on reduction and management of wastes through technological upgradation. The latter would be achieved through enforcement of stricter standards and by giving fiscal and other incentives. The plan lays emphasis on decentralized decision making and strengthening of organizations at all levels. As suggested in the beginning, environment policy is not confined to pollution alone. Consequently, the National Conservation Strategy and Policy Statement on Environment and Development, released in 1992, has a much broader scope. Following the principles agreed upon at the

Rio conference, it declared the government's commitment to a policy of sustainable development. To achieve that goal, it promised to reorient policies and actions in different sectors such as agriculture, forestry, and industrial development, keeping in mind the environmental perspective. Realizing that mere passing of laws was not enough, it laid stress on the joint role of the government, NGOs, industries, public and particularly women in preserving and protecting the environment. The statement also outlined strategies and action plans for protection of wildlife and preservation of biodiversity.

Recently a National Environmental Policy (NEP 2004) draft has been circulated by the MOEF for public debate. This is the most comprehensive and detailed policy statement on environment issues so far. Apart from elaboration of many sector-specific issues, covered in the statements mentioned in the preceding paragraph, it proposes a major rationalization of environmental laws and policies in India. In particular it promises to review procedures for granting environmental and forest clearances for development projects. These have been a source of delay for and a cause of complaints by investors in the past. The review will also extend to rules relating to development activities along the coasts to remove anomalies arising from their application in varying local conditions.

The NEP marks a major departure from the earlier policy framework in emphasizing increasing use of economic principles in environmental decision making. This implies that the costs associated with degradation and depletion of natural resources be reflected in the decision making of economic actors to prevent their overexploitation. Extending this to macro level, it proposes to institute a system of natural resource accounting so that macro aggregates like gross domestic product give a truer picture of economic growth.

The NEP promises to replace adversarial relationships in environmental management with cooperative ones. These would be based on partnerships between public agencies and local communities. This has special relevance to forestry. It advocates complementing and, wherever possible, replacing the fiat-based instruments for environmental compliance with economic instruments. In order to make compliance more effective, it advocates greater reliance on civil law in place of criminal law.

The draft NEP has brought to the fore the competing pulls of the economic and ecological approaches to environmental policy. Ecologists have faulted the policy draft for diluting concerns for biodiversity. Civil society groups have complained of inadequate provisions for protection of cultural identities, knowledge systems, and livelihood of indigenous communities that are directly dependent on ecological resources. Critics have derisively described it as a policy not on environment but an 'investor-friendly' policy on 'sustainable development'. Policymakers have used the same two terms with a sense of self-congratulation. A more valid criticism of the draft would be that it promises action on too many things in very general terms and fails to specify an enforceable agenda.

PURAN MONGIA

REFERENCES

Divan, Shyam and Armin Rosencranz. 2001. *Environment Law and Policy in India*, New Delhi, Oxford University Press.

Dwivedi, O.P. 1997. *India's Environmental Policies, Programmes and Stewardship*, New York, St. Martin's Press.

Government of India. 2004. Ministry of Environment and Forests, *National Environment Policy*, Draft for Comments (http://www.envfor.nic.in), New Delhi, October.

Farmer Distress and Suicides

Indian agriculture has gone through phases of stagnation and growth intermittently. The phase of growth is characterized by complacency and agricultural produce prices remain depressed under supply pressure, but even in the phase of stagnation when the prices rise, low level of production does not allow the net income of the farmer to increase expectedly. With this continuous cycle, the sector could not overcome its proverbial constraints on cash availability. As a result, the phases of stagnation are perpetually weakening the welfare of vulnerable farmers, each time making them increasingly sensitive even to the slightest economic shock. As a result, farmers are always at the receiving end in the factor, credit, and product markets. The decade of the 1990s witnessed a spate of such events compounded by complacency in policy. The situation became worse by the end of the 1990s, when the central government issued a first ever 'catch-all' agricultural policy document consisting of most of the perceivable 'catch phrases' without consulting the state governments. The situation was quite disturbing in Karnataka, Andhra Pradesh, Maharashtra, and Punjab. Agricultural production in these states stagnated along with prices. As distress in the sector became acute, a spate of farmer suicides

occurred in these states. Among other factors, the emergence of the World Trade Organization (WTO), genetically modified (GM) varieties, and spurious seeds also became prominent stressors. Certainly the accumulation of distress through all these was genuine but connecting it directly to suicides in every case may not be analytically correct.

Farmers, as an occupational group world over, face high risk and uncertainty in their income flow (Malmberg and Hawton 1999). In the factor market, farmers have to pay the prices dictated by the suppliers, whereas in the product market, the purchasers determine the prices with the farmers remaining mute observers. The role of farmers in influencing the prices in either market is astonishingly minimal. Thus farmers face not only weather risk along with constraints on access to inputs (water, fertilizer, pesticides, or seeds) but also perpetual price uncertainty. This is compounded by spurious inputs and domestic market imperfections. Further, even though farming is a free enterprise, state policies largely dictate its course of development. This is compounded by social stress caused by the collapse of the village as an institution and the strong current of commercialization. Distress among farmers in the country is genuine and the Suicide Mortality Rate for farmers is on an increase (Figure 1, Mishra 2007). The situation

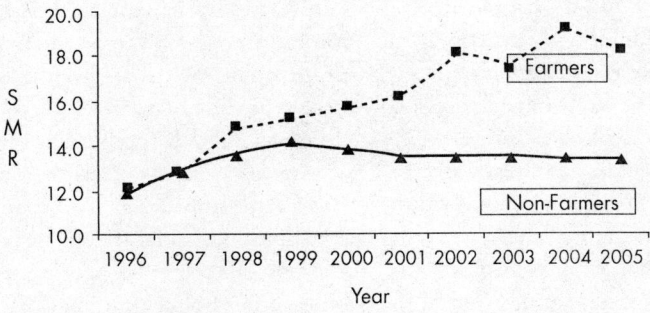

Figure 1   Suicide Mortality Rate for Farmers and Non-farmers

is quite depressing in Andhra Pradesh, Karnataka, Maharashtra, and Kerala.

THEORETICAL UNDERSTANDING

Studies on suicides failed to look at the phenomenon from an interdisciplinary perspective. Confronting pure psychological theories, Durkheim categorized suicides as egoistic, altruistic, anomic, and epidemiological based on the social response theory to distress (Durkheim 1952). An egoistic person is more prone to suicide as he has low tolerance of insult and this type can be observed in areas where semi-feudal production relations were prevalent. This is exactly the case of Northern Karnataka, Telangana, Rayalseema (Andhra Pradesh), and Vidarbha in Maharashtra. The 'altruistic' suicides involve individuals with inflated ambitions but unmatched capabilities. The mismatch between expectations and capability creates stress. Here again the historical emergences of production relations along with the process of commercialization play a role. 'Anomic' suicides are common among those who withdraw themselves from the group they belong to and it is largely ambitious farmers driven by the lure of high income who become this type of victim. According to some of the interpreters of Durkheim, distance of an individual from society is considered as an important reason for suicides. It is argued that a U-shaped relation could be established between suicide rates and the degree of integration of individuals with society and its norms. Lower assimilation may result in an 'egoistic' nature whereas total identification may provoke 'altruistic' suicides. 'Anomic' suicides are a result of a change in the social position of an individual due to socio-economic reasons.

Psychologists often explain a spate of suicides in terms of 'imitation effect' or the 'werther effect'. The latter refers to the victim copying another suicide that he/she knows about, following Goethe's novel *Die Leiden des jungen Werther* (The Sorrows of Young Werther) in which the main lovelorn character shoots himself. The suicides in Germany in 1774 arose out of similar reasons and followed the same method. More recently, in Kolkata a suicide by hanging provoked a number of similar cases.

Another way of methodically analysing the causes of suicides requires understanding the incidence as the culmination of four factors, namely, events, stressors, actors, and triggers. This categorization stems from the mental state of the victims (Deshpande 2002). Among 'events', crop loss, failure of borewell, price crash, daughters' marriage, family problems, and property disputes are included. These become 'stressors' (stress creators). Specifically, illness of a family member, heavy borrowings, continued land related or other disputes act as 'stressors'. These become lethal in combination with the 'events' but further provocation comes through the actors/catalysts and 'triggers'. The 'actors/catalysts' create a sense of 'insecurity' or 'insult' for the potential victim. These include the moneylender, banker, spouse, relatives, and close friends. Often the 'actors/catalysts' belong to the opposite sex of the probable victim. On the background of the 'events' and 'stressors', the 'actors/catalysts' instigate the final act by forcing an occasion to be the 'trigger' for the unfortunate incident. Given this complex nature of the phenomenon it certainly becomes difficult to pinpoint one particular reason for a suicide (Deshpande 2002). But a large number of studies rest the explanation of suicides on the immediate and obvious triggers, ignoring the build up. No wonder policy interventions have failed miserably to arrest the spate.

EMPIRICAL EVIDENCE

The decade of the 1990s witnessed a phase of complacency at policy level. The problems of the agricultural sector were treated casually. The situation became aggravated with successive droughts at the end of the 1990s when prices also stagnated along with low production. The situation was quite alarming in Karnataka, Andhra Pradesh, Punjab, and Maharashtra (Deshpande 2002; Sainath 2005, 2007; Mishra 2007). The spate of suicides that occurred in these states was immediately associated with the performance of the agricultural sector. Quite erroneously it was dubbed technological fatigue despite a huge yield gap. The technologically potential yield is way ahead of the achieved yield in the demonstration plots and the farmers' fields.

Agricultural production in these states was experiencing fluctuations and prices had stagnated despite supply stress. That brought down the gross income flow. On the other side, the cash component in the cost of cultivation had been increasing. As a consequence the net income flow to the farmer households had stagnated. Average farm business income of fourteen states (deflated by Consumer Price Index for Agricultural Labourers [CPIAL]) grew at 1.02 per cent per annum during 1990–1 to 1999–2000 as against 3.21 per cent per annum during 1983–4 to 1990–1 (Sen and Bhatia 2004: 241). The picture looks quite dismal when one plots the CPIAL along with the index of farm business income with the same base (Deshpande and Prabhu 2005). As a result farmers would borrow to meet the increased cost of cultivation or investment but the shrinking net income would result in non-repayment and indebtedness.

Farmer indebtedness should not be considered an inevitable or habitual condition, but during the 1990s the farm business income showed quite insignificant growth and thus increased farm indebtedness (NSSO 2005). During the 1990s indebtedness increased substantially and when farmers lose credit viability for institutional credit, they opt non-institutional credit. During the 1990s credit flow to the agricultural sector slowed down both as a result of policy and failure in the sector. The share of cooperative credit plummeted but it was not compensated for by commercial banks or Regional Rural Banks. As a result indebtedness became a major cause of distress and was quite erroneously treated as one in the policy corrections. Actually it was erosion of the repaying capacity of the farmer due to shrinking net income that caused distress and not borrowing per se. As a consequence the rates of suicides increased in these states.

The studies conducted on farmer suicides in India can broadly be grouped into three categories. The first group includes the reports prepared by committees to assist states in policy formulations. Three such reports are available for Karnataka, Andhra Pradesh, and Maharashtra. These reports essentially focus on the causes of suicides and policy to alleviate distress in the farming community. The Karnataka report focuses on the 'farmer consultation centre' approach to deal with the 'welfare domain', whereas the Andhra Pradesh report highlights inadequate public investment and need for agriculture technology mission. The Maharashtra report focuses on credit market, mitigating price risk, and post-suicide compensation. The second group of studies are citizens reports which focus on policy lapses and have ideological moorings. The third group consists of studies conducted by individual researchers, mostly using socio-anthropological methods. With the help of a few case studies these authors argue along the same lines. Among the issues highlighted by individual researchers are: indebtedness, borrowing from moneylenders, shift towards new technology, commercialization, crop failures due to spurious seeds and inputs, increased cost of production, overexploitation of natural resources, absence of safety nets, and collapse of the village as an institution. While all this makes it clear that all is not well in the sector, rarely do the studies suggest feasible policy options to mitigate the problem.

TOWARDS A POLICY FRAME

Examining the reasons of the spate of suicides has two objectives, first, to locate the probable areas of distress and second, to provide a policy frame to reduce the intensity of such distress. One can broadly group policy frames available in the literature into four important sub-systems. First, the 'production sub-system' includes correcting market imperfections, diversifying farm activities, providing non-farm production systems, promoting agro-processing, and upgrading technology. The 'input sub-system' focuses on amendments to legal impediments such as liberalizing the tenancy market, fixing the lower limit of holdings to arrest fragmentation of ownership holdings, high density sustainable agriculture, regular supply of electricity, and quality monitoring of other inputs. The 'input support system' includes providing information to farmers on a day-to-day basis through established farmer consultation centres. The 'welfare sub-system' through creation of a farmers' welfare fund, a nodal department for farmers, and a wide-ranging social security system with facilities for pension for aged farmers is being seriously considered in Karnataka. Health insurance, effective implementation of safety nets like crop insurance, and rationalization of a single window credit system, would go a long way towards strengthening the support system.

R. S. DESHPANDE

REFERENCES

Deshpande, R.S. 2002. 'Suicide by Farmers in Karnataka', *Economic and Political Weekly*, 37(26).
_____. 2005. 'Farmers' Distress: Proof beyond Doubt', *Economic and Political Weekly*, 29 October.
Durkheim, Emile. 1952. *Suicide: A Study in Sociology*, translated by John A. Spaulding and George Simpson, London, Routledge and Kegan Paul.
Malmberg, Sue Simkin and Keith Hawton. 1999. 'Suicides in Farmers', *British Journal of Psychitry*, 175: 103–5.
Mishra, Srijit. 2007. 'Suicides of Farmers', in *Maharashtra* (Research Report), Mumbai, Indira Gandhi Institute of Development Research.
Sainath, P. 2005. 'Six Out of Ten?'; 'Vidharbha: Whose Suicide is It Anyway?' 'As You Sow, So Shall You Weep', *The Hindu*, 31 May; 25 June; and 30 June.
_____. 2007. Presentation at Indira Gandhi Institute for Development Research, Mumbai.
Sen, Abhijit and M. S. Bhatia. 2004. *State of the Indian Farmer: A Millennium Study—Cost of Cultivation and Farm Income*, vol. 14, New Delhi, Academic Foundation.

Forest Policy

Forest policy in India faces a complex set of challenges. Massive deforestation in the past has drastically reduced the capacity of forests as a source of timber and other industrial raw materials. Further, degradation of standing forests has created serious ecological problems like soil erosion, reduction in the ability of soil to retain moisture, excessive water run-off during the monsoons, siltation of rivers, and the possibility of cycles of drought and flood. More critically, it has put at risk the livelihood of millions of people, particularly tribals, living within or around forests, who have for generations depended on forests for food, fuelwood, and fodder.

This state of Indian forests, and the ensuing policy dilemmas, can in part be traced to the advent of commercial forestry in India and the laws and policies initiated by the British in the nineteenth century. The British appropriated all forests which were not on private lands for state use. This step was motivated by revenue considerations and to ensure sustained supply of timber for shipbuilding and railway sleepers. The establishment of state control ended traditional property rights of village communities which had been in place for centuries. The resulting alienation and resentment ended the customary care of forests by these communities which had been part of their culture. They responded by non-cooperation in forest protection and, in many instances, even by hostile acts aimed at harming the state-owned forests.

Independent India inherited and continued with the colonial forest policy. In the Indian Constitution forests were originally placed in the state list of subjects. They were managed by the forest departments of respective states through laws enacted by them under the Indian Forest Act of 1927. This was a slightly amended version of a similar Act of 1878 conceived to assert exclusive state right on protection, production, and management of forests. The Act empowered state governments to declare forests on specified non-private lands reserved forests. This declaration had the effect of extinguishing any existing private rights of access to forests and their resources. From within these reserved forests, the state could declare certain areas village forests, where village communities had access to specified forest resources in exchange for forest protection duties. This access was a matter of privilege and not a right. The government could also declare certain areas on private lands protected forests where felling of trees, quarrying, and removal of forest produce were prohibited. The net result of these laws was that traditional forest dwellers came to be looked upon as encroachers on forest lands.

The Government of India announced a National Forest Policy in 1952. This policy did, in principle, recognize the ecological functions of forests. It stressed that at least one-third of the country's land area be brought under forests, partly in an effort to repair the extensive damage to forests in the inter-War period, primarily, however, to ensure the supply of timber and other raw materials for the emerging industrialization programme. It placed restrictions on grazing, shifting cultivation, and other local uses to promote conservation. Chopra (1995) recounts how, with regard to the needs of the local people, this was more restrictive even than the colonial forest policy of 1894, which had placed local interests above revenue needs.

The following two decades witnessed massive deforestation, as states were unable or unwilling to protect forests in the face of perceived needs of development. Major expansion of forest-based industries, aided by subsidized wood prices, put great stress on forests. Forests were cleared for cultivation, for extraction of timber, for mining and quarrying, to make way for industrial projects, and for construction of dams. As a result, forest cover was reduced to less than one-fifth of geographical area as against the recommended one-third. Apart from seriously endangering the ecological balance, it resulted in widespread uprooting of forest dwellers from their habitats.

An important development from the point of view of forest policy was the transfer of forests from the State to the Concurrent List through the forty-second amendment to the Constitution in 1976. This empowered the central government to act directly in the management of forests. To check rapid deforestation, it enacted the Forest Conservation Act in 1980. The Act mandated prior approval of the central government before a state government could de-reserve a reserved forest, use forest land for non-forest purposes, or assign forest land to a private person or corporation. The transfer of responsibility to the central government did not significantly improve the situation. At its core, forest policy still consisted of fencing off forests to protect them from the people! Over time, with the growth in population, scarcity of fuel and fodder assumed crisis proportions in different parts of the country and led to organized protests. It became clear that a policy based on centralized policing would be impossible to implement effectively.

The central government announced a new National Forest Policy in 1988. This policy marked a significant departure from the past in respect of conservation strategy. It stressed that henceforth forests would be maintained only for ecological functions and for meeting the subsistence needs of the people. It recommended that industry must meet its needs from farm forestry rather than from clear felling of forests. Most significantly, it recognized people's rights over forest resources. It suggested that forest departments should work together with village communities and voluntary agencies for management of forests. Following guidelines issued by the central government in 1990, most state governments took steps to establish Joint Forest Management (JFM) groups. Under the JFM programme, village communities were given conditional access to forest products like fuelwood, fodder, and non-timber products. In return, village

communities undertook to protect the forests against encroachment, poaching, and timber smuggling. JFM programmes have met with a fair degree of success. Apart from their geographical spread and increase in numbers, there is evidence that forest cover is beginning to respond.

But new sources of tension have emerged. While the earlier policy was production oriented, the new policy has tended to move too much towards conservation. It has led to resentment among states that are rich in forest cover but find that their development is hampered by not allowing forests to be cleared. They want compensation for providing the ecological benefits that accrue to the nation or even the globe.

As in the case of environmental policy, the Supreme Court has played a critical role in enforcing forest protection policies. Divan and Rosencranz (2001: 294–304) recount judgment in a forest conservation case that has had far-reaching consequences. A recent court order has the potential to make diversion of forest land for non-forest activities costlier and more difficult. The users must now pay an amount that must include, apart from the price of land and value of trees felled, the net present value (NPV) of a stream of ecological benefits, like soil protection, carbon sequestration, and flood and drought prevention, which would accrue in the future.

The conflict between the need for conservation and the needs of local people immediately affected by the policy persists. A proposed Scheduled Tribes (Recognition of Forest Rights) Bill has generated a lot of controversy. This bill seeks to accord legal recognition to the rights of tribals to forest lands and their produce. The Ministry of Environment considers this bill an obstacle in the way of forest protection. The Ministry of Tribal Affairs and social activists consider it necessary to 'undo the historical injustice

AGRICULTURE, RURAL ECONOMY, AND NATURAL RESOURCES 89

done' to tribal population and believe that it will ensure the survival and sustainability of forest ecosystems. There is clearly still a long way to go.

PURAN MONGIA

REFERENCES
Chopra, Kanchan. 1995. 'Forests and Other Sectors: Critical Role of Government Policy', *Economic and Political Weekly*, 24 June: 1480–2.
Divan, Shyam and Armin Rosencranz. 2001. *Environment Law and Policy in India*, New Delhi, Oxford University Press.

Green Revolution

The term 'green revolution' in India suggests two images. In the popular mind it is associated with a period in which India crossed the hump in terms of shortages of, and external dependence for, its grain and food requirements. The second more technical perception of the green revolution is one of a productivity breakthrough emerging from the high-yielding variety (HYV) of seeds in food grains, particularly wheat and then rice. These seeds initially imported from Mexico for wheat were adapted, replicated, and developed by Indian scientists. On account of their photo-insensitivity properties, they were shorter-duration crops as compared to the earlier varieties, and this property by itself led to more intensive use of land, in addition to water and nutrients. Technology and productivity improvement became the driving force in the green revolution areas.

The green revolution in India is seen as spanning four epochs (Alagh 2004). The first phase of the introduction of the high-yielding technology is attributed to the initiative of the political leader C. Subramaniam and civil servant B. Sivaraman in the second half of

the mid-1960s, a 'ship-to-mouth' phase of grain shortage and large grain imports as PL 480 aid from the USA. They took the risk of importing the dwarf varieties of wheat from the International Wheat Research Institute (IWRI) in Mexico and were assisted by Indian scientist M.S. Swaminathan and Indian Council of Agricultural Research (ICAR) teams in replicating the seeds.

The second was a phase in which the technology was internalized in what is called the favoured region, favoured crop period in the decade of the 1970s. However, in the early 1970s there was still considerable pessimism about the growth potential of Indian agriculture. Paddock and Paddock, in Famine 1975, argued:

Today, India absorbs like a blotter 25 per cent of the entire American wheat crop. No matter how one may adjust present statistics and allow for future increase in the American wheat crop... it will be beyond the US to keep famine out of India during 1970. The reason? Of all the national leadership the Indian comes close to being the most childish and inefficient, perversely determined to cut the country's economic throat (Paddock and Paddock 1968: 217).

This assessment was from a larger canvas. Other think tanks—the Hudson Institute, Keith Griffin, Francine Frankel, the Brettonwoods institutions, and at the Institute of Development Studies (IDS) Sussex, Paul Streeten and Michael Lipton— all had a dim view of India's agricultural prospects and some argued that India also did not have medium-term growth prospects since poor agriculture would lead to a wage goods constraint. The initial spurt of grain growth had petered out and the green revolution was seen as a misnomer. India's grain production after reaching 108 million tonnes in 1971, ranged between 101 and 104 million tonnes in the early 1970s. The World Bank, and in fact even the Indian Finance Ministry, felt that India would not achieve its target of 125 million tonnes of grain by 1978–9; estimates ranged between 118 and 120 million tonnes. It was at this time that policymaking in India focused on resource allocation and policy support to agriculture with priorities set by the then Prime Minister Indira Gandhi who saw food security as a central issue. The Planning Commission produced its first Agricultural Sub-Model (with the present author organizing the effort) and this model made conservative assumptions on land reserves and productivity assumptions so that resource allocation for agriculture, particularly irrigation, got high priority in the investment budget. Interestingly, public-sector capital formation of Rs 5566 crore at 1993–4 prices in the year 1976–7 was not reached in any year in the decade of the 1990s, reflecting the lack of strategic policymaking for agriculture in the reform period. By 1978–9, India was producing 127 million tonnes and was a net exporter of grains.

In the late 1960s it was the received wisdom from studies, amongst others by Keith Griffin, to state that the green revolution strategy would not impact on small farms, also such farms would not participate in diversified agriculture. In a large sample study of Haryana agriculture, G.S. Bhalla produced the counter-factual. Bhalla, an economist of avowed Marxist persuasion, hypothesized that small farms would not access the new technology, but since his data rejected the hypothesis, showed that the class of adopters was more equal than that of non-adopters (Bhalla 1974: survey in 1971). At roughly the same time, the economist Vijai S. Vyas, with his team at Vallabh Vidyanagar, showed with a field survey in the Charotar that small farms were viable in the sense that if given the necessary support, they could generate incomes above the poverty line. This was at that time, like all new ideas, neither intuitively felt nor accepted and yet soon became the orthodoxy at home and abroad. They also argued that with support of technology and credit, more small farmers would cross the poverty line, but after all that there would be some families left below the poverty line and a non-land-based non-farm growth programme was necessary for them (Vyas et al. 1969). Policymaking was to follow.

Meanwhile in the 1980s, in the third phase, Indian agriculture was growing faster and, as the economy picked up, non-food grains were leading. The growth rate accelerated in new crops, particularly rice, cotton, and oilseeds, and in new regions. The larger picture in terms of output and productivity growth and the shift away from food grains is shown in the estimates in Table 1.

Output growth rate went up since the 1980s for the agricultural sector as a whole. Output is now rising at 3.37 per cent

Table 1   Average Annual Growth Rates in Index of Area and Production

| | 1950/1–1996/7 | | 1950/1–1979/80 | | 1980/1–1996/7 | |
	All Crops	Non-food grains	All Crops	Non-food grains	All-Crops	Non-food grains
Prod.	2.7	2.99	2.46	2.70	3.37	4.39
Area	0.61	1.22	0.86	1.17	0.27 (NS)	2.02

Source: M. Alagh. 2004. 'Aggregate Supply Function of India', *Economic and Political Weekly*, 10 January.
Notes: Estimated by semi-log regressions on time. Estimates significant at 99 per cent confidence levels.(NS) implies not significant.

compound annual as compared to 2.46 per cent earlier. The contribution of area went down, yield being the major source of growth in the second phase. Growth of output in the non-food grains sector is only marginally higher than for the entire sector for the period up to 1980. However, since then the non-food grains sector grew at 4.39 per cent annual, which is significantly higher than the growth of the sector as a whole.

This also led to a change in the structure of employment.

A comparison of the 1999–2000 estimates with those of 1961 brings out this shift (Table 2).

Three points are notable. The first is that decline in the workforce engaged in crop production is higher than that in the

Table 2   Structural Change in Workforce in India 1961–2000

| | Per cent of workforce | |
Sector	1961	1999–2000
1. Agriculture, forestry, and fishing	75.9	59.9
of which		
2. Crop production	73.5	54.3
3. Livestock	2	4.1
4. Agricultural services	0	0.9
5. Logging forestry and fishing	0.5	0.5

Source: Census of India 1961; NSSO 2000, as quoted in Y.K. Alagh. 2004. *State of the Indian Farmers—A Millennium Study: An Overview*, New Delhi, Academic Press, p. 32.

Table 3   Shift in Employment in the 1990s

| | | Share of agricultural sector in in employment | |
S.No.	State	1991	2001
1.	Gujarat	56.3	51.0
2.	Haryana	57.8	51.6
3.	Karnataka	63.1	55.9
4.	Punjab	55.3	39.4
5.	Tamil Nadu	59.5	49.5
6.	India	64.8	58.4

agricultural sector as a whole. The second is that the increase in employment based on livestock is high. The third is that forestry is not absorbing a larger share of the workforce, because policies were not conducive to giving rise to a dynamic local production sector. In some fast-growing areas these trends are more pronounced, since either the share of non-farm employment is much lower than the national average and has fallen or the decline is faster than in the country as a whole, as the estimates in Table 3 show.

Since the mid-1990s, in the fourth epoch, the agricultural growth rate has gone down and employment growth in agriculture is low. Profitability of agriculture has fallen by 14.2 per cent in the 1990s and while public capital formation was falling, now even private investment is stagnant. Recently irrigation and fertilizer growth has slackened. Indian policymaking is attempting to develop a policy paradigm for a dynamic phase for an open agricultural economy. Farmer-managed infrastructure systems, reform for alternate channels for input supplies and marketing, improved access to credit and to markets are all being tried in an effort to reverse these trends causing concern to policymakers.

YOGINDER K. ALAGH

REFERENCES

Alagh, Y.K. 2004. *State of the Indian Farmer—A Millennium Study: An Overview*, New Delhi, Academic Press.

Bhalla, G.S. 1974. *Changing Agrarian Structure in India*, Delhi, Minakshi.

Paddock, William and Paul Paddock. 1968. *Famine 1975, America's Decision: Who Will Survive*, Boston, Little Brown & Co.

Vyas, V.S., D.S. Tyagi, and V.N. Misra. 1969. *Significance of the New Strategy of Agricultural Development for Small Farmers*, Vallabh Vidyanagar, Agro-Economic Research Centre.

Irrigation

Irrigation plays an important role in Indian agriculture. Currently nearly 45 per cent of the 175 million ha of the country's cropped area is irrigated. On a rough estimate, irrigated areas accounted for more than 60 per cent of the total crop output in the mid-1990s.

POST-INDEPENDENCE TRENDS

Irrigated area has nearly trebled since the early 1950s: from around 24 million ha in 1953–4 to nearly 75 million ha in 1998–9 (Table 1). According to one recent estimate, nearly three-fourths of the increment in total crop output between the early 1970s and early 1990s came from expansion of irrigated area and increase in per hectare yields on irrigated land. Unirrigated crop areas have actually declined and the rate of yield improvement in these areas has been far slower overall, compared to irrigated areas.

Expansion of irrigation has been central to the strategy for increasing agricultural production. During the second half of the twentieth century, the government has directly invested close to Rs 1000 billion at current prices (equivalent to Rs 2300 billion at constant 1996–7 prices) in irrigation and flood control. The bulk of it was for irrigation. By far the largest part of it was spent on construction of new reservoir-based canal systems and, to a much smaller extent, improvement of these systems. Substantial amounts were also spent on small-scale surface irrigation works (tanks, local stream diversions, and lift irrigation) as well as public tube wells. But these were much smaller than investments in large-scale surface works.

The government has also encouraged and stimulated exploitation of groundwater by farmers for irrigation by giving liberal credit at concessional rates of interest and by implementing a huge rural electrification programme and providing 'cheap' electricity and diesel oil for pumping. These public-sector initiatives were greatly reinforced by two other factors: reduction in the costs of lifting water brought about by the advent of energized pumps, followed, in the 1960s, by the high yielding variety (HYV) fertilizer revolution which greatly enhanced the potential for increasing yields. Both increased the private profitability

Table 1   Net Irrigated Area by Different Sources, India 1950–1 to 1995–6

| Source | 1950–1 | | 1995–6 | |
	Million ha	Distribution %	Million ha	Distribution %
Surface	14.9	71.3	23.7	44.3
Govt canals	8.3	39.7	17.5	34.0
Tanks	3.6	17.2	3.1	5.8
Other sources	3.0	14.4	3.5	6.5
Groundwater	6.0	28.7	29.8	55.7
All sources	20.9	100	53.5	100
GIA all sources	22.6		71.5	

Source: Government of India, DE&S. 2000. Statistics of Area Production and Yield of Principal Crops.

Notes: GIA = gross irrigated area; NIA = net irrigated area.

The latest year for which official estimates of source-wise NIA are available is 1995–6. Total NIA in 1997–8, according to official LUS data, was 55 million ha and total GIA 73 million ha.

of groundwater irrigation, which in turn stimulated a surge of private investment in wells and tube wells.

As a result, the importance of groundwater as an irrigation source has increased from less than 30 per cent in 1951 to nearly 60 per cent in the mid-1990s. The number of dug wells has increased from 4 million to over 10 million; over 70 per cent of wells now use electric and diesel pumps. This was also the period of the tube well explosion. Negligible in 1951, their number now exceeds 5 million serving 18 million ha, far exceeding the 10 million ha under dug wells (Table 2).

Compared to groundwater, the expansion of surface irrigation, though substantial, is considerably less both in absolute and relative terms. Practically all the increase has come from large reservoir-based canal systems. In the early 1950s surface systems consisted of several hundred thousands of traditional, locally managed small-scale tanks (collectively called 'minor' works) and some relatively large canal systems fed by anicuts and barrages across major rivers. Large storages were few. Since then there has been hardly any increase in the storage capacity of 'minor' surface works. The live storage capacity of reservoirs of more than 10,000 cubic million (called 'major and medium works') has increased to more than 175

billion cubic m (bcm). They now account for the bulk of the total water utilization and area irrigated by surface sources.

The quality of irrigation has also improved to some extent mainly because of the emergence of groundwater as the major source. Losses in taking water from source to fields are far less in the case of wells and tube wells. Users have much greater flexibility to adjust irrigation according to the actual condition of crops. In the case of surface irrigation, large reservoirs have wider catchments and therefore can provide larger, more reliable supplies than works that depend on small local catchments. The spread of conjunctive use of surface with groundwater also helps improve overall water use efficiency in surface irrigated areas as well. Available evidence points to an improvement in efficiency of irrigation water use in all major river basins of the country.

UNEVEN ACCESS TO IRRIGATION

Given the size and diversity of the country, it is not surprising to find much interregional variation in the extent and sources of irrigation and their development over time. Available data suggest that inter-state disparity in surface irrigation (relative to cultivated area) is considerably less than in groundwater irrigation and that, while the former has progressively declined over the years, the latter has

Table 2   Growth of Groundwater Irrigation 1951–94

		1951*	1968*	1994**
Open wells	No. 10^6	3.9	6.1	10.2
	Energized 10^6	neg.		
	Net area irrigated 10^6 ha	6.0	1.4	7.2
			8.0	12.4
Open wells	No. 10^6	neg.	0.4	5.1
	Energized 10^6	neg.	0.4	5.1
	Net area irrigated 10^6 ha	neg.	4.5	18.4

Sources: *Central Board of Irrigation and Power 1989.
**Central Water Commission 1998.

Table 3   Percentage of Operated Area Irrigated by Source, All India 1953–4 and 1991–2

	1953–4			1991–2			% Sample hhs with irrigation
	Surface	Ground	All	Surface	Ground	All	
<1 ha	18.5	8	26.6	19.8	21.8	41.6	40.0
1–2 ha	18	7.1	25.1	18.1	20.8	38.9	55.4
2–4 ha	14.3	6.8	21	15.9	20.9	36.8	61.5
4–10 ha	9.8	5.4	15.2	13.8	19	32.8	65.8
>10 ha	4.4	2.4	6.8	15.5	12.5	28.1	62.7
All	10	4.9	14.8	16	19.3	35.4	51
Cv %	41	33	38	17	18	14.4	

Source: National Sample Survey.

not. Disparity in the proportion of gross irrigated to total crop area has also been widening over the years.

Access to irrigation among the farming population is also unequal. For the country as a whole, there is a consistently positive association between size of holding and the proportion of households having access to any irrigation and a consistently negative relation of holding size to the proportion of irrigated to total operated area (overall and by major source). In other words smaller holdings have less access to irrigation but are able to irrigate a higher proportion of their land (Table 3).

The disparities in irrigation ratio, both overall and by source, have greatly narrowed during this period. This is because while the irrigation ratio has increased in all size classes, the rate of increase has been much higher in the larger holdings compared to smaller holdings. Expansion of irrigation has clearly favoured those with bigger holdings far more than those with smallholdings.

AREAS OF CONCERN

Government strategy for irrigation development and its implementation attracts criticism on several grounds. The bulk of public investment in the water sector has gone into construction of large surface irrigation projects. Inadequate preparatory investigations and laxity of pre-

clearance appraisal have resulted in serious underestimation of costs. Compounding this is the tendency to start far too many projects, unmindful of resources available to implement them. The result has been inordinate delays in completing projects, overcapitalization, underutilization of their potential, and accumulation of a huge overhang of incomplete projects.

The government strategy also attracts criticism for ignoring, at any rate grossly underestimating, the adverse impacts of these projects (by way of displacement of human population, submergence of forests, and effects on riverine and estuarine eco systems); the failure to so design them as to minimize these impacts and ensure that effective compensatory measures for unavoidable impacts and the costs involved are fully provided for in the project.

Depletion of groundwater is another major area of concern. Despite significant and increasingly widespread fall in the groundwater table, government policy continues to encourage and finance private investment in wells/tube wells and their energization and deepening. In this process, the distribution of access to groundwater is shifting in favour of larger farms at the expense of smallholders. Whether and to what extent they increase the quantum of water extracted is also in doubt. To the extent they do, they are dipping into the static reserve whose loss cannot be replenished easily or fast. Present levels of use already exceed sustainable limits in several areas and are likely to do so in more and more areas. The situation calls for major changes in the strategy and priorities of irrigation.

NEEDED CORRECTIONS

The potential for further expansion of water supplies for both surface and groundwater irrigation is strictly limited. In the case of surface water, nearly 60 per cent of the utilizable potential of surface water (690 bcm) is already being utilized and with the completion of projects under construction this proportion might reach 80–5 per cent. As the limits of the potential are nearing, new projects are becoming more difficult and more costly. These constraints will not be overcome by the interlinking of rivers. Apart from questions about its engineering aspects, there are serious concerns about its social and environmental impact, and its likely contribution to augmenting overall supplies relative to the costs involved. (The current status of this proposal and its main shortcomings are discussed in the entry on Water).

In the case of groundwater, there is growing evidence that groundwater exploitation is already at unsustainable levels in many areas and this is becoming more widespread. As the number of wells and tube wells continues to grow apace, they are getting deeper and deeper, and more and more powerful pumps are being installed to chase falling water tables. There is progressive decline in the area irrigated per well and per tube well. The Central Groundwater Board (CGWB) reports that in as many as 60 per cent of the districts in the country, water tables have fallen by more than 4 m over the twenty-year period from the early 1980s.

Scattered studies of wells and tube wells being used for irrigation show much larger long-term declines in groundwater levels.

The problem therefore is not just to check further increase in extraction but, in many areas, even reduce it to bring groundwater levels within sustainable limits. Since falling groundwater levels indicate mining of groundwater reserves, it is necessary to explore ways—including artificial recharge—to increase effective recharge rates from their current or perhaps even natural recharge rates.

IMPROVING WATER USE EFFICIENCY

Of necessity, therefore, the focus of irrigation programmes and policies has to shift to measures to facilitate and induce conservation and more efficient use of available supplies. The expansion of surface irrigation based on large reservoirs and the rapid growth of groundwater have no doubt led to considerable improvement in both technical efficiency of water use and in productivity per unit of water. But efficiency in both respects is considerably less than what is achievable by better water management with available agricultural technology. This has two components: (1) increasing the proportion of surface and groundwater drawn at source that is effectively available for consumption use of crops; and (2) flexible management of the timing and quantum of water application to crops to achieve higher yields per unit of consumption use.

In surface systems, substantial volumes are lost due to evaporation in the reservoirs and canals and seepage and waste in the distribution network and on farmers' fields. They contribute little to increased production of crops and useful biomass. No proper measurements of these losses are available. There is reason to believe that they are much higher than the notional working assumptions used by engineers. Ensuring that the distribution network right down to user level is properly laid and maintained in good physical condition can reduce leakages due to weak, breached, and porous banks. Lining of canals may also be desirable in some areas. The resulting reduction in seepage losses may increase supplies available for consumption use at the sub-basin or basin level but a part of it may simply result in a spatial redistribution of effective supply among the systems in the basin. Conjunctive use of surface and groundwater also increases the proportion of water let out of reservoirs that is effectively available for use by irrigated crops.

Productivity per unit water also depends on the extent to which the quantum and timing of irrigation can be managed flexibly to maintain an optimum soil moisture profile during crop growth. Surface irrigation systems have inherent limitations in this respect. In the Indian context, inadequate regulatory devices aggravate them. It is therefore essential to invest in installing appropriate physical structures at all levels of canal systems to enable better regulation of water deliveries to their different segments. Flexibility in water application can be increased by creating small ponds or other devices close to user level and/or by more extensive recycling of seepage in canal commands.

The scope for and potential contribution of this option depend on sub-surface geology and the extent to which it is already developed, both of which vary from system to system and region to region. Also, it is necessary to bear in mind that allowing unrestricted conjunctive use on an individual basis carries the risk of skewing the distribution of water access in favour of the larger farmers. Subject to this caveat, it is clearly important to explore and exploit all these possibilities.

This calls for a substantial shift in investment priorities in favour of improving physical facilities and control structures in existing systems and away from new constructions. But it calls for much more. Radical changes are needed in the institutional arrangements for water management and the way they function. They need to be complemented by measures to create strong incentives for more prudent and economical use of water.

WATER GOVERNANCE

That water governance is in serious disrepair is reflected in extensive violations of regulations regarding permissible crop patterns and groundwater extraction. Unauthorized and illegal tapping of canal water and pumping of water from under riverbeds to areas outside the commands of public systems have become widespread. Institutional mechanisms meant to prevent and penalize such violations have been largely ineffective. Regulations prohibiting construction of new wells and tube wells in areas classified by Ground Water Boards as 'overexploited' and restricting new wells and tube wells in 'grey' blocks that are close to exploiting their potential are practically ineffective.

The need for radical institutional reform to address these problems is widely recognized. But there are widely divergent views on its content. Some neo-liberals see water as a tradable commodity and consider property rights and market-mediated allocations as the solution. However: (1) clearly defined 'property' rights are impossible in the case of a fluid common pool resource open to pervasive mutual interference by different users; (2) being a limited but vitally important common pool resource serving multiple users and uses for several ends (especially externalities, non-tradable outcomes, and long-term sustainability), balancing of competing claims has to be seen and accepted as fair and equitable; (3) these tasks cannot be done through the market; they have to be based on a social consensus, arrived at through a political process.

A very different approach—and one which takes cognizance of the above compulsions—argues for redefining the role of the state to serve as a trustee of society in matters relating to water, leaving investment, management, and regulatory functions to autonomous organizations functioning within broad guidelines and legal framework defined by the legislatures. The desirability of user involvement and active participation in management of irrigation is gaining acceptance. Some states have taken significant steps to implement this concept by entrusting water users' associations with maintenance and collection of water charges at tertiary level. A couple of states have also provided for induction of elected user representatives on management committees of different tiers of canal systems. But they have little effective role in deciding or implementing rules of allocation and scheduling. These functions continue to vest with the government. Institutional reform clearly has a long way to go before it can make a significant impact on water management.

ECONOMIC INCENTIVES FOR EFFICIENT USE
It is moreover important to recognize that better laws, better enforcement of laws, and better management are necessary but not sufficient. But given that uses and users are numerous (running literally into millions), diffused, and connected in a complex network of interdependence, even the most competent, honest, and professional management cannot effectively monitor observance and enforce compliance of even properly designed rule systems. It is essential to complement them with strong economic incentives to induce individual users to behave in a manner conducive to achieving overall objectives. Pricing of irrigation and inputs used for irrigation (especially energy for pumping) is critical.

Wasteful and inefficient use of water by farmers as well as the overexploitation of groundwater, which is a glaring feature of the Indian scene, is due in large measure to the policy of keeping water charges and the prices of electricity and diesel oil at levels far below costs. This folly has been compounded by laxity in assessment and collection of dues, and by failing to adjust rates in the face of rising costs and output prices. With the effective cost of water relative to output prices falling progressively and steeply, users' interest in reducing waste and improving water use efficiency, already weak, has become weaker and weaker. But water pricing is a politically sensitive issue, which no government, irrespective of party affiliation, wants even to talk about. It is difficult to convince the politician or the farmer that improvement in efficiency and productivity that can come about with a combination of institutional reform and higher prices would largely, if not wholly, compensate the effect of higher prices. With few takers for price reform and anaemic interest in institutional reform, it is difficult to be optimistic about the prospect of achieving prudent, efficient, and sustainable management of irrigation.

A. VAIDYANATHAN

Land Reform

Land reform usually refers to redistribution of land from rich to poor. More broadly, it includes regulation of ownership, operation, leasing, sales, and inheritance of land (indeed, the redistribution of land itself requires legal changes). In an agrarian economy like India with great scarcity and unequal distribution of land, coupled with a large mass of below-poverty-line rural population, there are compelling economic and political arguments for land reform. Not surprisingly, it received top priority on the policy agenda at the time of Independence. In the decades following Independence, India passed a significant body of land reform legislation. The Constitution of 1949 left the adoption and implementation of land and tenancy reforms to state governments. This led to a lot of variation in the implementation of these reforms across states and over time, a fact that has been utilized in empirical studies trying to understand the causes and effects of land reform.

In this entry, I will briefly discuss the economic and political arguments in favour of land reform, and review the Indian evidence on the effects of land reform on agricultural productivity and poverty, and economic and political determinants of the speed and intensity of implementation.

ECONOMIC ARGUMENTS IN FAVOUR OF LAND REFORM

The most obvious argument in favour of land reform is equity. In a land-scarce country with a significant section of rural population below the poverty line, the case for ensuring that everyone has access to some minimum amount of land seems compelling from this point of view. However, this is a general argument in favour of redistribution, not necessarily redistribution of land. To make that case, one needs to understand the economic forces that govern the allocation of land.

I begin with two empirical observations. First, small farms tend to be more productive than large farms. This inverse farm size–productivity relationship is widely documented (see Banerjee 1999 for a review of the literature). Another empirical

regularity is that owner-cultivated plots of land tend to be more productive than those under sharecropping tenancy (Shaban 1987).

Given these observations, one could make an argument in favour of land reform based not only on equity considerations, but also efficiency. For example, the inverse relationship between farm size and productivity suggests that land reform could raise productivity by breaking (less productive) large farms into several (more productive) small farms. Also, lower productivity under sharecropping suggests that land reform could raise productivity by converting sharecroppers into owner-cultivators.

But then what prevents market forces from getting rid of the asymmetry and the resultant inefficiency? Saying that the inverse farm size–productivity relationship is driven by diminishing returns is not satisfactory, since that assumes that land cannot be sold or leased. For example, if a small farmer is more productive and a large farmer less productive, then the latter would be better off leasing some land to the former. Similarly, if sharecropping is inefficient relative to owner-cultivation, a landlord should sell the land to the sharecropper to make him an owner-cultivator, and get a share of the resulting productivity gains.

Clearly, an explanation of these facts must be based on some frictions in the operation of the land market, or some other input relevant for agricultural production.

A leading explanation of both these facts is based on incentives. A small farmer cultivates his land with own and family labour, while a large landowner uses hired labour which has lower incentives to put in effort. Similarly, a sharecropper effectively faces an income tax of 50 per cent (the most commonly observed sharing rule in the absence of tenancy legislation being 50:50) and naturally puts in less effort.

This, however, raises a deeper question: why cannot these parties design contracts that would get rid of the incentive problem?

A key assumption here is that some inputs such as effort, care, and maintenance of land are inherently difficult to monitor. As a result, unless the party that is supplying these inputs is full residual claimant (that is, retains 100 per cent of the profits), it will undersupply these inputs.

A landowner can offer a fixed rent contract that has this property. According to this contract, the landlord simply gets a fixed fee and the tenant keeps all the residual earnings. If everyone lived for one period, this would be equivalent to selling the land to the tenant. However, if the tenant is poor, then even though this contractual arrangement would be efficient, it might not be in a landlord's interest to offer it.

Consider a simple example. Suppose, given the scarcity of land, the fixed rent that would induce the landlord to lease out a given plot of land is Rs 100. However, since the tenant is poor and does not have enough liquid wealth, he may not be able to pay this rent upfront, or guarantee to pay it irrespective of whether the output is high or low. He may be able to pay a guaranteed fixed rent of only Rs 50. It is in the landlord's interest then to ask for a share of output, even though that would reduce effort, since he gets a higher expected rent. He would not ask for too high a share of output though, since at some point reduced effort would start reducing his expected rent (this is like the Laffer curve in the context of income taxes: if tax rates are too high, cutting taxes may actually raise revenue via increased labour supply).

This rent extraction versus incentives trade-off (see Banerjee et al. 2002 for a formal analysis) can explain the persistence of inefficiency in the land market. This would explain both the stylized facts mentioned earlier and why market forces will not necessarily get rid of the implied productivity losses.

An alternative form of friction that can explain these facts is that, due to an imperfect legal system, the market for land does not operate well. For example, if leasing out land entails a risk that it might be hard to evict the tenant if the landowner wishes to withdraw land for owner-cultivation at some later point, then the land-leasing market would not work well. Indeed, in their cross-state analysis of tenancy laws in India, Conning and Robinson (2005) show that tenancy laws, though designed with the aim of helping tenants, actually reduced the extent of tenancy.

So far we did not consider the issue of heterogeneity of farmers in terms of ability and/or in terms of soil quality. For example, a key econometric concern is whether the empirical observations mentioned above control for unobserved heterogeneity. If these observations are purely driven by unobserved variations in farmer quality or land quality, then the efficiency case for land reform is weakened. For example, if higher-ability farmers prefer to cultivate smaller plots of land (as opposed to being constrained to do so) or landowners prefer to lease out lower-quality plots to sharecroppers, then in the absence of any other frictions such as those mentioned earlier land reform will not raise average productivity.[1] However, there is some evidence (for example, Rosenzweig and Binswanger 1993 on farm size and

---

[1]Of course, heterogeneity combined with the frictions discussed earlier may accentuate or mitigate the loss of efficiency. For example, if land quality and effort are complements in the production function and landowners tend to lease out inferior-quality land, then reform that transfers land from landlord to cultivator will still raise efficiency, although to a lesser degree than if the land was of higher quality.

productivity; Shaban 1987 on sharecropping) to suggest that these empirical facts are not purely driven by heterogeneity in farmer quality or land quality. For example, Shaban (1987) finds, after controlling for land quality, that the same farmer puts in less effort in plots of land that he cultivates as sharecropper compared to plots of land that he cultivates as owner-cultivator.

To sum up, incentive problems and imperfect property rights are the leading explanations for distortions in the allocation of land. These arguments imply that land reform will raise productivity as well as serve the goal of equity.

As a matter of fact, redistributive policies that fall short of full-scale land reform can also have positive productivity effects. These include policies that increase the wealth or income of the rural poor or their bargaining power vis-à-vis landowners (Banerjee et al. 2002 refer to these as empowerment strategies).[2] Given that the loss of efficiency is due to the trade-off between rent extraction and incentive provision, any strategy that reduces the ability of landowners to extract rents will raise efficiency, even if it falls short of land reform, and will also serve the goal of equity. However, some of these strategies, such as regulation of tenancy, might have a negative effect from the point of view of reducing the incentive of landowners to lease out land. This is likely to be a particularly important concern for poorly implemented tenancy-reform legislation: the presence of the tenancy law would have the negative effect on the land lease market described earlier and at the same time the positive incentive effect on tenants may only be partially realized. I will return to this point

in the discussion of empirical work on land reform in India.

The above arguments also suggest that even if equity is the only consideration, there may be a case for redistribution of land as opposed to any other form of redistribution. For example, if because of imperfect property rights the market for land sales and rental is very thin, then a direct intervention in the land allocation method may be required to improve the conditions of the rural poor. This would typically require a combination of reforming property rights in land (for example, formalization of land records and legal protection of ownership rights) and redistribution (stipulating a land ceiling and redistributing surplus land).

INDIAN EVIDENCE ON THE CAUSES AND EFFECTS OF LAND REFORM

The two key empirical questions are: what is the effect of land reform on productivity and poverty, and what are the factors that drive its success? These are clearly interdependent: factors that affect the success of land reform are also likely to affect productivity and poverty. For example, if a left-wing administration comes to power, as it did in Kerala and West Bengal, it will implement land reforms more actively and also implement other reforms (for example, empowering local governments) that might have a direct bearing on productivity and poverty. The challenge is to isolate the effect of land reforms.

Land reform legislation in India consisted of four main categories: abolition of intermediaries who were rent collectors under the pre-Independence land revenue system; tenancy regulation that attempted to improve the contractual terms for tenants, including crop shares and security of tenure; a ceiling on landholdings with a view to redistributing surplus land to the landless; and finally, attempts to consolidate disparate

[2]Examples of the latter include tenancy laws that stipulate an upper bound to the share that can be charged as rent, or public works programmes that raise the rural wage rate.

landholdings.[3] Abolition of intermediaries is generally agreed to be one component of land reforms that has been relatively successful. The record in terms of the other components is mixed and varies across states and over time. Landowners naturally resisted the implementation of these reforms by directly using their political clout and also by using various methods of evasion and coercion, which included registering their own land under names of different relatives to bypass the ceiling and shuffling tenants around different plots of land so that they would not acquire incumbency rights as stipulated by the tenancy law. The success of land reform has been driven by the political will of specific state administrations, the notable achievers being the left-wing administrations in Kerala and West Bengal.

Besley and Burgess (2000) have used state-level data for the sixteen major Indian states from 1958 to 1992 and exploited the variation across states and over time in land reform legislation to identify the effect of land reform on productivity and poverty. They generate a cumulative variable that aggregates the number of legislative reforms to date in any particular state. Controlling for state and year fixed effects, and a number of time-varying economic and policy variables, they find that the lagged version of their cumulative land reform variable has had a negative and significant effect on poverty. Interestingly, they find that this is due primarily to the tenancy reform component of land reform. However, this also seems to have had a negative effect on agricultural productivity, suggesting an equity–efficiency trade-off. Abolition of intermediaries had a negative effect

on poverty, but no effect on productivity. Imposing a ceiling on landholdings does not seem to have had much effect on either poverty or productivity, while land consolidation had a positive effect on productivity without having any effect on poverty. The authors conclude that land reforms did not have much effect on the distribution of land and seem to have operated mainly through altering the contractual relations in agriculture.

The previous study takes land-reform legislation as the measure of land reform, and not its implementation. Given the widely acknowledged gap between the two, one concern is that, as discussed in the previous section, a poorly implemented tenancy reform may have a net negative effect on productivity by freezing up the land lease market even though it might improve the productivity as well as the income of some tenants. Indeed, a study by Banerjee et al. (2002) that focuses on West Bengal, a state where tenancy reforms were implemented very thoroughly, yields very different conclusions: tenancy reforms improved agricultural productivity. Within a year of being elected in 1977, the left-wing administration launched Operation Barga, a programme designed to implement and enforce the long-dormant agricultural tenancy laws that regulated rents and security of tenure of sharecroppers. Under these laws, if tenants registered with the Department of Land Revenue, they would be entitled to permanent and inheritable tenure on the land they sharecropped as long as they paid the landlord at least 25 per cent of output as rent. In the decade following the launching of Operation Barga, there was significant improvement in the terms of tenants' contracts and security of tenures.

The authors use two different approaches to estimate the effects of this reform on agricultural productivity.

[3]See Besley and Burgess (2000) who also provide a systematic description of these laws and their amendments that were passed in individual states over time.

Their first approach is to compare the growth in productivity in West Bengal districts with that of districts in the neighbouring country of Bangladesh. Except for religion and political boundaries, the two regions are very similar in most respects. This includes agro-climatic conditions, prevalence of tenancy, and agricultural technology and so we can expect technological shocks to agricultural yields to be similar between these two regions. Indeed, during this period agricultural productivity in both regions (and much of eastern India) grew in part due to the belated arrival of the green revolution permitted by the spread of a locally suited high-yielding variety (HYV) of rice, a fall in the price of fertilizers, and an increase in small-scale private irrigation. However, the authors find that even though the rate of adoption of HYV rice was faster in Bangladesh than in West Bengal, the rate of growth in rice productivity was higher in West Bengal. They attribute this difference to the implementation of tenancy reform. There are two concerns with this approach: first, that the data collection method concerning agricultural production underwent some changes under the new administration that could have inflated West Bengal's growth performance relative to Bangladesh. Also, during this period a number of other policy reforms were undertaken in West Bengal, such as decentralization of certain public programmes, and this approach could be picking up the effects of these other policies.

The second approach utilizes the fact that this reform was implemented in different districts of West Bengal at different rates due to bureaucratic frictions. The authors use inter-district variations in the rate of implementation of this programme (captured by the fraction of sharecroppers who were registered under this programme) as exogenous changes in the availability of a new contractual regime. That is, districts that received the programme earlier are the 'treatment' districts and districts that received it later are the 'control' districts. The resulting changes in productivity are attributed to the reform, after controlling for a number of other policy and economic variables that also changed during the period when the programme was implemented. Since this approach studies inter-district variation in agricultural productivity, it is not likely to be affected by concerns about any possible upward bias in the level of agricultural productivity due to changes in the data-collection methods. Also, since it looks at variation in the intensity of implementation of tenancy reform, it's less likely to pick up the effect of other programmes. This approach yields similar results regarding the effect of tenancy reform on agricultural productivity as the previous one, suggesting that tenancy reform did have a positive effect on agricultural productivity.

To sum up, it seems likely from the studies discussed here that tenancy reform had a direct positive effect on tenants who were directly affected by it, but the indirect effects of this reform on the rural land market as a whole are less clear. This explains why Besley and Burgess (2000) find that tenancy reform negatively affected rural poverty and Banerjee et al. (2002) find it positively affected agricultural productivity. However, both these studies are based on aggregate data (state or district level) and cannot distinguish between the direct and indirect effects of land reform. Only micro-level studies can throw more light on this question.

So far the effects of land reform have been discussed. Now I turn to the question of what determines its success.

Besley and Burgess (2000) find that political factors had a significant effect. In particular, Congress administrations had a negative effect on the passing of land-reform legislation, especially tenancy reform. In contrast, left-wing administrations had a significant positive effect. Besley and Burgess use these political variables as instruments for their land-reform measure to address the concern that land reform is endogenous and could be driven by factors that also affect the dependent variables of interest.

Conning and Robinson (2005) further pursue the investigation of determinants of land reform and find that, after controlling for other variables including state and year effects, the likelihood of reforms increases when land inequality is higher and where peasants have greater political power. Bardhan and Mookherjee (2005) study village-level data from West Bengal and find that land reform activity is highest where left-wing parties hold a larger number of seats in the state legislature and, interestingly, where they face greater political competition.

To sum up, land reform is clearly driven by political factors. One important ingredient is the strength of left-wing parties in the state. We can think of the support for left-wing parties as 'demand' for land reform. The 'supply' of land reform seems to depend on the electoral success of left-wing parties, as well as how tight the electoral competition is.

In this entry, the economic arguments in favour of land reform were reviewed and it was shown that they are based on frictions in the allocation of land. These frictions could either be due to agency costs or imperfect property rights. The evidence on land reforms in India was then evaluated. The evidence suggests that land reforms had a negative effect on poverty, while the effect on productivity is mixed. In states where these measures were strongly implemented, the effect of land reform on productivity seems positive.

MAITREESH GHATAK

REFERENCES
Banerjee, A.V. 1999. 'Prospects and Strategies for Land Reforms', in B. Pleskovic and J. Stiglitz, eds, *Annual World Bank Conference on Development Economics 1999*, Washington D.C., World Bank, pp. 253–84.
Banerjee, A.V., P.J. Gertler, and M. Ghatak. 2002. 'Empowerment and Efficiency: Tenancy Reform in West Bengal', *Journal of Political Economy*. 110(2): 239–80.
Bardhan, P. and D. Mookherjee. 2005. 'Political Economy of Land Reforms in West Bengal 1978–98', Working Paper, University of California, Berkeley and Boston University.
Besley, T. and R. Burgess. 2000. 'Land Reform, Poverty Reduction, and Growth: Evidence from India', *Quarterly Journal of Economics*, 115(2): 389–430.
Conning, J. and J.A. Robinson. 2005. 'Property Rights and the Political Organization of Agriculture', *Journal of Development Economics*.
Rosenzweig, M. and H. Binswanger. 1993. 'Wealth, Weather Risk, and the Composition and Profitability of Agriculture', *Economic Journal*, 103: 56–78.
Shaban, R.A. 1987. 'Testing between Alternative Models of Sharecropping', *Journal of Political Economy*, 95: 893–920.

Land Rights and Acquisition

LAND RIGHTS IN THE PRE-COLONIAL PERIOD

Codified rights to land date back at least to the time of Manu. In Manu's code, land rights are awarded to the first clearer. The king did not claim ownership of all the land in his kingdom then. Manu prescribed a maximum share of one-sixth of the gross produce to the king as recompense for giving protection. The code prescribes the duties for the four varnas (literally colours, which later formed the basis for all castes).

Commentators on Manu's code have elaborated on the different modes of acquisition advanced in it. In Sen (1918: 53–4), we find:

NARADA ... says that there are twelve different modes of acquiring wealth of which three are general (i.e.) open to all castes; and the rest are peculiar to the several castes. Succession, gifts of affection and marriage presents received with the wife—these are common to all the castes. There are three special cases of acquiring wealth in the case of brahmins which are free from stain, viz., acceptance of free gifts, performance of priestly duties and receipts from disciples; similarly there are three special sources of wealth in the case of kshatriyas, viz., revenue, gains of war and penalties of law; so the vaisyas acquire wealth in three distinct ways, viz., through agriculture, herdsmanship and commerce; and the sudras gain wealth by serving the aforesaid three castes.

The *avarna*s or 'untouchables' had no prescribed mode of acquisition: as near-slaves, they owned very little, and their masters could confiscate even that.

As it happens, custom could, and did, override the Sastric law. From the Gupta period onwards Sudras gained the right to acquire wealth through agriculture and animal husbandry. From this time on, all the four varnas owned land, though it was only the Sudras and avarnas who actually cultivated it.

In matters of succession, most of India followed the principles laid down in the *Mitakshara* of Vijnaneshwara. The *Mitakshara* allowed partition of ancestral joint-family property among offspring even when the father was alive. The *Dayabhaga*, written by Jimutavahana and Hemadri, and followed in West Bengal and Assam, permitted partition of joint family property only after the father's death. Marumakkathayam was a matrilineal system of inheritance that was unique to the state of Kerala: all family property was jointly owned, and among the liberties enjoyed by women was the right to property.

This multiplicity of succession laws in India made land rights a very complex affair. No female was allowed to be a member of the coparcenery[1] in the Mitakshara system. Joint-family property devolved by survivorship within the coparcenery. This meant that with every birth or death of a male in the family, the share of every other surviving male got either diminished or enlarged. Joint-family property or group property became the norm in India. Maine (1953: 305) observed the distinction between this form of ownership and the norm that prevailed in the West:

A Hindu may start with nothing, and make self acquired fortune by dint of his own ability and exertion; and he is the absolute owner of the estate. But in a couple of generations his offspring would have ramified into a joint-family, exactly like a banyan tree which started as a single shoot. Absolute unrestricted ownership, such as enables the owner to do anything he likes with his property, is the exception. The father is restricted by his sons, the brother by his brothers, the women by their successors. If property is free in the hands of its acquirer, it will become fettered in the hands of his heirs. Individual property is the rule in the West; corporate property is the rule in the East.

Land ownership was very prestigious. An individual member of the joint family could not easily borrow funds since the family's property could not easily be attached or foreclosed. Further, an individual's borrowings for illegal or immoral purposes were not binding on the other members of the joint family. So those who lent money were kept on the defensive. This acted as a fetter on the development of new contractual arrangements in agrarian land management and reinforced the continuance of subsistence agriculture for many centuries.

However, Hindu law did permit the *kartha* (head) of a vaishya joint family to

---

[1]Coparceners are persons with the right of joint inheritance or heirship to property. Coparcenery was a narrower body of persons within a joint family, and consisted of father, son, son's son, and son's son's son.

pledge its properties in order to raise loans. It also permitted interest collection. The fetters of group interests were relatively weak here, and this resulted in the development of many contractual forms, including negotiable instruments and insurance, in commerce.

In both the Hindu and Mohammedan systems, the king was by no means the owner of all land in his kingdom. When Islamic rule came to India, the sharia was applied to settle disputes among Mohammedans and between Mohammedans and Hindus. But the Hindu law continued to be applied in the settlement of disputes among Hindus. The sharia, as in the Hindu system, also discriminated against women in matters of succession. It held that 'the share of one male is equal to that of two females'.

With the fall of the Gupta Empire, there was an increase in the collection of land revenue. When Mohammedan rule came to India, the right to collect revenue from specified regions was conferred on intermediaries who maintained and supplied troops for the rulers. These intermediaries, who were subject to transfer from one region to another, tried to extract the maximum revenue they could from the regions under their temporary control. About one-half of the entire yield was collected as land revenue.

In the forests that covered more than a third of the territory of India, neither Hindu nor Mohammedan law applied. Land was collectively owned and jointly cultivated. Barter exchange prevailed. No particular type of work commanded special esteem there and there was also little evidence of gender discrimination. In the hills tracts of India such tribal communes have survived until quite recently.

BRITISH RULE: LAND RIGHTS AND FORESTS
The East India Company changed the land laws in India piecemeal and in stages. The Act of Settlement of 1781 preserved the personal laws of the 'Hindus' and 'Mohammedans' in matters of inheritance, succession, and contracts. But grouping all Indians under 'Hindu' and 'Mohammedan' was impractical (see Setalwad 1960: 9–10).

The Regulation of 1793 imposed the Permanent Settlement on Bengal, Bihar, and Oudh, and notified that the zamindars and independent *talukdars* were the actual proprietors of land (Field 1885: 515). This Regulation extinguished the property rights of hundreds of peasants and transferred them to a class of intermediaries.

Different experiments were tried out in different parts of India. The multiplicity of systems in British India included: (1) the *ryotwari* system (under which the owner paid land revenue directly to the state) in Madras, Bombay, and Berar; (2) the ryotwari-in-principle system (though not so named officially) in Assam, Coorg, and Burma; (3) the Permanent Settlement system (under which the owner paid revenue to an intermediary—with inheritable rights—who paid a fraction to the state) in parts of Bengal, Bihar and Orissa, Benares, and Madras; (4) the Temporary Settlement system (under which the intermediary's rights were not inheritable) in Oudh and parts of Bengal; and (5) the effectively, though not officially so-designated, *mahalwari* system (under which the village collective paid revenue to the state) in most parts of the United Provinces, Central Provinces, Punjab, and parts of Agra and Oudh. Common to all the systems in force was the fact that the British had unfairly distorted the land rights of the peasants in India.

While in theory, the ryotwari tenure conferred rights on the actual landowners, in reality, the actual cultivator was often different from the owner. The landowners were from all the four varnas; however, the actual cultivators were almost exclusively from the sudra and 'untouchable' castes. The British rulers completed a scientific survey of land and recorded the rights of the owners in their revenue records, while leaving unrecorded the entitlements of the actual cultivators, sharecroppers, tenants, and lessees. During British rule, the owner's land could be attached and sold to collect revenue, and the purchaser could obtain sound title to the land. The burden of land revenue became unbearable in the nineteenth century. Distress sales of land became a frequent occurrence. The golden age for the moneylender dawned.

After India was taken under the direct administration of England in 1858, the British quickly imported their own principles of jurisprudence into Indian criminal, civil, and commercial law, by way of a series of enactments such as the Code of Civil Procedure (1859), the Indian Penal Code (1860), the Code of Criminal Procedure (1861), the Indian Registration Act (1866), the Indian Contract Act (1872), the Indian Trusts Act (1882), and the Transfer of Property Act (1882). Section 205 of the Criminal Procedure Code made land liable to attachment and sale in the execution of a court decree. Inviolability of private property and rule of law were introduced in India step by step. The Land Acquisition Act of 1894 brought the American principle of eminent domain into India.

For railway expansion between 1855 and 1880 great chunks of forest were destroyed. In 1864, the British established the Indian Forest Department. The department incorrectly assumed that all land not actually under cultivation belonged to the state. Unless it had been expressly recorded in writing, customary use was deemed a 'privilege,' not a 'right'. The new Forest Act of 1878 divided the forests of India into three classes. The first, 'state or reserved forests', were meant for commercial exploitation. A legal settlement was made before constituting reserve forests which 'either extinguished customary rights of user, transferred them as "privileges" to be exercised elsewhere, or, in exceptional cases, allowed their limited exercise' (Guha 2001: 216). Millions of hill dwellers of India lost their land rights in reserve forests. In the second—'protected'—class of forests, rights and privileges were recorded but not settled. The third class—that of village forests—remained a 'dead letter.'

CONSTITUTIONAL PROTECTION TO PROPERTY RIGHTS

India did not have a written constitution till 1935. Sections 299 and 300 of the Government of India Act, 1936 (GI Act) were introduced to protect property rights including those of zamindars and other vested interests.

Land right is a state subject under the Indian Constitution. Article (19) (1) (f) granted all citizens the fundamental right to acquire, hold, and dispose of property. By a curious and tangled process, Section 299 of the GI Act, 1936—drafted by the British to protect vested interests—was modified and incorporated as Article 31: as a fundamental right to property in independent India!

After Independence, the state legislatures passed land reform legislations. The affected parties approached the courts. The Patna High Court held the Bihar Act abolishing zamindari interests invalid in Kameshwar Prasad vs. Bihar (1951) on the grounds that the compensation amount was inversely related to the size of the zamindari. The court held that this violated the 'equality before law' criterion of the Constitution. This necessitated the passing of the first amendment to the Indian Constitution. Articles 31A and 31B with the Ninth Schedule were introduced with effect from

18 June 1951. Acts placed in the Ninth Schedule were kept out of the judicial review prerogative of the courts.

The clash between the judiciary and the legislature continued. The court struck down the expropriation legislation as unconstitutional, and the state responded by amending the Constitution. The fourth and seventeenth amendments emerged through this route. The drastic twenty-fifth amendment to the Constitution followed the court's striking down of the bank nationalization of 1969 on the grounds of inadequate compensation. In Keshvananda Bharati vs. State of Kerala (1973) 4 SCC 225, a full bench of thirteen judges assessed the validity of the new amendment. Eleven judgments were delivered. The majority view upheld all the amendments related to property rights. However, property right was held not to be a part of the 'basic structure' of the Constitution which was declared inviolable (cf. Singh 2004).

The Forty-Fourth Amendment Act 1978 removed property as a fundamental right and deleted Articles 19(1) (f) and 31 from the Indian Constitution. Article 300-A—'No person shall be deprived of his property save by authority of law' (bearing a close resemblance to Section 299 (1) of the GI Act 1936) was introduced as a statutory right.

A unanimous Supreme Court judgment of 11 January 2007 reiterates the Kesavananda Bharati decision forewarning continued confrontation between the judiciary and the legislature.

LAND REFORMS AND THEIR IMPACT

P.S. Appu's comprehensive study of land reforms concludes (Appu 1996: 191):

Of the three programmes considered in this study, the laws for the abolition of intermediary interests were implemented fairly well. But in the case of tenancy reform and ceilings on holdings, the policies adopted were ambivalent and there were large gaps between policy and legislation and between legislation and implementation. We have seen that as a result of the implementation of the tenancy laws, tenants became owners of or acquired lands in only about 4 per cent of the operated area. The enforcement of ceilings led to the re-distribution of less than 2 per cent of the operated area. Thus these two measures taken together led to the re-distribution of only about 6 per cent of the operated area. This is insignificant.... In the People's Republic of China between the years 1950 and 1952 about 43 per cent[2] of the agricultural land changed hands.

Earlier [ibid.: 75], he laments: 'The worst consequence of the reform was the large scale ejectment of tenants-at-will, under tenants and share croppers.'

'Operation Barga' in West Bengal, in which the rights of sharecroppers were recorded, and Kerala's 'Kudiyiruppu' laws granting homestead land to agricultural labourers, were a few successes. The Task Force on Agrarian Reforms (1972–3) of the Planning Commission identified the reasons for the poor performance of land reforms as—'the lack of political will, absence of pressure from below, inadequacies of the administrative machinery, judicial intervention, the absence of correct and up-to-date land records and the lack of supporting facilities for the beneficiaries'.

Unenforced and partially enforced land reform legislation increases the transaction cost of effecting transfer of land rights. It provides enormous scope for the unscrupulous exercise of discretion by bureaucrats and politicians. Litigation is costly. The transfer of surplus land at considerable cost to 'benamis' (false substitutes) in order to evade ceiling

[2]Professor N. Krishnaji estimates that the percentage is much higher.

legislation is widespread. With increasing uncertainty, there is no incentive for the landlord or the 'benami' to make improvements on the land. Oral tenancies have become the norm, and landlords are ready to leave their lands uncultivated rather than to allow their tenancies to be recorded.

FORESTS, COMMON PROPERTY RESOURCES, AND TRIBAL LANDS

In 1998–9, government and forest departments owned 95.65 per cent of the recorded forest area. Sixty per cent of forest lands lay essentially in the adivasi-dominated regions of India.

Large-scale shrinkage of common property resources takes place through: (a) encroachments by big landholders and powerful vested interests at village level; (b) state appropriation of common lands for 'public purpose', mainly, that is, for development projects and commercial and industrial use; and (c) distribution to poor landless and agricultural labourers. Most distributed lands are subsequently purchased by the rich.

The present National Policy on Resettlement and Rehabilitation for Project Affected Families 2003 compensates only assets, not livelihoods. Compensation is given only to persons with undisputed legal title. It is not considered necessary to grant compensation for loss of access to community assets like grazing lands and forests. Inadequate rehabilitation of the displaced tribals compounds their woes, making them asset-less, unemployed, and trapped in debt bondage.

Constitutional provisions have not done much for tribal communities. The romantics from the outside world plead for preservation of tribal life. But tribals who get an opportunity to walk out of the quagmire vote with their feet and leave. The dilemma regarding the right tribal policy still persists.

GENDER DISCRIMINATION

In the past, family assets were apportioned almost exclusively among men (an exception being the Marumakathayam system). However, custom decreed that the returns from those assets be shared with women. During all life-cycle ceremonies associated with birth, puberty, marriage, and death and the festival of family deities, the male branches of the family were required to bestow gifts on the female branches.

In the Hindu law women had absolute ownership only over *stridhan* (property gifted by parents and relatives on marriage and other occasions). The Hindu Law of Inheritance Act 1929, The Hindu Gains of Learning Act 1930, and The Hindu Women's Right to Property Act 1937 were British legislations conferring limited property rights on women.

The framers of the Indian Constitution took note of the discrimination against women in society. Section 6 of the Hindu Succession Act 1956 hit at the ancient rule that property shall devolve by survivorship among the male members of the Hindu coparcenery. Till then, in Hindu Law, coparcenery was an exclusive male membership club. The aim of the 1956 Act was to mitigate gender discrimination in the Mitakshara coparcenery by including women in the system. The mother of the deceased, the widow, and the daughter were included as Class-I heirs along with the son. But the 1956 Act did not completely end gender discrimination. In a major blow to patriarchy, the Hindu Succession (Amendment) Act, 2005 has abolished discrimination between the son and the daughter in the matter of succession to coparcenery property. Whether this will be enforced or will suffer the same fate as land reforms is a matter for conjecture now.

EMINENT DOMAIN

The Land Acquisition Act of 1894 confers power on the government to compulsorily acquire land for public purposes or for a company on payment of compensation. Planned development, education, health, and other schemes are included as illustrations of 'public purpose'. Section 23 specifies the principles for computing compensation. A 'solatium' of 15 per cent of the market value of the land acquired is required to be added to the compensation in view of the compulsory nature of the acquisition. The Act makes no reference to rehabilitation. Since compensation is granted only to persons with legal title, tenants, sharecroppers, and wage labourers become ineligible.

Is it right for the state to expropriate land to advance private-sector development through schemes such as Special Economic Zones (SEZs) to correct India's 'infrastructure deficit'? There is mistrust that such schemes may do more for their promoters than for the country. Widespread opposition to expropriation of poor farmers at Singur and Nandigram stemmed from a felt sense of inequity.

Unless conversion of agricultural land for industrial use is permitted, all industries could be located only in deserts and desolate places! Normally, it is not necessary for the state to acquire private land and transfer it to private industry. The market is the proper channel for it, except to break hold-ups affecting the industrial development of an entire region. Sections 23 and 24 specify the principles to determine the amount of compensation. Section 23 states that 'increase in the value of land due to the new use' should not be taken into account. This is manifestly unfair since the sellers expect a substantial windfall after the setting up of major industrial projects on their lands.

Any practical solution should enable farmers whose lands are acquired to get cash compensation for a major portion (say, four-fifths) of their lands to meet their immediate obligations. They should be allotted an equivalent area for the balance of land (say, one-fifth) in the developed portion of the project area. That would give the landowners an opportunity to obtain a share in the possible future windfall gains. The promoters invest huge sums in these projects. They should be obligated to invest at least 5 per cent of the total project cost in construction of educational and health facilities to which the affected farmers and their children should have privileged access. In this way the future health and educational needs of the farmers' families would be taken care of and their children would grow to be employable anywhere (cf: Sau 2007).

S. NEELAKANTAN

REFERENCES

Appu P.S. 1996. *Land Reforms in India*, New Delhi, Vikas Publishing House Pvt. Ltd.

Field, C.D. 1885. *Landholding and the Relation between a Landlord and Tenant*, Calcutta, Thacker, Spint & Co.

Guha, Ramachandra. 2001. 'The Prehistory of Community Forestry in India', *Environment History*, 6(2): 214–26

Maine, John D. 1953. *Treatise on Hindu Law and Usage* (ed. N. Chandrasekara Aiyar) 11th edn, Madras, Higginbothams.

Sau, Ranjit. 2007. 'Second Industrialisation in India: Land and the State', *Economic and Political Weekly*, 42(7): 571–7.

Sen, Priyanath. 1918. *The General Principles of Hindu Jurisprudence, Tagore Law Lectures* (1909), Sri Krishna Tarkalankara: *Commentary on Dayabaga*, Calcutta, University of Calcutta.

Setalwad, M.C. 1960. *The Common Law in India*, London, Stevens and Sons.

Singh, Jaivir. 2004. '(Un)Constituting Property: The Deconstruction of the "Right to Property in India"', *CSLG Working Paper Series*, CSLG/WP/04–05, Jawaharlal Nehru University, New Delhi, August.

National Rural Employment Guarantee Act

Passed by the Lok Sabha on 23 August 2004 and signed by the President of India on 5 September 2005, the National Rural Employment Guarantee Act (NREGA) has been hailed as a major initiative in the Government of India's commitment to providing an economic safety net to India's rural poor. Data from 2002 show that 71.9 per cent of India's population still resides in rural areas, and coupled with the fact that the majority of India's poor also resides in rural areas, the NREGA can be thought of as a policy to boost rural income, stabilize agricultural production, and reduce population pressure on urban areas.

The NREGA extends to all rural areas of India, including Fifth and Sixth Schedule areas, except the state of Jammu and Kashmir. Among its provisions are the following: (i) every household in the rural areas of India shall have a right to at least 100 days of guaranteed employment every year for at least one adult member, for doing casual manual labour at the rate of Rs 60 per day; (ii) only productive works shall be taken up under the programme. The State Council shall prepare a list of permissible works as well as a list of 'preferred works'. The identification of preferred works shall be based on the economic, social, and environmental benefits of different types of works, their contribution to social equity, and their ability to create permanent assets; (iii) the programme may also provide, as far as possible, for the training and upgradation of skills of unskilled labourers; (iv) wages may be paid in cash or kind or both, taking into account the guidelines and recommendations of the state council on this matter as far as possible; (v) employment shall be provided within a radius of 5 km of the village where the applicant resides at the time of applying.

In cases where employment is provided outside such radius, it must be provided within the block, and transport allowances and daily living allowances shall be paid in accordance with programme rules; (vi) in cases where at least twenty women are employed on a worksite, a provision shall be made for one of them to be deputed to look after any children under the age of 6 who may be brought to the worksite, if the need arises. The person deputed for child minding shall be paid the statutory minimum wage; (vii) a proportion of the wages, not exceeding 5 per cent, may be deducted as a contribution to welfare schemes organized for the benefit of labourers employed under the programme, such as health insurance, accident insurance, survivor benefits, maternity benefits, and social security schemes.

The NREGA, as it stands, explicitly eliminates two important criteria inherent in Employment Guarantee Schemes (EGS), particularly those that have been instituted in the state of Maharashtra: (i) public works programmes should not compete with agricultural labour hiring decisions and (ii) public works programmes should generate a productive asset that directly impacts agricultural productivity (Basu 2005). However, with Indian agriculture largely characterized by seasonality—a slack/lean season when agricultural labour demand is low and a peak/harvest season when labour demand is high—it can be reasonably assumed that the public employment, guaranteed for at least 100 days, will be instituted during the lean season when the rural labour force is most vulnerable. By removing the constraint that productive assets must be created to impact agricultural productivity, the NREGA allows for a certain leeway regarding the location of public works programmes.

The operational dimensions of the NREGA are important and generate much of the debate about its efficacy. But equally important in the debate has been its conceptual basis, and whether the problem to which it is addressed, rural poverty, is in fact best addressed by such an Act. There has been considerable discussion, for example, on whether the employment will be targeted to those who are poor, or whether there will be leakages to those above the poverty line.

In this entry, we take a slightly different tack to the current extensive debate on poverty targeting. We consider the Act as an intervention in rural labour markets, and ask what the consequences of this are likely to be for wages and employment (Basu et al. 2006). We start with the presumption that rural labour markets in India do not conform to the classic competitive labour markets of economics textbooks. If they did, the arguments for the NREGA would be weaker. However, in our view agricultural labour markets in India exhibit a range of hiring arrangements, from sharecropping to seasonal spot wage labour demand and a variety of credit-labour-land contracts in between (Basu 2002). Thus, labour markets in rural India can best be characterized by imperfect competition with high costs on the part of workers to seek and to switch employment, and with elements of monopsony power that lead to low wages and above all to equilibrium unemployment.

Assuming the NREGA targets this latter group of unemployed workers, the possibility of an alternative source of income—call it the disposable income from public works employment calculated as the minimum agricultural wage paid in these programmes minus the cost incurred by workers in reaching and staying at the worksite—raises the reservation wage of all workers in the rural sector, and implicitly confers some bargaining power on to rural workers. Thus, apart from the provision of an analogue of unemployment benefits,

the fact of a guarantee of employment at a given wage through the NREGA introduces contestability in the rural labour market. In other words, private firms/landlords in rural areas need to raise the disposable income of the workers they hire—once again defined as the private wage minus the transportation/search cost of seeking private employment—in order to ensure the same number of available workers as before.

The key question then boils down to whether the NREGA can raise both private-sector wages and employment. The answer lies in how the labour supply schedule available to private employers in agriculture reacts to the opposing effects of the NREGA: in effect whether or not the unemployment benefit aspect that provides workers the option of an alternative source of employment and leads to a reduction in the pool of workers available for private employment dominates the contestability effect of the NREGA that makes private employment options more lucrative subsequent to a rise in private-sector wages. Intuitively, if the disposable income generated by public works programmes is low enough relative to the disposable income generated from private employment, then the contestability effect should dominate, leading to an increase in both private-sector wages and employment.

With the wage guaranteed in the NREGA at Rs 60 per day, the implicit discretion over transportation and other costs, and over various benefits at the point of employment, is thus revealed as a key factor in determining the efficacy of the NREGA.[1] What, then, should

[1]See Basu et al. (2006) for an analysis of minimum wage laws, wherein the issue of ex post policy discretion with respect to the enforcement of the minimum wage is once again key to the credibility of the law.

be the guaranteed optimal disposable income for public works employees? The answer lies in the efficiency versus equity trade-off from government intervention. The efficiency argument dictates that the disposable income should be low enough such that the contestability effect should dominate the unemployment benefit effect of the NREGA. On the other hand, the equity argument dictates that disposable income from public works employment should be high since the NREGA is a tool to redistribute income (through the NREGA fund) to the rural poor. Thus the equity criterion is inexorably tied to the government's aversion to income inequality. In general terms, if productivity of private-sector workers is low and hence there is low disposable income from employment in agriculture to begin with, then the disposable income from public works should be low. Needless to say, the opposite should be the case when productivity of workers in the private sector is high.

Finally, the ability of guaranteed public works employment can be thought of additionally as a policy that stabilizes employment levels in the rural sector facing productivity shocks. However, the extent to which such programmes can insure workers depends largely on the ability of the government to write and commit to complete contracts. In other words, if the government can credibly announce the wage and the location of public works programme for each and every possible productivity level, then the Employment Guarantee Act can in principle provide complete insurance to workers. But, as stated earlier, the nature of the NREGA leaves considerable discretion for the locational choice of public works programmes and other benefits at the worksite. This, coupled with the inability of the government to fully anticipate productivity shocks, may be viewed as providing only partial stabilization.

Conceptually, in order to better understand the ability of a public works programme to stabilize the labour market, the sequence of events from the announcement to the execution of a public works programme needs to be pinned down. As the NREGA is written, first the government announces the wage to be paid in public works programmes.

Next, productivity shock, positive or negative, to the private sector is revealed. Subsequent to the revelation of the productivity shock, private employers and workers form expectations regarding the location, and hence accessibility, of public works programmes ex post, and private employment contracts are signed. Finally, having observed private employment, the government decides on the location of public-works programmes and other benefits, and thus determines the disposable income of workers who seek public employment. In effect, with ex post discretion on the location of public employment, the government can act to either ration or encourage public works employment. During times when the productivity shock is positive, a location for public employment can be so chosen as to make the transportation cost high, and hence disposable income low from public employment while the opposite can be true when the productivity shock is negative. In this latter vein, it is worth noting that in the event where the agricultural sector specifically is exposed to a large negative shock, public works programmes can be instituted and productive assets created to directly dampen the level of unemployment in the agricultural labour market.

In the presence of labour market imperfections, an employment guarantee can improve both efficiency and equity. The key trade-off is between the unemployment benefit nature of the wage offered, and the contestability introduced into the labour market because of the employment guarantee. A conceptual cut at these issues reveals the key importance of the discretion embodied in the location of public works projects and various on-site benefits that can be made available to workers. While often seen as being 'merely' operational in nature, our argument shows that they are the counterpart to central features of the conceptual argument on the efficacy of employment guarantees.

ARNAB BASU, NANCY H. CHAU,
AND RAVI KANBUR

REFERENCES

Basu, Arnab K. 2002. 'Oligopsonistic Landlords, Segmented Labor Markets and the Persistence of Tied-Labor Contracts', *American Journal of Agricultural Economics*, 84: 438–53.

———. 2005. 'Labor Contracts and the Effectiveness of Rural Public Works Programs', processed, Williamsburg, VA, Department of Economics, The College of William and Mary.

———. 2005. 'Turning a Blind Eye: Costly Enforcement, Credible Commitment and Minimum Wage Laws', London, UK, Centre for Economic Policy Research, Discussion Paper 5107.

Basu, Arnab K., Nancy H. Chau, and Ravi Kanbur. 2006. 'A Theory of Employment Guarantees: Contestability, Credibility and Distributional Concerns', London, UK, Centre for Economic Policy Research, Discussion Paper 5784.

Panchayats

Panchayats or village governments have informally existed in India for many centuries, but as formal institutions of local democracy are only just over a decade old.

The British colonial authorities created some local administrative bodies (called union boards) in the nineteenth century, which were more of an effort to co-opt local elites into the colonial administration, rather than having any semblance of popular participation. The Constitution of the new Indian republic continued this tradition, recognizing state governments as the sole subnational units of government. The list of responsibilities was divided into the Union List (foreign affairs, defence, currency, income taxes, etc.), the State List (law and order, public health, agriculture, land reform, wealth tax, etc.), and the Concurrent List (electricity, newspapers, education, price controls, etc.) where both the centre and states had responsibility.

Nevertheless, the Constitution encouraged decentralization to village governments, but left the responsibility for implementing such a system on state governments. In order to assist this process, the central government set up the Balwantrai Mehta Committee in 1957, which provided a detailed set of suggestions for a three-tier system of local government. The recommendations of this Committee have formed a model that has substantially impacted the actual process followed in India in the subsequent half century. Village panchayats were to form the bottom-most layer, to be elected directly, with reserved seats for scheduled castes and tribes (SC/ST) and women. Above them would be the *panchayat samiti* (PS) at block level, with members indirectly elected from representatives of the village panchayats, and also with special provision for representation of women and SC/ST residents. The top tier of the system was to be composed of the *zilla parishad* (ZP) at district level. Panchayats were to rely principally on grants and aid from central and state governments. Responsibilities to be devolved excluded administration of public education (above primary schools). The system was insufficiently detailed on its definition of public health responsibilities to be assigned to local bodies. In other words, the system was to be part of a top-down centralized state, where the role of local governments would be to provide municipal services and implement development programmes mandated by state and central governments. It reflected the consensus in the 1950s that the centralized state would be the principal agent of economic development.

The Balwantrai Mehta Committee left room for state governments to experiment with the system as they saw fit, consistent with the Constitutional assignment of responsibility, and was endorsed in this respect by the National Development Council in January 1958. The central government created a Ministry of Community Development, Panchayati Raj and Cooperation in 1958, and issued a publication in 1962 entitled A Digest on Panchayati Raj reiterating its encouragement to state governments to implement a three-tier system of local government. In the absence of any concrete political pressure from the centre, state governments (with few exceptions such as Maharashtra and a Gujarat in the late 1960s, and West Bengal in the late 1970s) were unwilling to embark on any serious effort to devolve power to local governments.

CONSTITUTIONAL DESIGN

A set of landmark (seventy-third and seventy-fourth) amendments to the Constitution passed in 1993 finally mandated the creation of a three-tier structure of local government, quite close to the structure advocated by the Balwantrai Mehta Committee. It established in all states (with population less than 2 million) governments at village, block, and district levels, to be directly elected at all levels

once every five years. Reservations of seats and chairperson positions were mandated for SC/ST representatives on the basis of their demographic weight, in addition to one-third reservation for women. Two state-level commissions were also mandated—an election commission and a finance commission—to supervise the conduct of elections and devolution of finances. A District Planning Board was to consolidate plans from lower levels of panchayats.

The seventy-third and seventy-fourth amendments, however, did not mandate the pattern of be devolution, and left this to the discretion of the concerned state government. They merely suggested that panchayats were to be devolved the responsibility for preparing plans for local development and implementing a host of schemes (listed in Schedule XI) with regard to agricultural extension, land reforms, health and family welfare, primary and secondary education, and promotion of small-scale industry. They also suggested gram sabhas—village meetings constituted of the electorate—be endowed with powers and functions to oversee the panchayats. No legislative authority was delegated to local bodies.

IMPLEMENTATION

The mandatory requirements of holding elections have been followed by and large in most states, though the timing of elections has often been sought to be manipulated by state governments. Mandated reservation of one-third of panchayat positions for women had been successfully implemented by 2000 (except in Punjab and UP), while for SC/STs it has been somewhat less than their demographic weight in some states: the ratio was below 70 per cent in Gujarat, Orissa, and UP (Chaudhuri 2005).

On the other hand, the implementation of the discretionary provisions has been highly uneven across different states, with only a handful of states embarking on any significant devolution of functions or finances. A Government of India 2001 Report of Working Group on Decentralized Planning and Panchayati Raj Institutions revealed that only Karnataka had transferred (that is enacted legislation and passed government orders) functions, functionaries, and funds for twenty-nine different Schedule XI items. West Bengal and Kerala had by then transferred twenty-nine functions, but functionaries and finances for fifteen or less items. The remaining large states (Bihar, Gujarat, Haryana, Punjab, Rajasthan, Tamil Nadu) had transferred functionaries and funds for not a single item. State governments held significant powers over panchayats in various respects. Six large states (Andhra Pradesh, Haryana, Karnataka, Orissa, Punjab, and UP) imposed restrictions on the powers of panchayats to approve expenditures above Rs 25,000. Own revenue generated by panchayats constituted only 3.7 per cent of their total income for the period 1995–8, down from 4.5 per cent for the period 1990–5. Gram panchayats in ten out of fourteen major states reported own revenues of less than Rs10 per capita per year. Reports of State Finance Commissions were delayed in most instances, with the solitary exception of Kerala.

Nevertheless, some states have witnessed some meaningful devolution. In 1996 Kerala devolved 40 per cent of its development funds to panchayats, with the State Planning Board playing a key role in the implementation of discretionary components of the seventy-third and seventy-fourth constitutional amendments. It organized a massive training exercise for panchayat officials. Gram sabhas have witnessed widespread popular participation; civil society organizations such as the KSSP (People's Science Movement) have organized

presence in almost every village. Prior to the passage of the constitutional amendments, the Left Front government in West Bengal had created a mandatory three-tier structure of panchayats since 1978, directly elected every five years. These panchayats played a significant role in the implementation of land reforms, selection of beneficiaries of the Integrated Rural Development Programme (IRDP) credit programmes and various welfare assistance programmes, distribution of agricultural input mini-kits, administration of local employment programmes, and various community and cooperative projects. Since the 1990s, they have administered primary and secondary educational institutions, forming an alternative to the government-run schools that continue to remain under the state government.

Other states such as Rajasthan, Madhya Pradesh, and Karnataka have also witnessed some serious efforts at devolution. But for most of the country the general assessment is that the devolution has been de jure rather than de facto.

Detailed empirical data-based studies of the functioning and impact of panchayats have been restricted to a few states with some genuine devolution. Gram sansad (village meeting) attendance in twenty West Bengal panchayat constituencies as studied by Ghatak and Ghatak (2002) revealed 12–15 per cent attendance among voters, with representation of landless, marginal landowners, SC/ST groups, and Muslims more or less proportional to their population shares, but women and voters affiliated with the principal opposition party significantly underrepresented. Chattopadhyay and Duflo (2004) examine the effect of randomized reservation of gram panchayat positions in selected districts of West Bengal and Rajasthan. Reservation of panchayat pradhan positions for women was associated with a statistically significant shift in spending into areas favoured by women (drinking water and road maintenance).

Reservation of pradhan positions for SC/ST candidates, on the other hand, resulted in no discernible shift in composition of spending across different areas, but was associated with higher spending in the particular village in which the pradhan resided, at the expense of other villages administered by the same village panchayat. Bardhan and Mookherjee (2005) examine targeting of various programmes administered by West Bengal panchayats using a sample of eighty villages in fifteen major districts. They find high levels of intra-village targeting of IRDP credit and agricultural mini-kits to the landless, marginal landowners, and SC/ST groups, which did not vary with shifts in local poverty, land inequality, illiteracy, or caste composition of villages observed over the period 1978–98. On the other hand, pro-poor targeting of employment grants and all other fiscal grants exhibited a tendency to deteriorate significantly when local poverty, land inequality, or low-caste status of the poor grew. They argue that this was the result of political discretion among state government and panchayat officials, a problem which could be avoided with the establishment of direct formula-based allocation of grants to village panchayats.

AGENDA FOR FUTURE REFORMS

Much remains to be done to provide teeth to the seventy-third and seventy-fourth constitutional amendments and transform panchayat bodies into genuine institutions for democratic decentralization of development programmes. Aiyar (2002), amongst others, has stressed the need for reforms in the following areas: (i) significant devolution of functions and finances to panchayat bodies (responsibilities, functionaries and funds for local infrastructure, agricultural development

and development of small-scale industry; abolition of the the DRDA [Department of Rural Development and Aid], the arm of the state government bureaucracy traditionally responsible for administering development and welfare programmes); (ii) training of panchayat officials; (iii) direct formula-based grants to village panchayats and development of their capacity to raise local revenues; (iv) checks and balances over operation of village panchayats, including gram sabhas, audits by higher-level government officials, involvement of non-governmental organizations (NGOs), and disclosure rules for panchayat accounts; (v) conduct of elections, prevention of manipulation of timing of elections, voter lists, and vote counting by incumbents, law and order during conduct of elections, and rules governing electoral campaigns; and (vi) encouragement of local planning exercises based on popular participation. State governments have dragged their feet on these discretionary elements of the seventy-third and seventy-fourth amendments. To translate the intentions of the previous amendments into reality, perhaps another amendment is necessary.

DILIP MOOKHERJEE

REFERENCES

Aiyar, Mani Shankar. 2002. 'Panchayati Raj: The Way Forward', *Economic and Political Weekly*, 3 August.

Bardhan, Pranab and Dilip Mookherjee, eds. 2005. *Decentralization and Local Governance in Developing Countries: A Comparative Perspective*, Cambridge, MA, MIT Press: particularly chapters by Shubham Chaudhuri for India and Bardhan and Mookherjee for West Bengal.

Chattopadhyay, Raghabendra and Esther Duflo. 2004. 'Impact of Reservation in Panchayati Raj: Evidence from a Nation-wide Randomised Experiment', *Economic and Political Weekly*, 28 February.

Chaudhuri, S. 2005. 'What Difference Does a Constitutional Amendment Make? The 1994 Panchayati Raj Act and the Attempt to Revitalize Rural Local Government in India', in P. Bardhan and D. Mookherjee, eds, *Decentralization and Local Governance in Developing Countries: A Comparative Perspective*, Cambridge, MA, MIT Press.

Ghatak, Maitreesh and Maitreyee Ghatak. 2002. 'Recent Reforms in the Panchayat System in West Bengal: Towards Greater Participatory Governance?' *Economic and Political Weekly*, 5 January.

Government of India. 2001. *Report of Working Group on Decentralized Planning and Panchayati Raj Institutions*, Ministry of Rural Development.

Rural Credit

In 2000, over 70 per cent of India's population, and roughly three-quarters of its poor, lived in rural areas. The principal livelihood in rural India remains agriculture, an activity characterized by significant time lags in production and a high degree of sensitivity to weather conditions. These features of agricultural production make access to financial instruments critical to a rural household's ability to withstand income shocks and make long-term productive investments. However, as is well known, lenders' inability to perfectly identify the creditworthiness of potential borrowers and the cost of enforcing repayment place severe restrictions on rural households' access to credit. These problems are potentially more severe for the rural poor who are less able to reduce lender risk by providing collateral. This also has implications for the geographical distribution of formal credit lenders. Anticipating insufficient profits, lenders such as commercial banks may choose not to set up branches in relatively poor rural areas. This, in turn, by giving lenders in the informal sector monopoly power may further raise the interest rates the rural poor have to pay and restrict their access to affordable credit. Banerjee (2004) provides evidence that informal interest rates in India are high and exhibit significant variation.

A belief that the welfare costs of exclusion from the banking sector, especially for the rural poor, are high, has led to widespread government intervention in the banking sector of low-income countries. Examples of such intervention range from interest-rate ceilings on lending to the poor to state-led branch expansion in rural areas. India has witnessed some of the largest policy interventions aimed at providing banking for the poor. The motivation for the Indian interventions can be traced to the *All-India Credit Survey Report* (1954). This report showed that four years after Independence, the informal credit sector accounted for the bulk of rural lending, with moneylenders contributing close to 70 per cent of the total. The average annual interest rate on these loans exceeded 20 per cent. In contrast, less than 1 per cent of the borrowing was accounted for by commercial banks. Commercial banks remained confined to urban areas and geared towards the financing of trade and commerce. The survey data also showed a strong positive relationship between asset ownership and borrowing. The report concluded that financial backwardness was a root cause of rural poverty and that commercial banks needed to be harnessed to enhance formal credit in rural areas—both to enable poor rural households to adopt new technologies and production processes, and to displace 'evil' moneylenders who exploited their monopoly power to charge high rates of interest.

The conclusions of this report have guided the Indian government's policy towards rural credit markets. By 1991, according to the All-India Debt and Investment Survey, the share of moneylenders in total credit had declined to 15 per cent, and the share of commercial banks soared to 29 per cent. Equally striking is the fact that by 1991 the probability of a rural household having a formal loan was only weakly correlated with the amount of land it owned. At the same time, the total number of locations with at least one bank branch had increased from under 2000 in 1951 to over 30,000 by 1991. By the year 2000, the Indian rural banking sector accounted for the rupee equivalent of 26,768 million dollars as deposits and 10,834 million dollars as loans outstanding. In terms of population reached, the rural sector accounted for 125 million savings accounts and 25 million borrowings accounts.

A proximate reason for these changes in borrowing practices was the fact that the Indian government and central bank followed an aggressive policy of state intervention in rural credit markets, often described as 'social banking'. The policy instruments to achieve these objectives included the expansion of the institutional structure of formal-sector lending institutions; directed lending; and concessional or subsidized credit.

In 1969 the fourteen largest Indian commercial banks were nationalized, at which point they came under the direct control of the Indian central bank and were formally incorporated into the planning architecture of the country. Bank nationalization was intended to allow the state to target financial backwardness as a means of promoting social objectives. A central aim was to reduce and equalize the average population per bank branch across Indian states. To achieve this the Indian central bank adopted an area approach whereby unbanked locations—census locations with no prior presence of commercial banks—were targeted. The Indian central bank, however, still needed to coerce commercial banks to expand into unbanked rural locations, in particular in states where unbanked locations were remote and/or unprofitable. Under the Banking Regulation Act of 1949 commercial banks have to obtain a licence from the central bank in order to open a new branch. On 1 January 1977 the Indian central bank announced that to qualify to open a branch in an already banked location a commercial bank must open four in unbanked locations. This licensing rule was frozen in 1990 when India began liberalizing the economy, and was formally repealed in 1991. At this point it was deemed that future branch expansion should depend on 'need, business potential and financial viability of location'.

A second feature of the Indian social banking programme was an emphasis on directed bank lending towards sectors deemed as priority sectors (these included agriculture and small-scale industries), and within these sectors to individuals belonging to weaker sections of society. The latter included members of the historically disadvantaged scheduled castes and scheduled tribes. In 1980 the Indian central bank formalized its directed lending policy by requiring that, by 1985, 40 per cent of all bank lending go to priority sectors. Moreover, 25 per cent of this lending must go to individuals belonging to the weaker sections. While these targets remain in place to date, bank compliance with them fell sharply after financial liberalization.

The success of the Indian social banking programme in expanding the presence of commercial banks in rural India is incontrovertible. What is debatable is whether commercial banks in rural India affected the extent and type of economic activity in rural areas and whether they affected poverty and inequality. The extent to which credit disbursements by the banking sector were based on need rather than political power is also a matter of debate. Finally, the extent to which any economic gains were due to productive investments associated with credit provision, rather than simply attributable to the redistribution of resources through the banking sector, remains unclear.

Burgess and Pande (2005) use panel data for Indian states from 1961 to 2000 to examine whether the bank branch expansion programme affected state output and poverty outcomes. The typical problem with examining this relationship is that banks are prone to opening more branches in richer states. Not accounting for this fact can lead to biased estimates of the relationship between branch expansion and economic outcomes. Burgess and Pande address this problem by exploiting the fact that between 1977 and 1990 more bank branches were opened in financially less developed states. The opposite was true outside this period. This change in the trend relationship between a state's financial development and branch openings allows them to isolate the policy-driven part of branch expansion and to use that to examine how this expansion affected the Indian economy. They show that branch expansion was associated with an increase in the shares of rural credit and savings. In keeping with earlier studies, they also find that the branch expansion increased non-agricultural, but not agricultural, output. In a companion study, Burgess et al. (2005) used household data from the National Sample Survey to show that the simultaneous enforcement of directed bank lending requirements was associated with increased bank borrowing among the poor, in particular low-caste and tribal groups.

On the flip side, it is also true that commercial banking in rural India remained unprofitable. The average default rate for commercial banks during the 1980s stood at 42 per cent (as a share of all loans due for repayment). Default rates were very similar across types of borrower—a finding consistent with poor monitoring of borrowers at all levels, and the fact that large-scale loan defaults were very often politically condoned.

In the end, it was the relative unprofitability of rural banking that led to the demise of social banking in India. In 1991, at the outset of liberalization of the Indian economy, the *Report of the Committee on the Financial Sector* stated that redistributive objectives 'should use the instrumentality of the fiscal rather than the credit system' and that directed credit programmes be phased out and branch-licensing policy be revoked. As a result post-1991 rural branch expansion has been limited and multiple studies suggest that access of the rural poor to the banking sector has declined. The share of rural banks in total banks has fallen from 58 per cent in 1990 to under 50 per cent by 2000 and the share of total bank credit that went to rural areas has declined from 15.3 per cent in 1988 to 10.6 per cent in 2000. The policy recommendation is that this reduction in formal-sector lending be met by micro-credit institutions. Despite impressive advances by the Indian micro-credit sector, it is still unclear whether it will be able to achieve a mobilization of rural savings and a credit outreach to equal that achieved by the Indian social banking experiment in the 1970s and 1980s.

ROHINI PANDE

REFERENCES

Banerjee, Abhijit. 2004. 'Contracting Constraints, Credit Markets and Economic Development', in M. Dewatripont, L. Hansen, and S. Turnovsky, eds, *Advances in Economics and Econometrics: Theory and Applications*, Cambridge, Cambridge University Press.

Burgess, R. and R. Pande. 2005. 'Can Rural Banks Reduce Poverty? Evidence from the

Indian Social Banking Experiment', *American Economic Review*, 95(3): 780–95.

Burgess, R., R. Pande, and Wong. 2005. 'Banking for the Poor: Evidence from India', *Journal of the European Economics Association Papers and Proceedings*, 3(2–3), April–May: 268–78.

Government of India. 1991. *Report of the Committee on the Financial Sector*, chairman M. Narsimhan, New Delhi, Ministry of Finance.

Reserve Bank of India (RBI). 1954. *All-India Rural Credit Survey: Report*, Report of the Committee of Direction of the All India Rural Credit Survey, Mumbai.

Water

MAGNITUDE OF WATER RESOURCES

As everywhere else, the magnitude and characteristics of India's water resources are determined by topography, geology, and most importantly the quantum and seasonal distribution of rainfall. The average annual rainfall for the country as a whole is estimated at around 600 mm, ranging from less than 100 mm in the Thar desert to over 11,000 mm in parts of the north-east. On an average, the total quantum of rainfall over the country (including snowfall in the Himalayas) is estimated at some 4000 bcm.[1] Most parts of the country get the bulk of rainfall between June and October, the period of the south-west monsoon. The dates of onset and retreat of the monsoon, the quantum of rainfall during the season, and its contribution to annual rainfall vary across regions.

A part of the rainfall is absorbed and retained in the topsoil; a part seeps into the lower strata and recharges groundwater; and a third part constitutes surface run-off in streams and rivers. The Central Water Commission estimates the average annual

[1]1bcm = 1cu.km

surface flow at 1953 bcm; the Central Groundwater Board (CGWB) estimates average annual groundwater recharge from rainfall at around 430 bcm. The balance (around 1600 bcm) gives a measure of what is absorbed and retained in the topsoil. The balance is accounted for by evaporation from exposed water bodies (including natural streams and rivers) and wet surfaces, and by evapo-transpiration by forests, grasses, shrubs and other vegetation on uncultivated land and by crops grown on cultivated land. On a rough estimate the quantum of evapo-transpiration by cultivated crops from soil moisture derived from rainfall is estimated at around 460 bcm.

Rainfall is the ultimate source of replenishable water resources. In addition, there are stores of underground water accumulated in deeper strata over a long period in the past. Some estimates of its magnitude have been made by the CGWB based on the area and depth of different geological formations and their water-holding capacity. This so-called 'static reserve' is currently estimated at some 10,800 bcm.

These estimates, it must be noted, are only indicative. Surface flow estimates are based on measurements at selected observation sites in all major rivers. But not all rivers are covered and even in major rivers the measurement sites are too few and devices not sophisticated enough to give reliable estimates. No allowance is made for changes in the surface flow regimes due to changes in land-use pattern and, in particular, the reduction in the extent and quality of forest cover, soil erosion due to expansion of cultivation to marginal and fragile soils, and interruption of natural drainage networks due to urbanization and expansion of road and rail networks. Crop evapo-transpiration in different agro-climatic regions is computed on metereological observations of temperature, rainfall, and other climatic variables based on certain empirical formulae relating to evaporation rates under different climatic regimes. However, the low density of observation sites and the instruments and methods of recording do not make for reliable and representative data. Groundwater recharge estimates are based on infiltration rates under different soil and subsoil characteristics, rainfall levels, and intensities. No estimates of non-crop evaporation are available.

The volume of rainfall, magnitude of surface flow natural groundwater recharge, and static groundwater reserves for the country as a whole and for different river basins are given in Table 1.

UTILIZABLE RESOURCES

Diversion and impoundment of surface flow and exploitation of groundwater add to the quantum of water available for agricultural and non-agricultural uses (including domestic consumption). But it is neither possible nor desirable to use the entire surface flow for these purposes. Most of the surface flow in Indian rivers (90 per cent in the Himalayan rivers and 80 per cent in peninsular rivers) is concentrated during June to September. The peak monsoon flow can be used to augment supplies in the rest of the year only by storing it. The extent to which this is possible is constrained by the availability of suitable storage sites, the capacity of reservoirs

Table 1 Water Resources Potential of River Basins in India

(bcm)

		Surface water			Groundwater				
Basin	Precipi-tation	Sur-face flow	Utili-zable flow	Utili-zed flow	Stock total	Replen-ishable	Canal	Nat-ural	Estimated utilization
1 Indus	560	73.3	46	44	1338	26.5	12.2	14.3	18.2
2 Ganges	1160	525	250	145	7834	172	35	136	49.6
3 Brahmaputra–Barak	4080	677	24	1	1018	35	0.8	34	1
4 Basins between Ganges and Mahanadi	1470	41	25		54	5.8	0.8	5	0.5
5 Mahanadi, Godavari Krishna, Pennar	3370	254	191	156	226	88.4	17.4	71	14.6
6 Basins between Mahanadi and Pennar	1110	23	13		41	18.8	6	12.8	
7 Cauvery	990	21	19	18	42	12.3	3.5	8.8	5.8
8 Basins between Pennar and Kanyakumari	820	25	17	22	66	18.2	5.5	12.7	10.5
9 Tapi, Narmada, Mahi, Sabarmati	3580	75.3	54	25.5	59	26.7	3.8	22.9	6.6
10 Luni, Saurashtra–Kutch	380	15	15	2.5	113	11.2	2.1	9.1	11.4
11 All others	3700	231	36	11.4	11	17.7	2.1	15.5	3.3
12 Total	21,220	1953	690	425.4	10,812	432	89.2	342.1	121.5

Sources: GOI. 1998. *Water Related Statistics*, Central Water Commission. GOI. 1999. *Report of the National Commission on Integrated Water Resources Development 1999*, Ministry of Water Resources.

that can be built at these sites, geological conditions that determine the technical feasibility of constructing dams of acceptable safety standards, and of course the costs involved relative to the likely benefits that augmented supplies in the dry season can bring. According to the Central Water Commission, taking all these considerations into account, only about a third of surface flow is potentially utilizable. This assessment is necessarily tentative subject to the results of detailed site surveys and geological investigations. Some of the identified sites with huge storage capacities are in the seismically active sub-Himalayan regions. There are questions about the availability of cost-effective technology for exploiting these sites and ensuring that they can withstand high-intensity earthquakes.

Utilizable groundwater is taken to be equal to the annual recharge mostly from rainfall with an additional small quantity derived from recharge from seepage of water in canal-irrigated areas. This defines the level of use that is sustainable over time. Exploitation exceeding this level would mean dipping into the static reserve. And if it persists the reserve will get progressively depleted and eventually exhausted.

LEVELS AND PATTERN OF UTILIZATION

The last five decades have witnessed a concerted effort to increase the utilization of both surface water and groundwater resources. Surface water utilization has increased from 94 bcm in the early 1950s to 425 bcm in the late 1990s. Most of this increase has come from large, and some very large, irrigation and multipurpose reservoirs. Groundwater usage has gone up from 40 bcm to 120 bcm as a result of increase in the number of shallow wells (which has grown some two and half times) and the rapid spread of energized pumps to cover some three-fourths of wells. The major part of the

growth is due to the advent of tube wells in the 1950s and their phenomenal growth to 4 million in the 1990s.

At present about two-thirds of utilizable surface water potential is being used. With the completion of the large number of projects under construction, utilization may go up to 600 bcm, or nearly 85 per cent of the assessed potential. Further expansion would be both technically and economically more difficult. In the case of groundwater, official estimates shown in Table 1 would suggest that taking the country as a whole, current utilization is barely 30 per cent of the potential. This is, however, at odds with CGWB data, compiled from a sizable number of observation wells all over the country, showing a progressive and substantial fall in groundwater levels in nearly 60 per cent of the country's districts over the past twenty years. Sample surveys of some areas (Tamil Nadu, Gujarat, and Punjab) point to a much steeper decline in the depth of wells.

Available estimates of water utilization by use are given in Table 2. Being based on sketchy data and arbitrary assumptions, they are gross approximations. What they

Table 2   Gross Utilization by End Uses of Water

	1968–9*		1997–8**	
	Total	%	Total	%
Domestic	9.1	2.9	30	5
Industrial	2.7	0.7	30	5
Thermal power	6.9	1.8	9	1.5
Agriculture & livestock	356.8	95.0	524	88.5
	375.5	100	593	100

Sources: *Chaturvedi, M.C. 1976. Second India Series: Water, Delhi, Macmillan. **Government of India, Ministry of Irrigation and Power. 1999. Integrated Water Resource Development: A Plan for Action, Report of the National Commission for Integrated Water Resources Development, vol. 1, New Delhi, September.

point to is the predominance of agriculture and livestock as users of water mobilized by human intervention. While other uses are growing much faster—more than threefold for domestic use, more than ten times for industry in absolute terms—and their combined share has more than doubled, the bulk—close to 90 per cent—of water is used by agriculture and livestock.

EMERGING PROBLEMS AND RESPONSES

Agricultural demand for water has been increasing because of a large and growing differential between the productivity of irrigated and unirrigated land. Non-agricultural demand has grown even faster because of population growth, urbanization, and industrialization. There is ample evidence that the expansion in supplies, though large and historically unprecedented, has not kept pace with demand. Growing competition among farmers is reflected in (a) extensive violations of rules of allocation and use (including unauthorized tapping of canal water by farmers within and outside the command); (b) the proliferation of wells and tube wells and competitive deepening in the face of falling water tables; (c) growing complaints of water shortage in urban areas; and (d) the social and political tensions generated by attempts to meet non-agricultural demands by diverting supplies from irrigation.

Public policy response to the growth of demand has focused primarily on augmentation of supplies. Falling groundwater levels imply mining of static reserves and this is unsustainable. Groundwater policy is yet to recognize this and take measures to even arrest, let alone reverse, the trend. The notion that the utilizable surface flow can be substantially augmented, and the country's water problems solved, by diverting the monsoon floods of Himalayan rivers to the relatively drier regions of the south and the west was mooted several decades back by Visvesarayya and subsequently by K.L. Rao. It was not pursued in the face of strong criticism on technical basis, economic viability, and environmental consequences. But the idea has recently been revived and has become a live issue thanks to a directive from the Supreme Court that it be implemented within a period of fifteen years.

The latest project (estimated to cost Rs 5000 billion at late 1990s prices) has two components: one for harnessing the waters of the Ganges and Brahmaputra for hydropower generation and for diverting surpluses to the south; and the other for interlinking of (mostly east-flowing) peninsular rivers. The former, which involves international rivers and requires construction of huge storages in seismically active regions, is not being actively pursued. Following the Supreme Court directive, the Government of India set up a special task force to implement the peninsular component.

Almost every aspect of the project—the estimated magnitude of surpluses, the proposed modes and locations of transfer, the extent to which transferred water can be used to solve the domestic water problem and extend irrigation in water-short areas, the technical problems of transporting water over long distances in difficult terrain, the likely adverse impact by way of ecological disruption, forest submergence and human displacement, and the magnitude of investment relative to net additional supplies—has attracted criticism. So have the necessity for and wisdom of pursuing such a massive project without proper feasibility studies and assessment of its environmental and social consequences, and without semblance of open public scrutiny of all its aspects.

Partly because of this criticism, the taskforce has since been disbanded without abandoning the project. The government, evidently reluctant to confront the judiciary, has chosen to adopt a rather cautious and ambivalent posture on the matter. In the process attention and resources are being distracted, if not diverted, from urgently needed measures to complete the huge overhang of half complete projects and for improving the efficiency of existing irrigation systems.

CORRECTIVE MEASURES

The situation in all these respects is worsening. Corrective measures are thus imperative. These measures must recognize that, unlike other resources, water is in the nature of a common pool serving multiple uses and users. They must be such as to address the need to ensure that the distribution of access to and use of this limited resource among competing uses and users is seen to be fair and equitable and that the supply of water for future generations is not jeopardized. The neo-liberal prescription of privatization and market-mediated allocation is no solution. Property rights in a fluid common-pool resource prone to pervasive interference by users are difficult to define and impossible to enforce through markets. Private enterprises are primarily concerned with returns to their financial investment. Issues of overall productivity of water, fair distribution of cost and benefits, and long-term sustainability hardly enter their calculations. Public intervention is essential to address these concerns. Government therefore necessarily has a key role in water governance.

However, the present system of governance leaves much to be desired. Public irrigation and water supply systems are designed, constructed, and managed entirely by the government. Users have no stake or say in any of these functions. The various functions involved in the development and efficient management of water resources—such as defining the nature and basis of entitlements, laying down broad principles and institutional mechanisms for deciding and implementing projects, for regulatory functions and dispute settlement—are all conflated in the executive arm of government.

Rules are made and enforced by government fiat, guided more by considerations of political expediency than any serious concern for efficient use and equitable distribution of water. Extensive violations of rules of entitlement for access and use have not only been tolerated but in fact encouraged by the policy of providing water at far below cost. Water charges are so low, and collections so lax, that users have hardly any incentive to avoid waste and make prudent use of available water. Conflict resolution mechanisms do not exist or have become defunct or ineffective. In such a situation, there is no transparency, due process, or accountability in the discharge of these functions. The interests of the political executive and their parties and the bureaucracy, rather than the larger and longer-term public interest, dominate the whole process.

These trends cannot be arrested, much less reversed, without drastic changes in policies and institutional arrangements for water resource management. A shift in policy focus from supply augmentation to measures for conserving water and improving the efficiency of its use is imperative and urgent. This calls for (a) a change in investment priorities from construction of new projects to improvements in physical facilities and engineering structures needed for better control over quantum and timing of water deliveries in surface systems; (b) a change in the current policy of financing investments and pricing of canal water and energy inputs for pumping groundwater to create strong incentives for users to make prudent and efficient use of water. For this purpose users' stake in better management needs to be strengthened by requiring them to contribute at least a part of the cost of construction. Water and energy pricing policies should be geared to achieving full cost recovery with a rate structure that reflects the volume consumed for various purposes.

These measures have to be combined with a major restructuring of governance structure for water. There is clearly a great deal of room for improving the quality of project design, more economical and speedier construction of projects, and better coordination of programmes and policies relating to different sources and uses of water. These tend to be viewed primarily in terms of reorganizing government agencies concerned with water resource development. The creation of unified water resource organizations in some states, enactment of laws enabling user participation in management of irrigation systems, and integrated watershed development programmes reflect this approach. While these mark a significant and welcome change of approach, the 'reforms' are limited and piecemeal in both concept and implementation. They do not address the much wider and deeper weaknesses in water institutions and the way they are managed.

The following are some of the essential changes required: (1) limiting the government's role to laying down the broad principles regarding the nature and content of entitlements for water, the basis for determining entitlements of different uses and users within a basin and within individual systems, and intervention under specified contingent circumstances; (2) creation of autonomous and financially self-reliant organizations for integrated planning and management of water resource for different uses and difference sources in individual systems and for river basins with effective participation of users' representatives; (3) requiring that they levy and collect water charges to cover costs (including capital costs) without any state subsidy or subject to explicitly defined limits of budgetary subsidies and empowering them to decide and enforce rules of entitlement, access, and use as well as rates within their domains; and (4) redefining the law relating to private rights over groundwater towards community control and regulation.

Reforms of such far-reaching scope, however, figure nowhere as yet in the reform agenda. There is growing interest in integrated watershed development for rain-fed areas and creating water users associations and giving them a greater role in water management at the tertiary levels of public irrigation systems. Substantial investments for watershed development are being allocated under the public-sector plans. The idea of users' participation and turnover of management to water users associations has acquired wide currency. A few states have enacted and implemented legislation for this purpose. But the scope of these reforms is limited to tertiary levels of public canal systems. Water users associations are entrusted with limited functions (maintenance and, in some cases, recovery of water charges). They do not envisage empowering user-managed organizations to make, change, and enforce rules at the upper tiers and the system level. They have neither the freedom to decide water rates nor the compulsion to meet specified standards of cost recovery. There is little interest in pricing reform or in taking urgently needed but unpopular steps to check the depletion of groundwater. How to generate stronger pressures for reform and how to engineer them through the political process remains a challenge.

A. VAIDYANATHAN

INDUSTRY

Dhirubhai Ambani and Reliance Industries

If the story of Dhirubhai Ambani and Reliance Industries were told as fiction, it would appear too far-fetched to work as a credible plot. For a village schoolteacher's son, who started life as a gas-station attendant in Yemen, to lead a company that runs the world's largest grassroots oil refinery, would require many leaps of financial logic and a Bradmanesque tale set in the corporate world. And yet it is true that the company that Dhirubhai founded became the largest in India in terms of assets, sales, and profits within a quarter century of going public in 1977, and is now among the top 200 in the world when ranked on profits.

That is only the bare bones of the blood and thunder story of a man who created opportunity out of obstacles, started a love affair with the stock market (at one stage the company boasted the world's second largest retail investor base), thought global scale and vertical integration before his contemporaries, and innovated in financial structuring and made speedy project execution a trademark, both designed to keep capital costs low in a capital-intensive business.

Along the way, he redefined his business every decade: it was pure trading in the 1960s and then textile manufacture in the 1970s, before the principal business became petrochemicals in the 1980s and energy in the 1990s. The new century has belonged to diversification: first into telecom and now into healthcare and retailing. At every stage, outsize vision has been matched by project execution. So, imagine a BP or Shell also becoming a Wal-Mart. And bear in mind that the global healthcare business is bigger than information technology, with comparable opportunities for offshoring/outsourcing.

And yet, even that is only half the story, for Dhirubhai Ambani and Reliance have invited almost as much criticism as admiration, with a succession of controversies mirroring the scale of their achievements: violating import rules, dealing in duplicate shares, physically attacking a business rival, forgery, and upending the rules to gain delayed entry into the telecom market with a project that was breathtaking in conception but which, for the first time, faltered on delivery. In the late 1980s, the controversies swirling around Reliance became the subject of an intense media war that sucked in the government as well—the twists and turns in the plot would beat most thrillers.

So Dhirubhai and his two sons (Mukesh and Anil, who within three years of the father's death in 2002 have parted ways) have been feared as much for their lobbying power as for their business acumen. Yet, as if to answer critics who have argued that the company owed its stand-out success to its ability to exploit the 'licence-permit raj' era of controls on business, Reliance has done even better in the reform period post-1991.

Most of the allegations against Reliance have never been proved, with the exception of one adverse court judgment on some small imports using backdated bank letters of credit in the 1980s; and the company paid compounding fees in the duplicate shares case in the 1990s in order to buy peace without admitting guilt. But these have had no more effect than parking tickets. And while matters have been quieter under the two sons, the revelations that surfaced in the skirmishing that ended in the brothers parting ways did not speak of high governance standards.

Yet Reliance has been repeatedly voted among the country's most admired companies/industrial houses—not surprising when you consider that the company, a newcomer to the oil business, scored an exceptional 75 per cent success ratio in its exploratory drilling off India's east coast. When the government began selling state-owned enterprises, Reliance picked up Indian Petrochemicals Corporation (seen as a public-sector success story) and promptly improved its operating parameters. Also, those who argued that the company would not be able to maintain its growth record after Dhirubhai passed on, have seen the company trebling its value on the stock market in 2002–5 to cross Rs 100,000 crore (Rs 22 billion)—reflecting rapid growth (26 per cent in the last quarter) despite having reached global scale.

With annual cash profits in excess of Rs 20,000 crore, the company has started acquisitions abroad and is poised to double its refining capacity to 60 million tonnes (making it the world's single largest refinery), apart from adding to capacity that will build even greater dominance in polyester, polyester intermediates, and polymers—in almost all segments of which the company commands at least 50 per cent market share in India, going up to more than 75 per cent in some cases.

The profit margins that the company reports are better than normal in a 'commodity' business like petrochemicals or oil refining/marketing. Credit the Ambanis with focusing on value-added products that get better margins, for designing a refinery to maximize margins by having flexibility on crude quality, and for making sure that the company enjoys a significant sales tax concession in Gujarat and substantial import duty protection even today on oil refining. Critics who would focus on the last point have to reckon with the fact that Reliance intends to use its expanded capacity of a further 30 million tonnes to service mostly export markets—where the rules are the same for everyone.

While Mukesh plans his big moves into retailing and healthcare on the strength of huge cash flows, Anil Ambani runs two smaller businesses with long-term growth potential: power (Reliance Energy) and telecom (Reliance Infocomm). In addition, he has been using Reliance Capital to invest in different sectors, notably media (in which Anil has had a lasting interest—he started an unsuccessful business newspaper in the late 1980s). Anil has also bid for the Mumbai and Delhi airport privatization contracts.

Dhirubhai Ambani was unarguably the greatest Indian businessman of the last one-third of the twentieth century, adding his name to the league of the Tatas and Birlas who dominated the earlier two-thirds of the century. His sons continue to believe that their stage should be India, not the world, and that single-industry focus is for the management pundits; in a world full of diverse opportunities, they will grab everything that comes their way.

T.N. NINAN

Antitrust Law

Antitrust law (also known as competition law) is primarily concerned with the prohibition or regulation of restrictive business practices (RBPs, also known as anti-competitive practices) that firms undertake in order to limit competition. The most common RBPs include:

+ 'Horizontal' agreements between competitors selling the same or similar products to restrict competition among themselves. The most egregious are agreements to fix prices, restrict output, divide up markets, or make collusive bids in an auction or procurement process. Groups of firms that enter into such agreements are commonly known as 'hard-core cartels'.
+ 'Vertical' agreements between firms at different stages in the production and distribution chain that would limit competition. For example, agreements in which producers require distributors not to sell a competitor's product, not to sell outside a particular territory, or to maintain recommended retail prices.
+ Actions taken by a dominant firm to drive out rivals or prevent entry by potential competitors. This may involve temporarily charging prices below costs ('predatory pricing'), or denying rivals access to crucial raw materials or essential facilities such as a wire network (for telecommunications) that are owned by the dominant firm.

Apart from controlling RBPs, many countries regulate corporate mergers and acquisitions (M&As) that might have an adverse effect on competition. In most countries, only hard-core cartels are held to be illegal per se (with some clearly defined exceptions), while other RBPs and M&As that restrict competition may be approved under a 'rule of reason' on a case-by-case basis if they provide offsetting efficiency gains. The legal situation in India is currently in transition between the 1969 Monopolies and Restrictive Trade Practices (MRTP) Act and the 2002 Competition Act, which is yet to be brought into force. Hence both Acts are briefly described below.

THE MRTP ACT

The MRTP Act was passed in response to growing evidence of concentration of economic power in Indian industry. The Act originally required firms that were either 'large' (those that had, along with their 'interconnected undertakings', assets above a certain threshold) or 'dominant' (having assets above a lower threshold as well as a minimum market share) to register themselves with the central government, and to obtain its approval for substantial expansion, establishment of new undertakings, M&As, and appointment of their directors in other undertakings. The government could refer M&A applications to the MRTP Commission, but did not do so in most cases, and was not bound by the Commission's advice. All these sections of the Act were repealed by a 1991 amendment, on the grounds that they had hindered industrial growth. A section giving the government the power, after a referral to the Commission, to divide undertakings or to order severance of interconnections between them was retained, but was never used.

Although the MRTP Act had sections covering RBPs, the limited investigative resources of the Commission diluted its effectiveness. Also, its powers were limited to issuing 'cease and desist' orders; modest fines only could be imposed for non-compliance with these orders. Most of its orders under these sections pertained to vertical arrangements, and cartels were rarely brought to book. Overarching considerations of 'the public interest' and 'manipulation of prices', rather than a balancing of effects on competition and efficiency, were decisive in a large number of cases. A series of Supreme Court orders since 2000 have overturned many of these decisions, directing the Commission to focus on the effects of a particular RBP on competition.

The Act was amended in 1984 to include a new category of 'Unfair Trade Practices' (UTPs), dealing with misleading advertising and prize schemes. The same amendment gave the Commission the power to issue injunctions and compensation orders against suppliers of defective goods or deficiency in services. Despite the enactment of a Consumer Protection Act (COPRA) in 1986 with almost identical provisions, several advantages ensured that the MRTP Commission remained a favourite forum for such complaints. By the 1990s, the vast majority of cases pending before the Commission concerned such matters, further stretching its resources and diluting its ability to deal with RBPs that are usually the focus of antitrust law. In any case, the Commission sat only in Delhi, making it difficult to access for small complainants elsewhere in the country.

THE COMPETITION ACT

In December 2002, Parliament passed a new Competition Act to replace the MRTP Act. However, its implementation was held up by a legal challenge to the constitutional validity of several of its sections. Its substantive provisions were yet to be brought into force when this entry was written.

Unlike the MRTP Act, the Competition Act does not frown upon size or dominance as such, but on anti-competitive conduct or abuse of dominance. Instead of the categories of monopolistic, restrictive, and unfair trade practices, it follows the modern classification in terms of anti-competitive agreements, abuse of dominance, and 'combinations' (M&As). Its major features, in contrast to its predecessor, are: a per se prohibition of hard-core cartels; review (by the Commission, not the government) of combinations for firms above a certain asset or turnover threshold, with the authority to prevent, undo, or modify those having 'an appreciable adverse effect on competition'; long lists of factors the Commission should have 'due regard to' in its inquiries; and provision for substantial fines, which can be reduced for any party to a cartel agreement that discloses vital information about its functioning. There is also provision for regional benches and specialized merger benches, and for cooperation agreements with foreign antitrust authorities. The Commission has also been entrusted with competition advocacy, and may advise the government or any statutory body on matters that come under the Act. The Act does not have any counterpart to the UTP section of the MRTP Act; pending UTP cases are to be transferred to the National Commission constituted under COPRA.

Many of these features of the Competition Act are based on modern antitrust thinking and practice in advanced countries, but it remains to be seen whether the Competition Commission will be equipped with the expertise that is required to implement them. Concerns have also been expressed over potential conflicts between the Commission and sectoral regulators in areas such as telecommunications, financial markets and electricity, and over specific clauses in the Act that empower the government to issue binding policy directives to the Commission, or to supersede it entirely, thus threatening its autonomy. Experience with the existing sectoral regulators has not been encouraging in this regard.

ADITYA BHATTACHARJEA

REFERENCES

Basant, Rakesh and Sebastian Morris. Forthcoming. *Competition Policy in India: Issues for a Globalizing Economy*, New Delhi, Oxford University Press.

Bhattacharjea, Aditya. 2003. 'India's Competition Policy: An Assessment', *Economic and Political Weekly*, 38(34): 3561–74.

Chandra, Nirmal K. 1977. 'Monopoly Legislation and Policy in India', *Economic and Political Weekly*, 12(33/34): 1405–18. Reprinted in N.K. Chandra, ed., 1988. *The Retarded Economies*, Bombay, Oxford University Press.

Mehta, Pradeep, ed., 2005. *Towards a Functional Competition Policy for India*, New Delhi, Academic Foundation.

Sandesara, J.C. 1994. 'Restrictive Trade Practices in India, 1961–91: Experience of Control and Agenda for Further Work', *Economic and Political Weekly*, 29(32): 2081–94.

Singh, Jaivir. 2000. 'Monopolistic Trade Practices and Concentration of Economic Power: Some Conceptual Problems in MRTP Act', *Economic and Political Weekly*, 35(50): 4437–44.

G.D. Birla

Ghanshyamdas Birla (1894–1983) was an industrial pioneer, a generous financier of Mahatma Gandhi, and a key spokesperson and strategist of Indian big business. Born on 14 April 1894 in Pilani in the northern Indian state of Rajasthan, Birla belonged to the Maheshwari sub-caste of the trading community of Marwaris. His grandfather had migrated to Bombay in 1858 in search of fortune and by the time of G.D.'s birth, the family business of trading and speculation was based in both Bombay and Calcutta. The Birla family firm engaged in opium *satta*, carried out forward trading in several commodities such as cotton, piece-goods, wheat, rapeseed, and silver, and acted as a broker in the jute and gunny trade. Birla started his business career at the age of 12 after a traditional trader's and rudimentary English education. Within a few years, through astute leadership, he stood at the helm of the expanding family firm which made windfall profits during World War I from export of jute products, hedge transactions in raw jute and gunny, and speculative operations in silver and jute stocks. These profits led Birla to boldly venture into European-dominated jute manufacturing by establishing the Birla Jute Manufacturing Company Limited in 1919. G.D. Birla, with the support of his brothers Jugalkishore, Rameshwar Das, and Braj Mohan, led the transition of the family business from old-style trading to modern industry. Birla firms diversified into cotton textiles, sugar mills, publishing, paper, and insurance. By the mid-1930s the Birlas owned four textile mills, five sugar mills, and one jute mill. In the 1940s expansion followed in banking, textile machinery, automobiles, engineering, and plastics. Following Independence, Birla oversaw the family business move into challenging areas like chemicals, rayon fibre, engineering goods, aluminium, and fertilizers. These years saw enormous growth of the Birla business empire with a doubling of gross capital stock of the Birla public companies from Rs 65.26 crore in 1951 to Rs 152.14 crore by 1958, and a jump in the number of private companies controlled by the Group from sixty-one in 1951 to 105 by 1958. In the 1960s and 1970s, Birla encouraged the younger generation of his family to venture overseas and they set up factories in Nigeria, Kenya, Thailand, the Philippines, Indonesia, Malaysia, and Egypt to emerge as India's first multinational business house.

Alongside business, Birla always took keen interest in politics. A staunch nationalist, he became a strong financial supporter of leaders such as Madan Mohan Malaviya, Lala Lajpat Rai, and Mahatma Gandhi. Birla came to regard Gandhi as a *guru* and financed causes which the Mahatma espoused. From the 1920s onwards Birla also increasingly played the role of spokesperson of Indian big business. A propagator of solidarity among Indian business, he helped establish the Indian Chamber of Commerce in Calcutta in 1925. He also played a leading role in the formation in 1927 of the Federation of Indian Chambers of Commerce and Industry (FICCI), the first apex association of Indian business which brought together regional chambers of commerce. He was responsible for forging much of the solidarity that Indian capital displayed against the British colonial state before 1947. FICCI became a vehicle for the struggle of Indian big business against European domination of the Indian economy. For over three decades between 1927 and the 1960s Birla remained a powerful voice within FICCI as its chief strategist.

In the years following Independence Birla continued to provide visionary leadership to private enterprise. His abiding concern was that economic policies in free India must create an enabling environment for private enterprise so that it could contribute meaningfully to national development. However, Birla had lukewarm relations with Jawaharlal Nehru whose economic philosophy emphasized a predominant role for the state in economic life. While distancing himself from Nehru's economic philosophy, Birla was astute enough not to waver in his support of the Congress party as he was convinced that the interests of private enterprise could best be served through centrist parties. Notwithstanding his differences with Nehru, Birla was able to maintain his relationship with a range of Congress leaders. In 1957, at the height of Nehru's socialist rhetoric, he was awarded the Padma Vibhushan, one of the country's highest awards.

To his fellow industrialists, Birla advocated a flexible approach to accommodate diverse political interests, including the Communists. Thus, when a Communist government came to power in Kerala in 1957, he was the first businessman to invest in the state. Birla's vision was somewhat circumscribed under Nehru and the turbulent years of Mrs Gandhi's premiership, when big business faced political challenges and felt disadvantaged, but the astute political sense of his generation of business leaders enabled it to survive these years to re-emerge as an important player when conditions became favourable.

By the time Birla died in 1983 at the age of 89, despite the restrictive economic regime of his later years, his business empire had grown to be the largest family business in India. It consisted of over 200 companies under direct control and seventy under indirect control. The Birla group owned the country's biggest jute mills, the largest tea gardens, the second largest paper mill, the biggest car manufacturing unit, and produced 45 per cent of its aluminum and 3 per cent of the country's sugar. Its overseas business operations extended to a dozen countries. It also ran a large number of educational charities, one of the country's best regarded institutes of technology, charitable trusts, hospitals, more than forty temples, *dharamshalas*, and a planetarium. The business had passed into the hands of the fifth generation which had been ably trained to continue the tradition. Yet Birla failed to work out clear lines of succession within the family and his passing away left behind disputes over the division of assets and responsibilities which could never fully be resolved.

As India emerges as an economic power Birla's vision is being realized. This vision of an independent 'Hindustan' and a capitalist one is best epitomized in the names of two of the newspapers that he owned—the *Hindustan Times* and the *Eastern Economist*. Throughout his later public career, he had stressed the need for economic reforms, greater reliance on private enterprise, and a deeper integration with the world economy. It appears that Birla's vision has, at last, been embraced by the Indian political leadership. In a sense India of the twenty-first century, as it emerges as an economic power, represents a vision that was closer to Birla's than to Mahatma Gandhi's or Jawaharlal Nehru's.

MEDHA MALIK KUDAISYA

REFERENCES

Birla, G.D. 1953. *In the Shadow of the Mahatma: A Personal Memoir*, with a Foreword by Dr Rajendra Prasad, Bombay, Orient Longman.

Kudaisya, Medha. 2003. *The Life and Times of G.D. Birla*, New Delhi, Oxford University Press.

Business Policy

Business Policy is concerned with specifying and achieving an organization's objectives. It therefore involves (a) setting out the long-term goals for a firm in line with the expectations of its stakeholders, (b) formulating an action plan for meeting these goals, (c) allocating resources for the purpose, (d) implementing the action plan by modifying/building an appropriate structure within the organization, and (e) evaluating the end results through a review of results and future possibilities. Business policy is therefore dynamic and forward looking. It is the highest level of activity in a firm and usually falls in the domain of

decision making by the Chief Executive Officer and senior management team.

Two of the most important decisions facing a firm relate to scale and scope, that is size and range of activities. Size in turn is driven by growth. The famous PIMS study carried out over nineteen years seemed to yield the conclusion that the greater a firm's market share, the greater its rate of profit.[1] High market share enables a firm to gain from economies of scale through large volumes and, over time, provides experience and learning-curve advantages. The task of building up market share in turn forces a consideration of growth strategies. Should growth occur via diversification (related or unrelated), horizontal or vertical integration, mergers and acquisitions, strategic alliances and joint ventures, or franchises?

However, some research indicated that a low-market-share strategy focusing on niche segments could also be highly profitable, in other words that 'small is beautiful'.

The optimal range of activities, markets, and products was the second question that needed to be addressed. The theory of financial portfolios was extended to product portfolio decisions and operating division portfolios. As companies expanded their scope of operation, their organizations witnessed a transformation from U-form (unitary form) structures organized along functional lines to M-form (multidivisional form) structures organized along semi-independent profit centres called 'strategic

[1]The PIMS (Profit Impact of Market Strategy) of the Strategic Planning Institute is a large-scale study designed to measure the relationship between business actions and business results. The project was initiated and developed at the General Electric Co. from the mid-1960s and expanded upon at the Management Science Institute at Harvard in the early 1970s; since 1975 the Strategic Planning Institute has continued the development and application of PIMS research.

business units (SBUs). Each of these SBUs was viewed as an element in the corporate portfolio. In deciding the optimal portfolio, considerations of risk reduction had to be combined with considerations of market penetration and growth.

By the late 1970s, Japanese companies began to pose increasingly severe challenges to American companies. What was the secret of the Japanese success? In 1982 Pascale and Athos claimed that the Japanese success rested on the bedrock of superior management techniques. Rather than strategy, structure, and systems, the Japanese emphasized corporate culture, shared values and beliefs, and social cohesion in the marketplace. The end result was higher productivity. Moreover, the Japanese companies had a longer-term vision. Ohmae (1982) went further in claiming that strategy making in America was too analytical and had forgotten to be a creative art. These ideas were later complemented by authors who pointed out that successful companies often manage to develop a core ideology shared by all the employees. One can trace this line of thinking to Peter Drucker's belief that workers should be treated as resources rather than just as costs.

Michael Porter's work (1980) clearly identified the five forces that shape a firm's strategic environment. Analysis along Porterian lines enables a clearer articulation of SWOT (strengths, weaknesses, opportunities, threats) analysis. Porter also identified the three generic strategies of cost leadership, product differentiation, and focus. The highlighting of industry factors for a firm's success by Porter was countered by a number of authors who developed the resource-based view of the firm, arguing that it is only the possession of certain superior, scarce, and non-imitable intangible resources that can confer a sustainable competitive advantage on the firm. Hamel and Prahalad

(1994) saw a company as a portfolio of resources and competencies and focused on the need for a company to identify its core competencies.

THE INDIAN CONTEXT

For forty years after Independence, strategies of Indian companies were largely shaped by the industrial policy regime resting on the planks of industrial and import licensing, high tariffs, and tight regulation of technology imports. In an era of policy-induced entry barriers and low level of competition, Indian firms were not forced to develop capabilities for sustainable competitive strategies.

Corporate growth and diversification strategies were shaped by licensing policy and the ability of top management to lobby for licences and procure scarce foreign exchange and bank finance. Unrelated diversification was the norm rather than the exception. Even where entry was permitted through grant of an industrial licence, the government specified the size and location of the plant. Planners were guided by the concept of 'economic size' of plants and prevention of dominance through pre-empting of capacity. As a result, targeted capacity was fragmented between several medium-size units, unable to exploit scale economies.

The 1991 reforms combined macro-level changes with micro-level changes that lowered entry barriers for both domestic and foreign producers. From the early 1990s, therefore, Indian firms suddenly found themselves in a situation in which they were free to make investment, production, and pricing decisions. As a result, business policy formulation came to occupy centre stage. Even public-sector units that were earlier monopolies had to rethink their strategies in an era of greater competition and withering support from the government. For example, when the insurance sector was opened up, employees of Life Insurance Corporation, a public-sector enterprise that was previously a monopoly, came up with concrete proposals to improve customer service.

The growth and success of different firms under the new regime rested on different strategies. Thus Reliance Industries Limited became a giant in the petrochemicals industry by following the strategy of growth through backward integration and building up of 'world-scale' capacities that enabled it to reap economies of scale and achieve cost leadership. The Ispat International Group's growth was largely driven by a series of acquisitions in different countries of the world.

In contrast to companies like Reliance and Ispat International that have a relatively narrow range of product portfolio, one can cite Hindustan Lever Ltd. (HLL), the Indian subsidiary of Unilever, whose businesses were divisionalized in 1991 into Chemicals, Detergents, Agriproducts, Personal Products, and Exports. Again, while today we identify Wipro with its information technology division, in 1994, Wipro Corporation's activities spanned *vanaspati*, toilet soaps, toiletries, hydraulic cylinders, computer hardware and software, lighting, financial services, medical systems, diagnostic systems, and leather exports. Azim Premji described Wipro as a 'diversified integrated corporation', the integration being achieved through a set of shared beliefs and leadership values, and through people and through management processes' (Ghoshal et al. 2002: 421–2). All companies like HLL and Wipro are concerned with managing a diversified portfolio of products and at the same time protecting their core businesses.

Indian companies are also devoting attention to the softer set of issues of managing people in the workplace and revitalizing their organizations. It is now recognized that the 'internal behavioural

context' determines whether employees can be motivated to do their best. Ispat's success in being the lowest-cost producer of steel in country after country depends on motivating its employees to drive costs down. The HDFC (Housing Development Finance Corporation) has tried to foster a more open, entrepreneurial orientation, where shared responsibilities and sense of ownership are married to customer orientation.

The more competitive, liberalized regime has therefore forced Indian companies to pay attention to business policy formulation and implementation.

ANINDYA SEN

REFERENCES

Barney, J. 1991. 'Firm Resources and Sustainable Competitive Advantage', *Journal of Management*, 17(1).

Drucker, P. 1973. *Management*, New York, Harper and Row. Paperback 1983.

Ghoshal, Sumantra, Gita Piramal, and Sudeep Budhiraja, eds. 2002. *World Class in India*, New Delhi, Penguin Books.

Hamel, G. and C.K. Prahalad. 1994. *Competing for the Future*, Boston, Harvard Business School Press.

Ohmae, Kenchini. 1982. *The Mind of the Strategist*, New York, McGraw-Hill.

Pascale, Richard and Anthony Athos. 1982. *The Art of Japanese Management*, New York, Penguin.

Porter, M. 1980. *Competitive Strategy*, New York, Free Press.

Schumacher, E.F. 1973. *Small is Beautiful: A Study of Economics as if People Mattered*, Harper Collins. Paperback 1989.

Corporate Governance

It is strange but true that the first significant initiative to foster better corporate governance in India came neither from the government, nor the securities market regulator, nor even shareholder activists, but from least-expected quarters—an industry association. In 1996, the Confederation of Indian Industry (CII) set up a task force of industrialists and CEOs under Rahul Bajaj of Bajaj Auto Limited to draft a voluntary code of corporate governance for listed companies. As a person who had worked on the subject, I was inducted into the task force to raise the key issues, challenge the members, and help draft the report.

Almost a decade later, I still cannot fathom the proximate reasons for the CII to set up the task force and then arrive at a progressive consensus that allowed the publication of a state-of-the-art report in April 1998 (CII 1998). After all, there was neither any economy-wide crisis as it occurred in Southeast and East Asia in 1997–8 which led to a complete rethink on capital markets, banking, corporate governance, and the market for corporate control; nor at that point of time were there any embarrassing corporate or stock market scandals which could have induced an industry association to be seen cleaning the Augean stables. Notwithstanding occasional references by the financial press about the need for good corporate governance, there were no immediate reasons for a body representing industrial interests to advocate a series of enlightened, far-reaching proposals which could not have been gladly welcomed by its wider membership.

But it did. The strength of the CII code was that its provisions were incorporated two years later almost in toto by the securities market regulator, the Securities and Exchange Board of India (SEBI), as legally binding requirements for listed companies. As of today, a listed company in India is mandated to follow a number of corporate governance practices, many of which are from the CII code, and happen to be on a par with—and sometimes exceed—the best global practices. Let me begin the substantive part of this entry by stating some of these criteria.[1]

BOARD OF DIRECTORS AND COMMITTEES OF THE BOARD

+ At least half of the Board of Directors of any listed company must consist of non-executive directors. Moreover, if the chairman is a non-executive director, at least a third of the Board should comprise independent directors; and if the chairman is also an executive of the company, then independent directors must account for at least half of the Board.
+ 'Independent directors' are a sub-set of non-executive directors, and must fulfil several criteria, such as:
  – apart from receiving director's remuneration, must not have any material pecuniary relationships or transactions with the company, its promoters, its directors, its senior management, or its holding company, its subsidiaries and associates which may affect independence of the director;
  – must not be related to promoters or senior management;
  – cannot have been an executive of the company in the immediately preceding three financial years;
  – not being a partner or an executive currently or during the preceding three years of the statutory audit firm or the internal audit firm of the company, or any legal and consulting

[1]The mandating has been carried out by SEBI through what is known as Clause 49 of the Listing Agreement, which was initially introduced in 2001, and then updated with effect from 31 December 2005. In between, there have been three major committees to look into different aspects of corporate governance: the Naresh Chandra Committee (2002), the Narayana Murthy Committee (2003), and the J.J. Irani Committee (2005).

firm(s) that have had a material association with the company.

- cannot be a significant material supplier, service provider, customer, lessor, or lessee of the company; and
- is not a substantial shareholder of the company, that is owning 2 per cent or more of the block of voting shares.

+ Boards must meet at least once every three months, or at least four times a year, with a gap of no more than four months between meetings.

+ The attendance record of each director must be stated in tabular format in the company's annual report to its shareholders. So too must the remuneration of each director, including stock options. India is one of the very few countries that have these requirements. Moreover, directorial remuneration in any form has to be approved by the voting shareholders of the company at its annual general meeting.

+ No director can sit on the Board of more than ten Board-level committees of listed companies (specifically the SEBI-mandated compulsory audit committees and shareholder grievance committees), or serve as chairman of more than five committees.[2]

+ All listed companies must have an audit committee consisting of only non-executive and independent directors, with the majority as well as the chairman being independent. This committee must meet at least four times in a year, with no more than four months elapsing between

two meetings. The chairman of the audit committee must be present at annual general meetings to answer shareholder queries. Among others, the tasks of the audit committee are:

- Overseeing of the company's financial reporting processes and disclosures to ensure that the financial statement is correct and credible.
- Recommending to the Board, the appointment or replacement of the statutory auditor and fixing the audit fees, as well as the appointment, removal, and remuneration of the chief internal auditor.
- Approving payment to statutory auditors for any non-audit services.
- Reviewing with management the quarterly, half-yearly, and annual financial statements before submission to the Board.
- Reviewing with management the performance of both the statutory and the internal auditors as well as the adequacy of internal control systems.
- Discussing with internal and statutory auditors their annual audit plans, as well as any significant findings that have implications for control systems and financial reporting processes.
- Evaluating the instances and nature of related party transactions.

DISCLOSURES TO SHAREHOLDERS

+ In addition to disclosures regarding the Board of Directors, listed companies must, in the annual report, have a chapter on Management Discussion and Analysis, which is expected to deal with industry structure and developments, opportunities and threats, segment-wise performance, outlook, risks, internal control systems and their adequacy,

---

[2]This is doubtless too generous. Other than retired people, few can claim to have the time to serve on the Board of ten listed companies and carry out increasingly demanding fiduciary responsibilities. In the US, the median outside directorships for employees is around 2, and for retired people around 3.5.

financial and operational performance, and issues relating to human resources.

+ There must also be a corporate governance report which, among other things, must list the date, time, and venue of the company's annual general meeting, the financial calendar, date of book closure and of dividend payment if any, listing on which stock exchanges, market price data both in terms of monthly highs and lows as well as comparison of stock price with broad-based indices, distribution of shareholdings at the close of the financial year, the company's share transfer system and the extent of dematerialization of shares, and whether there are outstanding warrants or any convertible instruments, and what is their likely impact on equity.

+ Any listed company must frame its code of conduct for directors and employees, which must form a part of the annual report and be posted on the company's website.

+ Moreover, in a manner similar to the certification mandated in the US by the Securities and Exchange Commission (SEC) as a part of Section 404 of the Sarbanes-Oxley Act (popularly called SOX 404), the Chief Executive Officer (CEO) and Chief Financial Officer (CFO) of any listed Indian companies will be required from financial year 2005–6 to certify that:

  – they have reviewed financial statements for the year and to the best of their knowledge and belief these do not contain any materially untrue or misleading statement or omit any material fact and, hence, present a true and fair view of the company's affairs for the period under consideration;

  – there are, to the best of their knowledge and belief, no transactions entered into by the company during the year which are fraudulent, illegal, or violating the company's code of conduct;

  – they accept responsibility for establishing and maintaining internal controls, have evaluated the effectiveness of such systems, and have disclosed to the auditors and the audit committee, deficiencies in design or operations, if any, of which they are aware and the steps they have taken or propose to take to rectify these;

  – they have indicated to the auditors and the audit committee any significant change in internal controls during the year, significant changes in accounting policies which have also been disclosed in the notes to the financial statements, and any instance of significant fraud of which they have become aware, the involvement of the management or an employee in such an episode, and steps taken in this regard.

ACCOUNTING DISCLOSURES

In addition to the mandated requirements listed in the proceeding, the Institute of Chartered Accountants of India (ICAI) has set more stringent accounting disclosure standards over the last four years. These have, in large measure, brought the financial statements of Indian companies prepared according to Indian GAAP (generally accepted accounting principles) in line with best-in-class global accounting treatment. A few reforms need to be stated.

+ Over and above the balance sheet and profit and loss account with their schedules, listed Indian companies have to present a detailed cash flow statement.

+ Segment reporting is now mandatory.

Moreover, a company must disclose income, operating profits, as well as capital employed in each business segment for the year.[3]

+ Very detailed disclosures are mandated for related party transactions.
+ Consolidated balance sheets and profit and loss accounts are now mandatory. This gives shareholders an overall view of the reporting company as well as its subsidiaries.
+ Deferred taxes have now to be accounted for.[4]

WHY THESE CHANGES?

There can be little doubt that India's mandated corporate governance standards and disclosures rank among the best in the

---

[3]Incidentally, this is the most stringent segment reporting disclosure in the world because one cannot only calculate segment profitability per rupee of sale, but also return on capital employed. Many believe that in an increasingly globalized world, such a disclosure gives too much competitive information to non-Indian competitor companies, who do not have to give segment reports.

[4]This may be a bit abstruse for most economists and non-financial readers. But because it is a very important financial disclosure, let me explain it as simply as possible. In most countries, there are legally mandated differences in the treatment of depreciation between the accounts presented to the shareholders and those given to tax authorities for the purpose of calculating corporate income tax. Invariably, the latter get higher depreciation allowances (that is more tax breaks) than the former. India is no exception. Therefore, the profits presented to shareholders in the annual accounts are greater than those in the corporate income tax returns. From a purely disclosure point of view, the way of bridging the two over time is to account for deferred taxes. When this is done, a tax break under income tax laws (the difference between the two depreciation rates) will be treated as a deferred tax liability and provisioned for in the shareholders' balance sheet profit and loss account. It has no financial or cash flow implications; but it does help significantly in creating more transparent and better aligned accounts.

world. For almost every criterion, these are at least as good as the norms prescribed by the US and Australia; generally better than the UK; appreciably better than all the countries in continental Europe and Latin America; and, barring perhaps Singapore, significantly superior to any country in Asia. This is now recognized and acknowledged by corporate governance specialists throughout the world. This raises a question: Why has a nation with a per capita income of not much more than $700 created corporate governance standards that are superior to most OECD (Organisation for Economic Co-operation and Development) countries?

The answer has much to do with the enormous churning that has occurred in corporate India since the mid-1990s, and more so after 2000. Within a decade of the advent of economic reforms, India started witnessing a number of entrepreneurs who, unencumbered by the dirigiste protectionist baggage of their predecessors, wanted to prove their worth in a more competitive economy. They were the likes of Ratan Tata who wanted to create a more focused, cohesive conglomerate out of a loose confederation of independent satrapies; of Narayana Murthy of Infosys, Azim Premji of Wipro, Ramalinga Raju of Satyam, F.C. Kohli and S. Ramadorai of TCS (Tata Consultancy Services) who wanted to build internationally respected IT powerhouses; Parminder Singh and Davinder Brar of Ranbaxy and K. Anji Reddy of Dr Reddy's Laboratories; K.V. Kamath and his team at ICICI Bank, Deepak Parekh of HDFC, Sunil Mittal of Bharti, Baba Kalyani of Bharat Forge, Hari Bhartia of Jubilant, Kiran Mazumdar Shaw of Biocon, to name a few.

Facts bear this out over the last eight years. Consider the losers. The top 50 companies in terms of market capitalization in January 1997 dropped their average ranking by 30 notches in January 2005. Thus a company ranked

25th in 1997 fell to being 55th in 2005. For the top 100 companies, the average drop in rank was even more precipitous—a fall of 54 points. And for the top 200, it has been worse still—an average drop of 90 points. Here are some examples. Remember a blue chip called Bombay Dyeing? It was already heading south in 1997 and was ranked 95th; by January 2005, it had fallen by another 115 places. Or Century Enka, which fell in rank by 168 places. Or Escorts, which plummeted from being 84th in 1997 to 284th in 2005.

The power of this churning was not only in throwing out losers but in spewing winners with even greater force. Infosys was ranked 82nd in 1997; it rose to being in the top 5 in 2005. Wipro's rank went up from 92nd to 7th. Hero Honda raised its ranking from 85th to 30th; Ranbaxy from 28th to 14th; HDFC Bank from 62nd to 20th; and Bharat Forge from 114th to 70th. Bharti—ranked 8th today—wasn't even listed; as was the case with TCS (ranked 4th), ICICI Bank (ranked 12th), Maruti (ranked 23rd), or Biocon (ranked 58th).

What has this churning done to Indian business? At the bottom of the pack are companies that have become history. But the more exciting news is that corporations have re-engineered themselves to deal with a more competitive world. In the process, most of them have realized that fostering good corporate governance, having a strong board, and making the right kind of disclosures create powerful signals and are valuable tools for accessing international capital and best-in-class human resources and ultimately in increasing competitiveness.

Indeed, I would argue that the strong corporate governance signal has delivered results in terms of an unprecedented inflow of foreign portfolio investment in Indian equity. Between June 2003 and November 2005, cumulative investment in Indian equity has risen from $16 billion to $46

billion—a growth of $30 billion at the average rate of $1 billion per month. The market capitalization of the most actively traded 201 companies that are listed as Group A on the Bombay Stock Exchange was $369 billion on 1 November 2005, or 47 per cent of India's GDP and 79 per cent of total market cap. Foreign portfolio investors accounted for 16 per cent of the shareholding of these 201 companies; and for thirty-six of these, accounting for over a fifth of India's total market cap, foreign portfolio holding averaged 31 per cent—ranging from a high of 64 per cent to a low of 20 per cent.[5] Simply put, foreign portfolio managers are very comfortable in investing in Indian risk capital. And, I dare say, quite a bit of that comfort comes from India's good corporate governance practices and financial disclosures.

In fact, there is a massive disjunction between relatively high levels of foreign portfolio investor interest in India and absolutely low levels of foreign direct investment. My hypothesis is that it has much to do with substantial differences in governance. India regularly gets foreign portfolio investments because of high standards of corporate governance coupled with consistent corporate performance and shareholder value creation. In contrast, it gets barely $5 billion per year as foreign direct investment (compared to $55 billion for China) because of poor public governance.

THE DIFFICULTIES

For all its progress, it is necessary to highlight three major difficulties in corporate governance. The first has to do with the quality of supply. Strange as it

[5]The data are from *Prowess*, the electronic database of the Centre for Monitoring the Indian Economy (CMIE).

may seem for a country of over 1.1 billion people, corporate India is not being able to find enough independent directors who have the requisite qualifications, experience, and time to discharge increasingly more demanding fiduciary responsibilities, especially those required for audit committees. Even if one were to forget about the 10,000 plus listed companies and, instead, focus on the top 350 that account for over 95 per cent of India's market capitalization, and further assume an average board size of nine, there is still a need for 2500 independent directors, two-thirds of whom have to serve on audit committees. This is where there are severe quality supply bottlenecks. For one, the number of people who have both financial acumen and the time to serve on audit committees is limited. For another, with significantly greater fiduciary responsibilities and liabilities, a median compensation of Rs 72,500 per annum for independent directors of the top 350 companies is not good enough to attract the competent, leave aside the best.[6] Why most Indian corporates are not revising their compensation structure for independent directors is a different story altogether. Perhaps it says something about what many actually feel about the value of competent directors and real need for good corporate governance.

The second issue has to do with form versus substance.

[6]At over Rs 600,000 per annum, the compensation for independent directors by the top quartile of the 350-odd companies belonging to Groups A and B1 of the Bombay Stock exchange is quite adequate. Thereafter it drops very sharply:
Rs 140,000 per year for the second quartile;
Rs 42,000 for the third quartile; and a mere Rs 12,000 for the fourth. Data for 2319 non-executive directors for 2004–5 from the electronic database, *Capital Online*.

With such a vast array of mandated norms, there is real fear of a laundry list form of corporate governance, where the Company Secretary ticks a large checklist and where form overwhelmingly dominates substance. Not surprisingly, a thriving market is now developing for so-called corporate governance 'consultants', who are hired by companies at the end of each financial year to ensure that the annual reports follow the letter, not the spirit, of Clause 49. Given this high degree of mandating, the law does nothing to separate the wheat from the chaff. Today, as before, a serious analyst has to go beyond the legislated disclosures to get the real picture of actual corporate governance.

The third problem is that of enforcement. Neither SEBI nor the Stock Exchanges are equipped to carefully monitor the implementation of corporate governance and, therefore, cannot expeditiously enforce penalties for serious breaches. In fact, the extreme penalty is the threat of de-listing, which is hardly credible because if that were to happen, it would only hurt the minority shareholders—precisely the investors in risk capital whom good corporate governance seeks to protect.

Having said so, there is no doubt that India has made huge strides in corporate governance between 1998 and today. And more is bound to happen over the next few years. Credit for this goes not only to organizations like the CII and SEBI, some economists and policymakers, and a band of farsighted corporate chieftains, but also to a free and powerful financial press that has championed this cause. The progress makes one wonder when such reforms will spill over to the realm of public governance. Hopefully sooner, rather than later.

OMKAR GOSWAMI

REFERENCES

Capital Online, Database of Listed Companies.

Centre for Monitoring the Indian Economy (CMIE), Prowess.

Confederation of Indian Industry (CII). 1998. 'Desirable Corporate Governance: A Code', April.

Goswami, Omkar. 2003. 'The Tide Rises, Gradually: Corporate Governance in India', in Charles Oman, ed., *Corporate Governance in Development: The Experiences of Brazil, Chile, India and South Africa*, Paris, OECD Development Centre: 105–60.

Government of India, Department of Company Affairs. 2002. *Report of the Committee on Corporate Audit and Governance* (chair: Naresh Chandra).

———. 2005. *Report of the Expert Committee on Company Law* (chair: J.J. Irani).

SEBI. 2000 and 2005. Clause 49 of the Listing Agreement.

———. 2003. *Report of the SEBI Committee on Corporate Governance* (chair: N.R. Narayana Murthy).

Industrial Policy

Industry accounts for about 27 per cent of GDP in the Indian economy. This is significantly smaller than the average share of 35 per cent for developing countries as a whole. The share of manufacturing in India's industrial value added is 80 per cent. Textiles, chemicals including pharmaceuticals, and basic metals including steel are some of the major sectors in manufacturing. Software, pharmaceuticals, biotechnology, and auto components have emerged as the dynamic sectors in the post-1991 period. The electricity sector has been an area of major policy attention but reforms have been slow.

Indian industry experienced slow growth and poor productivity performance during the period from 1950 to 1980. The policy regime had strong preference for the public sector, extensive controls over private investment, a highly protective trade policy, and inflexible labour laws (especially after the mid-1970s). Promotion of the small-scale sector and regional balance were additional objectives of the industrial policy regime. Up to the mid-1960s, policy instruments were aimed at purposive diversification within the industrial sector and increased public investment. The period after the mid-1960s witnessed a marked deepening of the import-substitution regime and strengthening of domestic regulatory structures. This period witnessed a significant deceleration in growth to 4 per cent per annum compared to 6.1 per cent in the period from 1950 to 1965.

The decade of the 1980s witnessed some experimentation with domestic deregulation that yielded handsome dividends in productivity gains and acceleration in growth to 7 per cent per annum. In 1991, in response to a major balance-of-payments crisis, India made a radical shift away from its long-standing policy of inward orientation, and the subsequent reforms have moved the policy regime significantly towards market orientation, deregulation, and liberalization. Indian industry has responded to the increased competition—domestic as well as foreign—with significant restructuring, although the constraints arising from poor infrastructure, largely unreformed public sector, slowly reforming banking sector, inflexible labour laws, and other barriers to exit stand in the way of faster adjustment to the new and emerging policy regime which is inspired by market orientation.

THE PRE-REFORM REGIME

The pre-reform industrial policy regime relied heavily on the development of a public sector to cater to the infrastructure needs of development and to provide direction to the process of industrial development within a mixed economy framework. Besides 'reserving' certain strategic areas of industrial production, for example, iron and steel, coal, transport, power, mineral oils, atomic energy, arms and ammunition, and allied items of defence equipment, in the public sector, the state also acted as the leading entrepreneur in machine tools, non-ferrous metals, fertilizers, etc. Nevertheless, the private sector was expected to play a major role, especially in the provision of consumer goods and building up the small-scale sector.

Industrial licensing was a major instrument of control of the private sector under which central government permission was needed for both investment in new units and for substantial expansion of capacity in existing units. Licensing also controlled technology, output mix, capacity location, and import content. Large industrial houses needed separate permission for investment or expansion under the Monopolies and Restrictive Trade Practices (MRTP) Act so as to prevent the concentration of economic power. There were price and distribution controls in industries such as fertilizers, cement, aluminium, petroleum, and pharmaceuticals. Almost 800 items were reserved for production by small-scale units as a way of protecting the small-scale sector from competition from large-scale units. There were also barriers to industrial restructuring and exit of firms.

India's import tariffs were among the highest in the world, with duty rates above 200 per cent being fairly common and tariff rates being highly dispersed. Imports of manufactured consumer goods were completely banned. For the rest, only some goods were freely importable, and for most items where domestic substitutes were being produced, imports were only possible with import licences. The criteria for issuing these licences were non-transparent, delays were endemic, and corruption unavoidable. Policies towards foreign investment were quite restrictive, reflecting the general protectionist thrust of industrial policy.

The period from 1950 to 1980 experienced stagnant industrial growth at the rate of 5.5 per cent per annum. However, significant diversification of the industrial structure was achieved. But total factor productivity (a measure of the efficiency with which labour and capital are used in generating value added in the manufacturing sector) is estimated to have stagnated/declined during the period from 1960 to 1980. The high-cost industrial structure resulting from the heavily protectionist policy regime created an anti-export bias in the industrial sector. The erosion of competitiveness could be seen in the secular decline of India's share in global exports of manufactured goods from 1 per cent in 1950 to 0.4 per cent in 1980.

BEGINNING OF REFORMS IN THE 1980s

A central focus of the reforms was the improvement of industrial productivity. Some important features included selective removal of industrial licensing, import liberalization for exports, partial liberalization of trade policies and procedures, and changes in the foreign direct investment (FDI) regime for capital goods. However, the reservation of production for the small-scale sector continued even while it constituted an important hurdle in the way of developing export capability in labour-intensive sectors such as garments, leather products, and sports goods, where India has comparative advantage. Industrial policy in the 1980s also paid little attention to facilitating the restructuring of the industrial sector by removing the numerous barriers to exit.

Trade policies during the 1980s were consciously designed to improve efficiency and promote exports. The driving force for the reform was easier access to imported intermediate inputs to facilitate capacity utilization and modern capital goods for technological upgradation. Export subsidies were provided in order to offset the anti-export bias resulting from the protectionist regime.

The limited domestic deregulation and trade policy reforms were successful in creating conditions in which productivity in the Indian manufacturing sector grew at 2.7 per cent per annum in the 1980s compared to a growth rate of −0.5 per cent per annum in the earlier two decades. The industrial growth rate also accelerated to over 7 per cent per annum in the 1980s. Exports of manufactured goods grew at about 11 per cent per annum during the decade. A 45 per cent depreciation in the real effective exchange rate in the second half of the 1980s was one of the factors responsible for a significant acceleration in the growth of these exports from 4.5 per cent per annum in the first half of the 1980s to 21.7 per cent per annum in the second half.

The sustainability of the better growth and productivity performance of the industrial sector, however, was being put to test by a deteriorating macroeconomic environment, largely on account of the growing fiscal profligacy of the Government of India during the 1980s. The Gulf War of 1990 and the political instability at the turn of the decade further contributed towards a collapse of international confidence in the Indian economy. The result was the balance-of-payments crisis of 1991.

ECONOMIC REFORMS SINCE 1991
The response to the balance-of-payments crisis was to not only put in place policies for macroeconomic stabilization but seize the opportunity to launch wide-ranging economic reforms to realize the potential of the Indian economy for higher growth. Beginning in 1991 the policymakers

attempted to take significant steps towards integrating the economy with the world and improving the macroeconomic environment from the deterioration of the 1980s. The transformation in the policy regime away from extensive control and a strong inward orientation in the decade and a half since 1991 has been attained through incremental/gradualist changes, occasional reversals, and without any big ideological U-turns. Coalitions of various political parties at the centre and different political parties ruling the states have taken turns in moving the economic reform process forward, albeit in a haphazard manner.

The period from 1991–2 to 1996–7 saw rapid and wide-ranging reforms in industrial and trade policies, tax policies, and other policies impacting on macroeconomic management. There was a distinct slowing down of reforms after 1996–7 partly because of complacency at the favourable response to the early reforms, partly because of confusion resulting from change of government at the centre, and also because by the mid-1990s, the competition had begun to pinch and Indian industry was becoming less supportive of change including external liberalization. In 2001 India regained the momentum of change towards improving the environment for private investment, opening the economy to foreign competition, and infrastructure development. However, macroeconomic management (after an excellent start when the consolidated fiscal deficit of the centre and the states was brought down from 9.6 per cent of GDP in 1990–1 to 7 per cent in 1992–3) has been an area of weakness that could undermine the achievement of sustainable growth at high rates in the future.

The industrial policy reforms during the 1990s were bold in doing away with numerous barriers to entry, for example removal of industrial licensing for investment, opening up all but a few strategic areas to other than the public sector, and, more recently, replacing the earlier MRTP Act with a new Competition Law to regulate anti-competitive behaviour. Even on the policy of reservation for the small-scale sector, a beginning was made by dereserving a number of items, although the task remains essentially unfinished. Also, the microeconomic reforms and judicial reforms which would make the factor markets more flexible and enable individual firms to benefit from the more competitive environment were slow to come.

Trade policy reforms made a radical break with the past by discontinuing with the complex system of import licensing and making an open commitment to lowering the tariff rates on imports. At the outset, import licensing was dispensed with for most goods other than consumer goods, thereby removing a major source of corruption and inefficiency. In 2001 India finally began to remove the quantitative restrictions on consumer goods and agricultural products over a three-year period.

Import duties were reduced gradually if not always steadily. After a sharp decline from an average of 73 per cent in 1991–2 to around 25 per cent in 1996–7, the import-weighted import duty crept up again to 36 per cent in 2000–1 reflecting a revival of protectionist pressure from established Indian industry. Subsequently there was a reversal of this trend and the government reiterated the objective of reducing India's tariff protection rates to Association of East Asian Nations (ASEAN) levels. However, even at 18 per cent in 2005, import duty rates in India are still the highest among the developing countries.

In the 1990s the FDI rules were liberalized with a view to gaining improved access to technology and world markets and also helping release the resource constraints on investment. Many industries

were deregulated and opened to FDI. For others, the Foreign Investment Promotion Board was set up to expedite applications for foreign investment. As of December 2005, the FDI policy allows 100 per cent foreign ownership in a large number of industries and majority ownership in all except banks, insurance companies, airlines, and certain types of mining. In addition, the Indian stock market has been opened for investment in equity to foreign institutional investors (FIIs). These policy changes have led to a sharp increase in FDI flows from almost nothing in 1990 to over $5–6 billion, but the levels are still much below those in China.

A major challenge of the reforms was how to attract private investment into sectors such as electricity, telecommunications, roads, railways, ports, and airports, in order to meet the enormous investment requirements of upgrading infrastructure. These sectors were opened up to private investment at different times in the subsequent years with varying degrees of success.

Telecommunications is the area where reforms have been most successful, helped by the fact that pricing of telecom services (unlike that of power) was not uneconomic. Access to telecom services has expanded greatly, costs have come down, and quality improved as a handful of strong private-sector telecom service suppliers are competing effectively with the public-sector companies. Private investment has also been attracted in ports and more recently in airports. In roads, new investment has been dominantly in the public sector, as is the case in most countries, but there has been some limited private-sector involvement which could increase in future.

The biggest disappointment has been in the power sector, mainly because both the reform of the incumbent public sector and the setting up of an effective regulatory framework have been slow to come. The expectations of attracting large investments in generation capacity were belied by the continuing financial problems of the distribution segment which remains unviable because of a combination of unrealistically low tariffs for some sections of consumers (households and farmers) and very large inefficiencies in collection. In recent years, attempts have been made to depoliticize the process of fixing power tariffs. The Electricity Act of 2003 lays out a broad legal framework of regulation for the sector and effectively empowers state governments to accelerate power-sector reforms through fostering greater competition, increased involvement of the private sector, and better governance. But many details remain to be put in place.

Profit-making public-sector units (PSUs) were allowed greater autonomy and larger freedom to raise resources in the capital market, but the relatively less well-performing PSUs languished for want of public funds and political will to restructure, privatize, or close down. A Disinvestment Commission was set up in 1997, but privatization was not seriously put on the policy agenda until 2001. A few public-sector enterprises were privatized with the transfer of management control during 2001–3, the most important being BALCO (Bharat Aluminium Company Ltd), which was sold to a 'strategic' private investor. But resistance surfaced strongly when privatization of two oil companies was attempted. Further brakes were put on privatization by the new government which came to power in 2004. The current policy is that profit-making public-sector enterprises will not be privatized although sale of government equity can continue as long as the government retains 51 per cent.

The increased market orientation of the policy regime generated a favourable investment response from the private sector up to 1996–7. Indeed, the rate of private fixed investment increased from a low of 12.9 per cent in 1991–2 to 15.9 per cent in 1996–7. Following a two-year period of decline, private fixed investments resumed an upward trend, reaching 19.1 per cent in 2004–5.

The slowdown in reforms after 1996–7, together with a worsening of the external economic environment after the Asian financial crisis, resulted in slowing down of industrial growth rate. From 12.3 per cent in 1995–6, industrial growth rate dropped to 7.7 per cent in 1996–7 and 3.8 per cent in each of the successive two years. The subsequent period has shown industrial revival with the growth rate accelerating to 6.8 per cent, 7.9 per cent, and 8.9 per cent in the latest three years for which data are available, that is, 2002–3, 2003–4, and 2004–5 respectively. Moreover, the software boom has continued and created a new brand image for India in world markets.

There is substantial evidence to suggest that Indian industry has been restructuring and reducing costs in a slow but steady manner since the mid-1990s. The pace of adjustment and adaptation has been slow in some of the important traditional industries, for example textiles and garments which are facing new challenges of the competitive world market scenario after the end of the multi-fibre arrangement (MFA) in January 2005. On the other hand, pharmaceuticals and automotive components are examples of manufacturing industries that have successfully turned around and developed a global vision to penetrate world markets.

The Indian pharmaceutical industry currently has a global market share of 1 per cent, and the share of its exports in total output has increased from 32 per cent in 2000–1 to 35 per cent in 2004–5. While making inroads into the fast-growing generics market worldwide, the industry is also positioning itself under the new Intellectual Property Rights (IPR) regime through increased research and development (R&D) expenditures and strategic alliances to move up the value chain. With a more liberal foreign investment policy, multinational corporations and international generics companies have also been attracted to restructure their operations and increase their stakes in existing ventures in India and set up new ventures. The auto-components industry has also significantly improved its export orientation, having trebled its exports between 2001–2 and 2004–5 and increased its export share in output from 13 per cent to 16 per cent over the same period.

The post-reform era has also spurred the development of the biotechnology industry which is driven by new enterprise and new innovation. Skilled human resources, active government support, and increased investment—public as well as private—promises sustained growth of this industry with global orientation. India is emerging as the most favoured destination for collaborative R&D, bioinformatics, contract research and manufacturing, and clinical research as a result of growing compliance with internationally harmonized standards. Several states have taken steps to develop bio-clusters based on academic and entrepreneurial strengths.

Export performance of manufactured goods provides some indication of how Indian industry has fared in attaining global competitiveness. While data on India's penetration in world markets are not readily available, the trend growth of India's exports shows Indian industry on the move. Between 1991–2 and 2001–2 India improved its growth of manufactured goods exports to 11.8 per cent per annum from the 11.4 per cent per annum of the 1980s. This was significant as it came on the higher base of

the 1980s and was attained after allowing for adjustment to the balance-of-payments crisis of 1991. The subsequent two years for which data are available show even higher growth rates of manufactured goods exports, that is 22 per cent and 17 per cent respectively.

ISHER JUDGE AHLUWALIA

Intellectual Property Rights

The generation, valuation, protection, and valorization of intellectual property are becoming critically important issues all around the world. Why is this so? First, we have the phenomenon of increasing dominance of the new knowledge economy over the old 'brick and mortar' economy. Generation and protection of new knowledge assume importance in this context. Then there is the exponential growth of scientific knowledge. There is also the increasing demand for new forms of intellectual property (IP) protection as well as access to IP-related information. Additionally, we have also to address the emerging complexities linked to IP in traditional knowledge, community knowledge, and animate objects. All these pose a challenge in setting up the new twenty-first-century IP agenda, especially for a country like India.

While setting up the agenda for a balanced and progressive Intellectual Property Rights (IPR) regime in India, it needs to be realized that IP will no longer be seen as a distinct or self-contained domain, but rather as an important and effective policy instrument that would be relevant to a wide range of socio-economic, technological, and political concerns. The development of skills and competence to manage IPRs and leverage their influence will, therefore, need increasing focus in India.

Historically, the IP system has been divided into two main branches. One branch is concerned with industrial property. This deals with technological inventions providing new solutions to technical problems. These are registered as patents; utility models also known as 'petty patents' or 'utility innovations'; trademarks for goods and services; commercial names and designations; industrial designs; geographical indications or indications of source and appellations of origin; and layout designs of integrated circuits. The other branch deals with copyright and related rights that protect literary and artistic expression or works of culture, which, in the broadest sense, relate to creative expression of ideas. Copyright provides protection to literary, musical, artistic, photographic, and audiovisual works, computer programmes, software, multimedia creations, etc. The protection of confidential business information of commercial value, often called 'trade secrets', is also an important and distinctive form of IP. The protection of growers' rights in relation to new varieties of plants is another distinct form of IP.

The adoption of the Trade Related Aspects of Intellectual Property Systems (TRIPS) Agreement has meant certain obligations on all countries within which they have to circumscribe their laws. Every nation always needs a robust IP Act. It should be designed to facilitate innovation and growth as well as development. In particular, TRIPS has entailed significant changes for the protection of pharmaceutical products and processes. The Agreement not only made product patent protection binding on all member countries (Article 27.1); it also strengthened, inter alia, process patents (Articles 28 (b) and 34), narrowly defined the conditions for establishing exceptions to patent rights (Article 30),

and limited the possibility of applying special modalities of compulsory licences to pharmaceuticals (for example as provided for in Canada until 1993).

India has continuously evolved its IP laws. Several amendments to the Copyright Act, creation of a new Trademark Act, a new Designs Act, and amendments to the Patent Act show India's desire to change. New Acts have also been enacted covering semi-conductors and layout designs, which are of considerable importance to the electronics industry. Similarly, India's Plant Variety Protection Act and Farmers Rights Act will impact its agriculture and food industry. The Geographical Indications Act will protect the interests of groups in the different geographical areas of India.

Although IP covers diverse aspects, it is the aspect of patents that has attracted greatest attention. The first patents law in India was enacted in 1856. The Indian Patents and Designs Act was enacted in 1911. The need for a comprehensive law so as to ensure that patent rights are not worked to the detriment of the consumer or to the prejudice of trade or the industrial development of the country was felt as early as in 1948. After several attempts, the bill introduced in Parliament came on to the Statute Book as the Patent Act 1970.

India needed the 1970 Act, given its state of scientific, technological, and industrial development at the time. This Act did not allow product patents in the fields of drugs and pharmaceuticals, food, and agriculture. Only process patents were allowed. This allowed India to make use of its undoubted prowess in process chemistry and engineering. India would not have succeeded in having the drugs and pharmaceuticals industry that it has today without the Patent Act of 1970. In the 1950s, India was importing even formulations. Today, the Indian pharmaceutical industry is one of the most developed amongst the developing countries thanks to this Act.

During the 1995–2005 period, India has met its entire TRIPS obligations in various stages starting from providing mailbox applications in 1999 with retrospective effect from 1 January 1995, followed by a second amendment in the Patents Act, which was passed by the Parliament of India in 2002 and came into force on 20 May 2003. This amendment for the first time brought the Indian Patents Act more or less on a par with the developed countries by providing a twenty-year patent term and eighteen months publication and also safeguarding national interest by remodelling compulsory licence provisions and by introducing Bolar and Import Provisions. The third amendment in the Patents Act came into force from 1 January 2005, providing product patenting in pharmaceuticals, food, and chemicals, rationalizing and reducing timelines for processing of patent applications, and doing away with Exclusive Marketing Rights (EMR). The amended Act also provides pre-grant and post-grant oppositions and also safeguards generic producers from patent infringement suits by providing protection through EMR only from the date of grant.

There is concern about limiting the impact of the monopolies that will result from the enforcement of the new Act. Here, one must understand the way licences are issued. These are of three types— voluntary, automatic, and compulsory. A voluntary licence is the result of a negotiated arrangement between the patent holder and any other party interested in commercialization of the patent product. The patent holder gets a royalty payment and there is no state intervention. On the other hand, state intervention is needed in the case of automatic and compulsory

licensing, which can be used by the government in special circumstances. If AIDS poses the threat of a serious epidemic, then a compulsory licence can be issued for AIDS drugs, even if the drugs are under patent. Therefore such exigencies have been taken care of in India.

The greatest challenge is for the drugs and pharmaceuticals industry. This industry seems to be gearing up well to face this challenge. It is increasing its investment in research and development (R&D) severalfold. It is moving from 'imitative research' to 'innovative research' including research on the discovery of new molecules. Other knowledge-based industries in India, such as the information technology (IT) industry, biotechnology, and microelectronics, will also have to gear up to the new IPR regime. Indian IT industry will have to reduce the content of body shopping and move on to innovative IT products, which will need IP protection. The same is true of biotechnology. The Indian biotechnology industry now has a turnover of $1 billion, which is impressive. But there is no evidence of a spurt in creation of new IP barring a few exceptions. This needs to change.

Before Indians protect IP, we must generate IP that is worth protecting. Indian institutions, national laboratories, and industrial R&D laboratories, will have to gear up for this. Nurturing a strong innovation base through a balanced system of recognition and rewards is the need of the hour. India will have to invest liberally to enhance the skills and knowledge base of scientists through structured in-house and external professional training programmes, even abroad, on understanding, interpreting, and analysing the techno-legal and business information contained in IP documents and in drafting of IP documents.

Some organizations have achieved remarkable results by understanding and developing strategies to meet these challenges. The Council of Scientific and Industrial Research (CSIR) has been a pioneer. During 2002–4 the CSIR was granted 516 US patents, which is more than all the patents granted to it during its entire sixty years of existence! The precursor to the CSIR initiatives in the IP domain was the articulation of its Intellectual Property Management Policy in 1996.

Skills in filing, reading, and exploiting patents will be most crucial in the years to come. We must properly protect our inventions. We must fully understand the implications of the patents granted to our competitors. Many of the patents written by our professionals can be easily circumvented. Manpower planning for IPR protection needs priority. IPR must be made a compulsory subject matter in law courses in Indian universities. A number of patent-training institutes will have to be set up. Judicious management of patent information will require well-structured functioning of information-creating centres, information documenters and retrievers, information users, IPR specialists, and IT experts.

Monitoring national and international patents and other IP through access to online data bases to ensure effective protection and to ward off infringements and threats to India's IP portfolio will be crucial. Analysing and assessing techno-legal and business information and market intelligence to identify strategic alliances and exploit potential uncovered niche areas of opportunities itself will give rise to new knowledge-based business.

Further, in order to ensure that the courts deliver judgments that meet the ends of justice, there is need for further exposure for those in the judiciary to deal with the evolving new developments in the IP field. In our country the delay in the courts is a great cause of frustration for patentees and as such it would be desirable to have the members of the judiciary exposed to the decisions and the guiding principles that emerge from them.

Its rich traditional knowledge base, in particular its great strength in traditional medicine, is a special area of concern for India. Indeed, traditional medicine plays a crucial role in healthcare of serving the health needs of a vast majority of people in developing countries including India.

The grant of patents on non-original innovations (particularly those linked to traditional medicines), which are based on what is already a part of the traditional knowledge of the developing world, has been causing great concern in the developing world. It was the CSIR that challenged US patent No. 5,401,5041, which was granted for the wound-healing properties of turmeric. In a landmark judgment, the US Patent Office (USPTO) revoked this patent in 1997, after ascertaining that there was no novelty, the findings by the innovators having been known in India for centuries.

There was yet another case of revocation in May 2000. The patent granted to W.R. Grace Company and the US Department of Agriculture for *neem* (EPO Patent No. 436257) by the European Patent Office was quashed again on the grounds that its use was already known in India. India also filed a re-examination request for the patent on Basmati rice lines and grains (US Patent No. 5,663,484 granted by the USPTO), and the Ricetec Company of Texas decided to withdraw the specific claims challenged by India and also some additional claims.

There is a problem regarding the grant of such patents linked to the indigenous knowledge of the developing world that needs to be addressed jointly by the developing and developed worlds. To mitigate this problem, steps have been taken to create a Traditional Knowledge

Digital Library (TKDL) on traditional medicinal plants and systems. This has been done by the CSIR in partnership with the Department of Ayurveda, Yoga, Unani, Siddha, and Homoeopathy (AYUSH). The TKDL will also lead to a Traditional Knowledge Resource Classification (TKRC). Linking this to the internationally accepted International Patent Classification (IPC) System will mean bridging the gap between the knowledge contained in an old Sanskrit *shloka* and the computer screen of a patent examiner in Washington! This will eliminate the problem of wrongful grant of patents since the Indian rights to that knowledge will be known to the examiner.

Eventually the creation of the TKDL in India would serve the larger purpose of providing and enhancing its innovation capacity. It could integrate widely scattered and distributed references on the traditional knowledge systems of the developing world in a retrievable form. It could act as a bridge between the traditional and modern knowledge systems. Availability of this knowledge in a retrievable form in many languages will provide a major impetus to modern research in the developing world, as it can then itself get involved in innovative research to add further value to this traditional knowledge—an example being the development of an allopathic medicine based on a traditional plant-based medicine. Sustained efforts for the modernization of traditional knowledge systems in India will create higher awareness at national and international levels and will establish a scientific approach that will ensure higher acceptability of these systems by practitioners of modern systems and the public at large.

India expects to be a major global knowledge production centre by 2020. For this to happen, the Indian strategy will have to rest not only on the generation of new knowledge, but also its protection and valorization. Indian strategy has to evolve around bringing IP protection into the mainstream of its endeavours in education, science and technology, legal and judicial systems, trade and economics, etc. Several ongoing initiatives suggest that India is well on its way to achieving these objectives so that it can attain its rightful position in the emerging world dominated by knowledge economy.

R.A. MASHELKAR

Licensing

The evolution of industrial policy since Independence offers a fascinating window into India's long obsession with mixed economy methods, the philosophical and theoretical foundations of which are often traced back to Mahalanobis' two-sector model (which formed the basis of the Second Five Year Plan) that demonstrated the importance of preferentially channelling savings into the capital goods sector. As originally conceived, and articulated in the Industries (Development and Regulation) (IDR) Act of 1951 and later in the Industrial Policy Resolution of 1956, the role of the state in the industrial economy was to orchestrate this canalization of savings by itself undertaking production in the capital goods sector while exercising control over private investment so as to enable a 'balanced' industrial development, where

[1]The text of the IDR Act and the Industrial Policy Resolutions of 1948 and 1956 and subsequent amendments to the licensing policy may be found, for example, in Iyer (1982).

[2]A comprehensive list of industries de-licensed in different years may be found in various volumes of the *Handbook of Industrial Statistics* published by the Government of India.

'balance' was contemplated with respect to regional concentration as well as the relative rates of capacity creation in different sectors. In addition, controlling private investment flows was also considered crucial for keeping in check monopolistic tendencies and for protecting cottage industries and the small-scale sector. The policy of industrial licensing, whereby proposed investment projects were required to be vetted and approved by the state, arose naturally as a means of fulfilling these objectives.

In the immediate post-World War II period, this did not appear too burdensome a set of responsibilities for the planning authority to take upon itself—the apparent 'success', at the time, of the Soviet Union in shouldering an even more complex system of controls provided grounds for optimism.

Accordingly, the original scope of the licensing policy was fairly broad: industries were divided into two schedules (or lists), with industries in the first schedule being subject to licensing requirements. The first schedule was an expansive list, spanning industries from fertilizers to industrial machinery. Licenses were required for (a) opening new establishments, (b) expanding capacity, (c) changing the existing product mix, and (d) relocating to another region. Subsequent amendments to the policy designated certain industries as being reserved for the small-scale sector and, therefore, off-limits for large investment projects, while creating size-based exemptions for investment projects.

A Licensing Committee was set up to handle applications. Approval was subject to a consideration of whether projected demand warranted the additional installation of capacity as well as a feasibility assessment of the particular project, the former being based on Plan targets and the latter being a discretionary judgment on the part of the Licensing Committee. As a

preliminary stamp of approval for a project, the entrepreneur would be given a Letter of Intent (LOI), which he/she would then use to apply for separate licenses for importing raw materials and capital goods, for raising funds in the capital market, and so on. Once these auxiliary clearances had been obtained, the entrepreneur would be issued an industrial license. The actual enforcement of approved capacities was primarily achieved by means of limiting supplies of power, water, and raw materials, most of which were in the public sector.

An early and abiding emphasis was on conserving foreign exchange—projects that required importation of raw materials or capital goods were rationed, with the latter being further referred to the Capital Goods Committee (CGC), which would determine whether the capital goods in question could not have been purchased domestically.

The policy was also differentially restrictive with regard to foreign-owned firms (defined as firms in which foreigners held a majority equity share)—any project proposed by such a firm could be approved only if it did not crowd out a similar project proposed by a domestically-owned firm.

With the passage of time, administrative costs began to pile up and complaints from frustrated industrialists began to pour in. As a result, licensing policy went from being general to being extremely specific, embodying a veritable slew of provisions, exceptions, and exemptions, all of which were subjected to continual revision. At the end of the day, even the bureaucrats responsible for issuing licenses admitted to being perplexed about the procedures in effect at any point in time.

The first significant attempts to rationalize the system were in the 1970s, based on recommendations outlined in a report by Professor R.K. Hazari and the report of the Industrial Licensing Policy

Inquiry Committee (ILPIC). Both reports made the point that the licensing system was being gamed by the large corporate houses, who were obtaining licenses for capacity without actually installing it, thereby pre-empting their competitors. On the basis of an analysis of the Licensing Committee's (partial) records on applications and approvals, Professor Hazari came to the mildly-stated conclusion that 'one might, in a rash mood, hazard the statement that Birlas do not follow up about *one-half* of their licenses' (emphasis mine). The Hazari Report also pointed out that the size distribution of proposed projects was heavily skewed and, from the standpoint of administrative cost, it did not make sense to monitor the investments of a large proportion of applicants. Partly as a result, in 1973 the procedures were amended to make licensing mandatory for large industrial houses (defined under the Monopolies and Restrictive Trade Practices [MRTP] Act as being corporations with more than Rs 20 crore in assets), while increasing the size-based exemption limit for all other firms.

As Mohan and Aggarwal (1990) have noted, both the Hazari report as well as the ILPIC were extremely critical of the performance of the licensing system, but neither of them went so far as to challenge the basic ideological premises underlying it. On the contrary, their recommendations constituted little more than ad hoc adjustments to the policy with a view to fine-tuning it. In their view, it was not that the basic notion of the state replacing the market mechanism as a determiner of the merits of private investment projects was flawed, but that the feasibility of government oversight of private investment could not be guaranteed without a narrower focus on monitoring priority sectors and large-scale projects.

This policy inertia persisted well into the 1970s and the early 1980s, but by this time a long period of industrial deceleration (see Bosworth et al. 2007) was beginning to cast grave doubts on the ability of the state to steer the market. The 1980s witnessed a series of mini-reforms of policies ranging from foreign-exchange controls to industrial licensing. A large number of industries were freed from licensing requirements in 1985. This period is often hailed as marking a shift in ideology in favour of the market, although it was by no means as decisive as the massive liberalization of 1991. The New Industrial Policy of 1991 represented a clean break from the past—it practically abolished the system of industrial licensing (although it was retained in a handful of industries).

What is telling, though, is that neither of the two waves of reform was purely the result of an accumulation of a critical mass of opinion against the old ideology. The death of Indira Gandhi in 1984 and the unprecedented balance-of-payments crisis in 1991 unexpectedly brought to the helm progressive elements of the Congress party (Rajiv Gandhi in 1984 and Narasimha Rao and Manmohan Singh in 1991) who were able to seize the opportunity to effect a change in policy direction.

For scholars looking back in the hope of trying to assess the consequences of the 'License Raj' (as it came to be called in its day), the challenges are formidable. In the first place, it may not be particularly meaningful to consider a counter-factual world in which the License Raj did not exist, to the extent that the latter was only one of an interlocking set of policy controls, whose joint direction was determined by a unifying ideology. From a theoretical perspective, however, it is not difficult to imagine the kinds of distortions that industrial licensing in isolation might have created through its effects on product variety, competition, and efficiency. For instance, the regulation of entry and capacity expansion can easily have large effects on aggregate productivity, by protecting inefficient firms from competition and by limiting the expansion of efficient ones. Kochhar et al. (2006) observe that in 1981, the average manufacturing firm in India was more than ten times smaller than the average manufacturing firm in the US, although this may have been as much due to licensing regulations as to restrictive labour regulations that differentially affected larger firms. Of broader significance is the extent to which state intervention skewed the inter-sectoral allocation of investment, resulting in a manufacturing sector unusually (for a labour-rich country) concentrated in capital-intensive production (Kochhar et al. 2006).

Other consequences of the policy are worthy of mention: (a) The reservation of sectors for small industry is likely to have seriously undermined the export potential of some of these industries (see Gang and Pandey 2008); (b) foreign direct investment in India has also historically been pitifully low, due in no small part to the bureaucratic hurdles created by the licensing policy.

In conclusion, industrial licensing sounds anachronistic in this day and age, summoning up a vision of bureaucrats surrounded by files in dusty offices and money covertly changing hands, and it is truly fascinating that sixty years ago it was considered the instrument of choice for fulfilling the state's (well-intentioned) designs. That the policy, and to a greater extent, the overarching industrial programme that underpinned it, significantly shaped the current industrial landscape is indisputable. What the economy would have looked like today, and what its capabilities would have been had a different ideology prevailed at the time of Independence is, however, anyone's guess. But the one lesson that has emerged from India's forty-year-long experiment with state control is that it inevitably fosters rent seeking, whether in the form of bureaucrats

seeking bribes for issuing licenses, or in the form of industrialists trying to buy protection of one sort or another. This experience alone has arguably helped shape a strong consensus against eschewing the market mechanism in future policymaking.

A.V. CHARI

REFERENCES

Bosworth, B., S. Collins, and A. Virmani. 2007. 'Sources of Growth in the Indian Economy', NBER Working Paper 12901.

Gang, Ira N. and Mihir Pandey. 2008. 'Small-scale Industries', in Kaushik Basu, ed., *The Oxford Companion to Economics in India*, New Delhi, Oxford University Press.

Hazari, R. K. 1966. *Industrial Planning and Licensing Policy*, New Delhi, Government of India.

Mohan, R. and V. Aggarwal. 1990. 'Commands and Controls: Planning for Indian Industrial Development, 1951–1990', *Journal of Comparative Economics*, 14: 681–712.

Iyer, K.V. 1982. *Liberalization of Industrial Policy*, New Delhi, Indu Press.

Kochhar, K., U. Kumar, R. Rajan, A. Subramanian, and I. Tokatlidis. 2006. 'India's Pattern of Development: What Happened, What Follows', *Journal of Monetary Economics*, 53(5): 981–1019.

Patents

Patents are legal rights that are granted by national authorities in each country separately over new, inventive, and otherwise eligible products or processes. These rights give their owners the authority to prevent others from commercially exploiting their inventions without their permission within that country. Up to 2005 India granted only process patents for food, medicine, and chemical inventions while allowing product patents in all other sectors. In compliance with its World Trade Organization (WTO) obligations on intellectual property, India has made a paradigm shift, making available both product and process patents for all eligible inventions. The history of the evolution of this regime in independent India is replete with battles fought between representatives of foreign right holders and domestic interests. By 2005, this picture had changed somewhat with some in Indian industry and government advocating strong patent protection, while others, including international civil society groups, backing minimal changes necessary to implement international obligations.

PATENTS ACT 1970

The Patents Act 1970, which came into effect in April 1972, replaced the colonial Patents and Designs Act of 1911. The design of this law was the subject of at least three committees of inquiry over more than two decades since Independence, the most influential of which was the Ayyangar Committee set up in 1957 (Ayyangar 1959). The general philosophy underlying this long and complicated law was that patents should be used as industrial policy instruments to encourage industrialization and promote self-reliance. This was summed up in Section 82 (now 83) which stated inter alia that patents are granted to secure that inventions are worked in India on a commercial scale and that they are not granted merely to enable patent owners to enjoy a monopoly for the importation of the product.

One of the major changes introduced in 1970 was the virtual abolition of patents in the chemicals, food, and pharmaceuticals sectors through the use of four measures:

+ First, the 1970 law limited the grant of patents for chemicals, food, pharmaceuticals, and agricultural chemicals to process inventions only. This meant that inventors of products such as new human or veterinary medicines, vaccines, diagnostic products, agricultural chemicals, or food (as well

as their intermediate substances) could not obtain product patents in India, thus allowing anyone to manufacture and sell these products, using processes different from those patented, where necessary.

+ Second, while patents over methods or processes for the production of such products could be granted if they were eligible, the rights of the process patent owner were limited to excluding others from using the process within India and did not extend to prohibiting them from selling the product directly obtained through the use of the process. Thus anyone could import the end product from a jurisdiction where there was no such process or product patent and compete in the market with the patent owner or his authorized agent.

+ Third, the duration of the patent term was reduced from fourteen years from the date of filing of the patent application given to all other eligible inventions to seven years for food, pharmaceutical, or agricultural chemical process inventions. This was done despite the fact that it is in precisely these sectors that patents are important and where substances have to undergo long and expensive tests before obtaining marketing approvals from the national authorities. Thus, in reality, the term left for exclusive marketing of the product obtained from the patented process in India may have been negligible, if not negative.[1]

+ Fourth, in the unlikely event that third parties needed to use such patents during their short lifetime, they were automatically allowed to use these inventions through the licenses-of-right system applicable three years from the

[1] If the invention was a chemical process, the patent term allowed was fourteen years from the date of filing of the patent application.

grant of food, pharmaceutical, and agricultural chemical patents. They had only to pay a statutorily fixed royalty of a maximum of 4 per cent of the sales price. In addition, in keeping with the underlying philosophy, the law strengthened the general provisions for compulsory licensing and use of patents by government.

This regime is credited by some with the growth and international competitiveness of India's generic drug industry, with medicine prices consequently moving from one of the highest levels in the world to the lowest.

INTERNATIONAL OBLIGATIONS

Until 1995 India was not party to any international agreement on patents, although it was a member of the principal copyright treaties. As a founder member, India became bound by the agreement of the WTO on intellectual property known by its acronym TRIPS (Agreement on Trade-related Aspects of Intellectual Property Rights). TRIPS mandates, inter alia, the availability of process and product patents for eligible inventions in all fields of technology. Subsequently, in 1998, India joined two pre-existing treaties administered by the World Intellectual Property Organization (WIPO), the Paris Convention for the Protection of Industrial Property 1883 (as revised up to 1967), and the Patent Co-operation Treaty (PCT) 1970. Since the substantive provisions of the Paris Convention were already incorporated into the TRIPS Agreement, there were no additional changes in national legislation required on this account.

Joining the PCT, a subsidiary treaty of the Paris Convention that facilitates the work of patent filing internationally, made the task of filing of patents in India easier for foreigners and filing elsewhere easier for Indian residents.

The patent law of 1970 remained unchanged for more than twenty-five years until the process of implementing international obligations, notably the TRIPS Agreement, began—albeit with some delay—in 1999, was taken forward more substantially in 2002 and once again, more recently, in March 2005.[2] Given the very strong opposing interests trying to influence the content of the amendments, India availed itself of the grace period of ten years up to 2005 allowed under this Agreement to introduce product patents for sectors excluded earlier.

PATENTABLE SUBJECT MATTER

India introduced the extension of product patents to chemicals, pharmaceuticals, agricultural chemicals, and food, first through an executive ordinance in December 2004 and later, through a law that obtained the support of the left-wing parties, in March 2005. Earlier in 1999, having lost a WTO dispute, India introduced exclusive marketing rights (EMRs) that last five years—or less if a patent is granted or rejected in the interim—for patent applications covering pharmaceuticals and agricultural chemical product inventions filed from 1995 to 2004.

Confirming earlier patent office practice, chemical processes can be understood to include biochemical, biotechnological, and microbiological processes. However, any process for the medicinal, surgical, curative, prophylactic, diagnostic, therapeutic, or other treatment of humans, animals, and plants to render them free of disease or increase their economic value is excluded from patent grant.[3]

[2]See http://ipindia.nic.in/ipr/patent/patents.htm for the text of the amendments to the 1970 law and rules.

[3]This is a broader exclusion than that under the 1970 law. TRIPS allows diagnostic, therapeutic, and surgical methods for the treatment of humans and animals to be excluded.

Inventions that are plants and animals, in whole or any part, including seeds, varieties, species, and essentially biological process for the production or propagation of plants and animals, are excluded from patent grant.[4] Inventions that are micro-organisms are not excluded and, according to official explanations of the law, this term could cover plasmids, viruses, bacteria, fungi, and algae.[5] Through the provisions on exclusion of parts of animals or plants and discoveries of any living thing or non-living substance occurring in nature, it may be that India excludes patent grant with respect to genes and recombinant DNA, but this is not clear.

In addition, mathematical or business methods, algorithms or computer programmes per se are excluded. Although a move to clarify this was scuttled in 2005, the technical application of a computer programme to industry or its use in combination with hardware, if otherwise patentable, would not appear to be excluded.

CRITERIA FOR DETERMINING PATENT ELIGIBILITY

According to the TRIPS Agreement, an invention that meets three separate and cumulative criteria, not further defined, must be eligible to be granted a patent: it must be new, involve an inventive step (or be non-obvious), and be industrially applicable (or useful). These criteria were followed in the 1970 law, which defined an invention as essentially meaning any product or process that is new and useful and which allowed obviousness as a ground for opposition.

The amended law retains this and further specifies that a new invention is one that is not disclosed through publication or use in the country or elsewhere before the filing date.[6] The requirement of 'inventive step', the most important criterion in judging patent eligibility, was defined in 2002 as a feature that makes the invention not obvious to a person skilled in the art. This requirement was changed in 2005 and is now met where the invention is non-obvious to a skilled person as before and *either* represents a technical advance over existing knowledge *or* is economically significant.[7]

In theory, under the Indian law, EMRs, or product patents, cannot be granted for existing or known products that have been in the public domain before the filing or priority date of their application. The case of an EMR granted to a multinational company in 2003 raised a controversy about claims of 'evergreening' of pharmaceutical patents. This is a reference to attempts by patent owners to extend their effective period of exclusivity through obtaining new patents on formulations, dosage forms, or minor chemical variations of an earlier patented product. In 2005, exclusions from patent grant were extended to cover trivial inventions. The provision makes it clear, however, that any invention that enhances the known efficacy of the substance or results in a new product or employs at least one new reactant is patentable (provided it is otherwise eligible) and that only the 'mere' discovery of a new form or of any new

[4]Plant varieties are protectable in India through a different law, the Plant Variety Protection Act that was passed in 1999.

[5]However, at the time of passing the latest amendments in 2005, two issues (the definition and patentability of new chemical entities and micro-organisms) have been referred to a committee of experts by the government.

[6]The grounds for pre- and post-grant opposition, however, include publication in India or elsewhere but use or knowledge *only in India before the priority date*. Nonetheless, knowledge of the invention, oral or otherwise, within any local or indigenous community, whether located in India *or elsewhere*, is included.

[7]Some interpret this as a lowering of the standards of patentability. See Gopakumar and Amin (2005).

property or new use of a known substance or process is excluded. Some Indian pharmaceutical manufacturers who have just started down the R&D path may also find it easier to make minor improvement inventions that meet these criteria.

PRE- AND POST-GRANT OPPOSITION

The law now lays down that patent applications will not be examined unless this is requested by the applicant or other interested party. Only abstracts of applications, as submitted by the applicants, will be published eighteen months after their filing or earlier at the request of the applicant. The rights and privileges of the patent accrue to its owner from the date of publication, although infringement proceedings can only be instituted after grant. Pre-grant opposition is allowed to be filed by third parties, where applications have been examined, up to six months from the date of publication. In the absence of any opposition, and without any independent evaluation as allowed in the earlier law, the patent office must grant the patent without examination 'as expeditiously as possible' if the applicant has fulfilled all the procedural requirements of the law. The time given to an examiner to examine an application, where requested, is one to three months. If the patent gets granted before opposition proceedings are initiated, it can be opposed within one year after its grant, but there is no time limit prescribed for disposal of such proceedings.

RIGHTS OF A PATENT OWNER

As required by the WTO, the rights of the owner of a product patent exclude others from making, using, offering for sale, selling, or importing the product. The rights of process patent owners are extended from exclusive rights to use the process to rights over the product made through the process. The burden of proof of infringement of the

rights of the process patent owner is shifted to the defendant in certain circumstances.[8] India has taken advantage of TRIPS flexibilities to allow parallel imports,[9] use of the patent for obtaining regulatory approvals, and other limited exceptions.

PATENT TERM

The patent term for both product and process patents is now twenty years from the date of filing of the patent application and is applicable to both new and unexpired patents as of 2002. Renewal fees have been made progressively higher—albeit still low in dollar values—so that only economically significant patents are maintained up to the end of the patent term allowed.

COMPULSORY LICENCES AND USE BY GOVERNMENT

The licences-of-right system has been abolished as required but compulsory licences can be applied for and granted on a large number of grounds retained from the 1970 law three years from the grant of the patent, further extendable by one year on the grounds of non-working.[10] In emergency situations or public non-commercial use or use by government, such licences can be issued at any time even without first notifying the patent owner. There are no special expeditious procedures or prescribed time limits for the disposal of compulsory licence cases but six months has

[8]Both the optional circumstances available under TRIPS are included instead of choosing one or the other.

[9]In 2005 the definition of parallel imports was broadened from importation from any person 'duly authorized by the patentee' to 'duly authorized under the law'.

[10]This delay has been controversial as the Paris Convention limits this period of three years to compulsory licences granted on the grounds of non-working.

been accepted as the reasonable period that applicants have to first devote to attempting to obtain a voluntary licence from the patent owner on reasonable commercial terms. Three different standards of remuneration to be paid are applicable in case of general use of compulsory licences, emergency or public non-commercial use, and government use of patents. There is no prohibition of injunctions against use of the patent authorized by government, although this is provided for under the TRIPS Agreement. Compulsory licences can also be granted for export to countries without manufacturing capacity in the pharmaceutical sector, as permitted by the 2003 WTO decision.

In cases where there has been commercial exploitation of products covered by patent applications filed between 1995 and 2005, the patent owner is only entitled to get reasonable royalty provided that the manufacturer of the product has made significant investment and continues production up to the date of grant of the patent.[11]

The provision on the declaration of certain anti-competitive or restrictive conditions in contractual patent licences as null and void has been somewhat strengthened based on examples given in the TRIPS Agreement.[12]

REVOCATION

Revocation or invalidation of patents is provided for in cases where the patent is wrongfully obtained or where certain criteria or requirements are not fulfilled. One such requirement introduced in the law in 2002, both as a ground for opposition as well as

[11]It is not clear in how many cases this amendment made in 2005 will be applicable and whether or not this is compatible with WTO requirements.

[12]Some may argue that the TRIPS Agreement does not permit per se prohibitions and calls for a case-by-case analysis of the anti-competitive nature of these practices.

revocation, is the disclosure of the source or geographic origin of biological material used in the invention and a declaration that the invention is not anticipated by any traditional knowledge. The clause allowing the government to suo moto revoke a patent which is 'mischievous to the State or generally prejudicial to the public' has been retained, subject to judicial review. The patent can also be revoked two years after the first compulsory licence if it has failed to remedy the situation that warranted the grant and a decision has to be taken within a year of such application.

A new Appellate Board has been established to hear certain patent appeals, including those covering grant, opposition, compulsory licences, and revocation on the grounds of non-working or public interest.

India's revised patent law represents a compromise between opposing interests—those who wanted to retain the 1970 law with minimal changes and those who wanted to strengthen patent protection and procedures beyond what was required by international obligations. While the law now reiterates the philosophy of the 1970 law and retains several of its provisions, the procedural and substantive changes make it clear that India would like to go some distance in tilting the balance back in favour of the patent applicant in the hope of promoting research and development (R&D). Only time will tell what effect the new law will have on location of R&D in India or on India's ability to supply cheaper medicines to the world. What is clear is that by 2005 India had made a break with the past and had begun a new era in patent law and practice.

JAYASHREE WATAL

REFERENCES
Ayyangar, Justice N. Rajagopala. 1959. Report on the Revision of the Patents Law, September.

Gopakumar, K.M. and Tahir Amin. 2005.
'Patents (Amendment) Bill: A Critique',
Economic and Political Weekly, 9 April.
Available at www.epw.org.in.

Pharmaceutical Industry

The pharmaceutical industry is one of the
success stories of independent India. It has
developed at a phenomenal rate since the
1970s. India has become self-reliant in
drugs and has emerged as a major player in
the global pharmaceutical industry. It is a
source of low-cost quality drugs to the entire
world including developed countries such as
the USA.

The lessons that can be drawn from
the Indian experience are relevant for the
development of the pharmaceutical industry
in other developing countries. They also
have implications for the industrial policy
debate about the role of the government vis-
à-vis the market.

The patent system has played a very
important role in the pharmaceutical
industry. Globally the pharmaceutical
industry is dominated by a small number of
multinational companies (MNCs)—Pfizer,
GlaxoSmithKline, Merck, Johnson &
Johnson, for example. These MNCs develop
new drugs or in-licence those developed by
others and use the patent system to prevent
others from manufacturing and selling
them. They also use an elaborate marketing
infrastructure to promote the new drugs and
to maintain dominant market shares even
after the expiry of patents. The large number
of remaining pharmaceutical companies
are not only much smaller in size compared
to the MNCs, they primarily manufacture
products for which patents have expired, and
are known as generic companies.

But currently, the MNCs do not
dominate the pharmaceutical industry in
India. In fact India and Japan are the only
two countries in the world where Western
MNCs do not dominate the pharma
industry. Under the Patents and Designs
Act 1911, which was in force till 1972, India
effectively had a product patent regime
in pharmaceuticals. Under this regime,
while the MNCs prevented the indigenous
companies from producing the new drugs,
using the then existing patent law, they
themselves were more keen on processing
imported drugs rather than developing the
industry from the basics. As a result, on the
one hand, because of lack of competition,
drug prices in India were very high. On
the other hand, in the 1970s, India was
dependent on imports for many of the
essential drugs. The import dependence
constricted consumption in a country
deficient in foreign exchange and inhibited
the growth of the industry.

The 1911 Act was replaced by the
Patents Act 1970. This eliminated the
monopoly power of the MNCs by abolishing
product patent protection and providing only
process patent protection in pharmaceuticals.
The cost-efficient processes developed
by the Indian generic companies—Cipla,
Ranbaxy, Dr Reddy's Laboratories, and
others—could be used for manufacturing the
latest drugs, introducing them at a fraction
of international prices, and dislodging the
MNCs from their position of dominance in
the domestic market.

The Indian pharmaceutical industry shot
to international prominence when it started
supplying drugs at low prices for HIV/
AIDS. The price charged by the originator
company for a three-drug combination
(stavidine+lamivudine+nevirapine), which
dramatically reduced AIDS deaths in
developed countries, exceeded US$ 10,000
per patient per year till recently. Such pricing
made it almost impossible to treat all the
patients in developing countries. After Cipla

offered the three-drug combination at US$ 350 (per year), the international prices have crashed making the drugs more affordable and accessible.

It was not only the revision of the patents act, however, that contributed to the success of the indigenous pharmaceutical sector. It is important to note that many other countries, for example Ghana, Malawi, Pakistan, Uruguay, and Vietnam, did not provide product patent protection in pharmaceuticals. Despite that, the pharmaceutical industry remained underdeveloped in these countries because they basically lacked the entrepreneurial and technological skills to take advantage of the absence of product patent protection. India is different not only because of its long tradition of drug manufacturing. The entrepreneurial spirit of the indigenous private sector was actively supported through public investments in research and development (R&D) and manufacturing.

The number of laboratories set up by the Government of India under the Council of Scientific and Industrial Research (CSIR) helped the development of the technological skills necessary for the pharmaceutical industry. In fact, a distinctive feature of the pharmaceutical industry in India has been the close collaboration between government laboratories and the private sector.

The setting up of the two public-sector companies—Hindustan Antibiotics Ltd and Indian Drugs and Pharmaceuticals Ltd (IDPL)—was another important factor in the development of the industry. Though both the companies are now sick, they gave a tremendous boost to indigenous efforts in the private sector and contributed to its success. The city of Hyderabad, where the synthetic drug plant of the IDPL was located, has actually developed into the main bulk-drug-manufacturing centre in the country and founders of many bulk-drugs units originally worked for the IDPL.

Basic manufacturing by the MNCs too accelerated after the industrial policy restrictions imposed by the government in the 1970s that stipulated that unless they produced bulk drugs in specified ratios they would not be permitted to expand in formulations. But in the 1990s, as these restrictions were withdrawn, the MNCs started closing down or selling off the plants that they had set up.

Contrary to the common view, India's experience shows that the state can play a very positive role in the development of indigenous industry. It shows how a country can benefit by regulating the MNCs and supporting the indigenous sector. It exhibits how favourable state policy can help the indigenous sector realize its potential and be competitive vis-à-vis the MNCs.

While the state in India has been successful in realizing the industrial policy objective of developing a strong indigenous sector, it has basically failed in pursuing the health policy objective of ensuring accessibility of drugs to those who need but cannot afford them. For drugs to be accessible it is not enough that prices are lower than the patent-protected monopoly prices. If those who need them cannot afford even the lower prices, proper finances should be available to pay for the cost of the drugs. Purchase of drugs is financed by the consumers themselves, by the government, or through private or national insurance. Public-funded healthcare and/or subsidized insurance not only can counter the market power of the large firms and influence prices, it can also shift the financial burden from the poor who are unable to afford the cost themselves and hence can improve accessibility. But in India, the involvement of the government in healthcare is low and health insurance is underdeveloped.

It is true that the absence of product patent protection in India has not been associated with high accessibility of drugs. This does not mean that the presence or absence of such protection makes no difference. The absence of product patent protection and the presence of multiple producers and sellers provide opportunities that are not possible in a product patent regime. Even if public health and insurance facilities improve, it will be extremely difficult to ensure accessibility of drugs if the patent-protected prices are high.

Patents are mandatory in all fields including pharmaceutical products for a minimum period of twenty years under the Agreement on Trade Related Aspects of Intellectual Property Rights (TRIPS) of the World Trade Organization (WTO). In line with TRIPS, India has amended the Patents Act 1970 and again introduced a product patent regime in pharmaceuticals since 1 January 2005.

The product patent regime will result in a monopoly market structure and high prices as in the regime before the Patents Act 1970. After all the basic rationale of product patent protection is that it will prevent others from manufacturing the product and hence enable the patent holders to charge higher prices to recoup their R&D costs. This will adversely affect not only consumers in India but also in other countries that depend on low-cost supplies from India.

But the protection of the private rights of the patentees is not the sole concern of TRIPS. It also recognizes the underlying public policy objectives and the special needs of the developing countries to permit flexibilities in implementing its provisions. Compulsory licensing is the most important flexibility permitted under TRIPS. A compulsory licence (CL) is an authorization by a government to non-patentees to use the patent without or against the consent of the patentee but on payment of royalties to the latter. A properly administered CL

system is of vital importance in promoting competition and hence lowering prices while ensuring that patentees get compensation through royalties. In fact, CL is one of the ways in which TRIPS attempts to strike a balance between promoting access to existing drugs and promoting R&D in new drugs.

The Amended Patents Act has elaborate provisions on CL, but these have not been operationalized to have a simple and easy-to-administer CL system. The procedure is open-ended without any time limit imposed for the grant of CL. The entire process is excessively legalistic and provides patentees the opportunity to manipulate by litigation. The huge expenses involved in fighting the large pharmaceutical companies holding the patents may dissuade non-patentees from applying for licences in the first place.

The remarkable success of the Indian pharmaceutical industry has evoked the optimism that the growth in exports of patent-expired drugs will more than compensate for the decline in domestic opportunities as Indian companies are prevented from producing the new drugs developed abroad. But a steady and stable home market is of fundamental importance for success abroad. What is often not appreciated is that the remarkable export growth of the larger Indian companies in recent years has been accompanied by an equally remarkable domestic growth. It will be very difficult for Indian companies to sustain the export dynamism in the absence of a growing domestic market.

For the steady growth of the Indian generic companies, it is important to devise measures so that they can continue to manufacture and sell the new patented products in the domestic market. As mentioned earlier, this is possible within TRIPS by having a simple and easy-to-use

CL procedure. So far as new drugs are concerned, apart from CL, the option is for Indian companies to develop new drugs themselves or collaborate with the MNCs. Some Indian companies have started R&D for new drugs. But because they do not have all the skills and the funds, the model they have adopted is to develop new molecules and licence these out to the MNCs at early stages of clinical development. A number of Indian companies are very optimistic about the prospects of increasing marketing and manufacturing alliances with the MNCs in the new product patent regime. Outsourcing by the MNCs to Indian companies has started but the present size is still modest.

Both from the point of view of ensuring a competitive market structure and affordable prices and helping the growth of Indian generic companies, it is of fundamental importance to have a proper CL system, or better still to amend TRIPS and abolish mandatory product patent protection. But the MNCs are opposed to it. They consider exclusive patent rights as fundamental for earning profits for funding their R&D for new drugs. But it does not follow that patents are the best way to provide incentives for R&D. Arrow (1962), to whom much of modern economic theorizing on patents is attributed, did not consider patents the only possible incentive system. A number of alternatives have been mooted. If implemented, these can permit competition without adverse impact on innovation.

SUDIP CHAUDHURI

REFERENCES

Arrow, Kenneth J. 1962. 'Economic Welfare and the Allocation of Resources for Invention', in *The Rate and Direction of Inventive Activity: Economic and Social Factors*, Princeton, Princeton University Press.

Chaudhuri, Sudip. 2005. *The WTO and India's Pharmaceuticals Industry: Patent Protection TRIPS and Developing Countries*, New Delhi, Oxford University Press.

CIPR. 2002. *Integrating Intellectual Property Rights and Development Policy*, London, Commission on Intellectual Property Rights.

Correa, Carlos M. 2000. *Intellectual Property Rights, the WTO and Developing Countries: The TRIPS Agreement and Policy Options*, London, Zed Books and Penang, Third World Network.

Govindaraj, Ramesh and G. Chellaraj. 2002. *The Indian Pharmaceutical Sector: Issues and Options for Health Sector Reform*, Washington D.C., World Bank.

Power Sector and Regulation

It is common knowledge that the poor power situation in India is one of the principal impediments to economic growth and development. The statist strategy of public provisioning has failed: growth of coverage is dismal, quality of service is appalling, and operational inefficiencies are ubiquitous. What is to be done? Wherever commercial competition is feasible, the state should simply retreat, encourage private provisioning, and let the market allocate resources. However, for a variety of reasons, competition is unsustainable in many dimensions of the power systems and commercializing the functioning of state-owned providers is the feasible option, especially when private entry is limited. In dimensions where competition is unlikely to yield socially desirable outcomes, the state needs to regulate. A common rationale for the regulation of public utilities is that they are natural monopolies.[1] A natural

---

[1] However, some components (like generation) of the sector may in fact be highly competitive and should ideally be deregulated.

monopoly situation implies that given the cost structure of the firm a single firm can meet the entire demand for the output and no two firms can exist simultaneously and still be profitable. Thus it is unlikely that we can get competitive prices and allowing unfettered competition with pervasive natural monopoly characteristics may result in socially inefficient entry. Moreover, if the natural monopoly's product or service is also essential to the public, the government cannot rely on the operation of markets to prevent abuse of monopoly power.

Direct regulation by the state is not viable as it amounts to the fox guarding the chicken coop: it invites state actors (politicians and bureaucrats) to capriciously frame regulations to suit their ends, which are not necessarily congruent with the larger public interest and the commercial interests of the service providers. The fear of such draconian regulations will inevitably keep private players out since entry involves large sunk costs. So attracting the private sector requires the state to credibly pre-commit to not behaving in a capricious way once the private entry has been made. The creation of independent regulatory institutions is a way for the state to credibly tie its hands.

In this background I briefly analyse the performance of the Indian electricity regulators. In 1996, a conference of Chief Ministers approved the CMNAP (Common Minimum National Action for Power), which included the establishment of the Electricity Regulatory Commissions (ERCs) at central and state levels. Moreover, the reforming states were under considerable pressure from multilateral lending agencies to create ERCs; a state government that created ERC was in a better position to get large funding from them. The Government of India enacted the Electricity Regulatory Commissions Act 1998 (ERC Act 1998). The Act paved the way for the establishment

of the Central Electricity Regulatory Commission (CERC) at central level and State Electricity Regulatory Commissions (SERCs) at state level. Twenty-two states have already constituted SERCs. Prior to the enactment of the Act the regulatory function at central level was performed by the Central Electricity Authority (CEA) and the Government of India, and at state level by the State Electricity Boards (SEBs) and/or state government. There were some obvious drawbacks of the erstwhile regulatory framework. The foremost was the manner of setting tariffs, which lacked transparency at the very least. Though this anomaly has been corrected by the creation of these new regulatory institutions, the experience has been mixed.

Creation and sustenance of independent regulatory institutions requires a substantial degree of political and judicial maturity. Ultimately, the state actors have to forbear from routine interference in areas that they have hitherto considered to be a part of the state's (that is their own) eminent domain. The Indian political class has hitherto been unwilling to part with this fiefdom. Legitimate mandated regulatory functions are routinely compromised by the issuance of 'policy' directives.

Experience has shown that regulation is only one part of the reform story. Successful regulation requires complementary reforms, including the introduction of competition and encouragement of private participation. It is argued that regulation itself will discipline and improve the performance of state-run corporations, and entry of private entities is unnecessary. This view implicitly assumes that these corporations will respond to incentives in the same way as private firms. The regulator's ability to bring about desired outcomes depends on the regulated entity's sensitivity to financial incentives in the form of tariffs, transfers, penalties, etc. Historically, Indian state-owned entities have been motivated by myriad considerations, many of them of the non-commercial and non-financial kind. These considerations have been used as an alibi for poor commercial and financial performance by the managers of these entities and the political class that oversees and exploits these entities. Alibis of the 'social responsibility' variety are routinely seized upon by the political class to open the public purse to provide open-ended non-performance-related subsidies to these state-owned entities. Consequently, they face soft budget constraints and are unlikely to respond to regulatory incentives in the same way as private firms.

Moreover, there is insufficient institutional distance between the regulator and state-owned firms, especially when there is no firewall between the state actors and the regulator. Being two aspects of the same entity, namely the Indian state, it is not credible that the regulator is even-handed when private firms compete with state-owned firms. Regulatory capture by state-owned firms is a very real threat. The only way to have good regulatory outcomes when state-owned firms are involved is to make these firms very like private firms, thereby destroying their public-sector character: have similar employment policies and similar managerial and labour incentives, deny them budgetary hand-outs, and empower management to make commercially sensible decisions. Although such pronouncements are piously incanted every time public-sector reform is proposed, the political class is clearly loath to part with the milch cow fattened over decades. For India to benefit from the liberalization process, its government must convince the entrants that the regulatory environment will provide no special favour to the publicly owned incumbent. Till the government

solves this commitment[2] problem the future of independent regulation is bleak.

Experts recommend a variety of institutional arrangements to enhance the quality of regulatory governance: clarity of regulatory roles, objectives, and powers; a credible firewall between the regulator and state actors to guarantee the regulator's independence; participation in the regulatory process by interested parties such as consumers; and accountability of the regulator for his decisions. Yet, and here is the rub, the creation of institutions meeting these criteria and the implementation of complementary reforms is in the hands of the very political class that stands to lose the most from these changes. Slow and hesitant attempts to untangle the mess are under way in the face of pressure from consumers and other interested parties. However, rapid improvement in infrastructure regulation requires a statesman to rise above myopic political interests and cut the Gordian knot.

PAYAL MALIK

Special Economic Zones

Special Economic Zones or SEZs refer to areas within a country where some of the economic laws and restrictions of the land are relaxed with the purpose of giving incentives to investors. The usual relaxations are with respect to taxes, import and export duties, and labour laws. At present, an ever-increasing number of less developed

[2]These questions closely parallel questions that have long been considered in the macroeconomic policy literature as to whether governments that face elections every few years can commit to maintaining a low inflation policy, and if not, whether governments can effectively tie their own hands by installing an independent central bank charged with maintaining a pre-determined inflationary target.

countries all over the globe are finding the SEZs an integral part of their development programmes. Undoubtedly, the success of the Chinese SEZs in the 1980s has led other less developed countries to set up their own. According to World Bank estimates, as of 2007 there are more than 3000 projects taking place in the SEZs in 120 countries worldwide.

India is no exception to this general trend. In 2005, the Special Economic Zones Act was passed in the parliament with the purpose of establishing, developing, and managing SEZs in the country. By June 2006, there were eight functional SEZs in India located at Santa Cruz (Maharashtra), Cochin (Kerala), Kandla and Surat (Gujarat), Chennai (Tamil Nadu), Visakhapatnam (Andhra Pradesh), Falta (West Bengal), and Noida (Uttar Pradesh) and eighteen more were approved, waiting to become functional. By May 2007, the number of notified SEZs in the country after the passing of the SEZ Act of 2005 had reached one hundred. In addition to exemption from import and export duties, units in the SEZs get incentives in terms of benefits in income tax, service tax, and other obligations to the central and state governments. So it is not at all surprising that a large number of enterprises have queued up either to develop an SEZ or to enter an already established SEZ in India.

What are the advantages of having the SEZs? One major advantage is that an SEZ makes concentration of a number of similar production units within a small geographical area possible. This, in turn, has a number of well-known benefits. When similar firms are located together there is immense possibility of learning from one another, both directly and indirectly from the successes and failures of one's neighbours. This flow of knowledge improves technology, reduces costs of production, and makes each production unit

more competitive. Moreover, it is a lot easier to ensure uninterrupted supplies of inputs and a steady flow of demand for the final output if a firm is located in a zone specially designated for firms producing a particular type of product. Raw materials and other types of input-supplying firms know exactly where to go to sell their products. So is true for specialized labour. On the other hand, consumers and distributors of final products also find it convenient to find a number of production units located in one place ensuring variety, competition, and efficiency.

But while it is hard to deny the advantages of localization of any particular type of industry, the question remains as to whether the advantage deserves tax breaks and subsidies of such magnitude as are being offered in the SEZs. Indeed, industries have been observed to be naturally localized throughout recorded history without much incentive or enticement. The Manchesters, Sheffields, or Silicon Valleys of the world were formed not out of any conscious government endeavour, but simply because firms in those places found it worthwhile to stay together. In similar manner, one can argue that in India and elsewhere investments would have been forthcoming in any case if the investors found them profitable. Why then special incentives to form economic zones?

The objections against the SEZs do not end here though. In most cases, the firms that are getting the tax breaks and subsidies to form the SEZs are multinationals or large domestic players. One can certainly question the justification of giving economic incentives to these very rich enterprises at the cost of the common taxpayer. Indeed the tax structure implied by the SEZ Act looks regressive and unfair. One may perhaps argue in reply that these enterprises need to be initially subsidized to exploit potential gains from increasing returns. That would be reminiscent of the old infant industry argument. The trouble with this argument is that these big enterprises are not credit constrained. So if they can foresee potential gains from increasing investment, in order to exploit those gains they would go ahead with their investment even without any incentives offered to them.

Stricter proponents of free trade feel that the idea of the SEZs violates the very basic principles of a free market economy. According to them, India, which was imprisoned by the shackles of economic controls for a long period of time, was gradually emancipating itself from the chains through liberalization and globalization. It was a journey towards achieving efficiency. The SEZ Act is likely to reverse the process. To the liberals, building up the SEZs is equivalent to bringing back discretionary controls with all their evils and inefficiencies. The liberals apprehend that as industry houses will start competing with one another to get into the SEZs to appropriate the special benefits, the old licence raj with widespread lobbying and selective distribution of political favours might come back.

The more imminent problem, however, is related to the acquisition of land for the SEZs. Given that employment-wise, India is still a predominantly agricultural country, about two-thirds of the labour force being still dependent on the agricultural sector, and given that the land–man ratio is adverse in general, the available land is mostly cultivated. So a significant part of the land required for the SEZs must come from the agricultural sector. This has led some people to believe that indiscriminate land acquisition for the SEZs will jeopardize food security of the country.

A little reflection should, however, convince us that the fear about food security is ill founded. This is because of at least a couple of reasons. First, the land required for the development of the SEZs, though not small in absolute magnitude, is likely to be a negligible fraction of the total cultivable land in India. Acquisition of this land for building up industries and infrastructure is not going to affect the total food production in the country in any significant way.

Second, industrialization aided by the SEZs is likely to have a favourable effect on agricultural productivity. With industrialization, as more and more people shift to the industrial and the services sectors, pressure on agricultural land will fall and average landholding will increase as some of the emigrants going away from the rural sector will sell off their land to the people who would stay back. An increase in average landholding in the agricultural sector would, in turn, help consolidate fragmented pieces of landholding, which again would make possible the use of modern technology. Indeed, excessive fragmentation of land in India is one of the main constraints to the introduction of advanced methods of production. If land is consolidated, this constraint would be relaxed. It may be mentioned that in the advanced countries 2 to 4 per cent of the population is engaged in agriculture. But this small fraction of people is able to feed the entire country. This is made possible by the very high levels of productivity of labour in the agricultural sector, which again is the result of advanced technology. If a similar pattern can emerge in India, the increase in the productivity of labour in the agricultural sector can indeed compensate for the loss of production due to loss in acreage. That the level of productivity in the Indian agricultural sector is abysmally low is clearly borne out by the fact that about two-thirds of the labour force engaged in the agricultural sector is unable to contribute more than 21 per cent of the gross domestic product. Only large-scale exodus from the agricultural sector can increase this productivity.

The real problem of land acquisition is not macroeconomic but arises at the microeconomic level. When land is acquired for the SEZs, people lose their livelihoods. Moreover, those losing their livelihoods are among the least likely to get immediate jobs in the newly built SEZs simply because they would usually lack the education and training required for a job in the industrial sector. As a result, these displaced people would fight land acquisition tooth and nail unless they are properly compensated for their assets and livelihood.

Struggles over land acquisition, ranging from political rallies, demonstrations, and small riots right up to widespread conflicts leading to massive manslaughter, are taking place in West Bengal, Orissa, Uttar Pradesh, and other places. This simply indicates that compensations have been inadequate. State governments have so far proceeded to acquire land mainly on the basis of the Land Acquisition Act 1894. The Act empowers the government to acquire any land for a public purpose or for the purpose of use by a company by prior notification by paying a compensation to the owner. The problem is that there is no provision to compensate the other stakeholders of land including the landless labourers and share-croppers. In many cases, the owner of the land is an absentee landlord who is only too happy to sell off his land, the production of which he could not monitor and hence was being deprived of his just share. It is the other stakeholders who are the actual tillers and are truly losing their livelihoods. If land is to be smoothly acquired for the SEZs, these people are to be properly compensated. Some states, notably the state of Orissa, have come up with elaborate resettlement and rehabilitation packages for the displaced. But again these packages have

been so far limited to the owners of the land and have not been extended to the other stakeholders.

Is there any moral ground of compensating the labourers? After all one can argue that land acquisition does not rob the labourer of his labour power and so there is no need to compensate him. This is not true of the landowner who is certainly losing his asset, namely land, after the acquisition. But the point to note is that the agricultural labourer often has a very specific kind of expertise which has no use in other sectors. So with acquisition of land the value of this expertise is greatly reduced, which is equivalent to a fall in the value of his human capital. For this he needs to be compensated. Also, when a government factory closes down, the worker whose job is terminated is usually compensated through a retirement package. Why should the government not follow the same practice when it is acquiring land and making people jobless?

But then the question arises as to why governments are reluctant to pay compensation to all stakeholders, especially if it is generally understood that such an act would make land acquisition for the SEZs undeniably smoother. In my opinion, one should look for an answer in the recent competition between the state governments to attract investment. Indeed the SEZs have emerged as one of the primary avenues through which this competition is taking shape. To remain competitive, the states are trying to provide land for the SEZs at the lowest possible costs. On top of that various other subsidies and incentives are provided. In fact, so much money is spent to woo the investors that very little is left for compensation, rehabilitation, and resettlement. In fact, the competition is not confined to the Indian states alone. An intense competition is now developing between countries to woo multinationals.

This competition explains the emergence of a large number of SEZs all over the world.

The problem is one of adopting a long-run feasible policy for India. The so-called East Asian model of economic development, which has produced miracles in terms of growth, though not always in terms of human development, can hardly work in India even towards increasing the rate of growth. The East Asian model puts the entire policy emphasis on the investor, giving him all the incentives possible. In the process, humanitarian considerations are largely ignored, farmers are uprooted from their land and livelihood, and savage labour laws are implemented within the SEZs. But even though such coercive methods could work in authoritarian regimes like China, they are unlikely to work in India where, however faulty, we have a democracy.

This is amply clear from the growing discontent all over the country against the SEZs and land acquisition. If the discontent grows, the process of industrialization will be in jeopardy. Paying too much attention to investors and too little to workers and the displaced is morally wrong. But more important, as a long-run strategy it is untenable.

ABHIRUP SARKAR

REFERENCES

Krugman, Paul. 1995. *Development, Geography and Economic Theory*, Massachusetts, MIT press.

Land Acquisition Act, 1894. Government of India, Ministry of Law and Justice.

Orissa Resettlement and Rehabilitation Policy, 2006. Government of Orissa.

Sarkar, Abhirup. 2007. 'Development and Displacement: Land Acquisition in West Bengal', *Economic and Political Weekly*, 42(16), 21–7 April.

Special Economic Zones Act, 2005. Government of India, Ministry of Law and Justice.

Steel Industry

INDIAN STEEL INDUSTRY IN GLOBAL PERSPECTIVE

Steel is the largest metal industry and the second largest man-made material industry, after cement, in the world. Iron and steel provide the basic material needed for building the physical infrastructure of an economy as it grows into a mature developed one. Steel consumption has therefore been regarded as one of the basic indicators of an economy's state of development. The total world crude steel production increased from 28.3 million tonnes in 1900 to 696.4 million tonnes in 1973 and 964.8 million tonnes in 2003.

Since the end of the Cold War, the growth of the industry in the Asia Pacific region, with China emerging as a major player, has been a significant phenomenon. The share of the Asia Pacific region (excluding Japan) in global crude steel production increased from 28 per cent to 35 per cent during 1999–2003. China's crude steel output increased from 25.2 million tonnes in 1973 to 127.24 million tonnes in 2000 and a spectacular 220.11 million tonnes in 2003.

India, on the other hand, is now the ninth largest crude steel producer in the world and the fourth in the Asia Pacific region, after China, Japan, and South Korea. The production of crude steel and finished steel in India was 32.60 million tonnes and 36.91 million tonnes respectively in 2004. However, unfortunately, in spite of it being the ninth largest producer in the world in 2004, India is one of the poorest consumers of steel in terms of finished usable steel. In the absence of reliable data on stock changes every year, we take the apparent consumption of steel for measuring consumption and demand for steel, the

Table 1   Comparative Absorption of Steel by Major Asian Economies

	India	China	South Korea	Japan
GDP per capita in PPP $	2880	4990	17,930	28,620
Domestic savings rate (2003) in %	22	43	32	27
Gross domestic capital formation as % of GDP	24	42	29	26
Share of secondary sector (2003) in %	26	53	35	31
Finished steel consumption per capita (in kg)	28.9	178.1	574.9	955.4
Finished steel intensity of GDP in kg per PPP $ income	0.0098	0.036	0.053	0.02

Sources: SAIL. 2004. Statistics for Iron and Steel Industry in India, New Delhi, SAIL; World Bank. 2005. *World Development Report 2005*, Washington D.C., World Bank and New York, Oxford University Press.

apparent consumption being defined as domestic production plus imports minus exports = domestic sales plus imports. India's per capita apparent consumption of finished steel was as low as 28.8 kg while that of China, Japan, and South Korea was 178.1 kg, 574.9 kg, and 955.4 kg respectively in 2003.

The finished steel intensity of the gross domestic product (GDP) was also 0.0098 kg per PPP (purchasing power parity) $ of income, which is quite low in comparison with the other major steel-producing Asian economies (see Table 1). The steel intensity of GDP depends on the structural composition of the GDP since steel use in the material commodity or industrial sector is substantially higher than that in the services sector. The major use of steel in an economy is in the infrastructural construction of rail, roads and bridges, and buildings (residential and non-residential), in electricity supply and production of capital goods, and in production of automobiles and consumer durables. The growth of these sectors and spending on them would get reflected in changes in the share of the secondary sector in GDP and the rate of gross domestic capital formation (GFCF). A cross-country comparison of the stages of development, the GDP share of the secondary sector, the rate of GFCF, and the availability of domestic savings for financing such capital formation as given in Table 1, would explain

the relatively low rate of absorption of steel by the Indian economy in comparison with the other major Asian economies.

It may further be noted that the construction component of the GFCF has a higher steel usage than the other components. The relatively slow rate of growth of the GFCF, that is at 6.3 per cent, and particularly the construction component which was 4.2 per cent during the 1980s and 1990s explains to a large extent the erratic absorption of steel by the Indian economy (Sinha and Suri 2003). India's low steel intensity of GDP is not evidence of the efficiency of its steel use, but only indicates an inadequate pace of industrialization and infrastructure development which is supported by the growing share of the service sector in the GDP.

HISTORY AND GROWTH

From the pre-Independence period to the Third Plan, at the very start, it must be mentioned that unlike other developing countries, India's modern steel industry is quite old and dates back to 1907 when the Tata Iron and Steel Company (TISCO) was registered as an iron- and steel-making company. It represents the most important instance of entrepreneurship of Indian private capital in the twentieth century. It started producing pig iron in 1911 and ingot steel a year later and grew without any tariff protection. Besides TISCO, the

Indian Iron and Steel Company (IISCO) and the Mysore Iron and Steel Works came into existence in 1918 and 1921 respectively, to produce first pig iron and then steel. The Steel Corporation of Bengal was also floated in 1937 to produce steel using pig iron and service utilities from IISCO, the two companies being subsequently amalgamated in 1953.

The steel industry in India experienced its major growth after the Second Five Year Plan (1956–7 to 1961–2). Unlike the colonial period, the growth of the integrated steel plant sector during the period of planned development till 1991–2 took place mainly at the direction and initiative of the Indian state as per the Industrial Policy Resolution of 1956. This policy reserved the expansion of the integrated steel plant sector (that is the route of steel making via pig iron making, starting with iron ore as raw material in a single production establishment) in the public sector. TISCO and IISCO were, however, allowed to carry on their business as private steel-making companies.

In view of the inelasticity of India's traditional exports and the shortage of domestic savings and foreign exchange, the growth of the steel industry took place under a policy regime of industrialization by import substitution. This was characterized by heavy tariff protection, import control, and state control of both the domestic selling prices and the distribution of the products of the integrated steel plants.

In the Second Five Year Plan three steel plants of 1 million tonne capacity each in terms of crude steel were set up under the public-sector Hindustan Steel Limited (HSL) at Rourkela, Bhilai, and Durgapur, later expanded to capacities of 1.8 million tonnes, 2.5 million tonnes, and 1.6 million tonnes respectively. These plants were later merged into the Steel Authority of India (SAIL).

Second Phase of Planned Development of the Industry: Change in Government Policy and Deceleration of Growth

After the Third Plan (1962–3 to 1966–7) expansion programme, the growth of the steel industry decelerated because of financial resource constraint, long gestation lag due to indigenization of the plant and capital equipment of the projects, as well as some change in government policy regarding the priority of the steel sector in the central sector's plan investment allocation. The inefficiency of the public sector in absorbing foreign technology, low administered steel prices, and physical control of distribution resulted in a low rate of internal surplus generation in the steel industry in this period (Sengupta 2004). This period also saw a shift in the resource allocation policy of the government as a result of which the share of steel in public-sector plan outlay declined from 7.81 per cent in the Third Plan to 3.57 per cent in the Seventh Plan ending in 1996–7.

The constraint in the availability of finance due to low profits, inadequate plan resource allocation, and also non-availability of soft loans from other foreign sources left the Indian government with no choice but to depend on the Soviet Union alone for the new Bokaro Steel Plant (BSP) project of SAIL, the Bhilai Steel Plant's 4 million tonnes expansion project, and the Vishakhapatnam Steel Plant project of the Rashtriya Ispat Nigam Ltd. (RINL), which were the major integrated plant projects during the period 1967–8 to 1991–2. This phenomenon obviously constrained the country's range of choice of technologies.

This period of slowdown of expansion of steel capacity under state initiative in the integrated steel plant route, however, saw the emergence of a secondary sector in the industry which produced steel out of steel scrap in electric arc furnaces due to a demand–supply gap. Many entrepreneurs also reoriented their induction furnaces (IF) to steel making by just melting steel scrap without any refining. India is possibly the only country in the world today using IF units on a large scale for producing steel.

The Third Phase of Development: Economic Reforms, Market Orientation, and Technical Change

There has been a significant structural break in the development of the Indian steel industry since the announcement of a series of economic reforms by the Government of India in 1991–2. The new economic policy of the government and the policies attendant on it argue that the Indian state should, in principle, largely withdraw from investment in production. The production economy and the pattern of investment should hereafter be guided by domestic as well as global market forces, in order to make industries efficient as well as cost competitive. With reference to the steel industry, the supply-side considerations induced the government to dismantle state control over the industry by delicensing private investment and decontrolling distribution and prices of steel.

Besides, the new government policy dereserved the integrated steel-making sector from the public domain and decided that no new steel plant would be built at greenfield sites in the public sector. The government has also started privatizing public-sector steel companies by partly divesting their shares in the capital market. All these have basically opened up vast opportunities for the growth of the industry in the private sector.

STRUCTURE OF THE INDIAN STEEL INDUSTRY AND THE STEEL MARKET

The dynamics of change that followed economic reforms led to the emergence of the following structure in the steel industry.

(1) Large integrated steel plants that combine primary steel making and rolling of steel into semi-finished and/or finished products for sale. These plants produce steel out of iron which is extracted from virgin iron ore with the help of coal, coke, limestone, and other fluxing materials. These plants use mostly blast furnace (BF)-basic oxygen furnace (BOF) technology.

(2) Electric arc furnace (EAF) units using steel scrap and directly reduced iron (DRI) obtained by reducing iron ore with the help of non-coking coal or natural gas. Some of the plants combine DRI making from iron ore with EAF and also have rolling facilities. These plants of medium scale are often called midi plants. There are three major midi plants as in 2004–5, namely Essar Gujarat, Ispat Industries Ltd, and Jindal Vijayanagar.

(3) IF units that are normally of small size and melt steel scrap, DRI, and pig iron in such proportion that no refining is needed to produce steel, which is not of course of high grade. Some of these have rolling mills for forward integration.

(4) Stand-alone rolling mills which do not produce crude steel, but finished steel out of semi-finished steel like billets, blooms, or slabs produced by integrated steel plants, EAF units, or IF units, or imported from abroad, or ship-breaking scrap and other rerollable scrap generated in the country.

The integrated steel plant sector consists of the Steel Authority of India Ltd. (SAIL), IISCO (a subsidiary of SAIL), RINL, and TISCO. The segment of the industry comprising midi plants, EAF units, IF units, and stand-alone rolling mills is called the secondary sector and is entirely in the private sector in respect of ownership of capital invested. The distribution of steel-making capacity among the different segments is shown in Table 2.

The distribution of steel capacities as described in Table 2 implies that the secondary sector now has a 47 per cent share of the total capacity of crude steel making and 57 per cent of finished steel making in India. The share of the secondary sector in exports was 62.3 per cent in 2001–2. With reference to the pattern of ownership of capital assets, the share of the private sector is now 58 per cent in crude steel making and 66 per cent finished steel capacity. In the long run the industry would be driven more by the private capital flows,

the secondary sector playing a major role on the supply side. However, given the uneven size distribution of the different plants or company units, the main producers, that is the integrated steel plant sector, will continue to provide a leadership role in the market, particularly in the context of pricing.

In the initial phase of industrialization, the share of long or non-flat products is higher while the share of flat products goes up with the attainment of higher levels of development. In India the share of non-flat products is now approximately 48 per cent and that of flat products 52 per cent. If we look at the shortfall in our domestic supply that is met by imports, we find it to be

Table 2   Capacity of Steel Making as Assessed for 2003–4/2005

(million tonnes)

		Crude steel	Saleable steel	Finished steel
A	Integrated plant sector: SAIL including IISCO and its alloy steel plants	12.88	10.616	9.44
	RINL	2.82	2.656	2.41
	TISCO	4.0	3.83	3.21
	Sub total A	19.7	17.102	15.06
B	Secondary sector: midi plants	6.1	–	5.6
C	Secondary sector (other than midi plants) (i) EAF (other smaller units) on the basis of 35 working units*	6.7		(ii) & (iii) together
	(ii) IAF on the basis of production estimate in 2004–05**	4.9		4.0 million
	(iii) Independent rolling mills on the basis of 2001–2 production estimate	–		tonnes*** 10.4
	Sub total C	11.6		14.4
	Grand Total	37.4		35.06

Sources: SAIL. 2004. Statistics for Iron and Steel Industry in India, New Delhi, SAIL; *Steel Scenario Statistical Year book.* 2004. Kolkata, Spark Steel and Economy Research Centre (Pvt) Ltd., and author's own estimation on the basis of SAIL data and interviews with SAIL officials.

Notes: *Total capacity of all Electric Arc Furnaces installed—188 in number—would be 12.45 million tonnes.

**Total capacity of induction furnaces installed which are 934 in number in the country is 9.41 million tonnes. About 657 of them were working as in 2002–3.

***The estimate of 4.0 million tonnes, has been arrived at as the difference between the sub total C that is 14.4 million tonnes and the estimate for item C(iii), 10.4 million tonnes.

higher for flat products, at between 5 and 7 per cent of the total domestic consumption, and really negligible for non-flat products for which there exists substantive excess capacity in the industry.

PRICING OF STEEL AND GLOBALIZATION

The new economic policy of the government since 1991 has liberalized import of steel, by abolishing canalization of steel import and reducing tariff rates, and encouraged domestic competition by delicensing steel capacity creation. Domestic steel prices in India are now sensitive to price movement in the international market. The global business cycle in steel seriously affected the Indian steel industry in the late 1990s and early years of the present decade. It is only recently that the Indian steel industry has in fact emerged from a long stagnation of demand and restricted supply. However, it would be inappropriate to say that the global trend in production and consumption as well as in prices has impacted the Indian steel industry uniformly during the period. Besides, the linkage of global prices with India's domestic prices has been more prominent in the case of flat products. In long products the linkage has been indirect and with a time lag due to massive excess capacity in the country. While the European hot rolled coil (HR coil) prices went down by more than 36 per cent during June 2000–March 2002, the domestic prices in India went down by 20 per cent during the same period. Similarly, when the global market for HR coil rose by 180 per cent between March 2002 and June 2005, the corresponding increase in the Indian steel market was by 133 per cent. On the other hand, when the global prices of billets (of Commonwealth of Independent States [CIS] origin) went up by 143 per cent between March 2002 and January 2005, the Indian Mumbai-based market price rose only by

91 per cent. The domestic market for long or non-flat products with its excess supply situation, is in fact more dominated by the domestic suppliers.

The domestic market in Indian steel is, however, not one of perfect competition because of the varying sizes of the supplying companies. The three main producers with integrated plant technology who have a 43 per cent share of total supply, occupy a position of price leadership in the market. The finished steel market in India thus has some dualistic features, with the main producers, on the one hand, setting prices and optimizing scale and product mix in the short run on oligopolistic principles, and the secondary producers, on the other, taking the open market prices as given and supplying steel on competitive principles. However, while the open market prices can fluctuate from day to day and be influenced by the price leadership of the main producers along with demand conditions, the pricing decisions of the main producers are in turn influenced by import prices and open market price movements.

EXPORT ORIENTATION AND INTERNATIONAL COMPETITIVENESS

The Indian steel industry ignored the export market for a long time because of the import-substitution orientation of India's industrialization. However, the situation started changing after the introduction of economic reforms in 1991 and India has started exporting steel on a sustained basis and investments are being planned targeting the export market. The total export of steel increased from a meagre 0.373 million tonnes in 1991 to 5.8 million tonnes in 2003–4, the latter figure representing about 16 per cent of total steel production in that year. Expansion of export of a common variety of steel in the 1990s was possible for a host of reasons including devaluation of the rupee, full convertivity of the rupee on the trading account, and sluggish domestic demand coinciding with a boom in the world market, particularly an upsurge of demand in China and South East Asia. While the export market was very sluggish till 2001–2 following the economic crisis in East and Southeast Asia in the late 1990s, there has been a very recent upswing because of the spectacular growth in demand for steel in China and reduction in the flow of steel exports from the CIS countries due to the consolidation of their economies among other factors. This has enabled India to expand exports. Indian steel firms have also been making substantive profits for the last two years, with SAIL reaching a record profit figure of Rs 93.65 billion in 2004–5, particularly because the domestic steel prices have been moving along with international prices as mentioned earlier. While all this implies the competitiveness of Indian steel in terms of dollar cost of production, it does not necessarily reflect competitiveness in terms of technological efficiency or real factor productivity and quality (Sengupta 1994).

Further, the high ash content of Indian coal, high aluminia content of iron ore, and non-availability of good-quality fluxes (limestone and dolomite) offset part of the benefit of low factor prices. The productivity of labour is also substantially low for Indian steel plants, varying in the range of 39 to 228 tonnes of crude steel per man year for integrated plants as against 300 to 500 tonnes per man year for industrialized countries.

As far as technology and capital productivity are concerned, a significant section of the Indian steel industry is relatively inefficient due to its outmoded technology. This is immediately apparent from the fact that outmoded open hearth/twin hearth furnaces produced about 10 per cent of the total crude steel produced in the country in 2001–2 and induction furnaces, which can do no refining, another 15 per cent of low grade crude steel. Most blast furnaces in India are old and small. The productivity of the best furnaces of SAIL and RINL plants in terms of hotmetal (iron) output per m^3 of working volume per day is around 1.6 and the same for the best furnace of TISCO is around 2.2, while for any typical Japanese blast furnace it ranges between 2.3 and 2.8.

One of the major disadvantages the Indian steel industry suffers from is the high overall energy cost of its steel-making technology. Energy constitutes about 33 per cent of the total cost of steel making in India while the comparable figure for most major steel-producing countries is around 20 per cent. The high energy cost is explained by high energy usage per tonne of steel in India on account of obsolete technologies. However, the modernization of integrated steel plants since the 1980s has involved the replacement of the energy-inefficient open hearth process by the BOF process and ingot casting by continuous casting into slabs, blooms, or billets.

FUTURE PROSPECT OF THE INDIAN STEEL INDUSTRY

For sustained competitiveness of the Indian steel industry, the growth of real factor productivity and technical efficiency after duly internalizing the environmental externalities is crucial. This requires continuous human resource development for the absorption of all new technologies as well as India's greater participation in research and development (R&D) activities in steel.[1]

In a regime of global integration one may expect capital and technology to flow across national boundaries to facilitate the

[1]See Sengupta 1995 for the possibilities of new technological initiatives in steel for sustainable development.

setting up of steel capacity in a developing country like India. One should, however, be cautious in one's assumption of the flow of foreign direct investment in steel, particularly from the major industrialized steel-producing countries. It is important to note that the big steel producers of the OECD (Organisation of Economic Co-operation and Development) countries have not as yet chosen to locate investments in general in the developing countries with a view to relocation of their steel-making activities. However, POSCO (Pohang Steel Corporation) has signed an MOU (memorandum of understanding) for a joint venture of a 12 million tonne steel plant in Orissa very recently in order to produce steel primarily for export to South Korea. It may be noted that the advanced industrialized countries, in general, would not like to lose their market potential for the secondary export of steel to the developing countries in the form of engineering goods. India will therefore have to take dynamic initiatives in modernizing the industry and promoting R&D activities as well as develop human resources for achieving sustained competitiveness and the status of an important player in the global steel market.

RAMPRASAD SENGUPTA

REFERENCES

Sengupta, Ramprasad. 1994. *The Indian Steel Industry—Investment Issues and Prospects Part I: Market Demand and Cost Competitiveness,* New Delhi, Investment Information and Credit Rating Agency of India Ltd.
————. 1995. *The Indian Steel Industry— Investment Issues and Prospects Part II: Technology Choice and Investment,* New Delhi, Investment Information and Credit Rating Agency of India Ltd.
————. 2004. 'The Steel Industry', in S. Gokarn, A. Sen, and R.R. Vaidya, eds, *The Structure of Indian Industry,* New Delhi, Oxford University Press.
Sinha, R.K. and S.C. Suri. 2003. *Indian Steel Perspectives 2005,* Delhi, Shipra Publications.
Steel Authority of India. 2004. *Annual Report,* New Delhi, SAIL.
Steel Scenario Statistical Yearbook, 2002, 2003, 2004, Kolkata, Spark Steel and Economy Research Centre (Pvt) Ltd.
World Bank. 2005. *World Development Report 2005,* Washington D.C., World Bank, and New York, Oxford University Press.

Tata, The House of

The Tata Group was founded in the second half of the nineteenth century by Jamsetji Nusserwanji Tata, a leading industrialist of his time. Jamsetji believed that India would become truly independent only when it realized the full potential of its natural resources and became a modern, industrial nation. Over a hundred years after his death, as India still continues on that journey, his vision remains the Group's main guiding force.

Jamsetji saw disciplines such as medicine and science and industries such as energy and steel as building blocks in the emergence of a brave and bright new country. After creating the most modern textile mills— his mills were using ring spindles long before their use in Lancashire's mills—he committed the Group to setting up India's first steel plant and first hydroelectric power plant and distribution network, and bestowed half his personal wealth to found the Indian Institute of Science, the country's first institution of higher learning. He set up an endowment in 1892 to send the country's best minds abroad for higher studies. He pioneered several labour practices revolutionary for their time, instituting a Pension Fund in 1886 and paying accident compensation in 1895.

Thus did he set the mandate for the Group: to look beyond the generation of products and profits to serving the communities in which Tata companies functioned. Under his successors, the Group would align its growth plans with national priorities; it would be a pioneer; it would be technology driven; and, above all, it would be ethical in its conduct.

After Jamsetji's death, his elder son, Dorabji, became chairman, and with the help of Jamsetji's other son, Ratan, completed Jamsetji's unfinished projects: Tata Steel's plant at Jamshedpur, Tata Power's hydro-based power plants for Bombay, and the Indian Institute of Science in Bangalore. The late Mr J.R.D. Tata, a cousin of Dorabji and Ratan, became Group chairman in 1938 (and continued till 1991 when I succeeded him). Under his tenure the Group expanded into many new pioneering businesses, while it continued to retain its position as the country's premier business house.

Tata Airlines ushered in civil aviation to the country in 1932, later evolving into Air India before it was nationalized by the government of independent India in 1953. In the early 1950s Tata Chemicals cracked the technology for making synthetic soda ash, hitherto the preserve of a clutch of six international companies. Tata Motors signed a joint venture in 1954 with the then Daimler Benz to make commercial vehicles and Tata Consultancy Services (TCS) marked India's debut into information technology (IT) services way back in 1968.

In the heyday of the controlled economy in the 1960s and 1970s, however, the Group's plans did not always find favour with a socialist-minded government uncomfortable with 'Big Business'. The Group's plans to modernize a range of industrial sectors were repeatedly thwarted, none more prominently than the passenger car sector which the Group tried twice, in vain, to enter in partnership with Daimler Benz and Honda, but also in aluminium, paper, and fertilizers.

In the last twenty-five years, however, as the Indian economy has been opened up, the Tata Group has regained its momentum. When multinationals were reinvited to India in the 1980s, the Group brought in best-in-class technologies through joint ventures with multinational corporations (MNCs) in automobile engines (Cummins), industrial controls (Honeywell), computer hardware (IBM), and telecom equipment (Lucent Technologies). Around the same time Tata Motors' leadership in commercial vehicles was challenged by a spate of Indo-Japanese joint ventures but the company successfully managed to hold its own through innovative and competitively priced products in a convincing demonstration of the country's engineering expertise.

When telecom services were opened up to the private sector in 1994, the Tata Group was among the first to enter. Today, the Group offers a full suite of nationwide voice and data services in fixed line and CDMA-based wireless telephony. And in 1998 Tata Motors unveiled Indica, the country's first indigenously designed and manufactured passenger car, which marked India's entry into a club of developed nations only with the capability of creating a car from the ground up.

India's economy went into a prolonged slowdown in the latter half of the 1990s, affecting the Tata Group more than most, as its major companies are in basic industries. Along with the best of corporate India, however, the Tata Group focused on improving its productivity and efficiency during the slowdown years with the avowed target of making its companies globally competitive. Group companies have been helped in this endeavour by the adoption of the Tata Business Excellence Model, based on the US's Malcolm Baldrige Award, a proven template for charting a holistic improvement of companies' business performance.

Going forward, I believe Indian industry will need to produce goods and services of world class quality for the Indian market, and simultaneously develop an overseas strategy calculated to create a meaningful presence in select geographies. This is a challenge to which Group companies have been addressing themselves. For example, in India's most global sector, IT services, TCS, India's largest software exporter, stands first. Tata Steel is among the world's lowest-cost steel producers, and is today on a very robust expansion path on the twin strategic planks of scaling up the production of semi-finished steels in countries with a comparative advantage in that part of the steel value chain while acquiring finishing facilities in growth markets.

Similarly, Tata Motors, with strengths in the light and medium ranges of commercial vehicles, saw a strategic fit in the Daewoo Commercial Vehicles Company of South Korea with its range of heavy commercial vehicles, and acquired it; together the two are targeting a series of emerging markets with their full range of commercial vehicles and passenger cars. Similarly, other major Group companies like VSNL, Tata Chemicals, the Tata Tea-Tetley Group, Indian Hotels, Voltas, and Tata Power are pursuing aggressive overseas growth strategies.

As I look into the future, I am optimistic about the continued growth of Indian industry and the Tata Group. Indian industry has already demonstrated its ability to leverage the country's scientific and engineering talent pool to create value in a growing range of knowledge sectors. The country's manufacturing sector needs to aim much higher to attain the scale and size of a global player and it has the examples of Japan, South Korea, and now China before it. Certainly the ability is there; ambition and the right government policies are required in greater degree for the Indian manufacturing industry to take its place in the sun. The Tata Group, for one, intends to try to realize the full international potential of Indian industry in services and manufacturing in a manner that would earn for it the same trust it enjoys in India.

R.N. TATA

Technology Diffusion

Among the many technological innovations of the twentieth century few have had the impact of the agricultural green revolution. The green revolution is associated with the introduction of high-yielding varieties (HYVs) of wheat and rice in the late 1960s, which was followed by their widespread adoption, dramatically increasing farm productivity and rural incomes throughout the developing world. Wheat and rice are staple cereals in the Indian diet and these crops typically dominate the Indian farmer's investment (acreage) portfolio. HYVs suited to local growing conditions were successfully developed for both these crops and so the Indian economy benefited disproportionately from this new technology. The tremendous accumulation of rural wealth in the decades following the green revolution set the stage for a balanced and sustained pattern of growth that distinguishes India from other developing countries.

Despite the promise of the new technology, the diffusion of the HYVs was not entirely smooth. Two of the original wheat varieties imported from Mexico, Sonora 64 and Lerma Rojo 64A, were found to be particularly suited to Indian conditions. They were crossed with local varieties to yield the first generation of HYVs released for mass distribution in 1967. Four of the five varieties released in

1967 were very robust to growing conditions and were adopted throughout the Northern Plains where wheat was traditionally cultivated. Two of these varieties—Kalyan Sona and Sonalika—completely dominated in of overall coverage and even spread to areas that had traditionally grown rice, such as eastern Uttar Pradesh and other states in eastern India. Sonalika accounted for 65 per cent and Kalyan Sona another 25 per cent of the total supply of government-certified HYV seed in 1977–8. No other variety accounted for more than 2.5 per cent of seed supply in that year (ICAR 1978).

In sharp contrast with the smooth diffusion of HYV wheat, the story for HYV rice is one of setbacks and disappointments. The original semi-dwarf varieties, Taichung Native 1 and IR8, were imported from the International Rice Research Institute (IRRI) in the Philippines. The first cross-bred HYVs released for mass distribution, Padma and Jaya, were found to be unsuitable in a variety of stress conditions such as water logging, salinity, and drought. They were also found to be susceptible to pests and diseases. Indian agricultural scientists realized very early that the wheat experience would not be replicated with rice. Over the subsequent decades, the thrust of the research effort was to develop HYVs that were suited to specific local conditions. Despite these efforts, the diffusion of HYV rice was a slow process, extending well into the 1980s (ICAR 1985).

Why did adoption patterns for wheat and rice differ so widely? HYV wheat provided a much higher return than the traditional technology that it replaced. It was also a relatively stable technology, associated with fairly certain yields. It is well known that an innovation with these characteristics will diffuse more rapidly. My research on the Indian green revolution has explored an alternative—learning—dimension along which the diffusion patterns for

wheat and rice might have differed. When a farmer is faced with the choice between a traditional variety and a new variety, he will only adopt the new technology if he is sufficiently certain that it provides higher profits than the technology it is replacing. The farmer can learn about the performance of the new technology from the local agricultural extension agent. Perhaps more importantly, the farmer can learn from his neighbours' experiences—their acreage allocation decisions and subsequent yield realizations—about the new technology. A neighbour's (unexpected) decision to adopt the new technology indicates that he must have received a positive signal about its performance. His subsequent yield outcomes serve as an additional source of information. Such information received from neighbours' experiences is more credible than information provided by the local extension agent, since the neighbours have more to lose when they make a mistake, and social learning has been seen to have played an important role in the diffusion of agricultural technology, both during the green revolution and historically in US agriculture. Social learning generates natural lags in adoption because the set of neighbours the grower can learn from is restricted and because new information from them only appears each period. The point that I have tried to make in my previous research is that these learning lags may have been substantially greater for rice than for wheat, explaining in part the distinct adoption trajectories that were observed for the two crops.

Social learning is evidently weak, and diffusion rates will be slow, if the individual is unable to observe his neighbours' experiences perfectly. But this does not explain why some innovations diffuse faster than others, even when social information is readily available. It also does not explain why individuals or communities sometimes appear to persistently ignore their neighbours' (positive) experiences. For example, Ryan and Gross (1943), in an influential study that spawned an enormous diffusion literature in rural sociology, estimated that it took fourteen years before hybrid seed corn was completely adopted in two Iowa communities. I argue that such delays might arise because it is not enough to observe your neighbours' decisions and their subsequent outcomes when learning from them. The fact that a new technology worked well for a neighbour does not imply that it will work well for the farmer if characteristics that determine its performance vary in the population. The individual could control for differences between his own and his neighbours' characteristics when learning from their experiences, but only to the extent that these characteristics are observed. Social learning breaks down if unobserved, or imperfectly observed; individual characteristics are important determinants of neighbours' outcomes.

The rice-growing areas of Peninsular India are characterized by wide variation in soil characteristics, whereas conditions are fairly uniform in the Northern Plains where wheat is traditionally grown. The technological differences between the wheat and rice HYVs described earlier would have accentuated the differences between crops. The early rice HYVs were quite sensitive to soil characteristics such as salinity, as well as to managerial inputs, that are difficult to observe. The rice grower would thus have found it difficult to control for differences between his own and his neighbours' characteristics when learning from their experiences. The relatively stable HYV wheat technology, together with the uniform conditions in the wheat-growing areas of the country, would have resulted in conditions that were ideal for social learning. As we would expect, while slow diffusion rates were initially observed in the rice-growing areas of the country, the wheat HYVs spread rapidly and were ultimately adopted in areas that did not even traditionally grow wheat.

I have (Munshi 2004) statistically tested the link between unobserved heterogeneity and social learning by estimating the grower's response to his neighbours' decisions and outcomes, separately by crop. Wheat growers would have allotted relatively more weight to their neighbours' past acreage allocations and yield realizations, and relatively less weight to their own past decisions, if social learning was stronger for that crop. Although this would seem to be a simple test to implement, identifying social learning statistically is an extremely challenging problem. To understand the difficulties that could arise, suppose that each grower bases his acreage decision in part on an (unobserved) information signal that he receives in each period. If these information signals are correlated across growers in the village and over time, then neighbours' past decisions could simply proxy for the unobserved information signals. Manski (1993) points out more generally that a spurious correlation between the growers' current acreage decision and neighbours' past acreage decisions could be obtained if any unobserved determinant of acreage is correlated across neighbours and over time.

The prospects for identification of social learning improve considerably when we focus on the growers' response to lagged yield realizations in the village. Using data from a nationally representative sample of farm households over a three-year period at the onset of the green revolution, from 1968 to 1970, Munshi (2004) found that HYV wheat acreage responds strongly to lagged yield *shocks* in the village, whereas HYV rice acreage allocations do not. Consistent with the view that social learning was smoother for wheat, wheat growers also place relatively more weight on their neighbours' past acreage allocations and relatively less weight on their own past decisions, although as discussed earlier, the acreage effects are less easy to interpret.

I do not claim that the distinct diffusion patterns for HYV wheat and rice were driven entirely by differences along a single learning dimension. Nevertheless, the importance of social learning in generating variation in diffusion rates across these crops should not be minimized. If the view that rice growers are informationally disadvantaged is correct, then we would expect such growers to compensate for their lack of social information by experimenting on their own land. Agricultural production is divisible and so the grower can choose the precise level of HYV acreage that is optimal for him. Munshi's analysis concludes with the observation that rice growers who did adopt HYV allocated more land to the new technology than comparable wheat growers, despite the fact that average landholdings were smaller for rice growers than wheat growers and despite the fact that the likelihood of HYV adoption was significantly higher for wheat growers. Munshi shows formally that these empirical patterns are consistent with increased experimentation among rice growers to compensate for their lack of social information. In contrast, if diffusion rates were faster for wheat only because the new technology provided a higher relative return for that crop, or was more certain, then wheat adopters would have allocated more land to HYV as well. The fact that they did not, suggests that access to information significantly affected investment patterns across crops in this environment.

The Indian green revolution is now complete, but the lessons from that important historical episode could be applied in other settings in the future. Rice HYVs took at least a decade more than wheat HYVs to diffuse completely. This lag could perhaps have been shortened if information programmes that were responsive to the nature of the underlying social learning process had been adopted. Information was provided to growers in India through what is known as the Training and Visit (T&V) system of agricultural extension. Under the T&V system, extension workers focus their attention on a small group of contact farmers in each village. The implicit assumption here is that information will propagate from these farmers through the rest of the village. This system evidently worked very well with wheat. For rice, we would expect that the few contact farmers in each village had little impact on HYV adoption. In general, it may be necessary to invest in more concentrated external information programmes when the flow of social information is restricted.

KAIVAN MUNSHI

REFERENCES

Indian Council of Agricultural Research (ICAR). 1978. *Wheat Research in India*, New Delhi.
———. 1985. *Rice Research in India*, New Delhi.
Manski, Charles F. 1993. 'Identification of Endogenous Social Effects: The Reflection Problem', *Review of Economic Studies*, 60.
Munshi, Kaivan. 2004. 'Social Learning in a Heterogeneous Population: Technology Diffusion in the Indian Green Revolution', *Journal of Development Economics*, 73(1).
Ryan, Bryce and Neal C. Gross. 1943. 'The Diffusion of Hybrid Seed Corn in Two Iowa Communities', *Rural Sociology*, 8.

Technology Transfer

Economic growth is aided, stimulated, and catalysed by technology. Developing economies can exploit technological changes generated by spillovers from inventions and innovations at international level along with options like buying technology. Technology transfer is the process of acquiring technology from a country that has substantially superior technological knowledge. Two principal ways of utilizing technology transfer are gradual learning and leapfrogging. In comparison to leapfrogging, gradual learning is incremental, painstaking, long term, and cumulative.

The role and contributions of multinational companies (MNCs) in technology transfer through original equipment manufacturing (OEM) have generated considerable interest in the recent economic literature. The symbiotic relationship between local suppliers and their MNC OEMs has enhanced local suppliers' ability to adopt and assimilate foreign technology (Ernst et al. 1998, Lall 2000). This is particularly important for large economies like India, where it is possible for firms to survive and grow catering just to the domestic market. But the exposure to the international market, particularly selling to MNCs, helps them speedily upgrade their technology.

TECHNOLOGY TRANSFER

International technology transfer has become a major source of technology for developing economies. Even so, there are two areas of concern: one, the capacity of firms and countries to absorb and then to innovate; and two, to disperse the technological competence so acquired within the firm or country (Narula and Dunning 2000). Two alternate sets of observations have been made in this context. The predominant neoclassical 'accumulation theories' emphasize the role of physical and capital investments in moving these economies along their production functions. According to these, higher investments will increase the capital per worker and drive the upgradation of technology. The 'assimilation theories', on the other hand, focus on learning in identifying, adapting, and operating imported technologies. Put in a different way, these stress that learning is a key prerequisite to making such investment (Ivarsson and Alvstam 2005, Javorcik 2004).

Acquiring new technology may not be considered a one-time task. The process is continuous in the context of the dynamic status of knowledge development, human labour condition, market, institutions, and the role of government. A competitive firm may lose in the long run due to a competitor's upgradation of technology. It is thus argued that countries or firms must move into more advanced technologies in order to remain competitive. Herein lies the importance of the government's role that it can indirectly support the firms by providing infrastructure, institutions, and incentives.

In the Indian context, Lall (1983) found that Indian research and development (R&D) was basically adaptive and consequently import of technology would encourage in-house R&D. A number of empirical exercises including Katrak (1989) and Siddharthan (1992) have confirmed the complementary relationship between imported technology and local R&D. In view of these findings, it may be concluded that India's closed technology policies with respect to foreign direct investment and technology licensing had the desired effect of promoting indigenous R&D. We present a few case studies in an attempt to capture the Indian experience with technology transfer.

THREE CASE STUDIES

Case 1: Sundaram Fasteners Limited
Sundaram Fasteners Limited (SFL) is the largest manufacturer and exporter of high-tensile fasteners in India. Its wide product range caters to almost all the vehicle

manufacturers in India and many from outside the country. The company set up its first manufacturing plant in Padi, Madras, in 1965 and followed it up with a second fastener plant in Aviyur, a backward village of Ramnad district in Tamil Nadu in 1981. SFL commenced its first diversification venture in 1979 by setting up a unit for the manufacture of cold extruded components in Hosur, another backward district of Tamil Nadu, in technical collaboration with M/S Neumeyer Filespressen GmbH of Germany. In 1983, the company further diversified into powder metal (sintered) products in technical collaboration with Sintermetallwerke Krebsoege GmbH, also in Hosur.

An export-oriented unit to manufacture radiator caps, oil filler caps, and petrol filler caps was set up in 1992. Interestingly, this product category was a chance addition for SFL. SFL was exporting fasteners to the Opel plant of General Motors (GM) in Germany and during one of their visits, the GM technical auditors mentioned that GM was planning to close and sell a radiator caps plant in Britain. They enquired if SFL would be interested in making radiator caps for GM. Confident of its engineering and production capabilities and taking advantage of the liberalized economic environment in India, SFL bought the machinery from the plant in Britain, shipped it to Madras, and soon became a 100 per cent supplier of radiator caps to GM. SFL won the 'Supplier of the Year' award from GM five years in a row—from 1996 through 2000—and now supplies radiator caps to twenty-seven GM plants located across the globe.

SFL acquired Autolec, a leading manufacturer of oil pumps, fuel pumps, water pumps, and other automotive components in 1999 and the Cramlington precision forging unit of Dana Spicer Europe in 2003. Later in May 2004, SFL

inaugurated its China plant to manufacture fasteners, both standard and special. This plant would be used to meet the domestic demand for fasteners in China as well as to export to other countries.

SFL has built a reputation of being a low-cost high-quality supplier. It has not only increased its business with GM but also broken into other international markets like the German market where it secured a sizable contract from Daimler Benz AG and the Japanese market where it secured orders from Japanese engineering giant Komatsu for track shoe bolts and nuts. It has also secured orders from Cummins US for supply of fasteners. SFL continues as a 100 per cent Indian company with no foreign direct investment (FDI), although it has benefited from technology collaborations as described earlier.

Case 2: Moser Baer India Limited[1]

Moser Baer India Limited (MBIL) is the third largest producer of recordable optical media in the world with an 11 per cent share of the global market. It was established as a modest joint venture in collaboration with Moser Baer AG of Switzerland in 1983 to manufacture time-recording devices in India. As this product did not do very well in the market, the company entered the magnetic removable storage media industry and started the production of 8" and later 5.25" floppy disks in 1985.

With the government initiating economic reforms in 1991, MBIL sensed the need to be globally competitive by scaling up volumes and capacities and by cultivating a strong R&D team. Consequently, 5.25" floppy disk capacity was expanded in 1991 and 3.5" disk capacity in 1994. From 5

[1]This case is based on company Annual Reports and write-ups in *Business India* (14–27 October 2002) and *Economic Times* (14 January 2004).

million diskettes per year in the 1980s, production capacity increased to 120 million units by 1996.

Further expansion of production capacity was planned in 1996 but this was not implemented as the company realized that newer technologies were likely to affect the future growth of the magnetic media industry. Optical storage and retrieval technology was proving to be commercially viable and by 1997, the company decided to establish capacity for manufacturing CDs. The production of CDs actually started in 1999 and with this MBIL moved to another growth trajectory; it also signified a major strategic shift for the company.

With economic reforms gathering momentum, MBIL also slowly started developing the vision of being a world-class player in all the products it was manufacturing. The decision to quit the production of time-recording system was part of this vision as was the decision to expand capacities of 5.25" and 3.5" floppy disks. It already had a reputation for quality and it focused on achieving 'zero defect' manufacturing. MBIL also committed significant resources to its R&D which had the mandate of developing product and process technologies useful for the company.

R&D has emerged as one of the most important drivers of MBIL's success. Development of the company's PC12D process and its subsequent versions has helped the company's products achieve broad compatibility across a wide spectrum of drives with writing speeds from 1X to 52X along with significant cost reductions. The company developed the fastest CD-R line in the world in cooperation with a major German company in 2002–3. Its strength in R&D has helped it to develop the ability to design manufacturing facilities and fabrication equipment—as well as the ability

to develop highly flexible processes—thereby enabling the company to move quickly between different optical disk formats including customized disks.

MBIL is now setting up a manufacturing unit in Germany that will produce up to 17 per cent of its expanded capacity of two billion discs a year. This is a pointer to the fact that MBIL has graduated to a stage where it is not dependent on low labour cost processes to gain competitive advantages. In fact, it is confident of competing effectively with other global producers even with the discs being produced in Germany.

MBIL is an Indian company managed by Indian promoters and it has not benefited from any direct investment by another foreign optical media producer, although many foreign institutional investors and private equity firms like the International Finance Corporation (IFC), Warburg Pincus, and Electra Partners, have invested in the company.

Case 3: Sona Koyo Steering Systems Limited[2]

Sona Koyo Steering Systems Limited is the largest manufacturer of steering gears in India with a market share of 50 per cent. Its product range includes manual and power steering systems, rigid, tilt and collapsible steering columns, axle assemblies, and propeller shafts for the automobile industry. Besides being a large domestic player, it has entered the export market in a big way after setting up its 100 per cent export-oriented unit (EOU) in 2004. In a way, the progress of Sona Koyo represents that of the Indian automobile industry in recent times.

[2]This case is based on company website and Annual Reports and write-ups in *Outlook Money* (17 July 2004), *Deccan Herald* (7 September 2004), *Financial Express* (18 August 1998), and *Economic Times* (29 October and 23 November 2004).

With the entry of Maruti Udyog Limited in 1983 the automobile industry in India experienced a severe jolt from the low-volume, low-innovation, low-competition equilibrium it had settled into over the years. Set up as a joint venture between the Government of India and Suzuki Motors of Japan, Maruti was initially importing all its critical parts and components from its Japanese technical partner but it had massive indigenization plans. Sona Steering Systems Ltd. was set up in 1985 during this phase of indigenization to manufacture manual steering gear assemblies and steering column assemblies in technical collaboration with Koyo Seiko Co. Ltd. of Osaka, Japan. Sona Steering established its manufacturing plant in Gurgaon, in close proximity to the Maruti plant while Maruti also picked up a 10 per cent stake in its equity.

With a strong technical collaborator like Koyo Seiko, Sona Steering thrived in its initial years riding piggyback on the success of Maruti. As Maruti increased its market share in the growing but protected Indian automobile market, Sona Steering's sales also rose. However, Maruti continued to be its only large customer. For each steering assembly, Maruti paid Sona the unit cost plus a nominal profit. After the Indian government announced its policy of economic liberalization in 1991 and the automobile sector was opened up in the mid-1990s, Sona also had to upgrade its product mix and look beyond Maruti. In 1998 the company established its second plant in Chennai to cater to the requirements of car makers in southern India.

Sona Steering had established itself as a quality producer right from its early days. This reputation helped it increase its production and sales year after year. With rising demand, it increased its capacity in both the Gurgaon and Chennai plants, and in October 2004 it established a 100 per cent EOU in Sriperumbudur near Chennai to cater to the demand from its overseas customer, namely Koyo Seiko who is also its technical collaborator and financial partner.

As it caters to the OEM market, Sona Koyo realized that growth in volumes would be the key driver of earnings as there is limited scope for improvement in profitability. In fact, like others in the auto ancillary industry it finds itself unable to revise its price to completely offset any increase in input cost. Therefore it had to learn the skills required to continuously improve its business and manufacturing processes to simultaneously achieve lower costs and better quality. Even now Sona Koyo largely depends on its technical collaborator Koyo Seiko for its product and process technology but it has gone a long way in not only absorbing and assimilating that technology but also in improving it—particularly the shop-floor implementation—through continuous improvement.

Sona Koyo identified its core competency areas and decided to do away with the non-core activities. Outbound logistics was outsourced as was management and control of the receiving, storage, and issue functions. Sona Koyo has also outsourced several activities such as milk-run collections of parts from local suppliers and pick up, transport, storage, and delivery of parts to its Chennai plants on a Just-in-Time basis to its 3PL service providers. Operations at Sona Koyo also had strong support from TPM and TQM techniques, resulting in drastic improvement in profitability and quality of its products. Involvement of all the employees in these techniques contributed to lasting operating results. Subsequently, in 2003 Sona Koyo emerged as the first steering systems making company in the world to win the coveted Deming Application Prize. The prize acted as a shot in the arm for everyone at Sona Koyo and strengthened its brand equity.

The company no longer felt the need to establish its credentials with global auto majors looking out for low-cost world-class suppliers. It thought it could leverage the Deming Prize to scale up its export plans. Accordingly, it had to revise its investment and product development plans and established its 100 per cent EOU. The GM certification also helped as did the new production network concept of Koyo Seiko around the same time, utilizing cost-competitive units elsewhere as production hubs. The company, through Koyo Seiko, has already secured export orders worth US$ 35 million for manual steering gears to be executed over a five-year period. It has also been identified as the sole supplier of manual steering gear for Toyota's new vehicle to be launched globally. Sona Koyo also established a toehold in Europe through its 21 per cent equity stake in Fuji Autotech France Sas acquired in October 2004.

R&D expenses are only 0.8 per cent of net sales at Sona Koyo. This is low by international standards but Sona Koyo has the advantage of technical assistance from its partner Koyo Seiko. Sales of new products developed not more than three years ago accounted for about one-third of total sales at Sona Koyo.

The three case study firms reveal some characteristics of Indian manufacturing companies and their different approaches to technology acquisition, development, and assimilation. Most of them developed their technical skills in the domestic market and then included the export markets on their radar screens. MBIL represents a handful of Indian firms that developed global ambitions with the launch of its optical storage media and followed them up with domestic sales at a later date. However, the role of economic liberalization can be seen in all the three cases.

The evidence suggests that there is no easy or automatic transition from latecomer to leader or follower status. Indeed, products are grown extremely rapidly and successfully on the basis of subcontracting, OEM, and ODM. Once some basic capabilities are developed, it is relatively easy for such a firm to shift to new products based on those capabilities. This could be seen in the case of SFL when it entered the production of radiator caps, which was an entirely new line of products. Similarly, once it developed the capability to produce manual steering assemblies, Sona Koyo did not find it very difficult to produce power steering assemblies given the technological support of its technical collaborator.

A transition to leadership and followership on a broad front would require radical changes not only in the way latecomer firms operate but also in the environment in which they compete. For example, firms would have to develop strong marketing capabilities and invest heavily in creating brand images acceptable to worldwide consumers. Similarly, they would have to create a strong research culture within their companies and considerably increase their investments in basic and applied research to generate significant new innovations.

ARINDAM BANIK AND PRADIP
K. BHAUMIK

REFERENCES
Ernst, D., T. Ganiatsos, and L. Mytelka. 1998. *Technological Capabilities and Export Success in Asia*, London, Routledge.
Ivarsson, Inge and Claes Goran Alvstam. 2005. 'Technology Transfer from TNCs to Local Suppliers in Developing Countries: A Study of AB Volvo's Truck and Bus Plants in Brazil, China, India and Mexico', *World Development*, 33: 1325–44.
Javorcik, Beata Smarzynska. 2004. 'Does Foreign Investment Increase the Productivity of

Domestic Firms?: In Search of Spillovers
through Backward Linkages', *American
Economic Review*, 94: 605–27.

Katrak, Homi. 1989. 'Imported Technology and
R&D in a Newly Industrialising Country:
The Experience of Indian Enterprises', *Journal
of Development Economics*, 31: 123–39.

Lall, S. 1983. 'Determinants of R&D in a LDC:
The Indian Engineering Industry', *Economic
Letters*, 13: 379–83.

_____. 2000. 'Technological Change and
Industrialisation in the Asian Newly
Industrializing Economies: Achievements
and Challenges', in L. Kim and R.R. Nelson,
eds, *Technology, Learning & Innovation,
Experiences of Newly Industrialising Economies*,
Cambridge, Cambridge University Press.

Narula, R. and J.H. Dunning. 2000. 'Industrial
Development, Globalization and
Multinational Enterprises: New Realities for
Developing Countries', *Oxford Development
Studies*, 28: 141–67.

Siddharthan, N.S. 1992. 'Transaction Costs,
Technology Transfer, and In-house R&D:
A Study of Indian Private Corporate
Sector', *Journal of Economic Behaviour and
Organisation*, 18: 265–71.

Textile and Apparel Industry

The Multi-Fibre Agreement (MFA), that had
governed the extent of textile trade between
nations since 1962, expired on 1 January 2005.
It is expected that, post-MFA, most tariff
distortions will gradually disappear and firms
with robust capabilities will gain in the global
trade of textile and apparel. The prize is the
$360 billion market which is expected to grow
to about $ 600 billion by the year 2010—
barely five years after the expiry of the MFA.
An important question facing Indian firms
is whether their capabilities and their diverse
supply chain are aligned to benefit from the
opening up of the global textile market?

The history of textiles in India dates
back to the use of mordant dyes and printing
blocks around 3000 BC. The diversity of
fibres found in India, intricate weaving
on its state-of-the-art manual looms, and
its organic dyes attracted buyers from all
over the world for centuries. The British
colonization of India and its industrial
policies destroyed the innovative sector
and left it technologically impoverished.
Independent India saw the building up
of textile capabilities, diversification of its
product base, and its emergence, once again,
as an important global player. Today, the
textile and apparel sector in India employs
35 million people (and is the second largest
employer), generates one-fifth of the total
export earnings, and contributes 4 per
cent to the gross domestic product thereby
making it the largest industrial sector of the
country. This textile economy is worth US$
37 billion and its share of the global market
is about 5.90 per cent. The sector aspires
to increase its revenue to US$ 85 billion,
its export value to US$ 50 billion, and
employment to 12 million by the year 2010
(Texmin 2005).

THE TEXTILE AND APPAREL SUPPLY CHAIN

The textile and apparel supply chain
comprises diverse raw material sectors,
ginning facilities, spinning and extrusion
processes, the processing sector, weaving and
knitting factories, and garment (and other
stitched and non-stitched) manufacturing
that supply an extensive distribution channel
(see Figure 1). This supply chain is perhaps
one of the most diverse in terms of the raw
materials used, technologies deployed, and
goods produced.

This supply chain supplies about 70
per cent by value of its production to the
domestic market. The distribution channel
comprises wholesalers, distributors, and
a large number of small retailers selling
garments and textiles. It is only recently
that large retail formats are emerging,

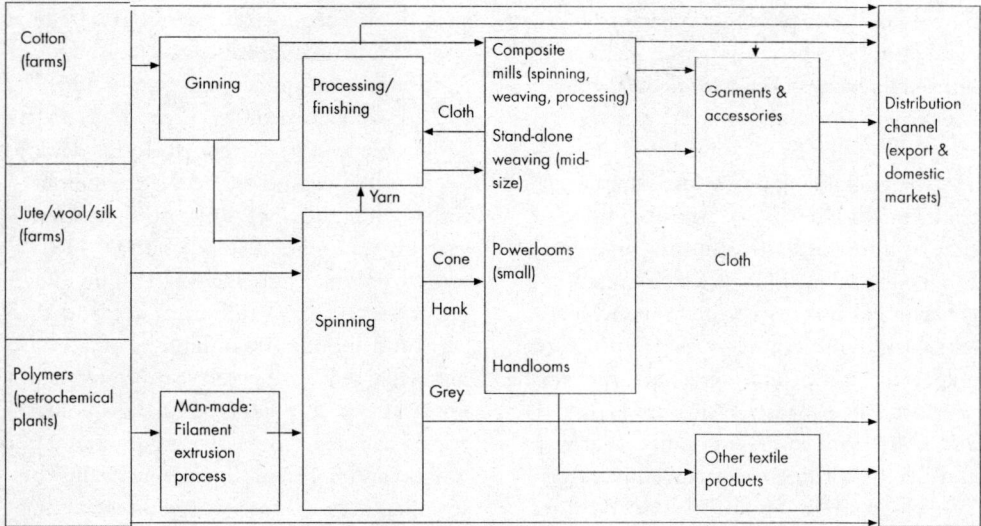

Figure 1   The Textile and Apparel Supply Chain

thereby increasing variety as well as volume on display at a single location. Another feature of the distribution channel is the strong presence of 'agents' who secure and consolidate orders for producers. Exports are traditionally executed through export houses or procurement/commissioning offices of large global apparel retailers.

It is estimated that there exist 65,000 garment units in the organized sector, of which about 88 per cent are for woven cloth while the remaining are for knits. However, only 30–40 units are large in size (as a result of long years of reservation of non-exporting garment units for the small-scale sectors—a regulation that was recently removed). While these firms are spread all over the country, there are clusters emerging in the National Capital Region (NCR), Mumbai, Bangalore, Tirupur/Coimbatore, and Ludhiana employing about 3.5 million people. According to my estimate, the total value of production in the garment sector is around Rs 1050–1100 billion, of which about 81 per cent comes from the domestic market. The value of Indian garments (for

example saree, dhoti, and salwar kurta) is around Rs 200–50 billion. About 40 per cent of fabric for garment production is imported—a figure that is expected to rise in coming years.

The weaving and knits sector lies at the heart of the industry. In 2004–5, of the total production from the weaving sector, about 46 per cent was cotton cloth, 41 per cent was 100 per cent non-cotton including khadi, wool and silk, and 13 per cent was blended cloth. Three distinctive technologies are used in the sector—handlooms, powerlooms, and knitting machines. They also represent very distinctive supply chains. The handloom sector (including khadi, silk, and some wool) serves the low and high ends of the value chain—both mass consumption products for use in rural India as well as niche products for urban and exports markets. It chiefly produces textiles with geographical characterization (for example cotton and silk sarees in Pochampally or Varanasi) and in small batches. Handloom production in 2003–4 was around 5493 million sq. m, of which about 82 per cent was using cotton fibre. Handloom production is mostly rural (employing about 10 million, mostly, household weavers) and revolves around master weavers who provide designs, raw material, and often the loom.

Weaving, using powerlooms, was traditionally done by composite mills that combined it with spinning and processing operations. Over the years, government incentives and demand for low-cost, high-volume, standard products (especially sarees and grey cloth) moved the production towards powerloom factories and away from composite mills (that were essentially full-line variety producers). While some like Arvind Mills or Ashima transformed themselves into competitive units, others gradually closed down. In 2003–4, there remained 223 composite mills that produced 1434 million sq. m of cloth. Most of these mills are located in Gujarat and Maharashtra. Most of the woven cloth comes from the powerlooms (chiefly at Surat, Bhiwandi, the NCR, Chennai). In 2005, there were 425,792 registered powerloom units that produced 26,947 million sq. m of cloth and employed about 4,757,383 workers. The weaving sector is predominantly small scale, has on average 4.5 powerlooms per unit, suffers from outdated technology, and incurs high coordination costs. Knits have been more successful, especially in export channels. Strong production clusters like Tirupur and Ludhiana have led to growth of an accessories sector as well, albeit slowly. The hosiery sector, on the other hand, has largely a domestic focus and is growing rapidly.

The spinning sector is perhaps most competitive globally in terms of variety, unit prices, and production quantity. Though cotton is the fibre of preference, man-made fibre (polyster fibre and polyster filament yarn) is also produced by about 100 large- and medium-size producers.

Spinning is done by 1566 mills and 1170 small and medium enterprises (SME). Mills, chiefly located in north India, deploy 34.24 million spindles and 0.385 million rotors while the SME units produce their yarn on 3.29 million spindles and 0.119 million rotors producing 2270 million kg of cotton yarn, 950 million kg of blended yarn, and about 1106 million kg of man-made filament yarn every year. Worsted and non-worsted spindles (producing woollen yarn) have also progressively grown to 0.604 million and 0.437 million respectively. The spinning sector is technology intensive and productivity is affected by the quality of cotton and the cleaning process used during ginning.

The processing sector, that is dyeing, finishing, and printing, is mostly small in scale. The largest amongst these would dye and finish about 5000 m of cloth per day. The remaining are independent process houses (or part of composite mills) that use automated large batch or continuous processing and have an average scale of about 20,000 m of cloth daily. About 82.5 per cent or 10,397 units are hand processors who dye cloth or yarn manually and dry in open sunshine. Of the remaining (and these use automated and semi-automated equipment), 2076 are independent process houses.

Cotton remains the most significant raw material for the Indian textile industry. In 2003–4, 3009 million kg of cotton was grown over 7.785 million acres. Other fibres produced are silk (15,742 tonnes), jute (10,985,000 bales), wool (50.7 million kg), and man-made fibres (1100.65 million kg). Cotton grows mostly in western and central India, silk in southern India, and jute in eastern India; wool comes mostly from northern India. Significant quantities of cotton, silk, and wool fibres are also imported by the spinning and knitting sectors.[1]

Managing such a complex supply chain requires coordination through excellent managerial practices, technology, and facilitating policies.

COMPETITIVENESS OF INDIAN TEXTILE AND APPAREL INDUSTRY

India is one of the few countries that owns the complete supply chain in close proximity from diverse fibres to a large market. It is capable of delivering packaged products to customers comprising a variety of fibres, diverse count sizes, cloths of different weight and weave, and a panoply of finishes. This permits the supply chain to mix and match variety in different segments to deliver new products and applications. This advantage is further accentuated by cost-based advantages and diverse traditions in textiles.

Indian strength in spinning is now well established—on unit costs on ring yarn, open-ended (OE) yarn, as well as textured yarn, Indian firms are ahead of their global competitors including China. The same is true of some woven OE-yarn fabric categories (especially grey fabrics) but is not true for other woven segments. India contributes about 23 per cent of world spindles and 6 per cent of world rotors (second highest in the world after China). In the last decade 55 per cent of total investment in technology has been made in the spinning sector. Its share in global shuttleless looms, however, is only about 2.8 per cent (and it is ranked ninth in the world). The competitiveness in the weaving sector is adversely affected by low penetration of shuttleless looms

(that is 1.69 per cent of Indian looms), the unorganized nature of the sector (that is fragmented, small, and, often, unregistered units and low investment in technology and practices especially in powerloom, processing, handloom, and knits), and higher power tariffs. There is, however, a recent trend of investment in setting up hi-tech, stand-alone mid-size weaving companies focusing on export markets. India also has the highest deployment of handlooms in the world (handlooms are low on productivity but produce specialized fabric). While production and export of man-made fibre (and filament yarn) has increased over the years, Indian industry still lags significantly behind the US, China, Europe, Taiwan, etc. (Texmin 2005.)

Indian textile industry has suffered in the past from low productivity at both ends of the supply chain—low farm yields affecting cotton production and inefficiency in garment sector due to restriction of size and reservation. Add to this, contamination of cotton with consequent increase in cost (as it affects quality and requires installation of additional process to clean and open cotton fibres before carding operations), poor ginning (most equipment dates back to the 1940s), high average defect rates in the production process (which also lead to increase in effective labour and power costs), hank yarn requirement, and its competitiveness gets severely compromised. Similarly, processing technology is primarily manual and small-batch oriented with visual colour matching and sun drying. This leads to inconsistency in conformance quality. Lead times across the sector continue to be affected by variability in the supply chain—defect rates average over 5 per cent, average of orders on time is about 80 per cent, variance in order size across firms is high (for example the coefficient of variability of average order

---

[1]Except for garments, all data in this section were obtained from OTC 2004 and Texmin 2005.

size for spinning firms is about 2.6)—and on an average sixteen days of sales as work-in-process (WIP) inventory (the highest for garment firms) and an average of thirty days of sales in raw material inventory (the highest for spinning firms) (Chandra 2004). Some of the hurdles (for example reservation in the garment sectors) including tariff distortions between the organized and unorganized sectors have now been systematically removed by policy initiatives of the Government of India and this has opened avenues for firms to compete on the basis of their capabilities.

Trade data of post-MFA performance reveal some interesting trends—Indian firms registered a 27 per cent growth in exports to the US (against China's 52 per cent) during the January–April 2005 time period. Most of this growth has been in textiles while apparels show marginal gains. Apparels and accessories constituted 78 per cent of global exports to the US (FICCI 2005). (India is still a relatively small yet growing player in the global apparel market.) It is expected that India will soon replace Mexico as the second largest apparel supplier to the US.

CHALLENGES FACING INDIAN TEXTILE AND APPAREL INDUSTRY

Textile supply chains compete on low cost, high quality, accurate delivery, and flexibility in variety and volume. Several challenges stand in the way of Indian firms before they can command a larger share of the global market.

Scale

Except for spinning, all other sectors suffer from the problem of scale. Indian firms are typically smaller than their Chinese or Thai counterparts and there are fewer large firms in India. Some of the Chinese large firms have 1.5 times higher spinning capacity, 1.25 times denim (and 2 times grey fabric) capacity, and about 6 times more revenue in

garments than their counterparts in India, thereby affecting the cost structure as well as ability to attract customers with large orders. The central tendency is to add capacity once the order has been won rather than ahead of the demand. Customers go where they see both capacity and capabilities. Large capacity typically goes with standardized products. These firms need to develop the managerial capabilities required to manage a large workforce and design an appropriate supply chain. For the size of the Indian economy, it will have to have bigger firms producing standard products in large volumes as well as small- and mid-size firms producing large variety in small- to mid-size batches (the tension between the organized and unorganized sectors will have to be addressed first, though). Then, there is the need for emergence of specialist firms that will consolidate orders, book capacities, and manage warehouses and the logistics of order delivery.

Skills

Three issues must be mentioned here: (a) there is paucity of technical manpower—there exist barely thirty programmes at graduate engineering (including diploma) level, graduating about thousand students—this is insufficient for bringing about technological change in the sector; (b) Indian firms invest very little in training their existing workforce and the skills are limited to existing processes (Chandra 1998); and (c) there is an acute shortage of trained operators and supervisors in India. It is expected that Indian firms will have to invest close to Rs 1400 billion by the year 2010 to increase their global trade to $ 50 billion. This kind of investment would require, by my calculations, about 70,000 supervisors and 1.05 million operators in the textiles sector and at least 112,000 supervisors and 2.8 million operators in the apparel sector (assuming a 80:20 ratio of investment between textiles and apparel). The real bottleneck to growth is going to be availability of skilled manpower.

Cycle Time

Cycle time is the key to competitiveness of a firm as it affects both price and delivery schedule. Cycle-time reduction is strongly correlated with high first-pass yield, high throughput times, low variability in process times, and low WIP and consequently cost. Indian firms have to dramatically reduce cycle times that are currently quite high across the entire supply chain (Chandra 2004). Customs must provide a turnaround time of half a day for an order before Indian firms can expect to become part of larger global supply chains. Indian firms need a strong deployment of industrial engineering with particular emphasis on cellular manufacturing, JIT, and statistical process control to reduce lead times on shop floors. Penetration of information technology for improving productivity is particularly low in this sector.

Innovation and Technology

A review of the products imported from China to the USA during January–April 2005 reveals that the top three products in terms of percentage increase in imports were tire cords and tire fabrics (843.4 per cent increase over the previous year), non-woven fabrics (284.1 per cent increase), and textile/fabric finishing mill products (197.2 per cent increase) (FICCI 2005). None of these items, however, figures in the list of imports from India that have gained in these early post-MFA days. Entry into newer application domains of industrial textiles, nano-textiles, home furnishings, etc. becomes imperative if we are to grow beyond 5–6 per cent of global market share as these are areas that are projected to grow significantly. Synthetic textiles comprise about 50 per cent of the global textile market.

The Indian synthetic industry, however, is not well entrenched. The Technology Upgradation Fund of the government is being used to stimulate investment in new processes. However, there is little evidence that this deployment in technology has accompanied changes in the managerial regimes—a necessary condition for increasing productivity and order-winning ability.

Domestic Market

The Indian domestic market for all textile and apparel products is estimated at $26 billion and growing. While the market is very competitive at the low end of the value chain, the mid or higher ranges are overpriced (that is 'dollar pricing'). Firms are not taking advantage of the large domestic market in generating economies of scale to deliver cost advantage in export markets. The Free Trade Agreement with Singapore and Thailand will allow overseas producers to meet the aspirations of domestic buyers with quality and prices that are competitive in the domestic market. Ignoring the domestic market, in the long run, will imperil the export markets for domestic producers. In addition, high retail property prices and high channel margins in India will restrict growth of this market. Firms need to make their supply chain leaner in order to overcome these disadvantages.

Institutional Support

Textile policy has gone a long way towards reducing impediments for the industry— sometimes driven by global competition and, at other times, by international trade regulations. However, few areas of policy weakness stand out—labour reforms (which is hindering movement towards higher scale of operations by Indian firms), power availability and quality, customs clearance and shipment operations from ports, credit for large-scale investments that are needed for upgradation of technology, and development of manpower for the industry. These are problems facing several sectors of industry in India and not this sector alone.

In conclusion, competitive strategies are developed by sector-level firms and it is their individual and collective initiatives that secure higher market share in global trade. While one has to be ever vigilant regarding non-tariff barriers in the post-MFA world, the new market will be won on the basis of capabilities across the supply chain. Policy will need to facilitate this building of capabilities at firm level and the flexible strategies that firms will need to devise periodically.

PANKAJ CHANDRA

REFERENCES

Chandra, P., ed. 1998. *Technology, Practices, and Competitiveness: The Primary Textiles Industry in Canada, China, and India*, Mumbai, Himalaya Publishing House.

———. 2004. 'Competitiveness of Indian Textiles & Garment Industry: Some Perspectives', a presentation, Ahmedabad, Indian Institute of Management, December.

Federation of Indian Chambers of Commerce and Industry (FICCI). 2005. 'Trends Analysis of India & China's Textiles and Apparel Exports to USA Post MFA', New Delhi, FICCI, July.

Office of the Textile Commissioner (OTC). 2004. 'Compendium of Textile Statistics', Mumbai, OTC, Ministry of Textiles, Government of India.

Texmin, Official website of Ministry of Textiles, Government of India. 2005. http://texmin.nic.in

SERVICES

Call Centres

Call centres are facilities that handle a range of business communications, involving one-on-one voice interaction between customers and employees of business firms. The most common form of interaction is customer service and is initiated by the customer, typically after a sale, including technical support, billing questions, warranty issues, and delivery queries. Customers may also initiate queries before a transaction. Business-initiated interactions include follow-up customer service calls, those related to payment and billing, and a wide range of marketing-related efforts.

A call centre is a specialized facility that may be owned by the firm that provides the relevant products or services, or be owned by a different firm, which provides the call centre services to its client. In the latter case, the call centre services are an example of outsourcing. In either case, if the facility is located in a different country from the main customers of the firm that relies on the services of the call centre, this is termed offshoring. Thus the two terms are conceptually distinct, and neither one necessarily implies the other, though they are often implemented together. Outsourced call centres are a special case of business process outsourcing (BPO) and, more broadly, IT-enabled services (ITES). BPO is a broad term including accounting, research and analysis, human resource management, and information technology (IT) infrastructure management. Call centres are an important sub-category of BPO, and often the most controversial because of their unique demands on employees. They may handle other BPO tasks, but are more likely to specialize in voice interactions, and even handle only certain kinds of these (for example just technical support, or just credit-card-related issues).

Call centres in India may serve domestic firms, but their greatest prominence arises in cases where their clients or owners are developed-country firms, chiefly those in the United States. The main motivation for offshoring call centres to countries like India has been cost savings. These savings may also be coupled with factors such as workforce availability and quality, expanded response availability due to differences in time zones, and diversification motives. In India, the growth of the software and IT services industry was crucial in paving the way for offshored call centres. The success of Indian firms in IT services accelerated the development of digital communications infrastructure linking India with the United States and Europe, developed and demonstrated the managerial competence of Indians, and proved the workability of providing global-quality services from India.

Statistics for Indian call centres are typically not broken out from overall ITES–BPO data. India's National Association of Software and Services Companies (NASSCOM) reported ITES–BPO export revenue of US$ 3.6 billion (two-thirds of which was from the US) in 2003–4, and employment of 250,000. Of these totals, the figures for customer care, which is mainly call centre based (but can include some analytical work), were US$ 1.2 billion and 96,000. Call centres might also be represented in areas such as payment services and finance. The overall numbers are small relative to the Indian economy, but recent growth rates have been well over 30 per cent. NASSCOM commissioned a 2002 study by consulting firm McKinsey, which predicted that this growth would continue for several years at least, with resulting projections of revenue and employment several times the current figures by 2008.

Call centres in India are run by independent domestic firms as well as subsidiary operations of major global firms. In some cases, such as Daksh by IBM, an independent Indian firm has been acquired by a multinational. In other cases, such as Spectramind by Wipro, the acquirer has been a larger Indian firm. Other examples of large Indian firms in ITES include the WNS Group, Convergys, and Zenta, as well as subsidiaries of ICICI, HCL, and Hinduja. There are numerous smaller firms as well, despite continuing consolidation and an ongoing shake-out of poor performers. Multinationals with call centre operations in India include firms such as AOL, Accenture, Dell, EDS, GE, and several financial-sector firms. Again, data on the call centre components of overall ITES are not available for individual firms.

Call centres, and ITES–BPO in general, are seen as contributing to the growth of the Indian economy and providing employment for educated urban youth who have otherwise found limited job opportunities, even after economic reform. The overall impact of this sector on the Indian economy is hard to quantify, but, in combination with the IT sector, may have contributed a percentage point or so to the economy's growth rate. There are also positives to be found in the training, skill formation, and workforce-entry opportunities that call centres and ITES–BPO in general provide. Call centre employees may welcome the freedom and new opportunities that come with their jobs.

On the other hand, call centres are singled out for criticism because of the relatively low level of skills required (versus some other BPO segments), and for their negative impacts on young people's lives. The latter, according to critics, include high pressure and stress; distortion of values, language, and culture; and possibly other forms of exploitation. These criticisms can be tempered by noting that employment is voluntary, that working conditions are subject to regulation, and that employers themselves have a strong incentive to make these jobs attractive, to reduce the high turnover rates (as high as 40 per cent a year) that do characterize the industry. Turnover imposes high training costs on employers and may also have negative spillover effects on morale and productivity of those who remain. One can conjecture that successful, growing Indian call centre firms will adjust their working conditions to overcome these problems. In some cases, NASSCOM may serve as a guiding force and industry self-regulator.

In conclusion, call centres in India and elsewhere are part of a growing globalization and disaggregation of work, enabled by the falling cost of using IT for communication and collaboration. They present challenges to existing industrial models, as well as to their host societies, but also provide substantial benefits by contributing to investment and employment. They are likely to be increasingly important over time, but represent just one aspect of globalization and economic change in India.

NIRVIKAR SINGH

REFERENCES
NASSCOM. 2005a. Facts and Figures, http://www.nasscom.org/artdisplay.asp?cat_id=811#2, accessed on 17 May 2006.
————. 2005b. Indian ITES–BPO Market, http://www.nasscom.org/artdisplay.asp?cat_id=412#2, accessed on 17 May 2006.
Singh, Nirvikar. 2004. 'Information Technology and India's Economic Development', in K. Basu, ed., *India's Emerging Economy: Performance and Prospects in the 1990s and Beyond*, Massachusetts, MIT Press; New Delhi, Oxford University Press, pp. 223–61.

IT-enabled Sectors

India's software services industry, begun in 1974, is one of the world's successful information-technology (IT)-exporting industries. For the fiscal year ended March 2007, it generated $23 billion in export revenue, or 4.3 per cent of global IT services expenditure. A further $8 billion in export revenue was earned from IT-enabled services such as call centres and back-office work. As of March 2007, the industry employed 1.25 million people in software and IT-enabled export services. The US is the largest export market, with a 68 per cent share, followed by Europe (23 per cent). Exports have grown at an average of 34 per cent annually for the last decade.

The Indian software story is little understood, in part because its clients are firms rather than retail consumers. Most retail users and small firms buy 'product software', that is, software that is written for general use and intended to be replicated in its original form across many users, such as the Windows operating system or Microsoft Word. While most large corporations also use product software for purposes such as managing hardware (operating systems, utilities, drivers, etc.) as well as for standardized applications such as word processing, they often need software customized to their needs for complex applications, such as software to automate an assembly line. This is 'custom applications software'. It is part of a larger category called software services, which includes simpler work such as deploying hardware and software, training and system maintenance, but also more complex work such as integrating different pieces of product and custom software into a working system and a range of outsourced managed services, such as email, network management, accounting, research and development (R&D), and customer care. Software services, a $475 billion industry worldwide, is a larger field than software products. Globally, software products had sales of $206 billion in 2006.

The Indian software success is particularly interesting because it is a rare case of services rather than manufactured goods being exported from a developing country. Also unusual is that it happened in custom software rather than product software: most software-exporting countries develop product software. India and Ireland are the only exceptions; but even Ireland's exports are almost entirely to Europe and the work is simpler than India's software services, consisting of localizing American software to European requirements. The third unusual thing is that IT is considered one of the most difficult items to export due to the requirement of staying regularly updated with rapidly changing customer requirements and requiring the ability to respond quickly to the latest technological changes. These have tended to deter technology-oriented service exports, as documented by Hobday (1995).

Several factors enabled India's software success. We shall discuss the key role played by domestic entrepreneurship but also argue that technological changes also mattered. We shall also later argue that, though India's software story has been a great success, it faces challenges as well.

ORIGINS AND GROWTH

The first software exporter was TCS (Tata Consultancy Services) which was founded in 1968 to serve the in-house data-processing requirements of the Tata industrial group. In 1969, it began offering data-processing services to outside clients on a Burroughs's mainframe and became Burroughs's exclusive India sales agent in 1970. In 1974, Burroughs, attracted by the India cost advantage, asked TCS to install its system software at Burroughs's clients' offices in the US. Thus started the export business termed 'body-shopping', that is, the export of programmers

for assignments typically lasting a few months. The Indian firms did little other than recruiting, while the overseas client decided on the work for the programmers. They initially focused on systems installation and maintenance. Later, they did 'conversion' of clients' existing applications software into (primarily) IBM-compatible versions. By 1980, the industry had export revenue of $4 million, shared by twenty-one firms, of which TCS and a sister firm accounted for 63 per cent (Heeks 1996: 88).

As Table 1 shows, the industry grew substantially after 1984 when the number of firms rose from thirty-five to 700 by 1990. This was enabled by three factors. First, the government, after a period of hostility to the private IT sector, turned around and announced the New Computer Policy in 1984. This substantially reduced import tariffs (on hardware from 135 per cent to 60 per cent, and on software from 100 per cent to 60 per cent), reallowed wholly owned foreign firms for exports, and (in a separate legislation) exempted all export income from tax in 1985. Second, the workstation with its sophisticated graphics and numerical

Table 1   Growth of the Indian Software Industry

Year	Total exports ($m)	No. of firms	Average revenue per firm ($)	Average revenue per employee ($)	Share of top 8 firms (%)	Average revenue per firm excluding top 8 firms ($)
1980	4.0	21	190,476	16,000	90.0	30,769
1984	25.3	35	722,857	18,741	78.0	206,148
1990	105.4	700	150,571	16,215	65.0	53,309
2000	5287	816	6,479,167	32,635	38.3	4,734,406
2003	8600	3031	2,837,347	33,076	64.8	1,711,214
2007	23,000	NA	NA	NA	NA	NA

Sources: Nasscom. 2004. *The IT Industry in India*, New Delhi, NASSCOM; Richard Heeks. 1996. *India's Software Industry*, New Delhi, Sage.

Notes: 1. Year refers to the fiscal year ending 31 March of that year. For example, 2007 refers to the period 1 April 2005–31 March 2007.

2. Figures are for software only and do not include IT-enabled services such as call centres.

computation capabilities was introduced in the mid-1980s. The workstation, unlike the PC which had been introduced a few years earlier, had the capacity for stand-alone programming for the mainframe and could run small business applications. Third was the widespread adoption of Unix as the standard operating system for workstations and mainframes from the mid-1980s. (We term these latter two developments the U-W standard.)

The U-W standard enabled programmers to develop programmes on any workstation in a common language (C), whereas earlier programmers needed to work on specific mainframes and write programmes in the language of that mainframe supplier. Thanks to the U-W standard and reduced tariffs, it became economical to write programmes in India.

A foreign firm, Texas Instruments (TI), was the first to do so, setting up a wholly owned subsidiary in Bangalore for software product development. Although several multinationals and Indian firms followed TI's lead in attempting to develop product software in India, they did not succeed.

TI's legacy lay in two other directions. First, it showed that a team of programmers working in India could do the same work as the team overseas, though at lower costs. Second, it showed the advantages of Bangalore, most importantly of being located close to the largest pool of engineers (the four southern states, Karnataka, Andhra Pradesh, Tamil Nadu, and Kerala produce 52 per cent of India's engineering graduates).

TCS pioneered the first complete custom software project for an overseas client done remotely, thus giving birth to a new way of working. Termed the 'remote project management model', it generated large new firm entry. It was to remain the industry's mainstay for the next two decades.

One of the outcomes of the U-W standard was that it allowed firms to focus on programming, whereas earlier they needed both system-specific skills and skills in the industries that they worked for (domain skills). This delinking of higher-paid system and domain skills from programming was accompanied by a decline in revenue per employee by 1990, as shown in Table 1.

It also played to Bangalore's strengths as a programmer base and enabled it to gain market share over the leader, Mumbai. Whereas in 1980 none of the top eight software exporters were from Bangalore and even by 1990, TI was the only Bangalore firm in the list (the rest were Mumbai-based firms), by 2000, there were two Bangalore firms in the list and Bangalore firms made up a quarter of the industry's exports.

In the 1990s, India went through major reforms. Apart from tariff reductions, a key reform was that firms were allowed to spend their export dollars on opening offices overseas, thus giving them access to more firms, particularly the mid-sized firms, and enabling them to offer both remote and proximate support—which was valuable for the larger clients.

In the 1990s, an important technological change led to another paradigm shift for the custom software industry. Variously termed the 'digital age' or the 'information age', it consisted of two components: the PC replaced the workstation as both the vehicle for programming and, through creating networks of computers, the vehicle for applications delivery for small businesses (large businesses continue to use mainframes for data management and use the PC only as a user interface). This allowed many more corporate users to directly access applications software than before. Second, the costs of transmitting information fell, particularly towards the end of the 1990s.

The digital age revolutionized (or, at least, allowed for) the conversion of service flows into stocks of information, making it possible to store a service. For example, a legal opinion that earlier had to be delivered to the client in person could now be prepared as a computer document and transmitted to the client over email or, better yet, encoded into software. Easy storage and transmission allowed for the physical separation of the client and vendor as well as their separation in time. It also induced the separation of services into components that were standardized and could be prepared in advance (such as a template for a legal opinion) and other components that were customized for the client (such as the opinion itself) or remained non-storable. Taking advantage of the possibility of subdividing tasks and the economies that come with a division of labour, this reduced costs by offering the possibility of preparing the standardized components with lower-cost labour and, possibly, at another location.

The second fundamental impact was the conversion of an increasing number of non-information service flows into information service flows. For example, sampling of tangible goods by a buyer visiting a showroom is increasingly being replaced by virtual samples delivered over the Internet. Once converted to an information flow, the service may also then be converted into a stock of information, as noted earlier, and subjected to the earlier mentioned forces of cost reduction through standardization of components and remote production.

Thus, by enabling transmission and storability, the digital age enabled the offshoring of services. As transmission costs continued to fall after 2000, even non-storable services, such as call centre services, could be offshored.

Whereas earlier, India's software industry was restricted to preparing custom software programmes, the digital age enabled the offshoring of what are termed 'managed services' or 'business process outsourcing', that is, functions such as bookkeeping, payroll, and customer care are part of an ever-increasing list of services that may now be offered remotely. Thus a large new industry has been opened up to offshoring. As in custom software, India is already the developing world's largest supplier of managed services to developed countries.

SUSTAINABILITY
Several scholars and policymakers have questioned the sustainability of India's IT-enabled sector. Of course, the record over the past three decades speaks for itself, but their critiques and some new issues need to be addressed.

Their reasons for future unsustainability are: the absence of domestic markets from which to acquire domain skills, lack of intellectual property (IP) protection, small firm sizes, migration of skilled IT professionals to developed countries, lack of R&D in universities and industry, limited involvement of a skilled diaspora, and the lack of clusters (see, for example, Schware 1992).

It turned out that these factors were not industry 'killers' but took the industry in a particular direction. For example, lack of learning from the domestic market and migration forced the industry to restrict the work to programming rather than higher-end work such as system design and integration. Similarly, the absence of venture capital discouraged start-ups but left large, well-capitalized firms unaffected. The lack of venture capital and R&D, non-involvement of the diaspora, and weak IP laws discouraged software product development but did not affect the custom software industry.

A bigger challenge is the quality of the labour force. This generally goes unnoticed due to the high employment growth in the industry, which hides issues of quality. According to NASSCOM (2000), only 27.12 per cent of the IT workforce has an undergraduate or graduate degree in computer sciences or electrical engineering.

Despite this, the industry has thrived. The credit must go to private enterprise. In the early days, when the government imposed high tariffs on imports, the industry responded by exporting programmers. When tariff walls were lowered, the work shifted to India. With the advent of the Internet, the industry expanded the scope of work to include business process work. It

is particularly remarkable that the industry, even when the government was hostile, managed to keep up with the work done in the US and other developed countries, albeit with a lag of about a decade. This is shown in Table 2.

Since 2004, the industry is headed in the direction of providing higher value-addition. Recent reforms, especially in telecommunications and venture capital and enabling access by domestic firms to overseas markets, have changed the direction of the industry significantly, moving it towards higher-value services such as managed services, software product development, and R&D. For instance, the world's largest contract IT R&D firm, is now an Indian firm, Wipro.

Looking ahead, outsourcing of software services remains a growth industry,

Table 2   Comparing Work Done in the US and India in Common Time-frames

Work type ⇒	US		India	
	More complex	Less complex	More complex	Less complex
Up to 1970	(In-house IT support (mainly conversion work)	O/S, software support for IT firm		EDP
1971–80	Applications prog-rammes and EDP	In-house IT support	In-house IT support (mainly conversion work); EDP	O/S, software support for global IT firm
1981–90	Systems integration (hardware with systems) and EDP	Applications and O/S programmes; Unix conversion work	Offsite conversion work and applications development; in-house product development by MNEs	Onsite conversion work and appli-cations development
1991–2003	Consulting, systems integration soft-ware, managed services	Applications prog-rammes, web services	Large applications development projects; engineering services; web services; in-house product development by MNEs	Onsite conversion (including Y2K) work, website maintenance

Source: Author's compilation.
Notes: EDP = electronic data processing, MNE = multinational enterprises, O/S = operating system, Y2K = Year 2000 work to convert old mainframe applications software containing 2-digit year codes to 4-digit codes).

entering its fourth decade. This is likely to be bolstered by a greater presence of multinationals, clusters, diaspora involvement, and access to risk capital. Only poor education puts growth at some risk.

RAFIQ DOSSANI

REFERENCES

Dossani, Rafiq. 2004. 'Origins and Growth of the IT Industry in India', Working Paper, Asia-Pacific Research Center, Stanford University.

Heeks, Richard. 1996. *India's Software Industry*, New Delhi, Sage.

Hobday, Michael. 1995. *Innovation in East Asia: The Challenge to Japan*, Cheltenham, Edward Elgar.

Ministry of Human Resource Development. 2001. 'Technical Education Quality Improvement Project of the Government of India', New Delhi, Ministry of HRD.

NASSCOM. Various years. *The IT industry in India*, New Delhi, NASSCOM.

Schware, R. 1992. 'Software Industry Entry Strategies for Developing Countries: A "Walking on Two Legs" Proposition', *World Development*, 20(2): 143–64.

Outsourcing

Some time ago, British Airways announced its plans to get all its accounting done in Mumbai. Many hospitals in the US are getting X-rays read by medical technologists in India. No matter where you live, your cries for 'Help' with your DELL computer may be answered by a technician in Hyderabad. These are the examples of outsourcing that consumers in the West are well aware of because they are a part of their everyday experience. However, this is only the tip of the iceberg. Many businesses use software (for example accounting, inventory control, marketing research) that needs to be customized for their own special needs. A

significant part of India's software exports comprises such software services. The term 'outsourcing' has come to mean all such services traded internationally over electronic media such as Internet, fax, and telephones.

In this entry we will first ask what factors may have been responsible for the advent of outsourcing. Second, we will probe the source of anxieties generated in the West on account of outsourcing and examine arguments about whether these are warranted. We will then consider the history of outsourcing to India, followed by an analysis of whether outsourcing is of any significance to the Indian economy and if so 'how'.

While anxieties about outsourcing to locations abroad are a new development, outsourcing itself is not a new phenomenon. Revolutionary developments in information technology (IT), particularly in the past two decades, made it imperative for informational structures within business and government organizations to be overhauled. New databases for inventory control, market research, and other management tasks were created. However, this was a monumental task and in most firms the expertise for such informational overhaul was unavailable among the ranks of existing employees. Further, in many cases, it made little sense to add to the payroll of permanent employees those who were needed for a one-time job. As a result, the one-time job of an informational overhaul was typically contracted out to specialist local firms. However, what initially seemed like a one-time addition of software invariably required further support and service, especially as information needs changed and technologies evolved to meet them. Over time, firms came to think of database management as a separate function that could be contracted to independent local firms. This was the beginning of outsourcing at local level.

Outsourcing dramatically picked up pace in the 1990s as technology became capable of handling tasks of increasing complexity and costs of computing fell. Further, as the Internet became ubiquitous and costs of transmitting information dropped, it was a small step from a local specialized firm to a firm located in India or Ireland. What mattered was that the same job could be done abroad for significantly lower cost. Once cost savings were realized, it was natural for firms to be on the lookout for further cost savings and for more tasks to be contracted out to specialized firms abroad.

It is well known that India had invested what seemed like excessive amounts of resources into post-secondary education. For a long time now, Indian engineers and technical graduates had been overqualified for the domestic labour market. The demand for specialized software assignments matched the excess supply of engineers and programmers, and the economic reforms of 1991 removed some of the obstacles in the way of these international business contracts. A number of software firms emerged in India to take advantage of these opportunities in the American market. Initially, many Indian firms got their foot in the door of the US market by helping fix the Year-2000 (Y2K) software glitch primarily by on-site placement of Indian software professionals. Riding on the initial success with Y2K, Indian firms began to provide other low-cost software services to US companies and developed 'off-shoring' business models where a large fraction of a project's software design, development, and testing took place in low-cost India. The result was a software boom in India with a myriad of firms designing customized software for American companies. From here it did not take long for the off-shore market in a range of outsourced services to develop. From manning call centres to

reading X-rays and processing of insurance claims, India's educated, low-cost, English-speaking workforce soon became an eager participant in the global service economy. Outsourcing from India had made a debut on the world stage in a noticeable way.

In the West, especially in the US and UK, the issue of outsourcing has created considerable anger and anxiety. In the US presidential debates during the 2004 election, the issue of outsourcing was given a lot of play. Leading media outlets such as *Time* ran cover stories on the issue and TV Networks such as CNN ran programmes that repeatedly highlighted the 'evils' of outsourcing. After all, outsourcing to India or China means that the jobs, whether existing or newly created, go to Indians or Chinese rather than to Americans.

It is legitimate to ask whether the phenomenon of outsourcing is essentially different from international trade in manufactured products. If Bangladesh can produce cheaper textiles than the US, then the imports from Bangladesh would drive American textile manufacturers out of business and consequently there would be similar sort of anxiety among American textile workers. Indeed, there was such anxiety vis-à-vis China in the 1990s and Japan prior to that, when cheap products manufactured in those countries posed a serious challenge to many segments of manufacturing industry in the US. What then is special about outsourcing?

International trade in any physical product, whether in textiles or automobiles, entails considerable shipping costs. Of course, they vary according to the product; they are reasonably small for textiles but quite high for autos. The greater the shipping costs, the less competitive are imports to domestically produced goods. However, when you think of services that can be sent over the Internet, the shipping costs are practically zero. An equally qualified programmer or a technician in India is able to do the job at a fraction of the cost of his or her American counterpart and ship the output over Internet. This is what has created the kerfuffle over outsourcing in the West.

Displacement of jobs may not be the only reason why outsourcing attracts so much discussion. Outsourcing may be breaking rank with history. There has always been a certain chronological pattern in the course of development across the world. As the labour force in low-wage countries develops skills in some industries—typically labour-intensive industries such as textiles—the comparative advantage in those industries passes on to low-wage countries. High-wage countries cannot compete anymore in those low-end industries. However, high-wage countries are typically also more technologically advanced and they have the advantage of a higher-skilled labour force. The capital in high-wage countries shifts to new products and new industries creating new jobs that require higher levels of skills. Thus there is a ladder of skills and jobs that the world keeps moving up, with high-wage countries leading and low-wage countries at their heels. When low-skill jobs are lost to low-wage countries, there is little to mourn for as long as much of the labour force can hope to climb the skills ladder and acquire high-end jobs. In other words, what one sees more explicitly through immigration, with menial and more 'dirty' jobs going to immigrants and migrant labour from less-developed countries, also happens indirectly through trade. Outsourcing, however, presents a clear break from this pattern. A fraction of the jobs lost in the US through outsourcing is clearly skilled. Acquiring higher levels of skills, it is feared, will no longer assure a secure future for an American worker.

Are fears about outsourcing voiced by many media commentators in the US warranted? We can try to address this question both theoretically and empirically. The most straightforward theoretical argument against the spectre of unemployment resulting from outsourcing is that any resultant unemployment is likely to be only a short-run phenomenon. As the jobs are outsourced to cheaper workers elsewhere, the production costs decline. The lowered costs and hence cheaper goods are a boon to domestic consumers; their real incomes rise. The rise in real incomes creates an increase in demand for other goods and services and hence in the supply of new jobs to produce them. The displaced workers take up the newly created jobs. Over time full employment is restored. Of course, the process takes some time to work and it is necessary to retrain the displaced workers. This theoretical argument invariably comes with a caveat that some workers are too old to retrain and some social insurance scheme may have to be provided for them.

The above argument is not specific to the consequences of outsourcing. It applies also to any job losses due to competitive imports or even to labour-displacing technical change. In fact, one could argue that the story of economic growth is very much a story of technological change, a large part of which consists of machines replacing human labour. The overall process has remained the same: the displaced workers have gone on to perform new activities created by a demand for a set of new goods and services. Essentially, there is little difference between a machine displacing local labour and a foreign worker doing the same.

Why then is there so much commotion about outsourcing when there is none at all about labour-displacing technical change? One reason is that the process of labour-displacing technical change is slow and continuous. The job losses come in trickles and it is difficult to attribute a big chunk of jobs lost to a specific event of technology adoption. Outsourcing, on the other hand, is easily noticed. An American company shifting its call centres or its accounting operations to India cannot fail to draw the attention of the American media. Outsourcing is very much in the public eye and therefore it provokes so much controversy. It is also easier to blame low-wage workers abroad for taking jobs away rather than assign responsibility to more abstract notions like technological change.

It has also been argued (Bhagwati et al. 2004) that the quantitative impact of outsourcing on the American labour market is insignificant and that very few high-end jobs have been lost as a result of outsourcing. Much of this debate is over future outcomes, so we can only examine arguments based on projections as in the following example. Bhagwati et al. use a much-cited Forrester Research report which estimates that slightly less than half of these jobs (43 per cent) can be classified as belonging to professions that may be subject to outsourcing and that 3.4 million jobs (roughly 300,000 per year) may be lost to outsourcing in the next decade (McCarthy 2004). Setting aside the question of whether such numbers will actually materialize, how one interprets these numbers becomes a matter of what they are compared with. Bhagwati et al. compare the average *annual loss* of jobs due to outsourcing with the *total* number of jobs in the vulnerable sectors and arrive at a small figure for outsourcing losses of 0.53 per cent. The same numbers can be interpreted as 17 per cent of the 20 million jobs the US economy is likely to *add* over the next decade, and jumps to 39 per cent of all *jobs added in the vulnerable sectors.* Thus whether you see job losses as small or significant may depend on the metrics you choose to apply.

It is often stated that many of the jobs being outsourced are low-skill, low-wage jobs and there is ample evidence that many outsourced jobs belong to this category. The current boom in relocation of call centres to India is a case in point. NASSCOM estimates that 95,000 of the 245,000 Indian workers employed in non-software outsourcing services work in call centres. Though some firms in India do high-end work such as patent application research, a majority of the remaining 150,000 workers are employed in relatively low-end jobs such as billing, payment processing, credit card services, and medical transcription. However, most software-related jobs in India cannot be so easily written off as being low end. It is true that in the mid-1990s Indian firms engaged in low-end software services such as fixing the Y2K bug. In recent years, however, the Indian software services sector has evolved to take on custom software of high complexity serving a diverse range of sectors. Examples abound: Infosys, Tata Consultancy Services (TCS), and Wipro, the big three Indian software firms, compete with IBM and Accenture for the accounts of Fortune 500 companies; a medium-sized Indian company, Mastek, was responsible for the IT infrastructure to manage the congestion charge for London's traffic system; Sasken is a Bangalore-based firm that supplies cutting-edge telecom software to many of the world's leading communication companies. A possible reason why Indian software continues to be seen as 'low end' is that no Indian company exports software products. Products have greater economic value than software services. Consequently, software services are seen as 'low end' in economic terms relative to software products. This does not mean that software services are provided by engineers with lower skills.

Increasingly, the distinction between Indian software companies and multinationals is being blurred as India offices of global software giants such as IBM, HP, and CSC (with 23,000, 13,000, and 5000 Indian employees respectively in 2005) perform software tasks in India that they might in offices in the US. Given the range of skills and the complexity of services offered by Indian firms and MNCs (multinational corporations) in India, it is silly to write-off India's software services as primarily 'low end'. This is reinforced by the recent opening up of dozens of product development and research and development (R&D) centres in India, as well as Indian companies specializing in 'outsourced product development'. In 2005, NASSCOM estimates that 25,000 engineers work in product development and R&D services in India employed in over 230 firms, primarily foreign, with product development offices in India. The number is expected to grow to 65,000 in three years. The list is impressive—Intel, Motorola, Sun, Oracle, Microsoft, SAP, Novell, Adobe, IBM, HP, GE, Google, Cadence, Yahoo, Amazon, Cisco, TI all have product development and R&D facilities in India. Some of these facilities are recent while others such as those of TI (225 patents filed, 1200 employees), Oracle (125 patents filed, 6400 employees), and Intel (65 patents filed, 2500 employees) have been operational for a long time. In addition to multinational corporations, numerous start-ups based primarily in Silicon Valley, the lifeblood of the US innovation system, do much of their product development in India.

Of course, none of the above has much significance for total levels of employment in the Indian economy. The entire software industry in India, of which outsourcing constitutes only a part, employs no more than 1 million workers in the total labour force of 450 million. Even the dramatic growth that is expected over the next decade is unlikely to change this picture by much. It is clear therefore that as a contributor to employment

in India, outsourcing could hardly have made much of an impact. Its contribution to Indian economy is channelled through indirect ways.

First, the software sector has been the fastest-growing sector in India's exports that make a twofold contribution to the process of growth in a developing country. Exports generate the foreign exchange that enables purchases of productivity-improving foreign machinery and technology. In addition, the foreign exchange reserves generated by software exports have given Indian policymakers a comfortable cushion to withstand any sudden changes in its balance of payments.

Perhaps, the most noteworthy effect of outsourcing on the Indian economy has been an intangible one: it has caused a change in entrepreneurial culture. Gone are the days when the business leaders in India came exclusively from leading business families. The founders of India's software-exporting firms are self-made millionaires who started out with their technological knowledge as their capital. This is a very healthy development as India's future growth depends on young people with talent and expertise entering the entrepreneurial arena.

Outsourcing has been a learning experience for both Indian and Western firms. The word has spread that India has technical expertise of respectable quality that could be tapped and that business relationships could be established with Indian firms. Also, Indian firms have learned a lesson or two in doing business in the West. All this is bound to stand India in good stead for further expansion of exports. The rapid expansion of foreign firms in India's software service sector, as well as the recent growth in R&D and product development, reinforce this point.

Moreover, there have been management spillovers through which the management approaches learned through outsourcing and interaction with foreign companies have been put to use in Indian firms. For example, corporate governance practices such as employee stock option plans, developed within leading companies in the IT sector, have come to serve as exemplars for other companies to follow.

A legitimate question that one might ask is whether outsourcing is relevant to the lives of almost one-third of India's population that is, below the poverty line. The answer is once again 'Yes, but only indirectly and only slightly'. A large component of the 'poor' (those under the poverty line) in India make a living in agriculture. Outsourcing could have an impact on their lives only if it created significant employment for them outside agriculture. It is difficult to sustain a claim that outsourcing has done so either directly or indirectly.

In sum, outsourcing of services emerged globally when cost of telecommunications began to drop in the mid–late 1990s. India, with its large pool of science and technology professionals, quickly became a major provider of these services. Outsourcing to India continues to grow rapidly both in the 'low-end' (for example call centres) and 'high-end' (for example product R&D) segments. However, the impact of outsourcing has largely been through indirect means and not through direct employment. Consequently, while outsourcing will continue to be an important contributor to the overall economic picture, its role in poverty alleviation is likely to be small.

MILIND KANDLIKAR AND
ASHOK KOTWAL

REFERENCES
Bhagwati, J., A. Panagariya, and T.N. Srinivasan. 2004. 'The Muddles of Outsourcing', *The Journal of Economic Perspectives*, Fall.

McCarthy, J. 2004. 'Near Term Growth of Offshoring Accelerating: Resizing US Services Jobs Going Offshore', Cambridge, Forrester Research Inc., May.

Services-led Growth

The Indian economy has undergone major macroeconomic and structural reforms since the balance-of-payments crisis of 1991. Trade, foreign direct investment (FDI), and industrial policies have been liberalized and many restrictions have been completely dismantled. Institutional, legislative, and regulatory measures have been undertaken to improve macroeconomic management in the context of monetary, fiscal, and external-sector policies. The liberalization of the economy has helped put India on a higher growth trajectory, with growth averaging around 5 per cent during the 1990s, as opposed to the Hindu rate of growth of 3 per cent during the 1980s and in the previous decade. India was among the fastest-growing economies during the 1990s. The country's external-sector performance has also improved post-liberalization, with an increase in its share in world trade as well as FDI flows over the past decade.

The services sector has played an important role in enabling this improved economic performance on the domestic growth as well as external fronts during the post-reform period. Services have been the fastest-growing sector of the Indian economy over the past decade and have thus helped accelerate the overall growth rate of the economy. Services have also facilitated India's integration with the world economy through trade and capital flows. The phenomenal growth and export performance witnessed in services like information technology (IT) and business process outsourcing (BPO) have placed India on the global map as a major supplier of knowledge-based services. Services have also helped improve productivity in other sectors of the economy, thus contributing to an improvement in overall competitiveness.

This entry provides an overview of the trends in growth, employment, trade, and capital flows in India's services sector in recent years. It highlights the case of specific services where India is highly competitive and services that have undergone significant liberalization and structural change in the post-reform period. The entry concludes by assessing the sustainability of services-led growth in India and underlines the close link between the services sector's prospects and the success of the overall economic reform process in India.

GROWTH IN THE SERVICES SECTOR[1]

The services sector has exhibited phenomenal growth rates during the 1990s. Its average annual growth rate rose from 6.6 per cent during the 1980s to 7.5 per cent during the 1990s, and was as high as 7.9 per cent between 1994 and 2004. This was in contrast to the average growth rates exhibited in other sectors during the 1990s, with agriculture growing at 3 per cent per year and manufacturing at 5.3 per cent per year. Growth has, however, been uneven within the services sector. The driving segments have been business services (which include software and IT-enabled services), banking, and communication, which have grown at over 10 per cent per year on average during the 1990s, while services such as railways, public administration, and legal and real-estate services have grown more slowly during the 1990s compared to the previous decade. Figure 1 highlights the

[1]Most of the statistics presented in this section are based on Banga (2005), unless otherwise mentioned.

overall as well as sectoral growth rates in India for the 1994–2004 period.

The high growth rate of services has contributed to the sector's growing share in the overall economy. Between 1950 and 1990, agriculture's share in the gross domestic product (GDP) declined by around 25 per cent with the corresponding increase in the share of services and industry being distributed roughly evenly. However, since the 1990s, the share of industry in overall GDP has remained at around 27 per cent while the entire decline in the share of agriculture from 32 per cent to 22

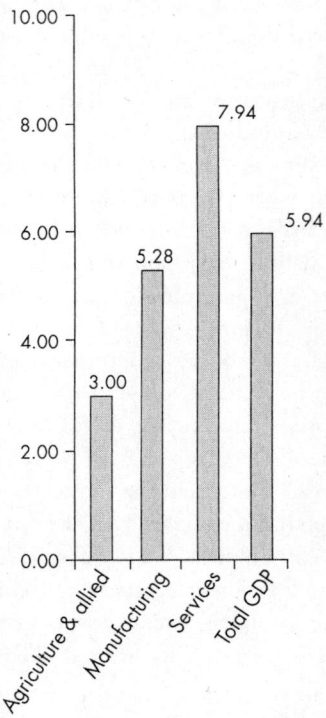

Figure 1   Average Sectoral Growth Rates in the Indian Economy 1994–2004 (percentage change)

Source: R. Banga. 2005. 'Critical Issues in Services-led Growth', Working Paper No. 171, New Delhi, Indian Council for Research on International Economic Relations, Figure 1, p. 8.

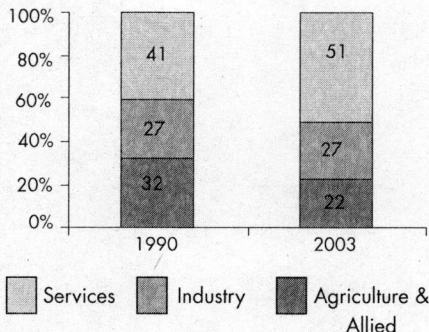

Figure 2   Composition of GDP across Sectors
(percentage shares)

Source: R. Banga. 2005. 'Critical Issues in Services-
led Growth', Working Paper No. 171, New Delhi,
Indian Council for Research on International
Economic Relations, Figure 3, p. 9.

per cent of GDP has been matched by a
corresponding rise in the share of services
in the economy. This is the contrast to other
developing economies, where the decline in
the share of agriculture in the GDP has been
followed by a corresponding rise in the share
of industry, in particular manufacturing,
and later in services. Thus, India seems to
be an aberration in terms of the services
sector having a much greater role in its
economy than in other countries at similar
or even higher levels of income. It appears
to have leapfrogged from the primary to the
tertiary sector. Figure 2 shows the relative
contributions of the primary, secondary, and
tertiary sectors to India's GDP and the shift
in this composition between 1990 and 2003
towards services.

The services sector's contribution to
overall employment has, however, lagged
behind its growth in output, and has in fact
declined during the 1990s. The share of
services in total employment was only 23
per cent in 1999–2000 compared to 35 per
cent in Thailand and 30 per cent in middle-
income economies. Thus growth in services
has not been accompanied by a concomitant

rise in service-sector employment. A
possible explanation for this trend is that
employment-intensive services, such as trade
and distribution or railways, have either
not grown that rapidly or have decelerated
while services such as communication
and business services, which are more
technology-intensive and which have
experienced productivity and technological
improvements, have grown more rapidly.

It is worth noting that Indian data on
services output and employment are subject
to many limitations. There are problems
with data collection, disaggregation, and
coverage. There is also no information
available on price indices for India's services
sector, as India's Wholesale Price Index
does not cover this sector. There are efforts
underway to improve statistical measurement
and coverage of services under the aegis of a
National Statistical Commission.

TRADE IN INDIA'S SERVICES SECTOR[2]

The contribution of services to India's
trade and FDI flows has also been growing
over the past decade, facilitating India's
integration with the world economy. India
has outperformed economies such as China
in the case of services trade. During the
1990s, India had the highest growth of
services exports among all economies, with
an average annual growth rate of 17.3 per
cent, compared to China at 15.8 per cent and
Taiwan at 8 per cent, and a world average of
5.6 per cent. Between 1997–8 and 2001–2,
India's services exports grew at an average
annual rate of 23 per cent compared to a
world average of 3.6 per cent. India's services
exports have grown from $9.7 billion in
1997–8 to $46 billion in 2004–5. Figure
3 highlights the rapid growth in India's

[2]Most of the statistics presented in this section
are based on World Bank (2004), unless otherwise
mentioned.

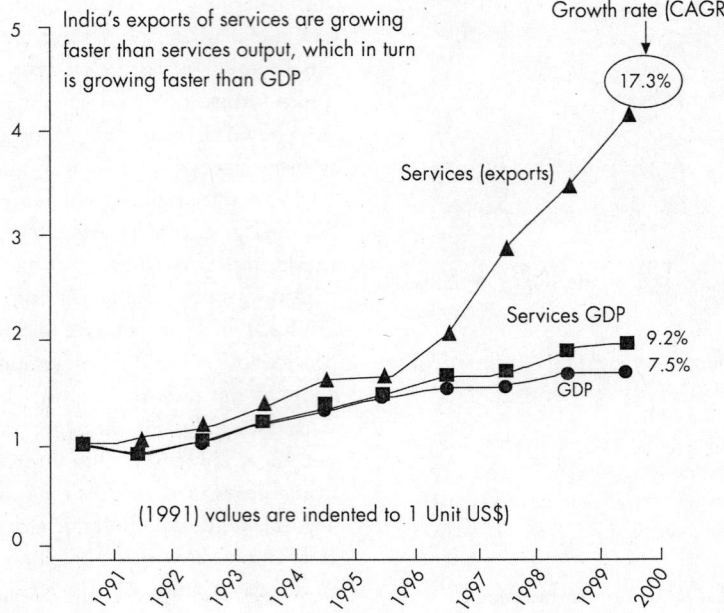

Figure 3   Trends in India's Services Output and Exports (1990s)

Source: World Bank. 2004. *Sustaining India's Services Revolution: Access to Foreign Markets, Domestic Reforms and International Negotiations*, New Delhi, Figure 1, p. 9. Based on World Bank Indicator and Balance of Payments Statistics Yearbook (2002).

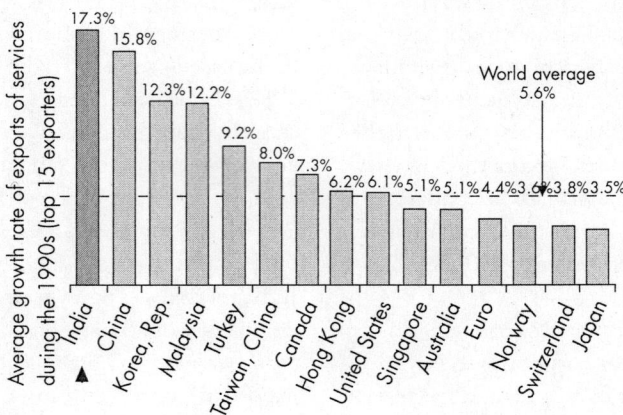

Figure 4   Relative Performance of India's Services Exports (1990s)

Source: World Bank. 2004. *Sustaining India's Services Revolution: Access to Foreign Markets, Domestic Reform and International Negotiations*, New Delhi, Figure 1, p. 9. Based on World Bank Indicator and Balance of Payments Statistics Yearbook (2002).

services output and exports and the strong export orientation of India's services sector over the past decade. Figure 4 illustrates the impressive export performance of India's services sector relative to other economies.

India's services exports have also grown much more rapidly than its merchandise exports. Between 1995 and 2000, India's services exports grew nearly six times faster than world exports of services (23.2 per cent compared to 3.7 per cent) while its merchandise exports grew much more slowly, at only 1.4 times the annual average growth rate for world exports of goods (5.4 per cent compared to 3.9 per cent). Segments such as software services registered growth rates of over 50 per cent in exports compared to less than 10 per cent for traditional exports such as textiles and clothing. Owing to such rapid growth in services exports, India has succeeded in raising its penetration of world markets more rapidly in the case of services than for goods. Its share in world services markets stood at 1.4 per cent in 2002–3 compared to 0.9 per cent for global merchandise exports.

Thus the evidence clearly indicates India's growing competitiveness in services relative to goods. This is supported by World Bank estimates of India's revealed comparative advantage (RCA) in services and goods, which show that between 1996 and 2000 the RCA for services increased by 74 per cent while that for goods declined by 15 per cent. Figure 5 illustrates the trends in India's RCA for services relative to goods.

India's services exports are quite broad based, including subsectors as varied as transport, travel, IT, business services, management, construction, communication, and financial services. There has, however, been a compositional shift in the structure of India's services exports away from traditional services such as transport and travel towards

India's RCA for goods and services export

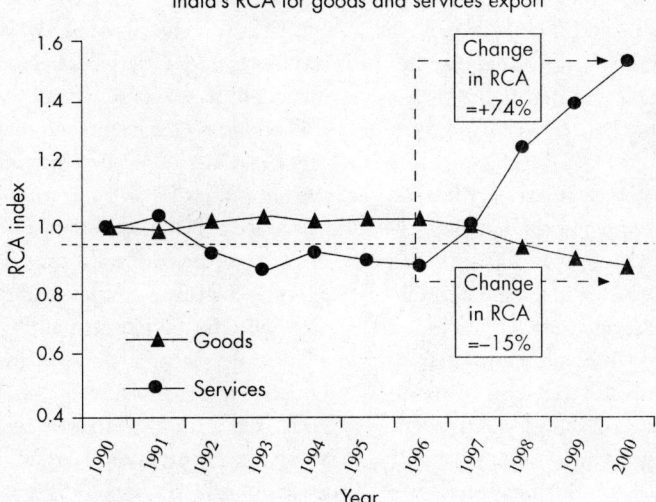

Figure 5   India's RCA in Services and Goods

Source: World Bank. 2004. *Sustaining India's Services Revolution: Access to Foreign Markets, Domestic Reforms and International Negotiations*, New Delhi, Figure 3, p. 11. Based on IMF's Balance of Payments Statistics Year Book (2002).

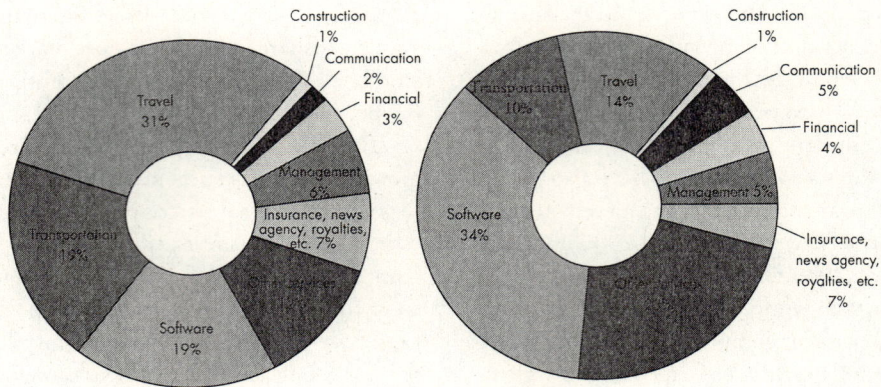

Figure 6   Composition of India's Service Exports 1997–8 and 2001–2

Source: World Bank. 2004. *Sustaining India's Services Revolution: Access to Foreign Markets, Domestic Reforms and International Negotiations,* New Delhi, Figure 4, p. 11. Based on RBI Bulletin.

emerging services such as software and other services, the latter mainly consisting of a wide variety of business services like advertising, exhibitions, engineering, accountancy, and health. The shares of services such as insurance, communication, and construction have remained more or less the same over this period. Figure 6 provides a breakdown of India's services exports in 1997–8 and 2001–2 and highlights the compositional shift that has occurred over this period.

The dissaggregated estimates for India's RCA for services exports explain this shift in the composition of India's services exports. The RCA index has risen sharply for other business services, which include software, consulting, management, financial, and communication services while it has fallen for traditional services like travel and transport. India's growing competitiveness in software services and business process outsourcing (BPO) has been particularly striking. Software services exports have risen from a mere $754 million in 1995–6 to $17.2 billion in 2004–5. BPO exports have risen from a mere $665 million in 1999–2000 to $6 billion in 2004–5 and are

projected to grow to $12 billion by 2008. These services have experienced growth rates of over 50 per cent in export earnings and turnover during the second half of the 1990s. Figure 7 provides the trends in the RCA index for different categories of services exports during the 1990s.

The growing role of software and business services in India's services-sector exports reflects India's comparative advantage in skill and knowledge-intensive labour-based services. On-site services provided through the temporary cross-border movement of service providers constitute around 40 per cent of the country's software service exports. Indian computer professionals accounted for 68 per cent and 63 per cent of all specialty occupation visas granted in the United States (alternatively known as H-1B visas, that is, non-immigrant visas given to persons with professional qualifications) in the computer-services category in 2001 and 2002 respectively. Even in other services, such as healthcare, architecture, engineering, and education, India is an important exporter through the movement of persons, featuring among the top five recipient countries in specialty occupation visas in the US for these

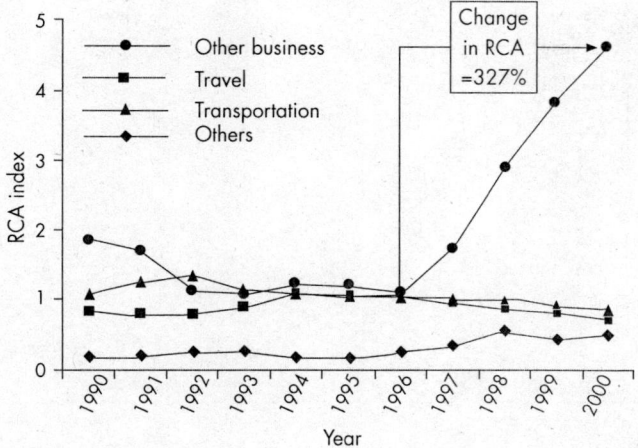

Figure 7   India's RCA for Selected Categories of Services Exports

Source: World Bank. 2004. *Sustaining India's Services Revolution: Access to Foreign Markets, Domestic Reforms and International Negotiations,* New Delhi, Figure 3, p. 11. Based on IMF's Balance of Payments Statistics Year Book (2002).
Notes: 1. Other business services include software exports, communication, management and consultancy services, financial services, construction, and news agency services.
2. Other services include insurance and government services.

service categories. India is also an important supplier of low- and semi-skilled services, especially to the Middle East and Gulf countries, in activities such as construction, transport operations, domestic help, nursing, and paramedical services.

India's growing presence in global BPO services is similarly based on its huge labour endowment, varied skill sets and low-cost but quality manpower coupled with a rapidly growing domestic IT industry. According to the *Financial Times*, half of the world's largest 500 companies and many government agencies contract out IT and business process work to India across a wide range of services, including medical and legal transcriptions, customer support, human-resource management and administration, financial and accounting processes, technical support, logistics, sales, and research and development (R&D), to name a few. According to a 2004 A.T. Kearney report,

India ranks highest among offshoring destinations.[3] Some Indian companies are also engaging in reverse outsourcing, offshoring part of their operations to other countries. The Indian BPO industry is projected to continue growing at double-digit annual growth rates over the medium term, raising India's share of the global BPO business from the current 2 per cent to 4.8 per cent by 2008.[4]

Apart from software and BPO services, there are emerging export opportunities in various other services, such as health, education, and tourism. There are concerted efforts underway to establish India as a hub for medical tourism services. Similarly, there is growing interest among Indian

[3]Discussion of India's attractiveness as an outsourcing destination and estimates of gains are largely based on the A.T. Kearney (2004) report.
[4]Based on NASSCOM Strategic Review Reports.

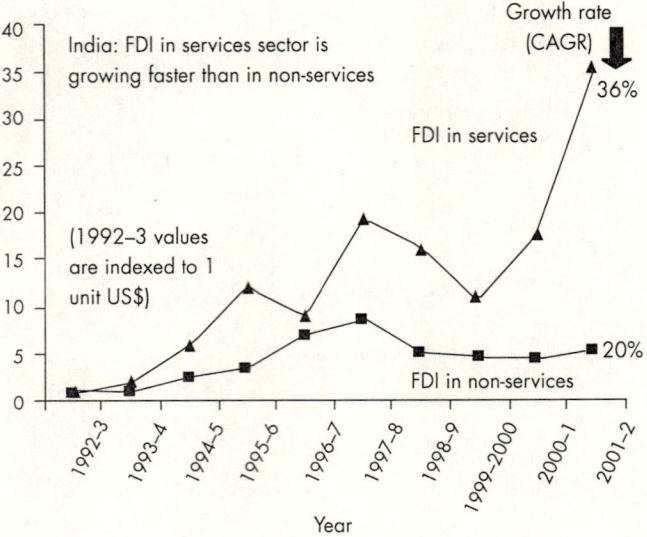

Figure 8   FDI in services and non-services (percentages)

Source: World Bank. 2004. *Sustaining India's Services Revolution: Access to Foreign Markets, Domestic Reforms and International Negotiations*, New Delhi, Figure 1, p. 9. Based on World Bank Indicator and Balance of Payments Statistics Yearbook (2002).

higher-education institutions in exporting education services through establishment of offshore campuses as well as twining and partnership arrangements. It is again worth noting that trade data on services are subject to problems of coverage and classification. Information is not available from the balance of payments at a sufficiently disaggregated level, particularly in the category of other services, to gauge trends and prospects for individual activities.

There are numerous domestic and external barriers to India's services exports. The main domestic barriers are in the form of infrastructural, financial, regulatory, technical, and standard-related constraints. The main external barriers are in the form of immigration and labour-market regulations, which limit India's ability to deliver on-site services. In addition, there has recently been a backlash against outsourcing in key markets like the US and

introduction of domestic regulations such as data privacy laws, which could affect India's BPO exports.

FOREIGN DIRECT INVESTMENT IN INDIA'S SERVICES SECTOR

As in the case of trade, there has also been a structural shift in FDI flows into India towards the services sector. The average share of services in FDI rose from 10.5 per cent for the 1990–4 period to 28.3 per cent during the 1995–9 period (World Investment Report 2004). FDI in services registered a cumulative average growth rate of 36 per cent between 1992–3 and 2001–2 compared to 20 per cent in the case of non-services. These inflows have, however, been directed to only a few services, namely telecommunication (mainly the cellular mobile segment) and financial services. Figure 8 illustrates the broad sectoral trends in FDI inflows in India over the 1992–3 and 2001–2 period.

Services are also accounting for a growing share of outward FDI flows from the Indian economy. Services constituted 45 per cent of total FDI outflows for the 1999–2003 period, with non-financial services, namely communication, software, and business services, being the main source sectors (World Investment Report 2004: 6). In segments like software and health services, Indian firms are increasingly emerging as exporters of capital, setting up overseas subsidiaries, establishments, and networks in developing and developed economies.

LIBERALIZATION OF SERVICES IN INDIA

Services have been a critical part of the overall economic reform and liberalization process in India. Much of the recent structural and institutional reforms as well as the liberalization/deregulation strategies have involved the opening up of key services such as telecommunications, banking, and insurance to attract much-needed foreign capital and technology, and to encourage competition and efficiency in these areas to induce positive externalities for the rest of the economy. Many services, including construction, tourism, health, and computer-related services, for instance, have been put on automatic approval route for FDI. Government monopoly in many critical services has been eliminated, with further liberalization planned or already announced.

Telecommunication services have experienced the greatest amount of liberalization. Today, fully owned foreign firms are allowed in some segments of the telecom sector, government monopoly in long-distance telephony and Internet has been eliminated, and there is no restriction on the number of providers. FDI in voice telephony services has been permitted with a ceiling of 49 per cent foreign-equity participation and a proposal to raise

the equity cap to 74 per cent. Similarly, government monopoly in the insurance-services sector has been eliminated and the sector has been opened up to private players, with a foreign-equity ceiling of 26 per cent through joint ventures and possibly 49 per cent in the near future. Banking services have also been liberalized with a 74 per cent ceiling on foreign equity in private banks and a 20 per cent ceiling on FDI and portfolio investment in public-sector banks (World Bank 2004).

However, there remain several services, such as distribution, legal, accountancy, and air transport, where policies towards foreign commercial presence as well as presence of foreign service suppliers, remain restrictive. For example, retail distribution until recently was closed to foreign firms and sensitivities in this sector still preclude speedy liberalization due to strong trader lobby opposition and concerns about employment and equity. Likewise, legal and accountancy services remain closed to foreign firms and service providers due to regulatory capture by concerned regulatory bodies. Although air-transport services have been partly opened up to FDI, current policy does not allow any equity stake by a foreign airline, in order to limit competition to the state-owned airlines. Thus there is considerable scope for further opening up of many parts of India's services sector.

Evidence suggests that services that have been liberalized most have typically experienced higher growth rates. Figure 9 indicates the positive correlation between the degree of liberalization in the services sector with regard to trade and FDI policies and its access to external markets, and the growth exhibited in that sector with regard to output and employment opportunities. Areas such as business services (mainly IT and IT-enabled services), communication, banking, and insurance, which have been liberalized,

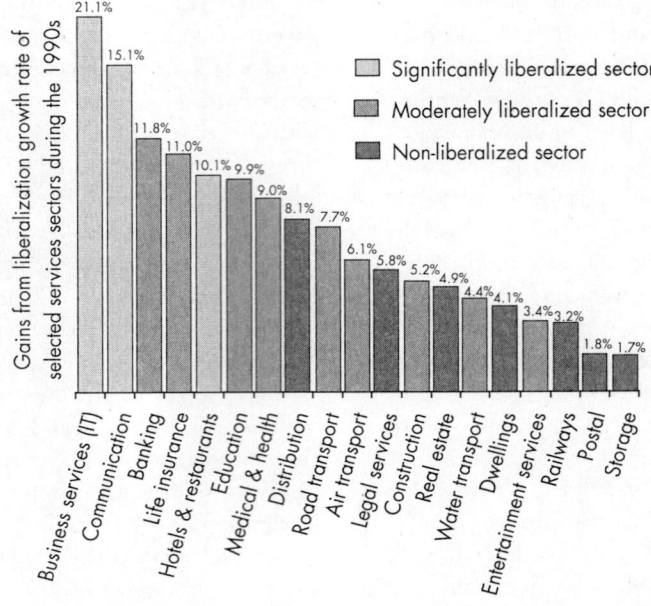

Figure 9   Liberalization and Growth Linkages in India's Services Sector

Source: World Bank. 2004. *Sustaining India's Services Revolution: Access to Foreign Markets, Domestic Reforms and International Negotiations*, New Delhi, Figure 6, p. 16. Based on staff estimates and CSO statistics.

have exhibited higher growth rates, with wider efficiency and growth benefits to the rest of the economy. On the other hand, services with limited opening, like air-transport, legal, and real-estate services, have grown much more slowly, with likely adverse effects on economy-wide competitiveness and growth performance.

Productivity estimates also corroborate the role played by competition and integration with global markets in improving efficiency in the services sector. Estimates by McKinsey indicate that telecommunications and software services have much higher productivity levels than other services sectors in India, owing to factors such as global and domestic competition and changes in ownership structure, which have in turn enabled technological externalities, knowledge spillovers, improved management practices, and technology diffusion. In

addition, liberalization in certain services has also impacted positively on export opportunities.

For instance, the opening up of areas like telecommunications to FDI has had a positive impact on export opportunities in IT and BPO services. Evidence also indicates increased usage of services in manufacturing and resulting productivity gains in India's manufacturing sector. Further liberalization of the services sector is likely to yield sector-specific and economy-wide gains in terms of growth, export, efficiency, and competitiveness.

INDIA AND TRADE NEGOTIATIONS IN SERVICES

India is actively involved in the World Trade Organization (WTO) negotiations on services. In view of the various barriers that affect India's key modes of export interest,

India has taken a proactive position in the services negotiations on temporary cross-border movement of service providers (mode 4) and cross-border supply of services (mode 1) under the General Agreement on Trade in Services (GATS). It has made a joint submission along with some other developing countries for a Service Provider Visa under GATS, which would expand and ensure more predictable and transparent market access for intracompany transferees, contractual service suppliers, and independent professionals. It has also submitted a joint proposal for securing market access in outsourcing through binding commitments in mode 1 across a wide range of services so as to pre-empt further protectionism in this area.[5]

There is in turn growing pressure on India by the main developed countries to make binding and more liberal commitments on commercial presence (GATS mode 3) across a wide range of services. India has received requests to multilaterally bind in the liberalization it has undertaken autonomously in sectors such as banking, insurance, and telecommunications and also to schedule other sectors such as distribution and education services, which it had not committed earlier. Several developed countries have requested India to open up areas like retail distribution, higher education, legal, and accountancy services to foreign commercial presence. Thus far India has taken a quid pro quo approach to the services negotiations, that is, exchanging commitments on foreign commercial presence against securing its market access interests in modes 1 and 4. However, in its latest services offer under the Doha round of

services negotiations, India has significantly improved upon its earlier commitments on commercial presence, despite its failure to secure its market-access interests in mode 4. India also endorsed plurilateral negotiations in services following the 2005 Hong Kong Ministerial Conference so as to expedite services negotiations.

The service sector is also playing an important role in India's bilateral and regional trade negotiations. The recently signed Indo-Singapore Comprehensive Economic Cooperation Agreement (CECA) attempts to facilitate investment by Singaporean companies in India in areas like financial, telecommunications, transport and real-estate services, and promote exports by India to Singapore in areas like IT, engineering, accountancy, healthcare, and BPO services through movement of service suppliers and outsourcing. The prospective Indo-ASEAN is similarly being perceived as a means for promoting the synergies of interests between India and ASEAN in the services sector.

The preceding discussion clearly highlights that the service sector has not only outperformed other sectors of the Indian economy, but has also played an important role in India's integration with world trade and capital markets. There is, however, growing debate within the country about the sustainability of a services-led growth process. No country in history has been able to grow rapidly in a sustained manner based on services alone. The manufacturing sector has always been part of the growth success. Hence it remains to be seen whether this model of growth also holds for India or not. The prevailing view today is that India needs broad-based growth as its services sector is largely driven by external demand. If high growth is to be sustained within services, then creation of internal demand is necessary and this is only

[5]Discussion of India's strategic interests in the WTO negotiations on services and proposals submitted is based on Chanda (2004)

possible with a vibrant manufacturing sector. Moreover, employment concerns cannot be addressed without concomitant growth in manufacturing since, as highlighted earlier, the faster-growing services are those that are not generating sufficient growth in employment opportunities for the masses. More broad-based growth *within* the services sector is required. Services such as trade and distribution, tourism, and construction, which have high employment intensities and large backward and forward linkages with other sectors need to grow more rapidly. In this regard, further infrastructural and regulatory reforms and FDI liberalization in services can help diversify the sources of growth within India's services sector and provide the required momentum.

RUPA CHANDA

REFERENCES

Banga, R. 2005. 'Critical Issues in Services-led Growth', Working Paper No. 171, New Delhi, Indian Council for Research on International Economic Relations.

Chanda, R. 2004. 'Movement of Natural Persons: A Case Study of South Asian Countries', Research Report, Jaipur, CUTS Centre for International Trade, Economics, and Environment.

NASSCOM. 2002, 2003. *The IT Industry in India: Strategic Review*, New Delhi.

World Bank. 2004. *Sustaining India's Services Revolution: Access to Foreign Markets, Domestic Reform and International Negotiations*, New Delhi.

World Investment Report. 2004. *The Shift towards Services*, New York and Geneva, United Nations.

Tourism

Tourism has come a long way from the luxury good it was perceived to be in the centrally planned Indian economy of the post-Independence era. It received little attention from the government until the 1960s, after which its foreign-exchange-generating potential was recognized in a closed economy severely short of foreign exchange. At the time, tourism infrastructure and services were limited and only the government had the resources, or indeed the incentive, to invest in these. But committing resources to tourism meant diverting them from areas such as agriculture and infrastructure, which were in dire need of investment. This called for very focused development of tourism, aimed mainly at generating foreign exchange, and an implicit decision was taken to attract high-end foreign tourists by investing in air capacity and luxury accommodation like the Ashok Hotel in New Delhi. In 1966, the government set up the India Tourism Development Corporation (ITDC) to promote the country as a tourist destination abroad, and to develop a hotel network for these tourists.

Domestic tourism at the time consisted mainly of pilgrimages and visits to relatives, with some of the wealthier people travelling to hill stations during summer to stay in circuit houses, summer rentals, or second homes. The government did little to actively encourage domestic travel, but took the more passive stance of setting up State Tourism Development Corporations and tourist offices, building some low-cost accommodation, and providing rail and bus services to the more popular destinations, mainly catering to lower-end travellers. It was the expansion of the leave travel concession (LTC) schemes—where government employees were encouraged to travel once a year with their families—which gave the initial boost to non-pilgrimage-based domestic tourism in the country.

Since then, the domestic tourism market has grown rapidly from an estimated 14 million in 1981 to 135 million in 1995, 220 million in 2000, and 309 million in 2003 (Ministry of Tourism 2004). (Domestic travel statistics are not as reliable as international arrivals data, as they are based on information collected by state departments of tourism, but they show a clear upward trend.) 'Attending social functions' has replaced 'pilgrimage visits' as the most common reason for travel, but this is followed closely by leisure and business travel (ibid.). The more recent rapid rise in domestic travel has been fuelled by the growing middle class, expansion in privately funded accommodation across all price ranges from *dharamshalas* to heritage palaces, and declining airfares in the wake of airline deregulation and competition.

International travel to India, in contrast, despite being the focus of tourism policy and programmes for the last forty years, has remained at almost the same level for the last decade. While domestic tourism within the country now accounts for a 4.6 per cent share of domestic tourism worldwide (2004), India's share of the world market has remained almost stagnant at 0.38 per cent since 1995 (Ministry of Tourism 2004). Between 1998 and 2003, international arrivals have hovered around 2.4 million to 2.7 million (of approximately 700 million total global arrivals), a large proportion of whom were non-resident Indians (NRIs) (ibid.).[1]

[1]International arrivals are used as a proxy for international tourism, but the data are an overestimate as they include all foreign visitors, both leisure and business, and refer to the actual number of arrivals into the country even if they are multiple trips made by one individual. The World Travel and Tourism Council (WTTC) estimates that around 8 per cent of international visitors come to India for business (WTTC 2004). However, Ministry of Tourism figures estimate that around 4 per cent visit for business.

Thus, despite its tremendous richness as a cultural, historical, and adventure tourist destination, India lags behind its neighbours such as Indonesia, which received around 4.5 to 5 million tourists between 1998 and 2003, Thailand, which received 7.8 to 10 million tourists, and Malaysia, which received between 5.5 and 13 million in the same period (World Tourism Organization website). Interestingly, for every foreign visitor to the country, more than twice as many Indians travel abroad. With the easing of travel permits and foreign exchange restrictions, the number of Indians going abroad has grown from 1.9 million in 1991 to 4.9 million in 2002 (ibid.).

Till recently, tourism was considered an elitist activity conducted primarily to earn foreign exchange. It is only recently, in the National Tourism Policy of 2002, that the industry's potential as a catalyst for growth and employment generation has been recognized. Strong linkages between tourism and almost all sectors imply that the multiplier effect of tourism-related expenditure is very high, especially till the mid-1990s when the leakage rate (through tourism-related imports) was one of the lowest in the world, as strict foreign exchange controls meant that almost all inputs were sourced domestically. Tourism-related services today (2004) directly and indirectly employ 25 million people (WTTC 2004).

India's low share in the world tourism market and its poor performance compared to other developing countries have largely been a result of infrastructural constraints. Most foreign tourists (more than 30 per cent in 2003) (Ministry of Tourism 2003) originate from the UK or US, and high airfares, relative to comparable Asian destinations are a major deterrent to travellers. Travel within the country is hampered by the poor road network linking many tourist circuits, overcrowded trains, and expensive air travel. Most large Indian cities have very little by way of budget accommodation, unlike Asian competitors such as Jakarta, Bangkok, and Kuala Lumpur, because of the high cost of commercial real estate and cumbersome land acquisition process. In Mumbai, for example, procuring a licence to build a hotel involves more than a hundred applications.

Many of these problems arise from the shared responsibility for basic tourism infrastructure between the central and state governments which has worked against the integrated development of the industry. Also, state governments control many areas crucial to tourism—local infrastructure, transport systems, municipal taxation, sanitation, law and order, and the preservation of local monuments—and their commitment has varied over time and across states. This lack of planning is most evident in the popular hill resorts of the past, many of which have lost their intrinsic tourist appeal by becoming sprawling urban clusters, facing major environmental problems. While private investment has increased in many parts of the industry such as hotels, airlines and road transport, and in areas that impinge on tourism services such as sanitation and telecommunications, bureaucratic red-tape and convoluted administrative procedures are still a strong deterrent.

Despite these drawbacks tourism continues to be an evolving, dynamic industry with new initiatives that have captured the interest of travellers. These include rural homestays combined with village tourism, which originated in Kerala but have been successfully replicated in Sikkim and other parts of the north-east; heritage tourism which has encouraged the restoration of *havelis*, forts, and palaces,

especially in Rajasthan and Madhya Pradesh; and mountain and adventure sports, such as river rafting, trekking, and rappelling. A 'Buddhist circuit' spanning several states is still evolving, but is becoming popular among visitors from the region, especially from East Asia. An emerging area that has received a boost through the new super-specialty hospitals is 'medical tourism', where patients visit the country for surgery and then recuperate in a resort of their choice. An estimated 150,000 medical tourists visited India in 2003. Changing demographics and widening price differentials in medical care between the US/Europe and India are expected to boost the Indian medical tourism industry to a $ 1 billion business by 2012 (CII–McKinsey Study on Healthcare 2004).

If managed well, these new ventures should lead to a more environmentally and culturally sustainable development of tourism than the random, unplanned path taken earlier, which has drastically affected the environment of the popular hill stations of the past.

ANURADHA BHASIN

REFERENCES

CII-McKinsey Study on Healthcare. 2004. Quoted in www.embassyofindia.com/IndiaNewsMay2004.

Ministry of Tourism. Various years. Tourism Statistics. Market Research Division, Government of India.

World Travel and Tourism website (wttc.org).

World Tourism Organization website (world-tourism.org).

World Tourism Organization. 2004. Compendium of Tourism Statistics 2004.

World Travel and Tourism Council (WTTC). 2004. *India Travel and Tourism: Forging Ahead 2004*, Travel and Tourism Economic Research.

FINANCIAL SECTOR

Banking

The banking structure that India inherited at Independence in 1947 suffered from two major drawbacks: (i) interlocking of directorships of industry houses and banks and (ii) paucity of credit to socially and economically important sectors of the economy. The numerous problems arising in the wake of these drawbacks provided the economic rationale for the momentous decision to nationalize fourteen private banks in 1969, as well as for the subsequent nationalization of six more banks in 1980. The post-nationalization phase was characterized by a strategy of massive expansion of the banking network coupled with stipulations on sectoral lending. Even today, when the euphoria over nationalization has given way to considerable skepticism, it cannot be denied that the liberal branch-licensing norms coupled with a system of directed credit stipulations, made a significant dent in rural and (to some extent) urban poverty and mitigated the dependence of the socially and economically disadvantaged groups on the indigenous moneylenders. Additionally, many would agree that the system did contribute to rapid growth by providing timely and concessional credit to several industrial sectors.

However, the strict regulation over banks' lending, combined with extensive regulation of interest rates across the entire maturity spectrum, also paved the way for the banking sector to be increasingly cast in the role of 'handmaiden' to government policies. The high cash reserve ratios (CRRs) and statutory liquidity ratios (SLRs), though ostensibly serving the purposes of credit regulation, financial stability, and inflation control, adversely impacted the profitability of banks and represented a substantial (about 63.5 per cent) pre-emption of bank resources. Additionally, the administered interest rate structure assumed, over time, an extremely complex character, with rates being distinguished according to bank size, maturity profile, and economic conditions, which permitted only a limited role for market forces in the pricing and allocation of credit. It was inevitable that such a highly regulated banking system should get riddled with administrative inefficiencies and red-tape. The constellation of economic features resulting from these developments is usually subsumed under the rubric of 'financial repression'.

A process of liberalization of the economy was initiated in India in 1991–2, which aimed at raising the allocative efficiency of available savings, improving the return on investments, and promoting accelerated and equitable growth of the real sector. Towards this end, a multi-pronged reform strategy was initiated, encompassing all areas of economic activity. In the financial sector, specifically, the thrust of the reforms was to promote a diversified, efficient,

Table 1 Structure of the Indian Banking System: Number of Institutions and Aggregate Assets

(as on March 2004)

Institution	Number of institutions	Total assets (Rs billion)	Per cent to total assets
Banking sector (1 + 2)		23,473	100.0
1. Commercial banks (a + b)	291	20,459	87.2
(a) Scheduled commercial banks	286	20,457	87.2
Public-sector banks	27	14,714	62.7
Private-sector banks	30	3672	15.6
Foreign banks	33	1353	5.8
Regional rural banks	196	707	3.0
(b) Non-scheduled commercial banks	4	2	0.01
2. Cooperative banks (a + b)	3111	3015	12.8
(a) Rural cooperative banks	1185	1790	7.6
(b) Urban cooperative banks	1926	1226	5.2

Source: Reserve Bank of India (RBI).

and competitive financial system. While these reforms were underway, the world economy also witnessed significant changes, coinciding with the movement towards global integration of financial services.

Before turning to an appraisal of banking reforms in India, it may be helpful to have a helicopter view of the Indian banking sector. Conventionally, the sector is classified into two broad categories: commercial banks and cooperative banks. The various sub-components of these two categories, together with two broad indicators of their relative significance (namely number of institutions and asset size), are presented in Table 1.[1] The exclusive focus of this entry is on the commercial banking system which currently accounts for over 85 per cent of the assets of the banking sector.

BANKING REFORMS: SOME GENERAL CONSIDERATIONS

The first phase of financial-sector reforms in India was guided by the recommendations of the Committee on the Financial System

[1]Cooperative banks belong to a different genre with distinct institutional and governance characteristics, and hence are not explicitly dealt with in our analysis.

(Chairman: Mr M. Narasimham). Several features of the reform process deserve mention (Reddy 2004). First, financial-sector reforms were undertaken early in the economic reform cycle. Second, reforms in the financial sector were initiated in a well-structured, sequenced, and phased manner and were not crisis induced, although the balance-of-payments (BOP) problems in 1991 did provide the wake-up call. Third, a consultative approach towards policy formulation was adopted, which not only enabled benchmarking of the financial services against international best standards in a transparent manner, but also provided useful lead time to market players for smooth adjustment to regulatory changes. Importantly, unlike the 'stop–go' approach adopted in several Latin American and Asian economies, the Indian approach to financial-sector reforms has been marked by 'gradualism' so as to ensure a smooth, non-disruptive, and transparent approach to the process (Ahluwalia 2002).

It seems useful to classify the liberalization process of Indian banking as the confluence of three distinct but mutually reinforcing sets of factors: (a) liberalization imperatives, (b) stimuli arising from domestic forces, and

(c) stimuli from external forces. This compartmentalization is, however, not watertight and more often than not, might reflect overlapping considerations. The details of Indian banking reforms are presented in Box I.

Box I: Banking Reforms in India

Liberalization Imperatives
+ Sharp reduction in CRR and SLR.
+ Dismantling of administered interest rates (with a few exceptions).
+ Market-determined pricing for government securities.
+ Measures to strengthen risk management through recognition of different components of risk, assignment of risk-weights to various asset classes, norms on connected lending, risk concentration, application of *mark-to-market* principle for investment portfolio, and limits on deployment of fund in sensitive activities.

Stimulus from Domestic Forces
+ Granting of operational autonomy and broad-basing ownership in public-sector banks by allowing them to raise capital up to 49 per cent of equity.
+ Enhanced transparency and disclosure norms to facilitate market discipline.
+ Introduction of pure inter-bank call money market, auction-based repos/reverse repos for short-term liquidity management, facilitation of improved payments and settlement mechanisms.

Stimulus from External Forces
+ Introduction of norms on risk-based capital standards, accounting conventions, income recognition, asset classification, provisioning, and exposure.
+ Transparent norms for entry of new private-sector banks, liberalized entry for foreign banks and insurance companies, permission for foreign investment in banks through foreign direct investment (FDI)/portfolio investment, permission to banks to diversify their product portfolios and business activities.
+ Setting up of *Lok Adalats* (people's courts), debt-recovery tribunals, asset-reconstruction companies, settlement-advisory committees, corporate-debt-restructuring mechanisms, etc. for quicker loan recovery/restructuring. The promulgation of the Securitization and Reconstruction of Financial Assets and Enforcement of Securities Interest (SARFAESI) Act and its subsequent amendment to ensure creditor rights.
+ Introduction of the CAMELS supervisory rating system, move towards risk-based supervision, consolidated supervision of financial conglomerates, and strengthening of off-site surveillance through technology-driven control returns.
+ Strengthening corporate governance, enhanced 'due diligence' on important shareholders, and 'fit and proper' tests for directors.
+ Institution of Credit Information Bureau for information sharing on defaulters as also other borrowers.
+ Establishment of Clearing Corporation of India Limited (CCIL) to act as the central counterparty for facilitating payments and settlement system relating to fixed income securities and money market instruments.
+ Setting up of INFINET as the communication backbone for the financial sector, introduction of Negotiated Dealing System (NDS) for screen-based trading in government securities and introduction of a Real Time Gross Settlement System (RTGS).

Source: Adapted from Rakesh Mohan. 2005. 'Financial Sector Reforms in India: Politics and Performance Analysis', *Economic and Political Weekly*, 40(12): 1106–21.

Table 2   Performance Indicators of Indian Commercial Banks

(as per cent of total assets)

Bank group	1980– 91	1992– 6	1997– 2001	2001– 2	2002– 3	2003– 4
Operating expense	2.53	2.74	2.64	2.19	2.24	2.20
Spread	1.90	2.94	2.87	2.57	2.77	2.86
Net profit	0.15	–0.16	0.61	0.75	1.01	1.13

Source: RBI.

The net impact of these policy changes is gradually getting reflected in the financial performance of banks. That banks have been able to cope successfully with the new liberalized environment is evident from the marked improvement in their standard performance indicators, as shown in Table 2.

Spurred by the gradual tightening of prudential norms over the years (reflecting an increasing convergence towards international best practices as detailed in Basel II), there has been considerable improvement in two other traditional areas of concern. The overall capital adequacy ratio of commercial banks, which was 10.40 per cent in 1996–7 has since trended upwards to reach 12.9 per cent in 2003–4. Likewise, improved recovery management and better risk assessment has resulted in a steady decline in the non-performing loans of banks, which, as a percentage of total loans, have halved over the last decade from 15.7 per cent to 7.8 per cent.

EMERGING ISSUES

Crystal ball gazers of the economy would have no difficulty in foreseeing that the Indian banking industry is poised for fundamental structural transformation in the coming years. The reasons for such a prognostication are manifold but could be condensed to four basic sets of factors: (1) liberalization of trade in financial services under World Trade Organization (WTO) auspices, (2) autonomous diffusion of information technology, (3) international harmonization of financial standards involving improved levels of transparency and disclosure, and (4) greater emphasis on governance through shareholder value creation. These four basic factors, acting singly and in combination, are the major drivers of the various changes that are being envisaged for the Indian banking sector in the future. We briefly survey some of these emerging issues.

Consolidation

The liberalization under way has as yet not impinged significantly on the structure of the Indian banking system. The consolidation process witnessed within the industry in recent years has primarily been confined to a few mergers in the private sector—often a response to localized bank failures. However, the rapid growth in global trade and investment flows has opened up avenues for cross-border financing of economic activities, propelling the inducement for cross-border mergers of banks, to avail of mutual location and business-specific complementarities. Technology developments have facilitated the integration of global transactions and in the process introduced substantial economies of scale. Recognizing the imperatives of consolidation, efforts have been initiated by the government and the RBI to iron out the various legal impediments inherent in the process.

Competition and FDI in the Banking Sector

The post-liberalization phase has also seen the emergence of newer competitive forces in the largely public-sector-dominated Indian banking scenario. So far these forces have been confined to a highly modernized and efficient domestic private banking sector, but in the wake of the WTO commitments to terminate most restrictions on foreign banks in a phased manner, these are very likely to exhibit a dramatic growth in their presence in India (going by the experience of other emerging market economies embarking on similar relaxations in the early 1990s). The WTO commitments would terminate most of these restrictions in a phased manner.

A related issue bears on the rules governing FDI in Indian banks, which have also been considerably liberalized in the last few years. Until recently, minority foreign participation by foreign banking companies as technical collaborators or co-promoters through the Foreign Investment Promotion Board (FIPB) route in private-sector Indian banks was restricted to 20 per cent. The limit was raised to 49 per cent in May 2001 (and subsequently to 74 per cent in 2004). Foreign banks having branch presence in India are also made eligible for FDI in private-sector banks subject to an overall cap of 49 per cent. One of the major demands of foreign investors has been the removal of the 10 per cent cap on their voting rights in the management of banks, and available indications point to the amendment of this limitation in the near future.

Several concerns, however, attend the issue of liberalization of the entry norms for foreign banks (and FDI in the banking sector). First, in view of the well-known tendency of foreign banks to 'cherry-pick' the loans market, a large foreign presence could leave domestic banks saddled with less creditworthy customers, increasing the overall risk of domestic bank portfolios. Second, the supervision of the more sophisticated activities of foreign banks and monitoring of their new products

entails a continuous challenge for regulatory authorities. Another important supervisory issue is whether depositors in foreign banks should be entitled to the same degree of protection as depositors in domestic banks and whether the central bank of the host country should extend the 'lender of last resort' umbrella to foreign banks facing illiquidity crises. There is also the possible threat of excessive concentration, since foreign subsidiaries backed by their parent corporations (often 'banking behemoths') could exert substantive market power and extract higher interest margins in the domestic market. Finally, it should be highlighted that the admission of foreign subsidiaries should be accompanied by the removal of all discriminatory practices vis-à-vis domestic banks.[2]

Credit Delivery

In recent years, it is being increasingly recognized that large segments of the rural population face 'financial exclusion' from the formal banking sector, and continue their traditional dependence on the informal sector. Two areas in particular have been of concern to policymakers: priority-sector lending and timely flow of credit to the needy and deserving.

As regards the first, over the years, the definition of the priority sector has been gradually enlarged, interest rates on priority-sector lending increasingly left to market forces (except for a cap on small loans), and alternate avenues of investment permitted, thus making priority lending far more flexible than before (at the cost of some deviation from its original avowed purpose), in line

[2]Some of the current discriminatory practices operate against foreign banks (for example, ban on accepting public-sector company deposits and higher tax rates), others operate in their favour (lower priority-sector lending requirements and exemption from rural-branching stipulation).

with the major recommendations of the Advisory Committee on Flow of Credit to Agriculture and Related Activities from the Banking System (Chairman: Mr V.S. Vyas).

As regards the issue of credit delivery, the 'lending inertia' on the part of mid-sized commercial banks has been well documented in an influential study (Banerjee et al. 2005). In recognition of this fact, recent policies have placed explicit emphasis on streamlining credit delivery through a gamut of measures including, inter alia, (i) widening the scope of infrastructure lending, (ii) revamping the rural credit-delivery system by envisaged restructuring of the rural banking segment, (iii) widening the scope of priority-sector lending, (iv) introduction of innovative instruments on the lines of *Kisan* Credit Cards buttressed with various value-added features, and (v) according all possible encouragement for forging of appropriate public–private partnerships in the field of micro-finance activities.[3]

Finally, there is the long-felt imperative to streamline and coordinate the activities of the four major institutions involved in the rural credit structure: (a) commercial banks, (b) a three-tier federal cooperative banking system (with the state cooperative banks at state level, district cooperative central banks at district level, and primary agricultural credit societies at village level), (c) the state cooperative agriculture and rural development banks with the primary cooperative agriculture and rural development banks affiliated to them, and (d) finally the regional rural banks (RRBs). Action on this front by the authorities is presently under way.

[3]Self-help groups (SHGs) formed by non-government organizations and financed by banks represent an important pillar of this development process.

Corporate Governance

The issue of corporate governance has come to the fore in the current liberalized environment where banks are expected to function as commercial entities with explicit emphasis on shareholder value creation. The commercial character of banks is getting increasing emphasis with more and more banks getting listed on the stock exchange, and the proposed lowering of government stockholdings in banks to a minimum of 33 per cent (first envisaged in the Union Budget 2000–1) would reinforce this character apart from providing bank boards with greater flexibility. The quality of corporate governance in banks in the emerging scenario would be crucially guided by their ability to find suitable qualified and independent professionals to serve on their boards.

Risk Management

In the highly regulated and protected financial environment of the pre-reform era, risk management was a secondary issue for the public-sector-dominated banking system. The picture has changed drastically with the deregulation and liberalization of the financial system.

So far as 'credit risk' is concerned, the envisaged introduction of 'core banking' solutions would enable banks to segregate the credit-sourcing (front office) and appraisal (back office) functions, which can, over time, build up expertise and monitor credit migrations on a bankwide basis, a key factor behind the application of the Basel II approach (Nacharre et al. 2005). The use of dynamic credit-scoring models coupled with the full-fledged operationalization of the Credit Bureau would enable banks to switch from traditional proprietary models to newer methods of credit evaluation to reflect the repayment and recovery experience across a spectrum of asset classes and spatial locations.

The recent reversal of the soft interest rate regime has also raised concerns about the interest-rate risks in banks' portfolios, in view of their large holdings of government securities. It appears very likely that banks will be exposed to increasing market risk on their debt investment portfolios. Additionally, in view of the increased regulatory capital allocation for market risk in the future, most banks would need to bolster their capital position. All these considerations underline the fact that banks need to put in place appropriate risk-management processes (such as Value-at-Risk models) to not only identify the risks, but also to effectively measure, monitor, and manage them.

TECHNOLOGY AND HUMAN RESOURCES

The success of Indian banks in capitalizing on future opportunities will critically depend on how well they are able to harness emerging trends in global technology to their advantage. The increasing sophistication, flexibility, and complexity of financial products and services makes the effective use of technology critical for managing the risks associated with banking business. Additionally, technology becomes the key factor in servicing almost all customer segments. Of course the rate of technology adoption is crucially constrained by the availability of trained personnel, so that investment in human resources by banks may be viewed as largely complementary to investment in technology.

The Indian financial system has exhibited a fair degree of resilience in responding to structural adjustments; nevertheless, a marked tendency towards slippages has also been evident with even slight relaxations of the regulatory leash. The 'bang-bang' approach to financial-sector liberalization, a hallmark of several Latin American and even Asian economies in the 1980s, was, more often than not, marked by reform reversals with substantial social and economic costs. Adoption of such an approach, in spite of being advocated by influential sections of domestic and global opinion could well prove counterproductive and impose 'collateral damage', especially on the poorer sections, with limited access to hedging opportunities. As in other areas of reforms, 'gradualism' seems the ideal prescription.

DILIP M. NACHANE, SAIBAL GHOSH,
AND PARTHA RAY

REFERENCES

Ahluwalia, M.S. 2002. 'Economic Reforms in India since 1991: Has Gradualism Worked?', *Journal of Economic Perspectives*, 16: 67–88.

Banerjee, Abhijit V., Shawn Cole, and Esther Duflo. 2005. 'Banking Reform in India', *India Policy Forum*, MIT, Brookings Institution.

Burgess, Robin and Rohini Pande. 2005. 'Can Rural Banks Reduce Poverty? Evidence from the Indian Social Banking Experiment', *American Economic Review*, 93(3): 780–95.

Caprio, G. and R. Levine. 2002. 'Corporate Governance in Banks: Concepts and International Observations', paper presented at the Global Corporate Governance Research Forum, April.

Nachane, Dilip M., Partha Ray, and Saibal Ghosh. 2005. 'The New Basel Capital Accord: Rationale, Design and Tentative Implications for India', in K. Parikh and R. Radhakrishna, eds, *India Development Report 2004–05*, New Delhi, Oxford University Press, pp. 171–90.

Reddy, Y. Venugopal. 2004. 'Monetary and Financial Sector Reforms in India: A Practitioner's Perspectives', in Kaushik Basu, ed., *India's Emerging Economy: Performance and Prospects in the 1990s and Beyond*, Cambridge, Massachusetts, MIT Press; New Delhi, Oxford University Press.

Reserve Bank of India (RBI). 1983. *Reserve Bank of India: Function and Workings*, Mumbai, RBI.

Credit Market Regulation, Evolution of

Development economists are well aware of several theoretical reasons why in an underdeveloped society the free hand of the market may fail to direct much-needed and scarce credit to its most productive use. Moreover, the asymmetry of power between the moneylender and borrower in such societies often results in the former enjoying excessive rents to the detriment of the latter. Hence, attempts to regulate usury[1] are pervasive in legal traditions around the world and India is no exception. In this entry I shall trace the origins and evolution of the legal framework under which the credit markets in India operate. The historical experience of credit market regulation is particularly instructive for the regulatory reforms currently underway. While the term 'credit market' can mean several things, I shall use it primarily to mean 'a market in which private persons (individuals and businesses) borrow money for consumption and investment'.

PRE-BRITISH PERIOD

The traditional Hindu Law, whose textual sources can be traced back to the *smrti* documents written around AD 200, laid down several rules governing the rights and duties of lenders as well as borrowers. These texts mention restrictions on rates of interest, permissible means of debt recovery, and punitive consequences of defaulting on a debt (Kane 1946). For instance, the rule of pious obligation required that a man's debts be paid with interest by his sons even when no property was bequeathed to

them. Another rule, the rule of Damdupat, required that the creditor cannot collect more than twice the original principal. Prescriptions laid out in the smrti texts supplemented by local customs formed the basis of the medieval law governing credit contracts in India. This practice continued even during the Mughal period notwithstanding Islam's summary ban on usury (Habib 1964). While there were important spatial and temporal variations in the functioning of credit markets, certain common features can be discerned. Indian society was predominantly an agricultural society and the demand for credit was occasioned by the investment and consumption needs arising out of the vagaries of monsoon-fed agriculture. In the pre-British period (and in some instances even afterwards) the enforcement of credit contracts was a local affair: the village councils often adjudicated disputes between the borrower and the moneylender; the state had a limited role in contract enforcement; and the informal forces of social custom and moral pressure, not to mention the moneylender's muscle power, often played a more important role. The mutual dependence between the moneylender and the village community helped, to some extent, in curbing the lender's rapacity. Even to this date, surveys of the informal credit sector in backward rural areas of India reveal a similar picture.

BRITISH PERIOD

The advent of British rule brought about important changes to the legal system in India. Influenced by the classical liberal views of political economy, the British sought to establish a legal system that would secure property rights and enforce private contracts. Several innovations were introduced that resulted in a significant change in the legal framework under

---

[1] In its original sense, the term 'usury' merely means the practice of lending at interest. It is only in subsequent usage that the term acquired the negative connotation of lending at exorbitant interest.

which credit contracts were enforced. For instance, the British introduced a system of civil courts that expedited the loan recovery process by granting ex parte decrees, that is, rulings in the absence of the defendant. Land titling converted communal land into private property and thus enabled the use of land as collateral. Moreover, overriding local customs, the British Law permitted seizure of land in lieu of loan repayment even if it had not been explicitly pledged as collateral. While these reforms succeeded in their goal of increasing competition among lenders, they destroyed the incentive of the lenders to insure farmers in times of adverse shocks. This in turn contributed to a dramatic increase in the incidence of rural indebtedness in the Bombay Deccan and Punjab provinces (Kranton and Swamy 1999). The point was brought home by the Deccan Riots of 1875. Following a period of growing indebtedness and loan defaults, villagers in the Poona and Ahmednagar districts of the Bombay Deccan rioted against the local moneylenders, seizing and destroying the bonds and decrees in the hands of their creditors. In some cases, shops and houses of moneylenders were targeted.

The Deccan Riots Commission of 1876 and its legislative sequel—the Deccan Agriculturists' Relief Act of 1879—mark an important juncture in the regulation of credit markets in India. In a decisive break from the laissez-faire approach of the earlier period, this Act gave the courts a right to go beyond the letter of the debt contract. The courts were given powers to determine and award only reasonable interest rates and to explicitly take into account the fairness of the contract in determining its validity. Among the specific provisions of this Act were the recognition of the traditional rule of Damdupat and a ban on seizure of land unless explicitly pledged. Other

acts imposing restrictions on the credit contracts that followed included the Punjab Alienation of Land Act 1900, the Usurious Loans Act 1918, and the Punjab Relief of Indebtedness Act 1934. These efforts met with mixed success. While they succeeded in providing specific relief, the general problem of rural indebtedness and lack of a well-functioning rural credit market remained unaltered.

By the turn of the nineteenth century, banking companies began to emerge in the urban centres of Bombay, Delhi, and Calcutta. Moreover, recognizing the limited success in regulating rural moneylenders, the British encouraged formation of cooperative credit societies as a means of providing rural credit. There was a definite change in thinking regarding the strategy for credit market regulation.

The minimalist approach of the earlier era, of providing a legal framework and then relying on market forces to do the rest, was set aside and the government took proactive measures to establish a modern banking sector as the mainstay of the credit delivery system. The regulatory infrastructure for this project was established by enacting the Reserve Bank of India (RBI) Act 1935 and the Indian Companies (Amendment) Act 1936. The RBI Act established the RBI as the apex bank of the country and provided it with powers to oversee the emerging banking sector. The amended Companies Act included several regulations pertinent to the operation of banking companies. However, there was growing consensus among policymakers that a separate legislation dealing exclusively with the regulation of banking companies was necessary.

POST-INDEPENDENCE PERIOD

One of the first legislations passed after Independence was the Banking Companies

Act 1949 which was subsequently renamed the Banking Regulations Act (BRA). Though enacted post-Independence, the BRA was in continuity of regulatory reforms of the preceding years. Since then, the BRA has been the main legal tool for regulating the formal credit sector. Under this Act, the RBI is given a wide range of regulatory powers over the banking sector, and until the reform era these powers grew with each amendment to the BRA. Cooperative banks were brought under the scope of the BRA in 1965. Every aspect of banking activity, from permission to operate and expand to details regarding the structure and rates of interest, comes under the purview of the RBI due to the various provisions of the BRA. Throughout much of the post-Independence period, the RBI has used these powers to channel credit in the direction commensurate with the socialist principles that governed the thinking of the planning era; it is under this Act that the RBI is able to determine how much of bank lending should go to the priority sector and how many rural branches a bank needs to open. In short, the BRA provides a regulatory framework that has helped consolidate much of the formal credit sector, that is the commercial and cooperative banking sector as well as many NBFCs,[2] under a unified authority. Social control over the banking sector was further consolidated following bank nationalizations in 1969 and again in 1980. It is only recently (after 1991) that the RBI has begun the process of granting banks greater operational discretion and inviting private competition, both domestic and foreign, into the credit markets. Hence the policy approach has once again started shifting in favour of a free-functioning credit market.

While the policy of social control over the banking sector has succeeded in increasing its share in the total lending operations vis-à-vis the informal sector, the latter still caters to a significant population, particularly in the backward rural areas. The regulation of the non-banking and informal sectors—local moneylenders, pawnbrokers, primary agricultural societies, etc.—is placed in the State List of the Constitution and hence falls under the authority of the respective state legislatures. In particular, the issues related to rural indebtedness, perhaps owing to regional variations in agricultural activities, are under states' jurisdiction. There are several laws such as Moneylenders Acts and Debt Relief Acts[3] that are enacted and enforced at state level for the purpose of controlling private moneylending and redressing rural indebtedness during adverse agricultural shocks.

The line demarcating the states' regulatory powers and those provided by central laws such as the BRA is sometimes fuzzy and that has led to some frictions. Under a provision added to the BRA in 1984 (Section 21-A), courts are precluded from scrutinizing loan contracts by banks to determine whether the interest charged is excessive. Moreover, this provision explicitly overrides the various state laws on this subject. The issue of the primacy of this provision vis-à-vis the states' constitutional prerogative to redress rural indebtedness is far from settled (Tripathi and Jaffree 2000: lvi–lvii). There are differences in opinions given by the various High Courts with regard to this matter. Moreover, with the growing incidence of rural indebtedness and

[2]NBFCs are non-bank financial companies. Their role in the credit market is discussed elsewhere in this volume.

[3]For example, the Karnataka Prohibition of Exorbitant Interest Act 2004 and the Maharashtra Debtor's Relief Act 1976.

farmer suicides in some states, this issue has gained salience.[4]

Another area of challenge, where the multiplicity of laws has become a hindrance is the regulation of the emerging micro-finance institutions. While the strategy of using self-help groups (SHGs) and other such channels has received much favourable attention in the policy circles, the magnitude of these activities is still limited and it is still far from clear if their success rate is invariant to scale. The micro-finance sector today operates under a myriad of state and central laws and its successful proliferation will be greatly aided by having a separate act governing micro-finance institutions.[5]

I have reviewed the laws regulating borrowing and lending and traced their evolution since the pre-British period. However, the efficacy of any law depends on the efficiency of its implementation; indeed, a delay in the delivery of justice is tantamount to its denial. There are monumental hurdles in the legal process of loan recovery. While some of these are placed intentionally with a view to protecting the welfare of the borrower, most are a result of the overload on the Indian court system and impose a hardship on the lender. Moreover, the unpaid debts and non-performing assets (NPAs) deprive other deserving borrowers of a chance to access the much needed credit. An important step towards reducing the backlog of pending debt recovery suits was taken with the passage of the Recovery of Debts due to Banks and

Financial Institutions Act 1993. This Act has helped set up legal machinery, the Debt Recovery Tribunals, to expedite the handling of recovery suits. While the process of legal reform is far from complete, early evidence suggests that it has had a favourable effect on credit market operations (Visaria 2005).

Finally, laws are effective only in so far as they are actually availed of by citizens. Particularly in the backward rural areas, knowledge of and access to the legal system are still limited. This is one of the reasons why rural moneylenders still play an important role in spite of the restrictive regulations intended to curb their usurious practices. Moreover, local powerbrokers and corrupt officials hinder access to the law even when information about it is available to the people. In that sense, the marginalized sections of the rural population are still in the pre-modern paradigm discussed earlier. It can only be hoped that the spread of literacy, local governance, and improved access to the formal as well as regulated micro-finance sector will eventually solve the age-old problem of indebtedness and servitude of the peasant.

MANDAR P. OAK

REFERENCES

Habib, I. 1964. 'Usury in Medieval India', *Comparative Studies in Society and History*, 6(4): 393–419.
Joshi, S. 2003. 'Politics of Farm Interest Rates', *Hindu Business Line*, Internet Edition.
Kane, P.V. 1946. *History of Dharmasastra: Ancient and Medieval Religious and Civil Laws*, vol. 3, Poona, Bhandarkar Oriental Research Institute.
Kranton, R. and A. Swamy. 1999. 'The Hazards of Piecemeal Reform: British Civil Courts and Credit Markets in Colonial India', *Journal of Development Economics*, 58: 1–25.
Tripathi, G.S.N. and S.I. Jaffree. 2000. *Seth's Commentaries on Banking Regulation Act, 1949 and Allied Banking Laws*, Allahabad, Law Publishers (India) Pvt. Ltd.

[4]In an editorial in *The Hindu* urging state intervention in bank interest rates, a prominent farmers' rights activist asks, 'Do we need a recurrence of Deccan riots to make the Government see reason?' (Joshi 2003)

[5]See http://www.nabard.org/roles/microfinance/index.htm for the views of the NABARD Task Force on Supporting Policy and Regulatory Framework for Micro-finance regarding this matter.

Visaria, S. 2005. 'Legal Reform and Loan Repayments: The Microeconomic Impact of Debt Recovery Tribunals in India', Working Paper.

Equity Premium

Equity premium is the return earned by a risky security, such as a stock, in excess of that earned by a risk-free security, such as a treasury bill (T-bill). It is a crucial input in financial decisions such as asset allocation, capital budgeting, and planning for retirement.

Historical data provide a wealth of evidence that over long periods of time, stock returns have been considerably higher than returns for T-bills. As Table 1 shows, the average annual real return (that is the inflation-adjusted return) on the US stock market for the past 115 years has been about 7.5 per cent. In the same period, the real return on a relatively riskless security was a paltry 1 per cent.

The difference between these two returns, 6.5 percentage points, is the equity premium. This statistical difference has been even more pronounced in the post-World War II period. Data on US stock and bond returns going back to 1802 reveal a similar, although somewhat smaller, premium for the past 200 years.

Furthermore, this pattern of excess returns to equity holdings is not unique to US capital markets. Table 2 documents that equity returns in other developed countries also exhibit this historical regularity when compared with the return to riskless debt holdings.

The annual return on the UK stock market, for example, was 5.7 per cent in the post-World War II period, an impressive 4.6 per cent premium over the average bond return of 1.1 per cent. Similar statistical differences have been documented for France, Germany, and Japan. Together, the United States, the United Kingdom, Japan, Germany, and France account for more than 85 per cent of capitalized global equity value.

Table 3 shows the equity premium for India in the 'post-liberalization' period, using both the Bombay Stock Exchange (BSE)

Table 1   US Returns 1802–2004

			(per cent)
	Mean real return		
Period	Market index	Relatively riskless security	Risk premium
1802–2004	6.9	2.9	4.0
1889–2004	7.5	1.0	6.5
1926–2004	8.0	0.7	7.3
1947–2000	7.5	0.5	7.0

Table 2   Returns for Selected Developed Countries

				(per cent)
		Mean real return		
Country	Period	Market index	Relatively riskless security	Risk premium
United Kingdom	1947–99	5.7	1.1	4.6
Japan	1970–99	4.7	1.4	3.3
Germany	1978–97	9.8	3.2	6.6
France	1973–98	9.0	2.7	6.3
Sweden	1919–2003	11.1	5.6	5.5
Australia	1900–2000	13.3	4.6	8.7

Table 3   India Returns 1991–2004

(per cent)

	Relatively riskless security	BSE 100	Equity premium (BSE 100)	Sensex	Equity premium (Sensex)
Mean real return	1.28	12.6	11.3	11.0	9.7
Standard deviation	1.73	37.2	37.7	32.6	33.2

100 and the Sensex as a proxy for the return on equity. Since participation in the T-bill market was highly regulated before 2000, the equity premium is calculated relative to the bank deposit rate, using the later as a proxy for the return on a risk-free security.

For the period prior to 1991 reliable data on dividend yields are not available. Table 4 gives the equity premium using the average annual stock price index as documented and reported by the Reserve Bank of India (RBI).

The dramatic investment implications of the differential rates of return are illustrated in Tables 5 and 6. Table 5 shows the enormous disparity in capital appreciation of $1 invested in different assets in the US for various time periods.[1] Table 6 displays a similar analysis for India.

Table 4   India Returns 1984–1991

(per cent)

	Relatively riskless security	BSE 100	Equity premium (BSE 100)
Mean real return	1.13	22.4	21.3
Standard deviation	0.74	28.1	27.9

Table 5   Real Terminal Value of $1 Invested

Investment period	Stocks	T-bills	Ratio
1889–2004	$4092.36	$3.14	1303.30
1926–2004	$407.56	$1.67	244.05
1947–2004	$61.70	$1.33	46.39

[1]The calculations in Table 5 assume that all payments to the underlying asset, such as dividend payments to stocks and interest payments to bonds, were reinvested and that no taxes were paid.

Table 6   Real Terminal Value of Re 1 Invested

Investment period	Stocks (BSE 100)	Bank deposit	Ratio
1984–2004	Rs 19.25	Rs 1.28	15.04
1991–2004	Rs 4.68	Rs 1.18	3.97

One can gain additional insights by examining what these differential rates imply for the time it takes to double one's money. Using rates in India over the 1991–2004 period, the doubling period for investments in stocks is about six years compared to fifty-five years for investments in a risk-free asset. This kind of long-term perspective underscores the remarkable wealth-building potential of equity premium and highlights why it is of central importance in portfolio allocation decisions, in making estimates of the cost of capital, and in the current debate about the advantages of investing social security trust or retirement funds in the stock market.

A PREMIUM FOR BEARING RISK?

Why has the rate of return on stocks in India and other countries been significantly higher than the rate of return on relatively risk-free assets? An intuitive answer is that stocks are 'riskier' than bonds and investors require a premium for bearing this additional risk. Indeed, the standard deviation of the returns to stocks in India (about 30 per cent a year historically) is larger than that of the returns to T-bills (about 2 per cent a year), so obviously stocks are considerably riskier than bills.

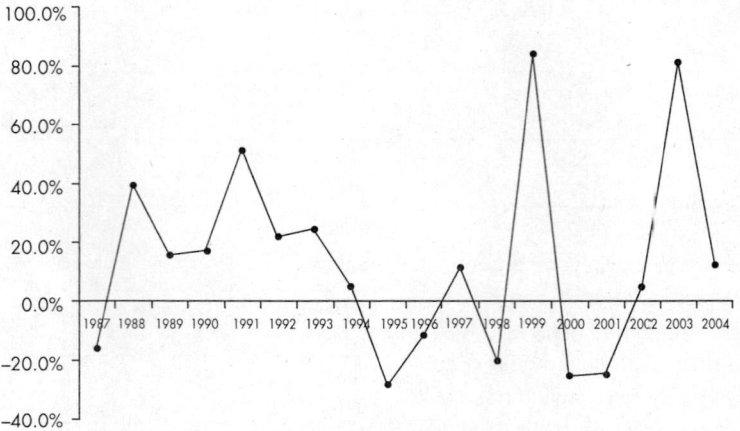

Figure 1   Annual Real Rate of Return—BSE 100

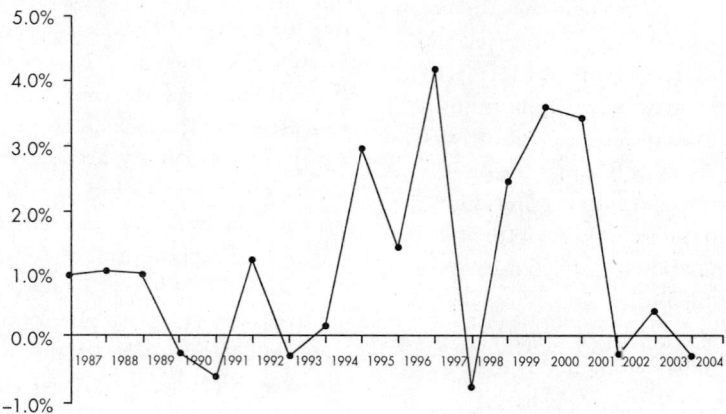

Figure 2   Commercial Bank Deposit Rate

But are they? Figure 1 illustrates the variability in the annual real rate of return on the BSE 100 index while Figure 2 shows the variability of a relatively risk-free security over the 1991–2004 period.

To enhance our understanding of the risk–return trade-off in the pricing of financial assets, let us make a detour into modern asset pricing theory and look at why different assets yield different rates of return. The deux ex machina of this theory is that assets are priced such that, ex ante, the loss in marginal utility incurred by sacrificing

current consumption and buying an asset at a certain price is equal to the expected gain in marginal utility contingent on the anticipated increase in consumption when the asset pays off in the future.

The operative emphasis here is the *incremental loss* or *gain* in well-being due to incremental consumption, which must be differentiated from the incremental consumption itself. This is because the *same* amount of incremental consumption may result in different degrees of well-being at different times. A five-course dinner after a heavy lunch, for example, yields considerably less satisfaction than a similar dinner when one is hungry!

As a consequence, assets that pay off when times are good and consumption levels are high, that is when the incremental value of additional consumption is low, are less desirable than those that pay off an equivalent amount when times are bad and additional consumption is both desirable and more highly valued.

Let us illustrate this principle in the context of the standard popular paradigm, the Capital Asset Pricing Model (CAPM). This model postulates a linear relationship between an asset's 'beta', a measure of systematic risk, and expected return. Thus high beta stocks yield a high expected rate of return. That is so because in the CAPM, good times and bad times are captured by the return on the market. The performance of the market as captured by a broad-based index acts as a surrogate indicator for the relevant state of the economy. A high beta security tends to pay off more when the market return is high, that is when times are good and consumption is plentiful; as discussed earlier, such a security provides less incremental utility than a security that pays off when consumption is low, is less valuable to investors, and consequently sells for less. Thus assets that pay off in states of low marginal utility will sell for a lower price than similar assets that pay off in states of high marginal utility. Since rates of return are inversely proportional to asset prices, the latter class of assets will, on average, give a lower rate of return than the former.

Another perspective on asset pricing emphasizes that economic agents prefer to smooth patterns of consumption over time. Assets that pay off a relatively larger amount at times when consumption is already high, 'destabilize' these patterns of consumption, whereas assets that pay off when consumption levels are low, 'smooth' out consumption. Naturally, the latter are more valuable and thus require a lower rate of return to induce investors to hold these assets. (Insurance policies are a classic example of assets that smooth consumption. Individuals willingly purchase and hold them, in spite of their very low rates of return.)

To return to the original question: are stocks so much riskier than bills as to justify a 7 per cent differential in their rates of return as observed in the US?

What came as a surprise to many economists and researchers in finance was the conclusion of a research paper that Edward Prescott and I wrote in 1979. Stocks and bonds pay off in approximately the same states of nature or economic scenarios and hence, as argued earlier, they should command approximately the same rate of return. In fact, using standard theory to estimate risk-adjusted returns, we found that stocks in the US on average should command, at most, a 1 per cent return premium over bills. Since, for as long as we had reliable data (about a hundred years), the mean premium on stocks over bills was considerably and consistently higher, we realized that we had a puzzle on our hands. It took us six more years to convince a skeptical profession and for our paper 'The Equity Premium: A Puzzle' to be published (Mehra and Prescott 1985).

For the purposes of this entry, I have done a similar analysis for India using the data in Table 7, which contains the sample statistics for the Indian economy for the 1991–2004 period.

My finding is that the theoretical equity premium should be in the range 0.02 per cent to 0.16 per cent if the coefficient of risk aversion is varied from 2 to 10. Since the observed risk premium in India is of a higher order of magnitude, there is a puzzle with respect to Indian data as well.

Table 7 Indian Economy Sample Statistics
1991–2004

Statistic	Value
Risk-free rate, R_f	1.0128
Mean return on equity, $E(R_e)$	1.126
Mean growth rate of consumption, $E(x)$	1.0227
Standard deviation of growth rate of consumption, $\sigma(x)$	0.0224
Mean equity premium, $E(R_e)–R_f$	0.113

I want to emphasize that the equity premium puzzle is a *quantitative* puzzle. Standard theory is qualitatively consistent with the notion of risk: stocks do, on average, return more than bonds in the theoretical model. The puzzle arises from the fact that the quantitative predictions of the theory are of an order of magnitude different from what has been historically documented. The puzzle cannot be dismissed lightly because much of our economic intuition and policy directives are based on the very class of models that fall short so dramatically when confronted with financial data. It underscores the failure of paradigms central to financial and economic modelling to capture the characteristic that appears to make stocks comparatively so risky. Hence the viability of using this class of models for any quantitative assessment—for example to gauge the welfare implications of alternative stabilization policies—is thrown open to question.

For this reason, over the past twenty years or so, attempts to resolve the puzzle have become a major research impetus in finance and economics. Several generalizations of key features of the Mehra–Prescott (1985) model have been proposed to reconcile observations with theory, including alternative assumptions about preferences, modified probability distributions to admit rare but disastrous events, survivorship bias, incomplete markets, and market imperfections. None has satisfactorily resolved the puzzle.

Recently some researchers and analysts have argued that ex ante equity premium is likely to be low. The data used to document equity premium (over the past 100 years in some instances) represent as reliable an economic data set as analysts have, and 100 years is a long series when it comes to economic data. Before the equity premium is dismissed, not only do researchers need to understand the observed phenomena, but they also need a plausible explanation as to why the future is likely to be any different from the past. Demographic shifts and changes in participation in equity markets will, of course, impact on the equity premium in India over time. For instance, greater stock market participation in particular by the younger generation is likely to reduce the equity premium. However, before these demographic factors play a role, on the basis of what is currently known, I make the following assertion: the equity premium in the future is likely to be similar to what it has been in the past and returns to investment in equity will continue to substantially dominate returns to investment in T-bills for investors *with long planning horizons*.

RAJNISH MEHRA

REFERENCES

Cochrane, J.H. 1997. 'Where is the Market Going? Uncertain Facts and Novel Theories', *Economic Perspectives*, 21(6), November: 3–37.

Constantinides, G.M. 2002. 'Rational Asset Prices', *Journal of Finance*, 57(4), August: 1567–91.

Kocherlakota, N.R. 1996. 'The Equity Premium: It's Still a Puzzle', *Journal of Economic Literature*, 34(1), March: 42–71.

Mehra, R. 2003. 'The Equity Premium: Why is It a Puzzle?', *Financial Analysts Journal*, January/February: 54–69.

_____. 2006. *Handbook of Investments: Equity Risk Premium*, Amsterdam, North Holland.

Mehra, R. and E.C. Prescott. 1985. 'The Equity Premium: A Puzzle', *Journal of Monetary Economics*, 15(2), March: 145–61.

———. 2003. 'The Equity Premium in Retrospect', in G.M. Constantinides, M. Harris, and R. Stulz, eds, *Handbook of the Economics of Finance*, Amsterdam, North Holland.

Finance and Law

The history of organized financial markets in India can be traced back to the year 1875 when the Bombay Stock Exchange (BSE) was founded, soon to be followed by two other stock exchanges in Calcutta and Delhi. However, for a century to follow, these establishments largely resembled clubs with privileged membership. Trading was primarily controlled by a handful of brokers, membership to the exchanges was fairly limited, and so were new issues, even in the post-Independence era.[1] Limited membership of the brokerage firms (which mostly run on a partnership basis), long settlement cycles, lack of transparency in trading, and absence of alternative stock exchanges exposed ordinary investors to risks attributable to illiquid markets and information monopoly of the brokers and traders. The absence of a mandatory requirement of information disclosures by listed firms added to the severity of the problem of informational asymmetry between a firm and its dispersed shareholders. Without a central and functionally independent body for overseeing activities of stock exchanges, small investors were left unprotected from losses due to both the selection of stocks

and the process of trading in them. This, in turn, discouraged small investors from participating in equity markets. At the same time, under the licensing regime of the post-Independence period, which prevailed into the mid-1980s, companies were restricted from freely entering the market to raise funds. Even for firms lucky enough to obtain a permit, it was not easy to raise finance because the office of the Controller of Capital Issues (CCI) determined the price of initial public offerings (IPOs) and monitored the number of shares issued, without paying much heed to informational issues that could hurt small investors. The yearly long-term capital raised by companies between 1957 and 1980 hovered around Rs 150 crore. The thinness of the market was reflected in a meagre stock market capitalization to gross national product (GNP) ratio of 5 per cent in 1980. Apart from stock market investors, creditors to firms were equally vulnerable due to a very time-consuming process for the resolution of bankruptcy as well as inflexible and archaic laws that prevailed during most of the post-Independence era.

Major legal, operational, and institutional changes began in the late 1980s. This entry will primarily concentrate on the relationship between the legal environment and financial markets in the pre- and post-reform periods and evaluate the performance of stock markets and bankruptcy procedures on the basis of some objective criteria that will shortly be outlined. It will also, in the Indian context, shed some light on the current debate in academics that makes a connection between legal origins of a country and finance.

MARKETS AND REGULATORY REFORMS

There were two major developments in the late 1980s and early 1990s that altered the functioning of the stock markets in India. First, in 1992, the government set up the

---

[1] In 1981, the BSE's annual turnover was Rs 4 million a day with 517 brokers. The corresponding figures in 1991 were Rs 23 million and 550 respectively. See Singhal (2004).

Securities and Exchange Board of India
(SEBI) with enhanced statutory authority
to enable it to perform a wide variety of
functions. These ranged from checking
information disclosure by firms and setting
guidelines for other financial institutions like
mutual funds to investigating insider trading
and related fraudulent transactions in the
market. Second, a National Stock Exchange
(NSE) was established with the objective
of reaching investors who are scattered
geographically through a computerized
trading system. An alternative to the BSE,
the NSE offered a wide range of choices to
investors including screen-based transactions
that increased the transparency in trades. It
also offered to become either a buyer or a
seller, thereby assuring completion of trades,
and helped in the floating of new financial
products such as derivatives and futures to
cater to the various needs of corporations
and investors.

Informational asymmetry between
investors and the possibility of default in
transactions are two major impediments to
the development of any financial market.
Prior to the 1990s, Indian stock exchanges
were monopolized by a few participants
who had captured enough informational
rent from the prevailing system and were
naturally very resistant to changes in daily
business practices. The launching of the
NSE directly created competition for other
stock exchanges and left them with no
option but to follow new trading practices
in order to retain their clientele. At the
same time, the creation of SEBI together
with its added emphasis on disclosures of
information was a step towards resolving
the concerns of small dispersed investors
due to informational asymmetry. Hence the
introduction of a new and modern stock
exchange curbed the monopoly power of
brokers and the initiation of a coordinating
body sent a strong message to participants

against manipulating markets or trading and
booking profits based on their privileged
information. These changes, together with
the abolition of industrial licences and
permits, created a flurry of activity in the
stock market almost immediately. The
number of shareholders and investors in
mutual funds rose from 2 to 40 million
between 1980 and 1993, the turnover of
shares increased from Rs 130 million in
1981 to Rs 3700 million in 1994. While
Rs 929 million was raised through corporate
securities in 1981, the figure reached Rs 225
billion by 1993–4 and out of nearly 1700
companies that raised funds in the equity
market in 1994–5, 369 were new.[2] Although
such phenomenal growth in numbers
decelerated later, primarily due to recessions,
it is on the rise again in recent years.

Contrary to the experience with
regulations, the pace of legal and legislative/
political reforms in the context of the credit
market is slow and laws and institutions
that are relevant for bankruptcy and
reorganization of firms have been weak.
Prior to the 1990s, the quasi-judicial body
responsible for overseeing liquidation or
reorganization was primarily the Board
of Industrial and Finance Reconstruction
(BIFR), instituted by the Sick Industrial
Companies (SIC) Act of 1985. Due to the
tremendous rise in volume of bad debts as
well number of sick organizations, a new
act came into force in 1993 that allowed
a creditor with more than Rs 1 million
outstanding debt to appeal to a Debt
Recovery Tribunal (DRT) for the speedy
recovery of loans. Then again, in 2002,
there was an amendment to the
Companies Act that sought to streamline
the procedures of bankruptcy and
reorganization. Hence, currently, the BIFR

[2]See Singh (2003) and Singhal (2004) for
details.

and DRT, together with the Company Law Board and High Courts, define the legal jurisdiction of bankruptcy procedures.

EVALUATION CRITERIA

In order to evaluate the impact of legal systems and institutions on financial markets, one needs some objective criteria. Since there have not been any extensive studies on the effects of reforms, I will resort to a combination of casual empiricism and some datum for evaluation and will use the following yardsticks for such judgements.

Efficiency

The legal system must ensure that it does not interfere with ex post efficient outcomes and at the same time must ensure ex ante efficiency. Early detection of insider trading in the stock market, and the assignment of more power to banks to investigate whether borrowers have violated covenants are examples of ex ante efficiency. Further, creditors should be able to get early redress from the legal system if debtor firms engage in activities that violate bond indenture agreements, such as payment of dividends. Ex ante efficiency can be measured by the combination time (and/or costs) spent in detecting such unlawful activities. That is, the longer it takes to detect occurrences of insider trading or fraudulent activity by controlling shareholders, the greater the inefficiency.

On the other hand, the concept of ex post efficiency deals with the issue of resolution of a crisis once it has taken place. An obvious example is when a debtor firm has already defaulted on loans. The major question is whether the firm should be liquidated or its assets and liabilities be organized for continuation as an economic entity. The legal framework must forestall liquidation when continuation is feasible and vice versa. In the context of equity markets, an example could be ex post default on delivery of shares on

a large scale, and whether the government would bail out or punish?

Fairness

The legal system should also ensure that minority shareholders and public debt holders' wealth is not expropriated by dominant insiders via either direct or indirect methods of coercion leading to violation of contractual agreements. Such a transfer of wealth could be the outcome of either privileged information of dominant stakeholders or loopholes in the legal system or both. Again, this issue is more important during unusual activities within a firm such as mergers and acquisitions and/or bankruptcy. For example, if there are different classes of creditors, fairness requires payments to senior and secured creditors first during bankruptcy.

However, it is not always easy to achieve efficiency and fairness because at times there could be a trade-off between ex post efficiency and fairness as illustrated by the following simple example. Suppose that a firm has failed to repay a loan of Rs 600 and liquidation value is Rs 300 and this sum will go to the creditor in the event the business of the firm gets wrapped up and assets are sold in the market. Alternatively the firm could have a new project that could generate a cash flow (cash available to its investors) of either Rs 800 or Rs 1200 and each could occur with equal probability. This project needs an investment of Rs 600 and the firm is cash starved. If the firm is allowed to raise finance for this project by issuing new debt and this debt is granted seniority over old debt, then it violates the seniority of old debt and could be unfair from the point of view of old creditors. On the other hand, if the project begins with new debt, old creditors could get either Rs 200 or Rs 600 with equal probability so that the expected value of what they might receive in the continuation of the firm is Rs 400 that exceeds their pay-off in liquidation. Though efficient, continuation of the firm violates original priority of payments. This simple example illustrates conflicts between fairness and efficiency. Of course, in the real world the problem is more complex but nevertheless, one could use this simple case to highlight problems that arise due to asymmetric information as well as from conflicts of interests between various parties in a legal dispute. For example, the dominant shareholders or managers may know more about the probability of success in the new project or the liquidation value of assets than the bank or the legal authority. In that case, a legal solution leads to an outcome which is both inefficient and unfair. Conflicts of interests could arise due to the presence of many classes of creditors such as senior and secured and the agents could play the game of chicken in which one class of agents expects the others to concede first. This results in a suboptimal outcome for everyone.

THE INDIAN FINANCIAL MARKET CONTEXT

Though there are a series of reforms in the stock-market rules and regulations, insider trading leading to default is still a nagging problem. The recent liquidity crisis of the Calcutta Stock Exchange offers evidence of serious violations of trading norms still going undetected ex ante. SEBI has undertaken a series of investigations in recent times against irregularities in trading and there has been a sharp rise in the number of investigations, prosecutions, and penalties. In the year 2003–4, SEBI initiated 287 enquiry proceedings against intermediaries compared to a figure of 185 in the preceding year with a concurrent 168 per cent increase in arbitration for imposing monetary penalties. The figures cited by SEBI are of course very insignificant in comparison to the overall volume of trading or potential violations. The main problems still lie with manipulation of the market,

rigging of prices, and insider trading and it is still not clear on what basis SEBI undertakes investigation. No comprehensive study exists so far to gauge the effect of efficient and fair handling of malpractices but indirect evidence points to an overall positive effect of the reforms. A wide variety of indicators suggests a positive connection between legal reforms and overall activity of the stock market. These include confidence of foreign mutual funds marked by large-scale entry (SEBI website), improved corporate governance norms for companies that have more than 25 per cent insider holdings, intensive monitoring of domestic financial institutions (Sarkar and Sarkar 2000), and overall increase in market capitalization.

However, similar changes in laws dealing with bankruptcy and reorganization pertaining to credit markets were very slow and had often led to both inefficient and unfair outcomes. As of March 2001, 3317 firms defaulted on loans equal to Rs 258 billion, which is nearly 2 per cent of the gross domestic product (GDP) (Kang and Nayar 2004). The definition of industrial sickness by the BIFR precluded the existence of ex ante inefficiency. According to the BIFR, the process of reorganization should begin once a registered company's accumulated losses exceed their net worth by the end of the year. Such a definition of sickness leaves no room for detection of financial trouble before companies lose their value. Hence a majority of the firms that appealed to the BIFR were liquidated and not reorganized. For example, out of 1711 active cases in 2002, liquidation was proposed for 63 per cent and only 22 per cent were successfully reorganized. The picture is even worse in the preceding decades. Second, huge delays in the resolution of bankruptcy hurt everyone except for the controlling shareholders and managers. In 2002, the BIFR's decision to reorganize took seven years and it recommended liquidation after 6.5 years.[3] Even a casual empiricism suggests that such a long time for resolution of bankruptcy and reorganization very often leads either to a drastic fall in net worth or in liquidation value of the firm and provides a sanctuary for the entrenched management or other parties with vested interests to keep the firm alive even when it should have been wrapped up. Hence the whole system has a bias towards ex post inefficiency and unfairness. Though the act of 2002 promised to deal with this situation, its effectiveness is yet to be assessed or seen.

AN ACADEMIC DEBATE

The discussion has so far highlighted the uneven pace of legal reforms relevant to transactions in the debt and equity markets. To what extent is performance linked to the legal origins of the country? Much of India's legal framework had its origin in the English Common Law due to the colonial legacy. An influential body of empirical research links a country's legal origin and development of its financial markets because of the influence that legal structure exerts on shaping contractual arrangements between outside investors and insiders of a firm. A spate of works, starting with La Porta et al. (1997, 1998), primarily made the distinction between the various legal regimes which had their origins in one of the following customs: (a) English Common Law; (b) French Civil Law; (c) German Civil Law; and (d) Scandinavian Civil Law.

According to La Porta et al. (1997, 1998), the English Common Law fares better in protecting small investors against the risk of appropriation by dominant shareholders and other influential insiders, in comparison with other legal systems. A

[3]See Kang and Nayar (2004) for details on bankruptcy procedures and relevant data for India.

major testable implication of this assertion is that in countries that adopted French or Scandinavian Civil Law, poor protection of investors must have led to costly outside financing as investors would factor out consequences of such poor protection and demand higher return. Moreover, costly outside financing also prompts excessive concentration of equity in the hands of the insiders of a firm, causing them to bear huge risks. This, in turn, discourages formation of entrepreneurial activities. Finally, dense concentrations in holding of equity by a few major players create poor liquidity in the secondary market since insiders' holdings of stock are very infrequently traded.

Hence, according to La Porta et al. (1997, 1998), poorer investor protection and inefficient legal systems put brakes on economic development as they make outside financing expensive, contribute to the thinness of the stock market, and act as an impediment to the formation of an entrepreneurial class. Based on this argument, La Porta et al. (1997, 1998) have run tests on many countries and have ranked their performance in terms of various indices. According to them, average creditors' rights index in countries with English Common Law is 3.11 and is the highest among the four systems, the same index for the French Civil Law countries being 1.58. In their measures of shareholders' protection, such as the anti-director rights index, common law countries score higher (4.0) than, say, French Civil Law countries (2.33).

Though an important piece of work, La Porta et al.'s classification could be overly simplistic because countries with similar legal origins vary significantly with respect to the workings of financial markets such as equity and credit markets. Second, La Porta et al.'s empirical assertions could be interpreted as too deterministic because while 'legal origin' of a country can be treated as an 'initial condition', development of and compliance with laws over time certainly depend upon the economic environment that determines the incentives of the various parties to implement or even to change the law through political processes. Hence, the view that 'initial condition' dominates the dynamic interactions of agents in terms of the implementation of rules as well as incentives to change laws is certainly a very strong assertion. In the Indian context, there has not been much change in the last fifteen years in the legal structure which is of English origin, but big bang reforms such as the introduction of the NSE and SEBI have had far-reaching impact on the equity market while things have remained more or less stationary in credit markets due to the absence of such reforms. My conjecture or maintained hypothesis regarding such uneven changes is that the introduction of strong legal institutions in one market has altered the incentives or even aligned the incentives of various parties while the lack of such changes in other markets has caused the status quo to prevail.

To sum up, though India's legal origin is in the English Common Law, its structure and effectiveness are not uniform across all markets. The World Bank Index of 'closing a business' for 2005 states that it takes almost ten years to resolve bankruptcies in India with 9 per cent cost of estate values, and the recovery rate is 12.8 cents a dollar. Similar figures for the South East Asia region and the Organisation for Economic Co-operation and Development (OECD) countries are 4.2 years, 7.3 per cent, 19.7 cents and 1.5 years, 7.4 per cent and 73.8 cents respectively. On the other hand, in the investors' protection index, primarily for shareholders' benefit, India's position is much higher and is comparable to that of the OECD countries. This index is 6

for India, 5 for the region, and 5.9 for the average OECD country. Though India has made significant gains in implementing legal and institutional reforms in the stock market, weak legal organization, lack of coordination with the labour laws, and overlapping jurisdiction of different statutory bodies are the primary weaknesses of the legal system. Two major deficiencies in India's legal reforms are worth mentioning. First, the reluctance to use market information contained in prices for the purpose of curbing illegal economic activities. For example, SEBI could use the information content of changes in price of stock induced by a huge volume of buying and selling, which could be either an outcome of pure information-based trading or a result of market manipulation. SEBI could announce and commit to investigation if the movements of prices cross a threshold limit. That is, combining information contained in price with its own information would not only reduce costs of investigation but also provide incentives to participants not to engage in market manipulation and rigging of prices. Second, the legal system and regulatory bodies very often ignore economic incentives of various individuals to engage in negotiations to make a deal to resolve financial crisis. Allowing agents to negotiate or renegotiate initial contracts implies flexibility and promotes efficiency. The legal authority could then intervene only to check whether renegotiation of contracts has led to unfair outcomes for a third party. This is very relevant for financially distressed firms that could float a new security (that could be traded in financial markets) while replacing old securities such as bonds. However, this requires a comprehensive change in the structure of bankruptcy and labour laws.

SANJAY BANERJI

REFERENCES

Kang, N. and N. Nayar. 2004. 'The Evolution of Corporate Bankruptcy Law in India', *ICRA Bulletin, Money and Finance*, 3 October–4 March.

La Porta, R., F. Lopez-de-Silanes, A. Shleifer, and R. Vishny. 1997. 'Legal Determinants of External Finance', *Journal of Finance*, 52: 1131–50.

———. 1998. 'Law and Finance', *Journal of Political Economy*, 106: 1113–55.

Sarkar, J. and S. Sarkar. 2000. 'Large Shareholder Activism in Corporate Governance in Developing Countries: Evidence from India', *International Review of Finance*, 1(3): 161–94.

Singhal R. 2004. 'Financial Sector Reform in India: Is There a Grand Design?', Occasional Paper Number 16, Centre for the Advanced Study of India, University of Pennsylvania.

Singh, Ajit. 2003. 'Corporate Governance, Corporate Finance and Stock Markets in Emerging Countries', Working Paper 258, ESRC Centre for Business Research, University of Cambridge.

Financial Crisis

A financial crisis is seen as occurring when the inability of one or a group of economic agents to meet commitments to creditors or investors in financial instruments leads to bankruptcies and/or the sale of assets, which in turn results in the collapse of asset prices and threatens the financial viability of related enterprises. Most often the event is accompanied by a freezing or slowing of the flow of credit that adversely affects the real economy. There have been a number of instances of financial crises throughout the history of capitalism. But concern over the phenomenon has increased substantially over the last three decades as a result of an increase in the periodicity and intensity of such crises when compared to the period between World War II and the early 1980s. While India has not faced financial difficulties since the debt-driven balance of payments crisis (BOP) it experienced in 1991, it has recently been adversely affected by the global financial crisis and sections of its financial sector do show signs of fragility.

A financial crisis could take many forms. It could, for example, take the form of a run on a group of banks resulting from a collapse of confidence in their ability to redeem deposits on demand because of the weaknesses of their balance sheets. It could appear in the form of a dramatic collapse in stock market valuations because of a flight out of equity, most often in the wake of an equally dramatic boom in stock values. It could be reflected in the actual or potential default on interest and amortization payments due on the external debt owed by a country or its private sector. Or, it could entail the collapse of a currency because of a speculative attack triggered by signs of difficulty a country is facing in obtaining the foreign exchange needed to meet commitments denominated in those currencies.

These crises have been experienced in rich, middle-income, and poor countries alike, belying the perceptions of some that, unlike in the period prior to World War II, the problem is one that is particularly acute in the so-called 'emerging markets'. In fact, a study of banking crises from the early nineteenth to the early twenty-first century (Reinhart and Rogoff 2008) found that the incidence of such crises was similar in the high to middle-to-low income countries, with the tally being particularly high for the world's financial centres', that is, the United Kingdom, the United States, and France.

The inter-temporal experience has also been characterized by much variation, as illustrated by the financial history of the US. For example, over the period 1955–81, failures of US banks averaged 5.3 per year, excluding banks kept from going under by official open-bank assistance. On the other hand, during 1982–90 failures averaged 131.4 per year or twenty-five times as during many as 1955–81 (Kareken 1992). Since then the US financial system has seen a variety of financial crises, culminating in the crisis of 2007–9 which was triggered by the sub-prime mortgage collapse.

CRISES AND REGULATION

The sharp increase in the number of failures has been traced to the shift in the regulatory regime in the United States starting in the 1970s. Prior to that banking in the US was highly regulated and shaped by the Glass-Steagall Act of 1933. That regulatory framework limited competition with deposit insurance, interest rate regulation, and entry barriers which together rendered any bank as good as any other in the eyes of the ordinary depositor. This preempted the tendency to push up deposit rates to attract depositors that would require risky lending and investment to match returns with costs. The regulatory framework went even further and imposed restrictions on investments that banks or their affiliates could make, limiting their activities to provision of loans and purchases of government securities. There was a ban on banks underwriting securities and serving as insurance underwriters or agents, besides limits on outstanding exposure to a single borrower and lending to sensitive sectors like real estate.

Even though this regulatory framework was directed at and imposed principally on the banking sector, it implicitly regulated the non-bank financial sector as well. It is not often recognized that the size, degree of diversification, and level of activity of the non-bank financial sector depends on the degree to which institutions in that sector can leverage their activity with credit delivered directly or indirectly from the banking system. Banks being the principal depository institutions are the first port

of call for a nation's savings. So if direct or indirect bank involvement in a range of non-bank financial activities was prohibited, as was true under Glass-Steagall, then the range and scope of those activities are bound to be limited. Not surprisingly, even by the 1950s, banking activity in the US constituted 80–90 per cent of that in the financial sector and trading on the New York Stock Exchange was limited to a daily average of three million shares as compared to as much as 160 million shares per day during the second half of the 1980s, when leverage became possible (Sametz 1992).

The regulatory shift began in the 1980s and the era of deregulation of interest rates and banking activity followed. The institutional landscape of the financial sector also changed. Initially money market funds grew in importance and stock market activity increased. The process of dismantling of the Chinese Walls separating different segments of the financial sector began in 1982, culminating in the Gramm-Leach-Bliley (or Financial Services Modernization) Act of 1999, which dismantled Glass-Steagall.

The transformation of the financial framework which followed had many features. To start with, banks extended their activity beyond conventional commercial banking into merchant banking and insurance. Second, within banking, there was a gradual shift in focus from generating incomes from net interest margins to obtaining them in the form of fees and commissions charged for various financial services. Third, related to this was a change in the focus of banking activity as well. While banks did provide credit and create assets that promised a stream of incomes into the future, they did not hold those assets any more. Rather, they structured them into pools, 'securitized' those pools, and sold these securities for a fee to institutional investors and portfolio managers. Banks transferred the risk for a fee, and those who bought into the risk looked to the returns they would earn in the long term. This implied a shift from a 'buy and hold' to an 'originate and distribute' model of banking and meant that those who originated the credit assets tended to understate or discount the risks associated with them. Finally, financial liberalization increased the number of layers in an increasingly universalized financial system, with the extent of regulation varying across the layers. Where regulation was light, as in the case of investment banks, hedge funds, and private equity firms, financial companies could borrow huge amounts based on a small amount of own capital and undertake leveraged investments to create complex products that were often traded over the counter rather than through exchanges. The system was one which put a premium on proliferating risk for profit.

Thus, by adopting a range of measures, the US state and federal governments and the Federal Reserve dismantled during the 1980s and 1990s the system of regulation and financial structure created by the policy framework put in place during and after the Great Depression. Threatened by regulatory arbitrage and the dynamic image of Wall Street, the United Kingdom and other countries followed the United States in liberalizing their financial sectors to differing degrees. The net result was an increasing proneness to crises, as illustrated starkly by the savings and loan crisis and the financial crisis triggered by the collapse of sub-prime mortgage market.

DEVELOPING COUNTRY EXPERIENCE

The experience in developing countries has been similar though not the same. Since the 1980s they too have been drawn into the world of global finance. Till the early 1970s the private international financial system played only a limited role in recycling financial surpluses to the developing countries. The period immediately after the first oil shock saw a dramatic change in this scenario. Since oil surpluses were held in the main as deposits with the international banking system controlled in the developed world, the private financial system there became the powerful agent for recycling surpluses. This power was indeed immense. Expenditure fuelled by credit in the developed and developing world generated surpluses with the oil producers, who then deposited these surpluses with transnational banks, that, in turn, could offer further doses of credit. As a consequence, there was a massive expansion of the international financial market.

Two other developments contributed to the increase in international liquidity during the 1970s and 1980s. First, the United States had built up large international liabilities during the Bretton Woods years, including those resulting from expenditures on the Vietnam War and its policing efforts elsewhere in the world (Sweezy and Magdoff 1972). The explosion of the Eurocurrency market in the 1970s reflected this. This was sustained by the confidence in the dollar stemming from the immediate post-War hegemony of the US, which made it as good as gold.

Second, the demographic structure in most of the advanced countries was changing, with baby boomers reaching the age when they would emphasize personal savings for retirement. This led to the accumulation of investible resources in pension funds, mutual funds, and the like, and created demand for greater variety in savings instruments as well as higher returns.

From the point of view of the developing countries, this growth in international finance appeared positive. Needing liquidity to finance their BOP deficits, they found it easier to negotiate with a relatively atomistic private financial system that could not openly impose conditions rather than with centralized multilateral financial institutions like the International Monetary Fund (IMF). This encouraged developing countries to liberalize their capital accounts and financial markets to attract such capital.

India too attempted to exploit this opportunity to 'escape' from the development impasse of the mid-1960s and after. The government opted to pump prime the system with deficit-financed spending and prevented this from spilling over in the form of an inflationary crisis or BOP crisis by borrowing from the international markets to import commodities in domestic short supply and finance the higher current account deficit that accompanied higher growth. The country's external debt to gross domestic product (GDP) ratio doubled during the 1980s, with short-term debt accounting for a rising share. However, creditors were soon reluctant to roll over past debt and provide new debt resulting in a collapse of reserves and a crisis which led to the reforms adopted in the early 1990s. The liberalization that followed resulted in an increase in inflows of portfolio capital into India's equity and debt markets, besides flows of foreign direct investment and commercial bank credit.

Though India has not faced a severe financial crisis since then, financial crises have been the norm in other developing countries that were discovered as 'emerging markets' by international financial capital.' This suggests that India too is vulnerable. There is an additional problem. If international finance is to use these markets as new avenues for investment and as a hedge against the risks in its own markets, the rules of the game in these 'emerging markets' have to correspond to those in their own markets. It was this which made financial liberalization of a kind that seeks to replicate the Anglo-Saxon

'model' a key demand of international finance. An excess of capital in the form of debt and equity investments began to flow into countries which were willing to change the regulatory regime applicable to the financial sector (including the entry and operations of international financial agents).

In India too, there are three broad forms that the process of financial liberalization has taken: (a) it has opened the country to new forms and larger volumes of international financial flows, in order to attract a part of the substantially increased flows of financial capital to the so-called 'emerging markets' since the late 1970s; (b) to facilitate these inflows it has liberalized to differing degrees the terms governing outflows of foreign exchange in the form of current account investment income payments and in the form of capital account transfers for permitted transactions; and (c) it has transformed the structure of the financial sector and the nature and operations of financial firms in a manner that makes the financial system resemble that in countries like the US and the UK.

However, while financial liberalization began early in the 1990s, the surge in foreign investment flows occurred much later. Liberalization was a necessary condition for such inflows, but not a sufficient one. Until 2003, net inflows were relatively low, reaching a maximum of $8.2 billion in 2001–2. This rose to $15.7 billion in 2003–4, partly encouraged by tax concessions offered to foreign investors in that year. Thereafter India was 'discovered' by foreign investors and effectively became the target of a capital investment surge. Foreign investment flows to India more than doubled from $29.2 billion in 2006–7 to $61.8 billion in 2007–8, even as capital was fleeing other Asian emerging markets (RBI 2009a).

Capital inflows rose also due to large increases in commercial borrowing by private-sector firms. As constraints on external commercial borrowing by domestic companies were relaxed and because interest rates ruled higher in the domestic market, large Indian firms at the margin took the syndicated loan route to borrow money abroad at relatively lower interest rates. They engaged in a version of the carry trade, borrowing money in foreign exchange from the international markets where interest rates were lower and making investments in India (besides financing investments abroad).

Not surprisingly, the 2007–8 crisis resulted in a sharp outflow of capital, especially capital brought into the stock market by foreign institutional investors (FIIs). Needing cash to meet commitments and cover losses at home, these FIIs were selling out in Indian markets and repatriating capital abroad (RBI 2009a, 2009b). One consequence of the capital outflow was a collapse of India's stock markets, just as the earlier capital inflows had triggered a speculative bubble in both stock and real estate markets. They had caused an unprecedented rate of asset price inflation in India's stock markets and substantially increased volatility in the movements of the Bombay Stock Exchange's (BSE) Sensitive Index (Sensex).

Another route through which integration has influenced the way in which the global crisis has affected India is its impact on the role played by credit in financing private consumption and investment. Three trends in the domestic credit market following internal financial liberalization are of note. The first was the scorching pace of expansion of total bank credit from 2005, at more than double the rate of increase of nominal GDP. The second was the evidence of a sharp increase in the retail exposure of the banking system, with personal loans increasing from 12.2 per cent of advances in 2000–1 to 22.3 per cent in 2006–7

(RBI 1993–2007). A significant but as yet unknown proportion of this expansion in retail lending could be 'sub-prime' in nature. Finally, the Indian financial sector too had begun securitizing personal loans of all kinds so as to transfer the risk associated with them to those who could be persuaded to buy into them. As the US experience shows, this tends to slacken diligence when offering credit, since risk does not stay with those originating retail loans.

Thus India could experience its own financial crisis for two reasons. First, there is the fragility that comes out of opening up its capital account to encourage the inflow of capital. Second, by institutionally transforming the financial sector it has unleashed a dynamic that endows the financial system with a poorly regulated, oligopolistic structure, which could again increase the fragility of the system. Greater freedom to invest, including in sensitive sectors such as real estate and stock markets, ability to increase exposure to particular sectors and individual clients, freedom to expand exposure to retail credit markets for purchases of housing, automobiles and durables, and increased regulatory forbearance could all lead to financial failure.

C.P. CHANDRASEKHAR

REFERENCES

Kareken, John H. 1992. 'Regulation of Commercial Banking in the United States', in Peter Newman, Murray Millgate, and John Eatwell, eds, *The New Palgrave Dictionary of Money and Finance*, vol. 3, London, Macmillan, pp. 315–19.

Reinhart, Carmen M. and Kenneth S. Rogoff. 2008. 'Banking Crises: An Equal Opportunity Menace', Working Paper 14587, National Bureau of Economic Research, Cambridge, MA. Available at http://www.nber.org/papers/w14587, accessed on 1 August 2009.

Reserve Bank of India (RBI). 1993–2007. *Basic*

Statistical Returns of Scheduled Commercial Banks in India, Mumbai, Reserve Bank of India.

RBI. 2009a. 'India's Overall Balance of Payments in Dollars'. Available at http://rbidocs.rbi.org. in/rdocs/Bulletin/DOCs/T43_TradeBal. xls, accessed on 21 March 2009.

————. 2009b. 'International Investment Position (IIP) of India as at the End of September 2008'. Available at http://rbidocs.rbi.org. in/rbiadmin/scripts/BS_PressReleaseDisplay. aspx?prid=20357, accessed on 21 March 2009.

Sametz, A.W. 1992. 'Financial Innovation and Regulation in the United States', *Palgrave Dictionary of Finance*, London, Macmillan, pp. 71–5.

Sweezy, Paul M. and Harry Magdoff. 1972. *The Dynamics of US Capitalism*, New York, Monthly Review Press.

Financial-sector Reforms

In the economic history of India, the crisis of June 1991 is very significant. The initial symptoms of economic difficulties, especially in the fiscal and external sectors, were apparent from the beginning of the 1980s—administered interest rates; underdeveloped debt and financial markets; rising fiscal, monetized, and current account deficits; increasing recourse to directed lending by state-owned banks; an overvalued domestic currency; a high and complex tariff structure; and a restrictive industrial policy. India was a financially repressed closed economy. In 1991, the current account underwent severe stress due to the Gulf War, and a difficult situation turned into a crisis in June, when foreign currency reserves dipped to an amount sufficient to cover only two weeks of imports. The Government of India had to ship 47 tonnes of gold to the Bank of England, amidst national humiliation, to secure a loan of about US$ 415 million

before support could be arranged from the International Monetary Fund.

The government's response to the short-lived crisis of June 1991 was the simultaneous implementation of measures to stabilize the economy and introduction of structural reforms. Although structural reforms designed to enhance productivity, efficiency, and international competitiveness of the economy were introduced in many sectors simultaneously, the most effective of the reforms have been those in the financial sector. The complexity of the economic situation spurred comprehensive reforms in fiscal management, banking, the external sector, and the financial markets. The general approach to financial-sector reforms was: (i) cautious sequencing of measures that are mutually reinforcing, and (ii) development of financial infrastructure—supervisory, institutional, technological, and legal.

Financial markets have developed significantly since 1991. This entry discusses the reforms in the money and government securities markets in the first section. Those reforms were supported by a number of complementary developments in related areas. The second section discusses the cessation of automatic monetization. The third section argues for the separation of debt from monetary management.

DEVELOPMENTS IN THE MONEY AND GOVERNMENT SECURITIES MARKETS

The development and regulation of the money and government securities markets are a responsibility of the Reserve Bank of India (RBI) that emerges from its role as the monetary authority and debt manager for the government, and its interest in maintaining stability of the financial system. The development of deep, liquid markets helps in efficient price discovery and effective transmission of monetary policy. The emphasis has been on removing structural rigidities, encouraging wider participation, and developing infrastructure for orderly market activity.

Money Market

Major reforms in the money market were introduced from 1991 onwards, though some measures had been initiated in 1987. The reforms included the introduction of new participants, instruments (commercial paper, certificates of deposit, and inter-bank participation certificates), and maturities of Treasury Bills. To regulate short-term liquidity in the system, the RBI introduced repurchase transactions (repo) on 10 December 1992 and a liquidity adjustment facility (LAF) on 5 June 2000 under which it absorbs (repo) or injects liquidity (reverse repo) in the system each day. The repo rate has become an important signalling instrument for the financial markets, and the LAF has succeeded in reducing volatility in the call rate.

In India, 91-day Treasury Bills have been in the market since 1917; 182-day Treasury Bills were introduced in November 1986, 364-day Treasury Bills in April 1992; and 14-day Treasury Bills in June 1997. After having experimented with different maturities and considered investors' choices, at present 91-day Bills are offered only by the central government in weekly auctions, and 182- and 364-day in fortnightly auctions. The longer-term bills provide varying maturities along the yield curve to cater to the needs of different investors.

The RBI mainly sold the 91-day Treasury Bills through weekly auctions until July 1965 and since then at a fixed discount rate until January 1993. The administered discount rate, generally lower than the prevailing market rate, resulted in concentration of their holdings with the RBI and inhibited the development of the secondary market in these bills. The auction system for placing Treasury Bills was re-introduced in January 1993. As a result, the ownership pattern has changed, with the bills becoming popular with the public, and the share of the RBI declining since 1993.

Government Securities Market

Fiscal-policy compulsions rendered debt management policy passive before 1991. The RBI, as a debt manager, had little control over such essential aspects of debt management as the volume issued, maturity profile, term structure, or time of floatation, but had to support the borrowing programme of the central government by participating in the primary market. Since 1981, the volume of outstanding long-term dated securities has expanded rapidly from Rs 185.4 billion (12.9 per cent of the gross domestic product [GDP]) at end March 1981 to Rs 11,088 billion (35.8 per cent) at end March 2005, with the share issued by the central government ranging between 80.8 and 83.8 per cent of the total, during the period.

To develop the government securities market, an active internal debt management policy has been pursued since 1991. To offer market-related yields to suit investor expectations, five-year and ten-year dated securities of the central government were auctioned for the first time on 3 June and 3 August 1992 respectively. Since then, auctions have increasingly been used for borrowings by the central government, and new instruments have regularly been introduced, including zero coupon, floating rate, and capital-indexed bonds. The maturity profile of government bonds has changed over the period with the reduction in maximum maturity from twenty years to ten years in 1992. As market conditions improved, and in consideration of the absorptive capacity of the market, the maximum maturity of central government securities was extended to 20 years in 1997,

25 years in 2001, and 30 years in 2002: the weighted-average maturity of fresh issuances has increased from 5.7 years in 1995–6 to 14.1 years in 2004–5. The state governments continue to raise resources from the market mainly through a traditional method (a non-auction method generally called 'tap sale') for a fixed maturity of ten years. The coupon on state government securities is fixed slightly higher (25 to 50 basis points) than central government securities of similar maturity trading in the secondary market, representing an illiquidity premium (due to lower volumes of outstandings and therefore low tradability)—thereby attempting to align the coupon rate to a market-related rate of interest. Since January 1999, some states have begun to raise a part of their allocated market borrowings through auctions.

The reforms in the government securities market have facilitated the active use of open market operations (OMO) as a tool of market intervention through auctions. The sale of government securities by the RBI increased from Rs 14 billion in 1995–6 to Rs 416 billion in 2003–4. Market-related rates, both in the primary auction as well as the OMO, have also helped achieve diversification of the investor base, with the share of non-captive investors increasing, though—statutorily—commercial banks, insurance companies, and provident funds continue to invest in government securities.

The reforms in the securities market were accompanied by two important developments in the economy. First, the statutory liquidity ratio (SLR), requiring the commercial banks to invest a specific proportion of their deposits in approved securities, mainly government, was reduced in quick phases to the lowest prescribed under the Banking Regulation Act. The SLR securities, mainly issued at low administered interest rates, adversely impacted the profitability and risk-taking capabilities of the captive market. Second, market-related interest rates have increasingly been adopted in various sectors of the economy, including money markets, government securities, bank deposits and credit, public-sector bonds, and small (postal) savings. The dismantling of the administered interest rate regime raised the efficiency of the intermediation process and ensured financing of projects based on commercial considerations.

A highly liquid and vibrant secondary market requires a transparent trading system and a secure system for payment and settlement. A negotiated dealing system (NDS), operationalized since February 2002, provides screen-based electronic dealing in the money and government securities markets, and connectivity to the Clearing Corporation of India and the Public Debt Office. The real-time gross settlement system has also been operational since March 2004.

To develop the secondary market, primary and secondary dealerships were established in 1995 and 1996 respectively, and trading of government securities on the stock exchange was initiated in January 2003. Self-regulatory associations of the primary and money market dealers played an important role in establishing codes of conduct and standards in the markets, while advisory committees, consisting of academicians and practitioners helped in benchmarking Indian practices to international standards. The smooth implementation of the reform process also benefited from a wider public debate on issues and the interplay of market forces.

Consequent upon the reforms, trading in the secondary market has increased from 10.7 per cent of GDP in 1995–6 to 87.7 per cent of GDP in 2004–5, with Treasury Bills (exclusively 91- and 364-day) increasing from 1.4 to 17.5 per cent and dated securities from 9.3 to 70.2

Table 1   Secondary Market Transactions in Government Securities

	Treasury bills						Dated securities					
	Outright			Repo			Outright			Repo		
Year end	Total (Rs bn)	Of which (%) 91-day	364-day	Total (Rs bn)	Of which (%) 91-day	364-day	Total (Rs bn)	Of which (%) Central	State	Total (Rs bn)	Of which (%) Central	State
1	2	3	4	5	6	7	8	9	10	11	12	13
1996	115	35.6	64.4	48	12.5	87.5	180	97.4	2.6	928	100	0
2005	1162	52.3	47.7	2877	42.5	57.5	9049	97.1	2.9	12,753	99.3	0.7

Source: RBI.

Table 2   Structure of Interest Rates—Short and Long Term

(per cent)

Year	Treasury bills, 91-day	Call money rate, Mumbai	Advances rate	Commercial bank rates* over 5 yrs	Coupon rates on market loans and bonds 0–5 yrs	6–10 yrs	over 10 yrs
1	2	3	4	5	6	7	8
1960–1	2.65	4.24	5.00	4.50	–	3.50	4.00
1970–1	3.08	6.38	8.50	7.25	–	4.50	5.75
1980–1	4.60	7.12	16.50	10.00	–	6.00–6.50	6.75–7.50
1990–1	4.60	15.85	16.50	11.00	10.50	10.75	11.25–11.50
2000–1	8.98	9.15	11.50	9.50–10.00	9.47–10.95	9.88–11.69	10.47–11.70
2003–4	4.59	4.33	10.25	5.25–5.50	4.69	4.62–5.73	5.18–6.35
2004–5	4.89	4.55	10.25	5.75–6.25	–	5.90–7.20	4.49–8.24

Source: RBI.

Note: * Since 1995–6 deposit rates refer to five major public-sector (state-owned) banks as in end March.

per cent (Table 1). The reforms have led to the emergence of a yield curve that is market related and is increasingly used as a benchmark for other instruments in the debt market (Table 2). The development of the markets has led to the convergence of interest rates in the economy (Jena 2004).

FISCAL DOMINANCE OF MONETARY POLICY AND TERMINATION OF AUTOMATIC MONETIZATION

In India, the RBI has been expected to automatically finance the fiscal deficit of the central government since the 1950s through subscription to government bills. The fiscal dominance of monetary policy, especially after the late 1970s, left little room for the RBI to pursue a monetary policy designed to foster financial markets and ensure price stability. The share of the monetized deficit in the gross fiscal deficit of the central government ranged from 30 per cent to 43 per cent during 1978–91. On average, the monetized deficit accounted for more than four-fifths of reserve money during 1970–99, and exceeded 100 per cent during 1980–91. In India, many studies have emphasized the applicability of monetarist theory, and also empirically tested the robustness of the money demand function whereby a rise in the money supply directly affects price level (Buiter and Patel 1992; and Singh 1999a).

The genesis of automatic monetization can be traced to the agreement between the central government and the RBI in January 1955, regarding creation of ad hoc Treasury Bills (91-day). This agreement, specified that the central government shall maintain a certain minimum cash balance with the RBI: if the balance should fall below the minimum agreed limit, the account would be automatically replenished by the creation of ad hocs in favour of the RBI. However, over time, issuance of such ad hocs became a permanent and increasing means of financial support to the central government from the RBI. The amount of ad hocs rose from a negligible amount to 2.4 per cent of GDP in 1982, 6.1 per cent in 1987, and 12.0 per cent in 1991. These ad hocs, held within the RBI, constituted a significant component of reserve money—19.0 per cent in 1982, 44.4 per cent in 1987, and 77.3 per cent in 1991. As a rising monetized deficit has implications for the price level, the central government and the RBI felt the need to place some limit on credit extended by the RBI to the central government. Consequently, the central government and the RBI signed an agreement in September 1994 to phase out the creation of ad hocs by the end of fiscal year 1996–7. The existing ad hocs, amounting to more than Rs 1200 billion by the end of March 1997 (9.6 per cent of GDP) and carrying a rate of discount of 4.6 per cent per annum, were converted into special perpetual securities and issued by the central government to the RBI.

PUBLIC DEBT AND ITS SEPARATION FROM MONETARY MANAGEMENT

In India, since 1951 when the five year plans were introduced, domestic debt has been incurred with the main objective of enhancing public investment for economic development. The impact of domestic debt on economic growth has been analysed theoretically in the context of two contrasting views—Keynesian, which considers it a

burden, and Ricardian (Barro 1978), which considers it neutral. In the Indian context, Rao (1953) argues that deficit financing is useful for economic development while Singh (1999b) concludes empirically that debt and growth are not co-integrated.

Public debt and contingent liabilities amount to 96.8 per cent of GDP in India (Table 3). Consequently, interest payments on public debt account for nearly 6 per cent of GDP and one-fifth of total government expenditure for the financial year ending March 2005. In India, the central government and state governments separately manage various components of debt through numerous offices spread across the country. The RBI plays a key role in managing a significant component of internal debt (mainly market loans and Treasury Bills, accounting for nearly half of domestic borrowings).

Table 3 Public Debt and Contingent Liabilities of the Government (per cent of GDP)

Year (end of March)	Domestic debt	External debt	Total public debt	Contingent liabilities
1952	30.8	1.4	32.1	NA
1990	55.5	10.5	66.0	13.9*
2000	59.2	9.4	68.6	11.2
2005	80.2	6.0	86.2	10.6**

Source: RBI.
Notes: *1992. **2004.

In India, the issue of separation of debt from monetary management was debated in the mid-1990s, when the conclusion was that such a separation would require well-developed financial markets and a credible commitment by the government to contain budget deficits. At that time, interest rates in India generally were still administered. In the past decade, consequent on reforms, financial markets have developed and the last remnants of interest rate controls are being dismantled. The borrowing requirements of the central government in recent years are successfully being met from the market, with minimal devolvement on the RBI or the primary dealers. Also, the Fiscal Responsibility and Budget Management Act 2003 places annual restrictions on the fiscal deficit of the central government as well as on participation by the RBI in the primary market for government securities. A number of state governments have enacted similar legislations to enforce fiscal responsibility.

The separation of debt management from monetary policy and the assignment of the debt management function to a separate office would help establish specific accountability and responsibility of the debt manager. This could lead to integrated and professional management of all government liabilities based on sound commercial principles. The development of a focused and transparent debt management strategy also would ensure that funds are available to government at competitive market interest rates, encouraging expenditure prioritization and fiscal discipline. The first step in the separation of the two operations—functional separation between debt management and monetary operations initiated within the RBI in April 2005—is expected eventually to culminate in a debt manager independent of the RBI.

Although India's fiscal deficits and debt continue to be high, the termination of automatic monetization and the enactment of the Fiscal Responsibility and Budget Management Act of 2003 gave confidence to the financial markets. The market-related rates of interest on government securities have diversified the ownership pattern and increased the absorption of government securities by the market.

The interest rates in the financial markets are converging and the markets are becoming integrated. Debt management functions and practices have developed substantially since 1991, though still being managed within the RBI. In view of the developments in the markets and the commitment on the part of the government to contain the fiscal deficit, the time has come to consider separating monetary and debt management. The government would then require a more independent RBI to meet an inflation target, as is common in most developed countries.

CHARAN SINGH

REFERENCES

Barro, R.J. 1978. 'Comment from an Unreconstructed Ricardian', *Journal of Monetary Economics*, 2: 1–32.

Buiter, W.J. and U. Patel. 1992. 'Debt, Deficits and Inflation: An Application to the Public Finances of India', *Journal of Public Economics*, 47(2): 171–205.

Jena, P.R. 2004. 'Integration of Financial Markets in India: An Empirical Analysis', *Indian Journal of Economics and Business*, 3(1): 63–77.

Rao, V.K.R.V. 1953. *Deficit Financing, Capital formation and Price Behaviour in an Under-Developed Economy*, Eastern Economist Pamphlets.

Singh, C. 1999a. 'Domestic Debt and Economic Growth in India', *Economic and Political Weekly*, 34: 1445–53.

———. 1999b. 'Monetized Debt, Monetary Aggregates and Price Level in India', *Prajnan*, 27(4): 1998–9.

Housing Finance

Since the turn of the twentieth century, home loans have grown at a rapid pace in India. The majority of the country's billion-plus population continues to live in rural areas where expansion of existing village homes has mostly serviced the needs of the expanding population. For a variety of reasons India has had a slower rate of urbanization than most developing economies, and certainly so relative to China. The 2001 Census of India found that 27.8 per cent of the population lived in urban areas, a modest increase from 25.7 per cent in 1991 and 23.3 per cent a decade earlier. By contrast, China saw urbanization rise from 26.9 per cent in 1991 to 41.8 per cent in 2004. However, even with the slower pace of urbanization, the need for new housing is large. The Planning Commission had estimated that during the Tenth Plan period (2002–7) there would be a need for constructing more than 22 million dwelling units.

In India, prior to the reforms of 1991, provision of housing was seen as part of the many social obligations of government and accordingly the agencies entrusted with the task were State (Provincial) Housing Boards and City Development Authorities. These agencies were specially mandated to service the needs of the lower-income sections of society. As a result, numerous small, congested, and aesthetically unappealing apartment blocks arose across the country, variously categorized as *janata* (people's), low-, and middle-income housing. That section of the middle class that did not qualify on the income criterion did have the option to buy housing plots from official agencies and build houses upon them or, since the late 1970s, to purchase ready-built apartments from the same agencies. While many of the apartments constructed under the lower income schemes were pre-financed by state agencies with easy repayment terms, the relatively higher-income middle class home buyer had to primarily rely on his or her personal financial resources once the considerable challenge of securing an allotment was overcome. Some financing from a variety of state agencies was, however, available for cooperative purchases, which was particularly useful for accommodating

employees of the government, including the armed and police services.

In 1970, the central government set up the Housing and Urban Development Corporation (HUDCO) which was mandated to finance the construction of urban economic infrastructure and also support housing schemes. The state-owned Life Insurance Corporation (LIC) and General Insurance Corporation (GIC) were also mandated to provide support for housing finance. This mandate was discharged indirectly by lending to social schemes that included housing and subsequently, since the late 1980s, directly, by the establishment of subsidiary housing finance companies.

The first private company established to provide home finance was the Housing Development and Finance Corporation (HDFC) set up in 1977. Historically in post-Independent India, both the legislation and legal system were not amenable to executing foreclosure, irrespective of the documentation securing the loan. To complicate matters, much of the property in the faster-growing urban areas was leasehold, with the state agency that was lessor having enjoined special prohibitions on resale. Under these circumstances, the mortgage of housing property at most served the role of a negative lien—prohibiting the borrower from selling the property without prior assent of the lender. The dread with which many Indians view their country's legal system was an added deterrent to the extent that most individuals would assess their own ability to navigate the court system very poorly compared to a corporation with its much greater resources.

The HDFC chose to focus on the salaried section of prospective home buyers, for that resolved several issues all at once. It immediately determined the income status of the borrower and subjected him/her to the additional discipline of the authority of his or her employer. The social reality also was that this section of Indian society was intrinsically risk-averse and hence loan-averse, with great fear of the social humiliation perceived to be associated with being named a defaulter and dragged to court. This made for a business where the borrower was most likely to have little or no debt other than the home loan and was under several obligations to observe the covenants of the loan. The economic environment of the era with its widespread shortages meant that the market price of the housing asset was always increasing and thereby the proportion of home equity (the difference between market price and the outstanding loan) was continually rising as a proportion of the outstanding loan.

It was therefore not surprising that the HDFC had assets with an enviable delinquency record and an even better loan loss record. Since the mid-1980s other non-banking housing finance companies (NBFC) also began to enter the market and the delinquency rates for individual salaried home owners continued to be sterling, with loan losses mostly restricted to credits given to companies in the construction business.

In the years after 1991, a market for personal loans began to rapidly develop, primarily focusing on the financing of cars. Foreign banks and some NBFCs that took the initiative found that the combination of credit discipline of one section of borrowers and the legislative initiatives easing repossession, made for a business with fairly low likely loan losses compared to the relatively higher yields prevalent. State-owned commercial banks, which had previously stayed away from personal finance, were increasingly attracted to it, and this at a time when their corporate portfolio was coming under considerable pressure. At the beginning of the second half of the 1990s, the personal finance business, and in particular home finance, was set to expand rapidly.

It needs to be remembered that India is a relatively under-leveraged economy. The proportion of bank credit to gross domestic product (GDP) at current market prices was 21.4 per cent in fiscal year 1995–6, which has since increased to 42.7 per cent in 2005–6. This is in considerable contrast to China for instance where the bank credit to GDP ratio at the end of calendar year 2005 was 136.2 per cent. In the USA, bank credit as a proportion of GDP is 56 per cent, up from 48 per cent a decade earlier. However, banks form a smaller source of credits in the US economy and the total outstanding debt of households was 85 per cent in 2005, with home loans at 64 per cent of the GDP.

In India at the end of March 1996, home loans issued by banks amounted to a mere 0.6 per cent of the GDP, which has since risen to 4.1 per cent at the end of 2004–5 and 5.3 per cent in 2005–6, forming about half of the stock of personal loans and little over 12 per cent of outstanding bank credit. In addition there are the independent housing finance companies and the small amount of mortgage-backed securitized (MBS) paper that is outside the balance sheet of the loan-originating institutions. The total of mortgage assets on the books of the banks, independent housing finance companies, and investing institutions was close to 8 per cent of the GDP at the end of 2005–6, compared to less than 0.7 per cent a decade earlier.

The environment of declining interest rates since 2001 helped the home finance business push out credit by making terms very attractive to prospective home buyers with variable rates as low as 6.5 per cent. The business, however, was careful in preferentially selling variable interest products and has thus largely excluded interest risk from its balance sheet. Some of the growth in the period 2001 to 2004 was due to refinancing of high-cost previously contracted debt, which added to business volumes. It also lowered perceived risk with previously existing lenders profiting from pre-payment fees and new lenders obtaining access to seasoned assets. The increase in interest rates in 2005 and 2006 is likely to curb the growth of the business, as home buyers find loan conditions becoming more expensive with interest rates on home loans having risen by 30 to 40 per cent in recent years. However, the pace of urban growth does not yet pose a serious downside risk on property prices and to that extent point to significant erosion of home equity. However, if property prices were to decline significantly following a severe economic downturn or some other crisis, pressure on delinquency is inevitable. Offsetting this is the fact that as loans mature, along with more stable loan growth the loan-to-value ratio would also ease, thereby reducing vulnerability.

The tightening of interest rates has energized the expected process of consolidation with marginal players choosing to exit from the loan-origination market. The four biggest players, namely ICICI, HDFC, State Bank of India, and LIC Housing, have well over 40 per cent market share; the next four have about 9 per cent market share. The concentration of the larger players is likely to increase in the next phase of expansion, which with high interest rates is likely to see slower growth and more cost pressure on margins.

The home finance business has also benefited from fiscal and regulatory encouragement. In 1999, the government provided an income tax shelter for interest payments of up to Rs 150,000 on housing loans. Initially designed to be operational for a few years, the provision continues to be in force. At about the same time,

housing loans extended by a bank, subject to loan size limits, were also qualified to count towards the bank's obligation under mandated priority-sector credit. The risk weight for purposes of computing capital adequacy of banks is set at 75 per cent, which is less than general commercial credits (100 per cent risk weight). The National Housing Bank (NHB), a wholly owned subsidiary of the Reserve Bank of India (RBI), acts as regulator and a source of refinancing for housing finance companies. However, by far the larger part of the business is with the commercial banks and remains regulated by the RBI.

Housing loans grew by 21 per cent in 1997–8 and maintained an average annual rate of expansion of 45 per cent over the next seven years to 2004–5. The year 2003–4 was the high point when housing credit grew by 74 per cent. The sharp expansion in housing credit (along with other retail loans) helped fuel the expansion of bank credit in 2002–3 and 2003–4 and contributed to lifting the pace of overall economic expansion. In 2004–5 and 2005–6, while retail loans including bank credit continued to play an important role, they yielded considerable ground to conventional industrial and infrastructure borrowing.

The delinquency and loan loss record of the housing finance business reveals many things. First that, as was expected, the generation of non-performing assets (NPAs) was low, estimated at 0.2 to 0.6 per cent (per annum) for established players. The overall stock of gross NPAs is estimated at around 2 per cent of outstanding advances on an average basis. Since the length of the asset is long and a large proportion of the loans are fresh, the possibility does exist that delinquencies will rise in coming years. While the careful way of feeling around credit quality of the 1980s may have been excessive, the rapid and competitive expansion of recent years may have imparted certain amount of avoidable credit risk. It is believed that some agencies, particularly in the state-owned sector, incurred above-average NPAs owing in part to inadequate credit selection resources and in part to collusive inaccurate documentation. On a static basis, that is over the lifetime of the credit, it is believed that the existing pool of mortgage credits would have loan losses of 3 to 5 per cent.

Initially there was little differentiation in interest spreads among customers of varying credit quality and the spreads in general were possibly thinner than what the credit risk should have implied. However, over the past couple of years, major lenders have been able to put in place differential pricing that is a more accurate reflection of the loan-adjusted profitability of the business, which is expected to be strengthened in the forthcoming period likely to be characterized by tighter monetary conditions and stable loan growth.

The home finance market in India is yet to penetrate the sub-prime markets in any significant fashion. Geographically too it has been concentrated in the larger cities, with metropolitan centres accounting for 47 per cent of outstanding loans in March 2005, and other urban centres another 27 per cent. Both vertical and horizontal expansion of the business is likely to increase the inherent credit risk, given continued weakness in institutional support for foreclosure. The further expansion of the business may encourage the development of innovations which try and get around the problems posed by the combination of sub-prime credit and the relative illiquidity of the underlying asset.

SAUMITRA CHAUDHURI

REFERENCES

ICRA Limited. 2004. 'Mortgage Loan Market', *ICRA Rating Feature*, October.

Karnad, Renu S. 2004. 'Housing Finance and the Economy: Regional Trends in South Asia—Perspectives', International Union for Housing Finance, 25th World Congress, June, Brussels.

Moody's Investors Service. 2005. 'A Primer on the US Residential Mortgage Market for Banks and Thrift Investors', *Global Credit Research*, March.

Reserve Bank of India (RBI). Various issues. *Banks Statistical Returns*, Mumbai, RBI.

———. 2005. *Report on Trends and Progress of Banking in India 2004–5* (also previous issues), Mumbai, RBI.

Monetary Policy

Monetary policy refers to that part of public policy pursued by a central bank that influences monetary and other financial conditions with the broader objectives of price stability, sustainable growth, and high employment. The role of monetary policy, as an arm of broad economic policy, has evolved over time in tune with developments in economic theory and empirical findings on changing perceptions of the role of money and interest rates in economic activity with advancements in technology, institutions, and financial markets. The evolution of monetary policy in India is no exception to this general trend.

The conduct of monetary policy is generally assigned to the central bank. The central bank responds to the evolving economic activity within an articulated monetary policy framework, which covers: (i) the objectives of monetary policy; (ii) the analytics of monetary policy focusing on the transmission mechanism; and (iii) operating procedures focusing on operating targets and instruments.

OBJECTIVES

Traditionally, central banks have pursued the twin objectives of price stability and growth. A number of central banks have additional objectives of exchange rate stability and financial stability. While these objectives are interrelated, there are trade-offs as well. Faced with multiple objectives that are equally desirable, there remains the problem of assigning to each policy instrument the most appropriate objective.

Accordingly, there is broad consensus, both in academic and policy circles, that monetary policy is best suited to achieving the goal of price stability. Price stability is generally defined as a low and stable order of inflation. For developed countries, such an inflation threshold is considered to be around 2 per cent which could be higher for developing countries depending on their stages of economic development.

A number of prominent central banks including the European Central Bank, Bank of England, and Bank of Japan have adopted price stability as the single objective of monetary policy. However, the Federal Reserve System of the US continues to pursue multiple objectives of monetary policy—maximum employment, stable prices, and moderate long-term interest rates. Central banks in several developing countries have made exchange rate management another important policy objective. In recent years, particularly after the financial crises of the 1990s, the concern for financial stability is an integral part of the central bank's activism.

Historically, in countries which have experienced high or hyperinflation, there is stronger public commitment to price stability as the primary objective of monetary policy. However, most central banks tend to operate on the golden mean of constrained discretion which takes the pragmatic view that within the objective of price stability, monetary policy has to stabilize swings in effective demand as well (Bernanke 2003).

The preamble to the Reserve Bank of India Act 1934 has spelt out the objectives of the Bank as being 'to regulate the issue of Bank notes and the keeping of reserves with a view to securing monetary stability in India and generally to operate the currency and credit system of the country to its advantage'. Although there is no explicit mandate for price stability, as is the current trend in many countries, maintaining price stability and ensuring an adequate flow of credit to the productive sectors of the economy have evolved as the objectives of monetary policy in India. In essence, monetary policy thus aims to maintain a judicious balance between price stability and economic growth. The relative emphasis on price stability or economic growth is governed by the prevailing circumstances and is spelt out from time to time in the policy announcements of the Bank.

Of late, considerations of financial stability have assumed greater importance in view of the increasing openness of the Indian economy and financial reforms. In the Indian context, financial stability could be interpreted to mean: first, ensuring smooth and uninterrupted payments and settlement system; second, maintenance of a level of confidence in the financial system amongst all the participants and stakeholders; and third, absence of excessive volatility in financial markets that unduly and adversely affects real economic activity. The Reserve Bank of India thus strives to pursue its monetary policy objectives by creating an environment of financial stability.

THE ANALYTICS OF MONETARY POLICY
The monetary policy framework largely depends on the underlying relationships between the relevant economic variables. It is also important to assess the stability of such relationships and the effectiveness of the various transmission channels. The transmission mechanism describes how monetary policy action affects output and

inflation, the final objectives of monetary policy. In the literature, four sets of transmission channels have been identified: one, the quantum channel, especially relating to money supply and credit; two, the interest rate channel; three, the exchange rate channel; and four, the asset price channel. How these channels function in a given economy depends on the stage of development of the economy and its underlying financial structure. There can be considerable feedbacks and interactions among the various transmission channels which need to be carefully assessed for a proper understanding of the transmission mechanism.

In the design of monetary policy, another important consideration is that since the central bank may not be in a position to directly achieve its ultimate objectives, monetary policy is often formulated in terms of an intermediate target. For example, in a monetary targeting framework, a suitable monetary aggregate is considered an intermediate target based on the basic relationship between money, output, and prices. Exchange rate as an intermediate target can be suitable for small open economies, setting the exchange rate against a low-inflation anchor country. This would, however, entail loss of independence in steering domestic interest rates. The 'impossible trinity', that is incompatibility between fixed exchange rate, open capital account, and independent monetary policy is well recognized by central banks world over. Direct interest rate targeting has been adopted in countries with higher levels of financial market integration. There have been attempts to combine both interest rate and exchange rate through the monetary conditions index (MCI).

In the context of improving transparency, the recent trend has been towards direct inflation targeting. Adoption of explicit inflation targeting as the final goal of

monetary policy involves the preparation of an inflation forecast, which, in a way, serves the purpose of both an intermediate target and final objective. The prerequisites for inflation targeting include a considerable degree of operational autonomy or independence for the central bank, flexible exchange rate conditions, well-developed financial markets, and absence of fiscal dominance.

In view of the growing complexities of macroeconomic management, several central banks, including the European Central Bank, have placed reliance on a broad set of economic and leading indicators rather than focusing on an intermediate target or a direct inflation target. The Federal Reserve has traditionally been following a more broad-based approach to the conduct of monetary policy in the US.

Monetary policy in India used to be conducted till 1997–8 with broad money (M_3) as an intermediate target, which amounted to regulating money supply consistent with the expected growth in real income and a projected level of inflation. In practice, the monetary targeting framework was used in a flexible manner with feedback from developments in the real sector. Questions were raised about the appropriateness of such a framework with the changing interrelationship between money, output, and prices in the wake of financial reforms and opening up of the economy. The Working Group on Money Supply (RBI 1998) sought to address some of these issues. The most significant observation of the Group was regarding the changing nature of the transmission mechanism as it highlighted that the interest rate channel was gaining in importance. In line with this thinking, the RBI has switched over to a multiple-indicator approach from 1998–9 wherein interest rates or rates of return in different markets (money, capital, and government securities), along with such data as on currency, credit extended by banks and financial institutions, fiscal position, trade, capital flows, inflation rate, exchange rate, refinancing and transactions in foreign exchange available on high-frequency basis, are juxtaposed with output data for drawing policy perspectives.

OPERATING PROCEDURES: INSTRUMENTS AND TARGETS

Operating procedures pertain to day-to-day implementation of monetary policy by central banks through various instruments that can broadly be classified into direct and indirect instruments. Typically, direct instruments include required cash and/or liquidity reserve ratios and directed credit and administered interest rates. The cash reserve ratio (CRR) determines the level of reserves (central bank money or cash) banks need to hold against their deposit liabilities. Similarly, the liquidity reserve ratio requires banks to maintain a part of their deposit liabilities in the form of liquid assets (for example government securities). Credit and interest rate directives take the form of prescribed targets for allocation of credit to preferred sectors/industries and prescription of deposit and lending rates.

The indirect instruments generally operate through the price channel which covers repurchase transactions (repos), outright transactions in securities (open market operations [OMOs]), standing facilities (refinance), and market-based discount window. For example, if the central bank desires to inject liquidity for a short period, it could do so by providing liquidity to banks in exchange for securities at a desired interest rate, reversing the transaction at a predetermined time. Similarly, if the central bank desires to influence liquidity on an enduring basis, it could resort to OMOs involving outright

purchase (and sale) of securities without any buy-back obligations.

While OMOs including repo transactions operate at the discretion of the central bank, standing facilities make available limited liquidity which could be accessed by eligible market participants (generally banks) at their discretion. Standing facilities can be of two types: uncollateralized deposit facility with the central bank and marginal collateralized lending facility by the central bank. A market-based discount window makes available reserves either through direct lending or through rediscounting or purchase of financial assets held by banks.

While direct instruments are effective, they are considered inefficient in terms of their impact on the financial market. On the other hand, the use of indirect instruments depends on the development of the supporting financial markets and institutions. These instruments are usually directed at attaining a prescribed value of the operating target, typically bank reserves and/or a very short-term interest rate (usually the overnight inter-bank rate).

The optimal choice between price and quantity targets would depend upon the sources of disturbances in the goods and money markets. In reality, it often becomes difficult to trace the sources of instability. Hence monetary policy is implemented by fixing, at least over some short time interval, the value of an operating target. In a single-period context, the choice of the level of the target amounts to setting a rule for monetary policy. However, in a dynamic context, the connection is less straightforward. Indeed, deviation from a target could occur, either intended or unintended, which may impart an inflationary bias when monetary policy is conducted with discretion (Kydland and Prescott 1977). In order to address the problem of dynamic inconsistency, rule-based solutions are emphasized in the literature, for example monetary rule (changes in money supply at a predetermined rate) and Taylor-type rule (changes in interest rate based on deviation of growth and inflation from their potential/ desired levels). While a rule-based system imparts transparency, providing certainty about future policy response, it becomes ineffective in its response to unanticipated shocks given its inflexibility. In practice, therefore, central banks follow an approach of constrained discretion.

The operating procedures of monetary policy of most central banks have largely converged on one of the following three variants: (i) a number of central banks, including the US Federal Reserve, estimate the demand for bank reserves and then carry out OMOs to target short-term interest rates (the Federal Funds Rate in the case of the USA); (ii) some other central banks, including the Bank of Japan, estimate market liquidity and carry out OMOs to target the bank reserves, while allowing interest rates to adjust; and (iii) a growing number of central banks, including the European Central Bank, modulate monetary conditions in terms of both the quantum and price of liquidity, through a mix of OMOs, standing facilities, and minimum reserve requirement and changes in the policy rate with the objective of containing overnight market interest rate within a narrow corridor of interest rate targets.

In the Indian context, reserve money was used as the operating target in the monetary-targeting framework until the mid-1990s. In the current monetary policy framework, with growing interlinkages in the financial market, reliance on direct instruments has been reduced and liquidity management in the system is carried out through OMOs in the form of outright purchases/sales of government securities and daily repo and reverse repo operations under the liquidity adjustment facility (LAF) (Reddy 2002). The LAF has enabled the Reserve Bank to modulate short-term liquidity under varied financial market conditions, including large capital inflows from abroad. In addition, it has enabled the Reserve Bank to set a corridor for the short-term interest rates consistent with policy objectives. This has also facilitated bringing down the CRR of banks without engendering liquidity pressure. These operations are supplemented by access to the RBI's standing facilities. In this new operating environment, changes in reverse repo/repo and/or the Bank Rate have emerged as interest rate signals.

Although there is no explicit interest-rate target in view of the evolving nature of the financial market and presence of nominal rigidities in determination of interest rates in certain segments of the market, a great deal of reliance has been placed in recent years on interest rates and exchange rates in the day-to-day conduct of monetary policy. In the context of increasing openness of the economy and a market-determined exchange rate, the large capital inflows witnessed in recent years have posed a major challenge in the conduct of monetary and exchange rate management. A critical issue in this regard is whether the capital flows are temporary or permanent in nature. The recent episode of large capital flows prompted a debate in India on the need for exchange rate adjustment. In a scenario of uncertainty facing the monetary authorities in determining temporary or permanent nature of inflows, it is prudent to presume that such flows are temporary till such time that they are firmly established to be of a permanent nature.

The liquidity impact of large inflows was managed till the year 2003–4, largely through the day-to-day LAF and OMOs.

In the process, the stock of government securities available with the RBI declined progressively and the burden of sterilization increasingly fell on LAF operations. In order to address these issues, the RBI signed in March 2004, a memorandum of understanding (MOU) with the Government of India for issuance of Treasury Bills and dated government securities under the Market Stabilization Scheme (MSS). The intention of the MSS is essentially to differentiate liquidity absorption of a more enduring nature by way of sterilization from the day-to-day normal liquidity management operations. The ceiling on the outstanding obligations of the government under the MSS is initially indicated but is subject to revision through mutual consultation. The issuances under the MSS are matched by an equivalent cash balance held by the government in a separate identifiable cash account maintained and operated by the RBI. The operationalization of the MSS to absorb liquidity of more enduring nature has considerably reduced the burden of sterilization on the LAF window.

In its monetary operations, the RBI uses multiple instruments to ensure that appropriate liquidity is maintained in the system so that all legitimate requirements of credit are met, consistent with the objective of price stability. Towards this end, the Bank pursues a policy of active demand management of liquidity through OMOs including LAF, MSS, and CRR, using the policy instruments at its disposal flexibly as and when the situation warrants.

EMERGING CHALLENGES

The major challenge currently faced is the conduct of policy in surplus liquidity conditions. Given the increasing openness of the economy, the stance of monetary policy in major economies and the direction of international interest rates have assumed significance for the conduct of monetary policy. Globally, volatile movements in asset prices have posed challenges to financial stability. In India, given the conservative lending and investment policies of banks, it has not been a major issue. However, with the current trend towards diversified lending, credit penetration, and liberalized investments, asset prices would need to be closely watched for their implication for maintaining financial stability. Another factor which would have significant impact on the conduct of monetary policy is the ongoing modernization of the payments system with the introduction of real-time gross settlement (RTGS). The gradual e-monetization can shrink cash demand and thus the monetary authority's balance sheet, reducing seigniorage revenue. However, the central bank's ability to influence the nominal rate of interest is eventually an issue of political economy and the government can always require settlement through central bank money.

Conduct of monetary policy, even in the best of times, is complex since it has to be forward looking and based on current and sometimes inadequate data relative to rapid changes. Additional complexities arise in the case of an emerging market like India, which is transiting from a relatively closed to a progressively open economy. In an environment of increasing capital flows, narrowing interest rate differentials, and surplus liquidity conditions, exchange rate movement tends to have strong linkages with interest rate movements and poses the challenge of an integrated view on interest rates and exchange rate developments for monetary management. Therefore policy coordination assumes greater significance in an increasingly synchronized business-cycle environment linked by trade and capital flows.

Y.V. REDDY

REFERENCES

Bernanke, Ben. 2003.'Constrained Discretion and Monetary Policy', *BIS Review*, 5.

Kydland, F.E. and E.C. Prescott. 1977.'Rules rather than Discretion: The Inconsistency of Optimal Plans', *Journal of Political Economy*, 85(3), June: 473–91.

Reddy, Y.V. 2002.'Monetary and Financial Sector Reforms in India: A Practitioner's Perspective', presented at the Indian Economy Conference, Program on Comparative Economic Development, Cornell University, 19–20 April.

Reserve Bank of India (RBI). 1998. Report of the Working Group on Money Supply: Analytics and Methodology of Compilation (Chairman: Y.V. Reddy), Mumbai.

Non-banking Financial Companies

A non-banking financial company (NBFC) is a company incorporated under the Companies Act 1956 and conducting financial business as its principal business. In contrast, companies incorporated under the same Act but conducting other than financial business as their principal business are known as non-banking non-financial companies. NBFCs are different from banks in that an NBFC cannot accept demand deposits, issue cheques to customers, or insure deposits through the Deposit Insurance and Credit Guarantee Corporation (DICGC).

In India, the non-banking financial sector comprises a multiplicity of institutions, which are defined under Section 45 I(a) of the Reserve Bank of India Act 1934. These are equipment-leasing companies (EL), hire-purchase companies (HP), investment companies, loan companies (LC), mutual benefit financial companies (MBFC), miscellaneous non-banking companies (MNBC), housing finance companies (HFC), insurance companies (IC), stockbroking companies (SBC), and merchant banking companies (MBC). A non-banking company which conducts primarily financial business and belongs to none of these categories is called a residuary non-banking company (RNBC). An overview of NBFCs together with relevant supervising bodies is given in Figure 1. Since banking, insurance, and stock markets are covered elsewhere in this volume, HFCs, ICs, SBCs, and MBCs will not be addressed in further detail here.

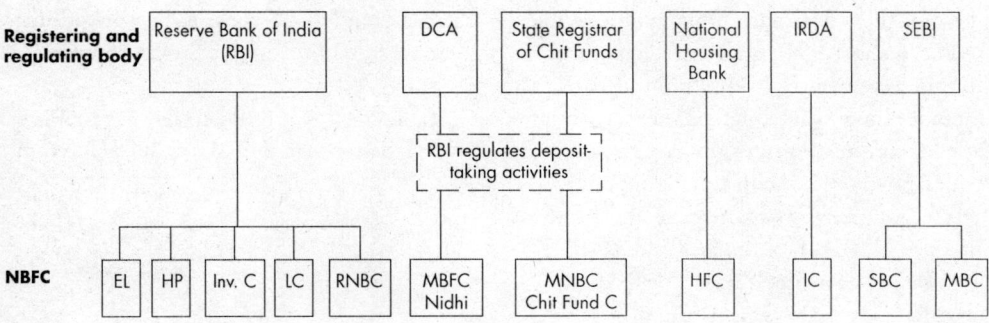

Figure 1   NBFCs and Supervising Bodies

Notes: Inv. C = Investment company.
DCA = Department of Company Affairs
IRDA = Insurance Regulatory and Development Authority
SEBI = Securities and Exchange Board of India

While most institutions of India's non-banking financial sector are also found in other countries' financial systems, two of them, MBFCs and MNBCs, better known as *nidhis* and chit fund companies respectively are genuinely Indian institutions and rarely found outside South Asia. Inside India, they are most popular in Tamil Nadu and Kerala, from where they have originated. A nidhi does business only with its equity shareholders. Much like a cooperative bank, a nidhi accepts deposits and makes loans, which are mostly secured by jewellery. A chit fund, in Kerala also known as *kuri*, is a particular form of a rotating savings and credit association (ROSCA), which is most easily explained by means of an example. Twenty people, say, agree to contribute a fixed amount, say Rs 1000, every month. So the group pools in Rs 20,000 each month, the prize money. Every month an auction is held. In each auction, the bidder who offers the highest discount is given the prize money minus the discount. For example, when a member bids Rs 4000, she will be paid Rs 16,000. The discount of Rs 4000 is equally shared by all members. In this example, each member thus earns a dividend of Rs 200. The winner of an auction continues to pay the monthly contribution but is not eligible to bid in subsequent auctions. According to this system, after twenty months each member has received the prize exactly once, at which point the chit fund comes to an end. An MNBC or chit fund company acts as commercial organizer of chit funds. In 1999, the Reserve Bank of India (RBI) mandated net owned funds (NOF) of at least Rs 2 crore for registration of a new NBFC. Companies that were already in business in 1999 had to prove net NDFs of at least Rs 25 lakh to register. Companies that failed to meet this requirement by 2003 have to phase out their business. This led to numerous mergers of existing NBFCs and

a considerable reduction in the number of NBFCs since the late 1990s after the sector had seen thriving growth throughout the 1980s and early 1990s. To illustrate, the number of companies monitored by the RBI increased from 7063 in 1981 to 51,929 in 1996. At the same time the share of non-bank deposits tripled. In 2003, the number of NBFCs monitored by the RBI had come down to 13,849, of which 710 were authorized to accept public deposits.

Between 1998 and 2003, the ratio of public deposits with NBFCs to commercial banks came down from 3.4 to 1.5 per cent. A profile (as of 2003) of deposit-taking activities within the NBFC sector is given in Table 1. Among the 710 registered and 165 unregistered deposit-taking NBFCs, the majority operated as HP companies. The bulk of deposits was held by RNBCs. It should be noted, however, that these numbers understate the importance of NBFCs for savings mobilization for at least two reasons. First, financial intermediation in chit funds takes place instantly and members' contributions do not appear as deposits on Chit Fund Companies' balance sheets. For 2004, the turnover in registered chit funds is estimated at Rs 20,000 crore. Second, deposits in nidhis by nidhi members do not count as public deposits.

Table 1 Profile of Public Deposits in the NBFC Sector as in End March 2003 (Rs crore)

	Number of reporting companies	Public deposits
EL	58	511
HP	439	3539
Investment and loan (IL)	173	329
RNBC	5	15,065
MNBC and MBFC	200	656
Total	875	20,100

Source: RBI. 2004. *Report on Trend and Progress of Banking in India 2002–03*, Mumbai.

Since the Department of Company Affairs (DCA), to which MBFCs report, does not publish statistics on nidhi operations, however, numbers on the volume of deposits in nidhis are not available. The number of nidhis was at 244 in 2004 and, according to conservative estimates, nidhi companies had lendings of about Rs 1500 crore in 2001.

Selected items of NBFCs' (excluding RNBCs) balance sheets are displayed in Table 2. The majority of liabilities of these NBFCs are borrowings from various sources, whereas public deposits contribute less than 20 per cent. The majority of assets are loans and inter-corporate deposits, and HP assets, which mostly consist of retail funding of cars, commercial vehicles, and consumer durables. While NBFCs excluding RNBCs have a deposit to net owned funds ratio of 1:2, the five RNBCs that report to the RBI are much more leveraged with a deposit to net owned funds ratio of 18:6. The RNBC sector is dominated by two companies, which, in 2003, held more than 99.9 per cent of RNBC deposits. While they offer a variety of financial products including insurance, their main business is to accept term deposits, which are invested into mainly government-issued securities.

Are NBFCs essential to a country's financial system or, put differently, could their functions not also be performed by banks? In this connection, several arguments can be made. First, NBFCs provide services not well suited for banks. Banks primarily provide payment services and liquidity. Since banks have to maintain the value of deposits, they tend to have mostly debt-type, as opposed to equity-type, items on both sides of their balance sheets. In contrast, NBFCs can finance riskier borrowers and intermediate equity claims. They thus offer a wider range of risks to investors, which encourages investment and savings and creates a market for risks. Second, NBFCs unbundle services that are bundled within a universal bank, and thus foster competition, which benefits customers.

Third, through specialization, NBFCs can gain informational advantages over banks in their narrowly defined fields of operation. Fourth, NBFCs diversify the financial sector, which may alleviate a systemic crisis.

Are the functions performed by NBFCs important for economic growth? Recent research with cross-country data sets has established that development of the financial sector has the potential to accelerate economic growth. However, no research on the particular role of NBFCs in this process has yet been undertaken. Nevertheless,

Table 2 Selected Assets and Liabilities of 870 NBFCs (excluding 5 RNBCs) as in End March 2003 (Rs crore)

Selected assets		Selected liabilities		
Equipment leasing	2011	Borrowings (by source)	Central and state governments	1570
HP	13,031		Foreign sources	694
Investments	4338		Banks and financial institutions	8959
Loans and inter-corporate deposits	13,296		Inter-corporate	2074
			Issue of convertible or secured debentures	5352
Bills	450			
		Public deposits		5053
		New owned funds		4141

Source: RBI. 2004. *Report on Trend and Progress of Banking in India 2002–03*, Mumbai.

international comparisons show that economies with lower per capita income tend to have a smaller range of equity-type claims and a smaller market share of NBFCs relative to banks.

An important and widely discussed issue in the context of financial institutions is regulation. NBFCs are particularly important for facilitating storage of value and intermediation of risk. Moreover, like other financial institutions, they are sensitive to runs and herding behaviour. If the financial sector does not work smoothly, high transaction costs, lack of confidence and short-sightedness of economic factors, as well as a culture of corruption may result. The objectives of financial-sector regulation are protection against systemic risks (like depositor runs), consumer protection, efficiency enhancement, and social objectives.

Regulation may be structured as either institutional or functional. Under the former, each financial institution has its own regulatory agency, for example one for each category of NBFCs. Under the latter, there are separate agencies for each function of an NBFC, for example one for deposit-taking activities, one for lending, one for market conduct, etc. India's legislators have chosen a mix of these two models. As illustrated in Figure 1, the RBI regulates ELs, HPs, investment companies, LCs, and RNBCs. Similarly, HFCs, ICs, SBCs, and MBCs report to the National Housing Bank, the Insurance Regulatory and Development Authority (IRDA), and the Securities and Exchange Board of India (SEBI) respectively. All these are instances of institutional regulation. In contrast, nidhis report to the DCA and chit fund companies to the State Registrar of Chit Funds for their general operations, as well as to the RBI for their deposit-taking activities, an instance of functional regulation.

To achieve the objectives of efficiency enhancement and protection against systemic risks, regulation has to be neutral. This means that institutions providing the same or similar services should be subject to identical regulatory requirements. Regulatory neutrality fosters efficiency-enhancing competition between institutions as each service will be provided by the institution that can provide it at the lowest cost. Deviations from regulatory neutrality, on the other hand, likely cause efficiency losses. Suppose that two institutions can provide a particular service at the same cost under regulatory neutrality but that, for no apparent reason, one of the two institutions is regulated less strictly. If regulatory requirements are costly to firms, that institution obtains a regulatory comparative advantage and will drive the more regulated one out of the market, an example of regulatory arbitrage. Moreover, if differences in regulatory requirements are big, less regulated institutions may drive out more efficient ones. In this worst case, the outcome will be both inefficient and fragile, as institutions that meet the lowest among all regulatory standards dominate the market. Much of the history of NBFCs in India over the last fifty years can serve as a case study of non-neutral regulation and consequent regulatory arbitrage. Before 1997, the RBI's supervision of NBFCs was limited to prescription of prudential norms and thus the structure of NBFCs' assets. No requirements were in place regarding minimum capital, amount and term structure of deposits, and interest rates on deposits and loans. At the same time the banking sector was heavily regulated through excessive statutory liquidity requirements, directed lending initiatives, and interest rate caps. NBFCs, which were not subject to any of these rules, thus enjoyed a substantial regulatory comparative advantage for several bank-type activities, most notably lending and deposit-taking. Consequently, between 1981 and 1996, the number of NBFCs grew more than sevenfold and the share of non-bank deposits increased from 3.1 to 10.6 per cent. Several companies were extremely leveraged and deposits-to-NOF ratio in excess of 40 were not uncommon. Numerous bankruptcies of NBFCs in the early 1990s prompted the RBI to take action. The measures sanctioned in 1997, most notably minimum NOF and a maximum deposits-to-NOF ratio of 1.5 and 4 (depending on the company's rating), brought NBFC standards closer to those of the banking sector. Subsequently the number of registered NBFCs shrank by 70 per cent between 1997 and 2003. Nevertheless, NBFCs continue to enjoy regulatory privileges. As of 2003, they can pay 11 per cent on deposits while the ceiling rate for banks is at 6.75 per cent.

The 1997 provisions were not applied uniformly across NBFCs. In particular, nidhis as well as RNBCs were exempt from maximum deposits-to-NOF ratios and, partly, from interest rate ceilings. Consequently, against the trend of a shrinking NBFC sector, the number of nidhis increased from 192 in 1996 to 244 in 2005 with instances where deposits amounted to eighty times the NOF. At the same time, insolvencies of major nidhi companies made it to national news. It was only in April 2004 that the DCA ruled nidhis to gradually reduce the deposits-to-NOF ratio to 20. The two main players in the RNBC sector have grown even more dramatically in response to the 1997 RBI initiative. As a share in total public deposits with NBFCs, deposits with RNBCs skyrocketed from less than 10 to 75 per cent between 1997 and 2003. The deposits-to-NOF ratio in the RNBC sector was at

116 in 2002 and improved to 19 in 2003 through a massive injection of capital. As one of the two large RNBCs continues to have weak financials, the RBI considers mandating a cap of 16, although no action had been taken by 2005.

As it stands, substantial deviations from regulatory neutrality and resulting inefficiencies continue to be common features of the NBFC sector. While the regulatory measures implemented over the last ten years are steps in the right direction, regulators still have to go a long way to create an environment in which banking and non-banking financial institutions compete on even grounds.

STEFAN KLONNER

REFERENCES

Carmichael, Jeffrey and Michael Pomerleano. 2002. *The Development and Regulation of Non-bank Financial Institutions*, Washington D.C., World Bank.

Pensions

A formal pension system existed in India even in the nineteenth century.[1] In its present avatar it is enshrined in the Central Civil Services (Pensions) Rules, from 1 June 1972 (Muthuswamy and Brinda 2002). These rules, with certain modifications (for example in the age of

[1]The earliest reference can be found in *Sukraniti*. In its modern form, see the Pensions Act 1871 (Act No. 23 of 1871) to consolidate and amend the law relating to the Pensions and Grants by Government of Money or Land Revenue. The scope, coverage, and benefits under the pension system continued to be liberalized periodically, with the award of the benefits by the Royal Commission of Civil Establishment (1881, 1920, 1924) and the Government of India Acts of 1919 and 1935.

retirement, the proportion of commutation, period for restoration of the commuted amount, etc.), were also adopted by the rest of the public sector. The original intent of the system, endorsed by a landmark judgement[2] by the Supreme Court of India, recognizes the need for the old-age consumption security system to be largely a self-insurance system, guaranteeing some desirable stream of inflow. However, the ruling also indicates that pensions be largely treated as deferred (and adequate) compensation, thus linking pensions to the salary or wages drawn by individuals while in active employment. In the absence of clearly laid down social security taxes, such a system qualifies as a completely defined benefit (DB) system.[3]

In India, the combined (centre and states) government expenditure on pensions and other retirement benefits (civil and defence) stood at Rs 403.21 billion in the year 2001–2 constituting 12.82 per cent of the total tax revenues (GOI 2004a). The total tax revenues constituted approximately 13.79 per cent of the gross domestic product(GDP) in that year. Note that this does not include payments to pensioners from statutory and commercial public-sector corporations.

Pensions were first introduced as a periodical allowance to individuals for meritorious work or service. Over time, their scope widened into a system of transfers to the elderly. Pensions metamorphosed into a system of social security, ushered in by Bismarck in Germany in 1891, encompassing the poor, retired elders, widow(er)s, orphans, the disabled, and destitutes.

[2]On a writ petition filed by D.S. Nakra vs the Union of India (1982).

[3]As opposed to a defined contribution (DC) system where only payments by individuals are (usually) mandatorily defined but their receipts are not.

Social security may be administered in several forms involving cash and non-cash transfers. In India, the former include enhanced interest payment and lower taxes for the elderly, and the latter include programmes for health, educational, nutritional and employment security, and subsidized transportation. These, however, do not form the core concern of pension reforms in India. The debate, in India, has concentrated on the narrow definition of pensions, focusing on employment-linked, post-retirement currency payments. These cover employees of:

(a) the public sector including government (central and state) civil service, defence, certain aided institutions, statutory, and public commercial corporations (including railways, posts, telecommunications, banks, and financial institutions) under a pay-as-you-go (PAYG) system where pensions are paid out of current revenues (that is either tax revenues or revenues from commercial operations), and

(b) private-sector companies, governed by the Employees Provident Fund (EPF) and Miscellaneous Provisions Act 1952, that extend a limited pension obligation under a largely funded (individual–employer) contributory system.

The total benefit payments, in the year 2003–4, from the employees pension scheme (EPS), administered by the Employees Provident Fund Organization (EPFO), amounted to Rs 23.55 billion (GOI 2004b). However, in contrast to a near-universal coverage in the public sector, there were only 1,758,841 pension beneficiaries (excluding beneficiaries from a few establishments operating their own pension funds), including 352,625 superannuation pensioners. Thus, despite registering the highest acceleration among the major items of government revenue expenditure in the past decade, the extant system of pensions does not cover a majority that is employed in the informal/unorganized sector.[4]

Demographically, India is favourably poised to expand coverage. According to the world population prospects (of the United Nations), assuming constant fertility (that is same as that between the years 2000 and 2005) the old-age dependency ratio in India in the year 2025 would be approximately 12. That is, there would be twelve elderly, aged 65 and above, for every 100 workers (workers are persons in the 15–64 age group), while in North America the old-age dependency ratio would be around 28 in that year. The presence of a larger number of workers in India is expected to bode well for growth in output and incomes and therefore government revenues.

Three policy parameters critically affect the sustainability of a pension programme. These are:

(a) the passivity ratio, the ratio of the number of post-retirement years (until death) to the number of working years,

(b) the dependency ratio, that is the ratio of the number of old (non-workers) to the number of young (workers), and

(c) the replacement ratio, the ratio of compensation or payment in old age (non-working years) to payment in youth (working years).

In particular, an unfunded PAYG social security system can be welfare enhancing if $(1+m)*(1+g)$ exceeds r, where m, g, and r denote respectively rate of growth of population, rate of growth of productivity or output, and interest rate (Samuelson 1958).

[4]According to the National Sample Survey Organisation (NSSO), there were 397 workers per 1000 persons in the year 1999–2000, of whom nearly 360 were engaged in the informal sector.

The design of the Indian pension system has, however, led to a perverse redistribution of public monies,[5] induced rigidities in the labour markets, adversely affected the motivation to raise productivity, and fostered informalization of the economy. The principal issues facing the Indian pension system pertain to

(a) rationalizing the benefits of those covered by introducing the appropriate changes to influence the critical parameters, and

(b) expansion of the coverage.

Recent changes in the pension system for central government civilian employees, joining service on or after 1 January 2004, have veered towards a completely DC system. Some state governments have also adopted the new system for their new recruits. Under this system, the individual and the government make an equal contribution of 10 per cent each of the individual's pay into that individual's retirement account (IRA). This is analogous to the EPF system. However, the new

[5]The average wage compensation to employees in the lower rungs in the public sector is significantly higher than the average wage in the private sector at an analogous level, while perhaps it is the opposite for those in the upper rungs of organizational hierarchy. The provisioning of pensions to public-sector employees, from a PAYG system, results in a substantially higher lifetime compensation as compared to employees in the private sector. A perception of high employment insecurity in the private sector as compared to fully secured employment in the public sector inhibits mobility of workers between the public and private sectors. It further depresses any incentives to raise productivity. Moreover, the absence of universal mandatory provisioning for retirement funds induces the expansion of the informal sector that can escape these costs. Of late, however, employment in the public sector has also seen an expansion in ad hoc or contractual appointments that are essentially designed to bypass the social security obligations.

system differs from the EPF system in the treatment of cumulations into the IRAs and the withdrawals therefrom. The EPF system is similar to a bank account where a pre-announced rate of interest on the balance is credited to the individual's account. The individual is assured of a ratcheting-up of the balances. It is here that the new system is perceived to differ significantly. The monies accumulating in the IRA are to be invested by pension fund managers (PFMs) under the surveillance of a regulatory authority.

This new system is a major shift from the erstwhile system, where retired workers are entitled to guaranteed payments, to a system where the individuals or workers bear all the risk with no guarantees. It raises some doubts about whether the suggested system continues to qualify as a system of 'security'. Is it admissible to enforce a mandatory but unsecured DC system? Further, does this reliance on market bode well for the stability of financial markets and is there a need to have a separate regulator for the pension funds, when most of their funds are expected to be invested in markets under other regulators (Reserve Bank of India [RBI], Securities and Exchange Board of India [SEBI], Insurance Regulatory and Development Authority [IRDA])? In particular, the market for pension and life insurance products may be complementary.[6]

The new recruits in the defence services, however, continue to be administered under the erstwhile system of pensions. While the number of defence personnel in active employment is significantly smaller than of those in civilian employment, the pool of retirees and benefit recipients from

the defence services constitutes a much larger share. The expenditure on defence pensions is more than twice that on central government civilian pensioners (excluding those with departmental commercial undertakings). The civilian employees of the central government constitute merely the head of the proverbial camel inside the tent that is almost certain to be uprooted when the camel decides to take to its feet.

The recent surge in interest in pensions was favoured by the effort to address the larger issue of poverty by distinguishing between the lifetime poor and those who fall into poverty upon retirement. It is generally hypothesized that the latter emerge due to lack of foresight (myopia) in contemplating loss of capacity to work and the corresponding decline in incomes. Myopia, however, is untenable as an argument to sustain pensions. As an example, consider two generations of persons. If the first generation is indeed myopic and provides inadequately for itself, then with hindsight (and increased literacy) this experience can easily be communicated to the next generation whereby for all subsequent generations the aforementioned short-sightedness ceases to exist. The nuclearization of the family system may aggravate the situation, but only for a trifle longer.

While the success of a defined contribution system in sustaining itself depends on participation and supervision, social security must have the attribute of an unambiguous, risk-free guarantee. Security is perceived from a feeling of being cared for. The continued preoccupation with the narrow domain of income security has resulted in high rates of replacement (of income) for those already covered and severely constrained coverage expansion. The role of markets and governments should supplement that of the family and not foster perverse incentives that eventually encourage

[6]A profit-maximizing insurance company would rather pray that the insured lives a long life (so that it may collect annual premiums), while on the contrary a pension provider would expect to minimize its payments by praying for early demise of the pensioner.

individualism bereft of the familial benefits. This crucial aspect was largely ignored, although it has now been recognized in the newly expanded approach of the World Bank (World Bank 2005). Rights and responsibilities of individuals, governments, and markets should be guided by ethical rectitude. This is crucial to minimize public-policy-induced distortions in choice of family, labour, and savings as well as in striking the correct balance between the roles of the government and the markets.

MUKESH ANAND

REFERENCES
Government of India (GOI). 2004a. 'Indian Public Finance Statistics 2003–4, Ministry of Finance', Department of Economic Affairs, Economic Division, August.
———. 2004b. '51st Annual Report 2003–4 of Employees Provident Fund Organization', Ministry of Labour, New Delhi.
Muthuswamy, P. and V. Brinda. 2002. *Swamy's Pension Compilation Incorporating Central Civil Services Pension Rules*, Swamy Publishers (P) Ltd.
Samuelson, P.A. 1958. 'An Exact Consumption-Loan Model of Interest with or without the Social Contrivance of Money', *Journal of Political Economy*, 66(6), December: 467–82.
World Bank. 2005. 'Old Age Income Support in the Twenty-first Century: An International Perspective on Pension Systems and Reform', 18 February, Web Version.

Reserve Bank of India

The Reserve Bank of India (RBI) is India's central bank. It manages India's monetary and exchange rate policies and the public debt, that is the borrowings of the central and state governments. The regulation of commercial banking is another key responsibility. Given India's rudimentary financial system in 1947, the efforts of post-Independence governments to promote rapid economic development within a mixed economy framework greatly widened the nature and scope of the RBI's responsibilities. The manner in which it interpreted and fulfilled these functions, and the constraints it faced, have consequently varied greatly in the seven decades of the RBI's existence.

None of this was on the agenda when the RBI was established under private ownership in 1935 where it remained until nationalization in 1949. The RBI came into existence for a distinctly political purpose, namely to insulate the colony's overvalued exchange rate and deflationary monetary policies from the pressures of representative government in India. But with 'finance' being made a 'reserved' subject in the 1935 Government of India Act, the RBI had no real role for the next decade and a half: monetary policy was made by the government, while the Imperial Bank of India (nationalized and renamed the State Bank of India in 1955) exercised much the greater influence on the money market.

In the first decades after Independence, the edifice of central banking in India rested on four pillars: monetary policy, developing an orderly and well-regulated banking system, establishing and financing the infrastructure for agricultural credit, and institutionalizing long-term lending to industry. For the RBI the institutionalization of savings and institutionalization of credit were inseparable from each other and its principal function, namely monetary policy. By providing channels for transmitting them, an organized financial system would lend greater effectiveness to the RBI's credit control measures. Second, growth in financial savings would reduce banks' dependence on RBI funds. Finally, the institutional mobilization of savings would enable a better match between demand and supply of investible funds. Therefore the RBI viewed its wider activities as an 'institutional' dimension of its monetary policy role. The wisdom and effects of the RBI's perceptions and priorities may be debated. But few would deny that in trying to adapt orthodox central banking principles and practices to the needs of an industrializing economy, the Bank was blazing a new trail.

In November 1951 the RBI made light of its constraints to unroll a new monetary policy marked by the abandonment of a cheap money policy whose historic symbol had been a 3 per cent lending rate. Thus began the RBI's efforts to assert greater control over the money market. However, whilst aspiring to follow a more active monetary policy from the 1950s, the Bank could ill-afford to ignore the longer-term needs of the planning and public-investment process that had meanwhile got under way. From 1956, the RBI loosened the reins of its lending to the government against ad hoc treasury bills, and its lending to government now came to account for a significant part of plan financing, for example almost a quarter of the Second Plan outlay. Such easy complaisance undermined the RBI's monetary policies that for the next three decades mainly sought to adapt the financial system to the needs of the central government, increasingly by forcing the private sector to trim investment and consumption expenditures. The RBI also deployed sectoral policies, notably selective credit control measures to check demand in specific sectors, and 'liquidity' instruments that boosted government securities as an investment destination for banks' funds.

The other three pillars of the Indian central banking edifice were built on rather stronger foundations, and despite several problems and setbacks helped expand and deepen India's financial system over the next five decades. Rural credit was a priority for the RBI from its earliest years. However,

it was not until it commissioned the All-India Rural Credit Survey in 1951 that any serious groundwork was laid for promoting a rural cooperative credit structure. Rural cooperative credit expanded rapidly in the 1950s, loans and advances on the books of village-level credit societies, for example, rising from less than Rs 230 million in 1950–1 to Rs 2180 million ten years later. But disagreements about the nature and design of cooperative credit institutions took some shine off this success, while shifts in agricultural programmes and priorities dictated experimenting with other ways of meeting rural credit requirements. In 1953, the RBI also commissioned a Committee on Finance for the Private Sector whose report marked an important stage in the evolution of ideas for providing institutional support for long-term industrial investment. The RBI followed this up by helping to establish national industrial financing institutions such as the Refinance Corporation for Industry (1958), the Unit Trust of India, and the Industrial Development Bank of India (both 1964). The RBI maintained close links with the last two institutions until 1976.

Apart from helping to channelize credit to agriculture and industry, the RBI's objective of institutionalizing savings and investment held direct implications for the second pillar of the central banking edifice, namely promoting and regulating the banking system. As potentially the most accessible destination for household savings, a sound banking system held the key to the development of the Indian financial system. However, in the 1940s panics and bank collapses were a recurring feature, as the Indian banking system was characterized by a large number of undercapitalized and poorly managed banking institutions. Consolidating banks and instituting sound licensing, management, and supervisory norms and procedures thus became important priorities. Following the RBI's efforts, an unwieldy banking arrangement comprising some 566 banks in 1951 was reduced by 1967 to a more homogenous and manageable system made up of ninety-one institutions. At the same time the reach of the banking system widened, offices of commercial banks rising from about 4000 in 1951 to over 7000 in 1967. This growth fuelled the nation's expectations by the late 1960s which saw a debate on the relative advantages of social control over banks and outright nationalization. The debate was settled in the realm of politics when Prime Minister Indira Gandhi decided to nationalize fourteen of India's largest private-sector banks in July 1969.

This one act dominated the 1970s. The issue in contention was basically sound: banking was not reaching the rural areas rapidly enough. But while critics argued that nationalization was an extreme measure taken in haste, it remains a moot point whether social control would have enabled the government to promote banking in rural and underdeveloped areas. To many observers, however, the latter did not appear immediately in prospect, even a modest 1967 proposal of the RBI Governor L.K. Jha to 'slow down ... branch expansion in urban areas', for example, going a begging because of mutual distrust among the banks. In the final analysis, the government saw the choice as one between a gradual if perhaps operationally more efficient spread of banking and a rapid extension that carried with it some danger of operational inefficiency and corruption.

There have been several criticisms of bank nationalization. One of the more potent is that it spelt the end of monetary policy, as captive banks became unquestioning subscribers to government paper. But this was already an issue from the early 1960s following the imposition of statutory liquidity ratios (SLRs). Nationalization was not without positive externalities, principally in the form of the rapid 'deepening and widening' of the financial system, and consequences of ambiguous import, such as the notion that market-based lending decisions would lead to inefficient forms of credit rationing in an economy in which many potential entrepreneurs and deserving borrowers did not possess adequate collateral. The latter notion was to become a source of corruption and weakness in later years. India's financial system would undoubtedly have been different without nationalization. Whether it would have been as wide or deep can never satisfactorily be answered. What is beyond doubt, however, is that nationalization led to a huge outpouring of ideas and initiatives to spread banking to all parts of the country. Whatever their provenance, including in bureaucratic attempts to micro-manage the quantity and price of credit, these initiatives greatly widened the distribution of credit in the economy and effected a sea change in India's economic sociology.

Nationalization also transformed the role of the RBI in ways that had never been envisaged. The Bank's autonomy, in particular, was further eroded, not merely as hitherto through the dominance of fiscal over monetary policies, but also because of greater government involvement in banking affairs.

Throughout the 1970s and the 1980s, fiscal policy and directed lending held centre stage. Indeed there was nothing 'monetary' about the RBI's policies: its department managing money and credit was called the 'credit planning cell', while its ritual twice annual announcements in April and in October were described as 'credit policy' announcements. Credit policy in these decades meant manipulating the cash reserve ratio (CRR) to affect banks' ability to lend, the SLR to influence the distribution of bank credit between the government and private sectors, and sectoral policies with sector-specific lending rates and quantitative controls. With the result, there were an estimated 200 interest rates in the mid-1980s. It was only from the end of that decade that the structure of rates at the short end began to be unified.

India faced persistent and severe foreign exchange shortages since 1956–7. The RBI played an important role in arranging short-term financing to tide over balance-of-payments (BOP) problems, and in preparing the ground for major policies such as the devaluation of the rupee in 1966. The RBI also contributed to the management of India's external sector after the collapse of the Bretton-Woods system of fixed exchange rates, and to developing India's positions in the international monetary reform negotiations that followed.

Though six more banks were nationalized at the beginning of the decade, the early 1980s were a period of austerity and consolidation under the shadow of the 1981 International Monetary Fund (IMF) structural adjustment loan. This period ended when within months of taking over as Prime Minister in 1984, Rajiv Gandhi inaugurated a reformist but expansionary fiscal policy. In the early 1980s the RBI set up a monetary policy committee headed by the late Sukhamoy Chakravarty that recommended, among other things, monetary targeting as an objective of monetary policy. In this reformist climate the RBI also attempted to loosen its rein on interest rates. But a mid-1986 experiment to allow banks to decide interest rates did not endure because of banks' erratic response. After this the RBI opted for slow and steady reform. That practice has continued, and financial reform since the 1990s has been steady more than spectacular.

The RBI's preoccupations in the 1990s extended in three main directions.

Monetary control has moved towards greater reliance on bank rate changes, open market operations, and repo auctions. This has been accompanied by greater discretion to banks to set deposit and lending rates and manage loan portfolios. These reforms have been accompanied by a steady decline in retail bank lending rates, with predictable effects on investment and consumer demand for credit. As regards the external sector, stress was laid in the early years on freeing up trade and current account transactions from unnecessary and counterproductive controls. The rapid growth in India's external reserves also encouraged the RBI to relax restrictions on capital account transactions. Restoring the soundness of India's banking system has been another major priority. Here the focus has been on stricter lending norms, accelerated recovery or writing off of non-performing assets (NPAs), speedy recapitalization whenever necessary, and the modification and implementation of risk-weighted norms of capital adequacy. Not surprisingly against the background of a rapidly liberalizing economy, relations between the RBI and the government have also been changing. A major development here was a 1996 agreement limiting the monetization of government debt which has helped increase elbow room for monetary policy.

Its control of inflation and management of the external sector, including through the 1997 Asian financial crises, represent important recent successes for the RBI. Liberalization has not, however, come without problems: the RBI has twice been caught napping, once over a stock market scam in 1993 and again in a 1998 bank collapse. In some parts of India non-banking financial institutions also suffered crises and collapse. The cooperative banking system is another potential source of financial instability, and remains in need of reform and rehabilitation.

The opening up of the Indian economy also has the potential to affect the future role and responsibilities of the Bank. A central bank's independence is usually defined in relation to the government. However, in recent years, pressure has grown from other quarters to weaken or disperse the regulatory powers of the RBI, notably in the area of bank regulation.

G. BALACHANDRAN AND
T.C.A. SRINIVASA RAGHAVAN

REFERENCES
Balachandran, G. 1998. *The Reserve Bank of India, 1951–1967*, New Delhi, Oxford University Press.
Reserve Bank of India. Various years. *Annual Report*, Mumbai.
———. Various years. *Report on Currency and Banking*, Mumbai.

Securities Markets

After the early 1990s, there has been a decline in price and quantity controls by the state in many parts of the economy, accompanied by major progress in trade liberalization. The role of the state in the allocation of capital has diminished. Firms have faced more competitive conditions. The financial sector has been increasingly called upon to engage in complex information processing, to make judgements about the future prospects of alternative firms, and shape resource allocation.

A far-reaching reforms programme on the securities markets in the 1990s complemented and supported the pro-competitive reforms in trade and industry. As described ahead, these policy initiatives on the stock market have been highly successful in fostering sound institutional development. India stands out when compared with most developing countries on the sophistication of securities markets, and in the prominent role of markets as opposed to banks in resource allocation.

COMPONENTS OF THE SECURITIES MARKETS

The term 'security' refers to a tradable instrument which has financial payoffs. India's securities markets comprise:
1. Corporate equity
2. Corporate debt
3. Corporate equity derivatives
4. Government bonds
5. Derivatives on government bonds
6. Commodity futures
7. Derivatives on currency

India has a fragmented regulatory architecture for addressing these components. The first three categories are regulated by the Securities and Exchange Board of India (SEBI). The Reserve Bank of India (RBI) plays a major role in government bonds and derivatives on interest rates. The Forward Markets Commission (FMC) regulates commodity futures. Finally, the RBI plays a major role in currency derivatives.

CORPORATE EQUITY AND EQUITY DERIVATIVES

The market for corporate equity is India's most sophisticated financial market. It works through the following elements.

Firms are incubated using the traditional approach, of capital from friends and family, or using the venture capital (VC) industry. There is a large industry comprising both foreign and domestic VC firms operating in the Indian market. Successful firms go on to sell shares to the public in an 'Initial Public Offering' (IPO). Roughly two IPOs per month took place in 2005. The IPO market works through a screen-based anonymous auction.

After the IPO, secondary-market trading commences, where there is competition between two exchanges, the National Stock Exchange (NSE) and the Bombay Stock Exchange (BSE). Both have member firms spread all over the country. Only 40 per cent of equity market turnover comes from Bombay. Roughly 7 million investors participate in the market, along with foreign investors. There is no separation between domestic and foreign investors, or between 'retail' and 'wholesale' investors: all price discovery takes place on unified electronic order-matching systems at the NSE and BSE. There are roughly 30,000 trading screens spread across the country, which are directly connected to the NSE, in addition to Internet access provided by many brokerage firms.

Two vital elements of the spot market are risk management and settlement. On the NSE, risk management is done by the National Securities Clearing Corporation (NSCC). Settlement is done using 'dematerialized' securities at the National Securities Depository Limited (NSDL) and the Central Depository Services Limited (CDSL).

The secondary market for equity is extremely active by world standards. The NSE and BSE are ranked 3 and 5 in the world by the *number* of transactions, with roughly 1 million to 2 million transactions per day on each exchange within the trading day of 5.5 hours. Annual spot market turnover works out to 107 per cent of end-year market capitalization. This is close to the value seen in market-dominated financial systems, such as the US (119 per cent).

India has complete unification between the equity spot market and the equity derivatives market in terms of brokerage firms, exchanges, and regulation. Futures and options are traded on 119 individuals stocks and on four market indexes. The 'Nifty' index is the biggest single underlying on which derivatives are traded. Index funds

and exchange-traded funds are also available on major indexes.

The equity market thus has a strong set of institutional mechanisms over the full life cycle of firms, from VC to IPO to secondary market, to index funds and derivatives.

While there is a broad range of investors who operate on the equity market, it is dominated by small investors. The average trade size on the NSE in 2004 was Rs 27,715 on the equity spot market and Rs 488,790 on the equity derivatives market. Gross equity market turnover is computed by summing across the NSE and BSE, across spot and derivatives, and across buyers and sellers. In 2004, gross equity market turnover was Rs 86 trillion. Of this, just Rs 5.5 trillion was by all institutional investors, domestic and foreign, put together. Foreign investors made up the bulk, with Rs 5 trillion of gross turnover.

The two weaknesses of the equity market are:

1. In keeping with a long tradition of financial repression, institutional investors such as banks, insurance companies, trusts, and pension funds are prevented by the state from participating in the corporate equity market.

2. While the equity spot market has achieved Organisation for Economic Co-operation and Development (OECD) levels of turnover ratio, the level of derivatives turnover is miniscule by world standards, when expressed as a ratio to the size of the spot market.

CORPORATE DEBT

When a company issues shares and bonds, both these are 'derivatives' on the cash flows of the company. There are direct relationships between the share price and the bond price. Hence, when there is active speculative price discovery on the corporate equity market, this should easily carry forward to the bond market.

However, India does not have an active corporate bond market. This failure derives from five factors:

1. Lack of screen-based auction for bond issuance (unlike the equity market).
2. Lack of nationwide electronic trading (unlike the equity market).
3. Foreign investors are permitted to lend to Indian firms through the banking channel, but are essentially prohibited from participating in the corporate bond market.
4. There are severe difficulties in credit recovery procedures when a company shuts down.
5. There is a bias in banking regulation, which gives banks incentives to disfavour bonds and hold loans instead, even though loans are more illiquid and more opaque than bonds.

The strong success of the equity market and the relative failure of the corporate bond market may have given firms an incentive to emphasize equity financing. The debt–equity ratio of Indian manufacturing dropped sharply from 1.995 in 1991–2 to 1.237 in 2003–4.

GOVERNMENT BONDS AND INTEREST RATE DERIVATIVES

Given persistent large fiscal deficits, the government has been a substantial issuer of government bonds. As of end 2004, the market capitalization of the government bond market was roughly Rs 10 trillion. However, there are many difficulties in market design which have inhibited liquidity and market efficiency. There is a narrow club of bond market participants, primarily located in Bombay. The RBI controls entry into the club. The RBI runs the depository. There is a fledgling exchange, also run by the RBI; however most transactions are as yet bilateral and not taking place on the exchange. The number of transactions observed per day is less than one-thousandth that seen on the equity market.

One modern element in the government bond market is the Clearing Corporation of India Limited (CCIL), which is a modern clearing corporation that has been placed outside the RBI. The CCIL is an innovation in market design, whereby counterparty credit risk is eliminated even though the transactions are themselves opaque. The RBI has started outsourcing some of the exchange operations work to the CCIL, which has resulted in improved efficiency and service quality.

There is a limited market for interest-rate derivatives. However, it is an opaque 'over-the-counter' market, where transactions are negotiated bilaterally, with severe entry barriers.

COMMODITY FUTURES

The FMC is an office of the Department of Consumer Affairs, which is charged with regulation of the commodity futures markets. It is not an autonomous regulator like SEBI.

In recent years, the FMC has permitted three entities to start nationwide commodity futures exchanges: the National Commodity Derivatives Exchange (NCDEX), the Multi Commodity Exchange (MCX), and the National Multi Commodity Exchange (NMCE). Turnover has risen dramatically to Rs 1.7 trillion in the first half of 2004–5.

There are many difficulties with the existing framework of commodity futures trading. For example, the present legal framework prohibits two fundamental tools of the derivatives market: cash settlement and options trading. More importantly, the universal international practice is of 'convergence' between commodity futures markets and securities markets, so as to exploit economies of scale and scope in securities firms, exchanges, and financial regulation. India is unusual in attempting to set up a separate regulator, exchanges, and securities firms for this narrow area.

DERIVATIVES ON CURRENCY

As with derivatives on interest rates, currency derivatives trading does not take place on the transparent exchange platform. It is negotiated bilaterally between members of a small club.

There is a fairly active currency swap and currency forward market, with maturities going out to one year. However, market access is supposed to be restricted to 'hedging transactions only'. Participants have to demonstrate currency exposure in order to trade on these markets. This inhibits the development of information-based speculative price discovery. The weaknesses on the domestic market have fuelled the growth of an offshore 'non-deliverable forwards' market, which now constitutes an important alternative to the domestic forward market.

Under normal circumstances, currency forwards are priced by covered interest parity (CIP). However, the RBI rules block the ability of banks to engage in CIP arbitrage. This induces large deviations between the fair price and the observed price of forwards and swaps.

ROLE IN RESOURCE ALLOCATION

Measurement of the *flow* of resources through alternative allocative mechanisms of the financial sector is fraught with methodological problems. In contrast, measurement of the allocation of the *stock* of financial capital is easier.

The non-food credit of the banking system measures the stock of credit given out by banks to big firms, small firms, and individuals. It constitutes an upper bound

for the stock of capital which firms obtained from banks. The true market value of bank credit is likely to be slightly smaller than the book value, reflecting the incidence of distressed debt.

This can be compared against the market value of equities and bonds. In order to improve the accuracy of measurement, we exclude the shares of companies where trading takes place for less than 75 per cent of the days. This is achieved by focusing on the market capitalization of the COSPI index.

In July 2005, non-food credit stood at Rs 11.4 trillion. The market value of equity of the 2550 companies in COSPI stood at Rs 19.6 trillion. The market value of corporate bonds was estimated at Rs 4 trillion. If we conservatively assume all non-food credit as being borrowings of firms, out of the stock of financial capital of Rs 35 trillion, 67 per cent came from markets and 33 per cent from banks. This relationship is not an artefact of a specific date of measurement. Over a thirteen-year time series ending in July 2005, there were only seven months (4.6 per cent probability) where non-food credit was larger than COSPI market capitalization. The median value of the ratio of non-food credit divided by COSPI market capitalization over this period was 68 per cent.

POLICY ISSUES

As argued in the preceding discussion, the market design of the equity market has been an outstanding success, in contrast with the policy failures in other areas. The policy agenda for the remaining six components of the securities industry consists of replicating the ideas and outcomes of the equity market. The four key elements that have induced success in the equity market are: (a) an arms-length separation between the focused regulator (SEBI) and competing firms that offer trading services (NSE, BSE, NSDL, CDSL, etc.), with a clear legal framework, (b) lack of entry barriers into either financial intermediation or exchange infrastructure, (c) price discovery driven by a heterogeneous mass of traders including foreign and domestic institutional investors and a large number of households from across the country, and (d) lack of trading on the market by the government.

There are important problems of market structure and competition policy in the securities markets that have inhibited the diffusion of ideas and prevented the other components from matching the success of the equity market. Securities trading is fragmented across three groups of firms: SEBI-regulated exchanges, RBI-regulated exchanges, and FMC-regulated exchanges. Efficiency gains will be obtained through (a) competition and (b) returns to scale if these three areas are unified, as is the international practice. This will require making SEBI the regulator of the entire securities industry.

In this difficult situation, the most awkward problems are posed by the RBI's operation of a monopoly financial exchange for bonds. As India's experience in sectors such as telecom has shown, there is merit in moving away from monopoly state production. The modern strategy consists of separating out the state function of regulation from production of services in a competitive market, with an arms-length relationship between the regulator and the competitors in the market. Further, a comparison with well-structured central banks such as the Bank of England does not suggest that running an exchange or regulating an exchange is the task of the central bank.

The second fundamental question that the securities markets face is that of global competition. Indian equities are now listed on foreign exchanges. This exerts limited competitive pressures in the domestic securities markets, by giving foreign investors an alternative venue where transactions can go. However, domestic investors, who account for the dominant fraction of transactions and particularly information-based speculation, have no alternative but to buy the services of local exchanges. The removal of capital controls that inhibit local households is required to bring competition to bear on this important industry.

AJAY SHAH

REFERENCES
Ministry of Finance. 2004. 'Securities Markets' (chapter 4), in *Economic Survey*, New Delhi.
Rajan, Raghuram and Ajay Shah. 2005. 'New Directions in Indian Financial Sector Policy', in Priya Basu, ed., *India's Financial Sector: Recent Reforms, Future Challenges*, New Delhi, Macmillan, pp. 54–87.
Thomas, Susan. ed. 2003. *Derivatives Markets in India 2003. Invest India*, Tata McGraw-Hill Series, New Delhi, Tata McGraw-Hill.
———. 2005. 'Agricultural Commodity Markets in India: Policy Issues for Growth', in Priya Basu, ed., *India's Financial Sector: Recent Reforms, Future Challenges*, New Delhi, Macmillan, pp. 176–96.

Stock Market Indexes

Stock market indexes traditionally served as a benchmark to measure the performance of equity portfolios. In recent decades, they have additionally come to prominence through their direct role in financial products, including index funds and index derivatives. In India, in the last decade, there has been considerable new work leading to improved stock market indexes.

The oldest and most prominent index in India is the Bombay Stock Exchange (BSE) Sensitive Index, known as the BSE Sensex. The BSE Sensex was created in

1986. The set of companies that formed the index was chosen by a committee. It was a market-capitalization weighted index of thirty listed firms. Daily data are available from April 1979 onwards, where the returns prior to 1986 were back calculated keeping the set of companies fixed for the seven-year period from 1979 to 1986. The committee was likely to have chosen firms which did well in the 1979–86 period. This probably generated an upward bias in the apparent returns on the BSE Sensex.

The index set that was selected in 1986 was held fixed till 1996. This is likely to have generated a downward bias in index returns during the 1986–96 period. In a substantial reshuffle of the index components in 1996, as many as thirteen of the thirty stocks were changed on one day. After 1996, the index set has been monitored and maintained on a regular basis. As of 31 March 2005, the index set covered 43 per cent of the market capitalization of active Indian equity.

In 2002, the BSE Sensex shifted from market capitalization weights to 'floating stock weights'. Here, the weightage of a company in the index is proportional to a subjective judgement about the shares held by investors who might possibly sell them.

The events of 1986, 1996, and 2002 imply that while the BSE Sensex has a long time series going back to April 1979, it suffers from inconsistencies in methodology. An additional difficulty when using the Sensex is that a 'total returns index', which incorporates capital gains and dividends, is not available.

The most important alternative to the BSE Sensex is an index published by the National Stock Exchange (NSE). Since 1995, the NSE has been India's biggest stock market. In 1996, a new index named the NSE-50 or 'Nifty' was released (Shah and Thomas 1998). This was calculated as a market-capitalization weighted portfolio containing fifty stocks. By virtue of using fifty stocks instead of thirty, this index covered 56 per cent of the market capitalization of active Indian equity as of 31 March 2005. The full name of the index is now 'S&P CNX Nifty', reflecting the involvement of Standard & Poors from 1999 onwards. While the BSE Sensex is calculated using prices from the BSE, the NSE-50 is calculated using prices from the NSE.

The fifty firms that go into the NSE-50 index are chosen using a methodology that focuses on liquidity. The stocks are required to deliver low transactions costs while doing portfolio (or 'basket') trades to buy or sell the index portfolio. Basket trades of Rs 5 million at a time are simulated for these computations. Basket trades are simulated using four snapshots of the limit order book every day on the NSE. Firms with a higher market capitalization naturally have bigger transaction sizes in these simulated baskets. The simulations use exact data from the NSE, and thus accurately measure the transactions costs associated with doing basket trades. This mechanism ensures that the index series is not contaminated by illiquid stocks, and that index returns are genuinely attainable to an investor who would have to implement such basket trades on the market.

The time series for the NSE-50 from March 1996 onwards consistently uses these rules and is hence an internally consistent time series. The time series was pushed back to July 1990, where high trading frequency was used as a proxy for low transactions costs. Through this imputation strategy, a time series of the NSE-50 index is available from July 1990 onwards.

Another useful index which uses the same methodology is 'Nifty Junior'. This contains the set of fifty stocks that satisfy the liquidity criteria, but are not big enough to qualify for inclusion into the NSE-50 index. The sets of stocks in Nifty and Nifty Junior are guaranteed to always be disjoint sets. It is hence easy to compute a composite index of the hundred most liquid firms of India, as a weighted average of the two returns, with weights proportional to the market capitalization.

The two major financial-sector applications of market indexes are in index funds and index derivatives. Derivatives based on the NSE-50 trade at the NSE in India and at the Singapore Exchange Limited (SGX) in Singapore. In India, over 99 per cent of the index derivatives trading volume in 2005 was based on the NSE-50 index. The NSE-50 is the largest single underlying on exchange-traded derivatives in India. The BSE Sensex has been more successful in the index fund market, where it had 7 per cent market share as of July 2005.

A comprehensive set of stock market indexes, spanning different sectors as well as the entire economy, comes from the Centre for Monitoring Indian Economy (CMIE). The CMIE indexes are calculated using a consistent methodology from 1990 onwards. The largest of the index portfolios calculated at the CMIE (called COSPI) recomputes a set of eligible stocks every day, containing all firms with a historical trading frequency of above 75 per cent. The number of firms in the COSPI index fluctuates over time, reflecting the contours of the economy. As of March 2005, COSPI consisted of 2500 stocks, which had a market capitalization of Rs 16.8 trillion, which constitutes the universe of 'actively traded equity' in India. This captures a substantial fraction of the total market capitalization of India which stands at Rs 20.6 trillion.

The CMIE releases COSPI and a detailed breakdown of 254 industry indexes organized in a tree structure. The CMIE also releases the daily time series of the number of stocks in COSPI, the market capitalization of COSPI, and the P/E of the index. The strengths of COSPI are that a single consistent methodology is in place from 1990 onwards, a large universe of stocks is captured, and a detailed range of industry indexes are available. The weakness of the COSPI family is that these index sets are relatively illiquid, which introduces noise in the index time series and impedes the direct utilization of the indexes in financial products such as index funds and index derivatives.

SUSAN THOMAS AND AJAY SHAH

REFERENCES

Shah, Ajay and Susan Thomas. 1998. 'Market Microstructure Considerations in Index Construction', in *CBOT Research Symposium Proceedings*, Chicago Board of Trade, pp. 173–93.

EXTERNAL SECTOR

Balance of Payments

This chapter describes the position of balance of payments (BOP) in India starting from the second oil shock of 1979 to the present. It is divided into two parts: before and after the BOP crisis of 1990–1.

BOP CRISIS

A rise in the gross domestic product (GDP) growth rate in the 1980s (relative to the 1970s) was accompanied by higher fiscal deficits, rising current account deficits, and larger external debt. The worsening fiscal situation, in the presence of inadequate flexibility of the exchange rate, led to a rising current account deficit. With foreign direct investment (FDI) and foreign portfolio inflows restricted, the higher current account deficit translated into rising levels of external debt. The low productivity of government expenditure contributed to external vulnerability by lowering the rate of return on the borrowed funds. The declining trend in concessional aid and the consequential recourse to private sources of external borrowing led to rise in the interest costs. The cost of servicing external debt was therefore rising faster than the return on its use.

As the perceived risk in international lending traditionally rises with outstanding external debt, this along with the increasing private sourcing of external borrowing made capital flows vulnerable and open to politically related perceptions. The proportion of long-term public and publicly guaranteed external debt sourced from private creditors rose sharply from 9.1 per cent of total long-term debt in 1980 to 31.2 per cent in 1990. From the user side, private non-guaranteed long-term debt more than doubled from 10.4 per cent of GDP in 1980 to 24.2 per cent of GDP in 1990. A substantial part of this debt was channelled to the central government, public-sector units, and public financial institutions during the 1980s. Thus, if the fixity of the exchange rate contributed to excessive external borrowing, the main borrowers so affected were the central government and public institutions.

There is evidence of growing overvaluation of the exchange rate in the late 1980s. During 1990–1, the BOP gap opened significantly and the need for devaluation was quite clear. The overvaluation manifested itself through the invisibles account and the capital account. The highly controlled external payments regime and the public banking oligopoly meant that the transaction costs of remitting money through the official markets were high. The ban on import of gold meant that the large domestic demand for gold could only be met through gold smuggling into India financed by underground ('hawala') markets for foreign exchange. Increased overvaluation of the exchange rate made the incentive for diversion greater and slowed the flow of remittances (private transfers) and service earnings through the official foreign-exchange market.

An unusual combination of external and domestic political developments between end 1989 and early 1991 accentuated all these vulnerabilities to produce the BOP crisis in India. This BOP crisis was more akin to the earlier (1980s) debt crises in Latin America than to the subsequent Asian crisis as it had its origins in government finances and functioning rather than in the private sector.

The crisis cannot be attributed to trade imbalances as many left-oriented economists did at that time. Though imports increased by 2.3 per cent of GDP (to 7.9 per cent of GDP), about one-third of this increase was due to the second oil shock (1979) which doubled the value (US$) of oil imports. Non-oil, non-customs imports that were the focus of import liberalization during the 1980s contributed about half the total increase in the import–GDP ratio. As exports increased by only 0.3 percentage point of GDP, the trade deficit increased from an average of 1.2 per cent of GDP in the 1970s to an average of 3.2 per cent of GDP in the 1980s. The current account deficit therefore rose sharply from an average of 0.1 per cent of GDP during the 1970s to an average of 1.8 per cent of GDP during the 1980s.

Both the sharp rise in trade deficit in the early 1980s and the declining trend thereafter were largely due to the second oil shock in 1979. The import–GDP ratio fell from an average of 8.2 per cent in the first half to 7.7 per cent during the second half of the 1980s, even though non-oil imports increased by 0.6 per cent of GDP between the two periods. The trade deficit therefore declined from 3.5 per cent of GDP in the

first half of the 1980s to an average of 3 per cent of GDP in the second half.

The current account deficit, which shot up to 1.5 per cent of GDP during 1980–4, increased further to 2.1 per cent of GDP during 1985–9, because of a shrinking surplus on the invisibles account, which followed an inverted U pattern during the 1980s. After rising from 1.1 per cent of GDP in the 1970s to an average of 2 per cent of GDP in 1980–4, it fell to an average of 0.8 per cent of GDP during 1985–9. Underlying the long-term deterioration in the invisibles balance were all three major sub-components. The non-factor service surplus increased from an average of 0.3 per cent of GDP in the 1970s to 0.6 per cent of GDP during 1980–4 and then declined again to 0.3 per cent of GDP during 1985–9. Similarly, private transfers rose from 0.6 per cent of GDP to 1.3 per cent of GDP and then declined to 0.9 per cent of GDP over the same periods. Finally, income deficit went from an average of 0.3 per cent of GDP (1970s) to 0.1 per cent of GDP (1980–4) and then to 0.6 per cent of GDP (1985–9). Thus in a medium-term perspective the invisibles balance was a much more significant element in the BOP crisis of 1990–1 than the trade deficit.

The declining invisibles surplus was driven by the income deficit, which was rising up to the crisis year. A fall in concessional (IDA) lending from the multilateral development banks led to rising average interest rates, and this coupled with a rising debt–GDP ratio led to rising interest payments.

BOP POST-REFORM

The comprehensive import control (QR) regime was gradually dismantled, starting with capital and intermediate goods and moving, after a period of slowdown, to consumer goods. Tariff rates were brought down over a decade from a peak rate of about 300 per cent to a peak rate of 35 per cent. The problem of overdependence on debt and the high proportion of short-term debt was addressed by liberalizing FDI and foreign equity inflows while keeping a very tight lid on short-term debt obligations and maintaining the control regime for external commercial borrowing. A comprehensive reform of the exchange control regime was undertaken based on thorough intellectual and administrative preparation. The illegal foreign exchange market and its link with smuggling and invisibles transactions were addressed by a comprehensive liberalization of gold imports.

The macroeconomic response to the BOP crisis as it existed at the start of 1991–2 was the classic textbook one of expenditure compression through a sharp fiscal correction and expenditure switching through devaluation. The fiscal deficit of the centre was reduced from 7.8 per cent of GDP in 1990–1 to 5.6 per cent of GDP in 1991–2. The nominal effective exchange rate (NEER) was depreciated by 18 per cent in 1991, resulting in a real effective depreciation of 12.4 per cent. The fiscal squeeze and the real depreciation reduced the current account deficit by 1.03 per cent of GDP and 0.97 per cent of GDP respectively. The total effect of these two measures was therefore to reduce the current account deficit by 2 per cent of GDP out of the total actual decline of 2.8 per cent of GDP. The decline of 1.6 percentage points in the private investment rate contributed about 0.5 per cent to the reduction. The remaining decline of 0.3 per cent of GDP can perhaps be attributed to the overall increase in private confidence arising from the major economic reforms initiated in 1991–2.

The trade policy of April 1992 freed imports of almost all intermediate and capital goods. Only 71 items remained restricted/licensed (3 banned, 7 canalized), most of which were either dual-use goods like office equipment or consumer goods. After this initial major step, further liberalization was slow, because the potential beneficiaries were fragmented and unorganized while the losers were few and organized. It was only the loss of the World Trade Organization (WTO) case against India that finally led to the complete elimination of QRs on consumer goods, previously justified on BOP grounds, on 1 April 2000.

The decontrol of FDI took the form of an 'automatic route'. FDI with up to 51 per cent (from 40 per cent) foreign equity was freed for a list of thirty-four 'priority' (intermediate and capital goods) industries and international trading companies (dividend-balancing condition remained). The 51 per cent level was chosen as this allowed foreign companies to amalgamate profits and losses from such a company into those of the parent company for tax purposes. Technology import was also put under the automatic route subject to conditions on royalty (< 5 per cent domestic, < 8 per cent export) and lump-sum payment (< Rs 1 crore). Any FDI or technology import outside these limits had to be approved by a newly created Foreign Investment Promotion Board (FIPB).

India was among the early openers of the equity market to foreign portfolio investment, with direct portfolio investment by foreign institutional investors (FIIs) allowed in 1992–3. At this time the degree of openness was greater than in almost all East and Southeast Asian emerging economies. Only Mexico started a country fund for foreign equity investment about six years prior to India, while the South Korean fund was set up only one year before India's. Both FDI and portfolio flows increased rapidly through the mid-1990s.

India introduced a 'dual exchange rate' system to ease the transition from a heavily controlled trade regime to a free market system encompassing both trade and payments. According to the 'Liberalized Exchange Rate Management System', exporters and remittances would surrender 40 per cent of exchange at the official rate (which was left unchanged at Rs 25.89 per US$), while the rest would be converted at the free-market rates. This effectively meant that export proceeds were taxed at 0.4 times the difference between the market and official exchange rates. Hundred per cent export-oriented units and export-processing zones could sell the entire amount at market rate and were thus not taxed in this way. All capital account transactions (except International Monetary Fund [IMF] multilateral flow against rupee expenditure) would also be at the market rate. Exporters could retain up to 15 per cent of earning in a foreign currency account with an authorized bank. The exchange surrendered at the official rate was to be used by the government for official transactions, thus effectively subsidizing these uses by the difference between the market and official rates. This represented a cross tax-subsidy scheme in which exporters subsidized certain types of government-related imports. This minimized the direct fiscal impact reducing the risk to macroeconomic balance.

The dual exchange rate mechanism was so successful that the official channel was abolished in 1993–4 leaving only a single market channel. On integration in February 1993, the exchange rate depreciated to Rs 32.43 per US$, but appreciated thereafter. Till August 1995 it remained below the peak reached in February 1993. Only in September 1995 did it depreciate to Rs 33.58 per US$. As the Reserve Bank of India (RBI) retains the right to intervene (and does intervene) to even out excessive volatility in the exchange rate, the system is classified as a 'managed float'.

Current account liberalization was initiated with an easing of rules for foreign exchange allocation to business travellers. This was followed in 1994 with indicative limits for travel, etc. on the basis of which foreign exchange could be bought by citizens directly from authorized foreign exchange dealers. In August 1994 India accepted the IMF Article VIII and thus the rupee officially became convertible on the current account.

A new Foreign Exchange Act was introduced in 1999–2000, based on a conceptual approach that current account convertibility must be codified in the new law and capital controls minimized and based on a regulatory rather than control approach.

Capital-flow liberalization led to an unprecedented surge in equity inflows between October 1993 and November 1994. Based on analysis and internal discussions, India developed a macro-management strategy for this 'Dutch Disease' problem that was quite different from the standard one proposed by the IMF. Though other countries in other time periods have undoubtedly used variants of the same policy, India's experience in this regard may also have useful lessons for others.

The invisibles account improved significantly in the post-crisis period, with inflows rising to 2.0 per cent of GDP compared to 1.4 per cent of GDP in the 1980s. Thus these invisible flows are back to the high levels seen during 1980–4. Part of the improvement was due to the reform of gold policy, which led to a big jump in remittances through official channels. Private transfers, which had averaged 1.1 per cent of GDP in the pre-crisis period, more than doubled to 2.5 per cent of GDP in the post-crisis period. The investment and other income outflows after rising to a peak of 1.4 per cent of GDP in 1991–2 and

1992–3 declined progressively to 0.8 per cent of GDP by 2000–1. In the earlier years external debt was the driving factor while in the latter years FDI and portfolio flows have also started playing a role.

Contrary to popular perception non-factor services, which include software exports, have not played a role in this improvement. This is primarily because software exports have offset declines in other non-factor services. The sharp increase in software exports is reflected in miscellaneous receipts (not net) from 0.6 per cent of GDP in the 1980s and in 1990–4 to 1.3 per cent of GDP during 1995–9.

As a result of the strengthening of the invisibles account, the current account deficit averaged 1.1 per cent of GDP in the post-crisis period. There is no evidence of deterioration in the current account over the decade, with the current account deficit being marginally lower (1.2 per cent) during 1995–9 compared to 1990–4 (1.3 per cent). The current account deficit is lower than the pre-crisis average of 1.8 per cent of GDP and the 1.5 per cent average of 1980–4. The position was even better (0.5 per cent) in 2000–1. The external reforms have therefore been successful in putting the current account balance on a sustainable path.

The capital account of the BOP has also shown corresponding improvement. Capital inflows (excluding 'other capital') increased from an average of 1.6 per cent of GDP in the pre-crisis decade to an average of 2.2 per cent of GDP in the post-crisis period. Foreign investment inflows averaged 1.1 per cent of GDP in the post-crisis period (nil earlier). The contribution of external assistance and rupee debt declined by 0.2 per cent of GDP (each), while that of external commercial borrowing increased by 0.1 per cent of GDP. Thus the objective of raising the equity–debt ratio of external liabilities was achieved.

The total fiscal deficit during the five years to 2001–2 is comparable to the fiscal deficit in the first half of the 1980s, while the current account deficit has declined dramatically. The difference in impact is due to the external sector (including the managed floating exchange rate) and other reforms that have improved the flexibility of the economy. They have reduced the external spillover effect of the fiscal deficit on the current account deficit as well as its effect on inflation (more open economy). The high fiscal deficit may in future, however, act as a drag on economic growth. Regression equations using a slope dummy for the post-crisis period suggest that the impact of the central fiscal deficit on the current account is a fraction of what it was till 1991–2.

Contrary to the perception of many outside observers, the Indian economy has become more open relative to other emerging economies. India's ranking with respect to trade, FDI, and portfolio flows has improved noticeably over the 1980s. In the case of tariffs, India was a complete outlier and only in 2005–6 is the peak non-agricultural tariff rate of 15 per cent beginning to move us up in the rankings. India's economy is, however, still relatively closed compared to its 'peer competitors' and there is a long way to go to attain a ranking in trade and FDI that is commensurate with the size of the economy. Further reduction of tariff protection and liberalization of capital flows will enhance the efficiency of the Indian economy and, along with reform of domestic policies, will stimulate investment and growth.

External-sector reforms have been the most successful of all the reforms that were undertaken in the 1990s, proving that a well-regulated market-based foreign trade and payments system would be more efficient and equally stable. Both the trade and invisibles accounts are now much more resilient than they were in the 1980s. Capital inflows are now much more diversified and therefore much less risky for the country. The strength of the external account rests substantially on the flexibility of the 'managed float' in responding to changes in demand–supply conditions in the exchange market.

The primary lesson of the 1990s is that liberalization of the current and capital accounts increases the flexibility and resilience of the BOP. This applies to trade, invisibles, equity capital, medium- and long-term debt flows, and the exchange market. A corollary lesson is that even though the balance of trade may not be the cause of BOP problems (excess demand for foreign currency), an exchange rate depreciation by improving the balance of trade and the invisibles account can help minimize the probability of a crisis. The analysis here confirmed that in India the exchange rate is a powerful instrument of adjustment in the current account deficit. It also confirms that equity outflows are very unlikely to be a major cause of BOP problems (unlike short-term debt).

ARVIND VIRMANI

REFERENCES
Virmani, Arvind. 1991. 'Demand and Supply Factors in India's Trade', *Economic and Political Weekly*, 26(6), 9 February.
———. 1992a. 'Trends in Current Account Deficit and the Balance of Trade: Separating Facts from Prejudices', *Journal of Foreign Exchange and International Finance*, 6(1), April–June: 72–8.
———. 1992b. 'Partial Convertibility of the Rupee (PCR) Implications for Exporters', *RBI Bulletin*, August: 1300–2.
———. 2001. 'India's 1990–91 Crisis: Reforms, Myths and Paradoxes', Planning Commission Working Paper No. 4/2001-PC, December. Available at http://www.planningcommission.nic.in/reports/wrkpapers/wp_cris9091.pdf.
———. 2003. 'India's External Reforms: Modest Globalisation Significant Gains', *Economic and Political Weekly*, 37(32), 9–15 August: 3373–90.

Convertibility

Before the development of modern banking, convertibility of a currency meant the willingness of a government to convert its currency into gold or silver at a fixed rate. Nowadays, convertibility is best defined negatively as absence of official restrictions on conversion of balances held in a home currency into foreign currencies. Table 1 lists thirteen major types of controls on transactions in foreign exchange levied by the number of member countries of the International Monetary Fund (IMF) (out of a total 184) that imposed such restrictions in 2004. Only thirty-five had independently floating currencies; the rest intervened in foreign exchange markets. Most of the latter controlled foreign exchange transactions

Table 1 Frequency of Occurrence of Types of Exchange Control across Countries in 2004

Controls on	Number of countries
Direct investment	143
Real estate transactions	136
Capital market securities	126
Financial credits	109
Money market instruments	105
Commercial credits	98
Collective investment securities	96
Personal capital transactions	95
Payments for invisible transactions	94
Guarantees, sureties, and financial back-ups	89
Derivatives and other instruments	79
Earnings surrender requirements	75

Source: IMF. 2004. *Annual Report on Exchange Arrangements and Exchange Restrictions 2004*, Washington D.C.

to prevent financial flows that would overwhelm official influence or profit from predictable, officially engineered exchange rate movements. Aside from this overriding motive of curbing private competition in the foreign exchange market, many countries controlled foreign exchange to prevent foreigners from buying or controlling too much of industrial, landed, or financial property.

After the British defeated the Marathas in 1818, they made the rupee coin of 180 grains of standard silver (11/12 purity) legal tender in south India. In 1835, it was made legal tender over all of India. The government thereby introduced a silver standard: it was prepared to do all its transactions in silver rupees, and to mint silver brought to it into rupees at a nominal charge. The government also kept the value of the rupee close to 1s 4d (that is 16 pence: it implied an exchange rate of Rs 15 to a pound of 240 pence). The exchange rate against the pound was maintained through the issue of Council Bills—bills of exchange that the India Office of the British government sold in London. They could be taken to India and sold to the Indian government at the fixed exchange rate.

Britain made gold legal tender in 1821; after that the exchange rate of the rupee into sterling depended on the relative prices of gold and silver. They varied little till 1871; but in the next twenty years, the price of silver in terms of gold fell sharply. The Government of India used to make large payments in sterling to service loans and to pay civil service pensions. It continued to convert its liabilities into sterling at 1s 4d a rupee whereas the gold value of the rupee fell much lower; the losses on exchange were borne by the Government of India and severely strained its budget.

Finally in 1892, the government refused to take in any more silver for minting. The stoppage of new supply led to a scarcity

of the silver rupee, until its exchange value came to correspond to the relative price of gold and silver by 1898. In the years that followed, the value of the metal in the rupee continued to be much below its market value; the rupee was a token currency, just like currency notes. But out of its trade surplus with the rest of the world, India built up sterling reserves in London, and used them to make payments in sterling at an exchange rate of 1s 4d. Sterling in turn was tied to gold. This arrangement, known as gold exchange standard, continued till 1931.

In 1931, the gold reserves of the Bank of England declined sharply, it could no longer support the gold value of sterling, and allowed the sterling to depreciate. After this date, the Government of India only supported the value of the rupee at 1s 6d; in effect, it placed the rupee on a sterling exchange standard. It announced that it would buy and sell sterling only for normal trade- and investment-related transactions; this was the first introduction of exchange control. The ordinance was withdrawn in January 1932. But for this brief period, the rupee remained convertible till 1939. The management of foreign exchange was taken over by the Reserve Bank of India (RBI) after it was set up in 1934 (Mathew 1992).

Full exchange control was introduced on 3 September 1939 following the declaration of war between Britain and Germany. During World War II, imports as well as capital issues were controlled. Foreign trade was also constrained by the shortage of shipping space, which the government allocated. The release of any foreign exchange to a private entity had to be cleared by one or other department of the Government of India. The function of exchange control then was to ensure that all payments in foreign exchange were backed by a document proving government approval. On the receipts side, the rule was that exporters must convert their export proceeds into rupees within a specified period; private entities were not allowed to hold foreign exchange unless they were authorized dealers approved by the RBI. Residents could continue to hold assets in non-sterling areas acquired before 3 September 1939, but not those acquired later. The same prohibition was introduced for assets in sterling area as from 8 July 1947 when the powers taken under the Defence of India Rules were replaced by the Foreign Exchange (Regulation) Act.

The chief source of civilian as well as military supplies to Britain and its Indian colony during the War was the United States. So the British government pooled all US dollar receipts of Commonwealth countries; they were credited with sterling for the dollars they paid into Britain's dollar reserves. In this way, the Government of India built up large sterling reserves in London. Between September 1939 and March 1946, the British government credited the Government of India with 1.632 billion pounds for War supplies; another 813 million was earned from export proceeds. Net of payments, the Government of India received 2026 million pounds, and was left with a balance of 2554 million pounds (RBI 1946).

Even after the War, however, these balances could not be used to increase imports because the United Kingdom continued to be short of both productive capacity and US dollars, and controlled the release of sterling balances. Hence, exchange control was continued in India. But after the War, the purposes for which foreign exchange was released became more diverse; for each, an official authority was appointed whose approval was required to get foreign exchange. Thus businessmen needed approval from the Commerce Ministry to travel and students who wished to go abroad for study, from the Educational Adviser

to the Government of India. Economic relations with countries that had been at war were restored, and the number of currencies in which there were dealings increased. The RBI kept its reserves in sterling; authorized dealers (holders of a licence to stock and trade in foreign exchange) were allowed to convert other currencies into sterling and to hedge them up to six months in the London market.

Despite Britain's restrictions on the spending of sterling reserves, sterling was less scarce and hence subject to less stringent exchange control than the US dollar. The rest of the world was divided into countries, chiefly of the Commonwealth, that maintained reserves and freely allowed transfers in sterling, and countries aligned to the US dollar. They came to be known as soft currency and hard currency areas; exchange control was more stringent vis-à-vis the latter. In 1958, Britain made the sterling held by non-nationals convertible; so did twelve European countries. The RBI then merged their accounts with those of the dollar account countries and termed them transferable accounts; the special concessions to sterling area in exchange control came to an end.

Beginning with Egypt in 1953, India made bilateral agreements with over twenty-five developing countries in the 1950s stipulating that proceeds of trade with each would go into non-convertible rupee accounts; the aim was to ensure that trade with those countries balanced. As an incentive, the countries were given rupee credits. In 1958, India made an agreement with the Soviet Union whereby their bilateral trade was conducted in rupees. Agreements with other communist countries followed; they came to be called rupee account countries.

A black market in the rupee account currency developed in the 1960s; a number

of East European countries were offering
the rupees they earned from their exports
to India at a discount to importers in
Western Europe (Batliwala 1998, Batliwala
and Balachandran 1998). A major dispute
erupted between India and East European
countries about revaluation of contracts
after India's devaluation in 1966. After it,
the latter lost interest in rupee trade, their
exports under rupee account agreements
declined, and so did the black market.

Facing a severe payments crisis in 1961,
the RBI permitted non-resident Indians
(NRIs) to invest in government securities
and to sell them and repatriate the proceeds
without its permission. The outbreak of
hostilities between India and Pakistan
in April 1965 worsened the balance of
payments (BOP); to augment foreign
exchange reserves, NRIs were permitted
to place deposits in special accounts
with banks in India. In 1968 they were
allowed to lend to private and government
companies and to set up partnerships with
residents. Approval was also extended
to portfolio investment by them in and
through government financial institutions.

These efforts to attract NRI money
were largely a failure till after 1973. Then
the emigration of Indian workers to the
booming oil economies of the Middle East
led to a flood of inward remittances. There
had been an informal market in foreign
exchange since 1958 when the RBI ceased
to release foreign exchange for travel other
than to businessmen and students; foreign
exchange diverted by underinvoicing
exports or overinvoicing imports was sold
to travellers abroad. This market expanded
considerably after the oil boom. Agents
sprang up in the cities where Indian workers
were concentrated, principally Dubai and
Abu Dhabi. They bought local currencies
from the workers on the promise that an
equivalent sum in rupees, converted at a

better than the official exchange rate, would
be delivered to their relatives in India. Most
of the foreign exchange thus intercepted was
used to buy gold and silver which were then
smuggled into India (bullion imports were
banned in 1939); profits from the smuggling
were partly used to give workers abroad who
used the smugglers to send money home
a premium that varied between 25 and 50
per cent. A substantial *hawala* trade, as
the illegal market in foreign exchange was
called, continued until gold imports were
liberalized in 1997.

To attract the remittances into legal
channels, the government allowed its own
banks to open branches in the Middle East
and allowed NRIs to keep money in savings
as well as deposit accounts with Indian
banks. The permission was then extended to
equity investment and residential property,
and to corporate bodies created by NRIs.
The RBI bore the exchange risk. Since
interest rates were considerably lower in the
industrial countries and Middle Eastern
countries where most NRIs were settled, the
banks found it profitable to borrow from the
NRIs at rates slightly above those in their
home countries and lend the money in India.
As a result, NRI deposits grew rapidly in
the 1980s.

These deposits were freely convertible.
When the BOP deteriorated in the late
1980s, the NRIs were the first to take
warning and withdraw their money; the
flight of these funds precipitated the
payments crisis of 1991. That crisis also
saw loss of foreign exchange from leads
and lags—that is from early payments
for imports and delayed realization of
export proceeds. It finally convinced the
government of the ineffectiveness of controls
for managing the BOP and began a process
of slow relaxation.

In 1990–1, the government issued
more than a million import licences and

gave Rs 30 billion in export subsidies. The new government which was voted to power in May 1991 printed import licences in standard denominations like currency notes, issued them to exporters in proportion to their exports, allowed them to sell the licences in the market, and stopped issuing import licences for commercial imports. The licences were soon counterfeited; but otherwise the arrangement worked so well that the government gained the confidence to permit a market in foreign exchange in which exporters were allowed to sell a part of their earnings and from which commercial importers had to satisfy their requirements. The market rate was higher than the official exchange rate. There was thus an incentive to obtain exchange at the official rate and sell it in the market. The possibility of exchange diversion led the RBI to unify the exchange rate, widen the market, and free all current transactions from exchange control in March 1993; official purchases and sales of foreign exchange were used to control the market exchange rate. Following commitments made at the conclusion of the Uruguay Round of trade negotiations in 1995, import licensing was abolished in April 2001. Since then, exchange control has applied only to capital account transactions. Foreign exchange releases for current account transactions are still subject to quantitative limits, but they have been raised to comfortable levels.

On the removal of restrictions on capital account transactions, however, the government has dithered. The RBI appointed two committees in the 1990s—the Sodhani Committee in 1994 and the Tarapore Committee in 1997—to prepare for relaxation of exchange control (RBI 1995, 1997). The first confined itself to measures to increase the depth of foreign exchange markets and the range of products

they traded in. The second explicitly addressed capital account convertibility, reviewed international experience, and proposed four preconditions: (1) the central and state governments should reduce their fiscal deficits and stop borrowing to repay old debt, and the central government must stop borrowing from the RBI; (2) the RBI should adopt explicit targets for the real effective exchange rate and for inflation; (3) banks' bad debts and the cash reserves they were required to hold must be brought down; (4) exchange reserves should exceed (a) six months' imports, (b) three months' imports plus half of annual debt service payments plus a month's commodity trade (sum of imports and exports), (c) one two-third times the sum of short-term debt and portfolio investment, and (d) 40 per cent of M_1. Of these conditions, there was never any difficulty with the second, the fourth was fulfilled even in 1997, and the third has been fulfilled since. But the government is no closer to fulfilling the fiscal deficit condition than it was then.

Since the introduction of current account convertibility, India's foreign exchange reserves have been comfortable, and have at times increased so rapidly as to flood the economy with liquidity, forcing the government to borrow more than it needed (Patnaik 2004). The excessive accumulation of reserves implies that the RBI prevented the rupee from appreciating, being concerned to keep export prices down. Undervaluation of the exchange rate, however, also raised inflation; so the gain to the real economy is not unequivocal.

Convertibility makes foreign funds available to finance state deficits; but such financing is subject to exchange risk, and governments that were unable to control deficits have been landed in a combination of fiscal and payments crises. Hence the Tarapore Committee stressed fiscal consolidation. In theory, convertibility can discipline a government prone to deficits. But as Kenneth Kletzer has pointed out, governments in India have derived considerable although diminishing cross-subsidies from banks, which are mostly owned by the central government, in the form of differential interest rates (Kletzer 2004). Their inability or unwillingness to forgo these subsidies makes the central government unwilling to relax its controls on banks; and unless banks are freed to compete with funds from abroad, convertibility could lead to both a banking and a fiscal crisis. This may be the overriding reason for India's failure to advance towards capital account convertibility.

ASHOK V. DESAI

REFERENCES

Batliwala, C.J. 1998. 'Administering Exchange Controls', Appendix E in G. Balachandran, ed., *The Reserve Bank of India 1951–1967*, New Delhi, Reserve Bank of India and Oxford University Press.

Batliwala, C.J. and G. Balachandran. 1998. 'Bilateral Rupee Payment Agreements', Appendix G in G. Balachandran, ed., *The Reserve Bank of India 1951–1967*, New Delhi, Oxford University Press.

Kletzer, Kenneth. 2004. 'Liberalizing Capital Flows in India: Financial Repression, Macroeconomic Policy and Gradinal Reforms', *India Policy Forum*, 1: 227–76.

Mathew, Joseph. 1992. *Exchange Rate Policy: Impact on Exports and the Balance of Payments*, Delhi, Deep Publications.

Patnaik, Ila. 2004. 'India's Experience with a Pegged Exchange Rate'. *India Policy Forum*, 1: 189–226.

Reserve Bank of India (RBI). 1946. *Report on Currency and Finance for the Year 1945–46*, Bombay.

———. 1995. *Report of the Expert Group on Foreign Exchange Markets in India*, Bombay.

———. 1997. *Report of the Committee on Capital Account Convertibility*, Bombay.

Exchange Rates

As India becomes more open and increasingly integrated into the world economy, the rupee's exchange rate is likely to play a very important role in defining the competitiveness of Indian goods and services in international markets.

A bilateral exchange rate, say of the rupee against the US dollar, is an incomplete measure of competitiveness for two reasons. First, a bilateral exchange rate only considers fluctuations against a single currency, whereas most open economies trade with many countries. Second, it does not adjust for the fact that the evolution of prices and costs in the home country could be quite different from that in the trading partners. To deal with this, economists compute 'effective exchange rates' (EERs). The nominal effective exchange rate (NEER) is a weighted average of various bilateral nominal exchange rates with the choice and associated weights of the bilateral rates depending upon the economic issue being analysed (for example competitiveness in international markets, determinants of domestic inflation, and demand for financial assets). The real effective exchange rate (REER) is the NEER deflated by a similarly weighted average of foreign prices or costs, relative to those in the home country.

The construction of an effective exchange rate depends on the definition of the exchange rate, the averaging techniques, and the weighting scheme used (see Zanello and Desruelle 1997). To fix ideas, define an exchange rate as the rupee price of a unit of foreign currency. Let us suppose that India trades with n foreign countries and the exchange rate for the ith foreign currency at time t is given by E_{it}, $i = 1, 2,..., n$; for each currency, an exchange rate index

$= (E_{it}/E_{i0})$ is constructed relative to a base period $(t = 0)$. For a given set of weights, $w, i = 1, 2,..., n$, we could use an arithmetic, a harmonic, or a geometric average to construct an NEER using the exchange rate indices for the n trading partners. The geometric mean is generally used because it treats appreciations and depreciations symmetrically. The weights w_i can be, for example, the share of India's exports going to country i, or the share of India's imports from country i, or a weighted average of Indian export and import shares, or something rather more complex, depending on the issue being studied. For India, the International Monetary Fund (IMF) uses weights based on trade in manufactured goods, primary commodities, and tourism services over the period 1988–90. The weights generally reflect both direct and third-market competition, that is the weights take into account competition between exported and imported goods and their Indian substitutes, and competition in third markets between Indian exports and the exports of other countries.

The NEER for India measures how India's exchange rate has changed vis-à-vis its trading partners relative to a particular base year. It is expressed as an index number relative to the base year, and using the geometric averaging method it is written as

$$\text{NEER} = 100 \cdot \prod_{i=1}^{n} (E_{it}^*)^{w_i} \qquad (1)$$

Movements in the NEER do not tell us anything about how the purchasing power of the rupee may have changed over time, because the evolution of prices in India and its trading partners could have been very different. For example, if the Indian price level has risen vis-à-vis those of its trading partners, then one rupee will buy relatively more abroad (compared with the base year)

than in India, and India's exports will have become more expensive relative to those of its trading partners. In this case, we say that the rupee has become overvalued, and this may have adverse consequences for India's competitiveness in world markets. To this end, economists calculate the REER index which is the NEER index deflated by a measure of relative price movements. Movements in the REER compared with the base period measure the effective change in national price or cost levels using a purchasing power standard. The REER index is defined as

$$\text{REER} = 100 \cdot \prod_{i=1}^{n} \left(\frac{E_{it}^*}{P_{it}^*}\right)^{w_i} \qquad (2)$$

where P_{it}^* is the ratio of the price index of the ith trading partner in period t to the Indian price index in period t (with the base year being the same as that used for the exchange rate indices).

What price measure should one use to compute the REER? The options fall into two broad categories: those based on aggregate price indices and those based on wage costs. There are four aggregate price indices that are commonly used to compute REERs—the consumer price index (CPI), the wholesale price index (WPI), the producer price index (PPI), and the gross domestic product (GDP) deflator. The REER-CPI is most commonly used and offers several advantages. The CPI is designed to reflect changes in the cost of living by comparing over time the cost of a fixed basket of goods purchased by a typical urban consumer. It is, by and large, comparable across countries and provides a relatively accurate measure of domestic price developments. Compared to other aggregate price series, the data are readily available and up to date. A disadvantage is that movements in the CPI could reflect price developments that are unrelated to the costs of production. For example, an increase in the price of electricity supplied to households may affect the CPI, but may have less of a direct effect on the cost of intermediate and capital goods used in production.

As an alternative to the CPI-based measure, REER indices based on the WPI and the PPI are also frequently computed. The main advantage is that these price series provide a closer approximation to tradable goods prices than the CPI. However, a number of disadvantages limit their usefulness. The data quality is often poor and not comparable across countries. In some countries, there is an emphasis on commodities and semi-manufactured goods that may not be traded. The REER can also be computed using the GDP deflator, which provides a broad measure of aggregate domestic costs. But the downside is that the data on deflators are available with a much greater time lag than for the CPI and are subject to more frequent revisions.

Because labour costs represent such a large share of the costs of production, the unit labour cost (ULC)-based REER measure is often preferred as a measure of competitiveness. Changes in ULCs are seen as having a direct effect on profitability. This interpretation of the REER-ULC index is based on two assumptions. First, the price of traded goods is equal across countries (so that increases in ULCs imply a direct and one-to-one decline in profits from production) and, second, there is no change in capital–labour ratios or in the share of non-traded intermediate inputs. ULCs can change owing to changes in productivity or the structure of production; under such circumstances, the relationship between changes in ULC and profitability may be difficult to decipher (see Lipschitz and McDonald 1992). A further drawback stems from the fact that ULC data are

often available across countries for only the manufacturing sector and, hence, manufacturing goods are used as a proxy for traded goods. With the growing international trade in services, this assumption may not be appropriate for many countries, including India. Another issue to keep in mind when using ULCs is the variation over the business cycle.

In general, interpretation of changes in the REER-ULC requires an understanding of the underlying products and markets. For example, excess wage demands could lead to increasing prices, with a negative effect on the ability to compete in international markets. In contrast, wage and price increases because of innovation and a move into higher value-added goods could be a positive development. In any event, a suitable ULCs data series is not yet available for India, and the IMF only calculates the REER-CPI.

Table 1 lists the currency regimes used by India in the last hundred years. Till 1975, with the exception of a brief period in 1971 when it was fixed to the US dollar, the Indian rupee was pegged to the pound sterling. Once afloat, the rupee had a de facto crawling band around the pound sterling between 1975 and 1979, and then a de facto crawling band around the US dollar between 1979 and 2003. India has had a managed float with no pre-announced path for the exchange rate since the beginning of 2004.

For the first five decades after Independence, a binding foreign exchange constraint was a constant feature of the Indian macroeconomic environment. It began to really bite as early as the Second Five Year Plan (1955–60), during which India's ambitious import-substitution strategy was unleashed. Draconian industrial and foreign exchange controls could not prevent the emergence of a shortage of foreign exchange, and a high parallel market

Table 1 India: Exchange Rate Arrangements 1914–2005

Date	Classification: primary/secondary/tertiary	Comments
August 1914	Peg to pound sterling	Convertibility into sterling is suspended
22 March 1927	Peg	Gold standard
24 September 1931	Peg to pound sterling	Suspension of gold standard adherence to sterling area
3 September 1939	Peg to pound sterling	Capital controls are introduced
November 1941	Peg to pound sterling/freely falling	
November 1943	Peg to pound sterling	
1 October 1965	De facto band around pound sterling/ parallel market There are multiple exchange rates	Band width is +/– 5%
6 June 1966	Peg to pound sterling	
23 August 1971	Peg to US dollar	
20 December 1971	Peg to pound sterling	
25 September 1975	De facto crawling band around pound sterling	Band width is +/– 2%. Officially pegged to a basket of currencies
March 1979	Managed floating	
August 1979	De facto crawling band around US dollar	Band width is +/–2%. Officially pegged to a basket of currencies
August 1989	De facto crawling peg to US dollar	
August 1991	De facto peg to US dollar	One devaluation on March 1993; parallel market premium rose to 27% in preceding February
July 1995	De facto crawling peg to US dollar	During this period, the parallel market premium has consistently been in single digits
January 2004	Managed float with no pre-announced path for the exchange rate	

Sources: Carmen M. Reinhart and Kenneth S. Rogoff. 2004. 'The Modern History of Exchange Rate Arrangements: A Reinterpretation', *Quarterly Journal of Economics*, 119(1), February: 1–48; IMF. 2005. *Annual Report on Exchange Arrangements and Exchange Restrictions*, Washington D.C., IMF.

premium remained in place during 1957–91. The premium reached a peak before the sharp devaluation in 1966, remained high and volatile till the rupee was floated in 1975, and only came down substantially after the financial crisis of 1991 (see Figure 1).

India's economic performance has been hampered by the reluctance of policymakers to vary the nominal exchange rate. External balance was maintained through import restrictions, concessional finance, and a build-up of external debt. This was most

evident in the first half of the 1960s and the 1980s. During periods of rapid growth and export expansion in the 1970s and 1980s, India's REER depreciated substantially: in the 1974–9 period, the REER (adjusted for export subsidies) depreciated by about 30 per cent; and during 1984–9, the fall was by about 40 per cent (Joshi and Little 1994).

Since the crisis of 1991, India's de facto exchange rate strategy has been one of keeping the REER stable; Figure 2 shows that the REER-CPI has fluctuated in a

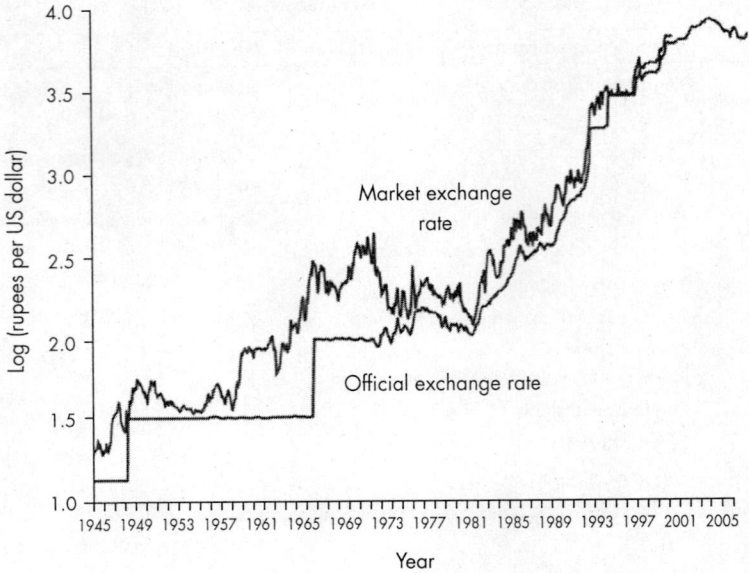

Figure 1 India: Official and Market-determined Exchange Rates

Sources: Background materials from Carmen M. Reinhart and Kenneth S. Rogoff. 2004. 'The Modern History of Exchange Rate Arrangements: A Reinterpretation', *Quarterly Journal of Economics*, 119(1), February: 1–48; International Financial Statistics, IMF.

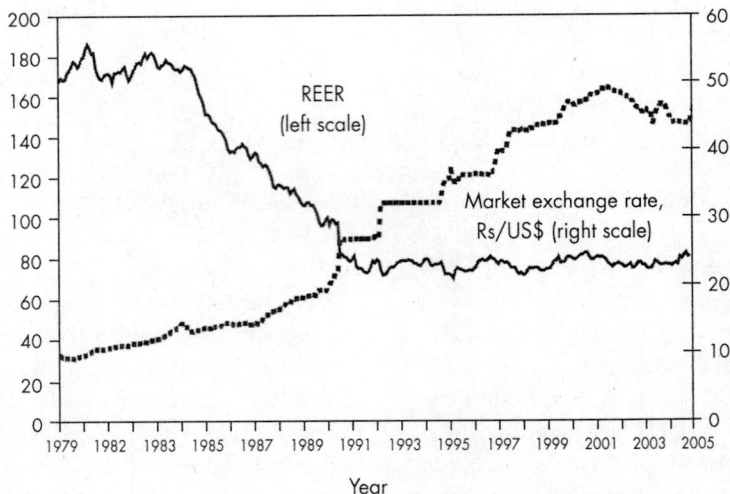

Figure 2 India: REER
(CPI-based weights, 1990 = 100)

Source: International Financial Statistics, IMF.

relatively tight band. In the last decade, India has seen a marked acceleration in export growth with a broadening of the export base, including services, and a diversification of trading partners. Despite increases in productivity, India's export performance has lagged behind that of China and other Asian countries, and its share of global exports remains low. Most commentators agree that poor infrastructure and a high regulatory burden have prevented India from capturing a greater share of world exports.

India removed all restrictions on the current account and accepted its obligations under Article VIII of the IMF's Articles of Agreement in 1994 (IMF 2005). Since the mid-1990s, it has also embarked on a strategy of gradually removing impediments to foreign direct investment and other capital flows (Ahluwalia 2002; Panagariya 2004). For now, the foreign exchange constraint is not binding; and as of December 2005, India had a comfortable foreign exchange reserve position. Going forward, a flexible and well-managed exchange rate is likely to be crucial for sustaining the increased outward orientation of policies and a higher growth path for the Indian economy.

SUNIL SHARMA

REFERENCES

Ahluwalia, Montek S. 2002. 'Economic Reforms in India since 1991: Has Gradualism Worked', *Journal of Economic Perspectives*, 16(3), Summer: 67–88.

International Monetary Fund (IMF). 2005. Annual Report on Exchange Arrangements and Exchange Restrictions, Washington D.C., IMF.

Joshi, Vijay and Ian M.D. Little. 1994. *India: Macroeconomics and Political Economy, 1964–1991*, Washington D.C., World Bank.

Lipschitz, Leslie and Donogh McDonald. 1992. 'Real Exchange Rates and Competitiveness: A Clarification of Concepts, and Some Measurements for Europe', *Empirica*, 19(1): 37–69.

Panagariya, Arvind. 2004. 'India in the 1980s and 1990s: A Triumph of Reforms', IMF Working Paper 04/43, Washington D.C., IMF.

Zanello, Alessandro and Dominique Desruelle. 1997. 'A Primer on the IMF's Information Notice System', IMF Working Paper 97/71, Washington D.C., IMF.

Exports and Export Policy

Exports typically refer to goods and services produced within a country, but consumed elsewhere in the rest of the world. For the past few decades issues related to export promotion, growth, and export-led development strategies have been occupying centre stage in discussions on policymaking everywhere in the world. This has widely influenced the theoretical and empirical literature in international trade and development. Primarily, the impetus for assigning a prime role to export-related strategies in the developing world comes from the tremendous achievement of the East and Southeast Asian countries in expanding their exports and gross domestic product (GDP) growth rates. While there has been a setback for some of them in the 1990s due to the well-known 'Asian crisis', their performance since the 1970s has been truly commendable. This entry takes a panoramic view of the theoretical aspects of export-promotional strategies, elaborates a few key concepts of the export-related problems of the developed and developing countries, and subsequently analyses the contemporary Indian scenario in a little more detail.

EXPORT-PROMOTION THEORY
Traditional trade theory suggests that left to themselves atomistic exporters within

a country are going to export too much, adversely affecting the country's terms of trade. The nation as a whole should act like a monopolist in the world market and restrict its exports accordingly. Thus, an export tax is prescribed (Caves et al. 2002). Such a theoretical assertion seems to be inconsistent with the actual policy scenario, since countries always pursue proactive export policies and what we observe are export subsidies, not taxes. James Brander and Barbara Spencer (1985) have argued that in an oligopolistic market structure, countries will subsidize exports to shift profits away from their rivals. For example, the USA and the European Union blame each other for providing fiscal support to the two large airline-manufacturing giants, Boeing of the USA and Airbus of France. Although such a policy is justified from the perspective of one particular exporting industry, it is not clear whether such subsidies are beneficial for the entire nation. Subsequently it was also pointed out that by restricting imports of a particular good, say automobiles, one could in fact push down its cost of production and increase export to other markets.

Another aspect of export-promotion strategy is related to its growth-augmenting impact. The earlier export pessimism, which was apprehensive of export-led growth of primary products because of low elasticity of demand and the resultant decline in terms of trade, has been convincingly dispelled thanks to the success of some of the Asian countries in the last few decades. Major expansion of manufacturing exports has been strongly correlated with growth in productivity and diversity of export items. Product differentiation, economies of scale, growth in infrastructure have all led to a sustained growth in export and real income. However, in spite of numerous efforts to prove the causal relation between export and GDP

growth, no one knows for sure which way the causality goes.[1]

Relatively recent literature on productivity and export focuses on the relationship between firm and productivity and the ability to export. Typically, it is shown that the most productive firms are likely to be exporters in a particular industry. Productivity-driven export also features in the analysis of intra-industry trade. Among labour-intensive products differentiated according to quality, the exported goods are likely to be more capital intensive and of better quality than those made available to the local market. This suggests that even relatively labour-abundant countries can export capital-intensive goods, contrary to the conventional view. Hence, a relatively capital-abundant country can export labour-intensive goods. More recent treatment of factors determining the pattern of exports takes into account the remarkable developments in the field of information technology (IT) and virtual trade across naturally separated time zones (Marjit forthcoming).

KEY EXPORT-RELATED ARRANGEMENTS
Voluntary Export Restraint
Unrestricted competitive exports can lead to serious problem in the importing countries. The recent public opinion in the USA against the import of cheap garments from China, earlier against cars from Japan, and also fairly recently against outsourced services from India, are some well-known examples. With Japan, the USA arranged a system called voluntary export restraints or VERs. VER is a policy which voluntarily restricts exports and raises the local price of exports relative to the world price. However, such a premium, interpreted as rent from imposing the export

[1]Francisco Rodriquez and Dani Rodrik provide an elegant analysis of the existing literature on trade and growth in one of their NBER Working Papers.

quota, goes to the exporting country. In case of an import tax, the importing country appropriates the margin.

Export-processing Zones

Another often-quoted term concerning exports from the developing world seems to be EPZs or export-processing zones. In their drive to promote exports, developing countries have built special zones where export-oriented industries are granted special favours in terms of duty exemption on imported materials and other tax deductions. Such effort has paid off well in China whereas in India it has not done so well. EPZs have recently lost some significance as tariffs and taxes have been declining all around and therefore special favours to some regions do not make much sense. However, EPZs are still thought to be a way of attracting foreign investment and export-oriented business in India.

Multi-fibre Agreements

Multi-fibre agreements (MFAs) refer to the export quota on textiles imposed to protect the textile industry in developed countries. Textile-exporting countries have specified quotas beyond which they are not allowed to export. The MFA has been criticized time and again as a severe protectionist device to block exports from the developing countries. For India these are related to a product group that accounts for around one-third of its exports. Interestingly, there is a feeling that the Chinese entry into the World Trade Organization (WTO) might make it difficult for other exporting nations to fulfil their quotas.

Anti-dumping Disputes

Disputes regarding the anti-dumping duties imposed to prevent exporters from selling cheap in the foreign markets relative to their local markets are quite common these days. The multilateral trade negotiations initiated by the WTO have generally accepted the abolition of non-tariff barriers, such as quantitative restrictions or non-price restrictions, but have allowed the provision that in case exporters are dumping their products in foreign markets, that is selling at a price lower than their average cost, they can be subjected to anti-dumping duties. This has hurt exporters from the developing world since they have to prove that their prices are legitimate in the sense that they are not artificially lowering prices to deter the entry of locals. In any case local cost and price estimates are hotly debated issues. Also such duties are often used as clear protection devices either to delay the entry of products or to force the exporters into arriving at some sort of settlement with local entities. India in recent times has successfully defended quite a few anti-dumping proceedings against European and American companies. But given the current scenario and competitive edge possessed by the cheap labour-abundant developing world, anti-dumping will be the most sought-after protection device in developed countries for years to come, notwithstanding the fact that it is local consumers or users who always suffer because of such duties.

THE INDIAN SCENARIO

After Independence India pursued a strategy of import substitution with a focus on self-reliance up to the mid-1980s. High import tariffs, both on final goods and intermediates, essentially taxed exports by channelling resources towards import substitutes and by making imported capital goods, technology, and raw materials quite expensive to use for potential exports. Since the mid-1980s, and especially since the early 1990s, there has been a radical change in India's external economic policies with increasing emphasis on export promotion and import competition. Substantial reduction in tariff and quantitative restrictions on imports have effectively made resources available for the export sector. A more flexible exchange rate policy, duty draw back on exportables, tax break for 100 per cent export-oriented units in software-related services, and rationalization of bureaucratic procedures are some of the policies that have positively impacted exports. India's volumes of trade and exports have grown commendably over the last decade (Marjit and Raychaudhuri 1997, Sinha Roy 2005). The resilient nature of our export growth is reflected in the fact that although in the last two years, the Indian rupee has experienced substantial appreciation, exports have not faltered both due to sustained world demand and easing out of tariffs on imported intermediates. As suggested in theory, tariffs of various kinds do act as a tax on exports and therefore even if no proactive measures are taken for exports, liberalization of trade itself acts as an incentive. However, non-price factors seem to have constrained export growth to some extent (Marjit 1998, Sinha Roy 2005).

The composition of India's exports is still heavily tilted towards traditional industries, although service exports have been growing at a fast pace. Growth of software and/or IT-related exports has been quite impressive. But their share in total exports is not very significant. While the share of agriculture and allied products in total exports has gone down from 44 per cent in 1960–1 to 15 per cent in 1999–2000, the share of manufacturing exports has increased from 45 per cent to 80 per cent. One can clearly associate a substantial jump in the average of growth of exports during 1985–99 (11 per cent) from 1973–84 (6 per cent) and 1960–72 (4 per cent), with policies directed towards a liberal trade regime.

Two major supply-side factors continue to adversely affect India's performance as an exporter. The first has to do with the bureaucratic control and transaction costs, related to procedural complexities and regulatory problems. These have been reduced to some extent in the 1990s but some problems persist.

The second has to do with infrastructural bottlenecks. Indian ports are rare examples of overutilized capacities. The loading and offloading of items, connection of ports to the hinterland, and roads and related transportation logistics usually create severe problems for the small exporters (Marjit 1998). A natural comparison between India and China is quite relevant here. Both have cheap labour and huge productive capacity and both seem to be doing well on the export front. China is well on its way to becoming the largest production hub in the world because of its infrastructure and labour-related costs of production; this is yet to happen in India. The Chinese advantage over India is also reflected in the fact that many Indian producers are setting up business in China.

On the demand side, it is felt that while Indian products have been doing well in spite of the appreciation of the Indian rupee, the pattern of India's exports does not really match with the transforming global demand—that is the pattern of growth in demand for various products at world level does not match with the pattern of growth in our exportables. There are also some genuine concerns regarding the desirability of export of agricultural goods when poor farmers are net buyers of food.

The following issues have often come up for debate in the public domain.

1. Is India's growth performance related to growth in exports? This is an unresolved issue. Working with data till the mid-1990s, Marjit and Raychaudhuri (1997) argued that exports are essentially residuals when we consider the overall growth in GDP and that growth in

GDP was not caused by export growth. However, the IT sector now commands a substantial fragment of our national income and therefore export growth in that segment is bound to boost our growth rate to some extent. One point to be noted here is that when we compare the Indian case with that of the other successful nations in Asia, a striking dissimilarity is the very high rates of saving and investment in most of these countries and a relatively stagnant rate of investment in India. Such information tends to blur the relationship between exports and growth unless one finds a link between exports and rate of investment.

2. Does a rise in exports widen the income gap between rich and poor in India? This is related to the popular debate on globalization and inequality. Increasing international trade and investment seem to have widened the skilled–unskilled wage gap almost everywhere in the world. Although no definitive empirical evidence points to trade as the only causal factor, there is a feeling that new technology enriches those who have the required human capital to absorb such technology and therefore it also leads to widening inequality. There is some evidence in India that the rising wage gap has coincided with the ongoing phase of economic reform. But the issue is still wide open.

SUGATA MARJIT

REFERENCES

Brander, J. and B. Spencer. 1985. 'Export Subsidies and International Market Share Rivalry', *Journal of International Economics*, 18: 83–100.

Caves, R.E., J. Frankel, and R.W. Jones. 2002. *World Trade and Payments*, Reading, MA, Addision-Wesley, 9th Edition.

Jones, R.W., H. Beladi, and S. Marjit. 1999.
'Three Faces of Factor Intensities', *Journal of International Economics*, 48: 413–20.

Marjit, S. 1998. 'Transaction Costs of India's Exports—An Analysis', Occasional Paper No. 64, Export-Import Bank of India.

———. Forthcoming. 'Trade Theory and the Role of Time Zones', *International Review of Economics and Finance*.

Marjit, S. and R. Acharyya. 2003. *International Trade, Wage Inequality and the Developing Economy—A General Equilibrium Approach*, Hiedelberg, New York, Springer-Verlag.

Marjit, S. and A. Raychaudhuri. 1997. *India's Exports—An Analytical Study*, New Delhi, Oxford University Press.

Sinha Roy, S. 2005. 'Factors in the Determination of India's Exports', Unpublished Ph.D. Thesis, Centre for Development Studies, Thiruvanathapuram.

External Debt

THE CURRENT DEBT SITUATION

By international standards, India's external debt is low. From being on the brink of defaulting on its debt in 1991, India has steadily improved its creditworthiness. All key indicators in Table 1 show that India's debt-carrying capacity has strengthened. The total external debt in US dollar terms increased moderately, by less than 50 per cent, between 1990–1 and 2004–5, whereas the economy's resource potential to repay the debt has grown much faster. As a result, debt-to-gross domestic product (GDP) has come down by over 20 percentage points from 38.7 per cent in 1991–2 to 17.8 per cent in 2003–4 and debt-to-external current receipts (excluding official transfers) has declined from 329 per cent in 1990–1 to 99 per cent in 2003–4. Measures of liquidity, such as the debt service ratio (DSR) (interest and principal payments as a proportion of exports of goods and services) and the extent of short-term debt in relation

Table 1   Key External Debt Indicators 1990–1 to 2004–5

As in end-March	CAB/ GDP %	Total debt $ bn	Debt/ GDP (%)	Debt/ curr rec. (%)	DSR (%)	Short-term debt/ total debt (%)	Short-term debt/ foreign exchange reserves (%)
1990–1	–3.1	83.8	28.7	328.9	35.3	10.2	382.1
1991–2	–0.4	85.3	38.7	312.3	30.2	8.3	125.6
1992–3	–1.4	90.0	37.5	323.4	27.5	7.0	98.5
1993–4	–0.4	92.7	33.8	275.6	25.4	3.9	24.1
1994–5	–1.0	99.0	30.8	235.8	25.9	4.3	20.5
1995–6	–1.7	93.7	27.0	188.9	26.2	5.4	29.5
1996–7	–1.2	93.5	24.6	169.6	23.0	7.2	30.1
1997–8	–1.3	93.5	24.3	159.8	19.5	5.4	19.4
1998–9	–1.0	96.9	23.6	162.1	18.8	4.4	14.5
1999–2000	–1.1	98.3	22.1	145.6	17.1	4.0	11.2
2000–1	–0.6	101.3	22.6	127.5	16.2	3.6	9.2
2001–2	0.7	98.8	21.2	121.6	13.7	2.8	5.4
2002–3	1.2	105.0	20.3	109.8	16.0	4.4	6.5
2003–4	2.3	111.7	17.8	98.5	16.2	4.0	4.1
2004–5	–0.8	123.3	–	–	6.1	5.7	5.5

Sources: Reserve Bank of India (RBI), Revised BOP Data, 30 December 2005; Revised MoF Sept. 2005: India's External Debt; RBI, *Handbook of Statistics on the Indian Economy.*

to foreign exchange reserves, also show dramatic improvement.

How does India compare with other countries? India ranks eighth among the debtor countries of the world by size of debt, but the burden of external debt depends less on its size than on a country's ability to service it. On such measures, India compares very favourably with both middle-income as well as low-income countries, as may be seen in Table 2. Indeed, the World Bank has classified India as a *less indebted country* since 1999. Since about one-third of India's debt is contracted on concessional terms, the nominal or face value of the debt overestimates the debt burden. Therefore, for comparability across countries, the present value (PV) of debt is used, which takes into account the degree of concessionality of the

debt by discounting the future stream of debt service obligations at a market interest rate. Some indicators of what is considered a sustainable debt threshold for low-income countries are: PV of debt to exports of 200 per cent, and debt service to exports of around 20–5 per cent. By these yardsticks, India is clearly comfortable.

BORROWING USED TO ENHANCE GROWTH RATE

Countries generally borrow when they are developing and industrializing and their investment needs exceed their domestic savings. As long as the rate of return on investment exceeds the interest rate at which they borrow, the capacity of the economy is enhanced and the debt is serviceable. Countries such as the United States and the

Table 2   External Indebtedness of Top Fifteen Debtors 2003

	Debt ($ bn)	Concessional to total debt (%)	PV of debt to GNI (%)	PV of debt to XGS (%)	Debt service to XGS (%)	Short-term/ total debt (%)	Short-term/ foreign exchange reserves (%)	Classification by	
								Indebtedness	Income
Brazil	235.4	1	50	323	72	8	40	Severe	Middle
China	193.6	17	14	48	9	38	18	Less	Middle
Russia	175.3	1	42	135	14	18	42	Moderate	Middle
Argentina	166.2	1	136	531	40	14	176	Severe	Middle
Turkey	145.7	4	62	243	45	16	68	Severe	Middle
Mexico	140.0	1	23	83	22	7	16	Less	Middle
Indonesia	134.4	27	68	200	27	17	66	Severe	Middle
India	113.5	38	19	106	22	4	5	Less	Low
Poland	95.2	7	46	147	30	20	62	Moderate	Middle
Philippines	62.7	23	72	147	23	10	47	Moderate	Middle
Thailand	51.8	19	37	59	17	21	27	Less	Middle
Malaysia	49.1	7	50	45	8	18	20	Moderate	Middle
Hungary	45.8	0	58	99	34	20	75	Moderate	Middle
Chile	43.2	1	63	178	34	17	49	Moderate	Middle
Pakistan	36.3	67	51	189	19	3	11	Moderate	Low

Source: World Bank. 2005. *Global Development Finance*, Washington D.C., World Bank.
Note: XGS = Exports of Goods and Services.

United Kingdom also relied extensively on external borrowing during earlier periods in their economic history. Britain financed much of its industrial revolution in the nineteenth century with borrowings from cash-rich Holland. Then Britain itself became a lender and financed much of the economic expansion of the United States, which in turn became a net lender only towards the middle of this century. Of course, countries also borrow to finance consumption. But then, unless the economy is growing at a faster rate than the real interest rate, it may run into a 'debt trap'.

In national accounting terms, the excess of a country's expenditure over national income is reflected in its current account deficit in the balance of payments (BOP), which in turn is financed by recourse to foreign savings either by way of non-debt-creating flows such as foreign investment or by way of debt flows in the form of bonds,

loans, and deposits. The actual transfer of resources from the rest of the world is the current account deficit before interest payments. Conversely, a primary (non-interest) current account surplus signifies a transfer of resources to the rest of the world.

An important issue here has to do with foreign-exchange availability. The government may be able to raise sufficient resources to service its debt but might not be able to transform them into foreign currency assets. If the exchange rate is inconvertible and there are insufficient foreign exchange reserves, it could lead to foreign exchange scarcity, as happened in 1991. Or, if the exchange rate is overvalued then there could be a speculative attack on the exchange rate resulting in a sharp loss of reserves, as happened in East Asia. If the exchange rate is managed flexibly, then imbalances in demand and supply for foreign exchange translate into exchange rate movements rather than foreign exchange shortages.

'Too little' borrowing?

For more than three decades India pursued extremely conservative borrowing policies. This was a direct outcome of the development strategy adopted after Independence based on self-reliance and import-substitution, whereby investment was almost entirely financed through domestic saving, with recourse to foreign flows only at the margin. The government accessed International Monetary Fund (IMF) facilities to meet extraordinary needs such as drought and oil shocks. Until the 1980s, therefore, the government borrowed mostly from official sources, bilateral and multilateral, and mainly on concessional terms. While this was prudent debt policy given the limited capacity to repay foreign currency loans, the inward-oriented approach was arguably at the cost of growth and poverty reduction, as GDP growth averaged a lacklustre 3.6 per cent between 1965 and 1980.

Too much borrowing relative to capacity to repay

On the other hand, during the 1980s borrowing accelerated and the cost of borrowing rose. The decade saw a large increase in public-sector deficit and a widening current account deficit. As aid inflows declined, the country turned to commercial sources of financing and the government started borrowing from private creditors, including non-resident Indian (NRI) deposits (at a higher cost). External debt quadrupled in ten years to $83.8 billion in 1990–1. Almost 40 per cent of the debt was owed to private creditors, up from negligible levels ten years previously.

A significant part of this increase during the late 1980s was short-term debt, in particular short-term NRI deposits. The East Asian financial crisis has shown that even if the total external debt burden is not high, the composition of debt is important. The greater the amount of short-term debt over and above trade credit, the greater is the vulnerability of the economy to external shocks and sudden reversals in capital flows. In 1990–1, $8.5 billion of short-term debt had accumulated. This was 382 per cent of the foreign exchange reserves. In fact, by the end of January 1991, foreign exchange reserves had been depleted to a mere $1 billion (equivalent to two weeks' imports). Throughout these difficulties India maintained full debt servicing, but it did so by various forms of financing, including by pledging its gold reserves and by an administrative squeeze on imports.

What were the fundamental causes of the crisis? Besides the rapid increase in the amount and cost of debt, there were other major problems that led to its unsustainability. First, the borrowing was driven by expanding government deficits, in large part due to a growth in unproductive expenditures. The fiscal deficit rose sharply due to an increase in current expenditures, not investments. The consolidated central and state government deficits increased from an average of 5.4 per cent of GDP in the second half of the 1970s to 10 per cent of GDP in the second half of the 1980s. Current expenditures rose by almost 7 per cent of GDP, outstripping increase in revenues of 2 percentage points, whereas investment remained about the same—at 7 per cent of GDP—over the same period. Thus the additional borrowing was not used to finance investment in growth-enhancing activities that would eventually help to repay the debt, but rather for expenditures such as subsidies and wage payments. Borrowing for consumption purposes cannot be sustained for a long time.

Second, the economy was still relatively closed and uncompetitive, mired in inefficiencies, notwithstanding the step up in the economic growth rate to 5.5 per cent in the 1980s. Until 1985 there was complete stagnation of exports, in turn largely the result of inappropriate exchange rate policy and limited deregulation of the industrial and trade regimes. The exchange rate became increasingly overvalued, rendering exports uncompetitive. Exports rebounded in the second half of the 1980s as exchange rate policy became more flexible and the exchange rate depreciated in real terms. But by then it was insufficient to offset the impact of rising interest payments on external debt and the rapid growth in imports induced by fiscal deterioration. Once the external finances had become so fragile, the country was vulnerable to exogenous shocks such as the Gulf War and concomitant oil price hike and disruption in worker remittances. Political uncertainties and a sovereign rating downgrade then precipitated a drying up of commercial financing, and ultimately a severe liquidity crisis ensued.

REFORMS AND EXTERNAL DEBT MANAGEMENT STRATEGY

Reforms were initiated in fiscal policy, industrial policy, the financial sector, and—perhaps mostly extensively of all—in the external sector, to make better use of resources including foreign borrowing. The framework for the external-sector reforms was provided by the Report of the High Level Committee on Balance of Payments chaired by Dr C. Rangarajan. External-sector reforms included exchange rate devaluation and the introduction of a market-determined exchange rate, reduction of anti-export bias through trade reform, and policies to encourage foreign direct investment (FDI) and portfolio flows through foreign institutional investors (FIIs).

Besides emphasizing non-debt-creating capital flows, the external debt management policies since 1991 have focused on reducing the cost of debt, encouraging long maturity loans, and controlling volatile components such as commercial borrowings as well as short-term debt. Accordingly, high-cost multilateral and bilateral loans were prepaid. This was facilitated by foreign exchange reserves rising and interest rates declining globally and domestically. The interest rates on NRI deposits were rationalized and schemes streamlined. Short-term debt was brought down and restricted to trade-related purposes, with NRI deposits of less than one year maturity phased out. Medium-term borrowing from private commercial sources was subject to annual caps, minimum maturity requirements, and end-use stipulations. Foreign exchange reserves were built up. In addition, external debt statistics were substantially improved in terms of coverage, classification, and consistency, consequent upon the recommendations of a Policy Group and Task Force on External Debt Statistics in 1992. Indeed, it is only thereafter that a reliable debt series is available.

SOME DEBT MANAGEMENT ISSUES AND CHALLENGES

The composition of external debt is changing, with borrowing increasingly by the private sector. Non-government medium- and long-term debt has expanded from 40 per cent in 1990–1 to over 60 per cent in 2004–5. Of this, 38 per cent is borrowing by the financial sector, 7 per cent non-financial public-sector borrowing, and 15 per cent non-financial private-sector borrowing. Improved access of corporates to international capital markets raised commercial borrowings sharply during 2004 and 2005. These borrowings mainly took the form of syndicated loans and issues of bonds, including foreign currency convertible bonds (FCCB) which are attractive due to lower spreads and conversion option to reduce the debt-servicing burden.

Private-sector borrowing brings in its wake different risks. As witnessed in the East Asian crisis, excessively risky private-sector behaviour can precipitate a crisis. This has been guarded against in India to a large extent by stipulations on the end use of such borrowing as well as annual borrowing limits. Another, perhaps more likely risk, is impact of exchange rate depreciation on the repayment of foreign currency loans. Since the exchange rate has been fairly stable or even appreciated over the recent past, much of this borrowing may have been unhedged. If, therefore, the rupee depreciates, debt servicing will become more costly and if the company does not generate foreign exchange earnings, it will have a net adverse impact on its profitability and ability to repay.

A second issue relates to the costs of excessive reserve accumulation. The large build-up of foreign exchange reserves over the past few years has certainly improved the country's creditworthiness, reduced vulnerability to external shocks and possible abrupt reversals of capital flows, and provided liquidity in exchange rate management. However, the current level of foreign exchange reserves exceeds, by a large margin, the conventional measures of reserve adequacy. As against a rule of thumb of three- to six-month import cover, India's foreign exchange reserves covered 14.3 months of imports. Moreover, the reserves exceed many times over the stock of short-term debt. Indeed, foreign currency assets of the RBI provided a cover of around 110 per cent of *total* external debt outstanding in end-March 2005. This means that India is a net creditor as net debt (foreign debt *minus* foreign assets) is actually less than zero.

A debate has been ongoing about whether India should hold such large reserves when our investment financing needs, especially for infrastructure, are so high. In addition, there are also significant costs in holding the reserves: these are the difference between what the foreign currency reserve assets earn and what the RBI must pay on domestic securities issued to offset their expansionary monetary impact.

A third, and related, issue is to consider a broader definition of external liabilities for monitoring volatile capital flows. Some economists and policymakers have pointed out that while equity flows provide a means of reducing debt levels, proper debt management should involve ensuring the cost effectiveness and sustainability of a stock of liabilities which includes both debt and non-debt elements. In particular, as foreign portfolio flows have become significant and they are relatively volatile, it is arguable whether foreign exchange reserves should also cover for a sudden outflow of such capital. Even if the stock of portfolio investment brought in cumulatively by FIIs is taken into account, the level of our existing foreign exchange reserves is more than necessary.

RITU ANAND

REFERENCES

Acharya, Shankar. 2002.'Macroeconomic Management in the Nineties', *Economic and Political Weekly*, 20 April.

Government of India. 2005. *India's External Debt: A Status Report*, June.

Joshi, Vijay and I.M.D. Little. 1994. *India: Macroeconomics and Political Economy, 1964–1991*, New Delhi, Oxford University Press.

———. 1998. *Report of the Technical Committee on External Debt*, May.

Report of the High Level Committee on Balance of Payments. 1992.

Report of Policy Group and Task Force on External Debt Statistics of India. 1992.

Vasudevan, A. ed., 1999. *External Debt Management: Issues, Lessons and Preventive Measures,* Mumbai, Reserve Bank of India.

World Bank. 2005. *Global Development Finance,* Washington D.C., World Bank.

Foreign Direct Investment

Foreign direct investment (FDI) involves foreign investors taking a controlling and lasting stake in productive enterprises unlike foreign portfolio investments that represent minor equity or debt holdings through stock markets by foreign investors only to seek returns on investments and not management control. FDI inflows are generally associated with multinational enterprises (MNEs) that have operations and production facilities across the world. FDI flows generally come as capital bundled with technology, skills, and sometimes even market access. Therefore, they are widely perceived as important resources for expediting the industrial development of receiving (or host) countries. Most developing countries, therefore, have a welcoming attitude towards MNEs and FDI. India's case is atypical in this context. After following a somewhat restrictive policy towards FDI in the first forty years of Independence, India has liberalized her FDI policy regime considerably since 1991 besides opening new sectors to FDI such as mining, banking, insurance, telecommunications, airlines, construction and management of ports, harbours, roads and highways, and defence equipment. This liberalization has been accompanied by increasing inflows. It has also been accompanied by changes in the sectoral composition, sources, and entry modes of FDI. The increasing recognition of India's locational advantages in knowledge-based industries among MNEs has also led to increasing investments by them in software development and in global R&D centres set up in India to exploit these advantages. This entry is a brief overview of the trends and patterns and impact of FDI in India in the context of reforms.

REFORMS AND FDI INFLOWS IN INDIA

With a progressively liberalized FDI policy regime since 1991, a large and growing domestic market, among other advantages, the investment climate has steadily improved with India moving up to second place in the A.T. Kearney FDI Confidence Index, from fifteenth in 2002 and sixth in 2003, only behind China and the US in 2005. FDI inflows received by India have shown a marked increase until 1997, when they peaked at US$ 3.6 billion. However, after stagnating for a few subsequent years at around US$ 2.5 billion they began to rise steadily again since 2001, reaching a level of US$ 19 billion in 2006–7.

The magnitude of FDI inflows received by India would appear too small, especially if compared with inflows received by other countries in the region such as China (around US$ 60 billion in recent years). However, the difference in the FDI to gross domestic product (GDP) ratio narrows if underestimation of FDI in India due to measurement problems and overestimation of FDI in China due to round tripping of Chinese capital are taken into account. The latter covers domestic Chinese investment registering as FDI through Hong Kong, Macau, or other countries to take advantage of more favourable tax treatment of foreign investors. An analysis of the role of liberalization in explaining the rising inflows of FDI suggests that only a part of the increase in FDI inflows in the 1990s could be attributed to liberalization, as the sharp expansion in the global scale of FDI outflows during the 1990s also played a role. Further analysis suggests that liberalization of FDI policy may be necessary but not sufficient for expanding FDI inflows. The overall macroeconomic performance continues to exercise a major influence on the magnitude of FDI inflows by acting as a signalling device for foreign investors about the growth prospects of the potential host economy. Hence, paying attention to macroeconomic performance indicators such as growth rates of industry through public investments in socio-economic infrastructure and other supportive policies, and creating a stable and enabling environment would crowd in FDI inflows. There has also been a discussion on the quality of FDI inflows in the post-reform period. A substantial proportion of FDI in the post-reform period has gone to services, infrastructure, and relatively low-technology intensive consumer-goods-manufacturing industries largely oriented to India's domestic market and very little to export-oriented production. As much as 40 per cent of FDI in the late 1990s in India has also taken the route of acquisitions rather than greenfield ventures. In China, in contrast, FDI is concentrated in export-oriented and high-technology manufacturing industry and has come largely in the form of greenfield ventures.

IMPACT OF FDI AND THE ROLE OF GOVERNMENT POLICIES

Although the importance of FDI as a source of capital and output generation has increased in the 1990s, its impact on direct investment and growth is mixed as some FDI inflows possibly crowd in domestic investments while some others crowd it out. One way to maximize the contribution of FDI to host development is to improve chances of FDI crowding in domestic investments and minimize the possibilities of it crowding out domestic investments. In

this context, the experiences of Southeast Asian countries such as Malaysia, Korea, China, and Thailand in channelling FDI into export-oriented manufacturing through selective policies and export performance requirements imposed at the time of entry deserve careful consideration. Export-oriented FDI minimizes the possibilities of crowding out of domestic investment and generates favourable spillovers for domestic investment by creating demand for intermediate goods. India's experience with respect to fostering export-oriented industrialization with the help of FDI has also been much poorer than that of East Asian economies. However, recent analysis suggests that MNEs are beginning to take a serious look at India's potential as a base for export-oriented manufacture.

Another policy that can help in maximizing the contribution of FDI inflows is to push them to newer areas where local capabilities do not exist as that minimizes the chances of conflict with domestic investments, as done by Malaysia through pioneer industry programmes. Similarly, because MNE entry through acquisition of domestic enterprises is likely to generate less favourable externalities for domestic investment than greenfield investments, some governments discourage acquisitions by foreign enterprises. Governmental intervention may also foster diffusion of knowledge brought in by foreign enterprises by promoting vertical inter-firm linkages with domestic enterprises through various means such as local content regulations or by creating sub-national or sub-regional clusters that facilitate the spillovers of knowledge through informal and social contacts among the employees besides traditional buyer–seller links. India is also attracting increasing attention from MNEs as a base for their knowledge-based activities such as software development and global

R&D activity. Studies suggest that India's success owes largely to the cumulative investments made by the government over the past five decades in building what is now termed as national innovation systems including higher education and centres of excellence, among other initiatives. Finally, in light of all this, it is clear that it is of critical importance for the host governments to preserve policy flexibility to pursue selective policy or impose performance requirements on FDI, if necessary. Some of the performance requirements have already been outlawed by the World Trade Organization (WTO)'s Trade Related Investment Measures (TRIMs) Agreement. Attempts have been made by developed countries to expand the scope of international trade rules beyond what is covered under TRIMs and the General Agreement on Trade in Services (GATS) and further limit the policy flexibility available to developing countries by creating a WTO multilateral framework on investment. However, due to resistance of developing countries, investment has been dropped from the ongoing Doha Round of WTO negotiations.

NAGESH KUMAR

REFERENCES

Kumar, Nagesh. 2002. *Globalization and the Quality of Foreign Direct Investment*, New Delhi, Oxford University Press.

_____. 2005. 'Liberalization, Foreign Direct Investment Flows and Development: Indian Experience in the 1990s', *Economic and Political Weekly*, 40(14), 2 April: 1459–69.

Kumar, Nagesh and Jaya Prakash Pradhan. 2005. 'Foreign Direct Investment, Externalities and Economic Growth in Developing Countries: Some Empirical Explorations', in Edward M. Graham, ed., *Multinationals and Foreign Investment in Economic Development*, New York, Palgrave Macmillan.

UNCTAD. 2006. *World Investment Report 2006*, New York, United Nations.

Foreign Exchange Markets

During 2003–4 the average monthly turnover in the Indian foreign exchange market touched about US$ 175 billion. Compare this with the monthly trading volume of about US$ 120 billion for all cash, derivatives, and debt instruments put together in the country, and the sheer size of the foreign exchange market becomes evident. Since then, foreign exchange market activity has more than doubled with average monthly turnover reaching US$ 359 billion in 2005–6, over ten times the daily turnover of the Bombay Stock Exchange (BSE). As in the rest of the world, in India too foreign exchange constitutes the largest financial market by far.

Liberalization has radically changed India's foreign exchange sector. Indeed the liberalization process itself was sparked by a severe balance-of-payments (BOP) and foreign exchange crisis. Since 1991, the rigid, four-decade-old, fixed exchange rate system replete with severe import and foreign exchange controls and a thriving black market is being replaced by a less regulated, 'market-driven' arrangement. While the rupee is still far from being 'fully floating' (many studies indicate that effective pegging is no less marked after the reforms than before), the nature of intervention and range of independence tolerated have both undergone significant changes. With an overabundance of foreign exchange reserves, imports are no longer viewed with fear and scepticism. The Reserve Bank of India (RBI) and its allies now intervene occasionally in the foreign exchange markets not always to support the rupee but often to avoid an appreciation in its value. Full convertibility of the rupee is clearly on the horizon. The effects of these developments are palpable in the explosive growth in the foreign exchange market in India.

FOREIGN EXCHANGE MARKETS IN INDIA— A BRIEF BACKGROUND

The foreign exchange market in India started in earnest less than three decades ago when in 1978 the government allowed banks to trade foreign exchange with one another. Today over 70 per cent of the trading in foreign exchange continues to take place in the inter-bank market. The market consists of over ninety authorized dealers (mostly banks) who transact currency among themselves and come out 'square' or without exposure at the end of the trading day. Trading is regulated by the Foreign Exchange Dealers Association of India (FEDAI), a self-regulatory association. Since 2001, clearing and settlement functions in the foreign exchange market are largely carried out by the Clearing Corporation of India Limited (CCIL) that handles transactions worth approximately US$ 3.5 billion a day, about 80 per cent of total transactions.

The liberalization process has significantly boosted the foreign exchange market in the country by allowing both banks and corporations greater flexibility in holding and trading foreign currencies. The Sodhani Committee set up in 1994 recommended greater freedom to participating banks, allowing them to fix their own trading limits, interest rates on Foreign Currency Non-resident (FCNR) deposits, and the use of derivative products.

The growth of the foreign exchange market in the last few years has been nothing short of momentous. In the last five years, from 2000–1 to 2005–6, trading volume in the foreign exchange market (including swaps, forwards, and forward cancellations) has more than *tripled*, growing at a compounded annual rate exceeding 25 per cent. Figure 1 shows the growth of foreign exchange trading in India between 1999 and 2006. The inter-bank forex trading

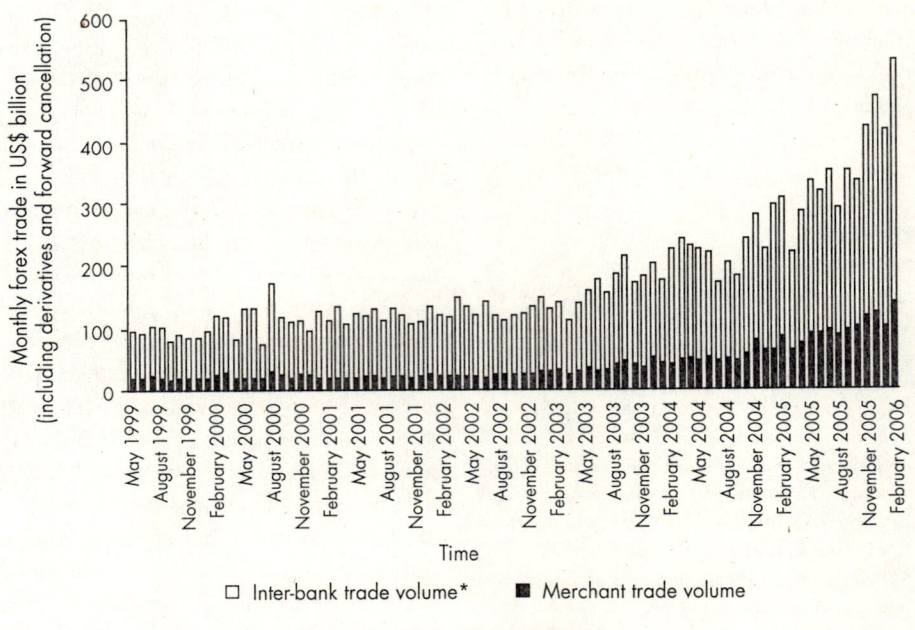

Figure 1   Forex Trading Activity

*Not corrected for double counting.
Source: RBI Bulletins.

volume has continued to account for the dominant share (over 77 per cent) of total trading over this period, though there is an unmistakable downward trend in that share. (Part of this dominance, though, results from double counting since purchase and sales are added separately, and a single inter-bank transaction leads to a purchase as well as a sales entry.) This is in keeping with global trends.

In March 2006, about half (48 per cent) of the transactions were spot trades, while swap transactions (essentially repurchase agreements with a one-way transaction—spot or forward—combined with a longer-horizon forward transaction in the reverse direction) accounted for 34 per cent, and forwards and forward cancellations made up 11 per cent and 7 per cent of transactions respectively. About two-thirds of all transactions had the rupee on one side. In 2004, according to the triennial central bank survey of foreign exchange and derivative markets conducted by the Bank for International Settlements (BIS 2005a), the Indian rupee featured at the twentieth position among all currencies in terms of being on one side of all foreign transactions around the globe, and its share had tripled since 1998. As a host of foreign exchange trading activity, India ranked twenty-third among all countries covered by the BIS survey in 2004, accounting for 0.3 per cent of world turnover. Trading is relatively moderately concentrated in India with eleven banks accounting for over 75 per cent of the trade covered by the BIS 2004 survey.

FEATURES OF THE FORWARD PREMIUM ON THE INDIAN RUPEE

The Indian rupee has had an active forward market for some time now. The forward premium or discount on the rupee (vis-à-vis the US dollar, for instance) reflects the market's beliefs about future changes in its value. The strength of the relationship of this forward premium with the interest rate differential between India and the US—the covered interest parity (CIP) condition—gives us a measure of India's integration with global markets. The CIP is a no-arbitrage relationship that ensures that one cannot borrow in a country, convert to and lend in another currency, insure the returns in the original currency by selling the anticipated proceeds in the forward market, and make profits without risk through this process.

Chakrabarti (2006) reports that between late 1997 and mid-2004 the average discount on the rupee was about 4 per cent per annum. During the period the average difference between 90–180 day bank deposit rates in India and the inter-bank US dollar offer rate was about 4.5 per cent for 3-month and 3.5 per cent for 6-month periods. With these two figures in the same ballpark (particularly given that bank deposit rates and inter-bank rates are not strictly comparable), annual averages of interest rate differences and the forward exchange premium also indicate a moderate degree of co-movement between the two variables. The interest rate differential explains about 20 per cent of the total variation in the forward discount. The deviation of the Indian rupee–US dollar from the CIP, however, exhibits long-lived swings on both sides of the zero line. This would indicate arbitrage opportunities and market imperfections provided we could be sure of the comparability of the interest rates considered. Therefore, while the behaviour of the forward premium on the Indian rupee is broadly in line with the CIP, more careful empirical analysis involving directly comparable interest rates is necessary to measure the strength of the CIP condition and the efficiency of the foreign exchange market.

Under market efficiency, the forward exchange rate is considered to be an unbiased predictor of the future spot rate, with random prediction errors. While the prediction errors of forward rates on the rupee appear to show some degree of persistence, any conclusion in this matter too must await more rigorous analysis.

INTERVENTION IN FOREIGN EXCHANGE MARKETS

The two main functions of the foreign exchange market are to determine the price of the different currencies in terms of one another and to transfer currency risk from more risk-averse participants to those more willing to bear it. As in any market, essentially the demand and supply for a particular currency at any specific point in time determines its price (exchange rate) at that point. However, since the value of a country's currency has significant bearing on its economy, foreign exchange markets frequently witness government intervention in one form or another, to maintain the value of a currency at or near its 'desired' level. Interventions can range from quantitative restrictions on trade and cross-border transfer of capital to periodic trades by the central bank of the country or its allies and agents so as to move the exchange rate in the desired direction. In recent years India has witnessed both kinds of intervention though liberalization has implied a long-term policy push to reduce and ultimately remove the former kind. It is safe to say that over the years since liberalization, India has allowed restricted capital mobility and followed a 'managed float'-type exchange rate policy.

During the early years of liberalization, the Rangarajan committee recommended that India's exchange rate be flexible. Officially speaking, India moved from a fixed exchange rate regime to a 'market-determined' exchange rate system in 1993. The overt objective of India's exchange rate policy, according to various policy pronouncements, has been to manage 'volatility' in exchange rates without targeting any specific levels. This has been hard to do in practice.

The Indian rupee has had a remarkably stable relationship with the US dollar. Meanwhile the dollar appreciated against major currencies in the late 1990s and then went into an extended decline particularly during 2003 and 2004. The lock-step pattern of the US dollar and the rupee is best reflected in the movements in the two currencies against a third currency like the Euro. The correlation of the exchange rates of the two currencies against the Euro during 1999–2004 was 0.94. Several studies have established the pegged nature of the rupee in recent years.[1] Based on volatility, India had a de facto crawling peg to the US dollar between 1979 and 1991 which changed to a de facto peg from mid-1991 to mid-1995, with a major devaluation in March 1993. From mid-1995 to end 2001, the rupee reverted to a crawling peg arrangement in practice. An analysis of the ratio of variance of the exchange rate to the sum of variances of the interest rate and foreign exchange reserves reveals a move even closer to the fixed exchange rate system. A comparison of the sensitivity (beta) of the dollar–rupee rate with the Euro–rupee rate for a three-year period (1999 through 2001), indicates that India had a dollar beta of 1.01—tenth highest among the fifty-three countries considered. More importantly, the US dollar–Euro exchange rate explained about 97 per cent of all movements in the Indian rupee–Euro exchange rate—*highest* among the fifty-three countries considered. Clearly the Indian rupee has been an excellent 'tracker' of the US dollar.

[1]See Chakrabarti (2006) for a more detailed discussion.

It is instructive to consider the rupee–dollar exchange rate in the light of purchasing power parity (PPP) holding that the exchange rate between two currencies should equal the ratio of price *levels* in the two countries. In its dynamic form PPP holds that that the rate of depreciation of a currency should equal the excess of its inflation rate to that in the other country. Over a reasonably long period of time, the devaluation in the Indian rupee vis-à-vis the US dollar does seem to have an association with the difference in the inflation rates in the two countries. Between 1991 and 2003, the two variables have had visible co-movements with a correlation of about 0.57 (Chakrabarti 2006). This may be a result of Indo-US trade flows dominating the exchange rate markets but it is perhaps more likely that it reflects the exchange rate management principles of the monetary authorities.

The RBI has used a varied mix of techniques in intervening in the foreign exchange market—indirect measures such as press statements (sometimes called 'open mouth operations' in central bank speak) and, in more extreme situations, monetary measures to affect the value of the rupee as well as direct purchase and sale in the foreign exchange market using spot, forward, and swap transactions (see Ghosh 2002). Till around 2002, the measures were mostly in the nature of crisis management of saving-the-rupee kind and sometimes the direct deals would be repeated over several days till the desired outcome was accomplished. Other public-sector banks, particularly the State Bank of India, often aided or veiled the intervention process.

The exact details of the interventions are shrouded in mystery, not unusual for central banks ever wary of showing too much of their hand to the currency speculators. The Tarapore Committee report had urged more transparency in the intervention process and recommended, in 1997, that a 'Monitoring Exchange Rate Band' of ± 5 per cent be used around an announced neutral real effective exchange rate (REER), with weekly publication of relevant figures, something yet to be implemented. In a recent survey on foreign exchange market intervention in emerging markets, the BIS (BIS 2005b) found that out of the eleven emerging market countries considered, India gave out the most complete information on intervention *strategy* (along with three others); no information on *actual* interventions (five others did the same); and did not cover foreign exchange intervention in annual reports (like two other countries). On the whole it ranked fourth most opaque in matters of foreign exchange intervention among the eleven countries compared.

REGULATION OF CROSS-BORDER CURRENCY FLOWS

A feature of the economy that is intricately related to the exchange rate regime followed is the freedom of cross-border capital flows. This relationship comes from the so-called 'impossible trinity' or 'trilemma' of international finance, which essentially states that a country may have any two but not all of the following three things—a fixed exchange rate, free flow of capital across its borders, and autonomy in its monetary policy. Since liberalization, India has been having close to a de facto peg to the dollar and has simultaneously been liberalizing its foreign currency flow regime.

Close on the heels of the adoption of market-determined exchange rate (within limits) in 1993 came current account convertibility in 1994. In 1997, the Tarapore committee, on capital account convertibility, defined the concept as 'the freedom to convert local financial assets into foreign financial assets and vice versa at market determined rates of exchange' and laid down fiscal consolidation, a mandated inflation target, and strengthening of the financial system as its three main preconditions. Meanwhile capital flows have been gradually liberalized, allowing, on the inflow side, foreign direct and portfolio investments, and tapping of foreign capital markets by Indian companies as well as considerably better remittance privileges for individuals; and on the outflow side, international expansion of domestic companies. In 2000, the infamous Foreign Exchange Regulation Act (FERA) was replaced with the much milder Foreign Exchange Management Act (FEMA) that gave participants in the foreign exchange market much greater leeway.

The ultimate goal of capital account convertibility now seems to be within the government's sights and efforts are on to chalk out the roadmap for the last leg, though it is not expected to be accomplished before 2009. Expectedly, the wisdom of the move has been hotly debated. Advocates of convertibility cite the 'consumption smoothing' benefits of global funds flow and point out that it actually improves macroeconomic discipline because of external monitoring by the global financial markets. Convertibility can spur domestic investment and growth because of easier and cheaper financing. It can also contribute to greater efficiency in the banking and financial systems. On the other hand, sceptics like Williamson (2006) point out that India is yet to fulfil at least one of the three major preconditions to capital account convertibility set out by the Tarapore committee, namely fiscal discipline, with a public-sector deficit of 7.6 per cent of the gross domestic product (GDP) and ratio of public debt to GDP of over 83 per cent in 2005–6. In any case, the argument goes, the benefits of convertibility do not necessarily outweigh the risks and cross-border short-term bank loans—usually the last item to be liberalized—are the most volatile. It is generally held that it was, in fact, the *lack* of convertibility that protected India from contamination during the Asian contagion in 1997–8.

THE DYNAMICS OF SWELLING RESERVES

An important corollary of India's foreign exchange policy has been the quick and significant accumulation of foreign currency reserves in the past few years. Starting from a foreign exchange reserves level barely enough to cover two weeks of imports in 1990–1 to about $ 32 billion at the beginning of 2000, India's foreign exchange position has rocketed to one of the highest in the world with over $ 155 billion of reserves in mid-2006. Since 2000, this implies a compounded annual growth rate of about 28 per cent with the years 2003 and 2004 having the most stunning rises at 48 per cent and 45 per cent respectively. During these two years the US dollar fell against the Euro by 19 per cent and against the rupee by 9 per cent. Without RBI intervention, the latter figure is likely to have been larger and the reserves accumulation less spectacular.

A sizable foreign exchange reserve acts as liquidity cover and protects against a run on the country's currency, and reduces the rate of interest on Indian debt in the world market by lowering the country risk perception by international rating agencies. However, beyond a point, it begins to affect the money supply in the country, and interest rates. There are significant 'sterilization costs' to avoid this and the RBI loses money by earning low returns on the safe assets used to park the reserves. Given this low rate of return, there has been discussion about the unique proposal to use part of the reserves to fund infrastructure projects.

Liberalization has transformed India's external sector and a direct beneficiary of this has been the foreign exchange market in India. From a foreign exchange-starved, control-ridden economy, India has moved on to a position of $ 150 billion plus in international reserves with a confident rupee and drastically reduced foreign exchange control. As foreign trade and cross-border capital flows continue to grow, and the country moves towards capital account convertibility, the foreign exchange market is poised to play an even greater role in the economy, but is unlikely to be completely free of RBI interventions any time soon.

RAJESH CHAKRABARTI

REFERENCES

Bank for International Settlements (BIS). 2005a. *Triennial Central Bank Survey: Foreign Exchange and Derivatives Market Activity in 2004*, Basel, Switzerland.

_____. 2005b. 'Foreign Exchange Market Intervention in Emerging Markets: Motives, Techniques and Implications', BIS Paper No. 24, Basel, Switzerland.

Chakrabarti, Rajesh. 2006. *The Financial Sector in India: Emerging Issues*, New Delhi, Oxford University Press.

Ghosh, Soumya Kanti. 2002. 'RBI Intervention in the Forex Market: Results from a Tobit and Logit Model Using Daily Data', *Economic and Political Weekly*, 15 June: 2333–48.

Williamson, John. 2006. 'Why Capital Account Convertibility in India is Premature', *Economic and Political Weekly*, 13 May: 1848–50.

Foreign Exchange Reserves

Any discussion of India's foreign exchange reserves immediately brings back unsavoury memories of April 1991 when India's foreign exchange reserves plummeted to $4.9 billion, which would suffice for barely two weeks of merchandise imports and brought the country to the precipice of an external payment default. Reserve Bank of India (RBI) had to physically airlift the required quantities of gold to London to ensure that credits were rolled over and the default avoided. Emergency access to standby facility with the International Monetary Fund (IMF) in June 1991 followed by wide-ranging structural reforms that included steep currency devaluation provided the much-needed breathing space and started the process of rebuilding the foreign exchange reserves. The traumatic events of 1991 have ensured that the economic policy stance has been focused on maintaining healthy external-sector balances in subsequent years. This is amply evident in foreign exchange reserves having risen to $309.7 billion by the end of 2007 and reaching a peak level of $314.6 billion in May 2008. While these reserves declined somewhat sharply in the wake of the Lehman Brothers collapse and the ensuing global financial meltdown and economic downturn, they provided the much-needed security to the Indian economy and helped it weather the storm without any palpable difficulties. By the end of July 2009 when the economic recovery was clearly visible both globally and in India, foreign exchange reserves (see Figure 1) were $271.6 billion. The decline of $43.0 billion from their peak in May 2008 was to a large extent due to valuation effects with the dollar having appreciated against the rupee as with other major currencies during this period.

It can be argued that India and the rest of the Asian economies were spared the more serious effects of the unprecedented global crisis of 2008–9, the worst since the Great Depression, primarily on account of the self-insurance that they had achieved by building up their foreign exchange reserves. This is in contrast to the Asian experience in the late 1990s and to the current experience of the East European and Baltic economies which did not have the comfort of large

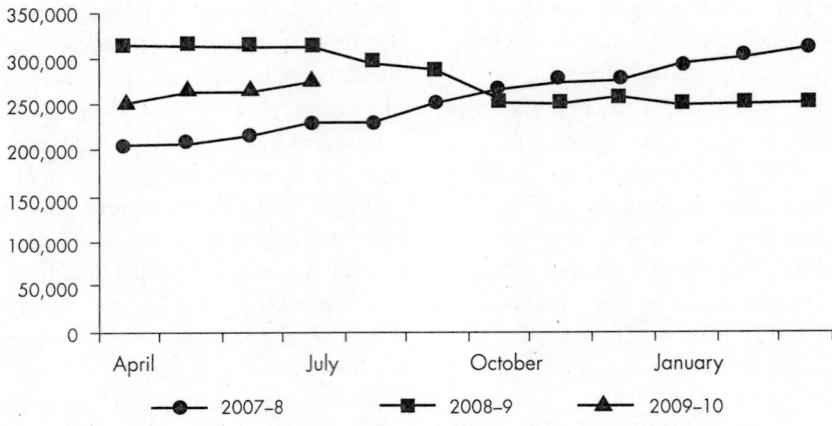

Figure 1   Stock of Foreign Exchange Reserves (US$ million)

Source: RBI.

reserves and had to rush to the IMF for large-scale emergency assistance. The experience of the Asian economies in the late 1990s and that of the East Europeans in the present downturn will reinforce the global trend towards building up national foreign exchange reserves as a self-insurance against acute external shocks. This is not a healthy development as these reserves represent a cost that could be avoided with the presence of an efficient multilateral agency that could be depended upon for bailing out countries during such emergencies. It is to be hoped that the IMF in its latest avatar, and armed with emergency and flexible credit facilities that can disburse urgent relief without conditionalities, will encourage its member countries to minimize the use of foreign exchange reserves for self-insurance. The question of the optimum level of foreign exchange reserves, which has been raised in the literature (Sengupta 2008), that provide a country with the required level of insurance is a difficult one as the answer clearly depends on the exchange rate policy (whether fixed, floating, or managed peg), the composition of the country's foreign exchange reserves, and the overall

macroeconomic stability that determines the foreign investors' stance and the consequent stability of foreign capital flows to and from the country. I address these issues in the Indian context later in this entry.

India's experience since 1991 has helped refute the earlier held belief that a country's economic vulnerability increases with greater openness and higher levels of integration with the global economy. As Table 1 shows, the share of external-sector transactions (exports and imports of merchandise goods and invisibles) in the gross domestic product (GDP) has increased from a low 27 per cent in 1991–2 to 35 per cent in 2000–1 and further to 60 per cent in 2008–9.

With a more than doubling of the external sector's presence in the economy, its resilience to external shocks has grown manifestly. Several measures are used for estimating the economy's resilience to external shocks. The ratio traditionally used is to estimate the cover provided by the foreign exchange reserves (or reserves) for total annual requirements of merchandise imports. This has improved from five months of import cover in 1991–2 to ten months in 2008–9. The second measure

Table 1   India's External Trade (US$ million)

Year	Merchandise exports	Merchandise imports	Invisibles exports	Invisibles imports	Total exports (2+4)	Total imports (3+5)	Total trade (6+7)	GDP	Trade as % of GDP (8/9)*100
1	2	3	4	5	6	7	8	9	10
1991–2	18,266	21,064	9502	7882	27,768	28,946	56,714	209,677	27.0
1992–3	18,869	24,316	9334	7413	28,203	31,729	59,932	240,942	24.9
1993–4	22,683	26,739	11,319	8422	34,002	35,161	69,163	275,976	25.1
1994–5	26,855	35,904	15,554	9874	42,409	45,778	88,187	322,516	27.3
1995–6	32,310	43,670	17,664	12,217	49,974	55,887	105,861	346,962	30.5
1996–7	34,133	48,948	21,405	11,209	55,538	60,157	115,695	383,855	30.1
1997–8	35,680	51,187	23,244	13,236	58,924	64,423	123,347	386,671	31.9
1998–9	34,298	47,544	25,770	16,562	60,068	64,106	124,174	412,678	30.1
1999–2000	37,542	55,383	30,312	17,169	67,854	72,552	140,406	447,663	31.4
2000–1	45,452	57,912	32,267	22,473	77,719	80,385	158,104	450,753	35.1
2001–2	44,703	56,277	36,737	21,763	81,440	78,040	159,480	466,998	34.2
2002–3	53,774	64,464	41,925	24,890	95,699	89,354	185,053	516,695	35.8
2003–4	66,285	80,003	53,508	25,707	119,793	105,710	225,503	634,048	35.6
2004–5	85,206	118,908	69,533	38,301	154,739	157,209	311,948	719,783	43.3
2005–6	105,152	157,056	89,687	47,685	194,839	204,741	399,580	804,113	49.7
2006–7	128,888	190,670	114,558	62,341	243,446	253,011	496,457	947,167	52.4
2007–8	166,163	257,789	148,604	74,012	314,767	331,801	646,568	1,181,293	54.7
2008–9	175,184	294,587	162,556	72,970	337,740	367,557	705,297	1,179,882	59.8

Source: RBI.

used is to estimate the cover offered by the reserves against not only merchandise imports but against total imports of both goods and services. On this count too, the cover has improved (Table 2).

Table 3, in addition, provides the factor income payments which is largely the interest payments on India's external debt during this period. Adding factor income payments to total imports of goods and services yields an estimate of expected current account liabilities facing the economy. As Table 2 shows, the foreign exchange cover on this basis increased from four months import cover in 1992–3 to thirteen months in 2003–4 before declining to a comfortable eight months in 2008–9.

The Asian financial crisis of the late 1990s demonstrated that countries which did not have sufficient reserves to cover their debt servicing and portfolio investment liabilities (for example, Indonesia) suffered a serious capital flight. Portfolio investment is distinct from foreign direct investment (FDI) because investors can encash and liquidate their portfolio holdings even while suffering an exchange loss if they are even slightly unsure of receiving their payments in light of the 'insufficient reserves holdings of the country'. Thus, in a world of self-insurance, central banks would be better off keeping an eye on their reserves position even in relation to portfolio investment liabilities that could be cashed at any point with foreign investors willing to bear the exchange rate loss that would invariably have to be incurred in such an eventuality. This leads us to also estimate the cover provided by reserves in relation to the total annual debt servicing requirements (included in factor income payments) and the stock of foreign institutional investments (FIIs, also

Table 2   Reserve Cover for Total Imports (Goods and Services)

Year	Merchandise imports (US$ million)	Imports of goods and services (US$ million)	Reserves (US$ million)	Reserve cover (in months) (3/4)
1	2	3	4	5
1991–2	21,064	24,879	9220	4
1992–3	24,316	27,917	9832	4
1993–4	26,739	31,469	19,254	7
1994–5	35,904	41,437	25,186	7
1995–6	43,670	51,214	21,687	5
1996–7	48,948	55,696	26,423	6
1997–8	51,187	59,297	29,367	6
1998–9	47,544	58,565	32,490	7
1999–2000	55,383	67,028	38,036	7
2000–1	57,912	72,488	42,281	7
2001–2	56,277	70,093	54,106	9
2002–3	64,464	81,584	76,100	11
2003–4	80,003	96,727	112,959	14
2004–5	118,908	146,731	141,514	12
2005–6	157,056	191,545	151,622	9
2006–7	190,670	234,981	199,179	10
2007–8	257,789	310,301	309,723	12
2008–9	294,587	345,993	251,735	9

Source: RBI.

Table 3   External Payments (US$ million) and Reserve Cover (in months)

Year	Merchandise imports	Service imports	Factor income payments	Stock of FII investment	Foreign exchange reserves	Reserve cover (in months) (6)/(2+3+4)
1	2	3	4	5	6	7
1992–3	24,316	3601	3799	4.2	9832	4
1993–4	26,739	4730	3665	1638.3	19,254	7
1994–5	35,904	5533	4317	3166.6	25,186	7
1995–6	43,670	7544	4634	5202.3	21,687	5
1996–7	48,948	6748	4380	7634.2	26,423	5
1997–8	51,187	8110	5081	9284.3	29,367	5
1998–9	47,544	11,021	5479	8898	32,490	6
1999–2000	55,383	11,645	5490	11,371.3	38,036	6
2000–1	57,912	14,576	7686	13,531.4	42,281	6
2001–2	56,277	13,816	7585	15,370.7	54,106	8
2002–3	64,464	17,120	6968	15,936.3	76,100	10
2003–4	80,003	16,724	8409	25,941.7	112,959	13
2004–5	118,908	27,823	9572	36,293.2	141,514	11
2005–6	157,056	34,489	12,263	45,656.5	151,622	9
2006–7	190,670	44,311	16,639	52,477	199,179	9
2007–8	257,789	52,512	19,185	68,918.5	309,723	11
2008–9	294,587	51,406	18,818	59,081.1	251,735	8

Source: RBI and Securities and Exchange Board of India (SEBI).

referred to as portfolio inflows). As Table 3 shows, the stock of FII into India increased from a mere $4 million in 1992–3 to $68.9 billion in 2007–8 before declining to $59.1 billion in 2008–9. With liberalization and reforms, the growth in reserves ensured that by 2006–7, they had reached 220 per cent of the total debt servicing and portfolio investment liabilities and thus provided the much-needed insurance against any external shock and consequent run on the currency. This ratio has gone up to 352 per cent in 2007–8 primarily because of the rapid build-up of reserves in that year. The build-up in reserves ensured that the economy could absorb, without much difficulty, a net outflow of nearly $10 billion from portfolio investments in 2008–9. As a result of these outflows, the ratio of foreign exchange reserves to total debt servicing and portfolio investment liabilities actually decreased to 323 per cent in 2008–9. It is thus evident that while the size of Indian reserves is much smaller than China's ($1.76 trillion), it has afforded India the necessary cushion against external shocks.

It is perhaps useful to point out that unlike in the case of China, whose current account surplus has contributed significantly to the reserves build up, India has built up its reserves exclusively with the help of a surplus on the capital account. As Table 4 shows, during 1991–2 to 2008–9, as also in previous decades, India's external sector has been characterized by a persistent current account deficit. In only three years (2001–2 to 2003–4) did India manage to generate a current account surplus over this period. India was successful in attracting sufficiently large capital inflows to generate a capital account surplus in every year since 1991–2. This has been steadily increasing and it peaked at 9 per cent of the GDP in 2007–8 when India added $110 billion to its reserves holdings.

Table 4   Current and Capital Account Balance (as per cent of GDP)

Year	Current account balance	Capital account balance
1	2	3
1991–2	–0.6	1.9
1992–3	–1.5	1.6
1993–4	–0.4	3.2
1994–5	–1.0	2.6
1995–6	–1.7	1.2
1996–7	–1.2	3.1
1997–8	–1.4	2.5
1998–9	–1.0	2.0
1999–2000	–1.0	2.3
2000–1	–0.6	2.0
2001–2	0.7	1.8
2002–3	1.2	2.1
2003–4	2.2	2.6
2004–5	–0.3	3.9
2005–6	–1.2	3.2
2006–7	–1.0	4.8
2007–8	–1.4	9.1
2008–9	–2.5	0.8

Source: RBI.

The composition of capital inflows used to build up the foreign exchange reserves is important in ensuring that these do not result in an unsustainable accumulation of external debt especially short-term debt. Table 5, therefore, gives us the annual stock of external debt in India including the share of short-term debt defined as debt of less than one year's duration. It is important to note that unlike many other emerging economies, India has managed to restrain the share of its short-term debt to less than 20 per cent of its total external debt. This gives the needed degree of comfort. More important, short-term debt has declined from nearly 93 per cent of total foreign exchange reserves in 1991–2 to less than 9 per cent by 2007–8 before rising to 18 per cent in 2008–9 when reserves declined in the aftermath of the global recession.

It is, therefore, evident that India today enjoys a comfortable foreign exchange

Table 5   External Debt and Foreign Exchange Reserves (US$ million)

Year	Total debt	Short-term debt	Foreign exchange reserves	Short-term debt as % of foreign exchange reserves (3/4)*100
1	2	3	4	5
1991–2	83,801	8544	9220	92.7
1992–3	85,285	7070	9832	71.9
1993–4	90,023	6340	19,254	32.9
1994–5	92,695	3627	25,186	14.4
1995–6	99,008	4269	21,687	19.7
1996–7	93,730	5034	26,423	19.1
1997–8	93,470	6726	29,367	22.9
1998–9	93,531	5046	32,490	15.5
1999–2000	96,886	4274	38,036	11.2
2000–1	98,263	3936	42,281	9.3
2001–2	101,326	3628	54,106	6.7
2002–3	98,843	2745	76,100	3.6
2003–4	104,914	4669	112,959	4.1
2004–5	111,645	4431	141,514	3.1
2005–6	132,973	17,723	151,622	11.7
2006–7	138,133	19,539	199,179	9.8
2007–8	169,669	26,376	309,723	8.5
2008–9	221,212	44,313	251,735	17.6

Source: RBI.

reserve position in relation to all relevant parameters. Its reserves are, however, only a fraction of the total reserves held by other Asian economies like China and Japan, or even much smaller economies like Taiwan and South Korea (see Figure 2). But these comparisons are not particularly relevant because the accumulation of reserves in other Asian economies has been primarily on account of pursuing an export-oriented strategy which has generated large current account surpluses that have to be absorbed through reserve accretion. The flip side of this strategy has been an imbalanced growth that has seen low levels of private consumption and extraordinarily high levels of savings in the economy. As the current global crisis has amply demonstrated, these imbalances, which are unsustainable, are having to be corrected and will force Asian economies to rely

more on domestic sources of demand in the coming years.

India, having successfully overcome its bias against exports and greater economic openness, has to persist with making its economy even more deeply integrated with global flows and further sharpen its competitive advantage to make better use of external demand. Its current growth strategy that has resulted in net exports (of goods and services) contributing –10.5 per cent to GDP growth between 2001/2–2007/8 also needs to be rebalanced so that net exports and external demand can be relied upon to a greater extent as a driver of growth. This is clearly feasible, given that India's present share in world trade of goods is 1.3 per cent and in services is 2.5 per cent. A higher contribution of net exports to GDP growth (or in other words a smaller negative contribution than at present) combined with policy initiatives

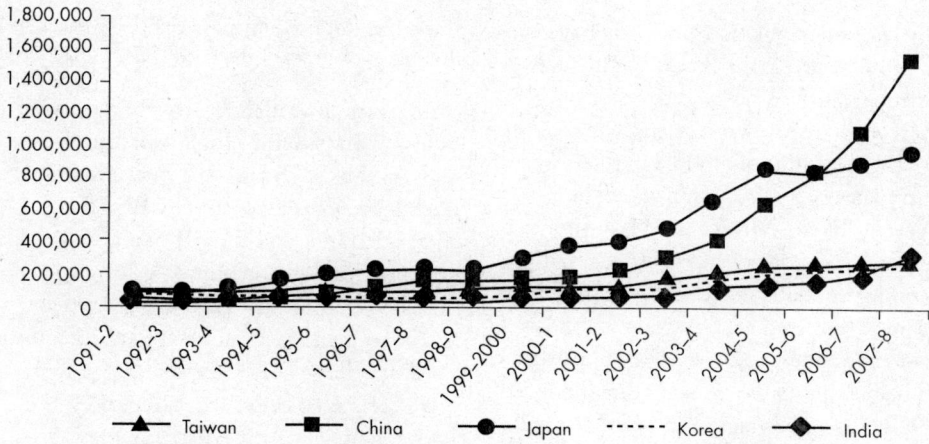

Figure 2   Foreign Exchange Reserves of Selected Countries (US$ million)

Source: IMF and RBI.

to make India an even more attractive destination for FDI will ensure that the country's overall external balance-of-payments position, which is summarily represented in the level of foreign exchange reserves, remains on a sound footing in the coming years.

RAJIV KUMAR[*]

REFERENCES

Acharya, Shankar. 2008. 'India's Macroeconomic Performance and Policies since 2000'.

Ahluwalia, M.S. 2002. 'India's Vulnerability to External Crisis', in M.S. Ahluwalia, S. Tarapore, and Y.V. Reddy, eds, *Macroeconomics and Monetary Policy: Issues for Reforming the Economy*, Oxford University Press.

Burke, D. and P. Lane. 2001. 'The Empirics of Foreign Reserves', *Open Economics Review*, 12(4): 423–34.

Department of Investment Services, Taiwan.

Financial Statistics of the Central Bank of China, Republic of China.

IMF, International Financial Statistics.

*Research assistance from Ritika Tewari and review by ICRIER colleagues is gratefully acknowledged. Mistakes are the author's responsibility.

Ministry of Finance, India.

Reserve Bank of India (RBI). 2009. *Handbook of Statistics and Bulletin*, September.

Sen Gupta, Abhijit. 2008. 'Cost of Holding Excess Reserves: The Indian Experience', March.

Foreign Institutional Investment

In 2004–5 portfolio investments in India accounted for about 62 per cent of total foreign investment in the country and at about 1.29 per cent of the gross domestic product (GDP) well exceeded the current account deficit (0.95 per cent of GDP). Foreign Institutional Investors' (FIIs) investments accounted for about 97.5 per cent of this. Ever since the opening of the Indian equity markets to foreigners, FII investments have steadily grown from about Rs 2600 crore in 1993 to over Rs 48,000 crore in 2005. At the end of June 2006, the cumulative FII flows to India accounted for a little over 9 per cent of the Bombay Stock Exchange (BSE) market capitalization.

While it is generally held that portfolio flows benefit the economies of recipient countries, policymakers worldwide have been more than a little uneasy about such investments. Often referred to as 'hot money', they are known to stampede out at the slightest hint of trouble in the host country leaving an economic wreck in their wake, like in Mexico in 1994. They have been blamed for exacerbating small economic problems in a country by making large and concerted withdrawals at the first sign of economic weakness. They have also been held responsible for spreading financial crises—causing 'contagion' in international financial markets.

International capital flows and capital controls have emerged as important policy issues in the Indian context as well. The danger of abrupt reversals and their destabilizing effects on equity and foreign exchange markets are always a concern. Nevertheless, in recent years, the government has been making strong efforts to increase FII flows in India. Some scholars (Rakshit 2006) have argued that, far from being healthy for the economy, FII inflows have actually imposed certain burdens on the Indian economy. Understanding the determinants and effects of FII flows and devising appropriate regulation therefore constitute an important part of economic policymaking in India.

FOREIGN INSTITUTIONAL INVESTORS— A BRIEF INTRODUCTION
Entities covered by the term 'FII' include

Overseas pension funds, mutual funds, investment trust, asset management company, nominee company, bank, institutional portfolio manager, university funds, endowments, foundations, charitable trusts, charitable societies, a trustee or power of attorney holder incorporated or established outside India proposing to make proprietary investments or investments on behalf of a broad-based fund (i.e., fund having more than 20 investors with no

single investor holding more than 10 per cent of the shares or units of the fund) [GOI 2005].

FIIs can invest their own funds as well as invest on behalf of their overseas clients registered as such with the Securities and Exchange Board of India (SEBI). These client accounts that the FII manages are known as 'sub-accounts'. A domestic portfolio manager can also register itself as an FII to manage the funds of sub-accounts.

A few large FIIs (less than 3 per cent of all registered ones, according to GOI 2005), issue derivative instruments called 'participatory notes' that are registered and traded overseas, backed by the FIIs' holdings of Indian securities. This arrangement has raised some concerns in regulatory circles since it makes it difficult to trace the ultimate beneficiary in the funds and may be used to bring in 'unclean' funds (funds generated out of illegal activities) into the Indian markets.

As of mid-July 2006, there were 932 FIIs registered with SEBI, of which 115 were registered in the first half of 2006 itself. US-based funds accounted for 39 per cent of all registered FIIs, followed by UK (16 per cent), Luxembourg (7 per cent), and Singapore (5 per cent) based ones. In terms of net cumulative investment, US-based funds accounted for 29 per cent at the end of October 2005 (GOI 2005) followed by UK-based ones at 17 per cent.

Though initially restricted to investing only in listed company stocks, FIIs are now allowed to invest in equity, bonds, and derivative instruments in India subject to limits of foreign ownership for various sectors as well as ceilings on total investment per FII. Regular FIIs follow what has come to be known as the '70:30 rule', that is they must invest no less than 70 per cent of their funds in equity-related instruments and may invest the remainder in debt-related instruments. There are also some FIIs that are registered as '100 per cent debt-fund FIIs' that are permitted to invest exclusively in debt instruments. Although equity holdings of FIIs have received maximum attention from the press, researchers, and policymakers alike, the debt holdings of FIIs are not wholly insignificant. As of 21 July 2006, the regular FIIs held US$ 224.25 million (about Rs 1009 crore) in government securities/treasury bills and US$ 82.02 million (about Rs 369 crore) in corporate debt. At the end of June 2006, the open interest of FIIs in stock and index futures and options exceeded Rs 22,000 crore.

WHAT WE KNOW ABOUT FII FLOWS TO INDIA
Over the last few years, research has brought to light a few important features of FII flows to India. The key question has been the relationship between FII flows and returns

in the Indian markets shown in Figure 1. Clearly FII equity investments and stock market performance in India have been very closely interlinked. Also, both variables experienced a sharp break around April 2003, after which they ramped up steeply. The association is unmistakable—the correlation of monthly net FII equity inflows and monthly Sensex returns is 0.61 since April 2003 and 0.33 in the overall sample.

FII flows are routinely depicted as a major driver of Indian stock market return in the financial press. However, research seems to suggest they are more of an effect than a cause of stock market performance. Analysing daily flow data during 1999, Chakrabarti (2001) concludes that in the post-Asian crisis period, stock market performance has been the sole driver of FII flows, though monthly data in the pre-Asian crisis period may suggest some reverse causality. This return-

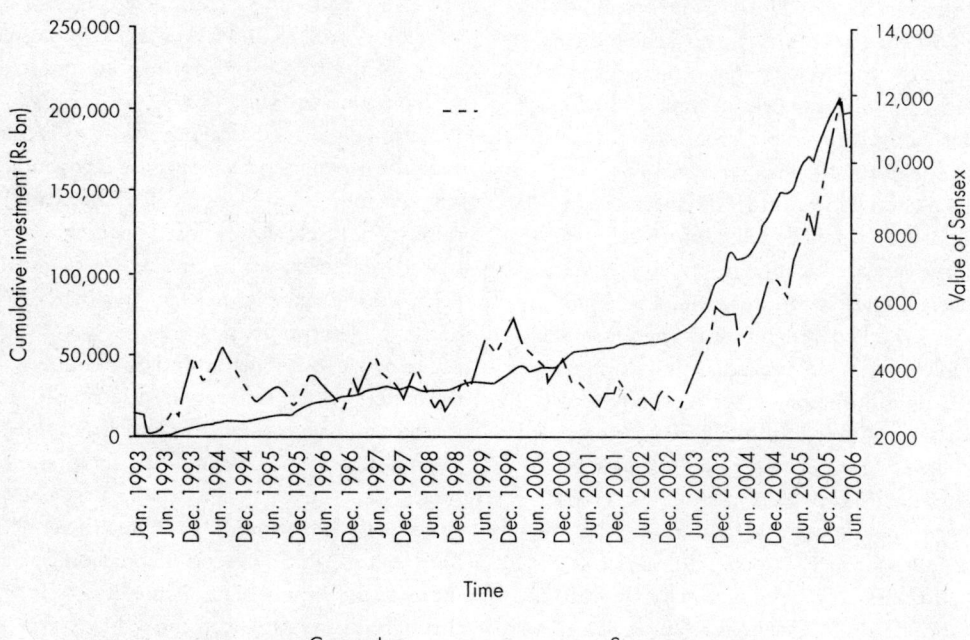

Figure 1 Cumulative FII Investment and the Sensex

Source: www.equitymaster.com

chasing behaviour has been confirmed using daily data during 1999–2002 in Mukherjee et al. (2002), who also find that the sales of Indian securities by FIIs are affected by returns but not purchases. On the other hand, Gordon and Gupta (2003) analyse monthly data over the period 1993–2000 to conclude that FII flows are *negatively* related to lagged stock market returns, suggesting negative feedback trading. There are, however, issues about the appropriateness of using monthly data in this analysis (Rakshit 2006). In any case, given that there is a structural break in the data around April 2003, careful analysis of more recent data would be instructive in understanding the nature of the relationship and causality, if any, between these two variables.

The largest single-month pull-out of FII funds happened in May 2006 when the FIIs withdrew over $1.7 billion (Rs 8247 crore) followed by May 2004 ($719 million, Rs 3250 crore). These were also the months with the fourth largest and the largest single-month per cent decline in the Sensex respectively (15.8 per cent and 18.8 per cent) in the post-reforms era.

As for other features, Chakrabarti (2001) finds no evidence of any informational disadvantage for foreign investors vis-à-vis their domestic counterparts. The Asian crisis marked a regime shift in determining FII flows. In the pre-crisis period, the beta (or co-movement) of the Indian market with the American S&P 500 index seemed to inversely affect FII flows to India, but the effect disappeared in the post-crisis period. India's country risk rating did not seem to affect FII flows. Mukherjee et al. (2002) have questioned the diversification motive behind FII flows to India and report auto-correlation or inertia in the flows. Gordon and Gupta (2003) report that FII flows are sensitive to the London Inter-bank Offer Rate (LIBOR) as well as India's

macroeconomic fundamentals. Coondoo and Mukherjee (2004) argue that both the stock market as well as FII flows in India have high and related volatility. Finally, in their analysis of the effects of regulatory measures on FII flows, Bose and Coondoo (2004) find that liberalizing policy changes have had expansionary effect on FII flows while restrictive measures aimed at giving regulators greater control over FII flows do not necessarily dampen them.

GOVERNMENT POLICY REGARDING FII FLOWS

In policy circles in India, FII flows are believed to have a positive impact on the country's development; so much so that encouraging FII flows—while reducing the financial sector's vulnerability to speculative capital flows—constitutes an objective of the National Common Minimum Programme. Accordingly, an expert group was set up in 2004 (in addition to a committee in 2002 which reported in 2004) to suggest ways to accomplish this goal. The group submitted its report in November 2005 (GOI 2005). Its rationale for encouraging FII flows is that such flows can increase domestic investment without increasing foreign debt. They can raise stock prices, lower cost of equity, stimulate investment by Indian firms, and lead to improvements in securities market design and corporate governance.

In order to further stimulate FII flows, the expert group has suggested setting FII investment caps, if any, over and above the foreign direct investment (FDI) sectoral limits. In cases where the limits have to be combined, they should be set at sufficiently high levels. Another recommendation is to increase the supply of 'good-quality equities' through disinvestment in the public sector and through encouraging companies with large projects like those in the infrastructure and telecom sectors to raise money in the domestic markets.

As for the companion objective of reducing the market's vulnerability to speculative flows, the group recommends participation of domestic institutional investors like pension funds in the equity markets. Entities from 'tax haven' countries should be barred from registering as FIIs. The practice of participatory notes (PNs) is acceptable provided SEBI has the powers to track down the final beneficiary for investigation or surveillance by making it obligatory for the FIIs to provide such information. PNs should not be issued to entities not regulated anywhere in the world and FIIs must follow the 'know-your-client' principle. Existing non-eligible PNs should be allowed to expire or wound down within five years, whichever is earlier. Further, to avoid abuse of the sub-account route to circumvent investment limits, the FII limits should be applied to total investments managed by an FII—directly and through its sub-accounts.

Rakshit (2006) has questioned the basic premise of beneficial effects of FII flows in India as well as the expert group's recommendations. Apart from the risks of financial instability, which he views as underestimated by the expert group, Rakshit (2006) points out that during the 1992–2002 period there has been little relationship between the capital account balance and aggregate investment in India and, except for a couple of years, the latter has exceeded the current account balance in all years since liberalization began. This indicates that FII flows are contributing primarily to the amassing of huge foreign exchange reserves at the Reserve Bank of India (RBI) rather than to real investment in the economy. Further, this accretion of reserves implies significant costs for the economy in terms of a fall in RBI profits through holding of lower-yielding reserves, loss of seignorage revenue, and the costs of sterilizing the inflows. In the presence of demand deficiency in the

economy, the real effects of enhanced FII flows are likely to be far from positive. Thus FII flows should be viewed not in isolation but as part of an integrated policy package for all capital receipts keeping in mind their role in the overall macroeconomic structure.

RAJESH CHAKRABARTI

REFERENCES

Bose, Suchismita and Dipankar Coondoo. 2004. 'The Impact of FII Regulations in India', *Money and Finance*, July–December.

Chakrabarti, Rajesh. 2001. 'FII Flows to India: Nature and Causes', *Money and Finance*, October–December. Reprinted in *The Financial Sector in India: Emerging Issues*, New Delhi, Oxford University Press, 2006.

Coondoo, Dipankar and Paramita Mukherjee. 2004. 'Volatility of FII in India', *Money and Finance*, October–March.

Gordon, James and Poonam Gupta. 2003. 'Portfolio Flows into India: Do Domestic Fundamentals Matter?', IMF Working Paper No. 03/20.

Government of India (GoI), Ministry of Finance. 2005. Report of the Expert Group on Encouraging FII Flows and Checking the Vulnerability of Capital Markets to Speculative Flows, New Delhi, November.

Mukherjee, Paramita, Suchismita Bose, and Dipankar Coondoo. 2002. 'Foreign Institutional Investment in the Indian Equity Market', *Money and Finance*, April–September.

Rakshit, Mihir. 2006. 'On Liberalising Foreign Institutional Investments', *Economic and Political Weekly*, 18 March: 991–8.

International Finance

Four major ways in which international finance affects India are, first, the increasing availability of foreign savings; second, their use; third, the changing effectiveness of macroeconomic policy; finally, the effect of macroeconomic policy on capital flows, their use, and associated risks, in the context of India's economic structure. I examine each in turn, drawing on insights from new research, and taking a nuanced view between ideological positions that emphasize only the risks or only the benefits of capital flows.

FOREIGN SAVINGS

India received some aid flows in the 1950s and the 1960s, and an influx of remittances started from the mid-1970s. But in the 1990s there was a large expansion of private capital flows due to changes in technology, markets, and liberalizing reforms in many parts of the globe, in which India participated. Capital inflows contribute to growth through technology spillovers and improvements in efficiency, but they also boost resources for investment. Using foreign savings to supplement domestic savings in this way requires an initial widening of the current account deficit (CAD) of the balance of payments (BOP), and for the widening to occur, investment must exceed savings.

It is a tautology that a CAD must equal the capital account surplus minus any rise in foreign exchange reserves. The latter is a balancing component which monetary and exchange rate policy affects directly and also indirectly, through effects on macroeconomic variables. The components of the BOP capital account are foreign investment, net commercial borrowings, net non-resident Indian (NRI) deposits, net external assistance, rupee debt service, and other capital. Foreign direct and foreign portfolio investments are non-debt-creating inflows. The first is the most stable of the various categories. Debt-creating inflows, and short-term debt in particular, carry a higher risk of reversal, but the share of short-term debt in India's total debt has been falling.

The current account (CA) is formally defined as the acquisition of foreign assets by domestic residents minus foreign residents' acquisition of domestic assets. If this is positive, the CA is in surplus. The basic macroeconomic identity, that income must equal expenditure, implies that the current account surplus (CAS) must equal both net exports of goods and services, and also gross national saving (GNS) minus investment. Subtracting income payments made abroad from gross domestic product gives gross national product. Subtracting consumption from the latter gives GNS. But the popular conception of CAS is identified with the net exports of goods and services.

Investment is the most volatile component of expenditure and expectations of the future can be particularly volatile in a reforming economy. Consumers would like to smooth consumption over time, if capital markets permit it. The modern intertemporal approach to the BOP (Sachs 1981) analyses this dynamic forward-looking behaviour. The new insight is that macro policies, savings and investment, and not only trade policies, affect the CA.

In a developing country with incomplete capital markets, forward-looking decisions will be severely constrained. Intertemporal optimization can give only a rough benchmark. Heightened uncertainty under reform may raise precautionary savings. But the associated positive productivity shock should raise investment and inflows that contribute to its financing. If incomes are expected to be higher in future, current consumption should rise towards higher smoothed levels. Therefore, although both savings and investment would rise together, the rise in investment would exceed that in savings (Goyal 2004). But the Indian CA moved into surplus at the turn of the century, and foreign exchange reserves rose rapidly. I turn to the effects of monetary policy in the Indian context to understand this.

IMPLICATIONS FOR MONETARY POLICY

Monetary policy affects the interest rate, and through it investment, savings, the current account and foreign inflows, but it was thought to have only short-run effects. What is known as the new International Finance or Open Economy Macroeconomics (Obstfeld and Rogoff 1996), however, emphasizes forward-looking expectations, with asset prices such as the exchange rate adjusting rapidly, and other sticky prices taking longer. The expectations congealed in the sticky prices give monetary policy persistent long-run effects. Changes in wealth in an open economy and shifts closer to potential output add to this impact of monetary policy.

In the workhorse open economy Mundell–Flemming model, however, monetary policy becomes ineffective under perfect capital mobility and a fixed exchange rate. A fall in money supply raises interest rates and invites more inflows, which raises money supply. Any differential between domestic and foreign interest rates reflects expected domestic currency depreciation plus country-risk premium. This is known as uncovered interest parity. If monetary policy and intervention keep the exchange rate undervalued (depreciated) on average, interest rates must also be low, otherwise capital will flow in to take advantage of higher domestic interest rates and a strong currency, creating conditions for a future reversal.

Capital mobility has risen in India but it is still far from perfect. There are now few restrictions on inflows, but domestic residents cannot easily hold foreign assets to diversify their portfolios. And the exchange rate is a managed float; it is not fixed. Monetary policy does have degrees of freedom. Under reserve accumulation and active sterilization of the resulting increase in money supply, the onus is on policy to minimize the interest differential.

Administrative restrictions on Indian interest rates are scaled down but have not completely gone. Banking spreads, prime lending rates, and savings deposit rates are difficult to decrease, partly for political reasons. But the gap between Indian and foreign interest rates now affects foreign inflows since the major restrictions left are only on domestic residents.

Aggressive sterilization, together with the rigidities, maintained positive interest gaps, attracting more inflows, but reducing the stimulus to activity that would have absorbed some of the inflows. A huge accumulation of forex reserves occurred partly due to arbitrage at different points of the interest rate spectrum.

The severe credit squeeze and rise in interest rates that followed the first episode of exchange rate volatility in 1995–6 helped trigger a sustained industrial slowdown. The Reserve Bank of India (RBI) shifted away from strict monetary targeting. The Bank Rate, which had been frozen, was activated as a benchmark for interest rates, and gradually brought down. The other prime aim of monetary policy was to prevent appreciation and volatility in the exchange rate. Reversals were carried out only during periods of exchange rate volatility, sometimes induced by fluctuations in foreign capital inflows. Since the late 1990s, policy committed to a soft interest rate regime, but steady softening of nominal interest rates occurred only after February 2001, with the fall in world interest rates. An upswing in activity followed. The response of spending to interest rates had risen. The fiscal deficit did not put pressure on interest rates because of large domestic savings and high foreign inflows.

High volatility of the exchange rate followed periods when it was almost static.

Such reversals disturb markets and can lead to panic attacks on the currency; both market players and policymakers overreact. The RBI intervened to limit volatility but did not maintain regular limited volatility, which may have mitigated the burst of high volatility and the defensive rise in interest rates.

REDUCING RISK AND ABSORBING CAPITAL INFLOWS

Following Tirole's (2002) position that the fundamental failure is the inability of governments to credibly contract with foreign capital, a number of authors argue that crises are inevitable where financial institutions are weak. Hausman et al. (2002) suggest the basic problem is that a developing country cannot borrow in its own currency. Markets do not exist for laying-off currency risk.

There are three ways to reduce risk associated with capital inflows: improvements in the international financial architecture, initiatives for regional cooperation, and improving own markets.

Limited exchange rate volatility around a trend competitive rate creates incentives for hedging and lowers exposure to currency risk, thus deepening and developing markets and reducing overreaction. Steady forex markets reform since 1995 has made more instruments available for hedging, but better incentives would contribute to their use. As long as policy credibly improves fundamentals, markets may help the RBI achieve targets. Changes in money supply should be sufficient for its purpose, but market intervention and announcements are additional tools available if necessary. The RBI has considerable clout to focus expectations in thin markets. Other benefits the exchange-rate policy has are:

+ It is consistent with encouraging trade and ensuring external balance over the long run.

+ It frees monetary policy to better implement smoother and more counter-cyclical interest rates to stimulate the real sector.

+ Higher activity allows more inflows to be absorbed.

+ It keeps inflation low as it counters supply shocks and anchors expectations.

In order to maintain a competitive real exchange rate and encourage exports, a benchmark real effective exchange rate (REER) set after the devaluations of the early 1990s has been largely maintained. This is a valid strategy as long as India, like China, has large reserves of labour yet to be absorbed into higher productivity employment to which exports contribute. Since the informal labour market accounts for about 90 per cent of the workforce, large numbers available to work at low wages prevent the substantial rise in average real wages required for a major currency appreciation. Such a rise in real wages is possible only with a rise in labour productivity in agriculture.

This labour market structure implies that if foreign capital can be used to alleviate specific bottlenecks and supportive reforms are undertaken, supply may not be a constraint on output since output is below its potential. As long as monetary policy is able to anchor nominal wages and inflationary expectations, it can stimulate demand. A rise in credit will finance an expansion in output, capital, and capacity.

An economy at full employment requires an appreciation of the exchange rate to absorb foreign inflows since a rise in domestic absorption can occur only through a rise in imports. If there is excess capacity, the rise in absorption can occur at an unchanged real exchange rate, through output and capacity expansion, but low interest rates are a necessary complement to such a strategy. Some exchange rate appreciation

would help to absorb inflows but it cannot
be the major part of the adjustment. Full
capital account convertibility, which allows
domestic residents to acquire foreign assets,
also absorbs reserves, but it raises the
risk of capital outflows and crises unless
markets and institutions are well developed.
Therefore it has to be introduced gradually
and in a correct sequence.

Short-term movements in the exchange
rate to counter temporary supply shocks,
such as oil price hikes, can achieve the
required limited volatility and pre-empt the
effect of these shocks on the domestic price-
wage process. As productivity rises, limited
nominal appreciation is feasible without
harming exports.

A large voting population whose wages
are not formally indexed to inflation implies
administrative restraints on prices of basic
consumption goods. Since political pressure
from farmers pushes up farm support
prices, consumption subsidies are given.
Since these are not complete, nominal wages
respond with a lag to a rise in food prices
leading to inflation. But with more openness,
world prices restrain domestic food prices.
An exchange rate policy that lowers food
price inflation reduces the necessity for
distorting subsidies and administered prices.
Improvement in efficiency releases surplus,
which enhances its political feasibility.
Therefore the policy is compatible with
political constraints and macropolicy
objectives to lower inflation and raise growth.

ASHIMA GOYAL

REFERENCES

Goyal, Ashima. 2004. 'Puzzles in Indian
    Performance: Deficits without Disasters',
    Kirit S. Parikh and R. Radhakrishnan, eds,
    India Development Report 2004–05, New
    Delhi, IGIDR and Oxford University Press.
Hausman, Ricardo, Barry Eichengreen, and
    Ugo Panizza. 2002. 'Original Sin: The Pain,
the Mystery and the Road to Redemption',
    mimeo, November.
Obstfeld, Maurice and Kenneth Rogoff. 1996.
    Foundations of International Macroeconomics,
    Cambridge, Massachusetts, MIT Press.
Sachs, Jeffrey D. 1981. 'The Current Account and
    Macroeconomic Adjustment in the 1970s',
    Brookings Papers on Economic Activity,
    1: 201–68.
Tirole, Jean. 2002. *Financial Crises, Liquidity
    and the International Monetary System*, New
    Jersey, Princeton University Press.

International Trade

Traditionally, India is viewed as a large,
self-contained economy with few links
with the outside world. Ancient evidence,
however, attests to the historical importance
of India's foreign trade. For millennia, India
has been the world's greatest sink of gold:
since not a grain of gold was produced in
India till the Kolar mines were sunk in the
nineteenth century, this mass of bullion
represented her accumulated trade surplus
with the outside world. Much data indicate
India's flourishing exports to the Roman and
Byzantine empires, originating in one of the
most extraordinary events in history: in 305
BC, a Bihari king marched his army across
the entire subcontinent and through the
mountain passes into Afghanistan to defeat
the Greeks in the shadow of the Hindukush
and link India with the Silk Road, the
highway of international commerce
between East and West. From this unique
episode emerged the first all-India empire,
the Mauryan empire. Nor was maritime
trade insignificant. Shore temples like
Mahabalipuram and Somnath arose in part
as banks financing the trade of south India
with Southeast Asia or of Gujarat with the
Middle East and Africa.

There was always, however, a tension
between coast and interior, a delicate

balance of power swayed by the relative contributions of each to the revenue and military capacity of the state. Land empires like the Mughal, rooted in river valley agriculture and defending a land frontier against north-western invaders, inevitably subordinated coastal interests to those of the hinterland. Well adapted to an age of land transport, they neglected maritime power and the technology of transport and defence at sea. From the sixteenth century, however, the world, particularly Western Europe, entered the age of open ocean navigation. By the eighteenth century, the sea was the primary avenue of international trade; continental regimes that, because of geography and consequent internal structure, faced landward, were gradually eclipsed and maritime powers, committed to ocean trade routes and their defence, came to dominate the world. The Pax Britannica now governed an 'empire of the sea' and an international trading network into which coasts everywhere were willy-nilly drawn.

The colonial system that evolved was dedicated, in principle, to free trade within the empire. In practice, it relegated India and other non-white colonies to the role of suppliers of primary products to Britain, 'the workshop of the world', and its trading hub. India exported opium and indigo in the nineteenth century, tea, cotton, jute, occasionally wheat and sugar, in the twentieth. Manufactured exports were limited to cotton textiles. The scene was set for prolonged stagnation as an overcrowded agrarian economy trapped in the vicious circle of poverty.

Over the century preceding 1950, similar scenarios were enacted all over the colonial world and this experience shaped policymakers' attitudes in the 1950s, when these colonies attained independence. Free trade was viewed as a design for reducing poorer countries to 'hewers of wood and drawers of water'. Their major exports, of primaries, faced low price and income elasticities of demand, threats from synthetic substitutes and from recycling of scrap (for example copper and tin) and consequently deteriorating terms of trade. Their manufactures could not compete with richer countries in the world market or indeed even at home. 'Export pessimism' fostered the belief that their development must necessarily be an autarchic process, based on import-substituting industrialization (ISI).

Nor was this entirely a prejudice born out of unfortunate experience. Before the 1960s, it had a solid economic basis. The populous low-wage countries had a labour cost advantage in manufacturing. But they also had low and inelastic domestic demand for manufactures: local producers could not achieve scale economies in home markets, while if they sought foreign markets, they ran into high distribution costs, political risks, and exchange rate volatility. Increasing returns were of course pervasive in industry, and in fact generally more important than unskilled labour costs. So low-wage economies could not realize the comparative advantage in labour-intensive manufacturing that neoclassical trade theory predicted on the assumptions of constant returns to scale and perfect mobility of goods.

If primary exports were inelastic and manufactured exports hopeless, growth had necessarily to be internally generated. And since growth shifts demand towards manufactures, self-sufficient growth involved industrialization. Industrialization in turn required protection from foreign large-scale producers located in affluent mass markets. It was also state sponsored, not market-driven. Such a development strategy dominated Indian planning since P.C. Mahalanobis, author of the Second Five Year Plan.

Particularly from the late 1960s, protection of manufacturing became a comprehensive and Byzantine system: the highest tariffs in the world (averaging 117 per cent) topped off total quantitative control and licensing of imports with complex and opaque procedures. Indeed, such an evolution was inevitable once government became the arbiter of import policy with the implied power to restrict entry and generate rents. Competition for these rents endowed administrators with enormous powers of patronage that could be exploited or encashed if dubious deals were veiled in official secrecy or by unintelligible regulatory procedure.

More generally, state-sponsored ISI was inherently limited in effectiveness and potential. It constrained productivity in many ways. It sacrificed comparative advantage and the economies of scale that accrue from specialization. It excluded foreign competition, thereby diluting pressures for efficiency. It denied India new technology embodied in imports. It raised the prices and reduced the quality of capital goods and intermediates. While all these were direct consequences of restricted trade, productivity effects just as severe flowed from the large role of government in production and economic administration under such a regime. Vast administrative resources were needed by government for formulation and enforcement of policy and by firms for compliance or evasion. As vast were the resources diverted from productive investment and innovation to rent seeking, the effort to influence the politicians and officials who doled out contracts and licences or enacted laws that set the parameters of economic activity. In a heterogeneous society dominated by organized interests, government decisions reflected these sectional pressures: this undermined productivity when, for instance, industrial location was determined primarily by these pressures or recruitment guided by non-

merit considerations. Equally damaging were the pressures of organized labour: these encouraged an approach to the public sector as an employment guarantee scheme rather than a productive element in the economy; they also perpetuated labour laws that eroded efficiency and ruled out quick exit for loss-making enterprises. Finally, there were the monumental delays of government decision making, a cost that was critical in markets requiring adaptation to rapid change or in a growth process where time is of the essence.

The main, though not exclusive, focus of this inefficiency was the public sector, which, in the ISI regime, occupied 'the commanding heights of the economy'. Its low productivity hampered supply of crucial infrastructural inputs—power, steel, coal, cement, railway and air transport, telecommunications, roads and port facilities—to the economy at large, undermining output and growth. It also implied low profitability: public enterprises became a chronic drain on the exchequer.

ISI favoured capital- and energy-intensive industries with high capital cost. Public investment also implied cost inflation due to corruption and cost escalation due to the dilatoriness of government decision making.

High cost of public investment, losses of public enterprises, and soaring salary bills in the public sector combined with vast subsidies extracted by organized interests from government to drive up public expenditure. Revenue, meanwhile, remained inelastic due to the low level and slow growth of income and the resistance of the same interest groups to tax increases. The initial response of government to these budgetary pressures was to curtail public investment. But this undermined infrastructure, creating interrelated crises in power, coal, steel, railways, cement, fertilizers, etc., that restricted growth until 1980 to a mere 3.2 per cent per annum. The

1980s saw a restoration of infrastructural investment, essentially debt-financed, with growth accelerating to 5.2 per cent. But budget deficits became endemic, a public prodigality contrasting with the frugal 22–4 per cent rate of private saving. Government borrowed massively, driving up public debt and interest rates. With debt service rising more than proportionally to the rapid growth of the debt and becoming a growing and incompressible budgetary commitment, government fashioned a debt trap for itself.

Excess demand created by budget deficits was partially absorbed by crowding out private investment through higher interest rates. In part, however, it overflowed abroad in trade deficits, financed by foreign loans at the exorbitant rates of the debt-crisis-ridden 1980s. The growth of foreign debt gradually eroded confidence in the rupee. A succession of unstable (therefore fiscally irresponsible) governments between 1989 and 1991, and the Gulf War of 1991, which imposed on government the cost of repatriating lakhs of Indian workers from the Gulf while depriving India of their foreign earnings, precipitated a crisis that drove India into the arms of the International Monetary Fund (IMF) and down the road of reform.

While in India the internal dynamics of ISI led to massive 'government failure', the international economy was changing. ISI was based on the assumed pervasiveness of scale economies in manufacturing and high distribution costs fragmenting the world market. From the mid-1960s, changes in tastes and technology and in the global distribution of wealth undermined these assumptions. Living standards rose worldwide: demand became more sophisticated and differentiated with quality, variety, and exclusiveness outweighing mere cheapness—so that the scale economies associated with long production runs and standardization dwindled in

importance. Increased uncertainty of the business environment (due to intensified global competition) made investment in specific fixed assets (which are the basis of economies of long runs) unjustifiable. Technology evolved instead towards 'flexible specialization', using microelectronically controlled general-purpose tools to produce small batches of differentiated products almost as cheaply as long runs. Distribution costs too dropped. Higher degrees of processing reduced the material and mineral intensity of output and therefore the share of transport cost in delivery price. A unipolar world economy centred on the Atlantic was replaced by a polycentric system with the Pacific and the Middle East as its other foci: this reduced spatial and cultural gaps that poor-country producers had to bridge in reaching rich markets. Ocean transport costs fell due to containerization, warehousing costs due to 'just-in-time' management technology. Above all, the information and telecommunications revolution not only demolished barriers of ignorance that had segmented markets in the past; it also created an international market in labour services that none had dreamt were tradable at all.

While technology, tastes, and economic geography combined to create a potential for globalization, its realization was facilitated by a dismantling of trade barriers beginning with the Kennedy Round in the 1960s and culminating in the World Trade Organization (WTO). Poor countries could now access rich markets at little cost and could realize their potential comparative advantage. In particular, densely populated, low-wage Asia could exploit its labour cost advantage to capture markets for manufactures and services hitherto beyond its reach. The initial consequence was the East Asian miracle—the upsurge in growth led by labour-intensive manufactured exports from the Pacific rim and, eventually,

China. South Asia followed. The labour surpluses of Asia were absorbed into the international economy much as the virgin land of the New World was in the late nineteenth century and the elastic supplies of fossil fuels were during the Industrial Revolution, and with similar consequences for the worldwide distribution of economic growth and potential economic power.

India was a latecomer to this process, its responses delayed by vested interests nurtured by ISI—in the bureaucracy, in protected industry, in organized labour in the public sector, and in large import-substituting enterprise. The crisis of 1991, however, made liberalization inevitable, paving the way for a retreat from quantitative controls and prohibitive tariffs. Liberalization also involved freer flow of capital and technology, a spectacular upsurge in exports and acceleration of growth (and consequently in developmental imports like oil and machinery) without accumulation of debt. India's recovery and transition to a high-growth trajectory were rapid, with only a minor blip between 1997 and 2000, a period when the Asian economic crisis abroad was compounded by domestic political instability.

In India, as elsewhere, accession to the WTO was a contentious issue. The WTO sets the framework for the international economy. It is not, however, a free trade system but only a forum for multilateral negotiation of the limits to trade restriction. The advanced West, concerned about slow growth, stagnant labour markets, and the threat from Asia to its economic ascendancy, has sought to negotiate a right to restrict trade on the plea of environmental or labour standards. It has tried to exploit existing clauses on quality and safety standards and against dumping to erect non-tariff barriers to imports. And it has pursued regional trading arrangements like the European Union (EU) and North American Free Trade Agreement (NAFTA) as alternatives to multilateral trade expansion over which it has less control. Protectionism in the West has changed its form but not its substance under the WTO. In India too, while Western protectionism is vigorously opposed, the government remains sensitive to the pressures of uncompetitive industries and their workers and has defended their interests through extensive anti-dumping action. Regional objectives like a South Asian free trade area have also been pursued—though fruitlessly, because of political constraints. Participation in the WTO has not, therefore, deterred protectionism—though protectionism is not the appropriate strategy for an economy that is expanding rapidly though trade.

While labour-intensive exports were the engine of growth throughout Asia, in India their expansion had its own distinctive features. These were shaped by comparative advantage that was partially a legacy of past policy. In most labour-abundant countries, traditional labour-intensive manufactures, in particular textiles, have spearheaded initial export expansion. In India, however, product reservation for small enterprise, supposedly for employment and equity, succeeded spectacularly in crippling the textile industry. And, while trade policy was being slowly reversed, interest group pressures ensured retention and reaffirmation of product reservations. The Abid Hussain Committee, appointed to re-examine industrial policy, recommended total dereservation, but its report was forgotten and India opted out of the world's mass market for traditional labour-intensive goods. The conquest of this market propelled China's stratospheric boom of the 1990s. India meanwhile was in dire peril of restricting itself to niche exports, cottage industry, exotica, and boutique products.

The effects of this quixotic industrial policy were reinforced by the neglect, particularly in the BIMARU states (Bihar, Madhya Pradesh, Rajasthan, and Uttar Pradesh), of primary education and health. This made it difficult to launch basic labour-intensive manufacturing with quality and productivity comparable to those of China where high literacy and health levels were inherited from the Maoist regime.

Fortunately for India, the advantage conferred by low labour costs is pervasive. It extends well beyond traditional labour-intensive goods into new industries and services not burdened by past legislation and well-organized interest groups. Further, in these new activities, India has been the fortunate beneficiary of historical accidents. The government's efforts to build up a large, university-educated middle class and its investment in science and technology education have created a labour force well equipped for the information technology (IT) and biogenetics booms. And its failure, despite its best efforts, to stamp out all vestiges of the knowledge of English that India had inherited from her colonial past has insured survival of an asset of incalculable value in an age of instant worldwide communication, basically in the English language. Thus, while China dominates the vast world market for traditional labour-intensive manufactures, new vistas are opening up for India in software and IT, biotechnology, basic pharmaceuticals, the export of higher education (particularly in technology and management) and of medical services and professionals and long-distance communication-based services like data transcription and business process outsourcing (BPO). In these fields, India's assets are complementary to China's (and most of East Asia's). These advantages, however, may be transient; with some effort, they can be replicated in other countries

and they can be irreparably damaged by unimaginative policy. Fortunately, electoral compulsions are forcing central and state governments to correct their most egregious policies: the West Bengal government, for instance, has been compelled by public pressure to recant on its earlier hostility to English education. The BIMARU states, however, unlike West Bengal, have not yet learnt their lesson.

Assuming that India maintains its existing pattern of comparative advantage, what will be the distributional consequences? Rapid expansion of IT and biotech, of BPO and similar services will mean an explosion in employment and incomes for the college-educated urban English-speaking population. It may also create incentives for upward mobility and opportunities for the less fortunate to climb the social ladder of absorption into the Great Indian Middle Class. Yet it is hardly an inclusive strategy of development. It emphasizes services performed by an educated middle class as the leading sector in growth—amidst an ocean of illiteracy and poverty. Income generated in this leading sector will eventually trickle down to the poor through increased demand for food and manufactures. But this is a process that raises mass aspirations and then fulfils them excruciatingly slowly. Not only is it inequitable in the extreme, it is also a prescription for political volatility. It is doubtful if it is a sustainable strategy in a democracy.

Contrast this with Chinese growth strategy. China began with the virtual dissolution of the communes, an institutional reform that doubled the per capita income of its 600 million farmers between 1978 and 1984. It followed it up by flooding the world market with the infinitely varied products of its raw, but literate and healthy, labour. The initial impact of expanding opportunity was distributed among hundreds of millions,

creating an ever-widening internal market for basic manufactures that supplemented external demand. The momentum of growth became independent of fluctuations in the world economy. The superiority of this strategy in terms of income distribution and of economic and political sustainability is evident.

Whatever the specific locus of opportunity that trade opens up for India, her future indisputably lies in increasing engagement with the outside world, an engagement that promises to end her millennial stagnation and poverty.

ASHOK GUHA

REFERENCES

Bhagwati, J.B. and P. Desai. 1970. *India: Planning for Industrialization: Industrialization and Trade Policies since 1951*, Oxford, Oxford University Press.

Bhagwati, J.B. and T.N. Srinivasan. 1975. *Foreign Trade Regimes and Economic Development: India*, New York, Columbia University Press.

Srinivasan, T.N. and S.D. Tendulkar. 2003. *Reintegrating India with the World Economy*, New Delhi, Oxford University Press.

Software and Services Exports[1]

The Indian economy has transitioned from an inward-looking economy to a more liberalized and export-oriented one. Software and services exports in particular, have had impressive growth, and have grown over 32 per cent annually between FY2002 and FY2007.[2] Exports are estimated to

[1]Software and services include (a) information technolgy (IT) services, (b) IT-enabled services (ITES), and (c) software products and engineering services.

[2]The fiscal year for the Indian economy follows a twelve-month cycle spanning April–March.

reach between US$ 58 billion and US$ 60 billion by 2010.

Today, Indian software and services exports stand at approximately US$ 32 billion. The share of software and services exports in India's exports increased from 3.2 per cent in 1996 to almost 25 per cent in 2006.

In 1981–2, India exported US$ 12 million in software and services. At the time, the sector faced significant challenges to growth. There was distrust of the private sector among policy makers. Imports were restricted and the corporate sector faced numerous bureaucratic hurdles. Business had difficulty accessing even basic infrastructure such as phones or data communication lines.

The economic reforms introduced in 1991 laid the foundation for the growth of the software sector in the country. The reforms decentralized power to regional and state offices—companies could now call on their local Software Technology Parks of India (STPI) offices with requests, instead of contacting Delhi. This increased the velocity of decision making in organizations, and reduced friction to business. The government's decision to allow 100 per cent ownership of subsidiaries by their multinational parents also brought several well-known multinational companies (MNCs) into India. They brought with them world-class technology, customer orientation, and employee orientation. The MNCs enhanced the competitive environment, forcing Indian companies to benchmark against global standards.

Market-determined pricing of initial public offerings (IPO) made equity a viable financing option for corporations. The reforms also introduced current account convertibility, which made it easier to hire foreign consultants and facilitated international brand building and overseas travel.

Another beneficial outcome of liberalization was easier and cheaper availability of data communication facilities. This made offshoring viable. The difference in time zones between India and North America is between 9.5 and 12.5 hours. Indian IT companies capitalized on this time difference to offer a twenty-four-hour virtual workday, and achieved efficient project execution and higher project productivity. Thus the industry pioneered the global delivery model (GDM) that envisages a substantial amount of value addition being done in India. The benefits of offshore delivery are now widely accepted around the world.

THE SOFTWARE AND SERVICES EXPORTS MARKET

Software and services exports are the dominating factor in the overall growth of the Indian IT industry. North America and Europe remain the key markets accounting for over 90 per cent of the total Indian software and services exports, with Europe accounting for 23 per cent of the total. This market poses challenges for Indian companies, due to both cultural and linguistic differences. The Asia-Pacific region accounts for about 8 per cent of all exports. It is predicted that demand from Latin America, Africa, and the Middle East will grow substantially in the coming years.

The level of IT investment varies widely across industry sectors. It is estimated that the financial services sector accounts for the largest share of investment. This includes spending by banks, insurance companies, and securities firms. Rapid changes in telecommunication technology, increase in mobile communications, and intense competition in the global telecom service and equipment markets have spurred IT expenditure in the telecom sector. Other sectors that spend strongly are manufacturing, retailing, healthcare, utilities, travel, and various governments.

GLOBALIZATION IS A KEY DRIVER FOR IT GROWTH

The world continues to witness the powerful effects of globalization. The broad range of products and services available, coupled with the information revolution, has raised customer expectations. Today, customers expect services at ever-greater speed. They demand quality services at reduced costs.

The dual pressures of competition and a knowledgeable customer are forcing companies to revamp their business models. Consequently, corporate strategies are increasingly focused on efficiency, discipline, cost control, and leaner operations. There is a need to increase productivity and efficiency by investing in IT.

As a result of these pressures—customer, competition, cost, and core—more companies are looking outside their walls, to outsource their operations to value-for-money destinations. Outsourcing exploits technology to achieve collaboration across company boundaries over activities which, earlier, would have had to be conducted within a single company.

In this context, India has established itself as the premier offshore destination for IT services. Recently, Gartner (2005) declared India 'unequivocally the global leader in offshore IT and process services' based upon a survey conducted across selected organizations in North America that are either currently outsourcing or planning on outsourcing in the future. Additionally, India has been ranked No.1 according to the recently published Global Services Location Index (2006) by the global consulting firm A.T. Kearney.

INDIA OFFERS SEVERAL ADVANTAGES

The basic business model of the Indian software industry is based on globalization. Globalization is sourcing capital from where it is cheapest, producing where it is most cost-effective, and selling where it is most profitable without being constrained by national boundaries. The Indian software and services export industry has pioneered the GDM, which leverages talent and infrastructure in different parts of the world. It enables Indian companies to deliver rapid time-to-market solutions, optimizing cost efficiencies.

The software development life-cycle tasks are partitioned to maximize those that can be taken up in cost-competitive, talent-rich, process-driven destinations such as India, and minimize those that have to be taken up at customer site. The GDM allows Indian vendors to capitalize on the time difference between India and the client location to achieve efficient project execution. This leads to lower cycle time with seamlessly integrated cross-border teams working on projects round the clock. Thus the GDM approach leverages the power of asynchronicity for fast and efficient execution.

The growth of the software and services industry has been largely driven by its knowledge professionals. The country has a huge base of highly qualified, English-speaking, analytically strong technical talent. According to Ministry of Human Resource Development, Government of India, there are close to 350 institutes of higher education and approximately 17,000 colleges in India. Collectively they produce 495,000 technical graduates,[3] 2.3 million other graduates, and over 300,000 postgraduates every year.

Indian companies quickly realized that securing the clients' confidence required them to have world class quality processes that were better than those of their global competitors. In fact, there have been several instances of clients upgrading their processes when working with Indian IT firms. Today, over 440 Indian companies have acquired quality certifications with ninety companies certified at SEI CMM Level 5—higher than in any other country in the world.[4]

The availability of a good communications infrastructure has helped Indian companies effectively implement the offshore development model. Further, a number of policy initiatives in the telecom sector, including privatization, have led to easier and cheaper availability of data communication facilities. For instance, the cost of an E1 line has decreased by nearly 50 per cent over the past five years.

Finally, as India grows into a knowledge-based economy, protection of knowledge capital becomes essential. India has a strong Intellectual Property Rights (IPR) regime and legal framework. India is a signatory to the Berne Convention, Universal Copyright Convention (UCC) and Trade-Related Aspects of Intellectual Property Rights (TRIPS) at the World Trade Organization (WTO).

However, the Indian software and services industry cannot afford to be complacent. It faces stiff competition from East Asian countries such as China and the Philippines, and from Eastern Europe. These destinations offer significant cost advantages. As the overall cost of offshoring increases due to reasons such as higher cost of operations, it is imperative that the Indian industry continuously innovate and move up the value chain. Companies should focus

[3]Including engineering degree and diploma holders and MCAs (NASSCOM Strategic Review 2007).

[4]As on December 2006 (NASSCOM Strategic Review 2007).

on acquiring better project management capability and deeper knowledge of business domains and improving both cost and quality with superior tools and methodologies.

INDIAN COMPANIES ARE MOVING UP THE VALUE CHAIN

Outsourcing relationships have become of long-term strategic importance. Hence, for global corporations, it is important to find a service provider who understands the business needs and IT goals. In response to this challenge, Indian service providers are shifting from being programming shops to becoming patent creators and mission-critical solution providers.

Indian companies are rapidly expanding their breadth by foraying into emerging and high-growth areas like Engineering Services, Bioinformatics, and Nanotechnology. These areas represent global growth avenues for the IT industry. Service lines like infrastructure management and testing are estimated to grow more than other services. Gartner estimates that the worldwide market for testing services will be close to $13 billion, with 45–50 per cent being outsourced (NASSCOM Strategic Review 2007). Also, according to a recent study by Booz Allen Hamilton, engineering outsourcing services alone present an opportunity of over $150 billion by 2020, primarily due to firms seeking access to new growing markets and quality manpower. The study estimates the potential for Indian IT services firms to be over $40 billion by 2020.

Additionally, many Indian companies have started providing end-to-end services to their clients, by introducing business process management and transitioning services. Consequently, clients have a one-stop shop for all their requirements. Value addition comes from continuous process improvement for clients and from implementation of

automation opportunities. Clients benefit from a common framework for shared services, built out of the experience of working with multiple clients and by leveraging technology. They have already started seeing measurable value in terms of increased productivity, reduced cycle time, and decrease in transaction costs. In India, the BPO (business process outsourcing) industry has grown from US$ 550 million in 1999 to over US$ 8 billion in FY2007. It is estimated that by 2010, this sector will be worth US$ 18–20 billion, providing direct employment to over one million Indians.

At the same time, the industry is also concentrating on optimizing and refining the existing GDM, and taking it to the next level. This includes extending the current GDM to all tasks from business process improvements, systems integration, knowledge management, and consulting to collaborating for the entire software lifecycle. Companies are now focusing on a process-driven approach with standardized solutions that increases the business effectiveness of IT. They are also enhancing productivity through a tools-based approach, while providing employees with world-class infrastructure.

Indian companies, aware of the changed business environment, have realized the need to expand their global presence. The number of overseas offices of Indian IT companies has increased from 167 in 1995 to over 800 today. These IT companies are diversifying their focus in the global marketplace— Europe, Asia-Pacific, and Latin America.

Today, the stakeholders—clients, partners, suppliers, investors, and employees—for Indian companies come from across the globe. Companies must learn to work in distributed, multicultural teams. In this context, Indian companies are working towards creating multicultural organizations, sensitive to local cultural issues in all countries. Indian firms now recruit talent from the best universities around the world. They also focus on instituting cross-cultural training programmes that sensitize managers to the issues involved in dealing with such a diverse environment.

CHALLENGES TO FUTURE GROWTH

At the same time, some basic challenges remain to be addressed. India has to make large social investments in order to sustain the basic building blocks of a knowledge economy. Education is fundamental for the growth of an industry like software. University-based research in India, a critical factor for innovation in the industry, remains low. Industry–academia partnerships are also weak. It is predicted that India will need approximately 2.3 million IT and BPO professionals by 2010 to maintain its current market share. India's education supply chain has proven to be remarkably responsive to market needs. However, by 2010, the supply of professionals is estimated to fall short by over 500,000 (NASSCOM-Mc Kinsey Report 2005). India has to ensure an adequate pipeline of 'English-speaking' graduates. To date, this has been one of our strong advantages over the competition.

The industry has to ensure that a larger section of the population gets training in basic IT skills. Unfortunately, India is increasingly getting divided into people who do and people who do not have access to—and the capability to use—modern information technology. Increasing access will help tap large talent pools across the country. However, a major problem in bridging the divide is the lack of infrastructure—both in terms of basic infrastructure issues and IT infrastructure.

If software services companies are to effectively implement the offshore delivery model, the country will need robust communication infrastructure and bandwidth. In this context, increased investments are necessary in optical fibre networks, telecommunications networks, and broadband IP networks. Another important challenge faced by the industry is shortage of quality infrastructure. Growth in the IT industry has so far outpaced the development of infrastructure in several cities. The need for creating integrated townships and developing Tier-2 cities is much greater than ever. Developing such townships and cities would add to the existing infrastructure in Tier-1 cities like Bangalore and Chennai. It is necessary to create multiple hubs for growth for the IT industry.

Today, countries and organizations globally are looking for partners who will bring in unique value, cost savings, and productivity. India has demonstrated unique strengths in terms of quality, efficiency, and rapidly scalable skills. Benchmarking globally, creating international brands, having a relentless focus on the customer, and learning to operate in a multicultural environment are key success factors for the future of the industry.

The software and services exports industry is now entering a critical phase of growth. The next ten years mark a time when the most innovative, competitive companies will pull ahead and dominate the global market. In the last decade, the Indian software and services industry has already helped change the way the world does business. Indian firms have had a great beginning, and we must not fritter away the advantages we have gained. Bill Gates spoke of India as the 'next software superpower'. I believe this goal is well within our reach. To achieve this, we must aspire higher than the status quo, and seize the opportunities ahead.

N.R. NARAYANA MURTHY

REFERENCES
Gartner, A.T. Kearney, IDC, JMS Research,
    NASSCOM Strategic Review (2007) and
    NASSCOM-McKinsey Report (2005).

Tariffs

External-sector policies in India can been broadly classified into three phases: 1950 to 1975 was the period of tightening controls; 1976 to 1991 a phase of slow but limited liberalization; and 1992 onwards when systematic liberalization was undertaken. The reduction in tariffs, along with the removal of quantitative restrictions in April 2002, has resulted in significant import liberalization in India. The discussion here is organized around the four themes of rates, structure, exemptions, and issues for reform.

RATES

Customs rates in India, which were amongst the highest in the world in 1991, are still high by world standards. This is conveyed by the evolution of the 'peak rate' over the last fifteen years. The 'peak rate', which applies for almost all manufactured goods, has dropped from 150 per cent in 1991 to 15 per cent in 2005. This was one of the most significant elements of economic reform in the recent period, one that has transformed the dynamics of domestic industry.

However, we have to be careful in the interpretation of the term 'peak rate', since in India, it is perhaps a 'median rate' and not the peak rate that is applicable for manufactured goods. Numerous tariffs for manufactured goods continue to be well above the 'peak rate' of 15 per cent.

One easily accessed measure of the extent of tariffs is tariff collections divided by imports. This was 11 per cent in 2004–5. However, we have to be careful in the interpretation of customs tax collections, since they reflect the summation of customs duty and the value-added tax (VAT) on imports. In India, the term 'countervailing duty (CVD)' is used for VAT on imports. In 2005–6, 43.4 per cent of the apparent customs collections is be on account of VAT on imports.

STRUCTURE OF TARIFFS

The structure of tariffs is biased towards providing higher protection to finished goods. As a consequence, the duties on raw materials, intermediate inputs, and capital goods are generally lower than those on finished products. As is well known, modest differences in apparent tariffs can imply very big differences in the effective rates of protection. This results in immense lobbying by firms, and a complex structure of tariffs. The government uses highly detailed control of the tariff structure to promote one or the other industry. While 'industrial policy', defined as the process of government choosing certain industries and promoting them, has faded away in the Indian context in many aspects, tariff setting continues to be an area where it has a place. For example, in his Budget Speech, 2005, the Finance Minister said:

For most textile machinery, I propose to reduce the duty from 20 per cent to 10 per cent, in order to help the textile industry acquire a competitive edge in the post-quota regime. Similarly, to encourage the food processing industry, I propose to reduce the duty on refrigerated vans from 20 per cent to 10 per cent. To give a leg-up to the leather and footwear industry, I propose to reduce the customs duties on seven specified machinery from 20 per cent to 5 per cent. The duty on ethyl vinyl acetate (EVA), an input for the footwear industry, is also proposed to be reduced from 20 per cent to 10 per cent.

The full text of the budget speech contains numerous paragraphs of this activist-style tariff setting. Such moves are inevitably rooted in dubious political economy.

EXEMPTIONS

Going beyond the issue of rate dispersion, when two different consignments of the same item are imported into India, they could encounter very different tariffs. This is because there are a large number of exemptions. These exemptions are based on who is importing, or why he is importing. If the imports are for defence, police, training, education, oil exploration, exhibitions, expeditions, for export purposes such as packaging materials, durable containers, by charitable institutions, for handicapped persons, or for sports-related activities, exemption from custom duty is given after due paper work. The list of items where such exemptions exist runs into nearly 2000. The importer gives the appraising officer the relevant literature and a certificate from one of the thirty-three approved certifying agencies such as the Director General of Foreign Trade, the Director of Vanaspati, Vegetable Oil and Fat, the Council for Leather Exports, or the Sports Authority of India.

The importer has to get a Bill of Entry from the appraising officer. These steps involve multiple contact points with the government and enormous costs of compliance, since appraising officers have to engage in questions of both valuation and end-use.

POLICY DIRECTIONS

The minimal agenda in reforms is the elimination of exemptions, which should ensure that no two consignments of a given product encounter different taxation rules or procedures. This would also serve to remove the involvement of all agencies external to the customs administration.

The second issue in reforms is identifying all goods with a rate above 'the peak rate' and bringing them down to the peak rate.

The third issue is the removal of rate dispersion, and the continued process of bringing down the peak rate from 15 per cent. A uniform rate is the best way to avoid the large dispersion of effective rates of protection, and the consequent political economy of tariff reform. Deficiencies of domestic taxation, however, pose an impediment against the move to uniform rate. There is a case for differential taxation of 'raw materials' and 'finished goods'—even though these terms are imprecise—given that domestic producers suffer state-level taxes that are not imposed on imports as part of VAT.

In the immediate future, the Vijay Kelkar FRBM Implementation Report has suggested that duty rates should be 5, 8, and 10 per cent for 'raw materials', 'intermediates', and 'finished goods' respectively. This is proposed as an interim solution until India is able to implement the goods and services tax (GST) in place of the various state sales taxes, state VAT, and so on. After the GST is in place, the next phase of tariff reform can commence—of moving to a uniform rate, and of going further down to a uniform rate such as 2 per cent.

ILA PATNAIK

REFERENCES

Ministry of Finance. 2002. Report of the Task Force on 'Indirect Taxes', Government of India, December.

Ministry of Finance. 2004. Report of the Task Force on 'Implementation of the Fiscal Responsibility and Budget Management Act, 2003', Government of India, July.

Mukhopadhyay, Sukumar. 2005. 'Proposals for Customs Reform in Budget 2005–06', *Economic and Political Weekly*, 15 January.

Panagariya, Arvind. 2004. 'India's Trade Reform', *India Policy Forum 2004*, NCAER, New Delhi and Brookings Institute, Washington D.C.

Union Budget, 2005–6. Ministry of Finance, Government of India.

Virmani, Arvind. 2004. 'Customs Tariff Reform', *ICRIER Policy Brief*, 1(1), December, New Delhi.

Trade Barriers in Manufacturing

The Nehru–Mahalanobis framework for Indian industrialization based on an import-substituting trade regime led to the emergence of trade barriers vis-à-vis Indian manufacturing. This regime of restrictions in trade continued for almost four decades after the initiation of planned development efforts in India in 1947. There have been several studies documenting the level of trade barriers in India's manufacturing sector. Evidence from these studies states that despite the prevalence of high import barriers, there have been conscious attempts since the mid-1970s to dismantle the complicated trade structure encompassing high and prohibitive levels of tariffs as well as a complicated licensing system for imports. In the 1990s, trade policies underwent major reforms. It was perceived that through widespread changes in rules and regulations that govern the trading of commodities and raw materials, Indian industries would be made competitive in global markets through better import conditions and easy export avenues. At the end of the 1990s, do we observe that the level of trade barriers for Indian manufacturing has declined substantially?

But first, what do we understand by trade barriers? In India, in the name of import-substitution-based trade strategy of industrialization, there were barriers to free trade (read imports) in the form of tariff and non-tariff measures. In simple terminology, an import tariff is a duty/tax on an ad valorem or specific basis levied on a product when it is imported into the country, whereas non-tariff barriers mean that there are various forms of restrictions on the import of a commodity. In India for the period before the 1991 trade policy reforms, not only were the peak tariff rates high but there were multiple tariff rates. Further, for a single commodity we could find several rates of tariff if we include the exemptions that were prevalent. The government levied three types of indirect taxes on goods imported into India—basic customs duty, auxiliary duty, and additional duty. After the 1991 reforms, the auxiliary duty was merged with the basic customs duty and there were considerable reductions in the number of notifications issued. The actual rate often called the effective rate was determined by the various exemption notifications announced by the government of India. The range of tariff rates extended from zero to almost 300 per cent in the pre-reform era and presently they are in the region of 15–20 per cent.

The second kind of trade barrier prevalent in the Indian economy was called the non-tariff barrier, which operated through the import licensing system put in place to regulate flow of imports to protect the domestic industries. This is a kind of quota that restricts the amount of commodity that can be imported into the country. The import licensing system divided imports into three broad categories: (1) intermediate goods raw materials, components, spare parts, and supplies; (2) capital goods, and (3) consumer goods. In India, there were four different types of restrictions on imports—banned, restricted, limited permissible, and canalized. Any item of import not covered by any of these four restrictions was categorized as open general licence (OGL) and was available for import without a licence and against payment of customs duties. Prior permission in the form of an import licence was required to import items that were classified under any one of the four categories listed earlier, subject to the importer satisfying some clauses, important amongst which were 'essentiality' and 'indigenous angle clearance' which meant that a product was an essential input and satisfactory specification and quality could not be supplied in a reasonable time by an Indian firm. Today, except for a small negative list consisting of items not allowed for import on account of health, environment, and social considerations, everything is available to industry against payment of restructured and low rates of tariffs inclusive of some items of consumer goods against special import licences.

TRADE BARRIERS

Trade barriers constituted an important impediment for the Indian manufacturing sector. It is held that due to trade restrictions in the form of high tariff rates and a complex import licensing regime, Indian firms were unable to develop into competitive and global units. In the following paragraphs I assess the extent of trade barriers in Indian manufacturing by looking at three well-known measures—effective rate of protection, import coverage ratio, and import penetration rate. The effective rate of protection captures the distortion introduced in domestic value added vis-à-vis world value added due to tariffs on input as well as output. Import coverage ratios are calculated by determining the value of imports of each commodity subject to non-tariff barriers, aggregating by applicable commodity groups and expressing the value of imports covered as a percentage of total imports in the commodity group.

The import penetration rate captures the impact of both tariff as well as non-tariff measures of protection and is calculated as the ratio of imports to domestic sales, with domestic sales defined as output of domestic industries minus exports plus imports.

The major sources of data for trade barriers are: (1) Monthly Statistics of Foreign Trade Volume 1 and II, Directorate General of Commercial Intelligence and Statistics, Ministry of Commerce, Government of India, (2) Customs Tariff Working Schedule, Directorate of Publication, Customs and Central Excise, Government of India, and (3) Export–Import Policy Documents, Ministry of Commerce, Government of India.

The assessment is over four five-year phases of trade reforms—Phase 1, which signifies ad hoc attempts at trade reforms; Phase 2, which signals the start of the process of trade reforms at moderate pace; Phase 3, which shows the major attempt at trade reforms in terms of tariff changes and abolishing of import licensing regime; and finally Phase 4, which shows the consolidation of the trade policy changes of 1991–2. The impact is documented on the use-based sectors to understand and appreciate the developments in line with the focus of policy in the Indian industrialization strategy, which gave priority to capital and intermediate goods sectors and sidelined the question of efficiency and competitiveness for consumer goods industries.

Effective Rate of Protection

A sharp fall in the level of protection across most industry groups can be observed in the 1990s as compared to the 1980s. The majority of industries belonging to the capital goods sector showed the maximum decline; for the intermediate goods industries, a decline could be observed from

Table 1   Trade Barriers in Indian Manufacturing: Effective Rates of Protection

Industry group	Phase 1 1980–5	Phase 2 1986–90	Phase 3 1991–5	Phase 4 1996–2000	All phases 1980–2000
	Effective rate of protection (per cent)				
Intermediate goods					
Average	147.03	149.18	87.58	40.13	112.36
SD	75.79	64.85	24.15	9.11	44.27
CV	52	43	28	23	39
Capital goods					
Average	62.77	78.45	54.23	33.30	61.87
SD	29.02	30.18	18.49	12.03	22.64
CV	46	38	34	36	37
Consumer goods					
Average	101.51	111.55	80.55	48.28	87.47
SD	19.87	33.77	10.50	5.53	16.60
CV	20	30	13	11	19
All industries					
Average	115.11	125.93	80.18	40.43	95.19
SD	67.62	63.48	23.77	10.71	40.96
CV	59	50	30	26	43

Sources: Author's calculations based on the (1) Customs Tariff Working Schedule, Central Excise and Customs, Government of India, (2) The Monthly Statistics of Foreign Trade, Ministry of Commerce, Government of India, and (3) Export–Import Policy Documents, Ministry of Commerce, Government of India.

Notes: 1. Period averages are computed as a value-added share weighted average of the yearly figures.
2. For all industries, the ERP is averaged over seventy-two three-digit industries.
3. SD stands for standard deviation and CV for coefficient of variation.

high levels of protection in the early 1980s to levels of around 40 per cent. A decline in the level of protection is noticeable even in the consumer goods sector. Thus protection by and large declined in the period after reforms, yet the degree of decline was uneven across different use-based sectors—capital, intermediate, and consumer as well as within each group. A glance at Table 1 shows the levels of effective rate of protection vis-à-vis Indian manufacturing industries.

Import Coverage Ratio

India had a complicated system of non-tariff barriers operating in the industrial sector of the economy till the overhauling of the trade regime in 1991, making it very difficult to quantify and assess the significance of non-tariff barriers. Using the import coverage ratio, I will assess the impact of non-tariff barriers on Indian manufacturing industries in the 1980s and 1990s. The percentage of imports subjected to non-tariff barriers remained close to 100 per cent in the early phases of trade reforms across all sectors—intermediate, capital as well as consumer goods industries. It was only in the first half of the 1990s that changes began to take place in terms of removal of import restrictions on products—that is freeing certain items of capital and intermediate goods industries from import licence requirements. It was, however, the second half of the 1990s that finally saw substantial decline in import coverage ratio across most manufacturing industries, be it capital or intermediate items of production. The last five years of the 1990s saw a marked

Table 2   Trade Barriers in Indian Manufacturing: Import Coverage Ratio

Industry group	Phase 1 1980–5	Phase 2 1986–90	Phase 3 1991–5	Phase 4 1996–2000	All phases 1980–2000
	Import coverage ratio (per cent)				
Intermediate goods					
Average	98.31	98.26	41.77	27.60	71.47
SD	12.89	12.65	42.63	37.88	20.43
CV	13	13	102	137	29
Capital goods					
Average	95.11	77.21	20.47	8.15	54.37
SD	21.56	26.94	25.36	16.96	16.69
CV	23	35	124	208	31
Consumer goods					
Average	98.69	87.85	45.69	33.43	68.77
SD	11.35	21.64	39.23	38.53	20.89
CV	12	25	86	115	30
All industries					
Average	97.59	91.64	37.97	24.82	67.11
SD	15.33	20.45	39.88	35.84	20.93
CV	16	22	105	144	31

Sources: Author's calculations based on the (1) Customs Tariff Working Schedule, Central Excise and Customs, Government of India, (2) The Monthly Statistics of Foreign Trade, Ministry of Commerce, Government of India, and (3) Export–Import Policy Documents, Ministry of Commerce, Government of India.
Notes: 1. Period averages are computed as a value-added share weighted average of the yearly figures.
2. For all industries, the MCR is averaged over seventy-two three-digit industries.
3. SD stands for standard deviation and CV for coefficient of variation.

decline in the percentage of imports covered by non-tariff barriers for consumer goods items—banned for most part of the 1980s and 1990s. Table 2 gives an idea of the extent of non-tariff barriers across different use-based industry groups.

IMPORT PENETRATION RATES
Table 3 provides data on the import penetration rates in different periods across industries; these data reveal that import penetration rates have improved only in the second phase of the 1990s, that is the 1996–2000 period. The trade policy changes of the first three phases are not reflected in an increase in the import penetration rates. Only in the case of the intermediate goods industries, do we find an improvement, albeit slow, in import

penetration rates in Phases 2 and 3. This is not difficult to comprehend as the 1980s saw some movement in products like industrial raw materials, and components and parts from banned, restricted lists to OGL lists. Another important finding is that across different industry groups import penetration rates are the lowest for consumer goods industries, which is in line with the trade stance towards that sector. The reason that import penetration did not increase despite lowering of tariffs and removal of non-tariff barriers is that tariff and non-tariff barriers are not equivalent when perfect competition does not characterize the domestic market, an argument put forward by economist Jagdish Bhagwati, which holds true for Indian industries that operate by and large in imperfectly competitive markets.

Table 3   Trade Barriers in Indian Manufacturing: Import Penetration Rates

Industry group	Phase 1 1980–5	Phase 2 1986–90	Phase 3 1991–5	Phase 4 1996–2000	All phases 1980–2000
	Import penetration rates (per cent)				
Intermediate goods					
Average	0.11	0.13	0.15	0.18	0.14
SD	0.12	0.11	0.15	0.15	0.12
CV	105	84	100	87	87
Capital goods					
Average	0.12	0.12	0.12	0.19	0.14
SD	0.15	0.12	0.11	0.15	0.13
CV	143	64	69	170	97
Consumer goods					
Average	0.04	0.04	0.04	0.10	0.05
SD	0.06	0.03	0.03	0.10	0.04
CV	143	64	69	170	74
All industries					
Average	0.10	0.11	0.12	0.16	0.12
SD	0.12	0.11	0.13	0.16	0.12
CV	119	97	112	98	98

Sources: Author's calculations based on the (1) Customs Tariff Working Schedule, Central Excise and Customs, Government of India, (2) The Monthly Statistics of Foreign Trade, Ministry of Commerce, Government of India, and (3) Export–Import Policy Documents, Ministry of Commerce, Government of India.

Notes: 1. Period averages are computed as a value-added share weighted average of the yearly figures.
2. For all industries, the MPR is averaged over sixty three-digit industries.
3. SD stands for standard deviation and CV for coefficient of variation.

Trade reforms attempt to relax the restrictions imposed on international trade. The data on trade barriers, however, show that only in the 1990s and after can we actually see changes taking place in the measures of the trade barriers discussed here. This holds across all use-based sectors and the direction of changes highlighted for each of the three measures reflects that there is perhaps a lagged impact of trade policy changes on the manufacturing sector, an issue that needs further investigation.

DEB KUSUM DAS

REFERENCES

Das, D.K. 2001. 'Some Aspects of Productivity Growth and Trade in Indian Industry', unpublished Ph.D. thesis, Department of Economics, Delhi School of Economics, University of Delhi, November.

———. 2003. 'Quantifying Trade Barriers: Has Protection Declined Substantially in Indian Manufacturing?' Working Paper #105, New Delhi, ICRIER, July.

GOVERNMENT POLICY

Defence Expenditure

The three wars India engaged in over the past four decades—with China (1962) and Pakistan (1965 and 1971)—and a state of tension with both countries during much of the period have made defence spending a high priority for the government and the political class. With the army drawn into fighting insurgency in Jammu and Kashmir and in the north-eastern states, military spending has also been influenced by the demands of internal security.

By the middle of the first decade of the twenty-first century, relations with China had vastly improved and there were signs that India and Pakistan were finally putting behind them half a century of open hostility. However, it is extremely unlikely that India will cut back on military spending in the short to medium term. Two new factors driving outlays have been India's ambitions of becoming a regional military power and the formal decision (announced in 1998) to acquire a nuclear weapons arsenal. Both are likely to take defence expenditure to a higher level.

In 2004–5, total (revenue and capital) defence spending, as officially defined and listed in the central government budget documents, was Rs 77,000 crore (US$ 17 billion at 2004 market exchange rates). In real terms (at 1993–4 prices), there was a fivefold increase from Rs 8364 crore in 1970–1 to Rs 41,100 crore in 2004–5. Estimates of outlays on the armed forces since the early 1960s show defence spending as a proportion of the gross domestic product (GDP) fluctuating between 2 and 3.5 per cent. After crossing 3 per cent of GDP in 1971–2 and 1972–3 (during and immediately after the India–Pakistan war of 1971), military spending gradually declined over the next decade, touching 2.6 per cent in 1983–4. It then rose again on large-scale acquisition of hardware and peaked at 3.4 per cent in 1987–8. Expenditure thereafter slid—partly on account of conditions imposed by multilateral institutions during India's fiscal crisis of the early 1990s—falling to 2.2 per cent of GDP in 1996–7 before growing moderately to around 2.5 per cent over the next decade.

When military expenditure is measured as a proportion of its GDP, India spends a relatively small amount on its armed forces. According to the Stockholm International Peace Research Institute in 2003, Pakistan, for instance, spent about 4.4 per cent of its GDP on defence in 2003 and the US 3.8 per cent. China's official figures, however, place military outlays at 2.3 per cent of GDP.

But there have always been questions about the appropriate measure of defence expenditure and how much the official data

Table 1 Defence Spending as a Proportion of GDP and Central Government Expenditure

(in per cent)

Year	Defence expenditure as a percentage of GDP		Defence spending as a percentage of central government expenditure	
	Official	Alternate	Official	Alternate
1995–6	2.3	2.9	15.1	19
1996–7	2.2	2.7	14.7	18.6
1997–8	2.4	3	15.6	19.9
1998–9	2.3	3.1	14.7	19.4
1999–2000	2.5	3.4	16.3	22.2
2000–1	2.6	3.4	16.7	20.7
2001–2	2.5	3.3	15.7	20.6
2002–3	2.3	3	13.5	18.1
2003–4	2.2	2.8	12.8	16.9
2004–5	2.5	3.2	15.2	19.5

Sources: Expenditure data from annual budget documents of Government of India, GDP data from Reserve Bank of India publications.
Note: 'Official' defence expenditure is total of spending under budget heads on army, air force, navy, capital outlay, and research and development. 'Alternate' is official plus defence pensions, budget heads on select paramilitary forces (Ministry of Home Affairs), border roads (Ministry of Surface/Road Transport), coast guard (Ministry of Finance), 25 per cent of spending on nuclear energy, excluding power (Department of Atomic Energy), and 25 per cent on space (Department of Space).

reveal of the true outlay. While India is far more transparent than most countries in presenting detailed statistics on funding for defence, the official definition does not cover all military and nuclear-weapon-related spending. The definition covers revenue and capital spending on the army, air force, and navy as well as research and development for the military. It does not include defence pensions (standard international practice is to include this item in military expenditure), paramilitary spending (much of which is

spent on securing India's external borders), and the outlays on nuclear research and space (which have fed into the assembly of fissile material and development of the missile programmes respectively). The intense debate following the India–US nuclear deal of July 2005 on the difficulties of separating military and civilian nuclear facilities is indicative of the strong overlap between the two. As Table 1 shows, an alternate and more inclusive estimate of India's defence outlays is 25–30 per cent higher than the official figure. The alternative estimate is only indicative, but the true level of India's defence spending is likely to be closer to the alternate than the official estimate.

Another and perhaps better indicator of the importance a government accords to defence is the defence–central government expenditure ratio. The figures for India are revealing. Over the decade 1995–6/2004–5, around 15 per cent of total central government expenditure was on defence. This consistently constituted the second largest item of government spending and was exceeded only by interest payments. It also dwarfed total central government spending on health and education (for example the respective figures in 2000–1 were an estimated 0.1 per cent and 0.5 per cent of GDP). Since the responsibility for government intervention in education and health rests more with the states, a better comparison may be with total central and state government spending: in 2000–1, defence consumed more than the combined allocations for health (1.2 per cent of GDP) but received less than the aggregate funding for education (3 per cent of GDP).

Global comparisons indicate that the central government in India spends relatively less on defence compared to many other large countries for whom military outlays are important, but India's figures are higher than the high-income and world averages. World Bank comparisons of the Scandinanian International Peace Research Institute (SIPRI) data for defence expenditure and International Monetary Fund statistics for central government spending show that in 2003 the defence–central government expenditure percentage for India was 14.2, compared to 23.9 in Pakistan, 19.4 in the US, 18.8 in Russia, 17.7 in Israel, 11.5 in Malaysia, and 5.8 in South Africa. The average for all low-income countries in the same year was 14.8, for high-income countries 10.8, and the world average was 10.7.

Since the mid-1990s, when global debates began to widen the notion of 'national security' beyond the conventional perspective of defence, there have been tentative attempts in wider public discourse to ask if India is spending too much on arms and the armed forces. However, the dominant view remains that defence allocations cannot be fundamentally questioned, especially at a time when insurgency in Kashmir was at its peak and India in a state of heightened tension with Pakistan. There are parliamentary debates on defence, media discussions on the choice of equipment, and periodic exposes about kickbacks in procurement. All these interventions have looked at the issue only on the margin, they have not questioned the basic premises of India's military outlays.

Since the mid-1990s, the larger force driving defence expenditure in India has been a focus on 'modernization', which has meant equipping the forces with superior and advanced arms technology and altering the machine–man ratio in favour of the former. As a consequence, from the middle of the last decade of the twentieth century to the middle of the first decade of the twenty-first century, India made very substantial purchases in the global market for the air force, army, and navy. According to SIPRI estimates, the

value of India's arms deliveries in the global market was the second largest in the period 2000–4 at $8.5 billion (at constant 1990 US$), second only to China's $11.2 billion. India's comfortable balance-of-payments position since the mid-1990s meant that these purchases did not strain its external finances, though they did earlier when the country was not so comfortably placed with regard to its external finances. India could still manage these purchases between the 1960s and 1980s, because the Soviet Union, which was the major supplier, provided soft credit and offered barter contracts. Global purchases by India have been supplemented by a major domestic defence production programme, including the development and testing of short- to medium-range missiles. India has a fairly large and well-developed domestic arms industry as well as research and development facilities, but the outlays on defence have not generated any measurable positive externalities.

India's decision, announced in 1998, to go openly nuclear will give an additional thrust to government outlay on defence. A considerable part of the infrastructure for assembling bombs and delivering them is in place, but major outlays for putting together a nuclear force are yet to be incurred. The draft nuclear doctrine of 1999 and India's stated policy of acquiring second-strike capability enjoin on it to develop a triad of bomb-delivery vehicles (aircraft, land and sea-based missiles, and nuclear-powered submarines) as well as a sophisticated command, control, and communication and intelligence (C3I) system that can withstand attack and retaliate in the event of a nuclear war. Much of this infrastructure has to be built up. The government has not made any public assessment of the cost of going nuclear. Independent and conservative estimates place the *incremental* cost of developing a second-strike nuclear weapon capability at 0.5 per cent of GDP a year, or an increase of 20–5 per cent over present spending levels. Media reports of internal government estimates confirm the size of this additional burden of nuclearization.

The acquisition of nuclear weapons is unlikely to reduce conventional arms spending. In the early years of global nuclear armament it was suggested that total defence spending would go down or at least increase more slowly because of the 'bigger bang per buck' that the weapons of destruction could deliver and the presumed strategic value of these arsenals in deterring external threats. Research into arms spending by the established nuclear powers shows no evidence of any such thinking or impact on total military spending. Conventional arms expenditure continued to grow alongside nuclear outlays, contributing to an expansion of the total. In India neither the government nor defence forces have discussed a reduction in aggregate expenditure. Spending on conventional arms has, if anything, increased after 1998 and this trend is likely to continue.

C. RAMMANOHAR REDDY

REFERENCES

Chari, P.R. 2000. 'India's Defence Expenditure: Can it be Reduced?', Colombo, Regional Centre for Strategic Studies Policy Studies 12.
Drèze, Jean and Amartya Sen. 2002. *India: Development and Participation*, New Delhi, Oxford University Press, ch. 8.
Navlakha, Gautam. 1999. 'Defence Spending: Cost of Fighting Imaginary Enemies', *Economic and Political Weekly*, 34(18), 1 May.
Reddy, Rammanohar C. 2002. 'Nuclear Weapons versus Schools for Children: An Estimate of the Cost of Nuclear Weaponisation', in M.V. Ramana and C. Rammanohar Reddy, eds, *Prisoners of the Nuclear Dream*, New Delhi, Orient Longman.
Singh, Jasjit. 2000. 'Reducing Defence Expenditure: Issues and Challenges for South Asian Countries', Colombo, Regional Centre for Strategic Studies Policy Studies 10.
Singh, Jaswant. 1999. *Defending India*, Bangalore, Macmillan.

Discretionary Centre–State Transfers

The allocation of grants from central to sub-national governments has always been an important issue of fiscal federalism. Central government grants help to break the linkage between revenue and expenditure assignments by levels of government, and permit the centre to pursue various objectives. While the traditional literature on fiscal federalism assumes that the central government is a 'benevolent planner', interested in maximizing social welfare, the more recent literature on political economy emphasizes that political considerations may influence the pattern of central grants to the states.

Case (2001) uses data on social assistance block grants from the central government to communes in Albania and concludes that politics does matter in determining the pattern of block grants. Johanssen (2003) analyses data on grants from the central government to municipalities in Sweden and finds limited support for the hypothesis that intergovernmental grants are influenced by political considerations. In the Indian context, Dasgupta et al. (2004), Khemani (2003), and Rao and Singh (2004) analyse whether *discretionary* grants—that is grants that are not governed by explicit formulae—are related to political considerations. The Indian evidence is discussed in greater detail here.

In India, there are *three* major channels through which the centre transfers funds to state governments. These are: (i) tax devolution and grants through the Finance Commissions; (ii) grants and loans given by the Planning Commission; and (iii) transfers or various central-sector and centrally sponsored schemes by different central ministries.

The Indian Constitution specifies that the states are entitled to a share of the tax revenues collected by the centre. The aggregate share as well as the distribution amongst the states is decided by Finance Commissions appointed at periodic intervals. Successive Finance Commissions recommend explicit formulae to determine the allocations amongst states. While Finance Commission awards have also been criticized from time to time, it is generally agreed that the formulae are *not* influenced by political considerations.

A sizable proportion of grants and loans is also channelled through the Planning Commission. From 1969, plan transfers have been carried out on the basis of a formula decided by the National Development Council. Since transfers on account of state plan schemes are based on this consensus formula, it is tempting to exclude them from the category of discretionary grants to the states. However, discretionary elements can enter into the determination of these grants for two reasons. First, while each state proposes its plan size to the Planning Commission, the final approval of the size rests with the Commission. So there is some scope for negotiation and 'persuasion'. Second, the formula explicitly sets aside 7.5 per cent of the grants on account of 'special' problems of states. Again, this allows for some subjectivity to creep into the determination of grants for state plan schemes.

The transfers given to states through central plan schemes and centrally sponsored schemes have attracted the sharpest criticism because these are essentially completely discretionary. Central plan schemes are funded entirely by the centre, the states merely exercising an agency role in executing these programmes. Centrally sponsored programmes involve some element of cost sharing between the centre and the concerned state.

Are central government transfers to state governments in India really motivated by political considerations? In order to examine this question, it is crucial to incorporate the fact that different political parties may be in control of government at different levels. This is important since the state government stands 'between' the central government and the voters in the state. Central grants relax the budget constraints of state governments and permit state governments to increase their expenditure. The increased expenditure in any state generates goodwill amongst the voters in the state. To the extent that voters in the state are unsure about how the additional expenditure is financed, the party in power in the state also benefits from increased central grants. So if the Congress party is in power at the centre, and the BJP in a particular state, then at least some of the benefits of central transfers 'leak' to the BJP.

Of course, if the incumbents in the state and the centre happen to be the same party (that is the state government is *aligned* with the central government), then that party derives the entire electoral benefit of any additional expenditure in the state. This suggests that the 'alignment effect'—the ruling parties (or coalition) being 'aligned' at the centre and in the state—should result in the aligned states receiving a disproportionately larger share of discretionary grants. Rao and Singh (2004) find some evidence in support of this hypothesis.

Dasgupta et al. (2004) propose a variant of the alignment hypothesis. Suppose the objective of the central incumbent is to maximize the *number of states* it can win, and it uses discretionary grants to further this objective. Assume that there are only two major parties or coalitions. They define a state to be *partisan* if one of the parties has a devoted 'vote bank' that constitutes more than half the electorate. In such states, there is no electoral compulsion to 'buy' votes since a majority of voters are *committed* to one of the parties. States that are not partisan are called *swing* states. The election is expected to be 'close' in these swing states, and so the marginal benefit from buying the extra vote is also correspondingly larger. Of course, the swing states that are aligned are in a particularly advantageous position. Dasgupta et al. (2004) find strong empirical support for the *aligned swing* effect.

Dasgupta et al. (2004) also focus on the possible influence of lobbying by members of parliament. More specifically, they assume that lobbying power is restricted to members of the ruling party. That is, if the BJP is in power at the centre, then members of parliament elected from say Uttar Pradesh and belonging to the BJP can exert pressure to get additional grants to their constituencies. Members of the opposition parties have less lobbying power because Cabinet Ministers perceive no benefit in increasing expenditure in constituencies where the incumbent belongs to the opposition. There is also some support for the lobbying hypothesis—ceteris paribus, states that elect relatively more MPs from the ruling party get higher discretionary grants.

BHASKAR DUTTA

REFERENCES

Case, Anne. 2001. 'Election Goals and Income Redistribution: Recent Evidence from Albania', *European Economic Review*, 45: 405–23.

Dasgupta, S., A. Dhillon, and B. Dutta. 2004. 'Electoral Goals and Center–State Transfers: A Theoretical Model and Empirical Evidence from India', mimeo., University of Warwick.

Johanssen, Eva. 2003. 'Intergovernmental Grants as a Tactical Instrument: Some Empirical Evidence from Swedish Municipalities', *Journal of Public Economics*, 87: 883–915.

Khemani, Stuti. 2003. 'Partisan Politics and Intergovernmental Transfers in India', mimeo, Development Research Group, World Bank.

Rao, M. Govinda and Nirvikar Singh. 2004. 'The Political Economy of Center–State Fiscal Transfers in India', mimeo, University of California at Santa Cruz.

Disinvestment, The Economics of

Public debates about economic policies in India have been very controversial ever since the early 1990s when India embarked on the reform process. Every major change has been intensely contested by opposition parties, professional economists, and trade unions. Even against this background, the discussions about the desirability of disinvestment of government holdings in public-sector enterprises stand out because they have been particularly heated. Is it sensible for the government to go in for privatization or should the public sector be allowed to survive 'as is'? If disinvestment is the right approach, what is the appropriate mechanism for the sale of shares? And how should the government utilize the revenues collected through disinvestment? Each of these aspects of disinvestment has been the subject of intense scrutiny.

The entire debate on disinvestment would have been only of academic interest if India did not have such a large public sector. The public sector played a central role under Nehruvian socialism and was instrumental in building up the economy in post-Independence India, in particular the heavy industrial base of the Indian economy. It is debatable whether private entrepreneurs would have shouldered the huge risks associated with setting up heavy industries in the immediate post-Independence period when the economy was in a fledgling state—the small size of the domestic market would have acted as a deterrent since the private sector would necessarily take uncoordinated decisions. Conceptually, centralized planning has tremendous advantage because the government can take *coordinated* decisions so that the steel industry demands the products of the capital goods industry while the capital goods industry demands the output of the steel industry. In other words, the simultaneous creation of several giant firms can circumvent the problem of small markets because each small firm would demand the products of the other firms.

In principle, centralized planning does not necessarily imply the existence of public-sector enterprises if the government has sufficient regulatory instruments allowing it to control the private sector. However, it is obviously easier to control the allocation of resources if the public sector occupies the commanding heights of the economy, and this provided the rationale for the emergence of the public sector in India.

Nation-building was the primary if not the only goal of the public sector. In particular, public-sector enterprises never had to achieve any hard financial targets. While this made sense in the initial stages of development, the absence of a stringent adherence to financial discipline was to prove disastrous for many public-sector enterprises in the long run. Even a cursory look at the balance sheets of these enterprises suggests that they produce paltry returns on the capital invested in them, and most of them are not commercially viable. Several of these units are now in sunset industries or operate with rundown machinery and obsolete technology, and only massive infusions of capital can possibly restore their viability.

The initial rationale for the growth of the public sector is no longer valid since the Indian economy now has a strong industrial base. So the continued existence of the public sector must depend largely on whether it utilizes scarce resources more efficiently than the private sector. Of course, even die-hard supporters of the public sector will concede that the public sector does not perform very well on the criterion of productive efficiency. Since they still believe that the public sector has a useful role to play in the Indian economy, it is important to examine possible objections to the use of (relative) productive efficiency as the principal criterion for the survival of the public sector in India. Much of the subsequent discussion focuses on the issue of whether it is right to use productive efficiency as the principal criterion in judging whether the government should go in for privatization of various public-sector enterprises. Before one does that, it is expedient to dispose of a relatively minor issue—there are a *few* sectors of tremendous strategic importance that should be outside the purview of the 'productive efficiency' criterion. The ordnance industry is an obvious example.

Perhaps, the *strongest*—though not necessarily *soundest*—opposition to the 'productive efficiency' criterion comes from the belief that the government should not sell its shares in *profitable* public-sector enterprises. The economic logic underlying this belief has never been very clearly spelt out, although analogies have often been drawn to the foolishness of selling off the family silver. Such analogies are misplaced because the proceeds from the sale of these enterprises can of course be used to build up other national assets such as economic and social infrastructure.

Perhaps a better or more appropriate analogy is to view the government's ownership of these enterprises as national assets. An owner often changes the composition of his portfolio of assets, selling off some assets in order to finance the purchase of others. This is very common practice, and no one labels the reallocation of asset portfolios as necessarily foolish or economically unsound. The correct principle here is that investment be changed in favour of assets that promise higher future social returns. Why should the government continue to own (say) Indian Airlines when private-sector airlines are offering the same type of service? Would it not be better for the government to use the proceeds from the sale of Indian Airlines to modernize Indian ports or build new highways?

Another strand of the arguments against disinvestment of profitable public-sector enterprises runs along the following lines. Public-sector enterprises have been built up with tax-payers' money, often in areas where the private sector would simply not have entered because of the initial risks associated with these ventures. If there are sectors and enterprises that are now profitable, then the public sector should be allowed to reap these profits. Why should the government allow private individuals to 'capture' the profits of enterprises built with public money?

However, the fallacy with this argument is that no one is advocating that the profitable public-sector enterprises be handed over on a platter to the private sector. The higher the prospective returns from a project, the greater is the present discounted value of the project. Hence the market value of an asset promising a million rupees every year is several times higher than that of an asset promising an annual return of only a few hundred rupees. Of course, this discrepancy in market valuations does not induce anyone to claim that the

former asset should not change ownership. It simply means that the more profitable asset should be sold at significantly higher prices. Similarly, the more profitable the public-sector enterprise, the higher the price at which it can be sold. So the government loses nothing by selling off a profitable enterprise provided it extracts an *appropriate* price from the buyer.

The price that can be extracted from prospective buyers is also linked to the *mode* of disinvestment. First, *when* should the actual sale take place? G.V. Krishnamurthy, Chairman of the erstwhile Disinvestment Commission, had argued that restructuring of the public-sector enterprises must precede any attempt at disinvestment. The rationale for this was that these enterprises would not find any takers unless they were first nursed back to health. Although there is some sense in this argument, the problem is that public management may never be capable of reviving the enterprises. External circumstances also influence the optimum time for disinvestment. The government should not attempt to sell its shares when the share market is in a slump. Indeed, the depressed state of the share market during the East Asian meltdown was a principal reason behind the United Front government's disinclination to proceed with disinvestment.

Second, *how* should the shares be sold? One school believes that there should be an immediate sale to a strategic partner, who would then obtain management control. The rationale behind this view is that the offer of management control would make the enterprises significantly more valuable to prospective bidders, and hence improve marketability of the enterprise. In other words, the offer of management control would enable the government to maximize the proceeds from disinvestment.

The downside to this argument is that in some sectors—petroleum being a prime example—economies of scale imply that there are only a few enterprises. Thus the strategic sale option carries with it the danger that the process will result in a couple of business houses capturing an entire sector. For instance, fears were expressed that the Reliance group would become a gigantic monopoly in the entire oil sector if the government had gone ahead with the privatization of HPCL and BPCL. Others feared that multinational groups such as Shell would capture the oil sector and hold the economy to ransom.

Those who hold these fears advocate a different route to disinvestment. They prefer the direct sale of shares in giant public-sector enterprises to retail or small investors, with the government retaining management control at least in the initial stages. This procedure will inevitably result in lower sale proceeds to the government because of the widely held belief that the government is less efficient in running businesses than the private sector. So these are very different policy options involving possible trade-offs—a potential loss of wealth in the form of lower sale proceeds versus benefits accruing from the prevention of private monopolies. However, both the central and state governments in India are armed with a diverse set of regulatory controls, and it is questionable whether a couple of giant business houses can hold the economy to ransom. This suggests the desirability of the strategic sale option.

The public sector has played a crucial role in building up the Indian economy. But the private sector has now come of age. If economic logic rather than nostalgia is to guide economic policies, then it is time for the government to privatize public-sector enterprises in a large number of areas.

The mode of disinvestment also involves important policy choices since this influences the prices at which the government can sell its shares.

BHASKAR DUTTA

Fiscal Federalism

India has twenty-nine states governed by their own elected parliaments. It has seven union territories which come under the jurisdiction of the central government. Fiscal relations between the centre and states are shaped by the seventh schedule in the Indian Constitution which describes the legislative, executive, and judicial powers of the centre and states through the *Union*, *State*, and *Concurrent* lists. The division of revenue and expenditure powers between the centre and states is specified by (a) the Union List, which states the powers that are exclusively under the purview of the central government and (b) the State List, which gives those powers exclusively under the state government. All residual powers rest with the centre.

In 1992, the seventy-second and seventy-third constitutional amendments introduced a third tier of fiscal authority, giving constitutional validity to existing rural and urban local governments.

Till that time, local governments acted as agencies of the state governments. Panchayati Raj institutions in the villages informally provided basic community and judicial services while in urban areas municipal authorities fulfilled this purpose. The constitutional amendments of 1992 gave these institutions an elective status and gave them powers to impose taxes—usually property taxes in urban areas. Education and housing and land use, development of industrial and commercial estates, and electricity distribution are some of the functions that have been decentralized in urban areas.

Most taxes with a broad tax base are assigned to the centre—for example income and wealth tax from non-agricultural sources, corporation tax, customs duties, and excise duties. Sales taxes, land revenue, alcohol excises, and agricultural income taxes are with the state government.

Out of these, the sales tax is the most significant source of revenue for states. On the expenditure side, the centre spends on defence and infrastructure while state governments spend mainly on internal security, law and order, and social and economic services. Among social services the largest proportion goes to education, public health, and family.

There is a well-documented vertical imbalance between the centre and states: in 2002–3, the state governments on average raised about 38 per cent of total revenues but accounted for 58 per cent of the expenditures. This imbalance has grown worse over the years: in 1955–6 these figures were 41 per cent and 59 per cent respectively. The imbalance was a direct result of the types of taxes that were assigned to the centre and the bias in favour of the centre which was an artefact of the colonial system and the subsequent emphasis on planned development and reducing inequalities between states. The Constitution recognized this imbalance and provided for the assignment of revenues between the centre and states as well as for the sharing of revenues from the proceeds of certain centrally levied taxes. In addition to this, the Constitution provides for grants from the centre to the states. The President of India appoints the Finance Commission, an independent body, to determine the shares of centre and states in shared central

revenues and their allocation between states. There have been twelve Finance Commissions till 2005. The members of Finance Commissions include academics and retired administrators. The Finance Commission also recommends grants to states in need on the basis of a formula that weights different states according to their population, income, area, infrastructure, tax effort, and fiscal discipline. After the seventy-second and seventy-third amendments to the Constitution, State Finance Commissions were set up analogous to the Finance Commission at national level.

Analogously to the asymmetry between centre and states, there is a marked asymmetry between states' and local governments' revenue-raising powers. If decentralization has taken place, it is more at the level of expenditure than revenue generation. In 1997 two-thirds of revenue was raised by the centre but it incurred one-third of the expenditures. A disproportionate share of expenditure at local level is incurred by urban local bodies compared to rural areas. Rural local bodies have so far mostly implemented grants from central ministries, usually in poverty alleviation and social and community services, but are heavily circumscribed by state governments and have yet to fulfil their potential as an independent tier of government.

As a consequence of the skewed distribution of taxing and expenditure powers, state governments typically run a deficit that is financed by central transfers (there are corresponding deficits noted at local government level). On average in 2000–1, states' own revenue to current spending was 49 per cent. State governments can rely on both tax and non-tax revenue sources. The latter comprise interest receipts from loans issued by the state government, dividends and profits from public-sector undertakings owned by states, and revenue from state lotteries. In 2000–1, states' share of central taxes was approximately 27 per cent while grants to states accounted for 11 per cent of total revenues. Hence states' dependence on central transfers is very high and causes many problems of fiscal indiscipline and low tax effort.

Transfers from the centre to state governments have been criticized for displaying a political bias. This criticism is especially directed towards *discretionary* transfers although even formula-based transfers have been suspect. The proportion of discretionary transfers has been increasing over time. There are three major channels through which the centre transfers funds to state governments. These are:

(i) Tax devolution and grants through the Finance Commissions (approximately 65 per cent of total transfers in 2000–1).

(ii) Grants and loans given by the Planning Commission (approximately 32 per cent of total transfers in 2000–1).

(iii) Transfers for various central-sector and centrally sponsored schemes by various central ministries (approximately 4.32 per cent of total transfers in 2000–1).

From 1969, plan transfers (that is transfers determined by the Planning Commission) have been effected on the basis of a formula called the 'Gadgil Formula' after the first chairman of the National Development Council. The formula is based on population, per capita income, and its deviation from an average of all states as well as from the highest per capita income, fiscal performance, and 'special problems'. The decision-making body is the National Development Council which is chaired by the Prime Minister, and contains all cabinet ministers at the centre, Chief Ministers of the states, and members of the Planning Commission. These are called transfers on account of *state plan schemes*. Although these transfers are based on a consensus formula,

discretionary elements can enter into the determination of these grants for two reasons. First, while each state proposes its plan size to the Planning Commission, the final approval of the size rests with the Commission. Hence there is some scope for negotiation and 'persuasion'. Second, the formula explicitly sets aside 7.5 per cent of the grants on account of *special problems* of states. This allows for some subjectivity to creep into the determination of grants for state plan schemes. In addition to grants, the Planning Commission also gives assistance in the form of loans. Major states get 70 per cent of all transfers by the Planning Commission at present and out of this 70 per cent is in the form of loans and the rest is in the form of grants.

Central plan schemes are funded entirely by the centre, the states merely exercising an agency role in executing these programmes. Centrally sponsored programmes involve some element of cost sharing between the centre and the concerned state. In principle, discretionary grants are meant to provide flexibility and responsiveness to states' contingencies. However, they have often been criticized for the political bias displayed in the disbursement of such grants. Indeed, the scope for politics to play a role in disbursement has only been increasing as the discretionary component of grants has grown at the expense of formula-based grants.

The transfers given to states through *central plan schemes* and *centrally sponsored schemes* have attracted the sharpest criticism because these are essentially completely discretionary. In financial year 1996–7, states' share of central taxes accounted for 23.3 per cent of states' total revenues, while grants on account of state plan schemes, centrally sponsored schemes, and central plan schemes (that is items (ii) and (iii)) jointly amounted to 15.9 per cent of states' total revenues (averaged over fifteen major states).

Political favouritism in discretionary grants may work through different channels. There may be favouritism by the incumbent party at the centre which is interested in furthering its re-election prospects, both at central and state levels. Transfers in this model are akin to 'pork' or targeted spending aimed at maximizing electoral support. There may also be lobbying by state governments, so that states with a higher representation in decision-making bodies get favourable treatment. Both models predict that *alignment* matters—that is it matters whether the incumbent party at state level is the same as the ruling party at the centre. The first type of model (see Dasgupta et al. 2004) predicts that the proportion of 'floating' voters in a state matters as well—this is the *swing* effect. Intuitively, a resource-constrained party that is interested in maximizing electoral prospects can decide to focus either on its core support group or on voters who are most easily 'bribed'. Dasgupta et al. (ibid) show that swing states which are aligned get more grants—the logic underlying this result is that transfers that add directly to the states' budget may not be attributed to the central ruling party, unless the two governments are aligned. The lobbying model (for example Rao and Singh 2002) predicts that states with higher representation in the central parliament get more transfers—hence that the *degree* of alignment should matter. Biswas and Marjit (2000) study a similar problem for loans from centre to states which are often at highly subsidized rates. Finance Commission transfers have mostly been immune to such criticisms. Khemani (2003), however, shows that Finance Commission transfers tend to compensate for the political bias in other transfers.

While there is emerging consensus in this recent literature on the political economy of transfers that politics matters, there is no such consensus as yet on the exact mechanisms through which it matters. Recent developments in Indian politics like the emergence of coalition governments at central level and regional parties in many states mean that the nature of transfers may change in the future.

The other notable feature of Indian fiscal federalism is the inter-state inequalities in revenue capacity and per capita expenditures. This is a natural consequence of the huge differences in per capita incomes between states, which are, moreover, increasing over time: in 1980–1 the per capita income of Punjab, the richest state was about three times that of Bihar, the poorest state, while in 1998–9 the per capita income in Punjab was five times that of Bihar. Hence differences in the ability to raise revenue have also increased over time. Per capita expenditures were 44 per cent higher than the all-India average in the high-income states while they were 36 per cent lower than the average in low-income states in 2000–1. Part of the rationale for transfers by the centre to states was to reduce the horizontal imbalance. The empirical evidence on the issue of whether Finance Commission transfers have resulted in lower inequality is ambiguous at best.

Reforms have been suggested by the Eleventh Finance Commission which would aim to reduce the role of the Planning commission vis-à-vis the Finance Commission and that would give higher powers to tax at state level. However, until now the trend has been the opposite.

AMRITA DHILLON

REFERENCES

Biswas, R. and Sugata Marjit. 2000. 'Political Lobbying and Discretionary Finance in India: An Aspect of Regional Influence in a Representative Democracy', mimeo, Centre for Studies in Social Sciences, Calcutta.

Dasgupta, S., A. Dhillon, and B. Dutta. 2004. 'Electoral Goals and Centre–State Transfers: A Theoretical Model and Empirical Evidence from India', mimeo, University of Warwick.

Khemani, S. 2003. 'Partisan Politics and Intergovernmental Transfers in India', mimeo, Development Research Group, World Bank.

Rao, M.G. 2000. 'Fiscal Decentralisation in Indian Federalism', mimeo, Institute for Social and Economic Change, Bangalore.

_____. 2004. 'Changing Contours in Fiscal Federalism in India', mimeo, National Institute of Public Finance, Delhi.

Rao, M.G. and Nirvikar Singh. 2002. 'The Political Economy of Center–State Fiscal Transfers in India', mimeo, University of California at Santa Cruz.

Fiscal Policy Reforms since 1991

India practices fiscal federalism with distinct demarcation of powers between the central and state governments. Since 1991, both the centre and states have initiated significant fiscal reforms as an integral part of ongoing initiatives launched in the aftermath of the balance-of-payments crisis in 1990. The reforms aim at improving efficiency, productivity, and competitiveness of Indian industries and imparting dynamism to the overall growth process.

The initial fiscal reforms were guided by the following factors and motivations:

+ Large fiscal deficits and automatic monetization of fiscal deficits leading to high inflation and interest rates and crowding out private investment.
+ High and irrational tax rates and tariff walls leading to industrial inefficiency, lack of competitiveness, high-cost economy, non-optimal allocation of resources, low compliance rate, and high degree of tax evasion.
+ Large variance and multiplicity of tax rates on the basis of end-uses leading to weak tax administration and rent seeking.
+ Narrow tax base and low buoyancy and elasticity of both direct and indirect taxes.
+ Complicated tax structure, laws, rules, and procedures.
+ Emphasis on social services and safety nets.
+ Need for public-sector enterprises reforms and disinvestments of government equity.
+ Integration of fiscal, monetary, exchange rate, and trade policies.
+ Demographic transition with an increase in life expectancy requiring old-age social security and healthcare and reforms in pensions and provident and insurance funds.

The basic objective of fiscal reforms since 1991 has been to reduce fiscal deficits to sustainable levels by expenditure management and resource mobilization through rationalization of taxes and duties, widening of tax base, modernizing of tax administration, focusing attention on contingent liabilities, and improving centre–states fiscal relations.

Like any other reforms, fiscal policies have perforce to be based on a gradual and step-by-step approach, rather than a big-bang or shock-therapy approach, and have a strong emphasis on human face and a bias towards poverty reduction and employment generation. Over the years, government has reduced its scope and gradually withdrawn from commercial sectors where private initiatives are more productive and efficient. But the need for enhanced public expenditure remains for the development of social and physical infrastructure. The government is also encouraging public–private partnership including foreign investment in crucial sectors. It is restructuring the public pension systems and insurance and provident funds with private participation so that these contractual savings with long-term maturity can be utilized for financing infrastructure projects. The government has increased allocations for poverty-alleviation and employment-generation programmes to fulfil its commitments under the UN Millennium Development Goals.

CENTRAL TAX REFORMS
Direct Taxes
Direct tax rates were gradually brought down over the years with reduction in the peak rate of personal income tax from 56 per cent in 1991–2 to 40 per cent in 1995–6, that of corporate tax from 57.5 per cent to 43 per cent, and that of surcharge from 15 per cent to 7.5 per cent over the same period. The Union Budget 1997–8 was a landmark in fiscal reform in attempting to align Indian tax rates with those in other developing countries. The maximum marginal tax rate for personal income was reduced to 30 per cent and that for corporate income to 35 per cent for domestic companies[1] and 48 per cent for foreign companies. Since then, till 2004–5, the emphasis on the direct tax front was to continue with moderate tax rates, widen the tax base, simplify and rationalize tax rules and procedures, continue incentives for infrastructure and housing, revive the capital market, and strengthen enforcement and tax compliance. Recent trends in direct tax collections indicate that these policies have paid rich dividends by enhancing compliance and tax productivity.

Indirect Taxes
In respect of indirect taxes, the focus was to reduce the multiplicity of duty rates by abolishing end-use specifications, move towards ad valorem rates, rationalize the tax

[1] In the Budget for 2005–6, the rate of corporate tax was reduced to 30 per cent.

structure, and drastically curtail the scope for discretion by abolishing the power to grant ad hoc duty exemptions except for charitable purpose or strategic reasons. In the Budget of 1998–9, eleven major ad valorem duty rates were reduced to three, namely a central rate of 16 per cent, a merit rate of 8 per cent, and a demerit rate of 24 per cent. Customs duty rates were also rationalized and simplified from seven to five ad valorem rates ranging from 5 per cent to 40 per cent.

These reforms resulted in reduction of peak rate of customs duty in a phased manner from 150 per cent in 1991–2 to 10 per cent in 2004–5 to make Indian industry globally competitive.

MODVAT
A modified value-added tax called MODVAT was introduced in 1986 for reducing industrial costs and prices by relieving taxes on inputs, thereby mitigating the cascading effect on final products. Since 1986, the MODVAT scheme has undergone significant changes with its extension to almost all commodities and introduction of input tax credit across goods and services.

Service Tax
The tax net was widened by introducing tax on a select number of services in 1994. With the share of the services sector growing in the gross domestic product (GDP), the coverage of the service tax has been widened to ensure greater equity and diversity in the tax system.

Fiscal Incentives
India provides fiscal incentives for the development of industry, infrastructure, and technology, which are equally applicable to both domestic and foreign companies. Tax holidays up to fifteen years are allowed for industries set up in backward regions and for infrastructure projects set up anywhere

in India. Incentives are given for exporters, research and development (R&D) activities, and units located in special economic zones (SEZs), export processing zones (EPZs), and science and technology parks. A number of incentives such as capital subsidy, tax breaks, exemption from state duties, and concessional land and power are also provided by the states. Regulatory authorities for telecom, ports, and power determine tariffs, which are important for enhancing the financial health of the public-sector enterprises within these sectors.

India allows World Trade Organization (WTO)-compatible tax exemption for exports, lower interest rates for export credits, and duty drawback on inputs used for exports. However, tax exemptions on exports are being phased out over time. Producers are allowed duty-free imports of capital goods subject to export obligations. Exporters of food grains are given WTO-compatible subsidies. India is a member of the Multilateral Investment Guarantee Agency and has signed comprehensive treaties for avoidance of double taxation with many countries. The so-called tax expenditures (that is revenue losses for most of these fiscal incentives) are not estimated in the budget.

PUBLIC DEBT MANAGEMENT

The outstanding domestic liabilities of the central government increased from 49.8 per cent of GDP at end March 1991 to 62.3 per cent of GDP at end March 2005, while the book value of outstanding external debt declined from 5.5 per cent to 1.8 per cent of GDP over the same period. An encouraging feature in recent years has been a decline in interest payments from 53.4 per cent of revenue receipts in 2001–2 to 41.8 per cent in 2004–5 and in the average interest rate on outstanding domestic liabilities from 10.5 per cent to 7.76 per cent over the same period.

The combined public debt of the general government (centre and states) as a percentage of GDP increased by 17 percentage points from 64 per cent at end March 1991 to 81 per cent of GDP at end March 2005. However, outstanding government guarantees of the general government declined from 13.4 per cent at end March 1993 to 10.6 per cent at end March 2004. The government is pursuing an active debt management policy with emphasis on appropriate maturity and interest rate minimization. It pre-paid $7.2 billion worth of high-cost external debt during 2002–3 and 2003–4.

Until 1990 India adopted a development strategy based on the predominant role of a public sector. Unlimited borrowings from the Reserve Bank of India (RBI) at subsidized rates enabled government to finance large fiscal deficits. The government initiated reforms in 1992 with the auction of government securities at market-determined rates, followed by gradual withdrawal of RBI support and cessation of automatic monetization of government deficit. The government also strengthened institutional infrastructure and the legal and regulatory set-up for the government securities market. The active public debt management strategy comprised minimizing refinancing risk and avoidance of issuing floating rate and short-term and foreign currency-denominated debt.

These policies paid dividends and protected India from the contagion effect of the East Asian crisis in 1997–2000. There was significant improvement in external debt indicators with external debt–GDP ratio declining from 38.7 per cent at end March 1992 to 17.4 per cent at end March 2005 and debt service ratio declining from 35.3 per cent in 1990–1 to 6.2 per cent in 2004–5. As per classification in the Global

Development Finance of the World Bank, India is now a 'low indebted' country.

CENTRAL FISCAL RESPONSIBILITY AND BUDGET MANAGEMENT (FRBM) ACT 2003

For fiscal consolidation, the central government enacted the Fiscal Responsibility and Budget Management (FRBM) Act 2003. The FRBM Act 2003 and FRBM Rules 2004 came into force with effect from 5 July 2004. The Act mandates the central government to eliminate revenue deficit by March 2009 and to reduce fiscal deficit to 3 per cent of GDP by March 2009. Under the Act, the central government is required to lay before both Houses of Parliament a Medium-term Fiscal Policy Statement, a Fiscal Policy Strategy Statement, and a Macroeconomic Framework Statement along with the Annual Financial Statement and Demand for Grants.

The FRBM Rules 2004 specify reduction of revenue deficit by 0.5 per cent of GDP or more and reduction of gross fiscal deficit by 0.3 per cent of GDP or more every year; no assumption of additional debt exceeding 9 per cent of GDP for 2004–5; progressive reduction of this limit by at least one percentage point of GDP in each subsequent year; and no central government guarantee in excess of 0.5 per cent of GDP in any financial year. The Rules also require quarterly review of the fiscal situation, greater transparency in the budgetary process, rules, accounting standards and policies, and projection of four fiscal indicators (namely revenue deficit, fiscal deficit, tax revenue, and total debt as a proportion of GDP) for the medium term.

The Rules mandate the central government to take appropriate corrective action in case the revenue and fiscal deficits exceed 45 per cent of the budget estimates, or total non-debt receipts fall short of 40 per

Table 1   Medium-term Rolling Targets for Fiscal Indicators as Percentage of GDP at Current Market Prices

Items	2004–5 RE	2005–6 BE	2006–7 Target	2007–8 Target
1. Revenue deficit	2.7	2.7	2.0	1.1
2. Fiscal deficit	4.5	4.3	3.8	3.1
3. Gross tax revenue	9.8	10.6	11.1	12.6
4. Year-end debt stock	68.6	68.6	68.2	67.3

Note: RE stands for revised estimate and BE stands for budget estimate.

cent of the budget estimates at the end of first half of the financial year. Medium-term projections presented along with the Budget for 2005–6 are given in Table 1.

STATES FINANCES

Side by side, there is a growing awareness that improvement in the economic management of the states is also critical for the country to sustain high rates of economic growth and accelerate the pace of poverty reduction. India's central challenge lies in more effective management of public finances at all levels of government. States have become more important in a liberalized environment. While the specific issues and remedies may differ between central and state governments, fiscal challenge and prudence are relevant for the states as well.

A state-level value-added-tax (VAT) has been introduced from 1 April 2005 to create a uniform, self-sustaining, and transparent tax system for the whole country. The state of Haryana started implementing VAT from 1 April 2003. Sixteen states and four union territories began to implement VAT from 1 April 2005. Assam and Meghalaya have joined the VAT states from 1 May 2005. Two union territories, Andaman and

Nicobar Islands and Lakshadweep, do not have any sales tax or VAT.

The central government is playing the role of facilitator for successful implementation of this significant reform by agreeing to bear the loss in revenue collection, if any, by the states. The government desires to move towards a uniform goods and services tax (GST), applicable to the whole country with a central share and a state share.

The Twelfth Finance Commission, while determining the revenue sharing between centre and states, has recommended the following measures for fiscal consolidation of the states:

+ Fiscal deficit to GDP for the centre and states be targeted at 3 per cent.
+ Revenue deficit of the centre and states be reduced to zero by 2008–9.
+ States' recruitment policy must ensure that salary bill as a percentage of revenue expenditure, net of interest payments, is within 35 per cent.
+ Each state must enact a Fiscal Responsibility Act to reduce fiscal deficit to SDP (state domestic product) ratio to 3 per cent and revenue deficit to zero by 2008–9.

RECENT FISCAL INITIATIVES

The Budget for 2005–6 highlights the need to maintain a growth rate of 7 to 8 per cent per annum as mandated by the National Common Minimum Programme (NCMP) of the coalition government, and at the same time provide a decisive thrust for reduction of poverty and unemployment at a faster pace. Towards this, the central government has enacted a National Rural Employment Guarantee Scheme to provide assured employment to rural poor households and has made significantly higher allocation to poverty-alleviation and employment-generation programmes. Thrust areas

identified include the mid-day meal scheme for schoolchildren, the Sarva Shiksha Abhiyan (universal education campaign), improved facilities for drinking water and sanitation, a roadmap for agricultural diversification and strengthening of agricultural marketing infrastructure, and the National Rural Health Mission.

Major reforms in direct taxes announced in the Budget for 2005–6 include higher exemption limit in the case of personal income tax with modified tax exemption for savings and elimination of tax rebate, reduction of the corporate tax rate from 35 to 30 per cent for domestic companies, introduction of a banking cash withdrawal tax for high-value transactions, and a fringe benefits tax (FBT) payable by the employers on certain benefits given to the employees.

The Budget has provided for measures towards fiscal consolidation, rationalization of customs duties with reduction of peak rate of customs duty from 20 per cent to 15 per cent, reduction in customs duty on petroleum products, and fixing of excise duties on petrol and diesel as a combination of ad valorem and specific duties, exemption of service providers whose gross turnover does not exceed Rs 4 lakh per year from service tax, and widening of service tax by including additional services.

FUTURE PERSPECTIVES

The process of fiscal correction needs to be sustained and strengthened. There is urgent need to improve the overall quality of fiscal adjustment, to change the composition of expenditure towards investment, and to restrain the growth in revenue expenditure. Expenditure management, including curtailing growth in non-plan revenue expenditure, is critical for better fiscal management. Capital expenditure needs to be focused more on non-tradable infrastructure sectors like transport, communications, and energy. These sectors are capable of stimulating private investment through 'crowding in' effect by improving the productivity of capital.

Fiscal policy is not only about correcting fiscal imbalances but also about developing and strengthening institutions and designs of expenditure programmes. There is enormous multiplicity in programmes covering a wide array of economic and social services. There is also the issue of how these programmes should be prepared and implemented. The government has to fund basic health services, for instance, but that does not mean that it also must deliver these itself. There is need to promote competitive and efficient delivery in these programmes, where possible, so as to reduce delivery costs and improve quality. It is also essential to establish systems that allow options for beneficiaries and promote transparent, accountable, and locally managed services. The role of grassroots institutions such as panchayats and dynamic non-governmental organizations (NGOs) in the management of the development process should be emphasized. Empowerment of panchayats, capacity building at local level, and greater transparency, accountability and participation in programmes are essential for improving the effectiveness of development funding.

Nevertheless, efforts must continue towards the goal of ensuring that expenditures, subsidies, and transfers reach the intended beneficiaries, by targeting subsidies to the poor and making the rest pay for the cost of public goods and services, cutting leakages, and reducing administrative overheads. There is also a need for concerted efforts to increase both the investment rate and savings rate to attain a consistent high-growth path.

P. CHIDAMBARAM

Government Subsidies

The term 'subsidy' is sometimes used to describe a financial transfer, for example scholarships to students, and sometimes to mean the unrecovered cost of publicly provided goods and services (henceforth collectively referred to as 'services'), that is the difference between the cost of providing a service and revenues realized from the provision of that service that is absorbed by the government budget. For purposes of this entry, we find it useful to make a distinction between transfers and subsidies, which are here interpreted to mean the unrecovered cost of publicly provided services. Such unrecovered costs can be calculated at conventional prices prevailing in the market or they can be calculated at their economic value, that is the outputs forgone on account of the inputs used up in the provision of the relevant service, what economists call 'opportunity cost' or 'shadow price'. Hence a further distinction has to be made between 'financial subsidies' computed at market prices and 'economic subsidies' computed in 'shadow prices'. Here we will mainly be discussing the volume and composition of financial subsidies in India.

A clarification is required here regarding the kind of publicly provided services for which unrecovered costs can be considered subsidies. At one end of the spectrum there are pure 'public services' that cannot be supplied by the market because they are characterized by 'non-rivalry' and 'non-excludability' in consumption. Non-rivalry implies that the service in question is jointly available to all consumers, and its consumption by one consumer does not reduce the supply available for other consumers. A good example is defence services that provide the same security to all citizens of a country simultaneously.

The enjoyment of such security by one citizen does not reduce the security available for other citizens. Citizens are not rivals competing for the enjoyment of such security. It is also evident that once such security is provided to the nation, it is not possible to exclude any citizen from this benefit. This non-excludability makes it impossible to 'sell' such a service to individual citizens at a price, since citizens know that once such security is provided to the nation they cannot be excluded from enjoying it even if they don't pay for it, that is they can free ride.

Such pure public services can only be provided by the government, and they have to be financed out of its general revenues. The question of recovering the cost of these services through user charges does not arise. Hence the concept of 'subsidies' as defined here will also not apply. Defence, maintenance of law and order, and general administrative services are typical examples of such pure public services. At the other end of the spectrum are pure private services, characterized by 'rivalry' and excludability' in consumption, that are generally provided by the market, though it may happen that these are also sometimes provided by the government. In between these two polar categories is also a range of quasi-public services that combine some characteristics of public services with some characteristics of private services. They are characterized by rivalry and excludability in consumption, and could therefore be supplied by the market. However, the market-determined supply may not be optimal for a variety of reasons that economists call 'externalities'. This is later discussed in greater detail. The concept of 'subsidy' applies only to the unrecovered cost of quasi-public and private services.

Unless such subsidies can be explicitly justified, they should be phased out or reduced as they lead to several undesired consequences. A large volume of subsidies generates macroeconomic pressures via its impact on the budget. Subsidies affect relative prices, thereby altering market signals and the allocation of resources via the market. Subsidies also alter the distribution of income since they enhance the effective income of beneficiaries relative to others in the economy, and this could be iniquitous. However, under some conditions subsidies are justifiable and desirable. First, there are services with positive externalities, where the social benefit of a service exceeds the private benefit accruing to the immediate beneficiary. In such cases, the cost of these services may have to be subsidized to increase the level of private demand for these services to the socially optimal level. Second, there may be services where unit costs decline as supply increases because of economies of scale in production or distribution. Costs would be minimized in such cases if a single 'natural monopolist' supplies the entire market. However, the 'natural monopolist' would be interested in maximizing profits not minimizing costs, and may have to be regulated as well as subsidized to minimize costs. Technological developments that enable unbundling of many such services and multiple-part pricing options have reduced the challenge of natural monopolies. Nevertheless, scale economies remain a valid justification for subsidies in some cases. Third, there may be 'missing markets' for some products that need to be nurtured and grown or a missing technology, for example cost-effective solar power, where subsidies may be justified.

Since subsidies affect income distribution, sometimes subsidies are provided for distributional reasons. However, as noted earlier, transfer payments are an alternative policy instrument for meeting this goal. If there is a social/political choice to support the income of a particular target group, for example the unemployed, this may be better accomplished by income transfers through the budget. Compared to subsidies they are more transparent, with less leakages to non-target groups, they do not distort relative prices, and do not encourage excess consumption of any particular service as a subsidy would.[1] A qualification arises in the case of some very basic needs of the poor such as food grains, potable water, basic education, or primary healthcare. Society may wish to ensure provision of a minimal quantity of these specific 'merit' items to everyone regardless of their income or personal preference. In such cases a subsidy would be preferred to a transfer payment. Finally, even when transfers are preferable to subsidies, policymaking has to be based on ground realities, including a history of widespread use of subsidies for distributional reasons. Hence, often the practical policy option is to gradually phase out inefficient subsidies and replace them by transfers wherever feasible.

Perhaps the most striking feature of government subsidies in India is their very large scale. The total volume of government financial subsidies was estimated for the first time for financial year 1987 by Mundle and Rao (1991) at the National Institute of Public Finance and Policy (NIPFP).[2]

They calculated the unrecovered costs (including annualized capital costs) of eighty-six out of 123 major categories of public services provided by the federal and state governments. This calculation excluded thirty-seven major services treated as pure public services, that is general administrative services in the functional classification of government expenditure, relief on account of natural calamities, general secretariat expenses of departments providing social and economic services, and compensation and assignment to Local Bodies and Panchayati Raj institutions. The authors also netted out pure transfer payments, and then arrived at an estimate of Rs 423 billion or 14.4 per cent of the gross domestic product (GDP) as the total volume of government financial subsidies, reflecting an underlying cost recovery rate of only 32 per cent for social and economic services. Of this Rs 161 billon or 5.5 per cent of GDP was provided by the federal government and Rs 262 billion or 8.9 per cent of GDP was provided by all the state governments taken together.

These estimates have turned out to be quite robust. In an updated NIPFP estimate for financial year 1994, Srivastava and Sen (1997) arrived at the same subsidy–GDP ratio of 14.4 per cent despite some changes in method and coverage. Unfortunately, combined estimates for the federal and state governments are not available for any other year. However, NIPFP estimates of federal government subsidies based on a

---

[1]Atkinson and Stiglitz (1976) also argued that under a set of strong assumptions direct transfers are superior to subsidies.

[2]Subsidy in a specific service (j) can be obtained by,

$$S_j = R_j + i\,(K_j + L_j + Z_j) + d\,K_j - y_j - r_j - t_j$$

S_j is the subsidy;

R_j is the variable cost or revenue expenditure on the services;

K_j is the capital stock in the sector;

L_j is the stock of loans advanced for the service;

Z_j is the stock of equity and loans advanced

to public enterprises classified within the service category;

i is an imputed interest rate representing the opportunity cost of money for government;

d is the depreciation rate;

y_j is revenue receipt by the sector;

r_j is income by way of interest or dividend on loans and equity; and

t_j is a transfer payment from the sector to individual agents.

broadly similar method are available for six additional years up to financial year 2003 and indicate that federal government subsidies have generally varied within a narrow range of 4–5 per cent of GDP since financial year 1987. Since there have been no marked changes in the cost recovery policy of most state governments during this period, it is possible that the total volume of subsidies has remained in the ball park of 14–15 per cent of GDP. However, with no actual estimates available after financial year 1994, this is a hypothesis that has to be tested. It would be very useful if the periodic updates of estimates of federal-level subsidies undertaken by the NIPFP at the behest of the Finance Ministry could be complemented by similar updated estimates of state government subsidies.

In their study Mundle and Rao (1991) noted that subsidies in social services, with an underlying cost recovery rate of less than 4 per cent, accounted for 40 per cent of total subsidies while economic services, with an underlying recovery rate of around 44 per cent, accounted for 60 per cent of total subsidies. They pointed out that less than 30 per cent of this large volume of subsidies was provided as visible subsidies and the rest was non-transparent, making it extremely difficult to identify the beneficiaries or assess whether these subsidies are justifiable in terms of the rationale outlined earlier. Based on a detailed analysis of the allocation of subsidies across social groups, sectors, and states they concluded that the distribution of subsidies was quite regressive, and that 'with greater transparency and better targeting it should be possible to increase the flow of services as well as subsidies to disadvantaged groups without any increase, perhaps even with a reduction, in the total bill of subsidies.'

Subsequent exercises have confirmed these broad conclusions. In their study Srivastava and Sen (1997) aggregated surplus-generating and deficit sectors separately to get a full measure of subsidy flowing in subsidized sectors without surplus offsets. They also introduced the concept of 'merit subsidies', which subsidies might be justified, and attempted to get at least a rough measure of the volume of 'unjustified' subsidies. They concluded that even non-merit services had an average recovery rate of less than 9 per cent and that 'non-merit' subsidies amounted to nearly 11 per cent of the GDP, the implication being that elimination of these unjustifiable subsidies could wipe out India's entire fiscal deficit. They also concluded that the overall allocation of subsidies was distributionally quite regressive. Brent (1995) used the Mundle–Rao state-level estimates to compare cost recoveries with his measure of socially desirable user charges in a cost–benefit analysis framework, and concluded that 'the application of the cost–benefit framework to India's state user price experience does therefore on the whole, support the Mundle–Rao conjecture that it is hard to justify the limited use of user pricing for government services in India'.

Available studies of government subsidies in India thus confirm that the total volume of such subsidies is very large, approaching around 15 per cent of GDP, that most of it is difficult to justify as 'merit goods' or in a social cost–benefit analysis framework, and that the incidence of subsidies is regressive and difficult to justify even on distributional considerations. This calls for a significant reform of subsidy policy in India. At the same time, in identifying a road map for subsidy policy reform that is feasible, it is important to recognize political economic ground realities. It is important to first freeze, and then reduce in a phased manner, subsidies that cannot be justified as 'merit subsidies' to both reduce the fiscal burden of unwarranted subsidies and also the distorting effects on resource allocation. Second, wherever feasible, subsidies should be substituted by other policy instruments that are less distorting for resource allocation, for example two-part or multiple-part pricing. Third, subsidies given for distributional reasons should be substituted by pure transfer payments that are more visible, and therefore can be better targeted, and that also do not distort price signals that impact on resource allocation. Finally, the shift to alternative policy instruments should be introduced alongside the phased reduction of subsidies so as to make these policy packages politically feasible.

SUDIPTO MUNDLE AND HIRANYA
MUKHOPADHYAY

REFERENCES

Atkinson, A.B. and J.E. Stiglitz. 1976. 'The Design of Tax Structure: Direct Versus Indirect Taxation', *Journal of Public Economics*, 6: 55–75.

Brent, R. J. 1995. 'Cost–Benefit Analysis, User Prices, and State Expenditures in India', *Public Finance*, 50(3): 327–41.

Srivastava, D.K. and Tapas Sen. 1997. *Government Subsidies in India*, New Delhi, National Institute of Public Finance and Policy.

Mundle, S. and M.G. Rao. 1991. 'The Volume and Composition of Government Subsidies in India', *Economic and Political Weekly*, 4 May.

Privatization

The past quarter century has witnessed a significant move towards privatization in economies across the globe. Several industrial countries have embraced it as have most of the transition economies of East Europe and large parts of the developing world. After the initial push received in the early 1980s during the Thatcher–Reagan era the process appears to have gathered momentum following the decline of communism in the erstwhile Soviet bloc. In India privatization or disinvestment of the public sector emerged as a major public policy option after the country embarked on a process of economic reforms in 1991.

Even though the question of the appropriate balance between public and private enterprise is one of the foundational issues in political economy, it has received relatively little attention in mainstream economic analysis until quite recently. In the past two decades there has emerged an appreciable literature that examines the diverse theoretical and empirical issues pertaining to privatization (Shleifer and Vishny 1994; Sheshinski and Lopez-Calva 2003, among others).

Privatization may be broadly defined as the transfer of various activities from the public to the private sphere. Specifically, it could mean the sale by government of state-owned enterprises (SOEs) to private economic agents. It could refer to a sale that is effected in full or in part. It can also mean a partnership between the public and private sectors through a transfer of responsibilities from the public to private sector. In terms of broad political economy it could also simply mean a shrinking of the welfare state.

It would be tempting to assume that since privatization has been accepted as a legitimate, and even a core, tool of statecraft by more than a hundred governments in the past two decades, its economic merits are firmly settled. There is in fact a widespread perception that privatization brings about outcomes that are superior from the point of efficiency in terms of resource allocation as compared to the situation under public ownership. However, these conclusions are without any firm basis either in theory or in empirical analysis.

In the following section I shall briefly review the theory of privatization that has emerged in the past two decades. This will be followed by a brief account of the rather large body of empirical work that has developed in recent years. I shall then consider the strategy of disinvestment that has been followed by the Government of India in the past decade and a half.

PRIVATIZATION: THEORY
Within the standard microeconomic literature, it is well established that under perfectly competitive conditions, absence of information asymmetries, and complete contracts, it does not matter whether one is operating under private or public ownership. The original arguments for government intervention come up in the context of market failure that can arise due to myriad factors. Under conditions of natural monopoly, denoted by decreasing average costs in the relevant range of demand, the possibility of monopoly power by a private owner created the rationale for public ownership.

Yet it is widely contended that public ownership brings about efficiency losses that are non-negligible (see, for example, Sheshinski and Lopez-Calva 2003). They could well be higher than the gains that may be ensured by solving a market failure problem. This comes about especially when the scope of competition becomes larger with an increase in the size of the market, with the economy possibly getting opened up to international trade and adopting higher levels of technology. The emergence of the theoretical work on regulatory mechanisms that examines their allocative as well as distributive properties has also prepared a rationale for seeking an alternative to public ownership.

There are two broad perspectives, namely, the managerial and the political, that may be used to explain the presence of inefficiency under the public sector. The managerial perspective holds that monitoring is poorer in publicly owned firms and therefore the incentives for efficiency are weak (Vickers and Yarrow 1988).[1] The argument here is that monitoring under the public sector is imperfect vis-à-vis the private sector. This is often, though not always, due to the fact that these firms are not traded in the market, unlike private firms. This eliminates the threat of takeover should the firm perform poorly.

The political perspective contends that it is political interference that distorts the objectives and brings in the possibility of soft budget constraints faced by public-sector managers (Shleifer and Vishny 1994). The possibility of soft budgets protects public-sector managers from the threat of bankruptcy. Using simple game theoretic tools it is possible to demonstrate that the political loss in closing a publicly owned company is greater than the cost of using taxpayer money or public debt to bail out a public-sector company. It is argued that privatization would effectively drive a wedge between politicians and managers and would make restructuring more likely by making it too costly for politicians to subsidize firms.

In a seminal paper Sappington and Stiglitz (1987) examine the choice between public and private provision of goods in a context where both modes involve significant delegation of authority. They argue that the main difference between the two modes concerns the transactions costs faced by the government when attempting to intervene in the delegated production activities. It is shown that such intervention is generally less costly under public ownership than private. They then proceed to put forward what they call the fundamental privatization theorem. The

[1]Vickers and Yarrow have analysed this in one of their books on privatization.

theorem specifies the conditions under which privatization is optimal. It focuses on the special concerns introduced by imperfect information about the productive environment. It provides conditions under which all of the government's objectives may be attained by an appropriately designed auction of the rights to produce a given product or service. It is shown that the conditions under which privatization is optimal are rather stringent. The authors conclude by emphasizing that neither public nor private provision can fully resolve the difficult incentive problems that arise when considerations of imperfect information result in the delegation of authority.

This leads to the position that it is not ownership, but the degree of competition, that ultimately matters for improving monitoring possibilities, and hence for productive efficiency. Major gains in efficiency can be expected by increasing market contestability via deregulation policies. Competition implies not only free entry into the market, but the freedom, especially on the part of SOEs, to fail. Competition also facilitates performance comparisons that can generally improve trade-offs between incentives and risk when several agents, or managers, facing uncertainties are being monitored.

In addition to the above micro-theoretic issues one needs to also consider the macroeconomic implications of privatization. Privatization may be used as a tool for improving the government's fiscal condition. When carried out through public offerings and mixed sales it can help increase the level of stock market capitalization and the development of the financial sector generally. The literature on the macroeconomic effects of privatization is not quite as rich from the theoretical perspective as that on the microeconomic effects.

PRIVATIZATION: EMPIRICAL EVIDENCE

In recent years a large body of empirical investigations has been carried out to assess the impact of privatization programmes in diverse settings (see, for example, Megginson and Netter 2001). There are several methodological problems with research in this area in addition to the problem of data availability and consistency. Some problems arise due to the nature of the accounting or stock data. One needs to determine the correct measure of operating performance, selecting an appropriate benchmark with which to compare performance, and to decide the appropriate statistical tests to be employed. Many of the studies on performance changes after privatization examine the effects on groups such as workers, but few examine the impact on consumers. Empirical studies on privatization may be broadly divided into three categories, (i) case studies, (ii) cross sectional comparisons of public- and private-sector performance, and (iii) statistical analysis of pre- and post-divestiture performance of enterprises. Both transition and non-transition economies have been studied. The conclusions obtained are diverse. In a study conducted to examine the performance of several British firms that were privatized in the 1980s, it was revealed that there is little evidence of any systematic improvement in performance, and promises made in political speeches remained unfulfilled. This is to be contrasted with the conclusion that Megginson and Netter (ibid.) come up with: 'Research now supports the proposition that privately owned firms are more efficient and more profitable than otherwise comparable state owned firms.'

In an important study Galal et al. (1994) compare actual post-privatization performance of twelve large firms, mostly airlines and regulated utilities, in the UK, Chile, Malaysia, and Mexico to predict performance if the firms remained SOEs. They capture the net change in welfare, defined as the sum of the changes in welfare of consumers, enterprise profits (including effects on buyers, the government, and other shareholders), the welfare of labour, and welfare of competitors. They document net welfare gains in eleven out of the twelve cases, which equal, on average, 26 per cent of the firms' pre-divestiture sales. In no case were workers worse off, and in three instances they were significantly better off. They therefore conclude that divestiture makes the world a better place.

Yet it is important to apply caution in drawing unqualified support for privatization. Most statistical analyses of pre- and post-privatization performance are marred by the failure to control for the economic environment. These could contribute to improved performance in the post-divestiture period and therefore need to be factored out. In many cases where privatization appears to have resulted in efficiency enhancement, one finds that there has actually been contemporaneous deregulation or other competition-enhancing measures.

Kalyuzhnova and Andreff (2003) provide a valuable assessment of the privatization experience in Eastern Europe and Russia now that more than a decade has passed since the end of communism there. There were several experts who had advocated overnight mass privatization programmes in the early 1990s. Many of these measures were simply 'robbery by the old elite and the new oligarchs'. It is very important to consider whether it is desirable to go in for a 'big bang' policy of massive overnight asset transfer, or whether one should not promote an evolutionist

and organic transformation of business enterprise. The first purports to ending state ownership in a drastic manner, using giveaway through voucher schemes and tolerating takeover by managers and management buyouts. The latter may be described as a bottom-up development of a new private sector but no giveaway of state property. The emphasis here is on consolidation and stability so as to make growth sustainable.

PRIVATIZATION: INDIAN EXPERIENCE SINCE 1991

A consideration of the privatization experience in India may well focus on the period after 1991, when the government embarked on a comprehensive process of economic reform and liberalization. At that time the public sector in India accounted for more than one-fifth of the country's GDP. Since a large number of public-sector enterprises (PSEs) regularly showed negative profit margins the government was keen on a programme of privatization, calling it disinvestment instead.

Data from the Department of Disinvestment, Government of India (2006)[2], reveal that the profit margins of manufacturing PSEs are systematically lower than the figures for manufacturing firms in the private sector. This is at least partly due to the fact that the expenditures on power and fuel, wages and interest as a fraction of net sales are all systematically higher than the corresponding figures for similarly placed private-sector manufacturing firms.

In the interim budget of 1991–2 the government took a policy decision to disinvest up to 20 per cent of the equity in selected PSUs in favour of mutual funds and financial or investment institutions

[2]http://divest.nic.in

in the public sector. The disinvestment, which was to broad base the equity, was to improve management and enhance the availability of resources for these enterprises. The Rangarajan Committee report on the Disinvestment of Shares in PSEs in April 1993 emphasized the need for substantial disinvestment, and recommended that the percentage of equity to be divested could go up to 49 per cent for industries especially reserved for the public sector. It recommended that in exceptional cases, such as enterprises that had a dominant market share or where separate identity had to be maintained for strategic reasons, the target public ownership level could be kept at 26 per cent, that is disinvestment could take place to the tune of 74 per cent. In all other cases it recommended 100 per cent divestment of the government stake. Holding of 51 per cent or more equity by the government was recommended only for six scheduled industries, namely (i) coal and lignite, (ii) mineral oils, (iii) arms, ammunitions, and defence equipment, (iv) atomic energy, (v) radioactive minerals, and (vi) railway transport.

In 1996 the government established a Disinvestment Commission. The purpose of this body was to formulate procedures so that any decision to disinvest would be taken and implemented in a transparent manner. The revenues generated from such disinvestment were to be allocated for education and health and for creating a fund to strengthen PSEs. By August 1999 the Disinvestment Commission made recommendations on fifty-eight PSEs. The recommendations indicated a shift from public offerings to strategic/trade sales, with transfer of management. The Commission also observed that the essence of a long-term disinvestment strategy should be not only to enhance budgetary receipts, but also to minimize budgetary support to unprofitable

units while ensuring their long-term viability. By 1998 government was of the view that 'in the generality of cases its shareholding in PSEs will be brought down to 26 per cent'. In PSEs involving strategic considerations, namely arms and ammunitions, atomic energy, and railway transport, government was to retain majority voting.

By 2000–1 the government's policy regarding privatization and public-sector restructuring comprised the following considerations: restructure and revive potentially viable PSEs, close down PSEs that cannot be revived, bring down government equity in all strategic PSEs to 20 per cent or lower, if necessary, and fully protect the interests of workers. The entire receipt from disinvestments and privatization was to be used for meeting expenditure in social sectors, restructuring of PSEs, and meeting public debt.

The Ministry of Disinvestment was converted into a department under the Ministry of Finance with effect from 27 May 2004 after the UPA (United Progressive Alliance) government headed by Dr Manmohan Singh as Prime Minister assumed office. From this point on, the disinvestment programme had to be in conformity with the National Common Minimum Programme. All privatizations were from now on to be considered on a transparent and consultative case-by-case basis. It was made explicit that the UPA would retain the existing 'navaratna' companies, which include the BHEL (Bharat Heavy Electricals Limited), in the public sector and that these would be permitted to raise resources from the capital market. The government constituted a 'National Investment Fund' in January 2005 into which the realization from sale of minority shareholding of the government in profitable PSEs would be channelized. This fund would be maintained outside the Consolidated Fund of India and the income from this

Fund would be used for the following purposes: (i) investment in social-sector projects that promote education, healthcare, and employment and (ii) capital investment in selected profitable and revivable PSEs that yield adequate returns, in order to enlarge their capital base to finance expansion or diversification.

The total quantum of receipts on account of privatization during 1991–2005 is Rs 49,214 crore. This is just a little above the half mark figure of the target receipts of Rs 96,800 crore for this period. Even though there is a strong reform lobby that calls for rapid mass privatization in India from time to time, it would be well to remember that the experience in Russia and Eastern Europe alluded to in the earlier section is far from reassuring.

After the initial phase of enthusiasm in the 1980s and then the onrush during the 1990s, we are now at a stage where we can take a more measured approach to privatization. There is certainly no clear superiority of private vis-à-vis public ownership from the standpoint of economic theory. More than ownership it would seem that the degree of competition and the regulatory environment are relevant to productive efficiency. The empirical evidence presents a mixed picture. As the world environment gets more competitive it would be necessary to put the sizable assets of the PSEs in countries like India to more productive use. Ultimately it is this consideration that should be of relevance rather than the simplistic presumption that the public sector is necessarily inefficient or that privatization is an all-purpose panacea.

PULIN B. NAYAK

REFERENCES

Galal, Ahmad, Leroy Jones, Pankaj Tandon, and Ingo Vogelsang. 1994. *Welfare Consequences of Selling Public Enterprises*, Oxford, Oxford University Press.

Kalyuzhnova, Yelena and Wladimir Andreff. 2003. *Privatisation and Structural Change in Transition Economies*, Basingstoke, Palgrave Macmillan.

Megginson, William and Jeffry Netter. 2001. 'From State to Market: A Survey of Empirical Studies on Privatization', *Journal of Economic Literature*, 39: 321–89.

Sappington, David and Joseph Stiglitz. 1987. 'Privatization, Information and Incentives', *Journal of Policy Analysis and Management*, 6: 567–82.

Sheshinski, Eytan and Luis Felipe Lopez-Calva. 2003. 'Privatization and Its Benefits: Theory, Evidence, and Challenges', in K. Basu, P. Nayak, and R. Ray, eds, *Markets and Governments*, New Delhi, Oxford University Press.

Shleifer, Andrei and Robert Vishny. 1994. 'Politicians and Firms', *The Quarterly Journal of Economics*, 109(4), Nov: 995–1025.

Vickers, John and George Yarrow. 1988. *Privatization: An Economic Analysis*, Cambridge, MIT Press.

Public Goods

For a country that calls itself both socialist and democratic, India has historically been remarkably comfortable with dramatic inequalities in access to public goods. In 1991, after, as discussed later, considerable narrowing of the gaps, rural populations in the southern state of Kerala had more than ten times as many hospital beds per head as those in the eastern states of Orissa and Assam. The fraction of people in rural Orissa with access to medical facilities in their village in 1981 was less than 11 per cent compared to 96 per cent in Kerala. In 1991, 93 per cent of villages in Kerala had a middle school but the corresponding figure in Orissa and Assam was less than 25 per cent, and in Uttar Pradesh, the largest northern state, it was less than 15 per cent. Disparities within most of these states are equally striking: according to the 1991 Census, less than 7 per cent of the villages in Vishakhapatnam district in Andhra Pradesh had middle schools and just over 46 per cent had some educational facility, as against 55 per cent and 100 per cent in Guntur. In the district of Rangareddy, in the same state, only 6 per cent of villages had primary health sub-centres as against almost 40 per cent in Anantapur. Less than 1 per cent of villages in Vishakhapatnam had tapped water as compared to 59 per cent in West Godavari.

In part this reflects our colonial legacy: in British India, it was almost a rule that public goods were only to be built where there was some commercial benefit to be had. This, not surprisingly, led to almost complete neglect of most villages.

Village India also did not have much of a place in the Nehruvian vision of development through heavy industry. Moreover, the Gandhians in the Congress were uncomfortable with bringing change too rapidly to rural India. As a result, villages were, for the most part, left to their own devices.

The obvious result of this was that by the end of the 1960s the villages that had relatively decent access to public goods tended to be either places that could afford to fund them out of their own resources or those that had enough political clout to extract them from a recalcitrant state.

This is clearly borne out by data from the 1971 Census on the correlates of access to public goods (Banerjee and Somanathan 2006). We use data on fifteen of the facilities that are classified as public goods in the census, which include various types of health and education facilities, water sources, and other types of infrastructure such as electricity, post offices and paved roads. Since the census does not distinguish between private and community government-owned facilities, it is not clear that all of these

deserve to be called *public* goods. Our best guess is that until the 1990s there were very few private education facilities in rural areas, while the power, transportation, and communication infrastructure continues to be in public hands. We are on weaker ground when we talk about hospitals and water tanks, and, especially, wells and dispensaries. The measure of access we use is the fraction of villages in a parliamentary constituency that have the particular public good.

We obviously need to be careful about possible sources of spurious correlation: We therefore only compare constituencies within the same state and include a range of geographical controls (rainfall, climate, whether on the coast, whether mountainous, sandy, or rocky, etc.) as well as controls for population density (it is easier to serve a denser population).

Our regression results are depressingly consistent with the conventional wisdom about who has power and influence in rural India. Among the fifteen goods for which we have 1971 data, scheduled tribe-dominated areas have significantly less of ten (and more of none) while scheduled castes have less of eight and more of two. As is well known, these are the groups that are at the bottom of the Hindu caste hierarchy. We also see that the largest religious minority, the Muslims, have less of seven public goods and more of none. And, strikingly, areas dominated by Brahmins, the group that is at least nominally at the top of the caste hierarchy, have more of all the goods we would expect them to especially value given their traditional role as the repositories of written knowledge—all kinds of schools and post offices.

We also see some evidence that could be interpreted to mean that social capital matters. Areas where the population is more fragmented along caste and religious lines do worse, raising the possibility that these areas are particularly ineffective in asserting their collective claim to public goods. On the other hand, places with more land inequality do better, consistent with Mancur Olson's view that the presence of an elite with a strong private stake helps alleviate collective action problems.

Unfortunately, few of these results survive when we compare what happened to access to public goods in places where the values of explanatory variables (say, share of scheduled castes) went up between 1971 and 1991, with places where they did not change or went down. We find, for example, that there is no systematic relation between the improvement in access to public goods and changes in either land inequality or socio-religious fragmentation. The most interesting contrast between the two sets of results is what we find for scheduled castes. Our results suggest that areas where scheduled caste concentration went up did better in terms of improvement in access than other areas. We do not find the same pattern when we look at scheduled tribe areas. Indeed, the evidence suggests that they may have fallen behind. There is no clear pattern with respect to Muslim areas.

What should we make of the contrast between these two sets of results? One possible interpretation is that the cross-sectional results are simply wrong. There could easily have been other things that are different about these constituencies we were comparing that were driving our results, and therefore we only get the right answers when we compare the same area over time. If this were the only explanation, it would suggest that historical/structural factors (like fragmentation and inequality) are perhaps much less important in determining access to public goods than we might have thought, except in some extreme cases such as that of scheduled tribes.

This may, however, be going too far. After all, both the Gini coefficient and the measures of fragmentation (especially given that they are measured at the parliamentary constituency level, which is not necessarily the domain within which all political competition takes place) are just proxies for the specific factors whose influence we are trying to capture. In addition, they change quite slowly, so it is not unlikely that the changes in these variables that we put into our regressions may be dominated by measurement error (the fact that what we measure only approximately captures what we really want). Therefore, it may not be surprising that they do not do very much in the regressions.

Indeed, there is some quite robust evidence that specific historical/structural factors do make a big difference. In Banerjee and Iyer (2005), we make the case that a key factor in understanding present-day rural India is the land tenure system it was assigned under British rule. Districts where an intermediary (usually called a zamindar) collected the land taxes do systematically worse than districts where the peasant directly paid the colonial state. Since the choice of the system was, to a significant extent, based on date of conquest in a quite specific and non-linear way, it is possible to make a strong case that what we are capturing is really the effect of the choice of the particular system and not something else about the district. While these systems were formally abolished in the 1950s (indeed, there is no land tax in India today) our results suggest that villages in non-landlord districts in 1981 were 15 per cent more likely to have a primary school, 30 per cent more likely to have a middle or high school, and 50 per cent more likely to have a primary health centre. While the mechanism underlying these effects is less easy to pin down exactly, our evaluation is that the history of the zamindari system (particularly the many instances of abuse of power by zamindars) created a political climate of class-based resentments, which continues to make these districts ineffective in their collective quest for public goods.

Iyer (2005) makes the case that another important historical influence on access to public goods is whether the district was under direct British rule or whether it was part of a princely state. She argues that the enforcement of the so-called Doctrine of Lapse under Lord Dalhousie, whereby the British annexed princely states where the king had died without having a male child, resulted in some districts being annexed for no reason other than the fact that the king happened to have died without an appropriate heir at an inconvenient time. When districts that got annexed in this way are compared to otherwise similar districts, they fare worse in terms of public goods, at least relative to British non-landlord districts. She argues that this might reflect the fact that the local elites in the princely states were much more directly concerned about public goods within their state while the elites elsewhere in British India were much more connected to the metropolitan cities of Calcutta, Mumbai, etc.

This is not to say that access to public goods is entirely determined by historical/ structural factors. By far the best predictor of change in access to public goods between 1971 and 1991 turns out to be the 1971 level of access. Places that had worse access in 1971 catch up quite rapidly over the intervening period. This would not be surprising if access to these goods was close to complete in most places at the start of the period—in fact, it would be mechanical. This was, however, very far from true. Half of the goods we consider were available in less than 5 per cent of Indian villages in 1971 and in less than 10 per cent of villages in 1991.

This strong tendency towards convergence in the 1970s and 1980s is

entirely consistent with political agendas of that period. Under Indira Gandhi's 'Garibi Hatao' (eradicate poverty) programme, first put forward during her election campaign in 1971, the Indian state, for the first time, made an explicit pledge to provide public goods to everyone; other, even broader commitments were made by subsequent governments. These results suggest that these commitments, once made, were relatively binding. The government also made additional specific commitments towards the scheduled castes, which echoes the finding reported here earlier, that scheduled caste-dominated areas catch up during this period, over and above the broader tendency towards convergence.

The natural reading of these results is that the structures of society are not entirely binding. They do permit the state and other individual actors to have a considerable degree of autonomy. Once there is governmental commitment towards delivering public goods, for example, the public goods do get built, even where the population is politically unable to claim them.

One should, however, be careful not to read this finding too optimistically. Building public goods and appointing people to work there is relatively easy. Indeed, bureaucrats may have a strong private stake in both. Getting the most out of these public facilities, by making sure that teachers teach and health workers show up to work, is harder. According to Chaudhury et al. (2006), 24 per cent of teachers and 40 per cent of health providers in government facilities are absent on any given day. Moreover, even when the teachers are present they are often not teaching. This problem is significantly worse in landlord areas (Pandey 2004). Problems may be even worse in other areas for items such as power supply, with many rural areas only getting supply once in two days.

The issue here is precisely that the natural tendency of the bureaucracy is not to take on these issues, in part because it requires them to confront other bureaucrats. While more popular control has been offered as the solution to these problems of agency, the evidence so far is, at best, mixed (Banerjee and Duflo 2006). In my opinion, this is one of the greatest challenges facing India as a nation today.

ABHIJIT V. BANERJEE

REFERENCES

Banerjee, Abhijit and Esther Duflo. 2006. 'Addressing Absence', *Journal of Economic Perspectives*, 20(1): 117–32.

Banerjee, Abhijit and Lakshmi Iyer. 2005. 'History, Institutions and Economic Performance: The Legacy of Colonial Land Tenure Systems in India', *American Economic Review*, 95(4): 1190–213.

Banerjee, Abhijit and Rohini Somanathan. 2006. 'The Political Economy of Public Goods: Some Evidence from India', *Journal of Development Economics*, 82(2): 287–314.

Chaudhury, Nazmul, Jeffrey Hammer, Michael Kremer, Karthik Muralidharan, and F. Halsey Rogers. 2006. 'Missing in Action: Teacher and Health Worker Absence in Developing Countries', *Journal of Economic Perspectives*.

Iyer, Lakshmi. 2005. 'The Long-Term Impact of Colonial Rule: Evidence from India', Harvard Business School Working Paper, No. 05–041.

Pandey, Priyanka. 2004. 'Are Institutions Malleable? Effects of History, Mandated Representation and Democratization on Public Schools in North India', mimeo., World Bank.

Rent Control Acts

The Rent Control Acts (RCAs) enacted in the various states of India were intended to restrict the increase of rent in certain premises situated within the urban areas and to regulate and control the eviction of tenants by landowners. The RCA was a piece of ameliorative legislation in the interest of tenants in urban areas. Historically, it was felt that the low degree of urbanization and development pressures immediately after Independence would lead to a gap in urban housing supply. The current owners could use this demand gap to charge exorbitant rents and displace current tenants who may not be able to pay these high rents.

Though each state enacted its own version of the Act, there are broad similarities among them. All of them impose two types of restrictions—on allowable increases in rent and on the conditions for eviction. The two are obviously related. First, as long as tenants paid the permitted increase in rents, there was no need to sign a fresh contract. Second, as long as they paid the rent, tenants could not be evicted unless they indulged in subletting, misuse of tenanted premises, non-use of the premises, or unless there was bonafide need of the landowner. In principle, the Act extended protection from eviction to a tenant even after determination of contractual tenancy so long as he or she paid, or was ready and willing to pay, the permitted increases and observed and performed other conditions of the tenancy consistent with the provisions of the Act.

Unfortunately, this is an instance of an Act gone horribly wrong. Tenants, taking advantage of the protection afforded them under the Act, continue residing in palatial houses by complying with the terms of the lease, paying in court the nominal/standard rent while eviction proceedings take years to culminate in eviction. This has led to two types of responses by landowners. First, they have stopped investing in the upkeep of their houses resulting in broken-down premises and urban decay. Second, new house owners find it safer to keep their houses locked till they move in rather than rent them out in the intervening period.

Indeed, the rent control legislations are to a certain extent responsible for the decline in the quality of living and supply of rental housing. Taking advantage of the law, tenants refuse to vacate property they had taken on rent. Landowners respond through inadequate maintenance, poor repairs, and grudging provision of services. The enjoyment a tenant can derive out of the dwelling space ultimately tends to be reduced to a level commensurate with the controlled rent. The dilapidated conditions of Mumbai chawls are ample proof of the adverse effects of the rent control legislation.

Importantly, this protection was extended to commercial properties also. The rent control legislations enacted throughout the country restricted the sale or transfer of commercial properties. This was responsible for the growth in pugree, the illegal institution of a one-time lump-sum payment to the landowner by the tenant, primarily to offset the low rents. It became a major source for the generation of black money in India. Visible instances of this counterproductive law are the famous Chawri Bazaar, Old Delhi, and Connaught Place shops that are worth millions but are still being rented out for as low as a few hundred rupees a month. This too has obvious consequences for real estate development and modernization of existing facilities for commerce and business.

In addition to landowners not spending sufficient amounts for the upkeep of assets, this also indirectly prevents the city municipalities from public spending on urban amenities. First, much of the tenancy is under the legal scanner. Landowners are unwilling to leave any record of tenancy so that tenants cannot claim as much in a court of law. This obviously means that there are no records of rents paid and hence no taxes collected either from rent income or from increased valuation of property. Second, property valuations are no longer driven by the market and property tax collections are below what they would have been were they to be valued at market prices.

The RCAs also laid the burden of proof on the owner. This essentially meant that tenants went to court. Given our court system, this meant long delays in case resolutions. Usually, an eviction proceeding is disposed of within a period of five to seven years. This is mainly because of a technical reason. For instance, the Delhi RCA is applicable only in cases of a pre-existing landowner–tenant relationship. Therefore, the determination of the jural relationship between the tenant and landowner at a preliminary stage is mandatory, and the same would entail appreciation and recording of evidence, trial, and arguments. Ordinarily it is for the civil courts to determine whether and, if so, what jural relationship exists between the litigating parties. However, the Act postulates that the relationship of landowner and tenant must be a pre-existing relationship. The remedy for a landowner where there is no existing relationship is to move to the civil court by way of a suit for ejectment, untrammelled by the provisions of the Act. Therefore, it has become standard practice, or a line of argument, by every tenant to challenge this relationship causing protracted delay in adjudication of the eviction proceedings. Not surprisingly, landowners take recourse to extra-legal methods in most cases.

Over the years, the courts have done their bit to redress the situation. In particular, they started acknowledging the rights of landowners. In 2002, the

Delhi High Court struck down three sections of the Delhi RCA 1958, which had virtually 'frozen' the rent of residential and commercial properties. The Court decreed Sections 4, 6, and 9 of the Act as 'ultra vires' and stated that these provisions were 'arbitrary and unfair' to landowners. It held these sections to be violative of the Constitution as they 'affect landlord's right to livelihood, right to life and avocation'.

In 1992, the central government announced the National Housing Policy and proposed amendments to the State Rent Control Laws to bring about uniformity in their application. The purpose of the model act was:

+ to regulate the availability of space at fair rents;
+ to facilitate accommodation to all classes of society;
+ to provide fair and equitable return on property investment;
+ to provide due and fair protection to tenants against landowners.

However, the states are yet to follow suit. For instance, a new Delhi Rent Act was introduced and approved by Parliament in 1995, but the Delhi government has not implemented it till date.

JUGNU BAGGA AND
SHUBHASHIS GANGOPADHYAY

INFRASTRUCTURE

Aviation

AIRLINES

Until a decade ago, aviation in India was a government monopoly. The Directorate General of Civil Aviation controlled every aspect of flying. The Airports Authority of India ran the airports and still does. The result was that for a country its size, India has a relatively poorly developed aviation industry. By international standards, the airports are primitive and the overall fleet, public and private sectors combined, is around 150 aircraft, largely medium-haul jets with around 200 seats. In fact, until 1993, when private operators were allowed, there were just around fifty aircraft in the domestic fleet. The reason was that from the mid-1970s air travel was regarded as an elitist indulgence and therefore starved of investment. The business had been nationalized in 1953 and only a public-sector monopoly, Indian Airlines (IA) for the domestic sector, existed. The foreign routes were served by another public-sector monopoly, Air India, which even now has only around thirty aircraft. Neither received much attention by way of investment and by the mid-1980s, both had become typical public-sector firms—inefficient, corrupt, and overmanned. To make matters worse, IA was required to service politically convenient routes on the pretext that this

served the cause of social justice, whereas in fact it only helped the ministers and members of parliament please their rich constituents. The volume of traffic was not at all a factor in the decision to ply on several routes, called category C routes.

In recent years, however, all this has changed. The government monopoly was dismantled in 1993 when the Air Corporations Act was repealed. Aviation is now seen as a major infrastructure requirement of travel and trade. The Airports Authority of India Act has also been amended to permit the privatization of the airports of Delhi and Mumbai. However, while foreign investment in airlines is allowed, incomprehensibly, foreign airlines are not allowed to invest beyond 49 per cent in an airline firm registered in India. They are also not allowed to fly on domestic routes.

On balance, however, it would be correct to say that India has now solved the airlines, fleet, and competition problems. At present there are nearly a dozen airlines that operate the domestic routes, several of them being low-cost, no-frills airlines. As a result of this competition, fares have fallen drastically without—so far at least—any major adverse impact on airline profits. This is largely due to efficiency gains and growing demand. The fact that the railways, another government monopoly, are no longer competitive for the business traveller has helped as well.

One noteworthy feature of the recent developments is that the new airlines are focusing on the short-haul markets, rather than the more crowded medium-haul ones. This is serving the same purpose as the old policy of Category C routes. Competition is achieving what the old monopoly could not, namely better air connectivity. An important factor that has contributed to this development is the reduction of government control on fleet acquisition. Unlike in the old days, airlines are now free to import whatever type of aircraft they need.

Even so, certain problems remain to be addressed, mostly in respect of operating costs. Landing charges, ground overheads, and government taxation are still very high, as is the cost of finance. Taxes on aviation fuel are especially high. More than 50 per cent of the revenue collected on airline operations goes to the government. This has raised the break-even point to a load factor of over 60 per cent. The international norm for comparable fleets is 45 per cent. In short, the policy focus has now shifted from aviation to tax policy.

Where the international aspect is concerned, flights into and out of India are governed by the internationally mandated system of bilateral agreements between countries. These bilaterals limit the flights to and from two pairs of countries to designated national carriers. The number of flights and destinations within a country are negotiated periodically. The system favours bigger airlines that have larger fleets. As a result, Air India, throughout the 1990s, because its fleet size did not increase, was forced not only to give up existing gateways, it also conceded its rights under the bilaterals to foreign airlines that increased their market share into and from India. This led to a demand from the private sector that it be allowed to take up the investment slack. This was recently permitted and it is expected that Indian carriers will now win back the market shares lost by Air India.

AIRPORTS

India has nearly a hundred airports. None of them is modern or large enough yet to accommodate the growing air traffic. But the airports in Delhi and Mumbai have been privatized and by 2010 will acquire additional capacity. To put it in perspective, Mumbai still handles less than a fourth of the air traffic that Heathrow does and Delhi just around 18 per cent. Delhi and Mumbai (and these are the best in the country) simply do not have the capacity to handle more traffic today. While terminal 1B at Delhi has the capacity to handle only 800 passengers an hour, it handles over 2000 now. Delhi also has additional problems caused by security needs after the attack on parliament in December 2001. Planes have to hold themselves at least twenty-five nautical miles away if they don't get landing permission. Overall, while the international norm for aircraft handling is 50–60 per hour, even if everything goes smoothly Delhi and Mumbai will not be able to handle more than thirty-five until the fresh capacity is added. They currently handle around thirty per hour. A second runway could be a solution but Mumbai does not have the space for it. The conservative approach of the air traffic controllers is also a problem because they have so far (June 2007) refused to accept a time separation of less than four minutes between aircraft that land or take off. This has had the effect of reducing runway capacity.

No wonder that the International Air Transport Association's (IATA) last airport survey of fifty-seven big international airports ranked Mumbai and Delhi as fifty-sixth and fifty-seventh respectively. China has seven airports in the world's top 150 while India has just two. The situation is especially bad at the metros of Mumbai and Delhi. However, the good news is that the idea that airports need not be a state monopoly has caught on and several states are now starting to privatize the smaller, feeder airports. It is only a matter of time before the major non-metro airports are also privatized.

Airports are expected to remain as they are for the next few years. A National Policy on Airports was enunciated in 2002, which said that 'no greenfield airport will normally be allowed within an aerial distance of 150 kilometres of an existing airport'. The expert committee has endorsed this. It is expected that by the end of 2007, aircraft may have to circle for as much as forty-five minutes at peak hours and about half that at off-peak hours because apron space and gates will continue to remain inadequate in spite of the additions to capacity in all major airports. A part of the problem is the poor management of existing facilities, as they are operated by the public-sector Airports Authority of India. Its strong unions have been preventing modernization.

T.C.A. SRINIVASA RAGHAVAN

Infrastructure-sector Reforms

The stabilization of 1992–3 in India was followed by major structural reform, an important part of which was opening up the infrastructure sectors to private capital and, with some lag, to foreign capital. Unlike in manufacturing, though, the entry of private capital necessitated regulatory and associated policy developments, given that the infrastructure sectors show varying degrees of market 'failure'. The report of the expert committee (GOI 1997) set up for the purpose, popularly called the Rakesh Mohan Committee (RMC) Report, set the agenda for reform of the infrastructure sector. The electricity sector has witnessed the so-called independent power producer policy that 'encouraged' the private sector to generate power to be sold to State Electricity Boards (SEBs) through long-term contracts as early as in 1994. The report and the discussions that followed created a virtual consensus that India's problem was that of poor infrastructure holding back development.

The RMC Report served to highlight the importance of bringing in the private sector into most areas of infrastructure. Following the Report, many states (Gujarat, Andhra Pradesh, Karnataka, Punjab, and Rajasthan) passed legislations that created umbrella organizations, typically Infrastructure Development Boards (IDBs), that have the mandate (but not necessarily the power) to develop infrastructure especially through private capital. Through enactments, participation by the private sector, typically on a BOT (build–operate–transfer) basis, was enabled in most states. And sometimes the frameworks even allowed for annuity contributions by the state to private builders. Nevertheless, after an initial spurt, private investments have petered out. The much-hoped for investments in urban areas have yet to materialize. More than fiscal stringency, several basic factors have ensured that the movement towards reform has been very slow.

The creation of IDBs did not give these organizations sufficient power, and the new laws did not address the issues emanating from consistency with past laws and authorities. Thus turf wars between the IDB and the PWD (Public Works Department), Irrigation Department, and Roads and Bridges Department were not uncommon.

Other more basic factors that were operative in the pre-reform period have continued to constrain infrastructure, the problem of land acquisition being one such.

The common perception is that India's democracy naturally makes land acquisition difficult while in China and elsewhere in East Asia the matter is easy since governments are not accountable. The reality though is very different. It is the continuation of the state's unmitigated control over land emanating from an 'imperial' law inherited from the colonial rulers that is at the root of the problem. Land values in areas surrounding urban centres incorporate, besides the rents in agricultural use, the value arising out of the probability that it would be used for non-agricultural purposes such as housing. But in India since government have discretionary control over land use, the latter value does not uniformly accrue to all lands surrounding an urban area. All of it would suddenly accrue to the land that is released by government for non-agricultural use. This would depress the prices elsewhere while raising them for the land released from agricultural use and acquired. Thus post-acquisition market prices are always very high, often by as much as five to ten times the pre-acquisition 'market' prices paid. Interesting ways of acquisition possible such as issuance of development rights to the ex-landowner, equity share in projects, re-mapping through town planning schemes, compensatory transfer of development rights are not part of the practice.

The unfairness introduces large risks in the form of post-acquisition litigation and social movements that have delayed large infrastructure projects. Indeed, many of the 'environmental' movements take place around land acquisition because the affected people have little recourse under the law. A less 'imperial' state would have attempted to limit the public purpose as arising when the land required is specific such as the site of a deep water port or a dam, or the land for the expansion of a road between two towns, since these tend to be unique.

The institutional framework for acquisition is also problematic. There is far too much discretion and power available to the administrator and the government of the day. Moreover, it is the government that decides both the lands to acquire and also their value. This creates a conflict of interest that acts against landowners who do not have contacts in high places.

Among the visible evidence of the country's infrastructure failure is its cities. In planning with very low floor space indices (very low built-up densities) that have little relationship with locational economics, the land cost share in infrastructure becomes too high. Similarly, since much urban infrastructure shows increasing returns to density it too becomes expensive. The poor get pushed into the 'illegal' spaces as a result, and most others are spread out in sprawl development, with increased travel times and densities that are not high enough to make mass transport systems viable. When combined with the state's limited capacities to invest and manage, the private response to poor public transport availability has been to acquire 'two-wheelers'. Once bought, the marginal private cost of their use is low enough to reduce the willingness to pay for public transport. Compounding this problem is the lack of organizational autonomy and authority of elected representatives in urban local bodies resulting in powerlessness to take on responsibilities credibly. This is despite the seventy-fourth constitutional amendment which provided autonomy to the urban local bodies.

Orthogonal to the town planners' low enforced densities, the central government is biased towards expensive long-gestation metro rail rather than other intermediate solutions such as bus rapid mass transport, far more suitable to the low to intermediate densities of most Indian cities. Overambitious standards in infrastructure, especially in the layout of townships have also been a cause of failure. Thus the excessive provision of open and public spaces in the design invite violations since they are often 'unaffordable'. Such violations then spread given the very high returns, so that the good chance of holding on to reasonable standards is lost. Violations become rampant, especially by those able to influence officials. Similarly, the Ministry of Urban Development's insistence on very high standards for post-treated solid waste (not possible in India given the inevitable contamination with faecal matter), has kept interested foreign investors away.

Despite more than ten years of 'reform' the electricity sector continues to be plagued by policy and regulatory uncertainty. In the oil and natural gas sector, the picture is no different with the system having moved from the earlier administered price mechanism to what is worse—ad hocism in prices and tax rates. Private investments continue to be negligible and overall rates of investment or capacity additions in these sectors have come down. The oil sector continues to extract its toll through massive adulteration, diversion, short-selling, and an impossible governance situation where managers get murdered if they really resist adulteration by dealers. In electricity the losses are astronomical. In oil and gas a new initiative to put distribution on open-access common carrier mode is in the offing. In electricity the Electricity Act 2003 attempts to bring in open access and competition for the market in generation with trading as a distinct business, and reduction in cross-subsidies. Yet improvements have not taken place.

The fundamental problem in these sectors emanates from the mode of subsidization. The price-based subsidization in lowering the allocative price of the service/ commodity causes many perversities. Low prices for electricity (zero prices for use

given horsepower-based tariffs) that apply for agriculture result in major distortions on the user and utility sides. The user-side distortions include excessive use and wastage, environmental problems including salinity ingress, destruction of aquifers, water-intensive crops being grown in dry areas, and cropping-pattern distortions more generally. While these are sometimes mentioned in the discussion, that they arise out of the near zero prices is not appreciated. Not surprisingly, India draws out more ground water than any other country by a wide margin. Similarly, the zero tariffs repel any investments in water-saving technologies such as drip and sprinkler systems with much potential since the costs here are private. The eastern region with abundant water is discriminated against in the national market for grain and this is one of the important reasons for the continued poverty in the region since it hurts the region's comparative advantage in water-intensive crops. Worse still are the utility-side effects, especially in electricity and oil. In electricity the large price difference between consumers of various categories creates the scope for 'price arbitrage', that is for the commercial officers to misreport consumption by various sectors to create rents, and loss of accountability.

In response, the government and regulatory bodies instead of eliminating the 'price arbitrage' try to work around it by having 'tamper proof' metres, 'armoured cables', separation of rural agricultural feeders from others, and mono-phase distribution, all of which are not only enormously expensive but also doomed to fail since fundamentally there cannot be an accountability to revenue in a situation of 'price arbitrage'. What is even more remarkable is that there are central programmes that give funds and grants for such investments which are essentially wasteful. The story is not very different in oil distribution. The tragedy is that remarkable political commitment and administrative energies, both rare in India, have been spent in these sectors against an impossible task—to overcome losses when the 'price arbitrage' is at large.

In many states electricity distribution officials have been given magisterial powers to resist theft under these conditions. So a simple task like management becomes quasi police and something that has to be monitored at the highest level—by the Prime Minister's office. Obviously private players would not enter the sector under these conditions unless the contracts are overly sweetened.

The risks from government decision making, which is often discretionary, hurt private investments. The government has far too much discretion that is not adequately constrained by the legislature. Thus it is only in the late 1990s that the centre and the Reserve Bank of India were able to place limits on state governments in their use of guarantees and contingent liabilities to incur expenditures that did not have the sanction of the legislature. The state-level public-sector units are largely a vehicle for government spending that bypass the legislature. Similarly, the central government too has used central public-sector undertakings (PSUs) to finance infrastructural and related expenditures that did not have the formal approval of Parliament.

Associated with this tendency is the poor record of contract adherence by the state in its internal dealings, with its own enterprises and parastatals and often with private contracting parties. Public–private partnerships and especially those that involve regular payouts—annuities, viability gap funding, shadow tolling, subsidy payment—that is private finance initiatives (PFIs), are problematic because when governments change there is an irresistible tendency to open up/question the previous

government's deals. Where the agreements follow due procedures and processes and are not purely commercial, the risk is much less. But few projects are so covered. The ex-ante effects of large risks have typically ruled out many otherwise possible PFIs. Irrigation, water supply and sanitation, city roads, sewerage services, which all have large asset lives or have excludability/appropriability problems, are so affected.

It is the compositional and coordination economies that have justified state intervention and planning in the late industrialization context, and herein the failure of the Indian state is most glaring. Thus today wagons and coal are allocated administratively literally on a daily basis at cabinet secretary level! Where multiple agencies/departments have to work together failure is almost guaranteed. Thus the new highways built under the NHDP (National Highway Development Programme) do not smoothly lead to city centres. So a large part of the total value of the vast investments in road construction otherwise possible is denied to society. The coordination among multiple agencies and authorities necessary for the seamless construction and management of a road, or in the realization of the benefits from multimodal design, has proved to be all but impossible to realize.

The problem is fundamental and lies in the nature of the accountability of the key managers within the state and its parastatals. Constitutional immunity to career bureaucrats and the conflicting allocation of powers and responsibilities between elected representatives and administrators are responsible for a situation of powerlessness among politicians (and the bureaucracy). Politicians cannot credibly promise to get a local road or water supplies fixed. They have, after all, to depend upon administrators who are not essentially answerable to them. As a result they cannot make 'political capital' which is the raison d'etre of politics. Nor can citizens demand accountability since the system makes them powerless. Not surprisingly, in a Darwinian sense, the situation has selected and created the irresponsible and corrupt politician. Administrative positions change with a rapidity that would prevent any firm and deep understanding of the problems, in essentially what are public management and policy tasks that increasingly demand specialist skills. A general belief in the power of 'leadership' to overcome hurdles, sanctified in the public image of a few successful bureaucrats, takes the attention away from the need to rewrite the rules, to restructure organizations and redefine budgetary process, to introduce competition for powerful positions in policymaking and administration by going outside the cadre to experts, and above all to make policies incentive compatible.

Regulatory developments in infrastructure with the notable exception of the TRAI (Telecom Regulatory Authority of India) in telecom have proved to be an added retardant to not only private investments but investments in general. The poor capacities and motivation of regulators to exploit the powers under the acts to push for reform are factors. Since many of the appointees are retired civil servants who are attuned to thinking from the government's perspective of having to 'manage' rather than reform a system, this behaviour is not surprising. Regulatory capture 'by government' of ostensibly independent regulators is a uniquely Indian phenomenon. Clauses empowering arbitrary government intervention are common in regulatory acts.

Regulators have tended to choose the much discredited and non-workable cost-plus regulation in the late 1990s! And in electricity they have attempted the impossible, that is to marry a cost-plus

regulation to market-determined prices! In not choosing the obvious—incentive regulation—such as price cap and its variants for sectors like transmission and wires business in distribution of electricity or in pipelines, they have further enhanced the regulatory risk.

Procurement failure is another important reason for poor infrastructural performance. PWDs, railways, and other parastatals of government with the significant exception of a few central public enterprises, have perverse contracting procedures and rules. Typically the tenets of good procurement are ignored. There is little flexibility to tailor procurement to suit the purpose or the nature of the good/service. Service contracts that attempt to shift all risks on to the private party, payment terms that do not recognize the experience nature of many goods and services, and frequent post-bid changes in scope, besides poor specifications are typical. Too many packages that enhance coordination risk and make monitoring all but impossible have taken their toll. Improvements have been slow despite models being available.

The idea of a development finance institution (DFI) to merely direct government funds to infrastructure was anathema in a liberalized financial environment. But the IDFC (Infrastructure Development Finance Company) which was set up in 1997, wisely interpreted its role to be market development, project structuring, viability gap financing, and leveraging private investments through crucial investments. Policy advice covering details to enable the creation of appropriate frameworks was a role that the IDFC took up but which overlapped with the turf of the state. Expectedly, the experiment had only a limited life, despite major gains. Again the government has mooted the idea of a special finance company to direct funds borrowed 'cheaply' abroad to private projects including public–private partnerships, and more recently of a special purpose vehicle (SPV) to finance the viability gap component of infrastructure projects. Both mercifully remain largely on paper. These initiatives reflect a tendency to get at least some projects going even if the core problems with policy and regulation that enhance risks and negate viability remain unaddressed.

Similarly guarantees are given to merely cover avoidable risks emanating from poor policies and inadequate contractual framework. Therefore in seeking private investments, very large costs and risk may ultimately be borne by the state. The worst example of this tendency is the framework that created the IPPs (independent power projects) under which cash-strung SEBs were encouraged to sign high-cost power purchase agreements (PPAs) that shifted most significant business risks on to the government, while taking over political risk. And to 'compensate' for this reversal the private parties charged high risk premium returns. Returns could therefore go as high as 30 per cent in generation!

The failure of the state in infrastructure and more generally in the provision of public services is systematically revealed. Development indicators that depend upon the state and its activities and where the public aspect is large do relatively poorly than do others that depend less on the state. Thus on infant mortality, or death during childbirth, both of which depend much more on the performance of public health and hygiene organizations, India's score is far below that of other countries with similar levels of income. But on adult mortality, which can be mitigated by a private health sector—India's low-cost doctors and medicines—the performance is significantly above that of its peers. In all primary education or basic literacy, or sanitation

and sewerage, and airports which are more public and state dependent than higher education, home sanitation, and airlines the performance is poor.

Success has eluded reform efforts in many sectors. But when realized, the effects have been revolutionary. Thus the National Highways Authority of India (NHAI) got the essentials of the road construction contracts nearly right—a road fund sealed from the general government budget, independent engineers to certify road quality, good designs that erred on the side of higher specifications, linking payment to maintenance, clarity in risk allocation, appropriate package sizes, and turnkey basis for the award of contracts. Similarly, the BOT and annuity frameworks were also essentially incentive-compatible though fewer stretches were to be built using these forms. The resulting investments were overwhelming and in a year or so more investments than in an entire decade flowed into the highway sector. The programme's economy-wide demand-side effects continue to be in force in the high growth of the economy since 2002. The approach and contract forms of the NHAI are also sought to be initiated by many state governments.

Airlines were thrown open to the private sector without much regulation except on the safety and technical aspects. Despite some major policy limitations such as not allowing private airlines (until recently) to operate on international routes, the airline industry has completely changed from the vantage point of the consumer. New segments have been added and air travel is no longer a luxury, and threatens to challenge an immovable railways in upper-class travel. Some improvements in roads, especially in the western and southern parts of the country, have suddenly made possible multiaxle trucks with their superior efficiency. 'Fast' buses on roads now challenge the railways in all classes of passenger travel.

Much the same is the story in overnight postal packages delivery. A private sector, despite the higher cost of duplication of services on account of numerous players, has made it nearly impossible for the high-priced state-owned carrier Speed Post to survive. In both airlines and posts, besides the superior operating efficiency of the private sector, the fact of significantly lower labour cost for the private sector is important. Unlike much of East Asia the long period of enclaved growth has created a schism in the labour market because of which the competitive labour market is not usually open to large firms or the state. Cost differences can be as high as eight times or more. So in privatization or in contracting out of services where competitive labour can be brought to bear, there are enormous cost savings.

In telecom, on the other hand, the basics of the regulation (price cap tariffs, independence, shift from licence fees to revenue sharing to lower risk, allowing multiple licencees to ensure competitive behaviour even if such entities were underscaled, but with no bar on merger and alliances) were right and the technology driver in reducing costs and increasing the coverage potential was high. For these two reasons telecom has grown very rapidly through both private and public investments. Telecom promises to cover all except the bottom 20 per cent or so of the population over the decade. For cellular telecom, India has the lowest tariffs in the world. Internet access has also grown by leaps and bounds and the much lower penetration of both telecom and Internet as compared to China is on account of factors that lie quite outside the sector (the income level in India being barely a fourth or less that of China, much better income distribution in China, besides higher levels of literacy and

education). Problems of quality especially in mobile services have surfaced, but are being systematically addressed by the regulator.

The political difficulties in reform of infrastructure have been overly highlighted in the discussion. The reality is otherwise. Where reasonable policy and institutional frameworks could be developed and put in place success has been spectacular. In almost all cases of slow movement or failure, the policy, regulatory, and subsidy frameworks, in creating perverse incentives for both consumer and service providers, are the core causes of failure. Corrections herein are also politically feasible. After all there is so much surplus hidden in the current deadweight losses that even vested interests could be overcome through innovative mechanisms that allow them benefits while avoiding the deadweight losses. Similarly the subsidies currently enjoyed by the genuinely deserving can be easily retained and even enhanced through reform. Thus today SEBs annually incur losses that are in excess of Rs 40,000 crore. Only a part, perhaps no more that Rs 12,000 crore, would be delivered to the farmer. The latter sum, if made available as a direct subsidy to farmers through coupons without distorting the allocative (use) price of electricity, would avoid these large losses and would be politically rewarding as well.

The ubiquitous poor have been the excuse to resist change. In the name of the poor the government's subsidy burden is of the order of 15 per cent of gross domestic product (GDP). In contrast, to correctly subsidize the poor all it would take is Rs 15,000 crore for infrastructure services, or about 0.75 per cent of the GDP. In infrastructure, the poor are the excuse to keep prices so low that they often get excluded. This happens in many ways. In drinking water in Delhi, despite the total production of more than 200 lpcd of water, as much as 30 per cent of the population uses less than 50 and some as low as 20. The price of water is low enough to make the large elastic demand of the rich compete with the inelastic (lifeline) demand of the poor to create denial, that is the non-availability of a necessity despite purchasing power. Large health losses and purchases of water in markets at prices that are many times the cost of production negate the large consumer surpluses in a necessity. Moreover, since producing entities are thereby starved of internal resources, there is underinvestment that creates permanent denial or 'outsiders' who have little hope of getting on to networks. The problem is further compounded by the usually high access charges when the use charges are so low. The misconception herein that the fundamental problem of lack of endowments can be solved by loading the problem on to infrastructure in the highly distortionary way of subsidizing use rather than access and that too through prices, is nevertheless shared widely among policymakers.

SEBASTIAN MORRIS

REFERENCES

Government of India (GOI). 1997. *The India Infrastructure Report*. Vols. I, II, and III, The Rakesh Mohan Committee, New Delhi, NCAER and GoI.

Morris, S., ed. 2001. *India Infrastructure Report 2001: Issues in Regulation and Industry Structure*, 3iNetwork, New Delhi, Oxford University Press.

———. ed. 2003. *India Infrastructure Report 2003: Public Expenditure Allocation and Accountability*, 3iNetwork, New Delhi, Oxford University Press.

———. 2004. *India Infrastructure Report 2004: Ensuring Value for Money*, 3iNetwork, New Delhi, Oxford University Press.

Morris, S. and Rajiv Shekhar, eds. 2002. *India Infrastructure Report 2002: Governance Issues for Commercialization*, 3iNetwork, New Delhi, Oxford University Press.

Raghuram, G., Rekha Jain, Sidharth Sinha, Prem Pangotra, and Sebastian Morris. 1999. *Infrastructure Development and Financing: Towards a Public Private Partnership*, New Delhi, Macmillan.

Ports and Shipping

PORTS

India has a coastline of over 5560 km. Twelve large and 185 medium and small ports serve it and 95 per cent of India's trade moves by sea. Major ports are controlled by the central government and minor ports by state governments. But there is immense potential for modernization and growth of Indian ports. The main problem is that, thanks to opposition from the unions, the government has not been able to modernize the major ports to the required extent. As a result, some experts believe that Indian ports are overmanned by as much as 90 per cent. This has a direct effect on efficiency. Political pressure, lack of autonomy, the absence of incentives, an excess of bureaucracy, and hierarchical rigidities have all contributed to the current state of Indian ports.

Compared to the larger international ports, India lags behind badly. Its ports handle only a fraction of the load—measured in TEUs (20-foot equivalent units)—that the world's biggest ports do. There are also problems with the average pre-berthing time which is about twice that in international ports. It can take a ship as many as four days to find a berth. These difficulties are primarily because of the poor road and rail container evacuation infrastructure from the port. The latter is not showing much signs of improvement, although, thanks to some sporadic reforms, there has been an increase in port and evacuation capacity. Nevertheless there is increasing congestion as a result of increased economic activity.

An attempt is now being made to develop satellite ports. The government intends to double the total capacity of major and non-major ports in the country by 2012—to 1500 million tonnes per annum (mtpa) from the current 750 mtpa.

Shippers also now have more choice and can choose between Mumbai Port, Jawaharlal Nehru Port (JNPT), and the privately owned ports of Pipapav and Mundra which have seen substantial investment by renowned players like Maersk, PSA, and P&O. These ports compete with each other, both on price and quality. It is fair to say that an era of real competition between ports has begun. But there is a long way to go before genuine efficiencies are induced.

Given the shortage of public funds, private participation is now being solicited. According to one estimate, as much as 85 per cent of the total investment requirement will have to come from private sources. Over a billion and a half dollars has so far been invested by foreign firms. The eventual potential is for around $35 billion. To make this possible, policies and procedures have also been significantly liberalized. The areas identified for private participation are leasing of existing assets of the port and allowing construction and creation of additional assets such as the construction and operation of container terminals, construction and operation of bulk, break bulk, multipurpose and specialized cargo berths, warehousing, container freight stations, storage facilities and tank farms, cranage/handling equipment, dry docking, and ship repair facilities. Leasing of equipment for port handling, leasing of floating craft, and captive facilities for port-based industries are also possible now. Foreigners can invest up to 51 per cent on an automatic basis in support services like operation and maintenance of piers and loading and discharging of vessels. Up to 100 per cent under the automatic route is permitted in projects for vehicular

tunnels, ports, and harbours. The BOT (build-operate-transfer) model is being used for private-sector participation, with assets reverting to the port after the concession period. Major ports have been permitted to form joint ventures with foreign ports, minor ports, and other companies to attract new technology and better management practices. Inputs and concessional import duty have been allowed. A ten-year tax holiday can be availed of in a block of fifteen years from 1 April 2002 under Section 80-IA of the Income Tax Act.

By amending the 1963 Major Ports Trusts Act, a tariff authority for major ports has also been set up. Some experts have argued that there is no longer any need for a regulator because the dismantling of the government monopoly over ports and the introduction of competition will take care of the pricing issues. But this argument has not found much favour, either in government or amongst operators.

The government has also decided to give a boost to coastal shipping by setting up a string of minor ports along the entire peninsula. This has met with a chorus of approval and disapproval. Objections vary from the economics of the project to the effect it will have on the ecology of the Mannar straits which would have to be deepened by dredging. Supporters say that by establishing small, low-cost ports with multi-modal connectivity to the hinterland at strategic locations along the coast, Sagarmala will give a fillip to coastal shipping and, therefore, to employment. The project is to be funded partly from the budget, partly by private investment, and partly by a cess meant for the purpose. The proposal for cess has been opposed by users.

SHIPPING
Between 1975 and 2005, like other capital-intensive businesses that required

large amounts of foreign exchange to be expended, the shipping business also became victim to the government's persistent worries over foreign exchange shortages. But the recent swelling in the volume of reserves has allowed the government to adopt more liberal policies. As a result, there has been a sharp increase in the tonnage owned by Indian shipping firms. The business has also started to return tidy profits.

A large and growing number of Indian nationals are now engaged in ship owning, management, and operations. But the falling share of the Indian shipping industry in the carriage of India's total overseas sea-borne cargo has been a cause of concern. The average age of the Indian fleet is almost seventeen. Over 31 per cent of the overseas fleet totalling 2.06 million gross registered tonnage (GRT) is more than 20 years old, while 26 per cent is between 15 and 19 years. Unlike ports, shipping has always been open to private investment but was constrained by illiberal operating rules and stringent financial procedures aimed at conserving scarce foreign exchange. However, in keeping with the spirit of the times, these have now been liberalized to facilitate the automatic approval of acquisition of ships and permission to retain sale proceeds for reinvestment. Cabotage laws have also been relaxed for container ships. Freight and passenger fares have been decontrolled to promote coastal shipping. Facilities on a par with the 100 per cent export oriented units are available for the ship repair industry. The results have been dramatic. In April 2004 the Indian shipping fleet was less than 7 million GRT. It has now crossed 8 million GRT and is growing. This growth comes after a hiatus of thirty years because between 1960 and 1975, GRT had grown from 0.50 million tonnes to 5 million tonnes. The surge in freight markets prompted Indian shipowners to go on an acquisition spree. The real fillip however, came from the introduction of tonnage tax, which considerably reduced the tax liability of shipowners. Certain things remain to be done, relating to depreciation and the taxing of personnel. These need to be reduced in line with international norms.

T.C.A. SRINIVASA RAGHAVAN

Railways

Railway transport in India began on 16 April 1853, with the passage of a train from Mumbai to Thane. In the century and a half since then, the railway network in India has grown to cover virtually all parts of the country. Only in the hilly regions of the north and north-east of India is the network relatively sparse. When India attained Independence in 1947, the total length of routes covered by the network was about 53,000 km, of which a meagre 388 km was electrified. From then until 2004, about 10,000 km have been added, not a very significant expansion over more than half a century. Obviously, much of the country had already been covered by the time of Independence. However, the total length of electrified segments has increased to over 17,000 km, almost 28 per cent of the total.

While the total length of the network remained relatively constant in the half century after Independence, its utilization increased manifold. Capacity expansions were achieved by a combination of factors—electrification, double lining, and increasing the number of wagons or coaches per train. Freight volumes carried by the system increased by about 8.7 times during the period 1950–2004. In the same period, the number of passengers carried increased by about 7.3 times. This growth in traffic was achieved on the basis of increases in the number of freight wagons and passenger coaches by multiples of 2.6 and 2.7 respectively, reflecting the importance of the other factors mentioned in the increased productivity of the system. One aggregate measure of productivity is 'train density', which is the ratio of total train kilometres operated to track kilometres. This parameter increased from 7.1 in 1950 to 15.2 in 2004.[1]

These magnitudes need to be viewed against the backdrop of aggregate changes to fully understand their significance. Over the 1950–2004 period, real gross domestic product (GDP) increased by a multiple of 10.2. Over the same period, the country's population increased by a multiple of 3. In proportion to GDP, therefore, railway freight traffic became a little less significant over the five decades. There is a very good reason for this. For the last two decades and more, the share of industry in GDP has remained stagnant at about a quarter. The share of agriculture has declined from about four-fifths to less than a quarter. Consequently, the share of services has risen from slightly over a third to over half of GDP. They have been by far the most significant contributor to GDP growth over the second half of the last century. Services, as a whole, are obviously far less dependent on commodity movements than industry. It is, therefore, not surprising that the growth in railway traffic has not kept pace with GDP growth.

By contrast, the growth in passenger traffic far outstripped the growth in population over the five decades. Clearly, as the significance of agriculture in the economy declined, more and more people felt the need to move out in search of employment. The railways met this need,

allowing people to travel longer distances at lower costs than other modes of mass transport. They played a significant role in creating a highly integrated national labour market, an important factor in the growth of the services sector.

AN ECONOMIC PERSPECTIVE

An economic perspective on the railways would have two broad components. One would address the causal relationships between railway activity and economic growth. The other would look at the organization and operation of the railway system in terms of its economic viability. Specifically, is the system as it is currently run able to generate resources adequate to maintaining operations as well as investing in maintenance, capacity expansion, and safety enhancement? In this entry, I take the first perspective as given and, having accepted the importance of the railways as a contributor to economic performance, focus on the second component, that is economic viability.

In recent years, many concerns have been expressed about the economic state of the Indian Railways. The essential problem is that the system is simply not generating adequate resources to fulfil the three critical objectives of maintenance, capacity expansion, and safety enhancement; in fact, it is barely able to meet its operating expenses. It is, therefore, quite dependent on transfers from the government to meet these objectives and, unless remedial steps are taken at once, this dependence will come sharply in conflict with the broader move towards fiscal discipline.

There are two main causes of this problem. First, operating as it does under persistent political compulsions, the system does not price its services on economic logic, with adverse consequences for revenue generation. Second, the system, despite the significant gains in productivity over the

[1] The data used in this paragraph are taken from various publications of the Ministry of Railways, Government of India and extracted from www.indiastat.com

last fifty years, discussed earlier, currently operates relatively inefficiently, which, apart from other factors, is itself a consequence of inadequate maintenance and investment.

PRICING AND REVENUES

A 'rational' pricing benchmark would require that the price of each of the services provided by the railways should reasonably reflect its costs. Within these constraints, there are various economic arguments for subsidizing one or more classes of consumers, either directly by way of transfers from the government or in the form of cross-subsidies from other classes of consumers. There are several practical lessons that have emerged from experience for the design of a viable subsidy mechanism that reasonably satisfies the combined interests of consumers (access to services), the system (financial viability), and the government (fiscal discipline). These lessons will undoubtedly influence the future course of the system and will be addressed in the concluding section. The fact, however, is that, historically, pricing decisions by the railways have generally tended to prioritize political objectives over economic ones. This has led to two major 'distortions'— departures from the benchmark.

First, pricing has tended to favour passenger traffic over freight traffic. Low-cost passenger transportation has been a high-priority objective for successive governments, a fact reflected in the discussion on relative magnitudes in the preceding paragraphs. In order to keep passenger fares as low as possible and still earn enough money to survive, freight rates have tended to be higher than the benchmark would warrant. As a result, freight customers have looked for substitutes and, over the years, many have shifted to road because of railway freight rates. Typically, rail freight is considered

to be more efficient for distances in excess of 250 km. Internal studies carried out in the mid-1990s revealed that a significant proportion of the freight traffic in the 250–700 km range had shifted to road, largely because of relative prices (Report of the Expert Group on Indian Railways 2001). One of the most important practical lessons on pricing is that it should take into account the availability of good substitutes. When these are there, raising prices will lead to declining revenues, as customers switch loyalties.

Second, within the passenger segment, lower class services have been underpriced, while upper class ones have been overpriced. For example, in 2003–4, lower class passengers constituted an overwhelming 98 per cent of the total, but contributed only 75 per cent of the revenues. Within this segment, the lowest service category, the 'second class ordinary', accounted for 71 per cent of the total passengers carried but only 16 per cent of total revenues. The last Railway Fare and Freight Committee, which made its recommendations as far back as 1993, had advocated a highest-to-lowest passenger fare ratio of 9.6. This ratio was as high as 14.4 in the late 1990s (Report of the Expert Group on Indian Railways 2001). Subsequent reductions in premium service fares have brought it down somewhat in recent years, but the impact of these discounts on revenues has been diluted by the steady increase in the affordability of air travel, which is the obvious substitute for potential upper class travellers.

Determining an optimal fare structure is obviously beyond the scope of this short entry, but it is obvious that the railways' earnings will always be constrained if it does not raise lower class fares. Equally obviously, there are significant political risks inherent in that move, which make it very difficult for any government to do so.

EFFICIENCY AND COSTS

The other dimension of financial viability is the cost of operating the system. As mentioned earlier, a key objective is to not only cover operating costs, but to generate enough surpluses to maintain assets in working condition, fund expansions where necessary, and continually enhance safety. One measure of the ability of the system to meet these multiple objectives is the 'operating ratio', which is the ratio of operating costs to total revenues. The lower this is, the larger the surplus left over to address the other critical objectives. This ratio was in the 80–90 per cent range in the early to mid-1990s, but increased sharply to 97 per cent in 2000–1, before coming down to around the 90 per cent mark in recent years.[2] The fact is, however, that at these levels, there is very little left over after meeting expenses to cater to the future. Maintenance slackens, reducing effective capacity of the system and the quality and safety levels it can offer its customers. This reinforces the movement towards road by shippers and towards air by travellers.

A discussion of specific parameters of productivity is beyond the scope of this entry, but one very important reason for the high burden of operating costs is the wage and salary bill of the system. Employment in the railway system peaked at around 1.6 million in the late 1990s; since then, there has been steady, if slow, attrition. However, attrition does not immediately reduce costs, because of lifetime pension commitments. Since the Indian Railways, like the rest of the government, used a 'pay-as-you-go' pension scheme until 2004, all pension commitments are paid out of general

[2]Railway financial performance indicators extracted from tables appearing on www.indiastat.com.

revenues. In the 2005–6 railway budget, the provision for pensions was Rs 7000 crore, almost 20 per cent of the 'ordinary working expenses', or operating costs (Ministry of Railways 2005). This commitment is unlikely to decrease in the foreseeable future, given the large number of retirees and increasing life expectancy. As an expenditure commitment, it dilutes the financial impact of any other efforts to increase efficiency and, through this, the pool of resources available to meet maintenance, investment, and safety objectives.

REFORMS AND THE FUTURE

Through all this, Indian Railways has been continuously attempting to deal with its problems, either directly or through by-pass solutions. Dramatic improvements may not have resulted, but the system continues to operate at some minimum acceptable standard of service delivery. In the freight business, value-added services were initiated through the Container Corporation of India, which provides a door-to-door service combining road and rail. In recent years, significant efforts have been made to realign the freight rates for a variety of commodities to the competitive situation in the marketplace. On the passenger side, expanding the premium services offered by the Rajdhani trains over long distances and the Shatabdis over short hauls has enhanced revenues, reinforced by more realistic pricing of these services.

However, the record shows that in the face of continuing resistance to a substantial adjustment of lower class passenger fares to more closely reflect the costs of providing them, the three critical objectives beyond merely keeping the trains running are elusive. The reform blueprint drawn up by the Expert Group on Indian Railways envisages the setting up of an independent tariff regulator to take political discretion out of the process of deciding fares. Once a 'rational' structure of freight tariffs and passenger fares is achieved and credibly managed by the regulator, the commercial viability that this induces will be able to attract private resources to make critical investments. Maintenance and safety will, of course, benefit from the increased flow of resources. Within this framework the government can, if it chooses, subsidize certain classes of customers on the basis of equity or regional development objectives, but persisting with the current emphasis on cross-subsidies is clearly at odds with revenue-enhancement objectives.

Given the importance of the railways for the country, providing the system the capability to meet the four objectives of operations, maintenance, investment, and safety is consistent with broader development objectives. This is not possible with marginal and peripheral changes. The core issue of rational pricing has to be tackled head on. If this is done, a system that has served the country for over a century and a half will get a new lease of life with a greater ability to meet the growing and evolving transportation requirements of the economy. If not, it will degenerate into a service used only by people who have no other choice and shunned by the rest, and find it increasingly difficult to live up to even the lowest expectations of quality and safety.

SUBIR GOKARN

REFERENCES

Report of the Expert Group on Indian Railways. 2001. The Indian Railways Report—2001: Policy Imperatives for Reinvention and Growth, New Delhi, NCAER and IDFC.

Ministry of Railways, Government of India. 2005. Railways Budget 2005–6, presented on 25 February.

Roads

The entire road network in India currently stands at 3.3 million km spanning the entire country, making it the second longest road network in the world behind the United States of America. The network includes national highways, state highways, major district roads, and other village roads. Use of the road network has increased dramatically throughout India's history with approximately 87 per cent of all passenger traffic and 65 per cent of all freight traffic currently on roads. However, despite this importance of roads for India, problems have plagued its infrastructure, including poor maintenance and inaccessibility of many villages.

India's oldest road is the Grand Trunk Road, which was built in the sixteenth century. Sher Shah Suri, the Emperor of India, attempted to link regional provinces for administrative and military purposes by building the road, which was at first called Sadak-e-Azam. After being used for transport and conquests, British rulers improved and renamed the road, sometimes calling it the 'Long Walk'. Today the road stretches for over 2500 km, connecting Calcutta with Kabul in Afghanistan, making it the longest road in the country.

Currently, expenditure on the road sector in India is approximately Rs 211 billion, accounting for less than 3 per cent of union and state government expenditures. However, the total tax revenue from the road sector amounts to 15.5 per cent of revenue, resulting in a revenue surplus of Rs 289 billion. The government's total tax revenue is composed of taxes on initial vehicle purchases, fuel, road freight and passengers, and collections from tolls. However, while the union and state governments' tax revenue from the road sector was Rs 500 billion, only 30 to 40 per cent was accounted for by annual road user charges (for example tolls).

The road network in India remains poorly funded for meeting the maintenance requirements for current roads. While the doubling of trucks on Indian roads has caused more extensive damage to the infrastructure, expenditure to improve and maintain roads has lagged behind. One of the major problems is the excessive expenditure on labour, which amounts to 60 to 70 per cent of expenditure on road maintenance. In addition to labour, asphalt, the dominant material in road construction, is produced by a few major oil companies, leaving very little production of other maintenance products. The government is beginning to use advanced materials, construct hot asphalt mix toll roads, and move towards less labour-intensive mechanized road maintenance, contributing to the creation of long-lasting all-weather roads. The cost for removing deficiencies in roads is extremely steep—removing deficiencies from National Highways would require Rs 1.65 trillion. Effort in expanding the road network has also lagged; the number of vehicles has grown by over 50 per cent, while the road network has grown by around 5 per cent. In order to keep up with the current rate of traffic growth, India would need to build 15,000 km of roads, costing Rs 1.5 trillion.

Of the 3.3 million km of roads in India, only 2 per cent, or 65,569 km are national highways, yet they carry 40 per cent of the traffic in India. A particular problem is the width of highways, of which only 2 or 3 per cent are four-laned and almost 15 per cent have only a single lane. In fact, only 34,298 km of national highways are actually suitable for speedy transportation.

In 1998, Prime Minister Atal Bihari Vajpayee launched the government's National Highway Development Project

(NHDP) to remove capacity constraints and improve all-weather connectivity. The funding for the NHDP comes from a Re 1 cess on each litre of diesel and petrol, amounting to Rs 20 billion per annum. On 9 December 1998, a Planning Commission task force decided on two components for the NHDP: a Golden Quadrilateral measuring 5846 km and the North–South and East–West Corridors measuring 7300 km. The Golden Quadrilateral consists of four major national highways connecting the four major regions of India: Delhi–Kolkata, Kolkata–Chennai, Chennai–Mumbai, and Mumbai–Delhi. Each of these highways is developed by Indian firms, joint ventures, and foreign firms. The North–South Corridor is designed to stretch from Kashmir to Kanyakumari, passing through major cities like Delhi, Hyderabad, and Bangalore. The East–West Corridor will begin in Silchar and end in Porbandar, passing through Lucknow, Udaipur, and Rajkot. Although many segments have been started between 1999 and 2001, much of the two highways still remains to be constructed. The first phase of the project was approved on 12 December 2000 at a cost of Rs 303 billion. The National Highways Authority of India predicts the majority of roads will be completed between 2005 and 2006.

The Pradhan Mantri Gram Sadak Yojana (PMGSY) programme was launched by the Government of India on 25 December 2000 to connect the 200 million people, or 330,000 habitations, lacking all-weather road access in India. The PMGSY programme was designed to further integrate the rural sector into the economy and allow easier access to healthcare and education services. On 23 September 2004, the World Bank Group approved a loan of US$ 400 million for the India Rural Roads Programme, which includes the PMGSY. By 2007, the government plans to provide all-weather road access to all habitations with population over 500, still leaving 50 million people without all-weather roads. The total cost for the project is estimated at just under US$ 600 million, of which almost two-thirds is in loans from the World Bank.

The Indian roads network stands to provide the country with great economic benefits if appropriately and quickly developed. According to the World Bank, the poor roads in India cause the nation an annual loss of between Rs 200 billion and Rs 300 billion. Development of India's road network should focus more on mechanizing road maintenance and continuing to provide tax incentives for private partnerships in road construction. However, at the same time there must be coordination in the government bureaucracy, as responsibility for roads spans several agencies and ministries. In addition, the road network in India must shift towards user charges through tolls and fuel taxes that are specifically used for road maintenance and construction, while encouraging further development of other transportation mechanisms, including the faltering railroad system.

PRITAL SAILESH KADAKIA

REFERENCES

Choudhary, Ajeet K., Deepak Dangayach, Prashant Dwivedi, Tarun Sharma, and P. Venu Madhav. 2001.'A Report on Road Sector in India', Ahmedabad, Indian Institute of Management, 24 August.
National Highways Authority of India, Government of India, http://www.nhai.org/.
World Bank Group.'Highway Sector Financing in India', http://www.highwayfinindia.org/.
———. 2004.'Project Appraisal Document on a Proposed Credit in the Amount of SDR 206 Million (US$ 300 Million Equivalent) and Proposed Loan in the Amount of US$ 100 Million to the Government of India for a Rural Roads Project', 16 August.

Space Satellites

India initiated a modest rocket-based space research programme in 1963 for carrying out basic scientific research in aeronomy and astronomy, but it soon embarked upon the development of a vibrant, totally self-reliant application-driven space programme, realizing the vast potential of space technology for tackling identified national tasks in the areas of communication, broadcasting, education, disaster management, weather forecasting, and management of natural resources. During the 1970s, the Indian Space Research Organization (ISRO) carried out a unique Satellite Instructional Television Experiment (SITE), using NASA's ATS-6 satellite, for regularly broadcasting developmental and educational programmes on health, hygiene, better agricultural practices, and family planning to 2400 remote villages in six clusters. A number of selected aerial remote-sensing surveys with multi-spectral and infra-red cameras were also conducted to demonstrate the potential of space remote sensing for agricultural and environmental monitoring, land-use planning, and forest management. ISRO took a major step in 1972 when it signed an agreement with the USSR Academy of Sciences to launch an Indian-built satellite on a Soviet rocket, which resulted in the establishment of the ISRO Satellite Centre at Bangalore, for the development and application of satellite technology.

The successful launching of Aryabhata, India's first satellite, weighing 360 kg, in April 1975, from Kapustin Yar near Volgagrad, established India's capability to design, fabricate, and launch space satellites. This was followed by the launch of two experimental remote-sensing satellites Bhaskara-1 and Bhaskara-2 in 1979 and 1981 respectively, each carrying a TV camera system for imaging at 1 km resolution and passive microwave radiometers for studying the dynamics and temperature distribution over the oceans. Parallelly ISRO undertook the development of a three-axis stabilized communication satellite called APPLE, weighing 670 kg and carrying two C-band transponders, which was launched into the geostationary orbit by the Arianne rocket in 1981 for communication and video broadcasting. The end-to-end experience gained from the design, fabrication, orbit raising, operation, and utilization of these experimental remote-sensing and communication satellites paved the way for India to emerge as one of the leading nations in satellite technology, capable of designing and launching state-of-the-art application satellites.

In order to achieve total self-reliance, parallel efforts were initiated at the Vikram Sarabhai Space Centre, Trivandrum, in the early 1970s, for the development of a modest launch vehicle SLV-3 which launched a 40 kg Rohini Satellite into a near-earth orbit. Sustained effort by ISRO scientists since then has enabled ISRO to develop a state-of-the-art PSLV (Polar Satellite Launch Vehicle) rocket capable of launching 2 ton remote-sensing satellites into a polar orbit and GSLV (Geostationary Satellite Launch Vehicle) rocket that can launch 2 ton satellites into a geostationary transfer orbit, making India totally self-reliant in space technology.

COMMUNICATION REVOLUTION THROUGH INSAT

Instead of following the conventional path of building separate communication and meteorological satellites, ISRO, from the start, decided to build cost-effective, multipurpose satellites combining all these services in a single geostationary spacecraft. To meet the immediate demand for nationwide TV broadcasting, ISRO decided to procure the INSAT-1 series of first-generation geostationary satellites from the Ford Aerospace Communication Corporation (FACC). These satellites weighing about 1150 kg carried 12 C-band communication transponders, two high-power S-band transponders for national TV coverage, and a Very High-Resolution Radiometer (VHRR) for meteorological imaging in the visible and thermal infrared bands over the Indian continent. Even though INSAT-1A built by the FACC failed within four months of its launch, the successful launch of INSAT-1B in August 1983 initiated a communication revolution in India. INSAT-1B was followed by two more first-generation INSATs for providing nationwide services in communication, broadcasting, and meteorological services in the 1980s.

With the experience gained from the successful design, fabrication, launching, and operation of APPLE, ISRO decided to indigenously design and fabricate the second-generation INSAT-2 series of satellites, weighing over 1900 kg and having much higher capacity than the first-generation INSATs. These satellites carried 12 C-band and 6 extended C-band transponders, 2 high-power S-band transponders, a data-relay transponder, and an improved VHRR with a resolution of 2 km in the visible and 8 km in the infrared. After the successful launch and operationalization of INSAT-2A in 1992, ISRO followed up with three more second-generation satellites, which, apart from the payloads launched on INSAT-2A, carried additional payloads for providing mobile communication, fixed satellite services, and Charge Coupled Device (CCD) cameras for augmenting meteorological capability. Growing requirement for fixed satellite services to address the communication needs of closed user groups resulted in the development of Very Small Aperture Terminals (VSAT), for receiving large volumes of data, audio, or video information directly from space. Rapid expansion of VSAT services and a growing demand from conventional communication and broadcasting services necessitated the development of third-generation INSATs. Since 2000, four third-generation INSAT-3 series of satellites, each weighing in excess of 2700 kg, have been launched to provide extensive communication capability in C, extended C, and Ku bands and also enhance the sensitivity of meteorological imaging. In addition, a dedicated meteorological satellite weighing 1 tonne and carrying meteorological imaging payload with water vapour channels, named Kalpana after astronaut Kalpana Chawla, was also launched on our indigenous launch vehicle GSLV, from the Satish Dhawan Space Centre, Sriharikota (SDSC) in 2002. The latest member of India's communication satellite fleet is Edusat, a dedicated satellite for the spread of education, which was launched from Sriharikota in 2003 on GSLV.

India, as of now, has one of the largest domestic communication satellite systems, with 150 communication transponders on eight satellites, providing a variety of communication and meteorological services to the country. With over 5500 two-way speech circuits covering about 143 routes and linking 704 earth stations of various sizes, the vast reach of INSAT satellites has been advantageously used for providing nationwide radio networking, administrative, business and computer communication, VSAT networking, and emergency communication services. More than 54,000 VSAT terminals including those installed by the National Informatics Centre (NICNET) are operating today to cater to the fast-growing requirements of both public and private closed user groups.

The most dramatic impact of INSAT has been in the rapid expansion of TV dissemination in India through the installation of about 1400 transmitters, providing 90 per cent of India's population access to national as well as regional services through sixty channels of telecasting. Use of transportable earth stations and Satellite News Gathering Vehicles now allows extensive real-time coverage of important events anywhere in the country. Recognizing the importance of the interactive communication system, a number of experiments have been conducted for imparting developmental education to target audiences of different types both in the rural and urban areas. Six developmental communication channels are being operated to broadcast programmes on technical education, agriculture, and vocational training, with the active involvement of state educational administrators and eminent teachers. The launch of Edusat, a dedicated educational satellite for broadcasting curriculum-based lessons to students and teachers in universities and technical institutions, has given a big boost to the expansion of the tele-education service.

Telemedicine, which extends specialized medical facilities even to people in remote rural areas by connecting them with medical experts located at specialty hospitals in major cities, has emerged as another major satellite application. Telemedicine consists of linking customized medical software integrated with computer hardware, at each rural location, with a super specialty hospital through satellite-based VSAT. The medical history of the patient including X-ray, ECG, and other diagnostic records is transmitted to specialist doctors, who can diagnose and advise on the course of treatment through videoconference with the doctor and paramedic at the patient's end. Since the establishment of ISRO's telemedicine network 18 months ago, it has already expanded to cover 88 remote area hospitals in several states, which are connected to 27 Super Speciality Hospitals, and has helped over 100,000 patients receive tele-consultation treatment.

REMOTE SENSING FOR NATIONAL RESOURCE MANAGEMENT

With the successful launch of its first operational Indian Remote-Sensing Satellite IRS-1A in 1988 from Bikonur, ISRO became the fifth country in the world to carry out remote sensing from space. Both the first-generation remote satellites IRS-1A and 1B, carried CCD cameras for taking multispectral imageries with a resolution of about 36 m, matching the capability of contemporary US-operated LANDSAT satellites. The second-generation IRS-1C and 1D launched in 1995 and 1997 respectively carried improved cameras with a resolution of 23 m in the multispectral and just 5.6 m in the panchromatic bands, the best available in the world at that time. The successful launch of the highly sophisticated technology satellite in 2001, capable of imaging at a resolution of just 0.8 m, and the subsequent launching of RESOURCESAT in 2003 and CARTOSAT in 2005, which in addition to very high-resolution and frequent revisit facilities also includes the capability to take three-dimensional images, have fully established India as a world leader in space remote sensing.

The IRS system has become invaluable for mapping spatial as well as temporal changes in soil characteristics, land-use patterns, forest resources, agricultural inventories, fisheries, and wastelands in the country. IRS imageries are now regularly employed to identify underground water aquifers, map surface water bodies, estimate snow melt run-off, delineate water-logged regions, and predict acreage and yield of all major crops. Regular bi-weekly bulletins demarcating potential fishing zones in the ocean, based on ocean temperature and phytoplankton distribution, are routinely distributed to all the fishing centres to help fishermen obtain improved fish catch. Space remote sensing has become the most important tool for urban planning, wasteland mapping, mineral prospecting, coastal monitoring, and environmental management. A unique application of IRS data has been in the Integrated Mission for Sustainable Development (IMSD), for generating locale-specific prescriptions to enhance agricultural productivity on a sustainable basis, using space and bio-technological inputs, and thus usher in the new Ever Green Revolution.

Since the 1980s, ISRO has been regularly monitoring cyclones, floods, and other natural disasters and providing advance warning wherever possible. Remote-sensing imageries have become invaluable in identifying and demarcating hazard-prone areas. Locale-specific advance warning on drought using space data on vegetation index, a measure of vegetation vigour, is now regularly transmitted to all drought-prone districts of the country. India's remote-sensing satellites have also been regularly mapping environmental pollution including forest fires, oil spills, and land degradation. While predictions of earthquakes and to some extent tsunamis are still far from being exact, remote-sensing imageries are extensively employed for disaster assessment and post-disaster rehabilitation. India was the first country to develop a comprehensive cyclone-warning system to provide locale-specific disaster alerts to areas likely to be affected by cyclones and floods, which has saved thousands of lives and livestock over the years, in the coastal areas of our country.

The Indian Space Programme, which had a modest beginning in 1963 has, over the last four decades, built up impressive capability and a high degree of self-reliance in the development and application of space technology. Space technology applications now encompass communication, TV broadcast, education, meteorological prediction, management of natural resources, agriculture, environment, disaster management, and sustainable integrated development, practically touching all aspects of human endeavour. ISRO has so far launched forty satellites, half of them from Sriharikota using its own indigenously developed rockets. The cumulative expenditure of the Indian Space Programme during the last four decades since its inception—including the vast infrastructure build-up of extensive test facilities, launch pads, control centres, tracking network, and regional centres for promoting application of space technology for a variety of national tasks—is a modest Rs 22,000 crore (US$ 8 billion), just about half of NASA's annual budget, which makes the Indian Space Programme a very cost-effective one.

U.R. RAO

Telecommunications

Spurred by rapid innovations in digital technology, the telecommunications sector has been one of the most dynamic areas of the Indian economy. Development of this sector has also been aided by policy reform, and, arguably, could have been even more impressive if this reform had taken place more smoothly and quickly. In 2005, India had 44 mainlines and 113 fixed and mobile line subscribers per 1000 people. As a benchmark, the corresponding figures for China were 266 and 565 respectively (International Telecommunications Union data). China's growth rates have also been considerably higher than India's, on average. This comparison may not be conclusive, but does indicate that telecommunications penetration in India has some distance to go. The particular interest in the telecommunications sector arises from its role in reducing transactions costs in the economy, democratizing information access, and spillover benefits for the rest of the economy. Modern telecommunications are a prime example of the power of digital technologies, simultaneously increasing the richness and reducing the cost of long-distance information exchange.

The historical case for regulation or for nationalized provision in telecommunications (telecoms) was based on economies of scale, implying that competition would be unstable or inefficient. India, like most countries, chose this route, with telephone provision under a department of a central ministry. Telephones were treated as a luxury good, their availability was severely rationed, and equipment and service quality were typically quite poor. Technological change removed the justification for monopoly in significant portions of the telecoms value chain, by lowering fixed costs and adding new technological options, allowing competition to become feasible. New technologies have included satellites, wireless, and fibre optics. Since market power may persist in portions of the value chain, in particular with respect to ownership of large networks, regulation of interconnection charges is still required to maintain a level playing field. However, directly managing technology choices and competition is difficult to justify on any grounds, economic or otherwise. The main policy objective should be to promote competition, and possibly innovation, though the former may well be sufficient to drive the latter.

POLICY REFORMS

India's telecoms reforms were pre-dated by successful efforts in the 1980s to expand rural access (and that of the urban poor) by allowing private operators of phone booths for local and long-distance calls. However, ownership of the network and provision of services remained a government monopoly. Telecoms connections with the rest of the world were particularly limited. Beginning in 1991, a general reorientation of government policy towards allowing more market-based allocation of goods was an important backdrop for telecoms reform. At the same time, the meteoric rise of the export-oriented Indian information technology (IT) services industry in the 1990s created pressure for improving telecoms infrastructure, in particular external access.

The IT industry uses international data links for accessing clients' hardware, communicating by e-mail, exchanging files among joint development teams, and carrying out remote diagnosis and maintenance work. IT-enabled services use voice lines for call centres, and data lines for transmitting electronic files back and forth. Internet-based media companies also require data links. While all economic activity requires good communications infrastructure, the rapid rise of the Internet increased such needs. Some physical infrastructure investments were made to serve IT industry needs, beginning in the 1990s. More importantly, two successive attempts were made, in 1994 and 1999, to reshape telecoms policy in a world where technological change in that sector was accelerating. Private firms were allowed into the nascent wireless/mobile telecoms sector, through auctions of licences. Despite corruption and mistakes in the design of licensing agreements, this, on the whole, significantly improved telecoms access for India's population. Liberalization and reform were extended to other aspects of the telecoms infrastructure, such as new fibre optic networks. The external gateway provider, Videsh Sanchar Nigam Limited (VSNL), was also eventually privatized.

As part of the reform process, India created a new regulatory institution for telecoms, the Telecom Regulatory Authority of India (TRAI). The TRAI was constituted in 1997, but was relatively ineffective due to lack of authority and interference by the Department of Telecommunications.

The TRAI was given greater and clearer authority in 2000 (Dossani 2002), and has evolved into a somewhat effective regulatory body. The scope of the TRAI includes establishing quality-of-service parameters, monitoring compliance, and examining technology choices. It is supposed to establish a level playing field and encourage competition, but it still lacks authority precisely where it needs it the most, in setting entry fees and some interconnection charges. Unfortunately, bringing quality of service, technology choice, and universal service obligations (USOs) into the regulatory mix has only served to muddy the waters and divert attention from what should be the core regulatory task of enabling and maintaining effective competition. The TRAI has also continued to struggle with political pressure that comes from the needs of the government-owned former monopoly provider of telephone services, now a state-owned enterprise christened Bharat Sanchar Nigam Limited (BSNL). There have been continued concerns about favourable treatment of this strong incumbent vis-à-vis private entrants.

RURAL ACCESS

Special treatment of the BSNL has been justified by its extensive penetration in rural India and its obligations to provide broader telecoms access. In fact, USOs were also built into licensing deals for the new private service providers. These have taken the form of (1) quantitative targets for installing rural telephones, and (2) funds created through a form of tax on basic service, to be used for proposed subsidies for rural users. However, it is not clear that the numerical targets have been of any use, in a situation where licensing and interconnection fees made it uneconomical for local access providers with lower-cost technology to enter. The distinction between rural users in general and shared access (through, for example, public call offices or Internet kiosks) is crucial, and was made clear in a dissenting comment by committee member Rakesh Mohan but not accepted by the majority of a TRAI committee that reported on the USOs (TRAI 2001).

An alternative to quotas, which are difficult to monitor and enforce, may be a narrowly targeted subsidy for enabling reliable rural telecoms access. Given the technological convergence that has taken place, with telephony, television, and Internet data all able to share large portions of the same infrastructure, a subsidy that allows Internet kiosks to be commercially viable may be least costly, since these kiosks may be in the best position to break even by providing a broad range of information and communication services. The greatest barrier to commercial viability is lack of access to low-cost, reliable connectivity to the network. The example of cable services in India, which are typically priced at Rs 100 to Rs 200 per month and have over 50 million subscribers, provides a useful benchmark. At this kind of price point, however, a rural telecoms operator in India cannot recover set-up costs for access, which are about Rs 40,000 using conventional technologies. Technological innovations alone may not bring down the cost of combined Internet and voice access to Rs 10,000, which would

make access affordable to 50 per cent of Indian households at current income levels. Unnecessary restrictions and high fees, including interconnect charges, licensing fees and deposit requirements for entry, restrictions on franchising, and limited bandwidth allocations, all work to raise rural telecoms access costs. Removing these institutional barriers, or providing some inframarginal subsidy for rural infrastructure build out, may be the best way to ensure acceleration of growth of telecoms in rural areas.

The available technological options for rural telecoms infrastructure have been multiplying. These include WLL (wireless-in-local-loop—these technologies can use single tall towers with line-of-sight, or more numerous, smaller towers; the former is currently the common approach but the latter is likely to replace it), fibre optic cables, and high-powered versions of Wi-Fi and Wi-Max (802.11 and 802.16 wireless standards respectively). The Internet boom of the 1990s pushed down costs and sped up innovation in fibre optics and wireless transmission. In some cases (in particular the *e-choupals* set up by the ITC, an Indian agribusiness conglomerate), VSAT (very small aperture terminal) satellite connectivity has been used for rural Internet access, but it is not cost effective. In any case, closed-ended subsidies to deploy these technologies may be justifiable in terms of social returns. One way to implement such a subsidy would be to use USO funds collected from telecommunications providers to finance improved rural ICT (information and communication technology) access (Dossani et al. 2005). This approach is distinct from government schemes to directly set up and operate rural Internet kiosks— those are more likely to suffer from incentive and cost problems than the hybrid private franchise models of organizations such as n-Logue and Drishtee. These organizations combine private income-earning motives at lower levels with high-level social objectives monitored by non-profit ownership.

Combining Internet and voice access in an economical manner through Internet kiosks also has the benefit of increasing the value of connecting to the network. The benefits would accrue not just to the poor, but also to the tens of millions of lower middle class households who are currently outside the affordability radius. Social returns can include better governance, as well as knowledge, which is an important enabler of 'empowerment' or 'development as freedom' (Sen 1999). A denser domestic network can increase the value of the network and of international links to it. Digital convergence means that separating voice from data in formulating policies for rural access no longer makes sense. Also, calls to focus on mobile phone access rather than Internet kiosks (*Economist* 2005) neglect the convergence in technologies as well as the different functions served by the two access modes. Shared mobile phones are very effective for certain types of communication, and their capabilities keep increasing. Hence they represent an important component of rural telecoms access. However, for many types of information access, where quantity and ease of reading and processing matter more than mobility, the use of desktop computers is more efficient. In addition, a desktop computer with a printer is able to provide a wide range of services that are not communication related, but just involve processing of information. Recently, the cost of desktop systems has fallen dramatically, making the economics of rural Internet kiosks more attractive, provided that telecoms infrastructure constraints can be overcome.

To summarize, telecoms have changed dramatically over the last two decades, due to rapid innovation centred on digital technologies. In addition to traditional voice communications, all kinds of data and information can now be exchanged through modern telecoms networks. In India, some of the benefits of these developments have been realized through policy reforms that have permitted more competition and private entry, leading to greater investment and cost savings that are passed on to consumers. Nevertheless, telecoms regulation in India has not been ideal, and government policy has not focused adequately on ways to stimulate cost-effective provision of telecoms access to rural India, where the majority of the country's population still resides. This makes sense from an economic perspective, if one accepts that there are positive externalities that can be reaped from wider telecoms access.

NIRVIKAR SINGH

REFERENCES
Dossani, Rafiq. 2002. *Telecommunications Reform in India*, Westport, CT, Quorum Books.
Dossani, Rafiq, D.C. Mishra, and Roma Jhaveri. 2005. 'Enabling ICT for Rural India', Project Report, Stanford University and National Informatics Centre, India.
Economist. 2005. 'The Real Digital Divide, Technology and Development Survey', *The Economist*, 10 March.
Sen, Amartya K. 1999. *Development as Freedom*, New York, Alfred Knopf; New Delhi, Oxford University Press, 2000.
Singh, Nirvikar. 2006. ICTs and Rural Development in India, Project Report for Rajiv Gandhi Institute for Contemporary Studies, New Delhi.
TRAI. 2001. TRAI Recommendations on Universal Service Obligation (USO), 3 October. Available at http://www.trai.gov.in/Recommendations_content.asp?id=61.

POPULATION, LABOUR, AND EMPLOYMENT

Agricultural Labour

Agricultural labourers constitute a large section of the rural population in India—26 per cent in 2001. A sizable proportion of female workers in rural areas are agricultural labourers—about 36 per cent in 2001. The proportion of agricultural labourers in the rural workforce has, however, declined—from 50 per cent in 1991 to 30 per cent in the 2001 Population Census. The Labour Force Surveys of the National Sample Survey Organisation (NSSO), however, do not show such a drastic decline of agricultural labourers in rural areas, in fact they remain more or less steady at 30 per cent of the workforce during the 1990s.

Agricultural labourers are drawn from the most socially and economically deprived sections of rural hierarchy and are hence doubly disadvantaged and vulnerable. About 49 per cent of scheduled caste households were agricultural-labour households in 1999–2000, though this proportion had declined from 52 per cent in 1983. The proportion of agricultural-labour households among the scheduled tribes, however, rose from 33 to 38 per cent during the period.

'ATTACHED' VERSUS 'FREE' LABOUR

An agricultural labourer may enter into a contract with an employer of his own free will, in which case he is a 'free' casual labourer. He may, however, enter into a contract due to a pre-existing obligation arising from customary social relations or on account of credit and/or land relations. This form of 'attached' or 'bonded' labour has its role in the functioning of the overall market for agricultural labourers. Several historical studies showed that as agriculture developed and became commercial there was a general tendency to move from labour contracts signifying relatively little freedom for the workers to freer, more impersonal forms of contract. Inter-generational bondage characterized by extra-economic coercions also tended to decline.

In recent times, however, other types of attachment, not necessarily of an unfree nature, arose due to the exigencies of the production process. Modernization of agricultural technology had increased the demand for a form of attached labour as it was seen as useful in overseeing the work of casual labourers (Bardhan 1984). The interlinking of labour and land markets through various forms of tenancy and sharecropping arrangements has been common in India. One of the most common sharecropping contractual arrangements was that output was shared equally between the tenant and landlord, and so were input costs, but labour and seeds were provided by the tenant. This is, therefore, in a sense a disguised 'attached' labour contract. Leasing out of small pieces of land to tenants on 'fixed' rent also exists, but is perhaps less common. A form of reverse tenancy has also been observed in some parts of India, where the small landholders, unable to cultivate their land, lease out to the large holders. 'Operation Barga' successfully conducted in the state of West Bengal was a legal recognition of various forms of tenancy arrangements and this has proved useful in increasing the productivity of farms.

LAND DISTRIBUTION AND DIVERSIFICATION

The decennial landholding surveys indicate an increase in semi-landlessness (less than 0.2 ha) from 37 to 42 per cent of rural households, and marginal landholdings (0.002 to 1.01 ha) from 62 to 72 per cent during 1972–92. Even though the proportion of completely landless households (11 per cent) has not increased much in the last decade, a large proportion of the semi-landless and marginal landholders would be working as casual agricultural labourers. The Rural Labour Enquiry data also showed that the proportion of labour households with cultivated land had increased over the period. This corroborates the earlier observation that these labour households are actually semi-landless and marginal landholders who are forced to enter the wage labour market often due to failure of the monsoon or because their small plots of poor-quality land do not yield enough to sustain the household (Unni 1997).

There has been increasing casualization of the total workforce in rural areas, with contradictory evidence on the decline in the proportion of agricultural labourers. The declining fortunes of agriculture discussed later could have resulted in a lack of demand for agricultural labour. An interesting feature of the labour households observed in the Rural Labour Enquiries was the decreasing proportion of wage earners despite casualization. This trend reflects an increasing diversification of economic activities among labour households. This diversification into non-wage activities is partly due to the increase in labour households with cultivated land. The avenues open for self-employment are obviously greater in such households. The diversification of economic activites in labour households over time was also reflected in the declining percentage of days in a year spent in wage employment (Unni 1997).

Overall this implied that the character of the recent entrants to the agricultural labour force had changed. The proportion of scheduled caste households in agricultural labour declined while that of scheduled tribe households increased. Agricultural labourers now also increasingly belonged to broader caste groups and were households with small landholdings and a diversified portfolio of economic activities.

MIGRATION: A SYMPTOM OF POOR AGRICULTURAL PERFORMACE

That all is not well with the agricultural sector in large parts of India is reflected in the shrinking share of the rural gross domestic product (GDP) and particularly rural GDP including agriculture in total GDP during the decade 1980 to 1990 (Unni and Rani 2005). This may of course also reflect increasing urbanization and the growth of the industrial and service sectors as is expected with economic development. The economic reforms since 1991 tended to concentrate on the secondary and tertiary sectors with less importance being accorded to agriculture. Massive public investments in agriculture occurred in the 1970s that supported the agricultural system, such as large irrigation projects. Such investments have declined considerably in the last decade.

Lack of water for irrigation and casual development of the semi-arid regions have led to increase in migration from rural to rural and urban areas.

Lack of irrigation facilities, low productivity of land, and uncertain monsoons lead to single-crop cultivation and strengthen the pressure to migrate. A circular mobility of labourers occurs as a consequence of unbalanced resource endowments and regional development. This is in the nature of distress migration. On the one hand, there is a net transfer of slack labour from the backward areas to relatively developed areas in the form of seasonal migration. In some areas the demand for labour in the peak season cannot be met by the local supply of labour and these areas attract agricultural labourers from outside. Such circular migration can also be to the urban areas where rural migrants do not settle permanently in cities and continue to maintain their links with the area of origin, where they return regularly. Another form of migration is of a more permanent nature with the settlement of migrants in urban areas.

POVERTY DEBATE

Debate on the changing economic conditions of agricultural labourers has raged since the 1970s and continues till today. While no one can deny that agricultural labourers form the lowest deciles of the poor, it is debated whether their conditions have improved over time. In the 1970s the discussion was on whether the conditions of the agricultural workers had improved since the advent of the green revolution. More recently the debate is on whether the economic reforms of the 1990s have benefited rural labourers.

Attempts at theorizing on the rural labour markets have focused on the process of wage determination. In attempting to empirically determine whether the status of agricultural labourers had improved, the arguments have focused on the real

wage rates. While many argued that the trickle-down effects of the green revolution were beginning to reach agricultural labourers reflected in a rise in real wage rates, others argued that the trickling of benefits was restricted to a few states where the organization of workers was strong. However, much of this debate was based on male wages alone. Jose (1978) argued that real wages alone did not tell the real story and the quantum of employment available in terms of days of work was important in determining the real incomes received by these workers. Further, the rise in real wage rates in the 1980s has been attributed to the massive public expenditures on public works (Sen 1996).

A similar argument showing that economic reforms had improved the economic condition of casual workers in the 1990s was also based on the real wage rates (Sundaram 2001). There have been few attempts to look behind these aggregate figures towards the declining capacity of the poor to obtain adequate nutrition or the lack of association between economic growth and poverty reduction and the declining employment elasticity of output.

ORGANIZATION OF LABOUR

The traditional organization of agricultural labourers in India was in trade unions, most of which were under a political party. These mainly concentrated on economic demands such as increase in the wage rates and implementation of statutory minimum wages. This strategy, however, yielded positive results only in some regions of the country such as Kerala, Andhra Pradesh, and Punjab. Mobilization of labour by the leftist political parties was along class lines. Agricultural labourers are deprived of land and resources, and organization helped them resist the oppression of the dominant classes. The Bahujan Samaj Party mobilized labourers around the understanding that caste-based oppression of the lower castes (dalits) is the root cause of exploitation of the poor. The traditional high castes deprived the lower castes of means of production and used the caste system to force them into adopting this occupation (Gill 1998).

A more recent form of organization has been through non-governmental organizations (NGO) and voluntary groups. These organizations take up more broad-based issues pertaining to agricultural labourers and other groups at grassroots level. Here the focus is not just on economic issues such as minimum wages, but also on acquisition of cultivable wastelands and forests for cultivation, supply of food grains, legal aid, healthcare, and social security issues. Only a few of these NGOs have taken up an anti-state position, while many of them have acted as agents for the government, taking up implementation of official programmes (Gill 1998). The limitation of NGOs and voluntary organizations is that they remain confined to local areas and are unable to mobilize a mass base at national level, unlike political parties, and hence rarely have much bargaining power.

A new strategy adopted in recent years is that NGOs often join together in loose networks of grassroots organizations linking local communities to one another (Fisher 2003). They join together to work on certain specific issues or a clearly drawn up agenda. This is done to improve their powers of negotiation. Networks are formed through alliances between NGOs, membership-based organizations, federations of trade unions, cooperatives, and savings and credit groups.

STATE RESPONSE TO ISSUES OF AGRICULTURAL LABOURERS

The Minimum Wages Act was adopted in India as early as 1948. The Act requires the government to fix minimum rates of wages in respect of employment specified in a Schedule, including agriculture. While the implementation of this Act is not monitored, it provides trade unions and NGOs with a legal weapon to fight for the cause of agricultural labourers.

The issue of lack of demand for agricultural labour and consequent seasonal migration is addressed by the government through rural public-works programmes. The government sponsors these public works as a form of insurance against the shock of drought. In theory the public-works programme can play multiple roles such as alleviation of poverty, construction of infrastructure, and environmental protection. All these together can help mitigate the problem of lack of demand for agricultural labour. However, in reality all these goals are rarely achieved.

In the state of Maharashtra, the Employment Guarantee Scheme initiated the public-works programme on a more permanent basis. It has been lauded as a successful programme where it works almost as a model of the right to work. The workers are entitled to paid work and can demand public employment on rural works.

The Government of India has recently sought to universalize this programme for the country by attempting to bring in an Employment Guarantee Act, which has been approved by the Cabinet. This Act has faced a lot of controversy regarding the resources needed to implement it on a countrywide basis. Currently the draft Act confines itself to providing 100 days of work per family in a limited set of backward districts.

In the early 1970s, the state started to address the problems of marginal and small farmers through the Integrated Rural Development Programme (IRDP), providing credit to farmers to undertake agriculture. This was meant to prevent marginal farmer households from deteriorating into agricultural labour. Several versions of this programme continue with varying degrees of success.

To address the problems of agricultural labourers the state needs to have a holistic policy towards investments in agriculture, particularly in semi-arid regions. In recent years the watershed development programme is an attempt in this direction, though with debatable success.

JEEMOL UNNI

REFERENCES

Bardhan, P. 1984. *Land, Labour and Rural Poverty: Essays in Development Economics*, New Delhi, Oxford University Press.

Fisher, J. 2003. *Non-governments: NGOs and the Political Development of the Third World*, Jaipur, Rawat Publications.

Gill, S.S. 1998. 'Unionising Agricultural Labour: Some Issues', in R. Radhakrishna and A.N. Sharma, eds, *Empowering Rural Labour in India: Market, State and Mobilisation*, New Delhi, Institute for Human Development.

Jose, A.V. 1978. 'Real Wages, Employment and Income of Agricultural Labourers', *Economic and Political Weekly*, 13(12): A16–A20.

Sen, A. 1996. 'Economic Reforms, Employment and Poverty', *Economic and Political Weekly*, 31 (35–7): 2459–77.

Sundaram, K. 2001. 'Employment and Poverty in India in the 1990s: Further Results from NSS 55th Round Employment-Unemployment Survey, 1999–2000', *Economic and Political Weekly*, 36(32): 3039–49.

Unni, J. 1997. 'Employment and Wages among Rural Labourers: Some Recent Trends', *Indian Journal of Agricultural Economics*, 52(1): 59–72.

Unni, J. and U. Rani. 2005. 'Gender and Non-farm Employment', in R. Nayyar and A.N. Sharma, eds, *Rural Transformation in India: The Role of the Non-farm Sector*, New Delhi, Institute of Human Development.

Brain Drain

The costs and benefits of the brain drain from India have been heavily debated with Indians having emigrated to a variety of countries including the United States, the United Kingdom, Australia, and the Middle Eastern and African countries. The magnitude of the brain drain has significantly increased from the 1970s onwards. Due to the current trend of skilled Indian professionals emigrating to the United States, research on the brain drain from India revolves largely around the United States and educated workers. In the 1990s, along with India's liberalization, the emigration of Indians to developed countries, particularly the United States, steadily increased. Prior to 1990, the United States issued only the H-1 visa, aiding domestic employers in finding temporary workers. This visa required an expression of intent to return by the recipient. However, with the Immigration Act of 1990, this provision was replaced by the H-1B visa which allowed the recruitment of foreign workers by employers in the United States for a duration of six years. The provision further included a limit on the number of visas issued annually, a number that rapidly increased throughout the 1990s. Though initially most of the H-1B visas were given to healthcare professionals, since 1999, 60 per cent of H-1B recipients have been from the information technology (IT) sector. In the same year, Indians received 48 per cent of the H-1B visas and comprised three-fourths of the IT-sector employees with H-1B visas that year, according to the US General Accounting Office in 2000. Half of the 400,000 H1-B visas provided by the United States were issued to Indians (Desai et al. 2004). As this number is continually high, it accounts for a significant loss of

Indian professionals and educated labour force within India. This disproportionate loss of educated people, it is argued, is a big cost for India. Others argue that the brain drain actually results in a brain gain through the remittances and information networks emigrant Indians provide to those in India. This has led to a revival of interest in the implementation of the 'Bhagwati Tax', which entails the taxation of all Indian nationals regardless of their location of residence, and the emergence of a reverse brain drain, with the entrance of Indians and foreign nationals into India.

The costs of the brain drain from India are substantial according to recent projections. In the United Nations Human Development Report 2001, the cost of the brain drain to India is estimated to reach $2 billion in lost resources annually. With more than 100,000 professionals leaving each year on average, particularly in the computer industry, the government loses the $15,000 to $20,000 it spends on every university student. In addition, there is loss of the income stream of the educated people, who disproportionately leave, leading to a decrease in the Indian tax base (United Nations 2001). The loss of educated workers would further have negative repercussions in India due to the scarcity of skilled workers to begin with. In addition, the trend of tertiary education professors, particularly in technological fields, and of teachers, teaching from grades kindergarten to the twelfth, emigrating to the United States and the United Kingdom, threatens the educational base of India and its future quality. As the number of postgraduates in India is very low, particularly in the technology sectors, this will exacerbate the issue of widely prevalent teacher vacancies, particularly in postgraduate schools. Furthermore, for the adaptation and development of new technologies, it is necessary for there to be a stock of well-educated individuals within India (Desai et al. 2004).

With regard to taxation, there are many possible policy implications that are currently being debated. The brain drain impacts the taxation base of the Indian economy, with significant losses of direct taxes on the high income of skilled workers who emigrate. This loss accounts for about 12 per cent of India's current tax base. In addition, a major part of India's tax revenue is derived from indirect taxes and the loss of skilled workers further emphasizes the importance of indirect taxes relative to direct taxes (Desai et al. 2004).

There are many ways that the Indian government could potentially attempt to tax Indian emigrants. The easiest way would be for the Indian government to charge an exit fee, which serves as a flat tax, which is paid when the visa is granted. The value of this exit fee could be equal to the charges of headhunters (two months' salary), which are estimated to be approximately $10,000. This fee could either be paid by the employee emigrating or the firm in the host country. Revenues from such a flat tax, which could add up to $1 billion annually, could be used towards more investment in higher education by the government to increase the skill base within India. In addition, a future policy implication would involve taxation on the basis of nationality, as the current United States taxation system operates. The Indian government can balance the costs of the brain drain by following the United States model of taxing by citizenship. In order for this to be executed, it would entail the negotiation of bilateral tax treaties. These tax revenues could be used to redistribute income and subsidize education for lower classes. In addition, university students could be required to take a loan, equal in value to the subsidy that the state provides, to be repaid if the student leaves the country.

In addition, countries such as South Korea are launching programmes with competitive incentives for skilled and educated workers to return through attractive wages and provisions. Hence they will return with skills they have acquired abroad (United Nations 2001). India could also consider such policies.

Even without such policies, there are benefits to the brain drain, primarily through the channels of remittances and network effects. Remittances are important in India because of credit and liquidity constraints due to imperfect local capital markets, particularly in rural areas. Hence remittances from Indians working abroad are a steady stream of financial resources which impact the education, investment, and consumption decisions made by those living in India (Docquier and Rapoport 2004). The importance of remittances has significantly increased with remittances accounting for 1.21 per cent of the gross domestic product (GDP) in 1991, rising to 2.21 per cent in 2001 (Desai et al. 2004). In addition, many returning emigrants bring back saved income which contributes to the Indian economy often in the form of innovation and entrepreneurship.

The network effects of the brain drain from India have been significant due to India's openness to innovation and rapid growth in the 1990s. They include increased trade between India and the host country, foreign direct investment, spread of technology, and migration. This impact has been referred to as 'brain circulation' and 'brain exchange' (United Nations 2001). For example, Indians from the Silicon Valley played an important role in the development of the IT sector in Bangalore and Indians from the Silicon Valley and other technology hubs make contributions to Indian universities, increasing their endowments. In addition, the success of

Indians, particularly in the IT sector and Silicon Valley, has created a worldwide image of Indian success in the sector, helping its growth in India. Furthermore, Indians in the United States play a significant role in the hiring of Indian nationals with ten of the top twenty-five employers of foreign workers being Indian companies or companies run by Indian nationals. In addition, Indians running 'front offices' in the United States have started manufacturing plants in India, providing valuable training in technology (Desai et al. 2004). Hence there is an increase in the exchange between India and the United States and other host countries through such network effects which is beneficial for India.

Another debated benefit is the incentive to invest more in education due to the opportunity to emigrate. As the wage premium ranges from two to five times higher, adjusting for purchasing power parity, for medical (2–4) and IT professionals (3–5), the prospect of emigration largely increases returns to education (Docquier and Rapoport 2004). With these increased returns, there will be increased investment in education. However, despite this increase, India is not able to reap the primary benefits of the educated population as the best-educated medical and IT professionals emigrate. Hence, though the education level increases among Indian nationals, once we account for emigration, the education level of the remaining population actually decreases as the most educated have left. There is evidence that most of the emigrants who leave are from the best institutions and are the most skilled. In 1980, only 3 per cent of Indian doctors emigrated to the United States. However, India's loss is worse than it seems as most of these doctors were from the best Indian medical schools, with the percentage being 56 per cent from 1956 to 1980 and decreasing only slightly to 49 per cent in the 1990s. In addition, they earn a disproportionate amount of income. Indians in the United States account for 0.1 per cent of the population of India but earn 10 per cent of the national income of India. Additionally, a majority of Indian students intend to stay in the United States and the percentage was highest for India in comparison to other countries such as China (*The Economist*. 2002). Hence there is strong reason to believe that the Brain Drain does not lead to a gain in India from increased investment in education despite increased returns to education.

However, there are two ways the prospect of emigration could still potentially increase the overall stock and quality of educated workers in India. If we assume that it is uncertain whether an individual will go abroad or not and investments in education are decided under the assumption of going abroad, if s/he does not go, this would increase the Indian educational base. In addition, if more temporary visas were issued then there would be a lesser threat of losing the most-educated population. Though the use of temporary visas could decrease the incentive to invest in education, it could also guarantee the return of emigrants, who bring back the skills they have learned working in foreign countries with higher technology (Docquier and Rapoport 2004).

Despite the gradual increase in the reverse brain drain, with Indians and foreign nationals coming to India, there are a large number of immigrant visas currently issued. While in places like Taipei many domestic companies have been started by returned emigrants, in the IT sector in Bangalore, the number of companies started by returned emigrants is limited reflecting the low return rate. The return of emigrants has largely been the *result* of

increased growth of the sector rather than the *cause* of it. However, that does not mean that Indian professionals living in developed countries such as the United States do not play a role in the growth of the sector. Their role is primarily through network effects, as Indian nationals in developed countries provide contacts for companies starting in India as well as the exchange of ideas within the IT sector. In addition, 30–40 per cent of the higher-level employees in the Indian IT sector are returned emigrants (Docquier and Rapoport 2004).

India, following the Philippines, has the second highest number of skilled workers, with 1,070,586 emigrants leaving India in 2000. However, due to its large population, the country has one of the lowest percentages of emigration of skilled workers—of 4.1 per cent (Docquier and Rapoport 2004). Therefore, the brain drain is not a phenomenon that will quickly subside. The brain drain essentially represents a trade-off for India: on one hand, India loses a scarce resource of educated and skilled workers while it gains financial resources through remittances and new opportunities through networks.

Hence the brain drain issue in the context of India has many diverse facets. One issue of focus has been a cost–benefit analysis of the phenomenon. On the cost side, India is losing the returns on its investment in education and its base of skilled workers. The negative repercussions of this loss of the educated labour force are even greater as they threaten the education system in India, from primary to tertiary education, with the outflow of educational professionals. On the benefit side, the outflow of Indians leads to network effects, which provide greater linkages with the host country, and remittances, which lead to greater financial resources within India. Another potential benefit is the increase in the investment in education due to the opportunity to emigrate. However, the extent of its benefit to India is questionable as the most-educated population is lost to emigration. There are policies that could be used to mitigate the costs of the brain drain such as taxation, whether it is a flat fee upon exit or a taxation system based on Indian nationality. This would increase the tax revenues in India which could significantly increase expenditure and access to education. Though the number of visas issued is still high, with the growth in sectors such as IT, there has been an increase in the return of Indians and the immigration of foreign nationals into India. In addition, there should be further emphasis on temporary emigration, which could decrease incentives to invest in education on the one hand but would lead to the increased retention of skilled workers along with the spillover of skills learned in foreign countries. The focus of research is primarily on skilled-labour emigration which is the bulk of the emigration out of India, particularly to the United States. But there are outflows of relatively unskilled labourers as well. However, there is no reason to believe that the brain drain from India will drastically decrease any time soon despite legislative moves on the United States front as well to restrain it. Hence the debates regarding the costs and benefits of brain drain will continue and lead to future legislative policy implications in both India and the host countries.

DIVYA MINISANDRAM

REFERENCES
Desai, Mihir A., Devesh Kapur, and John McHale. 2004. 'Sharing the Spoils: Taxing International Flows of Human Capital', *International Tax and Public Finance*, 11(5), September: 663–93.
Docquier, Frederic and Hillel Rapoport. 2004. 'Skilled Migration and Human Capital Formation in Developing Countries—A Survey', December.
The Economist. 2002. 'Outward Bound', 26 September.
United Nations. 2001. *Human Development Report 2001*. New York, United Nations.

Child Labour

Although scholarship and public policy have made it possible to clearly analyse the causes of and solutions to the problem of child labour, the lessons of such analysis have thus far been lost on the Indian state. There are more child workers in India than in any other country in the world. While the policy of modern states is based on a sociological view of 'childhood being,' *inter alia*, a period of learning through school, recreation, and other activity, not essentially a period of working at income-bearing tasks', policy in India is not based on such an understanding. As Myron Weiner points out in his landmark study *The Child and the State in India*, in India, neither is child labour illegal nor school education compulsory.

DEFINITION OF CHILD LABOUR

There are two immediate determinants of the definition of child labour: first, the age until which a person is to be considered a 'child' and second, the definition of 'work' itself.

The resolution of the International Labour Organization (ILO) 'Concerning Minimum Age for Admission to Employment' (Convention No. 138), passed in 1973, recommends that no person below 15 years be considered suitable for employment. For this reason, most scholars in the field take child labour to refer to workers below the age of 15. The UN Convention on the Rights of the Child (1989), however, refers to children as persons below the age of 18. The two major sources of data on the labour force in India, namely the Census of India and the National Sample Survey (NSS), define 'work' as participation in any economically productive activity.

The Census of India and the NSS tend to undercount the number of child workers for three main reasons. First, children working in factories and other urban locations may be hidden from enumerators and simply not be counted when data are collected. Second, it is difficult to identify child workers in an economy where subsistence production still occurs on a large scale and where many children work in homes or in the informal economy. Third, a substantial part of the child labour force is likely to be employed at housework and family-based work that lie outside the system of national accounts (and consequently outside the definition of 'work').

Thirty-one per cent of children in the age group 5 to 14 years in 2001 comprised children who were neither attending school nor participating in work. Such children numbered 92 million. A large proportion of such children may be employed in household and family-based work; those who are not, constitute potential child labour.

ESTIMATES OF CHILD LABOUR

According to the Census of India, there were 12.6 million workers in the age group 5 to 14 years in India in 2001. According to the NSS, there were 10.3 million workers in the same age group in 1999–2000 (5.5 million boys and 4.8 million girls), down from 13.1 million in 1993–4.

The ratio of child workers to all children aged 5 to 14 years in 2001 was 5.1 per cent among boys and 4.8 per cent among girls. These ratios were higher in 1991: 5.7 per cent among boys and 5.1 per cent among girls. Estimates of work participation rates among children in the same age group from the NSS also show a decline over time. In

rural areas, for example, work participation rates fell from 7.1 per cent in 1993–4 to 4.7 per cent in 1999–2000 for boys and from 7.2 to 4.9 per cent for girls during the same period. The rate was lower in urban areas and the decline was also smaller (from 3.6 to 2.7 per cent for boys and from 2.5 to 1.9 per cent for girls between 1993–4 and 1999–2000).

The all-India average hides large variations across states. In 2001, the rural work participation rate for children in the age group 5 to 14 years was 7.7 per cent in Andhra Pradesh and 0.5 per cent in Kerala. Some other states with a higher-than-average child work participation rate were Karnataka, Madhya Pradesh, Jharkhand, Chhattisgarh, and Rajasthan. The rural child work participation rate in states considered to be relatively backward such as Bihar and Uttar Pradesh was, in fact, lower (4.7 per cent and 4.1 per cent respectively). However, in terms of absolute size, 53 per cent of all child workers in 2001 were concentrated in the five states of Andhra Pradesh, Bihar, Madhya Pradesh, Rajasthan, and Uttar Pradesh.

Child labour is predominantly a rural phenomenon: rural areas account for 85 per cent of child workers and the incidence of child labour is higher in rural areas than in urban areas. Almost 80 per cent of estimated child workers are employed in agriculture. Nevertheless, there are some urban pockets with a high incidence and visible concentration of child labour in specific industries. These include gem polishing in Jaipur, fireworks in Sivakasi, diamond cutting in Surat, slate making in Markapur, and silk weaving in Varanasi.

CONDITIONS OF WORK, HAZARDOUS WORK, AND LEGISLATION

Child work in India is characterized by exploitative work contracts and abysmal conditions of work. Children work long hours (12–14 hours a day in the lock-making industry of Aligarh) for low wages (a child's wage was one-tenth an adult's in gem polishing in Jaipur), and in dangerous work environments (close to hot furnaces in the glass factories of Firozabad) (Burra 1995). Literacy among child workers is very low, they suffer ailments at an early age, and their life expectancy is unlikely to be high. There is also a sexual division of labour, with girls generally employed at lower wages than boys.

Current legislation in India does not ban all forms of child labour. The Child Labour (Prohibition and Regulation) Act, 1986, is concerned only with 'the engagement of children in certain employments' and accordingly lists specific occupations and processes in which the employment of children is banned or is to be regulated. The occupations specified in the Act include work in the railways, ports and the sale of fireworks, and the processes specified include, for example, bidi making, carpet weaving, and the manufacture of soaps, matches and cement. Recently, work as domestic servants and in hotels and teashops has been added to the list of hazardous occupations.

The ILO Convention (No. 182) on the Worst Forms of Child Labour, 1999, seeks the immediate elimination of certain types of child labour including slavery (sale of children, debt bondage, etc.), prostitution, drug trafficking, and other hazardous activity (or 'work which is likely to harm the health, safety, or morals of children'). While the objective of legislation and policy must be to illegalize all forms of child labour immediately, there is no doubt that bonded labour and other extremely exploitative forms of chid labour require specific and priority attention. It may be noted here that quite apart from the fact that all working children are exposed to a variety of hazards, only some of which are intrinsic to the work process, many 'dangerous processes' are actually excluded from the purview of the 1986 Indian Act (Burra 1995). Hazards arise from the work environment and conditions of work and the vulnerability of children (ibid.). Work in a carpenter's workshop or as field labour is not considered hazardous in India but can be dangerous for young children.

CAUSES FOR THE PERSISTENCE OF CHILD LABOUR

Why does child labour persist? Undoubtedly, income poverty is the seed-bed for child labour. It is the children of the poor, and of the socially and economically deprived sections of the population, who work. However, while 'poverty provides conditions for the supply of child labour it is not a sufficient explanation' for the prevalence of child labour in India today (Chandrasekhar 1997; Basu and Van 1998). There is no simple correlation between the incidence of child labour and that of income poverty across states. Surveys have also shown that the overwhelming majority of income-poor parents desire their children to go to school and not to work (PROBE 1999).

A central factor in the persistence of child labour is the demand for child labour. The demand for child labour is broadly of two types: first, from employers who attempt to make larger profits by employing cheap workers and second, from small employers or household enterprises attempting to survive in low-productivity activities (Chandrasekhar 1997).

A detailed study of the match-making industry in the Sivakasi–Sattur belt of Tamil Nadu found that the handmade match sector survived mainly because of cheap female and child labour (Chandrasekhar 1997). If child workers withdraw from the industry, adult wages would rise (thus increasing the earnings of worker households) but the costs of production would also rise. The latter costs, however, could be transferred to consumers (through price increases) or be taken from profit mark-ups and trader margins through a reorganization of the industry. The study showed that costs to employers of abolishing child labour are not excessive and can be met through technological and organizational change.

Two arguments are used to justify the continuation of at least some forms of child labour. The first argument is that children have certain special skills, for example 'nimble fingers', which help them perform certain activities and processes better than adult workers. This argument has been proved to be wrong. No occupation in India is wholly child-specific: in every activity at which children are employed, adults are also employed. There is no process where the labour power of children cannot be replaced by the labour power of adults, and no technological reason for the continuation of child labour (Chandrasekhar 1997). The 'nimble fingers' argument is in fact a mask for the demand for a low-cost and obedient workforce.

The second argument pertains to skill formation. It is argued that some traditional skills are acquired over time through the process of work itself. Early training, it is argued, leads to better skills and improved incomes and job mobility. This argument is also incorrect. There is evidence that starting work at an early age does not bring any additional economic benefits. A study of teenage workers in Bhavnagar, Gujarat, separated those who began work before the age of 14, the early starters, from those who started working at the age of 15 or later, and found that among boys, the early starters earned less and put in longer hours of work than the late starters (Swaminathan 1997). The primary determinant of wage differentials was not how early in his childhood a worker had

begun to work, but the level of education of the individual worker.

WHAT NEEDS TO BE DONE

It is time to recognize in practice that all children have a right to education and leisure and other means to develop their physical and mental capabilities during childhood, and consequently, to end all forms of child labour.

Some argue that child labour cannot be stopped (and even that it is harmful to stop child labour) until income poverty is eradicated. Their grounds are usually two: first, a concern for the household that depends on the earnings of the child worker, and second, the alleged impossibility of enforcing a ban on child labour in a situation of poverty.

History and comparative development experience clearly demonstrate that the achievement of universal school education and the abolition of child labour are not dependent on the level of per capita income or the level of industrialization or the socio-economic status of families (Weiner 1991). Even in India, the experience of Kerala shows that near-universal schooling and a very low incidence of child labour can be achieved at a relatively low level of per capita income. In almost all countries of the world, the spread of mass education and accompanying reduction in child labour *preceded* economic growth (and was, in fact, a *precondition* for economic development). The abolition of child labour does not have to wait for the end of income poverty.

With regard to enforcement, it is easier to ensure that children go to school than to enforce a ban on child labour by inspecting workplaces. The only way to ensure an end to child labour is to make schooling universal and compulsory. The task of ensuring universal compulsory schooling in a poor country is by no means easy. The state must commit itself to providing adequate school infrastructure and make primary and secondary education of good quality accessible to all children. Schools need trained teachers, teaching material, sports equipment, and other basic infrastructure. The majority of children need not just free tuition but books and uniforms as well as special incentives such as hot school meals.

It is also important to influence parents and their decision to send children to work, and while reducing poverty is essential, a direct impact on child labour participation can be expected from a rise in adult wages. To improve wages and working conditions, adult workers—and not child workers (as some would have it)—need to be organized.

On the demand side, governments must enforce a legal ban on all forms of child labour and punitive measures against employers of child labour. Trade sanctions are product- or sector-specific measures, and as such of limited relevance, besides often being disguised protectionism by advanced capitalist countries.

MADHURA SWAMINATHAN

REFERENCES

Basu, K. and P.H. Van. 1998. 'Economics of Child Labour', *American Economic Review*, 88(3): 412–27.

Burra, Neera. 1995. *Born to Work: Child Labour in India*, New Delhi, Oxford University Press.

Chandrasekhar, C.P. 1997. 'The Economic Consequences of the Abolition of Child Labour: An Indian Case Study', *Journal of Peasant Studies*, 24(3), April: 137–79.

PROBE Team. 1999. *Public Report on Basic Education in India*, New Delhi, Oxford University Press.

Swaminathan, Madhura. 1997. 'Do Child Workers Acquire Specialised Skills? A Case Study of Teenage Workers in Bhavnagar', *Indian Journal of Labour Economics*, 40(4): 829–39.

Weiner, Myron. 1991. *The Child and the State in India: Child Labour and Education Policy in Comparative Perspective*, Princeton, Princeton University Press.

Demographic Dividend

Over the past four decades India has undergone rapid demographic changes. The onset and speed of demographic transition—a process of change whereby societies move from a situation of high mortality and fertility to one of low mortality and fertility—differs from region to region within India. While the level of fertility in southern Indian states has already reached below replacement, it is still high in many states in north India because, though declining, the decline is at a slower pace. There are two important consequences of demographic transition. The first is population explosion due to a rapid decline in mortality rates amidst the maintenance of a high birth rate. This sudden and sustained increase in population size during the initial phase demographic transition directly impacts the economy. Another consequence of demographic transition is a shift in the age structure of the population resulting in broader and long-term age structural transition—changes in cohort sizes as they move through different age groups. In the first phase of the demographic transition the number of children increases both in relative and absolute size due to high fertility levels and a rapid fall in mortality. After some time lag, fertility rate also starts to decline, which then contributes to a decline in the relative share of the young population. The cohort size of the children born during this phase would be smaller than that of children born during the phase of high fertility. As children born during different phases of demographic transition move from youth to adulthood, and to old age, the age structure of the population undergoes major changes reflecting the varying cohort sizes resulting from past changes in fertility and mortality. During this process, there will be a period of—'window of opportunity' where child dependency ratio (ratio of child population to working age population) declines due to decline in fertility as well as increase in the working age population as children born during the high fertility regime move into working ages. If this window of opportunity is properly exploited, there is greater potential for demographic dividend through increased savings and investment for economic growth.

The period of 'window of opportunity' can be exploited in three ways to give demographic dividends: (i) by productive employment of the available labour force, which would raise total gross domestic product (GDP). It can also be shown algebraically[1] that output per capita would grow if the growth rate of workers exceeded the growth rate of total population even if the output per worker did not change (Bloom and Williamson 1997; Bhat 2001); (ii) by directing accumulated wealth and savings into productive investments. The window of opportunity may give higher incentives to save. Improved health, longevity, and smaller family size make savings easier and more attractive. Households tend to save less when there

are more children since a substantial part of the family income is spent on raising them. When fertility declines, the demand on household resources for raising children reduces, allowing households to save more of their income; and (iii) if appropriate investments are made for the formation of large supply of human capital. Fertility decline has immediate and direct impact on the school-going population and provides an opportunity to invest more on their education and health contributing to better-quality human capital in the future. Women with fewer children are more able and often more willing to participate in remunerative work, and are more likely to invest additional income in the health and education of their children.

This would be a one-time-only opportunity and its length would be determined by the speed of demographic transition. If appropriate interventions are not made during this period, it would have negative implications for the economy and society. Demographic dividend could explain as much as one-third of the per capita GDP growth rate of the East Asian economies during the period of their economic miracle.

'WINDOW OF OPPORTUNITY' FOR INDIA

The age structural transition for India since 1950 has been shown graphically in Figure 1. The age structure of the population has been classified according to the life-cycle stages and their impact on the general economy. The broad life-cycle stages are young (age group 0–14), youth (15–24), young working age (25–49), mature working age (50–64), and elderly (65+). As the young population (0–14) is dependent on the adults for their consumption, they incur health and education expenditures in the economy. The youth population (15–24) also consumes health and education; however, the pattern of consumption is likely to be different from

---

[1]The accounting identity that links income per capita (Y/N) to labour productivity (income per worker) and the labour force is as follows:

$$\frac{Y}{N} = \frac{Y}{L} \times \frac{L}{N}$$

where Y is the income, N is the total population, and L is the total number of workers. By differentiating the above equation, the expression can be converted to growth rates as $g_y = g_z + (g_l - g_n)$ where g_y is the growth rate of per capita income, g_z is the growth rate of income per worker, g_l is the growth rate of labour force, and g_n is the growth rate of total population (for more details, see Bhat 2001).

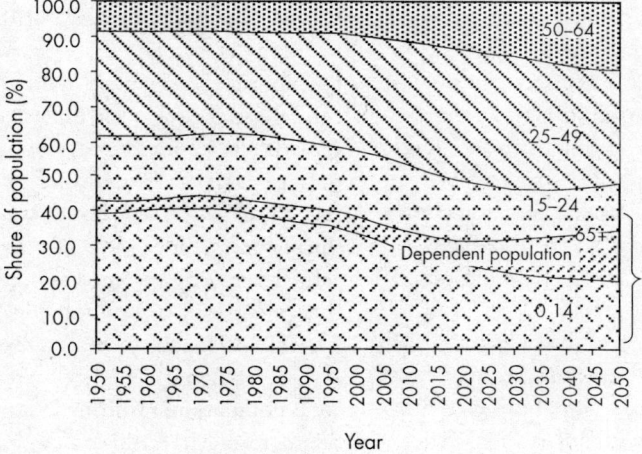

Figure 1   Age Structural Transition for India

Sources: Derived from UN Population Projection—United Nations. 1999. *Long Range Population Projection: Based on the 1998 Revision*, New York, United Nations; K. Navaneetham. 2004. 'Age Structural Transition and Economic Growth: Evidence from South and Southeast Asia', *Asian Profile*, 32(3).

that of children (0–14) due to differences in needs and services. The prime working age population (25–49) saves little. The population in the middle age group (50–64) is likely to earn higher income because of work experience and also to have a higher saving rate than the population aged 25–49. The old age people aged 65+ would mostly depend on others for their consumption needs such as healthcare and social support. As fertility started declining in India since the 1970s, the share of population under 15 years of age began to decline and this will continue until 2025–30. The decline is projected to be rapid after 2000. The child dependency ratio is concurrently declining since 1980 and this decline is likely to continue till 2030 due to the continuous decline in fertility and expansion of working-age population (in both absolute and relative terms). This is the greatest opportunity for India to improve the quality of its human capital and this will have greater impact on labour productivity and the economy when it enters into the labour force. Further, it

provides the opportunity to raise the saving rate if appropriate policies are pursued to promote it.

The share of the working-age population (15–64) has been increasing since 1980 and is expected to reach its peak by 2025. Generating new employment opportunities to meet the growing working-age population is a major challenge for India. If it is productively employed it will boost the economy. Among the working-age population, the share of the youth segment (15–24) will decrease from now on while that of the mature labour force will be increasing. This is also noted in the rapid decline in the ratio of youth (15–24) to working-age population (25–64) from 2010. This indicates that there will be less pressure on the economy to generate new employment opportunities and that can lead to a possible reduction in unemployment, which can be described as another window of opportunity for India. Further, this would increase the saving ratio as well as tax revenues, which may augment the capacity for investment and funding of social programmes. It is also likely that the increase in the share of middle working-age population (50–64) would contribute to higher saving rates as it tends to have a greater capacity to save due to higher income and reduced consumption. This opportunity would continue even after 2030 and this can be exploited for economic growth.

The size and share of the old-age population will continue to increase during the age structural transition. However, the increase would be greater after 2025. The old dependency ratio would also increase rapidly after 2025 (see Figure 2). Meeting the healthcare and social security needs of the elderly would be a major challenge for India particularly after 2025.

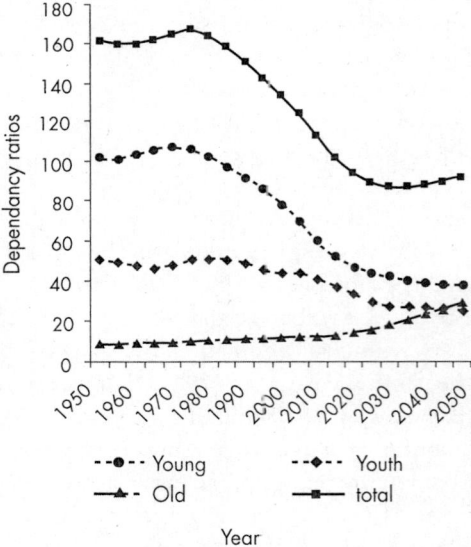

Figure 2   Trends in Dependancy Ratios for India 1950–2050

Source: Estimated from UN Population Projection (United Nations. 1999. *Long Range Populaton Projection: Based on the 1998 Revision*, New York, United Nations.)

ESTIMATED DEMOGRAPHIC BONUS FOR INDIA

From the identity equation mentioned in footnote 1, the extent of demographic bonus can be derived from the difference in the growth rate of working-age population and total population. Bhat (2001) estimated that the demographic bonus was negative during the decades 1951–71, as the growth rate of total population was higher than that of working-age population (see Figure 3). After 1971, the growth rate of working-age population was higher than that of total population, resulting in a positive demographic bonus. He also showed that the demographic bonus would be highest during the decade 2001–11—a contribution of 0.6 per cent GDP growth rate in the total per capita GDP growth rate. It is also clear from Figure 3 that the demographic bonus is likely to continue till 2031 and would be negative thereafter. It is also important to note that the extent and the process of age structural transition would be different in different states as the nature of demographic transition is different due to their socio-economic and cultural differences (Table 1). The bonus would be positive till 2011 among the demographically advanced states such as Kerala, Tamil Nadu, and Punjab and would be negative thereafter. It is interesting to observe that the BIMARU states where the process of demographic transition began later than in other states started getting greater dividend from 2001 and would be likely to continue to do so till 2031. As there are regional differences in age structural transition, internal migration could be of critical importance in the future as young workers move from underdeveloped to developed regions. The regional differences in age structural transition may also play an important role in terms of convergence in economic growth among the states in India, provided efforts are made to invest in human capital among the BIMARU states as a large share of labour supply in the future would come from them.

The demographic dividend is also likely to accrue from the expected increase in labour-force participation of women due to the shortening of the duration of child-bearing years. The total bonus derived from the labour supply during the period 2001–51 is estimated to be 1 per cent, out of which labour supply effect would be 0.2 per cent and the effect of the expected increase in labour-force participation of women would be 0.8 per cent, keeping labour productivity constant (Bhat 2001). The savings ratio would increase from 23 per cent in 2001 to 32 per cent in 2031 due to the expected decline in dependency burden, which would contribute to an increase in economic growth rate. It was estimated that the demographic transition would contribute 40 per cent of the per capita GDP growth rate during the period 2001–51. About 13 per cent of this increase would be due to the increase in labour supply, assuming output per worker remained constant, and the remaining 27 per cent would be due to an increase in the savings ratios, assuming per capita consumption did not change.

Table 1   Difference in the Growth Rate of Population Aged 15–64 and the Growth Rate of Total Population 1991–2031

State	Decade			
	1991–2001	2001–11	2011–21	2021–31
South				
Kerala	0.50	0.15	–0.20	–0.49
Tamil Nadu	0.77	0.32	–0.14	–0.21
Andhra Pradesh	1.02	0.91	0.11	–0.0
Karnataka	0.67	0.84	0.05	–0.22
West				
Maharashtra	0.69	1.01	0.08	–0.13
Gujarat	0.54	0.80	0.06	–0.26
East				
Orissa	0.40	0.76	0.14	–0.21
West Bengal	0.71	0.88	–0.05	–0.16
Assam	0.70	0.76	0.41	–0.22
North				
Himachal Pradesh	0.58	0.78	0.05	–0.13
Punjab	0.63	0.87	–0.13	–0.21
Haryana	0.47	1.06	0.42	–0.22
Rajasthan	0.38	0.71	0.68	0.14
Madhya Pradesh	0.31	0.79	0.62	0.01
Uttar Pradesh	0.09	0.58	0.58	0.56
Bihar	0.19	0.64	0.64	0.22
All-India	0.35	0.56	0.43	0.07

Source: P.N.M. Bhat. 2001.

INDIA'S RESPONSE TO 'WINDOW OF OPPORTUNITY'

The age structural transition does not give full dividend automatically and to get economic benefits, it is important to have a favourable economic setting and policy environment. The experience of India so far shows that the 'window of opportunity' has not been exploited though it has become available since the 1980s (Mitra and Nagarajan 2005; Chandrasekhar et al. 2006). It has been argued that the employment growth rate was low during the 1990s, particularly in the rural areas, and consequently the unemployment rate was high (Chandrasekhar et al. 2006). This was

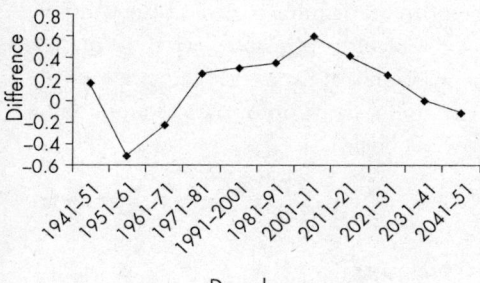

Figure 3   Difference between Growth Rate of Working-age Population and Total Population in India 1941–2051

Source: P.N.M. Bhat. 2001.

the period during which the growth of the youth population was also greater. As new employment opportunities did not grow at the same pace as the numbers of youth, the unemployment rate among the youth increased. But it is encouraging to see that the employment growth rate has increased significantly in both rural and urban areas. It is also likely that the increase in the share of middle working-age population (50–64) would contribute to higher saving rates as it tends to have greater capacity to save due to higher income and reduced consumption. This is likely to continue into the future when the relative share of youth population is expected to decline.

The East Asian success in economic growth was driven by the availability of high-quality human capital at the time when the demographic window of opportunity was emerging, thanks to the concurrently occurring demographic transition (Mason 2003; Navaneetham 2004). The East Asian countries' experience of demographic dividend underscores the importance of the quality of the labour force to maximize the benefits from the demographic transition. But the trend in India is not encouraging on this front. Chandrasekhar et al. (2006) showed that spread of education has been slow in India—the percentage of those with high school and higher educational qualifications has been very low in rural areas and only slightly better in urban areas. The educated unemployment trend among females was also not encouraging during the period 2000–5.

Though healthier populations are more productive and have greater incentives to invest in human capital and save more for their old age, in India, increased longevity may not be accompanied by increased savings due to increase in disease burden across all age groups and the consequent rise in healthcare expenditures (Chandrasekhar

et al. 2006). India will also face challenges in the areas of child and reproductive health as the numbers of women in the reproductive age group is projected to increase in the next two decades.

Age structural transition creates different opportunities and challenges across age groups. The relative share of childhood population will decline in the future. This provides an opportunity to improve the human capital through public policy measures with respect to nutrition, education, and healthcare. The relatively rapid growth of the labour force would benefit India, if employment opportunities increased with sufficient speed to match the growth in labour supply, maintained growth in labour productivity, improved public health, and invested in infrastructure. The size and share of the elderly population would increase rapidly after 2031 and this will pose several policy and programme challenges. To meet these challenges effectively there will be need for concerted efforts to devise appropriate public and social policies directed at the provision of social security and healthcare and encouraging the development of social networks. In order to meet the challenges in the future and to prepare for them, it is important for India to exploit the window of opportunity available for a short period, a one-time gift from the demographic transition, with appropriate economic and social policies.

K. NAVANEETHAM

REFERENCES
Acharya, S. 2004.'India's Growth Prospects Revisited', *Economic and Political Weekly*, 9 October.
Bhat, P.N.M. 2001.'A Demographic Bonus for India? On the First Consequence of Population Ageing', A Key note Address Presented on the Occasion of the 10th

Anniversary Celebration of the Population Research Centre, University of Groningen, The Netherlands, 22 November.

Bloom, D. and J.G. Williamson. 1997. 'Demographic Transition and Economic Miracles in Emerging Asia', Working Paper 6268, Cambridge, M.A., National Bureau of Economic Research.

Chandrasekhar, C.P., Jayati Ghosh, and Anamitra Roy Choudhury. 2006. 'The Demographic Dividend and Young India's Economic Future', *Economic and Political Weekly*, 9 December.

Mason, A. 2003. 'Population Change and Economic Development: What We have learned from the East Asia Experience', *Applied Population and Policy*, 1(1).

Mitra, S. and R. Nagarajan. 2005. 'Making Use of The Window of Demographic Opportunity: An Economic Perspective', *Economic and Political Weekly*, 10 December.

Navaneetham, K. 2004. 'Age Structural Transition and Economic Growth: Evidence from South and Southeast Asia', *Asian Profile*, 32(3).

Employment Trends

Employment has featured as an important priority in the development agenda in India. Approaches to it have, however, varied in different periods over the more than fifty years of Independence. In the initial years of development planning, unemployment was not expected to emerge as a major problem; yet some thought was given to ensure the generation of employment of a fair magnitude in the development process to productively employ the growing labour force. A reasonably high rate of economic growth combined with an emphasis on labour-intensive sectors like small-scale industry was envisaged to achieve this goal. The rate and structure of growth rather than technology were seen as the instruments of employment generation. Thus, while granting

that in 'an economy with relative abundance of labour, a bias in favour of comparatively labour intensive techniques is both natural and desirable', it was clearly recognized that 'considerations of size and technology should not be set aside to emphasise employment' (Planning Commission 1956: 112–13). Unemployment was estimated to be relatively low, as also the growth rate of the labour force, and a targeted economic growth rate of 5 per cent with some emphasis on labour-intensive consumer goods sectors was expected to generate enough employment over the years to prevent any increase in unemployment.

These assumptions and expectations continued from one Five Year Plan to the next during the 1950s and 1960s. Meanwhile the magnitude and rate of unemployment increased significantly. The economy grew at a rate of around 3.5 per cent as against the planned rate of 5 per cent per annum. Yet employment grew at a relatively high rate of 2 per cent per annum. However, since labour force growth was much higher at 2.5 per cent as against the less than 2 per cent per annum envisaged, the result was an increase in unemployment. The magnitude of unemployment had almost doubled during 1956–72, from around 5 to 10 million, and the unemployment rate from 2.6 to 3.8 per cent (Papola 1992). These figures are, however, only approximations as detailed data on employment and unemployment started becoming available from the National Sample Survey Organisation (NSSO) through its quinquennial surveys starting with 1972–3. They, nevertheless, do indicate overall trends during the first two decades of planned development in India.

With the availability of comprehensive data on levels of consumption, employment, and unemployment for 1972–3 which revealed a high incidence of poverty (54 per cent rural and 41 per cent urban) and high unemployment rates (8.4 per cent on current daily status [CDS] and 4.3 per cent on currently weekly status [CWS] basis), the official approach to the employment problem underwent a change in the mid-1970s. The Fifth Five Year Plan (1974–9) sought to address the employment issue by reorienting the pattern of growth in favour of employment-intensive sectors. At the same time, a strong view was emerging to suggest that growth alone cannot solve the problems of poverty and unemployment, and therefore a number of special employment and poverty-alleviation programmes were launched. They were mostly of two kinds: providing financial and other assistance for productive self-employment, and offering supplementary wage employment to the underemployed. Over the years, these programmes have been continued in one form or another with modifications or integrations, or new ones have been started while some old ones have been discontinued. The latest in the series is the National Rural Employment Guarantee Programme which aims at legally guaranteeing employment of up to 100 days annually to every rural household, under an act of Parliament.

While these programmes seem to have been able to reduce the degree of underemployment to a certain extent, the open unemployment rates have not declined over the years. This can be discerned from unemployment rates on CDS basis, which includes both open and underemployment and on CWS and usual principal status (UPS) bases given in Table 1. During the period 1993–4 to 1999–2000, however, unemployment rates, including those based on CDS, have increased.

Looking at different rates of unemployment, it is clear that underemployment is a problem of much larger magnitude than open

Table 1   Unemployment Rates
(% of labour force)

Year	UPS	UPSS	CWS	CDS
1972–3	3.80	1.61	4.32	8.35
1977–8	4.23	2.47	4.48	8.18
1983	2.77	1.90	4.51	8.28
1987–8	3.77	2.62	4.80	6.09
1993–4	2.56	1.90	3.63	6.03
1999–2000	2.81	2.23	4.41	7.32

Notes: UPS: usual principal status. A person is considered unemployed according to this concept if available for but without work for major part of the year.
UPSS: usual principal and subsidiary status includes, besides UPS, those available but unable to find work on a subsidiary basis, during a year.
CWS: current weekly status. A person is unemployed if available for but unable to find work for even one hour during the reference week.
CDS: current daily status measures unemployment in terms of person-days of unemployment of all persons in the labour force during the reference week.

unemployment. For example, in 1999–2000, the UPS unemployment rate was estimated to be only 2.81 per cent as compared to a CDS rate of 7.32 per cent. The problem, however, is not confined to these time-criterion-based rates; a large part of the employed people work at very low levels of income, as indicated by a much higher incidence of poverty (26 per cent in 1999–2000) than of unemployment. Thus the employment challenge in India consists not only of creating jobs for the unemployed, and providing additional work to the underemployed, but, to a much larger extent, of enhancing productivity and income levels of a large mass of the 'working poor'.

It is against this background that this entry presents an account of the trends in employment during the period 1973–2000 for which data are available from the quinquennial surveys of the

NSSO. Besides the slow growth rates of employment and its deceleration with higher economic growth in recent years, there are several other disquieting features of the Indian employment scene that are also covered briefly. They include a slow change in employment structure by sectors of economic activity, predominance of self-employment and increase in the share of the casual category of workers, predominance of the unorganized sector and stagnation and decline in organized-sector employment, and the issue of quality of employment which seems to have undergone a deterioration, in general, in recent years. The entry finally ventures to assess the prospects of employment growth and its qualitative aspects in the medium term.

EMPLOYMENT GROWTH

As noted earlier, employment growth has been over 2 per cent for almost thirty years since the early 1950s. In fact, it is recorded to be much higher during the 1970s. But since the 1980s there has been a declining trend in the growth rate of employment.

As Table 2 shows, the growth rate of employment declined continuously from one quinquennium to the next except for the period 1987–8 to 1993–4. Higher growth during the 1987–8 to 1993–4 period seems primarily to have been contributed by agriculture which has otherwise experienced a generally low and rapidly declining employment growth. Among other major sectors, manufacturing has also experienced a declining trend in employment growth, but construction, trade, and transport have had fluctuating trends and have recorded relatively high employment growth even during 1994–2000 when overall employment growth has been the lowest. In fact, the non-agricultural sectors together have registered a relatively high employment growth of 2.69 per cent during the 1994–2000 period, but because of a low growth of 0.06 per cent in agriculture, which had a weight of 60 per cent in total employment, the aggregate employment growth works out to be only 1.02 per cent. Construction, trade, and transport recorded employment growth rates of 6.61, 6.20, and 5.58 per cent respectively and manufacturing 2.05 per cent during 1994–2000.

What is particularly intriguing is the fact that while employment growth was reasonably high at around 2 per cent with a

Table 2   Employment Growth 1972–3 to 1990–2000 (% per annum)

Sector	1972–3 to 1977–8	1977–8 to 1983	1983 to 1987–8	1987–8 to 1993–4	1993–4 to 1999–2000
Agriculture	2.32	1.20	0.04	2.39	0.06
Mining	4.68	5.85	6.16	2.09	−3.27
Manufacturing	5.10	3.75	2.10	1.45	2.05
Construction	1.59	7.45	13.59	−1.10	6.61
Elasticity, gas, water supply	12.23	5.07	4.64	3.39	−5.25
Transport	4.85	6.35	2.67	3.58	5.28
Trade	3.71	4.12	4.42	3.20	6.20
Services	3.67	4.69	3.92	3.76	0.55
Total	2.82	2.22	1.55	2.37	1.02

Note: Growth rates are on UPSS basis, which defines a person as employed if carrying out economic activity on main or subsidiary basis during a year.

gross domestic product (GDP) growth rate
of just around 3.5 per cent during the earlier
decades, with GDP growth at over 6 per
cent, employment growth has been much
lower since the 1980s, particularly during
the period 1994–2000. It must, however,
be clarified that with the large weight of
agriculture, overall employment growth
has been mainly influenced by employment
growth in that sector. Thus, even though
employment growth in construction,
trade, transport, and manufacturing has
improved, aggregate employment growth
has significantly declined during 1994–2000
as compared to 1988–94 due to a steep fall
in employment growth rate in agriculture
(and to a certain extent a decline in the
growth rate of employment in community,
social, and personal services). Slowdown in
employment growth in agriculture has been
a result both of a low GDP growth and a
decline in employment elasticity (ratio of
employment growth to GDP growth).

Employment content of growth as
measured by employment elasticity has
been declining over the entire period since
1972–3, but has seen a particularly sharp
decline during 1994–2000 (Table 3).
Manufacturing, on the other hand, had a
reasonably high elasticity to begin with, but
has shown a continuous decline with slight

increase during 1994–2000. Construction,
transport, and trade have maintained
relatively high elasticities, and have even
shown an increase during 1994–2000 when
aggregate elasticity is estimated to have
sharply declined. Elasticity in other services
has continuously declined over the years
but the decline has been very sharp during
the last quinquennium. It may be noted
that the non-agricultural sectors on average
have shown an employment elasticity of
0.35, as against 0.02 in agriculture and 0.15
in aggregate.

EMPLOYMENT STRUCTURE
With differential growth of employment
among different sectors of the economy,
there have obviously been changes in the
structure of employment. Among the three
major sectors by broad division of economic
activity, namely agriculture, industry,
and services, there has been a decline, as
expected, in the share of agriculture and
increase in the share of industry and services
in total employment. The structural changes
have, however, been slow. In a period of
twenty-seven years, from 1973 to 2000,
the share of agriculture has declined by 17
percentage points only from 74 to 57 per
cent. The share of industry has increased
from 11 to 18 per cent and that of services

Table 3   Employment Elasticities in Major Sectors 1972–3 to 1999–2000

	1972–3 to 1977–8	1977–8 to 1983	1983 to 1987–8	1987–8 to 1993–4	1993–4 to 1999–2000
Agriculture	0.64	0.49	0.36	0.50	0.02
Mining	0.95	0.67	0.85	0.33	–0.63
Manufacturing	0.55	0.42	0.40	0.25	0.28
Construction	0.35	1.00	1.00	–1.10	1.00
Elasticity, gas, water supply	1.0	0.74	0.48	0.63	–0.76
Transport	0.76	0.92	0.45	0.64	0.56
Trade	0.78	0.75	0.70	0.58	0.68
Services	0.80	0.99	0.42	0.51	–0.06
All	0.61	0.55	0.38	0.41	0.15

Table 4 Employment Shares of Major Sectors 1972–3 to 1999–2000 (per cent)

	1972–3	1977–8	1983	1987–8	1993–4	1999–2000
Agriculture	74.0	72.3	68.4	65.5	60.38	56.70
Industry	11.4	12.3	13.7	15.5	15.82	17.56
Services	14.6	15.4	17.5	18.4	23.80	25.74

has risen faster from 15 per cent in 1972–3 to 26 per cent in 1999–2000, growing particularly fast during 1987–8 to 1999–2000 (Table 4).

The slow change in employment structure assumes the nature of a problem particularly when seen along with the change in the structure of the national GDP. During the period when the share of employment in agriculture declined from 74 per cent to 57 per cent, its contribution in GDP declined from over 40 per cent to 22 per cent; and while the share of the services sector in employment increased from 15 to 26 per cent, its contribution to GDP increased much faster from around 30 per cent to 52 per cent. As a result the asymmetry between the income and employment shares among different sectors has sharply increased, particularly between the agricultural and non-agricultural sectors. A sharper decline in the contribution of agriculture in GDP than in its share in employment implies a decline in its relative productivity and increase in income differentials between agriculture and the non-agricultural sectors. An opposite trend is seen in services, where the increase in GDP share has been faster than in employment, while industry has

retained its position in respect of relative productivity. That there would be a decline in the share of agriculture in GDP was expected, but a continuance of the heavy dependence of workers and population on agriculture as a source of income and livelihood is a matter of concern from the viewpoints of poverty and inequality. One hopes that a relatively higher employment growth in manufacturing, construction, transport, and services like trade, as experienced in recent years, will lead to some correction in this increasing imbalance.

INCREASING CASUALIZATION

Another aspect of employment trends and structure that is of interest in a developmental context is the distribution of workers by employment category as self-employed, regular wage, and salaried workers, and casual wage earners. It has been generally expected that with shift of workers from agriculture to non-agricultural activities and from footloose to enterprise-based employment, there will be an increase in the proportion of workers employed on a regular wage and salary basis. As Table 5 shows, there has been a decline, albeit slow, in the share of the self-employed, from 61 per cent in 1972–3 to 53 per cent in 1999–2000. The share of regular wage-salaried workers has, however, stagnated at around 14 per cent, while that of casual workers has increased from 23 to 33 per cent.

This situation has generally been interpreted to mean an increasing 'casualization' of workforce. Insofar as the term describes an increase in the share of

Table 5 Employment Status by Category of Employment 1972–3 to 1999–2000

	1972–3	1977–8	1983	1987–8	1993–4	1999–2000
Self-employed	61.4	58.9	57.4	56.0	54.8	52.9
Regular wage/salaried workers	15.3	13.9	13.9	14.4	13.2	13.9
Casual wage workers	23.3	27.2	28.7	29.6	32.0	33.2

casual workers, it is factually true. But if it is meant to imply a process of 'regular' workers turning 'casual', or a decline in employment and earnings, the trend needs to be carefully analysed. The shift is seen from the self-employed to casual workers category and most of it has taken place in rural areas, from agriculture to non-agricultural activities such as construction, trade, and services. There has, no doubt, been displacement of workers from large industries in urban areas, reducing regular workers to the status of casual workers. But the magnitude of such change has not been very significant in relation to the total numbers involved.

The phenomenon of casualization, therefore, needs to be seen in the overall perspective of employment trends in the economy. Agriculture is increasingly unable to productively absorb the growing rural labour force. At the same time, there has been some growth of non-agricultural activities in rural areas in construction, trade, and services which have generally offered better earnings than agriculture. Most of these employment opportunities have been of temporary and casual nature. But they have provided either full-time or supplementary employment, adding to the incomes of rural households. On the other hand, regular jobs have hardly increased in urban areas; in fact, there is evidence to show that such jobs have declined due to redundancy caused by technological and competitive compulsions in the larger industrial enterprises. So part of the regular workforce has been rendered casual and most new jobs have been in the casual category.

The increasing proportion of casual workers in total employment is thus mostly a result of structural shifts taking place in rural areas. To some extent, it is distress-driven, small and marginal landholders and the landless not finding gainful work in agriculture and taking up whatever work

they find in the non-agricultural activities, irrespective of earnings. But there is evidence to suggest that many are opting for non-farm work due to more regular employment and better earnings. This has been possible partly on account of various state-sponsored employment programmes, and partly because of an increase in the demand for labour in expanding construction, trade, and service activities in rural areas. In other words, 'casualization' of the nature observed does not necessarily imply a deterioration in the quality of employment. A small part of the real casualization that has taken place due to displacement of regular workers from large enterprise in urban areas, no doubt, indicates such deterioration.

Slow growth of employment in the organized sector has been a major factor in stagnancy in the proportion of regular wage and salary earners. This sector consisting of public services and enterprises and large private firms is the one that offers regular jobs. Employment growth in this sector has been just about 0.5 per cent during 1994–2000. In the post-2000 period, organized-sector employment has, in fact, shown an absolute decline—declining by about 1 million from around 28 million to 27 million during 2000–3 (GOI 2005a). Of around 21 million new employment opportunities generated during 1994–2000, only about 4 per cent have been in the organized sector and the remaining 96 per cent in the unorganized sector (Planning Commission 2002). As a result, the share of the unorganized sector in total employment has increased from around 92 per cent to 93 per cent. The high and increasing preponderance of the unorganized sector has been a matter of anxiety from the viewpoint of quality of employment as workers in this sector suffer from poor conditions of work, low earnings, and lack of employment and social security.

EMPLOYMENT PROSPECTS

What are the prospects for growth and quality of employment in India in the near future? The fact that a high economic growth rate has not been able to generate high employment growth, and it has, in fact, been accompanied by a slowdown in employment growth in recent years, has led many economists and others concerned to describe the recent experience as one of 'jobless growth'. A brief look at the performance of different sectors as attempted earlier, however, shows that but for the almost negligible employment growth in agriculture, growth in the non-agricultural sector has not really been jobless. Yet employment elasticities have declined in most sectors, though in some sectors like construction, trade, and transport, they continue to be relatively high (Table 3). And a faster growth of these sectors will lead to an increase in overall employment growth. Their share in employment, however, is still small as compared to manufacturing which has shown a relatively low employment growth and low and declining employment elasticity. Yet manufacturing still has an employment elasticity of around 0.3 and there are indications to suggest that it may improve. For example, its export-oriented sub-sectors have recently experienced higher employment growth and employment elasticity. During the 1990s, employment in export-oriented industries grew at 3.36 per cent per annum and showed an employment elasticity of 0.48 (Goldar 2003). A faster growth of manufactured exports, which now constitute over 75 per cent of total exports, as compared to 58 per cent in 1980, therefore, promises to be an important factor in reversing the declining trend in employment growth.

Employment growth is a function of growth of GDP and employment elasticity. The Indian economy has sustained a relatively high growth of over 6 per cent for about two decades and is expected to grow at that, if not a higher, rate in the coming years. There are indications towards a reversal of the declining trend in employment elasticities, particularly in manufacturing, and expectations of a growth structure in which sectors with higher employment elasticity will grow faster. Thus overall employment elasticity is likely to increase from the low of 0.15 experienced during 1994–2000. There is, therefore, a strong likelihood of the growth rate of employment getting restored to over 2 per cent during the first decade of this century. In fact, the evidence from the limited sample survey of the NSSO suggests a reversal of the trend already during 2000–4 when employment growth is estimated to be around 2.70 per cent. This, however, is still to be validated by the results of the larger sample survey (GOI 2005b).

The recent experience, however, suggests that most of the new employment opportunities are likely to be generated in the unorganized sector and will be characterized by poor conditions of work and lack of employment and social security. Even within the organized sector an increasing number of workers are being employed in a 'flexible' manner on casual or contract basis, without the social security benefits available to regular workers. Also, the problem of the 'working poor', namely of those fully engaged in work but earning less than poverty-line income, will persist. Thus the challenge of quality of work, in terms of earnings and social security, will continue. Tightening of the labour market with increase in the demand for labour may lead to improved earnings over time, but a vast majority of workers will continue to have no social protection against the risks of work-related hazards, unemployment, sickness, maternity, and old age. A measure of security against these risks is currently available to workers in the organized sector. With a decline in its share and increase in that of the unorganized sector, the share of unprotected workers will increase. Provision of a minimum social protection to this large mass of workers is, therefore, likely to emerge as a much greater challenge than that of expanding employment opportunities. It will require special attention of the state and society at large in coming years, as the market-driven high growth, even if accompanied by an expansion in employment opportunities, may not by itself be adequate to address the issue of social protection.

T.S. PAPOLA

REFERENCES

Goldar, B.N. 2003. 'Trade Liberalisation and Manufacturing Employment: The Case of India', Employment Paper 2002/3, 4, Geneva, International Labour Organzation.

Government of India (GOI). 2005a. *Economic Survey, 2004–2005*, Government of India, Ministry of Finance, Economic Division.

————. 2005b. *Employment and Unemployment Situation in India: January–June 2004*, National Sample Survey Organisation, Report No. 506.

Papola, T.S. 1992. 'The Question of Unemployment', in Bimal Jalan, ed., *The Indian Economy: Problems and Prospects*, New Delhi, Viking.

Planning Commission. 1956. *Second Five Year Plan*, New Delhi, Government of India.

————. 2002. *Report of the Special Group on Targeting Ten Million Employment Opportunities*, New Delhi, Government of India.

Informal Labour

Informal labour is labour whose use is not governed either by state regulations or by collective agreements between workers and employers. Though negative, the definition is nevertheless appropriate; for it is the existence of formal labour in the context of a dual economy, the *differentia specifica* of a developing country, that isolates informal labour as a category. A dual economy, first conceptualized by Arthur Lewis in a classic paper (Lewis 1954), is composed of two distinct segments—organized and unorganized. State regulations and collective agreements govern the use and remuneration of labour only in the organized segment, with the result that this remuneration is much higher than in the rest of the economy. The existence of this gap in labour income means an unlimited supply of labour from the unorganized to the organized segment. Thus it is the demand for labour in the organized segment that, together with the total supply of labour in the economy, determines the quantity of informal labour (and the level of unemployment, which affects only those who have the means to survive while waiting for formal-sector jobs).

Lack of clarity on this point has been a source of much confusion in the literature. Informal labour has, in different instances, been viewed as labour engaged in urban small-scale enterprises, as self-employment, as labour engaged in 'traditional' activities, as wholly unskilled labour, and as labour whose use is not subject to any rules or norms. None of this has any sound conceptual or empirical foundation. Informality does not imply a particular mode or location of labour use; informal labour can be in self-employment, in casual wage employment, and in regular wage employment, just as it can be in urban as well as in rural areas. There is little reason to think that informal labour must be confined to 'traditional' activities; it can be engaged in both 'traditional' and 'modern' activities. We do not need to assume that informal labour is unskilled; we only need to recognize that its skills are acquired outside the formal education system. There are rules and norms that govern the use and remuneration of informal labour; but these rules and norms reflect or derive from the prevailing social values and institutions (the currently fashionable term is 'social capital') and generally differ from those established by the state for the organized segment of the economy.

Informal labour is the overwhelmingly dominant form of labour in India.[1] The organized or formal segment of the economy, which is defined to include the entire public-sector and private-sector establishments with ten or more employees, accounted for just 7.6 per cent of the employed workforce of nearly 366 million in 1999–2000. Of the 338 million engaged in informal labour, 54 per cent were in self-employment, 37 per cent worked as casual wage labourers, and 9 per cent were regular wage employees. These workers were to be found in all production sectors of the economy: 64 per cent were in agriculture, 14 per cent were in industry, and 22 per cent were in services. An average self-employed worker had formal schooling of less than four years while an average casual labourer had formal schooling of less than two years.

The fact that the bulk of informal labour is either in self-employment or in casual wage employment is analytically significant. In both forms of employment, sharing of a given amount of work by a variable number of workers is possible. This ensures that informal workers rarely become wholly unemployed and that the market in informal wage labour can clear in the short run through variation in the level of underemployment rather than through variation in the wage rate. The wage rate,

therefore, is not market determined. What determines this wage rate? The question has received much attention in the literature, but a widely accepted answer does not exist.[2] The most plausible hypothesis is that the supply price of wage labour (casual and regular) is given by the average labour income of a marginal worker in self-employment. The assumption implicit in this view is that the self-employed, casual labourers, and regular employees do not form wholly distinct and rigid categories; a self-employed person could become a wage labourer just as a wage labourer could become self-employed.

While no attempt to test the hypothesis can be made here, the following facts are clearly consistent with it. In India, 12 per cent of the available workdays of the self-employed and 25 per cent of the available labour days of casual wage labourers remained unused for lack of work in 1999–2000. On the other hand, virtually no worker with less than five years of formal schooling was wholly unemployed, suggesting that unemployment was practically non-existent among informal workers. The problem confronting informal workers is not unemployment but poverty arising from a combination of underemployment and low reward from work. In 1999–2000, 35 per cent of these workers belonged to households with per capita expenditure below the official poverty line. The incidence of poverty among casual wage labourers (48 per cent) was higher than that among the self-employed (28 per cent) or among regular employees (29 per cent). Poverty forces some children to work; in 1999–2000, 2.5 per cent of informal workers were children (aged between 5 and 15).

In theory, economic growth is expected to steadily reduce the relative importance

[1] The facts and figures cited in this entry are taken from Ghose (1999, 2004).

[2] See Basu (1984) for a discussion of the theoretical possibilities.

of informal labour in a dual economy. In schematic terms, the organized segment, where formal labour and skills combine with modern technology and enterprise, is the source of capital accumulation and hence the engine of growth, while the unorganized segment is merely the source of labour. As growth occurs, therefore, the organized segment pulls labour out of the unorganized segment; informal labour is steadily transformed into formal labour. This, of course, is an overly simplified view; for growth in the organized segment requires not just labour but also goods (food grains and agricultural raw materials, for example) from the unorganized segment. So the unorganized segment must grow as well. But the organized segment can reasonably be expected to grow much faster than the unorganized segment. Moreover, while increased demand for labour in the organized segment translates into demand for additional workers, this does not happen in the unorganized segment where underemployment is pervasive. Thus there are good reasons to think that economic growth in a dual economy generates a process of transfer of informal workers into formal employment.

But India's experience does not bear out this expectation. During the twenty-two-year period between 1978 and 2000, the rate of economic growth was a decent 5.2 per cent per annum. Yet, as the data in Table 1 show, the relative importance of informal labour in the economy showed a tendency to rise rather than to decline. The reason, of course, is the slow growth of demand for labour in the organized segment: formal employment grew at a rate of only 1.3 per cent per annum while the labour force was growing at a rate of 1.8 per cent per annum. Why did formal employment grow at so slow a rate? Research suggests

three basic reasons. First, because India is a late developer, its organized segment uses technologies acquired from developed countries, which tend to be labour saving in character. Second, India pursued a development strategy that placed much emphasis on heavy industries, which are inherently capital intensive.[3] Finally, the regulations governing employment in the organized sector have been such as to encourage growth of wages rather than of employment. By placing excessive emphasis on protection of jobs of persons already in formal employment, these regulations serve to define the interest of formal workers in terms of growth of wages rather than in terms of growth of jobs. At the same time, the regulations also generate rather strong incentives for employers to move out of labour-intensive activities and to focus on technological change biased against the use of labour; for the interest of workers (growth of wages) remains consistent with that of employers (growth of profits) so long as output per worker rises steadily.

While the dominance of informal labour in the Indian economy remains undiminished, the pattern of its use has been changing. As Table 1 shows, the importance of self-employment has been declining while that of wage employment has been correspondingly rising. Informal workers have also been moving out of agriculture into industry and services. These are changes that economic growth is expected to generate in a developing economy. The surprise is that, in the case of India, we observe them in the unorganized part of the economy alone. In the organized segment, the pattern of employment as well as the change in this pattern has resembled

[3] See Chakravarty (1987) for an insightful discussion of India's development strategy.

Table 1 Informal Labour in India 1978–2000

	1977–8	1983–4	1987–8	1993–4	1999–2000
Informal workers as % of all workers	91.3	91.0	91.2	91.9	92.4
Percentage distribution of informal workers					
By type of employment:					
Self-employment	61.9	59.6	58.3	56.2	54.2
Casual wage employment	30.8	33.5	33.8	36.1	36.8
Regular wage employment	7.3	6.9	7.9	7.7	9.0
By sector of employment:					
Agriculture	75.2	72.4	67.9	66.4	63.6
Industry	10.7	11.9	14.1	14.0	14.4
Services	14.1	15.7	18.0	19.6	22.0

those in mature industrial economies. The available evidence suggests that the bulk of the employment in the organized segment was in services to begin with and that, over time, employment been shifting away from industry into services. India arguably has two parallel economies rather than a dual economy.

The changes in the pattern of employment of informal workers have been associated with significant growth of labour incomes. The clearest evidence is that the proportion of informal workers in poverty declined from 48 per cent in 1983 to 35 per cent in 1999–2000. The declining poverty also brought about a welcome decline in the incidence of child labour; the proportion of child workers in all informal workers declined from 6.8 per cent in 1983 to 2.5 per cent in 1999–2000.

These developments reflect the fact that the real daily wage rate for casual labourers in agriculture—the lowest wage rate in the economy—grew at a rate of 3 per cent per annum during 1978–2000. Yet there is little evidence to suggest that the degree of underemployment of informal workers was declining. It is clear, once again, that the wage rate is not market determined; it is linked to the average labour income

of a marginal worker in self-employment. The time trend in the informal wage rate essentially depends on the time trend in labour productivity in self-employment. If a change in the availability of resources or in production techniques increases the labour productivity in self-employment, the informal wage rate rises irrespective of what happens to the degree of underemployment. Similarly, population growth in the absence of any increase in productive resources or any change in production techniques drives down the informal wage rate, again irrespective of what happens to the degree of underemployment. The real wage rate for casual labour in agriculture rose because labour productivity in agricultural self-employment rose as a result of investments in irrigation, high-yielding varieties, chemical fertilizers, etc.

In short, the growth of the organized segment in India failed to generate a process of transformation of informal labour into formal labour. Fortunately, the growth of the unorganized segment, particularly of agriculture, was necessary for the growth of the organized segment. And it is agricultural growth that brought some modest improvements in the employment conditions of informal labour. That the improvements have been modest is clear from the fact that poverty still remains widespread.

Looking ahead, improving the conditions of informal workers must be regarded as a matter of urgency; widespread poverty and the associated ills have already been allowed to persist for too long. It is also important to recognize that programmes such as the recently launched employment guarantee scheme for rural areas, welcome though they are, can do little more than provide short-term relief to the poorer sections of informal workers. Achieving sustained improvement in the conditions of informal labour requires a growth strategy that emphasizes steady agricultural growth on the one hand and development of labour-intensive activities in the organized segment of the economy on the other. Adoption of such a strategy may be politically difficult as it will call for serious reforms of subsidy regimes and labour regulations. And there are easier alternatives. Agricultural stagnation is less of a constraint on the growth of the organized segment today than it had been in the past so that high economic growth can in principle be achieved simply by focusing on increasing the productivity of formal labour. But the temptation to adopt such a strategy must be resisted; for high economic growth of this type will largely bypass India's vast army of informal workers.

AJIT K. GHOSE

REFERENCES

Basu, Kaushik. 1984. *The Less Developed Economy*, Oxford, Basil Blackwell.

Chakravarty, Sukhamoy. 1987. *Development Planning: The Indian Experience*, Oxford, Clarendon Press.

Ghose, Ajit K. 1999. 'Current Issues of Employment Policy in India', *Economic and Political Weekly*, 34(36).

———. 2004. 'The Employment Challenge in India', *Economic and Political Weekly*, 39(48).

Lewis, W.A. 1954. 'Economic Development with Unlimited Supplies of Labour', *Manchester School*, 22: 139–91.

International Migration from India: Economic Impact

The first hundred years of migration from India since its modern inception in the 1830s was constituted largely of unskilled and low caste workers. Migrants in the nineteenth century came from poorer socio-economic groups, from poorer parts of the country, and went to (relatively poor) Southern countries. Between 1834 and 1937, 30.2 million people left India and 23.9 million returned, resulting in a net migration of 6.3 million (Davis 1951). A century later, international migration from India was starkly different in its selection characteristics. Migrants came from richer socio-economic groups, from wealthier parts of the country, and, with the significant exception of the large migration to the Middle East, went to industrialized countries. Post-Independence, an initial stream of unskilled and semi-skilled labourers migrated from Punjab and Gujarat to the United Kingdom (1950s to early 1960s). Another stream of unskilled and semi-skilled labourers went to the Gulf region (post-1973 oil shock) along with (for the first time) a substantial number of skilled labourers.

The latest stream has been high-skilled migration to the US following the liberalization of US immigration law in 1965. The large demand for information technology workers in the US in the late 1990s led to another wave of young professional immigrants and by 2003 immigrants from India emerged as the second largest group of legal immigrants to the US. This migrant stream has been the most highly educated, both compared to other immigrants into the US as well as to other Indian migrant streams abroad. Since the 1990s, increasing numbers of skilled emigrants from India have also been moving to Australia, Canada, New Zealand, and Singapore.

The impact of international migration depends critically on the magnitude and selection characteristics of migrating labour (including education, age, gender, vintage, and geographical and ethnic origins), the reasons for leaving, institutional features of the country of destination, and specific institutional features and policies to promote and harness these flows in the country of origin (Kapur and McHale 2005). The interaction of these factors in turn affects what aspects of the economy are most impacted by international migration and the mechanisms through which these impacts are amplified or attenuated. This entry focuses on three critical mechanisms that have most affected the Indian economy: financial capital, human capital, and reputational capital.

FINANCIAL CAPITAL

For nearly half a century Indian policymakers operated under conditions of foreign exchange scarcity. Attracting inflows from non-resident Indians (NRIs) has been part of the official thinking since 1970 when the first scheme to attract NRI flows was mooted. Inflows from the NRIs have come through the current account (remittances) and capital account (NRI banking deposits). Financial remittances emerged as an important part of India's balance of payments (BOP) since the oil-boom-induced Gulf migration in the 1970s. Remittances which were virtually negligible in 1970, rose to $ 0.43 billion in 1975 and jumped to $ 2.76 billion in 1980. However, they stagnated

during the 1980s, even dropping slightly to $ 2.4 billion in 1990. Since then they have climbed steeply to $ 11.1 billion in 1999 and $ 21.7 billion in 2003. As a percentage of India's gross domestic product (GDP), remittances grew from 1.2 per cent in 1991 to more than 3 per cent in 2003.

Paralleling the inflows of remittances have been NRI inflows in the capital account. Although schemes to attract the latter were introduced in 1970, a decade later deposits barely exceeded one billion dollars. During the 1980s, while remittances languished, deposits accelerated, growing to $ 12.4 billion by March 1990. Following the onset of the 1991 reforms, both remittances and NRI deposits grew rapidly in the 1990s with the latter totalling $ 35 billion by March 2006. This spurt has in part been due to the rapid growth in the stock of Indian citizens residing abroad (especially in North America) and the degree to which their earning power has increased. Policy changes including the large devaluation of the rupee and liberalization of gold imports have also made a difference, especially in bringing remittances from the Middle East through official channels rather than underground (hawala) markets.

In general NRI capital flows have been relatively stable and are comparable to portfolio equity flows, both exhibiting low volatility. They are influenced by standard risk and return variables, economic and political risk in the case of NRI capital flows, and the interest rate differential between deposit rates and LIBOR (London Inter-bank Offer Rate) in the case of portfolio equity flows (Gordon and Gupta 2004). The only significant behavioural difference between NRI capital flows and foreign portfolio investors is that the latter are much more sensitive to India's credit risk as assessed by foreign ratings agencies, while the former are more blasè about sovereign risk when they put money into India. The one clear case when NRI withdrawals amplified India's BOP crisis in 1991, appears to have been driven by the perception of an impending devaluation rather than credit risk per se. When storm clouds threatened, as in the aftermath of the Asian financial crisis in 1997 and India's nuclear tests in 1998, India raised funds from its diaspora: US$ 4.2 billion from the India Resurgent Bonds (RIBs) issued in 1998 and another US$ 5.5 billion from the India Millennium Deposit (IMD) scheme in 2000. In March 2006 NRI deposits accounted for 30 per cent of India's total long-term debt liabilities, exceeding even that owed to multilateral institutions. Together with remittances totalling $ 170 billion between 1991 and 2005, these inflows have been an important source of insurance, significantly contributing to India's burgeoning foreign exchange reserves and allowing the Government of India to retire multilateral debt prematurely and permitting Indian companies to refinance costly external borrowings.

In contrast to the large inflows in the current account and banking deposits in the capital account, NRI foreign direct investment (FDI) has been remarkably limited even controlling for low levels of FDI into India. Total NRI investment out of the total FDI approved since January 1991 to December 2003 was around 3.5 per cent. An oft-made comparison between the Chinese and Indian diasporas is that FDI from the former into China exceeds FDI from the latter into India twenty–twenty-five times over. During the 1990s annual average FDI flows into China as a share of gross fixed capital formation have exceeded 10 per cent while in India's case these have been barely above 2 per cent. Nearly 60 per cent of Chinese FDI (between 1978 and 1999) came from three ethnically Chinese

economies (ECEs)—Hong Kong, Macao, and Taiwan—while the diaspora's share in FDI in India has been under 4 per cent. However, overall financial inflows (that is remittances, NRI banking deposits, and diaspora FDI) from emigrants from the two countries are more comparable—with inflows into China being between two and four times those into India in absolute terms and roughly comparable as a fraction of GDP.

Despite their substantial size it is surprising how little we know of the macro and micro impacts of NRI financial inflows into India. There is considerable reporting confusion between inflows in the current and capital accounts and the RBI has been remarkably lackadaisical in revamping its statistical systems to better understand these inflows. Remittances have been much more important for some states than others. The most obvious case is Kerala where studies indicate that remittances now account for nearly a quarter of state net domestic product with wide-ranging economic and social consequences. Kerala's large investment in human capital, proximity and historical links to the Middle East, and the stagnation of the economy, all contributed to extensive international migration. Over time, migration, remittances, and return migration have transformed the state's economy, making it the most globalized of India's states—remittances are nearly a quarter of the state's economy. Remittances have fuelled a consumption boom and the resulting demand has driven growth in the service sector, most of which—such as transport, trade, and telecommunication—is non-tradables (Zachariah, et al. 2003). While much of the demand boom for consumer durables has spilled over to other states, one sector that has grown on the back of investments is the hospitality industry (tourism, transport, hotels, and restaurants), and private institutions in health and education have also mushroomed.

HUMAN CAPITAL

International migration has affected human capital formation in India in several ways. First, the *prospect* of migration current affects behaviour by changing forward expectations. For instance, at individual level the possibility of emigration leading to a higher expected return to human capital could lead to greater human capital investments. There are some indications that the burgeoning demand for private engineering, IT, and medical education in India and for English-language education are at least in part being fuelled by the prospects of higher returns from working abroad. Second, the so-called 'brain drain' results in an *absence* of scarce human capital. India has one of most positively selected emigration rates in the world. Recent estimates of the emigration rate from India for those with tertiary education are forty-two times those with primary and fourteen times those with secondary education. The implications of this loss are manifold, ranging from negative effects on institutions of higher education in India to the quality of health care and innovation. Nearly 60,000 Indian physicians (more than 10 per cent of the stock in India) practice abroad, and by all indications these come from the upper end of physician quality (Mullan 2006). An indication of the severity of the flight of scientific and engineering talent is the fact that the ratio of patents filed by Indians in North America to that by Indians in India (when normalized by population) is about 28,000:1 (Kapur n.d.). Third, there are human capital effects of the *diaspora* stemming from the flows of ideas from the diaspora. Some of India's most distinguished economists residing abroad have long been active participants and contributors to debates on India's

economic policies and a younger generation appears to be following suit. Increasingly, a large number of Indian-origin faculty in business schools abroad advise Indian firms. Fourth, *return migration* has augmented human capital through additional training, experience, and networks. Although financial flows resulting from international migration receive most attention, a potentially more important type of remittance is the flow of ideas be it technologies, theories, world-views, beliefs, or new ways of doing things. For instance, economic policymaking in India has been singularly affected by returning economists who have studied and worked abroad and have then worked in the economic policymaking institutions. However, while returning human capital in the 1950s and 1960s sought employment mainly in public-sector institutions, this is rarely the case in more recent years.

NETWORK AND REPUTATIONAL CAPITAL

The Indian diaspora has had important trade-enhancing and investment effects through its brokering role and by acting as a reputational enhancement mechanism. Firms and institutions in less developed countries (LDCs) are severely handicapped in the global arena because of reputational handicaps arising from a 'country-of-origin' effect.[1]

The success of the Indian diaspora has also made it possible for Indian diasporic networks to act as reputational intermediaries and credibility-enhancing mechanisms. This role has been particularly important in economic sectors such as software where knowledge, especially ex ante knowledge, of quality is tacit. Just as the Chinese diaspora played a critical role in the initial breakthrough of labour-intensive manufacturing exports from China the

[1] 'Reputation' here refers to prior beliefs of buyers of products and users of services.

Indian diaspora had a great role to play in the labour-intensive segment of IT—namely software and IT-related services. The destination of skilled labour flows from India to the US had important reputation effects. For instance, the Indian diaspora's success in Silicon Valley influenced how the world views India, reflecting the reputational spillover effects of success in a leading sector in a leading country. Of course once Indian IT's reputation was established, the role of the diaspora shifted to a brokering and human capital one.

In India's emergence as a leading exporter of cut and polished diamonds too, the Indian diaspora's reputational and brokering role has been critical. In 1968, India exported US$ 40 million in cut and polished diamonds. By 2003, India's exports of cut and polished diamonds had multiplied to US$ 7.1 billion, constituting 17 per cent of its total exports. India accounts for 55 per cent of world net exports of cut and polished diamonds in value terms, 90 per cent in terms of pieces, and 80 per cent in terms of caratage, making it the largest exporter of cut and polished diamonds in the world. Over 90 per cent of these diamonds were processed in Gujarat, employing over 1 million people in that state. India's rise as a world leader in the diamond industry over the past thirty-five years has been driven by the ascent of Indian èmigrè diamond traders (mostly Gujarati Palanpuri Jains) in Antwerp, the centre of the world diamond trade.

Despite the sizable flows of labour from India and the large India diaspora, data and analysis in this area are scant, hobbling our understanding of this complex issue. A major obstacle to understanding the economic impact of immigration on India is the lacuna in statistical systems commensurate with those that monitor the cross-border flows of capital and goods and services. While there are a host of potential statistical sources ranging from the National Sample Survey to visa and passport offices and the Protectorate of Emigrants, none have geared themselves up to collecting migration data that would lend themselves to analysis, perhaps because there is little external pressure from international organizations to do so.

DEVESH KAPUR

REFERENCES
Davis, Kingsley. 1951. *The Population of India and Pakistan*, Princeton, Princeton University Press.
Gordon, James and Poonam Gupta. 2004. 'Nonresident Deposits in India: In Search of Return?', IMF Working Papers 04/48.
Kapur, Devesh, n.d. 'Democracy, Death and Diamonds: The Domestic Impact of International Migration from India', unpublished book manuscript.
Kapur, Devesh and John McHale. 2005. *Give Us Your Best and Brightest: The Global Hunt for Talent and Its Impact on the Developing World*, Washington D.C., Center for Global Development and Brookings Institution.
Mullan, Fitzhugh. 2006. 'Doctors for the World: Indian Physician Emigration', *Heath Affairs*, 25(2): 380–93.
Zachariah, K.C., E.T. Mathew, and S. Irudaya Rajan. 2003. *Dynamics of Migration in Kerala: Dimensions, Differentials and Consequences*, New Delhi, Orient Longman.

Labour Laws in India

The intention of this entry is not to provide an exhaustive account of issues surrounding labour laws in general, but rather to critically describe some aspects of a significant law which acts as a metaphor for labour laws in general—The Industrial Disputes Act 1947 (IDA). I concentrate in particular on the scheme to resolve labour disputes and examine the IDA as an ostensible social security system. Among the many labour laws in India, the IDA probably reflects some of the most significant idiosyncrasies, one of which is the fact that it has a lineal connection with legislation aimed to further the British war effort during the Second World War. By legislating the IDA in 1947, Rule 81-A of the Defence of India Rules was formally inducted as law to become the key legislation associated with 'industrial relations', covering labour disputes, strikes, lock-outs, lay-offs, and retrenchments. These Rules were set up to ensure uninterrupted industrial production during the Second World War by structuring the role of both the executive and judicial arms of the state in a unique format to resolve 'industrial disputes'. Indian legislators at the time of Independence debated extensively on whether the labour legislation should be oriented towards a system where collective bargaining between unions and employers was encouraged or if a system should be developed that would emphasize state intervention in the resolution of conflicts. Protagonists favouring the latter, more paternalistic approach won on the grounds that this method would better serve the cause of social justice because a system of separate labour adjudication would keep in mind the 'power position and susceptibilities of workers' (Kennedy 1966).

THE INDUSTRIAL DISPUTE RESOLUTION SCHEME

The scheme elaborated in the IDA to settle a dispute can be summarized as follows. An industrial dispute, among other things, includes discharge or dismissal of workers, interpretation of standing orders, wages, bonus, rationalization, lay-offs, retrenchments, and conditions of work. The parties to a dispute have a couple of options open to them—they can set up a *Works Committee* consisting of representatives of the parties to the dispute and resolve the matter, but since the recommendations of such committees are not legally binding it is common practice to initiate a process referred to as *conciliation*, which involves the active participation of the executive branch of the government. The government steps into the picture if one of the disputing parties asks for intervention and the government considers the demand for such intervention valid. Alternatively, if a dispute appears to be persistent in the perception of the government, the government can also choose to intervene. Initially, if the dispute is particularly complex, a conciliation officer from the labour department or a Board of Conciliation appointed by the government is required to try working out a settlement. A settlement, though binding on all parties, is not as binding as a court order. As a consequence, it is widely held that conciliation is viewed merely as a stage before adjudication. If a settlement is not worked out, the conciliation officer or Board tables a failure report. At this point, parties to a dispute can ask for an arbitrator to resolve the conflict, but this again is not very common, as the award of the arbitrator does not have legal standing. Instead, proceedings then move to the final stage called adjudication, upon a reference being made by the government.

The IDA gives the government the power to appoint labour courts and tribunals to adjudicate disputes. There are three kinds of courts—labour courts, industrial tribunals, and national tribunals, structured in their inception, to conduct proceedings following inquisitorial methods. Labour courts deal with relatively minor matters—typically matters that affect less than 100 workmen, while industrial tribunals look after disputes of greater import and magnitude of workers involved. The judgments and awards of labour courts and tribunals are final and not subject to regular appeal. If some party to a dispute is not satisfied with the judgment or award, they can move for special leave appeal to the Supreme Court under Article 136 of the Constitution of India or seek writ jurisdictions of the relevant High Court under Articles 226 and 227 of the Constitution.

In this scheme, the role of trade unions is defined by the Trade Unions Act 1926, which allows any seven adults to gather and register themselves as a trade union. As a consequence, independent of the size of membership, all registered trade unions enjoy the same legal rights, powers, and privileges. Very broadly, these rights include the right to hold property, to contract, to litigate, and to be exempt from criminal liability if the union calls for a strike. However, the Act has no clause that obliges employers to recognize a particular union or even a set of unions as being representative of the workers' interests. This is a point that has been ratified by court decisions that have made it very clear that the law does not support obligatory recognition of a particular trade union as a bargaining agent.[1] At the same time Section 36 of the Industrial Disputes Act states that when a dispute arises, a worker can be represented by *any* registered trade union. This implies that while it is the volition of the employer to decide who is a representative bargaining agent; even the smallest union can bring up the grievances of its members into the dispute resolution process. As a consequence, multiple unions can exist, each winning the support of a fraction of the labour force employed in the concern, and the employer is obliged to deal with all of them.

[1]See for example *T.C.C Thozhilali Union* vs *T.C.C*, 1982 I L.L.J 425. In this judgment it is explicitly stated, 'Recognition by an employer of a trade union as a representative of its members and as their bargaining agent is a matter of volition on the part of the employer'.

Under this framework, the relationship between a union and an employer cannot be characterized by the usual understanding of the term cooperative bargain. Neither side is confined to a framework where a direct confrontation decides what each side will give and receive, because each side can always initiate or threaten to initiate the conciliation–adjudication process with the added ambiguity of who precisely are the players. As described in the preceding discussion, the conciliation–adjudication process involves participation by the executive arm of the government at many of the crucial stages of dispute resolution. The process of conciliation, initially placed in the hands of the labour department, may later end up involving the labour minister or even a higher executive functionary. Also, as noted earlier, if conciliation is not successful, the next stage involves the government as well. It is entirely the discretion of the government whether the dispute is referred for adjudication or not. Such involvement of the government at various steps of dispute resolution causes large-scale political interference in the resolution process. In fact prominent political parties control the bulk of union activity in India and the independent union movement is quite weak. A study based on a sample of dispute cases shows that unions affiliated to the ruling party were favoured by referring demands raised by them for adjudication, while reference of demands raised by rival unions was wilfully prevented (Saini 1993). As mentioned earlier, the adjudication process with respect to industrial dispute resolution was envisioned as being more inquisitorial rather than adversarial in nature. However, it is widely reported that in reality it is very much subject to standard adversarial procedures followed in most courts in India (Desai 1994). It appears that disputes get settled on the basis of legal norms and procedures rather than on particularities of the case, requiring unions to be represented by individuals who are conversant with legal procedures, to rebut employers who are represented by advocates. It has been observed that such considerations have given rise to the phenomenon of 'outsider union leaders' who man key positions in trade unions. These individuals, who are typically not workers, position themselves as having the requisite skill to see disputes through administrative, political, and legal hurdles. Such outsider union leaders may not have the interest of workers as their central objective and have been documented as being prone to working out underhand deals with employers that ultimately result in weaker unions (Saini 1995). Of course the exact orientation of such leaders would vary from case to case, but the overall point to note is that the relationship between workers and employers is not at all direct. Instead the relationship is mediated by a number of exogenous elements that include outsider union leaders, politicians, judges, and administrators.

One way of analysing this scheme is to perceive the intervention in a labour dispute by the executive and judicial arms of the state as resulting in an *exogenous contract*—termed so because bodies other than the contractors specify the 'contract' (Singh 2000). Though such a 'contract' is ostensibly driven by the concern to take into account the 'power position and susceptibilities of workers', the scheme described in the preceding paragraphs suggests such outcomes are clearly linked to the strategically engineered resources expended on the outcome, each party attempting a favourable outcome through the mediation of politicians, administrators, corporate lawyers, outsider union leaders, and judges. While all parties may be aware of such relations, in so much so as they are not able to simultaneously and precisely predict the exogenous contract— such outcomes are subject to the hazard of being inefficient. Such inefficiency arises from the fact that since each one of the parties functions with a set of tactical private information and networks which the other parties cannot be fully cognizant of, this structurally introduces agency problems that follow from the asymmetry of information across parties. This line of reasoning indicates that the idiosyncratic scheme of resolving industrial disputes encourages non-cooperative outcomes, where a structure that would encourage more direct relations between labour and its employers could support more cooperative results.

The scheme for industrial dispute resolution may not necessarily lead to equitable results either, particularly in the instance where employers have deep pockets, compounded by the endemic delays of the judicial system, a point that has been particularly stressed in the recent 'Report of the Second National Commission on Labour 2002' (SNCL, Government of India). The quest for equitable outcomes is possibly better met by giving workers rights that act to consolidate their bargaining power—the status of workers as a group could be influenced by a host of circumstances that can raise their well-being, say, by encouraging a framework that increases productive employment opportunities and by encouraging structures that favour collective bargaining. In this context the SNCL has very aptly, among other recommendations, suggested that the law be reoriented to encourage bipartite consultation at enterprise level and that disputes be resolved through voluntary arbitration rather than through adjudication. It is interesting to note that while India has signed some of the Conventions that form the 'ILO [International Labour Organization] Declaration on Fundamental

Principles and Rights at Work', it has not ratified the critical conventions regarding Freedom of Association, Right to Organize, and Collective Bargaining.

SOCIAL SECURITY

Apart from providing the scheme to resolve industrial disputes, the IDA also doubles up as a device to provide employment security to a class of workers employed in the formal sector. The IDA allows employers to layoff (temporarily severe the services of a worker) or retrench (permanently truncate the services of a worker) a worker only after they pay out a stipulated severance pay to the worker. However, in addition to this, 'large' employers are subject to further restrictions according to the stipulations laid down in Chapter V-B of the IDA: they have to actively seek permission from the government before they can layoff or retrench workers or even close the establishment. This Chapter is of comparatively recent vintage, having been added to the IDA in 1976 when it was legislated to cover establishments that employed 300 or more workers. Subsequently the Act was amended in 1984 to cover establishments employing 100 or more workers. Since labour legislation is in the Concurrent List of the Seventh Schedule of the Indian Constitution, amendments to the IDA at state level have resulted in further changes; for example in West Bengal, establishments employing fifty or more workers come under the aegis of Chapter V-B of the IDA. The adverse impact on the demand for labour in the organized sector on account of these laws has been widely noted (Fallon and Lucas 1993; Besley and Burgess 2004; and GOI 2001). However, the institutional change that is required to remedy the situation requires a wider discussion, not merely

calling for 'greater flexibility' in the labour market. It is important to appreciate that this is ultimately an issue of rights, and one way of initiating a discussion is to approach the problem using the frame provided by successive court judgments in response to a series of contestations that claimed that 'Chapter V-B of the IDA violated the fundamental right to carry on business and was therefore unconstitutional'.[2]

In the first judgment of this series, the Indian Supreme Court held in the *Excel Wear* vs *Union of India* case that the requirement that large concerns should seek permission from the government before they closed down was an 'unreasonable' restriction on the fundamental right to carry on business and that additionally the law was procedurally flawed because the government had the power to pass arbitrary orders.[3] In response to this, both the Indian state and subsequently the judiciary chose to interpret the judgment in a manner that diluted its intent. The 1984 amendment to the IDA translated the procedural objections raised in the Excel Wear case by merely requiring orders to state reasons for granting or refusing permission to close down, fixing a time frame within which an order had to be passed, and making provisions for review and/or appeal, while completely ignoring the substantial issues raised in the judgment. In the meanwhile, a series of High Court judgments also held the clauses pertaining to layoffs and retrenchments unconstitutional, which again resulted in relevant procedural changes being incorporated in the 1984 amendment to the IDA.[4] In addition,

[2] For a more detailed account, see Singh (2001).
[3] *Excel Wear* vs *Union of India* AIR 1979 SC 25.
[4] In *K. Gurumurthy* vs. *Simpson and Co.*, Madras (1981) II L.L.J. 360, Section 25-M (which

in *Workmen of Meenakshi Mills Ltd.* vs. *Meenakshi Mills Ltd.*, a Division Bench of the Supreme Court, in contrast to its earlier stance in the Excel Wear case, upheld the constitutional validity of the clause that requires employers to seek permission from the government before retrenching workers.[5] The decision was based on the argument that though the right to retrench is an integral part of the right to carry on business, the restriction imposed on this right by the law was justified because it protected the 'interests of the workers' which the state is obliged to guarantee according to the Preamble to the Constitution and the Directive Principles enshrined in it. The term 'interests of the workers' according to the judgment 'covers the interests of all workers employed in the establishment including not only the workers who are proposed to be retrenched but also the workers who are to be retained'.[6]

Translated into the language of economic analysis, it can be said that the rules governing the contract of employment under Common Law distribute the risk of an exogenous shock over both the

employer and the worker who runs the risk of being potentially unemployed, whereas the structure of rights under the IDA compels the employer to bear all the risks of a downswing. To make a normative judgment across these alternate states, the Pareto criterion is quite unhelpful; instead one needs to get some sense of the costs and benefits associated with each structure of rights. In a sense the Supreme Court in the Meenakshi Mills case, *did* perform a cost–benefit analysis while deciding whether the requirement that large firms should seek permission from the government before being allowed to retrench workers violates the fundamental right to carry on a business. To recall, the Supreme Court held that the requirement indeed violated the fundamental right to carry on a business, but such violation was justified in the interests of the workers. In other words, the implicit valuation was that the gains for workers from security of employment are far greater than the loss suffered by the employer. However, the crucial point to note is that in making this evaluation, the Supreme Court chose to perform the crucial evaluation over a very limited unit—a large employer and the workers who are employed in that concern. By ruling in favour of existing rights, the judgment sought to maximize social welfare over a very narrow domain of currently employed workers in large firms and their employers. The very limited domain taken into consideration allowed the ruling that the procedure of seeking permission from the government before retrenching workers is a fair requirement. While the allocation of rights and the procedure to implement these rights might be viewed as being just in the domain over which the Supreme Court has sought to maximize social welfare, once the domain is enlarged to include other effects and

---

deals with layoffs) was declared unconstitutional, while the Andhra Pradesh High Court in *General Industrial Society Ltd.* vs *Commissioner of Labour* (1980) I An. W.R. 92 held that Section 25-M was constitutionally valid. Turning to retrenchment, the Madras High Court in *K.V. Rajendran* vs *Dy. Commissioner of Labour Madurai* (1980) II L.L.J. 275 and the Rajasthan High Court in *J.K. Synthetics* vs *Union of India* (1984) 48 FLR 125 (Raj) held Section 25-N (which deals with retrenchment) to be violative of the Constitution, while the Andhra Pradesh High Court in *I.D.L. Chemicals Ltd.* vs *T. Gattiah* (Writ Appeal No 16 of 1981, decided on 4 December 1981) upheld the validity of Section 25-N.

[5] *Workmen of Meenakshi Mills Ltd.* vs *Meenakshi Mills Ltd.* (1992) 3 SCC 336.

[6] ibid. 377.

components of the economy, this position is less defensible.

The manner in which the rights of large employers have been curtailed has implications well beyond a particular enterprise and the workers employed in it. The retrenchment law forces an involuntary exchange on the employer in an attempt at redistribution; however, the consequences of this attempt are quite unlike the effects of more conventional schemes of redistribution such as taxation. Taxation might lower incentives, but it leaves agents free to participate in voluntary exchanges given their new asset positions. The scheme of redistribution sought by the retrenchment laws is to have a third party decide the outcome of what is essentially an exchange interaction, in the belief that the third party—in this case the labour department of the government—will only allow configurations that are in the interest of 'workers'. As employers are unsure of being given permission to retrench workers, they will plan in accordance with this anticipation, and as a result cut down on subsequent additions to their labour force—possibly substituting other factors of production for labour or plainly refusing to hire the labour that they might otherwise have hired. Thus, the law acts to pre-empt a number of strategies that producers might otherwise follow, but for the law.

To the extent Chapter V-B constrains the growth of employment that could absorb the substantial workforce that resides outside the formal sector, the laws are inimical to the spread of the benefits of growth and are therefore unjust. However, if the relevant domain is enlarged to include all workers, current and potential, the remedy has to engage with the fact that economic justice, in the final analysis, is associated with the allocation of risk across society.

Thus any process that aims to bring in the much-needed flexibility to the Indian labour market will have to engage with providing some security against risks of the market, by evaluating the possibilities of unemployment insurance or a social security system financed by a tax or a mix of both strategies.

JAIVIR SINGH

REFERENCES

Besley, Timothy and Robin Burgess. 2004. 'Can Regulation Hinder Economic Performance? Evidence from India', *Quarterly Journal of Economics*, 119, February: 91–134.

Desai, D.A. 1994. 'Industrial Adjudication and Social Justice in India', in Debi S. Saini, ed., *Labour Judiciary, Adjudication and Industrial Justice*, New Delhi, Oxford & IBH Publishing Co.

Fallon, Peter R. and Robert Lucas. 1993. 'Job Security Regulations and the Dynamic Demand for Industrial Labour in India and Zimbabwe', *Journal of Development Economics*, 40: 241–55.

Kennedy, V. D. 1966. *Unions Employers and Government*, Bombay, Manaktalas.

Government of India (GOI). 2001. Report of the Task Force on Employment Opportunities, Planning Commission, Government of India.

Saini, Debi S. 1993. 'Reference Power of State in Industrial Disputes Adjudication: A Study with Reference to Industrial Disputes in Faridabad', *Journal of the Indian Law Institute* 35 (Part II) (4): 233–52.

———. 1995. 'Leaders or Pleaders: Dynamics of Brief-Case Trade Unionism Under Existing Legal Framework', *Journal of the Indian Law Institute*, 37(1): 73–91.

Singh, Jaivir. 2000. 'Judicial Intervention in the Contract of Employment: Some Reflections on Labour Adjudication in India', mimeo., New Delhi, CDE, Delhi School of Economics.

———. 2001. 'Some Aspects of Industrial and Labour Markets in India: Perspectives from Law and Economics', unpublished PhD dissertation, Department of Economics, University of Delhi.

Mobility of Population

MIGRATION TRENDS AT MACRO LEVEL

Population mobility in the Indian subcontinent has historically been relatively low. Researchers like Kingsley Davis (Davis 1951) have attributed this to the prevalence of the caste system, joint families, traditional values, diversity of language and culture, lack of education, and predominance of agriculture and semi-feudal land relations. By the Davisian logic, improvements in

levels of education and in transport and communication facilities, shift of workforce from agriculture to industry and tertiary activities, etc. would increase mobility. Interestingly, however, an analysis of the trend in population mobility in post-Independence India reveals that, despite significant improvements in education, transport and communication facilities, growth of industries, diversification of the economy, and modernization of norms and values, population mobility at macro level has declined. A number of micro-level

Table 1   Internal Migrants in Various Categories 1961–2001

	Percentage to total population				Total migrants in millions	
	1961	1971	1981	1991	2001	2001
Total Migrants						
Intercensal	15.0	12.4	12.2	9.7	9.5	98.3
Intercensal inter-state	2.0	1.6	1.6	1.3	1.6	16.8
Lifetime	30.6	28.7	29.4	26.5	29.2	301.1
Lifetime inter-state	3.3	3.4	3.6	3.3	4.2	42.3
Male Migrants						
Intercensal	11.3	9.4	8.9	6.1	6.2	32.9
Intercensal inter-state	2.2	1.8	1.6	1.2	1.6	8.5
Lifetime	18.3	17.2	16.6	13.8	16.4	87.2
Lifetime inter-state	3.4	3.4	3.3	2.8	3.7	19.7
Female Migrants						
Intercensal	19.0	15.7	15.7	13.5	13.2	65.4
Intercensal inter-state	1.7	1.3	1.7	1.5	1.7	8.3
Lifetime	43.7	41.1	43.1	40.3	43.0	213.7
Lifetime inter-state	3.2	3.4	3.9	3.8	4.6	22.7
Rural Male Migrants						
Intercensal	8.4	7.1	6.3	4.2	4.0	15.2
Intercensal inter-state	0.9	0.8	0.7	0.5	0.6	2.3
Lifetime	13.9	12.9	11.5	9.4	10.5	40.2
Lifetime inter-state	1.4	1.3	1.2	0.9	1.1	4.4
Urban Male Migrants						
Intercensal	23.8	18.5	16.9	11.7	11.7	17.7
Intercensal inter-state	7.9	5.6	4.4	3.3	4.1	6.2
Lifetime	37.5	33.6	32.4	26.0	31.2	47.0
Lifetime inter-state	12.3	11.2	10.0	8.0	10.2	15.3

Note: Lifetime migrants are by their place of birth while intercensal migrants are by their place of last residence for reasons of temporal comparability.

studies have come to similar conclusions (Racine 1997).

The pattern of internal migration (excluding international migrants) has been presented in Table 1 using data from the population census. It may be seen here that mobility of population has declined systematically from 1961 to 2001, both in rural as well as urban areas. Focusing on mobility of men, wherein economic factors are likely to be relatively more important, the decline in the percentage of migrants can be seen to be significant in case of lifetime migrants, intercensal (shifting place of residence during the last decade) migrants, and inter-state intercensal migrants. Recently released data from the Population Census 2001 reveal that the percentages of lifetime migrants have gone up marginally both for men and women during the 1990s. The 2001 figures are nonetheless less than those of the 1960s or 1970s.

Importantly, the share of intercensal migrants has continued to fall almost continuously in all categories during 1961–2001. This implies that the growth rates of (male) intercensal migrants have been less than those of the rest of the population. The decline is markedly steep in the case of male migrants, both in rural as well as urban areas, which can be attributed, besides the rigidities of the agrarian system, growing regionalism, etc., to inhospitable environment in cities and towns. The share of (intercensal) migrants in the total incremental urban population was 22 per cent during the 1980s which has come down marginally to 21 per cent during the 1990s. A fall in the rate of urbanization during 1991–2001 also confirms the decline in population mobility in the country. The pattern is similar for female intercensal migrants, although the rate of decline is less than that for males.

National Sample Survey (NSS) data for the past two decades also confirm the declining trend of migration for males, both in rural as well as urban areas, although the fall is less than that reported in the census. The migration rates had declined to all-time lows in 1993, whereafter there has been a slight recovery. The fact that percentages of migrants in 1993 are marginally higher than the figures for 1999 (but less than those for 1983) may be attributed to the more liberal definition of migrants adopted in the 55th round of the NSS (see Kundu 2003). For women, the percentage of female migrants as per NSS data has gone up marginally during the past couple of decades. The general conclusion that thus emerges unmistakably is that mobility of men, which is often linked to the strategy of seeking livelihood, has gone down systematically over the past few decades. Unfortunately, the ghost of overurbanization has weighed heavily on the minds of demographers and urban planners. This has been backed by the phenomenal urban growth observed during the 1950s and 1970s that is now believed to be partly definitional. As a consequence, all official projections of urban population during the 1980s and 1990s, including those of the Planning Commission and the Expert Committee for Population Projections, have erred on the higher side. The recent projections of urban growth made by the United Nations (UNO 1995) are somewhat lower but still not untouched by the overurbanization hypothesis. The current data on urban population and migration seriously question all these projections.

MIGRATION DYNAMICS—THE REGIONAL DIMENSION

According to the neoclassical models of growth and labour mobility, spatial disparity in development, ceteris paribus, would result in migration from backward to developed states and regions which would help in bringing about optimality in the spatial distribution of economic activities. The mobility pattern observed in India fits well in these models. The analysis of inter-state migrants, attempted on the basis of census as well as NSS data reveals that the less-developed states report a high percentage of net out-migrants. The developed states, on the other hand, turn out to be in-migrating in character.

In recent decades, however, the migration pattern has been different. There has been a steep and consistent decline in the rates of net out-migration from backward states like Bihar, Rajasthan, and Uttar Pradesh. Importantly, Madhya Pradesh and Orissa stand out as exceptions as these report significant inflow of population. This could be explained in terms of massive public-sector investment, resulting in creation of job opportunities in industry and business. The local population, unfortunately, is not able to take advantage of these developments because of low levels of literacy and skills.

Developed states like Karnataka, Maharashtra, Tamil Nadu, and West Bengal that have been attracting large-scale in-migration, now report decline in in-migration rates. The state of Gujarat does not show this declining trend due to its growing dominance on the industrial map of India. Similarly, Haryana reporting high in-migration rates during recent decades can be explained in terms of migration from Punjab due to social instability and communal tensions in the 1980s.

Some scholars have explained the decline in inter-state migration (Mehrotra 1974) in terms of developmental programmes launched by the central and state governments in the post-Independence period. Furthermore, better transport, communication, and commutation facilities are supposed to have reduced the need to shift residence for employment or education, since people can now commute to neighbouring cities and towns. Undoubtedly, there is some truth in these arguments but they are not adequate to explain growing immobility. An analysis of the regional structure of development would discount the regional imbalances hypothesis since inter-state inequality in several dimensions of economic and social development has not declined and in many cases has gone up. A better explanation could possibly be found in the growing assertion of regional identity, education in regional languages up to high school, adoption of Master Plans and land use restrictions at city level, etc.; all these directly or indirectly discourage migration. This would discount the proposition that the mobility of labour, operationalized through market, would ensure optimal distribution of economic activities in space.

CHANGES IN THE COMPOSITION OF MIGRANTS

The most important change in the composition of migration is the sharp decline in the percentage of persons reporting economic factors as the reason for mobility. As many as 36 per cent of the recent rural male migrants (less than one-year duration) had reported new, better employment or transfer as the reason for their migration decision in 1983, as per the NSS data. This has come down to 25 per cent in 1999. For women, the percentage has declined from 5 to 3. Economic factors have become less important in migration decisions among urban migrants as well. For males, the percentage figure has gone down from 46 to 34 while the corresponding

Table 2   Percentage of Migrants across Monthly Per Capita Expenditure
(MPCE) Classes 1999–2000

	Rural			Urban	
MPCE class (Rs)	Men	Women	MPCE class (Rs)	Men	Women
0–225	4.3	31.6	0–300	10.5	32.1
225–55	3.7	34.2	300–50	13.0	35.6
255–300	4.0	38.0	350–425	13.4	37.3
300–40	4.6	39.8	425–500	19.7	39.9
340–80	4.9	41.3	500–75	21.1	40.9
380–420	5.8	43.2	575–665	23.9	41.2
420–70	6.3	44.3	665–775	27.8	45.3
470–525	7.3	46.1	775–915	30.7	43.6
525–615	8.6	48.6	915–1120	37.1	48.3
615–775	10.7	51.5	1120–1500	41.2	48.6
775–950	14.5	53.0	1500–1925	38.8	47.3
950 & above	23.3	57.0	1925 & above	43.3	49.3
All	6.9	42.6	All	25.7	41.8

figures for women are 8 and 3.[1] The increase in the share of women among migrants under all categories and durations is yet another indication of the growing importance of non-economic factors since marriage and joining the family are the major factors responsible for their mobility.

A related conclusion is that economic deprivation is less of a factor in migration of males now than in preceding decades. The migration rate in rural areas is as high as 23.3 per cent in the category with the highest monthly per capita expenditure (MPCE), going down systematically with expenditure levels. The rate is as low as 4.3 in the lowest class (Table 2). The same is the case in urban areas as well, the corresponding percentages being 43.3 and 10.5. The pattern is identical for women both for rural as well as urban

areas. It is important to point out that this is not clinching evidence that economically better-off people are more likely to migrate to avail of new economic opportunities elsewhere, since the expenditure levels reflect the post-migration situation. It is possible that people have moved to a higher consumption expenditure category *after* or *because of* the mobility. However, such post-migration upward movement may not be so high as to render the hypothesis that people in the high expenditure categories are more likely to migrate invalid. Also, the poor are unlikely to shift to top expenditure categories after migration where the percentage of migrants is very high.

The share of in-migrating households to total households in different per capita expenditure categories does not show a clear pattern. The figure happens to be high in some of the low, middle, and high expenditure categories. A similar mixed pattern can be observed in case of percentages of households reporting out-migrating members, outside the state or the country. At best, one could say that the distribution is bimodal, high

[1] There have been some classificatory changes, as far as the reasons for migration over various NSS rounds are concerned. This has rendered strict temporal comparison somewhat difficult. The definitions, however, have not changed in the last two NSS rounds which reveal that the share of all employment-related migration has gone down during 1993–9, except for urban males.

Table 3   Percentage of Migrants in Different Social Groups

Social groups	Rural			Urban		
	male	female	person	male	female	person
Scheduled tribe	5.6	35.7	20.4	28.2	41.1	34.5
Scheduled caste	6.4	43.4	24.4	22.5	39.3	30.5
Other backward caste	6.5	42.8	24.2	23.7	41.7	32.3
Others	8.1	44.3	25.9	27.6	42.6	34.7
All	6.9	42.6	24.4	25.7	41.8	33.4

values occurring at the lowest and highest expenditure classes. From these, one would infer that both poor and rich households are reporting mobility. This, too, would question the proposition that poverty is the key factor in migration.

Interestingly, migration rates among rural households do not vary linearly with size of their landholdings, as per NSS data. Indeed, households having virtually no land (less than 0.01 ha) report the highest migration rate. But then marginal farmers with the smallest landholdings—between 0.01 and 0.20 ha—report low migration. The rates are high again in the middle-level (between 1 and 3 ha) landowning category. Above that, the figures are once again low. The same pattern is observed to hold among scheduled caste (SC) and scheduled tribe (ST) households as well.

Migration rates for SC/ST or for other backward castes (OBC) are around 6 per cent among rural males in 1999–2000 (Table 3). The rate for other (non-backward) castes is over 8 per cent. For women, too, the migration rate for the non-backward classes is marginally higher than that of the others. In urban areas, however, the rates for SC/ST, backward, and other castes are not very different. One may infer that poverty and immiserization, often linked with SC, ST, and OBCs, and push-factor[2] migration do not provide major explanations for population mobility.

In a fast-globalizing economy like India, new employment opportunities are coming up in selective sectors and in a few regions/urban centres. While the poor constitute a large proportion of migrants, a substantial number belong to the middle- and high-income categories, grabbing new opportunities thrown up in the process of globalization. It would, therefore, be erroneous to consider all migrants as destitutes or economically and socially displaced persons, moving from place to place as part of their survival strategy. Furthermore, the fact that the percentage of migrants has declined and their economic and social status is better than that of non-migrants and has even improved over time, reflects barriers of mobility for the poor. With growing regionalism, service provision being based on market affordability, and changes in skill requirements in the urban labour market, the emerging productive and institutional structure has become hostile to newcomers. This has made the migration process selective wherein the poor who are unskilled labourers are finding it difficult to access the livelihood opportunities coming up in developed regions and large cities.

AMITABH KUNDU

---

[2]As per the forty-ninth Round of the NSS, the percentage of migrant households among STs was as high as 2.7 per cent in rural areas in 1993. The figure for SCs is 0.9 per cent against the national average of 1.1 per cent. Correspondingly, in urban areas, the percentage figure for STs is 2.9 against the SC and national figures of 2.1 and 2.2.

REFERENCES

Davis, Kingsley. 1951. *The Population of India and Pakistan*, New Jersey, Princeton University Press.

Kundu, A. 2003. 'Urbanisation and Urban Governance: Search for a Perspective beyond Neo-Liberalism', *Economic and Political Weekly*, 38(29).

Kundu, A. and S. Gupta. 2000. 'Declining Population Mobility, Liberalisation and Growing Regional Imbalances—The Indian Case', in A. Kundu, ed., *Inequality, Mobility and Urbanisation*, New Delhi, Indian Council of Social Science Research and Manak Publications.

Mehrotra, G.K. 1974. Birth Place Migration in India, Census of India 1971, *Special Monograph*, no. 1, New Delhi, Government of India.

Racine, Jean Luc, ed. 1997. *Peasant Moorings: Village Ties and Mobility Rationales in South India*, New Delhi, Sage.

United Nations Organization. 1995. *The UN Study of World Urbanization Prospects*.

Population Policy

Any textbook or discussion on population policy finds it necessary to acknowledge that India was the first country to officially have both a population policy as well as a family planning programme—the two are not necessarily the same thing, though they get equated in practice as well as in popular discourse. This happened as far back as 1951, when the rest of the world took either or both of two approaches—bemoaned the burgeoning populations of the developing world (and in the case of the United States, fretted about what this implied for the Cold War) and/or (except for a few loud pioneers like Margaret Sanger and Marie Stopes) acted coy about or downright hostile to the idea of its own women using contraception.

But while India is held up as the trailblazer in all discourses on population policy and family planning programmes, this must not be taken to imply a purely home-grown and home-sustained affair. For one thing, even if an 'official' interest in population and family planning was expressed in India before it was anywhere else in the world, this interest was in many ways a natural outgrowth of the intense non-governmental and popular interest in these matters in the Western world in the early and mid-twentieth century. Independent India's official position on the population question was also directly encouraged, funded, and technically supported by an increasingly aggressive international population control movement that saw the country both as a testing ground for family planning efforts and new contraceptive technology, as well as central to any attempts to reducing developing country population growth rates.

In any case, the earliest native proponents of population policy in India were all heavily exposed to and influenced by both neo-Malthusian debates as well as the arguments of women's health advocates in the West. And within India itself, the population and family planning question was by no means a post-colonial preoccupation—the London-based neo-Malthusian League had several Indian vice-presidents, a branch was established in Madras as early as in 1928—the population theme was repeatedly discussed in pre-1947 legislative assemblies, primarily by upper-caste members decrying the unbridled fecundity of the poor masses.

All these pre-Independence preoccupations with the population problem, well before there was actually any significant rise in population growth rate, meant that by the time of the First Five Year Plan, the country was ripe for an official policy. At this time, the Ministry of Health was allotted Rs 6.5 million by the Planning Commission for a family planning programme. The Commission also recommended further research on population issues. While the promotion of artificial birth control was opposed by some individuals, including the Health Minister Rajkumari Amrit Kaur, Prime Minister Nehru was able to overrule these objections. And since that time, population has remained a major subject in planning documents and on-the-ground operations in one form or another, often controversial, but never abandoned fully. Among the major policy instruments[1] that the country took a lead in promoting must be mentioned the drastic liberalization of its abortion laws through the Medical Termination of Pregnancy Act of 1972, a piece of legislation which made abortion available virtually on demand. Whatever the population control and/or women's welfare motives behind this Act, it is today one of the facilitators of the increasing practice of sex-selective abortions in the country.

What kinds of arguments have motivated and continue to motivate the very existence of Indian population policy? The 1994 Cairo Conference on Population and Development somehow gave the impression that earlier advocates of population policy were motivated solely by demographic, as opposed to individual, concerns. But any serious history of the population movement in India cannot fail to discern at least three parallel streams of concern that egged on government action in the form of policy statements, even if these 'ideological' streams were not equally strong or equally effective at all times. Nor were these three streams necessarily mutually exclusive in individuals or groups—it was all too common for more than one of them to motivate the same person.

The first (but not necessarily the FIRST) such openly stated support for

[1]For a detailed description of these instruments, see Visaria and Chari (1998).

official population policy came from the neo-Malthusians, from those who saw the rapid population growth unleashed by mortality declines in mid-century India as a serious drag on development and a serious impediment to poverty eradication. The Coale and Hoover (1958) text that became compulsory reading in undergraduate economics courses in the 1960s and 1970s was a formal attempt to demonstrate the ways in which economic growth would be hampered by rapid population growth in India. The arguments advanced in it influenced Indian planning in the 1960s and continue to haunt even the more individual-centred population policy documents of today. Note for example the slipping in of phrases to do with 'sustainable development' in the 2000 National Population Policy, which is otherwise explicitly centred on a reproductive health agenda. In fact, within the framework of this 'national' policy, several states continue to devise measures that have more or less explicit fertility control agendas. Incentives and disincentives, the bad words of the 1970s, are important parts of this promotion of supposedly voluntary birth control.

But alongside this population control (the currently fashionable phrase is population stabilization) agenda, there has always been a genuine advocacy of family planning services for the sake of women's health and freedom. In fact, it was this motive that justified the original creation of an official family planning programme in the 1950s, with a slower growing population being viewed as an additional benefit rather than the central goal (Visaria 2000). To be fair, even after the programme gained momentum for population growth reasons, there was always a stream of support for it that focused on the need for contraceptive access for women and children's welfare. The integration of the family planning programme with the maternal and child health programme in the mid-1960s was a reflection of this perspective, at the same time as the population growth rationale was used to introduce time-bound, method-specific targets into the programme.

In other words, at least two of the rationales for a national population policy were arguably less distasteful than later projections of them made them out to be (Basu 1997a). Often enough they ended up with their more distasteful ends being privileged, especially on the ground, but there is nothing *inherently* objectionable in concerns about the implications of high fertility and rapid population growth for women's welfare and/or national development. However, there is a third and continuing stream of support for an aggressive population policy that has always existed in some form or the other and is difficult to condone on either empirical or ethical grounds. This support takes the form of wanting the state to run a coercive or semi-coercive family planning programme so that the fertility of the 'other' may be curtailed. This is one kind of eugenics argument because it is concerned with changing the us-versus-them distribution of the population. Who this other is has varied with time and place—sometimes it is the poor that have too many children, at other times it is the lower castes, sometimes it is the uneducated, most often it is the minorities. Never is it us—those who would thrust family planning upon the other—who need to do anything about our own fertility or anything directly about the poverty or illiteracy or minority status anxiety that fosters high birth rates in these others.

This attitude is completely analogous to the Western world's push to bring down Third World birth rates which so regularly riles Third World elites. It is also this attitude that was expressed in the growing coerciveness of the Indian family planning programme which culminated in the excesses of the Emergency, when several parts of the country witnessed the forcible mass sterilization of men too old or poor or weak or unorganized to protest. The 1976 National Population Policy explicitly espoused legislation to make family planning compulsory. It is especially ironical that the Minister for Health and Family Planning at this time was the very person who had made history at the United Nations International Population Conference in Bucharest in 1974 by declaring that the Western world was mistaken in pushing birth control in the developing countries when in fact 'development is the best contraceptive'.

The nature of population and family planning policy during the Emergency brought down the government. In addition, it had one serious effect that has in fact now become somewhat institutionalized. Because of the severe backlash that the Emergency experience created against contraceptive acceptance, post-1977 the distribution of acceptors suddenly changed completely—from being something that focused on male sterilization, the family planning programme became entirely targeted at female acceptors and that too almost exclusively at female acceptors of sterilization, even though vasectomy is a much simpler and safer procedure than tubectomy and even though in principle the programme is committed to offering a cafeteria of methods (Basu 1985).

The target-driven, female-centred family planning programme that characterized Indian policy was an important source of the growing resentment against government-sponsored population programmes worldwide by all kinds of activist groups and the Cairo Conference on Population and Development at last gave these groups the clout to completely change the paradigm—'reproductive health' rather than population control or family planning became the new goal of population policy in international documents as well as in government policy statements. While many of these national policies began as little more than rhetorical documents, thanks to continued monitoring and pressure from a variety of international and domestic non-governmental organizations, population policy in India does seem to be making some real transition to a more women-friendly approach. Method-specific targets were abolished in 1996 (unfortunately interpreted in some places to mean that services are not provided even to women who want them); local institutions became increasingly more responsible for programme needs assessments and design; a Reproductive and Child Health Programme was launched in 1997; and a National Population Commission was set up in May 2000 (with a whopping 100 members), as envisaged in the new National Population Policy of February 2000.

And while the fertility question continues to be politicized by many groups (Basu 1997b), there are also more restraining voices. For example, while the Rashtriya Swayamsevak Sangh continues to officially (at least in the statements of its leaders like K.S. Sudarshan) exhort Hindus to have more children to avoid being outnumbered by Muslims, at the silver jubilee celebrations of the Bharatiya Janata Party in December 2005, party President L.K. Advani actually openly promoted the two-child family norm for all Indians.

All these are good portents. But no consideration of population policy is possible without some reflection on the r-vs-R problem. By which I mean the rhetoric-versus-Reality question. Like most policy documents that emerge from the Planning Commission or other agencies of the Indian government, especially the central government, successive versions of

population policy have also been articulate, well reasoned, reasonable, and often literary. Reading one of these versions, and especially reading post-Cairo versions, if one foolishly equated policy formulation with policy implementation, one would think that all India's population and reproductive health-related needs were being well taken care of by capable hands.

But, as scores of studies demonstrate, the ground reality is often totally disconnected from the rhetoric of these policy statements. If the policy statement proclaims its intent to address the contraceptive needs of adolescents and nulliparous married women, in reality, hardly ever does a family planning worker touch base with these categories of persons. Population policy may stress the need for a 'cafeteria' approach to the contraceptive methods it offers, but the bulk of family planning practice continues to consist of female sterilization. Policy statements may recognize the need for well-staffed primary health centres and may even lay down detailed staffing norms; but the vast majority of these centres do not have a female medical officer, a large number do not have any doctor at all, and a sizable proportion do not even have an auxiliary nurse midwife (and whether these functionaries, when they do exist on the rolls, actually exist in person on any given day is another matter altogether).[2] On all these matters, the pessimist shakes his head in despair, but the optimist sees teething problems that will be overcome, that must be overcome.

ALAKA MALWADE BASU

REFERENCES

Basu, A.M. 1985. 'Family Planning and the Emergency: An Unanticipated Consequence', *Economic and Political Weekly*.

[2]For empirical evidence on all these points, see the review by Santhya (2003).

_____. 1997a. 'The New International
Population Movement: A Framework for
a Constructive Critique', *Health Transition
Review*.

_____. 1997b. 'The "Politicization" of Fertility
to Achieve Non-demographic Objectives',
Population Studies.

Coale, A. and E.M. Hoover. 1958. *Population
Growth and Economic Development in Low
Income Countries: A Case Study of India's
Prospects*, Princeton, Princeton University
Press.

Santhya, K.G. 2003. 'Changing Family Planning
Scenario in India: An Overview of Recent
Evidence', The Population Council South and
East Asia Regional, Working Paper No. 17,
New Delhi, The Population Council.

Visaria, L. 2000. 'From Contraceptive Targets
to Informed Choice: The Indian Experience',
in R. Ramasubban and S.J. Jejeebhoy, eds,
*Improving Quality of Care in India's Family
Planning Programme*, New Delhi, Rawat
Publications.

Visaria, P. and V. Chari. 1998. 'India's Population
Policy and Family Planning Program:
Yesterday, Today and Tomorrow', in A. Jain,
ed., *Do Population Policies Matter: Fertility
and Politics in Egypt, India, Kenya and
Mexico*, New York, The Population Council.

Trade Unions

In the year 2000, there were about 65,000
registered trade unions with 5.4 million
members—constituting 19 per cent of
organized-sector employment, and less
than 2 per cent of the workforce.[1] Unions
are mostly functional in large factories and
offices; over one-half of the union members
work in utilities and in the tertiary sector,
mainly in government and publicly owned
entities. The unorganized sector remains

[1] The organized sector consists of public
sector, private corporate sector and cooperatives,
manufacturing units registered under the Factories
Act, 1948 or Bidi and Cigar Workers Act, 1966,
and recognized educational institutions.

largely outside the purview of trade unions,
except perhaps in Kerala. As unionized
workers largely represent educated and
skilled workforce employed in capital- and
knowledge-intensive sectors, their conduct
usually has economy-wide effects.

The Trade Unions Act 1926 permits
registration of a union with seven members
of a factory, firm, or trade, granting them
immunity against civil and criminal
proceedings to pursue their collective interest;
in return, unions are required to submit
annual reports of their membership and
audited accounts. But the registration does
not confer recognition as a bargaining agent
in bilateral negotiations with management.
Industrial relations in India rest on this law,
along with the Industrial Disputes Act 1947
and the Industrial Employment (Standing
Orders) Acts 1946. However, as labour is a
concurrent subject under the Constitution,
state governments can modify these laws,
subject to Presidential approval.

Introduction of modern factory
manufacturing during the second half of
the nineteenth century, mainly in cotton
and jute textiles, forms the genesis of the
Trade Union Act. In a short time the
cotton and jute mills became competitive
in the domestic market and posed a
challenge to the supremacy of the British
textile industry, partly based on the wage
differential between the two countries.
Rapid growth of these industries in an
unregulated environment also brought
in concerns about workers' welfare and
sporadic protests against long working hours
and inhuman working conditions in these
mills—especially for women and children.
The British textile interests endorsed a
similar view, as they were losing markets to
upcoming Indian mills. Thus, in response
to the growing concerns about labour
welfare as well as the British textile interests,
colonial government enacted many labour

laws in the late nineteenth century, the Trade Union Act of 1886 being the prominent one; amended in 1926, the law continues to be in force to this day.

Historically, middle-class philanthropists, social workers, politicians, and freedom fighters led trade unions—often justified on the grounds that uneducated workers are usually unaware of legal and technical matters for negotiating with employers. While such a leadership may have been advantageous initially, such leaders have less appreciation of workers' grievances arising on the shop floor, and issues arising out of technical change, work intensification and economic incentives. Unions are invariably affiliated to political parties and claim to leverage their political strength to bargain with the employers, in return for workers' loyalty and votes. The Indian National Trade Union Congress (INTUC), the federation of unions affiliated to the Congress party, is probably the largest 'umbrella' of trade unions in recent times.

In the pre-Independence period, union leaders were drawn into the freedom movement with the motive not only of improving the conditions of factory workers but also of involving the emerging working class in the struggle for national independence, and (as with some unions) struggle against colonialism and British imperialism. Therefore, the evolution of the trade union movement is closely intertwined with national politics—a link that still persists (as in many countries).

TRENDS IN TRADE UNIONS

While the number of the registered trade unions rose over the four decades since 1960–1, their membership declined by about 0.6 million in the 1990s. More seriously, the proportion of workers unionized declined from 33 per cent of the organized workforce in 1960–1 to less than

20 per cent four decades later; the average size of the union has fallen from about 354 members to eighty-three (see Figure 1) in this period. Though the declining trend is indisputable, these numbers need to be treated with caution. They are based on the returns submitted by the unions, an exercise which has fallen precipitously to 11 per cent of the total number of unions. However, there is more to these numbers, as will be discussed in the following pages.

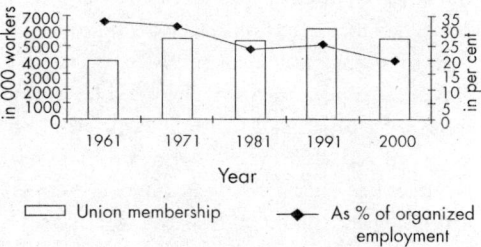

Figure 1   Trade Union Membership in India

Proliferation of trade unions in the existing organizations and their divisions along political lines are distinctive features of the trade union movement. Unlike in the advanced countries, there seems to be no institutionalized system of collection of dues, statutory audit of unions' accounts, and filing of the returns. Therefore, information on the registered unions and their strength is largely notional. While registering a union may be easy, it is hard to find effective trade unions in smaller establishments with, say, up to hundred workers, as employers can easily victimize the unionized workers and their potential leaders. In a situation of excess supply of labour in a heterogeneous society, employers can easily replace the 'troublemakers' with docile workers, effectively divided along caste, communal, and linguistic lines.

What explains the decline in trade unionism? Partly, it represents a worldwide trend in the second half of the twentieth century. However, there could be some specific factors relating to evolution of the Indian economy and its institutions that may also have contributed to the observed decline.

Despite being a large labour surplus economy (in contrast to many East Asian economies), the industrial sector in India was dominated by large factories, where it is easy to unionize the workers. But during the last half century, in response to a variety of policy initiatives and the development of capital market, spread of electricity and modern infrastructure, and growing inter-firm relations, industrial employment in India has moved into smaller-sized factories within the organized sector, and into the unorganized sector (employing ten or less workers per establishment), where employers exercise greater control over the workplace and employment contracts tend to be flexible and often personalized; hence it is difficult to unionize workers. However, the evolution of industrial relations may also have contributed to the fall in trade union strength.

INDUSTRIAL RELATIONS IN INDIA

India follows a tripartite industrial relations system wherein the state, in principle, mediates in all disputes between workers and employers. The law forbids workers or employers from going on strike or declaring lockout without giving a notice of fourteen days. When a strike or lockout notice is served, even if the labour department gets an inkling of a dispute, it initiates a conciliation process. If it fails, the dispute has to be referred for arbitration and finally for compulsory adjudication. On the face of it, the mechanism is highly interventionist, skewed towards labour to protect the weaker party, to ensure uninterrupted production and industrial harmony. But the reality seems different. The decision arrived at by the conciliation mechanism is not binding on the management or labour. The state does not

have judicial powers to enforce its decision on the parties in dispute. Evidence suggests that these state-mediated settlement efforts can drag on for years, often hurting the interests of labour as it cannot sustain a struggle with loss of income.

In the event of a dispute, the employer and all the registered unions are invited to the conciliation process. This procedure, by design, invites competition among unions, divided along political lines, and there can be as many unions as political parties in the region. Competition often leads to spurious membership claims and counterclaims, an added reason for the overestimation of trade union membership discussed earlier.

Such competition, expectedly, gives the management an edge. The employer need not necessarily negotiate with the union (or group of unions) claiming to represent the majority of workers, but is free to negotiate with any combination of unions. Quite conceivably, if the demand arises, employers can (and do) prop up a dummy union of loyal workers and choose to negotiate with it, to break the other unions. For instance, history suggests, the rise of the Shiv Sena, a militant regional party in Maharashtra, in Mumbai is attributed to such a tendency among employers, to break the stronghold of left-leaning unions in the 1960s. A minority union affiliated to a political party in power in the state can use its political links to compel the labour department to decisively intervene to persuade the management to negotiate with that union, ignoring the other unions. In such an event other unions would get discredited, causing workers to shift their allegiance to the minority union. Such inter-union rivalry and competition for membership with political objectives often leads to fluidity of union membership. In another instance, a recognized union (as per the Bombay Industrial Relation Act in Maharashtra), favoured by the management, that may have lost the support of the majority of workers could not be ousted as the sole bargaining agent, since there is no system of secret ballot to ascertain the strength of the incumbent union. If, for some reason, the employer persists with the incumbent union, then there is no mechanism available for a rival union to prove its majority except appeal in courts (as was the case in the famous Dutta Samant-led Bombay Textile strike in 1982).

Thus competitive politics of parliamentary democracy seems to be inhibiting evolution of healthy industrial relations practices. Many political parties, for fear of losing their labour constituency—perhaps the Congress party more than most—have opposed changes in labour laws to promote shop-floor democracy, union recognition, and an institutionalized mechanism for collection of membership fees to put the unions on sound financial footing.

In such a situation, workers' interests often seem to get reduced to wage demands; ignoring many issues like disputes on the shop floor, problem of work intensification, and sharing of productivity gains. Though employers gain an upper hand in such situations in dealing with labour, they bring in uncertainty and the need to 'manage' politics at local and state levels.

EMERGING TENDENCIES

Admittedly, trade unionism has not remained static in the shadow of competitive politics.

- Workers are increasingly economistic in their demands, shifting their allegiances to maximize their private gains, with decreasing interest in a political agenda.
- There has been a rise of factory- or company-based 'independent' unions not affiliated to political parties, though numbers are hard to come by. Such unions are often led by educated and experienced rank-and-file workers with

a better grasp of the shop-floor issues, and are often open to negotiations with managements on issues like automation and productivity-linked incentive systems.
- There has been decline of industry- and region-wide wage settlements, as productivity and manning levels have changed across factories in response to technological changes and market conditions.
- Although labour market reforms have not been initiated to any significant extent for lack of political consensus, the state has gradually withdrawn from getting involved in industrial disputes or has chosen to look the other way when the laws are violated. If we concede that the state was, contrary to the stated principle, dysfunctional and not in favour of the weaker agent—labour—then it can be considered a favourable development. However, such a decline in the absence of shop-floor democracy and a healthy bipartite bargaining mechanism would perhaps only weaken the bargaining position of the workers. This is perhaps well reflected in the sharp fall in employment in organized manufacturing since the second half of the 1990s without a murmur of protest from the trade unions which are perhaps not in a position to protect the interests of their workers.

What is the future of trade unions? Apparently, not bright. With intensification of competitive politics, prospects for genuine reform of labour laws that enhance collective bargaining and shop-floor democracy seem weak. Simultaneously, political parties have discovered that organized labour forms a numerically minor fraction of the total voters, and have therefore lost interest in organized labour. However, as collective bargaining is likely to grow in a decentralized manner with gradual withdrawal of the state, employers would get an upper hand. With deregulation and increased international competition even in many service industries, the role of trade unions could decline in these areas as well, as has happened in manufacturing during the last two decades.

If one agrees that trade unions have a positive role in countering oligopolistic power of employers in the workplace and in favourably influencing public opinion in a democracy, then the prospect of declining trade unions does not augur well for the economy and society in the long run.

R. NAGARAJ

REFERENCES

Bhaumik, Sharit K. 2004. 'The Working Class Movement in India: Trade Unions and the State', in Manoranjan Mohanty, ed., *Class, Caste and Gender*, New Delhi, Sage.

Nagaraj R. 2004. 'Fall in Organised Manufacturing Employment: A Brief Note', *Economic and Political Weekly*, 39(30): 24 July.

_____. 1994. 'Employment and Wages in Manufacturing Industries: Trends, Hypothesis and Evidence', *Economic and Political Weekly*, 29(4), 22 January.

Ramaswamy, E.A. and Uma Ramaswamy. 1981. *Industry and Labour: An Introduction*, New Delhi, Oxford University Press.

Seth, N.R. 1993. 'Our Trade Unions: An Overview', *Economic and Political Weekly*, 28(6), 6 February.

Unemployment, The Measurement of

The unemployed are those who are looking for work or are willing to work but cannot find it at the going wage. This notion of unemployment is motivated by the neoclassical conception of the labour market where wages clear the market and the failure to get work is voluntary. Deviations

from this ideal are measured by the above definition of involuntary unemployment. Other definitions have also been used. The influential two-sector development models (Lewis 1954, Fei and Rannis 1964) theorized non-neoclassical labour markets in sectors dominated by subsistence family enterprise (such as agriculture). As output was shared among family members, the family enterprise aimed to produce as much as possible without regard to the marginal productivity of labour. This led to the concepts of 'labour surplus' and 'disguised unemployment' both of which referred to people who were employed with low productivity in the subsistence sector and could therefore be transferred to the modern high-productivity sector without output loss in the subsistence sector. The early literature on unemployment in India attempted to measure such unemployment through measures that were defined with respect to low productivity or low incomes. However, they suffered from inconsistencies and were hard to implement operationally as well (Krishna 1976).

Unemployment is measured through labour force surveys that elicit the 'activity' status of the respondent for a given reference period. First, the respondent is identified as not working. Second, for those not working, the typical question is of the form: are you available for work, and have you made some effort to find work during the last x days? Those who answer in the affirmative are the unemployed while those who answer in the negative are the people who have opted out of the labour force. The labour force is the sum of the employed and the unemployed and the rate of unemployment is the proportion of labour force that is unemployed. The reference period could vary from a week to four weeks to a year. Such an approach works well when the activity status is invariant within the reference period, that is the person is either employed, unemployed, or out of the labour force. But what if an individual is unemployed for part of the reference period and is either employed or out of the labour force for the remainder? Should this person be counted as unemployed?

In India, employment–unemployment surveys are conducted by the National Sample Survey Organisation (NSSO). Beginning with the 27th round in 1972–3, labour force surveys have been conducted every five years using standardized concepts and procedures based on the recommendations of the Committee of Experts (Planning Commission 1970). The–'usual' status unemployment measure is defined with respect to a reference period of a year. The multiple activity status issue, which is more acute the longer the reference period, is resolved on the basis of majority time. This criterion is used first to classify a person as either belonging to the labour force (that is employed or unemployed) or not belonging to the labour force. If the person belongs to the labour force, then whether the person is to be classified as employed or unemployed is decided once again on majority time. The survey also uses a reference period of a week to compute a 'weekly' status unemployment measure. Here a person is regarded as employed if she or he worked for at least one hour during the reference week. It follows that a person is unemployed if she or he did not work for even one hour during the reference week and sought work or was available for work during the reference week.

Clearly, the usual status measure reflects only long unemployment spells. For instance, a male in the working-age group (who is never out of the labour force) would be unemployed on the usual status measure only if the unemployed spell during the year is longer than the employed period. While the weekly status measure captures short unemployment periods, it ignores unemployment for less than a week.

A third approach is to abandon the effort to assign every individual a unique activity status over the reference period. The NSS employment survey elicits an individual's time disposition during each day of the reference week. A day is split into two half units and an individual is assigned a unique activity status for that period (rather than the reference week). This information can be used to compute person days of unemployment in the economy. As households are surveyed uniformly throughout the year, the aggregates derived from weekly data are representative of annual aggregates. The 'daily' status rate of unemployment is the proportion of labour force (measured in person days) that is unemployed (also in person days).

Individuals with regular wage employment constitute only 14 per cent of the workforce. More than half of the workforce is self-employed (53 per cent), the great majority in agriculture and about one-third as casual wage workers (Papola 2006). Furthermore, over 80 per cent of female workers in unorganized manufacturing work out of their homes mostly in subcontracting relationships where the intermediary supplies raw material and buys back their output (Unni and Rani 2005). For most of the labour force, therefore, work is seasonal, short-term, and without tenure. Consequently, an individual's activity status can vary even within as short a reference period as a week. The daily status unemployment rate would therefore seem the appropriate measure for capturing their unemployment.

The data show a clear and stable ordering among these unemployment rates (Papola 2006). Between 1972–3 and 1999–2000, daily status unemployment rates are the highest (between 6 and 8 per cent), usual status rates are lowest (3–4 per cent), and weekly rates are in between (4–5 per cent). The data imply that while few are unemployed all through the year, unemployment spells are not uncommon. As the daily status measure is the only one that is immune to multiple activity status, it is widely agreed to be the most accurate measure of unemployment (Planning Commission 2001, 2002).

For instance, in the rural sector, among those who reported some unemployment during the reference week, 67 per cent reported a spell of less than a whole week and 50 per cent a spell of less than half a week (Table 1). Among rural labour households, 73 per cent of those who experienced some unemployment reported spells of less than a whole week and 55 per cent reported spells of less than half a week. None of these would be counted as unemployed even under the weekly

status. Therefore, from the point of view of designing poverty-alleviation programmes that target the unemployed, the daily status measure would seem to provide the best estimate of unemployment, since it is the poor who are likely to experience short spells of unemployment rather than the non-poor who can afford to stay unemployed longer. The rest of this entry will be restricted to daily status rates.

Table 2 presents the all India unemployment rates for 1983, 1993–4, and 1999–2000.[1] The data are also broken down by gender and by location (rural/urban). Two robust facts emerge from the tabulation. Unemployment rates in the urban sector are higher than those in the rural sector. While urban rates are in the range 8–9.5 per cent, rural rates are about one percentage point lower, fluctuating in the 7–8 per cent range. The second feature is that female unemployment rates are markedly higher than those for males in urban areas while they match those for males in the rural sector. Urban female unemployment rates have ranged between 9.5 and 11 per cent as compared to the 7–9 per cent range for males. In the rural sector, while the unemployment rate for women in 1983 was higher than that of males by more than one percentage point, the rates became similar in later years.

While there is not much variation in the unemployment rate across sectors in 1999–2000, there is considerable variation across states. Gujarat, Haryana, Karnataka, Madhya Pradesh, Punjab, Rajasthan, and Uttar Pradesh have unemployment rates much lower than the national average,

Table 1 Multiple Activities in the Rural Sector 1999–2000

Unemployment spell of	% of individuals who had some unemployment	
	All rural	Rural labour households
≤ half week	50	55
< full week	67	73
= full week	33	27

Table 2 All-India Unemployment Rate (%)

	1999–2000		1993–4		1983	
All	7.24		6.03		8.28	
	Rural	Urban	Rural	Urban	Rural	Urban
All	7.08	7.79	5.61	7.43	7.93	9.53
Males	7.09	7.45	5.64	6.72	7.51	9.22
Females	7.03	9.42	5.55	10.52	8.98	11.01

[1] The NSS surveys in 1999–2000 and 1993–4 were conducted during the agricultural year—July through June. In 1983, the survey was conducted during the calendar year—January through December.

ranging between 4 and 6 per cent. Andhra Pradesh, Assam, Bihar, Maharashtra, and Orissa have unemployment that is close to the national average. Finally, Kerala, Tamil Nadu, and West Bengal have rates far in excess of the national average, with unemployment in Kerala being greater than 20 per cent. These high unemployment rates pose a challenge to the understanding of labour markets. Why do wages not fall in the face of such unemployment? A generic explanation is the efficiency wage theory according to which wages higher than market clearing levels can be sustained if they elicit more effort from the employed. Other explanations have been offered in terms of societal norms and the workings of particular institutions such as trade unions and government laws on minimum wages. The latter set of factors would seem to be relevant for employment in the organized sector. But what of the labour force that does not have these protections? Would it have low unemployment rates?

It is often asserted that the poor cannot afford to remain unemployed. This is not borne out by the data, however. Table 3 presents the daily status unemployment rates in 1999–2000 for poor households and for labour households. Poor households are those with monthly per capita expenditures less than the official poverty line. Labour households are those whose major source of income is agricultural labour and other manual work in rural areas and casual labour activities in urban areas. There is a large overlap between poor and labour households. While 55 per cent of poor households are rural labour households, only about 39 per cent of rural labour households are poor. However, if we look at the average consumption expenditure of rural labour households, 75 per cent have expenditures less than 1.5 times the rural poverty line and 90 per cent have per capita expenditures less

than twice the poverty line. The figures are similar for casual labour households in the urban sector.

Table 3 shows significant unemployment among poor and labour households with rates approaching 12 per cent for labour households in both urban and rural areas. These rates are higher than those for the overall population (in Table 2). As the NSS surveys households throughout the year, we can also compute the distribution of the unemployment rate across different quarters for rural and casual labour households (Table 4). As one might expect, there is no particular seasonal pattern in the urban sector, while rural unemployment displays clear seasonality. The unemployment rate at 15 per cent is highest in the monsoon months from July to September when not much work can be done in the fields. Thus while agriculture-driven seasonality is part of the explanation for high unemployment rates among rural labour households, it cannot be the complete story as the unemployment in the busy *kharif* period (October to December) is as high as 10 per cent.

Table 3   Unemployment among the Poor 1999–2000

	Rural	Urban
Poor households	9.19	9.38
Labour households	11.74	11.61

Table 4   Seasonality in Unemployment 1999–2000

Quarter	Rural[*]	Urban[**]
July–September	14.95	12.10
October–December	10.10	10.70
January–March	10.64	10.79
April–June	11.20	13.02

Notes: * Rural labour households; ** Urban casual labour households

The overall all-India picture masks significant inter-state variation in the incidence of unemployment among labour households. Kerala, Tamil Nadu, and West Bengal are striking for unemployment rates of 20 per cent and more. Bivariate associations (not reported here) do not suggest any systematic relationship between real wages and the level of unemployment. A satisfactory theory of labour markets in India will have to reckon with persistent short-term unemployment among the poor.

WILIMA WADHWA AND
BHARAT RAMASWAMI

REFERENCES

Fei, John C.H. and Gustav Ranis. 1964. *Development of the Labor Surplus Economy: Theory and Policy*, Homewood, IL, Richard A. Irwin, Inc.

Krishna, Raj. 1976. 'Rural Unemployment—A Survey of Concepts and Estimates for India', Trivandrum, Centre of Development Studies, Reprinted in V. Krishna, ed., *Raj Krishna: Selected Writings*, New Delhi, Oxford University Press, 1995.

Lewis, W. Arthur. 1954. 'Economic Development with Unlimited Supplies of Labor', *Manchester School of Economic and Social Studies*, 22: 139–91.

Papola, T.S. 2006. 'Employment Trends', this volume.

Planning Commission. 1970. *Report of the Committee of Experts on Unemployment Estimates*, New Delhi, Government of India.

———. 2001. *Report of the Task Force on Employment Opportunities*, New Delhi, Government of India.

———. 2002. *Report of the Special Group on Targeting Ten Million Employment Opportunities per year over the Tenth Plan Period*, New Delhi, Government of India.

Unni, Jeemol and Uma Rani. 2005. 'Home Based Work in India: A Disappearing Continuum of Dependence?' Working Paper No. 160, Gujarat Institute of Development Research.

Women in the Labour Force

Measuring participation of women in economically productive work is an area fraught with huge estimation problems. This is true not only for India but for the entire developing world. Women are involved in all kinds of productive work both inside and outside the home, but tend to underestimate and deny their involvement. Women's evaluation of their own work is shaped by the low social evaluation of their work. Thus official and non-official statistics show low participation rates for women, but day-to-day observation, case studies, and simple common sense indicate otherwise. Given high levels of poverty in most of the developing world, sheer economic compulsion would drive women to work. However, especially in India, an admission of working for wages is seen as a mark of low status. Additionally, women's underestimation of their work stems from the fact that it is often unpaid, and when it is paid, women have very little control over their earnings.

Since women are engaged simultaneously in multiple activities, the main problem in documenting participation rates arises when defining what constitutes 'work' (as in economically productive work). For India, most survey questionnaires ask: 'In addition to your regular work, what activities have you been engaged in?' Often, women do not understand which of their activities constitute 'regular work' and which additional work. For example, most women in rural areas tend to view their unpaid agricultural work as a part of their regular household chores and do not realize that if the work had been done by someone outside the family, he would have to have been paid for the job.

TRENDS IN FEMALE LABOUR FORCE PARTICIPATION RATES

The major sources of data on labour force participation rates (LFPRs) for India are the decennial population censuses (Census of India) and surveys of the National Sample Survey (NSS) Organization, the largest, non-census sample of the Indian population. For comparable definitions of work, census figures give a lower estimate of workforce participation than the NSS. For instance, using the principal status definition of the NSS, the workforce participation rate of rural women was 23.4 per cent for 1993–4, whereas according to the census, for main workers (comparable to the NSS principal status) it was 18.8 per cent in 1991.[1] As the preceding discussion suggests, the NSS figure is an underestimate of the actual involvement of women in productive work—the Census underestimates it even further.

Table 1 shows the LFPRs for men and women according to the various rounds of the NSS. Predictably, female LFPRs are lower than male LFPRs for all the years. However, female LFPRs have fallen marginally since the late 1970s. For instance, the rural female principal status LFPR has fallen from 24.8 in 1977–8 to 23.1 in 1999–2000. This decline, for both rural and urban women, basically started in the late 1980s—the period that saw the introduction of the 'New Economic Policy'. The corresponding trends for males indicate that for rural areas, over the whole period, LFPRs have fallen

[1]Principal status is defined as the activity in which the person spent a relatively longer time (that is major time criterion) during the 365 days preceding the survey. Subsidiary status is one in which the person spent a relatively shorter time (minor time) during the reference period of 365 days preceding the survey. Prior to determining the usual/principal status, etc., it has to be first determined that the person belongs to the labour force.

Table 1   Labour Force Participation Rates Various Years (%)

Years	1977–8	1983	1987–8	1993–4	1999–2000
Rural					
Female					
main/principal status	24.8	24.8	24.5	23.4	23.1
marginal/subsidiary status	8.3	9.2	7.8	9.4	6.8
Male					
main/principal status	53.7	52.8	51.7	53.8	52.2
marginal/subsidiary status	1.5	1.9	2.2	1.5	0.9
Urban					
Female					
main/principal status	12.3	12	11.8	12.1	11.7
marginal/subsidiary status	3.3	3.1	3.4	3.4	2.2
Male					
main/principal status	49.7	50	49.6	51.3	51.3
marginal/subsidiary status	1.1	1.2	1	0.8	0.5

Source: NSSO. 2001. NSS 55th Round, July 1999–June 2000, National Sample Survey Organisation, Ministry of Statistics and Programme Implementation, Government of India, May.

by roughly similar percentage points. Male LFPRs show slightly greater fluctuation compared to female rates. This could reflect either a shrinking of employment opportunities in rural areas, or migration from urban to rural areas, or both. For urban areas, male LFPRs rose slightly over the whole period, but they stagnated over the 1990s. Looking at the figures by marginal/subsidiary status, the decline is similar for both men and women.

Table 1 also indicates consistently lower urban female LFPRs compared to rural rates, whereas the rural–urban LFPRs for males are comparable. This could be because labour relations in urban areas are marked by competition between individual units of labour rather than complementarity that is the hallmark of the traditional division of labour in rural areas. Thus women may be less able to compete because the technologically advanced urban settings require the acquisition of new skills that women possess to a lesser degree. Also, a large part of the work is outside wage jobs and there are fewer opportunities for working on family enterprises in or near one's own household compared to rural areas. Further, women need to combine household responsibilities with productive work, and that is easier to do in rural rather than urban settings.

The NSS has alternative definitions of work: usual status, daily status, and weekly status.[2] In view of the problems inherent in defining women's work, it is believed that definitions of work based on a shorter time span are better able to capture the workforce participation of women. For women, LFPRs with principal and subsidiary status combined are higher than those based on principal status alone, but the decline from the late 1980s is sharper for rural women based on principal status alone. Current weekly and daily status LFPRs are not higher than rates where principal and subsidiary status are combined, but they show an increase until 1993–4 and a decline thereafter for both urban and rural women.

[2]Usual status is defined in n. 1 (principal status). Current weekly activity status of a person is the activity status obtaining for a person during a reference period of seven days preceding the date of survey. It is decided on the basis of a certain priority-cum-major time criterion. Current daily activity status for a person is determined on the basis of his/her activity status on each day of the reference week using a priority-cum-major time criterion (day-to-day labour time disposition).

On the other hand, the male LFPRs show a near stagnation in rural areas and a slight increase in urban areas.

The age-decomposed LFPRs for men and women suggest that for both rural and urban women, the highest LFPRs occur between ages 30 and 45. In the productive years (roughly 30 to 50), the sex difference in the LFPRs is the sharpest, particularly for urban men and women. Over the entire period, there is a perceptible decline in female LFPRs in the age group 5–15. It has been argued that this reflects greater school enrolment of girls. However, there is a similar decline for boys as well, which leads us to think that there is greater school enrolment of both boys and girls. A similar trend is seen in the next age group, 15–19 years, but participation rates are much higher for this age group as compared to the younger girls, such that even in 1999–2000 the rural female LFPR in this group was about 30 per cent. Given that underestimation of total numbers would equally apply to this age group, this reveals the problem of high drop-out of girls in the secondary and higher secondary school levels.

It needs to be noted that there is considerable regional variation in both levels and trends of LFPRs. Abysmally low LFPRs are recorded for rural women, especially in the northern part of the country: Punjab, Haryana, Delhi, Jammu and Kashmir, Bihar, and Uttar Pradesh. These rates are particularly low in comparison with the western states (Maharashtra, Rajasthan) or the southern states (Tamil Nadu, Andhra Pradesh, or Karnataka). The only exception to the northern trend of low female LFPRs is Himachal Pradesh, a state that has shown exceptional advances in female literacy and total literacy in recent years. The same picture of regional variation is applicable to urban areas.

There are several factors that explain levels of female LFPRs. However, the existence of the underestimation phenomenon in the first place complicates the issue. Also, it must be noted that the explanatory power of most of the empirical work varies widely, calling for caution in formulating generalizations. However, some conclusions can be drawn:

a) The impact of poverty on labour force participation is striking.

b) Studies suggest that education seems to delay participation in the labour market, but subsequently increases LFPRs.

c) On the whole, studies that include socio-cultural factors such as caste and religion seem to indicate that these are relatively weak in explaining female LFPRs.

OCCUPATIONAL DISTRIBUTION OF WOMEN

For rural women, by principal status, there was a 4 percentage point decline in the self-employed category between 1983 and 1999–2000 and a similar rise in the casual labour category over the same period, which is a clear indication of 'casualization' of female labour. The same trend is seen when we look at principal and subsidiary status together. Again, the same trend is evident for men in rural areas, so there is evidence of casualization of the overall rural labour force for both men and women.

For urban women, the category of regular employees shows an increase, and there is a decline in both self-employed and casual labour. However, urban men do not share this trend in that the category of regular employees shows a decline by both activity status categories and there is a marginal increase in the other two employment categories.

Looking at occupational distribution by broad industrial categories, for rural areas, agriculture continues to be the sector providing employment to the majority of workers—both men and women. However, since 1983 the share of agriculture has declined more for men than for women. But in 1999–2000, agriculture continued to employ 85 per cent of rural women. For both men and women, rural manufacturing is the next largest employer. It has been argued that men are concentrated mostly in non-household manufacturing and women in household manufacturing. This is indicative of the fact that as industries are shifting from cities to nearby rural areas, more men than women tend to get absorbed in the new employment opportunities.

Agriculture is a significant employer of both men and women in urban areas too, but more for women than men. For urban women, the next most significant category that shows a rising trend until 1993–4 is public administration. However, in the 1990s this category has seen a decline. This could be due to the reduction in public-sector jobs as a part of the overall strategy to reduce the role of the government in the economy. If this trend continues, and it is likely to, it means that the only avenue open to urban women is the 'trade, hotel, and restaurant' sector since that is the only sector in which the percentage of women employees is rising. Urban manufacturing is the other significant sector of employment for women, but here again the employment trend is declining. The share of women in finance and business remains abysmally low, and is only marginally better in urban than in rural areas. The occupational distribution seems to follow stereotypical lines: that is the share of women in mining and quarrying, electricity, water, transport, and so forth, in other words, in the 'male' occupations, continues to be insignificant over the period. Liberalization and the strategy of neo-liberal globalization do not appear to be reversing this trend.

Underemployment

The proportion of person days of the usually employed utilized for work was quite low for women compared to men throughout the period 1987–8 to 1999–2000. During 1999–2000 this proportion was estimated at about 68 per cent and 79 per cent for women in rural and urban India respectively, versus 90 per cent and 94 per cent for men. In other words, women are underemployed in far greater measure than men. Also, when work is not available, large proportions of women simply withdraw from the labour force rather than report themselves as unemployed.

Wage Differentials

There is evidence of male–female wage differentials across broad occupational categories based on NSS data. Differences in human capital characteristics are often cited as the reason for the existence of these differentials. However, this differential is seen to exist within each educational category; in other words, men and women in similar occupational and educational categories earn disparate average salaries. This constitutes, prima facie, evidence of gender discrimination at the workplace. The picture holds true for both rural as well as urban areas, where the gap in the average wage for men and women increased from Rs 7 in 1987–8 to Rs 30 in 1999–2000. In addition to wage discrimination, the more important problem is that women are relegated to dead-end jobs and tasks with little scope for upward mobility.

ASHWINI DESHPANDE

HUMAN DEVELOPMENT

Affirmative Action

The affirmative action (AA) programme in India is primarily caste based (there is now some affirmative action for women in local self-governments). The caste system in India is believed to be over 2500 years old. The ancient manifestation of the system, the varna system, divided the population into first four, and later five, hereditary, endogamous, mutually exclusive, and occupation-specific groups: Brahmins, Kshatriyas, Vaisyas, Sudras, and later Ati-Sudras. The latter did the most menial jobs, were subjected to complete untouchability, in that even sight of them was considered polluting, and thus were victims of highly degrading segregation, discrimination, and exclusion. Over the years, this system metamorphosed into the contemporary jati system (also translated into English as caste), that has the same basic characteristics as the varna system. However, jatis (estimated to number between 2000 and 3000) are regional categories and are not clear subsets of the varnas, thus leading to claims and counterclaims of varna affiliation and the attendant status. In addition to the caste system, India is home to more than 50 million adivasis (indigenous tribes) who are subjected to extreme deprivation and discrimination.

Even before Independence, the British administration introduced a policy of AA for the untouchable castes and adivasis (called the 'depressed classes'). After Independence in 1947, the policy of reserving 22.5 per cent of seats in educational institutions, government jobs, and electoral seats at all levels was enshrined into the Indian constitution. The jatis and tribes entitled to these quotas were listed in a government schedule and are therefore called scheduled castes (SCs) and scheduled tribes (STs). These are official terms; the term dalit (meaning oppressed) is often used as a term of pride for these groups. The reservation programme for SCs–STs is comparatively less controversial and, being constitutionally guaranteed, cannot be challenged completely.

Since 1991, a further 27 per cent quota has been introduced for other low castes (called other backward classes, or OBCs) that, however, is not constitutionally guaranteed. The assignment of OBC status to jatis is fraught with difficulty, given the fluidity of the jati–varna link. The position of the OBCs in the caste hierarchy represents a situation of 'graded inequality', rather than a sharp distinction vis-à-vis upper-caste Hindus. Both the extension of the reservation system to the OBCs as well as the designation of jatis as OBC have been moves that are politically highly contentious. OBC lists typically comprise a range of jatis: some that are very close to SCs–STs in social and economic position, but also some jatis that are believed to be much more prosperous. Despite this mixed composition, latest national data (for instance consumption expenditure surveys from the National Sample Survey [NSS]) reveal clear disparities between the OBCs and upper-caste Hindus in 1999–2000. Also, since 1993, 33 per cent of seats in local self-governments have been reserved for women. In addition to the reservation policy, AA in India also takes the form of a provision for preferential treatment of SC-ST groups in other government schemes that are meant for the general population.

The case for a caste-based AA (particularly for SC-ST groups) is based on the following set of factors. One, continuing inter-caste disparities in all spheres: monthly per capita expenditure, educational attainment, occupational distribution, landownership, asset ownership, health indicators. There is evidence to suggest that this is not simply a hangover from the past, but that inequalities are being perpetuated in contemporary India. The evidence on trends in monthly per capita expenditure over the last twenty years (from the NSS) indicates that the gap between SC-STs and the 'others' is *not* closing. Two, dalits continue to suffer from a 'stigmatized ethnic identity' due to their untouchable past and there is corresponding social backwardness. Three, given the objective of equality of opportunity between castes, AA is needed to provide a 'level playing field'. Four, AA is needed to compensate for the historical wrongs of a system that generated systematic disparity between caste groups and actively discriminated against certain castes. It should be noted that unlike the much more radical Malaysian AA programme, AA in India does not really aim to rectify the disparities in wealth ownership that are directly the outcome of the caste system that prevented the untouchables from acquiring property.

Thus it is a much weaker programme of compensation than what would be construed fair, given the magnitude of wealth disparities. Five, there is evidence to suggest that caste-based discrimination in labour markets continues in both urban and rural areas, in the formal and informal sectors, and is manifested both as wage and job discrimination. There is evidence that points to a discriminatory gap in earnings between SC-STs and others.

Political reservations have an added, independent justification that is distinct from those for job and educational reservations. In the absence of proportional representation and the predominance of a first-past-the-post electoral system, there are special handicaps that minority groups face in terms of being guaranteed equality of political opportunity, even if theoretically they were not historically discriminated against. Another argument in favour of job and educational reservations is that individuals who manage to get better education and jobs could serve as role models and provide dynamic motivation to the rest of the community. On the other hand, critics of reservation argue that there might be more efficient ways of helping disadvantaged groups like special scholarships, credit subsidies, and job training. It is also argued that ideally these programmes should be time bound, as was provided for by the Constitution, but vested interests in the beneficiary communities would like the system to be perpetuated.

An assessment of these programmes suggests that their impact has been mixed. Quotas have been fully implemented in the electoral sphere but their implementation in education and jobs has been less than optimal. Moreover, reservations are often seen as the end and not the beginning of the AA programme. SC-ST quotas are constitutionally mandatory, but are often circumvented using loopholes in the system. Additionally, private-sector jobs are free from quotas, and with increasing liberalization of the economy, confining AA to the government sector is gradually making it redundant. Despite all these weaknesses, the AA programme has led to the creation of a dalit middle class and many more dalit families are freed from their traditional subservient roles. However, the case for AA continues to be strong for all the reasons listed here. Preliminary studies indicate that liberalization of the economy does not seem to be reducing inter-group disparities.

There are other countries, such as the USA, where the AA programme is not quota based. Comparative assessments of these programmes suggest that the key to the success of an AA policy may not lie in whether or not the programme is quota based. A successful programme would be one that is backed by the requisite political will. The Indian experience suggests that political reservations would be a crucial element to build that reservoir of political will.

ASHWINI DESHPANDE

Child Malnutrition and Feeding Practices

With one in every three malnourished children in the world living in India, malnutrition is one of India's largest development problems. Around 46 per cent of all children below the age of 3 are too small for their age, 47 per cent are underweight, and at least 16 per cent are wasted (UNICEF website on Nutrition in India). More than half of all child deaths are associated with malnutrition. The prevalence of malnutrition varies across states, with Madhya Pradesh recording the highest rate (55 per cent) and Kerala among the lowest (27 per cent).

Malnutrition that sets in during the first three years of a child's life has effects on the child such as stunted growth, weakened immune system, and lower IQ rate that persist long after infancy and into adulthood. The effects of malnutrition that sets in during this young period in a child's life are often irreversible and lead to severe health problems in adulthood as well. Malnourished children are less likely to perform well in school and more likely to grow into malnourished adults, at greater risk of disease and early death. 'Though quieter than famine, it [persistent undernutrition] kills many more people slowly in the long run than famines do' (Drèze and Sen 1989).

THE CAUSES OF MALNUTRITION IN INDIA

The reasons for the high rates of malnutrition in India are manifold. Some of the most common are: low birth weight which is attributed to the poor nutritional status of the mother, both in terms of food intake as well as high levels of anaemia (iron deficiency), high levels of disease often caused by poor hygienic conditions and poor water, lack of availability or adequate use of medical facilities to promote child's health and growth, and, finally, improper feeding practices including lack of exclusive breastfeeding and lack of proper supplementary feeding.

This entry focuses on the last aspect, namely how proper feeding practices can help prevent malnutrition. Practices that constitute 'proper' or 'best' feeding are defined in *Facts for Life*, a guide to proper nutrition and healthcare published by UNICEF, UNAIDS, UNDP, UNFPA, WHO, UNESCO, WFP, and the World Bank. These are:

1. The infant must be breastfed within thirty minutes of birth with the mother's colostrum. Colostrum is the thick, yellow breastmilk produced in the first three or four days of the baby's life, which is rich in vitamins and helps build the child's immunity.

2. The child should be exclusively breastfed at least five times a day for six months. This means that the baby should not be fed anything but breastmilk as water, other beverages, and solid foods are not easily digestible and may not be hygienically prepared. Breastmilk is superior to all other foods and breastmilk substitutes since it provides essential fatty acids and nutrients that assist the child's development and protect him/her from infection.

3. Supplementary foods must be introduced when the child is approximately 6 months old. *Dal*, rice, gruel, and *idly* are examples of nutritious Indian foods that are shown to facilitate normal growth of the infant.

4. The child should continue to breastfeed until it is about 24 months, gradually decreasing breastmilk intake until completely transitioned into solid foods.

There is some debate on the viability of the six-month exclusive breastfeeding period mainly due to the fact that many malnourished mothers are often deficient in breastmilk and therefore unable to breastfeed the baby as often as it should be during that six-month period (Anandaiah and Choe 2000). However, it is acknowledged that the above guidelines can help prevent child malnutrition. Moreover, these guidelines are relatively simple to follow and need no external agencies to implement.

POLICY IN INDIA: INTEGRATED CHILD DEVELOPMENT SERVICES

The Integrated Child Development Services (ICDS) scheme, a Government of India programme, is the largest programme for promotion of maternal and child health and nutrition in the world (ICDS website). UNICEF and the World Bank helped launch the ICDS in collaboration with the Government of India in 1975 and have provided it technical and financial assistance. The ICDS has now expanded to cover 4.8 million expectant and nursing mothers and over 23 million children under the age of 6 (UNICEF website on the ICDS). It is an integrated early childhood programme aimed at improving the development, nutrition, and education of children and comprises the following components: healthcare counselling for mothers, non-formal schooling for pre-school children, supplementary feeding for all children, pregnant and nursing mothers, growth monitoring and promotion, and links to primary healthcare services such as immunization and Vitamin A supplements.

The ICDS, at local level, operates through the *anganwadi* worker, a local woman resident of the village with at least seven years of education. She and one other female helper are trained by the government for seven months to perform the duties of the ICDS at village level. As part of the ICDS nutritional component, the anganwadi worker is supposed to distribute nutritional packages to mothers of young children and conduct house visits to give personal counselling and health-care education to pregnant and lactating mothers and encourage them to go to the hospital for delivery and health check-ups. Encouraging mothers to adopt the 'proper' feeding practices is supposed to be an essential part of the outreach, in-home counselling done by the anganwadi worker. Even though the successes of the ICDS have been rather uneven and heavily dependent on the character of each individual anganwadi worker, there have been moderate improvements in the nutritional status of children and a more widely adopted usage of the feeding practices. However, customs such as feeding the baby sugar water, animal's milk, or infant baby formula are still prevalent and are often more heavily influenced by other factors than the ICDS programme and therefore need to be accounted for in policymaking.

POLICY CONSIDERATIONS

It is widely acknowledged that an increase in the mother's status—her education, role in family decision making, and income-holding abilities—improves the health, nutrition, and educational levels of her children. Also, the mother's well-being determines the nutritional status of her children. Therefore, it is crucial that policies meant to address malnutrition go hand in hand with measures to improve women's status and nutritional health. Only then is a mother 'capable' (Sen 1999) of providing her child adequate care and nutrition.

The mother's exposure to mass media can also influence the child's nutritional status. Mass media is an important means of information dissemination. It can function as an educational medium enabling messages on child-care techniques to reach a much larger, more receptive audience. Therefore, alternative means of communication and information dissemination such as advertising, messages through popular media, and public-service announcements, need to be further developed and utilized to increase awareness of proper feeding practices and child care.

Finally, many pregnant and lactating mothers take advice from family members on how to raise their children. Yet many counselling services and outreach programmes fail to include the larger family in educating them about the feeding practices and other child-care techniques. Policies that aim at educating the mother must also educate the larger family as it forms the largest source of support, information, and advice for the new mothers.

ANANDITA PHILIPOSE

REFERENCES

Anandaiah, Ravilla and Minja Kim Choe. 2000. 'Are the WHO Guidelines on Breastfeeding Appropriate for India?', *National Family Health Survey Bulletin*, 16, May, Mumbai, International Institute for Population Sciences and Honolulu, East–West Center.

Drèze, J. and A.K. Sen. 1989. *Hunger and Public Action*, Oxford, Clarendon Press, New Delhi, Oxford University Press, 1998.

Facts for Life, Third Edition. 2002. Published by UNICEF, WHO, UNESCO, UNFPA, UNDP, UNAIDS, WFP, and the World Bank.

Integrated Child Development Services website. http:/www.indianembassy.org/policy/Children_Women/icds.html:Integrated Child Development Services.

Mishra, Vinod and Robert D. Retherford. 2000. 'Women's Education can Improve Child Nutrition in India', *National Family Health Survey Bulletin*, 15, February, Mumbai, International Institute for Population Sciences and Honolulu, East–West Center.

Sen, Amartya. 1999. *Development as Freedom*, Oxford, Oxford University Press, New Delhi, Oxford University Press, 2000.

UNICEF website on Nutrition in India. http://www.unicef.org/india/nutrition.html

UNICEF website on the ICDS. http://www.unicef.org/earlychildhood/files/india_icds.pdf

Education and Religious Minorities

Religious group affiliation is very clearly associated with different educational outcomes in contemporary India. The smaller minorities—Jains, Christians, Sikhs, and Buddhists—generally have more schooling and are more likely to be recorded as literate in the Census than the majority Hindu population, but the indicators for Muslims are worse than those for Hindus as a whole. The generalized stereotype of Muslim Indians is that they are 'backward';

that their lack of educational achievements is their own 'fault'; that Muslims are committed to a conservative view of Islam; and that their religious beliefs lead them to turn to madrasahs instead. This entry considers how far such views accord with reality.[1] Using data from a small-scale study I will also explore how current policy changes are affecting educational experiences for Muslim and Hindu children in western Uttar Pradesh.

The 2001 census results on literacy and religious-group affiliation are summarized in Table 1; holding sex and residence constant, Muslim literacy rates are below those of Hindus. National Sample Survey (NSS) data show similar patterns, with relatively small differences between male and female schooling achievements in rural areas, compared to urban areas. In general, however, the Muslims are catching up with the Hindu population, since the rate of change is fastest

Table 1 Literacy of Population Aged 7 and Above by Religion, for Persons, Males, and Females, India 2001

			(per cent)
Religious group	Persons	Males	Females
Others	47.02	60.80	33.19
Muslims	59.13	67.56	50.09
Religion not stated	61.34	71.23	50.31
Hindus; of which	65.09	76.16	53.21
Scheduled castes	45.20	55.10	34.62
Other Hindus	71.32	82.74	59.06
Sikhs	69.45	75.23	63.09
Buddhist	72.66	83.13	61.69
Christians	80.25	84.37	76.19
Jains	94.08	97.41	90.58
All religions	64.84	75.26	53.67

Source: Census of India, 2001, Tabulations made available electronically.

Note: The 'Other Hindus' are derived by subtracting scheduled castes (SCs) from 'Hindus'. Some SCs are non-Hindu, but this is unlikely to lead to significant errors.

[1] Another useful discussion of these issues can be found in Borooah and Iyer (2005).

for Muslims, then for Hindus, and then Christians (NSSO 2002: 24, 26, 28). Similar data from the 1994 National Council for Applied Economic Research (NCAER) data set on human development in rural India suggest that Muslim households spend the least on education per student, at all income levels, followed by Hindu households, Christians, and finally other minorities (Tilak 2002: 24). These data also suggest that less might be spent on Muslim girls than on girls from other religious backgrounds, though this is not statistically significant (ibid.: 68). This finding is unexpected, since the differences between Muslim and Hindu female literacy rates are relatively small and noticeably smaller than those for males, whether or not scheduled castes (SCs) are included in the 'Hindu' total.

Table 2 shows considerable variations across India in literacy for Hindu and Muslim women. Rural literacy rates for Hindu and Muslim women in Bihar are only about one-third of those in Kerala. In almost all urban areas, Muslim women are less likely to be literate than Hindu women (Tamil Nadu being the sole exception), but in seven states rural Muslim women are *more* likely to be literate than are rural Hindu women (Orissa, Gujarat, Maharashtra, Madhya Pradesh, Karnataka, Andhra Pradesh, and Tamil Nadu). Table 2 also brings out the extent to which, in rural areas, three states (Jammu and Kashmir, Assam, and Delhi) skew the overall results.

After the 2004 national elections, the Congress-led government made minorities, especially girls from minority groups, a focus for its educational concerns. Is there any point? What explains poor Muslim educational achievements? In part, Muslims invest less in boys' schooling because the returns are below those for other groups. In urban UP, for example, Muslim parents' motivation to acquire schooling for their children

Table 2   Literacy of Females Aged Seven and Above, by Religion and Residence,
India and Major States 2001

(per cent)

States	Urban			Rural		
	Hindu	Muslim	Difference	Hindu	Muslim	Difference
Jammu and Kashmir	77.4	52.4	25.0	52.0	29.7	22.3
Uttar Pradesh	67.9	47.3	20.6	37.7	31.6	6.1
West Bengal	78.3	59.2	19.1	55.7	47.9	7.8
Assam	82.6	65.6	17.0	56.9	38.4	18.5
Delhi	76.0	59.5	16.5	68.2	48.8	19.4
Rajasthan	66.3	50.4	15.9	37.2	31.2	6.0
India	73.9	63.2	10.7	45.7	42.7	3.0
Bihar	63.8	56.7	7.1	29.9	27.9	2.0
Orissa	73.1	66.3	6.8	46.9	59.6	−12.7
Gujarat	74.8	68.0	6.8	47.1	57.1	−10.0
Maharashtra	79.6	74.7	4.9	58.0	62.2	−4.2
Madhya Pradesh	70.2	65.9	4.3	42.3	49.5	−7.2
Karnataka	74.2	70.6	3.6	47.4	52.0	−4.6
Kerala	90.8	87.2	3.6	85.2	84.9	0.3
Andhra Pradesh	68.7	66.9	1.8	43.0	48.5	−5.5
Tamil Nadu	74.7	77.9	−3.2	53.8	71.8	−18.0

Source: Census of India, 2001, Tabulations made available electronically.

might be adversely affected by wage and job discrimination, though the data are not conclusive (Kingdon 1998: 49). If the beliefs and practices of the Muslim population, or their employment opportunities, are the major reasons behind the picture outlined here, then government policy might be fruitless; but if government policy (in how it is implemented or in how it is framed) is part of the problem, then change is essential.

Data from our study of Bijnor district can help answer some of these questions (Jeffery et al. 2006a; Jeffery et al. 2006b).[2] A 2001 database of primary schools shows that schools near Muslim villages, or with high proportions of Muslim pupils,

had fewer teachers, higher pupil–teacher ratios, and worse facilities than other schools. When faced with choices about which new school proposals to accept, or which schools to invest in, officials put schools serving Muslims down the list. When teachers have a choice of schools to work in, they vote with their feet, avoiding Muslim-dominated schools if they can. One result of this 'everyday' communalism is to increase Muslim girls' disadvantage. General problems of girls' access to education are exacerbated for Muslims when there are few schools in Muslim-dominated villages or muhallas and women teachers (predominantly Hindu) are scarce, because parents hesitate to enrol their daughters.

Accessibility is, however, only the start. In most schools in UP—whether government, government-aided, or Hindu-dominated private ones—the vernacular non-elite forms of Hindi spoken by most poor villagers, Hindu and Muslim alike,

[2]The research in Bijnor was carried out with Patricia Jeffery and Craig Jeffery and was funded by the Economic and Social Research Council in 2000–2 [Grant no. R000238495]; additional funding came from the Ford Foundation and the RGS/IGB: none of these bears any responsibility for the views expressed here.

are marginalized and denigrated by the dominance of Sanskritized Hindi. For Muslims, vocabulary and grammatical issues are compounded by those of script: Urdu facilitates children's access to Islam, but hinders access to the Hindi-based public sphere. Despite the Constitutional guarantee of 'mother tongue' primary schooling for minorities, Urdu is marginalized in school curricula and, as a medium of instruction is now largely restricted to madrasahs. Moreover, the formal and informal curricula in most UP schools (except the 'minority' institutions) presume that pupils are Hindu. Hindi literature courses contain narratives of Indian history and mythology in which Muslims are portrayed in a negative light. Hindu iconography and Sanskritized Hindi dominate daily assemblies and other functions. And teachers—not only those in Arya Samaj or Rashtriya Swayamsevak Sangh (RSS) schools—are often very unsympathetic to Muslim pupils and their concerns.

In sum, the education sector shows long-standing class, gender, and locational exclusionary biases that are especially disadvantageous to Muslims. However strongly Muslim parents in UP want to provide for their children's education, most have inadequate opportunities and resources to do so. How do Muslim parents try to provide their children with education in such situations? The answer is not straightforward: urban and rural, rich and poor, girls and boys, and low- and high-caste Muslim children follow different trajectories.

In villages and in some poor urban neighbourhoods, Muslim children are increasingly attending madrasahs, but in varying ways. Sometimes madrasahs teach children outside official school hours, and children move between schools and madrasahs: some pupils attend madrasahs full-time. Often boys are outnumbered

by girls in the lower classes, though some madrasahs are restricted to boys only. Increasingly, boarding madrasahs are springing up to provide higher Islamic education for girls. But madrasahs can go only some way towards addressing Muslim children's lack of access to formal education. Madrasah funding is erratic and unpredictable, most are poorly resourced, and this (rather than hostility from teachers or managers) explains why few madrasahs teach Hindi and other subjects. Most madrasahs charge no fees for teaching the Islamic curriculum, but they usually charge for 'secular' subjects—a serious deterrent for poor parents. Few madrasahs can contemplate 'modernizing' their curricula by introducing science and computing, purchasing teaching materials, or employing well-trained staff. Consequently, most madrasahs fail to equip Muslim children with the credentials and skills necessary in the local labour market. Muslim parents understand the costs of illiteracy: better, they say, a madrasah education than no education at all; better one that imparts Islamic values than one that marginalizes Muslims. Muslim parents' preference for madrasahs rests on their accessibility and low cost, their safe, user-friendly environment and conscientious teaching, as well as Islamic 'moral education'.

But madrasahs are only a part of the story of Muslim education in Bijnor. Some prominent Muslims simultaneously manage schools and madrasahs, and teachers in schools and madrasahs have similar educational philosophies and pedagogies. Most Muslim schoolchildren attend supposedly 'secular' schools. But most Muslim secondary schoolchildren do not follow an Islamic curriculum. In Bijnor town, schools established by Muslims teach the UP Hindi-medium curriculum, some offering Urdu as an optional subject, none teaching in Urdu. They recruit fair numbers of SC children—but very few pupils from other groups. Most urban Muslim children, however, go elsewhere, disproportionately to poorly funded government middle schools, leaving Muslim children under-represented in the better-funded, more expensive, competitive-entry government and aided intermediate colleges.

Muslim girls attend schools—especially single-sex institutions—in large numbers, but nearly three times as many Muslim boys as Muslim girls attend English-medium schools. Almost exactly the same number of Muslim boys and Muslim girls attend private Hindi-medium schools, but almost all the Muslim girls are in Muslim-run schools.

Middle-class Muslim boys, especially those in urban areas, are likely to continue in formal 'secular' education at least through secondary schooling. They might seem the most likely to integrate successfully into the Indian 'mainstream'—but they do not enter the labour market on completely equal terms with comparable Hindus. They face additional hurdles in accessing white-collar employment: they need 'pioneers' who can sponsor them, and Muslim kinship- and trust-based networks less often lead into such work, though they may help with obtaining comparable work in the Gulf states.

Poor Muslim parents rarely spend their scarce resources on educating their children in inadequate or failing schools: they know their children will not obtain credentials. These parents lack the social and financial resources to ease their children through a successful transition into employment. Their children rarely complete Class 5, let alone Classes 8, 10, or 12, and they will barely cope with the public sphere of newspapers, government offices, etc. In most respects, Muslim boys leaving schools and those leaving local madrasahs are in very similar circumstances, and they usually move straight

into work that does not depend on paper qualifications—for example the occupations of their fathers (farming, small businesses, or artisanal positions), apprenticeships for craft skills, or work as unskilled labourers. Some boys follow existing migration chains to places such as Delhi, Surat, or Kashmir. Here, poor Muslims seem to operate at a relative advantage compared to equivalent Hindus in Bijnor.

The few who take advanced Islamic training in Bijnor madrasahs often compete for admission to one of the larger Islamic seminaries (in Deoband or Saharanpur), where higher training may lead to respected (though not lucrative) careers as maulwis or imams. Other graduates from these seminaries then gain alternative credentials, or enter family enterprises. In general, these seminaries offer a learned and genteel Muslim alternative identity to 'secular' options, thereby making a public statement of commitment to Islam, and an implicit critique of westernization, consumerism, and modern India—perhaps why they provoke such hostility.

The hostility that madrasahs often face should not distract attention from the widespread and established processes of social and economic exclusion of Muslims, to which madrasahs themselves have been one response. Muslim parents enrol their children in schools, if they can afford to, if the schools are accessible and non-threatening for their children, and if there are realistic chances of schooling leading to good jobs. Muslim-friendly schools—in the right places, with sufficient facilities and committed staff, and with the worst excesses of saffronization removed—draw in Muslim children.

On 30 November 2006, the Justice Sachar Committee reported on the position of Muslims in India, and confirmed that Muslims in much of north India have lower levels of educational enrolment, largely as the result of state actions (or inaction). Segregation in school is growing, and non-state institutions are beyond the pockets of most north Indian Muslim parents. The Committee made a series of suggestions for reform. However, even if these proposals are all implemented, Muslim children will not immediately overcome the social and economic exclusion that perpetuates inequalities through the generations. Meanwhile, in the face of consumerism and with problematic access to employment, they are likely to be increasingly disaffected that the prizes of modernity and money elude them.

ROGER JEFFERY

REFERENCES
Borooah, V.K. and S. Iyer. 2005. 'Vidya, Veda and Varna: The Influence of Religion and Caste on Education in Rural India', *Journal of Development Studies* 41(8): 1369–1404.

Jeffery, P.M., R. Jeffery, and C. Jeffrey. 2006a. 'Investing in the Future: Education in the Social and Cultural Reproduction of North Indian Muslims', in M. Hasan, ed., *The Future of Muslims in India*, New Delhi, Manohar.

———. 2006b. 'Patterns and Discourses of the Privatisation of Secondary Schooling in Bijnor, UP', in K. Kumar and J. Oesterheld, eds, *Education in South Asia*, New Delhi, Orient Longman.

Kingdon, G. 1998. 'Education of Females in India: Determinants and Economic Consequences: A Case-study of Urban Uttar Pradesh'. http://www.economics.ox.ac.uk/Members/geeta.kingdon/Discussion Papers/min amararepoort98.pdf. Last accessed on 21 November 2005.

National Sample Survey Organisation (NSSO). 2002. *Employment and Unemployment Situation among Religious Groups in India, 1999–2000*, New Delhi, NSSO Report No. 468.

Tilak, J.B.G. 2002. *Determinants of Household Expenditure on Education in Rural India*, New Delhi, NCAER Working Paper 88.

Famines

Famine is one of the oldest scourges of mankind. Fortunately, in India today, we can claim with a reasonable degree of assurance that 'famine is history'—at least so it has been for over half a century. In spite of this success, or perhaps because of it, the study of Indian famines remains a matter of immense interest for a number of reasons.

First and foremost, the rich and varied literature that has emerged out of the study of Indian famines constitutes a valuable resource for advancing our understanding of how famines occur and how they can be prevented, relevant not just for those parts of the world where famines remain a recurrent scourge, for instance in large parts of Africa, but also for India itself, where, although famine might be history, sadly the threat of famine is not.

Second, the fierce debates that raged between the nationalist and colonial commentators over the famines that occurred during the British colonial period are singularly relevant for our understanding of the impact of colonial rule on the economic and social evolution of India. Third, the early colonial discourse on what would constitute an appropriate famine policy in India involved an intriguing interplay between economic theory and public policy that provides a striking example of how knowledge can be pressed into the service of power. Fourth, recent studies on the interaction between famine and epidemics in India shed valuable light on the nutrition–infection nexus—the synergistic relation that nutritionists believe to exist between food deprivation and infection. Finally, the study of Indian famines has great potential to contribute to the current research on famine demography—the study of the consequences of famine for fertility, mortality, and population growth.

AETIOLOGY OF FAMINES

The record of famines in ancient and medieval India is scant, although old literary sources and religious scriptures do testify that major famines occurred from time to time. More is known about famines that occurred after the onset of Muslim rule in the twelfth century, the major recorded ones being those in 1396 (in the Deccan and lasting twelve years), 1596 (almost the whole of India, and other parts of Asia, lasting three to four years), and 1660 (all of Aurangzeb's empire, excluding Bengal and Bombay).

Famines became more frequent with the advent of British rule. Soon after the East India Company established its dominion over Bengal in 1757, a severe famine decimated Bengal in 1769–70. This was followed by another major famine in 1803–4, which devastated most of India, excluding Bengal and the Deccan. The intensity and frequency of famines increased sharply in the second half of the nineteenth century, culminating in the Great Famines of 1896–1900, which engulfed almost all of India, and is known to be the greatest famine ever recorded in this land (Bhatia 1967). The situation improved in the twentieth century, but the improvement was rudely interrupted by the Great Bengal Famine of 1943—the last famine of the British period. Since Independence in 1947, India has managed to avoid a famine, despite a few close calls—Bihar in 1965–6, Maharashtra in 1972–3, and the whole of north India in 1979–80. Of the regions that were parts of British India, only Bangladesh has suffered a famine (in 1974) in the post-colonial period.

It is interesting that no major famine is recorded in Bengal until the arrival of the British. Bengal was often exempt when most of India was ravaged, as in 1660, and in 1343 during Mohammad-bin Tughlak's time people migrated to Bengal from the famine-stricken province of Delhi. All that was to change, however, after the British acquired the *Diwani* (revenue rights) of Bengal in the 1760s.

Until that time, the modus operandi of the Company was to purchase Indian commodities in exchange for precious metals imported from England and to sell them in international markets for profit. The acquisition of revenue rights in Bengal enabled the Company to enhance its profits enormously. Instead of using their own precious metals, they could now use the tribute collected from the peasants of Bengal to purchase the commodities for export, making the purchase virtually costless. Profits now consisted of the whole of the sales proceeds (minus trading costs), and not just the difference between selling price and purchase price. In a bid to maximize these profits, the Company set about extorting tributes at exorbitant rates. On paper, these rates were no different from the ones imposed earlier by the Muslim rulers, but the British collected the tribute more efficiently and more ruthlessly, with scant regard for the condition of the peasantry. They did not relent even after harvest failed repeatedly in the late 1760s, thereby reducing the peasants to a state of utter penury. This is what precipitated the famine of 1769–70, which killed nearly one-third of the population of Bengal, followed by another in 1783–4 and again in 1787–8. These famines were created not so much by the parsimony of nature as by the greed and callousness of men.

As famines and starvation ravaged Bengal, realization dawned on the British rulers that they were actually harming their own long-term future by killing the goose that laid the golden egg. Beyond a point, not much tribute could be extracted from a ruined peasantry, howsoever ruthlessly. This realization led eventually to the institution of the Permanent Settlement in eastern

India and *ryotwari* settlement in the south, whose objective was to trade off some land revenue in the short run in the hope of collecting more revenue from commerce in the long run. These institutions in turn had profound impact on the evolution of agrarian relations in India, with implications for not just the social and economic structures that emerged but also for the political alignments that characterized the nationalist movement in the later part of British rule. In this sense the Bengal famines of the early colonial era can be said to have played a catalytic role in shaping the entire course of Indian colonial history.

After the early shocks, Bengal was spared a major famine for nearly a century, but other parts of India continued to be ravaged. Indeed, famines became more frequent and more virulent in the second half of the nineteenth century. This was deeply embarrassing for the British government, as the period of more frequent famines started almost immediately after the East India Company's rule was replaced with direct rule by the Crown in 1858. Colonial administrators and other British commentators sought desperately to give a positive spin to this coincidence by describing the famines as an inevitable, if sad, by-product of their benevolent rule! To this end, the ideas of classical political economy, especially those of Malthus, were frequently invoked. Of the three positive checks—namely war, disease, and famine—that, according to Malthus, kept population down to the feeding capacity of land, the British claimed to have eliminated the first two through good governance. As a result, so the argument went, famines remained the only mechanism of nature to maintain parity between people and land. Famine was inevitable, the argument added, in the absence of preventive checks, in the form of conscious fertility control, allegedly not being practised by the Indians.

This view was hotly contested by the nationalist scholars (for example Dutt 1904) as well as some sympathetic British commentators. They argued that famines had become more frequent because British rule had actually reduced the living standards of the majority of Indians, making them more vulnerable than ever before to the vagaries of nature. Thus emerged a prolonged and heated debate on the economic impact of British rule in India whose reverberations can be felt even today (Habib 1985). The critics identified a number of policies that had exacerbated the vulnerability of Indian masses.

The most culpable of all was land tax policy. The example of the Permanent Settlement that was introduced in eastern India as a means of keeping land revenue down to a permanently fixed level was not followed elsewhere. Even the ryotwari system that was instituted in the south with a similar objective was subsequently modified to allow for more intensified extraction of rent. Thus the general experience of peasantry in most parts of India was one of high and uncertain demand for rent, which left it barely at the edge of survival.

No less pernicious was the policy of unrequited transfer of tribute to England. In the earlier era, when the rulers extracted tribute from the peasantry they used to spend most of it on local crafts and services. This had spawned a sizable urban-based industrial and services sector during the Mughal period. The policy of unrequited transfer during the British period ensured that this particular source of demand for industrial products and services dried up, setting in motion a secular process of deindustrialization and deurbanization.

This process was further exacerbated by the trade and industrial policy pursued by the colonial administration in support of the industrial revolution in England. First, it allowed free import of English cotton yarn, which destroyed the local spinning industry, and subsequently the British government imposed tariffs on the import of Indian cloth into England, which weakened the weaving industry as well (although the weaving industry revived somewhat in the twentieth century for other reasons).

The combined effect of these policies was to not only destroy existing jobs in the urban areas but also the possibility of absorbing surplus rural labour into off-farm activities. Thus, while on the one hand the peasantry was impoverished through rack-renting, it was at the same time deprived of the opportunity of escaping from rural misery by working outside. The result was a marked increase in rural landlessness, accompanied by declining real wages. It was little wonder that vulnerability to famine should have increased under these circumstances.

The problem was compounded by the unanticipated side effects of the expansion of irrigation and railways. By obstructing the natural flow of water, these developments created serious waterlogging problem, resulting in mosquito infestation and the spread of malaria. Repeated bouts of malarial fever combined with food deprivation to create a malnutrition–infection nexus, leading to serious debilitating effects. Modern research has demonstrated how this nexus contributed to raising the level of excess mortality when famines struck repeatedly in the late nineteenth century (Maharatna 1996).

Two hundred years of British rule in India started with a famine in Bengal and ended with another—the Great Bengal famine of 1943. The principal proximate cause of this famine, which took at least 1.5 million lives, was inflationary financing of India's involvement in the Second World War. The price spiral seriously eroded the purchasing power of the impoverished

segments of the population—landless agricultural labourers and all others who had to buy food from the market. As Amartya Sen has noted, the famine struck not so much because overall food availability had declined, but because millions of people had lost their 'entitlement to food' through loss of purchasing power (Sen 1981). The problem was aggravated by the government's failure to protect the entitlements of vulnerable groups through provision of work or food.

Sen's analysis of the 1943 famine led to the emergence of the celebrated entitlement approach to famine, which focuses on food entitlements instead of overall food availability as the chief explanatory variable in a famine analysis. Empirically, there has been some debate as to whether decline in food availability was a contributory factor or not in the famine of 1943. On the theoretical front, however, Sen's entitlement-focused analysis has made a lasting contribution to our understanding of famines in at least two ways. First, it has shown that famine can occur even without a decline in overall food availability—that is the Malthusian route is not the only one through which famine might strike. Second, even when decline in food availability plays a role, it is still necessary to look at the entitlements of different segments of population in order to understand why it is that in times of famine only some groups of people suffer while others don't, at least not to the same extent. At policy level too, the entitlement approach offers critical insights, as discussed in the following section.

FAMINE POLICY
Public policy towards famines in India has undergone remarkable metamorphosis over the centuries. In the pre-British period, the rulers would typically respond to famines by adopting various kinds of interventionist policies—for example debt forgiveness for

poor farmers, importation of food grains, and fixation of maximum prices. During the first half of British rule, however, a deliberate hands-off policy became the norm. The government would neither intervene in the market for food grains to relieve scarcity in the afflicted areas, nor would it take measures to provide subsidized food to the famine victims. Ostensibly, the rationale for this laissez faire policy was drawn from the doctrines of classical political economy (Ambirajan 1978).

The ideas of Adam Smith and John Stuart Mill were repeatedly invoked to justify the policy of non-intervention in the market for food grains. It was argued that the only sensible way of dealing with a situation of scarcity was to allow prices to rise, for any attempt to artificially keep prices down would only serve to prolong the period of scarcity as lower prices would discourage private traders from bringing additional food from outside. The faith in the ability of the private sector to deal with the problem was founded on the assumption of a competitive market, for which the existence of a very large number of small traders was adduced as evidence. The flaw with this argument was that a large number of traders was but one condition out of many that were needed for a market to function efficiently. Faced with serious transport bottlenecks and credit constraints, it was practically impossible for small traders to move large amounts of food grains from one part of the country to another quickly enough, even if they had the incentive to do so. As a result, even if the market behaved efficiently at normal times, it was bound to fail in times of acute scarcity. And so it did, costing millions of lives.

The non-interventionist approach extended to the issue of relief as well. Drawing inspiration from classical political economy's aversion to the Poor Laws in England, it was argued that giving charity

to the famine victims was not going to help in the long run, as it would only prolong the imbalance between population and food supply, which eventually must take its toll. The only tangible effect of charity would be to create a culture of dependency.

Apart from doctrinal influences, practical financial considerations also played a role in predisposing policy towards non-intervention. This became obvious during the famine that struck Madras and Bombay presidencies in 1875. Budgetary resources were dwindling at that time because of silver depreciation as well as repeal of certain import duties under pressure of British manufacturing industry. Severely handicapped by shortage of cash, and faced with the enormity of the famine, Governor General Lytton categorically declared that saving lives at any cost was not the responsibility of the government.

Within the general approach of non-intervention, the only action that the colonial government countenanced with some favour was providing temporary employment to famine victims. Contemporary analyses of famines had made it clear that the reason people suffered when harvests failed was not so much that there wasn't enough food around (in the country as a whole) as that they found themselves without work and thus without the purchasing power to buy food. As Baird Smith, commenting on the North Western Provinces Famine of 1860–1, put it in 1861, the famines in India were 'rather famines of work than of food'[1]—a clear precursor of the entitlement approach to famine that was to emerge later.

After much vacillation, the principle of providing work as a means of famine relief was operationalized under a system of 'Famine Codes' built on the suggestions of the Famine Enquiry Commission of

[1]Quoted in Loveday (1914).

1880. Even here, however, the bias towards minimalist intervention was manifest in at least two ways. First, workers were to be paid strictly in cash, not in food, so that the government didn't have to intervene in the grain market to procure the necessary food. Second, the wage rate was to be kept as low as possible consistent with survival. This was meant to act as a self-selection mechanism of targeting relief to the neediest of people, helping to keep expenditure down (Loveday 1914).

It would appear that, for all its limitations, the Famine Codes were reasonably successful in dealing with, and even preventing, famines during the subsequent seven decades of British rule, with two major exceptions. The first exception was the Great Famines of 1896–1900 and the second the Bengal famine of 1943. Each of these exceptions offers important lessons for famine policy. The famines of 1896–1900 demonstrate the folly of dogmatic refusal on the part of government to intervene in the grain market. Harvest failure was so widespread that unlike in earlier crises overall food production had declined drastically, so much so that private traders were simply unable to cope. In the absence of government efforts to augment food supply, provision of employment alone was not enough to stave off crisis, especially in view of the stinginess shown with respect to wages and the debilitating effects of the malnutrition–infection nexus referred to earlier.

The Bengal famine of 1943 highlights the political preconditions necessary for successful implementation of famine policy. Despite clear signs of distress before the famine became full-blown, the British government deliberately ignored the Famine Codes for political reasons. It was loath to acknowledge that its War efforts were creating vulnerabilities through inflation, nor was it willing to set aside resources for relief

operations at the expense of War-related expenditure. It was only after Independence and the establishment of a democratic polity that the principles embodied in the Famine Codes became fully operational in India. Every time a crisis loomed, the government intervened in multiple ways—by providing employment, importing food grains, and activating the public food grain distribution system—to forestall a full-blown famine (Drèze 1990). The existence of a democratic polity—characterized by electoral accountability, multi-party politics, and a free press—ensured that the government would spring into action to keep famines at bay by protecting the entitlements of vulnerable groups. Two major lessons regarding famine prevention thus emerge from the experience of Indian famines. First, governments must intervene actively to protect the entitlements of vulnerable people quite early in a crisis, and second, governments are more likely to do so in the presence of some form of effective accountability. These lessons remain valid as much for India today as for the rest of the world.

S.R. OSMANI

REFERENCES

Ambirajan, S. 1978. *Classical Political Economy and British Policy in India*, Cambridge, Cambridge University Press.

Bhatia, B.M. 1967. *Famines in India: A Study in Some Aspects of the Economic History of India 1860–1965*, Delhi, Asia Publishing House.

Drèze, J. 1990. 'Famine Prevention in India', in J. Drèze and A. Sen, eds, *The Political Economy of Hunger*, vol. II, Oxford, Clarendon Press.

Dutt, R.C. 1904. *The Economic History of India*, London, Routledge and Kegan Paul.

Habib, I. 1985. 'Studying a Colonial Economy—Without Perceiving Colonialism', *Modern Asian Studies*, 19(3): 355–81.

Loveday, A. 1914. *The History and Economics of Indian Famines*, London, A.G. Bell & Sons.

Maharatna, A. 1996. *The Demography of Famines: An Indian Historical Perspective*. New Delhi, Oxford University Press.

Sen, A. 1981. *Poverty and Famines: An Essay on Entitlement and Deprivation*, Oxford, Oxford University Press; New Delhi, Oxford University Press, 1998.

Food and Nutrition

According to Pierre Mac Orlan, artist and writer, 'Humanity is first and foremost a stomach'. The statement is based on Mac Orlan's personal experience of hunger during his childhood in France, but it would not be difficult to substantiate it in the Indian context. Folk songs, historical records, direct observation, consumer expenditure surveys, and a host of other sources point to the absorbing role of food in Indian culture. This popular concern, however, goes hand in hand with an extraordinary neglect of nutrition issues in public policy, in spite of the democratic nature of India's political institutions. Even the basic facts are poorly understood.

THE NUTRITION SITUATION

The first point to note about the food situation in India is that undernutrition levels are extremely high. To illustrate, according to the second National Family Health Survey (NFHS–2, conducted in 1998–9), 47 per cent of all Indian children below age 3 are underweight, 52 per cent of all adult women are anaemic, and 36 per cent have a 'body mass index' below the cut-off of 18.5 commonly associated with chronic energy deficiency (International Institute for Population Sciences 2000). This humanitarian catastrophe is not just a loss for the persons concerned, but also a tragedy for the nation as a whole. A decent society cannot be built on the ruins of hunger, malnutrition, and ill health.

Few countries fare so badly in this field. According to the *Human Development Report 2005*,[1] only two countries (Bangladesh and Nepal) have a higher proportion of underweight children than India, and another two (Sudan and Yemen) have a higher proportion of infants with low birth weight. Even after taking into account various gaps and inaccuracies in the international data, there is no doubt that undernutrition levels in India are among the highest in the world.

A wealth of further evidence on different aspects of the nutrition situation in India is available from NFHS–2. Consumption data, for instance, bring out the frugal nature of food intakes for a majority of the population. Only 55 per cent of adult women in India consume milk or curd at least once a week, only 33 per cent eat a fruit at least once a week, and only 28 per cent get an egg. The evidence on child morbidity is no less sobering. Among children under the age of three years, 30 per cent had fever during the two weeks preceding the survey, 19 per cent had diarrhoea, and another 19 per cent had symptoms of acute respiratory infection (International Institute for Population Sciences 2000). Even after allowing for some overlap between these different groups, this suggests that at least half of all Indian children below the age of 3 suffer from one of these conditions within any given interval of two weeks.

All these figures are national averages. It goes without saying that the situation gets worse—far worse—as we consider the poorer states (for example Jharkhand or Orissa), and the more deprived regions within these poorer states (for example Palamau in Jharkhand or Kalahandi

[1]UNDP 2005, New York.

in Orissa), not to speak of the poorer communities within these deprived regions. Among the Sahariyas, Musahars, Kols, Bhuiyas, and other marginalized communities, the nutritional situation can only be described as a permanent emergency. To illustrate, in a recent survey of twenty-one randomly selected households in a Bhuiya hamlet of Palamau district in Jharkhand, twenty reported that they had to 'skip meals regularly' (Bhatia and Drèze 2002). At the time of the survey, most of the households in this hamlet survived on *chakora* (a local spinach) and *gheti* (a wild root), supplemented with some broken rice on lucky days. Some had nothing to eat but plain chakora.

RECENT TRENDS

Recent nutrition trends in India present some interesting puzzles. Starting with anthropometric indicators, the situation seems to be improving, though rather slowly. For instance, anthropometric data from the National Nutrition Monitoring Bureau (NNMB) suggest a slow increase in the heights and weights of Indian children in the 1980s and 1990s, as well as a reduction in the proportion of adults with low 'body mass index'. The first two rounds of the National Family Health Survey (1992–3 and 1998–9) point in the same direction. To illustrate, the proportion of underweight children came down by about one percentage point per year between the two surveys—from 53 to 47 per cent. Both sources (NNMB and NFHS) suggest similar rates of reduction of undernutrition over time.

While anthropometric data present a fairly consistent picture of slow improvement, food intake data are harder to interpret. There has been much debate, for instance, about the steady decline in cereal intake. According to National Sample Survey (NSS) data, average cereal intake declined from 14.8 kg per month to 12.5 kg per month between 1983–4 and 2000–1 in rural areas, and from 11.4 to 10.2 kg per month in urban areas (Deaton 2006). The decline was particularly sharp among the higher income groups. For instance, among the top 20 per cent of the rural population in terms of monthly per capita expenditure (MPCE), cereal consumption declined from 18.8 to 13.4 kg per month in this period. Among the poorest 20 per cent, cereal consumption remained virtually unchanged (about 11.5 kg per capita per month in both years).

The issue is whether the decline of cereal consumption is a matter of concern. This decline has been associated with substantial increases in intakes of non-cereal food items such as milk, oil, fish, meat, eggs, and fruits, not just among the rich but also among the poor. Some experts have argued that this gradual substitution from cereal to non-cereal foods is a positive development. Indeed, a similar 'diversification' of food intake, away from cereals, has been observed in many other countries as levels of living improve.

What is puzzling, however, is that the diversification of food intake in India does not seem to be associated with an increase in nutrient intakes. According to NSS data, per-capita calorie intake in rural India declined from 2221 kcal/day in 1983–4 to 2149 kcal/day in 1999–2000 (NSSO 2001). In fact, per-capita intake of most nutrients declined in that period, with a few exceptions such as Vitamin C (Sharma 2006). This trend is broadly consistent with independent evidence from the NNMB (see Table 1). Here again, the decline was particularly sharp among higher MPCE groups; but it is fairly broad-based, and even among the poorer groups there is little indication of a significant rise in nutrient intakes in the 1980s and the 1990s.

Table 1   Recent Nutrition Indicators

Year	Average energy/protein consumption (per consumer unit' per day) Energy		Proportion (%) of adults with 'body mass index' (BMI) below 18.5 Protein	Proportion (%) of underweight children, age 1–5 years
	(kcal)	(g)		
1988–90	2283	58.4	49.2	66.6
1996–7	2108	53.7	46.8	62.4
2000–1	1954	50.7	38.6	60.1
2004–5*	1907	48.8	35.5	54.5

Source: NNMB (partially published data kindly supplied by Dr G.N.V. Brahman, Deputy Director). The reference region consists of Andhra Pradesh, Gujarat, Karnataka, Kerala, Madhya Pradesh, Maharashtra, Orissa, Tamil Nadu, and West Bengal. The 1988–90 and 1996–7 figures exclude Madhya Pradesh and West Bengal; the 2004–5 figures exclude Gujarat.
Note: *Provisional.

The simultaneous decline of cereal and nutrient intakes has been interpreted by some commentators as a symptom of the 'impoverishment' of the rural population. This interpretation, however, leads to further paradoxes and unresolved puzzles. First, there is little evidence of sustained, widespread impoverishment of the rural population in the 1980s and 1990s. This is particularly true of the 1980s (poverty trends in the 1990s are more controversial), when poverty indexes and related social indicators were steadily improving. Yet the decline of cereal and nutrient intakes was already in full swing in that decade. Second, this explanation jars with the fact that the decline of nutrient intakes has occurred mainly in the higher MPCE groups. There is strong evidence that these groups have enjoyed sustained increases in living standards in the 1980s and 1990s. Clearly, something else than impoverishment (for example a reduction in nutrient requirements associated with reduced activity levels or better health) needs to be invoked to explain the decline of nutrient intakes among these groups. And it is quite possible that this hidden factor, whatever it was, also played a role in the stagnation of nutrient intakes among lower-income

groups. Third, if impoverishment is the reason for the stagnation of nutrient intakes among lower-income groups, it is not clear why the consumption of superior foods such as milk, oil, eggs, and meat should have increased in the same period (changes in relative prices are unlikely to provide an adequate explanation).

As things stand, both the 'diversification' view and the 'impoverishment' view of recent trends in food intake leave important questions unanswered. The diversification view, which regards the substitution from cereals to non-cereals as a positive development, has to be reconciled with the decline of nutrient intakes. The impoverishment view, for its part, is hard to square with other recent evidence on food intakes and living standards.

A related puzzle is the relation between cereal intake and per capita income (the 'Engel curve' for cereals). NSS data suggest that cereal intake rises steadily with per capita income (more precisely per capita expenditure). According to NNMB data, however, this Engel curve is more or less flat, and, if anything, downward sloping except at very low levels of per capita income. The NNMB pattern is much easier to reconcile with recent changes over time—rising incomes and declining cereal intake. If this pattern applies, the decline of cereal intake over time may not be a matter of concern. On the other hand, it would also mean that there is something wrong with the NSS food consumption estimates, and cast doubt on a good deal of 'conventional wisdom' based on these estimates.

This is an important area for further research. Meanwhile, two useful lessons emerge from this debate. First, our understanding of 'nutrient requirements' seems to call for reappraisal. Food intake studies in India are typically based on rigid norms (such as the Indian Council of Medical Research's 'recommended daily allowances') that make little allowance for possible changes in activity levels, epidemiological environments, and so on. The steep decline in nutrient intakes among the better-off sections of the rural population in recent years suggests that nutrient requirements may, in fact, be highly context-specific. This would also help explain related 'anomalies' in food-consumption data, such as Kerala's very low calorie-intake levels, combined with excellent health and nutrition indicators.

Second, the fact that anthropometric indicators have apparently improved without any increase in average nutrient intakes draws attention to the role of 'non-food factors' in nutritional achievements—basic education, antenatal care, clean water, and sanitation, among others. There is strong evidence, for instance, that maternal education is one of the major determinants of child nutrition. Similarly, there is increasing recognition of the crucial role of appropriate breastfeeding and weaning for healthy child growth. Effective nutrition policies call for paying much greater attention to these non-food factors, along with a better understanding of the food factors.

FOOD POLICY RECONSIDERED

Until recently, food policy in India was mainly geared towards promoting higher cereal consumption. This was based on a particular interpretation of the food problem, which might be called the 'naive economic perspective'. In this perspective, calorie deficiency is taken to be the most important form of nutritional deprivation. Further, cereals are held to be the cheapest source of calories. From this it appears that the main issue is to raise calorie intake, and that raising cereal intake is the best means of achieving that goal.

This perspective translated into various policies aimed at boosting cereal intake. One example is state promotion of the green revolution, which led to major increases in the production of rice and wheat and helped make cereals more affordable. India's public distribution system (PDS) also focused on subsidizing the consumption of cereals. Even child nutrition programmes such as the Integrated Child Development Services (ICDS) (and, later on, mid-day meals in primary schools), in spite of their formal recognition of the need for an 'integrated' approach to child nutrition, quickly drifted in the direction of providing cereal-based food supplements to young children.

The preceding discussion raises important questions about this whole approach. Indeed, the evidence suggests that recent improvements in nutrition indicators have little to do with increases in cereal consumption. And there is a real possibility that further improvements depend overwhelmingly on food and non-food factors other than cereal intake. This does not detract from the usefulness of, say, subsidizing cereal consumption through the PDS, as a form of income support or social security. But it does suggest that the sharp focus on cereal intake as a means of nutritional improvement may be misplaced, and that more attention needs to be paid to other means of removing malnutrition: qualitative dietary improvements, better antenatal care, the promotion of effective breastfeeding, and the prevention of infectious diseases, to cite a few examples.

The naive economic perspective has been associated with another major bias in food policy: an excessive focus on households rather than individuals. If cereal intake is the main issue, focusing on household entitlements seems appropriate, since the intra-household distribution of cereal intake is hard to influence through public policy. But if nutrition is influenced by a wide range of food and non-food factors, the scope for individual intervention is likely to be much larger. This broader perspective draws our attention, in particular, to the possibility of intervening in early childhood. In India, the nutritional status of children deteriorates sharply between the ages of six months and two years, and this 'early childhood dip', which is very hard to reverse, has a lasting impact on nutrition and health achievements. Yet, little effort has been made to reach out to this crucial age group. There are well-known means of doing so, notably by expanding and revamping the ICDS—a national programme of integrated health, nutrition, and pre-school education services for children under the age of six years (Drèze 2006). Bringing young children (and their mothers) closer to the centre of attention would be a major step towards more effective nutrition policies in India.

Switching, then, to my activist hat, I cannot resist concluding with a reference to the case for a 'rights approach' to food and nutrition policies in India (Drèze 2004). The ability of the rights approach to bring about practical change in this field has been well demonstrated in recent years, notably with the mandatory introduction of mid-day meals in primary schools, the enactment of the National Rural Employment Guarantee Act, and, more recently the gradual 'universalization' of the ICDS. There is much scope for further extension of this approach, especially by putting in place legal safeguards for children's right to food.

JEAN DRÈZE

REFERENCES

Bhatia, Bela and Jean Drèze. 2002. 'Still Starving in Jharkhand', *Frontline*, 16 August.

Deaton, Angus. 2006. Special Tabulations of National Sample Survey Data, Department of Economics, Princeton University.

Drèze, Jean. 2004. 'Democracy and the Right to Food', *Economic and Political Weekly*, 24 April.

———. 2006. 'Universalization with Quality: ICDS in a Rights Perspective', *Economic and Political Weekly*, 26 August.

International Institute for Population Sciences. 2000. *National Family Health Survey 1998–9 (NFHS-2): India*, Mumbai, IIPS.

NSSO. 2001. 'Nutritional Intake in India, 1999–2000', Report 471, National Sample Survey Organisation, New Delhi.

Sharma, Rekha. 2006. 'Quantifying Malnutrition in India', Ph.D. thesis, Delhi School of Economics.

Food Procurement Policy

The Indian government's food procurement policy is geared to achieving the twin objectives of serving consumers through price subsidy and supporting the price for producers.[1] The policy has come under criticism not only for the increasing fiscal burden that it causes but also for administrative inefficiencies and creating market distortions. This entry provides a

[1] In this chapter, 'food' refers largely to grains, mainly rice and wheat and to some extent coarse grains.

brief overview of the functioning of the food grain procurement system, examines the roles of the public and private sectors in a scenario of restrictions on domestic and international trade, and comments on related policy changes under liberalized external trade. It ends with suggestions for directions of change.

PRICE AND DISTRIBUTION CONTROLS IN THE FOOD GRAINS MARKET

The major elements of the food policy are procurement of grain at minimum support price (MSP), maintenance of buffer stocks, and distribution at subsidized rates through the public distribution system (PDS). The Government of India (GOI)[2] allocates grains to states at central issue price (CIP) for distribution to consumers. The Food Corporation of India (FCI), an agency of the GOI, handles procurement, storage, and transportation of grains to states. The states in turn distribute to consumers at subsidized prices through a network of more than 460,000 fair price shops (FPSs). The 'food subsidy' comprises the cost of procurement incurred by the GOI net of sales realization (for rice, wheat, and sugar) and the carrying costs for maintaining the central pool of buffer stock incurred by the FCI and reimbursed by the GOI.

The concept of MSP was adopted for paddy, wheat, and various other crops in the early 1990s. The policy is effective for rice and wheat in major surplus states. For wheat, the government offers to buy all grain that comes forth for sale at the announced MSP. In the case of rice, part of the procurement is in the form of paddy at the MSP, which is custom milled, and the rest, which is the major part, is procured as rice in the form of a statutory levy imposed

[2]Alternatively referred to as the central government or just the government.

by all major rice-producing states on rice millers/dealers. The levy percentage varies widely from 10 per cent in Pondicherry to 75 per cent in Haryana, Punjab, and Orissa. Rice millers are paid levy rice prices fixed by the state government. The Commission for Agricultural Costs and Prices (CACP) recommends levels at which the MSP should be fixed based on several considerations. These include cost of cultivation, the overall shortage of grains as reflected by the trend in wholesale prices, and the need to keep in check the rate of inflation in the consumers' interest.

Fixing of the MSP to cover the full costs of cultivation imposes a heavy burden on the government's finances. Although the MSP is fixed supposedly based on a cost-plus formula, the actual price offered in practice is higher and influenced by high expectations of rich farmers represented by politically strong farm lobbies (Rao 2001). The high and rising MSPs provided by the GOI for wheat and more recently for paddy increased profitability of these crops and motivated farmers to shift greater area to these crops from coarse cereals, pulses, and oilseeds. Moreover, the income transfers accrued disproportionately to large farmers confined mainly to surplus states. Price distortions in the output market combined with distorted prices of inputs such as fertilizers, power, and irrigation had an added detrimental effect not only on the production of other crops but also on the environment such as decline in water tables. The policy also led to an accumulation of buffer stocks of grains and the credit blocked in these stocks put pressure on interest rates and possibly crowded out more productive investment. These adverse fiscal and environmental implications led to increased recognition of the need to reform farm support policies (see, among others, GOI 2001 and GOI 2002). As a short-term measure to reduce the physical and fiscal burden of storage, the government released some stocks at subsidized prices to exporters, revived the PDS, and introduced other food-based programmes. Recommendations were made to reduce the MSP so that it served as a price stabilization mechanism and not an income guarantee to farmers and to cover only the variable costs, namely the costs of inputs and wages (including family labour). The High-level Committee on Long-term Grain Policy (GOI 2002) examined the cost effectiveness and liabilities arising from some alternative programmes to support farmers in lieu of the MSP scheme (Box 1). Among other things, the Committee proposed removal of both the rice levy and restrictions on grain trade, limiting their use to emergencies.

Apart from supporting farmer prices, the government's policy of procurement helps

---

Box 1: Selected Recommendations of the High-level Committee on Long-term Grain Policy (GOI 2002)

- MSP policy should extend to all regions.
- The MSP should be national-level floor price, rather than remaining confined to surplus regions.
- The MSP should be reduced to levels of average capital costs (that is all costs including imputed costs of family labour, owned capital, and rental on land).
- Procurement should be at market prices and levy procurement of rice should be eliminated.
- The MSP should be supplemented with variable import and export tariff for effective price stabilization.
- When market price is greater than the MSP, government imports or makes open market purchases.
- There should be stable and predictable policy regarding open market sales.
- Private trade should be encouraged.

---

supply grain to the PDS, the scheme to distribute subsidized grain to consumers. In order to reduce the budgetary costs of this scheme as well as to redirect subsidy mainly to the poor (people below the poverty line), the government shifted from a universal PDS to a targeted PDS (TPDS) in 1997. However, in general the TPDS suffers from several deficiencies such as urban bias in coverage, leakage, and diversion of grain to the open market due to lack of transparent and accountable delivery systems (see, for example, Drèze 2001 and Deininger and Deininger 2001). The move by the government to decentralize the procurement and PDS operations to states is in part meant to rectify these problems.

ROLES OF THE PUBLIC AND PRIVATE SECTORS

The government plays a major role in the food grain marketing system in India. The FCI undertakes movement of grains from surplus to deficit areas by rail, road, and inland waterways, moving about 22 million tonnes annually or 400,000 bags daily. It procures almost two-thirds to three-fourths of marketed surplus from food surplus states. In the last two decades, procurement has increased from 4 million tonnes to over 25 million tonnes per annum. Share of official agencies in market arrivals is estimated to have steadily increased. Several factors caused the downtrend in private share in grain markets: lower rate of increase in retail than procurement and wholesale prices, expectation of low future prices due to a large build-up of public stocks, and subsidized sale from stocks for exports and for open market sales. Private traders found it more attractive to buy grain from the government agencies than from the market.

However, the government operations have proved to be costly. Labour, interest, and administrative costs constitute a significant proportion of FCI costs.

Procurement incidentals and distribution, administrative, and carrying costs put together form a high percentage of the actual purchase cost of grain. While rising costs of the FCI can partly be attributed to the government's support price policy, they are partly also due to inefficiencies in its operations (Gulati et al. 2000). Grain storage facilities with the FCI are inadequate and usually of poor quality. Grain losses are reported to be large during transit as well as under storage due to pilferage and damage.

The private sector is controlled in various ways in order to serve the government's procurement policy. There are formal and informal restrictions on trading, storage, and inter-state movement of grains. Restrictions such as limits on stocks under the Essential Commodities Act and Selective Credit Controls increase the cost of operations for private traders. Harassment by officials, corruption, and bribery add to the costs of marketing and trading, making domestic prices internationally uncompetitive. High levels of grain stored by government agencies further reduce incentives for private storage. In spite of such drawbacks, private operators operate with thinner margins compared to the post-procurement costs incurred by the FCI (Jha and Srinivasan 2004).

PROCUREMENT POLICY UNDER EXTERNAL TRADE LIBERALIZATION

Being a signatory to the WTO (World Trade Organization), India is moving towards more open trade in agriculture. This brings new opportunities as well as challenges to the food security system. The challenges are in terms of making appropriate changes in policy and developing appropriate marketing infrastructure and institutions to deal with trade in agricultural commodities. Liberalized external trade provides opportunities for reduced dependence on buffer stocks for price stabilization and in turn reduced

government costs. It also provides incentives to deregulate the domestic market and increase the role of private traders in the marketing of food grains.

Under a regime of liberalized trade, domestic buffer stock policy is closely related to external trade policy. Appropriate policy changes are required to avoid situations such as the following. In the post WTO period the international prices of rice and wheat plunged to the lowest levels while domestic prices in India rose upward largely due to continued hike in support price. This made it profitable to import wheat but adversely affected rice exports. As a consequence of this, according to an estimate, private traders imported 1.33 million tonnes of wheat during 1999–2000 despite record buffer stock levels in the country (Chand 2002). To counter this tendency, in 2000–1 the government introduced a 50 per cent tariff on imports of wheat and 80 per cent on imports of rice without any exemption even to official agencies. Moreover, decline in international prices and rise in domestic prices made it difficult to dispose of large public stocks for export at acquisition cost. The government was thus forced to subsidize grain export even though it charged domestic consumers a much higher price. For instance, in 2002–3 the government sold wheat to exporters for less than the procurement price and covered transport, storage, and other handling costs. A side-effect of this policy was that stocks sold for export at a subsidized price were diverted back to the domestic market fetching traders a higher price and bringing larger supplies for government purchase at the MSP. In 2000–1, as against the release of 1.6 million tonnes of wheat for export, actual export was estimated to be only 0.682 million tonnes.

As external trade is liberalized, the government can use new instruments such as variable tariffs to stabilize prices and depend less on physical procurement and storage of grain. In addition, if food grain required for the PDS is sourced from local open markets in a decentralized fashion rather than through a procurement system with price controls, it can reduce government costs substantially apart from providing a greater role for efficient private trade.

RECENT POLICY INITIATIVES AND THE STEPS FORWARD

In the last few years, the government initiated steps to encourage private participation in grain markets. The role of the FCI is proposed to be restricted to timely sales and purchases to maintain stability in food prices. In a scenario of trade liberalization, however, this needs to be complemented with appropriate trade and tariff policies. As part of a new strategy, the government plans to promote exports through long-term credit, removal of export restrictions, establishment of Agricultural Export Zones, and transport subsidies for export of wheat and rice from government warehouses. But it also needs to improve facilities for grading and measuring standards, and address quality problems. In order to take full advantage of growing exports, the exporters would need to have better ports and other domestic infrastructure facilities, which are currently very meagre. The ports are highly congested, have obsolete equipment, are managed by government-controlled port trusts, and marred by bureaucracy. Undertaking reforms in these areas would allow India to take on competition from major exporting countries such as Vietnam and Pakistan for rice and the United States for wheat.

Domestic marketing reforms also need to be undertaken so that there is one integrated market for food within India and restrictions do not prevent inter-regional flows in a timely and efficient manner. The private sector should be allowed to operate more freely in the market and to trade and store grains based on its expectations from the market. The public sector needs to play a facilitating role by providing the appropriate economic environment and creating a level playing field for private operators and traders. Several government committees have recommended the abolition of statutory and non-statutory charges such as *mandi* charges and purchase tax to reduce transaction costs and encourage free movement of grains domestically.

The high costs of maintaining public stocks can be reduced through encouraging private storage, which plays a complementary role to public storage. Support price should not be fixed at unduly high levels. The level of the MSP should be such that it provides protection against distress sales during surplus situations and not a guarantee for fixed returns on the costs incurred. The costs of operation of the FCI can be reduced by decentralizing procurement to local market, carrying out storage operations at state level, and by avoiding cross hauling of grain that takes place in the current centralized system (Jha and Srinivasan 2004). Decentralization would help to ensure market efficiency and reduce the economic costs of running the PDS. Efficient functioning of a decentralized system would, however, require support and cooperation from state governments. Reforms to the GOI's food procurement policy in these directions would help achieve its twin objectives more effectively.

SHIKHA JHA

REFERENCES
Chand, R. 2002. Government Intervention in Food Grain Markets in the New Context, Report prepared for the Ministry of Consumer Affairs, Food and Public Distribution, New Delhi, National Centre for Agricultural Economics and Policy Research.

Deininger, D. Umali and K.W. Deininger. 2001. 'Towards Greater Food Security for India's Poor: Balancing Government Intervention and Private Competition', *Agricultural Economics*, 25: 321–35.

Drèze, J. 2001. 'Starving the Poor', *The Hindu*, 26, 27 February, New Delhi.

Government of India. 2001. Report on Food Security, Expenditure Reforms Commission, Chairman: K.P. Geethakrishnan.

———. 2002. Report of the High Level Committee on Long-Term Grain Policy, Chairman: Abhijit Sen. Department of Food and Public Distribution, Ministry of Consumer Affairs, Food and Public Distribution.

Gulati, A., Satu Kähkönen, and P.K. Sharma. 2000. 'The Food Corporation of India: Successes and Failures in Indian Food Grain Marketing', in Satu Kähkönen and Anthony Lanyi, eds, *Institutions, Incentives and Economic Reform in India*, New Delhi, Sage Publications.

Jha, Shikha and P.V. Srinivasan, 2004, 'Achieving Food Security in a Cost Effective Way: Implications of Domestic Deregulation and Reform under Liberalized Trade', MTID Discussion Paper No. 67, International Food Policy Research Institute, Washington D.C.

Rao, V.M. 2001. 'The Making of Agricultural Price Policy: A Review of CACP Reports', *Journal of Indian School of Political Economy*, 13(1), Jan.–Mar.: 1–28.

Gender Inequality

Gender inequality, compared with other forms of inequality such as class or race, has some distinct features. It dwells not only outside the home but also centrally within it. It stems not only from differences in economic endowments between women and men but also from social norms and perceptions, that is the inequalities are ideologically embedded. While norms and perceptions also affect other inequalities like race and caste, gendered norms and perceptions cut across these categories and exist additionally. Moreover, gender inequality not only pre-exists, new forms can arise from the foundations of the old ones. For instance, those with prior advantage can formulate rules that perpetuate that advantage, such as rules governing new institutions now being promoted to manage common pool resources. These can effectively exclude significant sections, such as women, from their decision making and their benefits. In other words, gender inequality, unless specifically addressed, can be in the process of constant recreation in new dimensions.

In India, gender inequality is manifest in multiple forms, including basic survival (female adverse sex ratios); literacy and education; nutrition and healthcare (revealed especially in anthropometric indices and hospital admissions); employment (especially in the formal sector); wage rates and earnings; political participation and holding office; legal rights, especially in marriage and inheritance; and most particularly in command over property, and in social perceptions and social norms (Agarwal 1994, 1997; Drèze and Sen 2002). The geographic variability of these inequalities is also notable (Raju et al. 1999).

Some of these aspects are well studied, others remain neglected or hidden. In particular, inequality in command over property remains largely neglected, and the workings of social perceptions and norms are often hidden, albeit with visible economic outcomes. This entry focuses on these dimensions that are rather little addressed by economists. The former constitutes a significant material form of inequality, the latter a significant ideological form. Examining their interaction can illuminate the process of inequality creation, as also the means of its alleviation. The bargaining approach provides a promising analytical framework for understanding how both the material and the ideological aspects of gender inequality can be challenged, within the multiple arenas they are constituted—the family, the community, the market, and the state.

COMMAND OVER PROPERTY

Inequality in command over property is one of the most important forms of persisting economic inequalities between women and men, with a critical bearing not only on women's economic well-being but also on their social and political status.

The idea of 'command' over property implies not merely rights in law, but also effective rights in practice. Equality in legal rights to own property need not guarantee equality in actual ownership. The gap between inheritance law and its practice is especially wide. Indian women legally enjoy significant inheritance rights (even if unequal to men's). In practice, only a small percentage inherit. This is especially true of immovable property such as land or a house. A 1991 survey of rural widows by development sociologist Martha Chen found that only 13 per cent of the surveyed women with landowning fathers inherited any land as daughters; and only 51 per cent of widows whose deceased husbands owned land, inherited any (calculated by Agarwal: see Agarwal 1994).

Command over property also implies effective control. Ownership alone does not guarantee control, given social and legal obstacles. Moreover, command over property relates not only to private property but also to public property. A notable gender inequality lies in men as a gender (albeit not all men as individuals) largely controlling wealth-generating public property as managers of large corporations or heads of bureaucracies. In addition, those commanding property often control

the instruments through which existing property advantages get perpetuated, such as parliaments and law courts that enact and implement property laws; the mechanisms of recruitment into bodies which control property; and the institutions that shape ideas about gender, such as the media, and educational and religious bodies. Predominantly male control over these bodies can perpetuate negative ideas and assumptions about women's needs, work roles, and capabilities, which, in turn, affect women's economic outcomes.

Which form of property is important for economic and social security, however, can differ by context. In agrarian contexts, arable land has a pre-eminent position. In urban and industrialized contexts, housing and financial assets gain prominence.

In India, with its vast agrarian population, arable land is still the most valued form of property. It is wealth creating, livelihood sustaining, and status enhancing. For most rural households it provides security against poverty. Traditionally, it has been the basis of political power and social status. For many, it is linked with personal identity and rootedness. And it has a permanence that few other assets possess.

However, large-scale surveys such as the Agricultural census and the National Sample Survey do not collect gender-disaggregated data on land or other assets. Hence no comprehensive gender-specific assessment of access to these assets is possible. But small-scale surveys and village studies are indicative: they show that few women own arable land; even fewer effectively control any. Underlying this inequality is male bias in inheritance; in government land transfers largely to male household heads under various poverty-alleviation and resettlement schemes; and in women's restricted market access to land, especially due to financial constraints.

The welfare and efficiency implications of this inequality are wide-ranging. Many million rural women depend critically on land-based livelihoods. More men than women have moved to non-farm jobs, leaving women disproportionately dependent on farming. Relative to 53 per cent of male workers, 75 per cent of female workers are in agriculture. Over 1988–94, while 29 per cent of rural male additions to the labour force in the 15+ age group were absorbed into non-agriculture, less than 1 per cent of the additional female workers were so absorbed. And the gender gap is growing, as are de facto female-headed households, estimates for which range between 20 and 35 per cent. Many of these women bear primary responsibility for farming, but are constrained by their lack of independent land rights in their ability to procure secure livelihoods, or obtain production credit and inputs.

Without their own land, rural women face high risks of poverty in case of desertion, divorce, or widowhood. Propertylessness can also reduce entitlement to kin support. Many elderly people recognize that 'without property children don't look after their parents well'. In contrast, having land enhances the probability of getting supplementary employment and higher wages. Even a small plot can prove critical in a *diversified livelihood system*, by providing the means to grow crops, vegetables, fodder, or trees (for fruit or firewood), or to establish a micro-enterprise. The landed earn more than the landless, even in non-farm activity.

Moreover, assets in women's hands benefit the whole family. Women spend substantially more of their earnings on family needs than men. Children are found more likely to attend school and get medical care if the mother has assets, and to be better nourished where she cultivates a home garden and controls its produce. The best social indicators on health and education are found in Kerala (as also in neighbouring Sri Lanka) where many women historically enjoyed significant rights in immovable property.

Gender-equal land rights can also enhance production efficiency through better cross-farm distribution of inputs and incentive effects. On the latter, research on India is lacking but that from other countries is indicative. In Kenya, for instance, the introduction of new weeding technology raised crop yields by 56 per cent on women's plots, the output of which they controlled, but only by 15 per cent on men's plots where too women weeded but men controlled the proceeds (Elson 1995).

Land also empowers women socially, adding to their self-confidence and voice. This was graphically illustrated in the 1970s Bodhgaya movement in Bihar. When landless women in two villages received titles after an extended struggle, they movingly recounted: 'Now that we have the land, we have the strength to speak and walk.' Recent empirical work in Kerala also shows a significantly lower probability of marital violence if women own land or a house, than if they own neither (Panda and Agarwal 2005).

In private property, land and house appear key to women's economic and social security. In public property, decision-making control is critical, be it in government- or community-run institutions.

SOCIAL PERCEPTIONS
The second major source of gender inequality, largely neglected by economists, is ideological, embedded in social perceptions and norms. There is often a divergence between what a person actually

contributes, needs, or is able to do, and perceptions about her contributions, needs, or abilities. In particular, women's contributions and needs are usually undervalued. In the labour market, for instance, the work women do is often labelled as 'unskilled' and that which men do as 'skilled', even if both require equal skill. Or women are perceived as having lesser ability or commitment; or as being supplementary earners and men as the breadwinners.

Such assumptions underlie many discriminatory hiring and pay practices, with women not being hired or being paid less than men with the same abilities, for the same tasks.

Perceptions also guide intra-family allocations. Home-based or unwaged work done mostly by women is less valued than work that is more 'visible' in physical or monetary terms. Women and girls also do more poorly in nutrition and healthcare, because they are perceived as contributing less ('perceived contribution response': Sen 1990) or as needing less ('perceived need response': Agarwal 1997).

Perceptions similarly hinder women's community participation. They are often excluded from community decision-making bodies, such as for forest management, because men perceive them as making little contribution, or on the grounds that they are illiterate. Since the men who support such exclusion are themselves often illiterate (Agarwal 2001), their response has rather more to do with their *perceptions* about women's abilities than with *actual* gender differences in abilities.

Public policy is likewise influenced by perceptions. For instance, that the government transfers land almost solely to men, even when women are significant farmers, has much to do with perceptions about, rather than the universal fact of, male responsibility and female dependency.

Indeed perceptions underlie many assumptions in economic analysis and policy.

SOCIAL NORMS

Gendered social norms, like perceptions, embody an important ideological inequality and touch virtually every activity. They define housework and childcare as mainly women's work and, in rural areas, also firewood collection and cattle care. Hence firewood or fodder shortages adversely affect women more than men. In north India, norms determine that males eat first and/ or get more and better-quality food. This makes for gender differences in nourishment and growth. In most regions, social norms discourage women from asserting their property rights, by dictating, for instance, that 'good' sisters should forfeit their claims in parental property in favour of brothers.

Outside the household again, social norms restrict women's earning options by discouraging them from working outside the home, limiting the range of tasks they may perform, placing double work burdens on them, institutionalizing lower wages for them, having them relocate with husbands on marriage or job shifts, and so on. In rural north India, women of 'good character' are expected to avoid spaces where men congregate. Hence, while male farmers can sit in market spaces and strike deals with other men for hiring labour or selling crops, women farmers are socially restricted.

Social norms also affect economic outcomes by governing female behaviour. Women fish traders in parts of south India, if found haggling loudly, risk being dubbed 'masculine' and losing social status. Women attending public meetings are expected to listen rather than speak, even when livelihood or resource distribution issues that centrally affect them are discussed.

Basically gendered social perceptions and social norms embody inequalities that are largely invisible and difficult to quantify. Yet they centrally affect economic outcomes for women in multiple ways.

EMERGENT INEQUALITIES: COMMUNITY FORESTRY

Gender inequalities in property endowments, norms, and perceptions form the bedrock of pre-existing material and ideological disadvantage. And their persistence can create new inequalities, as revealed, for instance, by my recent research, based on extensive fieldwork, on community forest management (Agarwal 2001). Forests and commons are important sources of firewood, fodder, and other basic items for rural households. And since women usually lack private property resources such as land, and social norms make firewood and fodder collection mainly their responsibility, their dependence on the commons is greater than men's.

Traditionally, access to community resources such as local forests was based on village citizenship, thus mitigating, to some degree, inequalities in private property. Today, community forestry groups (CFGs), mostly falling under the state-initiated Joint Forest Management (JFM) programme launched in 1990, in which governments and villagers share the costs and benefits from protection, are largely excluding women from their decision making and benefit sharing.

There are over 65,000 JFM groups today. Their typical two-tier management structure has a general body (GB), meant to draw members from the whole village, and an executive committee (EC) of 9–15 persons. Both bodies, interactively, define the rules for forest use, the punishments for abuse, and the methods of protection and benefit distribution. Who has a voice in the GB and EC bears centrally on who gains or loses from these initiatives.

In many states the criteria for GB membership is one person per household. Although technically gender-neutral, usually only men—seen as the household heads—join. But even where women can become members, few attend or speak up at meetings due to restrictive social norms and perceptions. These 'participatory exclusions', that is exclusions within seemingly participative institutions, have other negative consequences. The rules framed for forest use, for instance, take little account of women's concerns.

CFGs typically ban or severely restrict forest entry. In some regions women's firewood collection time and distance travelled have doubled as a result. Everywhere women have switched in varying degrees to inferior fuels such as crop waste, which take more time to ignite and keep alight, and seriously increase smoke-related health risks, both for women and infants playing in smoky kitchens. Despite substantial forest regeneration, firewood extractions remain exceedingly low, sometimes less than 10–15 per cent of sustainable limits. Thus, despite several years into protection, firewood shortages persist, often to serious extent.

Benefits from the regenerated resource are, however, largely male controlled. In particular, any cash generated typically goes into a community fund, which is usually spent on items that bring women little benefit and do little to alleviate their fuel or fodder shortages. The new arrangements are thus creating a system of property rights in communal land which, like existing rights in privatized land, are strongly male centred and inequitable.

Here new gender inequality has emerged through male control of public property and the rules that govern its use. Gender-neutral rules become unequal when filtered through the prism of pre-existing inequalities. Hence membership by one person per household translates to one man per household. Women's lack of private property increases their dependence on common property, with associated fallouts. Both norms and perceptions restrict women's participation in rule making and implementation. And this remains largely invisible, since most evaluations deem the CFGs as success stories of decentralized management and participative community involvement.

ENHANCING BARGAINING POWER

Women's ability to reduce these inequalities is likely to depend on their bargaining power with the state, the community, the market, and the family, as the case may be. Traditionally, economists have applied ideas about bargaining within the game-theoretic mode and with little attention to gender. Recent interest in intra-household gender dynamics has yielded interesting formulations of bargaining models, as also of the less formal bargaining *approach* which extends the standard ideas to take account of qualitative factors. Unconstrained by the structure that formal modelling requires, a bargaining approach also allows freer application of concepts such as bargaining power to new arenas such as the state and the community.

What affects women's bargaining power? The determinants can vary by context and would include women's command over economic resources, support from external agents such as the state and non-governmental organizations (NGOs), and pre-existing social norms and perceptions (Agarwal 1997, 2001). For community forestry (as an illustration), two factors appear especially important: external agent support and women's group strength. Pressure from NGOs, donors, and key individuals has helped reshape JFM membership rules. Several states have instituted that one man and one woman

per household or all village adults can be members of the GB. Here village women did not need to bargain explicitly for change. External support gave them implicit bargaining power vis-à-vis the state.

However, bargaining with the community would require village women's more direct involvement. Ground experience suggests that for them to have more voice within mixed community forums would need, for a start, a critical mass of vocal women, and a sense of group identity.

On these counts women's credit and self-help groups have had mixed results. On the one hand, such groups enhance women's self-confidence and collective identity; improve male perceptions about women's capabilities through a demonstration effect; weaken restrictive social norms; and increase women's intra-family bargaining power. On the other hand, such groups often remain segregated from mixed gender forums such as mixed CFGs. Strategic interventions, as attempted by some NGOs, appear necessary to integrate separate women's groups into mixed groups and change the latter's gender dynamics. Also a deeper structural change appears necessary to uproot certain social norms, such as the gender division of domestic work, and to reduce gender inequalities in command over property.

In sum, gender inequality takes both material and ideological forms. A critical material form is embedded in who commands private and public property. Critical hidden dimensions of the ideological form are social norms and perceptions. The interactive effects of these pre-existing gender disadvantages can create new inequalities. Enhancing women's bargaining power could help challenge and undermine both forms of inequality.

BINA AGARWAL

REFERENCES

Agarwal, Bina. 1994. *A Field of One's Own: Gender and Land Rights in South Asia*, Cambridge, Cambridge University Press.

———. 1997. '"Bargaining" and Gender Relations: Within and Beyond the Household', *Feminist Economics*, 3 (1): 1–50.

———. 2001. 'Participatory Exclusions, Community Forestry and Gender: An Analysis and Conceptual Framework', *World Development*, 29 (10): 1623–48.

Drèze, Jean and Amartya Sen. 2002. *India: Development and Participation*, New Delhi, Oxford University Press.

Elson, D. 1995. 'Gender Awareness in Modelling Structural Adjustment', *World Development*, 23 (11): 1851–68.

Panda, P. and Bina Agarwal. 2005. 'Marital Violence, Human Development and Women's Property Status in India', *World Development*, 33(5): 823–50.

Raju, Saraswati, Peter J. Atkins, Naresh Kumar, and Janet G. Townsend. 1999. *Atlas of Women and Men in India*, New Delhi, Kali for Women.

Sen, Amartya K. 1990. 'Gender and Cooperative Conflicts', in Irene Tinker, ed., *Persistent Inequalities: Women and World Development*, New York, Oxford University Press: 123–49.

Globalization and the Poor

Globalization and economic reform have enormous potential for economic growth and poverty reduction. But there are at least three troubling features of these phenomena that have emerged over the last two decades—technical change which is biased in favour of capital and skilled labour; increased vulnerability and exposure to economic risks; and a shift of economic power towards more mobile factors of production. The benefits and the costs of globalization are seen in the ground-level experiences of SEWA (Self-employed Women's Association), which is primarily a movement of self-employed women workers, arising out of a confluence of three movements—the labour movement, cooperative movement, and women's movement based on a Gandhian philosophy.

We take as an example SEWA's experience in the construction sector. SEWA has many thousands of members in the construction sector, most of them in Ahmedabad city. These women are mainly 'unskilled' construction workers, working as casual labour. Here is how the issue appears to Madhuben Maganbhai, a 35-year-old construction worker, in her own words:

I started at the age of 15 and first carried loads of concrete on my head. Then I learnt to carry twelve bricks at a time. Later, I learnt to lay concrete and then do plastering. When I first started working we were attached to a contractor and would get work everyday. We only had one holiday on *amavas* (no-moon day). However, in the last ten–twelve years, the numbers of workers increased with the closure of the textile mills and the printing factories. Then workers started competing with each other, and we no longer had regular work. We all had to stand at the *kadiya-naka* [roadside site for construction workers] and contractors came and hired us by the day. Still, I used to get about twenty days of work a month. However, over the last five years things have become especially bad. I hardly get six- to seven-days work a month. This is the situation with all of us who stand at the kadiya-naka. Why? I don't know why. The work seems to have decreased overall. Some say it is due to recession. Others say it is due to new machines which have come in. In some of the bigger sites now, I have seen that all digging is done by machines, and even carrying bricks that we used to do, is now done by machines, and in some sites whole walls are made elsewhere and brought to the site.

The experience of Madhuben is multiplied manifold among the members of SEWA, across the many sectors in which SEWA works, and is documented in many detailed and rigorous studies. For example, take home-based garment workers. The products in the market have been changing rapidly. A decade ago, women were mainly making petticoats and children's wear for the local market. Now the demand is for more sophisticated items in the national and international markets, which they do not know how to stitch. Earlier, cotton cloth was the main raw material, but now there is a variety of synthetic materials including satin and velvet. These materials do not stitch well on the older sewing machines owned by the women. Most women have the simplest machines, and although many women have fitted these machines with motors, they still remain low in productivity. They would like to move to the next level of sewing machines but cannot afford the capital to do so. In addition, many types of work that used to be done by hand, such as making buttonholes and hemming, are now done by machines, or by add-ons to existing machines. One of the major problems of the garment workers is the lack of capital to expand their business if they are self-employed, or to upgrade the quality of their sewing machines.

SEWA's poor women members have always had tremendous vulnerabilities in their lives—the risks of accidents and illness, fire and theft, and periodic unemployment and loss of income through the vagaries of product and labour markets. In the late 1990s the Indian Parliament passed an Act allowing private insurance companies into the sector. Once the Act was passed, SEWA was keen to launch its own insurance company in the form of a cooperative. However, it was not allowed to do so because the Act seemed only to be promoting very large companies. The minimum capital required to register a company under the Act was Rs 100 crore for life insurance, and for general insurance. SEWA argued with the government that an insurance company for the poor did not require such a large capital base, and that Rs 30 crore would guarantee the safety and stability of such a company. However, this argument is not being heard and so far only the very large companies are being allowed to enter the market.

What can be done to help Madhuben, her sisters in SEWA, and the poor in India generally—to prepare her for the opportunities of globalization and economic reform, and to protect her against their ravages? Maximizing the benefits and minimizing the costs require active management of the process of globalization and economic reform with the outcomes for the poor in mind. A hands-off policy is not an option. Strategies for management should be developed by listening to the experiences of the poor and to their representatives. The actions need to address the three problems highlighted at the beginning—skills, vulnerability, and organization. Managing and mitigating the negative consequences of liberalization will require direct interventions to enhance the skills of the poor, and to develop insurance tools to manage the risks they face. Detailed policy recommendations on these, including for example reform of the national framework for skill training, and reform of the structure of insurance regulations to allow micro-insurance to expand, are presented in several SEWA policy papers.

These interventions need to combine government action and action by organizations of the poor. The poor, and especially unskilled poor women, need organization to counteract the growing economic power of capital and skilled labour as a result of their greater national and global mobility. Organization is also the sine qua non for representation of the interests of poor women in local, national, and global policy-making councils. Public policy can help by developing an enabling legal and regulatory environment in which membership-based organizations of the poor can represent their interests and provide them with the services they need.

RENANA JHABVALA AND
RAVI KANBUR

Health Indicators

The health sector as it exists today in India has many features that are the result of active planning, and some other features that have resulted from omission rather than commission. These features, in turn, have created a situation where the health outcomes are extremely heterogeneous, depending on the parameters being used and the units being analysed.

The health system as a whole, with its infrastructure, key inputs, and resources going into the health sector, affects to a large extent the health outcomes of the population. Thus, while the health outcomes are of interest to understand how India has performed over the years, these are not enough to complete the picture. A full discussion on the determinants of health outcomes would require an analysis of all the components that go to make up a health system.

This entry presents a brief analysis, based on selected indicators, of the progress India has made in improving the health status of its population. Added perspective is given by comparing India's achievements with those of other countries and regions, wherever possible.

HEALTH OUTCOMES

Mortality and morbidity statistics, presented across age, gender, residence, and economic categories, enable a proper understanding of a country's health outcomes. However, India has only a few sources of accurate information on the health outcomes of its population. The sources for the vital statistics are based on the Sample Registration System and are important indicators of the changing demography in the country. While demographic indicators are often seen as somewhat separate from health indicators, the two are intricately related—the values of birth and death rates in a way indicate whether the changes in the other health indicators are likely to be temporary or permanent. These, therefore, are core variables on which the rest of the health changes are predicated.

The other variables that determine the changing health outcomes of a population are the infant mortality rate (IMR), life expectancy (LE) at birth, and the maternal mortality rate (MMR). The Tenth Five Year plan, for example, uses the IMR and MMR as two monitorable targets.

The IMR is the number of children dying before age 1 divided by the number of live births that year. It is expressed as the number of infant deaths per 1000 live births. Life expectancy at birth (years) is defined as the number of years a newborn would live if prevailing patterns of age-specific mortality rates at the time of birth were to stay the same throughout the child's life. The MMR is defined as the number of maternal deaths per 100,000 live births. Finally, the under-5 mortality rate (per 1000 live births) is defined as the probability of dying between birth and exactly 5 years of age, expressed per 1000 live births. Various national and international sources are used here to present trends in these four basic indicators of health status. The UNDP's (United Nations Development Programme) Human Development Report calculates adjusted MMR (per 100,000 live births) to account for problems of underreporting and misclassification of maternal deaths, as well as estimates for countries with no data. This entry uses the adjusted MMR figure instead of the unadjusted figure.[1]

Since inter-state variations are critical to such analysis, some state-level analysis is presented as well. For ease of analysis, the states have been divided into four groups: major states, the newly defined Empowered Action Group (EAG) states, north-eastern states, and union territories. The EAG states broadly correspond to the BIMARU states—a term that was coined to describe the states of Bihar, Madhya Pradesh, Rajasthan, and Uttar Pradesh. The new list of EAG states additionally includes Chhattisgarh, Uttaranchal, Jharkhand, and Orissa.

Table 1 gives the values of four demographic/health indicators—LE, IMR, under-5 mortality rate, and MMR—for India for selected years over three decades.[2] Table 2 presents comparisons with three neighbouring South Asian countries (Bangladesh, Pakistan, and Sri Lanka), China, and high and medium human development countries. For two indicators, the comparison is done with an earlier year (1970) as well, and the percentage changes indicated.

Table 1   Trends in Selected Demographic and Health Indicators in India

Indicators	1982	1992	2003
LE	55.5 (1981–5)	60.3 (1991–5)	63
IMR	105	79	63
Under-5 mortality rate	152	94	87
MMR	–	–	540*

*This figure is for the year 2000.

[1]The MMR is the most problematic of all the indicators from the data point of view, and therefore here the trends are not presented, but the figure is discussed in the text.

[2]The rapid changes in the economy in the past three decades justify the choice of years.

The LE at birth was 30 years at the time of Independence; since then India has made rapid progress. In recent years, the LE increased significantly between 1982 and 1993, but slowed down between 1992 and 2003. The current figure of 63.3 in 2003 is still much lower than what many other countries have achieved: the figures are 78 and 67.2 respectively for high and medium human development countries, and 74 for Sri Lanka for the same year. Japan and Sweden are on top of the table with LE of over 80. As Table 2 indicates, the LE for females is significantly higher at 76.8 and 73.5 for Sri Lanka and China respectively in 2003, and India fares only marginally better than Bangladesh and Pakistan with female LE at 65.

While more will be said on male–female differentials in India later, it is important to note that the gender difference in LE is a very important marker for inequities that may exist between males and females in health and other related social well-being indicators. In the countries with the highest LEs, women tend to outlive men by 5 to 8 years; this difference is only 0 to 3 years in countries where the LE is low, as is the case with India (female and male LE are 65 and 61.8 respectively). In Sri Lanka the figures are 76.8 and 71.5 for females and males respectively.

As for IMR, again the progress seems to have slowed down in the later years; an IMR of 63 seems quite high when compared to 9 and 46 (2002) respectively for high and medium human development countries (UNDP). Sri Lanka has been able to achieve an IMR of 13, a figure much lower than even China's 30 and way below India's. Interestingly, Bangladesh currently has a lower IMR (46) than India. If one looks at the last thirty years, Sri Lanka, Bangladesh, and China have all achieved a more rapid decline in IMR than India.

Table 2 Demographic and Health Indicators in India and Selected Countries

Country	IMR 1970	IMR 2003	% change	MMR 2000	LE at birth–females 2003	Under-5 mortality rate 1970	Under-5 mortality rate 2003	% change
Bangladesh	145	46	68.3	380	63.7	239	69	71.1
China	85	30	64.7	56	73.5	120	37	69.2
India	127	63	50.4	540	65	202	87	56.9
Pakistan	120	81	32.5	500	63.2	181	103	43.1
Sri Lanka	65	13	80.0	92	76.8	100	15	85.0

Table 3 Rural–Urban and Male–Female Differentials in Selected Indicators

	Rural Male	Rural Female	Rural Total	Urban Male	Urban Female	Urban Total	Total Male	Total Female	Total Total
IMR (2002)	67	72	69	40	39	40	62	65	63
Crude mortality rate (2002)	9	8.4	8.7	6.5	5.6	6.1	8.4	7.7	8.1
LE at birth (1992–6)	58.9	59.8	59.4	64.9	67.7	66.3	60.1	61.4	60.7

As for under-5 mortality rates that stood at 242 in 1960, the decrease in over forty years to a figure of 87 is significant indeed. However, here too there remains huge scope for improvement: for example high and medium human development countries had figures of 11 and 61 in 2002 respectively. Sri Lanka had an under-5 mortality rate of 15 in 2003, close to what has been achieved by the high human development countries. China and Bangladesh had values of 69 and 69.2 respectively, again bettering India's figure of 87.

The MMR is a difficult parameter to estimate correctly, and it is indicated only for the latest available year in Table 1. The adjusted MMR for India has been calculated by the UNDP to be 540, whereas the unadjusted figure is significantly lower (400). Even this lower value is much higher than the levels existing in developed as well as some developing countries: for example USA and Sri Lanka have adjusted MMRs of 17 and 92 respectively.[3] As Table 2 indicates,

[3]Adjusted MMR figures for high and medium development countries are not available.

neighbour Bangladesh has done much better than India with an MMR of 380, not to mention China, which is way ahead at 56. Interestingly, Pakistan has an adjusted MMR of 500, lower than India's, though the difference is not large enough to draw conclusions.

No discussion on health indicators— or any other indicator for that matter— is complete without an exploration of inter-state, rural–urban, and male–female differentials in India. Table 3 presents the all-India values for some selected indicators to bring out the uneven progress in the country.

There is a large difference between IMR in rural and urban India (69 and 40), and also between male and female IMR in rural India (67 and 72). The difference between the two genders is not as much in urban India. Crude mortality rates are also higher for rural India, though females have a slightly better rate in both rural and urban areas. The LE is significantly lower in rural India, and the male–female differentials in rural and urban India indicate that there may be more gender inequality in rural areas.

Table 4   Demographic and Health Indicators across States in India

State group	IMR 1997 Male	IMR 1997 Female	IMR 2002 Male	IMR 2002 Female	MMR 1998	LE at birth 1992–6 Male	LE at birth 1992–6 Female	LE at birth 1993–7 Male	LE at birth 1993–7 Female
All India	70.0	72.0	63.0	62.0	407.0	60.1	61.4	60.4	61.8
Union territories	37.5	31.0	27.7	26.5	NA	NA	NA	NA	NA
N E states	51.6	40.3	34.3	35.7	NA	NA	NA	NA	NA
EAG states	84.2	89.0	66.3	63.0	538.8	57.7	57.1	58.1	57.5
Major states	50.5	48.5	46.8	46.0	151.3	57.7	59.8	58.1	60.1

Table 4 presents the averages of selected indicators for union territories, north-eastern states, EAG states, and major states. Some states like Delhi and Jammu Kashmir are omitted from the analysis. While the correct methodology would be to use weighted averages for calculating the group averages, this is not done here simply because the differences within these groups of states are not as marked as the differences across the groups.

It seems reasonable to state that the values of IMR and MMR for India are being driven by the EAG states. The highest IMR is recorded in Orissa, followed by Madhya Pradesh, Uttar Pradesh, and Rajasthan.

While estimates of LE at birth are not available for the north-east and union territories, the dominance of the EAG states in lowering the national average for LE seems true here as well.

The above analysis indicates that there is immense scope for improvement; the recent slowdown in the earlier momentum as well as continued inequality across gender, states, and residence make it doubtful whether India can meet the Millennium Development Goals (MDG) or even the goals of the Tenth Five Year Plan. The Tenth Plan target on IMR projects a decline of 34 per cent during 2000–7, which seems a bit overambitious if compared to the mere 12 per cent decline over 1991–2000. To give just one example, Rajasthan could achieve only 9 per cent decline in this period,

whereas it is predicted to improve its IMR by 37 per cent. Similarly, the inter-state variations in MMR are significant, with UP and Rajasthan having almost 7 deaths per 1000 live births. The Tenth Plan target is to bring MMR down to 2 per 1000 live births by 2007 and 1 per 1000 live births by 2012. The EAG states, which comprise almost half of India's population, are unlikely to be able to contribute enough to ensure a reduction of MMR by 50 per cent in the next five years (Deolalikar and World Bank 2005). Among the eight MDGs, three pertain to health: reduction in child mortality, improved maternal health, and combating diseases like HIV/AIDS and malaria. The poorest states, which are also experiencing rapid population growth, will contribute an even higher share of the country's population, and it is the performance of these states that would determine whether and when the country can expect to achieve the MDGs (ibid).

IMMUNIZATION

An effective immunization programme can eradicate much of the infant and childhood morbidities and mortalities. Table 5 indicates the status of immunization in India from a variety of sources: the National Family Health Survey (NFHS 1 and 2), the Reproductive and Child Health Survey (RCH), and a survey conducted by UNICEF (United Nations International Children's Education Fund). The numbers,

Table 5   Percentage of Children Fully Immunized, Based on Various Surveys

States/UT	NFHS 1 1992–3	NFHS 2 1998–9	RCH 1 1998–9	MICS 2000
India	35.4	42	54.2	37.9
Andhra Pradesh	45	58.7	74.5	46.1
Assam	19.4	17	46.7	22.2
Bihar	10.7	11	22.4	12.6
Gujarat	49.8	53	58.1	43.9
Haryana	53.5	62.7	66	33.5
Karnataka	52.2	60	71.8	68
Kerala	54.4	79.7	84	76.9
Madhya Pradesh	22.9	22.4	48.4	30.1
Maharashtra	64.3	78.4	79.7	63.7
Orissa	36.1	43.7	57.8	45.7
Punjab	61.9	72.1	72.9	43.5
Rajasthan	21.1	17.3	37	24.2
Tamil Nadu	65.1	88.8	91.5	80.8
Uttar Pradesh	19.8	21.2	43.7	16.6
West Bengal	34.2	43.8	51.5	57.2
Delhi	57.8	69.8	84.8	54.6
Goa	74.9	82.6	88.6	86.2
Himachal Pradesh	63.5	83.4	74.4	71.1
Jammu and Kashmir	54.2	56.7	52.9	54.9
Manipur	29.1	42.3	51	57.1
Meghalaya	54.9	42.3	32.7	30.2
Mizoram	56.9	59.6	68.4	37.5
Nagaland	3.8	14.1	26.1	23.4
Sikkim		47.4		60.7
Tripura	14.3	40.7	46.3	32.9
Arunachal Pradesh	22.5	20.5	30.6	28.6

Note: A Multiple Indicator Survey 2000 (MICS 2000) was undertaken by UNICEF in India to provide information on key indicators related to women and children and was conducted in all states and UTs.

while varying across surveys, indicate very clearly that India is unlikely to achieve universal immunization any time soon. At the very best, about 54 per cent of all children are currently immunized and at the very worst, 38 per cent are immunized.

Interestingly, the results continue to point towards the EAG and north-eastern states. No matter which data source one uses, Bihar, Rajasthan, Madhya Pradesh, Nagaland, Meghalaya, Tripura, and Assam seem to be performing relatively worse than many other states.

The performance on immunization indicates that child health continues to be a major source of worry for India. Thirty per cent of infants were born with low birth weight over 1998–2003, 47 per cent of children under 5 were from moderate to severely underweight, and 46 per cent of under-5 children suffered from moderate to severe stunting during the same period.

A few other important indicators add to the body of evidence on health outcomes. The number of births attended by skilled health personnel for 1995–2000 is 43 per cent for India, and 97 per cent for Sri Lanka (UNDP 2004). While it is not reported here, the rural and urban differences in the births attended by skilled personnel continue to be significant. The percentage of population with sustainable access to affordable essential drugs is reported to be between 0 and 49 per cent for India, and 95 and 100 per cent for Sri Lanka (UNDP 1995–2000 to 1995–2003). While no data readily exist on the rural–urban differences for access to drugs, it is easy to infer that rural India would be faring much worse than urban India in this respect.

COMMUNICABLE DISEASES

To complete the picture on health status, it is important to have reliable data on morbidities. Unfortunately, India does not have very good data on disease burden or morbidity. While the states do report cases and deaths due to major diseases (Directorate of Health Services),[4] there

[4]Central Bureau of Health Intelligence. *Health Information of India*. 2004. Director General of

is significant underreporting and poor coverage, and it is not clear whether these figures can be used to study trends or variations across states. Nevertheless, the various pieces of existing evidence indicate that India faces a policy challenge in the health sector due to the dual burden of communicable as well as non-communicable diseases. The changing patterns of disease burden calculated by the Commission on Macroeconomics and Health indicate that Category I health conditions which include HIV, TB, malaria, diarrhoea, acute respiratory infections, and maternal and prenatal conditions accounted for nearly half of India's disease burden in 1998. Maternal and child diseases are still about 17 per cent of the total disease burden. The Cause of Death statistics reported by the Registrar General of India's office indicate that diseases of the respiratory system and infectious and parasitic diseases are the major causes of deaths. Another set of statistics on the percentage of reported cases due to six major communicable diseases[5] indicates that in 2003, 66 per cent of the cases were due to acute respiratory infections, followed by acute diarrhoea (28 per cent). This profile of morbidity is associated with poverty, and is a result of conditions like malnutrition and anaemia.

As a cause of death, TB leads among the six diseases mentioned, and is a major public health problem in India, with an estimated 40 per cent of the population suffering from the infection. India accounts for nearly one-third of the global incidence of TB, with an estimated prevalence of 1.4 per cent (Tenth

Health Services, Ministry of Health and Family Welfare, Government of India.

[5]The diseases were TB, pneumonia, acute respiratory infection, acute diarrhoea, viral hepatitis, and enteric fever.

Plan, Planning Commission). TB has got an added impetus in the country now as the leading opportunistic infection of those infected with HIV.

NON-COMMUNICABLE DISEASES
Data on non-communicable diseases (NCDs) are scarce in India, but the available estimates indicate that India contributes substantially to the global burden of NCDs. In 1990, India accounted for 16 per cent of all NCD deaths in the world (Murray and Lopez 1996). It is estimated that the overall NCD burden will rise sharply by 2020 in India, imposing significant economic burden from mortality from NCDs. Changing lifestyle with changes in food habits, and rise in use of tobacco and alcohol, ensure that NCDs would pose difficult policy challenges in the near future. The Commission on Macroeconomics and Health reported that in 1998, the share of NCDs in total disease burden was 33 per cent.

NEWER DISEASES
India has also seen the emergence of newer diseases like HIV/AIDS (human immunodeficiency virus/acquired immune deficiency syndrome), and is fast approaching the dubious distinction of having the maximum number of HIV positive cases in the world. The National AIDS Control Organization reports an estimated 5.1 million HIV-infected cases in India in 2003, and the sentinel surveillance indicates that HIV has spread to all corners of India, and is also spreading into the general population. States like Andhra Pradesh, Karnataka, Maharashtra, Goa, Mizoram, and Nagaland report fairly high prevalence among antenatal clinic (ANC) attendees. However, the cause of concern is not so much the evidently high-prevalence states, but the states that are high on the list of vulnerability due to a variety of factors

like poverty, low education, low status of women, and high rates of migration. Thus the EAG states need to remain in focus in policies of control and prevention.

Another worrying trend has been the spread of hepatitis B in India; the WHO estimates that, assuming an HBsAg[6] carrier rate of 5 per cent, the total number of HBV carriers in the country is estimated to be about 50 million, which forms nearly 15 per cent of the entire pool of HBV carriers in the world. The estimates indicate intermediate to high endemecity for HBV infection. Again, there seems to be wide variation across states, with Maharashtra, Andhra Pradesh, and Karnataka reporting the bulk of the cases. Realizing the potential of hepatitis B to contribute significantly to the disease burden in the near future, hepatitis B vaccine has been included in the Universal Immunization Programme (UIP) in a phased fashion. In the absence of good epidemiological data, however, it is not easy to understand the exact burden of the disease or the effect of the vaccination programme on its incidence.

RE-EMERGING DISEASES

Finally, there has been a resurgence of vector-borne diseases like malaria and dengue. WHO reports on malaria indicate that in the Southeast Asia region, 80 per cent of malaria cases occur in India and it is second to only Myanmar in terms of total deaths from malaria. About 90 per cent of the population living in moderate to high risk of malaria in the Southeast Asia region lives in India, Indonesia, Myanmar, and Thailand.

As for dengue and dengue hemorrhagic fever, it is endemic in most of the countries

in Southeast Asia including India. The WHO categorizes India as a Category B country along with Bangladesh and the Maldives, where cyclical epidemics are becoming more frequent, multiple virus serotypes are circulating, and the disease is seen to be expanding geographically within the country.

Overall, the health situation in India seems to be pointing towards a mixed scenario. While significant progress has been made over the years, especially when compared to the situation in the early 1950s, India still has a long way to go. The progress has been neither spectacular nor equitable. India remains in the group of low achievers, and has been unable to step up the rate of improvement or distribute even this modest improvement fairly across regions and groups. The less developed states, rural areas, the poor, marginalized groups, and women continue to have poor health outcomes, which are made worse by their poor access to healthcare. While there are very few studies on the urban poor, the rapid urbanization and emergence of numerous slums across the major cities indicate that the urban poor are now a constituency that needs urgent focus as well. With countries like Sri Lanka and China galloping ahead, and even some other less developing countries catching up with and overtaking India, it is clear that major rethinking in terms of strategies is required to jump to the next level of health outcomes; else India will remain among the low achievers in the world.

The challenges of preventing and controlling communicable, non-communicable, new, and re-emerging diseases are acute. This brief overview of health outcomes in India is precisely meant to lead researchers, policymakers, and those concerned with the well-being of the population to ask the right questions: what are the critical factors that determine

[6]HBV, the cause of hepatitis B infection, is a DNA virus. The outer surface membrane of HBV contains hepatitis B surface antigen (HBsAg). Detection of HBsAg in the serum of an individual indicates that the person is currently infected with the virus (WHO 2002).

how quickly health outcomes can improve and how best to distribute those gains in a manner that is consistent with the goals of equity and welfare.

INDRANI GUPTA

REFERENCES

Deolalikar, Anil and World Bank. 2005. Attaining the Millennium Development Goals in India: Reducing Infant Mortality, Child Malnutrition, Gender Disparities and Hunger-Poverty and Increasing School Enrollment and Completion.

Family Welfare Programme in India. 2001. *Year Book 2001*, Department of Family Welfare, Ministry of Health and Family Welfare, Government of India.

Planning Commission. 2001. *National Human Development Report 2001*, Planning Commission, Government of India.

Sample Registration System. 2002. Statistical Report 2002, Report No. 3 of 2004, Office of the Registrar General, India.

United Nations Development Programme. 1995–2000 to 1995–2003 http://hdr.undp.org/reports/global/2005/pdf/HDR05_HDI.pdf

United Nations Development Programme. 2004. *Human Development Report. Cultural Liberty in Today's Diverse World*, UNDP, Oxford University Press.

World Health Organisation. http://w3.whosea.org/en/Section10/Section21/Section340_4018.htm
http://w3.whosea.org/en/Section10/Section332_1100.htm
————. 2002. *Prevention of Hepatitis B in India: An Overview*, New Delhi, World Health Organization, Regional Office for South Asia.

Higher Education

Higher education in India has been, in Stanley Wolpert's evocative words, 'the swiftest [of] elevators to the pinnacles of modern Indian power and opportunity'. At the time of Independence, while small relative to its population, India already had one of the largest and most sophisticated higher education systems among developing countries. Since then the system has expanded rapidly, with student enrolment growing at about two-and-half times the population growth rate, a result of both a population bulge in lower age cohorts as well as increased demand for higher education. By 2003 India had more than 15,000 colleges and about 10 million students. India's gross enrolment ratio in tertiary education was approximately 12 per cent of the age cohort. While considerably higher than developing country averages, it is lower than China's (16 per cent) and much lower than those of the OECD countries. Enrolment ratios vary across Indian states, with the southern and western states faring better than their eastern and northern counterparts.

Women account for about 40 per cent of enrolments (compared to just 10 per cent in 1950), varying from less than a quarter in Bihar to a high of three-fifths in Kerala. There has been a gradual increase in the enrolment of India's most marginalized social groups, namely scheduled castes (SCs) and scheduled tribes (STs): the ratio of general to SC/ST students in professional education dropped from almost 12:1 in the late 1950s to 8:1 during the late 1980s. There is strong suggestive evidence that the proportion of first-generation graduates in universities has been rising dramatically, belying the claim that state expenditure on higher education only subsidizes the privileged upper castes.

The bulk of students (about two-thirds) are enrolled in arts and science, with another 18 per cent in commerce/management. Recent growth—driven by the private sector—has been much greater in professional colleges (especially engineering, management, and medicine), as well as in private vocational courses. The fact that

India has 1253 medical colleges but just two in public health indicates the priorities and interests that shape Indian higher education. The private sector, which accounted for just 15 per cent of the seats of engineering colleges in 1960, accounted for nearly 87 per cent of seats by 2003. Data for business schools are even starker. In the case of medical colleges, private-sector dominance is less marked, but the trend is unambiguous: the proportion of private seats rose from 6.8 per cent to 41 per cent in the same period. Even as political parties rail against de jure privatization, de facto privatization continues unabated (Kapur and Mehta 2004).

There are considerable misconceptions regarding India's misplaced emphasis on higher education. There is no evidence that the neglect of primary and secondary education, however unconscionable, was *because of* an overemphasis on higher education. Higher education expenditure as a share of gross national product (GNP) declined from nearly 1 per cent during the 1970s to just 0.35 per cent in the mid-1990s before increasing modestly to 0.6 per cent by the end of the decade. Government expenditure on higher education as a percentage of total education expenditure declined from an average of 15 per cent during the 1980s to about 10 per cent during the 1990s. Since this occurred at a time when enrolment was rapidly increasing, the result was a sharp decline in real spending per pupil. A striking feature of higher education expenditure is that most of it goes to salaries resulting in very poor infrastructure and intense competition for scarce resources leading to greater politicization.

Indian higher education continues to be one of the most regulated sectors. Dirigisme and the licence raj may have been dismantled in industry, but are flourishing in higher education. The principal regulators are the University Grants Commission (UGC) and the All India Council for Technical Education (AICTE), and for specialized professional courses such as medicine, law and accountancy, the respective professional bodies. Although higher education is a concurrent subject, private universities (as distinct from private colleges) require approval from the federal regulator, the UGC. Although this was tested by the state of Chhattisgarh in 2002, the Supreme Court upheld the UGC's monopoly. The basic thrust of regulation is a deep reluctance to grant institutions the autonomy over the academic criteria that determine whom they wish to educate. Regulation has increased the cost of supplying education and resulted in adverse selection by deterring genuine educationists from investing, while encouraging those who are adept at manipulating the licence-quota raj in the system, one reason why many private colleges are run by politicians or their affiliates. A perceived need to curb 'exploitation' because of high fees has led to fee caps instead of empowering students directly by enhancing scholarships and loans. User costs (or costs recovered from students) have remained at roughly 5 per cent (compared to about a quarter in East Asia). Coupled with the severe fiscal crisis facing the state, the fee caps simply diminish the supply and quality of education rather than help the poor.

In 1948 the Radhakrishnan Commission had cautioned that the exclusive control of education by the state was a recipe for 'totalitarian tyrannies'. That warning went unheeded. From the 1980s while the state maintained tight official control over higher education, actual provisioning shifted to the private sector, a trend that accelerated in the 1990s. This de facto privatization was not a result of changing ideological commitments of the key actors—the state, the judiciary, or India's propertied classes—but instead resulted from a breakdown of the state system and an exit of Indian elites from public institutions, to both private-sector institutions within the country as well as abroad. The mushrooming of private higher education institutions (with the largest number in the southern states and Maharashtra) has been driven by four factors: fiscal exhaustion; diffusing the reservation conundrum by expanding supply; with earlier sources of patronage exhausted, the search for new sources of patronage; and inter-state competition and policy diffusion as states like Kerala and West Bengal realized that their students were fleeing—and spending large amounts of money—in neighbouring states. There is little doubt that while the mushrooming of private colleges has been driven by the profit motive, it has helped infuse dynamism in the economy over the long run. States that moved early in this direction (like Karnataka) benefited from this supply shock, whereas a state such as Kerala whose basic educational attainments receive so much attention, languished because of the limited supply of higher education.

The political economy of higher education defies easy explanations. Ideological considerations have played an important role. Rapid expansion without regard to quality has led to several low-level traps. One, it has had a diminishing signalling effect. With university degrees serving as formal minimal requirements but little else, competitive exams have virtually replaced performance at university level as a passport to further education or jobs. Consequently, there is no compelling demand for quality improvement in the bulk of higher education. Resources have shifted to those arenas that perform signalling functions—entrance exams, competitive tests, etc.—and those who can afford it have seceded from the system through a combination of private tuitions, private professional education, and study abroad. Although the last is a relatively small figure (about 1 per cent of tertiary education), the financial implications are more than an order of magnitude greater with estimates suggesting that expenditure on overseas consumption of education is to the tune of several billion dollars annually.

Two, even as private expenditures have increased dramatically, officially there continues to be enormous reluctance to see education as an industry or business or even as a service sector. Public institutions are severely proscribed from mobilizing private resources in any form—higher fees, licensing arrangements, or philanthropy. Prior to Independence private philanthropy in higher education played a critical role in its growth. This support not only built some of India's best liberal arts colleges and technology institutes but it also supported public institutions in significant ways. With private initiatives hostage to the discretionary actions of the state, private philanthropy's share in public higher education institutions withered, falling from 17 per cent just after Independence to less than 2 per cent half a century later. Although decline was natural as government expanded its role in higher education, the extent is striking. Moreover, philanthropy became increasingly conflated with creating not-for-profit, but financially sustainable institutions with beneficiaries charged for the services provided to them rather than funded through financial contributions of donors.

The proliferation of private institutions has been largely in the area of professional education driven by entrepreneurial activities of politicians. However, these private colleges are subject to roughly the same curricular guidelines as public institutions and hence lack the pedagogical innovation or excellence associated with private initiative.

The result is that Indian higher education is in a regulatory environment where the private sector will not be deregulated or foreign investment permitted and the state sector is strapped for resources because of the government's fiscal constraints and public education cannot mobilize higher funds because of ideological fetters.

Three, higher education policy is being driven less by a clear ideological vision or class interest than by the state's own interest (or perhaps its own ideological whims). While ideological battles over the curriculum in history capture attention, state bodies have sought to increase administrative control over institutions of higher education through a web of regulations—the setting up of an institution requires a gamut of clearances and it is required to conform to a set of norms set by state bodies. Over the course of the 1970s and 1980s, politicians acquired a great vested interest in the affairs of universities, seeing them as possible sites for not just political recruitment, but expanding patronage. The direct interference of the state has implied that in most states universities have become appendages of government offices.

As with other aspects of India's reforms, courts have played an important role in shaping the political economy of higher educational reforms, imperfectly filling in for the government and the statutory authorities that have been reluctant to clean up the Augean stables. In a series of judgements in the 1990s the court affirmed the state's right to interfere in admission policy and the fee structure of private professional institutions on the grounds that education being a fundamental right, could not be the object of profit-seeking activity. As a result poor service in education was effectively not justiciable in consumer courts with the courts and the Monopolies and Restrictive Trade Practices (MRTP)

Commission holding that education was not a service because the courts defined 'service' as covering only commercial transactions. More recently, there has been a distinct shift in the Supreme Court's stance, from undisguised suspicion of the private sector to grudging acceptance. In its landmark 'Inamdar' judgement in 2005, the Supreme Court reversed its earlier stance unshackling institutions that do not receive state funding from state diktats. However, this prompted Parliament to swiftly pass the 104th Constitution Amendment Bill that would allow for reservations in all private educational institutions.

The Court's interventions have been driven by an attempt to reconcile disparate principles of merit and social justice focusing more on the procedural aspects of equality and less on enabling higher education to be more widely available or improve quality. Like the government, courts have been reluctant to sanction fee hikes in public institutions reinforcing a peculiar public–private split. While the primary and secondary school sector has been left replete with freedoms, higher education is regarded as the arena where a formal principle of equality of opportunity is most vigorously asserted. The political and legal energies have overwhelmingly focused on professional education in medicine and engineering, neglecting both the majority of students enrolled in traditional science and arts courses as well as post high school vocational training institutions. India has a sizable system of Industrial Training Institutes (ITIs—vocational institutes), with enrolment of roughly three-quarters of a million. Most ITIs are of very poor quality, though there have been attempts to revive them through public–private partnerships. But the ITIs remain a neglected sector of higher education, with the result that the system is skewed towards degrees rather than skills.

India's higher education system remains neither fish nor fowl—suspended between over-regulation by the state on the one hand, and a discretionary privatization that is unable to mobilize private capital in productive ways, on the other. The success of narrow professional schools masks a deep crisis. The veneer of the few institutions of excellence masks the reality that the median higher education institutions in India have become incapable of producing students who have skills and knowledge. A few of the top institutions like the Indian Institutes of Technology (IITs) can free ride on the fact that they have little competition and can therefore get the best students out of a very large pool of available talent. But the bulk of the system does not provide adequate screening or signalling. Consequently, students are forced to spend more years (and, increasingly, large resources) in acquiring some sort of postgraduate professional qualification as they desperately seek ways to signal their qualities to potential employers. It would not be an exaggeration to say that India's current system of higher education is centralized and politicized and militates against producing broad analytical skills. The fact that the system nonetheless produces a noticeable number of high-quality students has to do with the sheer number of students and the Darwinian struggle at high school to get admission into the few good institutions.

The core problems in the sector are the mismatch of supply and demand and poor standards. The pressure on the state to expand higher education has been largely expressed as a demand for more seats rather than as a demand for higher quality or greater expenditure. There are too few institutions compared to the size of the demand and even fewer quality institutions, and the supply is locked into programmes that have not kept up with changing demands in labour markets. Over the long run, internal incentives and adverse selection effects within universities have undermined autonomy and professionalism.

The most acute weakness plaguing India's higher education is a crisis of accountability at all levels of the system, the result of a deeply flawed regulatory environment. The prevailing political ideological climate in which elite institutions are seen as being anti-democratic, finds its natural response in political control to influence admissions policies, internal organization, the structure of courses, and funding. Increasingly, even flagship institutions like the IITs and IIMs (Indian Institutes of Management) are suffering from growing shortfalls of faculty, the result of their inability to adjust to the increasingly global market for talent. Even the better Indian universities do little research, and that is one reason why India which once surpassed China in scientific research publications is now lagging behind. Except for a few elite institutions, the quality of teaching remains poor. As quality deteriorates, students are less and less willing to pay the very resources without which quality cannot be improved. Rigid regulation and underinvestment have ensured that there is not enough quality education to meet the skill demands of the economy.

Ironically, even as India is positioning itself as a global service provider, in higher education it is becoming an ever-larger consumer of overseas education. India will need a regulatory revolution to take full advantage of the knowledge economy but the political economy of reform of higher education poses more severe challenges than that of almost any other sector.

DEVESH KAPUR AND

PRATAP BHANU MEHTA

REFERENCES

Kapur, Devesh and Pratap Bhanu Mehta. 2004. 'Indian Higher Education Reform: From Half-baked Socialism to Half-baked Capitalism', Harvard University CID Working Paper No. 108, September.

Tilak, J.B.G. 1997. 'The Dilemma of Reforms in Financing Higher Education in India', *Higher Education Policy*, 10(1): 7–21.

HIV/AIDS, Economics of

Whilst sub-Saharan Africa remains the region most visibly blighted by human immunodeficiency virus/acquired immune deficiency syndrome (HIV/AIDS), India now also appears on the brink of a significant epidemic, which may represent a vastly different and perhaps more far-reaching challenge. India encompasses a large percentage of the world's population, with significant military strength, nuclear capability, and rapidly growing economic importance. The consequences of HIV/AIDS in India could have substantial repercussions worldwide.

The first serological evidence of HIV infection in India appeared in 1986 and HIV has since been detected in almost all of India's thirty-five states and union territories. Although for the most part contained within 'high-risk' groups, in seven Indian states the prevalence of HIV in women attending antenatal clinics exceeds 1 per cent, putting them in the 'generalized' epidemic category. With an estimated 5.134 million individuals living with HIV in 2004, approximately 0.9 per cent of adults are HIV positive, and in terms of absolute numbers, HIV prevalence in India is the second highest worldwide (NACO 2004). HIV/AIDS has become an established reality in India, and whilst it is impossible to forecast the long-term trajectory of the pandemic, the possibility of tens of millions of infections and AIDS

deaths is no longer remote. The National Intelligence Commission projects that India will have 20 to 25 million cases by 2010, the most in the world (NIC 2002). Given the manner in which the disease spreads and the disproportionate effects of its burden, there will be regional differences in the competency to handle this emergency, which may impact India's economic competitiveness and could potentially alter the political stability of the subcontinent. HIV/AIDS in India, as elsewhere, is no longer merely an infection; it is an economic and political factor, entrenched in the Millennium Development Goals, a prime source of international donor funding and a powerful driver of socio-economic reform.

Traditional thinking about HIV/AIDS has focused on the bio-medical aspects: the structure of the HIV virus, mechanisms of transmission, the management of opportunistic infections, and the quest to engineer an effective vaccine. Yet the effects of HIV/AIDS clearly extend far beyond health. HIV has profoundly influenced legal human rights and ethical frameworks, and has thrown up powerful debates regarding the strategies of prevention and treatment. In assessing the implications of the epidemic, it is necessary to account for local demography as well as family structure and gender roles, especially relevant in the case of India.

From the economist's perspective, it is important to note that HIV appears to be spreading without significant limitation, and given the lack of a cure in the near future, each case represents irreversible economic loss, albeit with variable time lags from diagnosis to death. When transmitted sexually—as is the dominant mode in most parts of India—HIV affects economically productive age groups and this impact is amplified by the consequences for families and dependents, who themselves are at high risk of concurrent infection. Given this compounded family burden, the costs of treatment can be prohibitively high especially in a country such as India where the great majority of all healthcare is sought within the private sector and is paid for out of a person's own pocket (Bloom et al. 2004). The Government of India has ambitious plans to provide free and subsidized anti-retroviral medications in the six highest-prevalence states, in line with current international thinking, but this represents a substantial strain on already overstretched health resources. Furthermore, social and cultural norms lead to a reluctance to acknowledge the spread of the disease or prevent it. Women are particularly vulnerable due to their lack of control over decision making, extending even to the lack of ability to negotiate safe sex.

IMPACTS OF HIV/AIDS
Micro-level Impacts
The adverse effects of illness and poor health at individual and household levels have been well established and can be intuitively extended to the consequences of HIV/AIDS. The most visible impact is on the financial expenses associated with medical treatment. In a study of several Asian countries including India (Bloom et al. 2004), annual treatment costs (not including anti-retroviral drugs) were estimated to be more than double the average per capita income.

Another immediate impact is on the earnings and incomes of households with members afflicted with HIV/AIDS. HIV/AIDS affects individuals at the age when they are likely to be working or providing in-kind support to the household. An International Labour Organization (ILO) study in four Indian states showed that households affected by HIV lost as much as one-third of their income while average monthly expenditures on food and treatment increased substantially (ILO

2003). One consequence is that these households have compromised on children's education; nearly 38 per cent of respondents said they were forced to withdraw children from school and send them to work. The study also indicates that stigma at the workplace complicates matters with many people living with HIV/AIDS (PLWHA) not disclosing their status to employers for fear of losing their jobs (ibid.).

Sectoral Impacts
Yet a society in aggregate may not be affected by a severe health crisis in the same manner as individual households. Economic assets may get transferred from one household to another and previously unemployed members of the labour force may take over from members of society unable to work. In societies with scarcity of food and educational resources, one family's loss may be another's gain. Moreover, communities and industries may have mechanisms to mitigate sustained household-level impacts—such as orphanages, public health systems, and extended family support.

There are few studies and thus limited information on sector-level impacts of HIV/AIDS in South Asia. Migrant workers who constitute a significant bulk of the unskilled labour force in both rural and urban areas are also at increased risk of HIV infection, presumably due to living far from their families with income to spare compounded by their low levels of education and awareness of HIV transmission risks (Gupta and Singh 2002). Sectors relying heavily on unskilled labour such as construction may face greater economic challenges from HIV. At the same time, the vast pool of underemployed labour that exists in India means that this threat is not likely to be significant in the immediate future.

To the extent HIV/AIDS is associated with declines in the rate of growth of per capita income, it is natural to suppose it will also thwart any decline in poverty. Cross-country evidence suggests that economic inequality and poverty rates, defined as the proportion of population living below US$ 1 per day, are positively correlated with HIV prevalence (Bloom et al. 2001). A causal impact of HIV on poverty (or inequality) has not been empirically demonstrated thus far, at least with national-level data.

Nonetheless, there is reasonable micro-evidence to support the assertion that the poor and less educated are at greater risk of infection than other groups (Bloom et al. 2001). Thus in the end it may be likely that the poor disproportionately bear the economic consequences of AIDS, contributing both to increased poverty as well as worsening economic inequality. With the poor in India, namely sex workers, truck drivers, and unskilled migrant workers, at higher risk for HIV infection, it seems inevitable that HIV will contribute to increased poverty and inequality. Whether this becomes evident in national-level statistics is less obvious, and depends crucially on the future scale of the HIV epidemic.

Macro-level Impacts

Even though India is projected to have the largest number of people infected with AIDS globally by 2010, the impact may be lessened because these individuals will remain diffused amongst a very large population, reflected by projected prevalence rates of 2–4 per cent (NIC 2002). Analysing the broader impact on economic growth and productivity is also difficult, because it depends largely on which demographic groups get hit hardest. Anand et al. (1999) estimated that AIDS cost India roughly 1 per cent of GDP per year because of lost productivity and treatment of secondary infections. The study did not include numerous factors, such as the cost of drugs

and retraining workers, and there is no consensus on a formula to calculate the economic costs. There is as yet no study on India that attempts to quantify the effects of the HIV/AIDS epidemic on growth and income in a general equilibrium framework.

From a purely economic perspective, in the case of such a populous nation, the more the disease remains confined to rural and lower skilled people, the more likely the abundant labour supply can fill the gap. However, if the disease spreads amongst young, educated, urban professionals, the economic costs will be much higher, especially given the premium on skilled labour. Most notably, by curtailing adult life spans, a widespread HIV epidemic alters the calculus of investment in higher education and technical skills, thereby undermining the local process of investment in human capital (Bloom and Mahal 1997).

In addition, burgeoning HIV prevalence could affect international decisions regarding direct investment, technology transfer, and personnel allocation in places perceived to be of high health risk, in effect cutting off afflicted countries from globalization. The long-term economic impact could be even more significant than the constraints imposed by the epidemic on local labour supplies or savings. Given its current economic resurgence, the Indian leadership fears the perception in global markets of a rising AIDS problem, which could discourage the huge flow of foreign investment into the country, vital to its continued growth (Anand et al. 1999, Bloom and Mahal 1997).

CONTRIBUTION OF THE PROCESSES OF ECONOMIC DEVELOPMENT

Studies have correlated several of the processes driving India's remarkable economic development with the spread of HIV, for example rural–urban and international migration, urbanization, and increases in income. This focus on the economic and political roots of the epidemic coupled with a study of societal culture and individual risk behaviours has a potentially vital role in promoting our understanding of the spread of HIV, and in designing policies that most efficiently limit its impact (Bloom et al. 2004).

First, economic deprivation and HIV/AIDS incidence are linked. Consider, for example, the supply side of the sex industry, which draws women and young girls from extreme poverty and thrusts them into high risk for HIV infection. A series of small-scale studies from sub-Saharan African countries, Haiti, Sri Lanka, and Brazil all show how poor women can be forced into sex work and into providing sexual favours in return for money, and may be less able to insist on condom use (Bloom et al. 2004, Bloom et al. 2001).

Second, the demand side of the sex industry is driven obviously by the fact that clients have the financial ability to afford the services of sex workers. Thus mobile populations, such as migrant labourers, truck drivers, merchant seamen, members of the armed forces, and possibly tourists, who often have considerable amounts of cash to spend, are especially likely to demand commercially available sex or engage in multiple-partner sex (Bloom et al. 2004). This connection seems strengthened by the fact that the behaviour of migrants is not easily subject to monitoring by their families and communities, and that they may be lonely due to separation from their families.

India has a huge migrant population, both internal and international; rural to urban migration is significant, especially in Maharashtra, Tamil Nadu, and West Bengal, as is the floating population of migrant workers. India is also experiencing substantial cross-border population movements with Bangladesh and Nepal, as well as strong migration flows to and from the Middle East and a growing influx of tourists and foreign business persons. Ongoing economic reform is likely to further promote the movement of people. Increasing economic inequality, another correlate of economic growth in its early stages, is also likely to contribute to increased risk of HIV transmission among Indians.

METHODS OF EVALUATION TO AID POLICY

By clarifying the underpinnings of behaviours at risk for HIV infection, economic analysis has also helped clarify the complexity of the mechanisms of HIV transmission, in particular explaining individual and organizational behaviour cost–benefit analyses that are extremely useful in providing policy insights.

Consider a policy of isolating or imprisoning HIV-positive commercial sex workers, as India did some years ago in a highly publicized case. This policy might seem a sensible way to curb HIV transmission, because it prevents HIV-infected sex workers from selling sex. However, it fails on two counts: it does not influence the demand side of the market for commercial sex and it neglects the deeper economic roots of the supply of commercial sex workers. Under the economic conditions prevailing in India the demand for commercial sex will be satisfied by a newly migrating group of women. Economic models of migration can be used to show that the likelihood of frequent arrests of commercial sex workers, and their consequent withdrawal, will only enhance work opportunities for new entrants into the industry. Moreover, the incarceration of sex workers in rehabilitation homes and prisons is likely to result in the industry remaining 'underground', which will hinder these women from accessing health messages.

Without information about HIV and the power to negotiate the use of condoms, they too will become infected and then infect others (Bloom et al. 2004, Bloom et al. 2001).

These examples illustrate a need for economic approaches to policymaking, to understand what is generating undesirable outcomes as a prelude to effective policy design and implementation. They also highlight the fact that many practical policies for HIV prevention may conflict with other social goals and policies. For instance, decriminalizing the use and possession of drugs and needles may promote drug use; promoting information about sex and condoms may enhance promiscuity; and policies promoting the use of condoms in brothels may accord prostitution a legal or at least a formally recognized status.

The operational objective of the National AIDS Control Organization (NACO) is to halt the prevalence of HIV at 3 per cent in the six states with a generalized epidemic and 1 per cent in the rest of the country (NACO 2004). At present India's strategy to deal with HIV/AIDS focuses first and foremost on prevention. The plan also aims to increase awareness amongst teenagers and other vulnerable sections of the population, and to vigorously promote condom usage, especially amongst high-risk groups. This programme in itself requires much greater resources than funds earmarked by the Indian government to combat HIV/AIDS. Treatment programmes have until recently been a low priority, but international pressures and increasing awareness of treatment success and cost-effectiveness have led to anti-retroviral roll outs being trialled in the six high-prevalence states.

India's private sector must also be encouraged to play its part in addressing the epidemic, from education programmes to financing treatment plans. Some companies such as Tatas and Bajaj have accepted some corporate social responsibility in instituting workplace testing and providing anti-retroviral drugs. These efforts should be replicated on a wide scale.

In reality it will be difficult for India to curb the epidemic in the near future without a dramatic shift in priorities: the disease has built up significant momentum, health services are inadequate, and the cost of education and treatment programmes will be overwhelming. Despite growing concern over the disease among senior leaders, the sheer size, resource constraints, widespread ignorance about AIDS, cultural taboos about discussing sex, and coordination problems between levels of government will make it difficult to check the spread of the disease. If the necessary research is conducted, economics can contribute usefully to thinking about the determinants of transmission and potential impacts of the HIV/AIDS epidemic in India, thereby leading to the development of optimal strategies to address this immense challenge.

BHARGAVI RAO, AJAY MAHAL,
AND DAVID E. BLOOM

REFERENCES

Anand, K., C.S. Pandav, and L.M. Nath. 1999. 'The Impact of HIV/AIDS on the National Economy of India', *Health Policy*, 47:195–205.

Bloom, D. and Ajay Mahal. 1997. 'Does the AIDS Epidemic Threaten Economic Growth?' *Journal of Econometrics*, 77:105–24.

Bloom, D., Ajay Mahal, Larry Rosenberg, Jaypee Sevilla, David Steven, and Mark Weston. 2004. *Asia's Economies and the Challenge of AIDS*, Manila, Asian Development Bank.

Bloom, D., Ajay Mahal, Jaypee Sevilla, and River Path Associates. 2001. 'AIDS and Economics', Harvard School of Public Health, Department of Population and International Health.

Gupta, K. and S.K. Singh. 2002. *Social Networking, Knowledge of HIV/AIDS and Risk-taking Behaviour among Migrant Workers*, Mumbai, Indian Institute of Population Sciences.

International Labour Organization (ILO). 2003. 'Assessing the Socio-economic Impact of HIV/AIDS on People Living with HIV/AIDS (PWLHAs) and their Families in India', New Delhi, International Labour Organization.

National AIDS Control Organization (NACO). 2004. Annual Report, New Delhi, National AIDS Control Organization.

National Intelligence Commission (NIC). 2002. *The Next Wave of HIV/AIDS: Nigeria, Ethiopia, Russia, India and China*, Washington D.C., National Intelligence Commission.

Human Development Index

The term 'Human Development' entered the lexicon of development economics in 1990 through the first Human Development Report (HDR) published by the United Nations Development Programme (UNDP). The concept, developed by Mahbub ul Haq and Amartya Sen, is defined as 'the process of enlarging people's choices'. Economic growth is considered only a means of capability expansion and not as an end in itself.

The Human Development Index (HDI), used in the HDRs to compare countries in the world, has been designed as an alternative to per capita income, the single most commonly used measure to evaluate development outcomes thus far. The index includes three important choices, namely to lead a long and healthy life, to acquire knowledge, and to have a decent standard of living. The distinguishing feature of the HDI is that, while developed as an alternative to the use of per capita income for evaluating development outcomes, it does not ignore the income dimension itself.

Several crucial decisions were taken with respect to the HDI by Mahbub ul Haq

and Amartya Sen, its principal architects. The first was that it should reflect human capabilities. Second, it should include only a limited number of variables to keep it 'simple and manageable'. Third, a composite index would be prepared rather than several separate indices. Fourth, the HDI would cover both social and economic aspects and, finally, the coverage and methodology of the HDI would be kept flexible (Haq 1995).

In developing the HDI, Amartya Sen and Mahbub ul Haq went beyond other similar attempts at measuring well-being, the most prominent of them being the Physical Quality of Life Index (PQLI), developed by Morris Davis Morris in 1979. The PQLI comprises three social indicators, namely basic literacy rate, infant mortality rate, and life expectancy at age 1. The HDI, on the other hand, includes both economic and social dimensions of development.

Three features of the HDI—its simplicity, universality, and plurality—have contributed to the emergence of the HDI as a strong alternative evaluative measure of development outcomes.

METHODOLOGY
Indicators
Since the HDI is an evaluation of development outcomes, it focuses on attainments in the realms of education, health, and real income per capita. Longevity is measured by life expectancy at birth. The knowledge dimension is measured using two indicators, (a) adult literacy rate, which is a crude reflection of access to education and (b) combined primary, secondary, and tertiary enrolment, with the former having a two-thirds weight and the latter, a one-third weight. The third dimension, command over resources needed for decent living, is represented by per capita income.

In order to reflect the diminishing returns that accrue while transforming income into human capabilities, the logarithm of per capita income is used as an indicator. However, to enable cross-country comparisons, per capita income is adjusted for purchasing power parity (PPP) reflecting the relative purchasing power of the currency and is expressed in US dollars. It is important to understand here that the income indicator represents a bundle of goods and services needed for the best use of human capabilities. All three dimensions are given equal weights as they are considered equally valuable in ensuring well-being. Equal weights, however, is an ad hoc procedure, in the absence of any obvious way of weighing the indicators. While the basic methodology of index construction has remained unchanged since 1991, there have been some changes in the indicators used in the education dimension and the method of transformation of the income variable.

INDEX CONSTRUCTION

In order to combine the three variables, a dimension index is prepared for each indicator using maximum and minimum values. Since 1995, fixed goal posts have been used, which are a minimum of 25 years and a maximum of 85 years for life expectancy, 0 and 100 for adult literacy, combined primary, secondary and tertiary enrolment, and purchasing power adjusted to US$100 and $40,000 for per capita income.

Performance in each dimension is expressed as a value between 0 and 1 applying the following general formula:

Dimension Index = [actual value − minimum value]/[maximum value − minimum value]

The HDI is then calculated as a simple average of the dimension indices. The values of the HDI vary between 0 and 1.

Countries with an HDI value of 0.8 and above are considered high human development countries, those between 0.5 and 0.79 belong to the medium human development category, and those below 0.5 are considered countries with low levels of human development.

CRITIQUE

As is evident, the index is simple to compute and has a strong appeal as advocating the cause of 'well-being' rather than only income. However, the index has been subject to much criticism both on conceptual and methodological grounds. Conceptually, its very simplicity, which has made it so successful, is its failing, for the expanse of the concept of human development is not fully captured by the HDI. Human development is increasingly being identified with improved education and health attainments alone. Important indicators like political and social freedom, participation in community life, environmental concerns, and crime and violence that could jeopardize the quest for sustainable development are excluded from the HDI.

More importantly, though it is positioned as an alternative approach, the focus continues to be on *average* levels of attainments and distributional concerns are bypassed. It has also been observed that there is a high correlation between the three components with per capita income explaining much of the variation in HDI values across countries rendering the HDI less useful as a replacement to gross domestic product (GDP) per capita. However, it has been observed that this applies only for the middle-income countries where the differential between economic and social attainments is higher than in either the high-income or low-income countries.

The HDI is also criticized for including both stock variables such as adult literacy and life expectancy and flow variables such as income per capita and gross enrolment ratios rendering difficult the evaluation of impact of policies on attainments within a short period.

INDIA

In India the HDI has been calculated officially for Indian states by the Planning Commission in the first Human Development Report, 2001. The HDI was computed separately for rural and urban areas for all states for the years 1981 and 1991 and for select states for the year 2001. While the methodology used was similar to that of the UNDP in terms of the dimensions used, process indicators, namely intensity of education to supplement adult literacy rate in the knowledge dimension, infant mortality rate to supplement life expectancy in the health dimension, and inequality-adjusted per capita consumption expenditure in the standard of living dimension, were used in each of the dimensions to enable frequent monitoring of the HDI within the country.

Several state-level HDRs have also been prepared in India, all of which compute district-level HDI. This level of disaggregation and the limitations of data have required some substitution and modification of indicators to compute district-level HDI. Most often, infant mortality rate is substituted for life expectancy and per capita income is reflected through per capita district domestic product. The computation of district-level HDI has shown severe data gaps and spurred efforts towards district-level estimation of domestic product, poverty, and demographic indicators.

POLICY IMPACT

Despite its many limitations, the HDI has proved to be very useful as a tool for policy analysis. It has enabled several developing countries in Asia, Africa, and Latin America to take explicit cognizance of human development issues and enabled a move away from excessively growth-centred strategies. The HDI has governed resource-allocation strategies in countries, for example Egypt and the Philippines, and in the states of Madhya Pradesh and Maharashtra within India. It has enabled examination of inter- and intra-country disparities with respect to HDI rankings, which, in turn, has spurred competition among countries and regions within a country to improve rankings on the HDI, giving rise to support for social sectors. This has been particularly valuable at a time when countries have been undergoing the process of economic reforms which typically lead to reduction in public resource allocation to these sectors. The HDI has also been a powerful advocacy tool and has rekindled debate and dialogue among various groups of people on the relevance of various development strategies and has spurred research on newer indicators and indices that are more relevant in capturing the multidimensional nature of development.

To quote Amartya Sen,

It would be a great mistake to concentrate on the Human Development Index. These are useful indicators in rough and ready work: but the real merit of the human development approach lies in the plural attention it brings to bear on development evaluation, not in the aggregative measures it presents as an aid to diverse statistics.

K. SEETA PRABHU

REFERENCES

Fukuda-Parr, Sakiko. 2003. 'Rescuing the Human Development Concept from the HDI: Reflections on a New Agenda', in Sakiko Fukuda-Parr and A.K. Shiv Kumar, eds, *Readings in Human Development*, New Delhi, Oxford University Press.

Fukuda-Parr, Sakiko and A.K. Shiv Kumar, eds, 2003. *Readings in Human Development*, New Delhi, Oxford University Press.

Haq, Mahbub ul. 1995. *Reflections on Human Development*, New Delhi, Oxford University

Press, Ch. 4, also reprinted in Sakiko Fukuda-Parr and A.K. Shiv Kumar, eds, *Readings in Human Development*.

Jahan, Selim. 2002. 'Measuring Living Standard and Poverty: Human Development Index as an Alternate Measure', Political Economy Research Institute (PERI), University of Massachusetts-Amherst, http://www.umass.edu/peri/pdfs/glw_jahan.pdf

Planning Commission, Government of India. 2002. *Human Development Report 2001*, New Delhi, UNDP.

Sen, Amartya. 2000. 'A Decade of Human Development', *Journal of Human Development*, 1(1).

United Nations Development Programme (UNDP). 1990. 'Defining and Measuring Human Development', *Human Development Report*, Ch. 1.

Human Rights

To have a 'right' means to have a claim to something of value on other people, institutions, the state, or the international community, which in turn have the obligation of providing or helping to provide that something of value (CDHR 2004: 47). As Amartya Sen put it, 'rights are *entitlements*[1] that require *correlated duties*. If a person A has a right to some X, then there has to be some agency, say B, that has the duty to provide A with X' (Sen 2000: 228). Right holders could be individuals, or groups behaving like individuals, capable of ordering 'things' or 'objects' in terms of 'value', 'utility', or

---

[1]Entitlement, as explained by Amartya Sen, is a very general concept. It implies the totality of things which a person can have by virtue of his rights. The 'things' referred to here need not be commodities but anything that a person can conceivably wish to have like non-molestation in the streets, or the freedom to lecture on the immorality of the modern age, or adequate means of livelihood (Sen 1982: 343–60).

'preference'. Duty bearers are agents whose actions or behaviours can influence or fulfil the enjoyment of those rights. Establishing this relationship between a right holder and one or more duty bearers is important for all rights—moral, legal, contractual, or any others—because rights imply accountability. The matching of rights with duties could be explained in terms of the Kantian concept of *perfect* and *imperfect obligations*.[2] Someone having a right does not mean anything unless agent-specific duties and ways of fulfilling the obligation of duty bearers can be identified. When such duties can be specified precisely for a particular agent responsible for the realization of a right, it is subjected to *perfect obligations* and could be legally enforced if that right is recognized in law. However, the duty bearers would have imperfect obligations wherein claims are addressed to anyone who can help without specifying the action that would deliver the rights. Thus imperfect obligations are essentially moral obligations that duty bearers ought to fulfil by trying to help but that cannot always be legally enforced.

This discussion on rights thus brings to the fore two crucial issues with respect to the realization of a right. These are: identification of the duty pertaining to a right and identification of the duty holders for that right.

However, identifying a duty corresponding to a particular right essentially presumes that the realization of that right is feasible. For if it were not feasible, there could be no duty that would lead to the realization of that right. So, in order to translate an aspiration or something that is desirable into a right with correlated duties, it would be necessary to establish that such a right is

---

[2]See *Stanford Encyclopedia of Philosophy*, 'Kant's Moral philosophy', http://plato.stanford.edu/entries/kant-moral

'feasible' and that taking some measure or creating some enabling conditions, by some agency in society, could pave the way for feasibly realizing the right.[3]

Thus, if we consider 'development' as a process of realizing all the rights and fundamental freedoms, then for development to be considered a right, it must be 'feasible', which implies that it should be possible to design a social arrangement to enable the claimants to enjoy those rights. Obviously, such development has to be 'progressively' realized as a process in time, as the instantaneous or immediate realization of all (or even most) of the rights will not be feasible. The obligation of the policymakers or the state authorities would be to expedite to the maximum extent the process of progressive realization of as many rights as possible depending upon the constraints of resources and institutions in a country. However, the process of progressive realization should not be at the cost of a denial or violation of any other rights that are inherent to human existence and dignity.

With regard to the identification of different duty bearers to specific duties it deserves to be mentioned that it may not always be the case that identifying a duty with respect to a right would automatically lead to unequivocal identification of the bearers of that duty. Sometimes more than

one agency may need to perform the same duty in parts or complementary to each other. Sometimes one agency may be the primary duty bearer, having the primary responsibility of carrying out the duty while others may have shared responsibility. These would in turn be contingent upon the institutional arrangements for exercising the rights. But until the duty bearers can be specified and the duties corresponding to a right assigned to specific agencies, a right holder's claim cannot be regarded as a right.[4]

Recognizing a 'right' as a 'human right' essentially lifts the status of the right to one with universal applicability to all human beings and at all places and articulates a set of norms governing the action by states and non-state actors, of individuals and groups, on which that claim is made. Realizing human dignity is the essential concern of human rights, which confers

---

[3]'It is quite possible that at a particular point of time or in a given state of affairs a right is not "feasible" to be realized, unless appropriate changes in the institutions and social arrangements are introduced. Feasibility would then imply that there exists a set of actions or policies adopted by the duty-bearers that will change the institutions and make it possible to realize the right. In other words, changing the institutions, or what is sometimes referred to as institutionalizing the right would be a part of the obligations of the duty-bearers' (Sengupta 2004: 188).

[4]'In the case of development, 'the primary duty-bearer will have to be the state-authorities who are in the position to design appropriate development policies and implement them. There will be other duty-bearers who will have responsibilities with respect to different aspects of development—taxpayers must pay taxes, multi-nationals must follow the appropriate conduct and the international community must cooperate. But the state-party would have the responsibility to ensure that these other duty-bearers fulfill their obligations. When these duty-bearers are subject to their domestic legal and administrative forces, the national states could hold them accountable. When the duty-bearers are other sovereign states and institutions, the national states will have to persuade them to cooperate to carry out those duties. But in either case, the exact responsibilities with respect to the different aspects of the development policies will have to be assigned to these duty-bearers. The design of the development policies must incorporate such assignments of specific responsibilities to all the different agents and methods of monitoring and enforcing the accountabilities' (Sengupta 2004: 201).

on the implementation of these rights a first-priority claim[5] and also obliges the state and non-state actors including the international community to take all steps to implement those rights. The most important characteristics of human rights as recognized by the international law of human rights are that they are universal, inviolable, indivisible, and interdependent.

HUMAN RIGHTS IN INTERNATIONAL INSTRUMENTS

The Universal Declaration of Human Rights (UDHR), adopted in 1945 by all members of the United Nations, including India, is the first declaration where an attempt has been made to encompass most of the human rights within its ambit. The UDHR lays down principles or standards of achievement to be followed by all nations and has been regarded as a benchmark in setting up the constitutional and legal systems of many countries including India. The UDHR has been followed by the adoption of a plethora of international instruments that seek to address issues relating to specific themes or sections of people. Out of these, six instruments that deserve special mention are as follows:

+ the International Covenant on Civil and Political Rights[6] (ICCPR)

+ International Covenant on Economic, Social, and Cultural Rights[7] (ICESCR)
+ Convention on the Elimination of all forms of Discrimination against Women (CEDAW)
+ Convention on the Elimination of all forms of Racial Discrimination (CERD)
+ Convention on the Rights of the Child (CRC)
+ Convention against Torture and Other Cruel, Inhuman, or Degrading Treatment or Punishment (CAT)

DEVELOPMENT AND HUMAN RIGHTS

The traditional development discourse evolved through various phases, focusing on maximizing gross national product (GNP), satisfying 'basic needs', incorporating 'structural adjustment', and so on. However, a focus on 'rights' was missing. The definition of 'development' earlier had a primary focus on 'economic growth' and material prosperity to the exclusion of the freedom, dignity, and overall 'well-being' of the people, and development was not usually linked to human rights standards.

The concept of 'Right to Development' (RTD)[8] provided the missing link between 'development' and 'human rights' discourses. The former Independent Expert on RTD[9] delineated the essence of RTD as the

[5]In human rights discourse a human right is a higher-order right with the expectation that it carries a peremptory character similar to John Rawl's idea of 'priority of liberty' or Ronald Dworkin's 'rights as trumps' that sets limits on state action whenever it encroaches upon individual liberty. Thus 'the fulfilment of such human rights gets overwhelming priority in the use of resources and public policy' (Sengupta 2004: 189)

[6]Civil rights basically guarantee a person's liberty and equality. Political rights allow persons to participate in the political life of their community and society by voting in their representatives, throwing them out, and restricting those elected in what they can do while they are in power.

[7]Economic and social rights guarantee the basic necessities of life like food, shelter, clothing, work, and social security. Cultural rights allow people to participate in cultural life of the community and in various traditional and cultural practices.

[8]The Senegalese jurist Keba M'Baye has coined the term in 1972 and it has been debated extensively in various international fora. On 4 December 1986, the United Nations General Assembly formally adopted the Declaration on the Right to Development.

[9]A/55/306, 'Second Report of the Independent Expert (Arjun Sengupta) to the Human Rights Commission', 17 August 2000, para 22 [republished in *Franciscans International* (2003): 160–85].

'*right to a process*[10] *of development*' where all human rights and fundamental freedoms are realized. He further clarified that the right to development as the *right to a process of development* is not just an umbrella right or the sum of a set of rights. It is the right to a process that expands the capabilities or freedom of individuals to improve their well-being and to realize what they value. He underscores that both the *outcomes* of the process and the *process* of development itself are human rights, which entail obligations.

The realization of the different rights (civil and political rights and economic, social, and cultural rights) is the specific outcomes of several policy programmes. But the right to those outcomes is not the same thing as the right to the process that produces those outcomes. In the RTD approach, the '*process*' is as important as the '*outcome*'. Just as different specific rights require specific policies to be implemented as obligation of the different duty bearers, the primary duty bearer being the state, the process requires designing and implementing appropriate programmes of coordinated policies of realizing the rights over the target period.

INDIA'S INTERNATIONAL COMMITMENTS ON HUMAN RIGHTS PROTECTION[11]

Of the six principal international human rights instruments, India has signed as well as ratified[12] five. Table 1 indicates India's

status of ratification of the principal human rights instruments.[13]

India, however, has not maintained a good record of reporting to the human rights treaty bodies[14] as mandated by the ratification of the instruments, as can be seen from Table 2. Apart from the CRC, for which it has submitted all its reports, India is lagging behind in its reporting commitments to all the other treaty bodies.

___

a treaty. 'Signature' merely expresses the willingness of the signatory state to continue the treaty-making process, though it does create an obligation to refrain, *in good faith*, from acts that would defeat the object and the purpose of the treaty.

[13]The six major international human rights treaties discussed here in the section on international instruments contain arrangements for a reporting system to monitor the way in which a government is fulfilling its treaty obligations. States parties to these treaties are required to submit a report to the relevant supervisory committee every four or five years (the reporting period for the Convention on the Elimination of All Forms of Discrimination is every two years). Such a state report should contain detailed information on the efforts the government of a state is making to respect of the human rights contained in the treaty, what progress has been made, and what obstacles and problems the state has encountered. After considering a state party's report, the committee will adopt so-called 'Concluding Observations', a public document that comments on the state's performance, recognizing positive developments, highlighting areas of concern, and providing suggestions and recommendations on specific issues.

[14]A committee of independent experts appointed to monitor the implementation by states parties of the core international human rights treaties. They are called 'treaty bodies' because each is created in accordance with the provisions of the treaty that it oversees. In many important respects, they are independent of the United Nations system, although they receive support from the United Nations Secretariat and report of the General Assembly. Also referred to as the 'committee' or 'treaty-monitoring body'.

___

[10]The *process* is a phased realization of the targeted outcomes with a corresponding programme or plan executed over time maintaining consistency and sustainability, which is expected to lead to the realization of the outcome [E/CN.4/1999/WG.18/2, 'First Report of the Independent Expert (Arjun Sengupta) to the Human Rights Commission', 27 July 1999, para 47–56, republished in *Franciscans International* (2003): 146–9].

[11]This section draws on CDHR (2004: ch. 4, 123–6).

[12]'Ratification' denotes an international act whereby a state indicates its consent to be bound to

Table 1 India's Status of Ratification of the Principal International Human Rights Treaties

Convention	Signature	Ratification/ Accession	Entry into Force
ICESCR	—	10 April 1979 (a)	10 July 1979
ICCPR	—	10 April 1979 (a)	10 July 1979
CERD	2 March 1967	3 December 1968 (r)	4 January 1969
CEDAW	30 July 1980	9 July 1993 (r)	8 August 1993
CRC	—	11 December 1992 (a)	11 January 1993
CAT	14 October 1997	—	—

Source: Treaty Body Database of the Office of the UN High Commissioner for Human Rights.

Table 2 India's Status of Reporting to the Human Rights Treaty Bodies

ICESCR

Report Number	Due	Submitted
4.	30 June 2001	Awaited
3.	30 June 1996	Awaited
2.	30 June 1991	Awaited
1.	NA, 1 September 1983, 1 September 1979	5 January 1989, 16 December 1985, 30 May 1983

ICCPR

Report Number	Due	Submitted
4.	31 March 2001	Awaited
3.	31 March 1992	29 November 1995
2.	9 July 1985	12 July 1989
1.	9 July 1980	4 July 1983

CERD

Report Number	Due	Submitted
17.	4 January 2002	Awaited
16.	4 January 2000	Awaited
15.	4 January 1998	Awaited
10, 11, 12, 13, 14.	4 January 1988	10 November 1994
8, 9.	4 January 1984	26 June 1986
7.	4 January 1982	16 August 1982
6.	4 January 1980	8 June 1981
5.	4 January 1978	5 March 1979
4.	4 January 1976	18 July 1977

CEDAW

Report Number	Due	Submitted
3.	8 August 2002	Awaited
2.	8 August 1998	Awaited
1.	8 August 1994	2 February 1999

CRC

Report Number	Due	Submitted
2.	10 January 2000	10 December 2001
1.	10 January 1995	19 March 1997

Source: Treaty Body Database of the Office of the UN High Commissioner for Human Rights.

With reference to the Five Year Implementation Review of the Vienna Declaration and Programme of Action,[15] the Government of India reaffirmed its commitment to the promotion and protection of human rights through national efforts and international

[15]In 1993, at the World Conference on Human rights held at Vienna, the Vienna Declaration and Programme of Action re-emphasized the status of the RTD as a universal and inalienable human right.

cooperation. In the statement submitted for the Secretary General's report on the review in 1998,[16] India views the RTD Declaration as 'an integral link between the UDHR and the *Vienna Declaration and Programme of Action* through its elaboration of a holistic view integrating economic, social and cultural rights with civil and political rights' (para 14). The statement further adds that India agreed with the Office of the High Commissioner of Human Rights that the RTD has the potential of providing the homogenous and integrated approach to human rights that the international community has been searching for over five decades, and that 'it bears all the necessary components to guide the human rights system into the new millennium' (para 15).

FRAMEWORK FOR HUMAN RIGHTS PROTECTION IN INDIA
The Constitution

Most human rights, which are identified in the UDHR and the main international covenants, are protected under the Constitution of India. Some of them are guaranteed as Fundamental Rights (Part III) and some form a part of the Directive Principles of State Policy (Part IV). The Fundamental Rights can be divided into six broad groups: right to equality; right to particular freedoms; right against exploitation; freedom of religion; cultural and educational rights; and right to constitutional remedies. The Directive Principles of State Policy (DPSP) set out certain socio-economic goals for the country and require that the state must make efforts to achieve these goals through its policies and laws. While the Fundamental Rights are enforceable in a court of law, the goals in the DPSP are not.

[16]See website: www.indianembassy.org/policy/Human_Rights/vdpa_india.html

The Judiciary

A citizen of India whose rights have been violated has the right to directly approach the Supreme Court and the High Courts for judicial intervention for redressal under Articles 32 and 226 of the Constitution.

The role of the judiciary since its inception has undergone a sea change, witnessing its emergence as a dynamic institution pioneering the expansion of the scope and content of individual and collective rights of the citizens. This changing role has evolved by virtue of a series of developments primarily through the innovation of public interest litigation[17] as an instrument to achieve social objectives by facilitating easy access to courts, particularly for the economically and socially disadvantaged sections of the community, through relaxation of the rules of standing and procedure as mandated by an ordinary litigation and freeing the litigants from the complexities of formal law. Some notable developments that evince the emergence of a more progressive judiciary are:

+ The declaration of the indivisibility of the fundamental rights on the one hand and the DPSPs on the other. The Supreme Court underscored, 'In building up a just social order it is sometimes imperative that the fundamental rights should be subordinated to the directive principles'[18] and that both

[17]Public Interest Litigation (PIL), in simple words, means litigation filed in the court of law for the protection of public interest such as pollution, terrorism, road safety, and constructional hazards. Public interest litigation is not defined in any statute or in any Act. Although the main and only area of PIL is 'public interest', there are various areas where a PIL can be filed. These includes among others: violation of basic human rights of the poor, content or conduct of government policy, violations of religious rights, and compelling municipal authorities to perform a public duty.
[18]*Kesavananda Bharati* vs *State of Kerala* (1973) 4 SCC 879.

are complementary, 'neither part being superior to the other'.[19]

• Attempts by the court in early PIL cases to rescue bonded labour from dehumanizing conditions of work,[20] ensuring availability of free legal aid to destitute undertrial prisoners,[21] protecting rights of pavement dwellers to due process while facing forced evictions.[22] More recently, the courts have been instrumental in specifying binding guidelines to deal with the problem of sexual harassment at the workplace,[23] have catalysed changes in law and policy relating to education in general and primary education in particular,[24] have delineated the right to emergency medical care for accident victims as forming a core minimum of the right to health,[25] and have emphasized the right of access to food supplies as bare non-derogable minimum and crucial to preserve human dignity.[26]

• Broadened interpretation of existing rights through judicial activism. For instance, the most fundamental human right—right to life and liberty—was widened in *Francis Coralie Mullin* vs. *Administrator, Union Territory of Delhi*[27] in 1981 with the Supreme Court observing that 'the right to life includes the right to live with human dignity and all that goes along with it, namely the bare necessaries of life such as adequate nutrition, clothing and shelter and facilities for reading, writing and expressing oneself in diverse forms'. Similarly, in *Bandhua Mukti Morcha* vs *Union of India* in 1984,[28] the Supreme Court held that the 'right to life' must include

protection of the health and strength of workers, men and women, and of the tender age of children against abuse, opportunities and facilities for children to develop in a healthy manner and in conditions of freedom and dignity, educational facilities, just and humane conditions of work and maternity relief. Neither the Central Government nor any State Government has the right to take any action which will deprive a person of the enjoyment of these basic essentials.

Despite its substantial autonomy and independence, the Indian judiciary has been plagued by innumerable problems that have dampened its effective functioning. There is paucity of courts, judges, and physical infrastructure. As a result, almost all courts have a huge backlog of cases. The National Commission to Review the Working of the Constitution (2001) notes that delayed hearings are 'a serious infraction of the right to speedy trials', and tantamount to violation of human rights.

HUMAN RIGHTS COMMISSIONS[29]
Human Rights Commissions have been established to protect human rights of the people in the country and to facilitate creation of an environment conducive to respect and understanding of human rights. The National Human Rights Commission (NHRC) was set up by the Protection of

[19]*State of Kerala vs N.M. Thomas* (1978) 2 SCC 310.
[20]*Bandhua Mukti Morcha vs Union of India* 1984 (Supp) 3 SCC 161.
[21]*Hussainara Khatoon vs State of Bihar* (1980) 1 SCC 81.
[22]*Olga Tellis vs Bombay Municipal Corporation* (1985) 3 SCC 545.
[23]*Vishaka vs State of Rajasthan* (1997) 6 SCC 241.
[24]*Unnikrishnan JP vs State of Andhra Pradesh* (1993) 1 SCC 645.
[25]*Paschim Banga Khet Majoor Samity vs State of West Bengal* (1996) 4 SCC 37.
[26]*Peoples Union of Civil Liberty (PUCL) vs Union of India* (2001) Indlaw SCC 196.
[27](1981) 2 SCR 516.

[28]*Kesavananda Bharati vs State of Kerala.*
[29]This section draws on CDHR (2004): 128–9.

Human Rights Act 1993. The Commission is an autonomous statutory body enjoying considerable operational independence. It has the powers of a civil court trying a case under the Civil Procedure Code 1908. Thus it has some degree of investigative power, can issue notices to people, can summon witnesses, and so on.[30]

The NHRC can inquire into complaints of violations of human rights or abetment in, and failure to prevent, such violations by a public servant. It can also intervene in any court proceeding involving an allegation of violation of human rights. The Commission has powers of reviewing the constitutional, statutory, and international safeguards for the protection of human rights. It has the power to recommend measures for their effective implementation, though it does not have the power to enforce its orders. The NHRC also undertakes and promotes research in the field of human rights and works towards spreading human rights literacy.

The Commission has, in its various recommendations relating to specific cases, urged the government to formulate policies that are responsive to the needs of the most vulnerable in society. Such action includes provision of free and compulsory education up to the age of 14 years, primary health facilities, potable drinking water, basic levels of maternal- and child-welfare facilities, and food and nutritional standards essential to fulfilling the potential of the human being.

The Protection of Human Rights Act, 1993, also mandated the establishment of human rights commissions in each state. A State Human Rights Commission (SHRC) can inquire into violation of human rights only in respect of matters in the State List (issues on which only state governments can take action) and Concurrent List (subjects on which both the centre and the states can take action) of the Constitution. Only twelve states have so far set up SHRCs. They are Assam, Chhattisgarh, Himachal Pradesh, Jammu and Kashmir, Kerala, Madhya Pradesh, Maharashtra, Manipur, Punjab, Rajasthan, Tamil Nadu, and West Bengal. Some SHRCs have taken up matters relating to food, education, and health.

HUMAN RIGHTS COURTS[31]

The Protection of Human Rights Act 1993 also stipulates the setting up of Human Rights Courts for providing speedy trial in cases of alleged human rights violations. In each district, a sessions court is to act as a Human Rights Court. The Court will have a public prosecutor or appoint an advocate who has been practising for not less than seven years, as a special public prosecutor for conducting cases in that Court. The state governments of Assam, Andhra Pradesh, Sikkim, Tamil Nadu, Uttar Pradesh, Meghalaya, Himachal Pradesh, Goa, Madhya Pradesh, and Tripura have notified Human Rights Courts.

NATIONAL COMMISSION FOR WOMEN[32]

The National Commission for Women (NCW) was set up as a statutory autonomous body in January 1992 under the National Commission for Women Act, 1990.[33] The mandate of the NCW is, among other things, to review the constitutional and legal safeguards for women; recommend remedial legislative measures; facilitate redressal of grievances; advise the government on all policy matters affecting women; investigate complaints; undertake promotional and educational research; inspect places of custody of women; and

[31]This section draws on CDHR (2004): 130–1.
[32]This section draws on CDHR (2004): 131.
[33]For more information on the NCW, see website http://www.nationalcommissionforwomen.org

[30]For detailed information on the NHRC, see website http://www.nhrc.nic.in

fund litigation. The NCW is, however, a purely recommendatory body with no powers to enforce its orders.

NATIONAL COMMISSION FOR MINORITIES[34]

The National Commission for Minorities is a statutory autonomous body set up under the National Commission for Minorities Act 1992. The central government has notified five communities as 'minority communities': Muslims, Christians, Sikhs, Buddhists, and Zoroastrians. A prominent member of each community is appointed to the Commission. The Commission's brief is to evaluate the progress of the development of the minority communities; to monitor the working of the safeguards provided in the Constitution and in laws; to recommend the implementation of safeguards for the protection of the interests of minorities; to investigate specific complaints regarding deprivation of rights of the minorities and take up such matters with the appropriate authorities; to undertake studies into problems arising out of any discrimination against minorities and related issues; and to recommend appropriate measures in respect of any minority to be undertaken by the central or state government. The Commission has all the powers of a civil court trying a suit but does not have the power to enforce its recommendations.

NATIONAL COMMISSION FOR CHILDREN[35]

The setting up of a National Commission for Children is also in the offing. The idea of a Children's Commission was proposed in 1998 and has been debated since then. The Department of Women and Child Development prepared the draft National Commission for Children Bill[36] in 2001.

---

[34]This section draws on CDHR (2004): 131–2.
[35]This section draws on CDHR (2004): 133.
[36]For the text of the National Commission for Children Bill, see http://wcd.nic.in/ncchildren.htm

The Commission is supposed to work as a statutory body for the protection of children's rights and also as an independent ombudsman for children, dealing exclusively with the status and development needs of children. The Commission will be a seven-member statutory body comprising specialists in the field of child welfare and headed by a retired judge of the Supreme Court, a sitting High Court judge, or a person of eminence in the field of child rights. It will be mandated to safeguard the interests of children, guide government policy on child-related issues, and review the laws and programmes relating to children's development.

ARJUN K. SENGUPTA AND KAUSHIK
RANJAN BANDYOPADHYAY

REFERENCES

Centre for Development and Human Rights (CDHR). 2004. *The Right to Development: A Primer*, New Delhi, Sage Publications.
Franciscans International. 2003. 'The Right to Development: Reflections on the First Four Reports of the Independent Expert (Arjun Sengupta) on Right to Development', Franciscans International, Geneva.
Sen, Amartya. 1982. 'The Right Not to Be Hungry', *Contemporary Philosophy: A New Survey*, The Hague, Martinus Nijhoff.
———. 2000. *Development as Freedom*, Oxford, Oxford University Press; New Delhi, Oxford University Press, 2000.
Sengupta, Arjun. 2004. 'The Human Right to Development', *Oxford Development Studies*, 32(2): 179–203.

Inequality

Inequality has been a key theme in the research agenda of economists because of (i) the intrinsic ethical attractiveness of equality and (ii) the significant implications of inequality for many macroeconomic variables like growth and poverty.

Although issues related to inequality can be analysed along several dimensions, I shall be dealing mostly with inequality in income or consumption and wealth.

Before undertaking a study of inequality one is always confronted with the issue of how to measure inequality. Since it is impossible to describe and compare the distributions of income of the whole population, it is necessary to have summary measures. One can get an idea of inequality by using rough measures like the share of the, say, bottom 10 or top 10 per cent of the population. However, such a measure ignores the intermediate 80 per cent of the population. There is now a large body of literature dealing with the measurement of inequality (Sen 1997).

One of the most commonly used measures of income or consumption inequality is the Gini coefficient. It measures the extent to which the distribution of income or consumption among individuals deviates from equal distribution. A high value of this coefficient signifies a more unequal distribution. Let us consider a population of N individuals with incomes $Y_1, Y_2, ..., Y_N$. We can plot the cumulative percentages of total income received by cumulative percentages of the population starting from the poorest. Such a plot is called the Lorenz curve. Obviously, for equal incomes, X per cent of the population will always enjoy X per cent of the total income and the Lorenz curve is the diagonal straight line. Otherwise, the curve always lies below this line since the bottom X percentage of population will always have less than X per cent of the total income. The Gini coefficient captures the gap between the actual Lorenz curve of the economy and the hypothetical equal distribution line.

Algebraically, the Gini coefficient can be computed using the following formula,

$$G = \frac{1}{2N^2Y^*} \sum_{i=1}^{N} \sum_{j=1}^{N} |Y_i - Y_j|$$

where Y^* is the mean income and $|Y_i - Y_j|$ is the absolute difference between incomes of individuals i and j. It considers differences over all pairs of incomes and there are N^2 such pairs of incomes. Hence it can be viewed as one-half of the mean of absolute values of differences between all income pairs. This measure of inequality has many desirable features.

In the Indian context, the consumption expenditure surveys (National Sample Survey, NSS) constitute the most basic source of inequality measurement. These surveys are conducted on a regular basis and cover a fairly large sample of households. Recently, individual tax return data have been used to analyse the income shares of individuals in the top earnings bracket. Since most of the population is exempt from income taxation, it is possible to look at only the top 1 per cent of the population.

Table 1   Inequality in India Computed Using Various Measures 1951–88

Year	Gini[*,***]	Consumption[**] shares of bottom 20%	Consumption[**] shares of top 20%	Income[***] shares of top 1%
1951	35.56	7.0	43.0	13.42
1960	32.59	8.4	41.4	12.31
1965	31.14	8.8	40.0	10.92
1970	30.38	8.8	39.5	10.02
1973	29.17	9.0	38.1	7.02
1977	32.14	8.5	40.9	6.18
1983	31.49	8.6	40.5	6.46
1986	32.22	8.5	41.1	8.64
1988	31.15	9.0	40.5	8.52

Notes: *In percentages (Gini Index for consumption); **Deininger–Squire (K. Deininger and L. Squire. 1996.'A New Data Set Measuring Income Inequality', *The World Bank Economic Review*, 10: 565–91); ***Banerjee–Piketty (A. Banerjee and T. Piketty. 2005. 'Top Indian Incomes, 1999–2000', *The World Bank Economic Review*, 19: 1–20).

The various measures in Table 1 provide a snapshot of inequality in India through the 1960s to the 1980s. Because of space limitation, information is provided for only a handful of years.

Historically, inequality levels (wealth as well as income or consumption) in India during the 1950s were quite high. The average Gini index for consumption in the 1950s would be in excess of 35, the Gini index for land distribution for this period would also be in excess of 40. However, through the 1950s and 1960s, there has been a steady (though not substantial) decline in all these measures. The Gini index falls from 35 to a lower level of 30. The consumption share of the bottom 20 per cent of the population goes up and the corresponding share of the top 20 per cent declines. The income share of the top 1 per cent also shows significant decline. Many scholars attribute this trend to the slower growth and socialist policies of this period.

However, the inequality measures have remained fairly stable during the 1970s and 1980s. There is no evidence of any clear increasing or decreasing trend. In fact the absence of trend is somewhat more pronounced if we look at the Gini coefficients for rural and urban households separately. Since inequality among urban households is greater than inequality among rural households, greater urbanization during this period could have led to a very small increase in overall inequality. This feature is observed in the early 1990s also (Datt 1999). However, the income share of the top 1 per cent does a turnaround in the 1980s after falling steadily for nearly three decades. It is interesting to note that this coincides with the beginning of the more pro-business orientation of the economy and higher growth rates. In fact some economists attribute the beginning of the higher growth phase in the early to mid-1980s to this shift in policy orientation.

While there is general agreement about the stable nature of inequality in the 1970s and 1980s, a different picture emerges in the 1990s. Two major rounds of surveys were undertaken in the years 1993–4 and 1999–2000 (NSS rounds 50 and 55). The inequality measures estimated using the basic data from these two rounds do not show any significant increase in inequality. In fact, inequality amongst rural households shows a slight decline over this period. However, as has been pointed out by many, these two rounds are not strictly comparable. A key difference between the two surveys is the use of different 'recall periods'. The 50th round uses (like all previous rounds) the thirty-days recall period for all types of consumption expenditures; respondents are asked to report expenditures incurred over the previous month. The 55th round uses the same recall period for many items but it also introduced a longer recall period (365 days) for consumer durables. Consequently, many poor households that would have reported no expenditure over the last month (in this category of items) end up reporting some expenditure over the past year. Deaton and Drèze (2002) point out that this effectively improves the reported expenditure pattern of poor households and gives a misleading picture of reduced inequality. After adjusting the basic recorded data of the 55th round, they find evidence of marked increases in inequality over these six years. While inequality in the rural sector stays the same, inequality in the urban sector shows considerable increase. This pattern is not just true at the aggregate all-India level, most states exhibit a similar pattern.

Deaton and Drèze (2002) point out that inequality seems to have risen on several fronts. There is evidence of greater regional inequalities. Compared to the 50th round, the adjusted data of the 55th round shows increasing inequality across states. States with higher average per capita expenditure in 1993–4 are also the states recording higher growth in these per capita expenditures. The wage gap across various occupations has also widened. While the real wages for agricultural labourers have grown at the rate of 2.5 per cent per year, the corresponding growth rate for public-sector employees is almost double.

A similar pattern is observed for the income share of the top earners. As mentioned earlier, the income share of the top 1 per cent has been rising since the mid-1980s. Apart from a brief decline in the early 1990s, it shows considerable increase from 1993 onwards. In fact the rise in the share of the ultra rich (the top 1 per cent of this 1 per cent) is much more striking. Within the richer section, the ultra rich have experienced a much larger growth in income over the 1990s. This suggests that inequality amongst the rich is also increasing. Though it is not possible to make sweeping generalizations, there is enough indication to worry about the growth process becoming increasingly pro-rich in its orientation.

As yet there is no clear causal explanation for this apparent rise in inequalities in the 1990s. One can argue that this is an inevitable consequence of the high-growth phase in a development process. The famous Kuznets hypothesis postulates that inequality should follow an inverse U-shape along the development process. The early phase of development is associated with greater urbanization and industrialization resulting in greater income inequality. However, after a stage, as a large proportion of the labour force is absorbed in the industrial sector, inequality starts falling. Until recently, some of the developed economies of the West were believed to have exhibited such a pattern. For example, in the US, the share of the top 10 per cent rose from 50 per cent around 1770 to about 75 per cent around 1870 and then fell to 50 per cent in 1970. Such a view could be comforting in the sense that the rising inequality need not be a matter of concern (though the time scale is still a matter of concern). However, this hypothesis has not been significantly supported by empirical research. Moreover, the sectoral shift in the Indian context took place in the 1980s, and the rise in inequality cannot perhaps be attributed to it.

It is important to recognize the rising inequality independently and seek proper causal explanation and not simply view it as by-product. If the growth process is highly uneven so that only a smaller section can benefit from it, it can have serious consequences for poverty reduction and further growth in the economy. For example, as Deaton and Drèze (2002) point out, the reduction in poverty over the 1990s has been significantly moderated by the rise in inequality. For the same level of inequality (same distribution of consumption), the growth in the 1990s would have implied a much larger reduction in poverty.

One can also draw several lessons from the recent research on inequality and growth. A traditional view suggests that rising income and wealth inequality fosters higher growth by generating greater incentives to save and invest. However, this view has come under scrutiny recently and a large body of empirical as well theoretical research shows that inequality can be harmful for growth. From a political economy perspective, higher inequality leads to social conflict and greater demands for redistribution. The effects of these outweigh the positive incentive effects of inequality and the end result could be lower growth. Inequality affects growth negatively through various other channels as well. In the presence of imperfect (credit) markets and limited financial development, higher (wealth) inequality leads to underinvestment in physical and human capital and hence lower growth. Given the imperfect nature of markets in India, there is danger of the full growth potential not being realized in the future if inequality levels continue to rise.

The causal relation between inequality and growth runs both ways. The process of growth can also have implications for income inequality. The experience of many OECD countries shows that growth does not necessarily entail a reduction in inequality. To the extent growth is achieved through trade and skill-biased technological and organizational changes, the growth process leads to a widening of earnings among the different sections of society. The widening of various wage gaps has already been observed in the Indian context as well.

In summary, though not alarmingly high, there is some evidence of rising inequalities in India in the 1990s. It is too early and premature to attribute this rise to the process of liberalization itself. However, inequality deserves a close watch and the rising trend has to be studied carefully. The uneven nature of the growth process has to be explored further so that policy actions could be taken to ensure relatively even access by different sections of the society to the benefits of growth in a liberalized and globalized India.

AJIT MISHRA

REFERENCES

Datt, G. 1999.'Has Poverty Declined since Economic Reforms?', *Economic and Political Weekly*, December: 11–17.

Deaton, A. and J. Drèze. 2002.'Poverty and Inequality in India—A Re-Examination', *Economic and Political Weekly*, September: 3729–48.

Sen, Amartya. 1997. *On Economic Inequality*, Oxford, Oxford University Press, expanded edition.

Infant and Child Mortality

In *Mother India*, her patently West-centric 1927 diatribe against the idea of independence for India, the American journalist Katherine Mayo pointed to the high levels of infant mortality in the country, which she attributed to the excessive sexuality and premature maternity that Hinduism encouraged in its followers. Seventy-five years later, high infant mortality is used as a major indicator, not of excessive and early sex (though demographers do attribute at least some of it to excessive and early childbearing—the two are not the same thing at all, especially in the age of modern contraception), but of unacceptably slow progress in a country's economic development whatever its income growth has been.

While the infant-mortality rate (or IMR—the number of deaths during the first year of life per 1000 live births) is a handy figure for all kinds of evaluations and comparisons, the more useful measure for policy purposes is probably the child mortality rate (the number of deaths in the first five years of life per 1000 live births). This is because the years immediately after infancy also represent a particularly vulnerable stage in life, sometimes even more vulnerable than infancy. This is especially so in populations that practice prolonged breastfeeding and that therefore delay exposure to the gastrointestinal and other infections that cause such a large proportion of early childhood deaths. In the following paragraphs I will therefore look interchangeably at levels and trends and differentials in infant and child mortality in India.

According to the best recent figures available, those from the second round of the National Family Health Survey (NFHS II—IIPS 2000), at the end of the twentieth century the IMR for India as a whole stood at around 68 deaths per 1000 live births. This is a big improvement from the figure of 134 in the early 1970s. But it is still a long distance from the single-digit figures for the IMR that characterize a society's transformation from a condition of high to low mortality. During the same period, under-5 mortality was 95 per 1000 live births. That is, the probability of dying before the fifth birthday is still around 10 per cent for the average newborn in India. More worryingly, there is some indication that gains in lowering infant and child mortality have begun to slow down since the 1990s.

These national averages hide gross inequalities in the life chances of infants and children in different parts of the country and in different socio-economic categories. For example, the rural–urban divide continues to be significant in spite of apparently deteriorating living conditions for the poor in urban areas. In the NFHS-II data set, in the late 1990s, child mortality was nearly twice as high in rural as in urban areas and post-neonatal mortality (deaths between the ages of 1 month and a year) was as much as 73 per cent higher. The national IMR of 68 was a result of an IMR of 73 in rural areas and 47 in urban areas. But before we celebrate health conditions in the towns and cities, it must be pointed out that this same survey finds that the IMR for the poor urban population (what the survey classifies as the 'low-standard-of-living', or SLI population) was as high as 76—obviously the proximity to health services and the greater direct and indirectly acquired health knowledge in the towns is not enough to compensate for the overcrowding and pervasive poverty that kills so many slum children before they can celebrate a first birthday.

Other kinds of differentials are just as pernicious and imply that egalitarianism and equity are somewhat hollow slogans in India. The NFHS data are particularly

revealing about differentials by caste, a category that is supposed to be unimportant in modern India. This same national average of an IMR of 73 hides a rate of 83 for the scheduled castes and 84 for the scheduled tribes. All these figures become even better contextualized if one looks at the unrealized potential by taking IMRs in economically or socially 'advantaged' populations in India. For example, compare 83 and 84 to a rate of 33 for high SLI urban Indians and a magically low 12 in Kerala for the children of women who have completed high school education or more.

Speaking of Kerala leads naturally to discussing all those geographical parts of the country that look as if they will never catch up with that state. Whatever the gloomy revisionist reappraisals of the Kerala model of development, the fact remains that for a range of social variables, it could just as well have been situated in Scandinavia as in southern India. The IMR in Kerala in NFHS-II stood at 16—note that this is not substantially higher than the figure for the children of well-educated women in the state, that is socio-economic differentials *within* Kerala are unimaginably, at least to our limited imaginations, small. In contrast, the IMR in Rajasthan was 80, Madhya Pradesh 86, Uttar Pradesh 87, and Orissa 81; in Bihar, the figure was (a suspiciously low) 73. Rates in the rest of the large states in the country were in the 40s, 50s, and 60s, with only Himachal Pradesh doing itself a little proud with a rate of 34.

These regional differences lead one next to an examination of the determinants of infant and child mortality. The large literature on the subject is best unravelled by classifying what have been called the 'proximate determinants' of infant and child mortality into those that arise from bio-demographic factors (to do with maternal age, parity, and intervals between births), environmental contamination (through the conditions of birth as well as the surroundings of life) affecting the exposure to infection, poor nutrition, injury, and what the authors of the proximate-determinants framework (Mosley and Chen 1984) call 'personal illness control' (those behaviours and attributes that rely on medical technology, both to prevent ill health as well as to cure it).

Whether one looks at trends in infant and child mortality in India or at contemporary differentials, all these factors come into play. To begin with, both over time as well as across regions (whether urban–rural or state-wise) bio-demographic factors have changed in the direction of improved prospects for child survival. High-risk births, as defined by very low or very high maternal age at birth or by a large number of siblings, have come down as a proportion of all births as the childbearing age has risen and fertility has declined. The only risky bio-demographic factor that has probably not changed much for the better is birth interval. Indeed, there is some evidence that as fertility has come down in India, there has been a compression of birth intervals—births to women have become more closely spaced. This has probably happened both because of involuntary reasons (to do with shortened breastfeeding and little use of birth-spacing contraception) as well as for voluntary reasons to do with wanting to get family size goals quickly met so that the demands of babies and young children can be more quickly dispensed with.

Environmental contamination continues to play havoc on young lives in the country. Whether due to poor public sanitation or poor household hygiene (fostered as much by poverty as by lack of knowledge), incidents of acute respiratory infections, fever, or diarrhoea in the two weeks before the survey were reported in about a quarter of children in morbidity surveys like the NFHS. Not

surprisingly, these illness rates were higher in rural areas, among the poor, among the lower castes, and among children of non-literate mothers. But these figures need to be interpreted with caution, based as they are on reporting by mothers. This caution is suggested by the finding that Kerala reported above-national-average levels of childhood morbidity, leading to the speculation whether the state's low infant and child mortality are not in fact an outcome of prompt recognition (and treatment) of illness. In other words, actual morbidity levels in the country may well be much higher than these reported levels because, in an environment of constant risk, coughs and diarrhoea may often be considered 'normal' enough not to merit mention in surveys.

Poor nutrition is certainly implicated in infant and child health and mortality in India, both as a determinant as well as an outcome of illness. Incidentally, maternal nutrition is as important here as is the level of child nutrition—in NFHS-II, over half the married women tested had some degree of anaemia, an important predictor of poor delivery outcomes. And there must be something 'cultural' about the poor nutritional levels in India—we seem to have much higher levels of malnutrition than many poorer countries in sub-Saharan Africa. In the NFHS survey of 1998–9, almost half the children under the age of 3 were *underweight* (as measured by weight for age), almost half were *stunted* (according to height for age), and about 16 per cent were *wasted* (according to weight for height). Each of these measures of poor nutritional status captures different aspects of food deprivation and illness prevalence; what is important here is to note that these figures are unacceptably high even by the standards of a poor country.

Finally, there is personal illness control, the use of medical technology to prevent as well as treat the many infectious illnesses that account for the high levels of infant and child morality in poor countries. In particular, there is the miraculous ORS (oral rehydration salts), which refers to the simple and inexpensive administration of a glucose and electrolyte solution to reduce deaths due to the dehydration caused by severe diarrhoeal disease. ORS packets are supposed to be routinely delivered by the national primary healthcare system but in NFHS-II, it was found that only 27 per cent of children below the age of 3 who had a bout of diarrhoea in the two weeks preceding the survey were given ORS packets, and about 40 per cent received some more traditional forms of oral rehydration such as extra fluid or gruel or home-made sugar and salt solutions. Worse, over half these children were treated with 'pills' or 'syrup'; 15 per cent even received an injection.

Of course it is better to prevent an illness than to cure it. And here too medical technology is a handy tool to overcome some of the disadvantages of poor environmental conditions. But in spite of the great publicity attending international and national universal immunization programmes, the fact remains that at the time of NFHS-II, only 42 per cent of children aged 12–23 months were 'fully' vaccinated (against tuberculosis, measles, DPT, and polio), and 14 per cent had not received any vaccinations at all. These figures are improvements from the levels found in the NFHS-I survey of five years earlier (when the respective figures were 36 per cent and 30 per cent) but far from a reason to boast of a successful immunization programme in the country.

Infant and child mortality in India cannot be discussed without touching upon gender differentials. Since Visaria's (1967) pioneering exploration of the unduly masculine juvenile (0–6 years) sex ratio of

the 1961 census, it has been increasingly clear that little girls face an 'unnatural' disadvantage in survival compared to little boys. Unnatural, because this disadvantage does not exist in many much poorer regions such as the countries of sub-Saharan Africa. In other words, the higher death rate of female children is being achieved with some effort—the effort needed to deny girls the same care as boys. What form this deprivation takes is debatable; at various points of time, discrimination in food allocation, healthcare, or even that elusive input, 'love', has been blamed (for example Miller 1981). While all these kinds of selective neglect are plausible, the largest single factor is probably the healthcare provided to girls—this healthcare is often too sub-standard, too little, and too late.

For a short while, it appeared that sex differences in child survival were narrowing; indeed life expectancies are now frequently greater for women than for men, in spite of a continuing high burden of reproductive mortality in the country. But more recent data clarify that this convergence of male and female child death rates is not really a cause for joy. In district after district, state after state, the juvenile sex ratio in the 2000 Census is much worse than in 1991. Given the gender convergence in death rates, this means that the female disadvantage in survival has got converted into a female disadvantage in initial existence. It is the sex ratio of *births* rather than the sex ratio of *deaths* that now works against girls. The increased resort to foetal sex-determination tests, followed by selective abortion of female conceptions, was at first reported only anecdotally. But there are now sufficient quantitative data to confirm this anecdotal evidence. Worse, this rising masculinity of births shows little signs of abating in spite of its proclaimed illegality through the Pre-natal Diagnostic Techniques

(PNDT) (Regulation and Prevention of Misuse) Act 1994, and the PNDT Amendment Act 2002, as well as the vast 'educational' campaigns to discourage sex-selective abortions. Moreover, whereas sex differences in child mortality in the past were predominantly a feature of north India, a masculine sex ratio of births has assumed virulent form in new parts of the country, the western states of Gujarat and Maharashtra in particular. The relative economic wealth of these states suggests that development is exacerbating gender differences in life prospects, if one considers sex-selective abortion as but one end of a continuum of discrimination against the girl child.

It is depressing to end on this negative note. But perhaps the third round of the NFHS, which is currently under way, will reveal that all this public and policy interest in and dismay about the life chances of children in general and girl children in particular has finally begun to pay off.

ALAKA MALWADE BASU

REFERENCES

Basu, A.M. 1997. 'Anthropological Demography in the Understanding of the Determinants of Child Mortality', in G.W. Jones, J.C. Caldwell, R.M. Douglas, and R.M. D'Souza, eds, *The Continuing Demographic Transition*, Oxford, Oxford University Press.

International Institute for Population Sciences (IIPS). 2000. *National Family Health Survey, India 1998–99*, Mumbai, IIPS.

Mayo, K. 1927 [1998]. *Mother India*, New York, Harcourt Brace and Company; London, Jonathan Cape [*Mother India: Selections Edited and with an Introduction by Mrinalini Sinha*, New Delhi, Kali for Women].

Miller, B.D. 1981. *The Endangered Sex; Neglect of Female Children in Rural North India*, Ithaca, Cornell University Press.

Mosely, W.H. and L.C. Chen. 1984. 'Child Survival: Research and Policy', *Population and Development Review*, supplement to vol. 10.

Visaria, P. 1967. 'The Sex Ratio of the Population of India and Pakistan and Regional Variations during 1901–1961', in A. Bose, ed., *Patterns of Population Change in India 1951–61*, Bombay, Allied Publishers.

Literacy

Literacy refers to an individual's ability to communicate through reading and writing. The literacy rate for any population measures the fraction of the population, above some cut-off age, that is literate. Based on the most-recent statistics compiled by UNESCO, more than one in three Indians above the age of 15 years is unable to read and write. Further, the roughly 268 million adult illiterates in India constitute one-third of the global population of illiterates. International comparisons show that the Indian literacy rate is well below those for other populous countries like China and also below those for developing countries in general.

The main source of information on literacy in India is the decennial census. The census enumerates a person as literate if he/she can 'read and write with understanding in any language'. Currently the census reports aggregate literacy rates for the population aged seven years and above. As Figure 1 shows, the literacy rate has risen significantly, especially in the post-Independence period. From a low level of 18.3 per cent of the population in 1951, it rose to 65.4 per cent in 2001. The recorded improvement in the most recent decade is notable in that with a 13 percentage point increase in literacy, the absolute number of illiterate people fell for the first time since Independence (from 328 million in 1991 to 296 million in 2001).

This data carries some caveats. One, the determination of literate status is based on self-reporting by respondents,

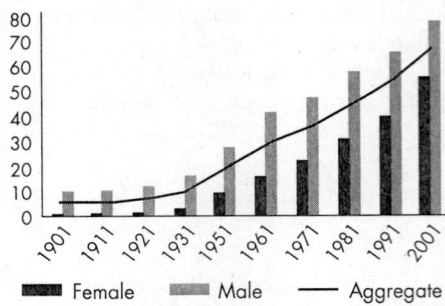

Figure 1 Trends in Literacy

Source: Census of India, various years.

or on inference by the census enumerator, with little attempt to verify actual literacy skills. Literacy tests administered as part of household surveys carried out by the National Sample Survey Organisation (NSSO) in 1991 found that more than a third of self-declared literates in the sample were illiterate (Govinda and Biswal 2005). This suggests that the estimates provided by the Census of India may be biased upwards. Two, the current '7+ years' threshold for computing aggregate literacy rates differs from that used by the Census till 1971 ('5+ years') and from that used commonly in international comparisons ('15+ years'). The difference matters. Aggregate literacy can be viewed as a weighted average of age-specific literacy rates. If the age-specific literacy of 5–6 year olds is lower than the average literacy of the '7+' age groups, a switch to the higher threshold can overstate improvements in literacy. Despite these caveats, estimates of the trends may be broadly accurate.

THE MANY DIMENSIONS OF DISPARITY

The distribution of literacy in India is uneven. As Figure 1 shows, the literacy rate for males has been consistently higher than that for females. In 1951 less than 9 per cent females were literate while the corresponding number for males was over 27 per cent. The gender literacy gap has

narrowed in recent decades, but remains large: in 2001, the female literacy rate of 54.2 per cent was significantly below the male rate of 75.9 per cent. Two, there is strong regional variation in literacy rates. Broadly speaking, the populous states of north India have lower literacy levels (and also greater gender disparity) than the southern states. Comparing states in 2001, Kerala had the highest literacy rate of 90.9 per cent (94.2 per cent for males, 87.9 per cent for females) while Bihar had the lowest with 47.5 per cent (60.3 per cent for males and 33.6 per cent for females).

Three, urban literacy is higher than rural literacy. In 1951, only 12.1 per cent of the rural population was literate relative to 34.6 per cent of the urban population. For 2001 the literacy rate was 59.4 per cent in rural areas compared to 80.3 per cent in urban areas. Four, literacy rates vary across age groups: younger cohorts, such as those aged between 10 and 20 years have higher literacy rates than older cohorts because of recent improvements in access to education. There is also a strong socio-economic dimension to literacy. Current literacy rates for scheduled castes (SCs, 54.7 per cent) and scheduled tribes (STs, 47.1 per cent) are significantly lower than for the population as a whole, though STs in the north-eastern states are an exception. Lastly, the 2001 Census released literacy rates by religion for the first time—literacy among the Muslim population (both men and women) was found to be lower than the national average.

While Census statistics are built around a simple, self-reported, binary classification (literate or illiterate), broader notions of literacy exist. For UNESCO literacy is 'the ability to identify, understand, interpret, create, communicate, compute, and use printed and written materials associated with varying contexts. Literacy involves a continuum of learning to enable an individual to achieve his/her goals, to develop his/her knowledge and potential, and to participate fully in the wider society.' Notions of functional literacy focus on the ability to use literacy in daily life. Unfortunately, there is no good quality, systematic assessment of such broader notions of literacy in India at the state or national level.

WHY DOES LITERACY MATTER?

Arguably literacy is an essential determinant of the quality of life. By enhancing cognitive skills, literacy enables fuller development of human potential, and helps promote a sense of self-worth and dignity. As such literacy is often proclaimed as a human right and measures of literacy are included directly in indices of human welfare. For instance, a country's adult literacy rate is a significant component of UN's Human Development Index. Literacy also plays a prominent role in social development. In India, literacy, especially female literacy, is the single most important factor associated with lower fertility and higher child survival, far outweighing in statistical significance other factors commonly associated with economic development such as income and urbanization. Female children have significantly higher chances of survival relative to male children in districts with high levels of female literacy and, more generally, greater female empowerment (Murthi et al. 1995).

In addition to its intrinsic value and wider social benefits, literacy is essential to economic transformation. A minimal level of literacy and numeracy is essential for participation in market transactions and fuller realization of economic potential. In particular, it enables greater and more effective participation in labour markets. Literacy is often a prerequisite for the acquisition of many other skills. The extent to which illiteracy poses a barrier to economic participation may depend on other considerations: for instance, an illiterate person with access to at least one literate household member (proximate illiterate) may not be as disadvantaged as one who belongs to a household where all members are illiterate (isolated illiterate). Also, while literacy can be achieved in any one of many languages, it may be advantageous to be literate in a language that is commonly used in economic interactions. At the aggregate level, there is considerable evidence of a positive link between investment in human capital and rates of economic growth. More specifically for India, there is evidence that states with higher initial levels of literacy have experienced stronger poverty reduction since the 1960s, other things being equal, than states with weaker starting positions (Datt and Ravallion 1998).

THE NEED FOR PUBLIC INTERVENTION

While these benefits of literacy seem self-evident, at least to those who are already literate, they can be less obvious to illiterate people. The acquisition of literacy requires sustained individual investment in time and effort to develop cognitive skills (to decipher written text) and fine motor skills (to be able to write). Such skills are more readily acquired at a relatively young age when learning is easier and the opportunity cost of time is low, but children themselves are not best placed to assess the merits of literacy. In many countries, cultural biases lead even parents to underestimate the benefits of literacy for their children, especially for girls. More generally, gaining literacy involves a beneficial externality in that others gain through enhanced communication possibilities with those who choose to become literate. If so, the social return to investment in literacy is likely to exceed the private return.

Not surprisingly, extension of literacy has been the subject of considerable effort around the world, both by the state and increasingly by non-state actors. Education for All, an international initiative, was launched in 1990 to accelerate progress with achieving universal primary education and raising adult literacy. Most countries around the world aspire to providing universal primary education, but in many cases the achievement of this goal has been limited by supply constraints (not enough schools and teachers) or less than universal take-up even in the absence of tuition fees. Governments have sought to make attendance at primary school level mandatory, or use other means to nudge the population to enrol. Incentives such as Conditional Cash Transfers (monetary payments made to households contingent on their children attending school regularly) and free school meals can enhance school attendance, especially in deprived sections of the population.

WHY HAS IT TAKEN SO LONG TO REDUCE ILLITERACY?

Addressing illiteracy in a population requires extension of literacy among the stock of illiterate adults (through adult education) and among the flow of entrants (via education of children). The relative size of the two populations determines the magnitude of effort and resources needed in each category. As listed in Table 1, in India roughly 263 million adults (those aged 15 years or above) and 33 million children of school-going age (7–14 years) were classified as illiterate in 2001. In addition, there were 164 million illiterate children between 0 and 6 years of age. Reducing illiteracy among children requires that the large cohort of children entering school-going age enrol and complete basic education. Helping the 33 million 7–14 year olds who are illiterate is important, as is encouraging the 167 million literate

Table 1   Age Distribution of Population by Literacy 2001

(in millions)

Age (in years)	Population	Literate population	Illiterate population
0–6 years	164	0	–
7–14	200	167	33
15+	664	401	263
All	1028	732	296

Source: Census of India 2001 for population totals and total number of illiterates. Age-specific literacy rates are not available from the 2001 Census, so we use estimates provided by Govinda and Biswal (2005) based on National Sample Survey and National Family Health Survey data.

7–14 year olds to complete school. But even with high enrolment and progression rates, aggregate illiteracy rate is likely to remain high without efforts directed specifically at reducing adult illiteracy. We review recent progress in each of these categories.

In India, a recent surge in enrolment rates of children of school-going age has begun to reduce flows into illiteracy. As part of the worldwide 'Education for All' programme, a range of initiatives launched by the government and various non-government organizations (NGOs) pushed the school enrolment of children aged between 6 and 14 years to 79 per cent in 2000. Enrolment rates have since risen further under the Sarva Shiksha Abhiyan (SSA) launched in 2001 to raise enrolment of children in this age-group to 100 per cent and encourage all children to complete eight years of school. The SSA is financed in part by a surcharge of 2 per cent on tax receipts collected since 2004. Central government funding of the SSA has financed improvements in school infrastructure, and the recruitment and training of more teachers. Related schemes have encouraged school attendance in other ways, notably through mid-day meal schemes. By some estimates enrolment of children aged 6–14 stood at over 95 per cent in 2004. It is expected to be boosted further by the recent enactment of the Right to Education Act which makes education compulsory and free for all 6–14 year olds.

Despite this surge in enrolment, learning outcomes remain weak. In part, this is because drop-out rates remain high. According to government statistics, over a third of enrolled children are estimated to drop out at the primary school level (Standards I–V), with the figure rising to over 50 per cent by the time students reach the lower secondary level (Standards I–VIII). Drop-out rates are even higher for categories such as SC and ST that are more vulnerable to the risk of remaining illiterate. Besides, there are questions of whether enrolled children are able to acquire basic literacy skills. There are no nationwide standardized assessments of learning outcomes at the primary level. However, non-official assessments such as the report series compiled by Pratham, an NGO, point to serious shortcomings in reading skills of rural children: in 2008 only 56 per cent of children in Standard V were found capable of reading a Standard II text (a short paragraph) with fluency.

What factors contribute to the poor learning outcomes of primary school students in India? A wide variety of factors come into play including the poor quality of schooling infrastructure, non-availability of textbooks, inappropriate curricula, and shortcomings in teacher competencies and effort. Of all these, teacher effort is the factor that has been the most widely studied. The *Public Report on Basic Education in India* (PROBE 1999) found teacher absenteeism to be a widespread problem. Even where the teacher is present, there is little reward (or punishment) for teaching effectively. Greater information—such as that provided

by standardized assessments—could help stimulate public debate and pressure for change from parents and NGOs. Greater monitoring of teacher presence, tied with financial incentives to reduce absenteeism, has been found to have beneficial effects on both teacher presence and learning outcomes in pilot studies. It remains to be seen if these successes can be replicated in the many state-level initiatives that aim to improve learning in schools.

NGOs can help too, by improving incentives and supplementing public effort. The Learning Guarantee Program in Karnataka, supported by the Azim Premji Foundation, provides financial rewards to schools where students achieve certain levels of learning or improvements in learning. Such schemes have to be carefully designed: where teachers' unions oppose schemes that measure performance of individual teachers, structuring incentives at the level of schools may help. But even when such schemes succeed in eliciting greater effort from schools that choose to participate, they run the danger of increasing inequality between schools by targeting 'out' some of the weaker schools that chose not to opt into the scheme. Using such schemes to improve student learning would need to go hand in hand with other schemes to improve performance of weaker schools. Where weak learning outcomes within schools can be attributed to weaknesses in pedagogy, it may help supplement teacher effort with remedial instruction. The Balsakhi programme organized by Pratham in urban areas provides additional support teachers (Balsakhis) to schools to augment instruction to weaker students during school hours. As Balsakhis are local secondary school graduates trained by Pratham, their services cost a fraction of those of regular teachers. The programme has been found to improve basic literacy and numeracy skills (Banerjee et al. 2007). Once again, the challenge is to sustain and scale up such programmes, especially as many NGOs rely quite significantly on volunteer effort.

The progress on addressing adult illiteracy has been weaker. The National Literacy Mission (NLM) was launched in 1988 to impart functional literacy to non-literates in the age group of 15–35 years. Its principal tool is the Total Literacy Campaign (TLC), an area-specific, time-bound, volunteer-based, mass-mobilization style programme inspired by the TLC from Ernakulum, Kerala. In the Ernakulum campaign, under the leadership of the Kerala Shastra Sahitya Parishad, careful efforts were made to identify every illiterate person in the district between 6 and 60 years, and then volunteers were used as instructors to help them attain literacy. Standards were set for literacy and numeracy and a primer, called *Aksharam*, was developed which imparted information on a range of socially-relevant issues. While TLCs have expanded nationwide and are followed by Post-Literacy Programmes to deal with relapse into illiteracy among the newly literate, to date Kerala remains the only state for which every district has been declared wholly literate by the NLM. For the other states, there are pockets of progress but systematic progress remains elusive. However, even when TLCs have been less than successful in raising adult literacy, they may have had indirect benefits through encouraging adults to enrol their children in schools. The Continuing Education Scheme provides further learning opportunities for those who graduate from TLCs and Post-Literacy Programmes.

Progress on adult literacy has been impeded by various factors. The pressure from civil society to improve adult literacy and the flow of public resources is not as strong as in the case of primary education. Also, where literacy contributes to social and economic empowerment of marginalized groups, efforts to sponsor adult literacy may face resistance from those who benefit from the prevailing order. Finding creative channels to enhance adult literacy and to prevent relapse of literate adults into illiteracy would benefit from careful research and systematic evaluation of current programmes.

To summarize, the ability to read and write is an essential skill, both for human development and economic transformation. While literacy has improved in India especially since Independence, a third of the population remains illiterate. Policy effort must focus not only on extension of primary education and improvement in its quality, but creative means to reduce adult illiteracy.

SANDEEP KAPUR AND MAMTA MURTHI

REFERENCES

Banerjee, A., S. Cole, E. Duflo, and L. Linden. 2007. 'Remedying Education: Evidence from Two Randomized Experiments in India', *Quarterly Journal of Economics*, 122(3): 1235–64.

Datt, G. and M. Ravallion. 1998. 'Why Have Some Indian States Done Better than Others at Reducing Rural Poverty?', *Economica*, 65(257): 17–38.

Govinda, R. and K. Biswal. 2005. 'Mapping Literacy in India: Who are the Illiterates and Where Do We Find Them', background paper for the Education for All Global Monitoring Report 2006, Literacy for Life, UNESCO.

Murthi, M., A-C Guio, and J. Drèze. 1995. 'Mortality, Fertility and Gender Bias in India', *Population and Development Review*.

The PROBE Team. 1999. *Public Report on Basic Education in India*, New Delhi, Oxford University Press.

Medical Care, Quality of

Health policy in India during the last twenty-five years has been driven by the desire to make basic healthcare accessible to all. Great strides have been made towards this goal: the average adult visits a doctor 6 times a year in rural Rajasthan and 6.1 times in Delhi compared to 3.5 times a year in the US.

The use of health services by the rich and poor is very similar. In Rajasthan, the poor visit doctors 5.2 times a year compared to 6.48 times for the rich; in Delhi, the poor visit doctors *more* than the rich (6.8 times versus 5.2 times a year). Even so, health indicators such as the infant mortality rate place India at the level of Kenya and Gabon and large differences persist between the rich and the poor—1 in 10 children born to poor families dies within 12 months compared to 1 in 26 among the rich (World Bank 2006).

Clearly the service that people receive from doctors is important. This entry summarizes the emerging literature on the quality of private and public doctors in India. We define alternate measures of quality, discuss recent findings, and suggest implications for health policy. Partly due to difficulties in defining and measuring quality, there is little country-wide evidence to rely on. The existing evidence, however, indicates that the quality of primary medical care is alarmingly low.

DEFINING QUALITY

Quality can be measured in three ways: (1) structure (tangible hardware such as infrastructure or consumables such as medicines); (2) process (quality of medical advice); and (3) outcomes (impact of care on patients' health).

Structural measures have dominated empirical work in economics and other social sciences that aim to make population-wide estimates of healthcare quality. This is understandable since large-scale surveys are confined to relatively quick and easily measurable variables. By far the most common measure has been availability of medicines (Collier et al. 2003).

Structural quality by itself provides an inaccurate picture of service delivery. For example, if a public facility gives free medicines, the stock of medicines measures subsidization of care, and is unrelated to the quality of advice. Prescriptions could just as easily be filled by the local pharmacy. Worse, insufficient drug availability may simply indicate 'stock-outs' at the most popular facilities, which could be inversely related to the quality of care. Other physical items in facilities are largely subject to the same criticism—the more 'tradable' a piece of equipment is, the worse it performs as an indicator of service.

At the other extreme, measures of quality based on health outcomes are still in their infancy even in developed countries. The data collection and analysis required for establishing causal relations between clinical service and health outcomes is limited. Moreover, the methodology adopted in these studies is unlikely to help in the analysis of Indian medicine, since the majority are done in rich countries (particularly the United States), where infectious diseases common to India are hardly ever observed.

Progress *has* been made on 'process' measures of quality that capture aspects of provider behaviour likely to result in better health outcomes. In addition, they respond quickly to medical education and incentives; collected over time they are a suitable candidate for assessing quality improvements in the country.

WHAT WE KNOW ABOUT PROCESS QUALITY

When a person visits the doctor, the quality of care s/he receives depends on (a) whether the doctor is present (the 'extensive' margin of effort), (b) what the doctor knows (competence), and (c) what the doctor does (effort); the latter two reflect the 'intensive' margin of care.

The Extensive Margin: Absenteeism in the Public Sector

Problems of provider absence arise from unfilled vacancies and absenteeism. These are problems specific to *public* providers since a private provider is not paid if absent, and is therefore making an efficient choice. By the same token, vacancies in public facilities are not as much a problem of quality as of access—not having a public health centre is the same as having one with all posts vacant.

The aspect of the 'extensive margin' that is a genuine problem in the public sector is the problem of absenteeism, since salaries are paid but the expected services are not delivered. A recent study measures absenteeism using a large, representative survey based on surprise visits to primary healthcare facilities (Chaudhury et al. 2005). On average, over 40 per cent of doctors employed at public facilities were not found when visits were made (after adjusting for all legitimate reasons for absence). For non-doctors, the problem was equally bad, with the average absence rate just under 40 per cent. Further, absenteeism was not confined to a few 'bad eggs'— researchers visited each facility three times and while 15 per cent were absent all three times (the bad eggs) only 22 per cent were present every time.

A more intensive study of one district of Rajasthan, which continuously monitored conditions in public facilities associated with 100 villages, found that sub-centres were closed 56 per cent of the time during regular hours. Absence rates were 45 per cent in sub-centres and 36 per cent in

primary centres (Banerjee et al. 2004). If closings follow an established pattern, such as always being closed on Tuesdays, then the welfare loss may be small. However, long queues were seen at facilities that never opened. However capable the providers, they cannot give high-quality advice in absentia.

The Intensive Margin: Competence

Even when providers are at work, problems on the intensive margin arise in terms of quality of advice, which can be measured in two ways. First, the quality of medical advice depends on how much doctors know— measured 'knowledge' or 'competence' reflects the *maximum* quality a doctor can provide. However, if effort is costly, the actual quality of care could be substantially lower than this upper-bound. Second, one can also observe the provider in actual clinical practice to evaluate what doctors *do*. In both cases, relating knowledge and practice to established benchmarks of good-quality advice provides a measure of the quality of medical care.

Nationally representative studies of this type have not been done, but a recent study in Delhi revealed disturbing patterns (Das and Hammer 2005a). Hypothetical questions for five common cases or 'vignettes' were posed to a representative sample of public and private doctors in Delhi. Several results are noteworthy.

The overall knowledge of medical practitioners in Delhi was very low. For four out of five typical cases, the average provider was more likely to *harm* than assist. For example, less than one-third of observed providers asked questions or undertook examinations that would help identify pre-eclampsia in a pregnant woman; the remainder gave advice that would, in high probability, lead to the death of the mother, child, or both.

The study also addresses the long-standing debate on the relative quality of care in the public and private sectors. One side sees the private sector as 'quacks'; the other sees the public sector as staffed by less-competent doctors. The data indicate that both views have valid empirical grounding. On average, competence in the two sectors was similar. However, if private-sector providers are divided into those with and those without an MBBS degree (Bachelor of Medicine and Bachelor of Surgery) and the public sector is divided between staff at hospitals (mostly elite institutions in Delhi) and at primary healthcare centres (PHCs), differences emerge.

Doctors in public hospitals were nearly as competent as private MBBS providers—they may well be the same people at different stages in their career or, given the prevalence of 'dual practice', the same people, period. Doctors in small public clinics were substantially less competent than public doctors in hospitals and private doctors with an MBBS degree, although they were more competent than private providers without an MBBS.

The most striking feature though, was the variation in competence across poor and rich neighbourhoods. In the private sector, more competent MBBS *and* non-MBBS doctors were practising in richer areas; indeed, private MBBS doctors in poorer areas were sometimes worse than non-MBBS doctors in richer areas. The government does nothing to equalize these differences in the private market. The difference in competence across rich and poor areas was very similar in both the public and private sectors. Poor people go to PHCs and to the non-MBBS private sector, receiving advice from providers with very low competence in either case. Richer people go to competent private doctors or to competent public doctors in hospitals and obtain better advice.

The Intensive Margin: What do doctors do?
Evidence on the quality of performance in clinical settings, or what doctors do, is thin. However, the same study included a component in which doctors were observed for one working day within a few weeks of the original study on competence (Das and Hammer 2005b). The amount of time, number of questions asked, examinations performed, medication prescribed, and advice for use of medications and follow-up were all recorded. An average interaction between a doctor and a patient in Delhi lasts 3.8 minutes; the doctor asks 3.2 questions, undertakes an examination 63 per cent of the time, and dispenses 2.6 medicines. These numbers are much worse than in Spain, Germany, or the UK, worse than in Tanzania, Paraguay, and Nigeria, but somewhat better than in Malawi.

Disaggregating the data further showed a number of patterns.
- What doctors knew (from the vignettes) had little to do with what they did (from observation). On average doctors performed less than one-third of the critical procedures that they *had said they would perform* in cases of diarrhoea and viral pharyngitis.
- More competent doctors exerted more effort—a combination of time, questions, and examinations.
- Public doctors put in far less effort, spending half the time and doing only 60 per cent as many examinations as private-sector providers. These results remain after adjusting for workload, competence, and location.
- Non-MBBS doctors did about as well as they could—their behaviour approximately matched what they said they would do on the vignettes. MBBS doctors did less in practice than what they said they would do hypothetically. In the private sector, the difference

was modest; in the public sector the difference was dramatic, particularly among doctors in small clinics.

Indeed, the difference in effort between the public and private sectors was so stark that people in poor neighbourhoods were *better off* visiting less-qualified private-sector doctors than their more-qualified public-sector counterparts, at least in terms of diagnostic abilities.

Even so, the private sector was not a panacea. In line with previous work (for instance Patel et al. 2005), the study also found that the incentives to exert effort can be 'too strong'. Doctors in the private sector cater to patient expectations by overmedication, and poly-pharmacy (prescribing multiple medicines for a patient) is higher in the private compared to the public sector. In many cases, a private-sector doctor would accurately diagnose viral diarrhoea, but still prescribe anti-cholinergics and antibiotics. The former is contra-indicated, and the latter develops antibiotic resistance, raising the cost of future treatment.

The evidence on the 'extensive' and 'intensive' margins leads to some frightening conclusions for the quality of care in the public sector: a poor person visiting a primary healthcare centre is likely to find the doctor absent 40 per cent of the time. When the doctor is present, what s/he knows is just enough to ensure a 60 per cent chance of *not* harming the patient *if s/he did all s/he knew to do*. Unfortunately, the gap between knowledge and practice is large for public-sector doctors—typically, the doctor will ask the patient two questions and spend 2.5 minutes before sending him/her off with medication for the day. The rich will see a doctor who is more likely to be there, knows more, and acts more conscientiously. As an added bonus, the rich will probably spend *less* on unnecessary medicines and treatments than the poor.

These patterns combined with information on patients indicate deep-seated problems in the healthcare sector. First, the wide variation in quality of providers can be maintained for a long time—low-quality doctors are not driven out of the market, though they may be driven out of rich neighbourhoods. Second, choices between where to seek treatment (public or private facilities) can lead to better or worse outcomes depending on the nature of the disease involved. If the disease is self-limiting, and therefore lack of effort is not a problem, it is better to go to a public clinic where the patient will not receive a number of unnecessary medicines. If the disease needs careful attention, the private sector is better. Unfortunately, people don't generally know a priori which type of problem they have.

POLICY OPTIONS

Policy options for improving the quality of care in the healthcare market are limited. The first option is to increase information *to the public* about how to decide when a problem is serious and therefore sort themselves into public and private sectors. Further, better information and public action on *prevention*, either through public hygiene campaigns or large-scale sanitation programmes would go a long way to keeping people from having to make these choices.

Additional training for *providers* is unlikely to improve the quality of service delivery. On the extensive margin, it is unlikely that doctors are not aware that they are expected to show up for work. Similarly, on clinical practice, many doctors know what to do but simply don't do it, responding to their direct incentives (public doctors are on salary and have very little incentive to provide service, private doctors want repeat business).

Policies to change the image of primary healthcare in the public sector could improve the entire market, but require substantial investments. Setting benchmarks of service that people can trust and rely on would be a good start. This would include providing incentives to public-sector doctors (perhaps through 'bonus' schemes or empowering local authorities to hire and fire) and developing trust with the population. Both are likely uphill political battles. Another is to closely monitor and certify providers in the private sector. But simply expanding the scope of the 'inspectorate raj' is not something that can be done without first improving the capacity and honesty of public service providers.

In some countries the threat of litigation for malpractice serves as a disciplinary device. This has its own problems, especially with private, third-party payment schemes in which defensive medicine could drive up overall costs. In India the court system is already so overburdened that this is not a practical route to fixing quality of healthcare problems. The challenge will be to improve healthcare performance under the set of currently existing institutions; this is a difficult task that first requires a systematic shift in the debate away from physical access towards the content of care.

JISHNU DAS AND JEFFREY S. HAMMER

REFERENCES

Banerjee, Abhijit, Angus Deaton, and Esther Duflo. 2004. 'Wealth, Health and Health Services in Rural Rajasthan', *American Economic Review, Papers and Proceedings*, 94(2): 326–30.

Chaudhury, N., J. Hammer, H. Rogers, K. Muralidharan, and M. Kremer. 2005. 'Causes of Absenteeism in Public Health Workers and Teachers in Eight Countries', World Bank, processed.

Collier, Paul, Stefan Dercon, and John Mackinnon. 2003. 'Density versus Quality in Health Care Provision: Using Household Data to Make Budgetary Choices in Ethiopia', *World Bank Economic Review*, 16(3): 425–48.

Das, Jishnu and Jeffrey Hammer. 2005a. 'Which Doctor? Combining Vignettes and Item Response to Measure Clinical Competence', *Journal of Development Economics*, 78(2): 348–83.

Das, Jishnu and Jeffrey Hammer. 2005b. 'Money for Nothing: The Dire Straits of Medical Practice in Delhi, India', Policy Research Working Paper #3669.

Patel V., R. Vaidya, D. Naik, and P. Borker. 2005. 'Irrational Drug Use in India: A Prescription Survey from Goa', *Journal of Postgraduate Medicine*, 51: 9–12

World Bank. 2006. *World Development Report: Equity and Development*, New York, World Bank and Oxford University Press.

Poverty

The UNDP's annual *Human Development Report* (HDR) is a major source of information on various aspects of global well-being and deprivation. According to HDR 2005, India is ranked 127th among 177 countries in terms of the 'Human Development Index', and 58th out of 103 developing countries according to the 'Human Poverty Index'. Employing data for the most recent year between 1990 and 2003 for which they are available, it emerges that the proportion of the Indian population with an income less than the international poverty line of two purchasing power parity dollars a day is nearly 80 per cent: only twelve countries have fared worse in this regard. India, with an estimated adult illiteracy rate of 39 per cent in 2003, ranks 94th in a field of 115 countries for which data are available. The gender gap in illiteracy rates is pronounced: 27 per cent for males, and nearly twice this figure, at 52 per cent, for females. From statistics relevant for specific years between 1995 and 2001, one learns that the proportion of women victimized by sexual assault in the city of Mumbai was of the order of 3.5 per cent: only four cities, from a list of thirty-six, had a worse record. The proportion of the population that had been asked or was expected to pay a bribe to a government official was 22.9 per cent in Mumbai, a figure exceeded in only five other cities from a list of thirty-two. In a study done by Abu Saleh Shariff (2001) for the National Council of Applied Economic Research, we find that, in 1994 the proportion of the population that was deprived in terms of a 'capability poverty measure' was in excess of 60 per cent for the scheduled castes and tribes, and of the order of 52 per cent for the population at large. The 18th Congress Resolution of the Communist Party of India (Marxist)[1] records:

[Between 1992 and 2000] about 77 crimes against dalits were reported every day and... on average, three dalit women are raped and six dalit women disabled every day. These figures however are a gross underestimation because a large number of cases of sexual assault do not get registered. Dalit women face the triple burden of caste, class, and gender oppression.

These limited and unsystematic statistics provided in the preceding paragraphs are nevertheless sufficient to provide confirmation of the known (but increasingly less acknowledged) dominant reality of India: that it is a country of large absolute and relative deprivations, with a disproportionate burden borne by identifiable sections of the population. These statistics, despite the apparent randomness of their selection, also suggest that three useful analytical categories in terms of which deprivation in any society—including India—can be appraised are those of *positive freedom, negative freedom*, and *discrimination*.

The notion of 'positive freedom' is best captured in what Amartya Sen (1985) has referred to as the *capability to function*. The reference here is to the ability which

human beings have to lead the 'good life', and the practical question is one of the power which individuals enjoy, or which they are enabled by society to acquire, in order to achieve various valued human 'functionings', a functioning being what Sen again calls a 'state of being or doing'. The notion of 'negative freedom', or 'liberty', is linked to the acknowledgement that each individual is entitled to what John Stuart Mill called a 'personal protected sphere', such that, within her or his protected sphere, the individual is in no way subjected to any let or hindrance in the pursuit of her or his desired goals, including the goal of avoiding deprivation. While positive freedom is concerned with 'enablement', negative freedom is concerned with 'absence of restraint' and 'protection from coercion'. If the extent to which positive and negative freedoms are secured for its citizens is an index of a society's achievement in avoiding capability failure and deprivation, then of comparable concern should be the *equitableness* with which such freedoms are distributed across the population. A society is subject to the charge of discrimination if it is one that presides over an inequitable distribution of freedoms across individuals on the strength of their group affiliation—where the grouping in question corresponds to some partitioning of the population on the basis, by way of example, of gender or caste or religion or age or geographical sector of origin.

In what follows, deprivation in India is assessed with respect to the aforementioned categories of positive freedom, negative freedom, and discrimination.

First, positive freedoms. A selective, and very largely non-quantitative, survey of the record suggests something like the following picture.[2] As Amartya Sen has

[1]See *People's Democracy*, 29(16), April 2005.

[2]For relevant facts and figures, the reader is referred to Planning Commission (2002: Statistical Appendix).

pointed out, there has been no large-scale famine in independent India, unlike in colonial India, whereas, on the other hand, there is still a great deal of persistent and endemic hunger in the country. Undernourishment is still an integral aspect of the socio-economic profile of India's population: the incidence of low birth-weight babies, and of stunting and wasting among children, continues to be disquietingly large in comparison with the record of neighbouring countries like China and Sri Lanka. The record of the last five years or so has been especially harsh: the coexistence of starvation deaths, agrarian distress, rural indebtedness, and farmer suicides in states like Orissa, Andhra Pradesh, and Maharashtra, on the one hand, with the phenomenon of bursting public granaries, on the other, must be seen to be a particularly unacceptable face of the recent regime of hunger and suffering.

The expectation of life at birth has increased from the early thirties over 1941–50 to the early sixties over 1991–2000, and yet lags behind the Chinese and Sri Lankan figures. The trends in the crude death rate and in infant mortality have been definitely declining ones, but their absolute levels are still such as to cause anxiety. In terms of guarding against child morbidity and mortality through elementary precautions such as oral rehydration therapy, there have been secular improvements, but at a pace so retarded as to cause India still to lag behind the global average.

Unemployment, which is intimately linked to poverty, continues to remain a major block to socio-economic development: joblessness, intermittency, seasonality, and sporadicity of employment, retarded rates of skill learning and segmentation of the labour market, casualization of the labour force, and depressed wage rates, are not ideal guarantors of the right to livelihood.

Income poverty levels, in terms of the headcount ratio and other more sophisticated measures of poverty, are reported to have registered a steady decline from about the end of the 1970s to the turn of the millennium. All too often, 'poverty' has tended to be interpreted almost exclusively in terms of income deprivation. A reportedly steady decline in the headcount ratio, placed alongside a reportedly increasing profile of growth in per caput gross national product (GNP), not to mention the remarkable (and persistently visible) advances made by a relatively 'enclave' sector of the economy like information technology, has played a major role in fostering the impression that India's development experience over the last quarter of a century has been outstandingly promising. In this connection, it is markedly pertinent to review the conceptual basis of India's official poverty statistics, with specific reference to the 'identification' problem in poverty measurement, namely the problem of fixing the poverty line.

Various rounds of the National Sample Survey Organisation's (NSSO) consumption expenditure surveys provide a remarkable time-series and cross-section database on the distribution of consumer expenditure across expenditure size-classes, together with detailed information on the quantity and value of commodity-wise consumption in each expenditure size-class. In the mid-1980s, the Union Planning Commission, employing NSSO data for 1973–4, fixed the rural and urban poverty lines at those levels of consumption expenditure at which the calorific norms of 2400 and 2100 kilocalories per caput per diem in the rural and urban areas respectively were observed to be achieved (a rough description of the exercise of 'inverting an Engel function'). The resulting poverty lines, in terms of monthly per person consumption expenditure levels, were approximately Rs 49 and Rs 56 in the rural and urban areas respectively, at current (1973–4) prices. The commodity bundles corresponding to these levels of consumption expenditure in 1973–4 were identified; and in subsequent years, the poverty lines were fixed by revaluing the 1973–4 commodity bundles at current (that is relevant year-specific) prices.

In performing time-series comparisons of poverty, it is important to get one's price indices as nearly 'right' as possible, as well as to ensure comparability across different rounds of the NSSO surveys, such as in terms of reconciling inter-round variations in reference periods of recall. The Indian poverty literature reflects much ingenuity in addressing these problems.[3] While these are necessary issues demanding attention, it is also true that, for the most part, the official procedure of identifying the poverty line has gone largely unchallenged. At the poverty lines compatible with the Planning Commission's suggested procedure, one notes that over time there has been an expanding divergence between actual calorific intake levels and the recommended norms. If consumer behaviour is taken to be explicable in terms of standard demand theory, then the 'price-updated' commodity bundles corresponding to the poverty line consumption expenditure level of 1973–4 would simply ignore (a) the possibility of preference changes in favour of 'non-food' over 'food' (necessitated, perhaps, by inter-temporally changing perceptions of what is called for—even in relation to something as basic as footwear, for instance—to 'live without shame'); (b) the possibility of differential rates of inflation for 'food'

and 'non-food'; and (c) the possibility of a dwindling availability of common property resources such as firewood for fuel and therefore of increasing involuntary reliance on the market for the consumption of such commodities. If the poverty line in any year were fixed at that level of consumption expenditure at which the calorific norm is actually observed to be achieved (as was done by the Planning Commission for 1973–4), instead of in terms of the price-updated value of the 1973–4 'poverty line commodity bundle', then the resulting time-trend of headcount ratios becomes an increasing rather than a declining one. Briefly, the Planning Commission procedure, which has been widely and uncritically accepted, is compatible with two highly questionable implicit judgements: (a) that, somehow, the 1973–4 pattern of consumption expenditure must be privileged as the only one with normative significance; and (b) that inter-temporal poverty comparisons are meaningful only if the poverty line consumption bundle is unvarying over time. In sum, it is—or should be—very hard to accept poverty trends deduced from the official approach to the identification problem. Even so, and taking these sorts of estimates at face value, one finds that more than a quarter of the country's population was in consumption expenditure poverty in 1999–2000 (Planning Commission 2002).

Additionally, one imagines the aggregate headcount ought also to matter in the scheme of things; and with something like 260 million poor persons in the country today, India has the dubious distinction of being the largest contributing country to the world's poor.

The country is far removed from a state where the absence of homelessness can be regarded as a routine aspect of everyday existence for an overwhelming majority of the population; and where housing

[3]The reader is referred to Deaton and Drèze (2002) and Sen and Himanshu (2004), two crucial contributions (among others) to the charged debate on whether poverty has or has not declined over the reform period of the 1990s.

is available, it is often of the semi-*pucca* or *kutcha* variety in rural areas, or of the type of shanties in urban slums. What of freedom from ignorance? The constitutional guarantee of universal mandatory primary education within the first decade of Independence continues to remain a promise unfulfilled. While literacy levels have gradually risen over time, with about two-thirds of the population now reported to be literate, this still leaves behind a third of a vast population unable to read or write a short statement on their everyday lives. Apart from the intrinsic importance of access to knowledge, literacy also has many instrumental advantages such as in being associated with lower levels of child labour and with declines in fertility, which latter can only be for the good in the context of population stabilization and an alleviation of the reproductive burden borne by women.

The public provisioning of aids to mobility—railways, roadways, transport vehicles, and subsidized travel—has improved gradually over time, but nowhere near extensively enough to suggest that shortages in connectivity are not, even now, a major bottleneck for freedom of movement. Despite repeated encounters with the forces of nature (like floods and cyclones), identifiable sections of the population in identifiable parts of the country (like the north-east and Orissa) continue to be predictably vulnerable to natural disasters.

Briefly, an un-severe assessment of India's track record in the matter of positive freedoms would be: 'not bad'; but not bad only in relation to historically very high levels of illfare. It is, unhappily, not good—in relation to the country's needs, in relation to its potential, and in relation to the record of other comparably income-poor countries. It must be emphasized that this diagnosis of inadequate state success is not intended to seek a replacement of the state by the market or civil society, but rather to seek enhanced levels of public pressure on the state for significantly better delivery and accountability.

Second, negative freedoms. How unfettered a citizen is, is reflected in the extent of her or his legal entitlements, and the extent to which these are protected. There are two issues to be considered here: first, the prospect of securing the positive freedoms of the disadvantaged sections of society must sometimes be predicated on limiting the negative freedoms of the advantaged sections of society; and second, the positive freedoms of the latter class are often better secured simply because of both the immunity and influence enjoyed by it as a consequence of its superior status in respect of negative freedoms. A considerable prevalence of deprivation must be expected to be an outcome of a socio-political system which is largely unprepared to disturb the settled weight of vested interests in a deeply stratified society. For example, India's poor record of land redistribution is a reflection of far greater concern for the negative right of private property for the few than for the positive right of a minimally decent standard of living for the many. In an important related context, budgetary resources for securing an improved quality of life for the many are severely compromised by the inability or unwillingness to deal effectively with the crime of undeclared wealth and incomes perpetrated by the few. Even so, it is sobering to note that the picture might have been so much worse without a (even if qualifiedly) free press and parliamentary democracy. The verdict of the 2004 General Elections is a case in point.

Third, discrimination. Objectivity must compel the conclusion that here, more than anywhere else, the country's experience of socio-economic development and deprivation has been acutely dispiriting.

Consider the distribution of positive freedoms across well-defined social groupings, effected on the basis of caste, sector of origin, or gender, for instance. Whether we speak of hunger or health or mobility or knowledge or income poverty, the scheduled castes and tribes are systematically and significantly worse off than the rest; people of rural origin are worse off than those of urban origin; and females are worse off than males. The picture is a faithful reflection of the group-wise distribution of personal liberties. Dalits are still subjected to caste atrocities; religious minorities are the victims of state-abetted genocide; women are discriminated against in the intra-family distribution of resources, in the intra-family allocation of work burdens, in the acquisition and utilization of skills in the labour market, in the payment of wages, and in the display of respect towards their privacy and their bodies, as reflected in the phenomena of rape, forced prostitution, dowry deaths and sex-selective foeticide and infanticide. If one accepts the philosopher John Rawls' criterion of reckoning the welfare of a society in terms of the welfare of its most deprived member, then India's achievement on the deprivation front, as crystallized in the predicament of an income-poor, landless, illiterate, rural, scheduled caste woman, is a matter of shame.

India's poverty, like that of many other developing countries, is explicable in terms of the effects of colonialism, the terms of international trade, external debt, the self- or other-inflicted burden of military spending at the expense of social-sector spending, structural adjustment, and both the niggardliness and capriciousness of international aid flows. These factors, however, do not exhaust explanation: a more complete account must also take stock of the fact that the opportunities which reside in the unfulfilled potential for fair, reasonably egalitarian, and democratic internal governance are still waiting to be exploited. State policy in combating deprivation has been deployed on a number of fronts: these have been comprehensively analysed, in terms of performance with respect to growth and to social justice, direct anti-poverty programmes, and programmes for the satisfaction of basic needs, by S. Guhan (2002), whose overall assessment (p. 39) is telling: 'Whatever might have been the rhetoric of planning or politics, poverty alleviation has been an *adjunct* to India's development plans and policies rather than the *core* of their purpose.'

The following are some ingredients of a broad anti-poverty campaign that could be implemented. First, a strong pro-poor and anti-corruption message can be sent out by recovering—at least in a few 'obvious' and egregious cases—unpaid taxes on income and wealth, and earmarking the proceeds specifically for poverty-alleviation purposes, and likewise by imposing a 'poverty surcharge' on personal and corporate income, with this component of direct taxation again set aside for anti-poverty measures. Second, rural India needs special and renewed efforts at raising agricultural productivity, relieving debt distress, expanding agricultural credit, and increasing the coverage of extension activities. Other special groups in need of specifically targeted assistance are women, children, and the disadvantaged castes. Third, food security is critical: the public distribution system must be restored and improved. Fourth, poverty is not just a matter of income deprivation: to address it in its more generalized forms, it would help to draw a district-wise map of India, with the colour red reserved for those districts displaying acute inadequacies in access to drinking water, energy for cooking, elementary health facilities, a school, and a road; and, on the basis of such a map, some prioritized effort at infrastructural development must be initiated and sought to be implemented under a reasonable time-frame. Fifth, the plethora of anti-poverty employment schemes must be rationalized and streamlined. Indeed, the principal merit of employment schemes resides in their property of 'self-selection', which obviates the necessity for costly targeting; but, often, employment schemes incur large administrative, overhead and material costs, are subject to the machinations of corrupt contractors, and do not result in the creation of durable assets. There may therefore be a strong case for preserving the 'self-selection' property of wage employment schemes while reformulating some of them as adult literacy programmes, which can result in the creation of a durable social and human asset and at the same time have a beneficent effect on fertility and child labour. Sixth, the 1991–6 Congress-led government was already in possession of a complete blueprint of a National Assistance Scheme, which is a feasible and affordable package of social security measures covering old age pension, survivor benefit, accident compensation, and disability relief, which should be dusted, aired, implemented, and given the widest possible publicity, both to inform potential beneficiaries of their entitlements and to advertise serious intent. Finally, and as distinct from specific anti-poverty policy, strategies for the macroeconomic desideratum of pro-poor growth must also be attended to.

These ingredients of state policy have all been informed by an appreciation of the centrality of bolstering positive freedoms, protecting negative freedoms, and reversing discrimination in any approach to the redress of deprivation.

What is called for is a massive effort at reforming governance, with key reference to the problems, as Dilip Mookherjee (2004: 54) lists them, of 'law and order, tax collection, infrastructure, environmental

control, education, health, and anti-poverty programmes'. Most importantly, the challenge of poverty redress is a matter that requires infinitely more urgent attention than any which stems from the presumption that India is already well on its way to becoming a superpower.

S. SUBRAMANIAN

REFERENCES

Deaton, A. and J. Drèze. 2002. 'Poverty and Inequality in India: A Re-examination', *Economic and Political Weekly*, 7 September: 3729–48.

Guhan, S. 2002. 'Rural Poverty Alleviation in India: Policy, Performance, and Possibilities', in S. Subramanian, ed., *India's Development Experience: Selected Writings of S. Guhan*, New Delhi, Oxford University Press.

Mookherjee, D. 2004. *The Crisis in Government Accountability: Essays on Governance Reform and India's Economic Performance*, New Delhi, Oxford University Press.

Planning Commission, Government of India. 2002. *India: National Human Development Report 2001*, New Delhi, Oxford University Press.

Sen, A. 1985. *Commodities and Capabilities*, Amsterdam, North-Holland.

Sen, A. and Himanshu. 2004. 'Poverty and Inequality in India—I & II', *Economic and Political Weekly*, 18 September: 4247–63 and 25 September: 4361–75.

Shariff, S.A. 2001. *India: Human Development Report—A Profile of Indian States in the 1990s*, New Delhi, Oxford University Press.

Poverty and Exclusion

About one-quarter of the Indian population is estimated to be living in poverty. This entry explores the role of state programmes in reducing poverty and also illustrates some of the biases inherent in using household consumption data to arrive at poverty estimates. Available evidence on the distribution of household consumption and public spending leads me to two main conclusions. First, that some types of spending can substantially raise household consumption and reduce poverty. Second, that the benefits from public programmes are spread unevenly, both across and within regions, and these benefits are not well captured by measures of household consumption typically used to estimate poverty. As a result, there is likely to be some misclassification of poor and non-poor households and regional differences in poverty may be larger than current estimates suggest. It appears, ironically, that the poor in India are often excluded from the benefits of state redistribution. In this sense, poverty and exclusion go together and an accurate assessment of poverty requires an understanding of the nature of this exclusion.

Historically, two types of public programmes have been important in redistributing national income: direct transfers to the poor and the expansion of public services. Poor relief first became sizable in England and Europe in the late eighteenth century while public education began somewhat later and expanded fastest in the United States (Lindert 2004). For countries that started to industrialize in the post-War period, direct transfers were relatively unimportant and the bulk of public welfare spending took the form of expansion in education, health, and physical infrastructure. This continues to be true of poor countries today: the provision of public goods and price subsidies on essential commodities are central components of policies aimed at reducing poverty. In addition, there has been a growing interest in schemes that transfer assets and provide credit for self-employment to families who are neglected by formal credit institutions.

I begin with an overview of state redistributive programmes in India. I examine the spatial distribution of public spending and the extent to which such spending has been directed towards the poor. At regional level, I find a close and positive association between per capita domestic product and the benefits from public goods, services, and transfers. Within regions, there appears to be very little targeting of state subsidies towards the poor. The next section considers the implications of these findings for poverty measurement and is followed by brief concluding remarks.

STATE REDISTRIBUTIVE PROGRAMMES
Food Subsidies

The public distribution system (PDS) was the first nationwide transfer programme introduced after Indian Independence. It began during the First Five Year Plan in the early 1950s and was based on the rationing schemes put in place by the British government during the War. The system functioned primarily to provide food security in the presence of fluctuating agricultural output and entitled all households to specified quantities of food grains and essential commodities at subsidized prices. It was not explicitly targeted towards the poor until 1997, at which stage a wedge was created between the prices paid by households listed as being below the poverty line and the others, with the poor paying prices that were about half the cost of provision and households above the poverty line paying close to cost prices. In December 2000 the Antodaya Anna Yojana (AAY) was introduced and the poorest 15 per cent below the poverty line were targeted for further subsidies. Those covered under the AAY pay Rs 2 and 3 per kg of wheat and rice respectively, and each household is currently entitled to a maximum of 35 kg per month of each of these.

There have been several studies of the PDS which document differences in take-up rates and coverage across regions and households. There are two principal sources of data on the distribution of food grains through the PDS. The Department of Food and Public Distribution publishes administrative data on the prices and quantities of each commodity distributed through the system. Household data on the consumption of these commodities can be had from the National Sample Surveys (NSS) which cover over a hundred thousand households across the country every five years and separately record the consumption of items from PDS and non-PDS sources. The last NSS round before the introduction of the targeted PDS scheme was in 1993–4. The data for that year show that many of the poorer states had very low rates of PDS participation and food subsidies through the system were generally higher in urban than in rural India. Bihar and Orissa were the two poorest states in that year, whether measured by poverty head counts or the poverty gap ratio and less than 5 per cent of the households in these states bought food grains from the PDS. By contrast, in each of the four southern states, poverty rates were much lower and over 80 per cent of households bought subsidized rice and wheat. Within almost all states, the programme was not targeted towards poor households in that the value of food subsidies was increasing in household expenditure over a wide range of expenditure levels in the bottom half of the expenditure distribution (Tarozzi 2000). The 55th round of the National Sample Survey in 1999–2000 allows an evaluation of the effectiveness of the targeted PDS introduced in 1997. The survey records commodity-wise quantities and values which can be used to calculate prices paid by each household. The data show very little variation in either participation rates or prices paid across consumption quartiles.

Participation rates rise slowly and prices paid fall slightly with expenditure. About one-third of surveyed households purchased some rice or wheat from the system and the corresponding figure was 30 per cent for those in the bottom expenditure quartile. This positive relationship between participation and consumer expenditure at national level could, in principle, arise from a dysfunctional PDS in some of the poorest states. This, however, is only part of the story because even within several states, participation is flat or rising in household expenditure. Most households paid prices that were a little above Rs 5 per kg (for both wheat and rice), which is fairly close to the issue prices for families below the poverty line. Administrative records on prices charged to those above and below the poverty line suggest that many states used funds from other sources to subsidize purchases by households above the poverty line.

There has been no major NSS round after the Antodaya scheme for the ultra poor began in 2000. In the relatively small sample surveyed in the annual consumption survey in 2004, only 1.6 per cent of all households and 3 per cent of the bottom expenditure quartile paid prices for wheat and rice that are stipulated under the scheme. Given the overall size of the scheme, its proper assessment requires much larger samples, yet these numbers suggest that its impact is still fairly marginal.

The overall picture with regard to food subsidies is one of substantial regional variation in outreach and very little targeting towards the poor within regions. Anecdotal evidence suggests that targeting may have improved under the AAY. Consumption data from the 61st NSS round (the first large one since the introduction of the scheme) will allow a more careful evaluation of this scheme.

Public Goods

Transfers by the Indian state in the form of increased access to public goods have been sizable relative to other spending programmes, although overall levels of provision are still very low by international comparison.

The earliest reasonably systematic evidence on village-level access to public goods for the Indian states is available from the 1961 Census. More than four-fifths of the Indian population at that time lived in villages, yet village access to public goods in most of rural India was severely limited. A little over 40 per cent of Indian villages had primary schools, though many of these were constructed and managed by religious and other social organizations. Only 1 per cent had high schools, less than 2 per cent had health centres, 3 per cent had electricity connections, and 8 per cent had post offices.

In the first half of the 1970s public good provision appeared, quite suddenly, in political speeches and policy documents. The Minimum Needs Plan introduced guidelines for rural access to clean water, schools and health facilities, electricity, and roads. Within this broad agenda, states differed in their priorities and in the rates at which they increased overall provision. Primary schools mushroomed in all states, and by 1991 over three-quarters of villages in most states had a local school. High schools expanded more gradually but steadily throughout the 1961–2001 period. Rural electrification was most rapid in states with commercial agriculture (in Haryana and Punjab coverage went from less than 10 per cent of villages in 1961 to 100 per cent by 1981) and piped water became widespread in the northern hill districts of Himachal Pradesh and what is now the state of Uttarakhand. Rural roads were relatively neglected until the 1990s, but expanded rapidly after that and by 2001 more than half of all Indian villages could be approached by a paved road. In contrast to the above changes, publicly funded health facilities have remained largely unavailable to the rural population. Primary Health Centres (the smallest facility with a trained doctor) were available in only 3 per cent of Indian villages in 2001 and no state, other than Kerala, had coverage of more than 10 per cent. The number of Primary Health Sub-centres (which house a trained nurse and provide immunizations) did increase substantially in south India and the 2001 Census indicates that these have spread to about a third of all villages in the southern states.

The foregoing discussion is not meant to suggest that the goods provided were of high or reliable quality—evidence on leaking school buildings, absent teachers and doctors, dry taps, and irregular power supply is now plentiful. The new facilities did, however, represent substantial expenditures, mostly by the state, that in some cases at least, reached those without wealth or political power. These investments also appear to have influenced social outcomes. Infant mortality rates are now roughly half of what they were in 1971. The gap in literacy between both males and females and urban and rural areas has been shrinking (at an increasing rate) and school attendance rates reported by the most recent census for scheduled castes and scheduled tribes are very similar to those for the rest of the population. States such as Rajasthan and Andhra Pradesh that invested in education have jumped from the bottom of the distribution of state literacy rates to the middle over the past thirty years. Even with large reporting errors and grossly inflated attendance rates, the trends in these outcomes are unmistakable.

An examination of the spatial distribution of public goods in 2001 shows that richer states had much better access, especially to those facilities that were relatively scarce at national level. This relationship is often blurred by the case of Kerala which, over the past century at least, has consistently had the greatest access to educational and health facilities accompanied by an unremarkable economic performance. If we ignore Kerala, we find a positive and surprisingly systematic relationship between the availability of social and physical infrastructure and state domestic product per capita. A single standard deviation change in per capita state domestic product is accompanied by a one-third increase in the proportion of villages with high schools and a 40 per cent increase in village access to piped water and bus services. In this descriptive sense, much of the variation in public goods access between, say, Bihar, Rajasthan, and Punjab (representing the bottom, middle, and top of the range of state domestic product) is 'explained' by differences in incomes. These patterns are important for assessments of regional poverty differences as discussed in the next section.

Have differences in public good access been important for recent reductions in poverty? Deaton and Drèze (2002) present state-level poverty estimates for poverty head counts and the poverty gap ratio based on NSS consumption data. The surveys in 1987–8 and in 1999–2000 are closest to the census years of 1991 and 2001. Matched in this manner, we find that changes in the availability of some public goods over the 1991–2001 period are highly correlated with declines in measured poverty. In fact, once we control for the expansion of public goods, changes per capita state domestic product seem to have very little to do with changes in poverty. These numbers, though rough and preliminary, suggest the absence of large trickle-down effects that did not operate through improved infrastructure.

Other Programmes

There are a large number of other programmes aimed at poverty reduction that have been introduced since the 1970s. Some of these, such as the Integrated Rural Development Programme (IRDP) started in 1978, were designed to encourage self-employment among the poor by providing them assets, often in the form of livestock. The IRDP, together with other self-employment schemes that were subsequently introduced, have come together under the banner of the Swarnajayanti Gram Swarozgar Yojana (SGSY). A major focus of the SGSY has been the promotion of small credit groups, known as self-help groups. Non-government organizations are funded and encouraged to promote the formation of these groups and nationalized banks are directed to provide them credit for self-employment activities. Other programmes include subsidized house construction under the Indira Awas Yojana and schemes that provide state funds to the unemployed for work on village infrastructure (the Jawahar Rozgar Yojana and, more recently, the National Rural Employment Programme).

Budgetary allocations to these programmes are sizable and have been rising. Little, however, is known about the composition of recipients and therefore the extent to which these programmes have been successful in reaching the poor. The limited evidence available suggests little or no targeting towards the poor. The 55th round of the NSS in 1999–2000 questions respondents on assistance received by them under the IRDP. About 5 per cent of respondent households had received such assistance during the five years prior to the survey and, remarkably, we observe no difference in this proportion across household expenditure deciles.

Public-sponsored micro-finance seems to have had better success in reaching the poor although destitute households do not appear to participate in the self-help groups that are now significant actors in rural credit markets (Somanathan 2005). The success of these institutions relative to other government subsidies probably owes much to the fact that a sizable fraction of public funds is routed through energetic and competent non-government organizations and state funds complement those given by external donor agencies who also independently monitor this sector.

IMPLICATIONS FOR POVERTY MEASUREMENT

Poverty estimates for India are based on the value of monthly per capita consumption expenditure obtained from the consumption surveys described earlier. Official poverty lines are defined in terms of a threshold level of monthly per capita consumption expenditure that was linked to food adequacy in the early 1970s. Since then, poverty lines are updated based on changes in general price level and, since prices vary across states and urban and rural areas, so do poverty lines.

How might benefits from public programmes be reflected in poverty estimates? Income transfers are likely to be reflected quite well in household consumption expenditure because they do not directly influence relative prices. Food subsidies are a different matter. Households with the same consumption expenditure would have different levels of real consumption based on whether or not they were receiving food subsidies through the PDS. This has implications for estimating regional differences in poverty and for the listing of poor households within regions. Households in states with a well-managed PDS would, on average, pay lower average prices for food. If we adjust the state-level poverty line to incorporate this lower average price level, we are more likely to misclassify poor households as non-poor if

they do not have access to state subsidies. So, paradoxically, errors in household listings could be larger in areas with higher coverage if the subsidies in question are not well-targeted.

One possible solution would be to create a set of price indices based on actual prices paid by households. We could estimate prices for each good as a function of household characteristics (state of residence, land possessed, household demographics, and any other relevant characteristics) and then construct household-specific price indices as functions of these predicted prices. The real consumption expenditure for a household would then be obtained by deflating observed expenditure by the index appropriate to that household. This procedure would, for example, use different price indices within regions for groups that are favoured by the state and those that are not. Poverty measures could then be based on the deflated consumption data obtained in this manner.

This procedure would work quite well for commodities and services that are consumed in well-defined units of reasonably uniform quality. In such cases consumption survey data report both values and quantities consumed and the implicit prices are easy to interpret. Unfortunately, this is not the case with expenditures on education, health, transport, and many other expenditure categories for which consumption units are not standard and surveys record only total expenditures. In such cases, useful adjustments to consumption data cannot be made without information on the types of services to which each household has access. In this sense, it is relatively difficult to arrive at accurate measures of real household consumption when there is variable access to public goods.

This entry has outlined the major types of interventions used by the Indian state to alleviate poverty. The public spending programmes described here are found to vary enormously in their coverage and average effectiveness across states and have, in general, performed badly in terms of targeting poor households. I have considered some implications of these findings for the measurement of poverty differences across regions and for the proper identification of poor households. Of these, I believe that the misclassification of poor households is by far the more serious issue. Most consumers of poverty data are aware that differences in governance and the availability of public goods across Indian states must be kept in mind when comparing differences in private consumption. In contrast, Indian policy makers are increasingly restricting the availability of public benefits to households they place below the poverty line. Inaccurate lists of such households can compound the targeting problems that have historically plagued poverty-alleviation efforts. A careful characterization of the poor needs much more attention than it has so far received.

ROHINI SOMANATHAN

REFERENCES

Banerjee, Abhijit and Rohini Somanathan. 2007. 'The Political Economy of Public Goods: Some Evidence from India', *Journal of Development Economics*, 82(2).

Deaton, Angus and Jean Drèze. 2002. 'Poverty and Inequality in India: A Re-Examination', *Economic and Political Weekly*, 7 September.

Lindert, Peter. 2004. *Growing Public: Social Spending and Economic Growth since the Eighteenth Century*, Cambridge University Press.

Planning Commission. Government of India, Tenth Five-Year Plan.

Somanathan, Rohini. 2005. 'Poverty Targeting in Public Programs: A Comparison of Alternative Statistical Tests', working paper.

Tarozzi, Allesandro. 2000. 'A Birds-eye View of PDS Utilization using the 50th Round of the Indian National Sample Survey (July 1993–June 1994)', working paper, Princeton University.

Primary Education

Despite the progress India has made in primary schooling since Independence, schooling attainment still remains very low. Household data from the National Sample Survey (NSS) for 1999–2000 reveal that 30 per cent of children between the ages of 12 and 15 have not completed primary school. While gender gaps have narrowed (the percentage of rural boys and girls between ages 12 and 15 with primary schooling in 1999–2000 was 66 per cent and 58 per cent respectively), caste and regional gaps remain significant. Only 51 per cent of scheduled caste (SC) and tribe (ST) children between ages 12 and 15 report completing primary school, as compared to 66 per cent of children of other castes. Comparing states, the figure varies from 97 per cent in Kerala to a low of 41 per cent in Bihar. Indeed, despite the fact that the figure for Kerala by 1999–2000 approached the ceiling of 100 per cent, the difference in this completion rate between Kerala and Bihar, at 56 per cent, *exceeded* that of rural adults of older cohorts in the two states. For example, primary school completion rates for adults between ages 45 and 50 in 1999–2000 were 65 per cent in Kerala and 23 per cent in Bihar, yielding a gap of 43 per cent. Finally, education quality, as reflected in the results of standard achievement tests, is very low.

In this brief entry, it is not possible to fully describe the research on the determinants of primary schooling in India. Instead, I focus on the role of policy in explaining schooling outcomes. I start by describing the constraints that shaped the formation of schooling policy in India, and the broad features of this policy. I then go on to discuss how schooling policy explains some of the features of schooling in India.

INDIA'S EDUCATIONAL POLICY

At Independence, India inherited a very weak system of primary education. In 1835, the British authorities decided that publicly funded education should only be provided in English, a policy that was adhered to until almost the end of the colonial era. Available funds were also primarily used to subsidize fee-charging private schools, rather than government schools. Consequently, popular primary education, particularly in rural areas, received scant support (Myrdal 1968). In 1950–1, at primary level there were only 211,071 schools and 537,918 teachers in the country, of whom over 40 per cent were untrained. Not surprisingly, schooling levels were low, with only 42 per cent of the 6–11 age group and 14 per cent of the 11–14 age group enrolled in school in 1950–1. And disparities in schooling attainment were large: across states, across urban and rural areas, across castes, and across boys and girls. In 1950–1, girls constituted only 28 per cent of primary school enrolments, even though they comprised roughly half of the school age population. Similarly, whereas 83 per cent of the population lived in rural areas in 1950–1, rural students constituted only 60 per cent of primary school enrolments.

Recognizing the importance of universal elementary schooling, the Constitution included a Directive which sought to ensure universal elementary schooling by 1960. Though this deadline was not met, the objective of universal elementary schooling has repeatedly been upheld, most recently in the ninety-third constitutional amendment which makes education for children between the ages of 6 and 14 a fundamental right.

This goal has been difficult to achieve, in part because of the country's very poor resource base. At the time of the First Five Year Plan, the Committee on the Ways and Means of Financing Educational Development in India estimated that the development of a national system of education would require an *annual* expenditure of Rs 400 crore, and an additional Rs 472 crore for teacher training and investment in buildings, adding up to a total of Rs 2472 crore over the five-year period. However, India's total tax revenue in 1950–1 amounted to only Rs 625 crore. As a consequence, the Plan restricted *total* outlays by the central and state governments to only Rs 2069 crore. As against the estimated requirement of Rs 2472 crore, expenditure on education was restricted to only Rs 152 crore for the Plan period. Allocations to education have consistently fallen short of the government's target of 6 per cent of national income.

The limited resources of the central government combined with the assumption that lower-level state governments could more efficiently deliver 'local' public goods such as schooling resulted in education being placed in the Constitution's 'State List', that is amongst the areas for which state governments are responsible. This decision effectively decentralized decisions relating to schooling resources and expenditure. Though the central government recognized that it nevertheless bore responsibility 'for helping, co-coordinating and guiding the work of the States', it admitted that it was unable to do much in this direction due to the shortage of funds (Government of India, First Five Year Plan). In 1976, education was shifted from the State List to the Concurrent List by the forty-second amendment to the Constitution, thereby formalizing a role for the central government in framing educational policies and providing central support for nationwide schooling schemes. However, individual states remain free to evolve and frame their own policies and structures within this broad framework, as also to determine their schooling budgets and the allocation of state expenditures.

The majority of schooling expenditure continues to come from state governments, which, in 2002–3, bore 82.2 per cent of the total budgeted expenditure on education. The central government primarily funds 'plan' investment in physical capital such as school buildings, while state governments finance 'non-plan' expenditure on teachers and other forms of working capital. However, the central government also supplements state-level funding through centrally sponsored educational programmes, such as Operation Blackboard and, more recently, the Sarva Shiksha Abhiyan, which frequently include components for working capital expenditure including teacher salaries.

Commitment to a decentralized framework was reiterated in two important policy documents, the 1986 National Policy on Education and the follow-up 1992 Plan of Action, which laid down a framework for utilizing decentralized political institutions, the *panchayati raj* institutions, for strengthening school decentralization. Since this period, the district is treated as the unit of educational planning, with district Boards of Education being responsible for teacher training, teacher allocations across schools, and a host of other administrative tasks. Village education committees were also set up to monitor investments at school level and to ensure local participation in the educational planning process.

The resource constraint also led the government to advocate a large role for the community and private funding, with the First Five Year Plan stating explicitly that 'in the context of prevailing conditions a larger

share of responsibility for social services will have to be borne by the people themselves'. This was accomplished by requiring even students enrolled in government schools to pay for tuition and other inputs. It was also achieved through a relatively liberal policy towards the growth of private schools.

Data from 1985–6 (NSS 42nd round) document that the average expenditure by households per student enrolled in elementary school was Rs 1205. In contrast, the average expenditure per elementary school student by the central and state governments combined was only Rs 338.72—private expenditures were approximately four times public expenditures! High household expenditures were not just a consequence of private school enrolments, but primarily reflected relatively high tuition fees, even in government schools (an average of Rs 994 per primary student in government schools). Most state governments subsequently abolished tuition fees in elementary schools, resulting in a decline in tuition expenditures by 1995, when the average tuition fee reported per primary student in government schools was Rs 52.

Nevertheless, total educational expenditures per elementary school student in 1995, at Rs 662, remained high, a consequence of the rapid growth in private schools. For India as a whole, the percentage of primary school students enrolled in private schools has increased from 15 per cent in 1986 to 21 per cent by 1995 (NSS, rounds 42 and 52 respectively). The corresponding percentages for urban India were as high as 36 per cent and 47 per cent. This growth has meant that private funding of elementary schools remains significant, with household expenditures amounting to 36 per cent of total expenditure on elementary schooling (1995–6).

The poor infrastructural base the country inherited combined with the shortage of funds also led the government to implement a 'step' approach, focusing initially on improvements in primary schooling facilities. Decisions regarding the number of schools and their location were, however, guided by the constraints placed on the system by the nation's existing socio-economic fabric. It is frequently stated that India is primarily a nation of villages. In reality, however, India is a nation of habitations within villages, with habitations generally being defined along caste lines. Because of the residential segregation of households and the unwillingness of parents to allow their daughters to walk relatively long distances to school, the government adopted an *extensive* policy, with the goal of providing a primary school 'within easy walking distance' from each home (Third Five Year Plan). This goal was formalized by the 1986 National Policy on Education and the follow-up 1992 Plan of Action, which stated that every habitation with a population that exceeded 300 should be provided with a primary school within 1 km radius. This population norm was relaxed to 200 for SC and ST habitations. As a consequence of this policy, the scarce resources available for primary schooling have principally been used to finance growth in schools. The number of primary schools has increased more than three times between 1950–1 and 1999–2000, from 210,000 to 642,000.

EFFECTS OF AN EXTENSIVE APPROACH: QUANTITY VERSUS QUALITY

Research has shown that the substantial growth in the number of schools, and the policy of providing schools within walking distance of households, has significantly contributed to the growth in primary school enrolment, particularly for SCs and STs (Kochar 2004). It has therefore contributed to the narrowing of schooling gaps.

However, the growth in the number of schools may have been at the expense of

improvement in the quality of schooling infrastructure and other schooling inputs, including teachers. As recently as 2002, data from the Seventh All-India Educational Survey (AIES) revealed that 20 per cent of rural schools lacked a *pucca* building. Indicators of poor schooling infrastructure abound: only 44 per cent of primary schools in 1993 had drinking-water facilities, while as few as 19 per cent of them had urinals. The percentage of primary schools having separate urinals for girls was as low as 9 per cent (Sixth AIES). And growth in the number of teachers has not kept pace with growth in student enrolment. Thus India has witnessed an *increase* in the primary school student–teacher ratio over the years, from 24 in 1950–1 to 43 by 1999–2000.

The extensive approach has also made it difficult to exploit economies of scale in schooling. In 1999–2000, the average student size of a primary school was 177, below the range most educationalists consider to be optimal. As many as 60 per cent of the nation's schools had an enrolment of less than 100 in 1993 (Sixth AIES). In fact, a quarter of rural schools have student populations of less than fifty. Such small school sizes means that multigrade instruction is the norm in most of the nation's schools, with teachers simultaneously providing instruction to students of several grades. This is also reflected in data on the number of teachers per school. In 2002, 28 per cent of rural schools had one or less teacher, while 64 per cent had two or less teachers.

Do indicators of quality such as student–teacher ratios, class size, and schooling facilities affect schooling quantity and quality? While the evidence from developed countries remains ambiguous, a significant body of research demonstrates that they do matter for schooling in developing economies. The policy of creating a large network of schools, each of relatively small size and with inadequate supporting inputs, may therefore have implied a vote for quantity over quality.

EFFECTS OF DECENTRALIZATION: EFFICIENCY AND EQUITY

It is widely believed that a primary advantage of a decentralized system of schooling is greater efficiency in input use, including the accountability of teachers. This has not been the case in India, as documented by several studies, including the PROBE report (1999) and Drèze and Sen (1995), which record considerable wastage of teaching time in several states. This may, however, not be a failure of decentralization but rather reflect the limited degree of school decentralization in India. For example, despite recent experimentation with 'contract teachers', the accountability of teachers in regular government employment to the community remains low.

Decentralization has, however, resulted in considerable variation in government allocations to schooling across states. In 2001–2, average expenditure on education was 24 per cent of total state budgeted expenditure, with expenditure on elementary schooling accounting for 52 per cent of this total. However, states such as Punjab devote only 17 per cent of budgeted expenditure to education, and only 30 per cent of the total educational budget to elementary schooling. In contrast, Madhya Pradesh devotes 27 per cent of its budget to education, and 64 per cent of its education budget to elementary schooling.

Average expenditures per student mirror this variation. While the budgeted average expenditure per elementary student across all states was Rs 2047 (2001–2), the amount was Rs 1166 in Chhattisgarh, Rs 1371 in Andhra Pradesh, Rs 2845 in Maharashtra, and Rs 4339 in Himachal Pradesh. And

data from the Seventh AIES (2002) reveal a commensurate variation in student–teacher ratios across states. Compared to the national average of 42, the student–teacher ratio is 19 in Jammu and Kashmir, 22 in Himachal Pradesh, 55 in Uttar Pradesh, and as much as 83 in Bihar.

Given administrative decentralization to the level of the district, it is no surprise that state-level variation in per student resources is mirrored by similar variation at district level, *within* a state. For example, in Bihar, data from the Seventh AIES reveal that the student–teacher ratio varies from 59 in Nalanda district to 100 in Gaya.

EFFECTS OF PRIVATIZATION: SUPPORT FOR GOVERNMENT SCHOOLS

Why has decentralization not resulted in greater efficiency of input use in India? Relatedly, what explains the low level of public expenditure on primary schooling and the variation in this expenditure across states? Many believe that low schooling budgets and the poor quality of government schools reflect the apathy of local elites—not towards schooling, but towards government schools (Weiner 1991).

This may, in turn, partly be a consequence of the combination of policies of administrative decentralization and the government's tacit support for private schooling. Researchers have argued that heterogeneity across a community in the value placed on schooling will reduce overall support for government schools that cater to all members of the population. Decentralization, which places some measure of control over schools in the hands of the community, will therefore generally result in poor-quality government schools in these communities. This effect will be exacerbated if private schools are encouraged, since those who care most about schools will have the option of 'exiting' from the government school system. If these are also the relatively influential households, government schooling communities may be singularly ill-equipped to ensure improvements in budgets for government schools.

The data suggest that the extent of schooling segregation between the rich and the poor is increasing. Dividing households by per capita expenditure, the percentage of primary school children attending private schools in 1995 was as high as 34 per cent for households in the highest per capita expenditure quartile (20 per cent in rural areas and as much as 76 per cent in urban areas). In contrast, 13 per cent of primary school students from the lowest per capita expenditure quartile attended private schools (8 per cent in rural areas, 29 per cent in urban areas).

Establishing a causal relationship between the growth of private schools and the consequent increase in schooling segregation, and the quality of government schools is difficult. However, the inverse correlation at state level between private school enrolments and the schooling attainment of the poor is suggestive of such a relationship. Private school enrolments at primary level are amongst the highest in the northern states of Punjab, Haryana, and Uttar Pradesh. For rural India, for example, data from 1995 (NSS 52nd round) reveal that 16 per cent, 23 per cent, and 26 per cent of the primary students in rural areas of these states respectively were enrolled in private schools, relative to the national average of 12 per cent. These states are also characterized by below-average schooling attainment of the poor. I define poor households as those whose per capita expenditure fell below state-specific poverty lines. By this definition, the percentage of poor rural children between the ages of 12 and 15 who reported completing primary school was

36 per cent, 34 per cent, and 39 per cent in Punjab, Haryana, and Uttar Pradesh respectively, below the (rural) national average of 42 per cent. In fact, only the states of Bihar (26 per cent) and Rajasthan (28 per cent) report lower primary school completion rates amongst poor households. Interestingly, primary school completion rates for the non-poor in Punjab (76 per cent) and Haryana (72 per cent) exceeded the national average (69 per cent), while it was 62 per cent in Uttar Pradesh. Correspondingly, the gap in primary school completion rates between the non-poor and the poor in Punjab (40 per cent) and Haryana (38 per cent) far exceeded the national average (27 per cent).

This necessarily short entry cannot do justice to the many issues that arise regarding primary schooling in India. Rather than attempt to be comprehensive, I have focused on identifying a few policy constraints on improvements in primary schooling in India.

India's poor resource base resulted in an extensive approach and in a decentralized schooling system with tacit support for private schools. While this approach has succeeded in increasing enrolment, and other measures of school quantity, the difficult task of improving school quality and achievement levels remains. The government has advocated further decentralization of school administration to village governments as a means of ensuring improvements in quality. Enhancing local accountability of schools and schooling staff is likely to generate some efficiency gains. However, it is unlikely that communities characterized by significant levels of private schooling will devote themselves to improving the quality of government schools. Improvements in school quality, as well as reductions in schooling inequalities and regional schooling gaps, may require a mix of centralized and decentralized control, with the extent of each varying with the socio-economic characteristics of the region.

ANJINI KOCHAR

REFERENCES

Drèze, Jean and Amartya Sen. 1995. *India: Economic Development and Social Opportunity*, Delhi, Oxford University Press.

Kochar, Anjini. 2004. 'Reducing Social Gaps in Schooling: Caste and the Differential Effect of School Construction Programs in Rural India', Stanford University, manuscript.

Myrdal, Gunnar. 1968. *Asian Drama: An Inquiry into the Poverty of Nations*, New York, The Twentieth Century Fund.

PROBE. 1999. *Public Report on Basic Education*, New Delhi, Oxford University Press.

Weiner, Myron. 1991. *The Child and the State in India*, Princeton, Princeton University Press.

Public Distribution System

The public distribution system (PDS) refers to a network of retail outlets (popularly known as 'ration shops') through which the government sells grain (principally rice and wheat) and kerosene. The scope of this entry is restricted to the PDS for grain. Grain sales occur at a fixed price called 'issue' price that is typically lower than market price. Two conditions govern the sale of subsidized grain. First, the buyer of grain must possess a 'ration card'. Second, grain purchases are subject to a quota. The PDS is supported by a procurement operation that obtains and funnels supplies to the PDS. Through the Food Corporation of India (FCI), the government procures grain at the 'procurement' price and then stores and transports it to the various consuming locations.

Till the late 1960s, the principal policy question was how food could be procured cheaply. Towards this end, the government imposed mandatory levies on rice mills, instituted zoning regulations on movement of grain from surplus to deficit areas (so that prices are lower in the surplus zones), prohibited external trade except on government account, and severely curtailed large trading operations through 'anti-hoarding' controls on stocks.

The food policy context changed in the 1970s with the technological breakthroughs of the green revolution. Earlier concerns about movements in inter-sectoral terms of trade adverse to industry faded away. With large food surpluses, declining real prices of food grains, and greater political clout of farmers, the emphasis of food distribution shifted to support of farmgate prices, stabilization, and subsidy for lower-income groups. Food subsidy as a major item of government expenditures made its appearance around this time. In recent years, the principal policy issue for the government has been to find acceptable ways to cap the food subsidy. Issues that are current in the policy debate are the efficacy and impact of food-subsidy expenditures.

ISSUES IN INTERVENTION

In principle, food market interventions are supposed to enhance the efficiency of food markets as well as improve the equity of food market outcomes. The efficiency effect arises from price stabilization. As private storage of food grains is typically unprofitable across years, markets do not provide price stabilization even though it is socially desirable, as poor risk-averse food consumers cannot obtain credit or insurance against crop failures. The reduction in risk is beneficial to producers as well. Even with stabilization, the market outcome involves unacceptably low food consumption for the poor. The equity objective of food market intervention is to augment the food consumption of such target groups by offering subsidies.

Both these goals could be achieved by procurement, storage, and distribution. To meet the equity goal, the government offers limited quantities of food to poor consumers at subsidized prices. Suppose this requires an annual distribution of 15 million tonnes of grain. The supply of this grain is secured by procurement. However, annual procurement could vary depending on the size of harvest and available stocks. In times of abundant supplies, the government will wish to procure more than 15 million tonnes (and build stocks) while the procurement target would be lower than the distribution target (drawing on stocks) in times of shortfall. Such a scheme could smooth out the inter-temporal variability in crop harvests with the exception of very unusual circumstances such as a sequence of record harvests or a series of disastrous crop failures.

In practice, food market interventions rarely approximate the ideal. The goal of stabilization is to steady prices around their mean. However, technological progress and Engel's law (that demand for food grows slower than income) typically tend to decrease the relative price of food. As a result, interventions that try to stabilize with reference to historical supply levels tend to carry too much stock. A greater difficulty is that price stabilization of foodcrops leads producers to allocate resources away from non-food crops to food crops. Such a supply response also calls for adjusting interventions to higher supply levels. However, as market interventions develop political interests, price stabilization is eroded by the politics of supporting producer incomes.

On the distribution side, the issue is that while the poor can be counted (by means of surveys), it is not easy to identify them. The difficulty is that the criteria to identify the poor cannot be those that can be claimed

or mimicked by the non-poor. Targeting schemes usually involve a trade-off between errors of exclusion (when some members of the target group are excluded from subsidies because of stringent targeting criteria) and errors of inclusion (when some members of non-target groups receive subsidies because of minimal targeting criteria). Subsidies with universal access (as was the case with the PDS prior to 1997) minimize exclusion errors but maximize inclusion errors.

THE FOOD SUBSIDY

The food subsidy arises from government procurement and distribution of two commodities: wheat and rice. Significantly, coarse cereals (*bajra* and *jowar*) do not receive subsidies even though, in some states, they are major components of food budgets of poor households. In the past subsidies have been offered on other commodities such as edible oils and most notably sugar. These are now unimportant. The food subsidy consists of two components. The first component is the distribution subsidy that comes about from the fact that the difference between the issue price (at which the government sells) and the procurement price is not enough to cover the costs of distribution. The second component is the cost of carrying buffer stocks.

Between 1971–2 and 2001–2, the food subsidy has averaged a little less than 0.5 per cent of the GDP. Broken up by decade, the food subsidy has increased over this period and is nearly 0.6 per cent of the gross domestic product (GDP) in the decade leading up to 2001–2. In recent years, the food subsidy has risen sharply above the historical averages (to nearly 0.9 per cent of the GDP) and it remains to be seen whether this rise is permanent or transitory. Relative to government expenditures on health and education (including all governments—states and central), the level of food subsidy is 46 per cent and 17 per cent respectively (in the 1990s). The food subsidy accounts for about 7.3 per cent of the tax revenues of the central government. This indicates the pressure of the food subsidy on central government finances, as it is an expenditure of the central government alone.

The division of the food subsidy into the distribution and buffer stock subsidy varies from year to year. However, it is not uncommon at all for the buffer stock subsidy to exceed the distribution subsidy. Indeed, this has been the typical pattern in the late 1990s. This happens whenever the government carries large stocks.

STABILIZATION

In an economy where the government stabilizes annual supplies, procurement and public distribution sales should balance over the span of a crop cycle (typically about five–six years). This was indeed the case over the two decades between 1972–3 and 1991–2. However, since 1992–3, procurement has been consistently larger than public distribution sales. As a result, grain stocks rose sharply towards the end of the 1990s. This in turn inflated the buffer stock subsidy and hence the aggregate food subsidy.

The failure of stabilization and the accumulation of stocks are commonly attributed to the political clout of the farm lobby. Grain surpluses are regionally concentrated—in Punjab, Haryana, Uttar Pradesh, and Andhra Pradesh. In the 1990s, it is argued, these states were able to exercise greater influence over the procurement prices determined by the central government because of the formation of coalition governments at the centre. While political interests have undoubtedly developed around the government's market intervention, there are other factors as well.

Once public stocks get large, it can be hard to get back to sustainable levels because

of price expectations. For a grain seller, the opportunity cost of sale to the government is the market price of grain but at a later point in time (as the procurement price is fixed at the same level throughout the year). Price expectations are in turn dependent on future government actions. When government stocks are large, it is natural to expect future sales from these stocks (open market sales is one of the ways by which the government brings down stocks from unwanted levels), which reduces private storage. Indeed, stocks can be so large that private stocks might not be carried at all as it happened in the wheat market in 2001 when the wheat stocks with the government were equivalent to the annual market supplies. Grain stocks were brought down by a combination of special measures including subsidized exports, expanded welfare programmes, and open market sales as well as the fortuitous circumstance of a drought in 2002–3.

REACHING THE POOR

In 1999–2000, 36 per cent of poor households (that is households with expenditures less than poverty line) report purchases of rice or wheat from the PDS. The corresponding figure for non-poor households is 31 per cent. If rural and urban sectors are considered separately, the PDS participation rate of poor rural households is no different from that of non-poor rural households (at 35 per cent). The small disparity in overall participation rates is driven by the urban sector where 37 per cent of poor households access the PDS as against 23 per cent of all non-poor households. These figures establish that while the PDS includes significant numbers of the non-poor, it also excludes the bulk of the poor.

Within this overall picture, there are noteworthy regional differences. More than 70 per cent of the poor use the PDS in Andhra Pradesh, Karnataka, Kerala, and

Tamil Nadu. Between 50 and 60 per cent of the poor use the PDS in Assam, Gujarat, Maharashtra, and Orissa. Participation rates of the poor vary between 6 and 22 per cent in Bihar, Madhya Pradesh, Rajasthan, and Uttar Pradesh. As for the non-poor, their participation rates are lower than those of the poor. Across states, the correlation between participation rates of the poor and non-poor is 0.98. This has led some analysts to conclude that the interests of the poor lie in universal subsidy schemes rather than targeted schemes.

Case studies have thrown up a variety of reasons for low participation rates of the poor such as the difficulty of obtaining ration cards, limited liquidity of poor households (as ration entitlements can be accessed only once every fortnight rather than continuously), uncertain ration supplies, inferior quality of PDS grain, inconvenient location of PDS shops, and the slender subsidy offered in most states. Lack of geographical access to the PDS network seems to be a powerful factor inhibiting participation. States where households have easy access to PDS shops are also the states with high participation rates.

Using expenditure surveys, researchers (Parikh 1994 and others) have computed the subsidy received by households as the product of the quantity purchased and the difference between the market price and PDS sale price. This is a partial equilibrium measure, as an ideal measure would use the market price that would have obtained in the absence of a PDS. Following the work of Dantwala (1967) and others, there is a presumption that a procurement plus PDS regime increases market prices. This essentially stems from the income effect on demand from subsidies. If this reasoning is correct, the partial equilibrium measure overestimates the subsidies received by households.

However, the bias is of no practical consequence as the partial measures show the received subsidy to be small. In rural areas and for the bottom four expenditure deciles, subsidies account for about 1–2 per cent of total household expenditure. The similar range for urban areas is 0.7–1.5 per cent. As a proportion of cereal expenditure alone, the subsidy is in the range of 6–7 per cent. The southern states depart significantly from the national picture. For instance, in Kerala, the state with the widest network of PDS outlets and the highest participation rates, the received subsidy is about 50 per cent of the cereal expenditure of poor households.

These figures suggest that if one is seeking to establish the impact of food subsidies on food consumption and nutritional status, then one should look at the southern states. Tarozzi (2005) investigates this question for Andhra Pradesh and concludes that even here the impact of the PDS on food security of poor households is likely to be limited.

POLICY RESPONSE

Prior to 1997, entitlement to the PDS was not contingent on household characteristics. The most significant policy initiative in reforming food policy was the introduction of the targeted PDS (TPDS) in 1997. In the TPDS, subsidies are restricted to below poverty line (BPL) households. Identification of the poor is the responsibility of state governments. A profound consequence of the TPDS is that it ties the central government subsidy to the BPL population within a state. Hence, with this arrangement, the government has bounded the distribution subsidy component of the food subsidy and can expect that it will decline with falling poverty. Very likely, the next reform will be that of the procurement process where the government will look to end its open-ended commitment to purchasing grain at the procurement price.

The impact of the TPDS on targeting is an open question as the consumption survey data that could answer it are not yet available. Critics of the TPDS, however, believe that identification is a difficult process and would lead to large exclusion errors. Moreover, by shrinking the PDS to serve the poor, they fear it would affect the economic viability of the PDS retail outlets. The TPDS also overlooks the possibility of subsidizing commodities particularly favoured by the poor such as coarse cereals. Targeting could improve as the non-poor voluntarily opt out (Dutta and Ramaswami 2004). Other analysis has shown that the food subsidy is expensive not just because of transfers to the non-poor but also because of fraud (because of illegal diversions of grain to the market) and excess distribution costs of the PDS (relative to the private sector) (Dutta and Ramaswami 2001). These findings question the deep involvement of the government and its agencies in physically handling the grain. Food coupons or food stamps are an alternative way to deliver food subsidies through the private sector.

The future of food subsidy programmes is unlikely to lie in a centralized PDS. A regionally differentiated safety net of food subsidies (but financed primarily by central government funds) is likely to offer more opportunities for designing and delivering subsidies appropriate to local consumption patterns and capabilities.

BHARAT RAMASWAMI

REFERENCES

Dantwala, M.K. 1967. 'Incentives and Disincentives in Indian Agriculture', *Indian Journal of Agricultural Economics*, 22: 1–25.

Dutta, Bhaskar and Bharat Ramaswami. 2001. 'Targeting and Efficiency in the Public Distribution System: Case of Andhra Pradesh and Maharashtra', *Economic and Political Weekly*, 36(18): 1524–32.

———. 2004. 'Reforming Food Subsidy Schemes: Estimating the Gains from Self-Targeting in India', *Review of Development Economics*, 8(2): 309–24.

Parikh, Kirit. 1994. 'Who Gets How Much from PDS—How Effectively Does it Reach the Poor?', *Sarvekshana*, January–March.

Tarozzi, A. 2005. 'The Indian Public Distribution System as Provider of Food Security: Evidence from Child Nutrition in Andhra Pradesh', *European Economic Review*, 49: 1305–30.

[Note: Owing to the limit on the number of references allowed per entry, the reader is referred for detailed references to the version of this entry on www.econ.worldbank.org.]

Public Health

WHAT IS PUBLIC HEALTH, AND WHY INVEST IN IT?

Public health services are conceptually distinct from medical services. Reducing a population's *exposure* to disease is their key goal—for example through assuring food safety and other health regulations; vector control; monitoring waste disposal and water systems; and health education to improve personal health behaviours and build citizen demand for better public health outcomes. Thus they involve such disparate activities as improving slaughterhouse hygiene and cattle-keeping practices, cleaning irrigation canals to discourage vector breeding, and applying public health regulations.

Public health services produce 'public goods' of incalculable benefit for facilitating economic growth and poverty reduction. Consider, for example, the long-term growth possibilities generated by draining the malarial swamps of Washington D.C. And conversely, consider the global economic costs imposed by the avian flu and SARS (severe acute respiratory syndrome) epidemics, emanating from poor poultry-keeping and health practices in a few Chinese localities. In India, the 1994 plague epidemic following poor municipal sanitation in Surat is estimated by the World Health Organization (WHO 2000) to have resulted in losses totalling up to $2 billion.

Poor public health conditions take economic toll in various ways, including reduced attraction for investors and tourists; continued expenditures on combating diseases which should have become history; and labour productivity losses. The poor pay a high price in debility, reduced earning capacity, and death. The rich suffer little mortality from communicable diseases, but nevertheless suffer repeated episodes of morbidity which are reflected in high rates of stunting amongst their children.

It has long been accepted that the most effective approaches to improving population health are those that prevent rather than treat disease. Moreover, they account for a small fraction of the total health budget in most countries. But in India public policies and programmes have focused largely on the provision of curative care and personal prophylactic interventions such as immunization, while public health activities have been relatively neglected. This helps explain why India's health indicators are so much poorer than those of East Asia and much of the rest of the world. Since communicable diseases remain the primary sources of ill-health in India, this discussion will focus on them.

THE EVOLUTION OF PUBLIC HEALTH SERVICES IN THE DEVELOPED WORLD

In developed countries, the need for effective public health services was triggered partly by military concerns, since army casualties from disease were far higher than from battle.

Elites also had a stake in disease control because cure was uncertain until antibiotics began to be mass produced in the mid-twentieth century. Besides, business interests were at stake, as illustrated by the massive business losses following a cholera epidemic in Hamburg in 1892.

In the last decades of the nineteenth century, scientists began to identify germs and learn how they cause disease. This led to the 'sanitary movement', which involved radical changes in citizens' health behaviours and private lives, including forgoing keeping livestock in urban areas. Protests arose, ranging from mass protests to the case of the incensed butcher chasing a sanitary inspector down a Chicago street with a knife. The changes had to be implemented not only rigorously (sometimes coercively), but with much attention to persuading citizens as to how better sanitation improved their well-being.

Much effort was devoted to building the organizational and technical infrastructure of public health services and public health engineering. Japan studied European public health services and moved early to emulating them as part of its preparation for becoming a world power, and applied similar measures in its colonies in Korea and Taiwan.

By the mid-twentieth century, the institutions and procedures for preventing exposure to communicable diseases had become well established in the developed world. They had brought about rapid declines in mortality and morbidity. Non-communicable diseases became the major source of ill-health, and the scope of public health services was broadened to control these through lifestyle changes and checking environmental pollution. Nevertheless, public health services continue to be highly successful at communicable disease control, and are overhauled periodically in response to changing circumstances.

PUBLIC HEALTH SERVICES IN COLONIAL INDIA

During the colonial period, public health measures were focused largely on protecting British civilians and army cantonments. There is much debate about whether this resulted from parsimoniousness where Indian well-being was concerned, or fear of triggering hostility by imposing alien practices. In any event, a series of measures ensured that the British lived in residentially segregated areas with good environmental sanitation. Municipal areas were privileged with machinery to assure good sanitary conditions, including the management of water, solid waste, and liquid waste. For towns and rural areas, the services were focused largely on early detection and control of outbreaks of contagious diseases with high fatality rates—such as cholera and the plague—before they could spread and even menace the more privileged populations.

Yet, even for these limited purposes, the colonial authorities built impressive capacity for delivering public health services:

+ Institutions for public health training and research, which ranked amongst the best in the world—most notably the All-India School of Public Health and Hygiene and the Calcutta School of Tropical Medicine. These conducted basic research such as discovering how malaria is transmitted; developed and tested vaccines; and provided technical leadership and support as well as training for the public health authorities.
+ Public health legislation along lines then current in Europe.
+ Sanitary Departments at national and provincial levels for civilian public health services, while military hygiene was under military medical officers. They were answerable directly to the government, and administratively separate from the Indian Medical Service (IMS) which provided medical services.
+ Policymaking and planning for public health services, done systematically to address all major threats to public health. The Sanitary Departments published annual reports with information on disease patterns and associated factors such as seasonal conditions and population movements, and analysed this information to extrapolate the potential for outbreaks for which advance planning might be necessary. Periodic Sanitary Conferences were convened to discuss and refine overall policy thrusts and coordinate policies and implementation between provinces.

The Sanitary Departments were tasked with ascertaining local sanitary conditions and improving them; vital registration; monitoring disease trends; providing technical advice on disease control; and carrying out vaccination programmes. They were expected to detect outbreaks early, trace them to their source, and extinguish them quickly. Their medical staff was on average better qualified and better paid, and had faster promotion avenues than Indian Medical Service staff. Municipal governments hired their own public health staff, consisting of medical doctors, and 'a small army' of supervisors and sanitary inspectors to enforce sanitary regulations. Municipal planning was designed to avert public health threats, for example an elaborate system of drainage in and around the city of Calcutta reduced the risk of malaria.

The spare but systematic colonial approach to public health service provision is reflected in its successes and failures. During the first half of the twentieth century, the mortality spikes from epidemics were sharply reduced. By the end of the colonial era mortality from diseases such as cholera and the plague had fallen sharply, but diseases such as malaria and gastroenteric infections continued to take heavy toll. Independent India's First Five Year Plan notes that only 3 per cent of households in India had toilets, and that much of the population lacked basic water, drainage, and waste disposal services.

PUBLIC HEALTH IN INDEPENDENT INDIA

Little remains of the colonial public health arrangements, beside an impressive capacity to control outbreaks once they have occurred. The capacity to *prevent* outbreaks has atrophied. By 1950, much had changed both globally and in India, which led to this atrophy.

+ Techniques for mass production of antibiotics were refined during the 1940s. This made it possible for local elites to protect themselves from dying of communicable diseases, without having to maintain rigorous environmental hygiene to prevent exposure to disease for rich and poor alike. The developed world also became better able to protect itself from the prospect of epidemics spreading from the developing world, and the focus of medical research shifted away from finding new technologies for communicable disease control—except when threatened by newly emergent diseases against which they have no protection, such as avian flu.
+ The public health successes achieved in the developed world meant that by the 1940s their main causes of death shifted from communicable to non-communicable diseases such as cardiovascular diseases and cancer. At the same time, advances in medical technology offered the promise of managing these diseases through clinical and surgical interventions. The glamour and status earlier accorded to public health authorities were now accorded to medical doctors. The intellectual cutting edge shifted from improving public health systems to improving curative technologies and methods of healthcare financing.
+ Multilateral and other donor agencies have encouraged creation of separate institutional structures and programmes for controlling specific communicable diseases, thereby facilitating the clear identification of project inputs and outcomes but discouraging the building of health systems that seek to use resources as they are needed to improve public health outcomes.
+ The spread of democratic institutions also affected public health services, because electorates typically prefer public funds to be used to provide private goods (such as medical care), rather than public goods (such as sanitary measures to protect the health of the population as a whole). Selling a public health success electorally requires creativity, since the successes are by nature negative ('no cases of typhoid last year' does not hit the headlines, while advances in surgical techniques is big news). In the developed world, this means that public health authorities have to fight to ensure adequate funding, while in the developing world it can lead to serious neglect of public health services. It is notable that the non-democratic regimes of East Asia were the most successful in the developing world in improving health outcomes, by focusing their scarce resources on public health measures rather than on providing advanced medical care.
+ Elite capture also plays a role. In India, more than in most developing countries, public funds for health and education have been funnelled towards tertiary rather than primary levels. Substantial proportions of the health budgets have been spent on expanding

subsidized medical training, public-sector employment for medical graduates, and high-end tertiary medical services—all of which largely benefit the middle classes and detract from the provision of public health services.

Several policy thrusts of the newly independent India also detracted from public health service provision. To begin with, the overarching policy vision emphasized developing heavy industry rather than health and education. Public health services were merged with the medical services in the 1950s. Qualifications in specialty curative skills became far better rewarded than public health qualifications, and attracted the best talent. Gradually senior positions were filled by people with no training or experience in public health, poorly equipped and poorly motivated to manage public health activities. The demand for as well as supply of public health training atrophied. The atrophy was further sped by the fact that it is politically much easier to respond to budget constraints by cutting (the relatively invisible) public health positions and activities, while expanding the curative services for which there is strong electoral demand.

Moreover, an inconsistency in Constitutional provisions starved public health systems of funds. Public health services were designated as the responsibility of the state governments, except for issues such as port quarantine and provisions relating to the spread of diseases between states. At the same time, the Constitutional fiscal provisions require states to hand over the bulk of their tax revenues to the central government. The central health authorities leverage their funds by requiring states to provide co-financing for many of their programmes. This leaves little fiscal room for states to operate programmes for which there is little support from the central government, such as assuring environmental sanitation and other core functions of a public health system.

The resulting atrophy of public health services is manifested in many ways, including:

a) *Neglect of public health regulations and their implementation:* Public Health Acts, which constitute the legislative framework for public health service provision, have not been updated and rationalized since the colonial era. For example, five decades after Karnataka state was created out of several contiguous kingdoms and provinces, it has not developed a unified and updated Public Health Act—those for each constituent part from the colonial era are still on the books. In Tamil Nadu, the Madras Presidency's Public Health Act of 1939 was still in place in 1999. The central government developed a Model Public Health Act in 1950 and revised it in 1987, but did not influence the states to adopt it. As in the colonial period, major municipal areas continue to be privileged, in that they still have public health regulations in place, and some staff and facilities for implementing them. These are much less in evidence in small towns, and even less in rural areas.

The Prevention of Food Adulteration Act is one of the few pieces of public health legislation that is still widely known to be in force. However, the Act has several serious deficiencies that prevent it from effectively ensuring food safety, not the least the fact that it focuses almost exclusively on food adulteration. In a large volume of detailed regulation, only a few paragraphs pertain to food hygiene. Besides, the Act is geared more towards punishing offenders than towards helping businesses understand and comply with the regulations. Given the very limited funds available to inspectors for purchasing food samples for testing, and the slow disposal of court cases, it is apparent to food sellers that the law is short on credibility. Food inspectors are also a shrinking category of staff, as they are of low priority for cash-strapped states.

b) *Diversion of funds from public health services:* The distortionary implications of the fiscal and planning regime are illustrated by the effects of the family planning programme. In the mid-1960s, the Indian government embarked on a massive effort to reduce population growth in the country, following some years of food shortages and census results showing that population growth rates had accelerated sharply. To deliver sterilization and other contraceptive services, the network of public clinics was rapidly expanded. The central government is generous in supporting the family planning programme, for example by covering the salaries of female outreach staff. The proportion of the central government health budget spent on this programme has risen sharply, at the expense of other health programmes. However, the states have to pay for maintaining the clinics and the salaries of doctors and other staff.

This heavy financial burden for the states has led to a progressive strangulation of funds for what ought to be routine public health services, to the point where these are often vestigial at best. For example, in West Bengal, the posts of Sanitary Inspectors are largely vacant. Across the country, there is a trend for the posts of male health workers also to be vacant, since their salaries have to be met by the state governments.

Unfocused labour policies add to the problems, with the emphasis often more strongly on protecting labour than on assuring an appropriately qualified workforce. For example, in West Bengal, malaria workers' job security was assured by absorbing them into the cadre of male health workers. Thus many of the precious

slots left in this important but underfinanced and dying cadre of public health staff are occupied by people who lack the required qualifications. Moreover, the staff suffers from the atrophying of public health training. For example, the District Sanitary Inspector of a large district said that in thirty-three years of service he had received almost no training in public health.

c) *Organizational changes inimical to maintaining public health:* Other problems arise from making health primarily a state responsibility, while building a 'command and control' framework of centralized planning backed by fiscal dependence of the states on the centre. The central government is the key actor in designing health policies and programmes, partly because state budgets are highly constrained as already described. However, the central government focuses on planning specific programmes, such as malaria eradication or family planning. This means that the bulk of the funds allocated by the central Health Ministry to the states is tied to specific programmes and categories of expenditure within those programmes, and states are not free to reallocate the funds to issues that may be of higher local priority.

A related problem is that there is very limited scope for making overall reviews of public health policies, fine-tuning their implementation, and rationalizing the use of resources, which had been done in the colonial era through forums such as the Sanitary Conferences. The demise of a public health system means that there is also inadequate inter-sectoral coordination, which further wastes resources. For example, the health department has limited recourse if the irrigation department generates malaria by leaving a canal half-finished and waterlogged, but once an epidemic breaks out it will be called in to step up clinical services to handle the problem. A multiplicity of agencies is able to work on parallel tracks or even at cross-purposes. These trends are further encouraged by donors, as discussed earlier.

Public health planning and implementation have become ad hoc in ways deeply inimical to effective functioning. For example, it quickly became the norm for health programmes to be conducted on a 'campaign' basis. This means, in practice, that when a specific issue enjoys high priority a lot of resources are diverted towards it, and the obverse. However, public health cannot be sustained on a 'campaign' basis. Much can be achieved in a campaign, but the benefits can be short-lived without continuing arrangements for identifying and responding to any remaining or imported threats. For example, there are a few cases of many communicable diseases every year in the US, but through constant vigilance they are confined and stamped out.

The history of public health since 1950 in India illustrates that the organization of services is conducive to successful campaigns followed by unsuccessful 'maintenance' phases of disease control programmes. For one thing, with the exception of female health workers (who are earmarked for family planning service delivery), other health personnel are considered to be 'multipurpose'. In principle this is a good idea, but in practice it means that they are allocated to whatever is deemed a priority at the time and discouraged from other activities such as maintaining the gains from earlier efforts.

This is searingly illustrated by the fact that India came very close to eradicating malaria through a highly successful campaign in the 1950s—but then the programme was put into a 'maintenance phase' and malaria resurged. This resurgence has often been attributed to the emergence of DDT-resistant strains of mosquitoes, though it

is clear that the government does not really believe this since it continues to use DDT as a main line of defence against malaria. Less attention has been paid to the shortcomings in programme design. In the 1950s, the malaria control programme was carefully organized, but attention to programme organization suffered subsequently. For example, the current programme is formulated such that the central government provides the DDT, drugs, and other supplies, while the state government is primarily responsible for the manpower costs. Not uncommonly the states are unable to afford the manpower to adequately supervise the spraying activities and prepare communities in advance so that they can plaster their homes before the spraying rather than plastering over the DDT. Besides, manpower is diverted: for example an ORG (Operations Research Group) study found that frontline staff was preoccupied with family planning work at the expense of malaria supervision at critical times.

The Five Year Plans document the rapid shift away from a public-health-oriented focus in independent India. Even though little was done on sanitation in the 1950s, the Plans clearly recognized its importance for controlling communicable diseases. Water and sanitation were an integral part of the chapter on health planning, and sanitary inspectors figured as an important cadre of frontline staff. By the 1960s, water and sanitation had been separated out as belonging outside the health sector, and there was little further mention of sanitary inspectors in the Plans.

The reduced focus on public health outcomes was also reflected in other ways in the Plans. For example, there is a striking difference between the discussions of the health programmes and of the high-priority family planning programme. In successive Plans, the sections on health are concerned with inputs and the current priority thrusts such as universal immunization. For the rest, there is a typically desultory account of policies and programmes. Analysis of shortfalls is often devoid of suggested remedies, as in the case of the Ninth Plan on malaria. Even lip-service ceases to be paid to important issues—for example the new strategies for malaria control make no mention of environmental management.

By contrast, the sections on family planning begin with a careful review of programme performance, reasons for shortfalls, and how to overcome them. The need for operational research is highlighted, as well as creative suggestions for generating greater demand for family planning. Indeed, the programme developed a highly successful Information, Education and Communication (IEC) campaign to change people's desired family size and bolster programme success. Similar efforts have been made in the health sector only sporadically, and typically to bolster campaign efforts such as immunization, rather than seeking to radically alter people's health behaviour to reduce their exposure to communicable diseases.

ENCOURAGING TRENDS FOR THE FUTURE

There are many reasons to be hopeful that public health may receive more attention in the near future. Financing is available through large programmes, for example the Rural Health Mission, National Sanitation Mission, and the renewed support for the Employment Guarantee Scheme. If implemented creatively, these programmes can be used to improve public health outcomes. For example in the US, the Depression era food-for-work programmes were used to eradicate malaria from large parts of the South. The success of this effort resulted from careful planning and overseeing of the work by teams of

sanitary engineers, entomologists, and administrators.

Institutions are also being built at local and national levels which can play powerful roles in public health. The Panchayati Raj Act has placed emphasis on building local government and devolving health activities to it. This makes it possible to build institutions for managing public health activities on the ground, with the requisite inter-sectoral coordination. States such as West Bengal and Kerala are experimenting with these possibilities in ways that can serve as models for other states.

At national level, a new thrust is to build an institution modelled on the US Centers for Disease Control. This model has been adapted across the world, most recently by China and the European Union; the latter recognizes that the public health systems of its component countries need to be coordinated and supported by a 'federal' authority. If designed creatively, this could transform the way that the central government shapes and supports public health services in India. In a large federal country, the key roles of such a central agency include monitoring trends, research, advocacy, and helping states fill specific service gaps with targeted financial and technical help.

India has exceptional capacity to deliver services, as evidenced by its smooth conduct of elections and censuses across a vast population including pavement dwellers and remote villages. Its inattention to public health is taking a large toll on its economy, as well as on the lives of its citizens, and it is time to recognize that public health is a key part of its development infrastructure.

MONICA DAS GUPTA

REFERENCES

Das Gupta, Monica and Manju Rani. 2005. 'How Well Does India's Federal Government

Perform its Essential Public Health Functions?', The World Bank Policy Research Working Paper No. 3447, Washington D.C., *Health Policy*.

Easterlin, Richard A. 2004. 'How Beneficient Is the Market? A Look at the Modern History of Mortality', in *The Reluctant Economist: Perspectives on Economics, Economic History and Demography*, Cambridge, Cambridge University Press.

Harrison, Mark. 1994. *Public Health in British India: Anglo-Indian Preventive Medicine 1859–1914*, Cambridge, Cambridge University Press.

Institute of Medicine. 2002. *The Future of the Public's Health in the 21ˢᵗ Century*, Washington, D.C., National Academy Press.

Jeffrey, Roger. 1988. The *Politics of Health in India*, Berkeley, University of California Press.

World Health Organization. 2000. 'The Hidden Cost of Outbreaks', *Bulletin of the World Health Organization*, 78(11). http://www.who.int/doestore/bulletin/Thismonth/november.htm.

Secondary Education

While much has been written about the problems and achievements of primary education in India, far less is known about secondary education, largely because the latter has not benefited from large-scale investment programmes such as the District Primary Education Programme or the Sarva Shiksha Abhiyan which have targeted primary grades. Yet, evidence suggests that secondary education is more important than primary for productivity and earnings: the wage increment from an extra year of secondary schooling is significantly higher than that from an extra year of primary schooling, that is, the pattern of returns to education is convex, with low returns at primary level and progressively greater returns at the secondary and tertiary levels of education in India. Presumably the

Indian government's increased attention to secondary education in the Eleventh Plan (2007) is a result of several factors: the recognition that prosperity increasingly comes from post-primary education; primary school enrolment having become close to universal (notwithstanding the acute problem of poor learning levels); and the disadvantageous comparison with countries in the BRIC grouping (Brazil, Russia, India, China) with which India is increasingly compared. For example, evidence in Kingdon (2007) shows that India's youth literacy rate in the early 2000s was 22.5 percentage points behind China's and the proportion of its population with completed secondary and post-secondary schooling is more than thirty years behind China's (that is, China achieved India's current level more than thirty years ago). India's secondary school net enrolment rates are 27 percentage points behind Brazil's and Russia's and 28 points behind China's.

While the base of India's education pyramid (primary and secondary education) may be weak, it has emerged as an important player in the worldwide information technology revolution on the back of substantial (absolute) numbers of well-educated computing and other graduates. The challenge now is to strengthen the base, without neglecting tertiary education.

ACCESS TO SECONDARY EDUCATION

Table 1 shows gross enrolment ratios (GERs) in lower and upper secondary education in India in 1999 and 2005. It shows a rapid increase of 10 percentage points in both lower secondary GER (from 61 to 71 per cent) and upper secondary GER (from 31 to 41 per cent). It also shows a great improvement in gender equity, particularly at the lower secondary level where girls' participation increased by 14 points over this short six-year period.

Table 1   Gross Enrolment Rates in Secondary
Education, India

	Total	Male	Female	Gender parity index
Lower secondary				
2005	70.5	74.9	65.7	0.88
1999	61.2	70.1	51.5	0.73
Upper secondary				
2005	40.9	46.4	35.0	0.75
1999	31.0	37.0	24.5	0.66

Source: Table 8, Statistical Tables from 2009
'Education for All' Global Monitoring Report,
UNESCO, Paris.

Demand for secondary education has
risen rapidly because it has high economic
payoffs in the Indian labour market, and
because these payoffs have been increasing
over time. Estimates based on National
Sample Survey (NSS) data from 1999 and
2005 find that the wage increment from each
extra year of secondary education (around 20
per cent) and from each extra year of tertiary
education (15 per cent) is significantly
greater than that from each extra year of
primary education (8 per cent) (Kingdon
2007). Moreover, the returns to higher
secondary and tertiary education have *risen*
consistently over time, while the returns to
primary education have fallen (for women)
or remained static (for men) (Riboud et
al. 2007). Finally, the non-market returns
to girls' secondary education (in terms of
lower fertility and infant mortality) are much
higher than those to girls' primary education.

The very high returns to secondary
education raise the puzzle why secondary
school participation is not higher in India.
It seems there are some supply-side barriers.
According to the Seventh All India Education
Survey, in 2002, there were only one-fifth
as many secondary schools (those with
Grade 10 classes) as the number of primary

schools. Thus, it seems likely that secondary
school enrolment rates are low partly because
of the lack of supply of nearby secondary
schools. A demand-side factor that likely
militates against higher secondary school
participation is the high cost of schooling.
Table 2 shows that households incur a great
deal of expenditure in educating a child even
in the government school sector which is
meant to impart free tuition, and that the
expenditure rises steeply with the level of
education. Expenditure on private tutoring is
important, constituting 13 per cent of total
education expenditure in government and
aided secondary schools and 10 per cent in
private schools. Given a national per capita
income of Rs 10,149 in 1995–6 (see http://
planning.up.nic.in/ annualplan0607/vol1/
Annex-chap-28.pdf), household expenditure
on a child's lower secondary education in a
government school (Rs 1058) was about 10
per cent of per capita income. At the upper
secondary level, it constituted 18 per cent of
per capita income. Expenditure on a child's
education in aided and private schools is
even greater. This suggests that even in the
publicly funded part of the schooling system,
private costs are an important barrier to
secondary schooling participation for those
from poor backgrounds. The poor may not
be able to borrow for secondary education
despite its high returns because of imperfect
credit markets.

Table 2   Annual Household Expenditure on
Education 1995–6
(in rupees, by level of education)

	Govt	Aided	Private	Total
Primary	269	1186	1431	507
Upper primary	639	1350	2159	921
Secondary	1058	1565	2759	1333
Senior secondary	1831	2553	3698	2257
Tertiary	2683	3416	5509	3164

Source: Author's calculations from National Sample
Survey 52nd Round, 1995–6.

INEQUALITY IN ACCESS TO SECONDARY EDUCATION

While gender inequality in secondary access has fallen over time (see Table 1), there is much inter-state variation in the size of the gender gap. The gender parity index is the female to male secondary school enrolment ratio. A ratio of 1 represents gender equality. States such as Bihar and Rajasthan have grotesque gender inequality: girls are only half as likely to enrol in secondary school as boys. Uttar Pradesh, Madhya Pradesh, Jharkhand, and Chhattisgarh also have severe gender inequality but, on the bright side, many states have gender parity or even slightly pro-female secondary enrolment rates, for example, Kerala and Tamil Nadu. Apart from the possibility of gender bias within the schooling system which may discourage girls' secondary school participation, an important part of the reason for gender inequality is to be found within the household itself. Using statistical analysis, Kingdon (2005) finds strong within-family pro-son bias in terms of both secondary school enrolment and educational expenditure. The persistence of these large gender inequalities appears not to reflect gender discrimination in the labour market since the rate of return to education is actually significantly larger for women than men in India (Riboud et al. 2007). Instead, gender inequalities in education more plausibly reflect the fact that some parents continue to believe in traditional gender roles, do not envisage daughters' participation in the labour market, and thus perceive it is futile to invest in girls' secondary education. Conservatism and concern for safety may also play a part in girls' attendance of distant secondary schools.

There is also a good deal of inter-state variation in the extent of *economic* inequality

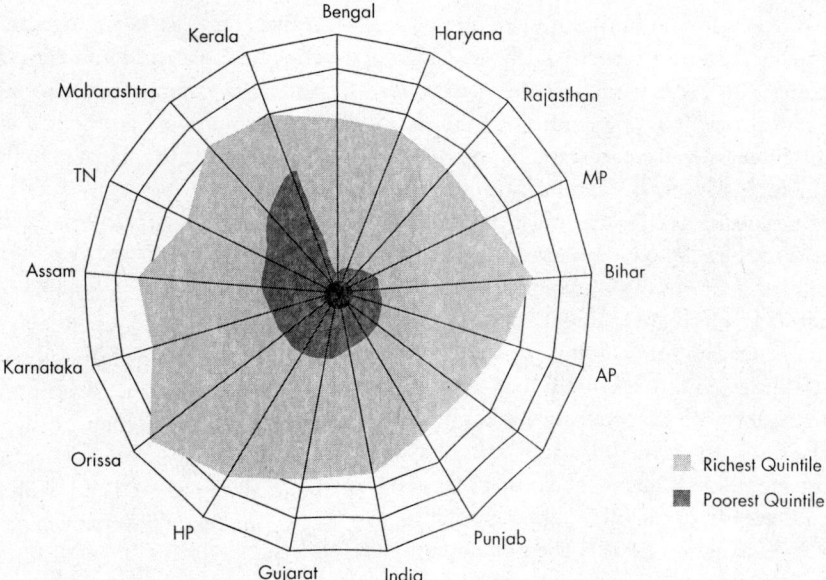

Figure 1   Differential Access to Secondary Schooling, India 1999–2000
(between the top and bottom income quintiles)

Source: World Bank 2009.

in access to secondary schooling, using NSS data for 1999–2000, as seen in Figure 1. The inequality (measured as the difference in access to secondary education among those in the top and bottom quintiles of the distribution of household per capita income) is greatest in Haryana, Andhra Pradesh, and the socially challenged states of Bihar, Madhya Pradesh, Rajasthan, and Uttar Pradesh. It is lowest in the left-leaning states of Kerala and West Bengal.

LEARNING ACHIEVEMENT LEVELS IN SECONDARY EDUCATION

Indian states have their own separate exam boards and set their own curricula; there are no national-level data based on a common standardized achievement test in India. While the Council of Boards of Secondary Education provides pass rates in the High School and Intermediate (senior secondary) examinations in different states (and pass rates in the 2004 High School exam varied from 37 per cent in Manipur to 80 per cent in Andhra Pradesh), such inter-state comparison is meaningless since curricula, exam papers, passing requirements, etc. all differ from state to state. In any case, the high school pass rates cannot be taken at face value as they are much inflated due to the phenomenon of widespread cheating. For example, when a reformist Uttar Pradesh government brought in an anti-cheating rule and installed police at all examination centres in 1992 to prevent the mass cheating that routinely takes place, the pass rate in the UP High School exam fell from 44–57 per cent in the previous four years to a pitiful 14.7 per cent in 1992 (Kingdon 2007). The policing order was withdrawn in later years and the pass percentage has crept back to the mid-40s. This suggests the extent of the problem of low achievement levels in secondary education, though it is possible that learning

achievement levels in Uttar Pradesh are lower than in other states.

India has not take part in any international tests of learning achievement levels since the early 1970s but recently the Ministry of Human Resource Development gave permission for items from the international TIMSS test[1] to be applied in two states. Based on data collected by Kin Bing Wu (World Bank 2009; Wu et al. 2009), Das and Zajonc (2008) place secondary students from Orissa and Rajasthan on a worldwide distribution of mathematics achievement. Tested one year further in school (ninth grade) than their international counterparts (who were tested in eighth grade), they find that India falls below 43 of the 51 countries for which data exists. But not all students test poorly. A proportion of Indian 14-year-olds pass the highest international benchmark and these, in absolute terms, constitute more students than in all but four of the other tested countries taken together. The authors conclude that 'the combination of India's size and large variance in achievement justify both the perceptions that India is shining even as *Bharat*, the vernacular for India, is drowning'.

ROLE OF THE PRIVATE SECTOR IN SECONDARY SCHOOLING

There are three main types of secondary schools in India: government, private aided, and private unaided. Aided schools in many states are like government schools because although they are nominally under private managements, their teachers are generally appointed and paid directly by the government, at government school salary

[1]For TIMSS, see http://nces.ed.gov/timss/. For PIRLS, see http://timss.bc.edu/pirls2001.html. For SACMEQ, see Southern and Eastern Africa Consortium for Monitoring Educational Quality http://www.sacmeq.org/.

Table 3   Enrolment Share of Different School Types at Secondary Level (by region and year)

Type	Rural				Urban			
	1978	1986	1993	2002	1978	1986	1993	2002
Govt	34	45	49	44	39	37	39	33
Aided	64	52	44	40	57	54	49	43
Private	2	4	7	16	4	9	11	24

Source: All India Education Surveys, various years.

rates. Unaided schools are truly private in the sense of having autonomy over hiring/firing and pay decisions.

There is little evidence on the quality of public, aided, and private schools at secondary level in India except for two recent World Bank surveys of secondary schools: a 2004 survey of 253 schools in Rajasthan and Orissa and a 2008 survey of 1400 private aided and unaided schools in nine states. The latter shows no major difference in school facilities (classroom infrastructure, laboratories, toilets) between aided and unaided schools, and reveals that teachers in unaided schools are equally qualified academically as peers in aided schools, though they are slightly less likely to have pre-service teacher training. However, the average salary of unaided school teachers in 2007 was one-third that of aided school teachers (Rs 5000 versus Rs 15,000 per month). Given that school costs are primarily driven by teachers' salaries, this suggests that overall unit costs of unaided schools are considerably lower than those of aided schools. At the same time, students in unaided schools did better in Board Examinations than their peers in aided schools, and were more likely to score in the first division, though this may partly be due to their better home backgrounds. Moreover, principals in unaided schools were less likely to cite any constraints or limitations to improving educational quality in their school (World Bank 2009). Unfortunately, no private–public comparisons are available of other indicators of school quality, for example, data on teacher attendance rates and teachers' time on task for secondary schools.

Perceived better quality of education in private schools is presumably what explains the steep increase in the share of private schools in total secondary school enrolment over time seen in Table 3. The increase in private secondary school demand is higher in urban than in rural areas. By 2002, 16 per cent of rural and about a quarter of all urban secondary students attended private unaided schools.

The growth of private schooling—though slower at the secondary than at primary education level—signals growing inequality of educational opportunity. The expansion of private schooling suggests not only that the quality of public education is poor but also that inequality (both in terms of access and quality of education) must be growing since the poor cannot afford private school fees.

PUBLIC POLICY TOWARDS SECONDARY EDUCATION

After decades of post-Independence focus on elementary education, the Indian government in its Eleventh Five Year Plan (2007–12) gave special attention to secondary education. The Eleventh Plan has seen the launch of the Rashtriya Madhyamik Shiksha Abhiyan (RMSA) or National Secondary Education Mission. This centrally sponsored scheme aims to (a) universalize access to secondary schooling in the age group 15–16 by 2015 by providing a secondary school within 5 km and a higher secondary school within 7 km of all habitations, and (b) universalize retention in secondary education by 2020. The strategies that have been laid down for the achievement of these goals are to upgrade upper primary schools and strengthen existing secondary schools through construction of classrooms, labs, computer rooms, separate toilets for girls and boys, and the appointment of additional teachers; the provision of special incentives to girls, minority groups, and other 'weaker section' groups—these could be freeships, scholarships, free uniforms, etc., as in primary education; and quality improvements via providing in-service training of teachers, curricular reforms, computer-aided education, teaching-learning aids, leadership training of school heads, and science and maths education. The central government has committed Rs 20,868 crore for non-recurring and Rs 35,567 crore for recurring expenditures related to the RMSA by 2012. By 2020, the requirement will be greater.

Increasing access without quality is meaningless and quality does not come from mere construction of classrooms and provision of inputs such as teachers and books: it is well known that despite these inputs, learning levels are extremely low in primary education. Accountability and incentive structures need to be re-thought. To the extent that private schools provide better accountability mechanisms for teachers, it is encouraging that of the planned 11,000 new schools in the country's 6000 blocks, those in 3500 blocks will be supervised by the government and in the remaining 2500 blocks through private–public partnership (PPP) arrangements, engaging the private sector and civil society. But there are different designs of PPPs around the world, some successful, others not, so the challenge is to choose the right type of PPPs for the Indian institutional context. Moreover, availability of comparable learning achievement data across the whole country is a necessary building block for ensuring that quality of secondary education can be tracked. At present due to different exam boards and the lack of a common standardized examination, there is no official mechanism to monitor learning levels in secondary education. Thus, while the RMSA provides an exciting opportunity for advancing secondary education in India, its modalities need to be carefully thought if it is to deliver quality secondary education for all.

GEETA KINGDON

REFERENCES

Das, J. and T. Zajonc. 2008. 'India Shining and Bharat Drowning: Comparing India to the Worldwide Distribution in Mathematics Achievement', Policy Research Working Paper, 4644, World Bank, Washington D.C.

Kingdon, G. 2005. 'Where has All the Bias Gone? Detecting Gender Bias in the Intra-household Allocation of Educational Expenditure in Rural India', Economic Development and Cultural Change, 53(2): 409–52.

———. 2007. 'The Progress of School Education in India', Oxford Review of Economic Policy, 23(2), Summer: 168—95.

Riboud, M., Y. Savchenko, and H. Tan. 2007. 'The Knowledge Economy and Education and Training in South Asia', Human Development Unit, South Asia Region, World Bank, Washington D.C.

World Bank. 2009. 'Secondary Education in India: Universalizing Opportunity', Human Development Unit, South Asia Region, World Bank, Washington D.C.

Wu, K., P. Goldschmidt, C. Boscardin, and D. Sankar. 2009. 'International Benchmarking and Determinants of Mathematics Achievement in Two Indian States', Education Economics, 17(3), September.

APPENDIX

This appendix (prepared by Annemie Maertens) presents a selection of statistics pertaining to the Indian economy and society. Such a short statistical appendix cannot but be idiosyncratic; yet it is our hope that it will be a handy source of reference for the students of India's development and, more generally, of development economics. The main sources for these data are: the *Handbook of Statistics on Indian Economy* published annually by the Reserve Bank of India (RBI), the reports published by the National Accounts Division at the Central Statistical Organisation (CSO), and the *World Development Indicators* (WDI) published annually by the World Bank. Other sources for macroeconomic data include the *Economic Survey*, published annually by the Ministry of Finance, the *Handbook of Monetary Statistics of India*, published annually by the RBI, the *IMF Balance of Payments Database*, and the various UN databases, including FAO Data, LABORSTA, Millennium Development Goals Database, and UNESCO's databases. For an overview of household-, firm-, and district-level data sets refer to the entry Data Sets by Badiani, Sharma, and Himanshu in this edition.

The first set of tables compares India today with the rest of the world in terms of its level of development, as captured by gross domestic product (GDP) as well as other basic indicators of well-being such as literacy and life expectancy. An often-neglected feature of development is its environmental concomitants. Accordingly, we have tried to present some data on the environmental aspects of India's development vis-à-vis other countries, as captured by land-use, energy-use, and emissions data.

The second set of tables presents time-series, macroeconomic aggregates of GDP, savings, investment, and balance of payments. This is followed by disaggregated data on output and employment in India's agricultural, industrial, and service sectors. Further, this section provides some inter-state data on total output, population, literacy, and infrastructure to highlight the regional diversity of India's development. The appendix also presents time-series data on some select indicators of human development, such as education, health, and the incidence of poverty.

In the post-liberalization period, policy emphasis has shifted towards improving the investment climate in the country in order to attract more foreign investment as well as encourage domestic competition. In recent years the World Bank has been collating data on how easy or difficult it is to conduct business in different countries. We present some of this data for India and, for reasons of comparison, Singapore.

Table 1 India among the Nations 2007

Country	Pop. (in 10,000)	GDP (current US$) (in millions)	per capita	Literacy rate, ages 15 and above (%) F	M	T	Life expectancy at birth (years) F	M	T
Afghanistan		8399[a]							
Albania	318	10,831	3405	99	99	99	80	73	76
Algeria	3385	135,285	3996	66	84	75	74	71	72
American Samoa	7								
Andorra	8								
Angola	1695	61,403	3623				44	41	43
Antigua and Barbuda	8	980[a]	11,664[a]						
Argentina	3950	262,451	6644	98	98	98	79	72	75
Armenia	301	9204	3059	99	100	99	75	68	72
Aruba	10			98	98	98			
Australia	2102	820,974	39,066				84	79	81
Austria	832	373,192	44,879				83	77	80
Azerbaijan	856	31,248	3652	99	100	100	71	64	67
Bahamas, The	33	6571	19,844				76	71	73
Bahrain	75	15,828[a]	21,421[a]	86	90	89	77	74	76
Bangladesh	15,857	68,415	431	48	59	53	65	63	64
Barbados	29	3044[b]	10,427[b]				80	74	77
Belarus	970	44,773	4615	100	100	100	76	65	70
Belgium	1063	452,754	42,609				83	77	80
Belize	30	1277	4200				79	73	76
Benin	903	5428	601	28	53	41	58	56	57
Bermuda	6	5855	91,490				82	76	79
Bhutan	66	1096	1668	39[b]	65[b]	53[b]	67	64	66
Bolivia	952	13,120	1379	86	96	91	68	63	66
Bosnia and Herzegovina	377	15,144	4014				77	72	75
Botswana	188	12,311	6544	83	83	83	51	50	51
Brazil	19,160	1,313,361	6855	90	90	90	76	69	72
Brunei Darussalam	39	11,471[a]	30,032[a]	93	96	95	80	75	77
Bulgaria	766	39,549	5163	98	99	98	76	69	73
Burkina Faso	1478	6767	458	22	37	29	54	51	52
Burundi	850	974	115				51	48	49
Cambodia	1445	8350	578	68	86	76	62	57	60
Cameroon	1853	20,686	1116				51	50	50
Canada	3298	1,329,885	40,329				83	78	81
Cape Verde	53	1434	2705	79	89	84	74	68	71
Cayman Islands	5			99	99	99			
Central African Republic	434	1712	394				46	43	45
Chad	1076	7085	658	21	43	32	52	49	51
Channel Islands	15	11,515	77,172				81	77	79
Chile	1659	163,913	9878	96	97	97	82	75	78
China	131,831	3,205,507	2432	90	96	93	75	71	73
Colombia	4399	207,786	4724	93	92	93	77	69	73
Comoros	63	449	714	70	80	75	67	63	65

(contd...)

Table 1 (contd...)

Country	Pop. (in 10,000)	GDP (current US$)		Literacy rate, ages 15 and above (%)			Life expectancy at birth (years)		
		(in millions)	per capita	F	M	T	F	M	T
Congo, Dem. Rep.	6240	8953	143				48	45	46
Congo, Rep.	377	7646	2030				57	54	55
Costa Rica	446	26,267	5887	96	96	96	81	76	79
Cote d'Ivoire	1927	19,796	1027				49	48	48
Croatia	444	51,278	11,559	98	99	99	79	72	76
Cuba	1126			100	100	100	80	76	78
Cyprus	85	21,277	24,895	97	99	98	82	77	79
Czech Republic	1033	174,998	16,934				80	74	77
Denmark	546	311,580	57,051				81	76	78
Djibouti	83	830	997				56	54	55
Dominica	7	314[a]	4331[a]						
Dominican Republic	973	36,686	3772	90	89	89	75	69	72
Ecuador	1334	44,490	3335	82	87	84	78	72	75
Egypt, Arab Rep.	7547	130,476	1729	58[a]	75[a]	66[a]	74	69	71
El Salvador	685	20,373	2973	80	85	82	75	69	72
Equatorial Guinea	51	9923	19,552				53	50	52
Eritrea	484	1375	284				60	56	58
Estonia	134	20,901	15,578	100	100	100	79	67	73
Ethiopia	7909	19,395	245				54	52	53
Faeroe Islands	5						81[a]	76[a]	79[a]
Fiji	83	3431	4113				71	67	69
Finland	529	244,661	46,261				83	76	79
France	6171	2,589,839	41,970				84	78	81
French Polynesia	26						77	72	74
Gabon	133	11,568	8696	82	90	86	57	56	57
Gambia, The	171	644	377				60	59	59
Georgia	440	10,175	2313				75	67	71
Germany	8227	3,317,365	40,324				82	77	80
Ghana	2346	15,147	646	58	72	65	60	60	60
Greece	1119	313,354	27,995	96	98	97	82	77	80
Greenland	6								
Grenada	11	605	5724				70	67	69
Guam	17						78	73	76
Guatemala	1335	33,855	2536	68	79	73	74	67	70
Guinea	938	4564	487				58	54	56
Guinea-Bissau	169	357	211				48	45	46
Guyana	74	1080	1462				70	64	67
Haiti	961	6715	699				63	59	61
Honduras	710	12,234	1722	83	84	84	74	67	70
Hong Kong, China	693	207,169	29,912				85	79	82
Hungary	1006	138,429	13,766	99	99	99	77	69	73
Iceland	31	19,963	64,190				83	79	81
India	112,479	1,176,890	1046	54	77	66	66	63	65

(contd...)

Table 1 (contd...)

Country	Pop. (in 10,000)	GDP (current US$)		Literacy rate, ages 15 and above (%)			Life expectancy at birth (years)		
		(in millions)	per capita	F	M	T	F	M	T
Indonesia	22,563	432,817	1918	89[a]	95[a]	92[a]	73	69	71
Iran, Islamic Rep.	7102	286,058	4028	77[a]	87[a]	82[a]	73	69	71
Iraq									
Ireland	437	259,018	59,324				82	77	79
Isle of Man	8	3438[a]	44,773[a]						
Israel	718	163,957	22,835				82	79	81
Italy	5937	2,101,637	35,396	99	99	99	84	79	81
Jamaica	268	11,430	4272	91	81	86	75	70	73
Japan	12,777	4,384,255	34,313				86	79	83
Jordan	572	15,833	2769	87[b]	95[b]	91[b]	74	71	73
Kazakhstan	1548	104,853	6772	99	100	100	72	61	66
Kenya	3753	24,190	645				55	53	54
Kiribati	10	78	817				63[b]	59[b]	61[b]
Korea, Dem. Rep.	2378						69	65	67
Korea, Rep.	4846	969,795	20,014				82	76	79
Kuwait	266	112,116	42,102	93	95	94	80	76	78
Kyrgyz Republic	523	3745	715	99	100	99	72	64	68
Lao PDR	586	4108	701	63[b]	82[b]	73[b]	66	63	64
Latvia	228	27,155	11,930	100	100	100	77	66	71
Lebanon	410	24,352	5944	86	93	90	74	70	72
Lesotho	201	1600	798				42	43	43
Liberia	371	735	198	51	60	56	47	45	46
Libya	616	58,333	9475	78	94	87	77	72	74
Liechtenstein	4								
Lithuania	338	38,332	11,356	100	100	100	77	65	71
Luxembourg	48	49,460	103,042				82	76	79
Macao, China	48	14,204[a]	29,744[a]	91[a]	96[a]	93[a]	83	79	81
Macedonia, FYR	204	7674	3767	95	99	97	77	72	74
Madagascar	1967	7382	375				61	58	59
Malawi	1392	3563	256	65	79	72	48	48	48
Malaysia	2655	186,719	7033	90	94	92	77	72	74
Maldives	31	1055	3456	97	97	97	69	68	68
Mali	1233	6863	556	18[a]	35[a]	26[a]	57	52	54
Malta	41	7449	18,203	94[b]	91[b]	92[b]	82	77	80
Marshall Islands	6	149	2559						
Mauritania	312	2644	847	48	63	56	66	62	64
Mauritius	126	6786	5383	85	90	87	76	69	72
Mayotte	19								
Mexico	10,528	1,022,815	9715	91	94	93	77	73	75
Micronesia, Fed. Sts.	11	236	2126				69	68	69
Moldova	380	4396	1156	99	100	99	72	65	69
Monaco	3								
Mongolia	261	3930	1507	98	97	97	70	64	67

(contd...)

Table 1 (contd...)

Country	Pop. (in 10,000)	GDP (current US$)		Literacy rate, ages 15 and above (%)			Life expectancy at birth (years)		
		(in millions)	per capita	F	M	T	F	M	T
Montenegro	60	3477	5804				77	72	75
Morocco	3086	75,119	2434	43	69	56	73	69	71
Mozambique	2137	7790	364	33	57	44	42	42	42
Myanmar	4878						65	59	62
Namibia	208	7015	3372	87	89	88	53	52	53
Nepal	2811	10,315	367	44	70	57	64	63	64
Netherlands	1638	765,818	46,750				82	78	80
Netherlands Antilles	19			96	96	96	79	71	75
New Caledonia	24			95	96	96	80	72	76
New Zealand	423	135,667	32,086				82	78	80
Nicaragua	560	5726	1022	78[b]	78[b]	78[b]	76	70	73
Niger	1420	4170	294	15[b]	43[b]	29[b]	56	58	57
Nigeria	14,798	165,469	1118	64	80	72	47	46	47
Northern Mariana Islands	8								
Norway	471	388,413	82,480				83	78	80
Oman	260	35,729[a]	14,031[a]	77	89	84	77	74	76
Pakistan	16,248	142,893	879	40[a]	68[a]	54[a]	66	65	65
Palau	2	164	8148				72[b]	66[b]	69[b]
Panama	334	19,485	5833	93	94	93	78	73	76
Papua New Guinea	632	6259	990	53	62	58	60	55	57
Paraguay	612	12,222	1997	93	96	95	74	70	72
Peru	2790	107,297	3846	85	95	90	74	69	71
Philippines	8789	144,062	1639	94	93	93	74	70	72
Poland	3812	422,090	11,072	99	100	99	80	71	75
Portugal	1061	222,758	20,998	93	97	95	82	75	78
Puerto Rico	394						83	74	78
Qatar	84	52,722[a]	64,193[a]	90	94	93	76	75	76
Romania	2155	165,976	7703	97	98	98	76	69	73
Russian Federation	14,210	1,290,082	9079	99	100	100	74	62	68
Rwanda	974	3339	343				48	45	46
Samoa	18	525	2894	98	99	99	75	69	72
San Marino	3	1703	55,681				85[a]	79[a]	82[a]
Sao Tome and Principe	16	145	916	83	93	88	67	64	65
Saudi Arabia	2416	381,683	15,800	79	89	85	75	71	73
Senegal	1241	11,165	900	33[a]	52[a]	42[a]	65	61	63
Serbia	738	40,122	5435				76	71	73
Seychelles	9	728	8560				78	69	73
Sierra Leone	585	1664	284	27	50	38	44	41	43
Singapore	459	161,347	35,163	92	97	94	83	78	80
Slovak Republic	540	74,972	13,891				78	70	74
Slovenia	202	47,182	23,379	100	100	100	82	74	78
Solomon Islands	50	388	784				64	63	64
Somalia	870						49	47	48

(contd...)

Table 1 (contd...)

Country	Pop. (in 10,000)	GDP (current US$)		Literacy rate, ages 15 and above (%)			Life expectancy at birth (years)		
		(in millions)	per capita	F	M	T	F	M	T
South Africa	4785	283,007	5914	87	89	88	52	49	50
South Asia	152,205	1,443,539	948	52	74	63	66	63	64
Spain	4488	1,436,891	32,017	97	99	98	84	78	81
Sri Lanka	2001	32,346	1616	89[a]	93[a]	91[a]	76	69	72
St. Kitts and Nevis	5	527	10,795						
St. Lucia	17	980	5834				76	73	74
St. Vincent and the Grenadines	12	553	4596				74	69	72
Sudan	3856	46,228	1199				60	57	59
Suriname	46	2241	4896	88	93	90	74	67	70
Swaziland	115	2894	2521				39	40	40
Sweden	915	454,310	49,662				83	79	81
Switzerland	755	424,367	56,207				84	79	82
Syrian Arab Republic	1989	37,745	1898	76	90	83	76	72	74
Tajikistan	674	3712	551	100	100	100	69	64	67
Tanzania	4043	16,181	400	66	79	72	54	51	52
Thailand	6383	245,351	3844	93	96	94	75	66	71
Timor-Leste	106	395	373				62	60	61
Togo	658	2499	380				60	57	58
Tonga	10	253	2474	99	99	99	74	72	73
Trinidad and Tobago	133	20,886	15,668	98	99	99	72	68	70
Tunisia	1023	35,020	3425	69	86	78	76	72	74
Turkey	7389	655,881	8877	81	96	89	74	69	72
Turkmenistan	496	12,933	2606	99	100	100	68	59	63
Uganda	3092	11,771	381	66	82	74	52	51	51
Ukraine	4651	141,177	3035	100	100	100	74	62	68
United Arab Emirates	436	163,296[b]	38,436[b]	91[b]	89[b]	90[b]	81	77	79
United Kingdom	6100	2,772,024	45,442				82	77	79
United States	30,162	13,751,400	45,592				81	75	78
Uruguay	332	23,136	6960	98	97	98	80	72	76
Uzbekistan	2687	22,308	830				70	64	67
Vanuatu	23	452	2001	76	80	78	72	68	70
Venezuela, RB	2748	228,071	8299	95	95	95	77	71	74
Vietnam	8515	68,643	806				76	72	74
Virgin Islands (U.S.)	11						82	76	79
West Bank and Gaza	371	4016[b]	1160[b]	90	97	94	75	72	73
Yemen, Rep.	2238	22,523	1006	40	77	59	64	61	63
Zambia	1192	11,363	953	61	81	71	42	42	42
Zimbabwe	1340	3418[b]	261[b]	88	94	91	43	44	43

Source: WDI 2009.

Notes: [a] 2006; [b] 2005

Table 2   The Bottom 45 Countries, Ranked by GDP per Capita, PPP 1980–2007

Rank	1980	1990	2000	2007
1	Swaziland	Honduras	Honduras	Morocco
2	Morocco	Philippines	Bhutan	Honduras
3	Thailand	Indonesia	Indonesia	Indonesia
4	Haiti	Cameroon	China	Vanuatu
5	Guyana	Sri Lanka	Philippines	Congo, Rep.
6	Cameroon	Cote d'Ivoire	Guyana	Philippines
7	Papua New Guinea	Nicaragua	Georgia	Guyana
8	Liberia	Bhutan	Nicaragua	India
9	Nigeria	Papua New Guinea	Papua New Guinea	Nicaragua
10	Mauritania	Pakistan	Pakistan	Pakistan
11	Sri Lanka	Haiti	Cameroon	Cameroon
12	Zambia	Solomon Islands	Cote d'Ivoire	Sudan
13	Senegal	Mauritania	India	Papua New Guinea
14	Kenya	Guyana	Mauritania	Nigeria
15	Indonesia	Nigeria	Solomon Islands	Mauritania
16	Madagascar	Kenya	Nigeria	Solomon Islands
17	Pakistan	Senegal	Senegal	Cote d'Ivoire
18	Comoros	Zambia	Kiribati	Senegal
19	Solomon Islands	Comoros	Sudan	Kenya
20	Kiribati	India	Kenya	Lesotho
21	Benin	China	Lesotho	Chad
22	Togo	Gambia, The	Haiti	Zambia
23	Gambia, The	Kiribati	Benin	Ghana
24	Sudan	Benin	Comoros	Benin
25	Ghana	Sudan	Zambia	Kiribati
26	Central Afr Republic	Madagascar	Gambia, The	Bangladesh
27	Niger	Chad	Ghana	Gambia, The
28	Bhutan	Guinea	Guinea	Haiti
29	Mali	Lesotho	Nepal	Comoros
30	Guinea	Ghana	Bangladesh	Guinea
31	India	Togo	Burkina Faso	Burkina Faso
32	Rwanda	Central Afr Republic	Chad	Mali
33	Sierra Leone	Mali	Madagascar	Nepal
34	Chad	Burkina Faso	Mali	Madagascar
35	Malawi	Nepal	Togo	Rwanda
36	Congo, Dem. Rep.	Bangladesh	Central Afr Republic	Mozambique
37	Lesotho	Rwanda	Malawi	Togo
38	Burkina Faso	Niger	Rwanda	Malawi
39	Bangladesh	Sierra Leone	Niger	Central Afr Republic
40	Nepal	Guinea-Bissau	Guinea-Bissau	Sierra Leone
41	China	Malawi	Mozambique	Niger
42	Guinea-Bissau	Congo, Dem. Rep.	Liberia	Guinea-Bissau
43	Mozambique	Liberia	Sierra Leone	Liberia
44	Burundi	Burundi	Burundi	Burundi
45	Mauritius	Mozambique	Congo, Dem. Rep.	Congo, Dem. Rep.

Source: WDI 2009.

Note: Of the 227 countries included in the WDI, 126 have data for all years selected. We ranked these 126 countries and present the bottom 45 countries of each year (1=least poor).

Table 3   Energy, Environment, and Land Use in an International Perspective, Selected Cross-country Comparisons

Country	Forest area (as % of land area) 2006	Nationally protected areas (as % of land area) 2006	Electric power consumption (kWh per capita) 2006	Electricity production from coal sources (% of total) 2006	Clean energy production (% of total energy use) 2006	CO_2 emissions (metric tons per capita) 2005	Other greenhouse gas emissions, HFC, PFC, and SF6 (thousand metric tons of CO_2 equivalent) 2006[a]	PM10 (micrograms per cubic metre) 2006[b]
Afghanistan	1.33	0.34			19.05	1.11		41.27
Argentina	12.07	6.34	2620	13.07	32.68	1.44	930	73.11
Australia	21.31	9.56	11,332	6.80	9.59	8.94	4580	15.39
Austria	46.84	28.47	8090	5.52	1.54	4.36	3310	33.03
Bangladesh	6.69	0.68	146	6.45		4.51	0	135.43
Belgium	22.06	3.22	8684	4.95		2.80	9380	22.47
Botswana	21.07	30.78	1419	14.88	14.99	1.74	0	67.10
Brazil	56.47	17.91	2060	16.82	0.00	15.76	7760	23.34
Canada	34.10	5.20	16,753	7.59		0.56	11,010	17.39
Chile	21.53	3.71	3207	12.40	2.95	4.26	10	47.80
China	21.15	15.41	2041	6.34	12.18	1.37	119,720	73.01
Colombia	54.73	25.48	968	19.25		0.15	330	22.41
Cuba	24.70	1.35	1231	15.78	1.64	8.39	110	17.48
Denmark	11.78	5.81	6864	3.19		0.46	1460	18.68
Ecuador	39.20	22.62	759	45.17	1.86	2.38	0	24.76
Ethiopia	13.00	18.62	38	10.00	8.11	7.01	0	67.74
Fiji	54.73	0.84			18.62	10.13		21.61
Finland	73.87	9.67	17,177	3.94	44.93	6.20	1030	17.80
France	28.27	10.11	7813	5.59		2.68	27,010	13.48
Germany	31.76	21.72	7174	4.58	5.08	0.32	41,980	18.58
Hong Kong, China			5883	12.04	13.16	5.59	330	
Hungary	22.05	5.82	3882	11.05	75.28	7.36	1540	18.64
India	22.77	5.10	503	25.39	3.66	1.90	9510	64.92
Indonesia	48.85	11.21	530	11.24	0.92	6.54	900	82.88
Iran, Islamic Rep.	6.80	6.38	2290	20.02	0.13		1560	50.61
Israel	7.90	15.58	6889	2.65	4.58	7.71	1140	31.47
Italy	33.93	6.58	5755	6.48	0.31	3.83	27,710	26.71
Japan	68.22	9.48	8220	4.61	1.38	3.79	70,570	29.64
Kenya	6.19	12.14	145	17.04		0.28	0	36.40
Korea, Dem. Rep.	51.38	2.62	797	15.80	18.07	9.39	860	68.18
Korea, Rep.	63.46	3.55	8063	3.63	0.00	36.91	8700	34.72

(contd...)

Table 3 (contd...)

Country	Forest area (as % of land area) 2006	Nationally protected areas (as % of land area) 2006	Electric power consumption (kWh per capita) 2006	Electricity production from coal sources (% of total) 2006	Clean energy production (% of total energy use) 2006	CO_2 emissions (metric tons per capita) 2005	Other greenhouse gas emiss-ions, HFC, PFC, and SF6 (thousand metric tons of CO_2 equiva-lent) 2006[a]	PM10 (micrograms per cubic metre) 2006[b]
Madagascar	22.08	2.62				0.08		33.84
Malaysia	63.58	18.18	3388	0.63		2.42	530	22.89
Maldives	3.00					0.05		31.61
Mexico	33.05	5.27	2003	16.06			3160	36.45
Mongolia	6.54	13.91	1298	12.11			0	110.45
Mozambique	24.49	5.76	461	14.08	2.00	0.24	0	28.00
Myanmar	49.00	5.40	93	27.13	8.81	1.26	10	57.72
Nepal	25.43	15.95	80	20.53	1.47	7.71	0	34.47
Nigeria	12.18	6.21	116	27.10			80	44.99
Norway	30.85	5.10	24,296	7.65	0.00	12.54	1770	14.80
Pakistan	2.47	8.48	480	22.38		5.70	620	120.26
Peru	53.70	13.74	899	9.32	22.93	0.89	80	54.48
Philippines	24.02	10.06	578	12.14	0.22	7.92	350	22.83
Russian Fed.	49.37	6.80	6122	10.83		0.07	56,600	17.74
Singapore	3.34	4.21	8520	4.92	27.50	6.80	1300	40.87
South Africa	7.58	6.07	4810	8.68	2.83	1.08	2600	20.54
Spain	35.89	8.29	6206	8.68	4.25	0.56	15,050	31.61
Sri Lanka	29.91	17.54	400	15.26		2.82	0	82.12
Sudan	28.43	4.80	95	15.18		5.25	0	165.03
Sweden	67.09	10.32	15,231	7.70	35.87	5.54	1620	11.62
Tanzania	39.80	38.69	59	20.89	0.68	4.30	0	25.39
Thailand	28.42	19.90	2080	8.06		0.18	940	70.90
Uganda	18.40	31.91			17.92	6.94		11.87
United Kingdom	11.76	19.64	6185	7.86	10.78	19.52	14,030	15.49
United States	33.08	15.05	13,564	6.23	7.57	5.47	108,420	21.34
Vietnam	41.70	5.16	598	10.98			10	55.32
Zimbabwe	45.34	14.80	900	7.22			20	26.81

Source: [a] International Energy Agency; [b] WDI 2009.

Notes: [a] Other greenhouse gas emissions are by-product emissions of hydrofluorocarbons, perfluorocarbons, and sulfur hexafluoride.

[b] Particulate matter concentrations refer to fine suspended particulates less than 10 microns in diameter (PM10) that are capable of penetrating deep into the respiratory tract and causing significant health damage.

Table 4   Components of GDP at Factor Cost 1950–2008

(Rs crore)

Year	Agriculture and allied activities		Industry		Service	
	Constant	Current	Constant	Current	Constant	Current
1950–1	1,23,884	5080	23,865	1153	76,349	3431
1951–2	1,25,732	5245	24,968	1283	78,827	3679
1952–3	1,29,697	5110	25,803	1218	80,144	3772
1953–4	1,39,685	5630	27,574	1361	82,487	3989
1954–5	1,43,791	4789	29,419	1415	87,143	4181
1955–6	1,42,549	4644	31,512	1458	93,071	4482
1956–7	1,50,298	5900	33,800	1737	98,369	4915
1957–8	1,43,547	5778	35,343	1869	99,712	5221
1958–9	1,58,010	6703	37,116	2001	1,04,911	5647
1959–60	1,56,420	6734	39,688	2238	1,10,424	6134
1960–1	1,66,954	7090	43,297	2608	1,18,316	6849
1961–2	1,67,095	7343	46,949	2870	1,24,354	7246
1962–3	1,63,771	7497	50,739	3209	1,31,135	8020
1963–4	1,67,602	8823	55,326	3652	1,40,222	8866
1964–5	1,83,062	10,781	58,850	4018	1,48,833	10,052
1965–6	1,62,848	10,751	60,423	4317	1,54,037	11,031
1966–7	1,60,532	12,506	61,287	4751	1,60,177	12,379
1967–8	1,84,404	15,650	62,124	5128	1,67,308	13,930
1968–9	1,84,112	16,132	65,650	5574	1,74,669	14,935
1969–70	1,95,946	17,644	72,138	6417	1,83,108	16,198
1970–1	2,09,843	18,192	73,235	7000	1,90,513	17,711
1971–2	2,05,903	18,584	75,839	7730	1,96,487	19,433
1972–3	1,95,570	20,440	79,016	8558	2,02,269	21,307
1973–4	2,09,655	26,936	82,119	10,251	2,05,731	24,158
1974–5	2,06,461	29,509	84,793	13,260	2,12,398	29,569
1975–6	2,33,074	29,249	88,311	14,125	2,28,688	33,755
1976–7	2,19,606	29,882	95,715	15,867	2,41,005	37,305
1977–8	2,41,646	35,380	1,01,219	17,782	2,54,546	41,361
1978–9	2,47,210	36,361	1,12,569	20,447	2,67,828	44,893
1979–80	2,15,630	37,616	1,09,864	23,584	2,71,303	49,957
1980–1	2,43,421	47,312	1,12,002	26,657	2,86,499	58,550
1981–2	2,54,622	53,327	1,21,997	32,733	3,01,413	69,098
1982–3	2,53,907	57,496	1,27,645	36,557	3,16,309	79,285
1983–4	2,79,605	68,613	1,39,098	42,995	3,33,966	91,142

(contd...)

Table 4 (contd...)

Year	Agriculture and allied activities		Industry		Service	
	Constant	Current	Constant	Current	Constant	Current
1984–5	2,84,037	73,989	1,45,294	48,610	3,53,153	1,05,095
1985–6	2,84,930	79,294	1,50,992	54,063	3,79,128	1,21,070
1986–7	2,83,763	85,108	1,61,250	60,348	4,05,204	1,38,226
1987–8	2,79,257	94,677	1,70,277	67,753	4,30,732	1,59,160
1988–9	3,22,932	1,16,925	1,86,578	80,841	4,60,192	1,86,024
1989–90	3,26,773	1,29,222	2,02,947	96,292	4,99,459	2,16,621
1990–1	3,39,893	1,50,800	2,14,552	1,10,760	5,29,127	2,53,472
1991–2	3,33,256	1,76,166	2,13,925	1,21,918	5,51,890	2,96,084
1992–3	3,55,421	1,97,569	2,20,880	1,42,566	5,81,723	3,41,382
1993–4	3,67,231	2,29,172	2,37,376	1,65,663	6,19,209	3,97,316
1994–5	3,84,549	2,63,895	2,62,164	2,02,888	6,55,363	4,58,456
1995–6	3,81,875	2,86,946	2,96,664	2,48,450	7,18,434	5,47,893
1996–7	4,19,759	3,45,020	3,20,266	2,80,247	7,68,353	6,35,444
1997–8	4,09,039	3,66,125	3,26,720	3,00,389	8,37,504	7,35,419
1998–9	4,34,892	4,20,486	3,38,369	3,32,464	9,05,148	8,63,133
1999–2000	4,46,515	4,46,515	3,50,233	3,50,233	9,89,778	9,89,778
2000–1	4,45,403	4,49,565	3,72,599	3,92,138	10,46,299	10,83,313
2001–2	4,73,249	4,86,617	3,81,366	4,10,667	11,17,991	12,00,442
2002–3	4,38,966	4,72,060	4,07,276	4,63,302	12,02,045	13,26,053
2003–4	4,82,676	5,32,342	4,31,724	5,09,106	13,08,358	14,96,722
2004–5	4,82,446	5,52,422	4,68,451	5,98,271	14,37,487	17,27,013
2005–6[P]	5,11,013	6,15,844	5,06,016	6,77,946	15,95,818	19,81,879
2006–7[QE]	5,30,236	6,95,424	5,59,801	7,90,333	17,74,272	23,04,307
2007–8[RE]	5,54,336	7,64,082	6,05,061	8,99,144	19,63,462	26,40,428

Source: RBI. 2009. *Handbook of Statistics on Indian Economy.*
Notes: Base for constant prices: 1999–2000.
P: Provisional; QE: Quick Estimates; RE: Revised Estimates.

Table 5   Employment with Sectoral Break-up, per 1000 Distribution of Usually Employed by Broad Groups of Industry for Various NSS Rounds

NSS survey period	Male						Female					
	Primary sector		Secondary sector		Tertiary sector		Primary sector		Secondary sector		Tertiary sector	
	PS	ALL	PS	ALL	PS	ALL	PS	ALL	PS	ALL	PS	ALL
1983	772	775	102	100	123	122	862	875	78	74	57	48
1987–8	739	745	123	121	138	134	825	847	112	100	63	53
1989–90	716	717	120	121	164	162	800	814	130	124	70	61
1990–1	705	710	123	121	172	169	842	849	83	81	75	70
1991	748	749	112	112	140	139	859	863	79	79	62	58
1992	753	757	106	104	141	139	858	862	78	78	64	60
1993	749	750	110	109	141	141	862	872	77	74	61	54
1993–4	739	741	113	112	148	147	847	862	91	83	62	55
1994–5	752	756	104	103	144	141	862	871	88	83	50	46
1995–6	746	748	115	114	139	137	854	868	87	80	59	52
1997	757	758	106	106	137	136	875	885	77	72	47	42
1998	755	757	103	102	142	141	876	885	70	66	54	49
1999–2000	712	714	127	126	161	160	841	854	93	89	66	57
2000–1	688	690	137	136	175	174	812	818	139	133	49	49
2001–2	672	678	148	145	180	177	819	840	124	109	57	51
2002	685	688	140	138	175	174	834	849	91	87	75	65
2003	704	708	143	141	153	151	841	852	99	95	60	53
2004	654	659	163	160	183	180	820	841	102	94	78	65
2004–5	662	665	157	155	181	180	814	833	108	102	76	66
2005–6	648	652	167	165	185	183	798	813	121	120	82	68
1983	97	103	344	342	551	550	255	310	307	306	430	376
1987–8	85	91	343	340	572	569	218	294	324	317	458	389
1989–90	95	100	323	319	582	582	214	241	297	303	489	456
1990–1	91	92	336	336	573	572	223	249	318	316	459	435
1991	95	95	306	307	599	598	217	237	278	282	505	481
1992	104	107	345	343	551	550	195	224	304	308	501	468
1993	101	102	345	344	554	554	232	258	306	306	462	436
1993–4	87	90	331	329	582	581	193	247	299	291	508	462
1994–5	86	88	330	329	584	583	154	205	354	343	492	452
1995–6	81	82	335	335	584	583	179	209	310	309	512	482
1997	76	78	343	340	582	581	165	200	328	324	507	476
1998	90	92	324	322	586	586	187	221	292	280	520	499
1999–2000	65	66	329	328	606	606	146	177	293	293	561	529
2000–1	63	66	359	356	579	578	136	183	342	342	522	475
2001–2	78	78	322	321	601	600	173	211	309	332	519	457
2002	69	70	338	337	594	593	156	171	298	315	546	513
2003	60	63	338	336	602	601	145	190	299	312	556	497
2004	61	63	348	347	591	590	126	161	289	309	584	530
2004–5	60	61	346	344	595	595	147	181	303	324	549	495
2005–6	62	63	345	343	594	594	123	148	313	330	564	522

Source: RBI. 2009. *Handbook of Statistics on Indian Economy.*

Notes: PS—Principal Status (the principal status approach counts a person among the 'employed' during a year if he or she has spent more time within the labour force than out of it and has spent more time in the 'working' state than in seeking or being available for work).

Primary sector: agriculture and allied activities.

Secondary sector: mining, manufacture, electricity, gas, water, etc., and construction.

Tertiary sector: trade, hotels, transport, storage, and communication.

Table 6   Savings Rate and Investment Rate 1950–2007
(at current prices, in percentage)

	Rate of gross domestic savings	Rate of net domestic savings	Rate of gross domestic capital formation	Rate of net domestic capital formation
1950–1	8.6	3.6	8.4	3.4
1951–2	9.0	3.7	10.7	5.5
1952–3	8.0	2.1	7.7	1.8
1953–4	7.6	2.1	7.5	2.0
1954–5	9.1	3.1	9.3	3.2
1955–6	12.3	8.3	12.6	8.7
1956–7	11.9	8.1	14.6	10.9
1957–8	10	5.7	13.5	9.4
1958–9	9.1	4.8	11.6	7.4
1959–60	10.8	6.3	12.3	7.8
1960–1	11.2	6.7	14.0	9.6
1961–2	11.2	6.5	13.1	8.4
1962–3	12.3	7.4	14.5	9.8
1963–4	11.9	7.6	13.8	9.6
1964–5	11.6	7.4	13.8	9.7
1965–6	13.7	9.1	15.8	11.4
1966–7	13.6	8.9	16.6	12.0
1967–8	11.6	6.8	13.8	9.2
1968–9	11.8	7.3	12.9	8.4
1969–70	14.0	9.3	14.5	9.9
1970–1	14.2	9.2	15.1	10.1
1971–2	14.7	9.4	15.7	10.4
1972–3	14.3	8.7	14.8	9.2
1973–4	16.4	11.0	17.0	11.6
1974–5	15.7	9.6	16.5	10.5
1975–6	16.9	10.4	16.7	10.2
1976–7	19.1	12.8	17.6	11.2
1977–8	19.5	13.4	18.0	11.8
1978–9	21.2	14.9	21.3	15.1
1979–80	19.8	12.7	20.3	13.2
1980–1	18.5	11.3	19.9	12.9
1981–2	18.1	10.7	19.6	12.4
1982–3	17.7	10.0	19.0	11.5
1983–4	17.1	9.6	18.3	10.8

(contd...)

Table 6 (contd...)

	Rate of gross domestic savings	Rate of net domestic savings	Rate of gross domestic capital formation	Rate of net domestic capital formation
1984–5	18.2	10.6	19.6	12.0
1985–6	19.0	11.0	21.2	13.4
1986–7	18.4	10.2	20.5	12.4
1987–8	20.2	12.1	22.1	14.2
1988–9	20.5	12.6	23.4	15.8
1989–90	21.8	13.7	24.3	16.5
1990–1	22.8	15.2	26.0	18.7
1991–2	21.5	13.3	22.1	13.9
1992–3	21.2	12.9	23.1	14.9
1993–4	21.9	13.9	22.5	14.5
1994–5	24.4	16.7	25.5	18.0
1995–6	24.4	16.6	26.2	18.6
1996–7	22.7	14.8	24.0	16.2
1997–8	23.8	15.9	25.3	17.5
1998–9	22.3	14.3	23.3	15.5
1999–2000	24.8	17.1	25.9	18.3
2000–1	23.7	15.6	24.3	16.3
2001–2	23.5	15	22.8	14.3
2002–3	26.4	18	25.2	16.7
2003–4	29.8	21.9	28.2	20.0
2004–5	31.8	23.8	32.2	24.3
2005–6[P]	34.3	26.5	35.5	27.9
2006–7[QE]	34.8	27.1	35.9	28.4

Source: RBI. 2009. *Handbook of Statistics on Indian Economy*.
Notes: P: Provisional; QE: Quick Estimates.
GDS and GDCF rates are percentages to GDP at current market prices; NDS and NDCF rates are percentages to NDP at current market prices

Table 7   Domestic Savings and Gross Capital Formation 1950–2007

(Rs crore)

Year	Savings				Gross capital formation			
	Household sector	Private corporate sector	Public sector	Gross domestic savings	Household sector	Private corporate sector	Public sector	Gross domestic capital formation
1950–1	578	93	200	871	516	227	294	1037
1951–2	546	136	287	969	532	265	342	1139
1952–3	599	64	182	845	527	88	296	912
1953–4	616	90	169	875	474	16	337	827
1954–5	671	118	199	988	389	161	508	1057
1955–6	991	134	231	1356	562	232	563	1357
1956–7	1108	155	298	1561	775	363	738	1876
1957–8	920	121	315	1356	629	423	908	1960
1958–9	934	140	305	1379	572	264	898	1735
1959–60	1205	185	330	1720	772	325	1000	2098
1960–1	1136	281	535	1952	680	572	1259	2512
1961–2	1143	320	611	2074	654	794	1272	2720
1962–3	1394	344	702	2440	895	579	1590	3063
1963–4	1439	394	870	2703	696	933	1852	3481
1964–5	1684	389	1004	3077	970	964	2146	4080
1965–6	2409	405	1019	3833	1337	745	2438	4519
1966–7	3019	424	885	4328	2155	671	2366	5192
1967–8	2993	410	890	4293	2128	873	2570	5572
1968–9	3122	439	1096	4657	2327	821	2422	5570
1969–70	4211	549	1284	6044	3292	721	2530	6543
1970–1	4371	672	1528	6571	3000	1107	3104	7211
1971–2	4917	769	1595	7281	3362	1282	3631	8275
1972–3	5263	806	1719	7788	3135	1432	4152	8719
1973–4	7590	1083	2239	10,912	3978	1757	5212	10,946
1974–5	7668	1465	3165	12,298	5294	2848	6083	14,225
1975–6	9163	1083	3950	14,196	5245	2344	8236	15,825
1976–7	11,223	1181	4916	17,320	6371	1437	9360	17,168
1977–8	13,619	1413	4963	19,995	7766	2530	8689	18,985
1978–9	16,300	1652	5649	23,601	9642	2403	10,805	22,850
1979–80	15,828	2398	5987	24,213	9747	3263	12,898	25,909
1980–1	18,724	2339	5818	26,881	10,114	3855	12,994	26,964
1981–2	19,659	2560	8677	30,896	10,045	9760	18,092	37,897

(contd...)

Table 7 (contd...)

Year	Savings				Gross capital formation			
	Household sector	Private corporate sector	Public sector	Gross domestic savings	Household sector	Private corporate sector	Public sector	Gross domestic capital formation
1982–3	21,230	2980	9577	33,787	8491	10,898	21,543	40,932
1983–4	26,122	3254	8715	38,091	12,828	7,726	22,810	43,364
1984–5	32,689	4040	8724	45,453	14,810	11,048	27,366	53,225
1985–6	36,942	5426	11,021	53,389	18,404	15,549	32,063	66,016
1986–7	41,653	5336	11,047	58,036	18,317	16,901	37,275	72,493
1987–8	55,907	5932	10,425	72,264	29,087	13,282	36,361	78,730
1988–9	66,907	8486	11,773	87,166	39,724	17,487	43,137	1,00,348
1989–90	82,765	11,845	11,482	1,06,092	44,767	21,215	49,707	1,15,689
1990–1	1,04,789	15,164	10,057	1,30,010	55,149	25,575	56,874	1,37,598
1991–2	1,03,495	20,304	17,290	1,41,089	41,394	40,439	62,052	1,43,885
1992–3	1,23,315	19,968	16,399	1,59,682	57,948	52,431	68,533	1,78,912
1993–4	1,49,534	29,866	10,533	1,89,933	54,796	53,008	75,923	1,83,727
1994–5	1,88,790	35,260	23,412	2,47,462	68,057	76,139	94,775	2,38,971
1995–6	2,01,015	59,153	30,834	2,91,002	95,296	1,23,899	97,749	3,16,944
1996–7	2,20,973	62,209	29,886	3,13,068	79,312	1,22,491	1,03,159	3,04,961
1997–8	2,70,308	65,769	27,429	3,63,506	1,22,531	1,34,643	1,07,830	3,65,005
1998–9	3,29,760	68,856	–8869	3,89,747	1,49,414	1,24,122	1,22,849	3,96,384
1999–2000	4,12,516	87,234	–15,494	4,84,256	2,05,914	1,43,475	1,44,610	5,09,518
2000–1	4,54,853	81,062	–36,882	4,99,033	2,39,634	1,09,013	1,44,638	5,08,009
2001–2	5,04,165	76,906	–46,186	5,34,885	2,56,689	1,23,628	1,56,537	5,51,041
2002–3	5,69,134	94,772	–15,936	6,47,970	3,15,879	1,40,255	1,49,399	6,19,490
2003–4	6,70,776	1,20,730	29,521	8,21,026	3,57,517	1,80,804	1,74,579	7,37,472
2004–5	7,25,110	2,06,363	68,951	10,00,424	4,06,846	3,31,081	2,16,962	9,95,943
2005–6[P]	8,66,756	2,68,329	92,263	12,27,348	4,45,916	4,77,490	2,72,002	12,36,800
2006–7[QE]	9,85,822	3,22,242	1,33,359	14,41,423	5,17,837	6,03,014	3,21,753	14,92,313

Source: RBI. 2009. *Handbook of Statistics on Indian Economy.*
Note: P: Provisional; QE: Quick Estimates.

Table 8 External Sector 1970–2008

(million US dollars)

Year	Exports	Imports	Trade balance	Balance of payments	FDI (net, in India)	Portfolio investment (net, in India)	Total foreign exchange reserves
1970–1	2031	2162	–131	–14	NA	NA	975
1971–2	2152	2442	–290	28	NA	NA	1194
1972–3	2569	2433	136	–43	NA	NA	1219
1973–4	3238	3793	–554	28	NA	NA	1325
1974–5	4192	5691	–1499	–599	NA	NA	1379
1975–6	4649	6064	–1415	707	NA	NA	2172
1976–7	5728	5652	77	1905	NA	NA	3747
1977–8	6299	7012	–713	2141	NA	NA	5824
1978–9	6960	8279	–1318	1308	NA	NA	7268
1979–80	7926	11,291	–3364	405	NA	NA	7361
1980–1	8485	15,867	–7382	–1140	NA	NA	6823
1981–2	8704	15,173	–6469	–2523	NA	NA	4390
1982–3	9108	14,787	–5679	–1319	NA	NA	4896
1983–4	9449	15,311	–5862	–561	NA	NA	5649
1984–5	9878	14,412	–4534	730	NA	NA	5952
1985–6	8905	16,067	–7162	–361	NA	NA	6520
1986–7	9745	15,727	–5982	–47	NA	NA	6574
1987–8	12,089	17,156	–5067	195	NA	NA	6223
1988–9	13,970	19,497	–5527	68	NA	NA	4802
1989–90	16,613	21,219	–4607	136	NA	NA	3962
1990–1	18,145	24,073	–5927	–2492	97	6	5834
1991–2	17,865	19,411	–1545	2599	129	4	9220
1992–3	18,537	21,882	–3344	–590	315	242	9832
1993–4	22,238	23,306	–1068	8535	586	3647	19,254
1994–5	26,331	28,654	–2324	5787	1343	3579	25,186
1995–6	31,795	36,675	–4880	–1222	2143	2660	21,687
1996–7	33,470	39,132	–5663	6793	2842	3312	26,423
1997–8	35,006	41,485	–6478	4511	3562	1828	29,367
1998–9	33,219	42,389	–9170	4222	2480	–68	32,490
1999–2000	36,822	49671	–12,848	6402	2167	3024	38,036
2000–1	44,560	50,537	–5976	5868	4031	2760	42,281
2001–2	43,827	51,413	–7587	11,757	6125	2021	54,106
2002–3	52,719	61,412	–8693	16,985	5036	979	76,100
2003–4	63,843	78,149	–14,307	31,421	4322	11,356	112,959
2004–5	83,536	1,11,517	–27,982	26,159	5987	9311	141,514
2005–6	103,091	1,49,166	–46,075	15,052	8901	12,494	151,622
2006–7[R]	126,362	1,85,749	–59,388	36,606	21,991	7004	199,179
2007–8[P]	159,007	2,39,651	–80,644	92,164	32,327	29,096	309,723

Source: RBI. *Handbook of Statistics on Indian Economy* (various issues).
Note: P: Provisional; R: Revised.

Table 9   Agricultural Performance 1950–2007

Year	Yield in kg/hectare					Area in million hectare			
	Rice	Wheat	Pulses	Cotton	Sugar cane	Net sown area	Gross sown area	Net irrigated area	Gross irrigated area
1950–1	668	663	441	88	33,422	118.75	131.89	20.85	22.56
1951–2	714	653	448	85	31,786	119.40	133.23	21.05	23.18
1952–3	764	763	463	89	29,495	123.44	137.68	21.12	23.31
1953–4	902	750	489	100	31,497	126.81	142.48	21.87	24.36
1954–5	820	803	500	100	36,303	127.85	144.09	22.09	24.95
1955–6	874	708	476	88	32,779	129.16	147.31	22.76	25.64
1956–7	900	695	495	104	33,683	130.85	149.49	22.53	25.71
1957–8	790	682	424	105	34,325	129.08	145.83	23.16	26.63
1958–9	930	789	541	104	37,658	131.83	151.63	23.40	26.95
1959–60	937	772	475	86	36,414	132.94	152.82	24.04	27.45
1960–1	1013	851	539	125	45,549	133.20	152.77	24.66	27.98
1961–2	1028	890	485	103	42,349	135.40	156.21	24.88	28.46
1962–3	931	793	475	122	40,996	136.34	156.76	25.67	29.45
1963–4	1033	730	416	119	46,353	136.48	156.96	25.89	29.71
1964–5	1078	913	520	122	46,838	138.12	159.23	26.60	30.71
1965–6	862	827	438	104	43,717	136.20	155.28	26.34	30.90
1966–7	863	887	377	114	40,336	137.23	157.36	26.91	32.68
1967–8	1032	1103	534	123	40,665	139.88	163.74	27.19	33.21
1968–9	1076	1169	490	122	49,236	137.31	159.53	29.01	35.48
1969–70	1073	1208	531	122	49,121	138.77	162.27	30.20	36.97
1970–1	1123	1307	524	106	48,322	140.27	165.79	31.10	38.20
1971–2	1141	1380	501	151	47,511	139.72	165.19	31.55	38.43
1972–3	1070	1271	474	127	50,933	137.14	162.15	31.83	39.06
1973–4	1151	1172	427	142	51,163	142.42	169.87	32.55	40.28
1974–5	1045	1338	455	161	49,855	137.79	164.19	33.71	41.74
1975–6	1235	1410	533	138	50,903	141.65	171.30	34.59	43.36
1976–7	1089	1387	494	144	53,383	139.48	167.33	35.15	43.55
1977–8	1308	1480	510	157	56,160	141.95	172.23	36.55	46.08
1978–9	1328	1568	515	167	49,114	142.98	174.80	38.06	48.31
1979–80	1074	1436	385	160	49,358	138.90	169.59	38.52	49.21
1980–1	1336	1630	473	152	57,844	140.00	172.63	38.72	49.78
1981–2	1308	1691	483	166	58,359	141.93	176.75	40.50	51.41
1982–3	1231	1816	519	163	56,441	140.22	172.75	40.69	51.83
1983–4	1457	1843	548	141	55,978	142.84	179.56	41.95	53.82

(contd...)

Table 9 (contd...)

Year	Yield in kg/hectare					Area in million hectare			
	Rice	Wheat	Pulses	Cotton	Sugar cane	Net sown area	Gross sown area	Net irrigated area	Gross irrigated area
1984–5	1417	1870	526	196	57,673	140.89	176.33	42.15	54.53
1985–6	1552	2046	547	197	59,889	140.90	178.46	41.87	54.28
1986–7	1471	1916	506	169	60,444	139.58	176.41	42.57	55.76
1987–8	1465	2002	515	168	60,006	134.09	170.74	42.89	56.04
1988–9	1689	2244	598	202	60,992	141.89	182.28	46.15	61.13
1989–90	1745	2121	549	252	65,612	142.34	182.27	46.70	61.85
1990–1	1740	2281	578	225	65,395	143.00	185.74	48.02	63.20
1991–2	1751	2394	533	216	66,069	141.63	182.24	49.87	65.68
1992–3	1744	2327	573	257	63,843	142.72	185.70	50.29	66.76
1993–4	1888	2380	598	249	67,120	142.34	186.58	51.34	68.26
1994–5	1911	2559	610	257	71,254	142.96	188.05	53.00	70.65
1995–6	1797	2483	552	242	67,787	142.20	187.47	53.40	71.35
1996–7	1882	2679	635	265	66,496	142.81	189.59	55.05	73.25
1997–8	1900	2485	567	208	71,134	142.08	190.57	54.99	73.00
1998–9	1921	2590	634	224	71,203	142.58	193.03	57.08	75.95
1999–2000	1986	2778	635	225	70,935	140.96	189.44	57.11	78.81
2000–1	1901	2708	544	190	68,577	141.16	185.70	54.84	75.82
2001–2	2079	2762	607	186	67,370	141.42[P]	189.75[P]	56.30[P]	78.07[P]
2002–3	1744	2610	543	191	63,576	132.66[P]	175.66[P]	53.88[P]	72.89[P]
2003–4	2077	2713	635	307	59,380	140.95[P]	190.37[P]	56.00[P]	77.11[P]
2004–5	1984	2602	577	318	64,752	141.32[P]	190.91[P]	58.54[P]	79.51[P]
2005–6	2102	2619	598	362	66,928				
2006–7 [AE]	2127	2671	616	422	71,081				

Source: RBI. 2009. *Handbook of Statistics on Indian Economy.*
Notes: AE: Advance Estimates; P: Provisional. Net sown area: area sown with crops and orchards. Area sown more than once in the same year is counted only once. Gross sown area: counts each plot as many times as it is cropped in a year. Net irrigated area: area irrigated through any source minimum once in a year for a particular crop. Gross irrigated area: counts each irrigated plot as many times as it is irrigated in a year.

Table 10   Industrial Activity, Formal Sector, Over Time 1973–2004

	Number of factories (units)	Number of workers	Gross value added (Rs lakh)
1973–4	64,133	46,59,523	5,40,225
1974–5	64,217	47,62,059	6,91,564
1975–6	71,705	49,96,223	7,34,081
1976–7	81,276	52,10,347	8,38,006
1977–8	84,924	55,41,830	9,33,930
1978–9	88,077	56,66,538	11,03,133
1979–80	95,126	59,62,288	12,54,173
1980–1	96,503	60,46,592	13,84,569
1981–2	1,05,038	61,05,622	16,72,345
1982–3	93,166	63,12,673	19,14,125
1983–4	96,706	61,58,837	23,52,048
1984–5	96,947	60,91,407	24,94,165
1985–6	1,01,016	58,19,169	27,66,699
1986–7	97,957	58,06,866	30,19,914
1987–8	1,02,596	60,61,786	34,58,578
1988–9	1,04,077	60,26,328	41,76,048
1989–90	1,07,992	63,26,541	52,03,683
1990–1	1,10,179	63,07,143	61,57,749
1991–2	1,12,286	62,69,039	66,16,778
1992–3	1,19,494	66,49,310	85,67,098
1993–4	1,21,594	66,32,323	104,88,911
1994–5	1,23,010	69,70,116	127,19,230
1995–6	1,34,571	76,32,297	163,02,304
1996–7	1,34,556	74,05,858	170,55,090
1997–8	1,35,549	76,04,907	187,77,820
1998–9	1,31,704	63,64,466	173,72,691
1999–2000	1,31,563	62,80,662	188,57,374
2000–1	1,31,269	61,35,246	178,35,037
2001–2	1,28,552	59,57,855	183,22,915
2002–3	1,27,964	61,61,497	214,37,556
2003–4	1,29,070	60,869,04	247,77,724

Source: EPW Research Foundation. 2007. *Annual Survey of Industries*.
Notes: For Annual Survey of Industries (ASI), the Collection of Statistics Act 1953 and the rules frame thereunder in 1959 provide the statutory basis. The ASI refers to the factories defined in accordance with the Factories Act 1948. The numbers presented in this table are all-India totals (manufacturing plus non-manufacturing sector).

Table 11   Industrial Activity, Unorganized Manufacturing Enterprises, across States 2006

State	Rural		Urban	
	Estimated number of enterprises	Estimated number of workers	Estimated number of enterprises	Estimated number of workers
Andhra Pradesh	1,085,242	2,026,591	447,997	912,354
Arunachal Pradesh	541	2299	318	1002
Assam	333,006	535,424	37,774	97,057
Bihar	663,379	1,205,694	109,018	247,379
Chhattisgarh	172,610	367,408	34,871	90,958
Delhi	3639	16,426	93,997	440,783
Goa	4546	13,227	5762	15,260
Gujarat	300,753	663,699	353,605	1,188,434
Haryana	119,687	224,349	110,423	319,674
Himachal Pradesh	100,437	146,389	7005	19,044
Jammu & Kashmir	140,468	252,259	32,944	66,610
Jharkhand	540,250	843,256	45,698	106,089
Karnataka	663,211	1,294,035	298,549	680,334
Kerala	492,777	1,008,614	165,914	382,393
Madhya Pradesh	564,463	1,117,202	290,097	623,444
Maharashtra	556,168	1,005,229	570,294	1,896,188
Manipur	35,797	52,991	16,721	28,379
Meghalaya	34,513	83,285	2474	7151
Mizoram	3291	4949	1810	4498
Nagaland	7167	10,939	2739	5369
Orissa	870,877	1,826,362	86,352	197,179
Punjab	150,208	232,288	143,029	368,521
Rajasthan	400,875	726,405	235,595	568,930
Sikkim	3684	6406	420	1219
Tamil Nadu	850,353	1,783,321	631,580	1,586,199
Tripura	38,900	131,651	6470	13,209
Uttaranchal	53,940	108,194	15,146	39,645
Uttar Pradesh	1,704,516	3,564,111	654,859	1,723,790
West Bengal	2,223,768	4,176,111	529,025	1,317,722
A & N Islands	1872	4390	444	1648
Chandigarh	753	1468	621	1131
Dadra and Nagar Haveli	797	1605	172	659
Daman and Diu	1464	6401	1175	2149
Lakshadweep	255	416	142	296
Pondicherry	4058	14,893	9513	29,816
All-India	**12,128,266**	**23,458,286**	**4,942,554**	**1,298,514**

Source: National Sample Survey (NSS), 62nd Round (July 2005–June 2006). December 2007. Report No. 524.

Table 12 Services, GDP at Factor Cost 1950–2008

Year	Construction		Trade, hotels, transport, and communication		Financing, real estate, and business services		Community, social, and personal services	
	Constant	Current	Constant	Current	Constant	Current	Constant	Current
1950–1	9931	249	25,409	939	17,238	1162	23,771	1080
1951–2	10,610	285	26,097	1017	17,635	1250	24,485	1126
1952–3	9841	265	26,940	1024	18,374	1320	24,989	1163
1953–4	10,144	266	27,943	1087	18,637	1424	25,763	1212
1954–5	11,399	295	29,738	1117	19,318	1526	26,686	1244
1955–6	13,558	368	31,907	1157	20,094	1638	27,512	1319
1956–7	15,117	416	34,262	1337	20,423	1776	28,567	1386
1957–8	13,268	382	35,392	1480	21,194	1903	29,858	1457
1958–9	14,827	441	37,206	1618	21,795	2041	31,083	1548
1959–60	15,844	491	39,532	1747	22,628	2190	32,420	1706
1960–1	18,324	635	42,885	1926	23,096	2360	34,012	1928
1961–2	18,968	666	45,687	2082	24,089	2411	35,610	2087
1962–3	19,674	702	48,421	2279	24,900	2768	38,139	2270
1963–4	22,076	803	51,833	2550	25,670	2994	40,642	2518
1964–5	23,850	953	55,287	2992	26,374	3254	43,322	2854
1965–6	25,442	1095	56,385	3245	27,171	3517	45,039	3174
1966–7	27,533	1291	57,880	3772	27,648	3765	47,116	3552
1967–8	29,513	1510	60,424	4311	28,401	4131	48,970	3977
1968–9	30,546	1638	63,185	4590	29,786	4422	51,152	4285
1969–70	31,495	1828	66,613	4954	31,024	4744	53,976	4672
1970–1	31,426	1934	69,816	5458	32,321	5169	56,950	5150
1971–2	31,563	2128	71,445	5919	33,987	5668	59,493	5718
1972–3	32,304	2319	73,226	6528	35,301	6203	61,439	6256
1973–4	30,206	2391	76,297	7814	36,165	6917	63,063	7036
1974–5	29,244	2618	81,054	10,319	36,049	7774	66,051	8858
1975–6	33,413	3271	88,357	11,701	38,534	8813	68,384	9971
1976–7	36,681	3871	92,449	12,673	41,590	9802	70,284	10,960
1977–8	40,394	4496	98,356	14,258	43,626	10,693	72,171	11,914
1978–9	39,493	4614	106,338	15,635	46,708	11,534	75,290	13,110
1979–80	37,408	4656	105,939	18,042	47,163	12,579	80,793	14,679
1980–1	42,339	6059	111,997	21,298	48,067	14,010	84,095	17,183
1981–2	44,658	6922	118,888	26,125	51,972	16,526	85,895	19,524
1982–3	41,522	7848	125,343	29,818	56,926	18,952	92,518	22,667
1983–4	43,764	9023	131,718	34,636	62,510	21,671	95,974	25,813

(contd...)

Table 12 (contd...)

Year	Construction		Trade, hotels, transport, and communication		Financing, real estate, and business services		Community, social, and personal services	
	Constant	Current	Constant	Current	Constant	Current	Constant	Current
1984–5	45,279	10,586	138,069	39,878	67,182	24,932	102,623	29,699
1985–6	47,843	12,355	149,032	46,567	73,741	28,557	108,512	33,591
1986–7	48,986	14,216	158,041	52,636	81,510	32,743	116,666	38,631
1987–8	51,795	16,854	166,349	60,107	87,487	37,422	125,102	44,776
1988–9	55,436	19,651	176,066	70,968	96,024	43,481	132,666	51,923
1989–90	59,336	22,805	189,043	83,065	107,962	51,238	143,119	59,513
1990–1	66,330	27,699	198,770	97,313	114,670	59,856	149,357	68,604
1991–2	67,696	31,133	203,897	112,119	127,079	73,112	153,219	79,721
1992–3	70,053	35,521	215,271	132,191	133,999	81,072	162,400	92,597
1993–4	70,452	39,240	230,141	156,202	148,962	97,928	169,654	103,946
1994–5	74,243	45,093	252,876	186,425	154,751	110,673	173,493	116,265
1995–6	78,683	53,042	286,232	224,259	167,276	133,235	186,244	137,357
1996–7	80,158	60,382	309,328	264,967	177,627	146,991	201,241	163,104
1997–8	88,553	74,999	332,580	303,755	198,423	167,381	217,948	189,284
1998–9	94,109	88,784	358,014	347,864	213,902	195,133	239,123	231,351
1999–2000	102,007	102,007	387,515	387,515	233,550	233,549	266,707	266,707
2000–1	108,362	111,999	415,650	428,855	243,048	254,772	279,239	287,688
2001–2	112,692	120,865	453,847	476,230	260,737	292,862	290,715	310,485
2002–3	121,650	135,172	496,692	525,968	281,550	330,685	302,153	334,228
2003–4	136,224	156,806	556,370	604,683	297,250	371,452	318,514	363,781
2004–5	158,217	212,812	615,848	706,073	323,080	405,081	340,342	403,047
2005–6[P]	184,255	264,616	686,738	815,698	359,942	452,593	364,883	448,972
2006–7[QE]	206,338	319,497	767,884	949,469	410,030	526,755	390,020	508,586
2007–8[RE]	226,579	366,946	860,212	1,085,468	458,364	614,066	418,307	573,948

Source: RBI. 2009. *Handbook of Statistics on Indian Economy*.
Notes: Base for constant prices: 1999–2000.
P: Provisional QE: Quick Estimates; RE: Revised Estimates.

Table 13   Inter-state Performance, Economy and Society

State/Union territory	NSDP (at factor costs, at current prices, 2004–5)[a]		% of villages electrified as on 31-03-09[b]	Population as of 2001 census (in thousands)	Literacy rate, ages 7 and above (%)		
	NSDP Rs crore	NSDP Rs per capita			T	M	F
Andhra Pradesh	1,88,855	23,755	100	76,210	60.5	70.3	50.4
Arunachal Pradesh	2590	22,542	56.8	1098	54.3	63.8	43.5
Assam	47,831	17,013	78.6	26,656	63.3	71.3	54.6
Bihar	66,202	7467	52.9	82,999	47.0	59.7	33.1
Jharkhand	50,143	17,493	31.1	26,946	53.6	67.3	38.9
Goa	10,039	66,135	100	1348	82.0	88.4	75.4
Gujarat	1,58,531	29,468	99.7	50,671	69.1	79.7	57.8
Haryana	85,488	37,648	100	21,145	67.9	78.5	55.7
Himachal Pradesh	20,262	31,139	98.2	6078	76.5	85.3	67.4
Jammu & Kashmir	20,724	18,630	98.2	10,144	55.5	66.6	43.0
Karnataka	1,31,943	23,848	98.7	52,851	66.6	76.1	56.9
Kerala	92,152	27,864	100	31,841	90.9	94.2	87.7
Madhya Pradesh	93,690	14,476	96.4	60,348	63.7	76.1	50.3
Chhattisgarh	40,292	18,068	95.6	20,834	64.7	77.4	51.9
Maharashtra	3,38,254	32,979	88.3	96,879	76.9	86.0	67
Manipur	4541	18,386	85.7	2167	70.5	80.3	60.5
Meghalaya	5319	21,915	59.3	2319	62.6	65.4	59.6
Mizoram	2181	22,417	80.6	889	88.8	90.7	86.7
Nagaland	4980	20,998	64.4	1990	66.6	71.2	61.5
Orissa	62,497	16,306	55.8	36,805	63.1	75.3	50.5
Punjab	86,250	33,158	100	24,359	69.7	75.2	63.4
Rajasthan	1,00,196	16,515	68.9	56,507	60.4	75.7	43.9
Sikkim	1356	23,791	94.4	541	68.8	76.0	60.4
Tamil Nadu	1,74,804	27,137	100	62,406	73.5	82.4	64.4
Tripura	7648	22,836	57.2	3199	73.2	81.0	64.9
Uttar Pradesh	2,14,506	12,023	88.3	166,198	56.3	68.8	42.2
Uttaranchal	19,915	22,093	96.5	8489	71.6	83.3	59.6
West Bengal	1,88,963	22,522	96.1	80,176	68.6	77.0	59.6
A & N Islands	1237	31,004	66.1	356	81.3	86.3	75.2
Chandigarh	7909	75,181	100	901	81.9	86.1	76.5
Delhi	84,992	55,215	100	13,851	81.7	87.3	74.7
Pondicherry	4679	44,908	100	974	81.2	88.6	73.9
Daman and Diu				158	78.2	86.8	65.6
Dadra and Nagar Haveli				220	57.6	71.2	40.2
Lakshadweep				61	86.7	92.5	80.5

Source: [a] RBI. 2009. *Handbook of Statistics on Indian Economy*; [b] Ministry of Power, India. 2009; remainder: Census of India. 2001.

Notes: [a] Owing to differences in methodology of compilation, data for different states/union territories may not be not strictly comparable. Literacy rates for Manipur exclude those of the three sub-division, namely, Mao Maram, Paomata, and Purul of Senapati district of Manipur as census results of 2001 in these three sub-divisions were cancelled due to technical and administrative reasons.

Table 14 Education and Health 1980–2005

Indicator	1980	1990	2000	2005
School enrolment, primary (% gross)	82	94	94	115
School enrolment, primary, female (% gross)	65	79	86	113
School enrolment, primary, male (% gross)	97	107	101	116
School enrolment, secondary (% gross)	33	41	46	54
School enrolment, secondary, female (% gross)	22	30	38	49
School enrolment, secondary, male (% gross)	44	52	54	59
School enrolment, tertiary (% gross)			10	11
School enrolment, tertiary, female (% gross)			8	9
School enrolment, tertiary, male (% gross)			11	13
Pupil–teacher ratio, primary	43	46	40	
Pupil–teacher ratio, secondary	21	29	34	
Population annual growth rate (%)		2.2	1.7	1.5
Population in urban areas (%)		26	28	
Total fertility rate (per woman)		4	3.3	
Infant mortality rate (per 1000 live births) both sexes		82	66	
Infant mortality rate (per 1000 live births) female		83	67	
Infant mortality rate (per 1000 live births) male		81	65	
Life expectancy at birth (years) both sexes		58	61	
Life expectancy at birth (years) female		58	62	
Life expectancy at birth (years) male		58	60	
Prevalence of tuberculosis (per 100,000 population)		568	464	310
Under-5 mortality rate, both sexes[a]		115	89	
Under-5 mortality rate, female[a]		122	95	
Under-5 mortality rate, male[a]		108	84	
Population with sustainable access to improved drinking water sources (%) rural		65	77	
Population with sustainable access to improved drinking water sources (%) total		71	82	
Population with sustainable access to improved drinking water sources (%) urban		90	94	
Population with sustainable access to improved sanitation (%) rural		4	13	
Population with sustainable access to improved sanitation (%) total		14	23	
Population with sustainable access to improved sanitation (%) urban		44	49	

Source: WDI 2009 (education indicators); WHO. 2009. *World Health Statistics* (health indicators).
Note: [a]probability of dying by age 5 per 1000 live births.

Table 15   Number and Percentage of Population below the Poverty Line

	Rural			Urban			Combined	
	No. of persons (lakh)	% of persons	Poverty line (Rs)	No. of persons (lakh)	% of persons	Poverty line (Rs)	No. of persons (lakh)	% of persons
1973–4	2612.9	56.44	49.63	600.46	49.01	56.64	3213.36	54.88
1983–4	2519.57	45.65	89.5	709.4	40.79	115.65	3228.97	44.48
1993–4	2440.31	37.27	205.84	763.37	32.36	281.35	3203.67	35.97
1999–2000[a]	1932.43	27.09	327.56	670.07	23.62	454.11	2602.5	26.1
2004–5[b]	1702.99	21.8	356.3	682	21.7	538.6	2384.99	21.8
2004–5[c]	2209.24	28.3	356.3	807.96	25.7	538.6	3017.2	27.5

Source: RBI. 2009. *Handbook of Statistics on Indian Economy*.
Notes: [a] Based on a thirty-day recall period.
[b] Based on a mixed recall period in which the consumer expenditure data for five non-food items, namely, clothing, footwear, durable goods, education, and institutional medical expenses are collected from a 365-day recall period and the consumption data for the remaining items are collected from a thirty-day recall period.
[c] Based on a uniform recall period in which consumer expenditure data for all the items are collected from a thirty-day recall period.

Table 16   Infrastructure 1970–2007

	1970	1980	1990	2000	2005	2006	2007
Households with television (%)	0.03	1.31	7.43	29.97	53.37		
Internet users (per 100 people)			0.00	0.54	3.84	6.85	7.20
Mobile and fixed-line telephone subscribers (per 100 people)	0.18	0.31	0.60	3.54	12.82	18.64	24.27
Passenger cars (per 1000 people)			2.42	6.00			
Mobile cellular subscriptions (per 100 people)	0.00	0.00	0.00	0.35	8.24	14.96	20.77
Personal computers (per 100 people)			0.03	0.45	1.55	2.79	3.29
Population covered by mobile cellular network (%)					30.50	60.90	
Railways, goods transported (milliard ton-km)		159	236	305	408	440	481
Railways, passengers carried (milliard passenger-km)		209	296	430	576	616	694
Roads, total network (1000 km)			2000	3316		3316	
Vehicles (per 1000 people)			4.31	9.00			
Container port trafic (1000 TEU)[a]				2451	4982	6141	7373
Passenger cars (per 1000 people)			2.42	6.00			

Source: WDI 2009.
Notes: [a] Port container traffic measures the flow of containers from land to sea transport modes, and vice versa, in twenty-foot equivalent units (TEUs), a standard-size container.

Table 17   Doing Business, Comparing India with Singapore 2006, 2009

Year		India		Singapore	
		2006	2009	2006	2009
Ease of Doing Business rank			122		1
Starting a business	Rank		121		10
	Procedures (number)	11	13	6	4
	Time (days)	71	30	6	4
	Cost (% of income per capita)	62	70.1	0.9	0.7
	Min. capital (% of income per capita)	0	0	0	0
Dealing with construction permits	Rank		136		2
	Procedures (number)	20	20	11	11
	Time (days)	224	224	102	38
	Cost (% of income per capita)	670.7	414.7	22.6	21.2
Employing workers	Rank		89		1
	Difficulty of Hiring Index	0	0	0	0
	Rigidity of Hours Index	20	20	0	0
	Difficulty of Firing Index	70	70	0	0
	Rigidity of Employment Index	30	30	0	0
	Firing costs (weeks of wages)	56	56	4	4
Registering property	Rank		105		16
	Procedures (number)	6	6	3	3
	Time (days)	62	45	9	9
	Cost (% of property value)	8	7.5	2.8	2.8
Getting CREDIT	Rank		28		5
	Legal rights index	5	8	10	10
	Credit information index	2	4	4	4
	Public registry coverage (% adults)	0	0	0	0
	Private bureau coverage (% adults)	1.7	10.5	38.6	48.3
Protecting INVESTORS	Rank	0	38	0	2
	Disclosure index	7	7	10	10
	Director liability index	4	4	9	9
	Shareholder suits index	7	7	9	9
	Investor protection index	6	6	9.3	9.3
Paying taxes	Rank		169		5
	Payments (number)	56	60	5	5
	Time (hours)	264	271	49	84
	Profit tax (%)		22.9		7.9
	Labour tax and contributions (%)		18.2		14.9
	Other taxes (%)		30.4		5.1
	Total tax rate (% profit)	65	71.5	27.7	27.9
Trading across borders	Rank		90		1
	Documents for export (number)	10	8	4	4
	Time for export (days)	36	17	5	5
	Cost to export (US$ per container)	864	945	416	456

(contd...)

Table 17 (contd...)

Year		India		Singapore	
		2006	2009	2006	2009
	Documents for import (number)	15	9	4	4
	Time for import (days)	43	20	3	3
	Cost to import (US$ per container)	1244	960	367	439
Enforcing contracts	Rank		180		14
	Procedures (number)	46	46	21	21
	Time (days)	1420	1420	120	150
	Cost (% of claim)	39.6	39.6	17.8	25.8
Closing a business	Rank		140		2
	Time (years)	10	10	0.8	0.8
	Cost (% of estate)	9	9	1	1
	Recovery rate (cents on the dollar)	12.8	10.4	91.3	91.3

Source: World Bank. 2009. *Doing Business*.

Notes: The 'ease of business' indicator ranks economies in terms of their 'ease of business', from 1 to 175, with 1 referring to the best. This index averages the country's percentile rankings on ten categories, giving equal weight to each category. Each category in its turn averages the country's percentile rankings on different sub-categories.

CONTRIBUTORS
(with entries)

BINA AGARWAL (*Gender Inequality*)
Director and Professor of Economics, Institute of Economic Growth, Delhi, India

ISHER JUDGE AHLUWALIA (*Industrial Policy*)
Chairperson, Indian Council for Research on International Economic Relations, New Delhi;
and Vice Chairperson, Global Development Network, New Delhi, India

YOGINDER K. ALAGH (*Green Revolution*)
Chairman, Institute of Rural Management Anand, Gujarat, India

MUKESH ANAND (*Pensions*)
Senior Economist, National Institute of Public Finance and Policy, New Delhi, India

RITU ANAND (*External Debt*)
Principal Adviser and Chief Economist, IDFC

REENA BADIANI (*Data Sets, co-authors Siddharth Sharma and Himanshu*)
PhD Student, Economic Growth Center, Yale University

JUGNU BAGGA (*Rent Control Acts, co-author Shubhashis Gangopadhyay*)
Formerly with India Development Foundation, Gurgaon, Haryana, India

G. BALACHANDRAN (*Reserve Bank of India, co-author T.C.A. Srinivasa Raghavan*)
Professor of International History and Politics, Graduate Institute of International Studies,
Geneva

KAUSHIK RANJAN BANDYOPADHYAY (*Human Rights, co-author Arjun K. Sengupta*)
Research Officer, Centre for Development and Human Rights and Researcher, Centre for
Economic Studies and Planning, Jawaharlal Nehru University, New Delhi, India

ABHIJIT V. BANERJEE (*Public Goods*)
Professor, Department of Economics, Massachusetts Institute of Technology,
Cambridge, USA

SANJAY BANERJI (*Finance and Law*)
Reader in Finance, Essex Business School, University of Essex

ARINDAM BANIK (*Technology Transfer, co-author Pradip K. Bhaumik*)
Professor of Economics, International Management Institute, New Delhi, India

PRANAB BARDHAN (*Political Economy*)
Professor of Economics, University of California, Berkeley, USA

ALAKA MALWADE BASU (*Infant and Child Mortality; Population Policy*)
Professor of Demography, Department of Sociology, Cornell University, New York, USA

ARNAB BASU (*National Rural Employment Guarantee Act, co-authors Nancy H. Chau and Ravi Kanbur*)
Associate Professor of Economics and Public Policy, College of William and Mary, Williamsburg, VA, USA

ANURADHA BHASIN (*Tourism*)
Consultant, National Council of Applied Economic Research, New Delhi, India

ADITYA BHATTACHARJEA (*Antitrust Law*)
Professor, Department of Economics, Delhi School of Economics, University of Delhi, Delhi, India

PRADIP K. BHAUMIK (*Technology Transfer, co-author Arindam Banik*)
Professor of Quantitative Techniques & Operations Management, International Management Institute, New Delhi, India

DAVID E. BLOOM (*HIV/AIDS, Economics of, co-authors Bhargavi Rao and Ajay Mahal*)
Clarence James Gamble Professor of Economics and Demography, Department of Global Health and Population, Harvard School of Public Health, Boston, Massachusetts, USA

C.P. CHANDRASEKHAR (*Financial Crisis*)
Professor, Centre for Economic Studies and Planning, School of Social Sciences, Jawaharlal Nehru University, New Delhi, India

RAJESH CHAKRABARTI (*Foreign Exchange Markets; Foreign Institutional Investment*)
Assistant Professor of Finance, Indian School of Business, Hyderabad, India

RUPA CHANDA (*Services-led Growth*)
Professor of Economics, Indian Institute of Management Bangalore, Karnataka, India

PANKAJ CHANDRA (*Textile and Apparel Industry*)
Professor of Operations & Technology Management, Indian Institute of Management Ahmedabad, Gujarat, India

A.V. CHARI (*Licensing*)
Allyn Young Post-Doctoral Fellow, Department of Economics, Cornell University,
New York, USA

NANCY H. CHAU (*National Rural Employment Guarantee Act, co-authors Arnab Basu
and Ravi Kanbur*)
Associate Professor, Department of Applied Economics and Management,
Cornell University, New York, USA

SAUMITRA CHAUDHURI (*Housing Finance*)
Member, Economic Advisory Council to the Prime Minister; and Member, Planning
Commission, New Delhi, India

SUDIP CHAUDHURI (*Pharmaceutical Industry*)
Professor of Economics, Indian Institute of Management Calcutta, Kolkata, India

P. CHIDAMBARAM (*Fiscal Policy Reforms since 1991*)
Union Minister of Home Affairs, Government of India

DEB KUSUM DAS (*Trade Barriers in Manufacturing*)
Reader, Department of Economics, Ramjas College, University of Delhi, Delhi, India

JISHNU DAS (*Medical Care, Quality of, co-author Jeffrey S. Hammer*)
Senior Economist, Development Research Group, World Bank, Washington D.C., USA

ARINDAM DAS-GUPTA (*Corruption*)
Associate Professor, Lee Kuan Yew School of Public Policy, National University of
Singapore, Singapore

MONICA DAS GUPTA (*Public Health*)
Senior Social Scientist, Development Economics Research Group (DECRG), World Bank,
Washington D.C., USA

BIBEK DEBROY (*Law and Legal System in India*)
Economist

ASHOK V. DESAI (*Convertibility*)
Consultant Editor, *Business World*, New Delhi, India

ASHWINI DESHPANDE (*Affirmative Action; Women in the Labour Force*)
Reader, Department of Economics, Delhi School of Economics, University of Delhi,
Delhi, India

R.S. DESHPANDE (*Farmer Distress and Suicides*)
Professor and Head, Agricultural Development and Rural Transformation Centre,
Institute for Social and Economic Change, Bangalore, India

S. MAHENDRA DEV (*Agriculture Development*)
Director, Centre for Economics and Social Studies, Hyderabad, India

AMRITA DHILLON (*Fiscal Federalism*)
Professor, Department of Economics, University of Warwick, UK

RAFIQ DOSSANI (*IT-enabled Sectors*)
Senior Research Scholar, Shorenstein Asia-Pacific Research Centre, Stanford University, Stanford, California

JEAN DRÈZE (*Food and Nutrition*)
Honorary Professor, Department of Economics, Delhi School of Economics, University of Delhi, Delhi, India

ESTHER DUFLO (*Dams, co-author Rohini Pande*)
Abdul Latif Jameel Professor of Development Economics and Poverty Alleviation, Massachusetts Institute of Technology, Cambridge, Massachusetts, USA

BHASKAR DUTTA (*Discretionary Centre–State Transfers; Disinvestment, The Economics of*)
Professor of Economics, Department of Economics, University of Warwick, UK

TATIANA FIC (*India's Growth Turnaround, co-authors Chetan Ghate and Stephen Wright*)
Senior Research Officer, National Institute of Economic and Social Research, London, UK

SHUBHASHIS GANGOPADHYAY (*Rent Control Acts, co-author Jugnu Bagga*)
Director, India Development Foundation, Gurgaon, Haryana, India

CHETAN GHATE (*India's Growth Turnaround, co-authors Stephen Wright and Tatiana Fic*)
Associate Professor, Planning Unit, Indian Statistical Institute, Delhi Centre, New Delhi, India

MAITREESH GHATAK (*Land Reform*)
Professor, Department of Economics, London School of Economics, UK

AJIT K. GHOSE (*Informal Labour*)
Senior Economist, Economic and Labour Market Analysis Department, International Labour Organization, Switzerland

SAIBAL GHOSH (*Banking, co-authors Dilip M. Nachane and Partha Ray*)
Assistant Adviser, Department of Economic Analysis and Policy, Reserve Bank of India, Mumbai, India

SUBIR GOKARN (*Railways*)
Deputy Governor, Reserve Bank of India, Mumbai, India

OMKAR GOSWAMI (*Corporate Governance*)
Chairman, CERG Advisory, New Delhi, India

ASHIMA GOYAL (*International Finance*)
Professor of Economics, Indira Gandhi Institute of Development Research, Mumbai, India

ASHOK GUHA (*International Trade*)
Professor, School of International Studies, Jawaharlal Nehru University, New Delhi, India

INDRANI GUPTA (*Health Indicators*)
Professor and Head, Health Policy Research Unit, Institute of Economic Growth, Delhi, India

JEFFREY S. HAMMER (*Medical Care, Quality of, co-author Jishnu Das*)
Charles and Marie Roberston Visiting Professor in Economic Development, Woodrow Wilson School of Public & International Affairs, Princeton University

HIMANSHU (*Data Sets, co-authors Reena Badiani and Siddharth Sharma*)
Assistant Professor, Centre for the Study of Regional Development, School of Social Sciences, Jawaharlal Nehru University, New Delhi, India

ROGER JEFFERY (*Education and Religious Minorities*)
Professor of Sociology of South Asia, School of Social and Political Studies, University of Edinburgh, Edinburgh, Scotland, UK

SHIKHA JHA (*Food Procurement Policy*)
Indira Gandhi Institute of Development Research, Mumbai, India; and Economist/Country Programs Specialist, Asian Development Bank, Manila, Philippines

RENANA JHABVALA (*Globalization and the Poor, co-author Ravi Kanbur*)
National Coordinator, SEWA, Ahmadabad, Gujarat, India

PRITAL SAILESH KADAKIA (*Roads*)
Department of Economics, Harvard University, Cambridge, Massachusetts, USA

RAVI KANBUR (*Globalization and the Poor, co-author Renana Jhabvala; National Rural Employment Guarantee Act, co-authors Arnab Basu and Nancy H. Chau*)
T.H. Lee Professor of World Affairs and Economics, Cornell University, New York, USA

MILIND KANDLIKAR (*Outsourcing, co-author Ashok Kotwal*)
Associate Professor, Centre for India and South Asia Research (Institute of Asian Research) and Liu Institute for Global Studies, University of British Columbia, Vancouver, Canada

DEVESH KAPUR (*Higher Education, co-author Pratap Bhanu Mehta; International Migration from India: Economic Impact*)
Director, Centre for Advanced Study of India; and Madan Lal Sobti Associate Professor for the Study of Contemporary India, University of Pennsylvania, Philadelphia

SANDEEP KAPUR (*Literacy, co-author Mamta Murthi*)
Reader in Financial Economics, Department of Economics, Mathematics and Statistics, Birkbeck, University of London, UK

GEETA KINGDON (*Secondary Education*)
Chair, Education Economics and International Development, Institute of Education, University of London, UK

STEFAN KLONNER (*Non-banking Financial Companies*)
Assistant Professor, Department of Economics, Cornell University, New York, USA

ANJINI KOCHAR (*Primary Education*)
Senior Research Scholar, Stanford Center for International Development, Stanford University, Stanford

ASHOK KOTWAL (*Outsourcing, co-author Milind Kandlikar*)
Professor of Economics and Director, Centre for India and South Asia Research (Institute of Asian Research), University of British Columbia, Vancouver, Canada

K.L. KRISHNA (*National Income*)
Professor, Centre for Development Economics, Delhi School of Economics, University of Delhi, Delhi, India

MEDHA MALIK KUDAISYA (*G.D. Birla*)
Professor, Department of History, Faculty of Arts and Social Sciences, National University of Singapore, Singapore

NAGESH KUMAR (*Foreign Direct Investment*)
Director-General, Research and Information System for Developing Countries (RIS), New Delhi, India

RAJIV KUMAR (*Foreign Exchange Reserves*)
Director and Chief Executive, Indian Council for Research on International Economic Relations, New Delhi, India

AMITABH KUNDU (*Mobility of Population*)
Professor, Centre for the Study of Regional Development, Jawaharlal Nehru University, New Delhi, India

AJAY MAHAL (*HIV/AIDS, Economics of, co-authors Bhargavi Rao and David E. Bloom*)
Associate Professor, Department of Population and International Health, Harvard School of Public Health, Boston, Massachusetts, USA

PAYAL MALIK (*Power Sector and Regulation*)
Senior Lecturer of Economics, PGDAV College, University of Delhi, Delhi, India

SUGATA MARJIT (*Exports and Export Policy*)
Reserve Bank of India Professor of Industrial Economics, Centre for Studies in Social Sciences, Kolkata, India

R.A. Mashelkar (*Intellectual Property Rights*)
FRS, Former Director General, Council of Scientific and Industrial Research, New Delhi, India

Rajnish Mehra (*Equity Premium*)
Professor of Finance, Department of Economics, University of California, Santa Barbara, CA

Pratap Bhanu Mehta (*Higher Education, co-author Devesh Kapur*)
President, Centre for Policy Research, New Delhi, India

Divya Minisandram (*Brain Drain*)
Graduate, Harvard University, Cambridge, Massachusetts, USA

Ajit Mishra (*Inequality*)
Senior Lecturer, Economics and International Development, University of Bath, Bath, UK

Puran Mongia (*Environment Policy; Forest Policy*)
Former Professor of Economics, Centre for Development Economics, Delhi School of Economics, University of Delhi, Delhi, India

Dilip Mookherjee (*Panchayats*)
Professor of Economics and Director, Institute for Economic Development, Boston University, Massachusetts, USA

Sebastian Morris (*Infrastructure-sector Reforms*)
Professor of Economics, Indian Institute of Management Ahmedabad, Gujarat, India

Hiranya Mukhopadhyay (*Government Subsidies, co-author Sudipto Mundle*)
Economist, Asian Development Bank, New Delhi, India

Sudipto Mundle (*Government Subsidies, co-author Hiranya Mukhopadhyay*)
Adviser, Strategy and Policy Department, Asian Development Bank, Manila, Philippines

Kaivan Munshi (*Technology Diffusion*)
Professor of Economics, Department of Economics, Brown University, Rhode Island, USA

Mamta Murthi (*Literacy, co-author Sandeep Kapur*)
Lead Economist, World Bank, Washington D.C., USA

N.R. Narayana Murthy (*Software and Services Exports*)
Chairman and Chief Mentor, Infosys Technologies Limited, Bangalore, Karnataka, India

Dilip M. Nachane (*Banking, co-authors Saibal Ghosh and Partha Ray*)
Senior Professor, Indira Gandhi Institute of Development Research, Mumbai, India

R. Nagaraj (*Trade Unions*)
Professor, Indira Gandhi Institute of Development Research, Mumbai, India

SUDHA NARAYANAN
PhD Student, Department of Applied Economics and Management, College of Agriculture and Life Sciences, Cornell University, New York, USA

K. NAVANEETHAM (*Demographic Dividend*)
Professor, Centre for Development Studies, Tiruvananthapuram, India

PULIN B. NAYAK (*Privatization*)
Professor of Economics, Delhi School of Economics, University of Delhi, Delhi, India

S. NEELAKANTAN (*Land Rights and Acquisition*)
Professor of Economics, Madras Institute of Development Studies, Chennai

T.N. NINAN (*Dhirubhai Ambani and Reliance Industries*)
Editor and Publisher, *Business Standard*, New Delhi, India

MANDAR P. OAK (*Credit Market Regulation, Evolution of*)
Assistant Professor of Economics, Department of Economics, Williams College, Williamstown, Massachusetts, USA

S.R. OSMANI (*Famines*)
Professor of Development Economics, School of Economics and Politics, University of Ulster, Jordanstown, UK

R.K. PACHAURI (*Energy*)
Director General, The Energy Research Institute, New Delhi, India

ROHINI PANDE (*Dams, co-author Esther Duflo; Rural Credit*)
Mohammad Kamal Professor of Public Policy, Harvard University, Cambridge, Massachusetts, USA

T.S. PAPOLA (*Employment Trends*)
Honorary Professor, Institute for Studies in Industrial Development, New Delhi, India

ILA PATNAIK (*Tariffs*)
Senior Fellow, National Institute of Public Finance and Policy, New Delhi, India

ANANDITA PHILIPOSE (*Child Malnutrition and Feeding Practices*)
Cornell Institute of Public Affairs, Cornell University, New York, USA

K. SEETA PRABHU (*Human Development Index*)
Head, Human Development Resource Centre, United Nations Development Programme, New Delhi, India

T.C.A. SRINIVASA RAGHAVAN (*Aviation; Ports and Shipping; Reserve Bank of India, co-author G. Balachandran*)
Consulting Editor, *Business Standard*, New Delhi, India

BHARAT RAMASWAMI (*Public Distribution System; Unemployment, The Measurement of,*
co-author Wilima Wadhwa)
Professor, Planning Unit, Indian Statistical Institute, Delhi, India

BHARGAVI RAO (*HIV/AIDS, Economics of, co-authors Ajay Mahal and David E. Bloom*)
Clinical Specialist, Harvard Medical School (Division of AIDS), Boston, Massachusetts, USA

U.R. RAO (*Space Satellites*)
Chairman, Governing Council, Physical Research Laboratory, Ahmedabad, Gujarat, India

PARTHA RAY (*Banking, co-authors Dilip M. Nachane and Saibal Ghosh*)
Former Director, Department of Economic Analysis and Policy, Reserve Bank of India,
Mumbai, India

C. RAMMANOHAR REDDY (*Defence Expenditure*)
Editor, *Economic and Political Weekly*, Mumbai, India

Y.V. REDDY (*Monetary Policy*)
Former Governor, Reserve Bank of India, Mumbai, India

ABHIRUP SARKAR (*Special Economic Zones*)
Professor of Economics, Economic Research Unit, Indian Statistical Institute, Kolkata, India

JAYATI SARKAR (*Corporate Ownership and Performance, co-author Subrata Sarkar*)
Associate Professor, Indira Gandhi Institute of Development Research, Mumbai, India

SUBRATA SARKAR (*Corporate Ownership and Performance, co-author Jayati Sarkar*)
Professor, Indira Gandhi Institute of Development Research, Mumbai, India

AMARTYA SEN (*Democracy and Social Welfare*)
Thomas W. Lamont University Professor and Professor of Economics and Philosophy,
Department of Economics, Harvard University, USA

ANINDYA SEN (*Business Policy*)
Professor of Economics, Indian Institute of Management Calcutta, Kolkata, India

ARJUN K. SENGUPTA (*Human Rights, co-author Kaushik Ranjan Bandyopadhyay*)
Member of Parliament (Rajya Sabha), and Former Chairman, National Commission for
Enterprises in the Unorganised Sector, Government of India

RAMPRASAD SENGUPTA (*Steel Industry*)
Professor of Economics at Centre for Economic Studies and Planning, Jawaharlal Nehru
University, New Delhi, India

AJAY SHAH (*Securities Markets; Stock Market Indexes, co-author Susan Thomas*)
Professor, National Institute of Public Finance and Policy, New Delhi, India

SIDDHARTH SHARMA (*Data Sets, co-authors Reena Badiani and Himanshu*)
Research Analyst, Middle East and North Africa Region, World Bank,
Washington D.C., USA

SUNIL SHARMA (*Exchange Rates*)
Director, IMF–Singapore Regional Training Institute, Singapore

PARTHASARATHI SHOME (*Savings and Investment*)
Former Adviser to Union Finance Minister, Government of India

CHARAN SINGH (*Financial-sector Reforms*)
Former Director, Department of Economic Analysis and Policy, Reserve Bank of India

JAIVIR SINGH (*Labour Laws in India*)
Assistant Professor, Centre for the Study of Law and Governance, Jawaharlal Nehru
University, New Delhi, India

NIRVIKAR SINGH (*Call Centres; Telecommunications*)
Professor, Department of Economics, University of California

ROHINI SOMANATHAN (*Poverty and Exclusion*)
Professor in Economics, Delhi School of Economics, Delhi University, Delhi, India

ARVIND SUBRAMANIAN (*Growth Experience*)
Assistant Director, Research Department, International Monetary Fund,
Washington D.C., USA

S. SUBRAMANIAN (*Poverty*)
Professor, Madras Institute of Development Studies, Chennai, India

MADHURA SWAMINATHAN (*Child Labour*)
Professor, Indian Statistical Institute, Kolkata, India

R.N. TATA (*Tata, The House of*)
Chairman, Tata Group, Mumbai, India

SUSAN THOMAS (*Stock Market Indexes, co-author Ajay Shah*)
Assistant Professor, Indira Gandhi Institute of Development Research, Mumbai, India

JEEMOL UNNI (*Agricultural Labour*)
RBI Chair Professor in Rural Economics, Institute of Rural Management Anand,
Gujarat, India

A. VAIDYANATHAN (*Irrigation; Water*)
Emeritus Professor, Madras Institute of Development Studies, Chennai, India

ARVIND VIRMANI (*Balance of Payments; Foreign Direct Investment for Media*)
Principal Adviser (DP/IE/SER), Planning Commission, Government of India

WILIMA WADHWA (*Unemployment, The Measurement of, co-author Bharat Ramaswami*)
Visiting Faculty, Planning Unit, Indian Statistical Institute, New Delhi, India, and
Department of Economics, University of California, Irvine, California

JAYASHREE WATAL (*Patents*)
Counselor, Intellectual Property Division, World Trade Organization, Geneva, Switzerland

STEPHEN WRIGHT (*India's Growth Turnaround, co-authors Chetan Ghate and Tatiana Fic*)
Reader in Economics, Department of Economics, Mathematics, and Statistics, Birkbeck
College, University of London, UK

'Eaton and Wagoner analyze the built landscape of the Deccan plateau during a period of intense political conflict, showing how the meanings of that landscape were contested and mobilized by succeeding rulers, who drew on both Sanskrit and Persianate cosmologies. Deploying an innovative, multidisciplinary methodology, shaped as much by on-the-ground analysis of historical remains as by the study of Sanskrit, Persian, and Telugu texts, their book provides critical new insights on the history of this era.'

—American Historical Association

'Truly collaborative, interdisciplinary work is a rarity in the humanities. Historian Eaton and Art Historian Wagoner have pooled their linguistic and methodological expertise to produce an adventurous, stimulating and innovative book. Employing archaeological survey methods over a large territorial expanse, the Deccan, with a time frame of three centuries, the authors read relevant chronicles and epigraphic texts against architectural evidence. The result is a significant reinterpretation of continuities and disruptions in kingship, state formation, and cultural interactions in a specific South Asian region.'

—Association for Asian Studies

'The book under review is an excellent interdisciplinary study that falls squarely in the shadowy space between art history and political history, and, given the present day academic scenario, there is virtually very little communication between such disciplines and their methodologies.... Stones and temples do have many tales to tell. The disruption of power centres and reestablishment of new nodes for dominion and rule have left several traces that resonate down the centuries for the attentive ear and eye to perceive and rearticulate—an intricate interplay of power, memory and architecture. This book is a treasure.'

—*The Hindu*

'With Eaton's training in history and Wagoner's in art history and archaeology, the book benefits from multiple disciplinary perspectives, and between the two of them, the authors bring to the table expertise in Persian, Telugu, and Sanskrit.'

—*South Asian Studies*